CONTRACT LAW AND PRACTICE
REVISED SECOND EDITION

CONTRACT LAW AND PRACTICE

Revised Second Edition

GERALD E. BERENDT
Professor of Law
The John Marshall Law School

REBECCA A. COCHRAN
Professor of Law
University of Dayton School of Law

DORIS ESTELLE LONG
Professor of Law
The John Marshall Law School

ROBERT J. NYE
Professor of Law
The John Marshall Law School

JOHN H. SCHEID
Professor of Law
The John Marshall Law School

ISBN:978–1–4224–2963–1

Library of Congress Cataloging-in-Publication Data

Contract law and practice / Gerald E. Berendt, [et al.]. — 2nd ed.
p. cm.
Includes index.
ISBN 978–1–4224–2963–1 (Hardbound)
1. Contracts-United States-Cases. I. Berendt, Gerald E.
KF801.C614 2009
346.7302-dc22
2009026371

To ensure that you are using the latest materials available in this area, please be sure to periodically check the LexisNexis Law School web site for downloadable updates and supplements at www.lexisnexis.com/lawschool.

Editorial Offices
121 Chanlon Rd., New Providence, NJ 07974 (908) 464-6800
201 Mission St., San Francisco, CA 94105-1831 (415) 908-3200
www.lexisnexis.com

MATTHEW◆BENDER

(2009–Pub.3526)

DEDICATION

The authors would like to dedicate this book to Marie A. Monahan, whose chapters in the First Edition of this casebook were an inspiration to her students and collegues.

Her wit, wisdom and humanity remain in our memories.

PREFACE

This casebook is unprecedented in legal education in that it represents the views of five faculty who have more than 150 years collective experience teaching and practicing law. The authors share the philosophy that in the study of law, particularly the law of contracts, the student cannot isolate theory or practice from one another, that theory and practice are not mutually exclusive concepts. In service of this approach, each of the authors brings her or his personal experience as a practitioner and an academic to the organization, content, and pedagogy of the casebook. We appreciate the willingness and cooperation of Matthew Bender & Company, Inc., a member of the LexisNexis Group, in embracing this project and seeing it through to completion.

We hope and expect that both faculty and students will find our book to be more valuable than the usual law school casebook. Our book emphasizes transactional and drafting considerations, law practice pointers, and recent court decisions. Hence, the title is CONTRACT LAW AND PRACTICE. Although the book is longer than the typical contracts casebook, the length reflects our conscious choice to provide depth of coverage and, presumably, the depth of understanding that should result.

We also hope that readers of this book will find it to be as interesting and helpful to them, as we found its preparation to be.

Gerald E. Berendt
Rebecca Cochran
Doris Estelle Long
Robert J. Nye
John H. Scheid

ACKNOWLEDGMENTS

The authors wish to acknowledge the support of their respective law schools for their cooperation and support during the research and writing of this casebook. And we owe a special debt of gratitude to Gwen Konigsfeld, Faculty Secretaries Supervisor, whose hard work and patience with the authors eased our labors substantially. Professors Cochran, Long, Nye and Scheid wish to thank Professor Berendt for his extra efforts in organizing the project and editing of the second edition of the casebook.

Professor Berendt thanks his research assistants Michael DeMarino, Anish Parikh, and Sanket Shah, students at The John Marshall Law School. And most important he wishes to thank his family, Emily, Sarah, Jack, Michael, Sherri, Joshua, and Tess for their patience over the years spent researching and writing his contribution to this book.

Professor Cochran thanks Mary Boston, Erin Glaser, Holly Horton, and Richard Freshwater for their assistance. She also gratefully acknowledges the support of Leo Chmielewski for his help and humor.

Professor Long thanks Anne Mudd, Teuta Bitucci, and Daniel Sullivan — students at The John Marshall Law School and research assistants extraordinaire. They found the needle in the haystack, even when it looked like the haystack never existed. Finally, but most importantly, she owes a special debt of gratitude to her sister Karen, who put up with the piles of paper around the house, and to Dad and Mom, who taught her nothing is impossible, not even finishing this project.

Professor Nye acknowledges the valuable assistance of Paul Kolbeck and Eugene Goryunov, who assisted in the revision and update of the contract breach and remedies chapters. He is also grateful for the assistance of his son, attorney Jonathan D. Nye, whose views contributed to the original design and re-design of those chapters. And finally, he thanks his wife Rebecca, son Howard, and daughter Dr. Elizabeth R. Nye for their support during preparation of both the original and update editions of the work.

Professor Scheid thanks his research assistants Matthew May and Daniel Saeedi, John Marshall Law School students, for their diligence in finding cases, points, and authorities. He also thanks his wife Nancy, for her encouragement that indeed there was light at the end of the tunnel, his children Mary Kay, Julie and Daniel for their understanding and patience, and his son, John, a fellow attorney, for bringing a fresh and insightful perspective to the study of contracts.

We express our thanks to the authors and publishers for permission to reprint portions of the following copyrighted material:

Richard A. Posner, ECONOMIC ANALYSIS IN THE LAW (4th ed. 1992). Copyright © 1992 by Richard A. Posner. Reproduced with Permission of Aspen Law & Business. [*See* chapter 1 pp. 27-31.]

Dennis M. Patterson, *The Philosophical Origins of Modern Contract Doctrine: An Open Letter to Professor James Gordley*, 1991 WIS.L. REV. 1432 (1991). Copyright © 1991 by Wisconsin University. Reprinted with permission. [*See* chapter 11 p. 547.]

John D. Calamari & Joseph M. Perillo, *A Plea For a Uniform Parol Evidence Rule and Principles of Contract Interpretation*, 42 IND L.J. 333 (1967). Copyright © 1967 by the Trustees of Indiana University. Reprinted with permission. [*See* chapter 12 pp. 597-598.]

John D. Calamari & Joseph M. Perillo, *The Parol Evidence, Is It Necessary?* 44 N.Y.U. L. REV. 972 (1969). Copyright © 1969 by New York University. Reprinted with permission. [*See* chapter 12 p. 642.]

Table of Contents

A COMPLETE SYNOPSIS FOR EACH CHAPTER APPEARS AT
THE BEGINNING OF THE CHAPTER

Table of Contents

Table of Contents

Table of Contents

Table of Contents

Table of Contents

PART I

CONTRACT FORMATION

This casebook is divided into two parts: Part I — Contract Formation and Part II — Honoring Contract Obligations. In Part I — Contract Formation, Section A is an Overview consisting of Chapter One, which is devoted to Legal Issues and Business Policy. There, we shall identify the sources of contract law. We shall also consider the multifold and sometimes interrelated public policies contract law may serve, including asking whether contract law should be applicable to all types of transactions and dealings in society. The issues and policies studied in this first chapter permeate the remainder of the study.

In Section B — Traditional Contract Formation, we shall study the process by which parties negotiate and reach binding agreements. Following the approach taken by many courts when deciding contract cases, we shall consider the basic elements of the contract in chronological sequence, paralleling the typical process, which leads to agreement. Thus, Chapter Two is devoted to Offers of Contractual Terms, since ordinarily the formation process begins with one party making an offer to the other. The next step in the bargaining process is usually acceptance. Therefore, Chapter Three concentrates on Acceptance of Offers. Chapter Four, Bargained-For Consideration, takes up another element which the courts frequently seek to identify before enforcing agreements, that is consideration. And Chapter Five deals with the judicial requirement of Reasonable Certainty of Terms before the court may enforce the agreement.

The traditional approach to contract formation addressed in Section B is not the only legal paradigm for the enforcement of promises or recovery for losses incurred during transactions. In Section C — Alternative Theories of Recovery, we shall explore these alternatives. In Chapter Six, we shall study the equitable principles associated with the Avoidance of Unjust Enrichment, including the cause of action in quasi-contract. And in Chapter Seven, we shall explore Reliance and Promissory Estoppel.

Having studied the basic elements for establishing the existence of a contract or an alternative theory for recovery, we then turn to reasons parties frequently assert for denying enforcement to agreements. Section D — Defenses to Contract Formation begins with Chapter Eight, which considers defenses associated with the Impairment of Free Will: Duress, Fraud, Unconscionability and Incapacity. Chapter Nine — Impact of External Law focuses on the defenses of illegality and returns to questions of public policy first encountered in Chapter One. In Chapter Ten, we shall consider the Statute of Frauds, which requires that some agreements be in writing to be enforceable.

SECTION A

OVERVIEW

The purpose of the Overview, which consists of Chapter One, is to identify the sources of contract law and to invite the student to consider why society has found it necessary to create and employ contract law. Here, we shall be introduced to contract law's possible policy objectives as well as its limitations with respect to societal dealings. Students should draw upon the materials encountered in the Overview during the remainder of their study of contract law, and the Notes & Questions in the remaining chapters call upon them to consider broader policy questions in their study of the various components of contract law.

CHAPTER 1

LEGAL ISSUES AND BUSINESS POLICY

A. INTRODUCTION

1.   Sources of Contract Law

Contract law, as it is manifested in most jurisdictions within the United States, is derived from two general sources, common law and statutory law.

The "common law" of contracts has evolved over hundreds of years, on a case-by-case basis, by judges applying generally accepted principles to actual disputes. In Anglo-American jurisprudence, the common law has been augmented by the doctrine of stare decisis under which judges generally consider themselves bound by prior judicial decisions. Under this doctrine, once a set of principles has been applied to a certain set of facts, the courts will strive to follow those principles in similar situations which later arise. This commitment of the judiciary to treat like cases alike has not, however, prevented the courts from modifying, adjusting or abandoning principles no longer in conformity with societal and commercial norms or expectations. Such departures are frequently gradual and characterized by the indirect erosion of long-accepted doctrine, with changes often initiated by courts forging exceptions to a general rule. The number of exceptions may increase, disclosing the irrationality or weakness of the previously prevailing principle, and eventually the courts may choose to abandon the old doctrine in favor of new principles. In a sense, the development of the common law has been a "trial and error" process under which the courts have embraced, modified, discovered and experimented with a wide variety of principles designed to serve society's needs. The courts tend to cling to principles which work while seeking substitute approaches for, and discarding, those which do not.

During the last century, another method of influencing common law developments has become prominent. Courts have become increasingly responsive to research and scholarly criticism in academic journals, treatises, and other authoritative publications. Although influential commentaries on the law were known to jurists and lawyers hundreds of years ago, the impact of such secondary sources on development of the law grew dramatically in the twentieth century with the proliferation of law journals, books and treatises easily acquired by judges, practitioners, scholars and law students. Among the many publications devoted to contract law published in the last hundred years, perhaps the most influential have been THE RESTATEMENT OF CONTRACTS, published in 1932, and THE RESTATEMENT SECOND OF CONTRACTS, published in 1981. Promulgated by the American Law Institute (ALI) under the supervision of Chief Reporter, Professor Samuel Williston, the original RESTATEMENT was designed to be an authoritative exposition of the subject. Professor Arthur L. Corbin, the other giant of contracts jurisprudence in the twentieth century, served as a Special Adviser and the Reporter on Remedies for the original RESTATEMENT.

Drafting of THE RESTATEMENT SECOND was supervised by Professor Robert Braucher and Professor E. Allen Farnsworth, with criticism and suggestions from Professor Corbin, who served as Consultant until his death in 1967. More than a simple restatement of prevailing "black letter" rules, the RESTATEMENT SECOND is the product of the combined efforts of noted judges, scholars and practitioners to refine the RESTATEMENT's analysis and incorporate new developments, particularly the impact of the Uniform Commercial Code. Careful not to denigrate the original document, the drafters of the RESTATEMENT SECOND produced a substantially new work which was more than a mere effort to restate the law, but also sought to incorporate bold suggestions for changes and refinements in the law in response to social changes. As of July 2006, the ALI's website reported no effort to draft a third RESTATEMENT OF CONTRACTS.

The Uniform Commercial Code (U.C.C.) contains statutory provisions which govern several commercial subjects, including sales of goods. Drafted by the National Conference of Commissioners on Uniform State Laws (NCCUSL) in 1952, the U.C.C. has been enacted with some variations by all states except Louisiana. The Code is prefaced by a "General Comment" section indicating that its purpose is to promote uniformity among the states. Of the now ten articles in the Uniform Commercial Code, three have significant effect on contract law: Article 2 governing the sales of goods; Article 2A concerning certain leases; and Article 9 dealing with the assignment of contract rights. Although the U.C.C. has successfully reduced to statutory form many of the common law rules of contract law, it has also modified traditional contract law in a number of ways, and in some areas yielding different rules for the sales of goods than for other contracts. Where the Code is silent, courts have continued to draw upon traditional common law principles for guidance when deciding disputes over contracts for the sale of goods. Similarly, there has been a noticeable tendency in the courts to borrow principles from the U.C.C. when deciding disputes over transactions outside the established coverage of the Code. Indeed, the drafters of the RESTATEMENT SECOND acknowledged that they revamped many provisions from the RESTATEMENT FIRST to harmonize them with the U.C.C.

In 2003, the NCCUSL approved a set of revisions to Articles 2 and 2A of the U.C.C. Some of the revisions were not as far-reaching as those proposed by consumer groups and the Reporter selected to draft the revisions. The draft that was approved is controversial and is considered by some to be favorable to business interests at the expense of consumers. The states have been slow to amend their existing versions of the U.C.C. to incorporate the changes in the revised Articles 2 and 2A. As of July 2006, the website for the NCCUSL reported that legislatures in only two states, Kansas and Oklahoma, had bills introduced to amend their existing versions of the U.C.C., but neither state had enacted the legislation.

2.   Purposes of Contract Law

According to Section 1 of the RESTATEMENT (SECOND) OF CONTRACTS (1981), "[a] contract is a promise or set of promises for the breach of which the law gives a remedy, or the performance of which the law in some way recognizes as a duty." It is often said that contracts are the product of a consensual relationship between the parties to the agreement; that is, the parties themselves enter into a bargain, setting the terms of their obligations to one another. It is also frequently said that for a contract to exist, the parties must have a meeting of the minds. Thus, contract law is sometimes characterized as "private law," wherein the parties, rather than the courts or legislature, are the source of the duties governing the relationship. Although our courts have to a great extent left the parties free to strike their own bargains, the parties sometimes fail to express their intentions unequivocally, both during the process of contract formation and in their agreement, once reached. Thus, when disputes arise over whether there is a contract or over a contract's terms, the parties may call upon the courts to resolve their differences. To deal with those instances in which the parties have not clearly expressed their intentions, the courts have devised a set of "default" rules or principles designed to serve a number of possible objectives. Although some jurists, lawyers and students are prone to applying such principles, like those found in the RESTATEMENT (SECOND) OF CONTRACTS, in a formalistic, mechanical manner, effective advocacy requires an understanding of their purposes and objectives.

The principles governing the law of contracts have evolved over many years through the process of common law decision-making and legislation, and those principles have been designed to serve many purposes. Sometimes, judges will take great pains to identify and explain the public policy or objective of a default rule employed to resolve a dispute in a given case. In other instances, the purpose of applied doctrine will remain unarticulated. In some situations, a selected principle may serve several purposes. In other instances, policy objectives may conflict with one another, inviting the court to choose among the competing policies and rules. Moreover, judges, academics and advocates may disagree over which policies should be pursued in a given situation.

Without purporting to be an exhaustive list of the possible purposes behind the default rules and principles of contract law, the editors offer the following purposes frequently identified by judges, advocates and academics:

1. Consent Theory. By manifesting their intention to be legally bound, promisors and promisees have consented to a legally enforceable agreement, a contract. Contract law should be designed to impose individual responsibility on those who make such promises (promisors). Randy E. Barnett, *A Consent Theory of Contract*, 86 COLUM. L. REV. 269 (1986).

2. Will Theory. Contract law should be designed to foster individual liberty, private autonomy, and freedom of transaction in the private sector, subject to minimum controls in the name of collective or public interests. Courts should vindicate the intentions of promisors and promisees who willingly exercise this "freedom of contract." Lon L. Fuller, *Consideration and Form*, 41 COLUM. L. REV. 799 (1941).

3. Promise Theory. Contract law is necessary to uphold moral values by recognizing the sanctity of promise. When a promisor invokes the norm of promising, he or she should be held to his commitment. Charles Fried, CONTRACT AS PROMISE: A THEORY OF CONTRACTUAL OBLIGATION (1981).

4. Reliance Theory. Contract law should be designed to protect promisees and their reasonable expectations. When promisees act in reliance upon others' promises, courts should protect them from injury due to broken promises to avoid injustice. Patrick S. Atiyah, THE RISE AND FALL OF FREEDOM OF CONTRACT (1979).

5. Utilitarian Economic Theory. The principles of contract law should be designed to maximize the potential gains from transactions by facilitating the process of voluntary trade. Contract law should be utilitarian and based on free market principles. Anthony T. Kronman and Richard A. Posner, THE ECONOMICS OF CONTRACT LAW (1979).

6. Critical Legal Studies Theory. Contract law based on any or all of the foregoing principles is not "value neutral," as some of the proponents of the foregoing principles would have us believe. From its inception, contract law has been designed to protect and promote particular vested interests and privileged classes, the "haves" at the expense of the "have nots." Private law, including contract law, should be deconstructed and then reconstructed to serve altruistic, societal interests in the pursuit of social justice rather than the venal interests of individuals. Duncan Kennedy, *Form and Substance in Private Law Adjudication,* 89 HARV. L. REV. 1685 (1976).

7. Relational Theory. Rather than concentrate on discrete transactions or isolated agreements as events between equally situated parties, adherents of this approach "emphasize the social and interpersonal relationships between the parties to the contract." James W. Fox Jr., *Relational Contract Theory and Democratic Citizenship,* 54 CASE W. RES. L. REV. 1, 5 (2003). Unlike the other schools of thought that embrace a neoclassical model and focus on offer and acceptance and the exchange of promises, this theory focuses on social practices, normative behavior, long-term relationships and how these factors operate together to influence transactions. There are many variations on relational theory. The founding spokesperson of this view is Professor Ian R. Macneil. Macneil, THE NEW SOCIAL CONTRACT: AN INQUIRY INTO MODERN CONTRACTUAL RELATIONS (1980). *See also* Stewart Macaulay, *An Empirical View of Contract,* 1985 WIS. L. REV. 465; Robert E. Scott, *The Case for Formalism in Relational Contract,* 94 NW. L. REV. 847 (2000).

The first four purposes of contract law identified above are associated with the traditional consensual, "freedom of contract" model of contract law. The fifth view has become increasingly influential in recent years and is championed by a number of academics and jurists associated with the "law and economics" movement. The sixth view emanates from developments in philosophy and literary criticism frequently characterized as postmodernism. Its proponents in legal academia are known as the "critical legal studies" movement. The seventh school of thought seeks to move beyond the "neoclassical" models of contract law represented in other views, moving beyond the bargain model to a model based on interpersonal relationships. Although the courts continue to rely on the traditional principles set forth in the first four purposes, other objectives, including those found in purposes five, six and seven, are influential in the development of the law as well.

The materials which follow invite us to consider the purposes and policies behind the law of contracts, whether one or more of those objectives should be given preference over the others, and whether the adoption and application of certain default rules in particular cases serve one or more of those principles.

B.   PUBLIC POLICY AND ENFORCING PROMISES

COHEN v. COWLES MEDIA CO.
457 N.W.2d 199 (Minn. 1990)

SIMONETT, Justice:

This case asks whether a newspaper's breach of its reporter's promise of anonymity to a news source is legally enforceable. We conclude the promise is not enforceable, neither as a breach of contract claim nor, in this case, under promissory estoppel. We affirm the court of appeals' dismissal of plaintiff's claim based on fraudulent misrepresentation, and reverse the court of appeals' allowance of the breach of contract claim.

Claiming a reporter's promise to keep his name out of a news story was broken, plaintiff Dan Cohen sued defendants Northwest Publications, Inc., publisher of the *St. Paul Pioneer Press Dispatch (Pioneer Press)*, and Cowles Media Company, publisher of the *Minneapolis Star and Tribune (Star Tribune)*. The trial court . . . jury then found liability on both claims and awarded plaintiff $200,000 compensatory damages jointly and severally against the defendants. In addition, the jury awarded punitive damages of $250,000 against each defendant.

The court of appeals (2-1 decision) . . . ruled, however, that misrepresentation had not been proven as a matter of law and, therefore, set aside the punitive damages award. The panel upheld the jury's finding of a breach of contract and affirmed the award of $200,000 compensatory damages. . . . We granted petitions for further review from all parties.

On October 27, 1982, in the closing days of the state gubernatorial election campaign, Dan Cohen separately approached Lori Sturdevant, the *Star Tribune* reporter, and Bill Salisbury, the *Pioneer Press* reporter, and to each stated in so many words: I have some documents which may or may not relate to a candidate in the upcoming election, and if you will give me a promise of confidentiality, that is that I will be treated as an anonymous source, that my name will not appear in any material in connection with this, and you will also agree that you're not going to pursue with me a question of who my source is, then I'll furnish you with the documents.

Sturdevant and Salisbury were experienced reporters covering the gubernatorial election and knew Cohen as an active Republican associated with the Wheelock Whitney campaign. Cohen told Sturdevant that he would also be offering the documents to other news organizations. Neither reporter informed Cohen that their promises of confidentiality were subject to approval or revocation by their editors. Both reporters promised to keep Cohen's identity anonymous, and both intended to keep that promise. At trial Cohen testified he insisted on anonymity because he feared retaliation from the news media and politicians. Cohen turned over to each reporter copies of two public court records concerning Marlene Johnson, the DFL [Democratic Farm Labor] candidate for lieutenant governor. The first was a record of a 1969 case against Johnson for three counts of unlawful assembly, subsequently dismissed; the second document was a 1970 record of conviction for petit theft, which was vacated about a year later. . . .

Both newspapers, on the same day, then interviewed Marlene Johnson for her explanation and reaction. The *Star Tribune* also assigned a reporter to find the original court records in the dead-storage vaults. The reporter discovered that Gary Flakne, known to be a Wheelock Whitney supporter, had checked out the records a day earlier; no one, before Flakne, had looked at the records for years. The reporter called Flakne and asked why he had checked out the records. Flakne replied, "I did it for Dan Cohen." The *Star Tribune* editors thereafter conferred and decided to publish the story the next day including Dan Cohen's identity. Acting independently, the *Pioneer Press Dispatch* editors also decided to break their reporter's promise and to publish the story with Cohen named as the source. . . .

The decision to identify Cohen in the stories was the subject of vigorous debate within the editorial staffs of the two newspapers. Some staff members argued that the reporter's promise of confidentiality should be honored at all costs. Some contended that the Johnson incidents were not newsworthy and did not warrant publishing, and, in any case, if the story was published, it would be enough to identify the source as a source close to the Whitney campaign. Other editors argued that not only was the Johnson story newsworthy but so was identification of Cohen as the source; that to attribute the story to a veiled source would be misleading and cast suspicion on others; and that the Johnson story was already spreading throughout the news media community and was discoverable from other sources not bound by confidentiality. Then, too, the *Star Tribune* had editorially endorsed the Perpich-Johnson ticket; some of its editors feared if the newspaper did not print the Johnson story, other news media would, leaving the *Star Tribune* vulnerable to a charge it was protecting the ticket it favored. Salisbury and Sturdevant both objected strongly to the editorial decisions to identify Cohen as the source of the court records. Indeed, Sturdevant refused to attach her name to the story.

Promising to keep a news source anonymous is a common, well-established journalistic practice. So is the keeping of those promises. None of the editors or reporters who testified could recall any other instance when a reporter's promise of confidentiality to a source had been overruled by the editor. Cohen, who had many years' experience in politics and public relations, . . . said this was the first time in his experience that an editor or a reporter did not honor a promise to a source.

The next day, October 28, 1982, both newspapers published stories about Johnson's arrests and conviction. Both articles published Cohen's name, along with denials by the regular Whitney campaign officials of any connection with the published stories. Under the headline, Marlene Johnson arrests disclosed by Whitney ally, the *Star Tribune* also gave Johnson's explanation of the arrests and identified Cohen as a "political associate of IR gubernatorial candidate Wheelock Whitney" and named the advertising firm where Cohen was employed. The *Pioneer Press Dispatch* quoted Johnson as saying the release of the information was "a last-minute smear campaign."

The same day as the two newspaper articles were published, Cohen was fired by his employer. The next day, October 29, a columnist for the *Star Tribune* attacked Cohen and his "sleazy" tactics, with, ironically, no reference to the newspaper's own ethics in dishonoring its promise. A day later the *Star Tribune* published a cartoon on its editorial page depicting Dan Cohen with a garbage can labeled "last minute campaign smears."

Cohen could not sue for defamation because the information disclosed was true. He couched his complaint, therefore, in terms of fraudulent misrepresentation and breach of contract. We now consider whether these two claims apply here. . . .

A contract, it is said, consists of an offer, an acceptance, and consideration. Here, we seemingly have all three, plus a breach. We think, however, the matter is not this simple.

Unquestionably, the promises given in this case were intended by the promisors to be kept. The record is replete with the unanimous testimony of reporters, editors, and journalism experts that protecting a confidential source of a news story is a sacred trust, a matter of "honor," of "morality," and required by professional ethics. Only in dire circumstances might a promise of confidentiality possibly be ethically broken, . . . and instances were cited where a reporter has gone to jail rather than reveal a source. The keeping of promises is professionally important for at least two reasons. First, to break a promise of confidentiality which has induced a source to give information is dishonorable. Secondly, if it is known that promises will not be kept, sources may dry up. The media depend on confidential sources for much of their news; significantly, at least up to now, it appears that journalistic ethics have adequately protected confidential sources.

The question before us, however, is not whether keeping a confidential promise is ethically required but whether it is legally enforceable; whether, in other words, the law should superimpose a legal obligation on a moral and ethical obligation. The two obligations are not always coextensive.

The newspapers argue that the reporter's promise should not be contractually binding because these promises are usually given clandestinely and orally, hence they are often vague, subject to misunderstanding, and a fertile breeding ground for lawsuits. . . . Perhaps so, and this may be a factor to weigh in the balance; but this objection goes only to problems of proof, rather than to the merits of having such a cause of action at all. Moreover, in this case at least, we have a clear-cut promise.

The law, however, does not create a contract where the parties intended none. . . . Nor does the law consider binding every exchange of promises. *See, e.g.,* MINN. STAT. CH. 553 (1988) (abolishing breaches of contract to marry); *see also* RESTATEMENT SECOND OF CONTRACTS §§ 189–91 (1981) (promises impairing family relations are unenforceable). We are not persuaded that in the special milieu of media newsgathering a source and a reporter ordinarily believe they are engaged in making a legally binding contract. They are not thinking in terms of offers and acceptances in any commercial or business sense. The parties understand that the reporter's promise of anonymity is given as a moral commitment, but a moral obligation alone will not support a contract. . . . Indeed, a payment of money which taints the integrity of the newsgathering function, such as money paid a reporter for the publishing of a news story, is forbidden by the ethics of journalism.

What we have here, it seems to us, is an "I'll-scratch-your-back-if-you'll-scratch-mine" accommodation. The source, for whatever reasons, wants certain information published. The reporter can only evaluate the information after receiving it, which is after the promise is given; and the editor can only make a reasonable, informed judgment after the information received is put in the larger context of the news. The durability and duration of the confidence is usually left unsaid, dependent on unfolding developments; and none of the parties can safely predict the consequences of publication. . . . Each party, we think, assumes the risks of what might happen, protected only by the good faith of the other party.

In other words, contract law seems here an ill fit for a promise of news source confidentiality. To impose a contract theory on this arrangement puts an unwarranted legal rigidity on a special ethical relationship, precluding necessary consideration of factors underlying that ethical relationship. We conclude that a contract cause of action is inappropriate for these particular circumstances. . . .

But if a confidentiality promise is not a legally binding contract, might the promise otherwise be enforceable? In *Christensen v. Minneapolis Mun. Employees Retirement Bd.*, 331 N.W.2d 740, 747 (Minn. 1983), we declined to apply a "conventional contract approach, with its strict rules of offer and acceptance" in the context of public pension entitlements, pointing out this approach "tends to deprive the analysis of the relationship between the state and its employees of a needed flexibility." We opted instead for a promissory estoppel analysis. The doctrine of promissory estoppel implies a contract in law where none exists in fact. According to the doctrine, well-established in this state, a promise expected or reasonably expected to induce definite action by the promisee that does induce action is binding if injustice can be avoided only by enforcing the promise. . . .

In our case we have, without dispute, the reporters' unambiguous promise to treat Cohen as an anonymous source. The reporters expected that promise to induce Cohen to give them the documents, which he did to his detriment. The promise applied only to Cohen's identity, not to anything about the court records themselves.

We are troubled, however, by the third requirement for promissory estoppel, namely, the requirement that injustice can only be avoided by enforcing the promise. Here Cohen lost his job; but whether this is an injustice which should be remedied requires the court to examine a transaction fraught with moral ambiguity. Both sides proclaim their own purity of intentions while condemning the other side for "dirty tricks." Anonymity gives the source deniability, but deniability, depending on the circumstances, may or may not deserve legal protection. If the court applies promissory estoppel, its inquiry is not limited to whether a promise was given and broken, but rather the inquiry is into all the reasons why it was broken.

Lurking in the background of this case has been the newspapers' contention that any state-imposed sanction in this case violates their constitutional rights of a free press and free speech. . . . Under the contract analysis earlier discussed, the focus was more on whether a binding promise was intended and breached, not so much on the contents of that promise or the nature of the information exchanged for the promise. *See* RESTATEMENT (SECOND) OF CONTRACTS, ch. 8, introductory note (1981) ("In general, parties may contract as they wish, and courts will enforce their agreements without passing on their substance."). Thus the court of appeals, using a contract approach, concluded that applying "neutral principles" of contract law either did not trigger First Amendment scrutiny or, if it did, the state's interest in freedom of contract outweighed any constitutional free press rights. . . . Because we decide that contract law does not apply, we have not up to now had to consider First Amendment implications. But now we must. Under a promissory estoppel analysis there can be no neutrality towards the First Amendment. In deciding whether it would be unjust not to enforce the promise, the court must necessarily weigh the same considerations that are weighed for whether the First Amendment has been violated. The court must balance the constitutional rights of a free press against the common law interest in protecting a promise of anonymity.

For example, was Cohen's name "newsworthy"? Was publishing it necessary for a fair and balanced story? Would identifying the source simply as being close to the Whitney campaign have been enough? The witnesses at trial were sharply divided on these questions. Under promissory estoppel, the court cannot avoid answering these questions, even though to do so would mean second-guessing the newspaper editors. *See, e.g., Miami Herald Pub. Co. v. Tornillo*, 418 U.S. 241, 258 (1974) ("The choice of material to go into a newspaper . . . constitute[s] the exercise of editorial control and judgment," a process critical to the First Amendment guarantees of a free press.). Of critical significance in this case, we think, is the fact that the promise of anonymity arises in the classic First Amendment context of the quintessential public debate in our democratic society, namely, a political source involved in a political campaign. The potentiality for civil damages for promises made in this context chills public debate, a debate which Cohen willingly entered albeit hoping to do so on his own terms. In this context, and considering the nature of the political story involved, it seems to us that the law best leaves the parties here to their trust in each other.

We conclude that in this case enforcement of the promise of confidentiality under a promissory estoppel theory would violate defendants' First Amendment rights. In cases of this kind, the United States Supreme Court has said it will proceed cautiously, deciding only in a "discrete factual context.". . . We, too, are not inclined to decide more than we have to decide. There may be instances where a confidential source would be entitled to a remedy such as promissory estoppel, when the state's interest in enforcing the promise to the source outweighs First Amendment considerations, but this is not such a case. Plaintiff's claim cannot be maintained on a contract theory. Neither is it sustainable under promissory estoppel. The judgment for plaintiff is reversed.

Affirmed in part and reversed in part.

. . .

YETKA, Justice (dissenting):

I would affirm the court of appeals and allow Cohen to recover on either a contract or promissory estoppel theory. The simple truth of the matter is that the appellants made a promise of confidentiality to Cohen in consideration for information they considered newsworthy. That promise was broken and, as a direct consequence, Cohen lost his job. Under established rules of contract law, the appellants should be responsible for the consequences of that broken promise. The first amendment is being misused to avoid liability under the doctrine of promissory estoppel. The result of this is to carve out yet another special privilege in favor of the press that is denied other citizens.

I dissent because I believe that the news media should be compelled to keep their promises like anyone else. If they did not intend to keep the promise they made to Cohen, they should not have made it or should have refused to use the proffered information. Alternatively, after accepting the information subject to the confidentiality agreement, the press could have printed the story without revealing the source or could have simply attributed the source to "someone close to the Whitney campaign" without revealing Cohen's name.

I find the consequences of this decision deplorable. First, potential news sources will now be reluctant to give information to reporters. As a result, the public could very well be denied far more important information about candidates for public office relevant to evaluating their qualifications than the rather trivial infractions disclosed here. Second, it offends the fundamental principle of equality under the law.

This decision sends out a clear message that if you are wealthy and powerful enough, the law simply does not apply to you; contract law, it now seems, applies only to millions of ordinary people. It is unconscionable to allow the press, on the one hand, to hide behind the shield of confidentiality when it does not want to reveal the source of its information; yet, on the other hand, to violate confidentiality agreements with impunity when it decides that disclosing the source will help make its story more sensational and profitable. During the Watergate crisis, the press published many pious editorials urging that the laws be enforced equally against everyone, even the President of the United States. Nevertheless, the press now argues that the law should not apply to them because they alone are entitled to make "editorial decisions" as to what the public should read, see, or hear and whether the source of that information should be disclosed. . . .

In the 19th century, the phrases "scandal sheet" and "yellow journalism" became common adjectives for disreputable publications. It would be tragic if these colorful descriptions regained popular usage because of the practices of a few of the more sensational "journalistic" enterprises which appear to be growing in number and popularity, replacing the great newspapers of the past.

Perhaps it is time in these United States to return to treating the press the same as any other citizen. Let them print anything they choose to print, but make them legally responsible if they break their promises or act negligently in connection with what they print — free of any special protection. . . . The decision of this court makes this a sad day in the history of a responsible press in America. Because I firmly believe that no one should be above the law, including the President of the United States or the news media, I would affirm the court of appeals.

KELLEY, Justice (dissenting):

A majority of this court recently held that a commercial media defendant, who the jury found had done a "hatchet job" with constitutional malice on a public official through distortion and/or omission of established facts and through unwarranted inference, was immune from tort liability, unlike the rest of the citizens of this state, corporate or private, who would undoubtedly be liable in tort for that type of conduct. I joined the dissent of Justice Yetka in that case. . . . In my opinion, the majority today, applying a somewhat different analysis, affords to that same commercial media immunity from liability from an unmistakable breach of contract, although any other corporate or private citizen of this state under similar circumstances would most certainly have been liable in damages for breach of contract.

While I agree with the majority that the trial court erred in not granting the defendants' post-trial motions for judgment notwithstanding the verdict on the misrepresentation claim, I remain unpersuaded by the majority's analysis that, notwithstanding that all of the elements of a legal contract and its breach are here present, the contract is unenforceable because "the parties intended none." It reaches this conclusion even as it concedes that the promises given by the agents and employees of these defendants was intended by them to be kept. . . . Rather than affording Cohen a remedy for the considerable damage he sustained . . . , the majority, it seems to me, engaged in or came very close to engaging in some inappropriate appellate fact finding, to-wit, that each of the parties did not intend a contract and assumed the risk "of what might happen." . . . I . . . join the dissent of Justice Yetka which highlights the perfidy of these defendants, the liability for which they now seek to escape by trying to crawl under the aegis of the First Amendment, which, in my opinion, has nothing to do with the case. . . . Today's decision serves to inhibit rather than to promote the objectives of the First Amendment by "drying up" potential sources of information on public matters. I dissent.

NOTES & QUESTIONS

1. Why did the Minnesota Supreme Court majority conclude that defendant newspapers and Cohen had no contract? Which contract law theory or theories does the majority opinion draw upon? Why do the dissenting judges disagree with the majority? Can their dissents be explained on the basis that they have different reasons for enforcing promises? *See* Barnett, *Some Problems with Contract as Promise,* 77 CORNELL L. REV. 1022, 1031–1033 (1992).

2. *Drafting exercise:* In light of the Minnesota Supreme Court's decision, could you draft an agreement under which a news source like Cohen could obtain an enforceable promise of anonymity from a newspaper in return for information? Would it make a difference if that agreement were written rather than oral, as it was in the actual case?

3. On appeal, the United States Supreme Court, by a 4–to–3 vote, reversed "[t]he Minnesota Supreme Court's incorrect conclusion that the First Amendment barred Cohen's claim . . . ," and remanded the case to the Minnesota courts for further proceedings including "consideration of whether a promissory estoppel claim had otherwise been established under Minnesota law and whether Cohen's jury verdict could be upheld on a promissory estoppel basis." 111 S. Ct. 2513 (1991). Whether the defendant newspapers breached a traditional contract with Cohen was not an issue before the United States Supreme Court, and the Court expressed no opinion on that matter. On remand, the Minnesota Supreme Court affirmed the trial court jury's verdict for the plaintiff Cohen on a promissory estoppel theory and affirmed the jury's judgment of $200,000 compensatory damages to Cohen. 479 N.W.2d 387 (1992).

C.   CONSENSUAL TRANSACTIONS AND THE MARKET

According to Professor Arthur Corbin, CORBIN ON CONTRACTS 185 (1 Vol. Ed. 1952):

> If there are willing buyers and sellers, there is a market; and it is their willingness that determines value. When two parties agree upon an exchange of this for that, they constitute a part of the market. We have a free market, under our common law, for the reason that the courts have left

it free. They do not require that one person shall pay as much as others may be willing to pay, or that one person shall receive for what he sells as little as others may be willing to receive for a like article. The contracting parties make their own contracts, agree upon their own exchanges, and fix their own values.

To what extent should the market be free to operate? Are there transactions which society should not permit or the courts should not enforce? Consider the facts in the following case, in which a husband agreed to his wife's wishes to adopt a child in return for her agreement that he would keep most of their marital property if they should divorce after the adoption.

STUTZ v. STUTZ
2005 Tenn. App. LEXIS 517 (Tenn. App. 2005)
Appeal denied, 2006 Tenn. LEXIS 33 (Tenn. 2006)

LEE, Judge:

This case involves a divorce and the validity of a postnuptial agreement. Mr. and Ms. Stutz were married more than twenty years. During most of the marriage, they wanted to have children but were unsuccessful. When a child became available for adoption, Ms. Stutz was elated and aggressive in her actions to secure the adoption of the child, but Mr. Stutz was opposed to the adoption of the child. Over the course of several weeks, Ms. Stutz attempted to change Mr. Stutz's mind regarding the adoption. Finally, she suggested that in exchange for his consent to the adoption, they would enter into an agreement dividing the marital estate, and in the event Mr. Stutz was unhappy being a father they would divorce and follow the agreement previously determined. The result was a lengthy postnuptial agreement, which among other things, divided the marital estate giving most of the marital property to Mr. Stutz. Within a few years of the signing of the postnuptial agreement and the adoption, Ms. Stutz filed for divorce. The trial court upheld the validity of the postnuptial agreement with the exception of a section which attempted to waive and/or significantly limit Mr. Stutz's child support obligation. The trial court also granted a divorce to the parties upon Mr. Stutz's motion without conducting an evidentiary hearing. Ms. Stutz appeals. We hold that the postnuptial agreement is invalid as it is contrary to public policy. We further hold that the trial court erred in granting a divorce to the parties in the absence of a stipulation to or proof of grounds for divorce. Accordingly, we reverse the trial court's decision and remand this case for a trial on the division of the marital estate, alimony, divorce, and any remaining issues.

I.

Linda Diane Stutz and David Larry Stutz were married on December 18, 1982. At the time of the marriage, Ms. Stutz, age 26, was working for a freight company and taking college classes at night. Later, she began working for the Tennessee Valley Authority. Mr. Stutz, age 34, had recently started a mechanical contracting business. Neither party had any significant assets or income. Ms. Stutz testified that Mr. Stutz was not drawing any income from the new company and that her salary paid their living expenses for a number of years. During the early years of this marriage, Mr. Stutz worked long hours away from the home at the new company in order to make it a success. Ms. Stutz was working full-time and going to school at night to advance her career. In short, much time was devoted by the parties to their respective careers. Mr. Stutz was an astute businessman and over the years, the company he started, Valley Mechanical, Inc., became very profitable. As the parties prospered financially, they began to travel extensively and acquire assets. In addition to their home in Chattanooga, they purchased a beachfront vacation home in Florida, lots on Watts Bar Lake, a boat, jet skis, diamond rings, other jewelry, and several mink coats.

At the time of trial, Ms. Stutz was a programmer analyst for TVA, earning approximately $50,000 per year, and Mr. Stutz operated Valley Mechanical, Inc, earning $1,082,552.00 in 1996, and $782,502.00 in 1995. The Stutzs had an adjusted gross income in 1997 of approximately $905,000 based on Ms. Stutz's salary at TVA, Mr. Stutz's earnings from Valley Mechanical, Inc., dividends, interest, real estate income, and other sources. During this marriage, Mr. and Ms. Stutz, by virtue of their perseverance and hard work, achieved great financial success and amassed a marital estate worth in excess of $11,000,000.

The parties wanted children, but were unable to conceive a child. Ms. Stutz testified that she had undergone three different surgical procedures in an attempt to become pregnant. She further testified that both parties underwent testing and sought help from two different fertility specialists. Ms. Stutz researched the possibility of *in vitro* fertilization, which they attempted, unsuccessfully, for a short period of time. Mr. Stutz testified that he was completely supportive of the many attempts to have a family and that he, too, desired to have children. At the age of 41, Ms. Stutz underwent a complete hysterectomy. After Ms. Stutz's hysterectomy in 1997, the parties ceased discussing the possibility of having a family.

However, this changed on February 27, 1998, when Ms. Stutz learned of a woman who was pregnant and wanted to surrender her child for adoption. Ms. Stutz was very enthusiastic about the prospective adoption, but was unable to discuss it with Mr. Stutz because he was in Europe on a business trip. On March 2, 1998, Ms. Stutz contacted Lane Avery, a Chattanooga attorney with the law firm of Gearhiser, Peters, Lockaby & Tallent, who had performed legal work for Mr. Stutz's business for many years. Ms. Stutz asked Mr. Avery if anyone in the law firm handled adoptions and was referred to another attorney within the same law firm, Terry Cavett. Ms. Stutz testified that she and Ms. Cavett had multiple telephone conversations over the next few days about the process of an adoption.

When Mr. Stutz returned from Europe on March 9, 1998, Ms. Stutz told him of the prospective adoption. Ms. Stutz was disappointed to learn that Mr. Stutz was not supportive of the idea of the adoption. Ms. Stutz began trying to convince Mr. Stutz to agree to the adoption, but he continued to resist the idea. Despite Mr. Stutz's opposition, on March 11, 1998, Mr. and Ms. Stutz went to the adoption agency handling the adoption and were interviewed. Mr. Stutz continued to disagree with the idea of the adoption and advised the adoption agency that he believed he was too old and that his health was too poor to become a parent. Meanwhile, Ms. Stutz continued to communicate with Ms. Cavett almost daily regarding her progress with locating the birth father and handling the legal aspects of the adoption.

On Friday, March 13, 1998, the couple spent the weekend at their Florida vacation home. Following that trip, Mr. Stutz still had not changed his mind about the adoption and remained adamantly opposed to the idea. On Monday, March 16,

1998, Mr. Stutz contacted Ms. Stutz about an opportunity for a business trip in Puerto Rico with some friends beginning March 18, 1998. Ms. Stutz testified that she agreed to go, but that before leaving Chattanooga she contacted both Ms. Cavett and the adoption agency to inform them of her plan to be out of town for several days.

During the trip to Puerto Rico, Ms. Stutz testified that she called both Ms. Cavett and Peggy Lowe, the director of clinical services at Bethany Christian Services, every morning and every evening for an update on the baby who was due on March 20, 1998. The parties talked about the adoption on several occasions while in Puerto Rico. Mr. Stutz continued to argue against the adoption citing his age, his poor health, the stress caused by his job, the limitations the child would place on their ability to travel, and the financial responsibilities the child would impose on them. Ms. Stutz, concluding that Mr. Stutz's opposition was primarily based on financial concerns, proposed a solution — the parties would enter into an agreement for the division of their assets in the event of a divorce in exchange for Mr. Stutz agreeing to the adoption. Ms. Stutz testified that she suggested an agreement for a fair and equitable property division pursuant to which, other than child support, Mr. Stutz would have no other financial obligation to Ms. Stutz or to the child. Ms. Stutz also testified that her proposal was for the agreement to last one year and that, if within that one year period Mr. Stutz "hated" being a parent, he could walk away, obtain a divorce and the assets would be already divided per the agreement. Mr. Stutz testified that Ms. Stutz set all the parameters for the agreement and that she was only interested in receiving the martial residence, her furs, her jewelry, the Watts Bar Lake lots, a car and one million dollars. Mr. Stutz agreed to this proposal. At the time Ms. Stutz made this proposal she had not seen a financial statement of the parties' net worth. According to Mr. Stutz, upon their return from Puerto Rico, Ms. Stutz contacted Mr. Avery and asked him to begin drafting the postnuptial agreement. Ms. Stutz denies contacting Mr. Avery and denies ever discussing the postnuptial agreement with him except on the morning the agreement was signed. Mr. Avery had no recollection as to whether he consulted with Mr. or Ms. Stutz regarding the drafting of the postnuptial agreement although Mr. Stutz's pager number was on Mr. Avery's handwritten notes.

The baby girl, whom the parties intended to adopt and whom they had agreed to name LaShawn Danielle Stutz, was born on March 20, 1998 while the parties were in Puerto Rico. When Mr. and Ms. Stutz returned home on March 23, 1998, they went to Bethany Christian Services to see the baby. Ms. Stutz bonded with LaShawn immediately upon the baby being placed in her arms. The first visit with LaShawn lasted approximately two hours. Ms. Stutz testified as follows regarding their first visit with LaShawn:

> Mr. Lawrence: Just tell the Court what happened, then, on the 23rd. You're there at Bethany Christian Services and they bring LaShawn in. Just describe what happens on that occasion.

> Ms. Stutz: I had already felt like Shawnee was mine, but when they put her in my arms, all 15 years of disappointment was gone. She was mine just as much as if I had just given birth to that baby. We bonded instantly and she was everything I had ever hoped for in a child.

And David was there, and I had asked him if he wanted to hold her, and he said he was nervous and afraid he would hurt her, and I said, "They're a lot tougher than you think," and he held her. And it was the family I had dreamed of my whole marriage and it was coming to pass right there. She put her little hand around one of his fingers and he just seemed so tender toward her. I mean, I knew that he would love her, if he didn't already. He just seemed to melt right there.

On March 24, 1998, a preliminary home study was conducted by the adoption agency and Mr. and Ms. Stutz were present in the home and participated. Ms. Stutz continued to visit with LaShawn on March 25th, and on March 27th, spending three to four hours with the child on each occasion. On March 29, 1998, Mr. and Ms. Stutz signed the application for adoption with Bethany Christian Services.

While the Stutzs were pursuing the adoption and represented by Terry Cavett, Lane Avery was drafting the postnuptial agreement. Lane Avery had represented Mr. Stutz's business interests since 1983, and done some estate planning for the parties. Mr. Avery was also a social acquaintance of the parties, had visited their Florida home on more than one occasion, and had accompanied them on a pleasure trip to San Francisco. From billing records of the law firm, it appears that legal work on the postnuptial agreement began on March 24, 1998. When asked who he was representing in the drafting of the postnuptial agreement, Mr. Avery responded that he did not represent either party, but that he merely drafted the parties' agreement. However, a letter was introduced into evidence from Mr. Avery to Mr. Stutz dated March 30, 1998, which outlined Tennessee law regarding postnuptial agreements and made references to their discussions regarding limitations on Mr. Stutz's child support obligation. Mr. Stutz testified that he did not seek independent legal advice because he knew he could rely on Mr. Avery. When asked whether he consulted with Ms. Stutz regarding this agreement, Mr. Avery testified as follows:

Mr. Lawrence: Do you have any memory of speaking with Linda Stutz about this agreement prior to its being drafted?

Mr. Avery: I have no particular memory of speaking with either Linda Stutz or David Stutz concerning this agreement during its preparation. However, I must have spoken to one or the other of them.

Mr. Lawrence: Is there any correspondence in your file addressed to Linda Stutz giving her a proposed draft of this Marital Property and Settlement Agreement to review and edit?

Mr. Avery: I have seen no specific letter addressed to Mrs. Stutz.

Mr. Lawrence: Insofar as your billing records are concerned, I understand your testimony to be that you can find no specific reference to the generation of this document?

Mr. Avery: I recall no specific reference to the generation of the document.

Pat Murchison, Mr. Stutz's accountant for many years, testified that he was contacted by Mr. Avery who asked him to meet with Mr. Stutz to prepare an "accurate financial statement." Mr. Avery stressed the importance of full disclosure. He further testified that he did meet with Mr. Stutz and that they put the financial statement together and then forwarded it to Mr. Avery.

According to Ms. Stutz, there had been no mention of the agreement by either party since their return from Puerto Rico, and she had not pursued the idea. However, on either March 30th or 31st, Mr. Stutz came home and presented Ms. Stutz with a postnuptial agreement. As to when she received the postnuptial agreement for the first time, Ms. Stutz testified:

> Ms. Stutz: I believe it was the following Monday or Tuesday night. We hadn't talked about anything about it. We had talked about LaShawn. I knew the court date. [Ms. Stutz is referring to the April 2, 1998, court date wherein the parties were to accept the surrender of LaShawn and receive physical custody of her.] I had told him when the court date was. We had all this stuff lined out. I had taken off from work. I mean, everything was set.
>
> And he came in from work one evening and just threw this agreement down on the couch, and he said, "This is the agreement."
>
> And I — "What?"
>
> And he said, "This is the agreement. This is all you're getting from me. You're not getting anything else. I suggest you read it." So I did.

Ms. Stutz further testified that she was shocked to see the financial disclosure and how much money they had. She said she was aware they had a high standard of living, but was surprised to see what they were worth. Ms. Stutz testified that while she had signed tax returns in the past she had never reviewed them prior to signing and that she had always trusted her husband to handle their finances and never felt the need to ask questions. When asked on direct examination about her reaction to the agreement presented to her by Mr. Stutz, she testified that it was nothing like the agreement she had suggested to him in Puerto Rico. Further, she testified that with respect to the parts she could understand, she knew the document was giving Mr. Stutz the bulk of the marital estate. On April 1, 1998, Ms. Stutz attempted to contact a lawyer to review the agreement, but was unsuccessful.

On the morning of April 2, 1998, the birth mother was to appear before the trial court and surrender her parental rights to the baby. Mr. and Ms. Stutz were to appear later that same morning to accept the surrender, receive guardianship and physical custody of the child. Before appearing in court, however, Mr. and Ms. Stutz went to the law office of Lane Avery for the purpose of signing the postnuptial agreement. Ms. Stutz testified that on the way to Mr. Avery's office she told Mr. Stutz that she had been unable to talk to a lawyer and asked that they postpone the signing of the agreement until she could consult with legal counsel. According to Ms. Stutz, Mr. Stutz said, "No. That kid is not coming in my house unless this is signed today." Ms. Stutz testified to the following regarding her emotional state upon arriving at Mr. Avery's office:

> Mr. Lawrence: So you arrived at the — you had this conversation with David in the car on the way to Lane Avery's office, correct?
>
> Ms. Stutz: Uh-huh. Yes. We drove and that was pretty much it. I mean, after he said no, I'm not postponing it, this kid is not coming into this house, I knew I had to sign or I would never see my baby again.
>
> Mr. Lawrence: How did you feel about that?

Ms. Stutz: I was sick. I was just — I remember feeling really light-headed and — just the emotion of the adoption would have been one thing. I was terrified the birth mother would not show; she might change her mind at the last minute, something. I had never been this close to being a mother. I had never been anywhere near. And Shawnee was literally an hour or so away from me being her mother, her being my little baby, I had originally thought, us being a family.

Mr. Lawrence: I want to focus, though, on what caused you to sign this agreement that you knew to be unfair.

Ms. Stutz: I had held Shawnee. She had my heart in her hand. I was her mother as much as any mother is to their child. Had David been holding a knife to her throat, I would have not felt any differently. I would have never seen that baby again. I know that. He was not going to postpone. That's — that was definite. I was at the crossroads. I could either sign this document, bring my child home, or refuse to sign and never see her again.

Once they arrived at Mr. Avery's office, Mr. and Ms. Stutz were escorted to a room to read and sign the postnuptial agreement. Present in the room with them were Mr. Avery, Mr. Murchison, attorney Jerre Mosley, and two women who were witnesses to the Stutzs' signatures. Mr. Murchison testified that Mr. Avery was clearly in charge of the meeting and that he asked both Mr. and Ms. Stutz to read each page of the agreement and execute the document. Before the agreement was signed, Ms. Stutz asked that the following sentence be added, "In the event of divorce, Mrs. Stutz shall be entitled to sole custody of any adopted child."

[The court reproduced the documents signed by the parties. Mr. Stutz agreed to pay Ms. Stutz $100,000 within 15 days of signing the postnuptial agreement. The agreements also provided that if the parties divorced, Mr. Stutz would receive the bulk of the marital estate, and Ms. Stutz would receive sole custody of any adopted child.]

Immediately following the execution of the . . . documents at Mr. Avery's office, Mr. and Ms. Stutz went to court to accept legal guardianship of LaShawn and then went to Bethany Christian Services to take physical custody of LaShawn.

Throughout this litigation, Mr. Stutz has admitted that he would never have agreed to the adoption of this child without Ms. Stutz signing the postnuptial agreement. Mr. Stutz testified at a deposition, which was read into evidence at the hearing, to the following:

Mr. Lawrence: Would you say that the adoption of LaShawn became conditioned upon the execution of this agreement, that were it not for the execution of this agreement you weren't going to participate in LaShawn's adoption?

Mr. Stutz: That's correct.

Mr. Lawrence: Did you make that known to Linda Stutz?

Mr. Stutz: I'm sure I did.

As per the postnuptial agreement, and in consideration for said agreement, Mr. Stutz forwarded to Ms. Stutz $100,000 within fifteen (15) days of signing the agreement.

The adoption proceeded and a final order of adoption was entered on March 15, 1999. On May 12, 1999, Mr. Mosley forwarded both packages to Mr. Avery with a letter stating that both Mr. and Ms. Stutz had requested their respective package be sent to him.

Despite his initial opposition to the adoption, Mr. Stutz testified at trial that he now believes LaShawn is, "the greatest thing that ever happened to me. She's the love of my life." It is abundantly clear that LaShawn is loved by both her parents.

Nearly three years after the adoption was final, on March 14, 2002, Ms. Stutz filed for divorce alleging irreconcilable differences and inappropriate marital conduct. In his answer, Mr. Stutz admitted that irreconcilable differences existed, but denied that he was guilty of inappropriate marital conduct. On February 24 and 26, 2003, the trial court conducted a hearing regarding the validity of the postnuptial agreement. Final arguments were heard on April 25, 2003, and the case was taken under advisement. Subsequently on June 2, 2003, the trial court issued an order, upholding the validity of the postnuptial agreement, but finding paragraph 22, the provision regarding child support, to be void and unenforceable. The trial court entered an order on July 2, 2003, declaring that Mr. and Ms. Stutz were divorced pursuant to Tenn. Code Ann. § 36-4-129(b), following a hearing on a motion filed by Mr. Stutz requesting that the parties be divorced. The order reserved for further hearing all other issues not previously addressed. On May 13, 2004, an order was entered on issues of child support and parenting. On May 27, 2004, an order was entered regarding summer vacation and parenting time. Ms. Stutz filed a notice of appeal on June 3, 2004 regarding the order upholding the validity of the postnuptial agreement and the order granting a divorce. On June 10, 2004, Mr. Stutz filed a motion to alter or amend and/or for a new trial regarding various matters including child support, attorney's fees, and counseling for the child. Mr. Stutz filed a notice of appeal on June 11, 2004, appealing the final judgment of May 13, 2004. On August 30, 2004, the trial court entered an order denying Mr. Stutz's motion to alter or amend stating that upon the filing of the notice of appeal by Ms. Stutz, the trial court was deprived of jurisdiction to determine the motion to alter or amend.

II.

Ms. Stutz raises two issues on appeal which we restate: (1) Whether the trial court erred in holding that the postnuptial agreement was valid and, (2) whether the trial court erred in decreeing a divorce to the parties absent proof of fault or stipulation by both parties.

III.

The parties in this appeal are well-represented by counsel and present compelling arguments in support of their positions. Ms. Stutz argues that the trial court erred in holding the postnuptial agreement valid. She asserts that the postnuptial agreement violates public policy because part of the consideration for the postnuptial agreement was Mr. Stutz's agreement to adopt the child. Further, she argues that the postnuptial agreement was invalid because it was obtained through duress and undue influence and is unconscionable due to its gross inequity. Also, Ms. Stutz argues that the trial court erred in decreeing a divorce between the parties without an evidentiary hearing or stipulation by both parties.

Mr. Stutz counters that the postnuptial agreement does not violate public policy in that TENN. CODE ANN. § 36-1-109 regarding illegal payments in connection with placement of a child for adoption does not apply to the situation before the court. He asserts that he was not compensating someone for surrendering a child but, rather, was entering into an agreement so that a third party could surrender a child to Ms. Stutz. Mr. Stutz submits that the agreement satisfies the requirements of *Bratton v. Bratton*, 136 S.W.3d 595 (Tenn. 2004). Finally, Mr. Stutz argues that the divorce decree was properly entered based upon Mr. Stutz's admission of grounds for divorce.

IV.

. . .

V.

As a general rule, postnuptial agreements are valid in Tennessee. . . . Postnuptial agreements seek to determine the rights of each spouse in the other's property, spousal support, and related issues in the event of death or divorce. . . . Postnuptial agree ments are generally treated in the same manner as antenuptial and reconciliation agreements.

Postnuptial agreements should be interpreted and enforced as any other contract. . . . As such, they must be supported by adequate consideration. . . . Generally, consideration for a contract may be either a benefit to the promisor or a detriment to, or an obligation upon, the promisee. . . . Marriage itself is sufficient consideration for a prenuptial agreement. . . . Reconciliation in the face of an impending separation or divorce may be adequate consideration. . . . However, the marriage itself cannot act as sufficient consideration for a postnuptial agreement because past consideration cannot support a current promise. . . . There must be consideration flowing to both parties as part of a postnuptial agreement.

Because of the confidential relationship which exists between husband and wife, postnuptial agreements are subjected to close scrutiny by the courts to ensure that they are fair and equitable. . . . Since a husband and wife do not deal at arm's length, a fiduciary duty of the highest degree is imposed in transactions between them. The *Bratton* Court stated:

> While it is lawful and not against public policy for husband and wife to enter into such contracts, yet they are not dealing with each other as strangers at arm's length. The relationship of husband and wife is one of special confidence and trust, requiring the utmost good faith and frankness in their dealings with each other. . . . Transactions of this character are scrutinized by the courts with great care, to the end that no unjust advantage may be obtained by one over the other by means of any oppression, deception, or fraud. Courts of equity will relieve against any unjust advantage procured by any such means, and less evidence is required in such cases to establish the fraud, oppression, or deception than if the parties had been dealing at arm's length as strangers. . . .

Bratton at 601 (quoting *In re Estate of Gab*, 364 N.W.2d 924 (S.D. 1985)).

As with any other contract, a postnuptial agreement must be made for a lawful purpose and must not be contrary to the public policy of the state. . . . With regard to public policy our Supreme Court has stated that, "the public policy of the State is to be found in its Constitution, its laws, its judicial decisions and the applicable rules of common law."*Nashville Ry. & Light Co. v. Lawson*, 144 Tenn. 78, 229 S.W. 741 (Tenn. 1921),*Home Beneficial Association v. White*, 180 Tenn. 585, 177 S.W.2d 545, 546 (Tenn. 1944).

The meaning of the phrase "public policy" is vague and variable; courts have not defined it, and there is no fixed rule to determine what contracts are repugnant to it. The principle that contracts in contravention of public policy are not enforceable should be applied with caution and only in cases plainly within the reasons on which that doctrine rests. It is only because of the dominant public interest that one who, like respondent, has had the benefit of performance by the other party will be permitted to avoid his own promise.

In determining whether this contract is void as being in violation of public policy it is proper to consider the situation of the parties at the time the contract was made and the purposes of the contract. *Hoyt v. Hoyt*, 213 Tenn. 117, 372 S.W.2d 300, 302–303 (Tenn. 1963).

We must now determine whether the agreement entered into by Mr. and Ms. Stutz meets the requirements for a valid and enforceable postnuptial agreement. It is clear from the evidence cited above that the postnuptial agreement in this case constitutes a contract whereby Ms. Stutz exchanges her promise to surrender her equitable share of the marital estate in return for Mr. Stutz's agreement to enter into an adoption to which he is opposed. In this regard, we have noted Ms. Stutz's testimony that Mr. Stutz stated to her "That kid is not coming to my house unless [the postnuptial agreement] is signed today." We have further noted Mr. Stutz's own testimony that the adoption of LaShawn was contingent upon the execution of the postnuptial agreement and that absent execution of the agreement he was not going to participate in the child's adoption.

It is well settled in our state that the best interest of the child is the paramount consideration in an adoption proceeding. . . . It is assumed that persons seeking to adopt a child are motivated by the desire to love and care for the child — motivations that are naturally consistent with the child's best interest. However, the best interest of the child is ignored and the adoption process is subverted when a prospective adoptive parent who is otherwise adamantly opposed to adoption, as was Mr. Stutz, enters into an agreement to effect an adoption for the sole reason that he will realize financial gain if he does so. Monetary enrichment should not be the motivating factor for a consent to an adoption.

Mr. Stutz's motivation for entering into the postnuptial agreement and the adoption was financial. He bargained his consent to the adoption for a larger share of the marital estate in the event of a divorce. An adoption should not be viewed as a business opportunity by an adoptive parent. Nor can we condone Ms. Stutz's actions in entering into the postnuptial agreement. Although in some sense her entrance into the agreement may appear to be less objectionable in that she was willing to sacrifice material goods for the opportunity to raise and nurture the child, she too placed the child's needs second to her own. She wanted a child and did not hesitate to resort to aggressive financial manipulation to get what she wanted without regard for the fact that she was bringing the child into a family in which the father was at the time strongly resistant to the child being a part of that family. We find the agreement arrived at by these parties to be both cynical and self-serving. We further find that it exposed an adopted child to the unreasonable risk of being placed in an environment that was not in that child's best interest. We do not contest the assertion that both parents have come to love the adopted child in this case; however, as noted above, in determining whether a contract violates public policy we consider the situation of the parties when the contract was made. . . . Our Legislature has expressed the public policy of the State regarding payments involved in the surrender of a child for adoption by making it a Class C felony to sell or surrender a child to another person for money or anything of value and to receive such child for such payment of money or thing of value. TENN. CODE ANN.§ 36-1-109. While we agree with Mr. Stutz that this statute is not directly applicable to the facts of this case, we do believe that it evidences the public policy of this State that a consent for a surrender or a consent to adopt is not to be bartered or sold and that an adoptive parent should not profit financially from an adoption. We cannot approve of and enforce an agreement in which a spouse in effect sells his or her consent to an adoption in exchange for a greater share of a marital estate in the event of a divorce. Accordingly, we find that the postnuptial agreement at issue to be invalid and unenforceable as against public policy.

VI.

The next issue we address is whether the trial court erred in granting a divorce to the parties based upon Mr. Stutz's "Motion to Grant Divorce" in which he admitted that he had been guilty of conduct that would entitle Ms. Stutz to a divorce and requested the trial court to declare the parties divorced. . . . We agree with Ms. Stutz that there should have been an evidentiary hearing before the divorce was granted. Because there was neither a stipulation to nor proof as to grounds for divorce, the trial court had no authority underTENN. CODE ANN.§ 36-4-129 to grant a divorce to the parties. We further hold that the issue of marital fault was not litigated during the hearing on the postnuptial agreement and that the notice of appeal was timely filed as to this issue. . . .

VII.

For the foregoing reasons, we reverse the decision of the trial court and remand for a trial on the division of the marital estate, alimony, divorce, any other remaining issues, and for further proceedings consistent with this opinion. The costs on appeal are taxed to Mr. Stutz. . . .

NOTES & QUESTIONS

1. In addition to asserting that the postnuptial agreement was unenforceable as against public policy, Ms. Stutz argued the agreement was invalid because it was the product of duress and undue influence, and she further maintained that the agreement was unconscionable due to the gross disparity in terms. Do these additional defenses to enforcement of the postnuptial agreement fall within the area of "public policy" defenses? Or do these defenses relate to the formation process itself and whether there was intent to contract in the first place?

2. Having read the court's decision in the *Stutz* case and the accompanying materials, which theory or theories of contract law do you prefer to guide the

decision in that case? Is your preference for that theory or theories a general one, applicable to all transactional disputes rather than exclusively to certain types of contracts, such as postnuptial agreements? Is it possible for the courts to consider all of these theories without slavishly following one or two and without eliminating any of these theories from consideration? Or are some of these theories irreconcilable with each other in general? For example, is it possible to reconcile the free market approach with the other public policy considerations?

3. Courts have viewed certain matters as largely outside the area of permissible contractual sales, including transactions in the custody or adoption of children. In *In re Baby M*, 109 N.J. 396, 537 A.2d 1227 (1988), the New Jersey Supreme Court declined to enforce a surrogacy agreement under which a biological mother agreed to be artificially inseminated with the semen of another women's husband, to carry the fetus to full term, and then surrender custody of the newly born child to the biological father and his wife. The court reasoned that the agreement was against the public policy of the state and was illegal because it conflicted with the state's statutory regulations governing adoption and laws which prohibit the payment of money for the purpose of adoption.

Should the market be permitted to operate in this and other areas in which technology, science and medical developments have opened up possibilities previously thought to exist only in science fiction? For example, should courts enforce agreements to clone human beings? Should courts permit people to sell their organs to others? Should the market be permitted to operate in these areas? Consider the thoughts of a leading federal jurist and law professor on the possible role of the free market in an area we have traditionally thought not to be subject to the market.

Richard A. Posner, Economic Analysis in the Law (4th ed. 1992)

§ 5.4 The Legal Protection of Children

In considering the appropriate role of the state in relation to children, we may begin with the assumption congenial to economic analysis that the state desires to maximize the aggregate welfare of all of its citizens, including therefore children. To realize their potential as adults in economic terms, to achieve a high level of lifetime utility — children require a considerable investment of both parental time and market inputs (food, clothing, tuition, etc.). Since costs as well as benefits must be considered in any investment decision, the optimal level of investment in a particular child is that which is expected to maximize the combined welfare of the child, his parents, and other family members. That level will vary from family to family depending on such factors as the child's aptitudes and the parents' wealth. It will also depend critically on how much the parents love the child; the more they love it, the higher will be the optimal investment, because the costs of the investment will be felt very lightly, even not at all, by the parents (can you see why?). Parents who make great "sacrifices" for their children are not worse off than those (of the same income) who make few or no sacrifices, any more than people who spend a large fraction of their income on housing are worse off than people who spend a smaller fraction of the same income on housing.

Even when parents love their children very much, there is a danger of underinvestment in children; and it is part of the explanation for free public education. Suppose a child is born to very poor parents. The child has enormous potential earning power if properly fed, clothed, housed, and educated, but his parents can't afford these things. This would not matter if the child or parents could borrow against the child's future earning capacity, but the costs of borrowing against a highly uncertain future stream of earnings, and also the difficulty (given the constitutional prohibition of involuntary servitude) of collateralizing a loan against a person's earning capacity (you cannot make him your slave if he defaults), make such loans an infeasible method of financing a promising child.

This problem, plus the fact that some parents love their children little or not at all[1]and the existence of widespread altruism toward children in general (i.e., not just one's own children), may explain why legal duties are imposed on parents to provide care and support, including education, for their children. Child labor laws, as well as the already mentioned provision of free public education . . . , are other social responses to the problem of underinvestment in children's human capital.

A serious practical problem with laws forbidding neglect is what to do with the child if the threat of fine or imprisonment fails to deter the parents from neglecting the child. The law's answer has been to place the neglected child either with foster parents or in a foster home. Both solutions are unsatisfactory because of the difficulty of monitoring the custodian's performance. The state can pay foster parents a subsidy sufficient to enable them to invest optimally in the care and upbringing of the child, but who is to know whether they have made that investment? The state cannot*trust*the foster parents: Because they have no property rights in the child's lifetime earnings, they have no incentive to make the investment that will maximize those earnings.

Another solution to the problem of the neglected or unwanted child is, of course, to allow the parents (or mother, if the father is unknown or uninterested) to put up the child for adoption, preferably before they begin to neglect the child. Provided that the adoptive parents are screened to make sure they do not want the child for purposes of abusing it sexually or otherwise, adoption enables the child to be transferred from the custody of people unlikely to invest optimally in its upbringing to people much more likely to do so. But the universal availability of contraception, the decline in the stigma of being an unwed mother (can you think of an economic reason for this decline?), and the creation of a constitutional right to abortion have reduced to a trickle the supply of children for adoption, since most such children are produced as the unintended by-product of sexual intercourse. Recent advances in the treatment of fertility (perhaps spurred in part by the decline in the supply of babies for adoption) have reduced or at least controlled the demand for babies for adoption, but the demand remains high, and is much greater than the supply. The waiting period to obtain a baby from an adoption agency has lengthened to several years and sometimes the agencies have no babies for

---

[1] [1] Even in an age of universal availability of contraceptive methods and a constitutional right to abortion, some children are produced as an undesired by-product of sexual activity, and in addition parents may have second thoughts once they begin coping with a baby. As a matter of fact the ready availability of contraceptive methods may not significantly reduce the number of unwanted children that are born. Contraception reduces the expected costs of sex and hence increases the incidence of sex; the fraction of unwanted births is thus smaller but the number of sexual encounters, by which the fraction must be multiplied to yield the*number*of unwanted births, is larger.

adoption. The baby shortage would be considered an intolerable example of market failure if the commodity were telephones rather than babies.

In fact the shortage appears to be an artifact of government regulation, in particular the state laws forbidding the sale of babies. The fact that there are many people who are capable of bearing children but who do not want to raise them and many other people who cannot produce their own children but want to raise children, and that the costs of production to natural parents are much lower than the value that many childless people attach to children, suggests the possibility of a market in babies. And as a matter of fact there is a black market in babies, with prices as high as $25,000 said to be common. . . . Its necessarily clandestine mode of operation imposes heavy information costs on the market participants as well as expected punishment costs on the middlemen (typically lawyers and obstetricians). The result is higher prices and smaller quantities sold than would be likely in a legal market.

This analysis is oversimplified in assuming that all babies are adopted through the black market. That of course is not true. Adoption agencies — private, nonprofit organizations licensed by the state — use queuing and various nonmarket criteria (some highly intrusive and constitutionally questionable, such as requiring that the adoptive parents have the same religion as the natural parents) to ration the inadequate supply of babies that they control. The principal objection to the agencies is not, however, the criteria they use to ration the existing supply of babies but their monopoly of adoptions, which ensures (given their profit function) that the supply will remain inadequate.

Most states also permit (subject to various restrictions) independent adoption of babies, wherein the natural parents (normally the mother) arrange for the adoption without using the facilities of an adoption agency. This avoids the sometimes irrelevant and demeaning criteria of the agencies, but since the mother is not permitted to sell the child, independent adoption does not create a real baby market. The lawyer who arranges the adoption, however, is permitted to exact a fee for his services plus payment for the mother's hospital and related childbearing expenses, and since these charges are difficult to police, in practice they will often conceal a payment for the baby itself. And if the mother breaks a contract to give up her child for adoption, the adoptive parents may be able to recover damages measured by the lying-in expenses they had advanced to her. Also close to outright sale is the "family compact," wherein the mother agrees to give up the child to a close relative in exchange for financial consideration running to the child; such contracts have been enforced where the court was satisfied that the arrangement benefited the child.

Should the sale of babies be made legal? The idea strikes most people as bizarre and offensive; the usual proposal for getting rid of the black market in babies is not to decriminalize the sale of babies but to make the criminal penalties more severe. However, economists like to think about the unthinkable, so let us examine in a scientific spirit the objections to permitting the sale of babies for adoption.

There is, it is argued, no assurance that the adoptive parents who are willing to pay the most money for a child will provide it with the best home. But the parents who value a child the most are likely to give it the most care,[2]and at the very least

---

[2] [6] The existence of a market in babies would also increase the natural mother's incentive to produce

the sacrifice of a substantial sum of money to obtain a child attests to the seriousness of the purchaser's desire to have the child. The reply to this is that the high paying adoptive parents may value the child for the wrong reasons: to subject it to sexual abuse or otherwise to exploit it. But the laws forbidding child neglect and abuse would apply fully to the adoptive parents (as they do under present law, of course). Naturally one would want to screen adoptive parents carefully for possible criminal proclivities — just as is done today.

A better objection to a market in babies is that the payment of a large sum to buy the child could exhaust the adoptive parents' financial ability to support the child. If so, the equilibrium price of babies would be low, since in deciding how much they are willing to pay for a child the adoptive parents will consider price. But this is not a complete answer to the objection. Few people would pay to adopt a child they could not afford to raise, but the more costly the child is to acquire the less will be the cost-justified investment in the child's upbringing, that investment being as we said a function of the parents' utility as well as the child's.

All this assumes that a free market would raise the price of babies. In fact it is unlikely that the price of babies in such a market would substantially exceed the opportunity costs (mainly the mother's time and medical expenses) that the adoptive parents would have incurred had they produced rather than purchased the child — and that they save by purchasing. For that would be the competitive price. The net cost to the adoptive parents would thus be close to zero, except that the adoptive parents would incur some costs in locating and trying to ascertain the qualities of the child that they would not have incurred had they been its natural parents. The black market price is high because it must cover the sellers' expected punishment costs for breaking the law and because the existence of legal sanctions prevents the use of the most efficient methods of matching up sellers and buyers.[3]

Opponents of the market approach also argue that the rich would end up with all the babies, or at least all the good babies. . . . Such a result might of course be in the children's best interest, but it is unlikely to materialize. Because people with high incomes tend to have high opportunity costs of time, the wealthy usually have smaller families than the poor. Permitting babies to be sold would not change this situation. Moreover, the total demand for children on the part of wealthy childless couples must be very small in relation to the supply of children, even high-quality children, that would be generated in a system where there were economic incentives to produce children for purchase by childless couples.

The poor may actually do worse under present adoption law than they would in a free baby market. Most adoptions are channeled through adoption agencies, which in screening prospective adoptive parents attach great importance to the applicants' income and employment status. People who might flunk the agencies' criteria on economic grounds might, in a free market with low prices, be able to adopt children, just as poor people are able to buy color television sets.[4]

---

a healthy baby and would reduce the demand for abortion.

   [3] [7] In one respect, however, the black market price is lower than a legal free market price would be. The buyer in the black market does not receive any legally enforceable warranties (of health, genealogy, or whatever), comparable to those that buyers receive in legal markets. The buyer in a legal baby market would receive a more valuable package of rights and it would cost more; the seller would demand compensation for bearing risks formerly borne by the buyer. But the resulting price increase would be nominal rather than real (can you see why?). . .

   [4] [8] A recent development in reproductive technology should be noted in connection with the

NOTES & QUESTIONS

1. Judge Posner's approach would permit individuals a great degree of autonomy in their transactions, allowing the market to operate with few restrictions, even in traditionally highly regulated areas that have been considered outside the marketplace. What limits, if any, should be placed on autonomy and the parties' freedom to determine a market?

2. Judge Posner proposes that market forces be permitted to operate with respect to adoption. Indeed, he points out that there is already a black market in babies. Do you agree that the "market's invisible hand" will provide solutions to the issues associated with adoption and abortion? Would society, particularly children, benefit from permitting the sale of children subject to minimal government regulation, as Judge Posner suggests?

3. Expressing an entirely different view of surrogacy agreements, Professor John Lawrence Hill has proposed a new defense to the enforcement of contracts, "exploitation." Professor Hill offers the following definition:

> Most essentially, I argue that exploitation is a psychological, rather than a social or an economic, concept. For an offer to be exploitative, it must serve to create or to take advantage of some recognized psychological vulnerability which, in turn, disturbs the offeree's ability to reason effectively. . . .

> One of the most frequent bases for the claim of exploitation in surrogate parenting arrangements is the fear that women may feel compelled for economic reasons to become surrogates. Poor women in particular may decide to bear children for others in order to augment their family income. . . . The danger is obvious: economic exigency may force some women to enter surrogate agreements when they might otherwise never have entertained the idea. . . .

> Another argument gaining currency, particularly among feminists, is the claim that the surrogate is unfree, coerced or compelled in some significant sense. This compulsion is not viewed simply as the function of economic factors, but rather as an inescapable result of the entire complex of social influences in a patriarchal society that serve to mold the personality, beliefs, motives, intentions and desires of women. Although a woman may choose to enter into a surrogate agreement, the argument runs, the decision is only superficially voluntary. Because she has grown up in a male-dominated society, which has conditioned her to view her primary function in that society in largely sexual, procreative and maternal terms, her choices are the legacy of this socio-psychological framework of social conditioning.

---

discussion in the text: artificial conception. Suppose a woman produces ova but cannot carry a fetus to term. Her fertilized ovum is transplanted to another woman. the surrogate mother, who carries it to term. Should the natural parents or the surrogate mother have the property right in the child? Should a contract between the surrogate mother and the natural parents whereby the latter pay the former to carry the fertilized ovum to term, and the former agrees to give the baby up to the natural parents when it is born, be legally enforceable? In what ways is the economic analysis different from that of baby selling? For background see Walter Wadlington, Artificial Conception: The Challenge for Family Law, 69 Va. L. Rev. 465 (1983).

Exploitation, 79 CORNELL L. REV. 631, 637–640 (1994).

According to Professor Hill, the court's decision in *In re Baby M* may be explained in part based on the court's concern that the surrogacy contract was exploitative of the biological mother. In its decision, the New Jersey Supreme Court suggested that the natural mother may have been coerced and exploited and may not have been capable of agreeing to give up her child because she could not anticipate the strength of her bond with her child before birth. Should the courts protect the biological mother from entering into such a bargain? If embraced by the courts, would the defense of exploitation be consistent or inconsistent with the purposes and theories of contract law set forth in this chapter? Does the concept of exploitation as a defense to contract fit comfortably within some approaches, such as critical legal studies and relational theory, but not in others?

4. Assuming for the sake of argument that "exploitation" should be a defense to contract enforcement, how should it be defined? Later in the casebook, we shall study established, traditional defenses to contract enforcement, including incapacity, duress, fraud, undue influence and others. After you consider those defenses, you may wish to reconsider the proposed definition of the defense of exploitation to determine whether it differs from the traditional defenses in a principled way. In particular, consider whether the proposed defense of exploitation is simply a manifestation of the relatively modern defense of "unconscionability."

PROBLEMS

1. Defendant Starks was indicted for armed robbery of a bank. Before the trial, the prosecutor promised Starks the charge would be dismissed if Starks submitted to a polygraph examination and passed the "lie detector" test. Starks allegedly passed the test, but the prosecutor proceeded with the criminal proceeding anyway. Stark, who was convicted and sentenced to 11 years' imprisonment, filed a motion for a new trial based on his contention that the prosecutor was bound by the pretrial agreement in which he agreed to dismiss the case if Starks took and passed the polygraph test. Is the pretrial agreement a contract enforceable against the prosecutor? *People v. Starks*, 106 Ill. 2d 441, 478 N.E.2d 350 (1985).

Recently, one of the authors was consulted by a prosecutor who asked the following question: A criminal defendant enters into a written pretrial agreement to take a polygraph test in return for the prosecutor's commitment to dismiss if the defendant passes the test. Is that agreement enforceable against the defendant if the defendant reneges and refuses to take the test? Are different policy considerations implicated when the defendant rather than the prosecutor reneges on such a polygraph test agreement? Is it possible that the defendant is free to renege on such an agreement but not the prosecutor?

2. A thirteen-year-old boy, who owned a collection of more than 40,000 baseball cards, entered a baseball card specialty store and inquired about a Nolan Ryan rookie card in the display case. Although the card was marked "$1200," the boy allegedly pointed to the card and asked an inexperienced, temporary clerk, "Is this worth $12?" When the clerk answered in the affirmative, the boy paid her $12 and took the card. According to one collector's publication, the card was worth between $800 and $1200 at the time. The store owner offered a reward for the return of the card and cruised local neighborhoods inquiring about the boy until the boy and his father came forward. The boy refused to return the card and the owner sued for

restitution. A local newspaper reported the boy as saying: "I didn't steal the card or do anything wrong. . . . It was a card I was looking for. I knew the card was worth more than $12. I saw prices for it of $150 and up. I just offered $12 for it and the lady sold it to me. People go into card shops and try to bargain all the time." Although the case went to trial, it was settled before decision when the boy and the store owner agreed to sell the card at auction with the proceeds to go to charity. *See Major League Dispute*, A.B.A.J., June 1991, p. 24. The card sold for $1500 at the auction.

Had the case not been settled, what should the court have done? Was the sale of the card a contract? Should the court have ordered the boy to return the card to the store owner? Did the boy do anything wrong? Does it matter that the boy was only thirteen years old?

SECTION B

TRADITIONAL CONTRACT FORMATION

The courts generally recognize three classes of contracts: express, implied in fact, and implied in law. *Legros v. Tarr*, 540 N.E.2d 257, 263 (Ohio 1989).

> An express contract occurs when the parties' assent to a contract's terms is expressed through an offer and acceptance. . . . A contract implied in fact occurs when a meeting of the minds is demonstrated by surrounding circumstances, allowing a factfinder to infer the existence of a contract by tacit understanding. . . . A contract implied in law occurs when there is no meeting of the minds, and the law creates an obligation on a person who received a benefit and would be unjustly enriched by the benefit. . . .

United Nat'l Insurance Co. v. SST Fitness Corp., 309 F.3d 914, 919 (6th Cir. 2002).

In addition, the courts have also enforced promises or provided relief for breach of promises under the doctrine of promissory estoppel. Promissory estoppel is available as an alternative theory where a traditional contract is not present, typically due to the absence of consideration in the transaction, but the promisee has reasonably relied to his or her detriment on the promisor's promise.

In Section B, we shall study the elements of traditional contract formation which give rise to the express contract and the contract implied in fact: offer, acceptance, consideration and certainty of terms. In Section C, we shall consider alternative theories for enforcement and relief, particularly the avoidance of unjust enrichment through the contract implied in law or "quasi-contract" and the doctrine of promissory estoppel or detrimental reliance theory.

CHAPTER 2

OFFERS OF CONTRACTUAL TERMS

A. CONTRACTUAL INTENT, ASSENT AND THE OBJECTIVE THEORY OF CONTRACTS

Before courts will enforce agreements or provide remedies for the breach of agreements, they must be satisfied that the parties intended to be bound by the agreements' terms. This mutual assent to the bargain is frequently called the "meeting of the minds." In the case of an express contract, this meeting of the minds is characterized by an "offer" made by the "offeror," followed by an "acceptance" made by the "offeree." Thus, whether an offer has been made is a significant prerequisite for the formation of an express contract.

The existence of an offer largely depends upon the intentions of the offeror. The courts consider the offeror to be "the master of the offer," that is, the offeror has the power to set forth the substantive terms of the bargain as well as the procedural terms by which the offeree may accept the offer. For example, on Wednesday, Sarah offers to pay Jack $50 if Jack will wash and wax Sarah's car by Saturday morning at 10:00 a.m. Sarah, the offeror, has exercised her mastery over the substantive terms of the offer by defining the subject matter of the transaction, i.e., washing and waxing her car, and by determining a price, $50. She has also set the procedural terms of the exchange by specifying the method and manner of acceptance, here requiring that the offeree Jack accept by performing by Saturday at 10:00 a.m. Is Sarah's requirement that Jack wash and wax her car before Saturday at 10:00 a.m. also a substantive term?

A *unilateral* contract is formed when an offeror makes a promise which the offeree accepts by *actual performance* of the act required under the terms of the offer. The courts have chosen to designate such agreements as unilateral contracts because only one of the parties has made a promise or promises. Is Sarah's offer to pay Jack $50 for washing and waxing her car an offer looking to unilateral contract? Is it reasonable for Jack to believe he could accept Sarah's offer by simply performing the work before Saturday at 10:00 a.m.? Is it also reasonable for Jack to believe he could accept Sarah's offer by promising to perform before Saturday at 10:00 a.m.?

An offer looking to a *bilateral* contract is made when the offeror offers a promise in exchange for the offeree's return *promise* instead of an actual act by the offeree. Had Sarah specified in her offer that she would pay Jack $50 if Jack PROMISED to wash and wax Sarah's car by Saturday at 10:00 a.m., her offer would have been a bilateral offer rather than a unilateral offer. Assuming Sarah extended a bilateral offer, would it be reasonable for Jack to believe he could accept either by return promise or actually performing before Saturday at 10:00 a.m.? Although the authors of the RESTATEMENT (SECOND) OF CONTRACTS sought to de-emphasize it, the distinction between unilateral offers and bilateral offers remains significant to the courts, particularly with respect to questions concerning acceptance, which we shall take up in Chapter 3.

The very existence and the nature of the offer depend on the purported offeror and whether she expressed contractual intentions or intent to be bound. However, the offeror's *actual* thoughts or subjective intentions are largely irrelevant when determining whether she has made an offer. Instead, the courts apply an "objective theory of contracts," determining whether an offer has been extended based on the offeror's outward manifestations of intent viewed from the perspective of a reasonable person in the offeree's place. Similarly, when deciding whether an offer has been accepted, the courts apply an objective theory, asking whether the reasonable person in the position of the offeror is warranted in believing the offeree has accepted based on the offeree's outward manifestations of assent. Under the objective theory, hidden intentions are generally irrelevant to a determination of contractual intent.

The following cases and materials invite us to study the offer, its characteristics and to consider the application of the objective theory of contracts.

Hawkins v. McGee, 84 N.H. 114, 146 A. 641 (1929). The plaintiff, a boy, suffered a severe burn which left substantial scar tissue on his hand. Nine years after the accident, the defendant doctor solicited the plaintiff's father to perform an operation to replace the scar tissue with a graft of skin taken from the plaintiff's chest. The doctor was apparently interested in performing a new procedure for skin grafting. When the father asked the doctor how long his son would be in the hospital, the doctor answered, "Three or four days, not over four; then he can go home and it will be just a few days when he will go back to work with a good hand." Before plaintiff's father agreed to permit the doctor to perform the operation, the doctor stated, "I will guarantee to make the hand a hundred percent perfect hand or a hundred percent good hand." The operation was less successful than expected and the boy sued. Held, the doctor's first statement, regarding when the plaintiff would leave the hospital, return home and be able to work again, "could only be construed as expressions of opinion or prediction as to the probable duration of the treatment and plaintiff's resulting disability," and therefore was not an offer. However, the doctor's second statement, guaranteeing a perfect hand, was sufficient to justify submission to the jury of the question whether the doctor had made an offer. The court rejected the doctor's argument that his words could only reasonably be understood "as his expression in strong language that he believed and expected that as a result of the operation he would give the plaintiff a very good hand." The court reasoned that the jury could conclude that the doctor's alleged statement should be accepted at its face value as an inducement for the plaintiff's and his father's consent.

NOTES & QUESTIONS

1. Is there a principled basis for the *Hawkins* court's distinction between the doctor's first statement deemed not an offer and his second statement, which the court held the jury could conclude was an offer?

2. The Uniform Commercial Code (U.C.C.), which governs sales of goods, contains several provisions dealing with express and implied warranties. *See*

U.C.C. §§ 2-312–2-318.

Lucy v. Zehmer, 196 Va. 493, 84 S.E.2d 516 (1954). Zehmer owned a farm that Lucy had been interested in for some time. One night, Lucy found Zehmer and Zehmer's wife in a restaurant where the two men shared some whiskey. Lucy stated to Zehmer: "I bet you wouldn't take $50,000 for that place." Zehmer replied, "Yes, I would too; you wouldn't give fifty." Lucy said he would and Zehmer wrote on the back of a restaurant check, "We do hereby agree to sell to W.O. Lucy the Ferguson Farm complete for $50,000. . . ." Zehmer and his wife signed the restaurant check. Later Zehmer failed to honor the agreement and Lucy sued for specific performance of the alleged contract. Zehmer argued that he had been joking, that he "was high as a Georgia pine," and that the transaction "was just a bunch of two doggoned drunks bluffing to see who could talk the biggest and say the most." Held, a contract had been formed. Employing the objective theory of contracts, the court reasoned that "[t]he law imputes to a person an intention corresponding to the reasonable meaning of his words and acts. If his words and acts, judged by a reasonable standard, manifest an intention to agree, it is immaterial what may be the real but unexpressed state of his mind."

NOTES & QUESTIONS

1. In the preceding two cases, the parties did not execute formal documents to mark their alleged agreements. Should they have reduced their agreements to writing? Consider the informal nature of the oral offer of $100,000 which is made in the next case.

2. In Chapter 10, Statute of Frauds, we will consider when agreements must be in writing to be enforceable and the prerequisites for satisfying the writing requirement of the Statute of Frauds. At that point, return to *Lucy v. Zehmer* and consider whether the writing requirement was satisfied in that case.

BARNES v. TREECE
15 Wash. App. 437, 549 P.2d 1152 (1976)

CALLOW, Judge: . . .

Vend-A-Win is a Washington corporation engaged primarily in the business of distributing punchboards. Warren Treece served as vice president, was a member of the board of directors, and owned 50 percent of the stock of Vend-A-Win. On July 24, 1973, Treece spoke before the Washington State Gambling Commission in support of punchboard legitimacy and Vend-A-Win's particular application for a temporary license to distribute punchboards. During the testimony, as stated by the trial judge, Treece made a statement to the following effect:

> I'll put a hundred thousand dollars to anyone to find a crooked board. If they find it, I'll pay it.

The statement brought laughter from the audience.

The next morning, July 25, 1973, the plaintiff Barnes was watching a television news report of the proceedings before the gambling commission and heard Treece's previous statement that $100,000 would be paid to anyone who could produce a crooked punchboard. Barnes also read a newspaper report of the hearings that quoted Treece's statement. A number of years earlier, while employed as a bartender, Barnes had purchased two fraudulent punchboards. After learning of Treece's statement, Barnes searched for and located his two punchboards. On July 26, 1973, Barnes telephoned Treece, announced that he had two crooked punchboards, and asked Treece if his earlier statement had been made seriously. Treece assured Barnes that the statement had been made seriously, advised Barnes that the statement was firm, and further informed Barnes that the $100,000 was safely being held in escrow. Treece also specifically directed Barnes to bring the punchboard to the Seattle office of Vend-A-Win for inspection.

On July 28, 1973, Barnes traveled to Seattle, met Treece and Vend-A-Win's secretary-treasurer in Vend-A-Win's offices, produced one punchboard, and received a receipt for presentation of the board written on Vend-A-Win stationery, signed by Treece and witnessed by Vend-A-Win's secretary-treasurer. Barnes was informed that the punchboard would be taken to Chicago for inspection. The parties next met on August 3, 1973, before the Washington State Gambling Commission. Barnes produced his second punchboard during the meeting before the commission.

Both Treece and Vend-A-Win refused to pay Barnes $100,000. Barnes then initiated this breach of contract action against both defendants. The trial court found that the two punchboards were rigged and dishonest, that Treece's statements before the gambling commission and reiterated to Barnes personally on the telephone constituted a valid offer for a unilateral contract, and that Barnes' production of two dishonest punchboards constituted an acceptance of the offer. . . .

The first issue is whether the statement of Treece was the manifestation of an offer which could be accepted to bind the offeror to performance of the promise. Treece contends that no contract was formed. He maintains that his statement was made in jest and lacks the necessary manifestation of a serious contractual intent.

When expressions are intended as a joke and are understood or would be understood by a reasonable person as being so intended, they cannot be construed as an offer and accepted to form a contract. However, if the jest is not apparent and a reasonable hearer would believe that an offer was being made, then the speaker risks the formation of a contract which was not intended. It is the objective manifestations of the offeror that count and not secret, unexpressed intentions. . . . If a party's words or acts, judged by a reasonable standard, manifest an intention to agree in regard to the matter in question, that agreement is established, and it is immaterial what may be the real but unexpressed state of the party's mind on the subject. . . .

The trial court found that there was an objective manifestation of mutual assent to form a contract. This was a matter to be evaluated by the trier of fact. . . . The record includes substantial evidence of the required mutual assent to support the finding of the trial court. Although the original statement of Treece drew laughter from the audience, the subsequent statements, conduct, and the circumstances show an intent to lead any hearer to believe the statements were made seriously. There was testimony, though contradicted, that Treece specifically restated the offer over the telephone in response to an inquiry concerning whether the offer was serious. Treece, when given the opportunity to state that an offer was not intended, not only reaffirmed the offer but also asserted that $100,000 had been placed in escrow and directed Barnes to bring the punchboard to Seattle for inspection. The parties met, Barnes was given a receipt for the board, and he was told that the board would be taken to Chicago for inspection. In present day society it is known that gambling generates a great deal of income and that large sums are spent on its advertising and promotion. In that prevailing atmosphere, it was a credible statement that $100,000 would be paid to promote punchboards. The statements of the defendant and the surrounding circumstances reflect an objective manifestation of a contractual intent by Treece and support the finding of the trial court.

The trial court properly categorized Treece's promise of $100,000 as a valid offer for a unilateral contract. The offer made promised that a contract would result upon performance of the act requested. Performance of the act with the intent to accept the offer constituted acceptance. The trial judge entered a specific finding that Barnes performed the requested act of acceptance when he produced a rigged and fraudulent punchboard. We concur with the trial court's holding that a binding unilateral contract was formed between Barnes and Treece and uphold the conclusions of the trial court in that regard. . . .

The judgment is affirmed.

NOTES & QUESTIONS

1. Is the objective theory of contracts consistent with all of the purposes and policies of contract law discussed in Chapter 1? Are there any arguments in theory which can be made for the adoption of a "subjective theory of contracts?"

2. In *Hotchkiss v. National City Bank*, 200 F. 287, 293 (S.D.N.Y. 1911), Judge Learned Hand stated:

> A contract has, strictly speaking, nothing to do with the personal, or individual, intent of the parties. A contract is an obligation attached by mere force of law to certain acts of the parties, usually words, which ordinarily accompany and represent a known intent. If, however, it were proved by twenty bishops that either party, when he used the words, intended something else than the usual meaning which the law imposes upon them, he would still be held, unless there were some mutual mistake, or something else of the sort.

3. How "objective" is the objective theory? Who is the "reasonable person?" Is the reasonable person "objective" in the sense of viewing the transaction as an outside, impartial observer would? Would the result in *Lucy v. Zehmer* be the same if Lucy had testified that he knew the Zehmers were joking, but the waitress observing the transaction testified that the Zehmers appeared to be serious. *See* RESTATEMENT (SECOND) OF CONTRACTS, § 20 (1981).

4. In *Barnes v. Treece*, the court reports that Treece's statement to the Gambling Commission "brought laughter from the audience." Is it clear whether Barnes was aware of that laughter? Does it matter?

5. Barnes reportedly had two "crooked" punchboards. Should he have been awarded $200,000 instead of $100,000? If others who heard Treece's statement before the Gambling Commission promptly tendered "crooked" punchboards after Barnes tendered his to Treece, would these other claimants be entitled to $100,000 for each punchboard they produced?

6. Had you been Treece's attorney, and you suspected his statement before the Gambling Commission was an offer, what would you have done to minimize your

client Treece's liability? *See* RESTATEMENT (SECOND) OF CONTRACTS, §§ 42, 43 & 46 (1981).

7. Courts will not enforce promises or transactions unless the parties may be said to have intended to be bound. Due to societal norms, custom and expectations, we presume that parties who make promises within the context of family transactions and social commitments do not intend contractual consequences. In addition to respecting the parties' intentions, the courts are generally reluctant to provide a remedy for the breach of such transactions for reasons of judicial economy. The courts' limited resources and time are better spent enforcing promises and agreements which the parties intend to be legally binding. *See* RESTATEMENT (SECOND) OF CONTRACTS, § 21, comment c. (1981). *Balfour v. Balfour*, 2 K.B. 571, 35 T.L.R. 609 (1919).

Kalavros v. Deposit Guaranty Bank & Trust Co., 158 So. 2d 740 (Miss. 1963). Theo Grillis immigrated from Greece to Mississippi where he prospered and became wealthy. Grillis' first wife, Themis Kalavros Grillis, died in 1948. In 1950, Grillis married his second wife, with whom he had a son. In 1952, he divorced his second wife and obtained custody of their son. On a visit to Greece in 1958, Grillis met and fell in love with his first wife's sister, Katherine Kalavros, whom he convinced to immigrate to Mississippi for the purpose of marrying him and caring for his son. However, after Katherine came to America and joined his household, Grillis could not convince his church's officials to lift their religious ban on marrying his sister-in-law. In 1961, Grillis died without marrying Katherine. Unprovided for in Grillis' will, Katherine sued his estate alleging an express contract to marry her or to make a will bequeathing half his estate or the money equivalent of half the estate to her. Alternatively, she asserted she was entitled to compensation for the services she rendered under a theory of contract implied at law. The state supreme court concluded there was no contract and affirmed the trial court's direction of a verdict for the executors of Grillis' estate, explaining:

> [T]here is a presumption of gratuity for mutual services growing out of a family relationship existing between persons living in the same household. . . . [W]e have reached the conclusion that the testimony shows that the services performed by [Katherine] were not under contract, express or implied, . . . but that her services were gratuitous and rendered in furtherance of the plan of the parties to marry. Death cut these plans short, leaving the estate of Theo Grillis to be administered according to his original plan and will, made before Katherine Kalavros came into his life. Courts may sometimes point out inequities and injustices created by thoughtlessness and carelessness of men, but courts do not have, and should not have, power to make contracts where none exists, nor take property from one person, like Robin Hood, and give it to another.

158 So. 2d at 745-746.

MORROW v. MORROW
612 P.2d 730 (Okla. App. 1980)

ROMANG, Judge:

The Plaintiffs-Appellants, Warren and Betty Morrow (husband and wife), brought this action to recover for services rendered to the decedent Maude Morrow, mother of Warren and Defendant-Appellee Woodye Morrow. They also sought to set aside a conveyance of certain mineral interests from Woodye to Defendant-Appellee Dennis M. Morrow, Woodye's son. This conveyance was made without consideration. Woodye had acquired title from Maude by warranty deed.

At trial the District Court, sitting without a jury as chancellor, found the evidence insufficient to support the Plaintiffs' claim for services and ordered the mineral conveyance set aside and the proceeds of the surface sale (less certain expenses) and mineral rights be evenly distributed to 8 surviving children of Maude. . . .

The Plaintiffs' theory was that after receiving title to Maude's real property, Woodye orally agreed with Plaintiffs that if they would care for Maude that on her death Woodye would sell the property and first pay the Plaintiffs for the care of Maude and divide the remainder equally among her heirs.

The District Court's Journal Entry indicated he found that Woodye had received the property in trust for the purpose of taking care of Maude and that "there is no clear and convincing evidence of an agreement for them to be paid for their services, and therefore, same are presumed to be gratuitous.". . .

Reviewing the record is confusing. The trial judge's journal entry indicates he did not find any "clear and convincing" evidence of an agreement. If he meant that as a technical statement of Plaintiffs' burden he was in error. The oral contract with Woodye need only be proven by a preponderance of evidence. It is also clear that he relied on the general principle that family arrangements are not presumed to be attendant with contractual consequences. Whether he viewed this as a factual presumption based on accumulated judicial experience but always susceptible to rebuttal, which it is, or a rule of law, which it is not, is unclear. . . .

Whether there was a contract is a matter as to which the party asserting the contract has the burden. . . . As part of the fact finders process, courts are convinced that in our society the vast majority of family arrangements are not expected to be attended with contractual consequences. . . . This expectation may be upset by any facts showing the parties expected to be bound legally, an element not normally relevant in agreements between nonfamily members. As Corbin says:

> The following statements may be of assistance in distinguishing between non-enforceable social engagements and contractual agreements: 1. If the subject matter and terms of a transaction are such as customarily have affected legal relations and there is nothing to indicate that the one now asserting their existence had reasons to know that the other party intended not to affect his legal relations, thus the transaction will be operative legally. 2. If the subject matter and terms are not such as customarily have affected legal relations, the transaction is not legally operative unless the expressions of the parties indicate an intention to make it so. . . .
> 1 CORBIN ON CONTRACTS § 34. See also RESTATEMENT (SECOND) OF CONTRACTS, § 21B comment c (T.D. 1973).

Nothing in our cases hold that family members may not make their arrangements contractual in nature. . . . Rather the point of our cases and scholarly comment is that there is a norm of societal expectation. The subject matter here involved is care for an invalid mother. Such arrangements are frequently gratuitous, founded in love and affection. But where there are a number of children, it is also frequently the case that one child and spouse will undertake primary care and the others will contribute financially in agreed amounts or as they can. Whether these arrangements are contractual or not depends on the intent of the parties. But in such cases the party asserting the contract has the burden of setting aside our belief that most such arrangements are not contractual.

It is also argued that Betty as a daughter-in-law is not "family" for purposes of the rule. . . . The Supreme Court [has] endorsed a factual definition of family not solely related to legal concepts of consanguinity. It is the reality that matters. Where a group of persons reflect reciprocal duties of a natural, or moral nature for support and care, there is a family relationship insofar as this factual presumption is concerned. Where this relationship exists our assumptions that the arrangement is not intended to be attended with contractual consequences is appropriate.

In this case the trier of fact was unpersuaded. Based on the record evidence we cannot say as a matter of law he was wrong. Accordingly, we affirm.

NOTES & QUESTIONS

1. Based on the record evidence, the reviewing court in Morrow affirmed the trial judge's conclusion that there was no contract between the plaintiffs and defendant. What sort of evidence would have persuaded the court that the parties intended contractual consequences to attach to their arrangements for the care of their mother?

2. Assuming that the courts' decisions in the Kalavros and Morrow cases reflect attitudes prevalent at the times of those respective decisions, have society's values and normative approaches to the relationships in those cases changed significantly since then? If so, do those changes justify different results if those disputes were brought before courts today?

3. A national news magazine reported that in 1978 a California certified public accountant, Tom Horsley, sued a waitress, Alyn Chesselet, for a broken date. In San Francisco Small Claims Court, Horsley alleged that he invited Chesselet to see the musical "The Wiz" ten days before the show. She agreed to meet him at a bar before going to the musical. After driving 50 miles from Campbell, California to San Francisco to meet her, Horsley found Chesselet there with a man she explained was an old flame. She claimed she tried to telephone Horsley to cancel their date and offered to reimburse him. When several months passed with no payment from Chesselet, Horsley demanded $15 for car expenses and $17 for his time based on his minimum hourly rate of $8.50 as a C.P.A. Chesselet replied that he could sue her, and he did. TIME MAGAZINE, June 5, 1978, at 25 (1978).

4. Was Chesselet's agreement to date Horsley a contract? If it was a contract, what remedy would be appropriate for Chesselet's breach?

5. Other than the broken date, was there another possible contract between Horsley and Chesselet? If so, what remedy would be appropriate for the breach of this second agreement?

PROBLEMS

1. Bill and Linda have always been proud of their eleven-year-old daughter, Ellen, but last fall her grades in school began to drop. To provide Ellen an incentive to improve her academic performance, Bill and Linda promised Ellen they would deposit $100 to Ellen's savings account after each month in which she

maintained "straight A's" in all her school subjects. The following month, Ellen received A's in all her subjects except physical education, which was graded pass/fail. Ellen received a "pass" in physical education. Bill and Linda promptly deposited $100 to Ellen's account. In each of the six months that followed, Ellen maintained a straight A average, but Bill and Linda ceased making the $100 deposits. Does Ellen have a cause of action for breach of contract against Bill and Linda?

2. Cobaugh, an avid golfer, was playing in a golf tournament when he observed a car at the ninth tee of the course. Next to the car was a sign stating:

> HOLE-IN-ONE Wins this 1988 Chevrolet Beretta GT Courtesy of KLICK-LEWIS Buick Chevrolet Pontiac $49 OVER FACTORY IN-VOICE in Palmyra.

Cobaugh made a hole-in-one on the ninth hole and claimed the car, but the automobile dealer Klick-Lewis refused to deliver it. Unknown to Cobaugh, the car had been a prize in another tournament held two days earlier, but Klick-Lewis had not yet removed the car or the sign when Cobaugh made his hole-in-one. Cobaugh sued Klick-Lewis for specific performance of an alleged contract. Klick-Lewis contended that the sign was not an offer but an announcement of a gift contingent on making the hole in one. Klick-Lewis also maintained that in the event the sign was an offer, the offer had expired at the end of the tournament two days before Cobaugh made the hole in one. Who will prevail? *See Cobaugh v. Klick-Lewis, Inc.,* 561 A.2d 1248 (Pa. Super. 1989).

B. PRELIMINARY NEGOTIATIONS AND INVITATIONS FOR OFFERS

Employing the objective theory of contracts, courts look for words of commitment by the purported offeror, at the offeror's conduct and at the surrounding circumstances to determine whether an offer has been unequivocally made in clear and uncertain terms. Preliminary negotiations and communications may lead to a cognizable offer, but until one party expresses an intention to be bound, such preliminaries are not offers and do not justify the other party's belief that he or she may strike a bargain by accepting. Advertisements, price list mailings and circulars, catalogues and other comparable publications are generally not considered to be offers but are invitations to the public to inspect, negotiate or consider purchasing the subject goods, services, etc. Ordinarily, the reader of the advertisement or circular makes the initial offer when placing an order with the advertiser. Nevertheless, normative assumptions concerning our understandings of advertisements and like publications may be overcome by an expressed intention to extend an offer. Consider the following cases in which courts addressed whether specific manifestations constituted offers.

Owen v. Tunison, 131 Me. 42, 158 A. 926 (1932). The prospective purchaser wrote to owner, "Will you sell me your store . . . for $6,000?" Owner replied, "[I]t would not be possible for me to sell it unless I was to receive $16,000 cash." The prospective purchaser then sent the following message, "Accept your offer. . . ." Held, no contract. The owner's response to the prospective purchaser's initial inquiry "may have been written with the intent to open negotiations that might lead to a sale," but it was not an offer to sell.

Harvey v. Facey, 1893 A.C. 552 (Privy Council 1893). The prospective purchasers telegraphed the owner of certain property, "Will you sell us Bumper Hall Pen? Telegraph lowest cash price — answer paid." Owner replied, "Lowest price for Bumper Hall Pen 900." Shortly thereafter, the prospective purchasers telegraphed: "We agree to buy Bumper Hall Pen for the sum of nine hundred pounds asked by you. . . ." Held, no contract. The first telegram asked two questions: first, the prospective purchasers asked whether the owner was willing to sell; second, they asked for the owner's lowest price. The owner's reply "gives only a precise answer to a precise question, viz, the price." An agreement to sell cannot be implied by the mere statement of the lowest price.

VOLKER COURT, LLC v. SANTA FE APARTMENTS, LLC
130 S.W.3d 607 (Mo. App. 2004)

SPINDEN, Judge:

Believing that one of the members of Santa Fe Apartments, LLC, had breached its agreement to sell an apartment complex to him for $4.6 million and had guaranteed that he could get the other member to agree to the deal, Brent Lambi and his limited liability company sued Santa Fe and its members for breach of contract and fraudulent misrepresentation when Santa Fe initially refused to go through with the sale. The circuit court granted summary judgment for Santa Fe and its members. Lambi and his company appeal. We affirm the circuit court's summary judgment.

Lambi was the sole owner and member of Volker Court, LLC. The limited liability company owned an apartment complex in Kansas City until, on September 19, 2001, it sold the complex for an $800,000 profit. To defer capital gains taxes, Volker Court entered into an Internal Revenue Service approved exchange agreement. To take advantage of the tax benefit, Volker Court had to identify three possible replacement properties within 45 days of the sale. In fulfillment of the agreement, Volker Court identified the Santa Fe apartments. The record does not indicate anything about any other properties.

On September 26, 2001, county government authorities sold the Santa Fe Apartments in an auction on the courthouse steps. David Atkins, on behalf N.B. Forrest Management, Inc., outbid Volker Court and purchased the complex for $3.9 million. N.B. Forrest later transferred title in the apartment complex by warranty deed to Santa Fe Apartments, LLC. David Atkins and Mark Atkins, brothers, were equal members and managers in Santa Fe.

After the auction, Lambi telephoned David Atkins and asked about buying Santa Fe Apartments, but Atkins refused to sell. Later, Lambi's real estate broker, Aandrea Carter, called Atkins and told him that Lambi was interested in buying the apartments for $4.1 million to $4.2 million. Atkins rejected the offer but solicited Lambi's formal, written offer.

On October 17, 2001, Carter sent Lambi's written offer to Atkins. Lambi offered $4.1 million for the apartments. Atkins rejected the offer. Two days later, Atkins sent Carter a letter, which said:

Thanks for the offers on Santa Fe. I know that you have spent a bit of time on the deal.

Here is my suggestion. Clearly $4.2M isn't nearly enough. Between your sales fee and my closing cost, I'd be out of pocket $200,000 which would mean I'd only net $100,000. After taxes I'd have been better off saving my time and waxing my car.

$4.4M is better, but again with the owner financing you've suggested, it would take me years to recoup my out of pocket expense, let alone realize some cash profit. With that in mind, here is my suggestion:

Price — $4.6M

I'll carry $580,000 at 10% for 6 years with interest only payments.

[Lambi] assumes my $3.9M or provides his own mortgage.

[Lambi] covers all closing cost, except title insurance (I'll pay for that), and pays the balance in cash.

As far as your fee goes, I'd be willing to chip in 1%; perhaps [Lambi] would be willing to pay the rest.

I'm willing to stay in this deal for 6 years as I believe in Santa Fe. I believe in the location and from everything I've witnessed [Lambi] can easily handle the management.

Let me know. I can't guarantee my lender will say yes, but I know they want to keep the loan. I spoke with him this afternoon and he was intrigued. *I also know that this is a deal I can force my partner[, Mark Atkins,] to sign off on.* Keep in mind this deal nets us about $22,000 per month as it is currently configured. I'm willing to give that up for roughly $5,000 per month and participate in the risk. [Emphasis added by the court.]

Bottom line: With some arm twisting [Lambi] gets into this deal for about $200,000 to $300,000 out of pocket. He'll earn that back within 2 years. Everyone wins.

/s/ David

PS. Ball is in your court.

Carter forwarded this letter to Lambi. In response, Lambi requested more information on income and expenses from Atkins, and he provided it.

On October 29, 2001, Atkins sent a letter to Lambi, which said:

It was good to speak with you this afternoon about Santa Fe. I've heard a lot about you and have been very impressed with your real estate business. I'm hoping that we'll have time to meet in the future and compare notes.

Since the very first day I started working on the Santa Fe numbers I realized what an opportunity this property represented. The previous management (prior to Yarco) was clearly out of their league. While Yarco did a much better job, they brought along a lot of management and receivership costs, which should not be applicable to our (yours and mine) type of management. While we have only been there for 20 days, I'm positive I'm right. Based upon the property's history and what we'll do to it, I'm confident that it is a $6M property, within 18 months. Frankly after that, I think the value could go as high as $7 to $8M. I don't know what you do at your other properties, but we are very aggressive with our Utility Bill Back system. Within 24 months I'm confident we'll have 50 to 100% of the units on the Utility Bill Back system which sends the NOI through the roof.

Bottom line (this week);

$4.4M all cash (you take care of Aandrea)

$4.6M, we'll carry $500,000 at 10% interest only, 5 year balloon (personal guarantees, lawyer stuff, etc. . . again you take care of Aandrea)

If you can do one of these two things, we have a deal provided everyone's lawyer and bankers are happy. Keep in mind that I do have a partner and I don't want to ask him if this is OK. What I want to have is a signed, secure contract to stick under his nose. The stronger the contract, the more likely he'll agree. He doesn't want to sell it. What I need to compel him is something in writing.

In all sincerity, the farther we dig into this property, the more we like it. A lot of the skeletons that we feared, are not in the closet after all. We acquired 5 leases just last week and hope to acquire 10 more by the end of next week. The point being that this property is becoming more valuable to us by the week.

Regardless, it has been a pleasure getting to know you a bit better throughout the last couple of weeks and I hope that we are able to work together on a different deal, if we can't come together on Santa Fe.

Lambi responded to Atkins' letter by sending him a certified letter on November 2, 2001, which said:

I hereby accept your offer dated October 29th, 2001, to purchase Santa Fe Apartment Complex located in Kansas City, MO, at 85th and Holmes Road, for 4.6 million dollars, as set out in your written offer dated October 29, 2001. I propose that we close this at the earliest time possible.

David, thank you for help making this happen. Please call me at your earliest convenience to schedule closing.

Atkins telephoned Lambi and told him that they did not have a contract. On November 7, 2001, David Atkins sent Lambi a letter, which said:

I can't understand why you feel you have a contract. I've been negotiating in good faith and have tried to make it amply clear that any offer that you might submit, or that I might suggest would have to be approved by my brother. My suggestions in my letter dated October 29th were simply suggestions.

Atkins told Lambi that he was unable to convince his brother to sell the property "in the mid $4M range" but that he thought he could get him "to accept $4.9M with a $500,000 mortgage with the same terms that [they] had outlined earlier." Atkins closed his letter by reminding Lambi that "all negotiations and any ultimately agreed upon sale contract [would] be subject to and contingent upon the review and approval of my partner and my attorney."

The Atkinses prepared a formal real estate purchase agreement on behalf of Santa Fe setting the sale price at $4.9 million, signed it, and sent it to Lambi. Lambi did not respond. On November 12, 2001, the Atkinses on behalf of Santa Fe delivered another contract to Lambi changing the terms and lowering the sale price to $4.6 million. Lambi did not respond again but, along with Volker Court, sued Santa Fe and the Atkinses for breach of contract and fraudulent misrepresentation. The circuit court granted summary judgment for Santa Fe and the Atkinses, and Lambi and Volker Court appeal.

Lambi and Volker Court assert that the circuit court erred in granting summary judgment for Santa Fe on the claim for breach of contract. They assert that genuine issues of material fact existed as to whether David Atkins' letter of October 29 was a binding offer to sell the apartments to Lambi for $4.6 million. We disagree.

When we review a summary judgment, we consider the evidence in the record in the light most favorable to the party against whom the circuit court ruled. We endeavor to do this by accepting only inferences in the evidence that favor the party against whom the circuit court ruled. . . . Before a circuit court can enter summary judgment, it must determine that the parties are not disputing any genuine issue of material fact and that the party seeking summary judgment is entitled to a judgment as a matter of law. . . .

Before a plaintiff can establish a breach of contract, he must establish the existence of a contract. . . . A contract does not exist without a definite offer and a "mirror-image" acceptance. . . . "An offer is made when the offer leads the offeree to reasonably believe that an offer has been made." *Brown Machine v. Hercules, Inc.*, 770 S.W.2d 416, 419 (Mo. App. 1989). RESTATEMENT (SECOND) OF CONTRACTS § 24 (1981), defines "offer" as "the manifestation of willingness to enter into a bargain, so made as to justify another person in understanding that his assent to that bargain is invited and will conclude it." *Brown Machine*, 770 S.W.2d at 419. A "manifestation of willingness to enter into a bargain," however, "is not an offer if the person to whom it is addressed knows or has reason to know that the person making it does not intend to conclude a bargain until he has made a further manifestation of assent." RESTATEMENT (SECOND) OF CONTRACTS § 26 . . . . Thus, the parties' negotiations, proposals, or preliminary steps do not constitute a contract. . . . Moreover, "whether a contract is made and, if so, what the terms of that contract are, depend upon what is actually said and done and not upon the understanding or supposition of one of the parties." *Gateway Exteriors*, 882 S.W.2d at 279.

Atkins' letter of October 29 was not an offer; it merely was an invitation to Lambi and Volker Court to negotiate further concerning the proposed sale. Atkins said in the letter that his brother's approval was necessary: "Keep in mind that I do have a partner[.] What I want to have is a signed, secure contract to stick under his nose. The stronger the contract, the more likely he'll agree. . . . What I need to compel him is something in writing." Such statements show that Atkins did not intend to conclude the bargain until he had made a further manifestation of assent because he still had to confer with his brother about the matter. Atkins merely was inviting Lambi to draw up a contract to present to Mark Atkins. The letter informed Lambi that David Atkins would recommend to his brother that they accept an offer on specified terms set forth in a strongly written contract. Without Mark Atkins' approval, Lambi did not have the power to close the contract by his acceptance. The letter made it clear that David Atkins did not have the sole authority to enter the contract on behalf of Santa Fe. David Atkins was not in a position to conclude any bargain given his express limitations of bargaining power. The letter merely was a part of the negotiations or preliminary steps to the formation of a contract.

[The appellate court then rejected Lambi's additional assertion that David Atkins had apparent authority to act on his brother's behalf. The appellate court also affirmed the circuit court's grant of summary judgment against Lambi's claim that Atkins made a fraudulent misrepresentation.]

We affirm the circuit court's judgment.

NOTES & QUESTIONS

1. The reviewing court held that Atkins' October 29 letter to Lambi was not an offer. Why would Atkins prefer to invite an offer from Lambi rather than make an offer to Lambi? Would you ordinarily prefer your client be in the posture of offeror or offeree? What are the advantages of being an offeror? What are the advantages of being an offeree?

2. *Drafting Exercise:* If you represented Atkins, who now wished to make an offer to Lambi, what changes would you make in Atkins' October 29 letter?

3. In his November 2 response to Atkins' October 29 letter, Lambi said he "accepted," restating the essential terms from Atkins October 29 letter, and then added, "I propose that we close this at the earliest time possible." If, contrary to the court's conclusion, Atkins' October 29 letter had been an offer, was Lambi's November 2 response an acceptance or a counteroffer?

Fairmount Glass Works v. Grunden-Martin Woodenware Co., 106 Ky. 659, 51 S.W. 196 (1899). The prospective purchaser wrote to owner: "Please advise us the lowest price you can make on our order for ten car loads of Mason green jars. . . . State terms and cash discount." The alleged seller replied: "We quote you Mason fruit jars, complete, in one-dozen boxes, delivered in East St. Louis, Ill.: Pints $4.50, quarts $5.00, half gallons $6.50, per gross, for immediate acceptance, and shipment not later than May 15, 1895; sixty days acceptance, or 2 off, cash in ten days." The prospective purchaser sent the following telegram: "Enter order ten car loads as per your quotation." In response, the alleged seller telegrammed: "Impossible to book order. Output all sold." Held, correspondence had formed a contract. "There are a number of cases holding that the transaction is not completed until the order so made is accepted. . . . But each case must turn largely upon the language there used. . . . The true meaning of the correspondence must be determined by reading it as a whole." In this case, the court identified an expression of intention by the seller to make an offer to sell on the terms indicated, emphasizing that the presence of the words "for immediate acceptance" in the seller's response to the purchaser's inquiry was strong evidence of a present offer.

ZANAKIS-PICO v. CUTTER DODGE, INC.
47 P.3d 1222 (Haw. 2002)

LEVINSON, Justice:

The plaintiffs-appellants/cross-appellees, Mary Zanakis-Pico and Thomas M. Pico (the Picos) appeal from the amended judgment of the first circuit court. . . .

We . . . hold that the circuit court correctly ruled that Cutter was entitled to judgment as a matter of law with respect to the Picos' contract claim. . . .

This dispute involves an advertisement by Cutter appearing in the September 12, 1997 editions of both of the Honolulu daily newspapers of general circulation — the Advertiser and the Star-Bulletin. In large print at the top, the advertisement announced a "**$13,000,000 INVENTORY REDUCTION**" and claimed, "**We're #1 For a Reason! Volume = Low Prices[.] Come on Down and find out why!! $0 cash Down!***" (outline and bold print in original). At the bottom were five lines of text, including two asterisks, in a much smaller type-face. The first asterisk was followed by the qualification: "$0 Cash Down on all Gold Key Plus pymnt. vehicles."

The main body of the advertisement, between the introductory text and the fine print, included pictorial depictions of and specific terms for fourteen different model vehicles. In each instance, the advertisement stated the number of vehicles of the particular model available at the stated terms or price and listed what appear to be their inventory identification numbers. Five of the models were listed with a cash price, while nine were simply advertised for "**$0 Cash Down**," subject to varying monthly payments over various periods of time.

The first and most prominently displayed vehicle was a "**NEW '97 GRAND CHEROKEE LAREDO**," priced at "**$229 Month* 24 Mos. $0 Cash Down or $20,988.**" A second asterisk in the fine print at the bottom of the advertisement read: "Rebate and APR on select models, not combinable, prices incl. $400 Recent College Grad, $750-$1000 Loyalty Rebate on Grand Cherokees & Loyalty Rebate on Caravans & Grand Caravans on pymnts & prices & all other applicable rebates. On approved credit. All pymnts/prices plus tax, lic. & $195 doc fee."

On October 16, 1997, the Picos filed a complaint in the first circuit court, based on the advertisement, and amended it several times thereafter. In their third amended complaint, the Picos alleged that they had traveled to Cutter's Pearl City lot in response to the advertisement. One of the advertised Jeep Grand Cherokee Laredos was still available, and the Picos test drove the vehicle. Finding it to their liking, the Picos advised Cutter's sales agent that they were ready, willing, and able to purchase the vehicle, whereupon the sales agent informed them that they would have to make a down payment of $1,400.00. The Picos protested, pointing out that, according to Cutter's advertisement, the vehicle could be purchased for no cash down and two hundred twenty-nine dollars per month, but the sales agent explained that the "$0 cash down/$229 per month" offer was only available to recent college graduates who were entitled to a "loyalty rebate." The Picos left the premises shortly thereafter without purchasing the vehicle.

The Picos' third amended complaint alleged [statutory, tort and contract causes of action, and among other forms of relief, sought] specific performance (i.e., the sale of the vehicle to them as advertised). . . .

Cutter filed a motion for partial summary judgment as to damages. On November 18, 1998, the circuit court . . . granted Cutter's motion in part and denied it in part. The circuit court ruled as a matter of law that the Picos were not entitled to damages for "benefit-of-the-bargain."

The Picos filed their more definite statement of claims on January 26, 1999. . . . On April 1, 1999, the circuit court . . . treated Cutter's motion as a motion for summary judgment and granted it, ruling that there were no genuine issues of material fact and that Cutter was entitled to judgment as a matter of law on all of the Picos' claims. . . .

D. There Being No Binding Contractual Agreement, The Circuit Court Correctly Ruled That Cutter Was Entitled To Judgment As A Matter Of Law With Respect To The Picos' Contract Claim.

The Picos urge that the circuit court erred in granting Cutter judgment as a matter of law with respect to their contract claim. The Picos argue that Cutter's advertisement amounted to a contractual offer that they were free to accept, thereby creating an enforceable contract. We disagree.

It appears that this court has never directly addressed the question whether an advertisement can constitute a contractual offer. *But see Sutton v. Hawaiian Trust Co., Ltd.*, 43 Haw. 310 (1959) (announcement that certain property will be sold at auction is not a binding contractual offer to sell but merely a declaration of intention to hold an auction at which bids will be received). There is substantial agreement among the courts that have addressed the question, however, that advertisements by merchants listing goods for sale at a particular price are generally invitations to deal, rather than binding contractual offers that consumers may freely accept. *See, e.g., Georgian Co. v. Bloom*, 27 Ga. App. 468, 108 S.E. 813, 814 (Ga. Ct. App. 1921) (holding that newspaper advertisements, " 'stating that the advertiser has a certain quantity of goods which he [or she] wants to dispose of at certain prices, are not offers which become contracts as soon as any person to whose notice they might come signifies his [or her] acceptance by notifying the [seller] that he [or she] will take a certain quantity of them[]' "); *Steinberg v. Chicago Medical School*, 69 Ill. 2d 320, 13 Ill. Dec. 699, 371 N.E.2d 634, 639 (Ill. 1977) (noting that advertisements for sale of goods at a fixed price are invitations to deal rather than binding offers); *Osage Homestead, Inc. v. Sutphin*, 657 S.W.2d 346, 351-52 (Mo. Ct. App. 1983) (holding that an advertisement offering a rig for sale at a specified price was not a contractual offer); *Ehrlich v. Willis Music Co.*, 93 Ohio App. 246, 113 N.E.2d 252, 51 Ohio Op. 8 (Ohio Ct. App. 1952) (noting that an advertisement for sale of a television at a specified price "was no more than an invitation to patronize the store"). *See also* 1 Williston, A Treatise on the Law of Contracts § 4.7 at 286-87 (4th ed. 1990) ("if goods are advertised for sale at a certain price, it is generally not an offer, and no contract is formed because of the statement of an intending purchaser that he will take a specified quantity of goods at that price"); Restatement (Second) of Contracts § 26 at 75 (1981) ("[a] manifestation of willingness to enter into a bargain is not an offer if the person to whom it is addressed knows or has reason to know that the person making it does not intend to conclude a bargain until he has made a further manifestation of assent"). Rather than make an offer, advertisements invite offers by prospective purchasers. "Only when themerchant takes the money is there an acceptance of the offer to purchase." *Steinberg*, 371 N.E.2d at 639; *see also Osage*, 657 S.W.2d at 351–52 (holding that a contract for sale of an advertised item was not complete until the seller accepted the buyer's offer to purchase based on the advertisement).

There is a very narrow, yet well-established, exception to this rule, which arises when an advertisement is "clear, definite, and explicit, and leaves nothing open for negotiation." *Lefkowitz v. Great Minneapolis Surplus Store*, 251 Minn. 188, 86 N.W.2d 689, 691 (Minn. 1957); *see also R.E. Crummer & Co. v. Nuveen*, 147 F.2d 3, 5 (7th Cir. 1945) (holding that advertisement inviting specific bond-holders to send their bonds to a designated bank for surrender pursuant to clearly specified terms constituted a binding contractual offer); *Leonard v. Pepsico*, Inc., 88 F. Supp. 2d 116, 124 (S.D.N.Y. 1999) (holding that "the absence of any words of limitation[,] such as 'first come, first served,' [rendered] the alleged offer [for a fighter jet in exchange for 'Pepsi-points'] sufficiently indefinite that no contract could be formed"); *Donovan v. RRL Corp.*, 26 Cal. 4th 261, 109 Cal. Rptr. 2d 807, 27 P.3d 702, 711 (Cal. 2001) (holding that a licensed automobile dealer's advertisement regarding a particular vehicle at a specific price constituted an offer in light of the California Vehicle Code, which rendered illegal the failure to sell the vehicle at the advertised price to any person while it remained unsold); *Izadi v. Machado (Gus) Ford, Inc.*, 550 So. 2d 1135, 1139 (Fla. Dist. Ct. App. 1989) (holding that car dealer's advertisement offering a minimum $3,000 "allowance" for any vehicle that a consumer traded in, regardless of its actual value, constituted a binding contractual offer); *Oliver v. Henley*, 21 S.W.2d 576, 578–79 (Tex. Civ. App. 1929) (holding that an advertisement, offering to "ship sacks of 3 bushels each, freight prepaid, to any point in Texas for $4 per sack, said sack tagged according to our state seed laws," constituted a binding contractual offer); *Chang v. First Colonial Sav. Bank*, 242 Va. 388, 410 S.E.2d 928, 930 (Va. 1991) (holding that bank's advertisement promising two free gifts and $20,136.12 upon maturing in 3½ years in exchange for a $14,000 deposit constituted an offer that was accepted when $14,000 was deposited). In such advertisements, "there must ordinarily be some language of commitment or some invitation to take action without further communication." RESTATEMENT (SECOND) OF CONTRACTS, § 26 at 76 (1981); *see also* 1 CORBIN ON CONTRACTS § 2.4 at 116–122 (1993) (noting that advertisements are not presumed to be offers unless they contain unusually clear words to the contrary).

We agree with the foregoing well-established principles. Accordingly, we hold that advertisements are generally not binding contractual offers, unless they invite acceptance without further negotiations in clear, definite, express, and unconditional language.

The provisions of Cutter's advertisement upon which the Picos rely in asserting their contract claim do not constitute a binding contractual offer. As described in detail [above], with the exception of the cash prices stated for five of the fourteen vehicles, the advertisement was hardly a model of clarity. The Picos themselves admitted that they were not certain what all of the fine print at the bottom of the advertisement meant. One of the few clear and intelligible statements located in the fine print, however, was that sales were "on approved credit." But a condition that a sale be "on approved credit" cannot constitute an offer that a consumer is free unilaterally to accept.[1] *See, e.g., Ford Motor Credit Co. v. Russell*, 519 N.W.2d 460, 463 (Minn. Ct. App. 1994) (holding that advertisement containing financing terms was not a binding offer because not everyone qualified for financing). Thus, the advertised "$0 cash down/$229 per month" financing terms could not constitute a binding contractual offer because they invited the public to apply for financing, not to accept financing without any further manifestation of assent on Cutter's part. . . .

---

[1] [26] Even if the advertised financing terms were an offer, acceptance would still have been conditioned upon credit approval. Because the Picos never submitted credit information to Cutter for its approval, they were not in a position to accept any alleged offer of "0 cash down." Indeed, it could hardly come as a surprise to a reasonable consumer that Cutter would need to run a credit check before extending financing.

Accordingly, we hold that the portion of Cutter's advertisement upon which the Picos rely did not amount to a contractual offer, but was merely an invitation to deal. . . .

IV. CONCLUSION

[For other reasons, the court vacated the amended judgment of the circuit court and remanded the case for further proceedings consistent with its opinion.]

NOTES & QUESTIONS

1. *Practice Tip*: Contracts for the sale of goods (such as mason fruit jars, coins and fur stoles) are governed by Article 2 of the Uniform Commercial Code. However, the Code does not address every feature or issue which may arise with respect to the sale of goods. Accordingly, the courts regularly draw upon basic principles of the common law of contracts when resolving issues involving the sale of goods. And in cases involving contracts which are not actually subject to the Code (such as real estate transactions and employment contracts), courts frequently look to the Code for guidance.

2. The reviewing court above acknowledged that there is a very narrow exception to the general rule that advertisements are not offers. How common is it for an advertisement to be an offer? Consider the following famous case.

Lefkowitz v. Great Minneapolis Surplus Store, 251 Minn. 188, 86 N.W.2d 689 (1957). The defendant store advertised one black lapin stole worth $139.50 for sale for $1.00 on a first-come, first-served basis when the store opened at 9:00 a.m. on a certain date. Although the plaintiff arrived first and sought to buy the stole, the store refused to sell it to him. The plaintiff then sued for breach of contract. The court held that this particular advertisement was an offer, reasoning:

> There are numerous authorities which hold that a particular advertisement in a newspaper or circular letter relating to a sale of articles may be construed by the court as constituting an offer, acceptance of which would complete a contract.

> The test of whether a binding obligation may originate in advertisements addressed to the general public is "whether the facts show that some performance was promised in positive terms in return for something requested." 1 Williston, CONTRACTS (Rev. ed.) § 27.

> The authorities above cited emphasize that, where the offer is clear, definite, and explicit, and leaves nothing open for negotiation, it constitutes an offer, acceptance of which will complete the contract.

> Whether in any individual instance a newspaper advertisement is an offer rather than an invitation to make an offer depends on the legal intention of the parties and the surrounding circumstances. . . . We are of the view on the facts before us that the offer by the defendant of the sale of the Lapin fur was clear, definite, and explicit, and left nothing open for negotiation. The plaintiff having successfully managed to be the first one to appear at the seller's place of business to be served, as requested by the advertisement, and having offered the stated purchase price of the article, he was entitled to performance on the part of the defendant. We think the

trial court was correct in holding that there was in the conduct of the parties a sufficient mutuality of obligation to constitute a contract of sale.

NOTES & QUESTIONS

1. In addition to clear, definite and explicit terms, is there language of commitment in the Great Minneapolis Surplus Store's advertisement? What is it?

2. Why are advertisements presumed to be invitations for offers rather than offers? Why is it ordinarily unreasonable for a potential buyer to regard a common advertisement as an offer empowering the buyer to accept, forming a contract?

3. Compare the following supermarket advertisements taken by the editor from a newspaper insert in May 2006:

"Fresh Broccoli — 68 Cents a Pound."

"12 Hour Meat Sale — Friday, May 5th — 8 am to 8 pm.
Prices Good for this 12 hour sale only.
Beef Tenderloin Filets — $6.48 per pound."

Is the reader warranted in believing he or she has the power to accept either or both of these proposals to form a contract? Are these advertisements offers?

SOUTHWORTH v. OLIVER
284 Or. 361, 587 P.2d 994 (1978)

TONGUE, Justice:

This is a suit in equity for a declaratory judgment that defendants "are obligated to sell" to plaintiff 2,933 acres of ranch lands in Grant County. Defendants appeal from a decree of specific performance in favor of plaintiff.

Defendants contend on this appeal that a certain "writing" mailed by them to plaintiff was not an offer to sell such lands; that if it was an offer there was no proper acceptance of that offer and that any such offer and acceptance did not constitute a binding contract, at least so as to be specifically enforceable.

Defendants are ranchers in Grant County and owned ranches in both the Bear Valley area and also in the John Day valley. In 1976 defendants came to the conclusion that they should "cut the operation down" and sell some of the Bear Valley property, as well as some of their Forest Service grazing permits. Defendant Joseph Oliver discussed this matter with his wife, defendant Arlene Oliver, and also with his son, and the three of them "jointly arrived" at a decision to sell a portion of the Bear Valley property. Joseph Oliver also conferred with his accountant and attorney and, as a result, it was decided that the sale "had to be on terms" rather than cash, for income tax reasons. Defendant Joseph Oliver then had "a discussion with Mr. Southworth (the plaintiff) about the possibility of . . . selling this Bear Valley property." Plaintiff Southworth was also a cattle rancher in Bear Valley. The land which defendants had decided to sell was adjacent to land owned by him and was property that he had always wanted.

The initial meeting between the parties on May 20, 1976.

According to plaintiff, defendant Joseph Oliver stopped by his ranch on May 20, 1976, and said that he (Oliver) was interested in "selling the ranch" and asked "would I be interested in buying it, and I said 'yes'." Mr. Southworth also testified that "he thought I would be interested in the land and that Clyde (Holliday, also a neighbor) would be interested in the permits" and that "I told him that I was very interested in the land. . . ."

Plaintiff Southworth also testified that at that time defendant Oliver showed him a map, showing land that he "understood them to offer for sale"; that there was no discussion at that time of price or terms of sale, or whether the sale of the land was contingent on sale of any of the permits, but that the conversation terminated with the understanding:

> That he would develop and determine value and price and I would make an investigation to determine whether or not I could find the money and get everything arranged for a purchase. In other words, he was going to do A and then I would B.

According to plaintiff Southworth, defendant Oliver said that when he determined the value of the property he would send that information to Southworth so as to give him "notice" of "what he wanted for the land," but did not say that he was also going to give that same information to Mr. Holliday, although he did say that "he planned to talk to Clyde (Holliday) about permits," with the result that plaintiff knew that Oliver "might very well be . . . talking to Clyde about the same thing he talked to you (plaintiff) about" and "give that information to Clyde Holliday as well as yourself."

According to defendant Joseph Oliver, the substance of that initial conversation with plaintiff was as follows:

> I told him we were going to condense our ranch down and sell some property and that we were in the process of trying to get some figures from the Assessor on it to determine what we wanted to sell and what we might want to do. Whenever we got this information together we were going to send it to him and some of my neighbors and give them first chance at it. . . .

Mr. Oliver also testified that plaintiff said that "he was interested"; that he had a map with him; that he mentioned to plaintiff that he "was going to sell some permits," but that there was no discussion "about the permits going with the land at that time" and that he (Oliver) "talked along the lines that Clyde (Holliday) would probably be interested in those permits." On cross-examination Mr. Oliver also answered in the affirmative a question to the effect that the property which he and Mr. Southworth "delineated on the map" during that conversation "was the property" that he "finally decided to sell and made the general offering to the four neighbors."

Plaintiff also testified that on May 26, 1976, he called Clyde Holliday to ask if he was interested in buying the land and Mr. Holliday said "no," that he was interested only in the permits, but would be interested in trading some other land for some of the land plaintiff was buying from defendants.

The telephone call of June 13, 1976.

Plaintiff testified that on June 13, 1976, he called defendant Oliver by telephone to "ask him if his plans for selling continued to be in force, and he said 'yes'," that "he was progressing and there had been some delay in acquiring information from the Assessor, but they expected soon to have the information needed to establish the value on the land." Defendant Oliver's testimony was to the same effect, but he also recalled that at that time Mr. Southworth "said everything was in order and that I didn't have to worry, he had the money available and that everything was ready to go."

The letters of June 17, June 21, and June 24, 1976.

Several days later plaintiff received from defendants a letter dated June 17, 1976, as follows:

Enclosed please find the information about the ranch sales that I had discussed with you previously. These prices are the market value according to the records of the Grant County Assessor. Please contact me if there are any questions.

There were two enclosures with that letter. The first was as follows:

JOSEPH C. and ARLENE G. OLIVER

200 Ford Road

John Day, OR 97845

Selling approximately 2933 Acres in Grant County in

T. 16 S., R. 31 E., W. M.

near Seneca, Oregon at the assessed market value of:

LAND 306,409

IMPROVEMENTS 18,010

Total $324,419

Terms available - 29% down - balance over 5 years at 8% interest. Negotiate sale date for December 1, 1976 or January 1, 1977.

Available after hay is harvested and arrangements made for removal of hay, equipment and supplies.

ALSO: Selling Little Bear Creek allotment permit__100 head @ $225 Big Bear Creek allotment permit__200 head @ $250

The second enclosure related to "selling approximately 6365 acres" in Grant County near John Day — another ranch owned by the Oliver family.

Defendant Joseph Oliver testified that this letter and enclosures were "drafted" by his wife, defendant Arlene Oliver; that he then read and signed it; that he sent it not only to plaintiff, but also to Clyde Holliday and two other neighbors; that it was sent because "I told them I would send them all this information and we would go from there," that it was not made as an offer," and that it was his intention that the "property" and "permits" be transferred "together."

Upon receiving that letter and enclosures, plaintiff immediately responded by letter addressed to both defendants, dated June 21, 1976, as follows:

> Re the land in Bear Valley near Seneca, Oregon that you have offered to sell; I accept your offer.

Plaintiff testified that on June 23, 1976, Clyde Holliday called and said he needed to acquire a portion of the land "that I had agreed to buy from Joe (Oliver), and I said I have bought the land," and that we would "work out an exchange in accord with what we have previously mentioned," but that "(h)e said he needed more land."

Defendant Joseph Oliver testified that after receiving plaintiff's letter dated June 21, 1976, Clyde Holliday told him that "they (Holliday and plaintiff) were having a little difficulty getting this thing worked out," apparently referring to the "exchange" previously discussed between plaintiff and Holliday, and that he (Oliver) then told plaintiff that:

> (T)here seemed to be some discrepancies between what I was getting the two parties and that I didn't exactly want to be an arbitrator or say you are right or you are wrong with my neighbors. I wished they would straighten the thing out, and if they didn't, I really didn't have to sell it, that I would pull it off the market, because I didn't want to get in trouble. I would have to live with my neighbors.

Finally, on June 24, 1976, defendants mailed the following letter to plaintiff:

> We received your letter of June 21, 1976. You have misconstrued our prior negotiations and written summaries of the lands which we and J. C. wish to sell. That was not made as or intended to be a firm offer of sale, and especially was not an offer of sale of any portion of the lands and permits described to any one person separately from the rest of the lands and permits described. The memorandum of ours was for informational purposes only and as a starting point for further negotiation between us and you and the others also interested in the properties. It is also impossible to tell from the attachment to our letter of June 17, 1976, as to the legal description of the lands to be sold, and would not in any event constitute an enforceable contract. We are open to further negotiation with you and other interested parties, but do not consider that we at this point have any binding enforceable contract with you."

This lawsuit then followed.

Defendants' letter of June [17], 1976, was an "offer to sell" the ranch lands.

Defendants first contend that defendants' letter of June 17, 1976, to plaintiff was "not an offer, both as a matter of law and under the facts of this case." In support of that contention defendants say that their testimony that the letter was not intended as an offer was uncontradicted and that similar writings have been held not to constitute offers. . . . Defendants also say that there is "authority for the proposition that all the evidence of surrounding circumstances may be taken into consideration in making that determination" . . . and that the circumstances in this case were such as to require the conclusion that defendants did not intend the letter as an offer and that plaintiff knew or reasonably should have known that it was not intended as an offer because:

1. Defendants obviously did not intend it as an offer.

2. The wording of the "offer" made it clear that this was "information" that plaintiff had previously expressed an interest in receiving.

3. It did not use the term offer, but only formally advised plaintiff that defendants are selling certain lands and permits and set forth generally the terms upon which they would consider selling.

4. The plaintiff knew of the custom of transferring permits with land and had no knowledge from the writing or previous talk that defendants were selling any cattle.

5. Plaintiff knew and expected this same information to go to others.

Defendants conclude that:

Considering the factors determined important by the authorities cited, these factors preponderate heavily that this was not an offer to sell the land only, or to sell at all, and should not reasonably have been so construed by the plaintiff.

In *Kitzke v. Turnidge*, 209 Or. 563, 573, 307 P.2d 522, 527 (1957), this court quoted with approval the following rule as stated in 1 WILLISTON ON CONTRACTS 49-50, section 22A (1957):

In the early law of assumpsit stress was laid on the necessity of a promise in terms, but the modern law rightly construes both acts and words as having the meaning which a reasonable person present would put upon them in view of the surrounding circumstances. Even where words are used, "a contract includes not only what the parties said, but also what is necessarily to be implied from what they said." And it may be said broadly that any conduct of one party, from which the other may reasonably draw the inference of a promise, is effective in law as such. . . .

As also stated in 1 RESTATEMENT OF CONTRACTS section 25, comment (A) (1932). . . :

It is often difficult to draw an exact line between offers and negotiations preliminary thereto. It is common for one who wishes to make a bargain to try to induce the other party to the intended transaction to make the definite offer, he himself suggesting with more or less definiteness the nature of the contract he is willing to enter into. Besides any direct language indicating an intent to defer the formation of a contract, the definiteness or indefiniteness of the words used in opening the negotiation must be considered, as well as the usages of business, and indeed all accompanying circumstances.

The difficulty in determining whether an offer has been made is particularly acute in cases involving price quotations, as in this case. It is recognized that although a price quotation, standing alone, is not an offer, there may be circumstances under which a price quotation, when considered together with facts and circumstances, may constitute an offer which, if accepted, will result in a binding contract. It is also recognized that such an offer may be made to more than one person. . . . Thus, the fact that a price quotation is sent to more than one person does not, of itself, require a holding that such a price quotation is not an offer.

We agree with the analysis of this problem as stated in MURRAY ON CONTRACTS 37-40, section 24 (1977), as follows:

> If A says to B, "I am going to sell my car for $500," and B replies, "All right, here is $500, I will take it," no contract results, assuming that A's statement is taken at its face value. A's statement does not involve any promise, commitment or undertaking; it is at most a statement of A's present intention. . . . However, a price quotation or advertisement may contain sufficient indication of willingness to enter a bargain so that the party to whom it is addressed would be justified in believing that his assent would conclude the bargain. . . . The basic problem is found in the expressions of the parties. People very seldom express themselves either accurately or in complete detail. Thus, difficulty is encountered in determining the correct interpretation of the expression in question. Over the years, some more or less trustworthy guides to interpretation have been developed.
>
> The first and strongest guide is that the particular expression is to be judged on the basis of what a reasonable man in the position of the offeree has been led to believe. This requires an analysis of what the offeree should have understood under all of the surrounding circumstances, with all of his opportunities for comprehending the intention of the offeror, rather than what the offeror, in fact, intended. This guide may be regarded as simply another manifestation of the objective test. Beyond this universally accepted guide to interpretation, there are other guides which are found in the case law involving factors that tend to recur. The most important of the remaining guides is the language used. If there are no words of promise, undertaking or commitment, the tendency is to construe the expression to be an invitation for an offer or mere preliminary negotiations in the absence of strong, countervailing circumstances. Another guide which has been widely accepted is the determination of the party or parties to whom the purported offer has been addressed. If the expression definitely names a party or parties, it is more likely to be construed as an offer. If the addressee is an indefinite group, it is less likely to be an offer. The fact that this is simply a guide rather than a definite rule is illustrated by the exceptional cases which must be noted. The guide operates effectively in relation to such expressions as advertisements or circular letters. The addressee is indefinite and, therefore, the expression is probably not an offer. However, in reward cases, the addressee is equally indefinite and, yet, the expression is an offer. Finally, the definiteness of the proposal itself may have a bearing on whether it constitutes an offer. In general, the more definite the proposal, the more reasonable it is to treat the proposal as involving a commitment. . . .

Upon application of these tests to the facts of this case we are of the opinion that defendants' letter to plaintiff dated June 17, 1976, was an offer to sell the ranch lands. We believe that the "surrounding circumstances" under which this letter was prepared by defendants and sent by them to plaintiff were such as to have led a reasonable person to believe that defendants were making an offer to sell to plaintiff the lands described in the letter's enclosure and upon the terms as there stated.

That letter did not come to plaintiff "out of the blue," as in some of the cases involving advertisements or price quotations. Neither was this a price quotation resulting from an inquiry by plaintiff. According to what we believe to be the most credible testimony, defendants decided to sell the lands in question and defendant Joseph Oliver then sought out the plaintiff who owned adjacent lands. Defendant Oliver told plaintiff that defendants were interested in selling that land, inquired whether plaintiff was interested, and was told by plaintiff that he was "very interested in the land," after which they discussed the particular lands to be sold. That conversation was terminated with the understanding that Mr. Oliver would "determine" the value and price of that land, i.e., "what he wanted for the land," and that plaintiff would undertake to arrange financing for the purchase of that land. In addition to that initial conversation, there was a further telephone conversation in which plaintiff called Mr. Oliver "to ask him if his plans for selling continued to be in force" and was told "yes"; that there had been some delay in getting information from the assessor, as needed to establish the value of the land; and that plaintiff then told Mr. Oliver that "everything was in order" and that "he had the money available and everything was ready to go."

Under these facts and circumstances, we agree with the finding and conclusion by the trial court, in its written opinion, that when plaintiff received the letter of June 17, with enclosures, which stated a price of $324,419 for the 2,933 acres in T 16 S, R 31 E., W.M., as previously identified by the parties with reference to a map, and stating "terms" of 29 percent down balance over five years at eight percent interest with a "sale date" of either December 1, 1976, or January 1, 1977, a reasonable person in the position of the plaintiff would have believed that defendants were making an offer to sell those lands to him.

This conclusion is further strengthened by "the definiteness of the proposal," not only with respect to price, but terms, and by the fact that "the addressee was not an indefinite group." . . .

As previously noted, defendants contend that they "obviously did not intend (the letter) as an offer. "While it may be proper to consider evidence of defendants' subjective intent under the "objective test" to which this court is committed, it is the manifestation of a previous intention that is controlling, rather than a "person's actual intent." . . . We do not agree with defendants' contention that it was "obvious" to a reasonable person, under the facts and circumstances of this case that the letter of [June] 17 was not intended to be an offer to sell the ranch lands to plaintiff.

We recognize, as contended by defendants, that the failure to use the word "offer," the fact that the letter included the "information" previously discussed between the parties, and the fact that plaintiff knew that the same information was to be sent to others, were important facts to be considered in deciding whether plaintiff, as a reasonable person, would have been led to believe that this letter was an "offer." . . . We disagree, however, with defendants' contention that these and other factors relied upon by defendants "preponderate" so as to require a holding that the letter of [June] 17 was not an offer.

The failure to add the word "offer" and the use of the word "information" are also not controlling, and, as previously noted, an offer may be made to more than one person. The question is whether, under all of the facts and circumstances existing at the time that this letter was received, a reasonable person in the position of the plaintiff would have understood the letter to be an offer by defendants to sell the land to him.

Defendants also contend that "plaintiff knew of the custom of transferring (Forest Service grazing) permits with the land and had no knowledge from the writing or previous talk that defendants were selling any cattle" (so as to provide such a basis for a transfer of the permits).[2] Plaintiff testified, however, that at the time of the initial conversation, Mr. Oliver told plaintiff that he thought plaintiff "would be interested in the land and that Clyde would be interested in the permits." In addition, defendant Joseph Oliver, in response to questions by the trial judge, although denying that at that time he told plaintiff that he was "going to offer the permits to Mr. Holliday," admitted that he "knew Mr. Holliday was interested in the permits" and "could have" told plaintiff that he was "going to talk to Mr. Holliday about him purchasing the permits."

On this record we believe that plaintiff's knowledge of the facts noted by defendants relating to the transfer of such permits did not require a holding that, as a reasonable man, he did not understand or should not have understood that defendants' letter of June 17 was an offer to sell the ranch lands to him.

For all of these reasons, the decree of the trial court is affirmed.

NOTES & QUESTIONS

1. Is the court's decision in *Southworth v. Oliver* driven by a desire to facilitate transactions, by a desire to vindicate the parties' intention, or by some other policy objectives?

2. Subsequent decisions have brought the validity of *Southworth v. Oliver* into question. In *Miller v. Ogden*, 134 Or. App 589, 896 P.2d 596, 599, ft. 9 (Or. App. 1995), an Oregon appellate court analyzed cases decided after *Southworth v. Oliver* and observed that Oregon courts no longer cite *Southworth*. Was *Southworth v. Oliver* wrongly decided?

3. Is it customary for the owner of real property to make an initial offer to sell that property? Should custom and practice have been considered by the court?

4. When an owner of real property lists the property with a real estate agent, is that listing ordinarily an offer?

5. *Practice Point*: What is an action for a declaratory judgment? Why would a plaintiff file such an action?

PROBLEMS

1. Purolator Filter Division mailed an advertising circular to its prior customers, including Rhen Marshall, Inc. The circular described premiums which customers could select with orders of Purolator products. With an order of 100,000 pounds of

---

[2] [7] Defendants offered testimony that Forest Service grazing permits could only be transferred with a sale of "commensurate land" sufficient to support the cattle subject to such permits or with a sale of such cattle to another party and that defendants did not desire to sell such cattle and had a policy against doing so. Defendants contend that, as a result, the value of these permits would be lost to them unless the permits were sold with the land and at a price to be added to the price for the land. Defendants also contend that plaintiff was aware of these facts.

Purolator products, Purolator would send the customer a new Buick automobile and 100 cameras and bill the customer $500 for the package, which had a retail value of $17,500. Rhen Marshall ordered 100,000 pounds of Purolator products and the premium package outlined in the brochure. Although Purolator's advertising circular contained no provisions for billing or for discounts, Rhen Marshall requested a five percent truckload discount and a "30-60-90 day billing." In their previous dealings, a "30-60-90 day billing" meant Rhen Marshall received a two percent discount if it paid for goods within 30 days, a one percent discount if it paid within 60 days, or payment in full at the end of 90 days. When it received the order, Purolator telephoned Rhen Marshall and stated the order was not accepted. In a suit by Rhen Marshall against Purolator for breach of contract and damages for nonfulfillment of the alleged contract, who will prevail? Why? *See Rhen Marshall v. Purolator Filter Division*, 211 Neb. 306, 318 N.W.2d 284 (1982).

2. On Sunday, this advertisement appeared in the newspaper:

> Read My Lips!
> Monday Morning Only!
> One 1939 Ferlinghetti Roadster!
> $30,000 (Valued at $100,000)!
> First Person Through the Showroom Door Gets it!
> Straight-Shooter George's Autos
> 1600 Pennsylvania Avenue

On Monday morning, several potential customers entered Straight-Shooter George's Autos, but were not interested in the Ferlinghetti Roadster, until Tex Payer entered and tendered $30,000 for it. However, George told Tex the car was no longer for sale. In a suit by Tex against George for specific performance, who will prevail?

3. Jodee Berry was a waitress at Hooters restaurant in Panama City, Florida, when on April 1, 2001 her restaurant manager, Jared Blair, announced a sales contest among waitresses at several Hooters in the geographic region. Blair orally announced that whoever sold the most beer at each participating restaurant during the month of April would be entered into a drawing for a "new Toyota." Blair sold the most beer at the Panama City restaurant. In early May, Blair informed Berry she had won the drawing and the sales contest. With other employees watching, Blair blindfolded Berry and led her out to the restaurant's parking lot. When Blair lifted the blindfold, Berry saw a toy Yoda doll (a character from the Star Wars movies), not a "new Toyota" automobile as she had expected. Blair and others observing the event laughed. However, Berry did not find the situation amusing, and she sued for breach of contract. Blair and Hooters claimed that it was an April Fool's joke. (For the purpose of this problem, the facts have been modified slightly from those reported by the press.) In the real case, the parties settled on undisclosed terms. Had the case been tried, who should have prevailed and why?

4. Pepsi-Cola (Pepsico) conducted a promotional campaign for its beverages, including a television advertisement that depicted a teenager preparing to leave for school in the morning. As the young man dresses, various items he uses or wears are identified by subtitles: "T-SHIRT 75 PEPSI POINTS"; "LEATHER JACKET 1450 PEPSI POINTS"; "SHADES 175 PEPSI POINTS". A voiceover then states, "Introducing the new Pepsi Stuff catalogue," and the camera focuses on the cover of the catalog. The scene then switches to three young men sitting in front of a high

school. Amid noise and high wind, the three young men observe a military jet plane landing next to the school. The narrator intones, "Now the more Pepsi you drink, the more great stuff you're going to get." The teenager from the first scene opens the cockpit of the airplane and quips, "Sure beats the bus." A subtitle appears: "HARRIER FIGHTER 7,000,000 PEPSI POINTS." Then the commercial closes with the script: "Drink Pepsi — Get Stuff." John D.R. Leonard, collected 7,000,000 Pepsi points and submitted an order form from the Pepsi Stuff catalog, claiming "a Harrier jet as advertised in your Pepsi Stuff commercial." Pepsico responded that the item Leonard sought was not part of the Pepsi Stuff collection. Leonard's attorneys continued to demand that Pepsico produce the Harrier jet, leading Pepsico to file suit against Leonard, seeking a declaratory judgment that it had no obligation to provide such a Harrier jet to Leonard. Does Pepsico owe Leonard a Harrier jet? *Leonard v. Pepsico, Inc.*, 88 F. Supp. 2d 116 (S.D.N.Y. 1999), *aff'd*, 210 F.3d 88 (2d Cir. 2000).

C. AUCTIONS

At auctions, would-be purchasers bid to buy goods, real estate or, less frequently, services. Courts treat auctions as contractual exchanges. However, auctions may not fit neatly into the "offer-acceptance" model we have studied thus far. Because parties to private transactions are generally free to design their own contracts, including the method by which any bargain is struck, they may invent a wide range of systems, some quite complex, for the purchase and sale of items. Over the years, auctions have evolved to the extent that two basic models predominate, although variations on these models are common.

First, and most commonly, there is the auction *with reserve*, in which the bidders are the offerors and the owner of the item at auction is the offeree who has the power to accept. It is said that the owner reserves the right not to sell the property. However, once the owner or the owner's agent, the auctioneer, brings the hammer down or otherwise signifies the sale of the item, the owner has accepted the offer of the last high bidder and a contract is formed. The bidder/offeror may effectively withdraw or revoke any bid/offer before the hammer falls, but such a revocation of a bid does not revive earlier bids. When a bid is revoked before the hammer falls, the bidding must start again to auction the item in question. Auctions are presumed to be with reserve and subject to the foregoing principles unless expressly designated otherwise.

In the less common auction *without reserve*, the roles of the owner and bidders are reversed, i.e., the owner is the offeror and the bidders are the offerees. The owner or the owner's agent, the auctioneer, declares the owner's commitment to sell to the highest bidder as long as bids are made within a reasonable time of the start of the auction. It is said that the owner has made an offer to sell the item without reserving the right to reject the highest bid. In the auction without reserve, the fall of the hammer identifies the highest bidder and signifies the owner's acceptance. Like the auction with reserve, bidders are free to revoke their bids before the hammer falls, and previous bids are not revived when a bid is revoked.

The owner of the item may expressly designate the auction as without reserve or subject to other conditions, such as a minimum bid at which the auction will begin. In the absence of clear, advance notice to the contrary, auctions are considered to be with reserve and free of special conditions.

MARTEN v. STAAB
4 Neb. App. 19, 537 N.W.2d 518 (1995)

Sievers, Chief Judge:

We are called upon in this case to review the law of auctions. The dispute arises from an auction of a 2,840-acre ranch located in Thomas and Cherry Counties, Nebraska, which was owned by the decedents, Fred J. and Ruthanna Marten.

This action was brought in the district court for Thomas County by Karl F. Marten and Adam J. Marten, who contended they were the successful bidders for the Marten ranch at the auction. Karl and Adam contended that they were entitled to a decree of specific performance conveying the ranch to them. . . .

Fred J. and Ruthanna Marten ranched on land located in Thomas and Cherry Counties, Nebraska. They had two sons, Karl F. and Herman, and two daughters, Barbara A. Staab and Judith M. Marten. Adam J. Marten, Karl's son, is the grandson of Fred and Ruthanna.

Fred died in May 1985, Ruthanna died in January 1991, and neither had a last will and testament. Although Karl had leased the ranch in partnership with his brother, Herman, prior to 1983, in 1983 Karl became the sole lessee of the ranch. Upon his father's death, Karl and his mother were appointed copersonal representatives of Fred's estate, and upon his mother's death, Karl and his sister Judith were copersonal representatives of that estate. The actual management of the estates was left to Karl, but he failed to properly perform his duties, and he was removed as personal representative of both estates in March 1993. Karl's sisters, Judith and Barbara, were appointed copersonal representatives and they, through their attorney, Tedd Huston, conducted the auction at issue to sell the Marten ranch. Huston was also a licensed real estate broker.

On September 30, 1993, an auction for the Marten ranch was held at the Thomas County courthouse in Thedford, Nebraska. The sale was tape-recorded by counsel for Karl and Adam and transcriptions of the tape are in the record before us, as well as the actual tape.

Huston began by describing the land and setting forth the legal description and improvements. In his initial remarks about the property and the sale, Huston stated, "This will be an auction with no protected bids, however, the sale is upon authority of the county court. . . ." Huston was asked before the bidding began if the tracts were going to be tied together, and the following exchange then occurred:

> HUSTON: It's going to be sold only by the tracts and we're not going to have one overall bid for all.
>
> ADAM MARTEN: Is this an absolute sale? . . .
>
> HUSTON: This is a sale subject to confirmation by the court, as I just read. It will have to be approved by the county court.

The land was offered in five separate tracts. As he called for bids on each separate tract, Huston announced a starting or minimum bid. The only bidder at the sale was Adam, who offered bids well below the starting bid for each tract.

At the conclusion of the sale, Mike Moody, a rancher and official with the Purdum State Bank, delivered his personal check for $52,200 to the clerk of the sale, Howard

Furgeson, and to Huston. This check recited bids of "$125" on Tracts 1 and 2 and "$75" on Tracts 3, 4, and 5, which were the amounts per tract bid by Adam. The memo portion of the check stated, "20% down on 2840 acres Fred J. Marten Estate."

Moody's involvement requires reference to exhibit 9, a document entitled "Agreement for Option to Purchase Real Estate," dated October 7, 1993. Moody is designated therein as "Seller," and Karl and Adam are designated as "Buyer[s]." This agreement recites:

> Seller and Buyer had on September 29, 1993 made an oral agreement that Adam J. Marten would bid at the sale of the real property of the Estates of Fred Marten and Ruthanna Marten on September 30, 1993 for Michael L. Moody as real purchaser, who would pay the consideration for the purchase, and in whose name the real property would be placed as buyer. . . .

This October 7 agreement further provided that Moody, the "real purchaser," granted "an option to buy the premises" to Karl and Adam on terms conforming to the terms of the purchase "of the real estate by Michael L. Moody from the Estates of Fred Marten and Ruthanna Marten." The option is said to be "severable and may be exercised in whole or in part," although there is no evidence in the record that the option was ever exercised. Paragraph 13 of the agreement provides in part, "This option may be exercised by Buyer, jointly or severally, with prior ten day notice to the other buyer, by payment of the consideration and costs set out herein."

. . .

Moody testified that he made the downpayment at the sale and that the check was returned to him thereafter, but he is ready, willing, and able to perform the contract once marketable title is established. Moody admitted hearing Huston state that Adam's bids were inadequate and could not be accepted. Furgeson and Huston testified that Moody and Adam were told that the proffered check would not be cashed. The check was never presented for payment, and Huston returned the check to Moody with a letter dated December 8, 1993.

Karl testified that he had an option agreement to purchase the real estate and that he had financing for that purpose through the Purdum State Bank or Moody. Karl testified that he was "ready, willing and able to purchase this property under the option if the deed is delivered to Adam Marten from that sale." The parties then stipulated that Adam's testimony would be the same as Karl's as to the option agreement and that Adam "was the sole bidder at the sale."

Huston testified that when conducting sales such as the one on September 30, he believes it is necessary at the end of the auction to secure a written contract of sale from a successful bidder and that is his typical practice. No contract was executed in this instance. . . .

After trial, the district court found in favor of Adam on his petition for specific performance and ordered the personal representatives to provide evidence of good title and, upon payment of the balance of the amount bid on the five tracts, to deliver the deeds to the tracts of land to the highest bidder at the auction, Adam. The district court reasoned that a valid sale of the land had occurred at the auction, since the only bids made and "marked down" were those of Adam. The court further found that the auctioneer and clerk accepted a check for the 20 percent downpayment on the property and that the auctioneer also stated that the bids would be submitted to the county court for confirmation. However, the district court noted that the auctioneer's statement that the matter would be submitted to the county court for confirmation was a "condition" that was really a "noncondition," since the county court had no authority to accept or reject any bids. The district court further reasoned that there was no evidence that there was a "protected bid" or that the personal representatives were reserving the right to reject any bids below a certain amount and thus the property was to sell absolutely to the highest bidder. The district court concluded that the action of the auctioneer and the clerk in marking down Adam's bids and in accepting the check for the downpayment signified that the land had been sold. Finally, the district court determined that the statute of frauds was satisfied by Moody's check. . . .

An auction is a public sale of property to the highest bidder by one licensed and authorized to do so and the goal is to obtain the best financial return for the seller by free and fair competition among bidders. 7A C.J.S. *Auctions and Auctioneers* § 1 (1980). There are essentially two kinds of auctions: those "with reserve" and those "without reserve." Although not specifically so stated, the import of the district court's decision was that this auction was without reserve and that, as a consequence, the land had to be sold to Adam — the only, and necessarily the highest, bidder. The facts are essentially undisputed as to what happened and what was said at the auction held September 30.

Although there is not a decided Nebraska case which comprehensively discusses the nature of auctions, our review of the literature leads us to the conclusion that the law of auctions is rather well established and does not vary in any appreciable degree from jurisdiction to jurisdiction. Nebraska has statutory provisions governing the sale of goods by auction under the Uniform Commercial Code, *see* Neb. U.C.C. § 2-328 (Reissue 1992), but none specifically addressing sales of real estate which impact this case.

One of the most complete discussions of the law of auctions is found in *Pitchfork Ranch Co. v. Bar TL*, 615 P.2d 541 (Wyo. 1980), and we rely extensively on the detailed analysis of the Wyoming court. In an auction with reserve, the bidder is deemed to be the party making the offer while the auctioneer, as agent for the seller, is the offeree. . . . The ramification of a with reserve auction is that the principal may choose to withdraw the property at any time, before the hammer falls, and if the bidding is too low — the auctioneer need do nothing and there is no contract between the seller and the bidder. . . .

In contrast, an auction without reserve, or a no reserve auction, is where the legal relationship between the seller and the bidder is reversed. This is also called an "absolute auction." In the without reserve auction, the seller becomes the offeror and the bidder becomes the offeree by reason of the collateral contract theory. . . . This role switching results in a significant readjustment of rights and obligations. For example, in a without reserve auction, the contract is consummated with each bid, subject only to a higher bid being received because the seller makes his offer to sell when he advertises or announces the sale as a without reserve sale to the highest bidder. Consequently, the seller may not withdraw his property once any legitimate bid has been submitted, as he may do at any time before the hammer falls in a with reserve auction. In the without reserve situation, the seller is absolutely committed to a sale once a bid has been entered, no matter what the level of bidding is or the property's true value. . . In a without reserve auction, once one bid has been made the seller's offer to sell is held to be irrevocable. . . .

The collateral contract present in a without reserve auction is simply the owner's agreement with all potential bidders that he will not withdraw the property from sale, regardless of how low the highest bid might be, and therefore the highest bona fide bidder at an auction without reserve may insist that the property be sold to him or that the owner answer to him in damages. . . .

An auction is deemed to be conducted with reserve unless there is an express announcement or advertisement to the contrary before the auction takes place. . . . When an auctioneer presents an article for sale, he ordinarily is not making an operative offer and such an auction is "with reserve." This is true even though the seller has advertised or made statements that the article will be sold to the highest bidder, as such statements are usually "merely preliminary negotiation, not intended and not reasonably understood to be intended to affect legal relations."

. . . .

What kind of auction was held on September 30 at the sale of the Marten ranch? The sale bill does not even advertise an auction, but, rather, advertises an "estate sale." The only terms set forth are "20% down on date of sale. Balance upon confirmation by the Court. Possession March 1, 1994." The legal notice, published once a week for 4 weeks before the sale, simply says "public auction" and sets forth the same terms quoted above, but does not contain any characterization of the auction as "absolute" or "without reserve." The legal notice also states that the sale is authorized by the county court. Thus, on the basis of the sale bill and the legal notice, this certainly was not a without reserve auction. In *Holston v. Pennington*, 225 Va. at 557, 304 S.E.2d at 290, the court noted that the words " 'subject to seller's confirmation' " would have negated an auction without reserve if they had been uttered before the sale. However, in that case, at the time those words were uttered, an absolute auction had already been announced, conducted, and terminated, and therefore, the words were too late to have any effect. In *Wilcher v. McGuire*, 537 S.W.2d at 847, a sale advertised as "subject to confirmation by the owner" provided recognition of the fact that the owner had only authorized a "with reserve" sale. In the instant case, the sale was clearly advertised as conditional, and it seems elementary that conditional sales are generally inconsistent with absolute auctions. . . .

We find on our de novo review that there was no advertised or announced intention to sell the ranch without reserve or at absolute auction. The evidence in this regard is quite clear.

Neither the sale bill nor the published notice advertised an "absolute" auction or a "without reserve" auction. We next look to the statements of Huston before bidding began. The principal statement of Huston relied upon by the appellees to show a without reserve auction is: "This will be an auction with no protected bids, however, the sale is upon authority of the county court. . . ." This statement must be reviewed with reference to the totality of the circumstances. Before the bidding began, Adam asked, "[I]s this an absolute sale?" Huston did not respond affirmatively, but, rather, stated, "This is a sale subject to confirmation by the court, as I just read. It will have to be approved by the county court." If this answer, clearly setting forth a condition of sale, does not negate any notion that this was an absolute or without reserve auction, then the announcement, before the bidding began, of the need for bids above the "starting bids" surely does so.

It makes no difference whether the sellers set starting bids, announced that they would not accept Adam's bids, or said that the sale was subject to confirmation by the court. The fact of the matter is that there was never any expressed intention or promise by Huston to hold an unconditional, absolute, or without reserve sale of the land to the high bidder on September 30, irrespective of the price bid for the land. The personal representatives on two occasions stated, through their agent, that it was not an absolute sale, advised what the "floor" was in terms of price for each tract, and stated that although they would submit Adam's bids to the court (which they probably were not obligated to do under the law of auctions), Huston nonetheless announced that they would not ask the court to confirm the bids. Finally, they asked those in attendance to contact them about a private sale. We find it difficult to conceive how it could be more clear that this was not an absolute, or without reserve, auction.

In this trial, the principal witness for Karl and Adam was Allan D. Woodward, a Broken Bow resident who has been an auctioneer nearly 33 years, handling both personal and real property. Bearing in mind the comments of Huston during the auction, we quote the following testimony from Woodward, elicited by the trial judge:

> Q: Okay. If I'm going to run an auction and say there are no protected bids, and I say I have a starting bid of a thousand dollars, and somebody bids $995, do I have to accept that bid?
>
> A: No. . . . .
>
> Q: . . . Let me back-up. I may not have asked that question very artfully: If I say this is not a protected bid sale, and I say, instead of saying I have a starting bid of X, I say "I will open the bidding at X" and somebody comes in below that, do I have to accept that bid?
>
> A: No.

We contrast the facts of this case with those of *Pitchfork Ranch Co. v. Bar TL*, 615 P.2d 541 (Wyo. 1980), which was unquestionably a without reserve auction. In *Pitchfork Ranch Co.*, Jerry Housel was selling the 70,000-acre Bar TL Ranch, and the brochure circulated to prospective bidders contained the following language: " '[The] 70,000 acre BAR TL RANCH properties will be offered at public auction by KENNEDY & WILSON AUCTIONEERS, INC., of Los Angeles, California in cooperation with George McWilliams, Auctioneer, Bozeman, Montana. There will be no minimums and no reserves. . . .' " The Wyoming court also recited that advertising placed in newspapers around the world stated that the sale was an " 'absolute no minimum auction.' " . . .

Pitchfork Ranch was the second highest bidder at the auction and sued for specific performance. Housel, doing business as the Bar TL Ranch, had secured an assignment of the rights of the highest bidder as a solution to the problem described by the Wyoming court in the following terms:

> In the no-reserves situation, the seller is absolutely committed to the sale once a bid has been entered, no matter what the level of bidding or the seller's notion of the property's true value. This is the catastrophic situation in which Housel found himself where $4,000,000 worth of his property was being bid at the $1,600,000 level. He could not extricate his property from the sale because he had committed it to sale to the highest bidder (no

matter how low the bid) — but that was his only commitment — that he would sell to the highest bidder. He was not committed to selling to the next highest bidder. . . .

Housel and the Bar TL did manage to extricate themselves from this catastrophe because they had acquired the rights of the high bidder, under an arrangement undisclosed in the Wyoming court's opinion, and thus Pitchfork Ranch did not get the Bar TL. The instant case is factually dissimilar from *Pitchfork Ranch Co.*, although the law extensively discussed and analyzed therein is applicable. Moreover, the facts of *Pitchfork Ranch Co.* are instructive on what is said or done before bidding begins in order to create an absolute auction. Since the seller is at the mercy of an uncertain bidding process, which may or may not be fair and open, it is logical that there be clear intent and express designation as such before absolute, or without reserve, auctions are held to have occurred. This is not present in the instant case.

Fundamental to a decree of specific performance is a meeting of the minds of the parties to the contract. . . . At the most elemental level, there was no meeting of the minds here. A with reserve auction was clearly conducted on September 30, and Adam's bids were all below the clearly announced bidding floor for each tract. There is no evidence of the sellers' acceptance of Adam's bids for any purpose except for submission to the county court, an unnecessary procedure in any event, since in a with reserve auction the sellers can reject — which was done in several different ways by Huston. Huston told Adam that they would not ask for confirmation and that the bids were inadequate. To establish a contract capable of specific enforcement it must be shown that there was a definite offer and an unconditional acceptance. . . . Unconditional acceptance of Adam's bids is absent, and thus, there was no sale. . . .

Reversed.

NOTES & QUESTIONS

1. The auction without reserve strains the offer/acceptance model with which we are familiar. For example, the bidders are the offerees, but are their bids truly "acceptances" because each bid is subject to an overbid by the next bid? Moreover, if the bidders are the offerees in an auction without reserve, how can it be said they are free to revoke their bids before the hammer falls, that is, after they have "accepted"?

2. Is it possible for an auctioneer to set a minimum starting bid in an auction without reserve?

3. Auctions of goods are governed by the provisions of the Uniform Commercial Code § 2-328. *See also* RESTATEMENT (SECOND) OF CONTRACTS § 28 (1981). Is it possible to conduct an auction of goods in a manner different from the provisions of the U.C.C.? For example, could the auctioneer in an auction with reserve deviate from U.C.C. § 2-328(2) by giving notice before the auction that the owner reserves the right to withdraw the goods after the hammer falls?

CUBA v. HUDSON & MARSHALL, INC.
213 Ga. App. 639, 445 S.E.2d 386 (1994)

POPE, Chief Judge:

Defendants are auctioneers who conducted an auction of real estate for the Resolution Trust Corporation ("RTC"). Plaintiffs attended the auction and were the high bidder for a particular parcel, Property No. 230. After the bidding was ended by the fall of the auctioneer's hammer, however, plaintiffs were told that the RTC rejected their bid. Plaintiffs sued defendants for damages, and after discovery, plaintiffs and defendants filed cross-motions for summary judgment. The trial court denied plaintiffs' motion and granted defendants', and plaintiffs appeal from both rulings.

The parties essentially agree on the facts. Defendants prepared an auction brochure listing and describing the various RTC properties to be auctioned. Some of the properties were listed with the word "absolute" next to them; others, including Property No. 230, were not. On the back cover, under the heading "AUCTION INFORMATION & TERMS," the brochure stated that properties without "absolute" next to them were being sold with reserve, and that "[f]or property being sold 'With Reserve,' the highest bid is subject to the approval of the seller." . . . Defendant Asa Marshall, who conducted the actual auction, stated in his introductory remarks that with respect to those properties being auctioned with reserve, "I can assure you you're not wasting your time. We have officials from RTC all over the country here. The only thing they want to make sure of is that they do have active bidding on those properties auctioned on reserve, and if they do they are going to sell them. I can assure you of that. They are not here to waste your time or to get this property appraised." Immediately following Asa Marshall's introductory remarks, however, another employee of defendant Hudson & Marshall, Inc. got up and pointed out to the audience that the terms of the auction were set forth on the back cover of the brochure. He held up a brochure and showed the audience exactly where the terms and conditions were and then said they would abide by those terms. . . .

Plaintiffs first argue that a contract for the sale of Property No. 230 was formed at the time the auctioneer's hammer fell, and that defendant auctioneers are liable for the breach of that contract. As a general rule, even if an auction is with reserve (and all auctions are presumed to be with reserve unless they are expressly stated to be without reserve), the seller must exercise his right to withdraw the property from sale before the auctioneer accepts the high bid by letting his hammer fall; immediately after the hammer falls, an irrevocable contract is formed. . . . Compare also OCGA § 11-2-328.[3] Yet at the same time, the seller has the right to establish any terms and conditions for the sale he wishes, and where the seller explicitly reserves the right to reject any bid made, the contract for sale is not formed until the seller actually accepts the bid. . . . We think the only way to reconcile these cases is to recognize, as other courts have, that there is a distinction between auctions which are merely conducted with reserve and those in which the seller explicitly reserves the right to approve, confirm or reject the high bid. . . ." [S]uch a reservation sets a sale apart from the garden variety of auctions with reserve." . . . . Where the seller explicitly reserves the right to reject or approve, the auctioneer is without authority to accept for the seller. Thus, the fall of the

---

[3] [1] This statute is part of our codification of Article 2 of the Uniform Commercial Code and thus does not directly apply to auctions of real property. *See* OCGA § 11-2-102. Courts in other states have recognized that this portion of the Article reflects common law principles applicable to land auctions as well as auctions of goods, however, and have borrowed rules from it or applied it to land auctions by analogy. *See, e.g., Chevalier v. Sanford,* 475 A.2d 1148 (Me. 1984); *Hoffman v. Horton,* 212 Va. 565, 186 S.E.2d 79 (1972).

hammer in such auctions merely ends the bidding, and no contract is formed until the seller actually accepts the high bid. . . .

The seller in this case explicitly reserved the right to reject or approve the high bid in the brochure. And Asa Marshall's "assurance" that all properties would be sold as long as the bidding was active did not modify this reservation since it was immediately followed by the announcement of another speaker who called the bidders' attention to the terms in the brochure and stated that "we will abide by those terms." Accordingly, the fall of the auctioneer's hammer merely ended the bidding and no enforceable contract was formed. . . .

Judgment affirmed.

NOTES & QUESTIONS

1. In *Cuba v. Hudson & Marshall, Inc.*, was the auction with reserve, without reserve, or something else?

2. Is the court's decision in *Cuba v. Hudson & Marshall, Inc.* consistent with *Marten v. Staab*?

3. May the owner of an item placed in auction bid on that item? *See* U.C.C. § 2-328(4).

4. Under U.C.C. § 2-328(2), the auctioneer has the discretion to reopen the bidding or declare the goods sold when a bid is made while the hammer is falling in acknowledgment of a prior bid. Should the law governing this situation be the same with respect to auctions not covered by the U.C.C., such as auctions of land? See the cases cited in the court's footnote 3 in *Cuba v. Hudson & Marshall, Inc.*, above.

PROBLEM

A secured lender, Greyhound Leasing & Financial Corporation, sought to sell an aircraft and two aircraft engines at an auction. The auctioneer announced that the sale would be to the highest bidder and no minimum bid would be required. Miami Aviation Service then bid $1 million for the items, but Greyhound bid $3.3 million and took the items. In a suit by Miami Aviation against Greyhound for breach of contract, who will prevail? Was the auction with or without reserve? Was Greyhound entitled to bid on the items? *See Miami Aviation Service v. Greyhound Leasing & Financial Corp.*, 856 F.2d 166 (8th Cir. 1988).

D. DURATION OF THE OFFER

There are several factors which may determine the duration of an offer or how long the offeree enjoys the power to accept. In *Akers v. Sedberry*, 286 S.W.2d 617 (Tenn. App. 1955), the court explained:

> An offer may be terminated in a number of ways, as, for example, where it is rejected by the offeree, or where it is not accepted by him within the time fixed, or, if no time is fixed, within a reasonable time. An offer terminated in either of these ways ceases to exist and cannot thereafter be accepted. . . .

The question what is a reasonable time, where no time is fixed, is a question of fact, depending on the nature of the contract proposed, the usages of business and other circumstances of the case. Ordinarily, an offer made by one to another in a face to face conversation is deemed to continue only to the close of their conversation, and cannot be accepted thereafter.

The rule is illustrated by RESTATEMENT OF CONTRACTS section 40, Illustration 2, as follows: "2. While A and B are engaged in conversation, A makes B an offer to which B then makes no reply, but a few hours later meeting A again, B states that he accepts the offer. There is no contract unless the offer or the surrounding circumstances indicate that the offer is intended to continue beyond the immediate conversation.". . .

Professor Corbin says: "When two negotiating parties are in each other's presence, and one makes an offer to the other without indicating any time for acceptance, the inference that will ordinarily be drawn by the other party is that an answer is expected at once. . . . If, when the first reply is not an acceptance, the offeror turns away in silence, the proper inference is that the offer is no longer open to acceptance." 1 CORBIN ON CONTRACTS (1950), § 36, p. 111.

"An offer is rejected when the offeror is justified in inferring from the words or conduct of the offeree that the offeree intends not to accept the offer or to take it under further advisement. . . ." 1 WILLISTON ON CONTRACTS, § 51.

The following cases and materials explore the various ways by which offers terminate.

1. Lapse by Express Terms

As master of the offer, the offeror may expressly limit the duration of the offer by requiring that any acceptance must occur before a certain date and time. *See, for example, Wheeler v. Woods,* 723 P.2d 1224 (Wyo. 1986). *See also* RESTATEMENT (SECOND) OF CONTRACTS § 60 (1981).

ELLEFSON v. MEGADETH, INC.
2005 U.S. Dist. LEXIS 545 (S.D.N.Y. 2005)

BUCHWALD, Judge:

The plaintiff, David Ellefson ("plaintiff" or "Ellefson"), has sued defendants Megadeth Inc., Majestic IV, Inc., Megamerch Inc., David Mustaine, LLC, Mustaine Music, Inc., David Mustaine, Gary Haber, Haber Corp., Pamela Mustaine, and "John Does" Nos. 1-5 (collectively "Megadeth defendants"), for fraud, violation of federal copyright and trademark laws, and several other claims. Asserting that any and all disputes between the parties were resolved by an agreement entitled "Settlement and General Release" (the "Agreement") and bearing the signatures of the parties, the Megadeth defendants have moved to enforce the settlement agreement and dismiss plaintiff's action. . . .

For the reasons stated below, that motion is granted.

Plaintiff [Ellefson] and defendant David Mustaine ("Mustaine") are original members of the heavy metal rock band Megadeth. The band was initially formed in

1983, with Mustaine as the lead guitarist, lead vocalist, and lead songwriter, and Ellefson as the band's bassist. In 1990, the parties formed a formal corporation, Megadeth, Inc., with Mustaine receiving eighty percent of the stock and Ellefson twenty percent. Underlying all of plaintiff's claims is the charge that defendant Mustaine, and collectively the Megadeth defendants, have defrauded plaintiff out of his share of the corporation's profits over the past fourteen years.

Beginning in October of 2003, plaintiff and defendants entered into negotiations to settle the various disputes between them. In these negotiations, plaintiff was represented by attorney Kenneth Abdo ("plaintiff's attorney" or "Abdo"), a partner in the firm of Abdo, Abdo, Broady & Satorius, and defendants by attorney Andrew Lurie ("defendants' attorney" or "Lurie"), a partner in the firm of Baker & Hostetler LLP. Initially the parties sought to reach a production agreement whereby plaintiff would continue to work with Megadeth. By April of 2004, however, these discussions began to focus on a buy-out of plaintiff's share of Megadeth, Inc. On April 16, 2004, plaintiff's attorney received an initial draft of a proposed "Settlement and General Release" whereby plaintiff's interest in the corporation and various other licensing/recording agreements would be purchased. Negotiations over this proposed settlement continued uneventfully over the next four weeks as defendants' and plaintiff's attorneys incorporated the parties' comments and changes.

The pace of negotiations quickened substantially during the week of May 10, 2004, due to Mustaine's imposition of five o'clock deadline on Friday, May 14, 2004, for completion of the settlement. To that end, Abdo and Lurie began working in earnest to put together a final draft of the Agreement by the end of the week. On the morning of Thursday, May 13, Abdo received an email reminding him "that Dave Mustaine has instructed us to pull the offer to Ellefson off the table and to terminate this deal as of 5PM PST on Friday 5/14/04, if we do not have a signed agreement in hand." Pl.'s Ex. B. In response, plaintiff's attorney Abdo emailed back that his client Ellefson "wants to get this behind him", but expressed some concerns that the deal might not close.

The following day, Friday, May 14, attorneys for both sides worked to finalize a draft of the Agreement in time to meet the five o'clock deadline. Early in the afternoon, plaintiff's attorney Abdo sent defendants' attorney Lurie an email with proposed language changes for a new draft. Pl.'s Ex. H. Later in the day, Lurie sent Abdo an email asking if his comments were complete, to which Abdo responded that he was faxing his final comments, and instructing Lurie to "[m]ake the changes and we are done." Approximately an hour later, Lurie sent Abdo a finalized, execution copy of the Agreement at 4:45 pm (PST), fifteen minutes prior to expiration of the offer. In a covering document to the final Agreement, Lurie stated that "[a]ttached is an execution copy (read only) of the above-referenced Settlement Agreement," reiterated the five o'clock deadline, and stated that defendants reserved "the right to make further changes pending our finalizing Exhibits A and B and the full execution of the agreement early next week." *Id.* In the final email of the day between the transacting attorneys, Abdo sent Lurie an email stating that "Dave Ellefson told me he signed and faxed the signature page to you. Thanks for the drafting work." Abdo's email is dated Friday, May 14, 2004 5:16 p.m.

There is no dispute that Ellefson did indeed sign and fax a completed signature page shortly after receiving the final Agreement at 4:45 p.m. on Friday. There is much dispute, however, over whether the fax was sent prior to the 5 p.m. deadline. While defendants' papers argue that the fax was received prior to the five o'clock deadline, defendants submit no evidence in the record to support the assertion that the fax was timely. Furthermore, because we find that a valid contract exists even assuming the fax arrived after 5 p.m., the exact time of the fax's receipt is inconsequential.

Plaintiff offers as evidence that the fax was sent after the deadline: 1) his own sworn declaration, 2) the register of his fax machine, and 3) an email from defendant Mustaine admitting that the fax was received late. While defendants have submitted objections to plaintiff's evidence, they have submitted no affirmative evidence to establish that the fax arrived on time. The sole evidence offered by defendants — the declaration of defendants' attorney Lurie — only states that he received Ellefson's signature page at "approximately 5:00 p.m. PST". As we find that a valid contract existed even though the fax arrived late, defendants' objections to plaintiff's evidence are inconsequential.

After receipt of the fax, communication between the parties slowed substantially. However, there are three more important dates and actions to consider in determining the enforceability of the contract. The first, and most disputed, concerns the events of the following Thursday, May 20, 2004. According to the defendants' attorney Lurie, he sent all the parties fully-executed copies of the Agreement by regular mail on that Thursday, four business days after Ellefson's signature fax was received. In his papers, plaintiff suggests that the alleged date of this mailing is suspicious and that the method of mailing, regular mail, is unreasonable.

Second, there was an email exchange between counsel on May 24, 2004, four days after Lurie attests he mailed the Agreement and ten days after Ellefson faxed the signed signature page. On that day, Lurie received an email from Abdo stating that Ellefson "withdraws from these negotiations and withdraws all proposals." In response to this email, Lurie stated "[w]e are not certain what you are talking about, but, as you know, there is a signed settlement agreement in place, which Dave [Ellefson] faxed to us more than a week ago."

Finally, nine days later, on June 2, 2004, Abdo states that he received the finalized Agreement that Lurie mailed on May 20, 2004. . . .

II. Offer and Acceptance

The issue presented by this motion is reminiscent of a first year law school contracts exam. We begin with the fundamental tenet: to have a valid contract, there must be both an offer and an acceptance. *Colonial Woolen Mills Co. v. Los Angeles County*, 15 Cal. App. 2d 536, 540, 59 P.2d 575, 577 (Cal. App. 2d Dist. 1936) ("It needs no citation of authority, because it is elementary in the law of contracts, that a contract is created by an offer from one party followed by an acceptance from the other."). These critical elements insure that there has been mutual assent by the parties to be bound by the terms of the contract. . . . One party makes an offer to enter into mutual obligations, and the other party can either accept or reject this offer. However, once the offer has been accepted, the parties have formed a contract and are bound by the terms of that agreement, even if later events make them regret their decisions. In the case at hand, the issue is whether the exchange between Ellefson and Mustaine fulfilled the requirements of offer and acceptance. Under California law, settlement agreements are governed by general principles of contract law.

A party making an offer can condition acceptance of that offer upon whatever terms he or she deems fit. . . . Many offers include terms concerning the length of time that the offer will remain open, or the method by which the offer may be accepted. . . . Failure of the offeree to comply with the terms of the offer voids the acceptance and prevents the formation of a contract. . . . Without an acceptance that conforms to the terms of the offer, the parties have not mutually agreed upon what terms are binding. . . . Therefore, courts generally find that there is no contract when an offer is followed by a defective acceptance that is equivocal or qualified in any material way. . . . Terms proposed in an offer must be met exactly, precisely and unequivocally for its acceptance to result in the formation of a binding contract.

Nonetheless, contracts are often formed after receipt of a defective acceptance. This is because an acceptance that does not unequivocally comply with the terms of original offer is considered a counteroffer. . . . Any new terms or modified terms in the defective acceptance are treated as new terms of the counteroffer, which the original offeror may then choose to accept or reject. . . .

A late acceptance is [a] form of defective acceptance, and therefore is considered a counteroffer which the original offeror can decide to either accept or reject.[4] *Sabo v. Fasano*, 154 Cal. App. 3d 502, 506–07, 201 Cal. Rptr. 275, 272–73 (Cal. App. 2d Dist. 1984). A late acceptance is defective in two ways. First, because the acceptance is late, it is not in compliance with the terms of the offer. Second, when an offer sets a specific time for acceptance, the offer lapses upon the expiration of that time, and therefore, a late acceptance cannot result in a contract because there is no longer an existing offer to accept. . . . Therefore, in order for a contract to exist after receipt of a late acceptance, the original offeror must accept the offeree's counteroffer. . . . Without a communication of acceptance of the counteroffer by the original offeror, there is nothing to show the original offeror's willingness to be bound by the terms of the contract.

In most situations, the end result is the same under either the waiver or the counteroffer approach. The leading California case on the issue of late acceptances, *Sabo*, 154 Cal. App. 3d 502, 506–07, 201 Cal. Rptr. 275, 272–73 (Cal. App. 2d Dist. 1984), noted as much in its opinion, and decided to employ the waiver terminology because it more accurately described what had transpired between the parties than the term counteroffer. However, use of the waiver terminology can imply that the original offeror may accept or reject the acceptance at his or her option "without communication to the offeree, and perhaps without any limitation on time," and therefore is "at best misleading and at worst incorrect." WILLISTON, *supra*, § 6:55 at n. 15 (criticizing the waiver doctrine for this defect and noting that in the *Sabo* decision, it "would clearly have been preferable to adopt the counteroffer rule").

---

[4] [9] We recognize that California law employs a variant on the counteroffer approach — the waiver doctrine — in its analysis of defective acceptances. *Sabo*, 154 Cal. App. 3d at 505–506, 275 Cal. Rptr. 271–72. . . . Instead of treating the late acceptance as a counteroffer, this approach suggests that the original offeror, having dictated the terms of the offer solely for his or her benefit, can decide to either to waive or enforce the deadline.

As we find that there is no genuine substantive difference between the waiver terminology as applied in California and the counteroffer approach, we employ the counteroffer terminology to prevent confusion regarding the existence of a contract upon receipt of a late acceptance. Referring to a late acceptance as a counteroffer clarifies that further conduct by the original offeror is needed for a contract to be formed, a position consistent with California law. *Sabo* (noting that the offeror's waiver was in fact communicated to the offeree, and expressly declining to rule that a contract exists without the communication of waiver to the offeree).

III. Ellefson's Late Fax

As noted above, it is undisputed that Mustaine conditioned his offer to Ellefson on the requirement that it be accepted by Ellefson by 5 p.m. PST on Friday, May 14. Further, as discussed above, there is no evidence to support the defendants' claim that Ellefson's fax was sent within that deadline; accordingly, Ellefson did not comply with the terms of the offer and no contract was formed upon its receipt.

Because Ellefson's acceptance did not fully comply with the terms of the original offer, it was not a valid acceptance and thus is viewed as a counteroffer. . . . Ellefson argues that his signature page was not a form of acceptance at all, but should be viewed as an invitation to continue further negotiations. Further, plaintiff asserts that his faxed signature page "cannot reasonably be construed as a counteroffer" since it was utterly silent as to the terms of the Agreement. We find plaintiff's arguments unpersuasive.

First, regardless of Ellefson's subjective intent, it is the objective significance of his actions that controls. . . . By faxing a signed signature page to an undisputed, execution version of the Agreement, plaintiff signaled his willingness to be bound by its terms, rather than, as he now claims, a desire to continue negotiations. Upon receipt of this fax, the defendants could reasonably infer that Ellefson offered to bind himself to the terms of the Agreement (sent to him just minutes earlier) if the defendants were willing to accept his counteroffer. *Sabo* (stating that late acceptance is full acceptance of offer by the offeree, even if untimely). The fact that the signature page did not contain the all of the terms is immaterial, as the terms of the contract are not disputed and were contained in the underlying Agreement. *See Robinson & Wilson Inc. v. Stone*, 35 Cal. App. 3d 396, 407, 110 Cal. Rptr. 675, 683 (Cal. App. 4th Dist. 1973) (noting that contract is enforceable as long as there is "evidence of a meeting of the minds upon the essential features of the agreement"). For these reasons, once defendants received the fax, defendants were free either to accept or reject Ellefson's counteroffer.

To the extent that defendants contend that no further action on their part was required for a contract between the parties to result, we reject their argument. While defendants could accept or reject Ellefson's counteroffer, defendants had to manifest their consent to be bound by the counteroffer. Without such evidence of mutual assent, no contract had been formed. . . .

We do, however, concur with the defendants' alternative contention that the mailing of the completed contract on May 20, 2004, constituted an acceptance of Ellefson's counteroffer. This act established the defendants' unequivocal intention to accept Ellefson's counteroffer and be bound by the terms of the Agreement. Under the mailbox rule, the defendants' acceptance is considered complete upon mailing. [California Civil Code section 1583 states that "[c]onsent is deemed to be fully communicated between the parties as soon as the party accepting a proposal has put his acceptance in the course of transmission to the proposor, in conformity to the last section."] Therefore, defendants accepted plaintiff's counteroffer prior to his May 24 withdrawal of that offer, and an enforceable contract was formed on May 20, 2004. *Glende Motor Co. v. Superior Ct. (United California Bank, et al.)*, 159 Cal. App. 3d 389, 395, 205 Cal. Rptr. 682, 686 (Cal. App. 3d Dist. 1984) (noting that unequivocal acceptance of counteroffer creates a binding contract).

Plaintiff urges the court to disregard the defendants' acceptance for two reasons. First, plaintiff asserts that the date of the mailing is highly suspicious, and suggests that the defendants "manufacture[d] an 'acceptance' pre-dating Abdo's withdrawal". This completely unfounded accusation is controverted by the sworn testimony of defendants' attorney Lurie. The only support for this wholly speculative accusation is the length of time the mailing took to reach plaintiff's counsel Abdo, thirteen days. In contrast, the affidavit of Lurie attests that he mailed the completed contract on May 20, 2004, as the postal meter stamp confirms. Therefore we conclude there is no genuine issue of fact concerning the date of the mailing.

Second, plaintiff argues that the Court should reject defendants' acceptance because the use of regular U.S. mail was an unreasonable method of acceptance in light of the parties' previous conduct. Prior communications between parties had been almost exclusively by fax or email. Therefore, "it [was] patently unreasonable [for defendants] to mail a purported acceptance by 'snail mail' without even advising Ellefson or Abdo that it was mailed.". . . . [California Civil Code § 1582 states that "[i]f a proposal prescribes any conditions concerning the communication of its acceptance, the proposer is not bound unless they are conformed to; but in other cases any reasonable and usual mode may be adopted."]

Whether a mode of acceptance is reasonable depends upon "what would reasonably be expected by one in the position of the contracting parties, in view of prevailing business usages and other surrounding circumstances." WILLISTON, *supra*, § 6:35; *see also* RESTATEMENT (SECOND) OF CONTRACTS § 65. Under California law, "any reasonable and usual mode of communication may be used to accept an offer unless a specific mode is prescribed." . . . Further, "the use of ordinary mail [is] a reasonable mode of communication" absent special circumstances. . . . Therefore, in the absence of any specific restriction, defendants' acceptance by mail is reasonable unless extraordinary circumstances exist.

Having examined all the surrounding circumstances, we find no impediment to defendants' acceptance by regular mail. First, the original offer and plaintiff's counteroffer contained no restrictions on the mode of acceptance. Second, the use of fax and email to negotiate the Agreement does not preclude the defendants from using mail to accept plaintiff's counteroffer by sending a fully-executed hard copy of the Agreement, and plaintiff offers no relevant authority to challenge this proposition. . . . *Lopez v. World Savings & Loan Assn.*, 105 Cal. App. 4th 729, 746–47, 130 Cal. Rptr. 2d 42, 56 (Cal. App. 1st Dist. 2003) (accepting for summary judgment purposes party's claim that fax "is *the* predominant" mode of communication between parties, but rejecting party's argument that therefore regular mail is an unreasonable mode of delivery); *Hofer v. Young*, 38 Cal. App. 4th 52, 56–57, 45 Cal. Rptr. 27, 29–30 (Cal. App. 3d Dist.1995) (finding that use of regular mail as mode of communicating offer does not preclude fax as method of acceptance). Third, defendants' last offer to plaintiff stated that defendants reserved the rights to make "further changes pending our finalizing Exhibits A and B and the full execution of the agreement early *next week.*" (emphasis added). Plaintiff's counteroffer signaled his willingness to comply with these terms, including completion by the defendants' the following week. Therefore Lurie's mailing of the fully-executed contract the following Thursday was consistent with these terms, and reasonable under the circumstances. We therefore find that an enforceable contract was formed on May 20, 2004, prior to plaintiff's attempted withdrawal.

For the foregoing reasons, defendants' motion to enforce the settlement agreement is granted, and plaintiff's action is dismissed. . . .

NOTES & QUESTIONS

1. Other courts agree with the *Ellefson* court that an offeror may not waive the lapse of its offer. *See Pakideh v. Franklin Commercial Mortgage Group, Inc.*, 540 N.W.2d 777 (Mich. App. 1995); *Houston Dairy, Inc. v. John Hancock Mutual Life Ins. Co.*, 643 F.2d 1185 (5th Cir. 1981). Why not?

2. The *Ellefson* court criticized the *Sabo* court for allowing an offeror to "waive" a late acceptance, forming a contract even though the offeree responded after the deadline for acceptance set by the offeror. Are there any good reasons to permit an offeror to waive a late acceptance? The *Sabo* court reasoned:

> It is well-settled a contracting party may waive conditions placed in a contract solely for that party's benefit. . . . The provision in an offer specifying the means of acceptance is such a condition and may be waived by the offeror. . . . We find no reason why this rule should not apply in the case of a time limit imposed by the offeror for acceptance by the offeree.

Which of the two competing approaches do you prefer to the question whether an offeror may "waive" a late acceptance? Which approach is more consistent with the objective theory of contracts? Are the objectives and purposes of contract law better served by one of the two conflicting approaches?

2.   Lapse After Reasonable Time

If the master of the offer, the offeror, does not specify the duration of the offer, the offer expires after a reasonable time. What is a "reasonable time" depends on the particular circumstances of the case, analyzed under the objective theory of contracts. For example, the reasonable time within which to accept an offer of a catch of fish is likely to be considerably shorter than an offer to sell a farm. Of course, additional circumstances may affect the duration of either of these offers. For example, what if buyer and seller knew the fish were already frozen at the time buyer made its offer? What if the market for farm land was fluctuating wildly due to rumors of a developer's plans to build a shopping center on adjacent land? In any event, the offeror's failure to exercise mastery over the duration of the offer may create risks for both the offeror and the offeree. Consider the following case.

JENNINGS v. HATFIELD
2005 Tex. App. LEXIS 8730 (Tex. App. Ct. 2005)

Memorandum Opinion

HEDGES, Chief Justice:

Appellant Dolores Jennings sued appellee Mark C. Hatfield after the parties were involved in a minor traffic accident. Appellant raises three issues on appeal, [including that] appellee's open-ended pre-trial settlement offer is enforceable despite the jury's having reached a verdict. . . . We affirm.

Background

The parties were involved in a minor traffic accident on May 24, 2001. Although the facts are disputed, the collision apparently occurred while the parties were driving through a construction zone in adjacent lanes, and one vehicle crossed into the other vehicle's lane. Appellant later complained of neck, back, and shoulder pain, and had surgery approximately two years after the accident. Appellant sued to recover the costs of her medical treatment, which she claims to be $83,976.00.

[In pre-trial discovery, appellee-defendant Hatfield requested that appellant-plaintiff Jennings produce certain documents, including information regarding the appellant-plaintiff's expert witnesses and her medical bills. In response to several demands for the documents, appellant-plaintiff repeatedly stated that the documents were available in her attorney's office. On April 19, 2004, appellee-defendant made yet another demand for the documents, and again appellant-plaintiff responded the documents were available in her attorney's office. In early May 2004, Appellee-defendant filed a motion to strike, asserting that appellant-plaintiff had not produced the requested documents.]

On May 11, 2004, appellee offered to settle for $50,000, the limits of appellee's insurance policy. Although the offer did not contain a specific time-frame, it referenced the impending hearing on the motion to strike and the trial. The offer also stated that "this offer is made with the understanding that the [appellant] will execute a full and final release of any and all claims which are or could have been asserted and for a full dismissal of the above-referenced lawsuit."

When the case proceeded to trial, the court excluded the expert testimony and documents referenced in appellee's motion to strike. The court also excluded the testimony of two doctors regarding the reasonableness of certain medical expenses, so that the jury heard evidence of $59,562.96 in damages instead of $83,976.00.

The jury awarded $3,673.00 in damages after finding that appellant and appellee were equally at fault. After the verdict, appellant purported to accept the settlement offer, and filed a motion for new trial and to enforce the settlement on July 9, 2004. The trial court denied this motion and appellant appealed, alleging three points of error, [including that] the settlement offer is binding and should be enforced. . . .

In her first point of error, appellant alleges that she properly accepted appellee's pre-trial settlement offer after the jury reached a verdict, and therefore that the settlement agreement is enforceable. We disagree. The Fifth Circuit has recognized Texas courts' definition of "settlement" as "the conclusion of a disputed or unliquidated claim, and attendant differences between the parties, through a contract in which they agree to mutual concessions in order to avoid resolving their controversy through a course of litigation." *McCleary v. Armstrong World Industries, Inc.*, 913 F.2d 257, 259 (5th Cir. 1990). Because settlements are contracts, basic contract principles apply. . . . One such principle is that the offeree's power of acceptance does not continue indefinitely, but terminates after a reasonable time. RESTATEMENT (SECOND) OF CONTRACTS § 41(1) (1981) ("An offeree's power of acceptance is terminated at the time specified in the offer, or if no time is specified, at the end of a reasonable time."). What constitutes a reasonable time depends on the circumstances in each case, including the nature and character of the thing to be done and the difficulties surrounding and attending its accomplishment. RESTATEMENT (SECOND) OF CONTRACTS § 41(2) (1981) ("What is a reasonable time is a question of fact, depending on all the circumstances existing when the offer and attempted acceptance are made."). Determining what constitutes a reasonable time may become a question of law where the significant facts are not in dispute. . . Furthermore, if an offer contains terms indicating that it expires at a certain time, the offer cannot be accepted after that time has passed. . . . In determining whether an offer contains a fixed time limit, the court must view the offer in light of all the surrounding circumstances. In cases of doubt, the court should adopt the meaning that is more favorable to the offeree.

Examining the offer in light of all the surrounding circumstances, we find that appellant's reasonable time for acceptance ended when she proceeded to trial; therefore, appellant's power of acceptance no longer existed when she tried to accept the settlement offer post-trial. Even when construed against the drafter, the offer's language clearly suggests that the purpose of the offer was to avoid a trial and its inherent variables and uncertainties. Although the offer does not mention a specific deadline, appellee states that "in light of the impending trial and the Motion to Strike Exhibits pending before the Court, I am hopeful that this case may be resolved." Appellee also explains that "this offer is made with the understanding that the [appellant] will execute a full and final release of any and all claims which are or could have been asserted and for a full dismissal of the above-referenced lawsuit." This language suggests that the offer would expire once trial began, or certainly once the jury reached a verdict. Therefore, the settlement offer had expired by its own terms by the time appellant attempted to accept. Furthermore, finding that appellant's power of acceptance terminated once the case proceeded to trial is consistent with the above-mentioned definition of a settlement: "a contract in which [parties] agree to mutual concessions *in order to avoid resolving their controversy through a course of litigation.*" *McCleary*, 913 F.2d at 259 (emphasis added). While we recognize that some cases settle post-trial, this not does affect our analysis in this case.

Appellant urges us to follow *Padilla v. LaFrance*, where the supreme court held that writings between the parties constituted a valid Rule 11 agreement. *See Padilla v. LaFrance*, 907 S.W.2d 454, 461, 38 Tex. Sup. Ct. J. 663 (Tex. 1995). However, we find that case distinguishable. In *Padilla*, the plaintiffs' attorney, Mr. Steidley, made a demand for policy limits on April 10th, and required payment by 5:00 on April 23rd. After trying unsuccessfully to contact Steidley to discuss medical liens, the insurance adjuster, Mr. Bradshaw, faxed a letter on April 23rd to confirm the settlement agreement; however, he did not mail any checks. That same day, Steidley responded that "this letter will confirm that the above referenced matter has been settled," and asked the insurance company to forward the checks. Bradshaw received Steidley's confirmation on the morning of April 24th, and defendant's attorney, Mr. Chandler, tendered the checks a week later. However, Steidley refused to accept the checks and claimed that the defendant had not timely accepted the April 10th offer. All of these communications took place before trial. The supreme court held that the writings constituted a binding settlement agreement, reasoning that Steidley's confirmation that "the above referenced matter has been settled" indicated that the defendant could timely accept without immediately tendering the checks, despite the language of the original offer.

However, in the present case, there were no such pre-trial settlement confirmations between the attorneys. As previously discussed, appellee made the offer before trial, but appellant attempted to accept only after the jury awarded a mere $3,673.00 in damages. Additionally, the offer explicitly referenced the impending trial and stated that it was made with the understanding that appellant would release all claims and fully dismiss the lawsuit. Unlike in *Padilla*, there is no indication that appellee consented to the alteration of any of the offer's terms; therefore, the offer expired according to its terms when trial commenced, as did appellant's reasonable time for acceptance. . . .

Thus, in light of all the surrounding circumstances, we find that a reasonable time for acceptance had passed and that appellant's power of acceptance had terminated by the time she attempted to accept the settlement offer. Accordingly, we overrule appellant's first point of error.

Accordingly, we . . . affirm the holding of the trial court.

NOTES & QUESTIONS

1. Why did the *Jennings* court employ the legal principle that an offer expires after a reasonable time?

2. Although appellee-defendant prevailed on this issue, what could his attorney have done to better protect him from the appellant-plaintiff's argument that she was still free to accept his settlement offer *after* the trial and the award of damages?

3. According to the appellate court, when did a reasonable time for acceptance of the settlement offer expire? Was the appellee-defendant's offer to settle still open in the morning before the trial began? Was it still open after the trial began but before the jury returned a verdict?

4. Could the appellant-plaintiff's purported acceptance after the jury's award have been a counteroffer? If so, what happened to that counteroffer?

3. Revocation of Offer

Ordinarily, the offeror retains the power to terminate the offer by revoking it. The offeror may exercise this power of revocation even if the offer has not expired according to an express duration term, unless revocation is prevented by an option in fact, an option at law, a firm offer subject to § 2-205 of the Uniform Commercial Code or some other statutory restriction such as laws governing bids for government work. As elsewhere in the law governing contract formation, the courts employ the objective theory to determine whether an offeror has successfully revoked an offer. To revoke, the offeror must explicitly or implicitly express the intent to revoke before the offeree accepts. Revocation is particularly important if a seller of a single item, real or personal property, is negotiating with more than one potential purchaser. If an offer is outstanding to a first offeree, the offeror should revoke that offer before agreeing to sell that item to someone other than the first offeree. That first offer terminates when the reasonable person in the position of the first offeree should know the offeror no longer wishes to sell to that first offeree. Without an effective revocation to the first offeree, the offeror hazards breaching a contract with one or more offerees when the offeror sells to a subsequent offeree.

Under ordinary circumstances, the offeror may terminate the offer by clearly and directly communicating to the offeree an intention to revoke or withdraw the offer. In addition, according to RESTATEMENT (SECOND) OF CONTRACTS § 43 (1981), "[a]n offeree's power of acceptance is terminated when the offeror takes definite action inconsistent with an intention to enter into the proposed contract and the offeree acquires reliable information to that effect."

Night Commander Lighting Co. v. Brown, 213 Mich. 214, 181 N.W. 979 (1921). Brown placed a written order for a generator with a salesman for Night Commander Lighting. The order form provided "this order is not subject to countermand" and is "subject to the approval of [Night Commander Lighting Co.] at its executive office." Night Commander Lighting's salesman then mailed Brown's order to the company's executive office. Before the order was received and approved by the company's executives, Brown's son explained to the salesman that he and his father wished to countermand the order, that they were unable to afford the generator, and that his father was incapable of doing business. The salesman failed to notify Night Commander Lighting of this conversation. Subsequently, the lighting generator was shipped to the Browns, who refused delivery. Night Commander Lighting sued to recover the price stated in the order, $275. Held, for defendant Brown. The court reasoned that Brown's offer was effectively revoked before Night Commander Lighting attempted to accept. According to the terms in the order form, acceptance would occur when the order was received and approved at the company's executive offices. "It is elemental that an order such as this, though it contain the words 'not subject to countermand,' may be countermanded at any time before acceptance. Until so accepted, [Mr. Brown's order] is simply an offer to purchase and in no way creates a binding agreement."

Hoover Motor Exp. Co. v. Clements Paper Co., 193 Tenn. 6, 241 S.W.2d 851 (1951). On November 19, 1949, the Hoover Company made a written offer to buy real estate from the Clements Company. On January 13, 1950, Williams, an agent of Clements Paper, contacted Hoover to discuss the property purchase and an additional term regarding an easement. Referring to Hoover's offer, Hoover told Williams, "Well, I don't know if we are ready. We have not decided, we might not want to go through with it." On January 20, 1950, Williams sent Hoover a letter in which Clements Paper purported to accept Hoover's offer. When Hoover refused to perform, Clements Paper sued for breach of contract. Held, for defendant Hoover. A revocation or termination of an offer need not be express. Rather, an offer is revoked where a communication "states or implies that the offeror no longer intends to enter into the proposed contract, if the communication is received by the offeree before he has exercised his power of creating a contract by acceptance of the offer." Hoover effectively withdrew the offer during the January 13 telephone conversation with Williams. Because Williams knew that Mr. Hoover "no longer consented to the transaction," on January 13, there was "no offer continuing up to the time of the attempted acceptance on January 20." Therefore, there was no contract.

GREENE v. KEENER
402 S.E.2d 284 (Ga. App. 1991)

BEASLEY, Judge:

In a bench trial, plaintiff Greene lost her suit to rescind the sale of an antique secretary, and to recover it. . . .

Viewed in favor of the judgment, the evidence showed the following. Greene placed on sale several pieces of antique furniture from her mother's estate in Valdosta. Because she lived in Atlanta she authorized her cousin to show the furniture. Keener inquired about the price of the secretary and was informed that it would be $4,200. Greene intended the price to be $6,000 and was unsure whether she wanted to sell it, but in conversation with Keener she agreed to sell it for $4,200. Keener said he was very interested and "the only thing I wanted to do was to be sure it blended in with the rest of our furniture." After some discussion it was agreed that Keener could take the secretary home and see if it matched his other furniture.

The night after Keener had the secretary taken to his home, Greene called and informed him that she no longer wanted to sell the secretary and asked that he return it. Keener said "hold on a minute," and went to speak with his wife. He inquired if she liked the piece and she responded yes. At the trial there was a dispute as to what Keener then told Greene. Taking the version favorable to the prevailing party, Keener informed her that "she liked the secretary" and "would like to keep" it.

The trial court determined that there was a valid binding contract for the sale. On appeal Greene contends that there was a mutual rescission of the contract. However, it was not necessary that the parties mutually rescind the contract because it was undisputed that Green revoked her offer before there was an acceptance by Keener.

"An offer to contract may be withdrawn by the offeror before its acceptance by the offeree." . . . This is true even where the contract provides that it remain open for a stated time. . . . "The consent of the parties being essential to a contract, until each has assented to all the terms the contract is incomplete. Until assented to, each party may withdraw his proposition." . . . To effectively terminate, there must be notification of the revocation by the offeror which is communicated to the offeree prior to acceptance by the latter. . . .

When the secretary was taken to Keener's home the contractual status was substantially equivalent to that found in *Stone Mountain Properties v. Helmer*, 139 Ga. App. 865, 229 S.E.2d 779 (1976). The sale was conditioned upon the item being satisfactory to the purchaser. At that point the contract was unenforceable on the part of the seller and lacked mutuality, but once Keener did agree that the secretary "fit in" with his furniture at home a contract could be formed. . . . The evidence unequivocally demonstrates that Keener had not made that determination prior to Greene's informing him that the deal was off. Her action revoked the offer before acceptance by the [buyer] could occur.

"[I]f both parties meet, one prepared to accept and the other to retract, whichever speaks first will have the law with him; and this question is one of fact to be decided by the jury." *Helmer, supra* at 870, 229 S.E.2d 779 *quoting* from 17 C.J.S. 708, *Contracts,* § 50(a). Both parties testified that Greene told Keener she did not want to sell and it was only afterwards that Keener discussed the issue with his wife and then relayed her assent indicating a desire to keep the secretary. As a matter of law, communication of the withdrawal of the offer occurred prior to acceptance.

[T]he trial court erred in determining that there was a valid contract for the sale of the secretary.

Judgment reversed.

NOTES

1. In order to revoke an offer made through the mass media or other form of public notice, the offeror must publish a revocation in a manner equal to the manner of notice given the offer. In other words, publicity given the revocation must be equal in time and treatment to that given the offer where "no better means of notification is reasonably available." *See* RESTATEMENT (SECOND) OF CONTRACTS § 46 (1981). Such constructive, public notice is effective even if the offeree does not receive actual notice of the revocation. The effect of revocation by public notice is illustrated by the court's decision in *Shuey v. United States*, 92 U.S. 73, 23 L. Ed. 697 (1875). On April 20, 1865, the United States government offered a $25,000 reward for the apprehension of John Surratt, an accomplice of President Abraham Lincoln's assassin, John Wilkes Booth. The offer of reward was published in newspapers and otherwise. On November 24, 1865, President Andrew Johnson published an order revoking the offer. Without knowledge that the offer had been revoked, Henry Ste. Marie learned where Surratt was while in Italy in April 1866, and provided government agents the information which led to Surratt's arrest. Ste. Marie brought suit claiming he was entitled to the $25,000 reward, asserting he was unaware of the revocation of the reward offer when he located Surratt in Italy. The Supreme Court concluded Ste. Marie was not entitled to reward because he merely provided information which led to Surratt's arrest but did not make the arrest. The Supreme Court also stated that the offer had been effectively revoked at the time Ste. Marie provided the information because President Johnson's revocation order of November 24, 1865, was published with the "same notoriety" as had been given the offer.

2. Return to *Barnes v. Treece* in Chapter 2, § A. Assuming that Defendant Treece's statement before the gambling commission was an offer, what course of action would you advise Treece take to revoke his offer?

Dickinson v. Dodds, 2 CH. D. 463 (1876). Dodds made an offer to sell real estate to Dickinson, with the offer to remain open for a certain specified time. Before the expiration of the specific duration of the offer, Dickinson learned that Dodds was planning to sell the same property to a third person. Prior to the expiration of the stated duration of Dodds' offer, Dickinson made several attempts to accept Dodds' offer, but Dodds refused to sell to Dickinson on the ground he had sold the property to the third party. The court held that Dodds' offer had been revoked before Dickinson's attempts to accept it. The court reasoned that Dodds did not have to make an express, actual statement that he withdrew his offer, but that under the circumstances, Dickinson "knew that Dodds was no longer minded to sell the property to him as plainly and clearly as if Dodds had told him in so many words, 'I withdraw the offer.' "

FORNEY v. TTX CO.
2006 U.S. Dist. LEXIS 10836 (N.D. Ill. 2006)

MEMORANDUM OPINION AND ORDER

CONLON, United States District Judge:

Reggie Forney brought this putative class action against TTX Company and Tim Loeffler, alleging violations of federal and state wage statutes as well as common law. Defendants move for approval and enforcement of a purported settlement agreement. For the reasons set forth below, the motion is denied.

BACKGROUND

This case arises from disputes over Forney's overtime wages and medical leave. Forney worked at TTX for seventeen years before she was terminated in September 2005. At the time of termination, she was a maintenance accountant; Loeffler was her supervisor. Her nine-count amended complaint alleges claims based on federal and state wage statutes (Counts I through V), the Family Medical Leave Act (Count VI), and common law (Counts VII through IV). This motion concerns the purported settlement of Counts I through V.

On October 28, 2005, Forney sent a letter to TTX demanding $2,989.40 for "all wages, salary, and compensation to which [she] is due" under the Illinois Wage Payment and Collections Act ("the IWPCA"). Three days after making the demand, she filed this case. As a putative class representative, she brought her wage claims under five federal and state statutes, including the IWPCA.

After the commencement of this case, the parties discussed settlement on several occasions. On November 11, 2005, defendants sent a letter to Forney requesting a settlement demand. In their letter, defendants questioned the jury value of this case, noting Forney demanded "less than $3,000" for her wage claims. They sent a second request on November 28, 2005. The next day, Forney offered to settle the entire case for $6 million. Defendants made a counter-offer of $17,000 on December 14, 2005. But Forney rejected defendants' counter-offer. At the status hearing on December 16, 2005, the parties informed the court that they failed to reach a settlement.

On January 6, 2006, defendants sent Forney a check in the amount of $2,989.40. They asserted the payment constituted acceptance of Forney's October 28, 2005 offer to settle her "entire wage, salary and compensation claim." Forney returned the check, stating the October 28, 2005 offer reflected an incorrect amount based on information obtained through discovery. Arguing their acceptance perfected the formation of an enforceable agreement, defendants move for approval of this purported settlement agreement.

DISCUSSION

I. Legal Standard

State law governs the formation of settlement agreements. Because the parties' briefs assume Illinois law governs, the court applies Illinois law. In Illinois, an enforceable settlement agreement requires offer, acceptance, and consideration. Questions of contract formation typically fall within the province of the jury. But if the relevant facts are undisputed, "the question of the existence of a contract is solely a matter of law for determination by the court." *Malcak v. Westchester Park Dist.*, 754 F.2d 239, 243 (7th Cir. 1985).

II. Offer and Acceptance

Defendants argue the parties formed a valid agreement to settle the wage claims. According to defendants' theory, Forney offered to settle her wage claims for $2,989.40 on October 28, 2005. Defendants accepted her offer by tendering payment on January 6, 2006. According to defendants, her return of the payment could not invalidate the settlement because she failed to withdraw her offer before defendants accepted.

Defendants' theory of contract formation is fatally defective because it ignores two events that took place after October 28, 2005. First, on November 29, 2005, Forney made a new settlement offer of $6 million for the entire case, including her wage claims. The new offer revoked the October 28, 2005 offer; as a result, defendants' power to accept the original offer was terminated. *Int'l Adm'rs Inc. v. Life Ins. Co. of N. Am.*, 564 F. Supp. 1247, 1256 (N.D. Ill. 1983), *aff'd*, 753 F.2d 1373 (7th Cir. 1985) (making of a later offer revokes an earlier offer); *see also* RESTATEMENT (SECOND) OF CONTRACTS § 42 (1981) ("[a]n offeree's power of acceptance is terminated when the offeree receives from the offeror a manifestation of an intention not to enter into the proposed contract"). Second, in response to the $6 million offer, defendants counter-offered $17,000 on December 14, 2005. This counter-offer terminated defendants' power to accept the $6 million offer, and a *fortiori*, the October 28, 2005 offer. *Sementa*, 595 N.E.2d at 692 ("a counter offer constitutes a rejection of the original offer"); *see also* RESTATEMENT (SECOND) OF CONTRACTS § 39(2) ("an offeree's power of acceptance is terminated by his making of a counter-offer"). Because defendants no longer had the power to accept the October 28, 2005 offer, their purported acceptance could not produce an enforceable agreement. *Sementa*, 595 N.E. 2d at 692 ("[a] rejected offer cannot be revived by a later acceptance").

Defendants' conduct clashes with their theory. In November 2005, they twice demanded a new settlement offer from Forney. These demands underscored defendants' understanding that as a result of the commencement of this case, Forney's October 28, 2005 offer was no longer valid. Moreover, defendants' correspondence with Forney and statements to the court gave no indication that they intended to settle the wage claims separately. Their conduct demonstrates post-filing settlement discussions superseded Forney's October 28, 2005 offer.

Because the lack of a valid offer precludes a finding of an enforceable contract, the court need not address defendants' arguments on acceptance, meeting of the minds, and public policy.

CONCLUSION

For the reasons set forth above, defendants' motion for approval and enforcement of the purported settlement agreement is denied.

NOTES & QUESTIONS

1. Did the plaintiff Forney expressly revoke her October 28, 2005 settlement offer? If not, how and when did she revoke it?

2. Were there other reasons that the plaintiff Forney's October 28, 2005 settlement offer terminated, besides the implicit effect of Forney's second settlement offer on November 29, 2005?

3. In November 2005, defendants twice demanded a new settlement offer from Forney. How would the reasonable person in Forney's position regard these demands? What effect would these demands have on Forney's October 28, 2005 settlement offer?

PROBLEM

On June 4, 1976, a public school teacher received an unsigned copy of a proposed employment contract from the school district at which he had been employed for several years. The unsigned contract (offer) provided, "If this contract is not signed by said employee and returned to the Secretary of the school district on or before June 14, 1976, the Board reserves the right to withdraw the offer." The school district's superintendent telephoned the teacher to remind him of the offer's time provision, but the teacher responded that he was considering other employment. Nevertheless, the teacher returned the contract with his signature on June 16, 1976. Two days later, the teacher received a letter from the superintendent stating the school district had decided not to accept contracts returned after the June 14, 1976 deadline and informing the teacher he would not be employed for the coming year. If the teacher sues the school district for breach of contract, what result? *See Corcoran v. Lyle School Dist.* No. 406, 20 Wash. App. 621, 581 P.2d 185 (1978).

4.   Irrevocable Offers: Option Contracts

The cases above illustrate that ordinarily the offeror is free to revoke the offer at any time before the offeree accepts. In order to ensure that the offeror does not revoke while the offeree considers the offer, the offeree may wish to negotiate for and purchase an option, providing the offeror consideration in return for the offeror's commitment not to revoke the offer for a stated time. In this situation, the offeror also becomes the optionor, that is the person who has extended the option, and the offeree is the optionee or option holder, that is, the person who enjoys the power to accept without fear of revocation for a specific time. Although the optionee/offeree is frequently a prospective purchaser, a prospective seller may also wish to obtain an option to sell to a prospective buyer, to ensure that the buyer/offeror does not revoke his or her offer for a specific time.

An option is a contract by itself, independent and apart from any agreement which may result from the offeree's acceptance of the offer held open under the option. And sometimes, the option may be contained within yet another contract, such as a lease with an option to buy. Indeed, in a simple lease with an option to buy, there could be three contracts: first, the lease of the property, which contains the option; second, the option itself; and third, the contract of sale, which would exist if the optionee/offeree accepted the optionor/offeror's offer held open under the option. *See* RESTATEMENT (SECOND) OF CONTRACTS § 25 (1981).

Options are increasingly employed in modern, complex transactions. For example, options to purchase real estate, automobiles and appliances are everyday transactions. In addition, the option to purchase or sell stock or commodities has become a staple in financial markets.

HAMILTON BANCSHARES, INC. v. LEROY
476 N.E.2d 788 (Ill. App. 1985)

MCCOLLOUGH, Justice:

Plaintiff brought this action for specific performance of two stock purchase options. Under each agreement the option period was 80 days. Within the option periods and prior to their exercise by plaintiff, defendants gave notice of withdrawal of the options. Thereafter, plaintiff sought to exercise the options, and subsequently commenced this action. Defendants maintained they had the right to withdraw the option offers before exercise, and plaintiff maintained they had no such right. The trial court granted defendants' motion for summary judgment, concluding that the consideration was insufficient to support the options, and thereafter denied plaintiff's post-trial motion. Plaintiff appeals from the judgment of the circuit court of Adams County. . . .

The suit is based on two option contracts, one between plaintiff and the Leroys for 2,068 shares of bank stock; and the other between plaintiff and the Gordens, Laveta Morris (trustee), and Eleanor Schrader (trustee), for 2,080 shares of bank stock. The agreements were by similar documents entitled "stock purchase option," each dated June 11, 1981, with 80-day option periods. Each option was purportedly granted "in consideration of the sum of One Dollar and other good and valuable consideration, in hand paid, the receipt whereof is acknowledged." Following the defendants' signatures, each option included the statement: "I Lloyd Edwards [plaintiff's president], have this day paid to the optionor the sum of $5,000 earnest money, to be applied to the purchase price of the shares subject to this option in the event that the option is exercised and to be refunded to me in the event that this option is not exercised."

By letters of July 17, 1981, signed for by plaintiff's president on August 12, 1981, defendants sent notice withdrawing the options. On August 19, 1981, plaintiff wrote to defendants, rejecting the purported withdrawal of the options and exercising them.

On December 11, 1981, plaintiff commenced this action for specific performance. Plaintiff admitted that the $1 consideration referred to in each option was not paid to defendants, but represented that the $5,000 earnest money was paid on each option on June 11, 1981. The record contains copies of the canceled $5,000-checks.

On May 18, 1982, defendants filed a motion for judgment on the pleadings, raising as one issue the adequacy of the consideration supporting the options. After hearing on June 21, 1982, the motion was denied as to consideration, the court finding a factual issue as to whether "other good and valuable consideration" existed to support the agreements; another matter was taken under advisement. Written authorities were filed as was an affidavit on behalf of the plaintiff. On February 2, 1983, the trial court denied the motion for judgment on the pleadings.

On April 26, 1983, plaintiff, by its president, Lloyd Edwards, filed answers to interrogatories wherein consideration given for the options was stated as including "the payment by Lloyd Edwards of $5,000 earnest money on behalf of the optionee as expressly set forth in the last paragraph on each Stock Purchase Option."

On July 29, 1983, defendants filed a motion for summary judgment stating that as a matter of law no consideration was given for the options, which were withdrawn prior to being exercised. On August 16, 1983, plaintiff filed the counteraffidavit of Edwards and documents, referring in part to the payment of earnest money to defendants per the terms of the options. After hearing on the motion on September 21, 1983, plaintiff by written brief argued (1) the adequacy of consideration was shown by the transfer of earnest money, and (2) the defendants had the use and benefit of plaintiff's $10,000 earnest money for a period, during which plaintiff was denied its benefit or use. Defendants' argued that the sum of $1 or other consideration, as stated in the option, was not in fact paid and, therefore, the document merely constituted an offer which could be withdrawn at any time prior to a tender of compliance. Defendants contended that since the $5,000 earnest money under each option was to be applied toward the purchase price if the option was exercised, but refunded if not exercised, it was of no "benefit" to them, and should be regarded as having been subject to a valid and enforceable trust rather than as consideration. On April 13, 1984, the court entered a written order granting summary judgment, reasoning that the earnest money was of no benefit to defendants as it had to be returned if the options were not exercised. On May 3, 1984, plaintiff filed a post-trial motion, which was heard and denied on July 13, 1984. This appeal followed. . . .

The general principles applicable to option contracts were reviewed in *Hermes v. Wm. F. Meyer Co.* (1978), 65 Ill. App. 3d 745, 749, 382 N.E.2d 841, 844–45:

> The general principles applicable to option contracts have been long established. An option contract has two elements, an offer to do something, or to forbear, which does not become a contract until accepted; and an agreement to leave the offer open for a specified time . . . , or for a reasonable time . . . . An option contract must be supported by sufficient consideration; and if not, it is merely an offer which may be withdrawn at any time prior to a tender of compliance. . . . If a consideration of "one dollar" or some other consideration is stated but which has, in fact, not been paid, the document is merely an offer which may be withdrawn at any time prior to a tender of compliance. The document will amount only to a continuing offer which may be withdrawn by the offeror at any time, before acceptance. The consideration to support an option consists of "some right, interest, profit or benefit accruing to one party, or some forbearance, detriment, loss or responsibility given, suffered or undertaken by the

other." [O]r otherwise stated, "Any act or promise which is of benefit to one party or disadvantage to the other."

Steinberg v. Chicago Medical School, 69 Ill. 2d 320, 330, 704, 371 N.E.2d 634, 639 (1977).

Consideration adequate to support an option is discussed at 1 CORBIN ON CONTRACTS § 127 at 550–51 (1950):

> A very small consideration is sufficient to support the promise of an option-giver, for a different reason. Suppose that A pays 25 cents in return for B's promise to sell and convey Blackacre for the price of $10,000 at any time within 30 days. The sum of 25 cents is not "inadequate" as an exchange for B's promise, although it would be exceedingly inadequate as an exchange for Blackacre. But it is not being exchanged for Blackacre, or even for a promise to convey Blackacre; it is being exchanged for a promise to exchange Blackacre for $10,000. B has bought a power to compel the exchange of Blackacre for $10,000, a power continuing 30 days; for this power he has paid 25 cents, a small sum. We can not say that it is an "inadequate" price to pay for such a power until we know the "market" for it — the opinions of other dealers as to its value in money. There may or may not be such a "market". It is true, however, under our existing law, that B's promise to A is enforceable even though it is proved that other dealers in land would gladly have paid $1,000 for the "option" that A got for 25 cents. Nor is B's promise made unenforceable by the fact that the other dealers would gladly have paid $50,000 for Blackacre. . .

1A CORBIN ON CONTRACTS § 263 at 501 (1950) states: "If, however, the consideration is nominal in fact as well as in amount — that is, it is merely named and is in fact neither given nor promised, then there is no consideration at all, and the option giver has power of revocation as in the case of other revocable offers.". . . The legal concepts of "detriment" and "benefit" are discussed at 1 WILLISTON ON CONTRACTS § 102A at 380–82 (3d ed. 1957):

> Both benefit and detriment have a technical meaning. Neither the benefit to the promisor nor the detriment to the promisee need be actual. "It would be a detriment to the promisee, in a legal sense, if he, at the request of the promisor and upon the strength of that promise, had performed any act which occasioned him the slightest trouble or inconvenience, and which he was not obliged to perform." Thus abstaining from smoking and drinking, though in fact in the particular case a benefit to the promisee's health, finances, and morals and of no benefit to the promisor, is a legal detriment and if requested as such is sufficient consideration for a promise. So obtaining signatures to a petition is a sufficient consideration though the petition is so defective as to be useless and the signatures are, therefore, of no benefit to the promisor. Detriment, therefore, as used in testing the sufficiency of consideration means legal detriment as distinguished from detriment in fact. It means giving up something which immediately prior thereto the promisee was privileged to retain, or doing or refraining from doing something which he was then privileged not to do, or not to refrain from doing. Benefit correspondingly must mean the receiving as the exchange for his promise of some performance or forbearance which the promisor was not previously entitled to receive. That

the promisor desired it for his own advantage and had no previous right to it is enough to show that it was beneficial.

This view of "benefit" and "detriment" as constituting valuable consideration has long been accepted in Illinois. It is not essential that it import a certain gain or loss to either party, but is sufficient if the party in whose favor the contract is made parts with a right which he might otherwise exert. . . . Common sense dictates that plaintiff's parting with $5,000 earnest money under each option contract for more than 30 days constituted a legal detriment to plaintiff.

Summary judgment should be granted only when the pleadings, depositions, and admissions, together with any affidavits, show there is no genuine issue as to a material fact, and the movant is entitled to judgment as a matter of law. . . . Therefore, the circuit court erred in granting summary judgment. Accordingly, the judgment must be reversed, and the cause remanded for further proceedings consistent with this opinion. . . .

NOTES & QUESTIONS

1. In *Hamilton Bancshares, Inc. v. Leroy*, the court indicates that a stated consideration which has not been paid provides no consideration for holding an offer open, and the offer may therefore be withdrawn at any time prior to acceptance. Some jurisdictions embrace a different view, enforcing such options. *See*, for example, *Berryman v. Kmoch*, 221 Kan. 304, 559 P.2d 790 (1977). What policy considerations explain this disagreement among the jurisdictions? RESTATEMENT (SECOND) OF CONTRACTS § 87(1)(a) (1981). *See also, 1464-Eight, Ltd. & Millis Management Corp. v. Joppich*, 154 S.W.3d 101 (Tex. 2004).

2. Many options are unilateral contracts, that is, a promise for an act; the optionor promises to keep the offer open for a specified time in return for actual payment of consideration by the optionee. Are bilateral options possible? Should courts enforce options where the optionee has promised to pay, but has not actually paid, the consideration for the optionor's promise to keep the offer open for a stated time?

3. Options which are the product of the parties' agreement are considered *options in fact*. Later in the casebook, we shall study other transactions which may be characterized as *options at law*, where the courts treat certain situations as if an option existed in order to avoid an injustice. *See* RESTATEMENT (SECOND) OF CONTRACTS §§ 45, 89 (1981).

4. With respect to the sale of goods, the Uniform Commercial Code provides for options in the form of "firm offers." § 2-205 of the U.C.C. states:

> An offer by a merchant to buy or sell goods in a signed writing which by its terms gives assurances that it will be held open is not revocable, for lack of consideration, during the time stated or if no time is stated for a reasonable time, but in no event may such period of irrevocability exceed (3) months; but any such term of assurance on a form supplied by the offeree must be separately signed by the offeror.

Is there any way a purchaser of goods could obtain a firm offer that exceeds three months irrevocability?

5. Termination of Offer by Rejection or Counteroffer

Under ordinary circumstances, when an offeree rejects an offer, that offer and the concomitant power of acceptance are terminated. The courts employ the objective theory of contracts to identify rejections, based on whether the offeree has exhibited outward manifestations of intent to decline to accept the offer. A rejection may be explicit, such as "No, I do not accept your offer." Or a rejection may be implied, as in the case of the "counteroffer" where the offeree responds to the original offer with a new offer, stating terms which differ from those made in the original offer. However, counteroffers which act as rejections must be distinguished from mere "inquiries," which do not terminate the offer.

NOTES & QUESTIONS

1. Sections 38 and 39 of the RESTATEMENT (SECOND) CONTRACTS, and the accompanying comments and illustrations are instructive concerning rejection, counteroffer and contrary statements. Section 38 provides:

Rejection

(1) An offeree's power of acceptance is terminated by his rejection of the offer, unless the offeror had manifested a contrary intention.

(2) A manifestation of intention not to accept an offer is a rejection unless the offeree manifests an intention to take it under further advisement.

Section 39 provides:

Counter-Offers

(1) A counter-offer is an offer made by an offeree to his offeror relating to the same matter as the original offer and proposing a substituted bargain differing from that proposed by the original offer.

(2) An offeree's power of acceptance is terminated by his making a counter-offer, unless the offeror has manifested a contrary intention or unless the counter-offer manifests a contrary intention of the offeree.

2. Consider whether the original offer has been rejected, and thus terminated, in the following hypothetical situations:

Smith offers to sell her land to Brown for $100,000. Brown responds, "Is $100,000 your lowest price?"

What if Brown responded, "Would you consider offering to sell your land for less, say $85,000?"

What if Brown responded, "Your price is too high"?

What if Brown responded, "I can't afford it right now, but I'll reconsider your offer next week."

3. If the offeror believes the offeree has rejected the offer, how might the offeror change his or her plans? For example, if Smith reasonably understood Brown to reject Smith's offer to sell Brown her land for $100,000, what might Smith do? How

would you advise offeror Smith to proceed in the event it was unclear whether Brown rejected the offer? (*See* RESTATEMENT (SECOND) OF CONTRACTS § 38, Comment a.)

4. If Smith stated her offer to sell was open until noon next Friday, but Brown rejected on the Monday before the expiration date, could Brown still accept before noon Friday? (*See* RESTATEMENT (SECOND) OF CONTRACTS § 38, Illustration 1.)

5. What If Smith states, "My offer to sell at $100,000 will remain open until noon next Friday, and I invite you to make counteroffers which will not terminate my offer before noon Friday"? Could Brown make a counteroffer/rejection before noon Friday without terminating Smith's offer? What policies influence your answer?

6. Rejection of an offer held open under an option contract may not terminate the offer. Consider the following cases.

RYDER v. WESCOAT
535 S.W.2d 269 (Mo. App. 1976)

TURNAGE, Presiding Judge:

This case poses the problem of a rejection on the part of an option holder and a subsequent acceptance within the time limited. The trial court held the rejection terminated all rights under the option. This court holds the option rights were not terminated.

Wescoat, for a valuable consideration, gave Ryder an option to purchase a 120 acre farm upon which Wescoat held an option. The parties agree the deadline for Ryder to exercise the option was September 1. This was prior to the time within which Wescoat had to exercise his option so that in the event Ryder exercised his option with Wescoat, Wescoat would have time in turn to exercise his option and acquire title to convey to Ryder.

The parties do not clash on any factual issue, but rather strongly disagree as to the effect of a rejection Ryder made of his right to purchase the farm.

It is tacitly agreed that on August 20, before Ryder's option expired on September 1, Ryder said he was going to 'pass' on the 120 acre farm. Wescoat testified he took this to mean Ryder was not going to exercise his option to purchase such farm, and thereupon talked with a bank about obtaining the necessary financing to purchase the farm himself under his option. Wescoat also stated he talked with a bulldozer operator and obtained a price for doing some work on the farm, and in addition, arranged to do some liming. Wescoat admitted he had not legally obligated himself under any of these arrangements, and stated if Ryder had actually purchased the farm on September 1, he would not have been obligated for any expenditure on the land.

On August 30, Ryder caused a contract to be prepared by which he agreed to purchase the 120 acre farm from Wescoat. This contract along with a down-payment was given to Wescoat on that day. Wescoat refused to sign the contract and stated he did not sell the land to Ryder because of Ryder's previous rejection of his right to purchase on August 20. . . .

No case has been cited, and diligent research on the part of this court has failed to locate any case involving this precise issue. However, text writers have dealt with the problem. In Simpson on Contracts, 2d Ed. section 23, the author states:

Where an offer is supported by a binding contract that the offeree's power of acceptance shall continue for a stated time, will a communicated rejection terminate the offeree's power to accept within the time? On principle, there is no reason why it should. The offeree has a contract right to accept within the time. At most rejection is a waiver of this right, but waiver not supported by consideration or an estoppel by change of position can have no effect upon subsequent assertion of the right. So an option holder may complete a contract by communicating his acceptance despite the fact that he has previously rejected the offer. Where, however, before the acceptance the offeror has materially changed his position in reliance on the communicated rejection, as by selling or contracting to sell the subject matter of the offer elsewhere, the subsequent acceptance will be inoperative. Here the rejection is a waiver of the offeree's contract right to accept the offer, binding the offeree to estoppel, so his power to accept is gone.

To the same effect is CORBIN ON CONTRACTS, Vol. I, § 94, p. 392, 1963.

It must be kept in mind Ryder had purchased for a valuable consideration the right to purchase this farm. This removes this case from the rule applied in those cases where an offer has been made, but the offeree has not paid any consideration for the making of the offer. In those cases, it is uniformly held that a rejection of the offer terminates the offer. Likewise, the making of a counter-offer terminates the original offer and places it beyond the power of the offeree to thereafter accept the offer.

However, the courts treat options which are purchased for a valuable consideration in a different manner. . . .

Since an option stands on a different footing from an offer which is made without consideration being paid therefor, and since it has been held that an option is irrevocable for the time stated, and that a counter-offer does not effect a rejection, it necessarily follows that a rejection standing alone would not end the rights of the option holder. This court adopts the rule stated in Simpson and Corbin and holds that a rejection of an option which has been purchased for a valuable consideration does not terminate the rights of the option holder unless the optionor has materially changed his position prior to a timely acceptance.

This rule fully protects the rights of both parties. It extends to the optionor the protection he requires in the event a rejection of the option is communicated to him and he thereafter changes his position in reliance thereon to his detriment. At the same time it protects the right of the option holder to have the opportunity to exercise his option for the full period for which he paid, absent the material change in position.

To apply this rule in this case, it must be held Ryder retained his right to exercise the option for the reason Wescoat has not shown any material change in his position between the time of the rejection and the later acceptance. The material change required by the rule adopted is the same as that in the well established rules of estoppel. This requires that a party must suffer a legal detriment or change his position for the worse and be prejudiced. . . .

Wescoat did not show that he had suffered any detriment, had changed his position for the worse, or had been prejudiced by any action he took between the time of Ryder's rejection and acceptance. Wescoat talked about obtaining a loan, doing bulldozing and spreading lime on the farm, but actually took no action which obligated him to pay prior to Ryder exercising his option to purchase. In that situation, Wescoat did not materially change his position prior to the acceptance by Ryder, and Ryder's acceptance prior to September 1 was a valid exercise of his right to purchase the farm. . . .

The judgment in favor of Wescoat is reversed and the cause is remanded with directions to enter a judgment in favor of Ryder. The court shall direct specific performance of the agreement between Ryder and Wescoat for the purchase and sale of the 120 acre farm. The court is also directed to enter judgment in favor of Wescoat and against Ryder for $1500 admittedly due Wescoat under the option. . . .

NOTES & QUESTIONS

1. The court's decision in *Ryder v. Wescoat* has been criticized. *See* Michael J. Cozzillio, *The Option Contract: Irrevocable Not Irrejectable*, 39 CATH. U. L. REV. 491 (1990). Would the policies behind contract law be better served by terminating the option/offer when the optionee rejects?

2. Assume you represent an optionor whose optionee has "rejected" the option/offer two weeks before the expiration of the option. If your client, the optionor, had another possible purchaser and asked you how to proceed, what would you advise in light of *Ryder v. Wescoat*?

3. Why do you suspect the court ordered Ryder, the optionee, to pay Wescoat, the optionor, $1500?

J.R. STONE COMPANY, INC. v. KEATE
576 P.2d 1285 (Utah 1978)

CROCKETT, Justice:

The controversy here arises from a lease and option to purchase a business property granted by plaintiff Stone Co. to defendant Raymond S. Keate in which the latter operated Fiber Glass Products Inc. . . . The trial court found in accordance with plaintiff's contention that the defendant's attempt to exercise the option to purchase was abortive, but ruled against its contention that the option is void and unenforceable. Plaintiff appeals.

In January 1971, the defendant Keate contacted Attorney Gerald R. Turner to get help in his plan to raise money to build a new plant and obtain equipment and working capital for his air-filter manufacturing business, all of which would require in excess of $400,000. They decided to take advantage of a program of the Small Business Administration (herein, S.B.A.). Under it, a third party could own a business property, lease it to the defendant Keate to operate his business therein, and the S.B.A. would guarantee payment of the rent to the landlord. Such an arrangement would make it easier to obtain financing by a bank, because both the building and the lease could be pledged as security.

Mr. Turner contacted his brother-in-law John R. Stone who agreed to participate in the transaction as the owner and lessor of the building. To do so, the plaintiff Stone Company Inc., was formed. On September 30, 1971, the plaintiff and

Fiber Glass Products, Inc., entered into a lease agreement prepared by Mr. Turner. They also executed a separate option agreement. Defendant Keate was given the option to purchase the building at any time after 1 year and within 14 years from that date for a purchase price of "the amount of the first mortgage . . . $125,000 plus 10 percent of the amount of said mortgage." And it further provided that the conveyance would be "subject to all liens and encumbrances of record.". . .

In February of 1972 Fiber Glass Products Inc. began occupancy of the completed building under the lease and continued to so occupy it and pay the rent until July of 1974, when it discontinued business and vacated the building. However, neither Fiber Glass nor Keate ever notified plaintiff Stone of that fact and he did not become aware of it until September 9, 1974, when so notified by S.B.A. When Fiber Glass moved out of the building there had been such substantial damage to the walls, doors and floors that it was unrentable. In order to clean up and renovate the building it was necessary for plaintiff Stone to obtain a further loan, secured by a trust deed, of $15,000 and also to advance an additional $4,606 for that purpose. This project was completed the following spring, in May of 1975.

That fall, on September 9, 1975, defendant Keate gave the plaintiff Stone a notice stating that he was exercising the option to purchase the building. However, this notice stated:

> It is my understanding that said mortgage is in the approximate amount of $117,000 at the present time and that 10 percent added to that amount equals $128,700. It is also my understanding . . . that there are at present two liens against the property . . . in the amount of $117,000 as stated above, plus a lien . . . of approximately $15,000, for a total of $132,000, which is $3,300 more than the purchase price under the option. Because the purchase price cannot exceed $128,700, the net difference which you are obligated to refund to me is $3,300, plus delivering to me a good and sufficient warranty deed.

In response thereto plaintiff Stone expressly rejected the terms stated by the notice. However, it also asserted that it accepted the defendant's exercise of the option, but only "in accordance with the terms of the Option" and demanded that he deliver "a check in the sum of $137,500.00 ($125,000 plus $12,500)" at which time "a warranty deed to the property subject to all liens and encumbrances of record" would be delivered "in accordance with the Option agreement."

September 18, 1975, was set as a time for the parties to meet to close the transaction, but this was not accomplished because, as the trial court found, the defendant Keate did not meet the terms of the option. The trial court's view, with which we agree, is that the terms of the option made the purchase price the basic mortgage amount of $125,000, plus 10 percent thereof, amounting to $137,500, as contended by the plaintiff. The unsoundness of the defendant's position is so obvious as to hardly require comment. E.g., if the mortgage had been paid down to one half, one third, or say even down to $10,000, how incongruous it would be to argue that the option was to purchase the property for what remained due on the mortgage plus 10 percent.

The law requires that one who desires to exercise an option must do so in accordance with its terms; . . . and where there is a substantial variance between the terms of the option and the offer to exercise it, the latter amounts only to a counter offer, which the optionor is at liberty to accept or to reject. From what has been said above it is plainly apparent that the trial court was justified in its finding that the plaintiff was ready and willing to deliver the proper conveyance upon performance of the conditions of the option by the defendant Keate, but the latter did not make a valid exercise of the option.

The next question of concern is whether the trial court was correct in refusing to declare the option void and unenforceable. Plaintiff's argument is that because the defendant Keate's purported exercise of the option was abortive, that constituted a rejection of the plaintiff's offer to sell and terminated the option. That argument represents a misconception of the distinction between an offer to sell and an option. The former, as any other offer, may be withdrawn at any time before its acceptance. Whereas, the granting of an option to sell, supported by a consideration, commits the offeror to sell according to the conditions of the option until the option by its terms expires. Under the circumstances shown the trial court was justified in its view that the option given the defendant was supported by consideration and therefore was binding according to its terms. . . .

[T]he judgment of the trial court is affirmed. . . .

NOTES & QUESTIONS

1. When did the option in *J.R. Stone Co., Inc. v. Keate* expire? In the typical lease-with-option-to-buy transaction, what conditions should be satisfied in order for the optionee to exercise the option?

2. Assuming Utah would follow the same law set forth in *Ryder v. Wescoat*, what argument would you make on behalf of Stone that the option should have been terminated even before Keate made his counteroffer?

3. *Drafting Exercise*: Had you represented Stone during the drafting of the lease agreement and option, how would you draft these documents to protect Stone in anticipation of the events which transpired in the case?

PROBLEMS

1. Betty Brown, who owns a farm in rural McHenry County, seeks your legal advice. This morning, her long-time neighbor, Otis McDonald, stopped by to tell her that he plans to sell his large spread, which is adjacent to Betty's property. McDonald told her he preferred not to sell to strangers and wished to give Betty the first opportunity to purchase his land. He produced a written document dated today, with the heading "Offer to Sell Farm to Betty Brown." The document contained a detailed legal description of the McDonald farm and stated: "I, Otis McDonald, offer to sell my farm described in this letter to Betty Brown for $650,000. Betty Brown may accept my offer by paying $650,000 cash or at least $200,000 cash and I will loan her the balance of the $650,000 purchase price for twenty years at 7% interest, secured by a personal mortgage with me." Neither McDonald nor his letter stated a duration for the offer. Betty thanked McDonald and said she would consider it.

Betty could put together $100,000 cash right now, but tells you she does not have access to $200,000. However, her Uncle Bob, who is on his deathbed, has indicated he plans to leave her a substantial sum which she could add to her savings to yield the $200,000 necessary to buy McDonald's farm. Betty has always wanted to buy McDonald's farm, but is now concerned the opportunity could slip away due to the circumstances. What alternative courses of action are available to her, and what are the relative advantages and risks of these alternatives?

2. Landlord rented commercial premises to Tenant in June 1985. The lease, which would expire on June 30, 1988, provided: "In the event that Landlord desires to sell or lease the premises and receives an acceptable offer during the lease, Tenant shall have the opportunity to match the conditions of the offer and to purchase or lease the premises." On May 17, 1988, Landlord notified Tenant that he had listed the property for sale for $450,000 cash. Tenant responded he was not interested in buying the property at that price because it was too high. On May 23, 1988, Landlord entered into an option contract with Oil Company under which Oil Company had the right to purchase the premises for $450,000 until September 19, 1988. Tenant learned about this option contract in June 1988, but waited until August 1988 to notify Landlord that he, Tenant, wanted to purchase the property. When Landlord refused to sell to Tenant, Tenant sued Landlord for injunctive relief; that is, an order preventing Landlord from selling to anyone else, and for specific performance of Landlord's obligation to offer him the opportunity to buy the property. Tenant also seeks recovery for any damages due to Landlord's breach of the "first refusal" provision in the lease. What, if any, relief should the court grant Tenant? *See Hewatt v. Leppert*, 259 Ga. 112, 376 S.E.2d 883 (1989).

6.   Termination of Offer by Death or Incapacity

Under the long prevailing common law, an offer terminates immediately upon the death of the offeror or offeree, even without notice to the other party. The courts have also held offers terminated in the event of the legal incapacity of the offeror or offeree. Is this approach consistent with the objective theory of contracts? If not, is an exception to the objective theory warranted? *See* RESTATEMENT (SECOND) OF CONTRACTS § 48, comment b (1981).

Jordan v. Dobbins, 122 Mass. 168, 23 Am. Rep. 305 (1877). On February 28, 1873, William Dobbins executed and delivered to the plaintiffs a written contract in which he made a continuing guaranty of payment up to $1000 for goods sold by the plaintiffs to Moore. According to its express terms, the guaranty was extended "until written notice shall have been given by [Dobbins] to [the plaintiffs] and received by them, that it shall not apply to future purchases." Dobbins died on August 6, 1873, but plaintiffs did not receive notice of his death until after goods were delivered to Moore between January and May, 1874. Plaintiffs demanded payment without success and sued for payment from the estate. Held, for the estate.

> [S]uch a guaranty is revocable by the guarantor at any time before it is acted upon. . . . Such being the nature of a guaranty, we are of the opinion that the death of the guarantor operates as a revocation of it, and that the person holding it cannot recover against his executor or administrator for goods sold after the death. . . . The provision, that it shall continue until written notice is given by the guarantor that it shall not apply to future purchases, affects the mode in which the guarantor might exercise his right

to revoke it, but it cannot prevent its revocation by his death. . . . We are not impressed with the plaintiff's argument that it is inequitable to throw the loss upon them. It is no hardship to require traders, whose business it is to deal in goods, to exercise diligence so far as to ascertain whether a person upon whose credit they are selling is living.

NOTES & QUESTIONS

1. In light of *Jordan v. Dobbins*, what would a trader have to do before extending credit to a purchaser to protect itself from revocation of the offer of guaranty without notice due to the death of the guarantor? Is it reasonable to expect modern businesspersons to do this? Does the *Jordan v. Dobbins* decision serve or conflict with any of the purposes and policies of contract law which we have previously identified?

2. Is the *Jordan v. Dobbins* decision consistent with the objective theory of contracts? *See* RESTATEMENT (SECOND) OF CONTRACTS § 48, comment b (1981).

3. If Dobbins had expressly written that his death would not terminate the guarantee until such time as the sellers became aware of it, would such a statement have been effective?

4. Should loss of mental capacity by either the offeror or offeree operate to terminate the offer without notice? Consider the following case.

SWIFT & COMPANY v. SMIGEL
115 N.J. Super. 391, 279 A.2d 895 (1971)

CONFORD, P.J.A.D.:

Plaintiff Swift & Company instituted an action in the Superior Court against Erwin Smigel, executor of the estate of Joseph O. Smigel, for $8,509.60, the amount of merchandise it supplied the Pine Haven Nursing Home & Sanitarium, Inc. ('Pine Haven') upon credit. Plaintiff held continuing guaranties by decedent Smigel and third-party defendant Abe Kraig for payment of the indebtedness. The trial court granted defendant Erwin Smigel's motion for summary judgment, and entered judgment dismissing Swift's complaint and Smigel's third-party complaint against Kraig. Swift appeals from that judgment.

The action of the trial court was predicated upon Joseph Smigel's adjudication as an incompetent prior to the delivery of any of the merchandise for which claim is here made, and upon the authority of the supposed rule that mental incompetency of an offeror prior to acceptance by the offeree terminates the offer whether or not the offeree had notice of the incompetency at the time of the acceptance. RESTATEMENT (SECOND) OF CONTRACTS § 48 at 56 (1932). The justification for any such rule, which has not heretofore been passed upon in any reported New Jersey case, is the main question before us for resolution.

The undisputed facts which emerge from the pleadings, motion papers, briefs and oral argument are these. To induce plaintiff to sell provisions to Pine Haven, the two equal owners of its stock, decedent Smigel and one Abe Kraig, on November 11, 1962 each entered into a written agreement of "continuing guaranty" with plaintiff undertaking to pay at maturity all indebtedness of Pine Haven for goods to be sold and delivered to it by plaintiff. Among other provisions, the agreement signed by Smigel purported to cover all liabilities the buyer might incur until ten days after receipt of notice from the guarantor or his legal representatives of withdrawal of the guaranty. No notice of withdrawal was ever given by Smigel or his representatives. Plaintiff asserts, and for the purpose of this appeal it must be accepted as a fact, that it never had knowledge of Smigel's incompetency during the period of delivery of the merchandise giving rise to the present claims, or previously.

We are without information on the basis of which it could be determined whether plaintiff reasonably should have known or been put on inquiry of facts which would have disclosed Smigel's incompetence. Smigel was adjudicated incompetent January 16, 1966, and letters of guardianship were issued to his son, the present defendant, on February 1, 1966. The unpaid-for merchandise was delivered during the period from January 4, 1967 to October 12, 1967. What the course of deliveries and payments therefor previously may have been is not disclosed by the record.

Smigel died November 19, 1967. Pine Haven filed a petition under Chapter XI of the Bankruptcy Act on December 20, 1967. Plaintiff made a claim against the decedent's estate, which was rejected, whereupon this action was instituted. . . .

Neither of the parties to this appeal disputes that the agreement upon which this action was brought was a continuing guaranty of the kind "which is not limited to a particular transaction . . . but which is intended to cover future transactions. . . ." A continuing guaranty is at its inception an offer from the guarantor and is accepted by the creditor each time the latter does a specified act (e.g., extending credit to the debtor). Typically, as here, such a guaranty reserves in the guarantor the power to revoke it unilaterally prior to action by way of acceptance by the creditor. . . .

The specific question which concerns us here — whether an adjudication of mental incompetency of a guarantor operates automatically to revoke a continuing guaranty — has not been decided in any American case disclosed by research of the parties or our own. . . .

The treatment of the question in the texts has been subsumed under the assumed analogy of death of the guarantor. Most of the few decided cases on the latter point have held that death terminates the guaranty without regard to knowledge by the creditor, on the purported general principle that the death of an offeror destroys one of the two essential assenting entities to a contract. . . . A New Jersey trial court followed the general rule. *Teplitz Thrown Silk Co. v. Rich*, 13 N.J. Misc. 494, 179 A. 305 (Cir. Ct. 1935). Other typical such cases are *Jordan v. Dobbins*, 122 Mass. 168 (Sup. Jud. Ct. 1877); *Aitken v. Lang*, 106 Ky. 652, 51 S.W. 154 (Ct. App. 1899). The leading case to the contrary is *Gay v. Ward*, 67 Conn. 147, 34 A. 1025 (Sup. Ct. Err. 1895), which stressed the diminished business utility of continuing guaranties if terminable without notice on death. Professor Corbin treats that case as representative of the preferred rule. 1 CORBIN, CONTRACTS (1963) § 54 at 229. . . .

The conceptual underpinning of the notion that an offer should be deemed automatically revoked upon death or insanity of the offeror despite good-faith action by way of acceptance thereof by an unknowing offeree has been criticized by the leading writers on the subject.

Corbin comments:

> It is very generally said that the death of the offeror terminates the offeree's power of acceptance even though the offeree has no knowledge of such death. Such general statements arose out of the earlier notion that a contract cannot be made without an actual meeting of minds at a single moment of time, a notion that has long been abandoned. The rule has also been supposed to follow by some logical necessity from the dictum that it takes two persons to make a contract. It is not contrary to that dictum to deny that death terminates the power to accept; the offer was made by a living man and is accepted by another living man.
>
> It has even been held, *and justly*, that the doing of the requested acts after the death of the offeror, but in ignorance thereof, consummates a contract. Thus, where through an agent an offeror orders the shipment of goods to the agent, and the offeree ships the goods in ignorance that the offeror has died, the offeree can collect the price from the offeror's estate. So, also, where one has given his promise to guarantee payment for goods to be sold, money to be lent, or service to be rendered to another, the sale or loan or service in ignorance of the promisor's death has been held to enable the promisee to enforce the promise of guaranty against the guarantor's estate. Some cases have held the contrary, however; and also it has been held that the offeree can not accept after he has knowledge that the offeror is dead. . . .

The case for terminating the offer on subsequent insanity of the offeror without knowledge of the offeree is found by Corbin "even more doubtful than the rule as to the offeror's death" as "[i]nsanity is far less easily determinable as a fact than is death, either by the contracting parties themselves or by a court. . . ."

Williston observes:

> Strong arguments have been advanced that, under the modern view of the formation of contracts which makes the expression of mutual assent the determining factor, notice of death should be required to end the offer, since until notice the apparent effect of the offer continues. A statute, however, would undoubtedly be necessary to bring about this result. . . .
>
> In all probability, insanity of either party would, more than a century ago, have been treated in the same way as death; but since the middle of the nineteenth century there has been a growing recognition of the capacity of insane persons to make contracts, at least under some circumstances, based on the apparent effect of the insane person's conduct and on the ignorance of any impropriety in the transaction by the other party. . . .

It is noteworthy, in the same vein, that the American Law Institute, although retaining in proposed RESTATEMENT (SECOND) OF CONTRACTS . . . the substance of section 48 of the RESTATEMENT, terminating an offeree's power of acceptance when the offeror (or offeree) dies or is deprived of legal capacity to enter into the proposed contract, apparently does so reluctantly and critically. Comment (a) to section 48 in RESTATEMENT 2D, reads:

> *Death of offeror.* The offeror's death terminates the power of the offeree without notice to him. *This rule seems to be a relic of the obsolete view* that a contract requires a "meeting of minds," and it is out of harmony with the

modern doctrine that a manifestation of assent is effective without regard
to actual mental assent. . . . Some inroads have been made on the rule by
statutes and decisions with respect to bank deposits and collections, and by
legislation with respect to powers of attorney given by servicemen. . . . In
the absence of legislation, the rule remains in effect. (Emphasis added)

See the comparable criticism of the rationale of the principle of automatic
revocation of offers on death or insanity of the offeror (*see* Oliphant, *Duration and
Termination of an Offer*, 18 MICH. L. REV. 201, 209–211 (1919); *see also* Note, 24
COLUM. L. REV. 294 (1924)) in both of which that rule is found to violate the
reasonable expectations of an offeree without knowledge of the offeror's death or
other disability. In the latter the observation is made:

> Contract and tort liabilities pass to personal representatives. Why not
> liability under an offer? If we adopt a test objective as to the offeror and
> ask, "What is the scope of the offeree's reasonable expectation?," it would
> seem that notice of the death should be required to terminate the
> offer. . . .

In view of the foregoing criticisms of the conventional approach, which strike us
as persuasive, we are not disposed, in determination of this first-instance litigation
on the point, routinely to follow existing standard formulations on the subject. The
search should be for the rule which will accord with the reasonable expectations of
persons in the business community involved in transactions of this kind. In that
regard, moreover, we bear no responsibility in this case for determining the rule in
the case of death of the guarantor but only in that of his adjudication of
incompetency. There may be material differences in the respective situations, as
noted in the excerpt quoted from CORBIN, *supra*. Furthermore, our New Jersey
cases on the effect of insanity on contract liability, as will be seen Infra, also call for
a special approach to the guaranty question in the insanity context.

> In broad terms, the law of contracts has been said to "attempt(s) the
> realization of reasonable expectations that have been induced by the
> making of a promise." . . . In the present instance decedent promised
> plaintiff to make good any bills for provisions incurred by a corporate
> business enterprise in which he had a one-half stock interest. Had he not
> done so plaintiff presumably would not have taken on the business risk of
> selling to the corporation. It would seem to us that if plaintiff neither knew
> nor had any reason to know of decedent's later adjudication as an
> incompetent during any portion of the time it was making the deliveries
> which gave rise to the debts here sued on, plaintiff's reasonable expecta-
> tions based on decedent's original continuing promise would be unjustifi-
> ably defeated by denial of recovery.

If the situation is judged in terms of relative convenience, it would seem easier
and more expectable for the guardian of the incompetent to notify at least those
people with whom the incompetent had been doing business of the fact of
adjudication than for the holder of a guaranty such as here to have to make a
specific inquiry as to competency of the guarantor on each occasion of an advance
of credit to the principal debtor. . . .

We have thus far been considering the problem presented on the theory that
decedent's accountability should soundly be appraised on the basis of reasonable
expectations and reliance of others stemming from his act of execution of the

guaranty. On that approach his subsequent incompetency would be irrelevant, for he was competent when he acted. The theoretical basis for the conventional view of automatic termination of the continuing guaranty on insanity, however, is that there is a renewal of the offer on each occasion of acceptance thereof by the offeree, and that renewal cannot be effected by one without legal capacity at the time. . . . But even if we adhered to that concept of the jural conduct of the guarantor in a continuing guaranty, immunity of defendant in the present situation as a matter of law would not square with existing New Jersey cases as to the liability of persons who, lacking mental capacity, contract with others having no knowledge of that fact and parting with valuable consideration.

In *Manufacturers Trust Co. v. Podvin*, 10 N.J. 199, 207–208, 89 A.2d 672 (1952), the court approved the rule declared in the early case of *Drake v. Crowell*, 40 N.J.L. 58, 59 (Sup. Ct. 1878), to the effect that:

> The law in this state is settled, that contracts with lunatics and insane persons are invalid, subject to the qualification that a contract made in good faith with a lunatic, for a full consideration, which has been executed without knowledge of the insanity, or such information as would lead a prudent person to the belief of the incapacity, will be sustained.

The qualification stated was applied by the court in the *Drake* case in favor of an unknowing party dealing with the alleged incompetent. . . .

It is thus clear that whatever view is taken as to the appropriate theoretical basis for determining the decedent's liability in this fact pattern, the decisive consideration should be the presence or absence of knowledge by plaintiff, actual or reasonably to be imputed, of decedent's incompetency at the time of each advance of credit pursuant to the guaranty.

Moreover, if at the trial plaintiff's knowledge is established by defendant, the issue of decedent's incompetency would not necessarily be concluded by proof of the fact of adjudication of incompetency. The decisions in this State leave no doubt that that fact is not conclusive but only prima facie evidence of legal incompetency.

The entire judgment . . . is reversed and the cause is remanded to the Law Division for further proceedings consonant with this opinion.

NOTES & QUESTIONS

1. The *Swift* court expressly declined to determine whether death terminates an offer without notice but suggested there may be material differences between death and loss of mental capacity that could yield a different result. Can you think of principled distinctions between death and supervening mental capacity which would justify a difference regarding whether revocation occurs without notice?

2. The *Swift* court reasoned that it is easier for the incompetent's guardian to notify the people with whom the incompetent has been doing business of the adjudication of incompetence than to expect the holder of the guaranty to make a specific inquiry as to competency each time before credit is advanced. Is the same reasoning applicable in the case of the guarantor's death?

3. The *Swift* court remanded for two reasons. What were they?

PROBLEM

Betty Brown paid Otis McDonald $500 for an option to purchase McDonald's farm for $650,000. Under the option, McDonald promised to hold his offer to sell open to Brown until July 16, 1997. On July 10, 1997, McDonald died. Unaware of McDonald's death, Brown exercised the option on July 12, 1997, by delivering a certified check for the agreed-upon down payment to an agent McDonald had previously designated. The agent, also unaware of McDonald's death, took the check and deposited it in an escrow account. Does Brown have a contract to buy McDonald's farm?

CHAPTER 3

ACCEPTANCE OF OFFERS

Mutual assent is essential to the formation of a binding agreement, that is, a contract. From the time an offeror extends an offer until that offer terminates, the offeree can create a contract by exercising the power of acceptance created by the offeror. To exercise this power of acceptance and close the bargain, the offeree must manifest agreement by words or actions evincing assent to the offeror's terms. *Crince v. Kulzer*, 498 N.W.2d 55 (Minn. App. Ct. 1993). An offer can be accepted only by persons who reasonably believe they are among the intended group of offerees. *See* RESTATEMENT (SECOND) OF CONTRACTS § 52 (1981).

Problems sometimes arise over when acceptance has occurred, whether the offeree had an obligation to notify the offeror of acceptance and whether notice was accomplished, particularly when the parties are dealing at a distance. The parties, particularly the offeror, may exercise control over the terms of the private bargain by setting terms governing the mode of acceptance, including dispensing with notice of acceptance from the offeree. In the absence of such mastery of the terms by the parties, the courts have developed default rules designed to vindicate the reasonable expectations of the parties, to facilitate their transactions and to apportion the risks inherent when the parties deal with each other over a distance and an extended period of time. In conceiving these default rules, the courts once again distinguish between unilateral and bilateral contracts.

A. THE MIRROR IMAGE RULE

In order to accept the offer and form a contract, the offeree must agree to the terms stated by the offeror. Courts applying the common law have traditionally required that the offeree's acceptance "mirror" the terms stated by the offeror in the offer. *See* RESTATEMENT (SECOND) OF CONTRACTS §§ 58, 59 (1981). In *Mike Schlemer, Inc. v. Pulizos*, 267 Ill. App. 3d 393, 642 N.E.2d 200 (1994), the court stated:

> As a general rule, in order to constitute a contract, an offer must be accepted. The acceptance must in every respect meet and correspond with the offer, neither falling short of nor going beyond the terms proposed, but exactly meeting them at all points and closing with them just as they stand. The acceptance must conform exactly to the offer, and it must be unequivocal.

An offeree who responds to an offer by varying the terms of the offer has not accepted. For example, Sarah offers to pay Jack $50 if Jack promises to wash and wax Sarah's car. Jack responds that he will wash but not wax Sarah's car for $50. Such a variance in the offeror's terms constitutes a counteroffer, which operates as a rejection of the offer. Rejection terminates an offer, and ordinarily the offeree cannot revive the offer and accept it after rejecting the offer. Were Sarah to reject Jack's counteroffer, he could no longer accept her now terminated original offer.

Minneapolis & St. Louis Ry. v. Columbus Rolling-Mill Co., 119 U.S. 149, 7 S. Ct. 168 (1886). On December 8, 1879, defendant sent a letter to plaintiff offering to sell plaintiff 50-pound iron rails. Under the terms of the defendant's letter, plaintiff could buy any quantity between 2000 and 5000 tons of the rails at the price of $54 a ton. On December 16, 1879, plaintiff telegrammed defendant with an order of 1200 tons of iron rails. On December 18, 1879, defendant responded by telegram that it could not fulfill plaintiff's order at the original price of $54 a ton. On December 19, 1879, plaintiff again telegrammed defendant, attempting to order 2000 tons of rails under the terms of the defendant's original offer. After repeated inquiries by the plaintiff, defendant denied the existence of a contract between the parties. The Supreme Court agreed, holding that the plaintiff rejected the defendant's offer in the plaintiff's December 16 telegram.

A proposal to accept, or an acceptance, upon terms varying from those offered, is a rejection of the offer, and puts an end to the negotiation, unless the party who made the original offer renews it, or assents to the modification suggested. The other party, having once rejected the offer, cannot afterwards revive it by tendering an acceptance of it.

Instead of accepting the offer in its December 16 telegram, the plaintiff varied the terms of the offer by requesting 1,200 tons on the same terms. Because the defendant did not accept the plaintiff's terms or renew its offer, the negotiations were ended. Consequently, the plaintiff's December 19 telegram attempting to revive the offer was ineffectual.

Poel v. Brunswick-Balke-Collender Co., 216 N.Y. 310, 110 N.E. 619 (1915). On April 4, 1910, Poel made an offer to sell rubber under specified terms to Brunswick. On April 6, 1910, Brunswick sent a letter accepting the offer according to Poel's terms, but added the following provision: "The acceptance of this order which in any event you must promptly acknowledge will be considered by us as a guarantee on your part of prompt delivery within the specified time." Poel did nothing to acknowledge receipt of the order. Brunswick later refused to purchase the rubber, and Poel sued for breach of an executory contract. The court held there was no contract. Brunswick's request of "prompt delivery within the specified time" added nothing of substance to the agreement because if Poel's offer were accepted, Poel would have already been obligated to deliver promptly. However, Brunswick's April 6 letter also provided that agreement was conditioned upon Poel promptly acknowledging receipt of Brunswick's order. By thus varying the terms of Poel's April 4 offer, Brunswick made a counteroffer. Since Poel failed to acknowledge receipt of Brunswick's order, Brunswick's counteroffer remained unaccepted. Therefore, Brunswick effectively revoked its counteroffer before Poel accepted it.

FINNIN v. BOB LINDSAY, INC.
852 N.E.2d 446 (Ill. App. 2006)

Lytton, Justice:

Plaintiffs Michael Finnin, D.J. McPherson and David Wright filed a breach of contract complaint against defendant Robert Lindsay, Jr., d/b/a Bob Lindsay Honda-Toyota (dealership), claiming that Lindsay failed to honor a written agreement to sell the dealership to plaintiffs. Both parties moved for summary judgment. The trial court found that plaintiffs' modifications to defendant's offer constituted a counteroffer which defendant did not accept. The court granted summary judgment in Lindsay's favor. We affirm.

In March of 2002, plaintiffs, Michael Finnin, D.J. McPherson and David Wright, approached defendant, Bob Lindsay, about selling his Honda-Toyota dealership. Negotiations continued over the next few months, and the agreement was eventually reduced to writing. Both parties then made several suggestions, modifications, and counter-proposals to the draft.

On August 13, 2002, a few final changes to the agreement were discussed between counsel for both parties. On August 13 or 14, defense counsel's legal assistant sent a letter to plaintiffs' attorney. Enclosed was a revised agreement for the sale of the dealership's stock which reflected the necessary changes. The copy was signed by Lindsay and contained all the corrections previously discussed.

Upon receipt of the agreement, plaintiffs' attorney noticed two errors which did not conform to the parties' intent. The parties previously agreed that plaintiffs would pay $ 1.1 million for the stock. The purchase price provision of the agreement stated the correct amount. However, exhibit A to the agreement still stated that the purchase price was $ 700,000. Second, the agreement made reference to another agreement for the sale of goodwill between the parties that had since been incorporated into the agreement for the sale of stock.

Plaintiffs' attorney contacted defendant's attorneys, and they discussed the errors. On August 19, 2002, Lindsay's attorney wrote to plaintiffs' counsel, suggesting that plaintiffs' attorney send the draft back and he would send plaintiffs a corrected version of the agreement. Plaintiffs' counsel did not return the contract.

On the morning of August 22, Lindsay telephoned Finnin and informed him that he had received another offer from a third party. During the conversation, Lindsay told Finnin that he intended to sell the car dealership to the interested party. Finnin stated that he did not want to "stand in [Lindsay's] way" but wanted to contact his partners before he made a decision. Finnin telephoned McPherson and Wright to inform them of the situation. Finnin also spoke with plaintiffs' attorney who recommended that the three partners sign the agreement and return it. Finnin called Lindsay and told him that plaintiffs intended to go through with the deal.

That same day, plaintiffs' attorney made the previously discussed changes to the written agreement by striking out the incorrect purchase price and inserting the correct amount in "Exhibit All" and by removing all references to the "agreement for the sale of goodwill" on page 14. Plaintiffs then initialed the corrections, signed the agreement, and returned the contract to Lindsay's attorney. Lindsay refused to sell the dealership to plaintiffs.

Plaintiffs filed a breach of contract complaint. During his deposition, defendant's attorney stated that the changes were "minor" and "basically corrected the written agreement to conform with the intent of the parties."

At the summary judgment hearing, Lindsay argued that no contract was ever formed between the parties because the plaintiffs made "material" modifications to the offer. Plaintiffs claimed that the modifications were not significant or material changes to the agreement, but rather corrections of clerical mistakes. Since the changes were consistent with the parties' intent, plaintiffs argued that a contract had been formed. In the alternative, plaintiffs claimed that the strict compliance rule should not be applied because the Uniform Commercial Code (U.C.C.) (810 ILCS 5/2-101 *et seq.* (West 2002)) applied to the agreement. The trial court held that the agreement signed by Lindsay was an offer and that plaintiffs' corrections constituted a counteroffer. The court granted summary judgment in favor of Lindsay.

ANALYSIS

I. Strict Compliance

On appeal, plaintiffs claim that the trial court erred in granting summary judgment in favor of Lindsay. Plaintiffs maintain that the modifications made after Lindsay signed the agreement were simply corrections to errors in the writing and did not change the terms agreed to by the parties; thus, a valid contract was formed.

It is well settled that in order to constitute a contract by offer and acceptance, the acceptance must conform exactly to the offer. . . . Under Illinois contract law, an acceptance requiring any modification or change in terms constitutes a rejection of the original offer and becomes a counteroffer that must be accepted by the original offeror before a valid contract is formed. . . . *Whitelaw v. Brady*, 3 Ill. 2d 583, 121 N.E.2d 785 (1954). . .

In the seminal case of *Whitelaw v. Brady*, our supreme court held that any changes to an offer, even minor changes, constitute a counteroffer rather than an acceptance. In 1950, decedent Ramm owned an apartment building. Shortly before his death he made an offer to Whitelaw to purchase the property. After consideration, Whitelaw decided to accept the offer. He typed in the date for performance in the blank provided by Ramm and typed in the date of acceptance as "12/26/51." Ramm died that same day. Whitelaw later changed the acceptance date to "12/26/50" to correspond to the actual date he signed the offer. The supreme court held that a valid contract had not been created because the acceptance did not conform unequivocally to Ramm's offer. . . .

Illinois' strict compliance rule of law was recently noted and applied by the Seventh Circuit in *Venture Associates Corp. v. Zenith Data Systems, Corp.* In that case, plaintiff and defendant were attempting to negotiate the sale of defendant's subsidiary company. The parties exchanged several drafts of a proposed agreement. After months of negotiations, the plaintiff returned a proposed purchase agreement "with minor, non-substantive changes on it in writing." The defendant seller eventually refused to proceed, and the sale was never completed. The plaintiff filed suit in federal court, alleging that the parties had entered into a binding agreement when it returned the agreement with only minor changes. The district court granted defendant's motion to dismiss. *Venture Associates Corp.*, 987 F.2d 429.

On appeal, the Seventh Circuit held that the plaintiff's conduct did not create a binding contract between the parties. The court concluded:

> Because Illinois law demands that an acceptance comply strictly with the terms of the offer (citations omitted), [Plaintiff's] modifications of [defendant's] proposed agreement, however minor, precluded formation of a contract at that point. Indeed, [plaintiff's] changes created a counteroffer which [defendant] never accepted. *Venture Associates Corp.*, 987 F.2d at 432.

Here, plaintiffs argue that they made only non-substantive, typographical modifications to the proposed agreement for the sale of stock. We agree that plaintiffs' changes were minor and that they apparently conformed to the agreement of the parties. Nevertheless, Illinois case law clearly mandates that any modification, however slight, prevents the creation of a valid contract. Plaintiffs' attempt to correct or modify the terms of the agreement formed a counteroffer that Lindsay refused to accept.

We recognize that many courts in other jurisdictions disagree with our disposition. *See* 17 Am. Jur. 2d *Contracts* § 87, at 112 (1964). Other states have found that immaterial or minor differences or variances between the offer and acceptance do not prevent the formation of a contract. Those courts have concluded that a modification of an offer constitutes a counteroffer only if the modification is a material one. *See Hollywood Fantasy Corp. v. Gabor*, 151 F.3d 203 (5th Cir. 1998) (applying Texas law); *State Department of Transportation v. Providence & Worcester R. Co.*, 674 A.2d 1239 (R.I. 1996); *Wallerius v. Hare*, 200 Kan. 578, 438 P.2d 65 (1968); *Richardson v. Greensboro Warehouse & Storage Co.*, 223 N.C. 344, 26 S.E.2d 897 (1943); and *Foster v. West Publishing Co.*, 1920 OK 44, 77 Okla. 114, 186 P. 1083 (1920). Although the material modification analysis may be more appropriately applied to the facts of this case, Illinois has yet to adopt that rule.

Plaintiffs argue that the rule of strict compliance is not meant to allow contracting parties to escape their obligations under the contract due to a mistake by the parties. In support of their position, plaintiffs cite *Farley v. Roosevelt Memorial Hospital*, 67 Ill. App. 3d 700, 24 Ill. Dec. 194, 384 N.E.2d 1352 (1978).

In *Farley*, the parties entered into an option agreement which granted the buyer the right to exercise an option to purchase real estate. The buyer later executed the option by signing a different real estate contract form which did not conform to the contract form attached to the option agreement. Defendant refused to honor the sale, informing the purchaser that the option had not been validly exercised due to the incorrect form. In construing the terms of the option agreement, the appellate court stated that the option agreement required only that the purchaser provide a timely option notice to the seller. The court found that the terms of the agreement did not require the purchaser to include with the notice a signed copy of the real estate agreement. The court concluded that "while the established rule is that where an option is granted, the exercise must in every respect meet and correspond with the offer, that rule should not be so inflexibly applied that it cannot accommodate an acceptance which mirrors the offer, but where a ministerial procedure was not carried out because of the mistake of one of the parties." . . . Therefore, the purchaser properly exercised the option to purchase the property.

Here, whether a valid agreement exists between the parties is still in dispute. Unlike the court in *Farley*, we are not operating under a valid contract and trying to determine if the parties' actions conformed with the contractual requirements to which they agreed. Plaintiffs made, albeit slight, changes to Lindsay's offer. Even assuming these changes were agreed to by the parties, the acceptance did not correspond with the offer in every aspect as required under Illinois law. Plaintiffs' corrections constituted a rejection of the initial offer and a simultaneous counter-offer. . . . As previously determined, a valid agreement was not created. Therefore, the trial court properly granted summary judgment in favor of Lindsay.

II. Uniform Commercial Code (U.C.C.)

In the alternative, plaintiffs argue that the trial court erred in concluding that the agreement is not controlled by the U.C.C. Plaintiffs claim that the sale of shares of stock in a corporation is governed by the U.C.C.; under the U.C.C., an acceptance need not strictly comply with an offer to form a valid contract.

Article 2 of the U.C.C. governs the sale of goods between merchants. *Section 104* of the U.C.C. defines "merchants" as "a person who deals in goods of the kind." 810 ILCS 5/2-104 (West 2002). Section 2-105 defines "goods" as "all things, including specially manufactured goods, which are movable at the time of identification in a contract for sale other than the money in which the price is to be paid, investment securities (Article 8) and things in action." 810 ILCS 5/2-105(1) (West 2002). Investment securities are excluded from the definition of goods, unless such application is "sensible and the situation involved is not covered by [Article 8]." 810 ILCS 5/2-105(1) (comment 1) (West 2002).

Plaintiffs and defendant are not merchants as defined by the U.C.C., and investment securities are expressly excluded from the definition of goods unless it is sensible to define them as such. In this case, the sale of the stock of Lindsay's closely held corporation doing business as a car dealership was a one time complex transaction. The application of the U.C.C. was intended to encourage the continuous transaction of goods that occur on a daily basis in the marketplace. *See* 810 ILCS 5/2-207 (West 2002) (battle of the forms provision). It is not sensible, nor is it necessary, to apply those rules to the lengthy, ongoing negotiations that occurred here. . . .

CONCLUSION

The judgment of the circuit court of Knox County is affirmed.

NOTES & QUESTIONS

1. To what extent does the common law "mirror image rule" apply to transactions in goods subject to the Uniform Commercial Code? *See* U.C.C. § 2-207.

2. Strict application of the "mirror image rule" has led to problems when parties use standard forms in their transactions with each other. A buyer may use its form to place an order (an offer) with a seller who responds by sending the buyer confirmation (acceptance?) on the seller's form, which differs significantly from the form of the buyer. Such exchanges have been characterized as "the battle of the forms." When a dispute over performance arises, the courts may have to determine whether the parties had an agreement and if so, on whose terms? See, for example, *Roto-Lith v. F.P. Bartlett & Co.*, 297 F.2d 497 (1st Cir. 1962). In *Northrup Corp. v. Litronic Industries*, 29 F.3d 1173 (7th Cir. 1994), Judge Richard A. Posner

explained how the solution to this problem differs depending on whether the transaction is governed by common law or is subject to the Uniform Commercial Code:

"Battle of the forms" refers to the not uncommon situation in which one business firm makes an offer in the form of a preprinted form contract and the offeree responds with its own form contract. At common law, any discrepancy between the forms would prevent the offeree's response from operating as an acceptance. *See Poel v. Brunswick-Balke-Collender Co.,* 216 N.Y. 310, 110 N.E. 619, 621–22 (1915). So there would be no contract in such a case. This was the "mirror image" rule, which Article 2 of the Uniform Commercial Code jettisoned by providing that "a definite and seasonable expression of acceptance or a written confirmation which is sent within a reasonable time operates as an acceptance even though it states terms additional to or different from those offered or agreed upon, unless acceptance is made conditional on assent to the additional or different terms." U.C.C. § 2-207(1). . . . Mischief lurks in the words "additional to or different from." The next subsection of 2-207 provides that if additional terms in the acceptance are not materially different from those in the offer, then, subject to certain other qualifications . . . , they become part of the contract, section 2-207(2), while if the additional terms are materially different they operate as proposals and so have no effect unless the offeror agrees to them . . . ; if the offeror does not agree to them, therefore, the terms of the contract are those in the offer. A clause providing for interest at normal rates on overdue invoices, or limiting the right to reject goods because of defects falling within customary trade tolerances for acceptance with adjustment, would be the sort of additional term that is not deemed material, and hence it would become a part of the contract even if the offeror never signified acceptance of it.

The Code does not explain, however, what happens if the offeree's response contains different terms (rather than additional ones) within the meaning of section 2-207(1). There is no consensus on that question. *See* James J. White & Robert S. Summers, Uniform Commercial Code 33-36 (3d ed. 1988); John E. Murray, Jr., *The Chaos of the "Battle of the Forms": Solutions,* 39 Vand. L. Rev. 1307, 1354–65 (1986). We know there is a contract because an acceptance is effective even though it contains different terms; but what are the terms of the contract that is brought into being by the offer and acceptance? One view is that the discrepant terms in both the nonidentical offer and the acceptance drop out, and default terms found elsewhere in the Code fill the resulting gap. Another view is that the offeree's discrepant terms drop out and the offeror's become part of the contract. A third view, possibly the most sensible, equates "different" with "additional" and makes the outcome turn on whether the new terms in the acceptance are materially different from the terms in the offer — in which event they operate as proposals, so that the offeror's terms prevail unless he agrees to the variant terms in the acceptance — or not materially different from the terms in the offer — in which event they become part of the contract. John L. Utz, *More on the Battle of the Forms: The Treatment of 'Different' Terms Under the Uniform Commercial Code,* 16 U.C.C. L.J. 103 (1983). This interpretation equating "different" to "additional," bolstered by drafting history which shows that the omission of "or different" from § 2-207(2) was a drafting error, substitutes a manageable inquiry into materiality for a hair-splitting inquiry into the difference between "different" and "additional." It is hair-splitting ("metaphysical," "casuistic," "semantic," in the pejorative senses of these words) because all different terms are additional and all additional terms are different.

3. The National Conference of Commissioners on Uniform State Laws has proposed an amendment to U.C.C. § 2-207 which is, in part, designed to end the confusion regarding the effect of additional or different terms included in an offeree's response to an offer. The amended section reads as follows:

> Subject to section 2-202, if (i) conduct of both parties recognizes the existence of a contract although their records do not otherwise establish a contract, (ii) a contract is formed by an offer and acceptance, or (iii) a contract formed in any manner is confirmed by a record that contains terms additional to or different from those in the contract being confirmed, the terms of the contract are:
>
> (a) terms that appear in the records of both parties;
>
> (b) terms, whether in a record or not, to which both parties agree; and
>
> (c) terms supplied or incorporated under any provision of this Act.

At the date of the writing of this note, the proposed amendment to the section had not been adopted in any states. How would the new § 2-207, if adopted, change the law of acceptance regarding sales of goods? Is the proposed new section a step back toward the traditional common law mirror image rule?

3. Although developments under the Uniform Commercial Code have influenced the application of the "mirror image rule" to transactions outside the U.C.C.'s coverage, in transactions governed by the common law the courts continue to require more strict conformity to the offeror's terms when determining whether an offeree has accepted. *See*, for example, *Sea-Van Investment Associates v. Hamilton*, 125 Wash. 2d 120, 881 P.2d 1035 (1994). Is this distinction between the law governing common law transactions and sales of goods justified? What public policy objectives support each of these competing approaches?

4. As indicated in *Finnin v. Bob Lindsay, Inc.*, the principal case above, Illinois takes the minority view that any departure from the terms of the offer in an offeree's response operates as a counteroffer and rejection of the offer. Courts in most other jurisdictions follow another approach. When applying the "mirror image rule," the courts conclude that an offeree has not accepted an offeror's terms when the offeree responds with different or additional terms which are "material." What makes some additional terms material while others are not?

B. MODE OF ACCEPTANCE

The master of the offer, the offeror, may expressly require that the offer can only be accepted if the offeree acts in accordance with specific terms. In *Crockett v. Lowther*, 549 P.2d 303 (Wyo. 1976), the Wyoming Supreme Court explained:

> If an offer prescribes the place, time or manner of acceptance its term in this respect must be complied with in order to create a contract. If an offer merely suggests a permitted place, time or manner of acceptance,

another method of acceptance is not precluded. *See also* WILLISTON ON CONTRACTS, 3d Ed., Jaeger, Vol. 1, § 76, p. 248: "Not only may the offeror dictate the consideration which he demands as the return for the promise in his offer, but he may also dictate the way in which acceptance shall be indicated."

The offeror creates the power of acceptance; and he has full control over the character and extent of the power that he creates. He can prescribe a single and exclusive mode of acceptance. It makes no difference how unreasonable or difficult the prescribed mode may be, if the offeror clearly expresses, in the terms of the communicated offer itself, his intention to exclude all other modes of acceptance. 1A. Corbin, CONTRACTS § 88 at 373 (1963).

However, frequently the offeror leaves the terms governing acceptance general rather than designate an exclusive mode of acceptance. Where the offeror has not required an exclusive mode of acceptance, the courts once again employ the objective theory of contracts and its corollary, the reasonable person, to determine whether the offeree has utilized a reasonable mode of acceptance and, thus, formed a binding agreement. The RESTATEMENT (SECOND) OF CONTRACTS § 30 (2) (1981), governing "Form of Acceptance Invited," provides, "Unless otherwise indicated by the language or the circumstances, an offer invites acceptance in any manner or by any medium reasonable in the circumstances." *See also* U.C.C. § 2-206.

Other sections of the RESTATEMENT (SECOND) OF CONTRACTS are instructive concerning whether an offeree has employed a reasonable mode of acceptance. Section 60 provides, "If an offer prescribes the place, time or manner of acceptance its terms in this respect must be complied with in order to create a contract. If an offer merely suggests a permitted place, time or manner of acceptance, another method is not precluded." And Section 65 provides: "Unless circumstances known to the offeree indicate otherwise, a medium of acceptance is reasonable if it is the one used by the offeror or one customary in similar transactions at the time and place the offer is received."

Depending on the circumstances, an offeree may effectively accept an offer of a bilateral contract in more than one way. For example, Sarah promises to pay Jack $50 if Jack promises to wash and wax Sarah's car this week. Jack could accept Sarah's offer by either promising to wash and wax her car or by actually performing the act of washing and waxing her car. The circumstances and the general language of Sarah's offer imply that Jack may accept in either manner. As the court explained in *Allied Steel & Conveyors, Inc. v. Ford Motor Co.*, 277 F.2d 907 (6th Cir. 1960), "[I]f the offer requests a return promise and the offeree without making his promise actually does or tenders what he was requested to promise to do, there is a contract if such performance is completed or tendered within the time allowable for accepting by making a promise." Nevertheless, circumstances and/or the expressed requirements of the offeror may preclude the offeree from a choice between return promise and actual performance. For example, if on March 1, Marcia promises to pay a florist $1000 for floral arrangements for her June 1 wedding, the reasonable florist should understand that Marcia seeks a return promise to deliver the flowers on June 1. It would be unreasonable for the florist to believe he could accept Marcia's offer by delivering the flowers on March 1 or any other time other than June 1 given the nature of cut flowers. And of course, the florist could not reasonably expect to accept by simply showing up on June 1 with the flowers. The reasonable person in the position of the florist understands that Marcia is seeking an advance commitment from the florist to provide the agreed-upon floral arrangements on June 1. Thus, this is an example of a situation in which circumstances limit the means by which the offeree may accept.

Allied Steel & Conveyors, Inc. v. Ford Motor Co., 277 F.2d 907 (6th Cir. 1960). Ford offered to purchase machinery from Allied on July 26, 1956. Ford's offer provided that Allied would install the machinery on Ford's premises and included an indemnity provision under which Allied would assume full liability for all damages resulting from the fault or negligence of either parties' employees during the installation of the equipment. (In a previous contract between the two parties, this provision had been voided out.) The offer also stated: "This purchase order agreement is not binding until accepted. Acceptance should be executed on acknowledgment copy which should be returned to buyer." Allied began installation without returning the acknowledgment copy to Ford. On September 5, 1956, an Allied employee was injured due to the negligence of Ford's employees. On November 10, 1956, Allied completed the acknowledgment copy which was received by Ford on November 12, 1956. The injured employee sued Ford, and Ford added Allied as a third-party defendant relying upon the indemnity provision. Allied argued that the agreement was not in effect at the time of the injury because it was not signed and returned until November 10, 1956. (Allied also contended that it was the parties' intention to void the indemnity provision as was done in their previous contract.) However, the court concluded Allied had accepted on Ford's terms. The court reasoned that an offeror may prescribe the manner in which acceptance shall be made by the offeree, and accepting in that manner will bind the offeror. However, if an offeror only suggests a permitted method of acceptance, then the offeree can use other methods to form the contract. Here, Allied's execution and return of the acknowledgment copy was merely a suggested method of acceptance and did not prevent Allied from accepting in another manner. Allied accepted, and a binding contract was formed, when Allied began performance with the consent and knowledge of Ford.

PANHANDLE EASTERN PIPE LINE CO. v. SMITH
637 P.2d 1020 (Wyo. 1981)

Brown, Justice:

Panhandle Eastern Pipe Line Company (Panhandle) appeals a district court judgment granting damages to its former employee Nowlin Smith, Jr., for breach of contract. Panhandle asserts that no contract ever existed.

Panhandle fired Mr. Smith in October 1979. Mr. Smith followed the grievance procedure provided by a collective bargaining agreement to the third and final level of intracompany proceedings, which was a meeting with company officials at the division office. After that meeting, Panhandle initially decided to uphold the decision to fire Mr. Smith, but changed its mind after Mr. Smith's union representative requested that it reconsider. By letter dated December 13, 1979, the company offered to withdraw the discharge if Mr. Smith would agree to comply with certain terms and conditions. Mr. Smith signed the letter under the typewritten words, "Understood, Agreed To and Accepted," added some handwritten notations, and again signed his name. The union representative also signed the letter and returned it to the company.

Because Mr. Smith wrote on the letter, Panhandle argues that no contract existed, claiming that Mr. Smith failed to use the mode of acceptance which it prescribed. As Panhandle conceded at oral argument, it would have contested any words being added to the letter, even ones as innocuous as, "Have a nice day." Panhandle also argues that Mr. Smith made a counteroffer by adding terms and conditions, which showed he was trying to modify the offer.

We think appellant's "mode of acceptance" argument was not directly raised in the district court. Panhandle's pleadings spoke to a counteroffer being made because Mr. Smith added terms and conditions to the proposed offer. The exhibits introduced at trial spoke to "modifications," and "added terms and conditions," implying that the content of the words mattered. No mention was made anywhere below of "mode of acceptance" or "method of acceptance." Appellant cautioned this court not to confuse the two theories of "mode of acceptance" and "counteroffer," although appellant tried to interweave them in its brief. Because we want to avoid any confusion, we have decided to address both the "mode of acceptance" argument and the "counteroffer" argument.

An offeror has the right to demand an exclusive mode of acceptance from an offeree. The mode of acceptance can be unreasonable or difficult if the offeror clearly expresses his intention to exclude all other modes of acceptance. This intention must be expressed in the communicated offer itself. *Crockett v. Lowther, Wyo.*, 549 P.2d 303, 309 (1976), *citing* 1 Corbin, CONTRACTS, § 88, at 373 (1963). The letter of December 13, 1979, contained the offer to withdraw Mr. Smith's discharge. The letter directed that both Mr. Smith and the union had to agree in writing to the terms of the offer, and that the signatures were a condition precedent to the withdrawal of the discharge.[1] It went on to reiterate that the withdrawal of the discharge was contingent upon receipt of written acceptance by Mr. Smith and the union.

Panhandle insists that it modified this offer by orally demanding of Mr. Smith during a telephone conversation that he just sign the letter and not add anything. Mr. Smith, however, does not remember the conversation that way, and we must view the evidence on appeal most favorably to him. Here, Mr. Smith testified he did not understand that any addition to the letter would be considered a rejection of the offer. Panhandle, therefore, did not orally modify the written offer of December 13, 1979; it failed to "clearly express, in the terms of the communicated offer itself," its intention to exclude all other modes of acceptance. *Crockett v. Lowther, supra.* Panhandle was explicit only in stating that the terms and conditions had to be agreed to in writing.

The offeror is master of the offer, but we think fairness demands that when there is a dispute concerning mode of acceptance, the offer itself must clearly and definitely express an exclusive mode of acceptance. There must be no question that the offeror would accept the prescribed mode and only the prescribed mode.

---

[1] "* * * The Company has, therefore, determined that Mr. Smith will be given one more opportunity to rehabilitate himself and his discharge shall hereby be withdrawn under the terms and conditions listed below, which terms and conditions must be agreed to in writing by both Mr. Smith and the Union as a condition precedent to the withdrawal of the discharge." The letter then said, "the terms and conditions are: . . ." and set out eight additional terms and conditions, some of which will be discussed later.

Corbin comments, "The more unreasonable the method appears, the less likely it will be that a court will interpret his offer as requiring it (a specific mode of performance) and the more clear and definite must be the expression of his intention in words." 1 CORBIN ON CONTRACTS, § 88, at 373 (1963). The only motivation we could surmise for the requirement that no handwriting be added to the paper, regardless of content, would be that the offeror had an inordinate fondness for tidy sheets of paper. The requirement strikes us as unreasonable, and strikes out as a prescribed mode of acceptance unless the offeror's intention is explicitly set out. We agree that the mode of acceptance rule "has been enforced with a rigor worthy of a better cause." Calamari & Perillo, CONTRACTS, § 2-22 (2d ed., 1977). We are not eager to enforce it if there is any question about the mode of acceptance or about the clarity with which the demand was made. Had Panhandle seriously been proposing an exclusive mode of acceptance calling for the absence of any writing on the paper other than signatures, the letter should have explicitly demanded that exact and exclusive mode of performance.

The requirement that no terms or conditions be added to change the contract is a different matter. The law of contract formation dictates that one who modifies an offer has usually rejected the offer and made a counteroffer, and that no contract exists unless the original offeror accepts the counteroffer. Panhandle contends that Mr. Smith made a counteroffer by adding a request on the letter to see his personnel file and to contest any mistakes he found there. An offer must be accepted unconditionally; but there is, as always, an exception to the rule. An acceptance is still effective if the addition only asks for something that would be implied from the offer and is therefore immaterial. 1 CORBIN ON CONTRACTS, § 86, p. 368 (1963). . . . A Panhandle supervisor, Mr. Smith, and a company machinist, who was also a union representative, all testified that all Panhandle employees had the right to see their personnel files. Panhandle's offer to withdraw its discharge and eventually reinstate Mr. Smith carried with it the implication that he would be able to see his personnel record when he was once again an active employee.

Besides reserving the right to see his personnel file, Mr. Smith wrote that his personnel file contained mistakes, and that he was having financial problems, apparently as a result of the company's actions. Williston has described the kind of acceptance Mr. Smith made as one showing "an abundance of caution," and Corbin has called it a "grumbling acceptance," which in this case it certainly appeared to be. WILLISTON ON CONTRACTS, § 78 (3rd ed., 1962); 1 CORBIN ON CONTRACTS, § 84 (1963). The acceptance was unenthusiastic to be sure, but it was an acceptance nevertheless. Mr. Smith signed his name under the words "Understood, Agreed To and Accepted." He wrote that he agreed to the terms and conditions. He began performance by seeking medical help and by sending in a check to keep his insurance current. Mr. Smith wanted to be sure that he would be able to see his personnel file when he returned to work. His effort to insure that right should not block him from benefits that Panhandle had already offered to him. His "grumbling acceptance" should stand . . . We therefore affirm.

NOTES & QUESTIONS

1. Which of the policy objectives we have identified are served by the "exclusive mode of acceptance" doctrine? Are different objectives served by the "reasonable mode of acceptance" approach applied in the *Panhandle* case?

2. In *Panhandle,* the court concluded that Smith did not reject Panhandle's offer when he asked to see his personnel file and for the right to contest any mistakes he found there. The court further concluded that Smith's "grumbling acceptance" was effective as acceptance of Panhandle's offer. Do you agree? Are the court's conclusions supported by the objective theory of contracts?

3. The offeror may specify that in order to accept, the offeree must do so in writing. However, the courts are generally reluctant to read a writing requirement into the terms of the offer without some express requirement in the offer. Section 27 of the RESTATEMENT (SECOND) OF CONTRACTS (1981) provides, "Manifestations of assent that are themselves sufficient to conclude a contract will not be prevented from so operating by the fact that the parties also manifest an intention to prepare and adopt a written memorial thereof. . . ." Thus, the courts distinguish those situations in which a written acceptance or document is a prerequisite for the formation of a binding agreement and those situations where the parties have entered into an oral contract or less formal document which they intend to memorialize later with a formal writing. Why? Consider the following case.

McCARTHY v. TOBIN
706 N.E.2d 629 (Mass. 1999)

ABRAMS, Judge:

We granted the interveners' application for further appellate review following the Appeals Court's opinion, concluding that the plaintiff was entitled to specific performance of a real estate purchase. The plaintiff, John J. McCarthy, Jr., claims that the defendant, Ann G. Tobin, agreed to sell certain real estate to him. He asserts that they created a binding agreement when they signed a standard Offer to Purchase (OTP) form. The DiMinicos intervened because they later agreed to purchase the property in question from Tobin. McCarthy and Tobin each moved for summary judgment and the DiMinicos for partial summary judgment. The motion judge allowed Tobin's and the DiMinicos' motions, declaring that Tobin had no obligation to sell to McCarthy and therefore McCarthy had no right to the specific performance of the real estate agreement. The Appeals Court vacated the judgment in favor of Tobin and the DiMinicos and remanded for entry of judgment in favor of McCarthy. The Appeals Court reasoned that the OTP was a firm offer that became a contract binding on the parties when it was accepted. . . .

The facts, which are undisputed, are as follows. On August 9, 1995, McCarthy executed an offer to purchase real estate on a pre-printed form generated by the Greater Boston Real Estate Board. The OTP contained, among other provisions, a description of the property, the price to be paid, deposit requirements, limited title requirements, and the time and place for closing. The OTP also included several provisions that are the basis of this dispute. The OTP required that the parties "shall, on or before 5 P.M. August 16, 1995, execute the applicable Standard Form Purchase and Sale Agreement recommended by the Greater Boston Real Estate Board . . . which, when executed, shall be the agreement between the parties hereto." In the section containing additional terms and conditions, a typewritten insertion states, "Subject to a Purchase and Sale Agreement satisfactory to Buyer and Seller." The OTP provided, "Time is of the essence hereof." Finally, an unnumbered paragraph immediately above the signature line states: "NOTICE: This is a legal document that creates binding obligations. If not understood, consult an attorney." Tobin signed the OTP on August 11, 1995.

On August 16, 1995, sometime after 5 P.M., Tobin's lawyer sent a first draft of the purchase and sale agreement by facsimile transmission to McCarthy's lawyer. On August 21, McCarthy's lawyer sent a letter by facsimile transmission containing his comments and proposing several changes to Tobin's lawyer. The changes laid out the requirements for good title; imposed on Tobin the risk of casualty to the premises before sale; solicited indemnification, for title insurance purposes, regarding mechanics' liens, parties in possession, and hazardous materials; and sought an acknowledgment that the premises' systems were operational. The next day, the two lawyers discussed the proposed revisions. They did not discuss an extension of the deadline for signing the purchase and sale agreement, and Tobin's lawyer did not object to the fact that the deadline had already passed. On August 23, Tobin's lawyer sent a second draft of the agreement to McCarthy's lawyer. On August 25, a Friday, McCarthy's lawyer informed Tobin's lawyer that the agreement was acceptable, McCarthy would sign it, and it would be delivered the following Monday. . . . On Saturday, August 26, McCarthy signed the purchase and sale agreement. On the same day, Tobin accepted the DiMinicos' offer to purchase the property.

On August 28, McCarthy delivered the executed agreement and a deposit to Tobin's broker. The next day, Tobin's lawyer told McCarthy's lawyer that the agreement was late and that Tobin had already accepted the DiMinicos' offer. In September, 1995, Tobin and the DiMinicos executed a purchase and sale agreement. Before the deal closed, McCarthy filed this action for specific performance and damages.

1. Firm offer. The primary issue is whether the OTP executed by McCarthy and Tobin was a binding contract. Tobin and the DiMinicos argue that it was not because of the provision requiring the execution of a purchase and sale agreement. McCarthy urges that he and Tobin intended to be bound by the OTP and that execution of the purchase and sale agreement was merely a formality.

McCarthy argues that the OTP adequately described the property to be sold and the price to be paid. The remaining terms covered by the purchase and sale agreement were subsidiary matters which did not preclude the formation of a binding contract. . . . We agree.

The controlling fact is the intention of the parties. . . . "It is a settled principle of contract law that '[a] promise made with an understood intention that it is not to be legally binding, but only expressive of a present intention, is not a contract' "; *Levenson v. L.M.I. Realty Corp.*, 31 Mass. App. Ct. 127, 130, 575 N.E.2d 370 (1991).

Tobin argues that language contemplating the execution of a final written agreement gives rise to a strong inference that she and McCarthy have not agreed to all material aspects of a transaction and thus that they do not intend to be bound. . . . If, however, the parties have agreed upon all material terms, it may be inferred that the purpose of a final document which the parties agree to execute is to serve as a polished memorandum of an already binding contract. . . . Mutual manifestations of assent that are in themselves sufficient to make a contract will not be prevented from so operating by the mere fact that the parties also manifest an intention to prepare and adopt a written memorial thereof. . . .

Although the provisions of the purchase and sale agreement can be the subject of negotiation, norms exist for their customary resolution. . . . If parties specify formulae and procedures that, although contingent on future events, provide mechanisms to narrow present uncertainties to rights and obligations, their agreement is binding. . . .

The interveners argue that McCarthy departed from the customary resolution of any open issues, and therefore manifested his intent not to be bound, by requesting several additions to the purchase and sale agreement. We agree with the Appeals Court, however, that McCarthy's revisions were "ministerial and nonessential terms of the bargain." . . .

The inference that the OTP was binding is bolstered by the notice printed on the form. McCarthy and Tobin were alerted to the fact that the OTP "created binding obligations." The question is what those obligations were. The DiMinicos argue that the OTP merely obligated the parties to negotiate the purchase and sale agreement in good faith. We disagree. The OTP employs familiar contractual language. It states that McCarthy "hereby offer[s] to buy" the property, and Tobin's signature indicates that "this Offer is hereby accepted." The OTP also details the amount to be paid and when, describes the property bought, and specifies for how long the offer was open. This was a firm offer, the acceptance of which bound Tobin to sell and McCarthy to buy the subject property. We conclude that the OTP reflects the parties' intention to be bound. . . . If parties do not intend to be bound by a preliminary agreement until the execution of a more formal document, they should employ language such as that suggested by the Appeals Court. The form may be redrafted if it does not reflect the intention of the parties.

The judgment is vacated. The case is remanded to the Superior Court for the entry of a judgment in favor of McCarthy's claim for specific performance. So ordered.

NOTES & QUESTIONS

1. There is a relationship between the parties' desire to have a written understanding, whether terms remain open and whether the parties intend to be bound. What is that relationship?

2. Oral agreements are enforceable *at common law*, unless the parties intend to have no contract without a writing. However, nearly all jurisdictions in this country have passed a version of the Statute of Frauds, which by *statutory provision* requires that certain agreements be in writing to be enforceable. Among the agreements subject to the Statute of Frauds' writing requirement are agreements for the sale of land and agreements not to be performed within one year of their making. In addition, the Uniform Commercial Code § 2-201 requires a writing for the enforcement of a sale of goods for a price of $500 or more. We shall study the Statute of Frauds in Chapter 10.

3. Under the objective theory of contracts, the offeree's failure to reply to an offer may not ordinarily serve as acceptance. RESTATEMENT (SECOND) OF CONTRACTS § 69 (1981). However, the courts do recognize a limited number of exceptions where the offeree may indeed accept by remaining silent. Consider the following cases.

VOGT v. MADDEN
713 P.2d 442 (Idaho App. 1985)

WALTERS, Chief Judge:

Harold and Betty Vogt sued Bob and Neva Madden for damages allegedly resulting from the Maddens' breach, as landlords, of a sharecrop agreement. A jury returned a verdict in favor of the Vogts. The Maddens appeal from the judgment. . . . They contend first that the evidence was insufficient to support the jury's implicit finding that a sharecrop agreement existed between the parties for the year 1981. . . .

It was undisputed that Harold Vogt had an oral sharecrop agreement with Bob Madden to farm seventy acres of land owned by the Maddens, for the year 1979. It also was undisputed that the parties renewed the agreement for the year 1980. Under their agreement, certain expenses would be borne solely by Vogt, other expenses would be shared equally between Vogt and Madden, and the net profits derived from crops grown on the land would be divided equally between them. When the Vogts eventually filed suit contending a sharecrop agreement existed for the year 1981, Vogt also sought recovery from Madden of $2,000 for the Maddens' share of expenses incurred by Vogt in the years 1979 and 1980.

The dispositive issue in this appeal is whether Vogt and Madden had a sharecrop agreement that Vogt could continue to farm the seventy acres, during 1981. Vogt testified that because no profits had been realized from wheat crops grown on the property in 1979 and 1980, he planned to raise beans on the land in 1981. He testified that he met with Madden several times in August and September, after the wheat crop had been harvested in 1980, concerning the expenses remaining for the years 1979 and 1980. He testified:

> [W]e also discussed the 1981 crop, of what to do then. We had several discussions on this. I met with him two or three, four times — I'm not sure how many — and we both agreed it wasn't the best ground. It isn't number one soil out there, because of the steepness, but I had raised grain for two years, and I had left the straw and stubble on the ground. And I had raised a — let the volunteer grain grow, watered it and plowed it under the first year. And I anticipated plowing under the second year and at that point I told him I thought it would raise a fairly decent crop of pinto beans. And at that time I told Bob [Madden] that I'd raised two years of grain, plowed under this straw and stubble, and I thought it would raise a crop of pinto beans. And at that time I had decided to do that. I was going to raise the pinto beans on there, along with possibly a few acres of garden beans.

> Q: And as a result of that conversation, it was your understanding that you were to farm that; is that correct?

> A: Yes. . . .

> Q: And when you were discussing the fact of growing the bean crop with Mr. Madden, did he have any objection to that type of crop being grown on his ground?

> A: No, not at all.

On cross-examination, Vogt testified as follows:

Q: You talked about beans, then?

A: Yes, sir.

Q: But Mr. Madden never told you that he wanted to grow beans, did he?

A: No.

Q: He never expressly told you that he would enter into another agreement in the spring of '81?

A: Yes. What we done, we just — I told him I had raised this crop, the wheat and grain for two years, and the third year we could raise a crop of pintos, a crop of beans. And the price of beans at that time was good, and as far as I know that was the way the discussion ended.

Q: But Mr. Madden never agreed one way or another, right?

A: I would say I was under the impression that we had an agreement.

Q: But he never said anything to give you that indication?

A: Honestly, I don't think he said, "Yes, go ahead." No, he didn't say that.

Madden disputed that he and Vogt had agreed to a sharecrop arrangement for the year 1981. He testified that, following one of their discussions over the expense bills for 1979 and 1980,

And I said at that time, I told him, I said, "I just had it. I don't want you to farm it any more. I'll send you what I think is right. . . ." "Harold," I said, "Life's too short to argue over these things, let's just-we're through."

In respect to that same discussion, Vogt denied on rebuttal that Madden had made any statement about Vogt not farming the Maddens' land the next year. In the late fall of 1980, Madden leased the property to another party for the 1981 crop year, thus preventing Vogt from pursuing his plan to raise beans on the land. This lawsuit for damages followed. By its verdict in favor of Vogt for $18,540, the jury concluded that a sharecrop agreement existed between Vogt and Madden for the year 1981. . . . In order to reach such a conclusion the jury must have disbelieved Madden when he testified he informed Vogt that their relationship was "through," and that he, Madden, did not want Vogt to farm the property any longer. Otherwise, had the jury believed Madden, then clearly the parties would not have had a contract for 1981. If Madden were disbelieved, then the only evidence regarding the creation of a contract between Vogt and Madden for the year 1981 would be Vogt's testimony that he informed Madden of his intent to raise beans on the property in 1981, that Madden did not say "yes" to this proposal, but that Vogt nonetheless was left with the "impression" that a contract had been created.

The question whether silence or inaction may constitute acceptance of an offer was an issue in this case. Over Madden's objection, the jury was given an instruction, No. 18, concerning silence as an acceptance of an offer, creating a contract between the offeror, Vogt, and the offeree, Madden. The instruction was requested by Vogt, demonstrating that Vogt was pursuing a theory that the evidence showed the creation of a sharecrop agreement for 1981 arising because of silence on Madden's part.

The instruction stated:

Silence and inaction may constitute acceptance of an offer to contract, where a party is under a duty to speak or to reject the offer. Such a duty may arise under any one of the following circumstances.

1. Where because of previous dealings it is reasonable that the offeree should notify the offeror if the offeree does not intend to accept.

2. Where an offeree takes the benefit of offered services with reasonable opportunity to reject them and reason to believe the offeror thought the offer was accepted.

3. Where the offeror has stated or given the offeree reason to understand that assent may be manifested by silence or inaction, and the offeree in remaining silent and inactive intends to accept the offer.

This instruction was a slightly modified version of the RESTATEMENT (SECOND) OF CONTRACTS section 69 (1981). In relevant part, RESTATEMENT (SECOND) OF CONTRACTS section 69 at 165 provides:

(1) Where an offeree fails to reply to an offer, his silence and inaction operate as an acceptance in the following cases only: (a) Where an offeree takes the benefit of offered services with reasonable opportunity to reject them and reason to know that they were offered with the expectation of compensation. (b) Where the offeror has stated or given the offeree reason to understand that assent may be manifested by silence or inaction, and the offeree in remaining silent and inactive intends to accept the offer. (c) Where because of previous dealings or otherwise, it is reasonable that the offeree should notify the offeror if he does not intend to accept.

The RESTATEMENT explains that silence by an offeree ordinarily does not operate as an acceptance of an offer. "The exceptional cases where silence is acceptance fall into two main classes: those where the offeree silently takes offered benefits, and those where one party relies on the other party's manifestation of intention that silence may operate as acceptance." *Id.* comment a, at 165.

Here, two of the exceptions stated in § 69, and in the court's instruction No. 18, are patently inapplicable because they are wholly unsupported by the evidence. There was no evidence that Madden received "the benefit of offered services" for which Vogt expected to be compensated. See *Id.* comment b, at 165 ("when the recipient knows or has reason to know that services are being rendered with an expectation of compensation, and by a word could prevent the mistake, his privilege of inaction gives way; under Subsection (l)(a) he is held to an acceptance if he fails to speak."). Vogt did not, in fact, farm the property in 1981. Nor does the evidence show that Vogt stated or gave Madden reason to understand that assent to Vogt's expectation to farm the property might be manifested by silence or inaction, and the evidence does not show that Madden, by remaining silent and inactive intended to accept Vogt's offer. *Id.* § 69(1)(b).

Finally, the exception arising from "previous dealings" between the parties is inapposite. In their prior dealings, 1979 and 1980, the parties expressly reached oral agreements for sharecropping the farm. After completion of the contract for 1979, a new contract for 1980 did not automatically follow. It was preceded by discussions between Vogt and Madden resulting in an express understanding that Vogt could farm the property in 1980 on a sharecrop basis. We do not believe those previous transactions could give rise to a legitimate conclusion that Vogt's offer to farm the property in 1981 would be accepted in the absence of affirmative notification from Madden that the offer would not be accepted. To the contrary, the previous dealings always resulted in a contract only when both parties expressly agreed.

Absent the applicability of the exceptions stated in RESTATEMENT § 69, it is a general rule of law that silence and inaction, or mere silence or failure to reject an offer when it is made, does not constitute an acceptance of the offer. *See generally* 17 AM. JUR. 2D *Contracts* § 47, at 385-86 (1964); J. Calamari and J. Perillo, THE LAW OF CONTRACTS § 2-21, at 63-68 (1977). Because none of the exceptions is applicable in this case, we conclude as a matter of law that no contract to sharecrop the Maddens' property in 1981 was created by Madden's silence in response to Vogt's offer to farm the property. We therefore set aside that portion of the judgment awarding damages to the Vogts based on the alleged 1981 contract. . . .

The judgment is reversed in respect to award of any damages for breach of the alleged 1981 contract. . . .

NOTES & QUESTIONS

1. Had Vogt farmed the property in 1981 and Madden received the benefit of the services Vogt offered, would the result have been different?

2. Where an offeror provides services which benefit the offeree, but there is no contract-in-fact due to the general rule that the offeree's silence does not serve as acceptance, is the offeree unjustly enriched? In *Weichert Co. Realtors v. Ryan*, 608 A.2d 280 (N.J. 1992), a commercial real estate broker brought suit for commissions against the buyers of certain property which he had procured for the buyers. The broker failed to prove the existence of a contract-in-fact because his offer to provide services in return for a specified commission had not been accepted by the buyers when he found the property the buyers bought. However, the court identified an alternative ground for recovery:

> In some circumstances, however, courts will allow recovery even though the parties' words and actions are insufficient to manifest an intention to agree to the proffered terms. Recovery based on quasi-contract, sometimes referred to as a contract implied-in-law, "is wholly unlike an express or implied-in-fact contract in that it is 'imposed by the law for the purpose of bringing about justice without reference to the intention of the parties.'" *Saint Barnabas Medical Ctr. v. County of Essex*, 111 N.J. 67, 79, 543 A.2d 34 (1988) (quoting *Saint Paul Fire & Marine Ins. Co. v. Indemnity Ins. Co.*, 32 N.J. 17, 22, 158 A.2d 825 (1960)). . . . Courts generally allow recovery in quasi-contract when one party has conferred a benefit on another, and the circumstances are such that to deny recovery would be unjust. Quasi-contractual liability "rests on the equitable principle that a person shall not be allowed to enrich himself unjustly at the expense of another."

> Applying that principle, courts have allowed quasi-contractual recovery for services rendered when a party confers a benefit with a reasonable expectation of payment. . . . That type of quasi-contractual recovery is known as quantum meruit ("as much as he deserves"), and entitles the performing party to recoup the reasonable value of services rendered.

Accordingly, a broker seeking recovery on a theory of quantum meruit must establish that the services were performed with an expectation that the beneficiary would pay for them, and under circumstances that should have put the beneficiary on notice that the plaintiff expected to be paid. Courts have allowed brokers to recover in quantum meruit when a principal accepts a broker's services but the contract proves unenforceable for lack of agreement on essential terms — for instance, the amount of the broker's commission. . . . Thus, a broker who makes a sufficient showing can recover fees for services rendered even absent express or implied agreement concerning the amount of the fee.

The New Jersey court concluded that although the broker was not entitled to a recovery based on the breach of a contract-in-fact, "[t]he record clearly establishes, however, that [he] is entitled to recover in quantum meruit for the reasonable value of his services. . . ." The court remanded to the trial court for a determination of the reasonable value of the services the broker rendered to the buyers.

Hobbs v. Massasoit Whip Co., 158 Mass. 194, 33 N.E. 495 (1893). Pursuant to a standing order, plaintiff Hobbs had earlier sent the defendant whip company four or five shipments of skins. The defendant had accepted and paid for each of these shipments of skins. However, in the transaction which led to their litigation, plaintiff sent defendant another shipment of skins which the defendant refused to accept. Without paying for them, the defendant retained the skins for months before they were destroyed. The plaintiff, who had received no notice that the defendant declined to accept the skins, sued to recover the price of the skins. Holding for the plaintiff, the court reasoned that the plaintiff properly sent the defendant the eel skins in conformity with the requirements understood between the parties. Noting that the parties were not strangers to each other, the court concluded that plaintiff's sending the skins imposed a duty on the defendant to act in light of their past dealings. Consequently, silence on the defendant's part, coupled with retention of the skins for an unreasonable time, justified the plaintiff's assumption that the skins were accepted. "[C]onduct which imports acceptance or assent is acceptance or assent in the view of the law, whatever may have been the actual state of mind of the party."

McGlone v. Lacey, 288 F. Supp. 662 (S.D. 1968). On May 8, 1964, plaintiff Margaret McGlone was seriously injured in a fall on the premises of William Chambley. On February 21, 1967, plaintiff sent a signed authorization to the defendant, attorney Charles Lacey, seeking to retain the defendant to represent her in her personal injury claim on a contingent fee basis. The plaintiff's daughter included a letter with the authorization, which contained information pertinent to her mother's injuries. On March 1, 1967, the letters were answered by defendant's partner, Parliman, who informed the plaintiff that defendant Lacey was away until the middle of March and that he would contact plaintiff upon his return. There was no further correspondence between the parties until May 11, 1967, when plaintiff sent a letter to the defendant reminding him that she would like to hear from him regarding her case. On May 17, 1967, defendant Lacey wrote plaintiff that he was "shocked" to learn that the statute of limitations on her cause of action had expired on May 8, 1967. He explained that he was heavily involved in several matters of pending litigation and had completely forgotten the deadline. Plaintiff sued the defendant for breaching the contract to represent her in her tort claim. The court held for the defendant on the ground that plaintiff had not contracted with defendant to represent her. Rejecting the plaintiff's argument that Lacey's silence from late February to early May constituted acceptance of plaintiff's offer to retain defendant, the court reasoned that "silence will not of itself constitute an acceptance." According to the court, there was no course of dealing between the parties from which it could be concluded that Lacey's silence and retention of the plaintiff's file amounted to acceptance. In addition, the court noted that the parties had not settled on the percentage of the defendant's contingent fee, which had the potential to vary greatly depending upon the expense of pursuing the intended litigation. Therefore, plaintiff's signed authorization merely invited a counteroffer from the defendant. Conversely, if the defendant sought a contingent fee which the plaintiff believed was unreasonable, the plaintiff could have withdrawn her offer to retain defendant. Accordingly, the court granted defendant's motion for summary judgment.

Austin v. Burge, 156 Mo. App. 286, 137 S.W. 618 (1911). The defendant received a two-year subscription to the plaintiff's newspaper, compliments of his father-in-law. However, after the two-year subscription expired, the defendant continued to receive copies of the newspaper for several years. On two separate occasions the defendant paid a bill for the subscription price, but both times requested that the delivery cease. However, the defendant still received copies of the newspaper and continued to read them until he eventually moved. Plaintiff newspaper sued defendant for the amounts due on the newspapers. Holding for the plaintiff, the court reasoned that a party may cause contractual relations to arise through conduct. Although defendant ordered the newspapers discontinued, plaintiff continued to send them, and defendant continued to take the newspapers from the post office to his home. "This was an acceptance and use of the property, and there being no pretense that a gratuity was intended, an obligation arose to pay for it."

National Union Fire Ins. Co. v. Ehrlich, 122 Misc. 682, 203 N.Y.S. 434 (1924). A broker for the plaintiff insurance company had contracted for fire insurance policies with defendant on numerous occasions. One of the policies had an expiration date on December 22, 1921. On that day, the plaintiff's broker sent the defendant a renewal policy issued by the plaintiff with a bill for the premium. The defendant retained the policy for two months without remitting a payment. Upon the plaintiff's demand for payment, the defendant rejected the policy. The plaintiff sought compensation for two months of insurance for the period prior to the defendant's rejection. The trial court dismissed the plaintiff's cause of action, but the appellate court reversed. Remanding for a new trial, the appellate court reasoned that the parties' previous relations justified the plaintiff's assumption that defendant's retention of the policy implied acceptance. "If a fire had occurred under these circumstances, plaintiff would not have been heard to say that defendant had not accepted the insurance, and defendant should pay the premium for the time he unreasonably retained the policy."

Indiana Mfg. Co. v. Hayes, 155 Pa. 160, 26 A. 6 (1893). Plaintiff shipped to defendant 64 refrigerators which defendant asserted he had not ordered. Upon receiving the refrigerators, the defendant ordered the railroad company to turn them over to defendant's agent instead of notifying the plaintiff of the mistaken delivery. Eventually, the defendant's agent delivered the refrigerators to the defendant's place of business, where they were stored. The defendant later sent a check to the plaintiff for other goods plaintiff purchased, but made no reference to the refrigerators. Plaintiff sued defendant for breach of contract to purchase the refrigerators. Holding for the plaintiff, the court reasoned that the defendant had appropriated the refrigerators for his own use and was therefore bound to pay for them whether he had bargained for them or not. Under the circumstances, the defendant had a duty to notify the plaintiff of the alleged mistake and failed to do so.

HOFFMAN v. RALSTON PURINA CO.
273 N.W.2d 214 (Wis. 1979)

HEFFERNAN, Justice:

The sole issue in this case is whether, where there is a dispute as to liability in tort between two parties and the alleged tortfeasor makes an offer of settlement accompanied by a check and credit memorandum, the retention of the check uncashed and the acquiescence in the fruits of the credit memorandum for a period of more than seven months constitutes an acceptance of that offer. We conclude that under these circumstances, where David Hoffman retained the check and credit memorandum for an unreasonable length of time with the knowledge that both instruments were offered in full settlement of the disputed claim, such retention in itself constituted an acceptance of the settlement offer.

In addition, the offeree, Hoffman, in this case had a duty to speak to reject the offer, because the parties, Hoffman and Ralston Purina, were engaged in settlement negotiations at the time the offer was made.

The facts revealed at trial show that Hoffman operated a ranch for the raising of Arabian horses. He purchased Purina horse feed through a dealer, Waldschmidt & Sons, Inc. In January of 1973, Waldschmidt delivered a load of Purina feed to Hoffman which allegedly resulted in the illness and death of a number of Hoffman's horses. It was determined that the feed was contaminated with highway-grade rock salt. In February of 1975, Hoffman commenced an action against the Ralston Purina Company, Waldschmidt & Sons, Inc., and Heritage Mutual Insurance Company.

The action for the injury to his horses was based upon theories of strict liability in tort, negligence, and breach of warranty. Ralston Purina answered, specifically denying the allegations in respect to the facts underlying each theory of recovery set forth in the plaintiff's complaint and, in addition, alleging the affirmative defense that, prior to the commencement of the lawsuit, the claim had been settled and that there had been a full satisfaction and discharge of the plaintiff's claim.

The case was tried to the court, and the action against Ralston Purina was dismissed on the basis of evidence which the trial court concluded was sufficient to show that the plaintiff and Ralston Purina Company had reached an accord and satisfaction upon the tendering and acceptance of the sum of $3,000.

The record shows that, when Hoffman's horses began to show signs of illness, he called Purina and Waldschmidt. Following a series of meetings, an employee of Purina, one Wuestenberg, visited the Hoffman ranch on March 26, 1973. He brought with him a release, which recited that for the sum of $3,000 the Ralston Purina Company was to be released of all liability as the result of the damage to the horses. Although the settlement on its face purported only to release Ralston Purina, Hoffman by interlineation added the sentence, "This agreement in no way releases the liability of Waldschmidt Feed and Supply Co." The release was signed by Hoffman and witnessed by Wuestenberg. Wuestenberg advised Hoffman at the time the release was signed that he did not know whether the release as amended would be acceptable to Purina. A day or two later, Wuestenberg informed Hoffman that the release as amended was not acceptable to Purina.

Shortly after Purina rejected the release as amended, it terminated its previous credit relationship with Hoffman and insisted upon cash for all future deliveries. The chief officer of Purina's Fond du Lac plant stated that this insistence upon cash was because Hoffman was two or three months past due on his account with Purina. Hoffman, however, was able to get feed from another source.

On May 2, 1973, Purina's director of claims and adjustments wrote to Hoffman and suggested that there be a further meeting between a Purina representative and Hoffman to resolve the situation. On May 9, 1973, a representative of Purina, Doyle L. Cook, wrote to Hoffman making an offer to settle for $3,000, with no reference to the amendment to the release which had been added by Hoffman. On May 11, 1973, Hoffman wrote to Purina stating his unwillingness to settle for the sum of $3,000 for the release of both Purina and the dealer, Waldschmidt. On May 15, the director of claims and adjustments for Purina again wrote to Hoffman, stating that, since Cook, the Fond du Lac representative of Purina, had in his possession the signed release of Hoffman (the release which excluded Waldschmidt from the release), a check would be sent to him shortly.

Although the trial court made the finding that Hoffman had in fact received this letter, Hoffman testified that he did not. On May 16, 1973, Cook, a Purina representative, wrote to Hoffman, stating:

> Since we had originally agreed to settle the claim with you for $3,000 and your signature was placed on the release, we would like to go ahead and settle this matter for once and for all. Attached is a credit memo in the amount of $2,624.36 that will clear your account in full with Ralston Purina and a check for $375.64. The total of these two come to $3,000.

Hoffman also testified that he had never received this letter nor the attached check for $375.64 and the credit memorandum in the amount of $2,624.36. The check was never cashed or returned. Hoffman acknowledged that a statement received from Purina dated May 15, 1973, showed that he had a balance due Purina in the amount of $2,650.60 and also acknowledged that a statement the next month dated June 17, 1973, showed his balance had been reduced to zero. He admitted that he never contacted anyone at Purina to determine why his indebtedness had been reduced.

At trial, Ralston Purina produced a document which it obtained from Hoffman in the course of pretrial depositions. That document was the May 15, 1973, Ralston Purina statement showing an indebtedness of $2,650.60. On that statement in handwriting, which Hoffman acknowledged to be his, was written, "Please forward difference for our consideration of your new offer as of 5/16/73."

While it is acknowledged that this statement with Hoffman's handwritten message was never sent to Ralston Purina, the fact that the notation was made upon the statement, referring to the offer of May 16, 1973, was taken as proof by the trial court that the plaintiff Hoffman knew the exact amount of the settlement check offered to him and that he had in fact received the settlement offer and the attached credit memorandum and check which accompanied the May 16 settlement offer.

In January of 1974 Purina found that the May 1973 check in the sum of $375.64 had not been cashed. When this was brought to Hoffman's attention, he stated that he had never received the check and that there was no settlement of the claim. Purina then sent him another check, which was returned.

On the basis of these facts, the trial court concluded that Hoffman had received the settlement offer dated May 16, 1973, and the accompanying check and credit memorandum. It concluded, as a matter of law, that the plaintiff's retention of the check and the credit memorandum for a period of more than seven months and the plaintiff's silence for that period of time was an acceptance of the offer and that, therefore, Purina and Hoffman had reached an accord and satisfaction of the prior controversy. He ordered judgment to be entered dismissing the plaintiff's complaint against Ralston Purina.

We conclude that the trial court's findings are not contrary to the great weight and clear preponderance of the evidence. Our analysis of the facts shows that Hoffman's offer to settle according to the amended terms of the release was indeed rejected by Purina. Purina, however, on May 16, 1973, made a new offer, which incorporated the terms of the release as amended by Hoffman. That offer, which was accompanied by a check and credit memorandum totaling the sum of $3,000, was received by Hoffman. The facts, then, demonstrate that Purina offered to settle the question of its disputed liability by the payment of $3,000, partially by crediting Hoffman's overdue account and partially by the check. Hoffman remained silent after the receipt of this offer and the attached instruments. He never cashed the check. He never returned either it or the credit memorandum. It was only in response to a query from Purina in January of 1974, more than seven months later, that he stated he was rejecting the offer.

The trial court properly concluded that these facts demonstrated that there was an "accord and satisfaction."

An "accord and satisfaction" is an agreement to discharge an existing disputed claim, whether the claim be one arising in contract, tort, or otherwise. An "accord and satisfaction" constitutes a defense to an action to enforce the claim. 6 Corbin, CONTRACTS, § 1276, p. 114.

Ordinary contract principles apply in determining whether an agreement of "accord and satisfaction" is reached. . . . Mere performance does not operate as a satisfaction unless offered as such to the creditor or claimant. There must be expressions sufficient to make the creditor understand or to make it unreasonable for him not to understand that the performance is offered in full satisfaction of the claim. . . .

The decisions of this court are in agreement with Corbin's analysis. In *Draper v. Rodd*, 185 Wis. 1, 200 N.W. 761 (1924), it was held that there could be no accord and satisfaction where the payment made could not be known to be in full satisfaction of the pre-existing liability. In the instant case, however, the record is clear that the payment of $3,000 was offered in full settlement of the pre-existing claim. The letter accompanying the check and the credit memorandum stated, "(W)e would like to go ahead and settle this matter for once and for all."

In order for a contract of accord and satisfaction to have been created, however, this offer of Purina must have been assented to by Hoffman. . . . Assent does not necessarily, however, require mental assent or a "meeting of the minds." . . . The question is not the actual intent of the offeree, but his manifested intent. Laufer, *Acceptance by Silence: A Critique*, 7 DUKE BAR ASSN. J. 87, 91 (1939). An assent or acceptance of a contract offer can be manifested by deed as well as by word.

Actions of the offeree can constitute acceptance even when accompanying words express a contrary intent. . . . When a creditor receives a check offered in full settlement of an obligation and cashes the check, but simultaneously writes to the debtor that he refuses to accept the check as in full satisfaction but will apply it only in reduction of the debt, the action of cashing the check will be considered an acceptance of the offer. . . . That same rule was followed in *Thomas v. Columbia Phonograph Co.*, 144 Wis. 470, 476, 129 N.W. 522, 524 (1911). We said, "(a) plaintiff could not accept the offer and avail himself of the funds without assenting to the condition upon which the offer was made." In the instant case, of course, Hoffman did not cash the check. Rather, he remained silent and retained the credit memorandum and the uncashed check.

Williston, *supra*, § 1854, pp. 5215-216, takes the position that there is no distinction between the cashing of a check or the retaining of a check for an unreasonable length of time. He states:

> It is said that the acceptance of the check necessarily involves an acceptance of the condition upon which it was tendered. A retention of a check, even for an unreasonable length of time has not always been given this effect, but as the creditor has no more right to retain the check an unreasonable time than he has to cash it, unless he accepts it as full satisfaction, there seems no propriety in distinguishing the two situations.

Corbin, *supra*, § 1279, p. 133, takes the same position:

> The retention of the check for an unreasonable time, even though not cashed, will have the same effect if no objection was made to the form of payment and if the check would have been honored on presentation at the bank. . . .

Whether a check is held for an unreasonable length of time obviously depends upon the facts and circumstances of the dispute and the status of negotiations between the adversary parties. What is a reasonable time under the circumstances is primarily a question of fact, and what is an appropriate and acceptable period of retention under one set of circumstances has no precedential effect in terms of what is reasonable under different circumstances. It cannot be disputed that in the instant case the retention of the check, the acquiescence in the receipt of the credit memorandum which had the effect of reducing Hoffman's balance to zero, and the maintenance of complete silence for over seven months was unreasonable.

Moreover, the RESTATEMENT (SECOND) OF CONTRACTS § 72(2) [69(2)] p. 142 (Tentative Draft 1972) provides that: "(2) An offeree who does any act inconsistent with the offeror's ownership of offered property is bound in accordance with the offered terms unless they are manifestly unreasonable. . . ."

Under the Williston and Corbin rationale, the **acceptance** or retention of a check without accepting the terms upon which it is offered **is an act** inconsistent with the offeror's ownership. In this case Hoffman retained not only the check but also retained the credit memorandum and accepted without objection the fruits of that credit memorandum the cancellation of his existing indebtedness. We are satisfied that such silence and acquiescence was a manifestation of assent, under the rationale of RESTATEMENT (SECOND) OF CONTRACTS § 72(2) [69(2)].

The RESTATEMENT (SECOND) furnishes still another rationale for our determination that Hoffman accepted Ralston Purina's contract of "accord and satisfaction." Section 72(1) [69(2)] provides: "(1) When an offeree fails to reply to an offer, his silence and inaction operate as an acceptance in the following cases and in no others: . . . (c) Where because of previous dealings or otherwise, it is reasonable that the offeree should notify the offeror if he does not intend to accept." Under this rationale, where Hoffman and Purina had been in a continuous process of negotiations, the silence of Hoffman in respect to the offer, even if no check and credit memorandum had accompanied the offer, could be construed as an acceptance of the offer.

The record shows that the parties had exchanged a number of letters concerning the settlement of the dispute over the contaminated horse feed. They had a prior existing credit relationship. When Purina made its offer of settlement on May 16, 1973, it had every reason to expect an answer if its offer was rejected. It was unreasonable for the offeree, Hoffman, to remain silent if he did not intend to accept the proposed settlement. Laufer, *supra*, explains the rationale relied upon by the RESTATEMENT: There is the desirable "privilege" to turn down offers summarily by silence, the "right" of inaction, There is, on the other hand, the steadily growing recognition that established business practices, standards of fair play often call for action upon offers. Letters of strangers may be ignored, and their writers reckon with this possibility but the same is not true of business friends, of parties with whom there are or have been contractual relationships. . . . Laufer, *Acceptance by Silence: A Critique*, 7 DUKE BAR ASSN. J. 87, 92 (1939).

* * *

We accordingly conclude that, under the facts found by the court, Hoffman, who knew of Ralston Purina's offer of settlement, retained the check and credit memorandum, and maintained silence in respect to the offer, accepted the contract of accord and satisfaction. . . . His tort claim against Ralston Purina was thereby settled, and his subsequent cause of action against Ralston Purina was properly dismissed.

Judgment affirmed.

NOTES & QUESTIONS

1. In *Hoffman v. Ralston Purina Co.*, the court concluded that Hoffman's silence and retention of Ralston Purina's check and credit memorandum constituted acceptance of Ralston Purina's settlement offer. The court relied in part on RESTATEMENT (SECOND) OF CONTRACTS § 69(1)(c), which provides that silence may serve as acceptance "[w]here because of previous dealings or otherwise, it is reasonable that the offeree should notify the offeror if he does not intend to accept." Compare the facts, and the relationships of the parties, in *Hoffman* with

those in *Hobbs v. Massasoit Whip Co.*, in which the Massachusetts court relied on past dealings to find acceptance by silence. Is there a difference between the parties' past dealings in these two cases which could be cited to justify a different result in *Hoffman?*

2. In *Hoffman*, the court also relied on RESTATEMENT (SECOND) OF CONTRACTS § 69(2), reasoning that Hoffman retained the check and credit memorandum in a manner inconsistent with Ralston Purina's ownership. However, what benefit did Hoffman derive from holding the check and credit memorandum? He did not cash or deposit the check. Why did Ralston Purina send Hoffman the second check if it was entitled to believe his retention of the first check and the credit memorandum served as acceptance of Ralston Purina's offer of accord and satisfaction?

3. Hoffman denied having received the first check and credit memorandum. However, the trial court considered Hoffman's notation on the May 15, 1973 statement from Purina to be evidence that Hoffman had in fact received Ralston Purina's settlement offer with the check and credit memorandum. Hoffman's notation on the statement read, "Please forward difference for our consideration of your new offer as of 5/16/73." Hoffman did not return this statement and notation to Ralston Purina. Is it clear that this notation on the statement disclosed that Hoffman had received the check and credit memorandum?

4. On March 26, 1973, Purina's agent, Wuestenberg, brought Hoffman a release which purported only to release Ralston Purina. Hoffman added a sentence refusing to release the feed dealer, Waldschmidt, and signed. Did the Hoffman and Ralston Purina have a contract on Hoffman's terms, that is, releasing Purina but not Waldschmidt at that time?

PROBLEM

In a state where casino gambling is legal, Dan decided to have a night on the town at Russ & Betty's Gambling Emporium. Dan went straight to the blackjack table where a sign prominently displayed over the table provided: "$25 MINIMUM BET. $1000 MAXIMUM BET." On each of his first three hands, Dan bet $350, losing each time. Before dealing Dan his fourth hand, the casino's dealer Bonnie announced, "For the next hand, the table limit will be $10 minimum and $100 maximum bets." Observing that several other patrons nevertheless placed bets over $100, Dan placed another $350 bet on the table. Without commenting on the players' bets, Bonnie then dealt Dan and the other players at the table their hands, and Dan drew blackjack, which would normally entitle him to win double his bet since Bonnie, the dealer, did not also have blackjack. Dan claimed his winnings were $700, but Bonnie refused to pay him that amount, offering to pay him $200. In the altercation which followed, Bonnie declared all bets off and asked the other players to remove their bets from the table. The other players, none of whom had been dealt blackjack like Dan, complied. In a suit by Dan against Russ & Betty's Gambling Emporium for the full amount of the winnings, who will prevail? *See Campione v. Adamar of New Jersey*, 643 A.2d 42 (N.J. Super. 1993).

C. DEALING AT A DISTANCE AND THE "MAILBOX RULE"

When parties deal in each other's presence, their expressions of intent are communicated instantaneously. An offeree's expression of acceptance is received by the offeror nearly simultaneously with the offeree's expression of that acceptance. Both parties become aware that they have a contract at virtually the same time, that is, when the offeree accepts. However, when parties deal with each other at a distance, the realities of time and space generally dictate that when the offeree accepts, the offeror at a distance may not learn of the offeree's acceptance until some time thereafter. Thus, such dealing at a distance raises risks for the parties.

For example, Sarah mails Jack an offer in which she promises to pay him $50 if he promises to wash and wax her car. Sarah's offer is effective when Jack receives it. Because Sarah has chosen the mail as her means of extending her offer to Jack, she has implicitly authorized Jack to accept by the same medium, the mail. However, if Jack accepts by mail, Sarah will not actually learn of his acceptance until she receives Jack's letter. During the time between Jack's mailing his letter of acceptance and Sarah's receipt, of that letter, several things could happen. Even though properly addressed and posted, Jack's letter could be lost in the mail, in which event Sarah would not actually learn he had accepted and could assume that her offer had lapsed. Believing that Jack had not accepted her offer, Sarah might enter into a contract with a third person to have her car washed and waxed. Alternatively, even if Jack's acceptance letter is not lost in the mail, Sarah might telephone Jack before his letter reaches her and withdraw her offer without knowing he had mailed an acceptance. These and other situations create problems for courts attempting to determine when parties dealing at a distance have entered into a contract. Who should assume the risks inherent in time and space when parties deal at a distance? When does acceptance take place between parties dealing at a distance? *See* RESTATEMENT (SECOND) OF CONTRACTS § 63 (1981).

MORRISON v. THOELKE
155 So. 2d 889 (Fla. App. 1963)

ALLEN, Acting Chief Judge:

Appellants, defendants and counter-plaintiffs in the lower court, appeal a summary final decree for appellees, plaintiffs and counter-defendants below. The plaintiff-appellees, owners of certain realty, sued to quiet title, specifically requesting that defendant-appellants be enjoined from making any claim under a recorded contract for the sale of the subject realty. Defendant-appellants counterclaimed, seeking specific performance of the same contract and conveyance of the subject property to them. The lower court, after hearing, entered a summary decree for plaintiffs.

A number of undisputed facts were established by the pleadings, including the facts that appellees are the owners of the subject property located in Orange County; that on November 26, 1957, appellants, as purchasers, executed a contract for the sale and purchase of the subject property and mailed the contract to appellees who were in Texas; and that on November 27, 1957, appellees executed the contract and placed it in the mails addressed to appellants' attorney in Florida. It is also undisputed that after mailing said contract, but prior to its receipt in Florida, appellees called appellants 'attorney and cancelled and repudiated the execution and contract. Nonetheless, appellants, upon receipt of the contract caused the same to be recorded. Additional factual allegations concerning demand for performance, tender of the purchase price and payment of taxes were disputed.

On the basis of the foregoing facts, the lower court entered summary decree for the appellees, quieting title in them. The basis of this decision was, in the words of the able trial judge: "[T]he contract executed by the parties hereto . . . constituted a cloud on the title of Plaintiffs. The Court finds said contract to have been cancelled and repudiated by Plaintiffs prior to its receipt by Defendants and that on this basis there was no legal contract binding on the parties. . . ."

Turning to the principal point raised in this appeal, we are confronted with a question apparently of first impression in this jurisdiction. The question is whether a contract is complete and binding when a letter of acceptance is mailed, thus barring repudiation prior to delivery to the offeror, or when the letter of acceptance is received, thus permitting repudiation prior to receipt. Appellants, of course, argue that posting the acceptance creates the contract; appellees contend that only receipt of the acceptance bars repudiation.

The appellant, in arguing that the lower court erred in giving effect to the repudiation of the mailed acceptance, contends that this case is controlled by the general rule that insofar as the mail is an acceptable medium of communication, a contract is complete and binding upon posting of the letter of acceptance. *See, e.g.* 12 AM. JUR. *Contracts* § 46 (1938, Supp. 1963); 1 Williston, CONTRACTS § 81 (3rd ed. 1957); 1 Corbin, CONTRACTS § 78 (1950 Supp. 1961). Appellees, on the other hand, argue that the right to recall mail makes the Post Office Department the agent of the sender, and that such right coupled with communication of a renunciation prior to receipt of the acceptance voids the acceptance. In short, appellees argue that acceptance is complete only upon receipt of the mailed acceptance.

Turning first to the general rule relied upon by appellant some insight may be gained by reference to the statement of the rule in leading encyclopedias and treatises. Accordingly, attention is directed to 12 AM. JUR. *Contracts* §§ 46, 49 (1938) for the following:

> § 46. Acceptance by Mail. — The formation of the contract may be made dependent upon the communication of the acceptance to the offerer, and in such a case there will be no contract if for any reason the offerer is not notified of the acceptance according to the agreement. In cases in which such an arrangement has not been made, the courts have been confronted by the rather difficult question whether the contract is completed when the letter of acceptance is mailed or when it is received by the offerer. There is no doubt that the implication that a complete, final, and absolutely binding contract is formed as soon as the acceptance of an offer is posted may in some cases lead to inconvenience and hardship. At the same time, it has been pointed out that an offerer, if he chooses, may always make the formation of the contract which he proposes dependent upon the actual communication to himself of the acceptance and that if no answer to his offer is received by him and the matter is of importance to him, he can make inquiries of the person to whom his offer was addressed. It has been suggested, moreover, that if the offerer is not to be bound by the acceptance until it is received by him, the party accepting the offer ought not to be bound when his acceptance is received, because he does not know

of the meeting of the minds, for the offer may have been withdrawn before his acceptance was received. Upon balancing convenience and inconvenience, the courts have deemed it more consistent with the acts and declarations of the parties to consider the contract complete and absolutely binding on the transmission of the acceptance through the post, as the medium of communication which the parties themselves contemplate, instead of postponing its completion until the acceptance has been received by the offerer. By treating the post office as the agency of both parties, the courts have managed to harmonize the legal notion that it is necessary that the minds of the parties meet with the equally well-established principle that a determination to accept is ineffectual if it is not communicated either actually or by legal implication. Accordingly, if acceptance by mail is authorized, the contract is completed at the moment the acceptor deposits in the post office the letter of acceptance directed to the offerer's proper address and with the postage prepaid, provided he does so within the proper time and before receiving any intimation of the revocation of the offer. Of course, a letter which is written, but remains in the writer's hands or under his control, is not an acceptance.

§ 49. — Effect of Withdrawal of, or Right to Withdraw, Letter from Mail. — Since 1887, at least, postal regulations have permitted the withdrawal, under certain conditions, of letters from the mail. . . . The authorities are not entirely harmonious as to the effect of such right to withdraw letters or of the withdrawal of letters pursuant to such regulations upon the acceptance of contracts. A leading authority on contracts states that it is not important that the acceptor has the power to withdraw his acceptance from the mail. Moreover, there are several decisions holding that an acceptance duly deposited in the mail is effective, although the acceptor intercepts the letter of acceptance and secures its return before it has reached the addressee. There are also numerous recent cases in which no question of withdrawal or the right to withdraw the acceptance from the mail arose, applying or recognizing the rule that a contract is complete at the time of the depositing of a proper letter of acceptance in the mail, where acceptance in this manner is authorized. On the other hand, the view is held that a contract is not deemed consummated by a deposit in the mail of a letter accepting an offer, so long as the sender has a right to withdraw the letter. The position has been taken that in view of the postal regulations permitting the withdrawal of a letter from the mail by the depositor, the post office should be regarded as the latter's agent, so long as the letter may be withdrawn by him, unless it appears, expressly or by implication, that the parties intended that the sender of the communication, after mailing, should have no right to withdraw it. . . .

Corbin (CONTRACTS §§ 78 and 80 (1950 Supp. 1961)), also devotes some discussion to the "rule" urged by appellants. Corbin writes:

Where the parties are negotiating at a distance from each other, the most common method of making an offer is by sending it by mail; and more often than not the offeror has specified no particular mode of acceptance. In such a case, it is now the prevailing rule that the offeree has power to accept and close the contract by mailing a letter of acceptance, properly stamped and addressed, within a reasonable time. The contract is regarded as made at the time and place that the letter of acceptance is put into the possession of the post office department.

Corbin negates the effect of the offeree's power to recall his letter:

> The postal regulations have for a long period made it possible for the sender of a letter to intercept it and prevent its delivery to the addressee. This has caused some doubt to be expressed as to whether an acceptance can ever be operative upon the mere mailing of the letter, since the delivery to the post office has not put it entirely beyond the sender's control. It is believed that no such doubt should exist. . . . In view of common practices, in view of the difficulties involved in the process of interception of a letter, and in view of the decisions and printed discussions dealing with acceptance by post, it is believed that the fact that a letter can be lawfully intercepted by the sender should not prevent the acceptance from being operative on mailing. If the offer was made under such circumstances that the offeror should know that the offeree might reasonably regard this as a proper method of closing the deal, and the offeree does so regard it, and makes use of it, the contract is consummated even though the letter of acceptance is intercepted and not delivered.

Significantly, Corbin expressly distinguishes cases involving bank drafts or bills of exchange from cases involving bilateral contracts. He writes:

> It should be borne in mind that whenever the receipt of the letter is necessary to produce some legal effect, the interception, and resulting nondelivery of the letter will prevent that effect. For almost all purposes, other than the acceptance of an offer, the mere mailing of a letter is not enough to attain the purpose. Unless it is clearly otherwise agreed, the mailing of a letter is not a sufficient notice to quit a tenancy, it is not actual payment of money that is inclosed, it does not transfer title to a check or other document, it will not ordinarily be sufficient notice required by a contract as a condition precedent to some contractual duty of immediate performance. . . .

The rule that a contract is complete upon deposit of the acceptance in the mails, hereinbefore referred to as "deposited acceptance rule" and also known as the "rule in *Adams v. Lindsell*," had its origin, insofar as the common law is concerned, in *Adams v. Lindsell*, 1 Barn. & Ald. 681, 106 Eng. Rep. 250 (K.B. 1818). In that case, the defendants had sent an offer to plaintiffs on September 2nd, indicating that they expected an answer "in course of post." The offer was misdirected and was not received and accepted until the 5th, the acceptance being mailed that day and received by defendant-offerors on the 9th. However, the defendants, who had expected to receive the acceptance on or before the 7th, sold the goods offered on the 8th of September. It was conceded that the delay had been occasioned by the fault of the defendants in initially misdirecting the offer.

Defendants contended that no contract had been made until receipt of the offer on the 9th. "Till the plaintiffs' answer was actually received there could be no binding contract between the parties; and before then the defendants had retracted their offer by selling the wool to other persons." But the court said that if that were so, no contract could ever be completed by the post. For if the defendants were not bound by their offer when accepted by the plaintiffs till the answer was received, then the plaintiffs ought not to be bound till after they had received the notification that the defendants had received their answer and assented to it. And so it might go on ad infinitum. The defendants must be considered in law as making, during every instant of the time their letter was traveling, the same identical offer to the plaintiffs, and then the contract is completed by the acceptance of it by the latter. Then as to the delay in notifying the acceptance, that arises entirely from the mistake of the defendants, and it therefore must be taken as against them that the plaintiffs' answer was received in course of post.

The unjustified significance placed on the "loss of control" in the cases relied upon by appellee follows from two errors. The first error is failure to distinguish between relinquishment of control as a factual element of manifest intent, which it is, and as the legal predicate for completion of contract, which it is not. The second error lies in confusing the "right" to recall mail with the "power" to recall mail. Under current postal regulations, the sender has the 'power' to regain a letter, but this does not necessarily give him the "right" to repudiate acceptance. The existence of the latter right is a matter of contract law and is determinable by reference to factors which include, but are not limited to the existence of the power to recall mail. In short, the power to recall mail is a factor, among many others, which may be significant in determining when an acceptance is effective, but the right to effectively withdraw and repudiate an acceptance must be dependent upon the initial determination of when that acceptance is effective and irrevocable.

From the foregoing it is clear that a change in postal regulations does not, ipso facto, alter or effect the validity of the rule in *Adams v. Lindsell*. To the extent that the cases relied upon by appellee mistakenly assumed that "loss of control" and "agency" were determinative of the validity of the rule they are not authority for rejecting the rule. Rather, the adoption of the rule in this jurisdiction must turn on an evaluation of its justifications, quite apart from the fallacious theories of agency and control sometimes advanced in its support.

Before discussing the justification of the "deposited acceptance" rule in contract law, it is important, to avoid confusion, to again distinguish between the rule in its application to offer and acceptance in contract and the application or nonapplication of an identical principle in other areas of the law. As the section from Corbin, quoted . . . supra, indicates, the courts and authors properly distinguish clearly between these applications, although often, as in the cases relied upon by appellee, the distinction is overlooked. *See* Annot. 9 A.L.R. 386 (1920); 92 A.L.R. 1062 (1934). . . .

The justification for the "deposited acceptance" rule proceeds from the uncontested premise of *Adams v. Lindsell* that there must be, both in practical and conceptual terms, a point in time when a contract is complete. In the formation of contracts inter praesentes this point is readily reached upon expressions of assent instantaneously communicated. In the formation of contracts inter absentes by post, however, delay in communication prevents concurrent knowledge of assents and some point must be chosen as legally significant. The problem raised by the impossibility of concurrent knowledge of manifest assent is discussed and a justification for the traditional rule is offered in Corbin (CONTRACTS § 78 (1950)).

> A better explanation of the existing rule seems to be that in such cases the mailing of a letter has long been a customary and expected way of accepting the offer. It is ordinary business usage. More than this, however, is needed to explain why the letter is operative on mailing rather than on

receipt by the offeror. Even though it is business usage to send an offer by mail, it creates no power of acceptance until it is received. Indeed, most notices sent by mail are not operative unless actually received. The additional reasons for holding that a different rule applies to an acceptance and that it is operative on mailing may be suggested as follows: When an offer is by mail and the acceptance also is by mail, the contract must date either from the mailing of the acceptance or from its receipt. In either case, one of the parties will be bound by the contract without being actually aware of that fact. If we hold the offeror bound on the mailing of the acceptance, he may change his position in ignorance of the acceptance; even though he waits a reasonable time before acting, he may still remain unaware that he is bound by contract because the letter of acceptance is delayed, or is actually lost or destroyed, in the mails. Therefore this rule is going to cause loss and inconvenience to the offeror in some cases. But if we adopt the alternative rule that the letter of acceptance is not operative until receipt, it is the offeree who is subjected to the danger of loss and inconvenience. He can not know that his letter has been received and that he is bound by contract until a new communication is received by him. His letter of acceptance may never have been received and so no letter of notification is sent to him; or it may have been received, and the letter of notification may be delayed or entirely lost in the mails. One of the parties must carry the risk of loss and inconvenience. We need a definite and uniform rule as to this. We can choose either rule; but we must choose one. We can put the risk on either party; but we must not leave it in doubt. The party not carrying the risk can then act promptly and with confidence in reliance on the contract; the party carrying the risk can insure against it if he so desires. The business community could no doubt adjust itself to either rule; but the rule throwing the risk on the offeror has the merit of closing the deal more quickly and enabling performance more promptly. It must be remembered that in the vast majority of cases the acceptance is neither lost nor delayed; and promptness of action is of importance in all of them. Also it is the offeror who has invited the acceptance.

The justification suggested by Corbin has been criticized as being anachronistic. Briefly, critics argue that the evident concern with risk occasioned by delay is premised on a time lag between mailing and delivery of a letter of acceptance, which lag, in modern postal systems is negligible. Opponents of the rule urge that if time is significant to either party, modern means of communication permit either party to avoid such delay as the post might cause. . . . At the same time critics of the rule cannot deny that even in our time delay or misdirection of a letter of acceptance is not beyond the realm of possibility.

Another justification offered for the rule, related to the argument of expediency discussed by Corbin, is the mixed practical and conceptual argument attributed to Holmes but in reality being manifest in *Adams v. Lindsell* itself. *See* Holmes, *The Common Law*, 305-307 (1881); Note, 38 Geo. L.J. 106, 110 (1949). This argument proposes that the making of an offer constitutes an expression of assent to the terms of the contract and that the "overt act" of depositing a written acceptance in the post represents the [offeree's] assent, whereupon the "concluding prerequisite" of a contract, mutual assent, is formed and the contract is complete. Critics of the rule respond by pointing out that the deposit of a letter in the mail is, in and of itself, a neutral factor, charged with legal significance only because the rule makes this particular "overt act" significant: signing a contract but then pocketing it could be, they argue, viewed as equally conclusive.

In support of the rule proponents urge its sanction in tradition and practice. They argue that in the average case the offeree receives an offer and, depositing an acceptance in the post, begins and should be allowed to begin reliance on the contract. They point out that the offeror has, after all, communicated his assent to the terms by extending the offer and has himself chosen the medium of communication. Depreciating the alleged risk to the offeror, proponents argue that having made an offer by post the offeror is seldom injured by a slight delay in knowing it was accepted, whereas the offeree, under any other rule, would have to await both the transmission of the acceptance and notification of its receipt before being able to rely on the contract he unequivocally accepted. Finally, proponents point out that the offeror can always expressly condition the contract on his receipt of an acceptance and, should he fail to do so, the law should not afford him this advantage.

Opponents of the rule argue as forcefully that all of the disadvantages of delay or loss in communication which would potentially harm the offeree are equally harmful to the offeror. Why, they ask, should the offeror be bound by an acceptance of which he has no knowledge? Arguing specific cases, opponents of the rule point to the inequity of forbidding the offeror to withdraw his offer after the acceptance was posted but before he had any knowledge that the offer was accepted; they argue that to forbid the offeree to withdraw his acceptance, as in the instant case, scant hours after it was posted but days before the offeror knew of it, is unjust and indefensible. Too, the opponents argue, the offeree can always prevent the revocation of an offer by providing consideration, by buying an option.

In short, both advocates and critics muster persuasive argument. As Corbin indicated, there must be a choice made, and such choice may, by the nature of things, seem unjust in some cases. Weighing the arguments with reference not to specific cases but toward a rule of general application and recognizing the general and traditional acceptance of the rule as well as the modern changes in effective long-distance communication, it would seem that the balance tips, whether heavily or near imperceptively, to continued adherence to the "rule in *Adams v. Lindsell*." This rule, although not entirely compatible with ordered, consistent and sometime artificial principles of contract advanced by some theorists, is, in our view, in accord with the practical considerations and essential concepts of contract law. *See* Llewellyn, *Our Case Law of Contracts; Offer and Acceptance II*, 48 YALE L.J. 779, 795 (1939). Outmoded precedents may, on occasion, be discarded and the function of justice should not be the perpetuation of error, but, by the same token, traditional rules and concepts should not be abandoned save on compelling ground.

In choosing to align this jurisdiction with those adhering to the deposited acceptance rule, we adopt a view contrary to that of the very able judge below, contrary to the decisions of other respected courts and possibly contrary to the decision which might have been reached had this case been heard in a sister court in this State. However, we are constrained by factors hereinbefore discussed to hold that an acceptance is effective upon mailing and not upon receipt. Necessarily this decision is limited in any prospective application to circumstances involving the mails and does not purport to determine the rule possibly applicable to cases involving other modern methods of communication. Cf. *Entores v. Miles Far East Corp.*, 2 Q.B. 327 (1955) (rejecting the application of *Adams v. Lindsell* to a case involving instantaneous communication). RESTATEMENT (SECOND) OF CONTRACTS § 65 (1932).

In the instant case, an unqualified offer was accepted and the acceptance made manifest. Later, the offerees sought to repudiate their initial assent. Had there been a delay in their determination to repudiate permitting the letter to be delivered to appellant, no question as to the invalidity of the repudiation would have been entertained. As it were, the repudiation antedated receipt of the letter. However, adopting the view that the acceptance was effective when the letter of acceptance was deposited in the mails, the repudiation was equally invalid and cannot alone, support the summary decree for appellees.

The summary decree is reversed and the cause remanded for further proceedings.

NOTES & QUESTIONS

1. The mailbox or dispatch rule applies only to acceptance. It does not apply to offers, counteroffers, rejections and revocations, which are all effective upon receipt. *See* RESTATEMENT (SECOND) OF CONTRACTS § 68 (1981).

2. Under the mailbox rule, acceptance is operative, and a contract formed, as soon as the acceptance is put out of the offeree's possession or control. Thus, the offeror may be bound at the time the offeree dispatches the acceptance without actually knowing the offeree has accepted. Is there anything an offeror can do to avoid this problem and the other risks associated with the mailbox rule?

3. A letter of acceptance is put out of the possession or control of an offeree when the offeree deposits the letter in a mailbox, hands the letter to a private messenger service or dictates acceptance to a telegraph company. In these situations, acceptance is effective upon dispatch. If the offeree entrusts a personal agent or servant with the written acceptance, will acceptance be effective upon dispatch or receipt?

4. If a letter of acceptance is properly dispatched, the offeror will be bound even if the letter is lost and never received by the offeror. Thus, if a postal service worker destroys a consignment of mail including a letter of acceptance, acceptance is effective and binds the offeror who has not received the acceptance. If a personal servant destroys a letter of acceptance without delivering it to the offeror, however, the offeror is not bound. Is there a principled reason for this difference?

5. There are a number of important exceptions to the mailbox rule. An offer held open under an option is accepted upon receipt of acceptance rather than dispatch. *See* RESTATEMENT (SECOND) OF CONTRACTS § 63(b) (1981). Ordinarily, an option holder has provided "valuable consideration" to the option giver for the right to exercise the option. Yet unlike the ordinary offeree who has paid nothing to the offeror, the option holder does not enjoy the advantage of the mailbox rule. Does this make sense? As the court explained in *Romain v. A. Howard Wholesale Co.*, 506 N.E.2d 1124, 1128 (Ind. App. 1987):

> Under an option contract . . . , the option holder has a firm and dependable basis for decision. His power of acceptance is absolute for the time agreed upon in the option contract. There is thus no reason to extend the rule that acceptance is operative upon mailing since the option contract

device itself fulfills the same purpose. . . . To impose such a rule, where the parties have not expressly provided, would alter the agreement by binding the option giver longer than originally agreed and would inflict upon the option giver the risk of delay avoided by entering into the option.

Another exception to the mailbox rule occurs where the offeror has permitted the offeree to insert important missing terms when accepting the offer. And acceptance is effective upon receipt when the offeror's obligation to perform is conditioned upon actual receipt of the acceptance. *See* RESTATEMENT (SECOND) OF CONTRACTS § 63, Comments (1981).

6. There is another exception to the mailbox rule in the situation where the offeree first rejects the offer by mail, and then before the offeror receives the rejection, the offeree dispatches an acceptance. In this situation, there is a contract only if the acceptance is received first. Why? *See* RESTATEMENT (SECOND) OF CONTRACTS § 40 (1981).

7. Another problem arises when the offeree dispatches an acceptance, but then changes his mind and sends a rejection. Assuming the acceptance arrives before the rejection, is there a contract? What is the effect of the rejection which the offeror receives after the acceptance? *See* RESTATEMENT (SECOND) OF CONTRACTS § 63, Comments (1981).

PROBLEMS

1. Seth has subscribed to an Internet server and has an electronic mail (e-mail) address for his computer. On Monday morning, he listed his car for sale on an Internet bulletin board and left his e-mail address. That afternoon, Betty, who subscribes to another Internet server, saw the listing and sent Seth the following e-mail message: "I offer to buy your car for $3000." Seth received Betty's message on Monday evening and replied by e-mail: "$3000 too low. I offer to sell you my car for $3500. Let me hear from you. If you accept, you can pay for it and pick it up anytime on Saturday. My address is 5600 Tron Trail, Bipville." Betty responded by e-mail on Tuesday morning, stating, "I accept your offer to sell me your car for $3500. I'll come by your place with the cash on Saturday morning." Due to a temporary shutdown of Seth's Internet server, Betty's e-mail acceptance was lost and never received by Seth. Had Betty checked her e-mail program for message confirmation she would have learned that Seth had not received her message, but she was busy the rest of week and did not check her e-mail. Having not heard from Betty, Seth sold his car to another on Friday. On Saturday, Betty showed up at Seth's house with the $3500, but Seth told her he no longer owned the car. In a suit by Betty against Seth for breach of contract, who will prevail? What relief should Betty seek?

2. On June 1, Alice mailed a written offer to sell her house to Bill. Bill received Alice's offer on June 4, and promptly wrote a letter accepting her offer, which he deposited in the mail the same day. However, on June 5, Bill changed his mind and telephoned Alice to tell her he rejected her offer. On June 6, Alice sold her house to Theo. On June 7, Alice received Bill's acceptance letter, which he had mailed on June 4. Having changed his mind again, Bill insists he has a contract with Alice to purchase her house. If Bill sues Alice for breach of contract, who will prevail?

D.   NOTICE OF ACCEPTANCE

When the offeree accepts by performance, must the offeree notify the offeror of that performance in order for the parties to be bound? Because the offeror is the master of the offer, the offeror could expressly require such notification as an antecedent to a contract. However, in the absence of such a requirement, whether notice is necessary depends on the circumstances. Section 54 of the RESTATEMENT (SECOND) OF CONTRACTS (1981) provides:

Acceptance By Performance;
Necessity of Notification to Offeror

(1) Where an offer invites an offeree to accept by rendering a performance, no notification is necessary to make such an acceptance effective unless the offer requests such a notification.

(2) If an offeree who accepts by rendering a performance has reason to know that the offeror has no adequate means of learning of the performance with reasonable promptness and certainty, the contractual duty of the offeror is discharged unless

(a) the offeree exercises reasonable diligence to notify the offeror of acceptance, or

(b) the offeror learns of the performance within a reasonable time, or

(c) the offer indicates that notification of acceptance is not required.

Where the offeror makes an offer looking to a bilateral contract and the offeree purports to accept with a promise, the need to notify the offeror is generally greater. Section 56 of the RESTATEMENT (SECOND) OF CONTRACTS (1981) provides:

Acceptance by Promise; Necessity of Notification to Offeror

Except as stated in section 69 [which governs acceptance by silence] or where the offer manifests a contrary intention, it is essential to an acceptance by promise either that the offeree exercise reasonable diligence to notify the offeror of acceptance or that the offeror receive the acceptance seasonably.

Carlill v. Carbolic Smoke Ball Co., 1 Q.B. 256 (1892). Defendants' medical preparation, "The Carbolic Smoke Ball," was advertised to the public in several newspapers. The advertisement provided: "100 pound reward will be paid by the Carbolic Smoke Ball Company to any person who contracts the increasing epidemic influenza, colds, or any disease caused by taking cold, after having used the ball three times daily for two weeks, according to the printed directions supplied with each ball. 1000 pounds is deposited with the Alliance Bank, Regent Street shewing our sincerity in the matter." After reading this advertisement, plaintiff purchased one of the smoke balls and used it according to the instructions provided. After using the product as directed for two months, plaintiff nevertheless contracted influenza. As a result, she brought a contract action against defendants to recover the 100 pound reward as stated in the advertisement. Initially, the court concluded that the advertisement was an "express promise" or offer and not a meaningless "puff." The defendants argued the promise was not binding because the promise was made to no one in particular. However, the court concluded that such advertisements offering rewards "are offers to anybody who performs the conditions named in the advertisement." Defendants also argued that plaintiff had not notified defendant of her acceptance of the offer. The court acknowledged that notice of acceptance is generally required to form a contract. However, the court observed that the offeror may dispense with the requirement that he be notified of acceptance. The court further explained, "if the person making the offer, expressly or impliedly intimates in his offer that it will be sufficient to act on the proposal without communicating acceptance of it to himself, performance of the condition is a sufficient acceptance without notification." Given the nature of this transaction, "common sense" dictates "that a person is not to notify his acceptance of the offer before he performs the condition, but that if he performs the condition notification is dispensed with." The court further concluded that the defendants' continuing offer was never revoked, and "if notice of acceptance is required — which I doubt very much — the person who makes the offer gets the notice of acceptance contemporaneously with his notice of the performance of the condition." Defendants also argued that plaintiff provided no consideration because contracting influenza was out of plaintiff's control. However, the court concluded that in order to accept the offer, the only obligation plaintiff had was to fulfill the requirements of defendants' advertised offer, and that since the acceptance was predicated only upon whether plaintiff contracted influenza, it was irrelevant that the act was out of her control. The court also noted that defendants were provided consideration for their promise to pay a reward in the form of the benefit the company received in convincing the public to use the Carbolic Smoke Ball.

International Filter Co. v. Conroe Gin, Ice & Light Co., 277 S.W. 631 (Tex. Com. App. 1925). On February 10, 1920, a traveling solicitor for International presented a paper proposal to Conroe for the sale of a steel tank water softener and filter. The proposal was to become a contract when it was "accepted" by Conroe and then approved by International's executive officer at its Chicago office. On the day Conroe received the proposal, Conroe made a notation on International's paper proposal, thus making an offer to International on the terms first proposed by International. On February 13, 1920, International's Chicago office received the paper, and International's president and vice-president approved Conroe's order. On February 14, International sent Conroe a letter acknowledging its agreement with Conroe. On February 28, Conroe sent a letter to International withdrawing its offer. International sued for breach of the contract. Conroe argued that neither the approval by the vice-president and president nor the February 14 letter, amounted to approval "by an executive officer of the International Filter Co., at its office in Chicago." Conroe further maintained that notice of acceptance by International was required to be communicated to Conroe. The court concluded that Conroe dispensed with the requirement of notice of acceptance by specifying a particular mode of acceptance. The approval by International's president and vice-president satisfied the mode of acceptance required by Conroe because it was made "by an executive officer of the International Filter Co., at its office in Chicago." The court also concluded that no requirement for notice of acceptance existed in the language of the contract.

NOTES & QUESTIONS

1. Was the offer in *Carlill v. Carbolic Smoke Ball Co.* a unilateral or bilateral offer? What was the requested act? Why did the court conclude the plaintiff offeree did not have to notify the defendant offeror of her performance of the requested act? Did the plaintiff nonetheless notify the defendant? If so, what was the issue?

2. Was the offer in *International Filter Co. v. Conroe Gin, Ice & Light Co.* a unilateral or bilateral offer? Why did the court hold that notice of acceptance was unnecessary for the formation of the contract? Who made the offer? Who really exercised mastery over the terms? Had Conroe not implicitly dispensed with notice of acceptance, what, if any, responsibility would International have had to notify Conroe of its acceptance?

3. What is the difference between the offeree's responsibility to notify the offeror of acceptance when accepting a unilateral offer as opposed to a bilateral offer? Does an offeree's failure to give notice when required have a different effect depending on whether the offer looks to a unilateral or bilateral contract? Why the distinction?

SEMENTA v. TYLMAN
595 N.E.2d 688 (Ill. App. 1992)

DUNN, Justice:

Anthony Sementa and Anthony Sementa, D.D.S., P.C., appeal from a judgment order of the circuit court of Du Page County. Sementa individually brought suit against Stanley Tylman. Tylman and his professional corporation, Dr. Stanley Tylman, D.D.S. (collectively referred to as Tylman), then filed a separate suit against Sementa and his professional corporation (collectively referred to as Sementa), and the two suits were consolidated. Over Sementa's objection, the circuit court entered a judgment order which had been signed by the individual parties. The court subsequently denied Sementa's motion to vacate the purported agreed judgment order, and Sementa now appeals. His contention on appeal is that the parties never reached a settlement agreement because Sementa's settlement offer was no longer in effect at the time Tylman's purported acceptance was communicated to Sementa. . . . We reverse and remand.

Sementa and Tylman are both engaged in the practice of dentistry. In January 1989, Sementa and Tylman entered into several written agreements pursuant to which Sementa purchased Tylman's dental practice in Lombard for a price of $215,000. In addition, Tylman was to work as a consultant in the office until December 31, 1994, unless the parties mutually agreed to an earlier termination date or one of them died, and was to receive compensation for his services. Tylman also agreed to refrain from practicing dentistry within a five-mile radius of his former office and soliciting patients of that office during the period of his independent contractor agreement with Sementa and for two years thereafter.

On April 16, 1990, Sementa filed a complaint alleging that Tylman had breached the above restrictive covenant by practicing dentistry within five miles of the Lombard office. Tylman filed a separate action against Sementa on June 20, 1990. He alleged that Sementa had failed to make certain payments due under the January 1989 agreements. The circuit court subsequently consolidated the two suits.

The case was originally set for trial on December 6, 1990. On that date, the attorneys for the parties advised the trial judge that a settlement was impending. They presented the judge a stipulation to dismiss the case with prejudice. The trial judge signed the stipulated dismissal order.

The parties did not execute a written settlement agreement at this time. On January 10, 1991, Tylman's attorney presented to the circuit court a motion to either enforce an alleged verbal settlement agreement or vacate the stipulated dismissal and set the case for trial. The trial judge vacated the dismissal order and set the matter for trial on March 28, 1991. The trial date was subsequently continued until April 4, 1991.

On April 4, Tylman's attorney presented a document titled "Agreed Order" to the trial court. This document set forth terms of a proposed settlement between Sementa and Tylman and contained the signatures of both. Over the objection of Sementa's attorney, the trial judge entered the order and stated that the document was "complete and regular on its face." The trial judge also stated that if Sementa's attorney had a valid objection, he could move to have the agreed order vacated.

On May 1, 1991, Sementa filed a motion to vacate the April 4 judgment order. Sementa's motion and Tylman's response contained affidavits establishing the following undisputed facts. On December 27, 1990, Tylman's attorney, John Garrow, sent a letter to Sementa's attorney, John McCluskey. The letter stated that Tylman's motion to vacate the December 6 stipulated dismissal order or to enforce the alleged verbal settlement agreement was enclosed. The letter also stated that Tylman would agree to a clause which would allow either party to terminate the agreement as of the beginning of 1992, 1993, or 1994. If Tylman terminated the agreement, he would be required to pay $15,000 to Sementa if the termination was to take effect in 1992, $10,000 for 1993, and $5,000 for 1994. The letter also stated that, in general, Tylman was willing to offer the same proposal contained in Garrow's letter of December 7, 1990.

On December 31, 1990, McCluskey delivered the document titled "Agreed Order" to Garrow's office. Sementa had signed the document earlier that day. At the bottom of the document, next to Sementa's signature, there was a signature line with Tylman's name printed below. The "agreed order" was seven pages long. Among other things, it stated that the independent contractor agreement could not be terminated until January 1, 1993. If Tylman wished to terminate the agreement as of that date, he would be required to pay Sementa $10,000, amortized over the period of remaining payments under the independent contractor and equipment lease agreements. If he wished to terminate the agreement as of January 1, 1994, he would be required to pay $2,000, amortized in a similar manner.

Enclosed with the "agreed order" was a check for $30,321.94 made payable to Tylman. Sementa wrote the words "Pursuant to Agreed Order" on the lower left corner of the check. Tylman cashed the check on January 3, 1991, but crossed out the above phrase.

On January 14, 1991, Garrow sent another letter to Sementa. This letter states that Tylman "was willing to settle this matter at any time upon the conditions set forth in my letter to you dated December 27, 1990." McCluskey informed Garrow that this proposal was not acceptable to Sementa.

When Garrow and McCluskey met at the Du Page County courthouse on March 28, 1991, Garrow showed him the "agreed order" dated December 31, 1990, which Tylman had now signed. McCluskey then telephoned Sementa, who was no longer willing to settle the case on those terms. This was the first notice Sementa had that Tylman had signed the agreement. According to Tylman's affidavit, he signed the "agreed order" on January 11, 1991. The attorneys were told to return to court on April 4 because the judge was not available on March 28.

The trial judge denied the motion to vacate. He ruled that, by accepting the check on January 3, Tylman created a contract between the parties. Sementa now appeals. . . .

Sementa contends that his December 31, 1990, "agreed order" was an offer that Tylman rejected several times prior to his purported March 28, 1991, acceptance, thereby rendering that acceptance invalid. The law of contracts is applicable to settlement agreements. . . . Settlement agreements are binding only if there is an offer, an acceptance, and a meeting of the minds as to the terms of the agreement. . . .

There is no dispute that the December 31, 1990, "agreed order" was an offer from Sementa to Tylman. The January 14, 1991, letter from Garrow to McCluskey proposed settlement on different terms than Sementa had proposed in the "agreed order." It therefore constituted a counteroffer. . . . Responding to an offer with a counteroffer constitutes a rejection of the original offer. . . . A rejected offer cannot be revived by a later acceptance. . . .

Tylman contends that he accepted the terms of the "agreed order" by signing it on January 11, 1991. There is no acceptance, however, until the offeree notifies the offeror of the acceptance or at least employs reasonable diligence in attempting to do so. (RESTATEMENT (SECOND) OF CONTRACTS § 56 (1981). . . .) The record reveals that Tylman made no effort to notify Sementa of his "acceptance" until March 28, 1991, long after he rejected the offer by making the January 14 counteroffer. Accordingly, there was no valid acceptance of Sementa's December 31 settlement proposal.

Tylman argues that Sementa ratified the December 31 agreed order by paying himself over $6,000 pursuant to it. This would not, however, remove the requirement of acceptance of the agreement by Tylman. The record reveals that no valid acceptance ever took place.

The trial court's conclusion that Tylman accepted the terms of the December 31 proposal by cashing the check was also erroneous. Under some circumstances, a tendered contract may be accepted if the offeree accepts benefits under the contract. . . . Here, however, although Sementa placed the words "Pursuant to Agreed Order" on the check, the agreed order did not specifically provide for a payment in that amount to Tylman. Instead, it provided that the sum due Tylman under the independent contractor agreement would be determined later. Thus, Tylman would not have been aware that he was accepting a benefit under the agreed order by cashing the check. Furthermore, by crossing out the above phrase before cashing the check, Tylman indicated he was not manifesting any intention to accept the terms of the "agreed order." We therefore conclude that Tylman's acceptance of the check did not constitute an acceptance of the terms of the agreed order. . . .

For the above reasons, the judgment of the circuit court of Du Page County is reversed, and the cause is remanded for further proceedings.

Reversed and remanded.

NOTES & QUESTIONS

1. The *Sementa v. Tylman* court concluded that there was no valid acceptance of Sementa's December 31, 1990 settlement offer because Tylman made no effort to notify Sementa of Tylman's acceptance until after Tylman had made a counteroffer on January 14, 1991. However, on January 3, 1991, Tylman cashed Sementa's check, albeit after striking the language "Pursuant to Agreed Order." If Tylman's cashing of the check was not acceptance of Sementa's offer, what was it? If Tylman's cashing the check was acceptance, would the reasonable person in Tylman's position be justified in believing that Sementa would receive the acceptance seasonably and thus learn in due course that Tylman had accepted Sementa's settlement offer?

2. Do you agree with the court's conclusion that Tylman did not accept Sementa's settlement offer when he cashed the check? Can Tylman have it both ways, that is, could Tylman reject Sementa's settlement offer with a counteroffer but still take the settlement money Sementa proffered in the check marked "Pursuant to Agreed Order"?

Bishop v. Eaton, 161 Mass. 496, 37 N.E. 665 (1894). The defendant, Frank Eaton, sent a letter to the plaintiff, Charles Bishop, regarding Frank's brother, Harry. In the letter, Frank wrote: "If Harry needs more money, let him have it, or assist him to get it, and I will see that it is paid." Relying on this letter, Bishop signed off as surety on a promissory note to permit Harry to obtain a loan. Harry would not have been able to secure the loan without Bishop's signing as surety. After signing the note, Bishop mailed a letter to Frank, informing him of the transaction. However, Frank later testified that he never received Bishop's letter. When Harry was unable to pay the note, Bishop fulfilled his obligation as the surety, paying the note. When Frank refused to reimburse Bishop for the amount Bishop paid on Harry's note, Bishop filed suit. The court held that a contract had been formed between Bishop and Frank Eaton. Frank's letter to Bishop was essentially a unilateral offer, Frank's promise of guaranty which Bishop could accept by acting to assist Harry in obtaining money. However, Frank claimed that he could not be bound to the agreement because he did not receive a timely notice of Bishop's act of surety. Regarding a requirement that the unilateral offeree notify the offeror of the performance of the act of acceptance, the court stated:

> Ordinarily, there is no occasion to notify the offeror of the acceptance of such an offer, for the doing of the act is sufficient acceptance, and the promisor knows that he is bound when he sees that the action has been taken on the faith of his offer. But if the act is of such a kind that knowledge of it will not quickly come to the promisor, the promisee is bound to give him notice of his acceptance within a reasonable time after doing that which constituted the acceptance.

Although Bishop's letter informing Frank he accepted never arrived, the court concluded that the letter satisfied the notice requirement. The court stated: "We are of opinion that the plaintiff [Bishop], after assisting Harry to get the money, did all that he was required to do when he seasonably sent the defendant [Frank] the letter by mail, informing him of what had been done."

NOTES & QUESTIONS

1. According to the court, when did Bishop accept Frank Eaton's unilateral offer: when he signed the promissory note as surety for Harry Eaton, or when he sent the notice of acceptance? In other words, was notice a prerequisite for acceptance and formation of the contract in the case?

2. If the *Bishop v. Eaton* court ruled that there could be no acceptance and unilateral contract until Bishop dispatched notice to Frank Eaton, what risk is created for the reasonable person in the position of Bishop, the offeree?

3. Sarah promises to pay Jack $50 if he washes and waxes her car by Saturday. Jack arrives at Sarah's home on Friday, and washes and waxes her car, which is parked in her driveway within view of Sarah's kitchen window. Must Jack give notice to Sarah that he has commenced or completed the job in order for Sarah to be bound? What if Sarah is away until Saturday? Does it matter whether Jack knows she is away?

4. What part does the "mailbox rule" play in *Bishop v. Eaton?*

5. For another case addressing the question of whether an offeree must notify an offeror of acceptance of an offer looking to a unilateral contract, refer to *Carlill v. Carbolic Smoke Ball Co.*, 1 Q.B. 256 (1892), which is synopsized earlier in this section.

LONG v. ALLEN
906 P.2d 754 (N.M. App. 1995)

BUSTAMANTE, Judge:

Defendant Allen (hereafter Seller) appeals from an order of summary judgment in favor of Plaintiff Long (hereafter Buyer) in an action for breach of a residential purchase agreement. Determining there were no genuine issues of material fact, the trial court found the purchase agreement enforceable and granted Buyer's motion to compel arbitration pursuant to the purchase agreement. Judgment was entered against Seller and his former wife, co-owners of the property at issue. Only Seller has appealed. We affirm.

DISCUSSION

Buyer made several offers to Seller and his former wife (collectively, Owners) to purchase their residence. Ultimately, Buyer made a written offer dated March 1, 1994, that was set to expire on March 3, 1994, at 6:00 p.m. unless the Owners delivered a written acceptance to Buyer before that time. The Owners signed the offer (the Agreement) on March 4, 1994, and returned it to Buyer on that date via her real estate agent. Both parties acknowledge that the Owners' execution of the Agreement on March 4 constituted a counteroffer. They dispute, however, whether uncontroverted facts establish that Buyer's performance constituted an "acceptance" that bound the Owners to the terms of the counteroffer.

The ultimate question of whether the Owners' counteroffer became a binding promise and resulted in a contract requires us to consider whether the evidentiary facts conclusively establish that Buyer accepted the counteroffer. *See Orcutt v. S & L Paint Contractors, Ltd.*, 109 N.M. 796, 798, 791 P.2d 71, 73 (Ct. App. 1990) (offeree's acceptance must be clear, positive, and unambiguous). Acceptance of an offer is a manifestation of assent to the terms of the offer, made by the offeree, in a manner allowed, invited, or required by the offer. *Id.* (*citing* RESTATEMENT (SECOND) OF CONTRACTS § 50 (1981)).

Seller initially contends that the specific terms of the Owners' counteroffer required a written acceptance. Seller refers us to paragraph 4.11 of the Agreement which states that "all notices and communications required or permitted under this Agreement shall be in writing." Paragraph 4.11 is a general provision which describes the mechanics for giving notice "required or permitted under this Agreement," including addresses and facsimile telephone numbers. The paragraph also defines the effective time of notices depending on the method of delivery. The paragraph does not on its face address the manner of acceptance or time within which acceptance of the counteroffer is required. We believe that the act of acceptance of the counteroffer is not a communication under the document as provided in paragraph 4.11. Rather, acceptance is an act creating an agreement. The Agreement does not otherwise address in any way Buyer's mode of response and, in our view, simply does not specify that the counteroffer can only be accepted in writing. The counteroffer thus invited acceptance by any manner reasonable under the circumstances, such as by promise or performance. *See* RESTATEMENT, *supra*, § 30(2) (form of acceptance invited) and § 32 (in case of doubt, offeree may accept by promise or performance).

The fact that the transaction involved the sale of land and thus was within the statute of frauds does not persuade us by itself that a written acceptance was required. The Agreement, already signed by Buyer on March 1, identified each party and the subject land and also specified the pertinent terms and conditions of the transaction. . . . Seller suggests that Buyer's actions were not the type of partial performance which would take the transaction out of the statute of frauds. We disagree. The Agreement satisfied the requirements [of the statute of frauds], and Seller, the party to be charged in this case, signed the document. Nothing more is required to satisfy the statute of frauds. . . . RESTATEMENT, *supra*, § 131.

We turn next to the facts bearing on the issue of Buyer's acceptance of the counteroffer by her performance. To the extent the pertinent facts are not in dispute and all that remains is the legal effect of those facts, summary judgment is appropriate. . . . The following facts are undisputed. Paragraphs 1.4(A) & 1.9 of the Agreement required Buyer to deliver a $5,000 earnest-money deposit to a named title company as soon as practical. The check was received by the title company on March 8, 1994. Buyer arranged for professional inspections of the property as urged in paragraph 2.5 of the Agreement. Pursuant to paragraph 2.1 of the Agreement, Buyer sought and obtained a financing commitment for her purchase of the property. Paragraph 1.10 specified that the closing take place within ten business days of April 8, 1994, and that the parties arrange for delivery and execution of the necessary documents and funds. Buyer appeared at the title company office on April 14, 1994, and signed all the documents necessary to close the transaction. In our view, these facts establish conclusively that Buyer accepted the Owners' counteroffer by performance of what the counteroffer requested. *See*

RESTATEMENT, *supra*, § 62 (where offer invites offeree to choose between acceptance by promise and acceptance by performance, beginning of invited performance is an acceptance by performance).

We recognize that Seller's affidavit states he never received any communication from Buyer specifically claiming or purporting to accept the counteroffer. However, the fact that Buyer may not have communicated her verbal or written promissory acceptance explicitly is not fatal to Buyer's position. The RESTATEMENT makes it clear that notification to the offeror of acceptance is not necessary unless the offeror requests notice or the offeree has reason to know the offeror has no adequate means of learning of the performance with reasonable promptness and certainty. RESTATEMENT, *supra*, § 54. We have already determined the offer did not require any particular form of acceptance. Further, Seller does not assert and has made no showing that he had no means of learning about Buyer's acceptance. Most tellingly, however, it cannot be disputed that Seller had actual notice of Buyer's acceptance.

The following facts are undisputed. On March 9, 1994, at Seller's request, Buyer's real estate agent faxed a copy of the Agreement to Seller's attorney. The cover sheet for the fax included the statement, "We are moving very fast to get everything done." Seller directed Buyer's agent to deliver Buyer's earnest-money-deposit check to the title company and Seller knew the check was delivered. Seller was kept informed regarding property inspections and Buyer's efforts to secure financing. Seller was aware that Buyer's real estate agent arranged for a survey of the property at the Owners' expense. Seller arranged for the April 14, 1994, closing appointment at the title company. Buyer was not aware of any obstacle to closing the purchase until she appeared at the title company to sign closing documents. These facts conclusively establish that Seller was aware in the normal course of business of Buyer's acceptance by performance.

[The court then summarily disposed of several other issues raised by the Seller.]

We hold as a matter of law that Buyer accepted the counteroffer by performance, thus making the Owners' promises binding. . . . Accordingly, we affirm the trial court's order of summary judgment for Buyer.

NOTES & QUESTIONS

1. Was the Seller's counteroffer in *Long v. Allen* a unilateral or bilateral offer? Was the nature of the counteroffer ambiguous? Did the counteroffer state an exclusive mode of acceptance?

2. How could the Seller in *Long v. Allen* have drafted its counteroffer to avoid the result in this case?

3. Besides the approach taken by the *Long v. Allen* court, which relied on § 54 of the RESTATEMENT (SECOND) OF CONTRACTS (1981), there are two other views regarding whether an offeree must notify the offeror that the act requested in a unilateral offer has been performed. One of these views, associated with Professor Williston, is that notice is not required unless requested by the offeror. *See Sunco Mfg. Co. v. Hargrove*, 581 P.2d 925 (Okla. App. 1978). Does this view serve any of the purposes and policies of contract law we have previously identified?

4. The third view, also summarized by the *Sunco* court and illustrated by *Bishop v. Eaton*, above, is that where notice is required, no contract exists unless and until notice is communicated to the offeror. Why is this considered to be the "least tenable view"? How is this third view different from the RESTATEMENT (SECOND) OF CONTRACTS § 54, which the *Long v. Allen* court chose to apply?

White v. Corlies & Tifft, 46 N.Y. 467 (1871). On September 29, 1865, the defendants, Corlies and Tifft, wrote plaintiff White, a carpenter, asking him to perform some remodeling work on their store. In their letter, defendants stated: "Upon an agreement to finish the fitting up of offices 57 Broadway in two weeks date, you can commence at once." The plaintiff received the defendants' note on September 29, but did not reply to defendants' letter nor did he otherwise contact the defendants. Instead, he immediately purchased lumber for the project and began to prepare that lumber away from the job site. On September 30, the defendants told the plaintiff that his services would no longer be needed. Plaintiff sued for a breach of contract. The court concluded that the plaintiff's act of purchasing and preparing the necessary materials did not constitute a valid acceptance of the offer made by the defendants' letter. Thus, the court held, no contract was formed because there was no meeting of the minds. The court explained:

> [W]here an offer is made by one party to another when they are not together, the acceptance of it by that other must be manifested by some appropriate act. It does not need that the acceptance shall come to the knowledge of the one making the offer before he shall be bound. But though the manifestation need not be brought to his knowledge before he becomes bound, he is not bound, if that manifestation is not put in a proper way to be in the usual course of events, in some reasonable time communicated to him.

Although plaintiff had arguably reached a mental determination to accept the defendants' offer, "he did no act which indicated acceptance to the defendants. He bought and prepared material for the work, but that material and preparation could have been done with respect to any other work." The court concluded, "There was nothing in his thought, formed but not uttered, or in his acts that indicated or set in motion an indication to the defendants of his acceptance of their offer, or which could necessarily result therein."

NOTES & QUESTIONS

1. Is the notice requirement enunciated by the court in *White v. Corlies & Tifft* the same as that applied by the court in *Bishop v. Eaton* synopsized earlier in this section? If White had sent a message accepting Corlies & Tifft's offer on September 29, after purchasing the lumber but before Corlies & Tifft withdrew their offer on September 30, would the result in the case have been different?

2. Was the offer in *White* one looking to a unilateral contract, to a bilateral contract, or something else? Does it matter with respect to the notice issue?

3. Refer to *Brackenbury v. Hodgkin* and § 45 of the RESTATEMENT (SECOND) OF CONTRACTS (1981) considered in section E of this Chapter. Do the circumstances in *White* justify protecting the offeree White with an "option contract at law"?

Ever-Tite Roofing Corp. v. Green, 83 So. 2d 449 (La. App. 1955). Defendant homeowners made a written offer to the plaintiff roofing company on June 10, 1953, to have the plaintiff reroof their house. The written offer detailed the work to be done and the price, and further provided: "This agreement shall become binding only upon written acceptance thereof, by the principal or authorized officer of the contractor, or upon commencing performance of the work." Because the work was to be performed entirely on credit, plaintiff sought a credit report from the lending institution, which was to finance the work. Defendants knew that the plaintiff would not begin work on the roof for some time until plaintiff received the credit report. The plaintiff received the lender's approval, and the plaintiff sent over workmen in two trucks loaded with the necessary roofing materials. When they arrived at the defendants' home, the workmen found other roofers already working on the house. At this time, the defendants told the plaintiff's crew that the job had been contracted to someone else and told them to leave. The plaintiff brought suit to recover for damages as a result of a breach of contract. The court held for the plaintiff, concluding that the plaintiff had commenced performance of the work by sending the workmen and the materials before receiving notice from the defendants that the offer had been revoked. The court reasoned that where an offer does not specify the time within which it is to be accepted, the offeree may accept within a reasonable time to be determined by the nature of the transaction and the circumstances. Here, the defendants made no attempt to notify the plaintiff of their decision to withdraw the offer until the plaintiff had already arrived. There was no unreasonable delay on the part of the plaintiff, who, in processing the credit check and approval, proceeded with due diligence. The court concluded that plaintiff commenced performance with the loading of the trucks and the transporting of the materials and workmen to the defendants' home. Thus, performance began before the offer was withdrawn, and a completed contract had been formed.

NOTES & QUESTIONS

1. Is it possible to distinguish the decisions in *White* and *Ever-Tite?*

2. Was the defendants' offer in *Ever-Tite* one looking to a unilateral contract, a bilateral contract or something else?

PROBLEMS

1. Wilson, who lived in Chicago, Illinois, owned a condominium in the Mississippi delta. After hurricane Nancy tore through the delta, Wilson learned that the condominium roof had been damaged and that the interior had suffered some water damage. Wilson telephoned Morrison Construction in Natchez, Mississippi, and after a brief discussion told owner Morrison, "I promise to pay you $2,000 if you repair my condominium's roof and paint the interior." Morrison said, "I've got so many other orders, I don't know. I'll have to think about it." The next day, Wilson entered into a contract with another Mississippi contractor, Baldwin, who promised to start repairs the following week. The day before Baldwin was scheduled to start work on the condominium, Morrison began work on the roof and the interior of the condominium. When Baldwin arrived at the site the next day, Morrison told Baldwin that she (Morrison) had already accepted Wilson's offer. Wilson later telephoned Morrison and told her that he had a contract with Baldwin,

not Morrison. Does Morrison have a contract with Wilson?

2. On March 1, Emily offered to pay Mike $2,000 to build a fence around her pasture if Mike would promise to complete the work by April 1. When Mike failed to get back to Emily by March 4, Emily made the same offer to Jack, who accepted and told her he would begin the work "in the next few days as soon as I can get my hands on what I need to do the job." In the meantime, without notifying Emily orally or in writing, Mike bought material and rented a tractor with a postdigger attachment. On March 5, Mike arrived at Emily's home at about 7:00 a.m. The tractor Mike rented arrived at 7:05 a.m., and shortly after, the wood posts and boards Mike ordered arrived. At about 7:15 a.m., Mike commenced digging the post holes for the fence around the pasture. The pasture is about thirty yards behind Emily's home and in plain view of Emily's kitchen window. Mike claims he saw Emily looking out of the kitchen window at about 7:30 a.m. and several more times later on March 5, that when he saw her he waved to her, and once she waved back. By the end of the day on March 5, Mike had dug 120 post holes and installed 60 posts. The next day, March 6, Mike arrived at 7:00 a.m. and continued installing post holes. However, at 8:00 a.m., Jack arrived with material and equipment. Jack and Emily went out to the pasture where an agitated Emily informed Mike she had entered into a contract with Jack, that Mike had no business being there, that she thought Mike was Jack when Mike started work the day before, and that Mike should take his equipment and material and get out. Does Mike have a contract with Emily?

E. UNILATERAL CONTRACTS

1. Rewards

Offers of reward are a common form of the offer looking to a unilateral contract. Typically, the offeror promises a sum of money for the return of lost or stolen property, for information leading to the apprehension of a fugitive, for the actual apprehension of a fugitive, for information about a missing person, etc. Ordinarily, offers of reward are made through the public media, such as, newspapers, television and radio. Sometimes an issue arises whether the person who claims to have accepted has performed the act requested by the offeror.

James v. Turilli, 473 S.W.2d 757 (Mo. App. 1971). Defendant operated the "Jesse James Museum," which featured a collection of memorabilia about the legendary outlaw. During an appearance on nationwide television, Defendant claimed that the man shot and buried in 1882 was not Jesse James, and that the real Jesse James lived under an assumed name at the Defendant's museum for many years and died in the 1950s. Defendant announced to the network audience that he "would pay ten thousand dollars to anyone . . . who could prove me wrong." Jesse James' daughter-in-law and two granddaughters convinced a judge and jury that Defendant was wrong. Affirming the trial court's judgment that the Plaintiffs had performed the act required in the Defendant's offer, the appellate court reasoned:

> [An] offer of a reward is a unilateral contract which becomes complete when accepted by performance of the act called for in the offer. A claimant to a reward needs only to show substantial performance. As with other contracts, literal performance is not required.

GLOVER v. JEWISH WAR VETERANS, POST NO. 58
68 A.2d 233 (D.C. App. 1949)

CLAGETT, Associate Judge:

The issue determinative of this appeal is whether a person giving information leading to the arrest of a murderer without any knowledge that a reward has been offered for such information by a non-governmental organization is entitled to collect the reward. The trial court decided the question in the negative and instructed the jury to return a verdict for defendant. Claimant appeals from the judgment on such instructed verdict.

The controversy grows out of the murder on June 5, 1946, of Maurice L. Bernstein, a local pharmacist. The following day, June 6, Post No. 58, Jewish War Veterans of the United States, communicated to the newspapers an offer of a reward of $500 "to the person or persons furnishing information resulting in the apprehension and conviction of the persons guilty of the murder of Maurice L. Bernstein." Notice of the reward was published in the newspaper June 7. A day or so later Jesse James Patton, one of the men suspected of the crime, was arrested and the police received information that the other murderer was Reginald Wheeler and that Wheeler was the "boy friend" of a daughter of Mary Glover, plaintiff and claimant in the present case. On the evening of June 11 the police visited Mary Glover, who in answer to questions informed them that her daughter and Wheeler had left the city on June 5. She told the officers she didn't know exactly where the couple had gone, whereupon the officers asked for names of relatives whom the daughter might be visiting. In response to such questions she gave the names and addresses of several relatives, including one at Ridge Spring, South Carolina, which was the first place visited by the officers and where Wheeler was arrested in company with plaintiff's daughter on June 13. Wheeler and Patton were subsequently convicted of the crime.

Claimant's most significant testimony, in the view that we take of the case, was that she first learned that a reward had been offered on June 12, the day after she had given the police officers the information which enabled them to find Wheeler. Claimant's husband, who was present during the interview with the police officers, also testified that at the time of the interview he didn't know that any reward had been offered for Wheeler's arrest, that nothing was said by the police officers about a reward and that he didn't know about it "until we looked into the paper about two or three days after that."

We have concluded that the trial court correctly instructed the jury to return a verdict for defendant. While there is some conflict in the decided cases on the subject of rewards, most of such conflict has to do with rewards offered by governmental officers and agencies. So far as rewards offered by private individuals and organizations are concerned, there is little conflict on the rule that questions regarding such rewards are to be based upon the law of contracts.

Since it is clear that the question is one of contract law, it follows that, at least so far as private rewards are concerned, there can be no contract unless the claimant when giving the desired information knew of the offer of the reward and acted with the intention of accepting such offer; otherwise the claimant gives the information not in the expectation of receiving a reward but rather out of a sense of public duty or other motive unconnected with the reward. "In the nature of the case," according to Professor Williston, "it is impossible for an offeree actually to assent to an offer unless he knows of its existence." After stating that courts in some jurisdictions have decided to the contrary, Williston adds, "It is impossible, however, to find in such a case [that is, in a case holding to the contrary] the elements generally held in England and America necessary for the formation of a contract. If it is clear the offeror intended to pay for the service, it is equally certain that the person rendering the service performed it voluntarily and not in return for a promise to pay. If one person expects to buy, and the other to give, there can hardly be found mutual assent. These views are supported by the great weight of authority, and in most jurisdictions a plaintiff in the sort of case under discussion is denied recovery."

The American Law Institute in its RESTATEMENT OF THE LAW OF CONTRACTS follows the same rule, thus: "It is impossible that there should be an acceptance unless the offeree knows of the existence of the offer." The RESTATEMENT gives the following illustration of the rule just stated: "A offers a reward for information leading to the arrest and conviction of a criminal. B, in ignorance of the offer, gives information leading to his arrest and later, with knowledge of the offer and intent to accept it, gives other information necessary for conviction. There is no contract." (RESTATEMENT (SECOND) OF CONTRACTS, § 53. . . .)

We have considered the reasoning in state decisions following the contrary rule. Mostly, as we have said, they involve rewards offered by governmental bodies and in general are based upon the theory that the government is benefited equally whether or not the claimant gives the information with knowledge of the reward and that therefore the government should pay in any event. . . . We believe that the rule adopted by Professor Williston and the RESTATEMENT and in the majority of the cases is the better reasoned rule and therefore we adopt it. We believe furthermore that this rule is particularly applicable in the present case since the claimant did not herself contact the authorities and volunteer information but gave the information only upon questioning by the police officers and did not claim any knowledge of the guilt or innocence of the criminal but only knew where he probably could be located. Affirmed.

NOTES & QUESTIONS

1. The preceding case follows the majority rule that a person must know of a private offer of reward in order to accept. *Gadsden Times v. Doe*, 345 So. 2d 1361 (Ala. App. 1977). *See also* Annotation, *Knowledge of Reward as Condition of Right Thereto*, 86 A.L.R.3d 1142; RESTATEMENT (SECOND) OF CONTRACTS § 23 (1981). What public policy objectives underpin this majority rule? Are there public policy considerations which militate toward a different rule? Consider the following statement from the dissenting opinion of a Tennessee judge:

> [T]o base the payment of a reward on "prior knowledge" ought to be against the public policy of this State. . . . What public policy could be more fraught with impediments to justice and with fraud than one that says to the public, "Citizens, if you come forward and do your civic duty promptly as you should without knowledge or thought of reward, you shall forfeit all claims to any funds which have been offered by other public-minded citizens."

Stephens v. Memphis, 565 S.W.2d 213 (Tenn. App. 1977).

2. Should the prior knowledge requirement apply to an offeree claiming a reward offered by a governmental body? Are there public policy considerations which may justify a rule that the offeree need not know of the government's offer of reward in order to claim the reward? *See 86* A.L.R.3d 1142.

Simmons v. United States, 308 F.2d 160 (4th Cir. 1962). The sponsors of a fishing derby tagged a particular fish, "Diamond Jim III," which was then placed into the Chesapeake Bay. The derby sponsors offered a $25,000 reward if "Diamond Jim III" were caught on a hook and line. Simmons caught the $25,000 fish and presented it to the contest sponsors, who awarded him with the cash price. Soon after, the Internal Revenue Service assessed an income tax on the prize, asserting that Simmons earned the money through a contract with the sponsors. Claiming a refund of the tax, Simmons argued that he had not entered into a contract, that the prize was a gift and therefore not taxable under the Internal Revenue Code. Although he admitted he was aware of the contest and the prize when he went fishing in the bay, Simmons maintained that he had not entered into a contract because his intention that morning was not to catch the prize fish. He asserted that, as an experienced fisherman he knew that his chances of catching the prize fish were remote and that the idea of winning the contest was not on his mind when he went fishing that day. Thus, Simmons asserted, the act of catching the fish did not constitute acceptance of an offer. The court, however, held that a contract was formed between Simmons and the sponsor. According to the court, "[f]or the offer to be accepted and the contract to be binding, the desired act must be performed with knowledge of the offer." Even if Simmons went fishing for reasons unrelated to the offer, he knew of the offer. By rendering performance and receiving the prize, Simmons entered into a unilateral contract.

Sheldon v. George, 132 App. Div. 470, 116 N.Y.S. 969 (1909). Defendant, a jeweler, placed an advertisement in the Watertown Daily Times which read: "$100 reward for the return of a pair of diamond earrings lost from my store during the past two weeks. No questions asked. S.L. George, The Jeweler." Plaintiff returned the earrings, but the Defendant refused to pay the $100 reward. Plaintiff filed suit to recover the reward. Defendant, however, claimed that the diamond earrings were actually stolen from the store by an acquaintance of Plaintiff. Defendant further alleged that Plaintiff knowingly purchased the earrings from the thief and only returned them because the reward offered was higher than the price he had paid for the stolen jewelry. Defendant also contended that Plaintiff returned the earrings after Defendant threatened to inform the police about Plaintiff's criminal activities, not because of the advertisement. The court held for Defendant, stating that no contract was formed if the service for which the reward was offered was not rendered voluntarily. The court reasoned that because the diamonds were returned out of fear and compulsion, the act did not constitute acceptance of the offer.

PROBLEMS

After losing her cat, Emily, a first-year law student, posted a notice of reward on lampposts and trees in her neighborhood. Her signs read: "$100 reward for anyone who finds and returns my lost cat, Lincoln. Emily Brent, 193 Roscoe Street. 555-5555." Consider the following questions based on this offer of reward:

1. Without seeing the posted signs, Emily's neighbor, Michael, discovered the lost cat in his backyard across the alley from Emily's house. Recognizing the cat,

Michael returned the cat to Emily who said, "I guess you expect the reward." Michael asked, "What reward?" Emily responded, "Never mind," and closed her door on him. Walking home, Michael discovered and read the posted offer of reward. Is Michael entitled to the reward?

2. Michael found Emily's lost cat in his yard without recognizing it and without knowledge of the reward. Michael took the cat into his house to care for him. The next day, Michael discovered and read the posted notice. He then returned the cat to Emily, who declined to give him the reward because he admitted finding the cat before he learned of the reward. Is Michael entitled to the reward?

3. Michael read the posted notice of reward, found the cat and returned it to Emily, who refused to pay him the reward. In small claims court, Emily asked Michael, "Did you know the cat was mine when you found it?" Michael answered, "Yes." Emily then asked him, "Would you have returned the cat to m even if there had been no reward?" Michael answered, "Of course." Is Michael entitled to the reward?

4. Michael is fifteen years old and, therefore, a minor. Initially unaware of the posted reward, he discovered Emily's lost cat in his backyard and brought the cat into his house where he asked his mother if he could keep it. Michael's mother instructed him to check with each of their neighbors to see whether the cat belonged to one of them before deciding whether Michael could keep the cat. On his way to Emily's house, Michael read the posted notice of reward. Michael then returned the cat to Emily, telling her that his mother instructed him to return the cat. Emily refused to give Michael the reward. Is Michael entitled to the reward?

2. The Effect of Part Performance

Where an offer looks to a unilateral offer (that is, a promise offered in exchange for a performance), the offeree may accept by performing the act the offeror has requested. The offeror could theoretically revoke before the offeree performs that act, and under ordinary circumstances, such revocation operates to terminate the offer. *See Greene v. Keener,* 402 S.E.2d 284 (Ga. App. 1991); *Night Commander Lighting v. Brown,* 213 Mich. 214, 181 N.W. 979 (1921), noted in Chapter 2. However, where the offeree begins performance of the act requested in the offeror's offer, it would be unfair to the offeree to permit the offeror to revoke before the offeree has a reasonable opportunity to complete performance. For example, on Monday, Sarah promises to pay Jack $50 if he washes and waxes Sarah's car by Saturday. On Friday, Jack arrives at Sarah's house and washes her car in the driveway. Before Jack can wax the car, Sarah emerges from her house to tell Jack, "I revoke my offer to pay you $50 to wash and wax my car." Because Sarah's offer induced Jack to commence performance, it would be unfair to permit her to revoke the offer before he has a reasonable opportunity to complete performance. Should the courts regard part performance by the offeree as acceptance of the offer, creating a binding agreement as soon as the offeree commences performance? Or should the courts simply limit the offeror's power to revoke once the offeree begins performance of the requested act? Consider the following cases.

Brackenbury v. Hodgkin, 116 Me. 399, 102 A. 106 (1917). On February 8, 1915, Sarah Hodgkin, a widow living alone on her farm in Maine, sent a letter to the

Brackenburys, her daughter and son-in-law who lived in Missouri. In her letter, Mrs. Hodgkin stated that if the Brackenburys would move to her farm in Maine, care for her during her life, and pay their own moving expenses, she would permit them to use the farm and its household goods and keep the income from the farm. In closing, Mrs. Hodgkin wrote "you have the place when I have passed away." In response to Mrs. Hodgkin's offer, the Brackenburys moved from Missouri to Maine in April of 1915. However, relations between Hodgkin and the Brackenburys deteriorated a few weeks after their arrival. Hodgkin brought two suits against her son-in-law, and ordered the Brackenburys to leave. The Brackenburys refused to leave. On November 7, 1916, Hodgkin delivered a deed for the farm to her son, Walter Hodgkin. The Brackenburys then sued to compel Walter Hodgkin to reconvey the property to Mrs. Hodgkin and for a declaration that Mrs. Hodgkin held the farm in trust for the Brackenburys under the alleged contract. The court held that a legal and binding contract had been formed. Hodgkin's written offer did not require a verbal acceptance. Instead, her offer looked to a unilateral contract requiring the Brackenburys to act in return for Mrs. Hodgkin's promise. The Brackenburys accepted the offer by moving from Missouri to Maine and performing the specified acts to the extent they were permitted to perform by Mrs. Hodgkin. The court concluded, "The existence of a completed and valid contract is clear."

NOTES & QUESTIONS

1. The Brackenburys lived on the farm with Mrs. Hodgkin for many years after the decision reported above. It is reported that Mr. Brackenbury sometimes read aloud to Mrs. Hodgkin from the transcript in the case.

2. If the Brackenburys had left the Hodgkin farm after the reported decision rather than staying, what recourse would Mrs. Hodgkin have had? What if the Brackenburys had remained but failed to care for her properly?

3. Under the court's decision, when were the Brackenburys entitled to ownership of the farm? When they arrived at the farm? By the time they filed suit? When the court ruled in their favor? After the court issued its order, could the Brackenburys have moved to evict Mrs. Hodgkin?

4. Do you agree with the *Brackenbury* court's conclusion that the Brackenburys had accepted Mrs. Hodgkin's offer? *See* RESTATEMENT (SECOND) OF CONTRACTS §§ 32, 45 & 62 (1981).

TAYLOR v. MULTNOMAH COUNTY DEPUTY SHERIFF'S RETIREMENT BOARD
510 P.2d 339 (Or. 1973)

HOLMAN, Justice:

Plaintiff brought a mandamus proceeding to force defendants, custodians of the Multnomah County Deputy Sheriff's Retirement Board, to include plaintiff in the retirement system for sworn law enforcement personnel of the Department of Public Safety. The trial court granted the writ and defendants appealed to the Court of Appeals. That court reversed the trial court and dismissed the application for the writ. The Supreme Court granted review.

Plaintiff has been employed since 1956 by the Department of Public Safety or its predecessor, the Multnomah County Sheriff's Office. Her job classification until 1968 was that of Jail Matron, after which time she was reclassified as a Corrections Officer, which position she presently holds. At all times plaintiff has performed her duties under a commission and oath as a deputy sheriff.

On July 10, 1969, the Board of County Commissioners enacted Ordinance No. 25. The ordinance provided: "An Ordinance providing for a retirement system for deputy sheriffs of Multnomah County." Multnomah County ordains as follows:

A retirement system for sworn law enforcement personnel of Multnomah County is hereby established in accordance with and under the authority of Section 7.50 of Chapter VII, Multnomah County Home Rule Charter, as prescribed in the following articles:

ARTICLE I. DEFINITIONS. (1) Sworn law enforcement personnel as used in this ordinance shall mean such employees of Multnomah County assigned to the Department of Public Safety who perform their duties, under an oath administered to law enforcement personnel, and who are required to render service as such to the County.

Pursuant to Ordinance No. 25 plaintiff demanded admission to coverage under the new retirement plan and the demand was refused by defendants. Plaintiff performed all the acts which were precedent to her right to make contributions and to have contributions made on her behalf by the county if qualification requirements were met. Prior to the enactment of Ordinance No. 25, plaintiff was contributing to an existing retirement plan under Multnomah County Civil Service. Because of the refusal of admission to the new plan she has continued to do so.

Subsequent to plaintiff's application and defendants' refusal to accept her, Ordinance No. 25, after being in effect for nine months, was amended by Ordinance No. 29, which identified sworn law enforcement personnel as employees of the Department of Public Safety within the following job classifications: (a) Captain (b) Lieutenant (c) Sergeant/Detective (d) Identification Technician (e) Deputy Sheriff (Patrolman). Clearly, plaintiff was excluded from participation by the amendment.

Defendants first contend that plaintiff performed no services as a law enforcement officer and, therefore, did not qualify under Ordinance No. 25. Defendants assert that Black's Law Dictionary, 4th edition, defines a law enforcement officer as one "whose duty it is to preserve the peace." We agree with the trial judge in that we are not sure that a jail matron does not "preserve the peace." We also agree with the trial judge that, in any event, the definition in the ordinance controls eligibility under the plan. Those eligible are, ". . . employees of Multnomah County assigned to the Department of Public Safety who perform their duties, under an oath administered to law enforcement personnel, and who are required to render service as such to the county." It seems clear that plaintiff meets the definition. Eligibility was dependent upon the kind of oath that was required as a prerequisite to the performance of the employee's services. It was changed by Ordinance No. 29 to depend upon the particular type of work usually performed

This brings us to the principal question in this case; that is, whether plaintiff acquired any contractual rights under Ordinance No. 25 prior to its amendment by Ordinance No. 29. Plaintiff did not undertake employment with the county with the expectation that she would be entitled to the advantages of Ordinance No. 25

because the ordinance was not then in existence. She continued in her employment after having been refused coverage by defendants and, thus, it cannot be said that she continued her employment, at least after such refusal, upon the expectation she would receive the advantageous pension authorized by Ordinance No. 25. Therefore, the usual basis for contractual relations in such cases is lacking in the present case. In addition, defendants argue that plaintiff made no contributions under Ordinance No. 25 which would constitute consideration. The absence of contributions was one of the principal bases for the opinion of the Court of Appeals which stated: "Unlike the police officers in Adams, petitioner's application was never accepted; she paid no money into the new retirement fund and none was deducted from her regular pay."

However, we believe that plaintiff did establish a contractual right to participate in the pension plan. The adoption of the pension plan was an offer for a unilateral contract. Such an offer can be accepted by the tender of part performance. It was stipulated that plaintiff complied with all the prerequisites to coverage under the plan if she came within the definition of sworn law enforcement personnel. Therefore, we must assume that an adequate tender of part performance was made in this case, i.e., that the plaintiff tendered the required contributions from her wages and asked to participate in the plan. Such a tender furnished consideration. Section 45 of the RESTATEMENT OF THE LAW OF CONTRACTS, states as follows:

> If an offer for a unilateral contract is made, and part of the consideration requested in the offer is given or tendered by the offeree in response thereto, the offeror is bound by a contract, the duty of immediate performance of which is conditional on the full consideration being given or tendered within the time stated in the offer, or, if no time is stated therein, within a reasonable time.

Comment:

> b. Tender, however, is sufficient. Though not the equivalent of performance, nevertheless it is obviously unjust to allow so late withdrawal. There can be no actionable duty on the part of the offeror until he has received all that he demanded, or until the condition is excused by his own prevention of performance by refusing a tender; but he may become bound at an earlier day. The main offer includes as a subsidiary promise, necessarily implied, that if part of the requested performance is given, the offeror will not revoke his offer, and that if tender is made it will be accepted. Part performance or tender may thus furnish consideration for the subsidiary promises.

RESTATEMENT (SECOND) OF CONTRACTS (Tent. Draft No. 1, 1964) treats section 45 somewhat differently but with the same result. It reads as follows:

OPTION CONTRACT CREATED BY PART PERFORMANCE OR TENDER.

(1) Where an offer invites an offeree to accept by rendering a performance and does not invite a promissory acceptance, an option contract is created when the offeree begins the invited performance or tenders part of it.

(2) The offeror's duty of performance under any option contract so created is conditional on completion or tender of the invited performance in

accordance with the terms of the offer.

An option contract is defined by section [25] . . . as a promise which meets the requirements for the formation of a contract and limits the promisor's power to revoke an offer. As applied to the present circumstances, plaintiff's tender of the contributions and acceptance of the plan terminated defendants' power to revoke the offer, and plaintiff would be entitled to the benefits of the plan if she continued to work for the requisite period necessary for retirement.

After all, if plaintiff came within the classification provided by the ordinance (the trial judge, the Court of Appeals and this court all agree that she has), it does not make much sense or meet equitable considerations to allow the defendants to contend that her right to participate under the plan has not "vested" because she has not made contributions or served under the plan, when defendants have prevented plaintiff from doing so by their wrongful refusal of her contributions. . . .

The opinion of the Court of Appeals is set aside and the decision of the trial court is reinstated. Reversed.

NOTES & QUESTIONS

1. Both *Taylor v. Multnomah County Deputy Sheriff's Retirement Board* and *Brackenbury v. Hodgkin* deal with the issue of protecting an offeree from an offeror's revocation of the offer after the offeree has engaged in part performance of an act requested under an offer looking to a unilateral contract. Does the *Taylor* court's approach differ significantly from the *Brackenbury* court's approach? Which is preferable?

2. Is the option contract created under § 45 of the RESTATEMENT (SECOND) OF CONTRACTS really an option? What is the difference between an "option in fact" and an "option at law"?

3. Under § 45 of the RESTATEMENT (SECOND) OF CONTRACTS, the offeror may not revoke the offer looking to a unilateral contract for a reasonable time after the offeree commences performance. Is the offeree obligated to complete performance? *See* RESTATEMENT (SECOND) OF CONTRACTS § 45, Comments (1981).

4. If an offeree under a unilateral offer commences performance, thus creating a § 45 option contract, but fails to complete performance within a reasonable time or discontinues performance for an unreasonable time, what is the likely consequence? *See* U.C.C. § 2-206(2).

5. Is the law the same where the offer invites the offeree to accept either by promise or performance? Section 62 of the RESTATEMENT (SECOND) OF CONTRACTS (1981) provides:

> Effect of Performance by Offeree Where Offer Invites Either Performance or Promise
>
> (1) Where an offeror invites an offeree to choose between acceptance by promise and acceptance by performance, the tender or beginning of the invited performance or a tender of a beginning of it is an acceptance by performance.

(2) Such an acceptance operates as a promise to render complete performance.

How does § 62 differ from § 45 of the RESTATEMENT (SECOND) OF CONTRACTS? How are the offeror's and offeree's obligations any different?

6. Section 32 of the RESTATEMENT (SECOND) OF CONTRACTS (1981) provides:

Invitation of Promise or Performance

In case of doubt an offer is interpreted as inviting the offeree to accept either by promising to perform what the offer requests or by rendering the performance, as the offeree chooses.

If an offeror makes such an ambiguous offer and the offeree chooses to accept by performance, does the offeree's commencement of performance create an option contract at law as under § 45 or a bilateral contract as under § 62? According to the commentary to § 32 of the RESTATEMENT (SECOND) OF CONTRACTS (1981), where performance will take time, the offeree's commencement of performance may operate as a promise to complete performance. Is this rule fair to the offeree who was not responsible for the ambiguity in the offer?

7. The § 45 option contract is created when an offeree tenders or begins performance in response to an offer looking to a unilateral contract. However, mere preparation for performance does not operate to create the option at law under § 45. *But see* RESTATEMENT (SECOND) OF CONTRACTS § 87 (1981). How easy or difficult is it to distinguish between commencement of performance and preparation for performance? Consider the following case.

RAGOSTA v. WILDER
592 A.2d 367 (Vt. 1991)

PECK, Justice:

Defendant appeals from a judgment ordering him to convey to plaintiffs a piece of real property known as "The Fork Shop." . . .

In 1985, plaintiffs became interested in purchasing "The Fork Shop" from defendant, but preliminary negotiations between the parties were fruitless. In 1987, plaintiffs learned that defendant was again considering selling the "The Fork Shop," mailed him a letter offering to purchase the property along with a check for $2,000 and began arrangements to obtain the necessary financing. By letter dated September 28, 1987, defendant returned the $2,000 check explaining that he had two properties "up for sale" and that he would not sign an acceptance to plaintiffs' offer because "that would tie up both these properties until [there was] a closing." In the letter, he also made the following counter-offer:

I will sell you The Fork Shop and its property as listed in book 35, at page 135 of the Brookfield Land Records on 17 April 1972, for $88,000.00 (Eighty-eight thousand dollars), at anytime up until the 1st of November 1987 that you appear with me at the Randolph National Bank with said sum. At which time they will give you a certified deed to this property or to your agent as directed, providing said property has not been sold.

On October 1st, the date plaintiffs received the letter, they called defendant. The court found that during the conversation plaintiffs told defendant that "the terms and conditions of his offer were acceptable and that they would in fact prepare to accept the offer." Defendant assured plaintiffs that there was no one else currently interested in purchasing "The Fork Shop."

On October 6th, plaintiffs informed defendant that they would not close the sale on October 8th as discussed previously but that they would come to Vermont on October 10th. On October 8th, defendant called plaintiffs and informed them that he was no longer willing to sell "The Fork Shop." The trial court found that, at that time, defendant was aware plaintiffs "had processed their loan application and were prepared to close." Plaintiffs informed defendant that they would be at the Randolph National Bank at 10:00 a.m. on October 15th with the $88,000 purchase price and in fact appeared. Defendant did not. Plaintiffs claim they incurred $7,499.23 in loan closing costs.

Plaintiffs sued for specific performance arguing that defendant had contracted to sell the property to them. They alleged moreover that defendant knew they would have to incur costs to obtain financing for the purchase but assured them that the sale would go through and that they relied on his assurances.

The trial court concluded that defendant "made an offer in writing which could only be accepted by performance prior to the deadline." It concluded further that defendant could not revoke his offer on October 8th because plaintiffs, relying on the offer, had already begun performance and that defendant should be estopped from revoking the offer on a theory of equitable estoppel. It ordered defendant to convey to plaintiffs "The Fork Shop" for $88,000. This appeal followed. . . .

Plaintiffs claim that defendant's letter of September 28, 1987 created a contract to sell "The Fork Shop" to them unless the property was sold to another buyer. Rather, defendant's letter contains an offer to sell the property for $88,000, which the trial court found could only be accepted "by performance prior to the deadline," and a promise to keep the offer open unless the property were sold to another buyer. Defendant received no consideration for either promise. In fact, defendant returned plaintiffs' check for $2,000 which would have constituted consideration for the promise to keep the offer open, presumably because he did not wish to make a firm offer. Thus, the promise to keep the offer to sell open was not enforceable and, absent the operation of equitable estoppel, defendant could revoke the offer to sell the property at any time before plaintiffs accepted it. . . .

Plaintiffs argue that the actions they undertook to obtain financing, which were detrimental to them, could constitute consideration for the promise to keep the offer to sell open. Their argument is unconvincing. Although plaintiffs are correct in stating that a detriment may constitute consideration, they ignore the rule that "[t]o constitute consideration, a performance or a return promise must be bargained for." RESTATEMENT (SECOND) OF CONTRACTS § 71(1) (1981). "A performance or return promise is bargained for if it is sought by the promisor in exchange for his promise and is given by the promisee in exchange for that promise." *Id.* at § 71(2). Plaintiffs began to seek financing even before defendant made a definite offer to sell the property. Whatever detriment they suffered was not in exchange for defendant's promise to keep the offer to sell open.

The trial court ruled that the offer to sell "The Fork Shop" could only be accepted by performance but concluded that in obtaining financing plaintiffs began performance and that therefore defendant could not revoke the offer to sell once plaintiffs incurred the cost of obtaining financing. Section 45 of the RESTATEMENT

(SECOND) OF CONTRACTS provides that "[w]here an offer invites an offeree to accept by rendering a performance and does not invite a promissory acceptance, an option contract is created when the offeree tenders or begins the invited performance or tenders a beginning of it." However, "[w]hat is begun or tendered must be part of the actual performance invited in order to preclude revocation under this Section." *Id.* at comment f.

Here, plaintiffs were merely engaged in preparation for performance. The court itself found only that "plaintiffs had changed their position in order to tender performance." At most, they obtained financing and assured defendant that they would pay; plaintiffs never tendered to defendant or even began to tender the $88,000 purchase price. Thus, they never accepted defendant's offer and no contract was ever created. *See Multicare Medical Center v. State Social & Health Services*, 114 Wash. 2d 572, 584, 790 P.2d 124, 131 (1990) ("under a unilateral contract, an offer cannot be accepted by promising to perform; rather, the offeree must accept, if at all, by performance, and the contract then becomes executed"). . . .

On remand the court shall consider the case under promissory estoppel only and determine what remedy, if any, is necessary to prevent injustice. In making this determination the court should consider the fact that plaintiffs incurred the expense of obtaining financing although they could not be certain that the property would be sold to them. . . .

Reversed and the cause remanded for further proceedings consistent with the principles expressed herein.

NOTES & QUESTIONS

1. In *Ragosta v. Wilder*, what was the act the defendant offeror sought from the plaintiff offeree? Was the court unduly formalistic in its interpretation of the parties' intentions? Was the court's interpretation of their intentions consistent with the purposes and policies of contract law we have previously considered?

2. Assuming the court's holding was correct, was there anything the plaintiff offeree could have done in order to commence performance and acquire the protection of the § 45 option contract at law?

3. Is there any way to interpret the defendant's counteroffer and subsequent communications with the plaintiff as inviting acceptance by either promise or performance? If yes, would the result in the case be different?

4. *Drafting Exercise*: Had you represented the plaintiff in *Ragosta v. Wilder*, how would you have responded to the defendant's counteroffer of September 28, 1987? Is there a way to protect the plaintiff from the vulnerable position in which it found itself? Draft a letter for plaintiff responding to the defendant's counteroffer.

5. Although the court in *Ragosta v. Wilder* concluded there was no traditional contract between the parties, it remanded the case for further consideration under the alternative theory of promissory estoppel. We shall take up reliance theory and promissory estoppel in Chapter 7.

CHAPTER 4

BARGAINED-FOR CONSIDERATION

A. CONSIDERATION DEFINED

In addition to requiring mutual assent, common law courts have traditionally required that the parties' promises be supported by "consideration" before finding a contract between them. Although it is difficult to discern the origin of the consideration element, the requirement may have evolved as a method of distinguishing binding agreements from non-binding transactions, such as gifts. If consideration's presence is evidence of the parties' intention to keep their bargain, then the requirement appears to duplicate contractual intent. Moreover, the vagaries of the definition of consideration and a judicial tendency to resort to a formalistic, uncritical application of the doctrine have led to conflicting court decisions, some of which are palpably unjust. These concerns have led some scholars to observe that the doctrine of consideration is redundant at best, confusing at worst. Professor Arthur Corbin suggested that the consideration requirement be abandoned as a means of distinguishing between enforceable and unenforceable promises in favor of other ways of providing evidence that the parties intended to be bound. CORBIN ON CONTRACTS § 111 (1 vol. ed. 1952).

Although the courts stubbornly cling to the consideration requirement for traditional contracts, scholarly criticism has led to the development of alternative theories for relief and restitution where strict application of the requirement could yield unjust results. While retaining consideration as a fundamental element of the contract, modern courts have moved away from a strict, formalistic application of its requirements in an effort to facilitate rather than inhibit the parties' transactions. The doctrine itself has been modified to permit courts to find consideration based on implications and circumstances surrounding the parties' transactions. And in those cases where the element of consideration is missing, the courts have developed alternative bases for enforcing promises and avoiding unjust enrichment, such as promissory estoppel and quasi-contract.

Whether it serves as further evidence of the parties' intent to be bound or as a discrete and separate prerequisite for a contract, consideration is not easily defined due to the many qualifications the courts have attached to it. Nevertheless, the courts still require consideration before enforcing promises based on traditional contract theory, and therefore, we must adopt a working definition. At its most fundamental level, consideration may be broken into two elements: 1) something of legally recognized value; 2) which the parties have intentionally exchanged through their bargain. A Pennsylvania court has provided this basic definition: "[V]alid consideration confers a benefit upon the promisor or causes a detriment to the promisee and must be an act, forbearance or return promise bargained for and given in exchange for the original promise." *Cardamone v. University of Pittsburgh*, 253 Pa. Super. 65, 72 n.6, 384 A.2d 1228, 1232 n.6 (1978). *See* RESTATEMENT (SECOND) OF CONTRACTS § 71 (1981). Judicial determination of whether something of legal value has been exchanged has often invited an abstract inquiry, sometimes yielding puzzling and inequitable results.

At traditional common law, the courts did not require consideration for promises made under "seal." Historically, parties making promises melted wax on their documents which contained their commitments, applied some personal or family insignia to the wax by ring or other jewelry impression, and delivered the sealed document to the other party. The practice of applying the seal and delivering the document under seal was akin to swearing an oath on the Bible, and has now been largely abandoned in favor of less formalistic evidence of the parties' intentions. Although the seal's significance is substantially diminished, many legal forms, such as deeds and mortgages, still contain the language "Seal" or the abbreviation "L.S." (Locus Sigilli) next to the space for the parties' signatures.

It has been said that the seal "imports a consideration" (*see, e.g., Thompson v. Bescher,* 176 N.C. 622, 97 S.E. 654 (1918)), but this is not quite correct. Professor Fried notes that "the effect of a seal may range from a complete substitute for consideration to a substantive though rebuttable presumption of consideration, to an allocation of pleading requirements and burdens of proof on the issue, to mere allocation of the issue to judge or jury." Fried, CONTRACT AS PROMISE: A THEORY OF CONTRACTUAL OBLIGATIONS 139-140 (1981). Whatever its meaning, most states have abolished the common law effect of the seal. § 2-203 of the Uniform Commercial Code has likewise abolished the seal's effect with respect to sales of goods. Today, the seal is hardly more than a quaint reminder of an earlier time when transactions were frequently accompanied by solemn, formal ceremonies derived from traditional folkways no longer relevant to modern dealings.

Thomas v. Thomas, 2 Q.B. 851, 114 Eng. Rep. 330 (1842). Shortly before he died, John Thomas declared in front of witnesses that he wanted his wife, Eleanor, to have his house during her life so long as she remained his widow. John died without reducing his wishes to writing, but his two executors were aware of his wishes. The co-executors agreed that the house would be conveyed to Eleanor for her life or as long she remained unmarried. In return, Eleanor was to pay one pound's rent yearly and committed to keep the house in good and tenable repair. After one of the co-executors died, the remaining executor refused to convey the property to Eleanor and had her ejected from the premises. Eleanor sued to enforce the agreement and prevailed. The appellate court judges agreed that Eleanor provided consideration for the co-executors' promise to convey the life estate "quite independent of the moral feeling which disposed the executors to enter into such a contract." One judge explained,

> Motive is not the same thing with consideration. Consideration means something which is of some value in the eye of the law, moving from the plaintiff [Eleanor]: it may be some detriment to the plaintiff, or some benefit to the defendant [the executor]; but at all events it must be moving from the plaintiff. Now that which is suggested as consideration here — a pious respect for the wishes of the testator — does not in any way move from the plaintiff; it moves from the testator; therefore, legally speaking, it forms no part of the consideration.

However, the appellate court concluded that Eleanor provided legally sufficient consideration in the form of the promise to pay rent and the promise to keep the house repaired.

Hamer v. Sidway, 124 N.Y. 538, 27 N.E. 256 (1891). Uncle William Story, Sr. promised his 15-year-old nephew William Story II that if the nephew would refrain from drinking, using tobacco, swearing, and playing cards or billiards for money until he became 21 years old, the uncle would pay him $5000. When he turned 21, the nephew wrote his uncle to tell him he had performed and was therefore entitled to the $5000. The uncle wrote back acknowledging the nephew's performance and stating the money was being held in a bank and drawing interest. The nephew consented to this arrangement, but the uncle died without the nephew collecting. The nephew assigned his interest to others who made a claim for the money from the uncle's executor who rejected the claim. In a suit by the assignee for the $5000 and interest, the executor maintained that the nephew provided no consideration in return for the uncle's promise to pay because the nephew was not harmed but actually benefited from his abstinence. The court disagreed and held the agreement enforceable. Quoting from the exchequer chamber, the court stated, "A valuable consideration, in the sense of the law, may consist either in some right, interest, profit, or benefit accruing to the one party, or some forbearance, detriment, loss, or responsibility given, suffered, or undertaken by the other: The court continued, " 'Consideration' means not so much that one party is profiting as that the other abandons some legal right in the present, or limits his legal freedom of action in the future, as an inducement for the promise of the first." Here, the court reasoned that the nephew abandoned what he had the legal right to do, restricting his lawful freedom of action, in return for his uncle's promise to pay him if he performed according to their agreement. The court therefore held that "the abandonment of the use was a sufficient consideration to uphold the promise."

Kirskey v. Kirskey, 8 Ala. 131 (1845). After his brother's death, the defendant wrote his brother's widow, the plaintiff, who lived with her children sixty or seventy miles away on land she owned. The defendant advised the plaintiff to sell her land and stated, "If you will come down and see me, I will let you have a place to raise your family. . . ." A month or two after receiving defendant's letter, plaintiff abandoned her land without selling it and moved her family to the defendant's residence where defendant gave her comfortable houses and land to cultivate. However, after two years, defendant required plaintiff to leave. Plaintiff sued for breach of contract and was awarded $200 by a trial court. The Alabama Supreme Court reversed. Although one judge believed that the loss plaintiff sustained in breaking up and moving her home some sixty miles was sufficient consideration, the court majority concluded that the defendant's promise was a mere gratuity for which no cause of action for breach was available.

Newman & Snell's State Bank v. Hunter, 243 Mich. 331, 220 N.W. 665 (1928). The defendant's husband died without funds to pay off his debts, including a note for $3,700 held by the plaintiff bank. The defendant widow paid interest on her husband's unenforceable note and gave her personal note to the bank in return for the bank's surrendering her husband's note to her. The bank sued to collect on the widow's note, and the widow defended on the ground that the bank gave no consideration in return for her promise to pay her husband's debt. Holding for the widow, the court reasoned:

> Here we have the widow's note given to take up the note of her insolvent husband, a worthless piece of paper. When plaintiff surrendered this worthless piece of paper to the defendant, it parted with nothing of value, and defendant received nothing of value, the plaintiff suffered no loss or inconvenience, and defendant received no benefit.

NOTES & QUESTIONS

1. In *Hamer v. Sidway*, the court concluded that the nephew, the promisee, provided consideration in return for the uncle's promise by refraining from acts he had a legal right to do. Had the nephew promised to refrain from acts which would have been illegal for a minor to engage in, would the nephew have provided consideration for the uncle's promise to pay?

2. In its opinion, the court raised but did not address the issue of whether the uncle received a benefit from the nephew's performance. Did the uncle receive any benefit which the courts would legally recognize? Given the court's conclusion that the nephew suffered a detriment, does it matter whether the uncle received a benefit?

3. What element of the definition of consideration is missing in *Kirskey v. Kirskey?* Do you agree with the court's analysis of the facts and its characterization of the transaction as a gratuity? Does the *Kirskey* court's decision yield a harsh result?

4. In *Newman & Snell's State Bank v. Hunter*, the court held that the deceased husband's note was of no legal value. If courts should not ordinarily inquire into the adequacy of consideration, why should the market value of the note matter? The widow apparently wanted the note to protect her late husband's good name, and the bank was under no obligation to give up the note. Did the court thwart the parties' intentions by disregarding their bargained-for exchange?

Hamilton Bancshares, Inc. v. Leroy, 131 Ill. App. 3d 907, 476 N.E.2d 788 (1985). On June 11, 1981, the plaintiff purchased 80-day options from the defendant bank, under which the plaintiff had the right to buy bank stock for "$5000 earnest money, to be applied to the purchase price of the shares . . . in the event this option is exercised and to be refunded . . . in the event that this option is not exercised." After the defendant bank attempted to withdraw the options on July 17, 1981, plaintiff nonetheless sought to exercise the options on August 12, 1981. The trial court granted summary judgment for the defendant on the ground that the plaintiff provided no consideration for the options. The appellate court reversed and remanded. The appellate court reasoned that, ordinarily, a small consideration is sufficient to support the promise of an optionor, but that consideration must be actually given or promised rather than merely named. Quoting from 1 Williston, CONTRACTS § 102A at 380-82 (3d ed. 1957), the court explained:

> Both benefit and detriment have a technical meaning. Neither the benefit to the promisor nor the detriment to the promisee need be actual. "It would be a detriment to the promisee, in a legal sense, if he, at the request of the promisor and upon the strength of that promise, had

performed any act which occasioned him the slightest trouble or inconvenience, and which he was not obliged to perform." Thus abstaining from smoking and drinking, though in fact in the particular case a benefit to the promisee's health, finances, and morals and of no benefit to the promisor, is a legal detriment and if requested as such is sufficient consideration for a promise. So obtaining signatures to a petition is a sufficient consideration though the petition is so defective as to be useless and the signatures are, therefore, of no benefit to the promisor. Detriment, therefore, as used in testing the sufficiency of consideration means legal detriment as distinguished from detriment in fact. It means giving up something which immediately prior thereto the promise was privileged to retain, or doing or refraining from doing something which he was then privileged not to do, or not to refrain from doing. Benefit correspondingly must mean the receiving as the exchange for his promise of some performance or forbearance which the promisor was not previously entitled to receive. That the promisor desired it for his own advantage and had no previous right to it is enough to show that it was beneficial.

The court concluded that "[c]ommon sense dictates that plaintiff's parting with $5,000 earnest money under each option contract for more than 30 days constituted a legal detriment to plaintiff."

BROWNING v. JOHNSON
70 Wash. 2d 145, 422 P.2d 314 (1967)

LANGENBACH, Judge:

This is the tale of two osteopaths who attempted a business transaction. The heart of the case is a certain promise which Dr. Browning made to Dr. Johnson. The sole issue is whether Dr. Browning is to be bound by his promise.

Browning and Johnson entered into a contract of sale whereby Browning was to sell his practice and equipment to Johnson. Both parties and their attorneys believed the contract made to be completely valid and enforceable. Before the contract's effective date, Browning changed his mind about selling and sought to be released from the obligations he had undertaken. Johnson, at first, demurred. Later, however, upon Browning's promise to pay Johnson $40,000 if Johnson would give up the contract of sale, the parties entered into a contract (the contract here in issue) canceling the contract of sale.

Some months later Browning tired of his bargain and brought this action for declaratory judgment and restitution. In the course of this action the trial court concluded that the canceled sale contract had lacked mutuality and had been too indefinite in its terms for enforcement. Nevertheless, it concluded that the contract canceling the sale contract was supported by "adequate consideration." Browning has appealed from that decision. . . .

We should first say a word about terminology. Courts are loath to inquire into the "adequacy" of consideration, that is, into the comparative value of the promises and acts exchanged. As we said in *Rogich v. Dressel*, 45 Wash. 2d 829, 843, 278 P.2d 367 (1954):

[W]e must apply the rule followed in this state that parties who are competent to contract will not be relieved from a bad bargain they make

unless the consideration is so inadequate as to be constructively fraudulent. . . . But "adequacy" of consideration, into which courts seldom
inquire, is to be distinguished from the legal "sufficiency" of any particular
consideration. The latter phrase is concerned not with comparative value
but with that which will support a promise. "[A]nything which fulfills the
requirements of consideration will support a promise whatever may be the
comparative value of the consideration, and of the thing promised." 1
Williston, CONTRACTS § 115, cited in *Puget Mill Co. v. Kerry*, 183 Wash. 542,
558, 49 P.2d 57, 64, 100 A.L.R. 1220 (1935). "[T]he relative values of a
promise and the consideration for it, do not affect the sufficiency of
consideration." RESTATEMENT, CONTRACTS § 81 (1932).

This distinction is sometimes lost sight of. In the instant case, Browning
bargained for Johnson's act of giving up the contract of sale. The issue is whether
the law regards Johnson's act of giving up that contract as legally "sufficient"
consideration to support Browning's promise to pay him for such an act. The trial
court concluded that giving up the contract of sale was "adequate" consideration for
Browning's promise. . . .

We hold that Browning's promise was supported by sufficient consideration[,]
and there is nothing in this case which induces us, under the Rogich formulation, to
consider the relative values of the things exchanged.

This is a unilateral contract. . . . A unilateral contract is one in which a promise
is given in exchange for an act or forbearance. Here, Browning gave Johnson a
promise to pay $40,000 in exchange for Johnson's act of giving up the contract of
sale. Sufficiency of consideration in unilateral contracts is discussed by Professor
Williston in his treatise, CONTRACTS § 102 (3d ed. 1957). There he indicates that the
requirement of sufficient consideration to support a promise is met by a detriment
incurred by the promisee (Johnson) or a benefit received by the promisor
(Browning) at the request of the promisor. "That a detriment suffered by the
promisee at the promisor's request and as the price for the promise is sufficient,
though the promisor is not benefited, is well settled." Williston, *supra*. This has
been the law in Washington for over 50 years. *Harris v. Johnson*, 75 Wash. 291, 294,
134 P. 1048 (1913). The question then becomes the nature of a detriment. Detriment
is defined by Williston as the giving up of "something which immediately prior
thereto the promisee was privileged to retain, or doing or refraining from doing
something which he was then privileged not to do, or not to refrain from doing."
Williston, *supra*, § 102A. . . . We have employed the definition for many years, *see*,
e.g., Harris v. Johnson, supra, where we said: "Indeed there is a consideration if
the promisee, in return for the promise, does anything legal which he is not bound
to do, or refrains from doing anything which he has a right to do, whether there is
any actual loss or detriment to him or actual benefit to the promisor or not.". . .

The problem presented by this case is not a new one. Over a century ago, in
England, Brooks obtained a certain document from Haigh believing that it was a
guarantee, and promised to pay a certain sum of money in consideration of Haigh's
giving it up. The guarantee proved to be unenforceable. Haigh sued Brooks for the
money promised. The court said:

> [T]he plaintiffs were induced by the defendant's promise to part with
> something which they might have kept, and the defendant obtained what he
> desired by means of that promise. Both being free and able to judge for

themselves, how can the defendant be justified in breaking this promise, by discovering afterwards that the thing in consideration of which he gave it did not possess that value which he supposed to belong to it? It cannot be ascertained that that value was what he most regarded. He may have had other objects and motives; and of their weight he was the only judge. *Haigh v. Brooks*, 10 A. & E. 309, 320 (1839).

Similarly here, of Browning's objects and motives, he was the only judge. . . .

In 1935 the case of *Puget Mill Co. v. Kerry, supra*, came before this court. The following discussion (appearing in 183 Wash. 556, 559, 49 P.2d 63, 64), while not entirely necessary there is persuasive here. So much so that we feel justified in quoting at some length. [*sic*]

> It clearly appears that appellants, represented as they were by able counsel, procured respondent's consent to their purchase of the lease. . . . Appellants state that at the time of their purchase of the lease all parties believed that respondent still had the right to object to an assignment thereof, and that its consent was necessary to a valid assignment. . . . [A]ppellants [argue] that the giving of an unnecessary consent by respondent cannot be held sufficient consideration for appellants' promise. In the first place, this assumes that the consent which respondent accorded was unnecessary. . . . In determining the question, the position of the parties in 1923 must be considered, not the situation as it exists now. Appellants then, of course, believed that they were making a good bargain, and anything which tended to make their position more secure would appear to them to be to their advantage. Then, it is well settled that a consideration sufficient to support a promise need not always, in the last analysis, have an actual value. In this instance, it may be assumed that whether or not respondent had the right to refuse its consent to an assignment of the lease could only ultimately be determined by the courts. The giving of its consent by respondent would constitute a valuable consideration for a promise, even though a possibility existed that at the end of protracted litigation, it might be held that respondent had lost its right to accept or reject a new tenant. Of course, a consideration cannot be sham or frivolous or manifestly false; but in the case at bar, we are satisfied that a real controversy might have been waged before the courts as to the rights of respondent as they existed in 1923.

The matter is discussed in 1 Williston on Contracts, §§ 102, 102A and 115. The Supreme Court of the United States case of *Sykes v. Chadwick*, 21 L. Ed. 824, 18 Wall. 141, 149, is in point. In the case cited, the court used the following language:

> At all events, the defendant when he was endeavoring to negotiate the sale of his property deemed it of sufficient importance to give the note in question in consideration of the plaintiff joining in the deed, and releasing any contingent right she might have. This very act of hers may have been necessary, and we have a right to infer that it was deemed important, to the closing up of the transaction and securing the sale of the property. If any release is deemed requisite to confirm the title of lands with which one has been connected, though by a proper construction of the law he has no interest in them whatever, still such release will be a good consideration for a promise or for the payment of money.

That the parties cited none of the above cases in their briefs makes these cases no less appropriate. It is clear that at the time of contracting, the parties, equally informed, of equal bargaining power and equally assisted by able counsel, freely bargained for, and freely settled upon an exchange which each felt would be beneficial to him. Their mutual assent proved this mutual expectation of benefit for the law must presume that no man bargains against his own interest. Subsequent events revealed that the contract, fully acceptable to both parties when made, was less beneficial to the promisor than he and his attorney had, at the time of contracting, thought. But this alone can not be reason enough for allowing the promisor to avoid it. There was no misrepresentation, no fraud, and no duress. The promisor Browning wanted Johnson to give up the sale contract and to secure the performance of that act, he solemnly promised to pay Johnson $40,000. Johnson, induced by Browning's urgent pleas and solemn promise, gave up the sale contract. The legal detriment suffered by Johnson through Browning's inducement will support Browning's promise to pay. . . .

The judgment is affirmed.

NOTES & QUESTIONS

1. What is the difference between "sufficiency" of consideration and "adequacy" of consideration? Why do courts ordinarily decline to evaluate the "adequacy" of the parties' consideration? Is this disinclination to consider adequacy consistent with the purposes and policies of contract law we identified in Chapter One?

2. Is a promise to exchange unequal sums of money supported by consideration? What about an exchange of corporate stock in two different companies where the stock is presently of equal value? *See Emberson v. Hartley*, 762 P.2d 364 (Wash. App. 1988).

3. Courts are particularly reluctant to consider the adequacy of consideration when the plaintiff seeks ordinary, legal remedies for the breach of a contract, such as compensation for damages based on the plaintiff's reasonable expectations under the lost bargain. However, courts may inquire into the adequacy of consideration when the plaintiff seeks an equitable remedy, such as an injunction or specific performance. And courts may regard shockingly disparate terms or grossly inadequate consideration as probative of other defenses to contract enforcement, such as duress, incapacity, fraud or unconscionability. *See Ryan v. Weiner*, 610 A.2d 1377 (Del. Chanc. Ct. 1992).

McKinnon v. Benedict, 38 Wis. 2d 607, 157 N.W.2d 665 (1968). Defendants, the Benedicts, sought to purchase an eighty-acre resort from the Dorseys. The Dorseys' resort was surrounded by another larger tract owned by the plaintiffs, the McKinnons. When the Benedicts had difficulties obtaining a downpayment to buy the resort from the Dorseys, the Dorseys' agent directed them to the McKinnons, who loaned the Benedicts $5,000 with the understanding that the Benedicts would continue to operate the tract as a resort. The Benedicts also promised that for a period of 25 years no trees would be cut between the McKinnons' land and the resort or between the resort and a nearby highway, and no construction would be placed any closer to the McKinnons' property than the buildings then in existence. The McKinnons promised to help generate business for the resort and to otherwise assist the Benedicts in organizing the resort's operation. However, the McKinnons made no effort to help the Benedicts organize the operation, and the Benedicts decided to add a trailer park after encountering financial difficulties. The court denied the McKinnons' request for an injunction preventing the Benedicts' use of the land as a trailer park. The court held that the extraordinary equitable relief sought by the McKinnons was not available because the detriment to the McKinnons was minimal and inadequacy of consideration was so gross as to be unconscionable. The court explained:

> No action at law has been commenced for damages by virtue of the breach of the restrictions; and, in fact, the plaintiffs in their complaint claim that they have no adequate remedy at law. We are thus not confronted with the question of damages that may result from the breach of this contract and confine ourselves solely to the right of the plaintiffs to invoke the equitable remedy of specific performance, in this case the enjoining of the defendants from the breach of the contract. 28 AM. JUR., *Injunctions* § 35, pp. 528, 529, points out that: "Courts of equity exercise discretionary power in the granting or withholding of their extraordinary remedies, and this is particularly true in a case where injunctive relief is sought. . . . The relief is not given as a matter of course for any and every act done or threatened to the person or property of another; its granting rests in the sound discretion of the court to be exercised in accordance with well-settled equitable principles and in the light of all the facts and circumstances in the case. . . ." The court in *Mulligan v. Albertz* (1899), 103 Wis. 140, 143, 144, 78 N.W. 1093, 1094, summarized policies of the Wisconsin court in this regard, and we consider these principles applicable to this case: "An action for the specific performance of a contract is an application to the sound discretion of the court. It does not come as a matter of course. The jurisdiction to compel it is not compulsory. A court of equity must be satisfied that the claim for a deed is fair and just and reasonable, and the contract equal in all its parts, and founded on an adequate consideration, before it will interpose with this extraordinary assistance. . . ."

> Considering all the factors — the inadequacy of the consideration, the small benefit that would be accorded the McKinnons, and the oppressive conditions imposed upon the Benedicts — we conclude that this contract failed to meet the test of reasonableness that is the sine qua non of the enforcement of rights in an action in equity. 5A Corbin, CONTRACTS, § 1164, p. 219, points out that, although a contract is harsh, oppressive, and unconscionable, it may nevertheless be enforceable at law; but, in the discretion of the court, equitable remedies will not be enforced against one who suffers from such harshness and oppression.

PROBLEM

Under state law, a spouse has the right to dispose of marital property during the marriage without the other spouse's concurrence. Husband and wife James and Jeannette DeLaney owned a valuable Rubens painting. In 1970, James purportedly sold the painting to his friend O'Neill "for $10 and other valuable consideration, including the love and affection we have for each other." James did not tell Jeannette of the sale to O'Neill, and the painting remained at the couple's home for the next four years. During that period, O'Neill did not insure the painting. In the divorce proceedings, Jeannette claimed an interest in the painting, prompting O'Neill to file an action for a declaratory judgment that he owned the painting. Who owns the painting? *See O'Neill v. Delaney*, 92 Ill. App. 3d 292, 415 N.E.2d 1260 (1980).

B.   PAST CONSIDERATION AND MORAL OBLIGATION

Courts have difficulties identifying consideration when a party provides a valuable service or goods before the recipient of the services or goods promises to pay for them. Strictly speaking, such transactions are missing the element of the "bargained-for exchange," and the conferral of the benefit is considered a mere gratuity which cannot serve as consideration to support a subsequent promise to pay for that benefit. Put another way, what could have served as consideration had it been bargained for may no longer serve as consideration after it has been conferred. Past consideration is no consideration, and any moral obligation the recipient of the gratuity has to the donor will not support the recipient's promise to compensate the donor. The results of this strict application of the consideration doctrine have sometimes been so harsh that courts have strained to characterize gratuitous acts as bargained-for exchanges, inventing fictions to avoid unjust results. And in the absence of a traditional contract remedy, courts have recognized other grounds for relief, promissory estoppel and quasi-contract. We shall take up these alternative theories for recovery in Chapter Six, Avoidance of Unjust Enrichment, and Chapter Seven, Reliance and Promissory Estoppel.

Mills v. Wyman, 3 Pick. 207 (Mass. 1825). Defendant's adult son returned from a sea voyage and became ill. After the plaintiffs nursed the son back to health at considerable expense, defendant wrote the plaintiffs that he would pay them for the cost of that care, but he did not pay. The court dismissed plaintiffs' suit against defendant for the cost of the care on the ground that plaintiffs provided no consideration in return for the defendant's promise to pay. The court held that any moral obligation incurred by the defendant could not serve as consideration. "[T]here must have been some pre-existing obligation . . . to form a basis for an effective promise."

Harrington v. Taylor, 225 N.C. 690, 36 S.E.2d 227 (1945). Defendant-husband entered the plaintiff's house and began to assault his wife who had fled there from him. Defendant's wife knocked defendant down and was about to hit him with an axe when the plaintiff saved the defendant's life by taking the blow with her hand, which was badly mutilated. After the incident, defendant orally promised to pay plaintiff for her damages, but after paying a small amount, he paid no more. Plaintiff sued for breach of contract, but the court held there was no cause of action, stating, "however much the defendant should be impelled by common gratitude to alleviate the plaintiff's misfortune, a humanitarian act of this kind, voluntarily performed, is not such consideration as would entitle her to recover at law."

Webb v. McGowin, 27 Ala. App. 82, 168 So. 196 (1935). Plaintiff was employed at McGowin's lumber mill. As he prepared to drop a 75–pound wooden block from an upper level of the mill, plaintiff saw McGowin walking below directly under the block's course. To prevent McGowin from being hit by the block, plaintiff held onto the block and fell with it, diverting it away from McGowin. Although McGowin was not injured, plaintiff suffered severe injuries and was crippled for life. Nearly a month later, McGowin, in consideration of plaintiff's preventing his injury, promised to care for and maintain plaintiff for the rest of his life at a rate of $15 every two weeks. McGowin paid that sum until his death some eight years later after which his estate stopped the payments. The court enforced McGowin's promise. The court observed that McGowin received a valuable benefit from the plaintiff's services, for which he became morally bound to compensate the plaintiff. The court further noted that McGowin recognized his moral obligation to plaintiff, expressly agreed to pay him and did so for over eight years. "In such cases the subsequent promise to pay is an affirmance or ratification of the services rendered carrying with it the presumption that a previous request for the service was made. . . ." The court then concluded that McGowin's express promise to pay the plaintiff was an affirmance or ratification of what plaintiff had done, raising a presumption that the services had been rendered at McGowin's request.

Feinberg v. Pfeiffer Co., 322 S.W.2d 163 (Mo. App. 1959). Mrs. Feinberg had worked for the defendant pharmaceutical company for 37 years when in 1947 the company's directors adopted a resolution acknowledging her long and faithful service and stating that "provision should be made to afford her retirement privileges and benefits which should become a firm obligation of the corporation to be available to her whenever she should see fit to retire . . . upon a retirement pay of $200 per month for life. . . ." When she retired a year and one half later, the corporation began the $200 monthly payments, but after seven years, the corporation decided the amounts sent her were gratuities and sent her a check for $100. Mrs. Feinberg refused to accept the smaller checks and sued for breach of contract. The court concluded that Mrs. Feinberg had provided no consideration for the corporation's promise to pay her $200 per month in retirement benefits. Her past services could not serve as consideration for the corporation's promise, and since she was not required to continue working under the resolution, she made no commitment in return for the corporation's promise. However, the court concluded she was entitled to recover under a promissory estoppel theory because she retired from a lucrative position in reliance upon the corporation's promise to pay her the pension.

NOTES & QUESTIONS

1. Is the *Webb* court's presumption, that a subsequent promise is ratification of a previous request for the services, realistic? Do the facts in the case support the presumption?

2. Is there a principled distinction between the *Webb* decision and the other note cases? *See* RESTATEMENT (SECOND) OF CONTRACTS § 86 (1981).

DEMENTAS v. ESTATE OF TALLAS
764 P.2d 628 (Utah 1988)

ORME, Judge:

Plaintiff Peter Dementas appeals from a judgment dismissing his claim against the Estate of Jack Tallas. Dementas seeks reversal of the trial court's decision and the entry of judgment in his favor. . . . Jack Tallas came to the United States, as an immigrant from Greece, in 1914. He lived in Salt Lake City for nearly seventy years, residing at Little America Hotel during the last years of his life. Tallas achieved considerable success in business, primarily as an insurance agent and landlord. Over a period of fourteen years, Peter Dementas, who was a close personal friend of Tallas, rendered at least some assistance to Tallas.

On December 18, 1982, Tallas met with Dementas and dictated a memorandum to him, in Greek, stating that he owed Dementas $50,000 for his help over the years for such things as picking up his mail, driving him to the grocery store, and assisting with the management of Tallas's rental properties. Tallas also indicated in the memorandum that he would change his will to make Dementas an "heir for the sum of $50,000."

Tallas kept the Greek document, retyped it in English, notarized the English version with his own notary seal, and, three days later, delivered the documents to Dementas. Tallas died on February 4, 1983, without changing his will to include Dementas as an "heir." He left a substantial estate. Dementas filed a timely claim for $50,000 with Tallas's estate, pursuant to UTAH CODE ANN. § 75-3-803 (1978). A copy of the memorandum given to him by Tallas was attached to the claim. The estate denied the claim and Dementas brought this action to recover $50,000.

In its pretrial order, the trial court disposed of the issues of quantum meruit; a contract to make, change or modify a will; and gift causa mortis. The court found, as a matter of law, that the memorandum was at best "an acknowledgment of a previously existing debt resulting from the performance of a previously existing oral contract," and the case proceeded to trial. Following trial, in which the court heard extensive testimony from witnesses and received numerous exhibits, the court concluded that the memorandum was executed by Tallas free from fraud, duress, or undue influence. However, the court did not find the memorandum to constitute an enforceable contract. Rather, the court found that the memorandum was an expression of Tallas's appreciation for services gratuitously performed by Dementas. The court concluded that the memorandum, both in its Greek and English versions, showed that Tallas intended — at some time in the future — to include Dementas in his will or to otherwise compensate him, but that Tallas failed to complete the transaction prior to his death. . . . The court also ruled that Dementas's "account stated" theory was barred since no such claim was articulated in the notice of claim filed with the estate. Alternatively, the court concluded no "account stated" had been proven. . . .

The English version of the memorandum, as translated and revised by Tallas, reads exactly as follows:

> PETER K. DEMENTAS, is my best friend I have in this country and since he came to the United States he treats me like a father and I think of him as my own son. I visit his house and have dinner with his family twice a week. He takes me in his car grocery shopping. He drives me to the doctor and has also takes me every week to Bingham to pick up my mail, collect the rents and manage my properties. For all the services Peter has given me all these years, for the use of his automobile, for the money he spent on gasoline and his time, I owe to him the amount of $50,000 (Fifty

Thousand Dollars.) I have already mentioned Peter in my will for all the services and love he has offered me during all these years and I will shortly change my will to include him as my heir.

Salt Lake City Utah
December 18, 1982
Jack G. Tallas

"A generally accepted definition of consideration is that a legal detriment has been bargained for and exchanged for a promise." *Miller v. Miller*, 664 P.2d 39, 40-41 (Wyo.1983). "The mere fact that one man promises something to another creates no legal duty and makes no legal remedy available in case of non-performance." 1A Corbin, CORBIN ON CONTRACTS § 110 (1963). "[A] performance or a returned promise must be bargained for." *Miller v. Miller*, 664 P.2d at 41 (*citing* RESTATEMENT (SECOND) OF CONTRACTS § 71 at 172 (1981)).

In determining whether consideration to support a personal service contract exists, the focus is not whether the amount promised represents the fair market value for the services rendered. On the contrary, "[a]s a general rule it is settled that any detriment no matter how economically inadequate will support a promise." J. Calamari & J. Perillo, CONTRACTS § 55 at 107 (1970). *See Gasser v. Horne*, 557 P.2d 154, 155 (Utah 1976) ("It has further been held that there is consideration whenever a promisor receives a benefit or where promisee suffers a detriment, however slight."). Thus, while the estate introduced extensive testimony as to whether the services Dementas claimed to have rendered were actually performed, the court expressly admitted this testimony only insofar as it bore on Dementas's credibility and not to prove that the services were worth less than the amount Tallas promised to pay. While the testimony suggested that Dementas did not actually perform all the services he claimed to have rendered, this testimony had no relevance to the question of whether there was consideration for Tallas's promise since the testimony suggested Dementas did at least some work. In this regard, the court correctly stated: "If Tallas thought it was worth 50,000 bucks to get one ride to Bingham, that's Tallas' decision. . . . The only thing you can't do is take it with you.". . .

Even though the testimony showed that Dementas rendered at least some services for Tallas, the subsequent promise by Tallas to pay $50,000 for services already performed by Dementas is not a promise supported by legal consideration. Events which occur prior to the making of the promise and not with the purpose of inducing the promise in exchange are viewed as "past consideration" and are the legal equivalent of "no consideration." 1A Corbin, CORBIN ON CONTRACTS § 210 (1963). This is so because "[t]he promisor is making his promise because those events occurred, but he is not making his promise in order to get them. There is no 'bargaining'; no saying that if you will do this for me I will do that for you." . . . *See also County of Clark v. Bonanza No. 1*, 96 Nev. 643, 615 P.2d 939, 943 (1980) ("A benefit conferred or detriment incurred in the past is not adequate consideration for a present bargain."). This rule can surely work unfair results and has accordingly been criticized[1] and the object of legislation. . . . Some courts have sought to enforce promises supported only by past consideration by invoking a "moral obligation" notion to make at least some of these promises enforceable. *See*

---

[1] [7] "One may question the adequacy of a legal system which refuses to enforce a promise such as this: 'In consideration of your forty years of faithful service, you will be paid a pension of $200.00 per month.' " J. Calamari & J. Perillo, CONTRACTS § 54 at 106 (1970).

Manwill v. Oyler, 11 Utah 2d 433, 361 P.2d 177, 178-79 (1961). Although the "moral obligation" exception has not been embraced in Utah, . . .[2] Other courts apply the exception in cases where services rendered in the past were rendered with the expectation of payment rather than gratuitously. Even if the "moral obligation" doctrine applied in Utah, Dementas would not prevail. The trial court found that the services rendered by Dementas to Tallas were not rendered with the expectation of being compensated, but were performed gratuitously. That finding has not been shown to be erroneous. . . .

Dementas failed to prove there was any valid consideration for Tallas's promise to pay $50,000. Even if the "moral obligation" exception applied in Utah, the court found that the services Dementas performed were rendered without the expectation of payment. . . . We acknowledge, as have other courts in disregarding contracts for lack of consideration, that "[a]ppell[ant] will probably remain convinced [he] should be paid. Nevertheless, [he] failed to meet [his] burden of proof" and "this court will not find a contract where one has not been proved to exist." *Miller v. Miller*, 664 P.2d 39, 43 (Wyo. 1983). The judgment appealed from is affirmed. . . .

NOTES & QUESTIONS

1. Could the *Dementas* court have reached a different result relying on the "fiction" used by the court in the *Webb* case? Are the facts in *Dementas* as compelling as those in *Webb?*

2. If the courts abandoned the doctrine of consideration entirely, as Corbin has suggested, in favor of simply finding evidence of contractual intent before enforcing promises, would the results in the preceding cases be different? Would the purposes and policies of contract law be better served by abandoning the consideration requirement?

3. Courts have recognized certain limited exceptions to the general rule that a moral obligation cannot serve as consideration for a promise. For example, a debtor's promise to pay a debt barred by a statute of limitations is enforceable. *See, e.g., Kopp v. Fink*, 204 Okla. 570, 232 P.2d 161 (1951). And in some situations, a party who may avoid a promise due to incapacity or some other traditional ground for avoidance, may make a new, enforceable promise to perform the voidable obligation. For example, courts will enforce the promise of an adult to perform an obligation which was originally voidable because entered into when the promisor was a minor. *See* RESTATEMENT (SECOND) OF CONTRACTS §§ 7, 12 & 85 (1981).

---

[2] [8] The logical flaw in the "moral obligation" concept was accurately summarized by Justice Crockett in *Manwill*:

> The difficulty we see with the doctrine is that if a mere moral, as distinguished from a legal, obligation were recognized as valid consideration for a contract, that would practically erode to the vanishing point the necessity for finding a consideration. This is so, first because in nearly all circumstances where a promise is made there is some moral aspect of the situation which provides the motivation for making the promise even if it is to make an outright gift. And second, if we are dealing with moral concepts, the making of a promise itself creates a moral obligation to perform it. It seems obvious that if a contract to be legally enforceable need be anything other than a naked promise, something more than mere moral consideration is necessary. . . .

PROBLEM

On June 1, 1984, Mr. Price purchased a bait shop in East Peoria, Illinois. In March 1985, Price decided to remodel the premises as a donut shop, obtained the necessary building permit, and commenced remodeling. On August 1, 1985, Price hired an employee who was to learn donut-making skills. On August 6, 1985, Price ordered a sign for the donut shop. Sometime in July or August, he ordered paving work for the parking lot. On Friday, August 16, 1985, the mayor of East Peoria announced that a $1,000 reward was being offered for the establishment of a new business in East Peoria hiring 10 or more people. Price learned of the reward offer that same day and hurried to get the shop open on Monday, August 19, so as to be the first to claim the reward. The shop opened on August 19, 1985, despite the fact that it was not fully completed. The parking lot and sign were not completed until September 1985. On the afternoon of August 19, Price went to the city hall to claim the reward, but was told that he did not qualify because the reward was for the opening of new businesses and he had already decided to open his donut shop when the reward was extended. Price sued the City, alleging he had accepted the City's offer and was due the $1,000 reward. At trial, Price testified that he did not plan on opening the business until September 1985, but opened early so as to be the first person to claim the reward. Until he learned of the City's reward offer, he did not plan on opening until the sign was in place and the parking lot was completed. Further, Price argued that he did not intend to employ 10 people, but did so in order to comply with the terms of the reward offer. Is Price entitled to the reward? *Richard D. Price, Jr. & Associates, Ltd. v. The City of East Peoria,* 154 Ill. App. 3d 725, 507 N.E.2d 228 (Ill. App. 1987).

C. PRE-EXISTING DUTIES

At traditional common law, past consideration is no consideration. It follows that the performance of a pre-existing legal duty, that is, doing something one is already obligated to do, may not serve as consideration. Section 73 of the RESTATEMENT (SECOND) OF CONTRACTS (1981) provides:

> The performance of a legal duty owed to a promisor which is neither doubtful nor the subject of honest dispute is not consideration; but a similar performance is consideration if it differs from what was required by the duty in a way which reflects more than a pretense of bargain. Once again, strict adherence to this corollary of the consideration doctrine has led to some questionable decisions and caused the courts to engage in sometimes arcane, abstract analysis or to embrace legal fictions to avoid unjust results. As is frequently the case in the evolution of the common law, the need to devise legal fictions discloses a more fundamental flaw in the relevant legal doctrine. Eventually, the scholars, judges and attorneys recognize the flaw, reconsider, and adjust or abandon the doctrine entirely. This process is illustrated by the development of the law governing settlements, disputed claims and contract modifications which is the subject of this and the next section.

McDevitt v. Stokes, 174 Ky. 515, 192 S.W. 681 (1917). McDevitt, a jockey, was employed by Shaw to ride Shaw's horse, Grace, in the Kentucky Futurity in 1910. Stokes owned a number of horses in Grace's lineage and would profit handsomely if Grace won the race. Stokes therefore offered McDevitt $1,000 if he rode Grace to a win in the race. McDevitt agreed and won the race. When Stokes failed to pay him, McDevitt sued for breach of contract. However, the court denied McDevitt's claim, reasoning McDevitt had a pre-existing duty to ride Grace and to use his best efforts to win for his employer Shaw.

Denney v. Reppert, 432 S.W.2d 647 (Ky. App. 1968). The Kentucky Bankers Association offered a reward of $500 for information leading to the apprehension and conviction of three men who robbed a member bank of $30,000. After the robbers were apprehended and convicted, a number of individuals claimed the reward, leading the Bankers Association to petition a court to determine who was entitled to the reward. Four bank employees provided details of the crime and descriptions of the robbers to peace officers who used that information in capturing the robbers. However, the court concluded they were not entitled to the reward because they were acting within the scope of employment with the bank and were already obligated to cooperate with the police. Similarly, the state police officers who arrested the criminals were merely performing duties they were already obligated to perform and could not collect the reward. However, a deputy sheriff, who made an arrest outside of his jurisdiction, was under no duty to make the arrest outside of his county of employment and was therefore entitled to the reward.

DeCicco v. Schweizer, 221 N.Y. 431, 117 N.E. 807 (1917). Blanche Schweizer and Count Oberto Gulinelli were engaged to be married. At the time, engagements were binding contracts in New York state. Blanche's parents later entered into an agreement with the Count under which Blanche's father promised to pay Blanche $2,500 annually in consideration for Blanche and the Count marrying. After the marriage in 1902, Blanche's father made annual payments until 1912 when the couple's assignee (DeCicco) sued for that year's installment. The defendant, Blanche's father, contended that the promise to pay was unenforceable because the Count was already engaged to Blanche and that the Count merely fulfilled an existing legal duty by marrying her. However, Justice Cardozo, speaking for the court, held there was consideration for the defendant's promise to pay Blanche the annuity. Justice Cardozo reasoned:

> [A] promise by A to B to induce him not to *break* his contract with C is void. . . . We have never held, however, that a like infirmity attaches to a promise by A, not merely to B, but to B and C jointly, to induce them not to *rescind* or *modify* a contract which they are free to abandon. . . . The situation . . . is the same in substance as if the promise had run to husband and wife alike, and had been intended to induce performance by both. They were free by common consent to terminate their engagement or to postpone the marriage. If they forebore from exercising that right and assumed the responsibilities of marriage in reliance on the defendant's promise, he may not now retract it. (Emphasis in original.)

NOTES & QUESTIONS

1. Should the court in *McDevitt v. Stokes* have enforced Stokes' promise in favor of Shaw, Grace's owner and McDevitt's employer, on the ground that McDevitt accepted Stokes' offer as agent for Shaw, who had no pre-existing duty to have

McDevitt ride to win? *See* Restatement (Second) of Contracts § 73 (1981).

2. Does the pre-existing legal duty rule serve the purposes and policies of contract law? Are other public policy considerations present in cases such as *Denney v. Reppert?*

3. If one of the bank employees in *Denny* had pursued one of the robbers outside the bank and physically restrained him until the police arrived, would she have been entitled to the reward? If the bank employee had tackled one of the robbers inside the bank and held him until he was arrested, would she be entitled to the reward?

4. Although Justice Cardozo's dazzling analysis in *DeCicco v. Schweizer* avoids the trap of the pre-existing legal duty rule, it may obscure more important reasons for enforcing the defendant's promise to Blanche and the Count. What are those reasons? Are there any reasons to deny enforcement of the promise?

KUDER v. SCHROEDER
110 N.C. App. 355, 430 S.E.2d 271 (1993)

Wells, Judge: . . .

Plaintiff and defendant were married in March of 1978. One child was born to their marriage in June of 1984. After plaintiff and defendant were married, they entered into an oral agreement that plaintiff would forego her career as a veterinarian and would work as a teacher in a local community college to support their family in order that defendant might pursue his undergraduate education at the University of North Carolina in Chapel Hill. Defendant agreed that upon the completion of his undergraduate studies, he would provide the family's total support, so that plaintiff could then give up her employment and devote her full time to being a wife and mother. Pursuant to this agreement, plaintiff did work and provide the sole support for their family. Plaintiff and defendant subsequently amended or extended their agreement to allow defendant to obtain a master's degree and a law degree. Following his graduation from law school, defendant was unable to earn sufficient income to fully support the family, but in December of 1989, defendant obtained a position with a law firm which provided him with sufficient income to fully support the family. Three months later, in April of 1990, defendant told plaintiff he no longer loved her and that there was no hope for their marriage; whereupon, the parties separated.

Plaintiff contends that the oral agreement asserted by her in her complaint is a valid and binding contract, entitling her to damages for its breach. Taking plaintiff's allegations as true, we are sympathetic to her apparent dilemma, and certainly would not condone defendant's apparent knavish ingratitude, but we do not find support in the law of this State for such a claim and therefore hold that the trial court correctly dismissed plaintiff's claims. Under the law of this State, there is a personal duty of each spouse to support the other, a duty arising from the marital relationship, and carrying with it the corollary right to support from the other spouse. . . . So long as the coverture endures, this duty of support may not be abrogated or modified by the agreement of the parties to a marriage. . . .

Plaintiff's reliance on our decision in *Suggs v. Norris*, 88 N.C. App. 539, 364 S.E.2d 159, *cert. denied*, 322 N.C. 486, 370 S.E.2d 236 (1988), is misplaced. In that case, we sanctioned a claim for remuneration for services performed in a business (farming) enterprise by a person who was cohabiting with, but not married to, a deceased cohabitor. The facts and ruling in that case are in no sense relevant to the facts and issues presented in the case now before us.

For the reasons stated, the trial court's order must be and is

Affirmed.

*   *   *

GREENE, Judge, dissenting.

I agree with the majority, but for a different reason, that the trial court correctly dismissed plaintiff's breach of contract action. I, however, would reverse the trial court's dismissal of plaintiff's claim for unjust enrichment.

I reiterate the allegations of plaintiff's complaint in order to provide a fuller appreciation of the facts at issue. Plaintiff and defendant were married on 17 March 1978, in Sanford, North Carolina. On 19 June 1984, the parties' only child was born. During the entire course of the marriage, plaintiff, a veterinarian, worked as a teacher at a local community college. She provided total financial support for the family. Upon their marriage, plaintiff and defendant agreed that plaintiff would remain in her teaching position in order to ensure a steady source of income for the family while defendant returned to school full-time to complete his undergraduate education at the University of North Carolina. Plaintiff also agreed that she would have only one child while defendant was in school. In return, defendant agreed that he would provide the family's total financial support upon the completion of his undergraduate studies, at which time plaintiff could achieve her goal of becoming a full-time wife and mother. Pursuant to this agreement, plaintiff taught and provided the family's sole source of income, including the income for defendant's education, with the expectation that she would soon be able to remain at home and raise a family.

Defendant obtained his undergraduate degree as planned; however, defendant decided upon graduation that he wanted to earn a Master's degree as well. The parties decided to extend their original agreement for a period which would allow defendant to achieve this goal. After two years, however, defendant discontinued his efforts to obtain a Master's degree and decided instead to enroll in law school at UNC. Again, the parties extended their original agreement in order to allow defendant to complete law school. Plaintiff continued to work and provide all of the family's income. Defendant continued to devote his time to completing his education.

Upon graduation from law school, defendant told plaintiff that, instead of entering the private practice of law, he wanted to start his own legal research business. The parties, plaintiff reluctantly, once more extended their original agreement, with plaintiff continuing to work in order to ensure a steady income for the family until defendant's business became profitable. Plaintiff, who by this time had reached the age of forty, also agreed to forego having more children. In his first two years of self-employment, defendant failed to earn enough money to fully support the family.

In December, 1989, defendant obtained a position with a law firm in Charlotte, North Carolina, with a starting salary of approximately $38,000 per year. For the first time during eleven years of marriage, defendant was able to provide total financial support for the family. Three months later, however, in April, 1990, defendant told plaintiff that he no longer loved her and that there was no hope for their marriage, and the parties separated. . . .

I agree with the majority that arising out of the marital relationship there is the equal duty of each spouse to support the other spouse, and that a spouse may not recover for support provided in the discharge of the duties imposed by the marital status. It has long been observed by our Courts, however, that a husband and wife are free to contract for the performance of services or the rendering of support outside those duties. *See Dorsett v. Dorsett*, 183 N.C. 354, 356, 111 S.E. 541, 542 (1922) (wife entitled to compensation where, pursuant to an agreement with her husband, she renders services outside the home);. . . *see also* N.C.G.S. § 52-10 (1991) (contracts between husband and wife not inconsistent with public policy are valid). In my opinion, the type of support furnished by plaintiff in the instant case is outside the scope of the marital duty of support as recognized by our Courts. Therefore, plaintiff and defendant were not precluded from entering, as husband and wife, into the agreement at issue.

Even assuming, as the majority apparently does, that plaintiff's contribution to defendant's educational endeavors falls within her spousal duty of support, I question the continued validity of the rule that the duty of support arising out of the marital relationship cannot be modified by the agreement of the parties. Our Legislature currently recognizes the validity of contracts which modify or abrogate the marital duty of support, provided that such contracts are entered into before marriage and are in contemplation of marriage, or are entered into upon separation of the parties. *See* N.C.G.S. § 52B-1 *et seq.* (1987); N.C.G.S. § 52-10.1 (1991). Parties are also permitted before, during, or after marriage to provide in a written agreement for distribution of marital property in a manner deemed by the parties to be equitable. N.C.G.S. § 50-20(d) (Supp. 1992). Moreover, our Courts recognize the validity of an agreement of the type at issue provided that the parties to such agreement are unmarried cohabiting partners. *See Suggs v. Norris*, 88 N.C. App. 539, 364 S.E.2d 159, *cert. denied*, 322 N.C. 486, 370 S.E.2d 236 (1988) (*citing Marvin v. Marvin*, 18 Cal. 3d 660, 557 P.2d 106 (1976)). I find it incongruous that, given a cohabiting partner on the one hand and a spouse on the other hand, both of whom pursuant to an agreement provide total financial support for their partner in order for that partner to obtain a degree, an advanced degree, or a professional license with the expectation that both parties would benefit therefrom, upon the dissolution of the relationship, the cohabiting partner is entitled to compensation for such contribution to the educational achievements of his partner, but a spouse who made the same contribution is not. I am at a loss to understand the "public policy" supporting such a rule.

In the instant case, I agree with the majority that the trial court properly dismissed plaintiff's claim for breach of contract, but for a different reason. It is a basic principle of contract law that, even if the parties intend to contract, an agreement which is not reasonably certain as to its material terms is indefinite and will not be — because it cannot be — enforced by our Courts. . . . Generally, "material terms" include such items as subject matter, price, payment terms, quantity, quality, duration, time and place of performance, and so forth.

A review of the allegations in plaintiff's amended complaint relating to the terms of her alleged express oral contract with defendant, taken as true, reveals the agreement's pervasive and fatal lack of definiteness. Among other things, plaintiff fails to allege that the parties agreed on any specific time period during which defendant was to complete his various educational efforts and plaintiff was to begin her pursuit as a full-time wife and mother. Nor is there any mention of the intended duration of plaintiff's role as full-time wife and mother. In addition, the parties never agreed on what amount of financial support plaintiff was obligated to provide for the parties' living expenses while defendant was in school or for defendant's educational expenses. Likewise, the complaint fails to allege the amount of financial support defendant was expected to provide once the parties switched breadwinner roles. Therefore, I would affirm the trial court's order dismissing this claim. *See Pyeatte v. Pyeatte*, 135 Ariz. 346, 661 P.2d 196 (Ariz. App. 1983). Even though plaintiff's contract claim was properly dismissed, however, I believe that the trial court erred in dismissing plaintiff's claim for unjust enrichment, an issue which the majority fails to address. . . .

WYNN, Judge, concurring:

I concur fully in the majority opinion and write separately to point out that the law provides different protection for married couples and unmarried cohabitants. . . .

First, the dissent submits that there is something incongruous in allowing an unmarried but cohabiting partner to enter into a valid contract regarding the support of the other partner, but not affording a married partner this same privilege. The marital relationship is bestowed special protections by the laws of North Carolina, protections that a cohabiting partner cannot claim. These include, for example: the right to have property held as tenants by the entireties, N.C. GEN. STAT. § 39-13.6 (1984); the right, upon the death of one's spouse, to dissent from an unfavorable bequest in the deceased's will, in favor of a larger portion of the estate, N.C. GEN. STAT. § 30-1 (1992); an entitlement to a year's allowance upon the death of one's spouse, N.C. GEN. STAT. § 30-15 (1992); and numerous rights arising from the dissolution of the marital relationship that are not available to a cohabiting partner when his or her relationship comes to an end. *See generally* N.C. GEN. STAT. Chapter 50 (1987, Supp. 1992). Quite simply, the rules are different for married couples. *See Ritchie v. White*, 225 N.C. 450, 453, 35 S.E.2d 414, 416 (1945) (the moment the marriage relation comes into existence certain rights and duties spring into being). The dissent chooses to focus on one aspect of the law which does not grant a married person the same privilege as an otherwise similarly situated unmarried cohabitant in an effort to illustrate that the married couple is unduly restrained by our laws. The fact that the law does not allow a married couple to contract regarding spousal support, however, is not indicative of a general trend in the law to deprive married individuals of otherwise valid legal rights. . . .

NOTES & QUESTIONS

1. All of the judges on the *Kuder* court agreed that marriage creates a legal duty in spouses to support each other. Do you agree? Does this legal duty arising from marriage foster or interfere with the purposes and policies of contract law? Does this legally recognized duty serve other public policy considerations?

2. Assuming that marriage does create a legal duty of mutual support, where does that duty end and a spouse exceed the scope of that duty? For example, if Father Brady and Mother Brady each bring three children from a previous marriage to their union, are mutual promises to contribute money to the college

education of each other's biological children enforceable in contract? Do you agree with the *Kuder* dissenter that Mrs. Kuder's contribution exceeded the scope of the marital duties?

3. Assuming the existence of the marital duty of mutual support, should the couple be free to modify that duty, as suggested by the dissenter? Why should unmarried, cohabiting partners be free to enter into enforceable agreements like the one at issue in *Kuder*, while married couples are denied that freedom? Is the concurring Judge's opinion persuasive?

4. The dissent would deny enforcement to the Kuders' agreement on the ground it was fatally indefinite. We shall consider questions concerning missing or indefinite terms in Chapter Five, Reasonable Certainty of Contract Terms. In a portion of the dissent edited out, the dissenter would permit Mrs. Kuder to recover to avoid unjust enrichment. We shall consider this alternative theory for recovery in Chapter Six, Avoidance of Unjust Enrichment.

PROBLEMS

1. Kistler solicited O'Brien to work for Kistler's company, which sold fire prevention equipment. O'Brien quit his other employment and went to work for Kistler on oral terms governing wages, benefits and duties, but no mention was made of any covenant under which O'Brien would commit not to compete with Kistler were he to leave employment with Kistler. The day he began work for Kistler, O'Brien asked a clerk about his insurance benefits and was given various forms to complete and sign. One of the forms was entitled "Employment Contract" and contained a clause stating that in return for $1.00 O'Brien promised he would not compete in a 50-mile area with Kistler's business for two years after leaving employment with Kistler. O'Brien signed this form next to a space marked "Seal." Three years later, Kistler discharged O'Brien, who then went into business servicing fire prevention equipment. If Kistler sues to enjoin O'Brien from competing with Kistler's business in violation of the covenant, what will be the result? *George W. Kistler, Inc. v. O'Brien*, 347 A.2d 311 (Pa. 1975).

2. According to an Illinois statute, municipalities must administer a physical agility test to any applicant for a job as a firefighter. Angela White applied to work as a firefighter for the Village of Homewood, Illinois. Before the Village of Homewood would permit White to take the physical agility test, the Village required White to sign an "exculpatory agreement" under which she agreed that she would release the Village of any and all claims or liability for any injury she might suffer while taking the physical agility test. After suffering an injury during the test, White sued the Village for alleged negligence in administering the test. The Village moved to dismiss White's claim based on the exculpatory agreement. Is that agreement enforceable? *White v. Village of Homewood*, 628 N.E.2d 616 (Ill. App. 1993).

D. DISPUTED CLAIMS, SETTLEMENTS AND MODIFICATIONS

Rather than litigate their differences, parties to a disputed transaction may wish to enter into a settlement. Settlement agreements are also executed by parties who have disputes unrelated to contracts, such as tort claims, property disputes or domestic matters. Such settlement agreements are contracts, subject to the ordinary law of contracts including the consideration requirement. If a claim turns out to be invalid, a question may arise as to whether relinquishing that claim may serve as consideration for a return promise. Issues may also arise over whether the pre-existing legal duty prevents the enforcement of a settlement agreement because one party is already obligated to perform in some fashion.

For example, Sarah promises to pay Jack $50 if he washes and waxes her car. Jack washes and waxes her car, but Sarah is dissatisfied with the quality of Jack's work and refuses to pay him. Jack would prefer to be paid the full $50, but rather than receive no pay for his work, Jack compromises. Sarah would prefer to pay Jack nothing, but rather than be sued, Sarah compromises. In return for Sarah's promise to pay him $30, Jack promises to drop his claim for the remaining $20, accepting her promise of $30 in full settlement of his claim. However, Sarah refuses to pay Jack the $30 she promised to pay in settlement of his claim. If Jack sues for the $30, Sarah may defend on the ground that the settlement is unenforceable because Jack's original claim for $50 was invalid due to the shoddy job he did.

Alternatively, if Sarah pays Jack the $30 in settlement of his claim, but Jack nonetheless sues for the $20 balance, Sarah could interpose the settlement agreement as her defense, claiming an accord and satisfaction. Jack may counter that Sarah provided no consideration for Jack's agreement to drop his claim for $20 because Sarah had a pre-existing duty to pay him $50 for the job. In addition to § 73 governing Performance of Legal Duty, § 74 of the RESTATEMENT (SECOND) OF CONTRACTS (1981), addresses these problems:

Settlement of Claims

(1) Forbearance to assert or surrender of a claim or defense which proves to be invalid is not consideration unless

(a) the claim or defense is in fact doubtful because of uncertainty as to the facts or the law, or

(b) the forbearing or surrendering party believes that the claim or defense may be fairly determined to be valid.

(2) The execution of a written instrument surrendering a claim or defense by one who is under no duty to execute it is consideration if the execution of the written instrument is bargained for even though he is not asserting the claim or defense and believes that no valid claim or defense exists.

Fiege v. Boehm, 210 Md. 352, 123 A.2d 316 (1956). Plaintiff, an unwed mother, alleged that defendant agreed to pay support for her illegitimate child in return for her promise not to bring a paternity action against him. Although he claimed he had never had sexual intercourse with the plaintiff, defendant paid her $480 over a nearly two-year period until blood tests disclosed he could not possibly be the child's father. Plaintiff then filed a paternity action against the defendant and sought enforcement of the alleged contract with defendant. Defendant argued that even if he had entered into the alleged contract, plaintiff's forbearance to prosecute was based on an invalid claim since he could not possibly be the father, and therefore the contract lacked consideration. The court, however, held that the contract was based on sufficient consideration. The court noted that "the surrender of, or forbearance to assert, an invalid claim by one who has not an honest and reasonable belief in its possible validity is not sufficient consideration for a contract." But here, the court concluded, there was no evidence of fraud or unfairness, and the plaintiff made her claim in good faith. "[F]orbearance to sue for a lawful claim or demand is sufficient consideration for a promise to pay for forbearance if the party forbearing had an honest intention to prosecute litigation which is not frivolous, vexatious, or unlawful, and which he believed to be well founded."

NOTE

Do you agree with the *Fiege* court's finding that the plaintiff acted in good faith and had a reasonable belief in the claim's possible validity? What must the plaintiff have known that the defendant apparently did not know? Does it matter whether she told him?

DYER v. NATIONAL BY-PRODUCTS, INC.
380 N.W.2d 732 (Iowa 1986)

SCHULTZ, Justice:

The determinative issue in this appeal is whether good faith forbearance to litigate a claim, which proves to be invalid and unfounded, is sufficient consideration to uphold a contract of settlement. The district court determined, as a matter of law that consideration for the alleged settlement was lacking because the forborne claim was not a viable cause of action. . . .

On October 29, 1981, Dale Dyer, an employee of National By-Products, lost his right foot in a job-related accident. Thereafter, the employer placed Dyer on a leave of absence at full pay from the date of his injury until August 16, 1982. At that time he returned to work as a foreman, the job he held prior to his injury. On March 11, 1983, the employer indefinitely laid off Dyer.

Dyer then filed the present lawsuit against his employer claiming that his discharge was a breach of an oral contract. He alleged that he in good faith believed that he had a valid claim against his employer for his personal injury. Further, Dyer claimed that his forbearance from litigating his claim was made in exchange for a promise from his employer that he would have lifetime employment. The employer specifically denied that it had offered a lifetime job to Dyer after his injury.

Following extensive discovery procedures, the employer filed a motion for summary judgment claiming there was no genuine factual issue and that it was entitled to judgment as a matter of law. The motion was resisted by Dyer. The district court sustained the employer's motion on the basis that: . . . (2) there was no forbearance of any viable cause of action, apparently on the ground that workers' compensation provided Dyer's sole remedy.

On appeal, Dyer claims that consideration for the alleged contract of lifetime employment was his forbearance from pursuing an action against his employer. Accordingly, he restricts his claim of error to the second reason advanced by the district court for granting summary judgment. Summary judgment is only proper when there is no genuine issue of any material fact. . . . Dyer generally contends that an unresolved issue of material fact remains as to whether he reasonably and in good faith forbore from asserting a claim against his employer and his coemployees in exchange for the employer's alleged promise to employ him for life. Specifically, he asserts that the trial court erred because: (1) the court did not consider the reasonableness and good faith of his belief in the validity of the claim he forbore from asserting, and (2) the court considered the legal merits of the claim itself which Dyer forbore from asserting.

The employer, on the other hand, maintains that workers' compensation[3] benefits are Dyer's sole remedy for his injury and that his claim for damages is unfounded. It then urges that forbearance from asserting an unfounded claim cannot serve as consideration for a contract. For the purpose of this discussion, we shall assume that Dyer's tort action is clearly invalid and he had no basis for a tort suit against either his employer or his fellow employees. We recognize that the fact issue, as to whether Dyer in good faith believed that he had a cause of action based in tort against the employer, remains unresolved. The determinative issue before the district court and now on appeal is whether the lack of consideration for the alleged promise of lifetime employment has been established as a matter of law. Preliminarily, we observe that the law favors the adjustment and settlement of controversies without resorting to court action. . . . Compromise is favored by law. . .Compromise of a doubtful right asserted in good faith is sufficient consideration for a promise. . . . The more difficult problem is whether the settlement of an unfounded claim asserted in good faith is consideration for a contract of settlement. Professor Corbin presents a view favorable to Dyer's argument when he states:

> [F]orbearance to press a claim, or a promise of such forbearance, may be a sufficient consideration even though the claim is wholly illfounded. It may be ill-founded because the facts are not what he supposes them to be, or because the existing facts do not have the legal operation that he supposes them to have. In either case, his forbearance may be a sufficient consideration, although under certain circumstances it is not. The fact that the claim is ill-founded is not in itself enough to prevent forbearance from being a sufficient consideration for a promise. 1 CORBIN ON CONTRACTS § 140, at 595 (1963).

Further, in the same section, it is noted that:

> The most generally prevailing, and probably the most satisfactory view is that *forbearance is sufficient if there is any reasonable ground for the claimant's belief that it is just to try to enforce his claim. He must be asserting his claim "in good faith"*; but this does not mean he must believe that his suit can be won. It means that he must not be making his claim or threatening suit for purposes of vexation, or in order to realize on its "nuisance value." *Id.* § 140, at 602 (emphasis added).

---

[3] [1] It is undisputed that the employee was covered under workers' compensation. The Iowa workers' compensation act states in pertinent part that:

> The rights and remedies provided in this chapter . . . for an employee on account of injury . . . for which benefits under this chapter . . . are recoverable, shall be the exclusive and only rights and remedies of such employee . . . at common law or otherwise, on account of such injury . . . against: (1) his or her employer. . . . IOWA CODE § 85.20 (1983). . . .

Indeed, we find support for the Corbin view in language contained in our cases. *See White v. Flood*, 258 Iowa at 409, 138 N.W.2d at 867 ("[C]ompromise of a doubtful right asserted in good faith is sufficient consideration for a promise."); *In re Estate of Dayton*, 246 Iowa 1209, 1216, 71 N.W.2d 429, 433 (1955) ("The good faith assertion of an unfounded claim furnishes ample consideration for a settlement."); *Messer v. Washington National Insurance Co.*, 233 Iowa 1372, 1380, 11 N.W.2d 727, 731 (1943) ("[I]f the parties act in good faith, even when they know all the facts and there is promise without legal liability on which to base it, the courts hesitate to disturb the agreements of the parties. . . ."); *Lockie v. Baker*, 206 Iowa 21, 24, 218 N.W. 483, 484 (1928) (Claim settled, though perhaps not valid, must have been presented and demanded in good faith.); *First National Bank v. Browne*, 199 Iowa 981, 984, 203 N.W. 277, 278 (1925) (Settlement of a disputed or doubtful claim in good faith is sufficient consideration for a compromise, even though judicial investigation might show claim to be unfounded.).

The RESTATEMENT (SECOND) OF CONTRACTS section 74 (1979), supports the Corbin view and states:

Settlement of Claims

(1) Forbearance to assert or the surrender of a claim or defense, which proves to be invalid is not consideration unless

(a) the claim or defense is in fact doubtful because of uncertainty as to the facts or the law, or

(b) *the forbearing or surrendering party believes that the claim or defense may be fairly determined to be valid.*

*   *   *

Comment: . . .

b. Requirement of good faith. The policy favoring compromise of disputed claims is clearest, perhaps, where a claim is surrendered at a time when it is uncertain whether it is valid or not. Even though the invalidity later becomes clear, *the bargain* is *to be judged as it appeared to the parties at the time;* if the claim was then doubtful, no inquiry is necessary as to their good faith. Even though the invalidity should have been clear at the time, the settlement of an honest dispute is upheld. But a mere assertion or denial of liability does not make a claim doubtful, and *the fact that invalidity is obvious may indicate that it was known.* In such cases Subsection (1)(b) requires a showing of *good faith.* (Emphasis added.) . . .

However, not all jurisdictions adhere to this view. Some courts require that the claim forborne must have some merit in fact or at law before it can provide consideration and these jurisdictions reject those claims that are obviously invalid. *See Bullard v. Curry-Cloonan*, 367 A.2d 127, 131 (D.C. App. 1976) ("[A]s a general principle, the forbearance of a cause of action advanced in good faith, which is neither absurd in fact nor obviously unfounded in law, constitutes good and valuable consideration."); *Frasier v. Carter*, 92 Idaho 79, 437 P.2d 32, 34 (1968) (The forbearance of a claim which is not utterly groundless is sufficient consideration to support a contract.); *Charles v. Hill* 260 N.W.2d 571, 575 (Minn. 1977) ("[A] wholly baseless or utterly unfounded claim is not consideration for a contract."); *Agristor Credit Corporation v. Unruh*, 571 P.2d 1220, 1224 (Okla. 1977) (In order to constitute consideration for a contract, "claim forborne must be reasonably doubtful in law or fact."); *see generally* 15A C.J.S. *Compromise and Settlement* § 10, at 201 (There are many decisions holding that a claim which is entirely baseless does not afford consideration for a compromise.)

In fact, we find language in our own case law that supports the view which is favorable to the employer in this case. *See Vande Stouwe v. Bankers' Life Co.*, 218 Iowa 1182, 1190, 254 N.W. 790, 794 (1934) ("A claim that is entirely baseless and without foundation in law or equity will not support a compromise."); *Peterson v. Breitag*, 88 Iowa 418, 422-23, 55 N.W. 86, 88 (1893) ("It is well settled that there must at least be some appearance of a valid claim to support a settlement to avoid litigation."); *Tucker v. Ronk*, 43 Iowa 80, 82 (1876) (The settlement of an illegal and unfounded claim, upon which no proceedings have been instituted, is without consideration.); *Sullivan v. Collins*, 18 Iowa 228, 229 (1869) (A compromise of a claim is not a sufficient consideration to sustain a note, when such claim is not sustainable in law or in equity, or, at least doubtful in some respect.). Additionally, Professor Williston notes that:

> While there is a great divergence of opinion respecting the kind of forbearance which will constitute consideration, *the weight of authority holds that although forbearance from suit on a clearly invalid claim is insufficient consideration for a promise*, forbearance from suit on a claim of doubtful validity is sufficient consideration for a promise if there is a sincere belief in the validity of the claim. 1 WILLISTON ON CONTRACTS § 135, at 581 (3rd ed. 1957) (emphasis added).

We believe, however, that the better reasoned approach is that expressed in the RESTATEMENT (SECOND) OF CONTRACTS § 74. Even the above statement from Williston, although it may have been the state of the law in 1957, is a questionable assessment of the current law. In fact, most of the cases cited in the cumulative supplement to Williston follow the "good faith and reasonable" language. 1 WILLISTON ON CONTRACTS § 135B (3rd ed. 1957 & Supp. 1985). Additionally, RESTATEMENT (SECOND) OF CONTRACTS § 74 is cited in that supplement. As noted before, as a matter of policy the law favors compromise and such policy would be defeated if a party could second guess his settlement and litigate the validity of the compromise. The requirement that the forbearing party assert the claim in good faith sufficiently protects the policy of law that favors the settlement of controversies. Our holdings which are to the contrary to this view are overruled.

In the present case, the invalidity of Dyer's claim against the employer does not foreclose him, as a matter of law, from asserting that his forbearance was consideration for the alleged contract of settlement. However, the issue of Dyer's good faith must still be examined. In so doing, the issue of the validity of Dyer's claim should not be entirely overlooked:

> Although the courts will not inquire into the validity of a claim which was compromised in good faith, there must generally be reasonable grounds for a belief in order for the court to be convinced that the belief was honestly entertained by the person who asserted it. Sufficient consideration requires more than the bald assertion by a claimant who has a claim, and to the extent that the validity or invalidity of a claim has a bearing upon whether there were reasonable grounds for believing in its possible validity, evidence of the validity or invalidity of a claim may be relevant to the issue

of good faith. 15A Am. Jur. 2d *Compromise and Settlement* § 17, at 790.

We conclude that the evidence of the invalidity of the claim is relevant to show a lack of honest belief in the validity of the claim asserted or forborne.

Under the present state of the record, there remains a material fact as to whether Dyer's forbearance to assert his claim was in good faith. Summary judgment should not have been rendered against him. . . .

REVERSED AND REMANDED.

NOTES & QUESTIONS

1. Dyer's claim was clearly invalid at the time he made it due to the state's workers' compensation law, and Dyer and/or National By-Products could have learned of the invalidity of the claim before they entered into their settlement by contacting an attorney. In light of this, do you agree with the court's decision? Is the court's decision consistent with the objective theory of contracts? Does the *Dyer* court's decision serve any of the public policy objectives of contract law?

Whittaker Chain Tread Co. v. Standard Auto Supply Co., 216 Mass. 204, 103 N.E. 695 (1913). The plaintiff sold and delivered to the defendant goods in the amount of $80.03. The defendant sought to return some of the goods said to be worth $50.02, but the plaintiff refused to receive the returned goods. The defendant then sent the plaintiff a check for $30.01, the amount admittedly due for the goods defendant had kept, but the defendant stated the check was in full settlement of the account. After cashing defendant's check, the plaintiff demanded a further payment of $50.02. When defendant refused to pay the additional amount, plaintiff sued for the $50.02. Defendant argued that plaintiff's claim was barred because plaintiff cashed the check for $30.01, but the court held that plaintiff was entitled to the $50.02. The court explained:

> In the case at bar there was no express agreement by the creditor to forego the balance of his claim on receiving payment of the amount admitted without dispute to be due. The only way in which such an agreement can be made out in the case at bar is on the ground that the plaintiff had to take the check sent him on the condition on which it was sent, and that by cashing the check he elected to accept the condition and so took the part admittedly due in full discharge of the whole debt. But while the doctrine of election is sound where a check is sent in full discharge of a claim no part of which is admitted to be due, it does not obtain where a debtor undertakes to make payment of what he admits to be due conditioned on its being accepted on discharge of what is in dispute. Such a condition, under those circumstances, is one which the debtor has no right to impose, and for that reason is void. In such a case the creditor is not put to an election to refuse the payment or to take it on the condition on which it is offered. He can take the payment admittedly due free of the void condition which the debtor has sought to impose.

2. If the buyer in *Whittaker Chain Tread* had sent the seller a check for $30.02 marked "In full settlement of all claims," would the settlement have been enforceable if the seller cashed that check? What if the check were for $30.03, $30.04, etc.?

FIELD LUMBER CO. v. PETTY
9 Wash. App. 378, 512 P.2d 764 (1973)

FARRIS, Judge:

Field Lumber Company initiated action on January 20, 1971 to recover the sum of $1,264.73 which it alleged is due and owing from Robert A. Petty, a general contractor doing business with his wife as Pacific Profile Homes. Hartford Accident & Indemnity Company as surety on the contractor's bond was joined as a party defendant. . . . Petty admits that he refused to pay the $1,264.73 but asserts that the claim is unliquidated and was settled by an accord and satisfaction in October, 1970. The trial court agreed. Field Lumber Company appeals. Petty made numerous purchases from Field Lumber Company during the period June 6, 1968 through January 23, 1970. Field Lumber Company's ledger statement showed a balance of $1,752.21 in October, 1970. Petty acknowledged a balance of $1,091.96 but disputed the difference of $660.25 which represented an allegedly unauthorized $292.60 purchase by an employee and a 1 percent per month finance charge. In early October, 1970, a check in the amount of $500 was mailed to Field Lumber Company with a letter, clear and definite in its terms, indicating that the check must be accepted in full settlement of the claim or returned. The letter also recited that the funds had been borrowed.

[The court's decision included an appendix reproducing the letter to Field Lumber Company as follows.]

October 2, 1970
Field Lumber Company
10234 S.E. 256th
Kent, Washington 98031
Attn: Larry
Re: Robert A. Petty d/b/a Pacific Profile Homes
Gentlemen:

Our client, above named, has asked us to transmit to you the enclosed check in the sum of $500.00 in full settlement of your claim against him. We realize this check represents a little less than 50% of your claim, but in the present market, Mr. Petty has been unable to sell his real estate, or unable to obtain an offer in excess of his cost, or to obtain a figure representative of his equity. He has been able to borrow the amount enclosed herewith, which is tendered to you, solely upon the condition that it is accepted in full settlement of your claim and your endorsement and collection of the enclosed check will evidence your agreement to that effect. If the above is not acceptable, will you please return the check without delay.

Yours truly,
COOK, FLANAGAN & BERST
/s/ George S. Cook
George S. Cook
GSC:sk Encl.

In response, Field Lumber Company notified Petty by telephone that it would require full payment but cashed the $500 check. The trial court found that this discharged Petty from any further liability on the account. . . .

We recognize the general rule that where a sum due is unliquidated or disputed and a remittance of an amount less than that claimed is sent to the creditor with a statement explaining that it is in full satisfaction of the claim, the acceptance of such a remittance by the creditor constitutes an accord and satisfaction. . . . However, this rule is not applicable where a portion of the alleged debt in excess of the amount paid is acknowledged and not in dispute. . . . In such a case a debtor cannot unilaterally tender a lesser sum than that which it is agreed is due and owing and rely upon the retention of that sum as full settlement of the debt unless there is some additional consideration given therefore. An accord and satisfaction is founded on contract, and a consideration therefore is as necessary as for any other contract. . . .

The recognition of a debt in a fixed amount and in excess of the $500 which was tendered under the circumstances here precludes the finding of an accord and satisfaction unless there is proof of new consideration. It has long been the rule in this state that payment of an amount admitted to be due can furnish no consideration for an accord and satisfaction of the entire claim. . . . Here we cannot find a scintilla of evidence indicating that any new consideration was given. Petty did not borrow the sum after agreeing with Field Lumber Company that he would do so if it would be accepted as full settlement. He borrowed the money of his own volition and then simply mailed the check with a letter after efforts had been made and were continuing to be made to recover the full amount. To find an accord and satisfaction here where a definite portion of the alleged debt was acknowledged to be due and owing and therefore liquidated and undisputed would place a creditor at a disadvantage in accepting partial payments from a reluctant debtor, since by doing so he would be jeopardizing his right to receive the balance, even though in law that balance was in fact due him. It is true that courts look with favor on compromise, but this means genuine compromise, arrived at through mutual agreement.

The payment of $500 here was a payment on account; whether the disputed sum of $660.25 is due and owing is a proper subject for litigation. The cause is remanded for determination of the question of the balance due on account. Reversed and remanded.

PROBLEMS

1. In 1970, Simpson entered into a written employment contract with Norwesco under which Simpson would sell the company's agricultural equipment. The employment contract, which was terminable by either party at will upon six months' written notice, specified that Simpson would receive a 10% commission on sales of proprietary sprayer tanks and a 6% commission on other sales. In 1972, Norwesco encountered economic difficulties and decided to reduce Simpson's commissions on proprietary sprayer tanks from 10% to 7%, but to increase his commissions on other sales from 6% to 7%. Simpson protested the change and wrote the company, "I plan to continue with the same efforts in accordance with the terms of the original agreement." Rather than notify Simpson that he must accept the new terms or leave its employment, Norwesco began to send Simpson commission checks reflecting the new terms. Simpson cashed the checks. In 1976, Norwesco terminated Simpson in accordance with their contract, giving him six months' notice. Simpson sued for back commissions ($90,381.68) based on the original commission terms. Who will prevail? Would your answer be the same if the checks had been marked "In full settlement of all commission claims"? *Simpson v. Norwesco*, 583 F.2d 1007 (8th Cir. 1978).

2. Carte Blanche sued Segal, an attorney, for his unpaid credit card debt and obtained a default judgment of nearly $13,000 against him. Segal then moved to have the judgment vacated for lack of notice. While his motion was pending, Segal then mailed a check for $95.60 directly to Carte Blanche, bypassing Carte Blanche's attorneys. The check was marked "acceptance, negotiation or endorsement of this draft shall constitute a full and final release in settlement of all claims and causes of action for [Segal's account]." Carte Blanche cashed the check. Is the suit by Carte Blanche against Segal settled? Has Segal acted unethically? *In re Segal,* 117 Ill. 2d 1, 509 N.E.2d 988 (1987).

NOTE

To be enforceable, a modification of an existing contract must be bilateral and uncoerced. Once the parties have entered into a contract, its terms govern their respective obligations to one another, and the pre-existing legal duty rule prevents one of them from unilaterally imposing different terms on the other. In this context, application of the pre-existing duty rule prevents the "hold up game" where one party to an executory agreement withholds a promised performance to extract additional payment or consideration from the other party.

For example, in *Alaska Packers' Association v. Domenico,* 117 F.2d 99 (9th Cir. 1902), a group of seamen entered into an agreement with a company to sail from San Francisco, California, to Alaska, to catch salmon on the way, and to can the salmon at the company's Alaska canning plant. Upon arrival in Alaska at the start of the short salmon season, the seamen refused to work unless they were given a substantial raise over the wage terms of their original agreement. Unable to find replacements for the seamen, the company promised to pay them the additional amount, but reneged when the ship returned to San Francisco. The court held that the employer's promise to pay the additional amount was unenforceable due to the pre-existing legal duty rule.

Although application of the pre-existing legal duty rule prevents the enforcement of coerced unilateral modifications as illustrated in the *Alaska Packers'* case, its broader application has been criticized for preventing enforcement of good faith modifications where coercion is absent but no new consideration is provided by one of the parties. Courts have sometimes resorted to fictions rather than permit the strict application of the pre-existing legal duty rule to yield unfair results. And these fictions have drawn attention to the fundamental weaknesses of the pre-existing legal duty rule, leading to changes in the law governing modification. Under § 89 of the RESTATEMENT (SECOND) OF CONTRACTS (1981), additional consideration is unnecessary to support a modification where the parties voluntarily enter into a fair and equitable modification due to unanticipated circumstances.

Schwartzreich v. Bauman-Basch, Inc., 231 N.Y. 196, 131 N.E. 887 (1921). Plaintiff was employed by defendant under a one-year, written contract to serve as a coat designer in return for a salary of $90 per week. Another company then offered plaintiff more money. After learning that plaintiff planned to leave for the better offer, defendant called plaintiff into his office and asked how much the other company was going to pay plaintiff. Plaintiff answered that the other company offered him $115 per week. Defendant then offered plaintiff $100 a week if he would stay. Plaintiff agreed. Defendant then dictated to a typist the new contract, which was identical to the first contract except for plaintiff's salary, which was now $100 a week. When the parties signed the new contract, plaintiff left his old contract with defendant and tore off the signatures from the old contract. Defendant discharged plaintiff two months later and plaintiff sued for breach of the second contract. Defendant argued the second agreement lacked consideration because plaintiff had a pre-existing duty to work for defendant for the lesser salary under the first contract. However, the court held the second contract enforceable, reasoning that the parties had simultaneously rescinded their first agreement when they executed the second agreement in its place. "We are . . . of the opinion . . . that both transactions can take place at the same time."

Goebel v. Linn, 47 Mich. 489, 11 N.W. 284 (1882). In November 1879, Belle Isle Ice Co. entered into a contract with Goebel, a large brewery, to supply Goebel with all the ice it would need in 1880 at $1.75 a ton, or $2 a ton if ice were scarce. The winter was so mild, however, that the ice crop was a failure. In May 1880, Belle Isle notified Goebel and other brewers that it could no longer furnish ice at the stipulated price. At a meeting with the brewers, Belle Isle initially demanded $5 a ton for its ice, but then agreed to accept $3.50 a ton. Because Goebel could find no other supplier and had a large stock of beer that would be spoiled without ice, it paid Belle Isle $3.50 per ton for the ice by giving Belle Isle its note from time to time. Goebel paid all of these notes except the October note, and Belle Isle's assignee sued Goebel for payment on that note. Goebel defended on the ground that the notes were obtained without consideration and under duress. The court, however, held that the parties were free to enter into the new arrangement, that the note was supported by consideration, and that Belle Isle's refusal to perform and its extraction of the higher price was not legal duress. The court reasoned:

> If the ice company had the ability to perform their contract, but took advantage of the circumstances to extort a higher price from the necessities of the defendants, its conduct was reprehensible, and it would perhaps have been in the interest of good morals if defendants had temporarily submitted to the loss and brought suit against the ice company on their contract. No one disputes that at their option they might have taken that course, and that the ice company would have been responsible for all damages legally attributable to the breach of its contract. But the defendants did not elect to take that course. They chose for reasons which they must have deemed sufficient at the time to submit to the company's demand and pay the increased price rather than rely upon their strict rights under the existing contract. . . . [I]t is plain that then, whether they chose to rely upon their contract or not, it could have been of little or no value to them. Unexpected and extraordinary circumstances had rendered the contract worthless; and they must either make a new arrangement, or, in insisting on holding the ice company to the existing contract, they would ruin the ice company and thereby at the same time ruin themselves. It would be very strange if under such a condition of things the existing contract, which unexpected events had rendered of no value, could stand in the way of a new arrangement, and constitute a bar to any new contract which should provide for a price that would enable both parties to save their interests.

Watkins & Sons, Inc. v. Carrig, 91 N.H. 459, 21 A.2d 591 (1941). Plaintiff entered into a written contract to excavate a cellar for Defendant for a specified price calculated on the basis of the units of material to be excavated. When Plaintiff began digging, he quickly hit solid rock and notified the Defendant. Plaintiff and Defendant then orally agreed that Plaintiff would continue the excavation but at a new, higher rate for any rock removed. Ultimately, two thirds of the excavation was rock subject to the higher excavation rate. When Defendant refused to pay the higher price, Plaintiff sued to enforce the oral agreement. A referee concluded that the oral agreement superseded the original written agreement, that in effect, the parties agreed to rescind the written agreement and then entered into the oral agreement as though it were the only agreement. Accordingly, the referee recommended a judgment for the Plaintiff. Defendant appealed, arguing that the record did not support the referee's finding that the parties had two separate transactions, but that they had one, the written agreement. Defendant further argued that the oral agreement was not enforceable because Plaintiff was already obligated to excavate "all material" under the written contract, and any oral modification lacked new consideration from Plaintiff in return for Defendant's promise to pay more. The court, however, held for the Plaintiff, concluding that the oral agreement to pay the higher price was enforceable. The court stated that it was unimportant whether the new agreement followed rescission of the written agreement or was a modification of the written agreement. The court reasoned:

> On insistent request by the plaintiff, the defendant granted relief from the burden by a promise to pay a special price which overcame the burden. The promise was not an assumption of the burden; the special price was fair and the defendant received reasonable value for it. . . .

> The basic rule that a promise without consideration for it is invalid leads to its logical application that a promise to pay for what the promisor already has a right to receive from the promisee is invalid. The promisee's performance of an existing duty is no detriment to him, and hence nothing is given by him beyond what is already due the promisor.

> Conceding that plaintiff threatened to break its contract because it found the contract to be improvident, yet the defendant yielded to the threat without protest, excusing the plaintiff, and making a new arrangement. Not insisting on his rights but relinquishing them, fairly he should be held to the new agreement. The law is a means to the end. It is not the law because it is the law, but because it is adapted and adaptable to establish and maintain reasonable order. If the phrase justice according to law were transposed into law according to justice, it would perhaps be more accurately expressive.

NOTES & QUESTIONS

1. Although the *Watkins & Sons* court considered the distinction unimportant in that case, modifications of contracts should generally be distinguished from "rescissions." A rescission occurs when parties agree to release each other of their respective obligations under an existing contract. The rescission itself is another contract. The consideration for such a rescission is each party's agreement to forbear from enforcing the obligations incurred under the original contract, although additional consideration is sometimes provided. Modification, on the other

hand, occurs when the parties agree to alter the terms of their agreement, but retain a commitment to be bound albeit on somewhat different terms. Courts also use the term "rescission" to describe a possible remedy; that is, restoring a party to the position the party occupied before consideration was exchanged. However, this use of "rescission" is a misnomer, and in fact the proper term for the remedy is "specific restitution."

2. Is *Schwartzreich v. Bauman-Basch, Inc.* an example of a rescission or a modification? Is the court's characterization of the facts, specifically its finding that the parties simultaneously rescinded their old agreement and entered into a new one, a fiction designed to avoid the pre-existing legal duty rule?

3. Do you agree with the court's decision in *Goebel v. Linn*? Did Belle Isle Ice Company engage in the "hold up game" against Goebel? What public policy objectives does the court's decision serve or disserve?

4. Do you agree with the court's decision in *Watkins & Sons, Inc. v. Carrig*? Were the circumstances significantly different from the situation in *Goebel?* What public policy objectives are served or disserved by the court's decision?

5. At traditional common law, an employment contract for an indefinite or undetermined duration is presumed to be "at will"; that is, the employee is free to quit for any reason at any time and the employer is free to terminate the employee for any reason at any time. *See* G. Berendt, Employment Contracts in Illinois, Contracts and Sale of Goods (IICLE 1990, 1993). The at-will employment relationship was extensively qualified during the twentieth century by legislation and case law. For example, many employees are now protected by legislation which prohibits their discharge due to race, religion, ethnic and national origin, gender, age, disability, union activity and, in some locations, sexual orientation. Although the basic common law doctrine of employment at will remains valid in the absence of these specific statutory prohibitions, employment at will has been eroded in some jurisdictions by recognition of the tort of retaliatory discharge, implied covenants of good faith, and/or employer commitments found in employment manuals, handbooks or policies. *See* M. Polelle & B. Ottley, 1 Illinois Tort Law, Retaliatory Discharge and Good Faith Dealing, §§ 13.01-13.11 (2d ed. 1993).

In *Duldulao v. St. Mary of Nazareth Hospital,* 115 Ill. 2d 482, 505 N.E.2d 314 (1987), the Illinois Supreme Court held that an employee who would otherwise have been at will enjoyed certain rights recited in an employment manual. The employer had discharged the employee without following the employment manual's provisions, which stated that after a probation period employees could only be terminated after progressive discipline, proper notice and investigation. The court stated:

> [W]e hold that an employee handbook or other policy statement creates enforceable contractual rights if the traditional requirements for contract formation are present. First, the language of the policy statement must contain a promise clear enough that an employee would reasonably believe that an offer has been made. Second, the statement must be disseminated to the employee in such a manner that the employee is aware of its contents and reasonably believes it to be an offer. Third, the employee must accept the offer by commencing or continuing to work after learning of the policy statement. When these conditions are present, then the employee's contin-ued work constitutes consideration for the promises contained in the

statement, and under traditional contract principles a valid contract is formed.

Applying these principles, the court concluded the employee handbook in question created an enforceable right to the recited disciplinary procedures before discharge and that the employer had breached a contract by terminating the employee without adhering to those procedures. The court noted that "the handbook contains no disclaimers to negate the promises given."

After *Duldulao,* some Illinois employers attempted to insert disclaimers into employment manuals they had already delivered to their employees, raising issues of proper modification and the pre-existing legal duty rule. Consider the following case.

DOYLE v. HOLY CROSS HOSPITAL
682 N.E.2d 68 (Ill. App. 1997),
aff'd, 708 N.E.2d 1140 (1999)

CAHILL, Justice:

Plaintiffs appeal a trial court dismissal of their complaint. . . . They allege defendant terminated their employment in violation of the terms of defendant's employee handbook. The trial court relied on the second district decision in *Condon v. American Telephone & Telegraph Co.,* 210 Ill. App. 3d 701, 569 N.E.2d 518 (1991), which held that an employer could unilaterally modify an existing contract to claim a contract no longer exists. . . .

Plaintiffs are nurses and former employees of Holy Cross Hospital. Mary Doyle and Leni Serra were hired in 1960 and 1968, respectively. Susan Valderrama and Valerie Zorek were hired in 1972. In 1971 Doyle and Serra received employee handbooks which set out certain policies of the hospital. These policies were in effect when the handbooks were given to Valderrama and Zorek in 1972. Plaintiffs' complaint relies upon policy number 7-G titled "Economic Separation," which reads in part:

> Holy Cross Hospital is committed to providing a working environment where employees feel secure in their job. We understand that job security is important to an employee and to that employee's family. There are instances, though, that for economic or other reasons it becomes apparent that the permanent elimination of departments, job classifications and/or jobs must be made, and there is no reasonable expectation that employees affected could be placed in other positions in the hospital or be recalled for work in one year or less. To ensure that the economic separation is handled in an objective, structured and consistent way, the following policies will be followed in determining which employees will be affected. 1. Job Classification 2. Length of Continuous Hospital Service 3. Ability and Fitness to Perform the Required Work

> *   *   *

> Because of the special needs of our patients, the following factors will be used in an economic separation affecting R.N.'s: 1. Nursing Areas of Expertise 2. Length of Service Within Each Area of Expertise 3. Ability and Fitness to Perform the Required Work

* * *

Employees affected by an economic separation will be placed on a priority rehire list and will be contacted by the Human Resources Department if a position becomes available for which the separated employees may be eligible through experience, training, education and/or other qualifications. Priority rehire consideration shall be for a period of one year.

In 1983 Holy Cross added policy 5-I. That policy, titled "Employment Relationship," reads:

The Personnel Policies and other various Hospital employee and applicant communications are subject to change from time to time and are not intended to constitute nor do they constitute an implied or express contract or guarantee of employment for any period of time. The employment relationship between the Hospital and any employee may be terminated at any time by the Hospital or the employee with or without notice.

In November 1991 Holy Cross terminated the plaintiffs. Plaintiffs filed a complaint for wrongful discharge, alleging breach of contract and promissory estoppel. They allege in their complaint that Holy Cross violated policy 7-G because:

a) there was in fact no permanent elimination of any departments, job classifications or jobs; b) there were other positions available on November 1, 1991, which plaintiffs could fill, but Holy Cross failed and refused to employ them in these positions; c) other employees with less continuous hospital service were retained; and d) more than one year has passed since plaintiffs were terminated, and subsequent to November 1, 1991, Holy Cross has had positions for which they were eligible through experience, training, education and qualifications, but Holy Cross has failed and refused to offer them any such positions.

Holy Cross filed a motion to dismiss the complaint. . . . Holy Cross argued that plaintiffs were at will employees and that economic separation policy 7-G no longer constituted an enforceable contractual right because the hospital amended its handbook. The trial court followed the decision in *Condon v. American Telephone & Telegraph Co.*, 210 Ill. App. 3d 701, 569 N.E.2d 518 (1991), and granted defendant's motion to dismiss.

The plaintiff in *Condon* argued that his employer breached an employment contract when it demoted him without following the procedures set out in personnel and management training manuals. After the plaintiff was hired, the employer inserted disclaimers in the manuals. The plaintiff argued that the disclaimers were invalid because they were not contained in the original manuals he received when hired. The second district court rejected the plaintiff's argument and held "an employer may unilaterally alter existing policies to disclaim those policies in order to prevent contractual obligations from arising under *Duldulao*." *Condon*, 210 Ill. App. 3d at 705. The *Condon* court reasoned that, because the plaintiff continued to work after the disclaimers were inserted in the handbook, he was bound by them. Explicit in the court's holding is that the plaintiff's continued performance constituted consideration for the contract modification. The court reached this conclusion based upon a reading of *Duldulao* in which it found implicit support. The *Condon* court wrote:

The implied contract which arises under the *Duldulao* doctrine is unilateral in nature. In setting out its test for contract formation, the *Duldulao* court states in part three of the test that the employee accepts the offer by working or continuing to work. [Citation.] The only way an employee could accept an offer by continuing to work is if the employee was already employed and the employer altered an existing policy. Implicit in this requirement is that the employer may unilaterally change its own policies. *Condon*, 210 Ill. App. 3d at 708.

We respectfully disagree with this analysis of *Duldulao*. In that case, our supreme court applied traditional requirements for contract formation to determine whether an employee handbook creates an enforceable contract-offer, acceptance, and consideration. *Duldulao v. St. Mary of Nazareth Hospital Center*, 115 Ill. 2d 482, 505 N.E.2d 314 (1987). The court held "an employee handbook or other policy statement creates enforceable contractual rights if the traditional requirements for contract formation are present." *Duldulao*, 115 Ill. 2d at 490. Three requirements must be met for an employee handbook or policy statement to form a contract. First, the language of the policy statement must contain a promise clear enough that an employee would reasonably believe an offer has been made. Second, the statement must be disseminated to the employee in such a manner that the employee is aware of its contents and reasonably believes it to be an offer. Third, the employee must accept the offer by: "commencing or continuing to work after learning of the policy statement." . . . The *Duldulao* court then held: "When these conditions are present, then the employee's continued work constitutes consideration for the promises contained in the statement, and under traditional principles a valid contract is formed." *Duldulao*, 115 Ill. 2d at 490.

The *Condon* court read the . . . language above to implicitly include a subsequent disclaimer of the policy statement, followed by the employee remaining on the job. There was no reason for the supreme court in *Duldulao* to so infer or hold. The issue of a subsequent disclaimer was not an issue in the case. . . . We turn now to whether the language of the employee handbook in this case contains a promise which is sufficiently clear and definite to constitute a contractual offer. It is a question of law. . . .

We find that policy 7-G of the employee handbook set out above, as a matter of law, meets the test in *Duldulao* for contract formation. Policy 7-G can be understood to convey a clear offer by Holy Cross to relinquish the right to terminate at will. The requirements for contract formation were met for plaintiffs Doyle and Serra in 1971 and plaintiffs Valderrama and Zorek in 1972. Under *Duldulao* their work constituted their acceptance and the consideration to form the contracts. The defendant does not dispute this.

The issue before us is whether the disclaimer, added in 1983, which stated that Holy Cross could terminate "any employee . . . at any time," is a legally binding change which altered plaintiffs' employment status and returned them to the status of employees at will. Plaintiffs argue that defendant's unilateral modification of the contract is unenforceable because the requisite consideration is lacking. Defendant, citing *Condon*, argues that plaintiffs' continued work after the unilateral modification of the contract in 1983 constitutes the consideration to make the disclaimer binding.

When an employment agreement is terminable at will, it may be modified by the employer as a condition of its continuance. . . . This principle is the foundation of the reasoning in *Duldulao* that an employee's continuation of work constitutes consideration for the employer's offer to modify the employment contract. But, in this case, plaintiffs' employment contracts were not terminable at will. When they were given their handbooks, the hospital gave up the right to terminate plaintiffs at will and promised to follow handbook policy in job termination. That promise became a contractual obligation as we read *Duldulao*.

The 1983 disclaimer, which stated that Holy Cross employees were once again terminable at will, was an attempt to modify an existing contract between Holy Cross and plaintiffs. Traditional contract principles allow parties to modify their contract, if there is consideration to support the modification. . . . Consideration consists of some right, interest, profit or benefit accruing to one party, or some forbearance, detriment, loss or responsibility given, suffered or undertaken by the other. . . . If parties to a contract agree to a modification, consideration is usually found to exist where the obligations of both parties are varied. A modification solely for the benefit of one of the parties is unenforceable.

We do not reach the conclusion of the court in *Condon*. The court never explains how it is possible, under traditional contract principles, for an employee to revert to at will status through the unilateral act of the employer. We are not the first court to question *Condon*'s reasoning. *See Robinson v. McKinley Community Services, Inc.*, 19 F.3d 359 (7th Cir. 1994). The court in *Robinson* stated:

> The *Condon* court relied on *Duldulao*. But *Duldulao* did not alter basic rules of contract modification. *Duldulao* merely held that if an employer embodies a clear and definite promise in its employee handbook, then an offer has been made. *Condon* also relied on *Bartinikas v. Clarklift of Chicago North, Inc.*, 508 F. Supp. 959 (N.D. Ill. 1981). However, *Bartinikas* recognized that in Illinois, "an employer acting ex parte, without the consent of the employee, cannot modify the terms of the employment contract." *Bartinikas*, 508 F. Supp. at 961. *Robinson*, 19 F.3d at 364.

We will not infer, as suggested in *Condon*, acceptance and consideration because the plaintiffs continued to work. Plaintiffs were not then employees at will. If, as Holy Cross argues, plaintiffs' continued work amounts to acceptance and consideration for the "loss" of their right under the Economic Separation policy, then the only way plaintiffs could preserve and enforce their contractual rights would have been to quit working after Holy Cross unilaterally issued the disclaimer. This would make the promise by Holy Cross not to terminate, except under the terms of the Economic Separation policy, illusory. The illusion (and the irony) is apparent: to preserve their right under the Economic Separation policy the plaintiffs would be forced to quit.

We believe this analysis avoids an illogical result: by continuing to work, plaintiffs continued to perform their duties and assert their rights under the existing contract, which promised that Holy Cross would follow specific procedures for job termination. Plaintiffs received no benefit and Holy Cross suffered no detriment when Holy Cross modified the employee contract to attempt to make plaintiffs terminable at will. There was no bargained for exchange to support plaintiffs' purported relinquishment of the protections they were entitled to under the existing contract. The modification by Holy Cross was solely for the benefit of

Holy Cross and is unenforceable as to plaintiffs.

Reversed and remanded.

NOTES & QUESTIONS

1. *Drafting Exercise*: If you represented the employer in *Doyle v. Holy Cross Hospital*, how would you advise your client to proceed with respect to employees hired in the future? Redraft the separation policy to accomplish your client's objectives.

2. *Drafting Exercise*: If you represented the employer in *Doyle v. Holy Cross Hospital*, how would you advise your client to proceed with respect to its employees hired when the separation policy was in force? Is there anything the employer can do to modify or eliminate the commitments it entered into under the separation policy? Draft a letter to the present employees proposing a modification.

ANGEL v. MURRAY
113 R.I. 482, 322 A.2d 630 (1974)

ROBERTS, Chief Justice:

This is a civil action brought by Alfred L. Angel and others against John E. Murray, Jr., Director of Finance of the City of Newport, the city of Newport, and James L. Maher, alleging that Maher had illegally been paid the sum of $20,000 by the Director of Finance and praying that the defendant Maher be ordered to repay the city such sum. The case was heard by a justice of the Superior Court, sitting without a jury, who entered a judgment ordering Maher to repay the sum of $20,000 to the city of Newport. Maher is now before this court prosecuting an appeal.

The record discloses that Maher has provided the city of Newport with a refuse collection service under a series of five-year contracts beginning in 1946. On March 12, 1964, Maher and the city entered into another such contract for a period of five years commencing on July 1, 1964, and terminating on June 30, 1969. The contract provided, among other things, that Maher would receive $137,000 per year in return for collecting and removing all combustible and noncombustible waste materials generated within the city.

In June of 1967 Maher requested an additional $10,000 per year from the city council because there had been a substantial increase in the cost of collection due to an unexpected and unanticipated increase of 400 new dwelling units. Maher's testimony, which is uncontradicted, indicates the 1964 contract had been predicated on the fact that since 1946 there had been an average increase of 20 to 25 new dwelling units per year. After a public meeting of the city council where Maher explained in detail the reasons for his request and was questioned by members of the city council, the city council agreed to pay him an additional $10,000 for the year ending on June 30, 1968. Maher made a similar request again in June of 1968 for the same reasons, and the city council again agreed to pay an additional $10,000 for the year ending on June 30, 1969.

The trial justice found that each such $10,000 payment was made in violation of law. His decision, as we understand it, is premised on two independent grounds.

First, he found that the additional payments were unlawful because they had not been recommended in writing to the city council by the city manager. Second, he found that Maher was not entitled to extra compensation because the original contract already required him to collect all refuse generated within the city and, therefore, included the 400 additional units. The trial justice further found that these 400 additional units were within the contemplation of the parties when they entered into the contract. It appears that he based this portion of the decision upon the rule that Maher had a preexisting duty to collect the refuse generated by the 400 additional units, and thus there was no consideration for the two additional payments. . . .

It is generally held that a modification of a contract is itself a contract, which is unenforceable unless supported by consideration. In *Rose v. Daniels*, 8 R.I. 381 (1866), this court held that an agreement by a debtor with a creditor to discharge a debt for a sum of money less than the amount due is unenforceable because it was not supported by consideration.

Rose is a perfect example of the preexisting duty rule. Under this rule an agreement modifying a contract is not supported by consideration if one of the parties to the agreement does or promises to do something that he is legally obligated to do or refrains or promises to refrain from doing something he is not legally privileged to do. . . . In *Rose* there was no consideration for the new agreement because the debtor was already legally obligated to repay the full amount of the debt.

Although the preexisting duty rule is followed by most jurisdictions, a small minority of jurisdictions, Massachusetts, for example, find that there is consideration for a promise to perform what one is already legally obligated to do because the new promise is given in place of an action for damages to secure performance. *See Swartz v. Lieberman*, 323 Mass. 109, 80 N.E.2d 5 (1948). . . . *Swartz* is premised on the theory that a promisor's forbearance of the power to breach his original agreement and be sued in an action for damages is consideration for a subsequent agreement by the promisee to pay extra compensation. This rule, however, has been widely criticized as an anomaly. *See* Calamari & Perillo, *supra*, § 61; Annot., 12 A.L.R. 2d 78, 85-90 (1950).

The primary purpose of the preexisting duty rule is to prevent what has been referred to as the "hold-up game." . . . A classic example of the "hold-up game" is found in *Alaska Packers' Ass'n v. Domenico*, 117 F. 99 (9th Cir. 1902). There 21 seamen entered into a written contract with Domenico to sail from San Francisco to Pyramid Harbor, Alaska. They were to work as sailors and fishermen out of Pyramid Harbor during the fishing season of 1900. The contract specified that each man would be paid $50 plus two cents for each red salmon he caught. Subsequent to their arrival at Pyramid Harbor, the men stopped work and demanded an additional $50. They threatened to return to San Francisco if Domenico did not agree to their demand. Since it was impossible for Domenico to find other men, he agreed to pay the men an additional $50. After they returned to San Francisco, Domenico refused to pay the men an additional $50. The court found that the subsequent agreement to pay the men an additional $50 was not supported by consideration because the men had a preexisting duty to work on the ship under the original contract, and thus the subsequent agreement was unenforceable.

Another example of the "hold-up game" is found in the area of construction contracts. Frequently, a contractor will refuse to complete work under an unprofitable contract unless he is awarded additional compensation. The courts have generally held that a subsequent agreement to award additional compensation is unenforceable if the contractor is only performing work which would have been required of him under the original contract. . . .

These examples clearly illustrate that the courts will not enforce an agreement that has been procured by coercion or duress and will hold the parties to their original contract regardless of whether it is profitable or unprofitable. However, the courts have been reluctant to apply the preexisting duty rule when a party to a contract encounters unanticipated difficulties and the other party, not influenced by coercion or duress, voluntarily agrees to pay additional compensation for work already required to be performed under the contract. For example, the courts have found that the original contract was rescinded, *Linz v. Schuck*, 106 Md. 220, 67 A. 286 (1907); abandoned, *Connelly v. Devoe*, 37 Conn. 570 (1871), or waived, *Michaud v. MacGregor*, 61 Minn. 198, 63 N.W. 479 (1895).

Although the preexisting duty rule has served a useful purpose insofar as it deters parties from using coercion and duress to obtain additional compensation, it has been widely criticized as a general rule of law. With regard to the preexisting duty rule, one legal scholar has stated:

> There has been a growing doubt as to the soundness of this doctrine as a matter of social policy. . . . In certain classes of cases, this doubt has influenced courts to refuse to apply the rule, or to ignore it, in their actual decisions. Like other legal rules, this rule is in process of growth and change, the process being more active here than in most instances. The result of this is that a court should no longer accept this rule as fully established. It should never use it as the major premise of a decision, at least without giving careful thought to the circumstances of the particular case, to the moral deserts of the parties, and to the social feelings and interests that are involved. It is certain that the rule, stated in general and all-inclusive terms, is no longer so well-settled that a court must apply it though the heavens fall. 1A Corbin, *supra*, § 171; *see also* Calamari & Perillo, *supra*, § 61.

The modern trend appears to recognize the necessity that courts should enforce agreements modifying contracts when unexpected or unanticipated difficulties arise during the course of the performance of a contract, even though there is no consideration for the modification, as long as the parties agree voluntarily.

Under the Uniform Commercial Code, § 2-209(1), which has been adopted by 49 states, "[a]n agreement modifying a contract [for the sale of goods] needs no consideration to be binding." *See* G.L. 1956 (1969 Reenactment) § 6A-2-209(1). Although at first blush this § appears to validate modifications obtained by coercion and duress, the comments to this § indicate that a modification under this § must meet the test of good faith imposed by the Code, and a modification obtained by extortion without a legitimate commercial reason is unenforceable. The modern trend away from a rigid application of the preexisting duty rule is reflected by [§ 89(a)] of the American Law Institute's Restatement Second of the Law of Contracts, which provides:

> A promise modifying a duty under a contract not fully performed on either side is binding (a) if the modification is fair and equitable in view of circumstances not anticipated by the parties when the contract was made. . . .

We believe that [section 89(a)] is the proper rule of law and find it applicable to the facts of this case. . . . It not only prohibits modifications obtained by coercion, duress, or extortion but also fulfills society's expectation that agreements entered into voluntarily will be enforced by the courts. . . . section [89(a)], of course, does not compel a modification of an unprofitable or unfair contract; it only enforces a modification if the parties voluntarily agree and if (1) the promise modifying the original contract was made before the contract was fully performed on either side, (2) the underlying circumstances which prompted the modification were unanticipated by the parties, and (3) the modification is fair and equitable. . . .

The evidence, which is uncontradicted, reveals that in June of 1968 Maher requested the city council to pay him an additional $10,000 for the year beginning on July 1, 1968, and ending on June 30, 1969. This request was made at a public meeting of the city council, where Maher explained in detail his reasons for making the request. Thereafter, the city council voted to authorize the Mayor to sign an amendment to the 1964 contract which provided that Maher would receive an additional $10,000 per year for the duration of the contract. Under such circumstances we have no doubt that the city voluntarily agreed to modify the 1964 contract.

Having determined the voluntariness of this agreement, we turn our attention to the three criteria delineated above. First, the modification was made in June of 1968 at a time when the five-year contract which was made in 1964 had not been fully performed by either party. Second, although the 1964 contract provided that Maher collect all refuse generated within the city, it appears this contract was premised on Maher's past experience that the number of refuse — generating units would increase at a rate of 20 to 25 per year. Furthermore, the evidence is uncontradicted that the 1967-1968 increase of 400 units "went beyond any previous expectation." Clearly, the circumstances which prompted the city council to modify the 1964 contract were unanticipated.[4] Third, although the evidence does not indicate what

---

[4] [4] The trial justice found that section 2(a) of the 1964 contract precluded Maher from recovering extra compensation for the 400 additional units. Section 2(a) provided: "The Contractor, having made his proposal after his own examinations and estimates, *shall take all responsibility for, and bear, any losses resulting to him in carrying out the contract;* and shall assume the defence of, and hold the City, its agents and employees harmless from all suits and claims arising from the use of any invention, patent, or patent rights, material, labor or implement, by or from any act, omission or neglect of, the Contractor, his agents or employees, in carrying out the contract.". . . The trial justice, quoting the italicized portion of § 2(a), found that this section required that any losses incurred in the performance of the contract were Maher's responsibility. In our opinion, however, the trial justice overlooked the thrust of § 2(a) when read in its entirety. It is clearly a contractual provision requiring the contractor to hold the city harmless and to defend it in any litigation arising out of the performance of his obligations under the contract, whether a result of affirmative action or some omission or neglect on the part of Maher or his agents or employees. We are persuaded that the portion of § 2(a) specifically referred to by the court refers to losses resulting to Maher from some action or omission on the part of his own agents or employees. It cannot be disputed, however, that any losses that resulted from an increase in the cost of collecting from the increased number of units generating refuse in no way resulted from any action on the part of either Maher or his employees. Rather, whatever losses he did entail by reason of the requirement of such extra collection resulted from actions completely beyond his control and thus unanticipated.

proportion of the total this increase comprised, the evidence does indicate that it was a "substantial" increase. In light of this, we cannot say that the council's agreement to pay Maher the $10,000 increase was not fair and equitable in the circumstances. The judgment appealed from is reversed, and the cause is remanded to the Superior Court for entry of judgment for the defendants.

NOTES & QUESTIONS

1. Were the circumstances which led to the distress of Maher in *Angel v. Murray* truly unanticipated? If not, are there any good reasons for enforcing the parties' modified contract? Are there any good reasons for denying enforcement to the modified agreement?

2. *Drafting Exercise*: Could the parties in *Angel v. Murray* have avoided the need to modify their contract by drafting it to make allowance for the changed circumstances? Had you represented Maher or the city of Newport, how would you have drafted the refuse collection contract to avoid the costly litigation they incurred in the taxpayers' suit?

3. Had Maher performed the refuse collection services for the entire contract term before requesting the additional $10,000 for collection at the 400 new dwelling units, would a promise by the city to pay the additional $10,000 be enforceable?

4. If Maher had refused to collect any refuse during the term of the original contract until the city agreed to pay $10,000 for collection at the additional dwelling units, would a promise by the city to pay the additional amount be enforceable?

5. If Maher had picked up refuse everywhere in the city but at the additional dwelling units, but demanded an additional $10,000 for collection at those additional dwellings, would a promise by the city to pay the additional amount have been enforceable?

PROBLEM

Barry Landers may be the best running back in professional football. For nearly ten years he has led the league in rushing yards and he has been selected to the starting all-pro team every year. However, under the long-term contract he signed with his team, the Cheetahs, he is not among the five highest paid running backs in the league. Now, the Cheetahs have re-signed their under-achieving quarterback to a contract which will pay him more than Landers, and Landers is incensed. Landers has refused to suit up for the new football season until the Cheetahs tear up his old contract, which has three more years to run, and sign a new contract paying Lander's more than the second-rate quarterback and as much as another top running back, Emmitt Schmidt, earns for the Cheetah's rivals, the Cowguys. The Cheetahs relent, tear up Lander's old multiyear deal and sign a new agreement paying him as much as Emmitt Schmidt for the next three years. Landers rejoins the Cheetahs but suffers a career-ending leg injury in the season's first game when the Cheetahs' quarterback backs into him during a blitz. The Cheetahs continue to pay Landers but only what he would have earned under his original contract. If Landers sues for the additional amount he would be paid under the new contract, who will prevail?

E. ILLUSORY PROMISES

A statement or manifestation which appears to be a promise but in fact is empty of commitment is said to be "illusory" and cannot serve as consideration. For example, your contracts professor says, "In return for your promise to pay me $100, I promise to teach you the law governing illusory promises tomorrow if I feel like it." Your professor has retained the volition or discretion not to perform at all, therefore, her promise lacks commitment and cannot serve as consideration. On the other hand, if your professor promises to teach you the law of illusory contracts tomorrow "unless it rains," the condition governing her performance is outside her control and her promise may serve as consideration for your promise to pay her.

Sections 76 and 77 of the RESTATEMENT (SECOND) OF CONTRACTS are instructive concerning illusory promises. They provide:

Section 76. Conditional Promise

(1) A conditional promise is not consideration if the promisor knows at the time of making the promise that the condition cannot occur.

(2) A promise conditional on a performance by the promisor is a promise of alternative performances within Section 77 unless occurrence of the condition is also promised.

Section 77. Illusory and Alternative Promises

A promise or apparent promise is not consideration if by its terms the promisor or purported promisor reserves a choice of alternative performances unless:

(a) each of the alternative performances would have been consideration if it alone had been bargained for; or

(b) one of the alternative performances would have been consideration and there is or appears to the parties to be a substantial possibility that before the promisor exercises his choice events may eliminate the alternatives which would not have been consideration.

In an effort to facilitate transactions and vindicate the parties' intentions, some courts have moved away from strict application of the illusory promise doctrine by implying commitments from the circumstances surrounding transactions which would otherwise be unenforceable due to one or more illusory promises.

Strong v. Sheffield, 144 N.Y. 392, 39 N.E. 330 (1895). The defendant's husband had a debt which was past due to the plaintiff. Defendant signed and delivered a promissory note to the plaintiff as security for her husband's debt. Plaintiff agreed that in return for defendant's note he would "hold [the note] until such time as I want my money." The plaintiff did not attempt to collect for about two years, but when plaintiff sought to collect, defendant claimed they had no contract because plaintiff's promise to forbear from collecting was illusory. The court agreed and held there was no contract. The court explained:

It would have been no violation of the plaintiff's promise if, immediately on receiving the note, he had commenced suit upon it. Such a suit would have been an assertion that he wanted the money, and would have fulfilled the condition of forbearance. The debtor and the defendant, when they became parties to the note, may have had the hope or expectation that forbearance would follow, and there was forbearance in fact. But there was no agreement to forbear for a fixed time, but an agreement to forbear for such time as the plaintiff should elect. The consideration is to be tested by the agreement, and not by what was done under it. . . .

DiBennedetto v. DiRocco, 372 Pa. 302, 93 A.2d 474 (1953). Defendants entered into a written agreement to sell certain real estate to the plaintiff. Their agreement contained the following provision: "In the event that the buyer cannot make the settlement, he may cancel this agreement, without any further liability on his part, and deposit money returned." When the defendants refused to convey title, plaintiff sued for specific performance. Defendant argued that the agreement was unenforceable because plaintiff's promise to buy the property was illusory. However, the court found plaintiff's promise not to be illusory and granted specific performance. The court explained:

> The . . . question in the case is whether plaintiff. . . had an absolute, arbitrary right to cancel the agreement without any further liability on his part. We think that he had no such right. The determinative, crucial word in that regard is "cannot". "Cannot" connotes, not unwillingness, but inability. . . . If defendants had brought action against plaintiff to compel performance of his agreement to purchase the property he could have successfully defended only by proving that he was unable to complete the transaction, not merely that he did not desire to do so. . . . The agreement constituted, therefore, a contract binding on both parties alike, and did not lack mutuality of obligation.

OFFICE PAVILION SOUTH FLORIDA, INC. v. ASAL PRODUCTS, INC.
849 So. 2d 367 (Fla. App. 2003)

WARNER, Judge:

Appellee, ASAL Products, Inc. ("ASAL"), an office supply wholesaler, sued appellant, Office Pavilion, an office supply company, for breach of a contract to supply chairs. Office Pavilion contended that the contract was unenforceable, as it was not supported by consideration and was indefinite. The trial court denied all motions directed to the enforceability of the contract, and after trial, the jury returned a substantial verdict in favor of ASAL. We hold, however, that the contract for the purchase of chairs was not enforceable and reverse.

Office Pavilion ("Pavilion") is a subsidiary of Herman Miller, Inc., a corporation which manufactures and distributes office furniture throughout the United States and Europe and is the exclusive distributor of Herman Miller office products in South Florida. Bernd Stier is a German wholesaler and reseller of office furniture and equipment mainly in Germany but also in other parts of Europe. Stier hired Oliver Asel, a former employee of Pavilion, and the two formed ASAL in Florida in order to facilitate purchasing Herman Miller keyboard trays from Pavilion to resell to Stier's customers in Europe.

Asel contacted Pavilion's sales manager, Gary Kemp, to negotiate a contract for the sale of keyboards. After months of negotiations, on December 23, 1998, they entered into a two-year contract for keyboard trays. The contract provided, in part:

2. Purpose of Contract:

The parties agree that the purpose for entering into this agreement is for Pavilion to supply and ASAL to purchase from Pavilion products known as keyboard trays, and accessories for those keyboard trays.

3. Delivery Times:

Pavilion agrees to supply ASAL with keyboard trays & accessories ordered by ASAL within 30 days of receipt of any orders up to 2,000 units per month and any accessories ordered by ASAL to supplement ordered units.

A "unit" is defined, for purposes of this contract as a keyboard tray. An accessory is not a "unit" for purposes of calculating minimum and maximum order quantities.

4. Quantities:

ASAL agrees to order a minimum of 1,000 units per year. Pavilion agrees to supply ASAL with any and all quantities ordered by ASAL up to a maximum of 2,000 units per month plus the accessories for those ordered units.

The contract further provided that the unit price would be established by a separate writing, which included volume discounts. ASAL placed three orders for keyboard trays in amounts between 100 and 150, for which ASAL timely paid and Pavilion timely delivered.

Approximately a month after the contract was signed, ASAL became interested in expanding its contract to include Herman Miller's Aeron chair, and Asel commenced negotiations with Kemp for this modification. While these negotiations were proceeding, ASAL marketed the chair in January and February, in addition to the keyboard tray, to determine demand for the chair. On March 11, 1999, Kemp forwarded ASAL a letter regarding amending the parties' contract for the keyboard trays to include the Aeron chairs. The letter included the price for two Aeron chair models and indicated:

The terms and conditions of the December 23, 1998 Contract and Amendment will apply to these chairs except for Paragraph 3 and 4, Delivery Times and Quantities. The following paragraph shall be added to the Contract and Amendment:

Aeron Chair Delivery Times:

Pavilion agrees to supply ASAL with Aeron chairs ordered by ASAL within its established manufacturing lead times. The lead time will normally be 6 weeks from receipt of orders until shipment to Pavilion. Shorter lead times are also available depending upon order quantity and fabric selection.

Like the keyboards, the attached price list allowed for volume discounts on the chairs. Later, the parties signed an addendum memorializing the pricing structure.

After the letter regarding the chairs was sent, ASAL purchased six chairs from Pavilion to display at a trade show in Germany. The show was such a success that ASAL immediately reevaluated its sales forecast and requested a meeting with Kemp. Asel wanted 2,450 chairs to cover sales orders from the show plus 30 chairs to use as samples. However, while ASAL wanted the chairs, it did not include a deposit with its order or specify model numbers for the chairs. Kemp replied that it could not fill the order because Herman Miller International would not approve the sale. Pavilion had authority from Herman Miller to supply its products to ASAL only for sale in Germany, and ASAL was expanding outside of Germany, contrary to Kemp's understanding of their original contract negotiations.

ASAL filed a breach of contract action, claiming as damages its lost profits for all expected sales under the contract for its two-year duration. While Pavilion admitted the existence of the keyboard contract, it defended against the much larger chair contract, contending that the agreement lacked consideration.

At trial, Kemp testified that he drafted the letter and addendum to expand the contract between the parties to include the chairs. He explained that the quantity paragraph from the keyboard tray contract was specifically excluded in his March 11th letter because "there was no minimum order quantities that were promised or that we agreed to for pricing for discounting purposes." He further explained that:

> Furniture industry agreements to purchase. [sic] They are not — They don't require you to purchase unless it would specifically say you agree to by [sic] X amount. So historically what it is is [sic] it's a license — it's a hunting license, if you will, is what we used to call them in the industry, to try to go after business, but with no promise that you'd ever see any business from it.

However, Kemp said that even with the lack of a quantity term provision, if Pavilion received an order from ASAL, Pavilion would fill it "within whatever terms." Basically, with a hunting license, Pavilion "had no expectations of what would come from it." Based upon his negotiations with Asel, Kemp did not know when or if ASAL ever was going to place these orders because Asel had been indicating for several months that the "orders were coming."

Asel testified that he brought an order for 2,480 chairs and a check for $633,000 to the meeting with Kemp regarding the chairs. However, Kemp informed him that Herman Miller would not approve the agreement. Kemp then advised Asel to submit a smaller order, and Asel modified the amount to 1,000 chairs with a $255,000 deposit. However, that order also was not accepted. Kemp denied that Asel ever presented the $633,000 check at the meeting at which Kemp informed Asel of Herman Miller's rejection of his order. As to the smaller order, Asel's check for $255,000 was returned for insufficient funds, after which Pavilion rejected the order.

After the trial court denied Pavilion's motion for directed verdict with regard to the enforceability of the contract and on the speculative nature of the lost profits, the jury awarded ASAL $4,000,000 in damages. From this verdict and resulting judgment, Pavilion appeals.

Pavilion contends that the chair contract between the parties was legally unenforceable for lack of consideration. We agree. While the contract for keyboards obligated ASAL to purchase a minimum of 1,000 keyboards a year from Pavilion, there was no minimum quantity term for the chairs. Essentially, Pavilion agreed to fill orders as made by ASAL, but ASAL had no obligation to place any orders at all. As Kemp said, the "agreement" was a "hunting license" which allowed ASAL to look for customers of Pavilion's merchandise and then to place orders when it found them.

It is a fundamental principle of contract law that a promise must be supported by consideration to be enforceable. *See* RESTATEMENT (SECOND) OF CONTRACTS § 17 (1981) ("The formation of a contract requires a bargain in which there is a manifestation of mutual assent to the exchange and a consideration"). Moreover, a modification of a contract must be supported with consideration. . . . In a contract where the parties exchange promises of performance, "if either of those promises is illusory or unenforceable then there is no consideration for the other promise." *Allington Towers N., Inc. v. Rubin*, 400 So. 2d 86, 87 (Fla. 4th DCA 1981). As stated by the Court of Appeals for the Eleventh Circuit applying Florida law:

> If, however, "one of the promises appears on its face to be so insubstantial as to impose no obligation at all on the promisor — who says, in effect, 'I will if I want to' " — then that promise may be characterized as an "illusory" promise. . . . An illusory promise does not constitute consideration for the other promise, and thus the contract is unenforceable against either party. *Johnson Enter. of Jacksonville, Inc. v. FPL Group, Inc.*, 162 F.3d 1290, 1311 (11th Cir. 1998) (citations omitted).

The RESTATEMENT OF CONTRACTS illustrates these contract principles. Section 75 acknowledges that "a promise which is bargained for is consideration if, but only if, the promised performance would be consideration." RESTATEMENT (SECOND) OF CONTRACTS § 75 (emphasis added). However, the RESTATEMENT further provides in section 77, "[a] promise or apparent promise is not consideration if by its terms the promisor or purported promisor reserves a choice or alternative performances." The commentary to this section explains:

> Words of promise which by their terms make performance entirely optional with the "promisor" do not constitute a promise. . . . Where the apparent assurance of performance is illusory, it is not consideration for the return promise. RESTATEMENT *supra* at § 77 comment a (citation omitted).

As appellant noted in its brief, the RESTATEMENT contains an example of illusory promises explaining this principle which is analogous to the alleged contract between Pavilion and ASAL.

> A offers to deliver to B at $2 a bushel as many bushels of wheat, not exceeding 5,000 as B may choose to order within the next 30 days. B accepts, agreeing to buy at that price as much as he shall order from A within that time. B's acceptance involves no promise by him, and is not consideration. RESTATEMENT, *supra* at § 77 comment. a, illus. 1.

Similarly, Pavilion agreed to sell to ASAL any chairs it chose to order at the price set forth in the price list. While ASAL may have agreed, its acceptance involved no promised performance and therefore did not constitute consideration to support the contract modification for the Aeron Chairs.

ASAL responds by maintaining that mutuality of obligation is unnecessary where other consideration is present in the contract; yet, it fails to point to any other consideration. It first cites to the parties' mutual promises in paragraph two of the contract for Pavilion to supply, and ASAL to buy, the chairs. Without the ensuing quantity term or price term, however, this "mutual promise" is illusory and unenforceable. Next, it maintains the consideration was the benefit Pavilion received from ASAL's ongoing marketing efforts and sales of the chairs. This "benefit" also does not constitute consideration. First, the contract does not obligate ASAL to market the chairs. Second, marketing the chairs actually benefits ASAL where it obtains orders from it. ASAL's marketing efforts did not obligate Pavilion to sell the chairs. *See, e.g., Gull Lab., Inc. v. Diagnostic Tech.,* Inc., 695 F. Supp. 1151, 1154 (D. Utah 1988) (holding agreement to actively market product did not supply consideration where contract failed to include requirement that purchaser had any obligation to buy a minimum quantity of product). Finally, ASAL asserts its implied promise to place future orders was consideration. Were that the case, then any promise to place orders with no obligation to do so would constitute consideration. The case law cited above rejects such an illusory promise.

Next, the parties' contract is unenforceable for lack of an essential term, the quantity of chairs ASAL must order. That a quantity term is essential to a contract for the sale of goods is illustrated by Florida's statute of frauds provisions adopted from the Uniform Commercial Code. § 672.201(1), FLORIDA STATUTES (1997), provides that a contract for the sale of goods in excess of $500 must be in writing to be enforceable. "A writing is not insufficient because it omits or incorrectly states a term agreed upon but the contract is not enforceable under this paragraph beyond the quantity of goods shown in such writing." *§ 672.201(1)* (emphasis added). Therefore, without a quantity term, this contract would be unenforceable under this section. *See Merritt-Campbell, Inc. v. RxP Products, Inc.,* 164 F.3d 957, 962 (5th Cir. 1999) ("The only term that must appear in a writing to support an enforceable contract for the sale of goods is the quantity term."). Contrary to ASAL's argument, that pursuant to the statute the contract may still be enforceable if the parties admit the existence of the contract, the statute actually provides that a contract is enforceable, "if the party against whom enforcement is sought admits in his or her pleading, testimony or otherwise in court that a contract for sale was made, but the contract is not enforceable under this provision beyond the quantity of goods admitted." *§ 672.201(3)(b)* (emphasis added). Not only did Pavilion not admit to an enforceable contract with respect to the sale of chairs, it did not admit any quantity of chairs governed by the contract. Therefore, the contract could not be enforceable under this exception.

Because the chair contract was illusory and unenforceable, and Pavilion did not breach the keyboard contract, the trial court erred in denying Pavilion's motion for directed verdict. We therefore reverse the final judgment and direct entry of a judgment in favor of Pavilion.

NOTES & QUESTIONS

1. In *Office Pavilion South Florida, Inc. v. ASAL Products, Inc.,* the court concluded that the chair contract was illusory and unenforceable. What was the controlling difference between the acknowledged contract for sale of keyboards and the unenforceable contract for sale of chairs?

2. Did the court thwart the parties' intentions by denying enforcement of the chairs sales agreement? Are there good reasons to deny enforcement of this agreement? Are there better reasons to enforce the chairs sales agreement?

3. Strict observance of the illusory promise doctrine may hinder modern transactions. For example, requirements or needs contracts under which a purchaser promises to buy all its needed materials, goods or services from a single provider, have become common in modern trade, but would be unenforceable under a strict application of the illusory promise doctrine because the purchaser might decline to buy anything from the seller. The trend in twentieth-century jurisprudence was to facilitate transactions by identifying the parties' intentions and then enforcing them to the extent possible. Consistent with this objective, courts have devised methods and rationales for enforcing many agreements which would have been denied enforcement for lack of "mutuality" under the traditional common law.

Wood v. Lucy, Lady Duff-Gordon, 222 N.Y. 88, 118 N.E. 214 (1917). Defendant, Lucy, Lady-Duff Gordon, was a fashion designer who was much in vogue in the early twentieth century. In an effort to profit from her fame, she employed the plaintiff, Otis F. Wood. Under their agreement, Wood had an exclusive right, subject to approval, to place her name on the designs of others, and he also had the exclusive right to sell her designs and to license others to market her designs. In return, Wood promised her one-half of all profits from any contracts he made and to provide her a monthly account of all money he received. Their contract was for a one-year term, and then year to year unless terminated by ninety days notice. Wood sued Lucy, Lady Duff-Gordon alleging she breached their contract by placing her name on other products without sharing the profits with him. Lucy, Lady-Duff Gordon defended on the ground that Wood did not bind himself to do anything. The court disagreed and held for plaintiff Wood. Justice Cardozo, speaking for the court, wrote:

> It is true that he does not promise in so many words that he will use reasonable efforts to place the defendant's endorsements and market her designs. We think, however, that such a promise may fairly be implied. The law has outgrown its primitive stage of formalism when the precise word was the solemn talisman, and every slip was fatal. It takes a broader view to-day. A promise may be lacking, and yet the whole writing may be "instinct with an obligation," imperfectly expressed. . . . If that is so, there is a contract. . . .

Reviewing the terms of the parties' agreement, Justice Cardozo continued:

> Her sole compensation for the grant of an exclusive agency is to be one-half of all the profits resulting from the plaintiff's efforts. Unless he gave his efforts, she could never get anything. Without an implied promise, the transaction cannot have such business "efficacy as both parties must have intended that at all events it should have." . . . His promise to pay the defendant one half of the profits and revenues resulting from the exclusive agency and to render accounts monthly, was a promise to use reasonable efforts to bring profits and revenues into existence.

BONNER v. WESTBOUND RECORDS, INC.
76 Ill. App. 3d 736, 394 N.E.2d 1303 (1979)

SIMON, Presiding Justice:

The defendants Westbound Records, Inc. (Westbound) and Bridgeport Music, Inc. (Bridgeport) appeal from a summary judgment in favor of the plaintiffs. The circuit court held that two contracts dated March 24, 1972 between the defendants and a rock music performing group known as The Ohio Players, of which the plaintiffs were members, were void and unenforceable. Westbound's business is making master recordings and selling them to others for production and distribution. The agreement between Westbound and The Ohio Players (the recording agreement) required The Ohio Players to make records exclusively for Westbound for a 5-year period. Bridgeport is in the business of owning and licensing copyrights to music compositions. The agreement between Bridgeport and The Ohio Players (the publishing agreement) provided that Bridgeport would employ The Ohio Players as authors and arrangers so long as the recording agreement was in existence, and that The Ohio Players would render these services exclusively for Bridgeport. Both agreements provided they were to be governed by and construed in accordance with Michigan law. The capital stock of both Westbound and Bridgeport was owned by the same person.

In the 21 months immediately following the execution of the recording agreement, The Ohio Players recorded four single records and two albums for Westbound. They were successfully distributed on a national basis, and one of the records, FUNKY WORM, was the recipient of a gold record, which in the record industry symbolizes sales in excess of $1,000,000. During the months these recordings were being made, Westbound advanced $59,390 for costs of recording sessions for The Ohio Players, artwork, travel expenses, and recording session wages paid to The Ohio Players. In addition, Westbound and Bridgeport advanced $22,509 to enable The Ohio Players to pay income taxes they owed and to settle litigation against them. Neither of the defendants was obligated to make the latter advances. The Ohio Players had no personal obligation to repay these advances; under the recording agreement and the publishing agreement, Westbound and Bridgeport could recoup the advances they made only out of royalties payable to The Ohio Players.

In January 1974, five of The Ohio Players, the plaintiffs in this case, repudiated the recording agreement, and signed an agreement with Phonogram, Inc. and Unichappell (hereinafter collectively referred to as Mercury Records), competitors of Westbound, to record exclusively for Mercury Records under the "Mercury" label. On March 8, 1974, they filed this action seeking a judgment declaring that the recording agreement was invalid and unenforceable, and that, consequently, they were no longer obligated to record for Westbound. . . . Proceeding to the merits, the plaintiffs contend that the recording agreement is unenforceable because no consideration passed from Westbound to The Ohio Players for their agreement to record exclusively for Westbound. Plaintiffs emphasize especially that the recording agreement lacked mutuality because even though The Ohio Players were obligated to make a minimum number of recordings, Westbound was not required to make even a single recording using The Ohio Players. . . .

Contrary to the conclusion reached by the circuit court judge, it is our view that consideration passed to The Ohio Players when they accepted $4,000 to enter into the agreements. The fact that this payment was made by Westbound and Bridgeport by a check containing the notation that it was "an advance against royalties" does not disqualify the payment from being regarded as consideration. If sufficient royalties were not earned to repay Westbound the $4,000, The Ohio Players would not have been obligated to return it. By making the $4,000 advance, Westbound suffered a legal detriment and The Ohio Players received a legal advantage. . . . Therefore, under both Michigan and Illinois law, the $4,000 payment constituted valid consideration. . . . It is not the function of either the circuit court or this court to review the amount of the consideration which passed to decide whether either party made a bad bargain . . . unless the amount is so grossly inadequate as to shock the conscience of the court. . . . The advance The Ohio Players received, taken together with their expectation of what Westbound would accomplish in their behalf, does not shock our conscience. On the contrary, to a performing group which had never been successful in making records, Westbound offered an attractive proposal. The adequacy of consideration must be determined as of the time a contract is agreed upon, not from the hindsight of how the parties fare under it. . . .

Even had the defendants not made the $4,000 advance, the plaintiffs could not prevail. The circuit court judge erred in finding that "there was no obligation on the part of the defendants to do anything under their respective agreements" with The Ohio Players. During the first 21 months after the date of the recording agreement, Westbound expended in excess of $80,000 to promote The Ohio Players and to pay their taxes and compromise litigation against them, and during this period the performers recorded four single records and two albums. The consistent pattern of good faith best efforts exerted by the parties during the first third of the term of the agreements demonstrates that they intended to be bound and to bind each other. Even contracts which are defective due to a lack of mutuality at inception may be cured by performance in conformance therewith.

Disregarding the performance under the agreements, the conclusion that the parties intended to be and were mutually obligated is also compelled by the rule that the law implies mutual promisees to use good faith in interpreting an agreement and good faith and fair dealing in carrying out its purposes. . . . *Wood v. Lucy, Lady Duff-Gordon*, 222 N.Y. 88, 118 N.E. 214 (1917). In *Wood v. Lucy*, an often cited decision, the plaintiff, a dress manufacturer, obtained exclusive rights to market dresses designed by the defendant, a prominent designer, in return for the plaintiff's agreement to pay the designer one-half of its profits. The designer endorsed fabrics and dresses of plaintiff's competitors, and defended the plaintiff's suit for damages by contending, as the plaintiffs in this case argue, that the contract lacked mutuality because it did not require the plaintiff to do anything. Mr. Justice Cardozo speaking for the New York Court of Appeals rejected this argument, saying:

> [The defendant insists] that the plaintiff does not bind himself to anything. *It is true that he does not promise in so many words that he will use reasonable efforts to place the defendant's indorsements and market her designs. We think, however, that such a promise is fairly to be implied.* The law has outgrown its primitive stage of formalism when the precise word was the sovereign talisman, and every slip was fatal. It takes a broader view today. A promise may be lacking, and yet the whole writing may be "instinct with an obligation," imperfectly expressed. . . . If that is

so, there is a contract. . . . (Emphasis added.)

Justice Cardozo relied upon features identical with those included in the recording agreement as a basis for implying that the manufacturer had a contractual obligation. Referring to the manufacturer's exclusive privilege to market the designer's creations, the court reasoned that absent the manufacturer's efforts, the designer would have had no right to market her own fashions. Justice Cardozo explained the significance of this factor: "We are not to suppose that one party was to be placed at the mercy of the other.". . .

The court noted that it was to be assumed that the plaintiff's business organization would be used for the purpose for which it was adapted, to manufacture and distribute the designer's creations. The court also regarded as relevant that the designer's compensation depended upon the manufacturer's efforts. The court next stressed the duty of the manufacturer to account for profits, commenting that this obligation supported the conclusion that the manufacturer had an obligation to use reasonable efforts to bring profits and revenues into existence. . . .

Courts in Illinois have consistently required contracting parties to use their best efforts to effectuate the intent of the parties. In *Dasenbrock v. Interstate Restaurant Corp.* (1972), 7 Ill. App. 3d 295, 287 N.E.2d 151, a lease conditioned the obligation to pay rent upon the tenant obtaining certain licenses and permits for the premises. The tenant justified his nonpayment of rent by his failure to obtain the required permits and licenses. The court held that the lease contained an implied promise by the tenant to act in good faith and use reasonable efforts to obtain such licenses and permits within a reasonable time. The court went on to hold that the tenant's failure to make any effort to obtain such permits over a 2-year period while paying no rent was a breach of the lease which rendered him liable for all of the accrued rent. And in *Martindell v. Lake Shore National Bank* (1958), 15 Ill. 2d 272, 154 N.E.2d 683, the court said:

> Every contract implies good faith and fair dealing between the parties to it, and where an instrument is susceptible of two conflicting constructions, one which imputes bad faith to one of the parties and the other does not, the latter construction should be adopted.

The plaintiffs attempt to distinguish *Wood v. Lucy*. . . . First, they contend that the agreements in this case resulted in the transfer of their total creative efforts, while the designer in *Wood v. Lucy* transferred only limited rights. The reverse is true. The designer transferred not only endorsement rights, but the exclusive right to sell her designs and to license others to sell them. In other words, she transferred the identity of her creative efforts and her major source of livelihood as a dress designer. In this case, The Ohio Players retained the right to perform in nightclubs and in concerts. This is significant, for at the time these agreements were signed, the major portion of The Ohio Players' income was from their live performances rather than their recording or song-writing efforts.

Finally, plaintiffs, relying upon provisions of the recording agreement and the publishing agreement, argue that those agreements expressly negated any implied promise by defendants to perform in good faith, and *Wood v. Lucy* is, therefore, not applicable. The recording agreement provided:

Company is not obligated to make or sell records manufactured from the master recordings made hereunder or to license such master recordings or to have Artist record the minimum (number) of record sides referred to in paragraph 2(B).

The publishing agreement provided:

The extent of exploitation of any Musical Composition, including the publication of sheet music or other printed editions, or the decision to refrain therefrom, shall be entirely within the discretion of Publisher.

Plaintiffs' argument is inconsistent with the meaning of the agreements, taken in their entirety, and also is at odds with the interpretation placed upon the agreements by the parties. Neither of the above quoted provisions states that Westbound and Bridgeport may sit idly by for 5 years, and they did not. Neither agreement states that Westbound and Bridgeport may act in bad faith. Neither provision quoted above contradicts the implied promises of good faith which we attribute to the agreements.

As we interpret the provision of the recording agreement quoted above, it states only that Westbound is not obligated to record the full minimum number of records set forth in another provision of the contract which The Ohio Players were obligated to record, or after going to the expense of making master recordings, to license them or make or sell records from the master recordings in the event the master recordings proved not to be suitable for that purpose. It does not mean, as plaintiffs urge, that Westbound is not required to make even one recording with The Ohio Players. And, the Bridgeport provision merely left to the discretion of the publisher the amount of advertising and publicity that would be given to any musical composition written by The Ohio Players. These provisions reserve to Westbound and Bridgeport discretion to control the content of recordings and the timing and number of releases. Flexibility of this type was essential in order to achieve the greatest success for The Ohio Players as well as Westbound and Bridgeport. Nothing in either the recording agreement or the publishing agreement or in the conduct of the parties demonstrates that Westbound or Bridgeport could or did use this discretion arbitrarily or in bad faith.

This interpretation of the recording agreement finds support in a seemingly unrelated provision of that agreement. The agreement was to run for an initial term of 5 years, but Westbound had the option to extend it for 2 years. If, as the plaintiffs contend, Westbound had absolutely no obligations under the contract, that extension would be practically automatic, for Westbound would have nothing to lose by exercising its option, and perhaps something to gain. The agreement would be essentially for one 7-year term, and the "option" phrasing a meaningless complication. Under our interpretation of the contract, however, the option provision makes perfect sense: Westbound could extend its right to the plaintiffs' services, but only at the cost of renewing its own obligation to use reasonable efforts on their behalf. The law prefers an interpretation that makes sense of the entire contract to one that leaves a provision with no sense or reason for being a part of a contract. . . .

In *Furrer v. International Health Assurance Co.* (1970), 256 Or. 429, 474 P.2d 759, the contract gave one of the parties absolute discretion regarding the amount of time he would spend in the performance of his duties; nevertheless, the Oregon court relied on *Wood v. Lucy* to hold there was an implied promise of good faith performance. The doctrine announced in *Wood v. Lucy* involving an implied promise of good faith performance has become such an integral part of contract law that contractual terms should not be construed to negate it where they are ambiguous or subject to a contrary interpretation. We do not regard *Wood v. Lucy* as distinguishable from this case on the grounds advanced by the plaintiffs. . . .

Because the agreements which this action involves were valid and enforceable and not susceptible of division and apportionment, the circuit court erred in granting summary judgment in favor of the plaintiffs on the various counts of the complaint seeking a declaratory judgment. . . . Order vacated and cause remanded.

NOTES & QUESTIONS

1. The Illinois appellate court's decision in *Bonner v. Westbound Records, Inc.* has been criticized by a federal court of appeals in *Beraha v. Baxter Health Care Corp.*, 956 F.2d 1436, 1445 n.7 (7th Cir. 1992). In *Beraha*, the court stated:

> In *Bonner v. Westbound Records, Inc.*, 76 Ill. App. 3d 736, 31 Ill. Dec. 926, 394 N.E.2d 1303 (Ill. App. 1979), the Illinois Appellate Court seemed to merge the concept of an implied best efforts clause and an implied covenant of good faith and fair dealing. In *Bonner*, the plaintiffs argued that their publishing and exclusive recording agreement lacked mutuality. The court relied on *Lady Duff-Gordon* (an implied best efforts clause case) as well as *Martindell* (an implied good faith and fair dealing case) and its progeny to find that even absent an advance royalty payment to the plaintiffs and the course of dealing between the parties, an implied best efforts clause would prevent the contract from failing for lack of mutuality. . . . The court also relied on the implied covenant of good faith and fair dealing to interpret other express provisions of the agreement in a manner consistent with the implied obligation to exert best efforts. Although the court correctly found that an implied best efforts obligation would have saved the contract in the absence of the advance royalty payment or course of dealing, the court's reasoning unnecessarily confused a principle of construction, good faith and fair dealing, with an independent implied obligation, best efforts. To more incisively reach the same conclusion, the court should have first reasoned that the implied best efforts obligation provided mutuality even in the absence of advance royalties and only then turned to the implied covenant of good faith and fair dealing to construe the other provisions of the contract consistent with the implied obligation to exert best efforts.

2. Is the decision in *Bonner* reconcilable with the court's decision in *Office Pavilion South Florida, Inc. v. ASAL Products, Inc.*? Could the court in *Office Pavilion South Florida, Inc. v. ASAL Products, Inc.* have used any of the devices employed by the *Bonner* court to enforce the alleged contract under which the distributor promised to sell the manufacturer's products?

Sylvan Crest Sand & Gravel Co. v. United States, 150 F.2d 642 (2d Cir. 1945). The plaintiff, a quarry owner, contracted with the United States to provide all the trap rock the government needed for an airport project. Specifically, the agreement recited that the rock was "[t]o be delivered to project as required," and "[c]ancellation by the [government] may be effected at any time." When the government failed to accept delivery of the rock, plaintiff sued for breach of their agreement. The United States argued that its promise was illusory because it could cancel the agreement at any time. The court, however, decided to give the agreement's language a "reasonable interpretation" in order to give effect to their intentions. Holding for the plaintiff, the court reasoned:

> [W]e cannot accept the contention that the defendant's power of cancellation was unrestricted and could be exercised merely by failure to give delivery orders. The words "cancellation may be effected at any time" imply affirmative action, namely, the giving of notice of intent to cancel. . . . While the phrase "at any time" should be liberally construed, it means much less than "forever." If taken literally, it would mean that after the defendant had given instructions for delivery and the plaintiff had tendered delivery in accordance therewith, or even after delivery had actually been made, the defendant could refuse to accept and when sued for the price give notice of cancellation of the contract. Such an interpretation would be not only unjust and unreasonable, but would make nugatory the entire contract, contrary to the intention of the parties, if it be assumed that the United States was acting in good faith in accepting the plaintiff's bid. The words should be so construed as to support the contract and not render illusory the promises of both parties. This can be accomplished by interpolating the word "reasonable," as is often done with respect to indefinite time clauses. . . . Hence the agreement obligated the defendant to give delivery instructions or notice of cancellation within a reasonable time after the date of its "acceptance." This constituted consideration for the plaintiff's promise to deliver in accordance with delivery instructions, and made the agreement a valid contract.

McMichael v. Price, 177 Okla. 186, 58 P.2d 549 (1936). Defendant McMichael agreed to supply sand to plaintiff Price for a period of ten years. Their written agreement specified, "in consideration of the mutual promises herein contained, [McMichael] agrees to furnish all of the sand of various grades and qualities which [Price] can sell. . . ." When McMichael failed to provide the sand, Price sued for breach of the contract. McMichael defended on the ground that there was no consideration since plaintiff had no obligation to sell sand to third parties and, therefore, did not have to buy any sand. The court, however, held there was a valid contract and affirmed a judgment for Price. The court noted that the "agreed predicate" for the parties' agreement was the fact that Price was engaged in the business of selling sand. Quoting an Illinois decision, the court stated the applicable law:

> A contract wherein defendant agreed to buy of plaintiff all its "requirements", of coal for the season at a specified price is not void for uncertainty, in that the actual amount of the requirement was not stated, it being, manifestly, the amount of coal defendant needed and used in his business during the season. If the word "requirements," as here used, is so interpreted as to mean the appellee was only to furnish such coal as appellant should require it to furnish, then it might be said that appellant was not bound to require any coal unless he chose, and that, therefore, there was a want of mutuality in the contract. But the rule is that, where the terms of a contract are susceptible of two significations, that will be

adopted which gives some operation to the contract, rather than that which renders it inoperative. A contract should be construed in such a way as to make the obligation imposed by its terms mutually binding upon the parties, unless such construction is wholly negatived by the language used. It cannot be said that appellant was not bound by the contract. It had no right to purchase coal elsewhere for its use in its business, unless, in case of a decline in the price, appellee should conclude to release it from further liability.

With respect to the agreement between McMichael and Price, the court observed that Price was an experienced sand salesman and that both parties expected him to sell a substantial amount of sand to their mutual profit. And Price did indeed make a profit on the sale of sand in the nine months immediately after the agreement was executed. The court reasoned:

> By the terms of the contract the price to be paid for sand was definitely fixed. Plaintiff was bound by a solemn covenant of the contract to purchase all the sand he was able to sell from defendant and for a breach of such covenant could have been made to respond in damages. The argument of defendant that the plaintiff could escape liability under the contract by going out of the sand business is without force in view of our determination . . . that it was the intent of the parties to enter into a contract which would be mutually binding.

Propane Industrial, Inc. v. General Motors Corp., 429 F. Supp. 214 (W.D. Mo. 1977). Plaintiff Propane Industries accepted defendant GM's purchase order, under which Propane Industries would provide GM with propane GM needed at its Fairfax plant. However, a shortage of propane and government regulations led Propane Industries to notify GM that it could not provide the propane. After the government granted GM's application for a hardship permit to be shipped propane, Propane Industries shipped propane to the Fairfax plant but charged a higher rate than the rate stated in the parties' original agreement. GM paid at the lower rate, and Propane Industries sued for the difference. Defendant GM argued that the original purchase order was a valid requirements contract whose terms governed the parties' transaction. The court disagreed, noting that:

> A "requirements" contract is generally defined as a contract in which the seller promises to supply all the specific goods or services which the buyer may need during a certain period at an agreed price in exchange for the promise of the buyer to obtain his required goods or services exclusively from the seller. Although the buyer does not agree to purchase any specific amount, the requisite mutuality and consideration for a valid contract is found in the legal detriment incurred by the buyer in relinquishing his right to purchase from all others except from the seller. . . .

> An essential element of the valid requirements contract is the promise of the buyer to purchase exclusively from the seller. . . . In the absence of such a promise, or some other form of consideration flowing from the buyer to the seller, the requisite mutuality and consideration for a requirements contract is absent. . . . The promise of the seller becomes merely an invitation for orders and a contract is not consummated until an order for a specific amount is made by the buyer. . . .

Here, GM's purchase order stated that it covered GM's "possible requirement," and that delivery was to be made "within 24 hours of Release on 'As Required' Basis." However, the court concluded that the purchase order did not contain an express promise from GM to purchase exclusively from Propane, nor could such a promise be implied from the parties' ambiguous terms. The court explained:

> A promise to purchase exclusively from plaintiff cannot be implied solely from use of the terms "requirement" and "as required" because "requirement" can mean either "all needed by defendant for the Fair-fax plant" or only "all desired by defendant from plaintiff."

> "[T]he word 'requirements' . . . is not a word of art" having the meaning attributed to it by the defendant.

LACLEDE GAS CO. v. AMOCO OIL CO.
522 F.2d 33 (8th Cir. 1975)

Ross, Circuit Judge:

The Laclede Gas Company (Laclede), a Missouri corporation, brought this diversity action alleging breach of contract against the Amoco Oil Company (Amoco), a Delaware corporation. It sought relief in the form of a mandatory injunction prohibiting the continuing breach or, in the alternative, damages. The district court held a bench trial on the issues of whether there was a valid, binding contract between the parties and whether, if there was such a contract, Ammo should be enjoined from breaching it. It then ruled that the "contract is invalid due to lack of mutuality" and denied the prayer for injunctive relief. The court made no decision regarding the requested damages. . . .

On September 21, 1970, Midwest Missouri Gas Company [now Laclede], and American Oil Company [now Amoco], the predecessors of the parties to this litigation, entered into a written agreement which was designed to provide central propane gas distribution systems to various residential developments in Jefferson County, Missouri, until such time as natural gas mains were extended into these areas. The agreement contemplated that as individual developments were planned the owners or developers would apply to Laclede for central propane gas systems. If Laclede determined that such a system was appropriate in any given development, it could request Amoco to supply the propane to that specific development. This request was made in the form of a supplemental form letter, as provided in the September 21 agreement; and if Amoco decided to supply the propane, it bound itself to do so by signing this supplemental form.

Once this supplemental form was signed the agreement placed certain duties on both Laclede and Amoco. Basically, Amoco was to "[i]nstall, own, maintain and operate . . . storage and vaporization facilities and any other facilities necessary to provide [it] with the capability of delivering to [Laclede] commercial propane gas suitable . . . for delivery by [Laclede] to its customers' facilities." Amoco's facilities were to be "adequate to provide a continuous supply of commercial propane gas at such times and in such volumes commensurate with [Laclede's] requirements for meeting the demands reasonably to be anticipated in each Development while this Agreement is in force." Amoco was deemed to be "the supplier," while Laclede was "the distributing utility." For its part Laclede agreed to "[i]nstall, own, maintain and operate all distribution facilities" from a "point of delivery" which was defined to be "the outlet of [Amoco] header piping." Laclede also promised to pay Amoco "the Wood River Area Posted Price for propane plus four cents per gallon for all amounts of commercial propane gas delivered" to it under the agreement.

Since it was contemplated that the individual propane systems would eventually be converted to natural gas, one paragraph of the agreement provided that Laclede should give Amoco 30 days written notice of this event, after which the agreement would no longer be binding for the converted development.

Another paragraph gave Laclede the right to cancel the agreement. However, this right was expressed in the following language:

> This Agreement shall remain in effect for one (1) year following the first delivery of gas by [Amoco] to [Laclede] hereunder. Subject to termination as provided in Paragraph 11 hereof [dealing with conversions to natural gas], this Agreement shall automatically continue in effect for additional periods of one (1) year each unless [Laclede] shall, not less than 30 days prior to the expiration of the initial one (1) year period or any subsequent one (1) year period, give [Amoco] written notice of termination.

There was no provision under which Amoco could cancel the agreement.

For a time the parties operated satisfactorily under this agreement, and some 17 residential subdivisions were brought within it by supplemental letters. However, for various reasons, including conversion to natural gas, the number of developments under the agreement had shrunk to eight by the time of trial. These were all mobile home parks.

During the winter of 1972-73 Amoco experienced a shortage of propane and voluntarily placed all of its customers, including Laclede, on an 80% allocation basis, meaning that Laclede would receive only up to 80% of its previous requirements. Laclede objected to this and pushed Amoco to give it 100% of what the developments needed. Some conflict arose over this before the temporary shortage was alleviated.

Then, on April 3, 1973, Amoco notified Laclede that its Wood River Area Posted Price of propane had been increased by three cents per gallon. Laclede objected to this increase also and demanded a full explanation. None was forthcoming. Instead Amoco merely sent a letter dated May 14, 1973, informing Laclede that it was "terminating" the September 21, 1970, agreement effective May 31, 1973. It claimed it had the right to do this because "the Agreement lacks 'mutuality.'" . . .

The district court felt that the entire controversy turned on whether or not Laclede's right to "arbitrarily cancel the Agreement" without Amoco having a similar right rendered the contract void "for lack of mutuality" and it resolved this question in the affirmative. . . .

A bilateral contract is not rendered invalid and unenforceable merely because one party has the right to cancellation while the other does not. There is no necessity "that for each stipulation in a contract binding the one party there must be a corresponding stipulation binding the other." *James B. Berry's Sons Co. v. Monark Gasoline & Oil Co.*, 32 F.2d 74, 75 (8th Cir. 1929). . . .

The important question in the instant case is whether Laclede's right of cancellation rendered all its other promises in the agreement illusory so that there was a complete failure of consideration. This would be the result had Laclede retained the right of immediate cancellation at any time for any reason. 1 S.

Williston, Law of Contracts § 104, at 400-401 (3d ed. 1957). However, Professor Williston goes on to note:

> Since the courts . . . do not favor arbitrary cancellation clauses, the tendency is to interpret even a slight restriction on the exercise of the right of cancellation as constituting such legal detriment as will satisfy the requirement of sufficient consideration; for example, where the reservation of right to cancel is for cause, or by written notice, or after a definite period of notice, or upon the occurrence of some extrinsic event, or is based on some other objective standard. . . .

Professor Corbin agrees and states simply that when one party has the power to cancel by notice given for some stated period of time, "the contract should never be held to be rendered invalid thereby for lack of 'mutuality' or for lack of consideration.". . . 1A A. Corbin, Corbin on Contracts § 164 at 83 (1963). The law of Missouri appears to be in conformity with this general contract rule that a cancellation clause will invalidate a contract only if its exercise is *unrestricted*. . . .

Here Laclede's right to terminate was neither arbitrary nor unrestricted. It was limited by the agreement in at least three ways. First, Laclede could not cancel until one year had passed after the first delivery of propane by Amoco. Second, any cancellation could be effective only on the anniversary date of the first delivery under the agreement. Third, Laclede had to give Amoco 30 days written notice of termination. These restrictions on Laclede's power to cancel clearly bring this case within the rule. A more difficult issue in this case is whether or not the contract fails for lack of "mutuality of consideration" because Laclede did not expressly bind itself to order all of its propane requirements for the Jefferson County subdivisions from Amoco.

While there is much confusion over the meaning of the terms "mutuality" or "mutuality of obligation" as used by the courts in describing contracts, 1 S. Williston, *supra*, § 105A, at 420-421; 1A A. Corbin, *supra*, § 152, at 2-3, our use of this concept here is best described by Professor Williston:

> Sometimes the question involved where mutuality is discussed is whether one party to the transaction can by fair implication be regarded as making any promise; but this is simply an inquiry whether there is consideration for the other party's promise. . . .

As stated by the Missouri Supreme Court:

> Mutuality of contract means that an obligation rests upon each party to do or permit to be done something in consideration of the act or promise of the other; that is, neither party is bound unless both are bound. . . . *Aden v. Dalton*, 341 Mo. 454, 107 S.W.2d 1070, 1073 (1937)

We are satisfied that, while Laclede did not expressly promise to purchase all the propane requirements for the subdivisions from Amoco, a practical reading of the contract provisions reveals that this was clearly the intent of the parties. In making this determination we are mindful of three pertinent rules of contract law. First, the contract herein consisted of both the September 21, 1970, agreement and the supplemental letter agreements, for a contract may be made up of several documents. . . . Second, "the consideration for a contract will not be held uncertain if by the application of the usual tests of construction, the court can reasonably discover to what the parties agreed." . . . Finally, "[w]here an agreement is susceptible of two constructions, one of which renders the contract invalid and the other sustains its validity, the latter construction is preferred." . . .

Once Amoco had signed the supplemental letter agreement, thereby making the September 21 agreement applicable to any given Jefferson County development, it was bound to be the propane supplier for that subdivision and to provide a continuous supply of the gas sufficient to meet Laclede's reasonably anticipated needs for that development. It was to perform these duties until the agreement was cancelled by Laclede or until natural gas distribution was extended to the development.[5]

For its part, Laclede bound itself to purchase all the propane required by the particular development from Amoco. This commitment was not expressly written out, but it necessarily follows from an intelligent, practical reading of the agreement. Laclede was to "[i]nstall, own, maintain and operate all distribution facilities from the point of delivery as defined in paragraph 3(b) . . . ." paragraph 3(b) provided: "the point of delivery shall be at the outlet of [Amoco] header piping." Also under paragraph 3(b) Amoco was to own and operate all the facilities on the bulk side of that header piping. Laclede thus bound itself to buy all its requirements from Amoco by agreeing to attach its distribution lines to Amoco's header piping; and even if a change of suppliers could be made under the contract, Laclede could not own and operate a separate distribution system hooked up to some other supplier's propane storage tanks without substantially altering the supply route to its distribution system or making a very substantial investment in its own storage equipment and site. As a practical matter, then, Laclede is bound to buy all the propane it distributes from Amoco in any subdivision to which the supplemental agreement applies and for which the distribution system has been established.

When analyzed in this manner, it can be seen that the contract herein is simply a so-called "requirements contract." Such contracts are routinely enforced by the courts where, as here, the needs of the purchaser are reasonably foreseeable and the time of performance is reasonably limited. . . . We conclude that there is mutuality of consideration within the terms of the agreement and hold that there is a valid, binding contract between the parties as to each of the developments for which supplemental letter agreements have been signed. . . .

For the foregoing reasons the judgment of the district court is reversed and the cause is remanded for the fashioning of appropriate injunctive relief in the form of a decree of specific performance. . . .

NOTES & QUESTIONS

1. *Drafting Exercise*: Although Laclede prevailed in the suit, it incurred substantial litigation expenses. If you represented Laclede, how would you redraft the agreement with Amoco to eliminate the issues which led to this costly litigation?

2. *Drafting Exercise*: Conversions to natural gas and other circumstances apparently led Amoco to conclude that the contract with Laclede was no longer profitable. If you represented Amoco, how would you redraft the agreement with

---

[5] [2] The evidence indicates that Laclede contemplates converting all of the subdivisions within 10 to 15 years, although it could not and would not commit itself to this timeframe.

Laclede to better protect Amoco's interests?

ANDREOLI v. BROWN
35 Ohio App. 2d 53, 299 N.E.2d 905 (1972)

VICTOR, Judge:

This appeal is from an order of the Court of Common Pleas of Medina County sustaining a motion filed by Donald I. Brown and Elizabeth Brown to dismiss the amended complaint filed against them, and dismissing them as parties defendant in this action.

The amended complaint alleges that:

(1) On September 13, 1961, an option agreement was entered into between the plaintiff, A. J. Andreoli, appellant herein (for convenience referred to as Andreoli), and one Herman Crane, wherein Crane agreed to sell, and Andreoli agreed to purchase, some thirty acres of land in Sharon Township, Medina County, Ohio, for $12,000; (2) the consideration for the agreement was $10; (3) the agreement contained the following provision:

> This agreement to be at the election of the seller anytime during his lifetime upon 60 day notice. At that time buyer shall complete the transaction and pay over the purchase price agreed upon. If this agreement is not exercised during seller's lifetime the buyer shall have the right to buy at the agreed price immediately thereafter. In the event of death of optioner, this option expires unless the optionee has given written notice of his exercise of the option to the executor or administrator within ninety (90) days after the appointment of such executor or administrator;

(4) during 1965 and 1966, Crane transferred the property to the defendants, Donald I. Brown and Elizabeth C. Brown, appellees herein; (5) "said defendants paid no consideration or an inadequate consideration for such conveyances to them," (6) had knowledge, at the time the deeds were given, of the agreement between Andreoli and Crane; (7) therefore, the Browns were not bona fide purchasers for value; (8) Crane died testate in 1968 and, on October 3, 1969, the defendants, Henry E. Laribee and Donald I. Brown, were appointed executors of the estate of Herman L. Crane, and are still acting as such executors; (9) on October 27, 1969, Andreoli notified the executors of his election to exercise the option, and offered to deposit the purchase price of $12,000; (10) the executors refused to convey the real property; (11) Andreoli demanded specific performance, and judgment in the amount of $50,000.

The executors did not file an answer. The Browns moved for dismissal of the action against them and, as previously indicated, the motion was sustained. It is this action in which it is claimed the trial court erred. . . .

In the case before us, Crane promised to sell the real estate in question to Andreoli for $12,200, only if he saw fit to do so, or at his "election." This is not a promise to ever sell it to Andreoli. Andreoli would only have the right to purchase if Crane desired to sell the property to him, or if Crane died still owning the property, and Andreoli gave proper notice. Nothing precluded Crane from divesting himself of the property by deed of gift, sale, or otherwise, to some person other than Andreoli. Crane's promise, under the circumstances, was not an enforceable promise, but entirely illusory in character. The judgment of the trial court that the complaint failed to state a cause of action against the appellee, Donald I. Brown and Elizabeth Brown, for which relief can be granted, is proper. We, therefore, affirm that order.

NOTES & QUESTIONS

1. Under § 202(2) of the RESTATEMENT (SECOND) OF CONTRACTS (1981), "[A] writing is interpreted as a whole, and all writings that are part of the same transaction are interpreted together." And § 203(a) of the RESTATEMENT (SECOND) states that "an interpretation which gives a reasonable, lawful, and effective meaning to all terms is preferred to an interpretation which leaves a part unreasonable, unlawful, or of no effect. . . ." Applying these aids to interpreting agreements, did the *Andreoli* court reach a correct decision?

2. The option in *Andreoli v. Brown* is peculiar. Usually, the option holder has the right to buy at a specific price during a set period, but the option holder makes no commitment to buy during the option period. Here, Andreoli was apparently committed to buy at the specified price during Crane's lifetime at Crane's election. If Crane died without having elected to sell to Andreoli during his lifetime, Andreoli could then buy the property for the agreed-upon price from Crane's estate. Is it possible to discern the intentions of the parties in *Andreoli v. Brown* based on the court's terse statement of the facts? What possible reason could Crane have had to enter into this option contract?

3. Assuming the *Andreoli v. Brown* court erred in concluding the option was unenforceable due to an illusory promise, is there some unarticulated reason to explain the court's reluctance to enforce the option?

PROBLEM

In 1966, Moe, a 79-year old widower, enticed Penny, an 83-year old married woman, to leave her husband and apartment and move in with him in a house which he owned in fee simple. In 1967, Moe deeded the fee simple title to Penny, reserving a life estate for himself. Moe and Penny continued to live together until 1970 when they argued and Penny attempted to leave the house. In a spirit of reconciliation, Moe requested that Penny remain, and they entered into a written reconciliation agreement under which they promised that during the remainder of their lifetimes, they would live together in harmony in the house, and that neither would have the right to dispossess the other from the premises. The agreement also provided that should either of them desire to separate, there was no inhibition against that person leaving the premises on his or her own volition. In 1973, Moe changed the locks and dispossessed Penny, who then sued to enforce their agreement to permit her to reside in the house. Is the reconciliation agreement enforceable? *Maszewski v. Piskadlo,* 318 So. 2d 226 (Fla. App. 1975).

CHAPTER 5

REASONABLE CERTAINTY
OF CONTRACT TERMS

Courts may be reluctant to enforce agreements if the parties have omitted material terms or left their terms uncertain, indefinite or ambiguous. When seeking to discern the parties' intentions, the courts may regard missing, uncertain, indefinite or ambiguous terms as evidence that the parties' negotiations may not have matured to the point that they possess contractual intent or have achieved mutual assent. Nevertheless, the judicial approach to uncertainty and indefiniteness has not been uniform, and in an effort to facilitate transactions, some courts show a greater willingness than others to fill in what the parties have left out or left uncertain. *See* U.C.C. § 2-204.

Some commonly found terms are material to nearly all agreements, but often the nature and circumstances surrounding the transaction, as well as the parties' expressed understandings, dictate on a case-by-case basis which terms are essential for contract formation. Once again, reasonableness is the touchstone for the determination of whether an agreement is definite in its terms. This usually means that the parties to the transaction must be identifiable along with the subject matter, quantity, duration, price, and payment provisions. Although these terms are usually set out by the offeror in the offer, they may be left to the offeree to supply in the acceptance by return promise or performance. *See* RESTATEMENT (SECOND) OF CONTRACTS § 34 (1981). Litigation of these issues most commonly arises when a party accused of breaching a contract maintains that a material term is missing or that a fatal uncertainty or ambiguity exists.

Section 33(2) of the RESTATEMENT (SECOND) OF CONTRACTS provides a two-part test for determining whether the terms of an agreement are sufficiently certain for a court to find a contract:

> The terms of a contract are reasonably certain if they provide a basis for determining the existence of a breach and for giving an appropriate remedy.

Even where the court is inclined to provide missing terms or to further define uncertain terms, a question remains concerning how the court should do so. In an effort to facilitate transactions and afford the parties the benefit of their bargain, the courts sometimes fill in the missing or uncertain terms by drawing upon common trade practices to complete the agreements. For example, the courts may examine the local custom in a particular area, previous dealings between the parties, and/or industry-wide standards. However, the courts do not always agree on the extent to which they should strive to identify the parties' intentions where the parties have failed to do so themselves. An attorney drafting an agreement must be aware of the law governing certainty of terms in the relevant jurisdiction.

Wilhelm Lubrication Co. v. Brattrud, 197 Minn. 626, 268 N.W. 634 (1936). On January 24, 1934, Wilhelm and Brattrud entered into an agreement in which Brattrud agreed to purchase 11,500 gallons of four brands of oil, and 4,000 pounds of lubricating grease. Although the agreement stated the quantity for each of the four brands of oil, it did not indicate what weight of oil would be purchased. There were seven different levels of weight to choose from, with each weight selling at a different price ranging from 21¢ to 31¢ per gallon. Approximately three weeks after making the agreement, Brattrud repudiated the agreement and Wilhelm sued for damages. The court held that there was no meeting of the minds or mutual assent of the parties to the contract with regard to the oil. The court declared that "[t]he subject matter of a contract must be definite as to quantity and price." Here, the weight of the oil controlled the price, and therefore, the price Brattrud was obligated to pay could not be ascertained under the contract until he chose a particular weight of oil. The court considered it impossible to apply any measure of damages for breach because such an action would have to rely on a missing contract price. The court concluded, "This indefiniteness and uncertainty in the contract, is fatal to the plaintiff's cause of action." However, the court did enforce the portion of the contract for 4,000 pounds of lubricating grease because the parties clearly indicated the brand, price, and quantity to be purchased.

NOTES & QUESTIONS

1. *Drafting Exercise:* If you represented the plaintiff Wilhelm, how would you draft the parties' agreement to avoid the uncertainty problem which led the court to conclude that the portion of the parties' agreement dealing with oil was unenforceable?

2. Would *Wilhelm Lubricating Co. v. Brattrud* be decided the same way today under the Uniform Commercial Code? *See* U.C.C. § 2-311.

PYEATTE v. PYEATTE
135 Ariz. 346, 661 P.2d 196 (1983)

CORCORAN, Judge:

This is an appeal by the husband from an award of $23,000 in favor of the wife as ordered in a decree of dissolution. Two issues are before us:

(1) The validity of an oral agreement entered into by the husband and wife during the marriage, hereby each spouse agreed to provide in turn the sole support for the marriage while the other spouse was obtaining further education; and, (2) whether the wife is entitled to restitution for benefits she provided for her husband's educational support in a dissolution action which follows closely upon the husband's graduation and admission to the Bar. The word "agreement" is used as a term of reference for the stated understanding between the husband and wife and not as a legal conclusion that the agreement is enforceable at law as a contract.

The husband, H. Charles Pyeatte (appellant), and the wife, Margrethe May Pyeatte (appellee), were married in Tucson on December 27, 1972. At the time of the marriage both had received bachelors degrees. Appellee was coordinator of the surgical technical program at Pima College. Appellant was one of her students. In early 1974, the parties had discussions and reached an agreement concerning postgraduate education for both of them.

Appellee testified that they agreed she "would put him through three years of law school without his having to work, and when he finished, he would put [her] through for [her] masters degree without [her] having to work." Appellant concedes the existence of an agreement. Although there was a claim by appellant that his agreement with appellee was qualified by certain contingencies, there is substantial evidence in the record to support the findings made by the trial court after the trial:

> The Court is of the opinion that there was a definite agreement that the respondent [appellant] would pay for the support of petitioner [appellee] while the petitioner [appellee] obtained her master's degree without her having to work. The Court is further of the opinion that there was no contingency expressed or implied that this would not be carried out or enforced in the event of a divorce. Petitioner [appellee] carried out her part of the agreement in supporting the respondent [appellant] while he obtained his law degree.

Appellant attended law school in Tucson, Arizona, from 1974 until his graduation. He was admitted to the State Bar shortly thereafter.

During appellant's first two years of law school appellee supported herself and appellant on the salary she earned at Pima College. During the last year, appellee lost her job, whereupon savings were used to support the couple. Although each spouse contributed to the savings, a significant amount was furnished by appellee.

After appellant's admission to the Bar, the couple moved to Prescott, Arizona, where appellant was employed by a law firm. Both parties realized that appellant's salary would not be sufficient to support the marriage and pay for appellee's education for a masters degree simultaneously. Appellee then agreed to defer her plans for a year or two until her husband got started in his legal career. In the meantime, she obtained part-time employment as a teacher.

In April, 1978, appellant told appellee that he no longer wanted to be married to her, and in June of 1978, she filed a petition for dissolution. Trial was had in March of 1979, and a decree of dissolution was granted. At the time of the trial, there was little community property and no dispute as to division of any community or separate property. Spousal maintenance was neither sought by nor granted to appellee.

The trial court determined that there was an agreement between the parties, that appellee fully performed her part of that agreement, that appellant had not performed his part of the agreement, and that appellee had been damaged thereby.

Based on appellee's expert testimony on the cost of furthering her education, in accordance with the agreement, the trial court awarded judgment of $23,000 against appellant as damages for breach of contract, with additional directions that the judgment be payable through the court clerk on a quarterly basis in a sum of not less than ten percent of appellant's net quarterly income.

The trial court directed appellant to use his best efforts to produce income and to keep accurate records of his income-producing activities, which records would be available to appellee upon request but not more frequently than on a quarterly basis. The court also retained jurisdiction of the case for the purpose of supervising the administration of the payment of the judgment and the keeping of records by the appellant. Appellant filed a timely notice of appeal from the judgment.

On appeal, appellant argues that the agreement did not rise to the level of a binding contract because, among other things, the terms thereof were not definite and could not be legally enforced. Appellee advances three theories as grounds upon which the trial court's award should be upheld:

1. The agreement between the parties was a binding contract. Appellant's failure to perform after appellee had fully performed her obligations renders appellant liable in damages. . . .

3. If the agreement is not enforceable as a binding contract, appellee is nevertheless entitled to restitution in quantum meruit to prevent appellant's unjust enrichment because he received his education at appellee's expense.

Although the terms and requirements of an enforceable contract need not be stated in minute detail, it is fundamental that, in order to be binding, an agreement must be definite and certain so that the liability of the parties may be exactly fixed. Terms necessary for the required definiteness frequently include time of performance, place of performance, price or compensation, penalty provisions, and other material requirements of the agreement. . . . In *Savoca Masonry Co. v. Homes and Son Construction Co.*, 112 Ariz. 392, 542 P.2d 817 (1975), the court found that a contractual relationship based upon an oral agreement did not exist between a general contractor and a subcontractor because "[o]nly the price and work involved were agreed upon; other provisions which might in the end have proven critical were not."

Upon examining the parties' agreement in this instance, it is readily apparent that a sufficient mutual understanding regarding critical provisions of their agreement did not exist. For example, no agreement was made regarding the time when appellee would attend graduate school and appellant would be required to assume their full support. Both parties concede that appellee could not have begun her masters program immediately after appellant's graduation because his beginning salary was not sufficient to provide both for her education and the couple's support. Appellee told appellant she was willing to wait a year or two until he "got on his feet" before starting her program. Nothing more definite than that was ever agreed upon. Furthermore, although appellee agreed to support appellant while he attended law school for three years, no corresponding time limitation was placed upon her within which to finish her education. Even if we assume that the agreement contemplated appellee's enrolling as a full-time student, the length of time necessary to complete a masters degree varies considerably depending upon the requirements of the particular program and the number of classes an individual elects to take at one time. Such a loosely worded agreement can hardly be said to have fixed appellant's liability with certainty.

The agreement lacks a number of other essential terms which prevent it from becoming binding. Appellee's place of education is not mentioned at all, yet there are masters programs available throughout the country. Whether or not they would be required to relocate in another state should she choose an out-of-state program was not agreed upon. Appellant testified at trial that "that particular problem was really never resolved." Nor was there any agreement concerning the cost of the program to which appellee would be entitled under this agreement. There can be several thousand dollars' difference in tuition, fees, and other expenses between any two masters programs depending upon resident status, public versus private institutions, and other factors. Appellant testified that at the time of the "contract," neither he nor his wife had any idea as to the specific dollar amounts that would be involved.

Appellee urges us to enforce this agreement because contracts should be interpreted, whenever reasonable, in such a way as to uphold the contract, and that this is particularly true where there has been performance by one party. We are aware of these general legal concepts, and also note that reasonableness can be implied by the courts when interpreting agreements.

The court's function, however, cannot be that of contract maker. . . . Nor can the court create a contract simply to accomplish a purportedly good purpose. . . . Our review of the record persuades us that the essential terms and requirements of this agreement were not sufficiently definite so that the obligations of the parties to the agreement could be determined: A party will not be subjected to a contractual obligation where the character of that obligation is so indefinite and uncertain as to its terms and requirements that it is impossible to state with certainty the obligations involved.

Based on its ruling that the agreement was enforceable, the trial court awarded appellee $23,000, the amount established by expert testimony as necessary to further her education in accordance with the agreement. On the basis of our determination that the agreement in this case is unenforceable, there can be no recovery for amounts necessary to further appellee's education.

NOTES & QUESTIONS

1. At the time the Pyeattes agreed to the arrangement which was the subject of their litigation in the above case, they were apparently happily married. Did they intend "contractual consequences" when they reached their understanding regarding their respective educational plans? Does the absence of definite terms suggest they had no contractual intent at the time they reached their understanding? Is the enforcement of their understanding, before or after divorce, a proper subject for judicial intervention?

2. Although the *Pyeatte* court held the parties' terms were too indefinite for an enforceable contract, the court provided a lesser recovery for Mrs. Pyeatte under an alternative theory for recovery in a portion of the decision omitted here. We shall consider that alternative in Chapter 6, Avoidance of Unjust Enrichment.

3. Although the *Pyeatte* court found the couple's terms too indefinite to enforce, many modern courts strive to facilitate transactions and to vindicate the parties' intentions by enforcing their agreements whenever possible. The courts have embraced several approaches when dealing with uncertain, ambiguous and missing terms. Consider and compare the approaches taken by the courts in the next three cases.

DEADWOOD ELKS LODGE NO. 508 v. ALBERT
319 N.W.2d 823 (S.D. 1982)

HENDERSON, Justice: . . .

William J. Albert, a/k/a W. Alberts and WABEC, Inc., (appellant) appeals from a judgment of the trial court which awarded Deadwood Lodge No. 508 Benevolent and Protective Order of Elks (appellee) $1,050 stemming from a bench trial over a dispute between the parties concerning the renewal clause of a lease agreement.

The parties to this appeal entered into a lease agreement whereby appellant would lease from appellee a building previously known as the "Ben Franklin Store" located in Deadwood, South Dakota. This lease was for a period of five years (commencing on May 31, 1975) providing for a $400 monthly rental. The main issue on appeal concerns the following provision in the lease. . .:

> Lessor [appellee] specifically agrees that Lessees [appellant] shall have the option to renew this Lease for an additional Five (5) year period from and after May 31, 1980 upon all the same terms and conditions, except for the rental consideration which the parties agree to negotiate a mutually acceptable monthly rental.

During the course of this lease, appellant made several thousand dollars worth of improvements and renovations to the leased building, which appellant used as a retail store. These improvements consisted of paneling, carpeting, refurbishment of display areas, new air conditioning and shelving.

In February of 1980 appellee informed appellant that the rent would be increased to $1,000 per month commencing at the expiration of the present lease. This being unacceptable to appellant, negotiations occurred but the parties were unable to reach a mutually acceptable agreement for renewal. The negotiations continued until the latter part of May 1980. A finding of fact was made by the trial court which specifically stated that the parties had negotiated in good faith.

A notice to quit was served upon appellant by appellee on June 3, 1980. Due to the presence of inventory in the building, however, appellant was not able to vacate until June 30, 1980, six days after appellee filed its complaint praying for $30,000 in damages to the property, possession, and $1,600 rent for willful holdover. Appellant filed an answer and counterclaim for damages in the amount of $85,000 for loss of good will, lost profit, moving expenses, business losses and additional rent incurred plus $21,000 in damages for loss of fixtures. Did the trial court err by ruling that the option to renew provision contained in the lease was unenforceable?

Appellant contends that the trial court erred by holding that the aforementioned option to renew was unenforceable. It is appellant's position that when, as here, the parties cannot agree on the amount of rent for the renewal period, the judiciary should intervene to determine and provide a reasonable amount of rent based upon current market conditions. The rationale of this position is that the parties to the lease intended, at the time the lease was entered into, to use a reasonable figure to effectuate the option to renew and, when the parties are unable to agree, a reasonable figure will be determined by the courts. By providing this figure, argues appellant, the courts will be preventing the lessor from not allowing the lessee to renew the lease by offering him an unreasonable amount (which is refused by the lessee) and then claim that the option to renew cannot be enforced due to vagueness. Appellant does not deny, however, that he is advocating a position adopted by a minority of the judiciary.

In holding that the option to renew clause was unenforceable, the trial court adhered itself to the majority school of thought which, in essence, promulgates the view that it is not a function of the courts to fix the terms of a lease for the contracting parties.

This court in *Engle v. Heier*, 173 N.W.2d 454, 456 (1970), was confronted with a situation where the parties had allegedly reached an oral agreement to enter into a written lease. In *Engle* we upheld the trial court's summary judgment that there was no oral agreement for a lease between the parties because there was no showing that the terms of the alleged oral agreement were ever settled and agreed upon. In reaching our decision, we stated:

> If it appears that any of the terms of the future lease are left open to be settled by future negotiation between the lessor and lessee "there is no complete agreement; the minds of the parties have not fully met; and, until they have, no court will undertake to give effect to those stipulations that have been settled, or to make an agreement for the parties respecting those matters that have been left unsettled." (citation omitted).

Here, the lease provides that the parties negotiate "a mutually acceptable monthly rental." The parties, however, could not agree upon a mutually acceptable monthly rental. The trial court expressly found that "the parties negotiated in good faith, but were unable to reach an agreement for renewal." We are not disposed to say that this finding was clearly erroneous. . . .

We believe that *Engle v. Heier, supra*, is dispositive of appellant's contention. Furthermore, an agreement to agree does not fix an enforceable obligation. It is indefinite, vague, and uncertain. An agreement must be sufficiently definite to enable a court to give it an exact meaning. *See* 1 WILLISTON ON CONTRACTS § 37 (3d ed. 1957). Accordingly, we hold that the trial court was not erroneous in ruling that the option to renew contained within the lease was unenforceable and, by so doing, we align ourselves with the majority view. . . .

The judgment of the trial court is affirmed.

FOSHEIM, Justice (dissenting):

While a majority of states have held that a clause giving the lessee an option to renew with the rent to be negotiated is unenforceable, the minority view has gained credible support in recent years. Courts enforcing such clauses stress that it is not a matter of rewriting or making a contract for the parties, but rather of giving effect to their obvious intent, that the rent for the renewal period be reasonable. Therefore, the majority's reliance on *Engle v. Heier*, 84 S.D. 535, 173 N.W.2d 454 (1970), is misplaced in this case where the only question is the enforcement of one clause in an existing written contract.

Courts enforcing such clauses also rely on the long-standing principle that a lease is generally construed against the landlord where the provision was obviously intended for the benefit of the lessee. Another legal principle justifying enforcement is estoppel. Often, as here, the lessee made costly improvements and worked hard to establish good will in reliance on the renewal clause. Additionally, the renewal clause is part of the consideration offered to induce the lessee to enter into the lease. The lessor benefits from this clause by receiving a higher initial rent in consideration for its inclusion in the lease and from the improvements to the property the lessee makes in reliance on, and in anticipation of his rights under, such clause. Since the lessee has paid valuable consideration for the clause it follows that he should receive the benefit of the clause upon renewal. . . .

166 MAMARONECK AVENUE CORP. v. 151 EAST POST ROAD CORP.

575 N.E.2d 104 (N.Y. 1991)

WACHTLER, Chief Judge:

In this case, we consider whether a lease renewal option that provides for arbitration if the parties cannot agree on rent for the renewal period is indefinite and therefore unenforceable. We agree with the Appellate Division that the option is not an invalid "agreement to agree" because the arbitration clause provides an objective standard for determining the amount of rent. Accordingly, the order of the Appellate Division should be affirmed.

The appellant in this proceeding is the landlord, 151 East Post Road Corp., and the respondent is the tenant, 166 Mamaroneck Avenue Corp. Both are successors in interest to parties that signed a 42-year commercial lease in 1946 for a parcel in White Plains. The term ran from January 1, 1947 to January 1, 1989. The lease gave the tenant, its successors, or assigns the "right, option and privilege" to renew the lease for another 21-year term on the same conditions and terms as those contained in the original lease except for the amount of rent. According to the agreement, if the parties were unable to agree to the rent, "the same shall be fixed by arbitration as provided for by the Civil Practice Act of the State of New York."

The tenant notified the landlord of its intention to exercise the option and renew the lease. The parties entered into negotiations but were unable to agree on a new rent for the renewal period. In November of 1986, the landlord filed a demand for arbitration with the American Arbitration Association seeking determination of the market rental value of the parcel for the 21-year renewal period. The demand was later withdrawn. In September of 1988, the landlord notified the tenant that it deemed the tenant's rights and interests in the parcel as terminating on January 1, 1989, the original expiration date set forth in the lease.

By service of notice of petition and petition verified October 19, 1988, the tenant commenced a proceeding in Supreme Court, Westchester County, for appointment of an arbitrator pursuant to CPLR 7504. The landlord cross-moved for dismissal of the proceeding for failure to state a cause of action "in that the renewal provision contained in the lease [was] an agreement to agree and [was] therefore void and unenforceable". Supreme Court granted the landlord's cross motion to dismiss the petition. The court found that the renewal term was indefinite and therefore unenforceable, relying upon this Court's holding in *Martin Delicatessen v. Schumacher* (52 N.Y.2d 105) and upon the decision of the Appellate Division in *Cobble Hill Nursing Home v. Henry & Warren Corp.* (144 A.D.2d 518). The Appellate Division reversed and granted the tenant's petition, also relying upon *Cobble Hill*, which had in the interim been reversed by this Court (74 N.Y.2d 475). We now affirm.

The doctrine of definiteness or certainty is well established in contract law. In short, it means that a court cannot enforce a contract unless it is able to determine what in fact the parties have agreed to (*see* 1 Corbin, CONTRACTS § 95 at 394). As we noted recently in *Cobble Hill*, "[i]f an agreement is not reasonably certain in its material terms, there can be no legally enforceable contract" (74 N.Y.2d, at 482, citing *Martin Delicatessen v. Schumacher*, 52 N.Y.2d, at 109; RESTATEMENT (SECOND) OF CONTRACTS § 33 [1981]). Further, "a mere agreement to agree, in which a material term is left for future negotiations, is unenforceable" (*Martin Delicatessen v. Schumacher, supra*, at 109).

This Court, however, has not applied the definiteness doctrine rigidly. Contracting parties are often imprecise in their use of language, which is, after all, fluid and often susceptible to different and equally plausible interpretations. Imperfect expression does not necessarily indicate that the parties to an agreement did not intend to form a binding contract. A strict application of the definiteness doctrine could actually defeat the underlying expectations of the contracting parties. Thus, where it is clear from the language of an agreement that the parties intended to be bound and there exists an objective method for supplying a missing term, the court should endeavor to hold the parties to their bargain. Striking down a contract as indefinite and in essence meaningless "is at best a last resort."

In *Martin Delicatessen* (*supra*), we identified two ways in which the requirement of definiteness could be satisfied in the absence of an explicit contract term: (1) an agreement could contain "a methodology for determining the [missing term] . . . within the four corners of the lease, for a [term] so arrived at would have been the end product of agreement between the parties themselves"; or (2) an agreement could "invite[] recourse to an objective extrinsic event, condition or standard on which the amount was made to depend." (*Id.*, at 110.)

We looked to these principles for guidance when we revisited the definiteness doctrine in the *Cobble Hill* case. There, the tenant had an option to purchase a nursing home owned by the defendant "at a price determined by the Department [of Health] in accordance with the Public Health Law and all applicable rules and regulations of the Department" (*Id.*, at 480). The defendant refused to sell the facility to the tenant, contending that the price term contained in the option was void for indefiniteness (*Id.*, at 481). We held the option enforceable, concluding that the parties' intent that a third person fix the sales price for the nursing home "itself provid[ed] an objective standard without the need for further expressions by the parties" (*Id.*, at 483). We noted that it was apparent from the agreement that the parties rested discretion in the Department of Health to calculate the sales price, "limited only by the requirement that it apply provisions that were suitable, pertinent and appropriate for the task at hand." (*Id.*, at 484.)

In the case now before us, we examine a contract in which the parties have expressly provided that a third party, an arbitrator, is to determine the price term in the event they are unable to reach an agreement on their own. As in *Cobble Hill*, the contract does not spell out the precise manner in which the amount of rent is to be calculated. The landlord argues that this renders the clause unenforceable. We disagree. The original parties to the lease themselves selected a process for the calculation of rent for the renewal term. They clearly intended to be bound by the arbitrator's determination. Arbitration, while a process and not a methodology per se, implicates the participation and decision making of a neutral third party. We conclude that by providing for this eventuality and agreeing to be bound by the result, the parties "invited recourse to an objective extrinsic event, condition or standard on which the amount was made to depend" (*Martin Delicatessen v. Schumacher, supra*, at 110), and that the renewal term is consequently definite and enforceable.

That the third party in this case is an arbitrator and not a governmental subdivision is of no consequence. Just as the Department of Health was circumscribed by applicable law and regulations in *Cobble Hill*, so too would the authority and discretion of an arbitrator be mapped out by State statutory and common law.

Arbitration is a favored method of dispute resolution in New York, as this Court has repeatedly held, and New York courts interfere "as little as possible with the freedom of consenting parties" to submit disputes to arbitration. . . . Additionally, the cases grant arbitrators broad authority to resolve disputes, unfettered by formal rules of law or the constraints of the traditional litigation model. . . . When the original parties to this lease consented to arbitration of a rent dispute, they necessarily entrusted the dispute to the considerable discretion of the arbitrator.

Thus, while this case is not identical to *Cobble Hill*, we believe that our reasoning in that case applies with equal force here. We do not doubt that the original parties to the lease fully intended to be bound by their agreement. The decision of these parties to submit any dispute as to the amount of rent payable during the renewal period to an arbitrator — a third party with considerable discretion, but whose discretion is delineated by law — provides an objective standard that renders the renewal clause definite and enforceable.

We have considered appellant's remaining arguments and we find them to be without merit.

Accordingly, the order of the Appellate Division should be affirmed, with costs.

MOOLENAAR v. CO-BUILD COMPANIES, INC.
354 F. Supp. 980 (D.V.I. 1973)

WARREN H. YOUNG, District Judge:

This case involves the proper construction of the renewal clause in a lease. Briefly stated, two issues are presented. First, is a valid and specifically enforceable renewal option created by a clause which leaves the rent for this period to be determined by subsequent agreement between the parties? And secondly, if the clause is valid but the parties are unable to agree on the rent, how is this rental figure to be determined? Here I must decide whether the court must look to fair market value at the time when the option is exercised, or whether the court may take a lower figure if it is shown that the parties contemplated that the land would be put to less than its most remunerative use.

The facts of this case are not in dispute. In October of 1967, plaintiff Moolenaar, a sheep and goat farmer, leased 150 acres of land from one Aurea Correa. His leasehold was to run for a period of five years with an option to renew for an additional five. Moolenaar was to pay $375 per month during the initial term, but the rent for the renewal period "shall be renegotiated."[1] Moolenaar took possession under this lease and expanded his sheep and goat farm onto the demised premises. Before the time came to exercise the renewal option, however,

---

[1] The renewal clause provides in full as follows:

> 4. OPTION OF RENEWAL: Provided that Tenant shall not be declared in default at any time during the term hereof, the Tenant shall be entitled to an option to extend the term of this lease for an additional period of FIVE (5) YEARS upon the same terms and conditions except that the rental shall be renegotiated.

Mrs. Correa sold the land to real estate speculators who in turn sold it to West Indies Enterprises, the predecessor corporation to the defendant Co-Build Companies, Inc. ("Co-Build"). The new owners nonetheless took subject to Moolenaar's rights under the pre-existing and duly recorded lease. At this point I should mention that the testimony disclosed, and I so find, that the representatives of Co-Build negotiating the purchase of the land had actual knowledge of the lease and its renewal clause. They discussed its validity or purported lack of validity with their counsel and accepted title insurance with an exception taken by the title insurer to the rights of the tenant in possession, including the lease renewal clause.

In April of 1972, some six months before the first five year term expired, Moolenaar informed Co-Build of his intention to exercise the renewal option. Co-Build expressed its willingness to extend the lease at a "renegotiated" rent of $17,000 per month. Co-Build justified this figure by the high price it had paid for the land, and by its unquestionably great value if put to industrial use. [The land is presently zoned 1-2, for light industrial use. It has considerable potential in this role, since it adjoins the Hess and Martin Marietta plants and has been appraised at $2,775,000 as of December 20, 1972. Report of Juan B. Gaztambide & Associates, Defendant's Exhibit B. Moreover, it is included in the parcel of land on which the second oil refinery may be built, and if this plan is implemented the land will automatically be rezoned I-1 for heavy industrial use.] Such a rent, however, is obviously beyond the resources of the less profitable goat husbandry business. Moolenaar therefore proposed a considerably lower figure and indicated his desire to meet for direct negotiations. All such offers were declined. Upon Co-Build's refusal to recede from its initial position, Moolenaar filed the present action for a declaratory judgment setting out the rights of the parties under the lease.

The threshold question is, of course, whether Moolenaar possesses a renewal option at all. A number of jurisdictions would hold that he does not, reasoning that a clause which neglects to stipulate the rent is void for uncertainty and indefiniteness. . . . The better view, however, would hold that such a clause intends renewal at a "reasonable" rent, and would find that market conditions are ascertainable with sufficient certainty to make the clause specifically enforceable. A number of policy considerations support this result. First, it will probably effectuate the intent of the parties better than would striking out the clause altogether. A document should be construed where possible to give effect to every term, on the theory that the signatories inserted each for a reason and if one party had agreed to the clause only in the secret belief that it would prove unenforceable, he should be discouraged from such paths. Secondly, a renewal option has a more sympathetic claim to enforcement than do most vague contractual terms, since valuable consideration will often have already been paid for it. The option of renewal is one factor inducing the tenant to enter into the lease, or to pay as high a rent as he did during the initial period. To this extent the landlord benefited from the tenant's reliance on the clause, . . . and so the tenant has a stronger claim to receive the reciprocal benefit of the option. . . . Finally, I might take note of the policy of construing ambiguities in lease agreements against the landlord, or, with more theoretical justification but little difference in practical result, against the party responsible for drafting the document.

It then remains to be determined only whether this resolution is within the powers of the Court. In the absence of an applicable statute, the RESTATEMENT OF

CONTRACTS has been designated as positive law in this jurisdiction. V.I.C. section 4 provides as follows:

> The rules of the common law, as expressed in the restatements of the law approved by the American Law Institute, and to the extent not so expressed, as generally understood and applied in the United States, shall be the rules of decision in the courts of the Virgin Islands in cases to which they apply, in the absence of local laws to the contrary.

Section 32 of the RESTATEMENT provides that a contract is valid if it is "so definite in its terms" that the "performances to be rendered by each party are reasonably certain." Under this standard the renewal clause would appear sufficiently definite to be binding. Illustration 7 in the RESTATEMENT provides as follows:

> A promises B to execute a conveyance in fee or a lease for a year of specified land and B promises A to pay therefor. Although the terms of leases and conveyances vary, the promises are interpreted as providing for documents in the form in common local use, and are sufficiently definite to form contracts.

It should be noted that this illustration refers to the promises of both parties and that B has not, unlike his practice in other illustrations, agreed to pay "a specified price." Rather, this example seems to assume that a "reasonable rent" is contemplated and that the local real estate market is well enough developed to permit this figure to be determined with fair accuracy. Illustration 10, relied upon by Co-Build, is distinguishable in that it deals with a contract for personal labor which is less susceptible to market valuation. With the blank in the renewal clause thus filled in, it becomes definite enough to be not only valid but also specifically enforceable.

Even if it were thought that the RESTATEMENT is ambiguous or silent on the precise issue sub judice, Moolenaar would still recover. In that case we must make our determination under the common law "as generally understood" in courts of other jurisdictions. . . . The rule which I have followed here is admittedly the minority view. But for the reasons which I gave in an earlier opinion, I think it is appropriate to give greater weight to recent decisions rather than weighing the authorities on a strictly numerical basis. Briefly, the common law is in a state of perpetual evolution and recent decisions will more accurately reflect the current understanding on an issue. For the issue at hand the minority view is nonetheless a widely followed one and has been gaining adherents at a rate which indicates that the common law is moving in that direction. And while, of course, not controlling here, the U.C.C. provisions on the Sale of Goods also illustrate the approach of the modern law, with its emphasis on reasonable commercial dealings and its rejection of technical requirements. 11 A V.I.C. § 2-305 provides as follows:

> (1) The parties if they so intend can conclude a contract for sale even though the price is not settled. In such a case the price is a reasonable price at the time for delivery if (a) nothing is said as to price; or (b) the price is left to be agreed by the parties and they fail to agree.

The comments to this section are also informative, and state in part as follows:

> This article rejects in these instances the formula that "an agreement to agree is unenforceable" . . . and rejects also defeating such agreements on the grounds of "indefiniteness." Instead this Article recognizes the dominant intention of the parties to have the deal continue to be binding upon

both. For all the above reasons, I hold that the renewal clause is valid and enforceable.

Given that the clause is enforceable, there remains the question of what rent Moolenaar should pay during the additional five years. As a general rule the "reasonable rent" will be established at its "fair market value," which is to say, at the highest rent which a responsible bidder is apt to offer. This in turn suggests that the leasehold should be valued at its "highest and best use," for a lessee using the land in the most intensive and remunerative way possible will be able to outbid a person who would use it less efficiently. From this Co-Build asks us to conclude that the rent should be many times higher than it had been, since the 150 acres are now zoned 1-2 and may be subdivided for light industry.

Nonetheless, I believe that Moolenaar is entitled to have the rent established at its fair value for the land as used for agricultural or animal husbandry purposes only. I conclude that this will most accurately reflect the intent of the original signatories to the lease. From the testimony presented at trial, I find that Mrs. Correa intended that Moolenaar be able to use the land for the purpose of raising sheep and goats during the renewal period, and that the rent be set at a fair value for this purpose. It is true that under this arrangement she will lose the possibility of a higher rent if circumstances changed to make a more profitable use practicable. But one purpose of a long-term lease, or of a renewal clause, is precisely to insulate the parties from such changes in circumstances. Co-Build then took title to the land subject to the provisions of the lease as outlined above.

Since the parties have been unable to agree on a fair rental value for agricultural purposes, that figure will now be determined by the Court. The testimony at trial indicated that the present rental of $375 per month is, if anything, somewhat high for grazing use. Nonetheless I must take this figure as a freely bargained one, and hence fair. I also feel that I should make a rough adjustment for intervening inflation. A round figure of $400 per month would seem appropriate in the circumstances.

For the reasons set forth in the Memorandum Opinion above, it is hereby adjudged and declared as follows: 1. The renewal clause is valid and enforceable. 2. The clause contemplates a rent for the additional term at a reasonable rate, as calculated by the value of the land for agricultural and animal husbandry purposes. 3. The fair rental in this case is $400 per month, retroactive to the end of the original five year term.

NOTES & QUESTIONS

1. Is it possible to reconcile the approaches of the courts in the preceding three cases, *Deadwood Elks Lodge*, *166 Mamaroneck Avenue Corp.* and *Moolenaar*, with each other? Are the issues the same or different in the three cases? Is it possible to explain the diverse approaches employed by the courts on the basis of factual differences in those cases?

2. The effect of missing or indefinite terms on a purported contract covered by the Uniform Commercial Code may be entirely different. Consider the following case.

NEBRASKA BUILDERS PRODUCTS CO. v. THE INDUSTRIAL ERECTORS, INC.

478 N.W.2d 257 (Neb. 1992)

HASTINGS, Chief Justice:

Appellant, Nebraska Builders Products Co. (Nebraska Builders), brought this action against the appellee, The Industrial Erectors, Inc. (Industrial), to recover the excess costs of substitute performance on an alleged purchase contract for cranes. Nebraska Builders appeals from a judgment of the trial court declaring that there was no enforceable contract between the parties but that, instead, the parties contemplated a written contract which was never executed. We reverse, and remand for further proceedings.

In early 1985, the Omaha Public Power District (O.P.P.D.) invited bids for the construction of a service center near Elkhorn, Nebraska. William Hawkins, on behalf of Nebraska Builders, an Omaha-based company engaged in the business of selling construction products, obtained the plans and specifications which identified supplies, materials, and equipment to be used in the construction of the service center. Nebraska Builders intended to submit its bid as a subcontractor or material supplier to the companies bidding for the general contract for the construction of the service center later that year. Hawkins identified many items in the plans and specifications which Nebraska Builders could potentially supply for the project, including several types of crane systems. Previously, Nebraska Builders had purchased such cranes from Industrial. Industrial is a Chicago-based company which manufactures various types of cranes and also sells cranes manufactured by others.

Hawkins contacted Timothy Brennan, Industrial's sales manager, in February 1985, to inquire if Industrial was interested in submitting a bid on the cranes. Brennan traveled to Omaha on February 28, 1985, to review the plans and specifications for the crane systems. Brennan obtained the information necessary to prepare a bid, including Section 11520 of the specifications — Material Handling and Associated Equipment. The specifications were very detailed, specifying manufacturer, model number, electrical requirements, capacity, speed, control system, and other performance characteristics. Variance in equipment had to be approved in writing by the project engineer pursuant to a procedure set forth in the specifications. Both Brennan and Hawkins were aware of this procedure.

On March 12 or 13, 1985, Brennan telephoned Hawkins and told him that Industrial would sell and install the crane systems as per specifications for a total sum of $449,920, which consisted of $399,935 for materials and $49,985 for installation. Brennan stated that there were some minor exceptions to the specifications, but those could be worked out with the O.P.P.D. engineer. Nebraska Builders submitted a bid based, in part, on Industrial's bid. On March 26, 1985, Brennan confirmed the telephone conversation with a letter to Hawkins stating Industrial's proposal.

By this letter, exhibit 14, Industrial "proposed to furnish all Crane Systems, Jib Cranes and Monorail Systems per Specification #11520 dated 2/26/85 including the three Addendums." Then followed a detailed listing of the specific items which Industrial agreed to furnish at a total material cost of $399,935, plus $49,985 if Industrial was to install the listed equipment.

William Hawkins contacted Hawkins Construction Company (Hawkins Construction), the general contractor with the lowest bid, to see if Nebraska Builders was the low bidder on any of the items Hawkins Construction had bid on. This conversation led to a period of negotiations between Industrial and Nebraska Builders. During the negotiations, Nebraska Builders put together a "package bid" and gave Hawkins Construction a lump-sum price on several items, including the cranes. Nebraska Builders alleges that upon its request Industrial reduced its bid twice. Industrial disputes the second reduction and argues that the bid was only once reduced, by $4,500. However, exhibit 46 consists of a series of adding machine tapes including notations admittedly made by Brennan of Industrial. These tapes indicate a second reduction of $26,937, with additions of $2,400 for each interlock device. As testified to by Hawkins, there were four interlock devices, and this total reduction was therefore $17,337.

At the time Nebraska Builders submitted its package bid to Hawkins Construction, William Hawkins had reviewed Industrial's proposal and knew that the items proposed were different models made by different manufacturers than those called for in the specifications; however, the proposal stated that Industrial would furnish all crane systems as required by Section 11520 of O.P.P.D.'s specifications. Hawkins was also aware that any deviations needed specific approval. He was not concerned about the deviations, since O.P.P.D. was required to accept alternatives if they were of equal quality. Since Industrial was in the business of manufacturing and selling cranes and had stated that the proposal was per specifications and any deviations from the specifications were "minor," Hawkins believed that the cranes set forth in Industrial's proposal were of equal quality, and thus, approval of the deviations would not be a problem.

During early May, Hawkins was informed by Hawkins Construction that Nebraska Builders' bid on the crane systems, as well as on various other items, was accepted. Hawkins testified that he immediately telephoned Industrial to accept Industrial's offer. He does not remember whether he talked to Brennan or Jerry Cole, the president of Industrial. Brennan testified that he did not have that conversation with Hawkins. Cole did not testify at the trial.

Although Brennan denies his having the conversation in which Nebraska Builders accepted Industrial's bid, Industrial and Nebraska Builders exchanged correspondence concerning the variance approval and exceptions to the specifications between May 31 and August 9, 1985. In a letter dated May 31, 1985, Brennan assured Nebraska Builders that Industrial had adhered to all of O.P.P.D.'s specifications in preparing its bid and that all equipment "will be equal to or better than" the equipment specified in the plans and specifications. Brennan also sent a letter dated June 10, 1985, which starts as follows: "This letter is to confirm our telecon regarding the above subject." The above-named subject in the letter was "Jib Crane, Monorails and Crane Equipment." The letter states further that Industrial is "trying to alleviate the confusion of the materials that Industrial is supplying." Brennan went on to describe the cranes "to be furnished" and concluded by stating that he hoped "this letter will alleviate any confusion regarding the materials to be furnished and we look forward to working with you on this project." The O.P.P.D. engineers for the district ultimately approved Twin City Monorail (Twin City) and Crane Manufacturing & Service Corporation, Industrial's subcontractors, as crane manufacturers.

During this same time period, Industrial repeatedly requested Nebraska Builders to issue a purchase order, written contract, or letter of intent. Nebraska Builders denied these requests, stating that a written contract would be forthcoming upon its signing a contract with Hawkins Construction. Nebraska Builders never provided Industrial with a written contract. Industrial, in turn, did not issue any written contract or purchase order to any of its suppliers and, in fact, told one supplier that a written purchase order could not be given until Industrial received one from Nebraska Builders.

Despite the fact that there was no written contract, Brennan visited Nebraska Builders' office on August 8, 1985, on behalf of Industrial. Industrial also prepared and submitted shop drawings showing the recommended foundation design and bolt locations for the various floor-mounted jib cranes included in Industrial's proposal.

Brennan sent Hawkins a letter dated July 23, 1985, to confirm a verbal conversation concerning a list of deviations from the specifications, which deviations, if changed to meet the specifications, would constitute an additional cost of an unspecified amount to Industrial's bid. Hawkins testified that he was confused when he received the letter because he had not spoken to Brennan about any deviations to the specifications other than when he got Industrial's oral bid in March 1985. Hawkins discussed the letter with Brennan during Brennan's trip to Omaha on August 8, 1985. Brennan stated that he had not included in Industrial's bid the hoists for the jib cranes and that he had forgotten to include the footwalks and handrails for the largest overhead crane. Hawkins told Brennan that he expected Industrial to supply everything called for in the specifications in accordance with its bid.

Brennan had prepared another letter, dated August 7, 1985, which purported to confirm a telephone conversation between Hawkins and Brennan. The letter informed Hawkins that in order to provide the cranes in accordance with the specifications "with no exceptions" there would be an additional cost of $167,500 to the original quotation. Brennan testified that the letter was never sent to Hawkins. Brennan further stated that he could not recall the telephone conversation referred to in his letter to Hawkins.

In September 1985, Brennan told Hawkins that Twin City, the company from which Industrial was to purchase some of the cranes, did not want to furnish the cranes. According to Brennan, Twin City felt that the specifications had been drawn up for one manufacturer.

Hawkins became concerned that Industrial was not going to perform under the alleged contract. He telephoned Cole, Industrial's president, to discuss his concerns. Cole assured Hawkins that he would discuss the matter with Twin City and attempt to get it resolved. Brennan informed Hawkins sometime between October 7 and 9 that Twin City had taken several exceptions to the specifications and that as a result Twin City's price to Industrial was going to increase by more than $100,000.

Hawkins went to Chicago on October 14, 1985, to meet with Brennan and Cole to discuss Industrial's problem with Twin City. During the meeting, Brennan and Cole showed Hawkins a breakdown of the original bid and the new costs in view of Twin City's price increase. Hawkins was informed that strict compliance with the specifications would increase the original bid by approximately $150,000, which included extra costs for the jib crane hoists and Twin City's price increase. Hawkins told Industrial that a price increase was not possible. Brennan stated that Industrial would not perform without the price increase. Discussions between Industrial and Nebraska Builders terminated. Nebraska Builders claims to have obtained performance of the contract elsewhere at an additional cost of $136,136.11.

Industrial and Nebraska Builders had no written agreement regarding the time of performance, necessity or amount of a performance bond, time of payment, or whether Industrial would be bound by the terms and conditions of the general contract. However, some of these items were discussed in Industrial's proposal letter. Nebraska Builders and Industrial contemplated entering into a written agreement which would have addressed such concerns. Hawkins testified that Nebraska Builders has a standard subcontract form which includes such terms as a complete description of work, approved variances, price, terms of payment, time of performance, performance bond, and adherence to the terms of the general contract.

The parties stipulated at trial that the dispute would be governed by the Uniform Commercial Code. Following a trial and submission to the court without a jury, judgment was entered in favor of Industrial.

In order for one to more clearly understand the issues in this case, it may be helpful to set forth that portion of the district court's order, which contains its findings:

> The Court finds that no contract existed between Nebraska Builders Products and Industrial Erectors. The Court finds that the parties had negotiated to enter into an agreement at a later time which would include among other items the delivery dates, payment schedules and specific waivers of general contractor's written requirements and specifications. In fact, each of the parties contemplated a written contract which was never entered. *Fleming Co. of Nebraska v. Michals*, [sic] 230 NW 2d (1988), 230 Neb. 753, 433 N.W.2d 505 (1988), *Nebraska Seed Co. v. Harsh*, 98 Neb. 89, [sic] 154 NW 310, 152 N.W. 310 (1915). A contract was not present in this case as a matter of law and facts.

Nebraska Builders' assignments of error can be summarized as follows: (1) The decision of the trial court is not supported by the evidence and is contrary to law; (2) the trial court erred in deciding there was no enforceable contract because the parties intended to execute a written contract at some point in the future; and (3) the trial court misapplied the Nebraska U.C.C. in its determination that no valid enforceable contract existed between Nebraska Builders and Industrial in that there was no agreement on incidental terms.

Since the parties stipulated at trial that the U.C.C. governed the dispute, this court will presume that the U.C.C. controls the case. Because of its citation to *Michals* and *Harsh* in its order, it is quite apparent that the trial court decided this case on common-law grounds and not under the U.C.C. In doing so, the district court erred.

This court has previously decided that if a contract involves both the sale of goods and services, and the parties have presented the case to the trial court and the Supreme Court on the theory that the sales article of the U.C.C. applies, this court will dispose of the case on appeal on that theory.

The first issue to be determined is whether a contract was formed between the parties. NEB. U.C.C. § 2-204 (Reissue 1980) on formation of a contract states:

> (1) A contract for sale of goods may be made in any manner sufficient to show agreement, including conduct by both parties, which recognizes the existence of such a contract.

> (2) An agreement sufficient to constitute a contract for sale may be found even though the moment of its making is undetermined.

> (3) Even though one or more terms are left open a contract for sale does not fail for indefiniteness if the parties have intended to make a contract and there is a reasonably certain basis for giving an appropriate remedy.

A contract may be found in the bargain of the parties by their language or by implication from other circumstances, such as course of dealings or usage of trade.

The conduct of the parties in the case before us would support a finding that a contract existed. Industrial submitted an oral proposal to Nebraska Builders to supply cranes for the service center in telephone calls on March 10, 1985, and on March 12 or 13. Later, Industrial confirmed the offer in a letter dated March 26, 1985, written to Hawkins by Brennan, as sales manager of Industrial. That letter consisted of seven pages and was quite explicit.

The next issue to be decided is whether the contract fails for indefiniteness. The trial court in the case at hand found that the parties had negotiated to enter into an agreement at a later time which would include among other items the delivery dates, payment schedules, and specific waivers of the specifications, and that as a result there was no contract. The trial court cited the cases *Fleming Co. of Nebraska v. Michals*, 230 Neb. 753, 433 N.W.2d 505 (1988), and *Nebraska Seed Co. v. Harsh*, 98 Neb. 89, 152 N.W. 310 (1915);. *Michals* and *Harsh*, however, are not controlling in determining what constitutes an enforceable contract under the U.C.C., since they construe contracts formed under common law.

According to § 2-204(3), a contract does not fail for indefiniteness because a term is left open, as long as the parties have intended to make a contract and there is a reasonably certain basis for giving an appropriate remedy. Cf. *Zimmerman v. Martindale*, 221 Neb. 344, 377 N.W.2d 94 (1985) (when an agreement not covered by the U.C.C. stipulates that certain terms will be settled later by the parties, such terms will not become binding unless and until they are settled by later agreement). The U.C.C. allows the courts to supply reasonable terms for those that are missing. *See* NEB. U.C.C. §§ 2-305 (Reissue 1980) (price), 2-308 (Reissue 1980) (place of delivery), 2-309 (Reissue 1980) (time of delivery), 2-310 (Reissue 1980) (payment terms), 2-503 (Reissue 1980) (tender by seller), 2-509 (Reissue 1980) (risk of loss), 2-511 (Reissue 1980) (tender by buyer), and 2-513 (Reissue 1980) (buyer's inspection). The official comment to § 2-204 states:

> If the parties intend to enter into a binding agreement, this subsection recognizes that agreement as valid in law, despite missing terms, if there is any reasonably certain basis for granting a remedy. The test is not certainty as to what the parties were to do nor as to the exact amount of damages due the plaintiff. Nor is the fact that one or more terms are left to be agreed upon enough of itself to defeat an otherwise adequate

agreement. Rather, commercial standards on the point of "indefiniteness" are intended to be applied, this act making provision elsewhere for missing terms needed for performance, open price, remedies and the like.

The only necessary term to satisfy the definiteness requirement under the U.C.C. is the quantity. *See* NEB. U.C.C. § 2-201(1) (Reissue 1980). But see NEB. U.C.C. § 2-306 (Reissue 1980). In the case at bar, the quantity requirement was satisfied, since the proposal letter listed the materials to be furnished, i.e., 14 cranes and 1 monorail. Since the conduct of the parties indicated that the parties intended to make a contract, the requirements of § 2-204(3) have been met, and the contract is not indefinite. The fact that the parties intended to execute a written agreement in the future is immaterial in this case, since the U.C.C. focuses on the parties' conduct. The trial court was therefore clearly wrong in finding that no enforceable contract existed.

The district court's finding that no contract existed was based on an erroneous application of the law controlling this case. As previously mentioned, the parties stipulated at trial that the case was governed by the U.C.C. Even if the parties had not made this stipulation, the case should have been decided under the U.C.C., since the predominant factor of the alleged contract was the sale of goods. . . . Therefore, the judgment is reversed and the cause remanded for further proceedings consistent with this opinion. Reversed and remanded for further proceedings.

NOTES

1. As illustrated by *Moolenaar,* a court willing to provide a missing term or to resolve an ambiguity in an agreement must still decide which terms govern the parties' transaction. When the parties disagree about the meaning of the terms of their agreement, Section 20 of the RESTATEMENT (SECOND) OF CONTRACTS (1981) is instructive concerning whether there is an agreement, and if there is, whose terms will prevail.

§ 20. Effect of Misunderstanding

(1) There is no manifestation of mutual assent to an exchange if the parties attach materially different meanings to their manifestations and

(a) neither party knows or has reason to know the meaning attached by the other; or

(b) each party knows or each party has reason to know the meaning attached by the other.

(2) The manifestations of the parties are operative in accordance with the meaning attached to them by one of the parties if

(a) that party does not know of any different meaning attached by the other, and the other knows the meaning attached by the first party; or

(b) that party has no reason to know of any different meaning attached by the other party, and the other party has reason to know the meaning attached by the first party.

Other sections of the RESTATEMENT (SECOND) OF CONTRACTS (1981) are also instructive when parties contest the meaning of their agreement. *See* RESTATEMENT (SECOND) OF CONTRACTS §§ 201-204 (1981).

Hurst v. W.J. Lake & Co., Inc., 141 Or. 306, 16 P.2d 627 (1932). Plaintiff and defendant were in the business of selling and buying horsemeat scraps. Plaintiff offered to sell defendant 350 tons of horsemeat scraps containing a minimum of 50% protein. Defendant accepted the offer in writing. The contract specified that the agreed-upon price was to be reduced by five dollars per ton on any scraps that were less than 50% protein. The plaintiff delivered 349.25 tons of horsemeat scraps containing the following percentages of protein: 180 tons contained in excess of 50%; 29.25 tons contained 48.66%; and 140 tons contained protein varying from 49.53% to 49.96%. The defendant paid a discounted price on 169.25 tons. The plaintiff then sued to recover the full, undiscounted value of the horsemeat scraps. The plaintiff argued that the meaning of term "minimum 50% protein" should be determined based on trade usage, which the plaintiff maintained meant no less than 49.5% protein. Holding for the plaintiff, the court required the defendant to pay the full-undiscounted price on the 140 tons of scraps containing between 49.53% and 49.96% protein. The court noted that the plaintiff and defendant were members of a trade group in which the term "minimum 50% protein" was a trade term understood to mean 49.5% or more of protein. Absent evidence to the contrary, "when tradesmen use trade terms in their dealings, they attach to them their trade significance." If the parties had no intention of using the terms for their special, trade significance, they should have so stated in their agreement. Here, they did not. The court further explained:

> In addition to the multiplicity in meaning of words set forth in the dictionaries, there are the meanings imparted to them by trade customs, local uses. . . . Thus it must be evident that one cannot understand accurately the language of such sciences and trades without knowing the peculiar meaning attached to the words which they use. It is said that a court in construing the language of the parties must put itself into the shoes of the parties. That alone would not suffice; it must also adopt their vernacular.

Frigaliment Importing Co. v. B.N.S. International Sales Corp., 190 F. Supp. 116 (S.D.N.Y. 1960). On May 2, 1957, plaintiff Frigaliment purchased a specified quantity of "U.S. Fresh Frozen Chicken, Grade A, Government inspected" from defendant International. The parties had negotiated their transaction by telegrams, mostly in German. When the first shipment arrived, Frigaliment refused to accept delivery because it expected young chickens suitable for broiling and frying, but instead the birds were "fowl" or stewing chicken. Frigaliment brought this action against International for breach of warranty. International, which had only recently entered the poultry trade, contended that the term "chicken" meant any bird of that genus that met contract specifications on weight and quality, which could include "stewing chicken" and "fowl." The court held for the defendant International. The court observed that this case illustrated Justice Holmes' remark "that the making of a contract depends not on the agreement of two minds in one intention, but on the agreement of two sets of external signs — not on the parties' having meant the same thing but on their having said the same thing." *The Path of the Law*, in Collected Legal Papers, at 178. Reviewing the evidence, the court concluded that it was clear that International believed it could meet the contract requirements by delivering stewing chicken. However, International's subjective intent would not otherwise have been significant had it not coincided with an objective meaning of the term "chicken." Here, International's subjective intent coincided with one of the dictionary meanings of "chicken," the definition in the Department of Agriculture Regulations to which the parties obliquely referred in the contract, some trade usage, and market realities. Although Frigaliment made it clear that its subjective intent was to obtain broilers and fryers, there was evidence that the market price for such birds would have been higher than the contracted price, and Frigaliment should have been aware of this. Frigaliment failed to sustain its burden of showing that the term "chicken" was used in the narrower rather than the broader sense.

2. Consider the applicability of § 20 of the RESTATEMENT (SECOND) OF CONTRACTS (1981) to the following case. You may wish to refer to the Comments and Illustrations to that section when answering the questions following the case.

Raffles v. Wichelhaus, 2 H. & C. 906 (Ex. 1864). Plaintiff Raffles agreed to sell 125 bales of Indian cotton at 17 pence per pound to defendant Wichelhaus, with payment to be made within a specified time after the arrival of the cotton in Liverpool, England. The parties' agreement provided that the cotton was "to arrive ex Peerless from Bombay." However, there were two different ships named "Peerless" regularly sailing from Bombay to England, one leaving in October and the other in December. Plaintiff Raffles shipped the cotton on the December Peerless, and defendant Wichelhaus refused to accept the cotton. Raffles sued on the alleged contract. Wichelhaus argued that it understood shipment would be on the October Peerless. Raffles argued that it was immaterial which Peerless was used, "so long as it was a ship called the 'Peerless.'" Plaintiff also argued that the words "to arrive ex Peerless" only meant that if the vessel were lost on the voyage, the contract was ended. Holding for defendant Wichelhaus, the court concluded there was "no binding contract." Because the parties meant different ships, "there was no consensus *ad idem*."

NOTES & QUESTIONS

1. Would the result in the case have been different had defendants/buyers known there were two ships "Peerless" but plaintiff knew only of the ship leaving in December?

2. If both parties knew there were two ships "Peerless" but nevertheless did not designate which ship would carry the goods, would the result have been different?

3. In the actual case, should we presume that October Peerless arrived in England before December Peerless? Does it matter? Would the result have been different if plaintiff/seller had proved December Peerless arrived first?

4. Would the result have been different if plaintiff/seller had introduced evidence that October Peerless was a luxury ship not appropriate for shipping cotton?

5. The court concluded there was no enforceable agreement in *Raffles* because of lack of mutual assent. Could the court have reached the same conclusion by finding mutual assent based on mistaken facts? What is a mutual mistake and how does it differ from a misunderstanding? Consider the following case.

SHRUM v. ZELTWANGER
559 P.2d 1384 (Wyo. 1977)

RAPER, Justice:

"What is a "cow?" This appeal comes here as an ultimate result of a dispute between plaintiffs-appellees contract buyers and defendants-appellants contract sellers of 134 "cows," over the answer to that question. The trial judge granted summary judgment to the plaintiffs for return of $6,700 they paid as a deposit on purchase of the cows and by the same summary action denied defendants' counterclaim.

While the parties fail to hone their arguments into definitive issues, there is only one question as we see it. Do the depositions in support of the motion before the district court really disclose no issue of material fact?

One significant fact is not in dispute. The parties entered into a written agreement as follows:

> Aug. 3, 1973
>
> LIVESTOCK BILL OF SALE AND CONTRACT
>
> This Certifies, that Howard Shrum of Sheridan has this day bargained and sold to Heinhold Cattle Mkt., 134 head of Cows to be delivered F.O.B. cars, on or before 17 day of Sept., 1973 at $450. per head or at $_____ per cwt., to be weighed on twelve hours overnight stand and hauled at _____ with _____ cut back. Received as part payment $6,700 balance of $53,600 to be paid on delivery. I hereby guarantee title thereto, viz:

No Hd.	Description	Brands	Location of Brands	Per Head Price
134	Hereford-Few BB Cows	9		RH

> All of above stock to be free from encumbrance, including taxes for year of delivery, and to pass federal and state inspection for interstate shipment. Health and brand certificates to be furnished purchaser, free of charge, on delivery. Above to be free of contagious disease and in merchantable condition.
>
> (Seal) /s/ Howard A. Shrum, Seller
> Witness /s/ Steve Harris
> /s/ Wm. Zeltwanger, Jr. Purchaser

Steve Harris, shown as a witness on the document, was the agent-buyer for the plaintiffs as purchasers. He negotiated the contract and was the active participant for the plaintiffs. Defendant Shrum negotiated the sale for the defendants.

From depositions on file, other peripheral circumstances are apparent. Prior to and when time for delivery arrived, defendants' cattle were in two groups, 54 at Story, Wyoming, and 80 at Otter, Montana. About two weeks before the delivery date, Harris went to Story along with a prospective buyer from his principal to look at the animals. Harris, though requested, did not inspect the Story group at the time of signing the contract. Defendant Shrum claims that at the time of the pre-delivery visit Harris said they were better than he expected. Harris claims he saw no yearling heifers. The visit is not in dispute. At the date of delivery, however, at that site, there were six or seven that had not been bred.

Harris made no examination of the cattle at Otter at any time prior to the delivery date, though at the time the contract was signed, Shrum asked Harris to inspect them, as well as those at Story. Harris said he trusted Shrum and thought no inspection necessary. Of all the cattle, at both Story and Otter, Harris refused to accept 72, as being heifers, which he claimed were not "cows" under the contract. Shrum, when testifying by deposition, claimed that at the time the contract was signed, he told Harris that he "had 134 heifers and some young cows on them"; "I told him they weren't cows, they were heifers and some young cows on them. And he said that took care of the female end of the bovine family. So, I trusted his word and left it go." Harris deposed that Shrum represented all were cows that had lost calves and he assumed he was buying bred cows.

Harris, in his deposition, further testified as follows:

> Well, it's always been my thought that a cow is a female bovine that's already had a calf. Normally they're not referred to as a cow until after they've weaned their first calf. Even at that time they were often referred to as first-calf heifers. Harris offered to take what he considered to be cows under the contract but refused the others. Shrum refused, claiming all were cows under their agreement.

The trial judge entered an order granting summary judgment for plaintiffs for the recited reason that: "There was a mutual mistake in the formation of the contract and the Plaintiffs should be entitled to judgment as a matter of law." As we read the depositions and as outlined in the foregoing narration, the district judge apparently decided that since the plaintiffs assert they intended one thing and the defendants assert they intended another, there was mutual mistake. That is not mutual mistake.

As nearly as we can determine, through search of West's Wyoming Digest, this court has not undertaken to define the expression "mutual mistake," though it has recognized that a contract may be cancelled on that ground. . . . Mutual mistake makes a contract voidable. . . . In this tribunal it has likewise been recognized that an instrument may be reformed on that ground.

"Mutual mistake" is a common utterance in the law of contracts, however, and has come to have a universal meaning. A mutual mistake is one which is reciprocal and common to both parties, each alike laboring under the same misconception in respect to the terms of the written instrument. . . . More briefly stated, it means a situation where both parties share the same misconception. 13 WILLISTON ON CONTRACTS, 3d Ed. (Jaeger) § 1550A, p. 168, and, in the same volume § 1543, p. 75, pulling its effect into play, it is said:

> Where both parties assume the existence of a certain state of facts as the basis on which they enter a transaction, the transaction can be avoided by a party who is harmed, if the assumption is erroneous.

Some courts have worded their definitions in different ways and it is probably well to set out some of those because they are clarifying. If the intention of the parties is identical at the time of the transaction, and the written agreement does not express that intention, then a mutual mistake has occurred. . . . Mutual mistake may be defined as error in reducing the concurring intention of the parties to writing. A mutual mistake exists where there has been a meeting of the minds of the parties and an agreement actually entered into but the agreement does not in its written form express what was really intended by the parties. *Sierra Blanca Sales Company, Inc. v. Newco Industries, Inc.*, 505 P.2d 867 (N.M. 1972).

The New Mexico court has used the expression "meeting of the minds." We cite the case for an occasion to update and supersede use of that well-known old contract phrase with the modern expression "mutual assent." In order for there to be a binding contract, there must be mutual assent — a mutual manifestation to the same terms. Calamari & Perillo, LAW OF CONTRACTS, HB, §§ 11 & 12, pp. 13-14. 13 WILLISTON ON CONTRACTS, 3d Ed. (Jaeger), § 1536, p. 33, refers to "meeting of the minds" as a "quaintly archaic expression." When there is mutual mistake, then there can be no mutual assent.

Since there was no mutual mistake the trial judge stated an erroneous ground for granting summary judgment. There remains a genuine dispute as to the meaning of the contract term "cows." One says it means one thing, the other, another. It must be realized that all that is before the court is the subjective expressions of the plaintiffs' buyer agent and the defendants and those expressions are at opposite poles. One or the other may or may not represent what the parties really intended by their transaction. The intent of the parties can only be ascertained by an objective not subjective approach in contract situations. The subjective intent of the parties is ordinarily irrelevant. An objective test is applied. A party's intention will be held to be what a reasonable man in the position of the other party would conclude his manifestations to mean.

The only way to shake out what the parties intended or did not intend is by the adversary process of a trial. There may have been mutual mistake but from what we have examined it seems unlikely, though we would not foreclose that conclusion. The cancellation of a written agreement is a drastic interference with the right of parties to contract. While we have authority to do so, in a proper case, a court should not compel a party to relinquish the fruits of an honestly-made contract and deprive him of its benefits in the absence of clear, convincing and well-founded evidence. The burden of proving mistake is upon the party asserting it.

Another possibility exists and that is there was unilateral mistake but even in that case, a mistake by only one of the parties ordinarily does not offer ground for avoidance of the contract or relief unless the mistake or relief is known by the other and particularly if caused by the other.

Since we decide that there was no mutual mistake as a matter of law, we must now see whether the summary judgment can be sustained on other grounds.

The whole case revolves around what the parties intended by the use of the word "cows" in describing the subject matter of the contract. Taken by itself, it has any number of meanings: WEBSTER'S THIRD NEW INTERNATIONAL DICTIONARY, UN-ABRIDGED:

> Cow: 1 a; . . . the mature female of wild or domestic cattle of the genus Bos of any of the various animals the male of which is called bull . . . b: a domestic bovine animal regardless of its sex or age (bring home the_____s).

BLACK'S LAW DICTIONARY, 4th Ed. 1951:

> "Cow. Female of bovine genus of animals. Strictly, one that has calved. Often loosely used to include heifer, or young female that has not calved. (Citing cases.)

BALLANTINE'S LAW DICTIONARY WITH PRONUNCIATIONS, 2d Ed., under the word "cow," the volume states: "See heifer." "Heifer. A female calf of the bovine species, from the end of the first year until she has had a calf; a young cow. (Citing case.)" *See also* WEST'S WORDS AND PHRASES, p. 516, under the word "cow." We can conclude that it has within the corral of this case, no plain and ordinary meaning. From the definitions, the positions of either plaintiffs or defendants could be supported. Since the term 'cows' is not clear, there must be a trial.

There are material questions of fact requiring resolution. Summary judgment should only be granted when there are no issues of material fact. . . .

Reversed and remanded for trial of the issues as we have noted and may otherwise appear.

NOTES & QUESTIONS

1. What sort of evidence would you expect the parties to introduce into the record on remand in *Shrum v. Zeltwanger*? Does Section 20 of the RESTATEMENT (SECOND) OF CONTRACTS (1981) suggest who will likely win this case on remand?

2. The *Shrum* court suggests that the parties' disagreement over the meaning of the term "cow" may have been a unilateral rather than a mutual mistake. Is the effect of a unilateral mistake different from a "misunderstanding"? *Compare* §§ 20, 152, & 153 of the RESTATEMENT (SECOND) OF CONTRACTS (1981).

3. Consistent with its heavy emphasis on facilitating commercial transactions, the U.C.C. makes it easier for a court to enforce contracts where terms are uncertain, ambiguous or even missing. *See* U.C.C. §§ 2-205, 2-208, 2-305, 2-306, 2-308, 2-309, and 2-310.

PROBLEMS

1. Architect provided professional services to Developer, designing a planned residential apartment project called Sugar Creek. Under their written agreement, Developer "agrees to pay Architect for its services a fee of $500 per apartment constructed." Although not in their written agreement, the parties understood that between 68 to 100 apartment units were to be built. Developer agreed to pay Architect periodically as construction progressed. The agreement also provided that no payment would be made unless the project proceeded into working drawings. Architect submitted preliminary drawings for use in bidding by contractors, and the Developer instructed Architect to proceed with final drawings and specifications. Initial bids from contractors were higher than expected, leading Architect to alter the final working drawings. Developer then sought new bids from interested building contractors. When the second sets of bids were also too high for Developer's budget, Developer abandoned the project without paying Architect for its services. Architect sues Developer for breach of contract. Did the parties have a contract? What, if anything should Architect recover from Developer? *See Goebel v. National Exchangors, Inc.*, 88 Wis. 2d 596, 277 N.W.2d 755 (1979).

2. Owner and Painter signed a simple, written agreement provided by Painter, which stated:

> Paul Painter agrees to paint *Otis Owner's house* at *109 Grant Street, Volo, IL.*
>
> In return, *Otis Owner* promises to pay Paul Painter $3,000.
>
> *(Otis Owner) 11/12/96*
>
> *(Paul Painter) 11/12/96*
>
> (The italicized portions of the agreement were inserted in Painter's handwriting, except for Owner's signature and the date that followed it, which were in Owner's handwriting.)

Painter asked Owner what color paint he wanted. Owner responded "The same as it is." Owner assumed Painter would paint the interior as well as the exterior, but Painter assumed he would only paint the exterior. When Painter completed the exterior he demanded payment, but Owner refused to pay until Painter painted the interior. Painter refused. Owner then hired another contractor who painted the interior for $1,000. Painter sued Owner for $3,000 and Owner countersued for $1,000. Did the parties have a contract? If so, on whose terms? Who will prevail in the suit and countersuit?

SECTION C
ALTERNATIVE THEORIES FOR RECOVERY

The materials presented to this point have focused our attention on the process of formation of traditional contracts, characterized by the prima facie elements of offer, acceptance, certainty of terms, and consideration. Throughout this next section of the book, we will put aside much of that specific analysis in order to examine two alternative theories for recovery of contract or contract-type remedies. We are about to see that under some circumstances the parties will not have arrived at a true contract, and yet the equities will suggest that recovery akin to contract remedies is in order.

CHAPTER 6

AVOIDANCE OF UNJUST ENRICHMENT

A. OVERVIEW

Traditional common law courts will enforce agreements and provide remedies for breach when they conclude that offer, acceptance, mutual assent, certainty of terms and consideration are all present. Yet courts will also confront contract disputes where the parties attempted to create a traditional contract meeting all these requirements, but have failed in that effort. In addressing these attempted, but failed contracts, courts sometimes recognized that to leave the disputing parties as they are would allow a defendant to be unjustly enriched. From this setting, courts defined and developed a legal doctrine to address and prevent such unjust enrichment. The doctrine of unjust enrichment holds that one who has been unjustly enriched at the expense of another should be required to make restitution to the other. *See* RESTATEMENT OF RESTITUTION § 1 (1937); RESTATEMENT (SECOND) OF RESTITUTION § 1 (Tent. Draft 1983).

In this same effort to prevent unjust enrichment, courts will also apply the doctrine of unjust enrichment where the parties in court made no attempt to enter into a traditional contract. Again, courts determined that leaving the parties as they were would unjustly enrich the defendant.

The doctrine shifts the courts' attention away from the traditional contract requirements and measuring the recovery of expectation or reliance losses suffered. Instead, the focus is upon what benefits were conferred upon a party and if the party retained those benefits unjustly. Thus, a majority of jurisdictions allow an injured party to recover benefits unjustly retained as an alternative remedy to a breach of contract recovery.

As you read the cases that follow, work to articulate how the doctrine of unjust enrichment is applied in each case. How is the recovery described and calculated? How does the process differ from calculating a breach of contract award or formulating an equitable remedy?

The doctrine of avoiding unjust enrichment appears under many different labels, such as quasi-contract and quantum meruit. These labels, however, hurt more than they help. For example, the label quasi-contract suggests that a type of contract has been formed when in fact, under the doctrine, a contract has failed or has never been attempted.

B. WHERE THERE HAS BEEN AN ATTEMPT TO CONTRACT

Most frequently, courts apply the doctrine of avoiding unjust enrichment where the parties' attempt to enter into a contract fails for some reason. Indeed, the legal question of whether a contract exists may be a close one. Therefore, the doctrine of avoidance of unjust enrichment is regularly brought as an alterative theory of recovery in traditional breach of contract cases.

CALLANO v. OAKWOOD PARK HOMES CORP.
219 A.2d 332 (N.J. Super. 1966)

COLLESTER, Judge:

Defendant Oakwood Park Homes Corp. (Oakwood) appeals from a judgment of $475 entered in favor of plaintiffs Julia Callano and Frank Callano in the Monmouth County District Court.

The case was tried below on an agreed stipulation of facts. Oakwood, engaged in the construction of a housing development, in December 1961 contracted to sell a lot with a house to be erected thereon to Bruce Pendergast, who resided in Waltham, Massachusetts. In May 1962, prior to completion of the house, the Callanos, who operated a plant nursery, delivered and planted shrubbery pursuant to a contract with Pendergast. A representative of Oakwood had knowledge of the planting.

Pendergast never paid the Callanos the invoice price of $497.95. A short time after the shrubbery was planted Pendergast died. Thereafter, on July 10, 1962 Oakwood and Pendergast's estate cancelled the contract of sale. Oakwood had no knowledge of Pendergast's failure to pay the Callanos. On July 16, 1962 Oakwood sold the Pendergast property, including the shrubbery located thereon, to Richard and Joan Grantges for an undisclosed amount.

The single issue is whether Oakwood is obligated to pay plaintiffs for the reasonable value of the shrubbery on the theory of *quasi*-contractual liability. Plaintiffs contend that defendant was unjustly enriched when the Pendergast contract to purchase the property was cancelled and that an agreement to pay for the shrubbery is implied in law. Defendant argues that the facts of the case do not support a recovery by plaintiffs on the theory of *quasi*-contract.

Contracts implied by law, more properly described as *quasi* or constructive contracts, are a class of obligations which are imposed or created by law without regard to the assent of the party bound, on the ground that they are dictated by reason and justice. They rest solely on a legal fiction and are not contract obligations at all in the true sense, for there is no agreement; but they are clothed with the semblance of contract for the purpose of the remedy, and the obligation arises not from consent, as in the case of true contracts, but from the law or natural equity. Courts employ the fiction of *quasi* or constructive contract with caution. 17 C.J.S. *Contracts* § 6, pp. 566–570 (1963).

In cases based on *quasi*-contract liability, the intention of the parties is entirely disregarded, while in cases of express contracts and contracts implied in fact the intention is of the essence of the transaction. In the case of actual contracts the agreement defines the duty, while in the case of *quasi*-contracts the duty defines the contract. Where a case shows that it is the duty of the defendant to pay, the law imparts to him a promise to fulfill that obligation. The duty which thus forms the foundation of a *quasi*-contractual obligation is frequently based on the doctrine of unjust enrichment. It rests on the equitable principle that a person shall not be allowed to enrich himself unjustly at the expense of another, and on the principle of whatsoever it is certain a man ought to do, that the law supposes him to have promised to do. . . .

The key words are *enrich* and *unjustly*. To recover on the theory of *quasi*-contract the plaintiffs must prove that defendant was enriched, *viz.*, received a benefit, and that retention of the benefit without payment therefor would be unjust.

It is conceded by the parties that the value of the property, following the termination of the Pendegast contract, was enhanced by the reasonable value of the shrubbery at the stipulated sum of $475. However, we are not persuaded that the retention of such benefit by defendant before it sold the property to the Grantges was inequitable or unjust.

Quasi-contractual liability has found application in a myriad of situations. *See* Woodruff, CASES ON QUASI-CONTRACTS (3d ed. 1933). However, a common thread runs throughout its application where liability has been successfully asserted, namely, that the plaintiff expected remuneration from the defendant, or if the true facts were known to plaintiff, he would have expected remuneration from defendant, at the time the benefit was conferred. *See Rabinowitz v. Mass. Bonding & Insurance Co.*, 119 N.J.L. 552, 197 A. 44 (E. &A. 1937). . . . It is further noted that *quasi*-contract cases involve either some direct relationship between the parties or a mistake on the part of the person conferring the benefit.

In the instant case the plaintiffs entered into an express contract with Pendergast and looked to him for payment. They had no dealings with defendant, and did not expect remuneration from it when they provided the shrubbery. No issue of mistake on the part of plaintiffs is involved. Under the existing circumstances we believe it would be inequitable to hold defendant liable. Plaintiffs' remedy is against Pendergast's estate, since they contracted with and expected payment to be made by Pendergast when the benefit was conferred. . . . A plaintiff is not entitled to employ the legal fiction of *quasi*-contract to 'substitute one promisor or debtor for another." *Cascaden v. Magryta*, 247 Mich. 267, 225 N.W. 511, 512 (Sup. Ct. 1929). . . .

Recovery on the theory of *quasi*-contract was developed under the law to provide a remedy where none existed. Here, a remedy exists. Plaintiffs may bring their action against Pendergast's estate. We hold that under the facts of this case defendant was not unjustly enriched and is not liable for the value of the shrubbery.

Reversed.

ADVANCE LEASING & CRANE CO. v. DEL E. WEBB CORPORATION
573 P.2d 525 (Ariz. App. 1977)

JACOBSON, Judge:

On this appeal from summary judgment we are asked to determine whether appellant is entitled to recover rental charges for a crane used in the construction of a building for which appellee was the general contractor.

In 1974, the appellee, Del E. Webb Corporation (Webb) contacted Meyeres and Sons Crane Service, Inc., (Meyeres) to obtain necessary crane rentals for the construction of the Physics and Geology Building at Arizona State University. Webb's agreement with Meyeres provided that the crane to be supplied would be changed from time to time as the building took shape and the need arose for larger capacity cranes. In July of 1974 it was apparent that the 45 ton crane then on the construction site would require an extension in order for work to proceed on higher levels. Meyeres' arrangements to obtain the needed extension fell through. Meyeres informed Webb that it would rent a crane from another rental company until Meyeres obtained its own equipment. Webb had no objection as long as it was still billed according to the rate originally agreed upon for the 45 ton crane plus extension. Meyeres consented and informed Webb that Meyeres would arrange and pay for the temporary crane and absorb any loss.

Meyeres then leased a 125 ton crane from appellant, Advance Leasing & Crane Co., Inc. (Advance) to temporarily service the Webb project. This crane far exceeded the capacity necessary for the work to be done and the rental cost to Meyeres substantially exceeded the rates at which Meyeres billed Webb.

Advance's crane was on the ASU job for approximately ten days. All billings for the rental were made by Advance to Meyeres. Webb's construction supervisor directed the work done by appellant's crane on the job site. However, the record shows and counsel for Advance concedes that no contractual relationship existed between Advance and Webb.

Meyeres failed to pay Advance for rental of the 125 ton crane and Advance brought suit against both Meyeres and Webb. The trial court granted Webb's motion for summary judgment.

The record fails to show the existence of any genuine issue of material fact that would preclude summary judgment. Therefore, we must decide as a matter of law whether appellant was entitled to recover based upon the legal theories presented to the trial court.

Appellant first seeks recovery based upon a theory of quantum meruit. Appellant contends that it conferred a benefit resulting in unjust enrichment to Webb. . . .

It was undisputed that a contract existed between Meyeres and Advance whereby Meyeres was to pay Advance at a fixed rate for the rental of the crane. The doctrine of quantum meruit has no application where an explicit contract exists. *Brown v. Beck*, 68 Ariz. 139, 143, 202 P.2d 528, 530 (1949); *Ashton Co., Inc., Contractors and Engineers v. State*, 9 Ariz. App. 564, 570, 454 P.2d 1004, 1010 (1969). These cases are consistent with the applicable section of the RESTATEMENT OF RESTITUTION, which reads as follows:

§ 110 RESTITUTION FROM BENEFICIARY OF A CONTRACT WITH THIRD PERSON WHO HAS FAILED TO PERFORM.

A person who has conferred a benefit upon another as the performance of a contract with a third person is not entitled to restitution from the other merely because of the failure of performance by the third person.

The Arizona courts have made it clear that they will follow the sound reasoning of the RESTATEMENT in the absence of contrary Arizona law. *Waddell v. White*, 56 Ariz. 525, 109 P.2d 843 (1941).

Additionally, the theory of quantum meruit is inapplicable because Webb paid Meyeres the contractual price for use of the crane. The fact that the contractual price between Webb and Meyeres fell far below the rate at which Meyeres promised to compensate Advance is immaterial. Webb gave consideration for the benefit received and thereby was not unjustly enriched. . . .

Quantum meruit is an equitable remedy not warranted by the facts presented to the trial court. Webb did not contemplate incurring the cost of hiring a crane of a size that far exceeded its needs. Webb merely gave permission to Meyeres to substitute a crane at Meyeres' expense until Meyeres could bring in its own crane. Webb specifically conditioned its permission upon being billed at the original rental rates for the smaller crane. This was known to Advance at the time of its agreement with Meyeres. Meyeres had assumed the risk of making sufficient profit from remaining on the ASU job to make up its loss on the rental of the Advance crane. Likewise, Advance assumed the risk that Meyeres would be able to pay. This risk cannot now be shifted to Webb. . . .

The judgment is affirmed.

NOTES & QUESTIONS

1. In *Callano*, the court denied the plaintiff recovery based on the doctrine of avoiding unjust enrichment. What alternative remedy could the plaintiff pursue? Draft allegations that would appear in the Complaint to state the available claim and the recovery sought.

2. Both cases involve third parties (Pendergast; Meyeres) in the disputes. In each case, how does their presence affect the operation of the doctrine of avoiding unjust enrichment?

3. In later chapters, you will learn about additional theories of recovery: contract theory (Chapter 16) and promissory estoppel (Chapter 7). Compare recovery under the doctrine of avoiding unjust enrichment with these two theories of recovery.

WEICHERT CO. REALTORS v. RYAN
608 A.2d 280 (N.J. 1992)

Stein, Justice:

Plaintiff, Weichert Co. Realtors (Weichert), sought damages from defendants, Thomas Ryan and Jay Saunders, based on defendants' failure to pay Weichert for brokerage services rendered by William Tackaberry, a Weichert employee. Weichert based its claim on defendants' alleged breach of contract, or, in the alternative, on a theory of quantum meruit. The Appellate Division upheld the trial court's determination that Weichert was entitled to recover damages for breach of contract. . . .

In late March 1987, Socrates Kyritsis, a property owner, met with Robert Olpp, the manager of Weichert's Chatham office, and Tackaberry, a real estate agent in that office, and told them he wished to sell the "William Pitt property" for $3,000,000, with the sales commission to be paid by the buyer. Shortly after that meeting, Tackaberry telephoned Ryan, a local developer, and informed him that he knew of a property that Ryan and Saunders, his partner, might be interested in purchasing. Tackaberry also stated that the purchaser would have to pay Weichert a ten percent commission. Ryan indicated that he was interested in knowing more about the property, and Tackaberry disclosed the property's identity and the seller's proposed price. Ryan ended the conversation by agreeing to meet with Tackaberry to obtain more information.

As a result of his telephone conversation with Ryan, Tackaberry met with Kyritsis to acquire information concerning the property's current leases, income, expenses, and concerning plans for its eventual development. Tackaberry also collected tax and zoning documents relevant to the property. In a face-to-face meeting held on April 4th, Tackaberry gave Ryan the data and information he had procured. Tackaberry began that meeting by presenting Ryan with a letter dated April 3, 1987, that stated in part, "As compensation for this information. . . there will be a ten percent finders fee to be paid by your group upon successfully completing and closing of title." Ryan testified that he had refused Tackaberry's request that he sign the letter, and had explained to Tackaberry that he needed more information about the property before he could commit to the broker's fee, and therefore they would discuss that fee later. Tackaberry, however, testified that he had not asked Ryan to sign the letter, although on cross-examination he admitted that he had been intent on memorializing the agreement in writing. According to Tackaberry, after Ryan had read the letter, he had indicated only that he was concerned about the method and timing of the commission payment. Tackaberry did not pursue that point, apparently assuming that the parties would resolve that issue at a later date. Ryan ended the meeting by instructing Tackaberry to arrange a meeting between Ryan and Kyritsis. Ryan took the letter and the information with him, and later used the information to evaluate the project.

On April 7th, Ryan and his attorney met with Kyritsis to discuss the sale of the property. Although Ryan initially refused to allow Tackaberry to attend that meeting, he relented when Tackaberry insisted. Before the meeting began, Tackaberry offered unsolicited advice concerning how to negotiate effectively with Kyritsis. The meeting was successful, and afterwards Ryan instructed his attorney to prepare a draft contract for the purchase of the William Pitt property for $3,000,000. At that time Ryan informed Tackaberry that he had discussed the commission issue with Saunders, and they both agreed that ten percent was too much to pay for Tackaberry's services. Tackaberry insisted that Ryan had already agreed to pay ten percent. After some discussion the two parted without resolving the issue.

At trial, the parties did not dispute that from the April 7th meeting until the closing, Ryan consistently had told Tackaberry that he would not agree to pay a ten percent commission. Ryan testified: "We had several discussions about the amount of the fee, the method of payment of the fee, but we were not able to be in agreement as to the amount of the fee. Mr. Tackaberry was insistent on the $300,000 amount. I indicated to him on several occasions, verbally that I would not sign his $300,000 letter, . . . the April 3rd letter, [ ] and that it was just too much money[. T]o pay out as the property was developed was discussed and was, I felt, agreeable to Mr. Tackaberry. But we were not and have not been able to agree on the amount of a finder's fee."

Tackaberry's subsequent involvement in the transaction was unsolicited by Ryan and Saunders. At trial he acknowledged that "there were no phone calls coming in my direction." Nevertheless, he continued to participate in the sale by carrying draft contracts back and forth between the parties, and offering negotiating advice. When Kyritsis eventually decided to raise the price of the property by $250,000, he informed Tackaberry, who broke the news to Ryan and Saunders. After Kyritsis signed the final contract, Tackaberry delivered it to Ryan and Saunders for their signature. The final contract, signed by Ryan and Saunders on April 27th, stated: "Both parties represent to each other that they have not dealt with any broker or other person entitled to a commission in connection with this transaction except Weichert Realtors ("Weichert"). Buyer agrees to pay any broker's commission due Weichert as per separate agreement between Buyer and Weichert. Buyer agrees and covenants to protect and indemnify Sellers against and/or with regard to such commissions."

On May 4th, Tackaberry wrote to Ryan and Saunders, bringing to their attention some errors in the contract. He again requested that they sign his April 3rd letter indicating that they would pay a ten percent broker's fee, and informed them that the fee would be due and payable by certified or attorney's check at the closing. The letter had two spaces for Ryan's and Saunders' signatures underneath the caption "Acknowledgement of Commission Agreement." Tackaberry personally delivered the letter to Ryan, who said he would have to talk to Saunders. Neither Ryan or Saunders signed or otherwise responded to that letter.

Throughout May, Tackaberry continued his efforts to obtain a written agreement. During that time, Ryan and Saunders offered to pay him a $75,000 commission on an installment basis as they developed the property. Tackaberry refused to consider anything less than ten percent. Tackaberry testified that he had met with Ryan again on May 15th, but they were still unable to agree on the commission amount. Thereafter, Tackaberry testified, Ryan had ceased to return his phone calls, and he had cancelled a meeting scheduled for May 29th. On that date, Tackaberry drafted another letter, stating in part: "I have forestalled processing my paperwork on this transaction for almost a month in hopes that when I did process it the commission issue would be resolved. This complicates the issue in that I may not have as much flexibility in the manner of payment of the commission as I would have, had we resolved this issue prior to the file being processed." On June 5th, Ryan and Tackaberry met once more to discuss the commission. Ryan offered Tackaberry $150,000, and Tackaberry again refused to consider less than $300,000. On June 26th, Ryan made Tackaberry a final offer of $150,000, which Tackaberry again refused. Tackaberry subsequently delivered to Ryan a bill for $325,000, ten percent of the final purchase price. On September 29, 1987, Ryan and Saunders closed on the property but did not pay Tackaberry for his services.

Weichert brought this action to enforce an alleged oral agreement between Tackaberry and Ryan for the payment of a ten percent brokerage fee, or, in the alternative for damages based on quantum meruit. At trial, Kyritsis surprised counsel on both sides by testifying that he had agreed to sell the property to Saunders for $3,000,000 before Tackaberry had first contacted Ryan. Saunders testified and corroborated Kyritsis' testimony. Subsequent to that revelation, defendants argued that Tackaberry deserved no commission because he had not been the procuring cause of the sale.

The trial court found that Ryan and Saunders had contracted to pay Tackaberry a $300,000 broker's fee. The court first found that Tackaberry was the efficient and procuring cause of the sale, and expressly rejected Kyritsis' testimony that he had independently agreed to sell the property to Saunders: "It is not logical or credible that [Ryan and Saunders] would have their attorney . . . prepare a contract and later sign a revised contract . . . referring to Weichert as the only broker 'entitled to commission,' providing that 'buyer agrees to pay any broker's commission due Weichert as per separate agreement between buyer and Weichert,' and further arranging to indemnify the sellers as to any commissions claims, unless Ryan and Saunders believed Weichert Realtors was the efficient cause of the sale."

The court also found that Ryan had orally contracted to pay Tackaberry a broker's fee totaling ten percent of $3,000,000 (the original price for the property), and that the statute of frauds did not apply to that oral contract. Finally, the court ordered Ryan and Saunders to pay interest on the commission beginning six months after the closing. Because the trial court found an enforceable contract, it did not reach the issue whether Weichert could recover on a quantum meruit theory.

The Appellate Division affirmed in an unpublished opinion, finding that Ryan had entered into a binding agreement with Weichert when he had availed himself of Tackaberry's services knowing that the broker expected a ten percent commission. Relying on § 69(1)(a) of the RESTATEMENT (SECOND) OF CONTRACTS (1981), the court concluded that although Ryan might have orally rejected the ten percent figure, he had implicitly contracted to pay a ten percent commission because he took the benefit of Tackaberry's services with a reasonable opportunity to reject them.

We consider two issues: whether Ryan and Tackaberry entered into an enforceable agreement, and, if not, whether Weichert is entitled to recover the reasonable value of Tackaberry's services on a theory of quantum meruit. A contract arises from offer and acceptance, and must be sufficiently definite "that the performance to be rendered by each party can be ascertained with reasonable certainty." *West Caldwell v. Caldwell*, 26 N.J. 9, 24–25, 138 A.2d 402 (1958). . . . Thus, if parties agree on essential terms and manifest an intention to be bound by those terms, they have created an enforceable contract. *See West Caldwell, supra*, 26 N.J. at 24–25, 138 A.2d 402. . . . Where the parties do not agree to one or more essential terms, however, courts generally hold that the agreement is unenforceable. . . .

In some circumstances, however, courts will allow recovery even though the parties' words and actions are insufficient to manifest an intention to agree to the proffered terms. Recovery based on quasi-contract, sometimes referred to as a contract implied-in-law, "is wholly unlike an express or implied-in-fact contract in that it is 'imposed by the law for the purpose of bringing about justice without reference to the intention of the parties.' " *Saint Barnabas Medical Ctr. v. County of Essex*, 111 N.J. 67, 79, 543 A.2d 34 (1988) . . . *see also Callano v. Oakwood Park Homes Corp.*, 91 N.J. Super. 105, 108, 219 A.2d 332 (App. Div. 1966) ("In the case of actual contracts, the agreement defines the duty, while in the case of quasi-contracts the duty defines the contract."). Courts generally allow recovery in quasi-contract when one party has conferred a benefit on another, and the circumstances are such that to deny recovery would be unjust. *See, e.g., Shapiro v. Solomon*, 42 N.J. Super. 377, 383–86, 126 A.2d 654 (App. Div. 1956); RESTATEMENT OF RESTITUTION § 53 (1937). Quasi-contractual liability "rests on the equitable principle that a person shall not be allowed to enrich himself unjustly at the expense of another." *Callano, supra,* 91 N.J. Super. at 108, 219 A.2d 332.

Applying that principle, courts have allowed quasi-contractual recovery for services rendered when a party confers a benefit with a reasonable expectation of payment. *See, e.g. Hardin v. Hunter,* 174 Ga. App. 756, 331 S.E.2d 83, 85 (1985). . . . That type of quasi-contractual recovery is known as quantum meruit ("as much as he deserves"), and entitles the performing party to recoup the reasonable value of services rendered. *Marta v. Nepa,* 385 A.2d 727 (Del. 1978). . . .

Accordingly, a broker seeking recovery on a theory of quantum meruit must establish that the services were performed with an expectation that the beneficiary would pay for them, and under circumstances that should have put the beneficiary on notice that the plaintiff expected to be paid. *Marta, supra,* 385 A.2d at 729. . . . Courts have allowed brokers to recover in quantum meruit when a principal accepts a broker's services but the contract proves unenforceable for lack of agreement on essential terms — for instance, the amount of the broker's commission. *See, e.g., Marta, supra,* 385 A.2d at 729 . . . cf. *Traylor v. Henkels & McCoy, Inc.,* 99 Idaho 560, 585 P.2d 970 (1978) (holding that contractor could recover in quantum meruit where parties did not agree on price of services). . . . Thus, a broker who makes a sufficient showing can recover fees for services rendered even absent express or implied agreement concerning the amount of the fee.

Application of the foregoing principles to the transaction between Weichert and Ryan demonstrates that the record is insufficient to support a finding that Tackaberry and Ryan mutually manifested assent to the essential terms of the contract. First, Ryan never expressly assented to the terms of Tackaberry's offer. Although Ryan expressed interest in learning more about the Pitt property during the initial March phone call, neither his expression of interest nor his agreement to meet with Tackaberry to learn more about the transaction was sufficient to establish the "unqualified acceptance" necessary to manifest express assent.

. . . Moreover, Ryan refused to agree to the ten-percent figure during the April 4th meeting, and thereafter consistently rejected that term. Thus, the parties never formed an express contract.

The closer question is whether Ryan implicitly assented to Tackaberry's terms when he accepted information concerning the property and proceeded to act on that information. That Ryan's actions evinced a willingness to compensate Tackaberry is uncontested. Ryan accepted Tackaberry's services with a reasonable opportunity to reject them and with the knowledge that Tackaberry expected compensation. Moreover, Ryan admitted throughout the trial that he had intended to compensate Tackaberry.

As the Appellate Division noted, had Ryan remained silent after reading the April 3rd letter, such silence combined with his acceptance of Tackaberry's services might have been sufficient to manifest assent to the ten percent commission proposal. Ryan, however, was not silent when presented with Tackaberry's offer. He not only withheld his assent to the terms of the offer, declining to sign the April 3rd letter, but also expressed some reluctance about agreeing to pay the full commission on closing. Shortly after the April 4th meeting, Ryan stated that a ten percent commission was too high, and he consistently sought to negotiate that term. In fact, the record indicates that Tackaberry was not sure that Ryan had assented to the ten percent fee, accounting for his persistent attempts to induce Ryan to indicate his acceptance in writing.

Although the trial court concluded that the proofs were sufficient to establish agreement to pay the full commission, the court made no findings of fact inconsistent with the evidence of Ryan's rejection of the ten percent commission. In our view, the circumstances surrounding their negotiations did not justify Tackaberry's belief that Ryan had assented to the terms of his offer.

The Appellate Division's conclusion that Ryan had agreed to pay the ten percent commission was based on its assumption that § 69 of the RESTATEMENT (SECOND) OF CONTRACTS "does not require that the offeree agree with the expected compensation, but takes the benefit of the services with a reasonable opportunity to reject them." We are persuaded, however, that proof of "silence and inaction" — the indispensable predicate to a finding of acceptance under § 69 — cannot be found in this record. Ryan's initial unwillingness to agree to the ten-percent commission, and his subsequent express rejection of that term, hardly constitutes the passive acquiescence to an offer contemplated by § 69. Implication of an agreement to pay Weichert a ten percent commission under those circumstances would impermissibly expand the rule allowing an offeror to treat silence as acceptance.

Arguably, Tackaberry should have cemented the terms of the agreement before conferring the benefit of his services. We note that in the ordinary real estate brokerage transaction in which the seller pays the commission, the broker's right to payment depends on the existence of a writing specifying the rate or amount of the commission. . . . Although a writing is not mandated in transactions in which the buyer pays the commission, Tackaberry's testimony was consistent with the common understanding that real estate brokerage agreements ordinarily are committed to writing. In proceeding to render services despite Ryan's refusal to agree, either in writing or orally, to an essential term, Tackaberry apparently elected to pursue consummation of the transaction on the assumption that Weichert's fee would eventually be paid. That choice, although perhaps commercially reasonable, did not result in the formation of a binding contract because the parties had never agreed on the amount of the fee. . . . Thus, Ryan's implied promise to pay a commission is unenforceable because of the parties' failure to agree on the amount of the commission.

The record clearly establishes, however, that Tackaberry is entitled to recover in quantum meruit for the reasonable value of his services. The trial court's factual finding that Tackaberry was the procuring cause of the sale is supported by substantial evidence. Further, the proofs adduced at trial firmly establish that Tackaberry furnished Ryan with information about the Pitt property with an expectation that Ryan would pay a brokerage fee, and Ryan himself admitted throughout the trial that he had always intended to compensate Tackaberry for his services. Given those circumstances, to deny Tackaberry compensation for services rendered would unjustly enrich Ryan and Saunders. . . .

Accordingly, we remand to the Law Division to determine the reasonable value of Tackaberry's services. By remanding, we do not imply that the reasonable value of Tackaberry's services is less than ten percent of the purchase price, nor do we imply any view concerning the value of such services. The commission amount should be determined on the basis of proofs tending to show the reasonable value of Tackaberry's services, including evidence of customary brokers' fees for similar transactions. . . .

NOTES & QUESTIONS

1. Even though Tackaberry "should have cemented the terms of the agreement before conferring the benefit of his services," he failed to do so. Yet the court still remanded the case to permit him to prove and recover the reasonable value of his services. Does this result demonstrate that the doctrine of avoiding unjust enrichment undermines traditional contract requirements or that at least the doctrine encourages informality and casual practices?

2. In its analysis, the court distinguishes among a number of types of "contracts." Can you distinguish among: an express contract; an actual contract; an implied-in-fact contract; an implied-in-law contract; a quasi-contract; recovery in quantum meruit?

PYEATTE v. PYEATTE
135 Ariz. 346, 661 P.2d 196 (App. 1983)

CORCORAN, Judge:

This is an appeal by the husband from an award of $23,000 in favor of the wife as ordered in a decree of dissolution. Two issues are before us: (1) The validity of an oral agreement entered into by the husband and wife during the marriage, whereby each spouse agreed to provide in turn the sole support for the marriage while the other spouse was obtaining further education; and, (2) whether the wife is entitled to restitution for benefits she provided for her husband's educational support in a dissolution action which follows closely upon the husband's graduation and admission to the Bar. The word "agreement" is used as a term of reference for the stated understanding between the husband and wife and not as a legal conclusion that the agreement is enforceable at law as a contract.

The husband, H. Charles Pyeatte (appellant), and the wife, Margrethe May Pyeatte (appellee), were married in Tucson on December 27, 1972. At the time of the marriage both had received bachelors degrees. Appellee was coordinator of the surgical technical program at Pima College. Appellant was one of her students. In early 1974, the parties had discussions and reached an agreement concerning postgraduate education for both of them.

Appellee testified that they agreed she "would put him through three years of law school without his having to work, and when he finished, he would put [her] through for [her] masters degree without [her] having to work."

Appellant concedes the existence of an agreement. Although there was a claim by appellant that his agreement with appellee was qualified by certain contingencies, there is substantial evidence in the record to support the findings made by the trial court after the trial:

The Court is of the opinion that there was a definite agreement that the respondent [appellant] would pay for the support of petitioner [appellee] while the petitioner [appellee] obtained her master's degree without her having to work. The Court is further of the opinion that there was no contingency expressed or implied that this would not be carried out or enforced in the event of a divorce. Petitioner [appellee] carried out her part of the agreement in supporting the respondent [appellant] while he obtained his law degree.

Appellant attended law school in Tucson, Arizona, from 1974 until his graduation. He was admitted to the State Bar shortly thereafter.

During appellant's first two years of law school appellee supported herself and appellant on the salary she earned at Pima College. During the last year, appellee lost her job, whereupon savings were used to support the couple. Although each spouse contributed to the savings, a significant amount was furnished by appellee.

After appellant's admission to the Bar, the couple moved to Prescott, Arizona, where appellant was employed by a law firm. Both parties realized that appellant's salary would not be sufficient to support the marriage and pay for appellee's education for a masters degree simultaneously. Appellee then agreed to defer her plans for a year or two until her husband got started in his legal career. In the meantime, she obtained part-time employment as a teacher.

In April, 1978, appellant told appellee that he no longer wanted to be married to her, and in June of 1978, she filed a petition for dissolution. Trial was had in March of 1979, and a decree of dissolution was granted. At the time of the trial, there was little community property and no dispute as to division of any community or separate property. Spousal maintenance was neither sought by nor granted to appellee.

The trial court determined that there was an agreement between the parties, that appellee fully performed her part of that agreement, that appellant had not performed his part of the agreement, and that appellee had been damaged thereby.

Based on appellee's expert testimony on the cost of furthering her education, in accordance with the agreement, the trial court awarded judgment of $23,000 against appellant as damages for breach of contract, with additional directions that the judgment be payable through the court clerk on a quarterly basis in a sum of not less than ten percent of appellant's net quarterly income.

The trial court directed appellant to use his best efforts to produce income and to keep accurate records of his income-producing activities, which records would be available to appellee upon request but not more frequently than on a quarterly basis. The court also retained jurisdiction of the case for the purpose of supervising the administration of the payment of the judgment and the keeping of records by the appellant. Appellant filed a timely notice of appeal from the judgment.

On appeal, appellant argues that the agreement did not rise to the level of a binding contract because, among other things, the terms thereof were not definite and could not be legally enforced.

Appellee advances three theories as grounds upon which the trial court's award should be upheld:

> 1. The agreement between the parties was a binding contract. Appellant's failure to perform after appellee had fully performed her obligations renders appellant liable in damages. . . .

> 3. If the agreement is not enforceable as a binding contract, appellee is nevertheless entitled to restitution in quantum meruit to prevent appel-

lant's unjust enrichment because he received his education at appellee's expense. . . .

Although the terms and requirements of an enforceable contract need not be stated in minute detail, it is fundamental that, in order to be binding, an agreement must be definite and certain so that the liability of the parties may be exactly fixed. Terms ne*cessary* for the required definiteness frequently include time of performance, place of performance, price or compensation, penalty provisions, and other material requirements of the agreement. 17 C.J.S. *Contracts* § 36(2) at 647–61 (1963); 17 Am. Jur. 2d *Contracts* § 75 at 413–15 (1964). In *Savoca Masonry Co. v. Homes and Son Construction Co.*, 112 Ariz. 392, 542 P.2d 817 (1975), the court found that a contractual relationship based upon an oral agreement did not exist between a general contractor and a subcontractor because "[o]nly the price and work involved were agreed upon; other provisions which might in the end have proven critical were not." . . .

Upon examining the parties' agreement in this instance, it is readily apparent that a sufficient mutual understanding regarding critical provisions of their agreement did not exist. For example, no agreement was made regarding the time when appellee would attend graduate school and appellant would be required to assume their full support. Both parties concede that appellee could not have begun her masters program immediately after appellant's graduation because his beginning salary was not sufficient to provide both for her education and the couple's support. Appellee told appellant she was willing to wait a year or two until he "got on his feet" before starting her program. Nothing more definite than that was ever agreed upon. Furthermore, although appellee agreed to support appellant while he attended law school for three years, no corresponding time limitation was placed upon her within which to finish her education. Even if we assume that the agreement contemplated appellee's enrolling as a full-time student, the length of time necessary to complete a masters degree varies considerably depending upon the requirements of the particular program and the number of classes an individual elects to take at one time. Such a loosely worded agreement can hardly be said to have fixed appellant's liability with certainty.

The agreement lacks a number of other essential terms which prevent it from becoming binding. Appellee's place of education is not mentioned at all, yet there are masters programs available throughout the country. Whether or not they would be required to relocate in another state should she choose an out-of-state program was not agreed upon. Appellant testified at trial that "that particular problem was really never resolved." Nor was there any agreement concerning the cost of the program to which appellee would be entitled under this agreement. There can be several thousand dollars' difference in tuition, fees, and other expenses between any two masters programs depending upon resident status, public versus private institutions, and other factors. Appellant testified that at the time of the "contract," neither he nor his wife had any idea as to the specific dollar amounts that would be involved. . . .

Appellee urges us to enforce this agreement because contracts should be interpreted, whenever reasonable, in such a way as to uphold the contract, and that this is particularly true where there has been performance by one party. We are aware of these general legal concepts, and also note that reasonableness can be implied by the courts when interpreting agreements. . . .

The court's function, however, cannot be that of contract maker. . . . Nor can the court create a contract simply to accomplish a purportedly good purpose. *Stearns-Roger Corp. v. Hartford Accident and Indemnity Co.*, 117 Ariz. 162, 571 P.2d 659 (1977). Our review of the record persuades us that the essential terms and requirements of this agreement were not sufficiently definite so that the obligations of the parties to the agreement could be determined:

> A party will not be subjected to a contractual obligation where the character of that obligation is so indefinite and uncertain as to its terms and requirements that it is impossible to state with certainty the obligations involved.

Aztec Film Productions v. Tucson Gas and Electric Co., 11 Ariz. App. 241, 243, 463 P.2d 547, 549 (1969).

Based on its ruling that the agreement was enforceable, the trial court awarded appellee $23,000, the amount established by expert testimony as necessary to further her education in accordance with the agreement. On the basis of our determination that the agreement in this case is unenforceable, there can be no recovery for amounts necessary to further appellee's education. . . .

Appellee's last contention is that the trial court's award should be affirmed as an equitable award of restitution on the basis of unjust enrichment. She argues that appellant's education, which she subsidized and which he obtained through the exhaustion of community assets constitutes a benefit for which he must, in equity, make restitution. This narrow equitable issue is one of first impression in this court. . . .

Restitution is available to a party to an agreement where he performs services for the other believing that there is a binding contract.

When Restitution for Services is Granted.

> A person who has rendered services to another or services which have inured to the benefit of another. . . is entitled to restitution therefor if the services were rendered . . . .

> (b) To obtain the performance of an agreement with the other therefor, not operative as a contract, or voidable as a contract and avoided by the other party after the services were rendered, the one performing the services erroneously believing because of a mistake of fact that the agreement was binding upon the other. . . .

RESTATEMENT OF RESTITUTION § 40(b) at 155 (1937).

In order to be granted restitution, appellee must demonstrate that appellant received a benefit, that by receipt of that benefit he was unjustly enriched at her expense, and that the circumstances were such that in good conscience appellant should make compensation. *John A. Artukovich & Sons v. Reliance Truck Co.*, 126 Ariz. 246, 614 P.2d 327 (1980); RESTATEMENT OF RESTITUTION § 1 at 13 (1937). In *Artukovich*, the Supreme Court discussed unjust enrichment.

Contracts implied-in-law or quasi-contracts, also called constructive contracts, are inferred by the law as a matter of reason and justice from the acts and conduct of the parties and circumstances surrounding the transactions . . . and are imposed for the purpose of bringing about justice without reference to the intentions of the parties. . . .

RESTATEMENT OF RESTITUTION § 1 provides, "A person who has been unjustly enriched at the expense of another is required to make restitution to the other." Comment (a) to that section notes that a person is enriched if he received a benefit and is unjustly enriched if retention of that benefit would be unjust. Comment (b) defines a benefit as being any form of advantage. . . .

. . . Unjust enrichment does not depend upon the existence of a valid contract, . . . nor is it necessary that plaintiff suffer a loss corresponding to the defendant's gain for there to be valid claim for an unjust enrichment. . . .

A benefit may be any type of advantage, including that which saves the recipient from any loss or expense. . . . Appellee's support of appellant during his period of schooling clearly constituted a benefit to appellant. Absent appellee's support, appellant may not have attended law school, may have been forced to prolong his education because of intermittent periods of gainful employment, or may have gone deeply into debt. Relieved of the necessity of supporting himself, he was able to devote full time and attention to his education.

The mere fact that one party confers a benefit on another, however, is not of itself sufficient to require the other to make restitution. Retention of the benefit must be unjust.

Historically, restitution for the value of services rendered has been available upon either an "implied-in-fact" contract or upon quasi-contractual grounds. D. Dobbs, REMEDIES § 4.2 at 237 (1973); 1 Williston, CONTRACTS § 3 and 3A at 10–15 (3d ed. 1957). An implied-in-fact contract is a true contract, differing from an express contract only insofar as it is proved by circumstantial evidence rather than by express written or oral terms. . . . In contrast, a quasi-contract is not a contract at all, but a duty imposed in equity upon a party to repay another to prevent his own unjust enrichment. The intention of the parties to bind themselves contractually in such a case is irrelevant. 1 Williston, CONTRACTS § 3A at 12–15 (3d ed. 1957). To support her claim for restitution on the basis of an implied-in-fact contract, appellee must demonstrate the elements of a binding contract. For the reasons we have previously discussed, we cannot find the necessary mutual assent or certainty as to the critical terms of the agreement sufficient to establish such a contract. . . .

Restitution is nevertheless available in quasi-contract absent any showing of mutual assent. While a quasi-contractual obligation may be imposed without regard to the intent of the parties, such an obligation will be imposed only if the circumstances are such that it would be unjust to allow retention of the benefit without compensating the one who conferred it. . . . One circumstance under which a duty to compensate will be imposed is when there was an expectation of payment or compensation for services at the time they were rendered.

> [A]n obligation to pay, ordinarily, will not be implied in fact or by law if it is clear that there was indeed no expectation of payment, that a gratuity was intended to be conferred, that the benefit was conferred officiously, or that the question of payment was left to the unfettered discretion of the recipient.

Osborn v. Boeing Airplane Co., 309 F.2d at 102.

Although we found that the spousal agreement failed to meet the requirements of an enforceable contract, the agreement still has importance in considering appellee's claim for unjust enrichment because it both evidences appellee's expectation of compensation and the circumstances which make it unjust to allow appellant to retain the benefits of her extraordinary efforts.

We next address the question of whether restitution on the basis of unjust enrichment is appropriate in the context of the marital relationship. No authority is cited to the court in support of the proposition that restitution as a matter of law is inappropriate in a dissolution proceeding. . . . Where both spouses perform the usual and incidental activities of the marital relationship, upon dissolution there can be no restitution for performance of these activities. . . . Where, however, the facts demonstrate an agreement between the spouses and an extraordinary or unilateral effort by one spouse which inures solely to the benefit of the other by the time of dissolution, the remedy of restitution is appropriate.

Arizona courts have traditionally utilized the equitable restitutionary device of the constructive trust to prevent unjust enrichment between spouses upon dissolution when there is property to which such a trust may attach. . . . We see no reason in law or equity why restitution should not be available in an appropriate circumstance to prevent the unjust enrichment of a spouse when a constructive trust is not available, as here, when no property exists. We analogize the two restitutionary devices solely to the extent of illustrating their common essence — prevention of the unjust enrichment of one spouse at the expense of the other. . . .

The Oklahoma Supreme Court in *Hubbard* [v. *Hubbard*, 603 P.2d 747 (Okla. 1979)] held that, while a degree is not "property" subject to valuation and division upon dissolution, equitable relief is not thereby precluded. The court then ordered that the wife be reimbursed in quasi-contract for the amounts she expended during the 12 years in which she supported her husband while he obtained his medical training.

> While it is true that Dr. Hubbard's license to practice medicine is his own to do with as he pleases, it is nonetheless also true that Ms. Hubbard has an equitable claim to repayment for the investment she made in his education and training. To hold otherwise would result in the unjust enrichment of Dr. Hubbard. He would leave the marriage with an earning capacity increased by $250,000 which was obtained in substantial measure through the efforts and sacrifices of his wife. She on the other hand would leave the marriage without either a return on her investment or an earning capacity similarly increased through joint efforts. . . . All the resources of the marriage had been dissipated on Dr. Hubbard's education. There is no reason in law or equity why Dr. Hubbard should retain the only valuable asset which was accumulated through joint efforts . . . free of claims for reimbursement by his wife.

603 P.2d at 750.

The Minnesota Supreme Court in *DeLaRosa* [v. *DeLaRosa*, 309 N.W.2d 755 (Minn. 1981)] similarly affirmed an award of restitution to the wife for the financial support she provided her husband while he attended medical school, in a dissolution which occurred shortly after the husband's graduation.

> The case at bar presents the common situation where one spouse has foregone the immediate enjoyment of earned income to enable the other to pursue an advanced education on a full-time basis. Typically, this sacrifice is made with the expectation that the parties will enjoy a higher standard of living in the future. Because the income of the working spouse is used for living expenses, there is usually little accumulated marital property to be divided when the dissolution occurs prior to the attainment of the financial rewards concomitant with the advanced degree or professional license. Furthermore, the working spouse is not entitled to maintenance . . . as there has been a demonstrated ability of self-support. The equities weigh heavily in favor of providing a remedy to the working spouse in such a situation, . . .

309 N.W.2d at 758. . . .

The record shows that the appellee conferred benefits on appellant — financial subsidization of appellant's legal education — with the agreement and expectation that she would be compensated therefor by his reciprocal efforts after his graduation and admission to the Bar. Appellant has left the marriage with the only valuable asset acquired during the marriage — his legal education and qualification to practice law. It would be inequitable to allow appellant to retain this benefit without making restitution to appellee. However, we need not decide what limits or standards would apply in the absence of an agreement. Commentators have discerned in various statutory enactments and the developing case law a renewed and expanded recognition of marriage's economic underpinnings. *See Comment, The Interest of the Community in a Professional Education*, 10 CALIF. W. L. REV. 590 (1974); Erickson, *Spousal Support Toward the Realization of Educational Goals: How the Law Can Ensure Reciprocity*, 1978 WIS. L. REV. 947. By our decision herein, we reject the view that the economic element necessarily inherent in the marital institution (and particularly apparent in its dissolution) requires us to treat marriage as a strictly financial undertaking upon the dissolution of which each party will be fully compensated for the investment of his various contributions. When the parties have been married for a number of years, the courts cannot and will not strike a balance regarding the contributions of each to the marriage and then translate that into a monetary award. To do so would diminish the individual personalities of the husband and wife to economic entities and reduce the institution of marriage to that of a closely held corporation.

Generally, where claims are made by the working spouse against the student spouse, the trial court in each case must make specific findings as to whether the education, degree or license acquired by the student spouse during marriage involved an unjust enrichment of that spouse, the value of the benefit, and the amount that should be paid to the working spouse. A variety of methods of computing the unjust enrichment may be employed in ascertaining the working spouse's compensable interest in the attainment of the student spouse's education, degree or license.

The award to appellee should be limited to the financial contribution by appellee for appellant's living expenses and direct educational expenses. *See DeLaRosa v. DeLaRosa*, 309 N.W.2d 755.

Under the agreement between the parties, the anticipated benefit to appellee may involve a monetary benefit in a lesser amount than the benefit conferred by appellee on appellant. In that event, the award to appellee should be limited to the amount of the anticipated benefit to appellee. Appellee should not recover more than the benefit of her bargain. RESTATEMENT OF RESTITUTION, § 107, Comment b, at 449 (1937). . . .

The portion of the judgment in the amount of $23,000 is reversed and remanded for proceedings in accordance with this opinion.

NOTES & QUESTIONS

1. Ms. Pyeatte's recovery was limited to her financial contribution to her husband's living and educational expenses. But she could not recover "more than the benefit of her bargain." How can she be limited to the contract when the court held the couple's contract was unenforceable for lack of definiteness and certainty?

What is the measure of recovery when a court is acting to avoid unjust enrichment? The court awarded the wife recovery by the measure of her contribution to her husband's living and educational expenses. Did the court here focus on the defendant's gain or the plaintiff's loss?

2. Does the *Pyeatte* case really raise contract issues or is it an issue of purely family law? The court stated that marriage should not be viewed "as a strictly financial undertaking upon the dissolution of which each party will be fully compensated for the investment of his various contributions." But doesn't the court adopt this view in its decision to allocate the spouses' financial contributions?

3. When courts find that parties entered into an illegal contract and hold the contract void, should one or both parties be able to invoke the doctrine of avoiding unjust enrichment? What if the violation of the law were unintentional or inadvertent?

DECK v. JIM HARRIS CHEVROLET-BUICK
386 N.E.2d 714 (Ind. App. 1979)

LOWDERMILK, Judge:

Defendant-appellant Diana L. Deck (Mrs. Deck) brings this appeal after the Putnam County Court entered judgment in favor of plaintiff-appellee Jim Harris Chevrolet-Buick (Harris) in the amount of $134.40 as payment for labor performed by Harris on Mrs. Deck's automobile.

FACTS

The trial court entered the following findings of fact and conclusion of law:

. . . 2. Defendant, Diana Deck, brought her 1976 Buick Regal automobile to Plaintiff's establishment because of a problem with the transmission.

3. Defendant was told that an attempt to fix it with a particular modulator valve would be made and that it would probably cost less than $50.

4. Defendant was told she would be called if the repair work would cost over $50 and she requested that this call be made.

5. Defendant was subsequently told the next day that the first valve did not repair the problem and Defendant was told another valve would have to be replaced and that she could pick the car up that day at 5:00 p.m.

6. Defendant arrived at 5:00 p.m. but her car was not finished so she was given a loaned auto to drive.

7. Defendant, through some breakdown in communications, was never contacted about further work that was required to be done to repair the transmission.

8. Defendant was presented with a bill for considerably more than $50 for an overhaul of the transmission that effected the necessary repairs, specifically $388.98.

9. The automobile was technically out of warranty but the Plaintiff contacted Buick and managed to have them pay for the parts for the transmission and presented Defendant with a bill for the labor, only $134.40.

10. The Court finds no evidence of fraud in this matter but that repairs over and above what Defendant was originally told were necessary and were accomplished without notification to Defendant.

CONCLUSION OF LAW

The Plaintiff is entitled to recover judgment in this cause for its labor bill on the legal theory of quantum meruit since there was no express agreement by Defendant to allow further repairs to be made in excess of $50 but Plaintiff in apparent good faith effected the repairs and to allow Defendant to have the benefit of such repairs without paying for them would unjustly enrich Defendant at Plaintiff's expense.

We deem it necessary to consider only one issue presented by Mrs. Deck: Did the trial court err in allowing Harris to recover for work done in direct contradiction of the agreement made by Mrs. Deck and Harris? . . .

. . . [W]e must determine whether Harris can recover payment for work not authorized on the theory that denial of recovery would leave Mrs. Deck unjustly enriched.

In 66 AM. JUR. 2D *Restitution and Implied Contracts* § 27 (1973) appears the following summary:

Restitution for services rendered under mistake is not permitted as freely as for money paid or things given. Frequently it would be unfair to the person benefited by services to require payment, since although benefited he reasonably may be unwilling to pay the price; he does not have the opportunity of return, which usually exists in the case of things received, nor the definite and certain pecuniary advantage which ensues where money has been paid. Thus, where services are rendered to another without intent or agreement by the other party to pay for them, the hardship to the person called upon to pay for the services ordinarily is sufficient to prevent restitution because of mistake.

Where one by mistake in good faith has expended labor and materials on the property of another, not destroying its identity, nor converting it into something substantially different, nor essentially enhancing its value, he cannot recover compensation therefor from the owner, although the owner has availed himself of the benefit. *Nothing could more encourage careless-ness than the acceptance of a principle that one who by mistake performs labor on the property of another should lose nothing by his error, but should have a claim on the owner for remuneration. . . ."* (Footnotes omitted, our emphasis)

The testimony presented at trial reveals that Mrs. Deck expressed her displea-sure as soon as she was presented with a repair bill of $388.98. The trial court entered judgment against Mrs. Deck solely for the purpose of preventing unjust enrichment. Yet Harris was in a far better position to prevent misunderstanding than was Mrs. Deck. Harris used a work order form which provided for written authorization for work to be performed. Harris failed to obtain written authoriza-tion; and Harris, due to "some breakdown in communications," never obtained any authorization for its extra work. Mrs. Deck did not ask that work exceeding a cost of $50 be done, and Mrs. Deck could not return the services rendered.

98 C.J.S. *Work and Labor* 36 (1957) provides this statement:

There can be no recovery for extra work in the absence of an express or implied agreement to pay therefor, where it is performed without the knowledge or consent of the other party, or where recovery for the extra services is precluded by a provision of the contract. It has been held that no quantum meruit recovery may be had for extra work beyond the scope of the contract, or for additional services rendered after expiration of the contract term. . . . (Footnotes omitted)

Finally, in *Engelbrecht v. Property Developers, Inc.*, (1973) 156 Ind. App. 354, 296 N.E.2d 798, 801, this court emphasized that "[w]here there is a contract controlling the rights of the parties there can be no recovery on the theory of quantum meruit." Mrs. Deck and Harris agreed that Harris would not do work exceeding a cost of $50. Harris did not contact Mrs. Deck about further work. Harris, therefore, must be limited to a recovery of $50.

We acknowledge once again that the evidence could have supported different findings of fact. The findings of fact entered by the trial court, however, are not consistent with the judgment entered. Accordingly, this cause is remanded to the trial court with instructions that the judgment be reduced to $50.00. As modified in accordance with these instructions, the judgment is affirmed.

NOTES & QUESTIONS

1. In some cases, a contract fails to be enforceable and the injured party turns to the doctrine of avoiding unjust enrichment. Note, however, that here, the contract between Deck and Harris was valid and enforceable. The court held that "[w]here there is a contract controlling the rights of the parties there can be no recovery on the theory of quantum meruit."

2. *Practice Point*: This fact pattern — a situation where some kind of additional work may be required to complete a task — is quite common in the construction industry and various service industries. And in these settings, courts tend to insist

that there be a traditional contract in place for such additional work.

3. In *Kittyhawk Landing Apts. III v. Anglin Construction Co.*, 737 S.W.2d 90 (Tex. App. 1987), the court considered quantum meruit for "extra" work in the context of a construction contract. First, it determined if the work was properly labeled as "extra" services or materials; second, it determined if the contract provided for this type of "extra" work:

> The right to recover in *quantum meruit* does not grow out of contract, but is based upon the promises implied by law to pay for beneficial services rendered and knowingly accepted. The existence of an express contract does not preclude recovery in *quantum meruit* for the reasonable value of services and materials not covered by a contract. The central issue is whether providing the "extra" 9,000 cubic yards of fill was required in the contract. If providing the fill was part of the contract, then appellee must look to the contract for compensation. *Id.* "In determining whether the work was required by the contracts we must determine (1) whether the work was extra and (2) whether the contracts made provision for the type of extra work performed."

The contract is composed of twenty-five pages of General Conditions of the Contract for Construction (AIA Document A201 1976), five pages of particular terms dealing with the relationship between the contractor Wildwood and the sub-contractor Anglin, and an addendum giving specifications for compacting fill. The description of the work quoted above is found in the five-page segment. Paragraph 5 of this second segment states:

> The Contractor shall be liable to pay in accordance herewith only for work and materials furnished by the Sub-Contractor at the direction of the Contractor pursuant to the terms hereof; and the Sub-Contractor shall not be entitled to payment or damages in connection with any work not done or material not furnished though included herein; the Contractor may order changes in the work, the contract sum being increased or decreased accordingly. All orders and adjustments for any extra work of any kind must be in writing and signed by the Contractor. Sub-Contractor shall have no claim for extra work unless an order in writing is secured from the Contractor, signed by their authorized agent prior to commencement of the work for which such extra charge is claimed, setting forth the exact cost or basis of cost to be allowed for extra work. Any unit price or prices which may be stipulated herein shall govern in determining the value of such additions, substitutions and/or omissions to which said units apply. In case of disagreement as to the adjustment of the contract price, the Sub-Contractor shall proceed with the work pending the determination of such amount.

Appellee contends that the written contract is for *work* of cutting streets and parking areas and constructing building pads and *material* amounting to 6,000 cubic yards of fill. Therefore, the extra 9,000 cubic yards were materials provided outside the contract. Appellee reads paragraph 5 as requiring written orders for extra *work*, not extra *materials*. Thus, under appellee's construction of the contract, his claim for payment for the 9,000 "extra" yards of fill can be based on *quantum meruit*.

We cannot accept appellee's construction of the contract. Reading the contract as a whole, it is clear that the "work" to be provided by appellee included fill. Under article one of the general conditions portion of the contract is this definition: "The Work comprises the completed construction required by the Contract Documents and includes all labor necessary to produce such construction, and all materials and equipment incorporated or to be incorporated in such construction." Even if we were to read the 6,000-cubic-yard figure as a definite amount rather than an estimate, providing fill clearly falls under the general term "work" as used in the contract, and the additional 9,000 cubic yards provided amounted to "extra work" as the term is used in paragraph 5. The contract made provision for the type of extra work performed, and thus appellee must look to the contract for compensation. *Quantum meruit* is not available. [citations omitted]

C. WHERE THERE HAS BEEN NO ATTEMPT TO CONTRACT

COTNAM v. WISDOM
104 S.W. 164 (Ark. 1907)

Action by F.L. Wisdom and another against T.T. Cotnam, administrator of A.M. Harrison, deceased, for services rendered by plaintiffs as surgeons to defendant's intestate. Judgment for plaintiffs. . . .

Instructions 1 and 2, given at the instance of plaintiffs, are as follows:

(1) If you find from the evidence that plaintiffs rendered professional services as physicians and surgeons to the deceased, A.M. Harrison, in a sudden emergency following the deceased's injury in a street car wreck, in an endeavor to save his life, then you are instructed that plaintiffs are entitled to recover from the estate of the said A.M. Harrison such sum as you may find from the evidence is a reasonable compensation for the services rendered.

(2) The character and importance of the operation, the responsibility resting upon the surgeon performing the operation, his experience and professional training, and the ability to pay of the person operated upon, are elements to be considered by you in determining what is a reasonable charge for the services performed by plaintiffs in the particular case. . . .

HILL, C.J. (after stating the facts): The reporter will state the issues and substance of the testimony and set out instructions 1 and 2 given at instance of appellee, and it will be seen therefrom that instruction 1 amounted to a peremptory instruction to find for the plaintiff in some amount.

The first question is as to the correctness of this instruction. As indicated therein the facts are that Mr. Harrison, appellant's intestate, was thrown from a street car, receiving serious injuries which rendered him unconscious, and while in that condition the appellees were notified of the accident and summoned to his assistance by some spectator, and performed a difficult operation in an effort to save his life, but they were unsuccessful, and he died without regaining consciousness. The appellant says: "Harrison was never conscious after his head struck the pavement.

He did not and could not, expressly or impliedly, assent to the action of the appellees. He was without knowledge or will power. However merciful or benevolent may have been the intention of the appellees, a new rule of law, of contract by implication of law, will have to be established by this court in order to sustain the recovery." Appellant is right in saying that the recovery must be sustained by a contract by implication of law, but is not right in saying that it is a new rule of law, for such contracts are almost as old as the English system of jurisprudence. They are usually called "implied contracts." More properly they should be called "quasi contracts" or "constructive contracts." *See* 1 PAGE ON CONTRACTS, § 14; *also* 2 PAGE ON CONTRACTS, § 771.

The following excerpts from *Sceva v. True*, 53 N.H. 627, are peculiarly applicable here:

> We regard it as well settled by the cases referred to in the briefs of counsel, many of which have been commented on at length by Mr. Shirley for the defendant, that an insane person, an idiot, or a person utterly bereft of all sense and reason by the sudden stroke of an accident or disease may be held liable, in assumpsit, for necessaries furnished to him in good faith while in that unfortunate and helpless condition. And the reasons upon which this rest are too broad, as well as too sensible and humane, to be overborne by any deductions which a refined logic may make from the circumstances that in such cases there can be no contract or promise, in fact, no meeting of the minds of the parties. The cases put it on the ground of an implied contract; and by this is not meant, as the defendant's counsel seems to suppose, an actual contract — that is, an actual meeting of the minds of the parties, an actual, mutual understanding, to be inferred from language, acts, and circumstances by the jury — but a contract and promise, said to be implied by the law, where, in point of fact, there was no contract, no mutual understanding, and so no promise. The defendant's counsel says it is usurpation for the court to hold, as a matter of law, that there is a contract and a promise when all the evidence in the case shows that there was not a contract, nor the semblance of one. It is doubtless a legal fiction, invented and sued for the sake of the remedy. If it was originally usurpation, certainly it has now become very inveterate, and firmly fixed in the body of the law. Illustrations might be multiplied, but enough has been said to show that when a contract or promise implied by law is spoken of, a very different thing is meant from a contract in fact, whether express or tacit. The evidence of an actual contract is generally to be found either in some writing made by the parties, or in verbal communications which passed between them, or in their acts and conduct considered in the light of the circumstances of each particular case. A contract implied by law, on the contrary, rests upon no evidence. It has no actual existence. It is simply a mythical creation of the law. The law says it shall be taken that there was a promise, when in point of fact, there was none. Of course this is not good logic, for the obvious and sufficient reason that it is not true. It is a legal fiction, resting wholly for its support on a plain legal obligation, and a plain legal right. If it were true, it would not be a fiction. There is a class of legal rights, with their correlative legal duties, analogous to the obligations quasi ex contractu of the civil law, which seem to lie in the region between contracts on the one hand, and torts on the other, and to call for the application of a remedy not strictly furnished either

by actions ex contractu or actions ex delicto. The common law supplies no action of duty, as it does of assumpsit and trespass; and hence the somewhat awkward contrivance of this fiction to apply the remedy of assumpsit where there is no true contract and no promise to support it. . . .

The defendant sought to require the plaintiff to prove, in addition to the value of the services, the benefit, if any, derived by the deceased from the operation, and alleges error in the court refusing to so instruct the jury. The court was right in refusing to place this burden upon the physicians. The same question was considered in *Ladd v. Witte*, 116 Wis. 35, 92 N.W. 365, where the court said: "That is not at all the test. So that a surgical operation be conceived and performed with due skill and care, the price to be paid therefore does not depend upon the result. The event so generally lies with the forces of nature that all intelligent men know and understand that the surgeon is not responsible therefor. In absence of express agreement, the surgeon, who brings to such a service due skill and care, earns the reasonable and customary price therefor, whether the outcome be beneficial to the patient or the reverse.". . .

NOTES & QUESTIONS

1. In *Cotnam*, the parties made no attempt to contract for services. Further, Mr. Harrison was unable to express his consent to receive the physician's services. The court relied upon the doctrine of avoiding unjust enrichment; this doctrine depends neither on a contract or a party's consent.

However, if Mr. Harrison were conscious and by his words or acts gave his consent to treatment, could there be a contract implied in fact?

See Prudential Ins. Co. v. U.S., 801 F.2d 1295 (Fed. Cir. 1986) (". . . contract implied in fact is not created or evidenced by explicit agreement of the parties, but is inferred as a matter of reason or justice from the acts or conduct of the parties. However, all of the elements of an express contract must be shown by the facts or circumstances surrounding the transaction. . . .").

2. If Mr. Harrison had survived his surgery, how would the court have measured the physicians' recovery? Would it be measured by Mr. Harrison's net worth? By the plaintiff physicians' usual fees? By the amount Mr. Harrison would have had to pay for comparable services?

JEFFS v. STUBBS
970 P.2d 1234 (Utah 1998)

ZIMMERMAN, Justice:

This case involves a dispute over the occupancy of land between twenty-one individuals ("the claimants") and the United Effort Plan Trust ("the UEP"). The claimants built improvements on land located in Hildale, Utah, and Colorado City, Arizona, which they occupy but which is owned by the UEP. Claimants filed an action in Washington County, Utah, to determine their rights in the UEP land they occupy.

Sometime in the late nineteenth century, some members of the Church of Jesus Christ of Latter-Day Saints organized a movement called the Priesthood Work

("The Work") to continue the practice of plural marriage outside that church. In the early part of this century, The Work's leadership — the Priesthood Council — decided to settle its membership in an isolated area to avoid interference with their religious practices. In approximately the 1930s, The Work selected an area composed of Hildale, Utah, and Colorado City, Arizona — an area now known as Short Creek. The Priesthood Council secured a large tract of land in this area, and adherents of The Work began to settle there.

The Work continued to secure additional land in the area. Commonly, its adherents bought land and deeded it to The Work. Eventually, the leadership of The Work formed a trust to hold title to the land. This trust failed, and, for the most part, the land was deeded back to those who contributed it. In 1942, the Priesthood Council signed and recorded in Mohave County, Arizona, a Declaration of Trust for the United Effort Plan. After the Priesthood Council formed the UEP, adherents deeded most of the land that had been held by the first trust to the UEP. Over the years, the UEP acquired more land as adherents obtained and deeded it to the trust. The UEP currently owns all the land occupied by the claimants.

From its inception, the UEP invited members to build their homes on assigned lots on UEP land. Through this system, the UEP intended to localize control over all local real property and to have the religious leaders manage it. Members who built on the trust land were aware that they could not sell or mortgage the land and that they would forfeit their improvements if they left the land. However, the UEP did encourage its members to improve the lots assigned to them and represented to its members that they could live on the land permanently, by using such phrases as "forever" or "as long as you wanted." The leaders also told members that having a home on UEP land was better than having a deed because creditors could not foreclose upon the land for members' debts.

Sometime during the late 1960s or early 1970s, dissension over a doctrinal issue arose among adherents of The Work, causing a split in the Priesthood Council. The dissension broke into the open in 1984 when adherents of The Work split into two groups: One group, led by Rulon T. Jeffs ("Jeffs"), acquired control of the UEP. A second group, led by J. Marion Hammon and Alma Timpson, includes most of the claimants in the present case.

In 1986, Jeffs declared that all those living on UEP land were tenants at will. Before this declaration, neither the UEP nor any of its representatives had told the claimants that they were tenants at will. In 1987, the claimants filed an action in the Federal District Court for the District of Utah, asking the court to determine their rights in the property.

The UEP, in turn, filed an unlawful detainer action and several quiet title actions against some of the claimants in state court in 1989 and 1993. The state court stayed these cases pending resolution of claimants' federal action. In 1993, the federal district court dismissed the federal claims for lack of subject matter jurisdiction and dismissed the pendent state law claims without prejudice. Shortly thereafter, the claimants filed an action in Utah's district court in Washington County. The state court consolidated their action with the UEP's previously filed unlawful detainer action and several quiet title actions.

In these consolidated actions, the claimants presented a number of claims. . . [Including one] that the UEP has been unjustly enriched by their improvements to the land. After a bench trial, the judge made findings of fact and granted claimants relief only on their unjust enrichment claim. We address each issue in turn.

* * *

The UEP's second argument is that because the claimants knew they did not own the land, there is nothing inequitable about the UEP's keeping the improvements without compensating claimants.

* * *

We now turn to our analysis of the trial court's application of the law. Arizona recognizes the equitable remedy of unjust enrichment and generally provides that " '[a] person who has been unjustly enriched at the expense of another is required to make restitution to the other.' " *Murdock-Bryant Constr.*, 703 P.2d at 1202 (quoting RESTATEMENT OF RESTITUTION § 1 (1937)). A person is unjustly enriched if (i) he received a benefit, and (ii) his retention of that benefit would be unjust. *See Flooring Systems, Inc. v. Radisson Group, Inc.*, 160 Ariz. 224, 772 P.2d 578, 581 (1989) (*en banc*). We find that the trial court correctly concluded that claimants proved both elements. Regarding the first element, the trial court found: "There can be no doubt from the evidence presented that [claimant] has conferred a benefit on the UEP by improving the lot." Arizona law defines a benefit as "any form of advantage." *Artukovich & Sons, Inc. v. Reliance Truck Co.*, 126 Ariz. 246, 614 P.2d 327, 329 (1980) (*en banc*). In making its finding, the court relied on evidence showing that the claimants spent a considerable amount of money and time improving the UEP land, that these improvements increased the value of the land, and that the UEP will benefit from the increased value. We agree that this evidence supports the finding that the UEP received some advantage, and, thus, a benefit.

The claimants must also show that the UEP's retention of these benefits would be unjust. The UEP argues that because the claimants knew that the UEP owned the land and because the claimants intended to "donate" the improvements, they cannot recover. We disagree.

In determining whether it would be unjust to allow the retention of benefits without compensation, Arizona law provides that:

> a court need not find that the defendant intended to compensate the plaintiff for the services rendered or that the plaintiff intended that the defendant be the party to make compensation. This is because the duty to compensate for unjust enrichment is an obligation implied by law without reference to the intention of the parties. *What is important is that it be shown that it was not intended or expected that the services be rendered or the benefit conferred gratuitously, and that the benefit was not "conferred officiously."*

Murdock-Bryant Constr., 703 P.2d at 1203 (emphasis added) (internal citation omitted) (quoting *Pyeatte v. Pyeatte*, 135 Ariz. 346, 661 P.2d 196, 203 (Ct. App. 1983)); *see also Flooring Systems*, 772 P.2d at 581.

Thus, under Arizona law, the trial court had to find that (i) services were conferred, (ii) the services were not conferred "officiously," and (iii) it was not intended that the services were "gratuitously" conferred. As we explained above, the trial court found that the claimants conferred a benefit on the UEP — they rendered services by improving the UEP lots.

As to the second element, the claimants plainly did not confer the services officiously. "Officiousness means interference in the affairs of another not justified by the circumstances under which the interference takes place." RESTATEMENT OF RESTITUTION § 2 comment a (1937). Thus, an officious person is one who "thrust[s] benefits upon others." *Id.* Here, the claimants did not interfere or thrust benefits on the UEP. To the contrary, the UEP encouraged the claimants to improve the land. The trial court found: There can also be no doubt that the trust was aware of the benefit as its representatives encouraged the construction and the improvement of the lot by the occupant and watched the building going in. The issue is whether, given the facts of this case, it would be inequitable to allow the UEP to retain the benefit without compensation. . . . The Court is of the opinion that such a result would be inequitable.

Finally, the claimants did not confer their services gratuitously. One renders services gratuitously if at the time they were rendered, there was no expectation of "a return benefit, compensation, or consideration." WEBSTER'S NEW INT'L DICTIONARY 992 (3d ed. 1961); *see also* 66 AM. JUR. 2D *Restitution* § 26 (1973). We conclude that because the claimants built the improvements with the intention that they could occupy them for their lifetimes, they did not confer them gratuitously.

The RESTATEMENT OF RESTITUTION, which Arizona courts follow in the absence of contrary authority, *see Bank of America v. J. & S. Auto Repairs*, 143 Ariz. 416, 694 P.2d 246, 248 (1985), is instructive in determining whether one rendered services gratuitously. Section 40 provides:

> A person who has rendered services to another . . . is entitled to restitution therefor if the services were rendered . . . in the mistaken belief, of which the other knew or had reason to know, that the services would inure to the benefit of the one giving them. . . .

RESTATEMENT OF RESTITUTION § 40 (1937). Thus, one who renders services with the reasonable expectation of a returned benefit does not render the services gratuitously. Section 42 of that RESTATEMENT, which limits a party's right to recovery for improvements to land,[1] specifies that section 40 applies when the true owner, "having notice of the error and of the work being done, stands by and does not use care to prevent the error from continuing." *Id.* § 42 comment b. A comment to section 40 clarifies that an owner "cannot retain a benefit which knowingly he has permitted another to confer upon him by mistake." *Id.* § 40 comment d.

---

[1] [10] Section 42(1) of the RESTATEMENT OF RESTITUTION, governing improvements upon land or chattels, provides:

> Except to the extent that the rule is changed by statute, a person who, in the mistaken belief that he or a third party on whose account he acts is the owner, has caused improvements to be made upon the land of another, is not thereby entitled to restitution from the owner for the value of such improvement; but *if his mistake was reasonable*, the owner is entitled to obtain judgment in an equitable proceeding or in an action for trespass. . . only on condition that he makes restitution to the extent that the land has been increased in value by such improvements, or for the value of labor and materials employed in making such improvements, whichever is least.

RESTATEMENT OF RESTITUTION § 42(1) (1937) (emphasis added). Thus, if a person who made improvements had a reasonable belief of ownership, the true owner may eject the party who made the improvements only after paying restitution for the improvements.

The trial court concluded that the claimants "expected to use the property into the foreseeable future" and "[a]s a result [they] invested lots of money and time in the improvement of the property." The court also found that the claimants improved the land with the knowledge and encouragement of the UEP and with the understanding that they could remain on the land for their lifetimes. The court further indicated that the UEP failed to disabuse claimants of their beliefs that they could remain on the land for their lifetimes. The court stated:

> The UEP must bear a large share of the blame for the confusion as to the terms of occupancy since it did not communicate to [claimants] directly the conditions of [their] occupancy . . . even though the trust was engaged in a long term and wide spread program of settling its people on UEP lands. It would have been easy to prepare a list of conditions of occupancy and to distribute the list to those preparing to invest heavily in improvements with the encouragement and agreement of the trust.

Applying the law to these facts, we conclude that the trial court's disposition was adequately supported by the evidence and was consistent with the Arizona substantive law. We therefore find that the trial court did not abuse its discretion in requiring the UEP to allow claimants to live on the land for their lifetimes or to compensate them for the improvements.

We next consider the trial court's unjust enrichment ruling under Utah law, as that law governs the claims of any Utah residents. . . for whom an equitable remedy is more favorable. Utah law, like Arizona's, recognizes the remedy of unjust enrichment. A party may prevail on an unjust enrichment theory by proving three elements:

> "(1) a benefit conferred on one person by another; (2) an appreciation or knowledge by the conferee of the benefit; and (3) the acceptance or retention by the conferee of the benefit under such circumstances as to make it inequitable for the conferee to retain the benefit without payment of its value."

American Towers Owners, 930 P.2d at 1192 (citations omitted). Although these elements are phrased differently than Arizona's, we find the analysis to be much the same.

Regarding the first two elements, the trial court, as discussed above, found that claimants conferred a benefit by improving the property and that the UEP knew about, and, indeed, encouraged the improvements.

We addressed the third element in *Baugh v. Darley*, 112 Utah 1, 184 P.2d 335 (1947). This court stated:

> Unjust enrichment of a person occurs when he has and retains money or benefits which in justice and equity belong to another. The benefit may be . . . beneficial services conferred. . . . Services officiously or gratuitously furnished are not recoverable. Nor are services performed by the plaintiff for his own advantage, and from which the defendant benefits incidentally, recoverable.

Id. at 337 (internal citations omitted).

Here, the claimants improved the land in reliance upon the UEP's representations that they could live on the land for the rest of their lives. Even though the claimants intended to benefit from the improvements by occupying them during their lifetimes, the claimants' services still conferred a direct, not incidental, benefit on the UEP. Thus, we uphold the trial court's equitable remedy for all claimants, both those occupying land in Arizona and Utah.

*   *   *

In conclusion, we uphold the trial court's equitable ruling allowing claimants to remain on the land for their lifetimes or requiring the UEP to compensate claimants for the benefit it received if it seeks to remove claimants.

*   *   *

NOTES & QUESTIONS

1. The *Jeffs v. Stubbs* court addressed another challenge to the lower court's use of the doctrine of avoiding unjust enrichment. The UEP argued that "the religious context of this case should prohibit a court from applying unjust enrichment principles. Essentially, the UEP argues that balancing the equities between the UEP and claimants is tantamount to judging the fairness of the UEP's religious practices and is therefore prohibited." 970 P.2d at 1243. The court rejected the argument and concluded that UEP had cited no law "suggesting that a court should limit the application of the doctrine of unjust enrichment solely because of the religious nature of the relationship and motivation of the UEP and claimants." *Id.*

2. Both cases present the doctrine of avoiding unjust enrichment in settings where labor or services were performed in the absence of contract. The benefits received by defendant, whether medical attention or improvements upon land, however, cannot be ones that the plaintiff conferred gratuitously or officiously thrust upon the defendant.

3. The employment setting has also provided examples of the doctrine of avoiding unjust enrichment. An employee submitted a useful new idea in the employer's suggestion box, but if the employer uses that idea and reaps savings from it, should the employee have a claim based on unjust enrichment? *See Schott v. Westinghouse Electric Corp.*, 259 A.2d 443 (Pa. 1969). An exemplary employee volunteers his idea to solve a defect found in the employer's product. The employer did not ask for the employee's solution; he learned of the product's defect from talk among employees. His solution to the problem proved effective enough that his employer used it and saved costs that would have been expended to replace the defective products. When the employee asked to be compensated for the use of his idea, the employer was advised by its attorneys that it could make full use of the idea without compensating the employee. Is this a case of unjust enrichment? *See Dewey v. American Stair Glide Corp.*, 557 S.W.2d 643 (Mo. App. 1977).

PROBLEMS

1. Claire Collins retained Maria Alvarez, Esquire, on a one-third contingency fee contract to represent her in a personal injury action. For several months, Alvarez diligently pursued discovery as well as settlement negotiations. Then Collins terminated Alvarez. She then retained Frank Barnett, Esquire, to represent her in the case, also under a one-third contingency fee arrangement. After Barnett had

pursued the case diligently for several months, Collins terminated him also. Collins then promptly settled the case for $300,000.

Both Alvarez and Barnett have demanded one-third of the $300,000 recovery. In the alternative, they have each demanded an amount that represents the reasonable value of the legal services each provided to Collins.

Should the terminated attorneys be able to recover from Collins? Under what theory of recovery — the contingency fee contract or unjust enrichment? How should the recovery be calculated?

The seminal case addressing the recovery available for a contingency fee attorney discharged by a client before settlement or judgment is *Fracasse v. Brent*, 494 P.2d 9 (Cal. 1972).

2. What if, after discharging both Alvarez and Barnett, Collins had not settled the case, but instead permitted the statute of limitations to run on the personal injury claim? Now the discharged attorneys again seek to recover compensation for their work. What should be the result in this situation?

3. Allan Weltner operated an auto wrecker service. He received a call from the state police to go to Ann Owen's home and to remove her vehicle and tow it to Weltner's storage garage. Weltner did so and the police came to his business and inspected the Owen automobile there. Police were investigating an auto accident they believed Owen had been involved in. Owen's automobile was later released from Weltner's garage.

Weltner then sought to recover from Owen the costs he incurred in towing and later storing her automobile. Weltner argues that the court should use the doctrine of avoiding unjust enrichment or quasi contract to permit his recovery of the towing and storage costs. How should the court rule on this request?

See Connors v. Wilkinson, 387 A.2d 568 (Conn. Common Pleas 1978).

4. Hotel owner Marge Olney was approached by Todd Workman with an offer to have him lease and operate the hotel. Workman moved into the hotel and with Olney's knowledge, he undertook extensive remodeling of the hotel. For the first six months he lived and worked in the hotel, Workman's monthly rent was excused because of his improvements on the hotel. But after those six months, Workman and Olney had a falling out and when the next month's rent was due and went unpaid, Olney notified Workman that he had to vacate the hotel premises. Workman could not pay rent; the remodeling work he engaged in had exceeded the amount of rent due.

Workman left and then brought a claim for unjust enrichment against Olney to recover the amount he spent on the remodeling work. How should the court rule on Workman's claim?

See Hertz v. Ficus, 567 P.2d 1 (Ida. 1977).

CHAPTER 7

RELIANCE AND PROMISSORY ESTOPPEL

A. OVERVIEW

A contract and promissory estoppel are two separate and distinct legal theories. They "are two different creatures of law; they are not legally synonymous; the birth of one does not spawn another." *Duke Power Co. v. S.C. Pub. Serv. Comm'n*, 284 S.C. 81, 100, 326 S.E.2d 395, 406 (1985). This chapter will primarily focus on when a person can recover damages caused by another's promise, which is usually a spoken promise.

Chapter 2 through Chapter 5 of this text delineate the elements required to form a traditional contract. At minimum, to form an enforceable contract, there must be an offer, an acceptance, some form of bargained-for consideration and reasonable agreement as to the terms of the contract. If these elements are present, and one party is in breach, then recovery can simply be based on a claim of breach of contract.

There are times when one party induces another to take steps in reliance upon the first party's promise, although the parties have not agreed to a contract. And, there are times when as a matter of sound legal policy, the promisor should be held responsible for such a promise. This situation may arise, for example, when the aggrieved party is unable to prove each element required of a formal contract, or when the parties are acting upon a less than complete contract. In other words, the first party should be estopped to deny its promise and the reasonably expected consequences (the reliance by the promisee).

The doctrine of promissory estoppel, which was developed out of sound legal policies and has evolved over the past hundred years, "is one which supplies a needed tool which courts may employ in a proper case to prevent injustice." *Hoffman v. Red Owl Stores, Inc.*, 26 Wis. 2d 683, 133 N.W.2d 267 (1965). The doctrine of promissory estoppel was set out in the Restatement (Second) of Contracts § 90 (1932) as follows:

> A promise which the promisor should reasonably expect to induce action or forbearance of a definite and substantial character on the part of the promisee and which does induce such action or forbearance is binding if injustice can be avoided only by enforcement of the promise.

The later Restatement (Second) of Contracts § 90 (1981) provides as follows:

> (1) A promise which the promisor should reasonably expect to induce action or forbearance on the part of the promisee or a third person and which does induce such action or forbearance is binding if injustice can be avoided only by enforcement of the promise. The remedy granted for breach may be limited as justice requires.

(2) A charitable subscription or a marriage settlement is binding under Subsection (1) without proof that the promise induced action or forbearance.

The doctrine of Promissory Estoppel can be viewed in at least two ways. It can be viewed as a sort of substitute for consideration. The plaintiff has reasonably relied on the defendant's promise and taken steps to his detriment in that reliance. When the plaintiff then sues to enforce the contract, the defendant asserts the defense that because there was no consideration exchanged, there can be no contract to enforce. Promissory estoppel would estop, or prevent, the defendant from using this defense and would substitute consideration with the plaintiff's detrimental reliance and create a valid, enforceable contract. So the promisor is estopped from pleading in defense that there was no consideration.

Promissory estoppel can also be viewed as an affirmative right or claim the plaintiff brings against the defendant to enforce the defendant's promise. The plaintiff shows he has met the elements of promissory estoppel and can then recover on that claim.

While reading this chapter, contemplate the following example: While at a family gathering, Steve's uncle, Red, who is disappointed that Steve is a heavy smoker at the age of 15, tells Steve that if he quits smoking for two years, he will give Steve his Corvette, which happens to be red. Two years later, Steve approaches Red and tells him that he is ready to pick up the Corvette because he has not smoked in two years. What rights, if any, does the doctrine of promissory estoppel confer on Steve?

B. THE BASIC ESTOPPEL DOCTRINE

As a matter of fundamental fairness, people should be accountable for the intended and expected consequences of their actions. But how far should the law go to protect individuals who rely on the promises of others? Should it make a difference whether the promise is pronounced in a commercial setting, or in other settings such as a family gathering or a dark alley? Consider those questions as you read the following section.

RICKETTS v. SCOTHORN
57 Neb. 51, 77 N.W. 365 (1898)

SULLIVAN, Judge:

In the district court of Lancaster county the plaintiff, Katie Scothorn, recovered judgment against the defendant, Andrew D. Ricketts, as executor of the last will and testament of John C. Ricketts, deceased. The action was based upon a promissory note, of which the following is a copy: "May the first, 1891. I promise to pay to Katie Scothorn on demand, $2,000, to be at 6 per cent. per annum. J. C. Ricketts." In the petition the plaintiff alleges that the consideration for the execution of the note was that she should surrender her employment as bookkeeper for Mayer Bros., and cease to work for a living. She also alleges that the note was given to induce her to abandon her occupation, and that, relying on it, and on the annual interest, as a means of support, she gave up the employment in which she was then engaged. These allegations of the petition are denied by the administrator. The material facts are undisputed. They are as follows: John C.

Ricketts, the maker of the note, was the grandfather of the plaintiff. Early in May — presumably on the day the note bears date — he called on her at the store where she was working. What transpired between them is thus described by Mr. Flodene, one of the plaintiff's witnesses:

> A. Well, the old gentleman came in there one morning about nine o'clock, probably a little before or a little after, but early in the morning, and he unbuttoned his vest, and took out a piece of paper in the shape of a note; that is the way it looked to me; and he says to Miss Scothorn, "I have fixed out something that you have not got to work any more." He says, none of my grandchildren work, and you don't have to.

> Q. Where was she?

> A. She took the piece of paper and kissed him, and kissed the old gentleman, and commenced to cry.

It seems Miss Scothorn immediately notified her employer of her intention to quit work, and that she did soon after abandon her occupation. The mother of the plaintiff was a witness, and testified that she had a conversation with her father, Mr. Ricketts, shortly after the note was executed, in which he informed her that he had given the note to the plaintiff to enable her to quit work; that none of his grandchildren worked, and he did not think she ought to. For something more than a year the plaintiff was without an occupation, but in September, 1892, with the consent of her grandfather, and by his assistance, she secured a position as bookkeeper with Messrs. Funke & Ogden. On June 8, 1894, Mr. Ricketts died. He had paid one year's interest on the note, and a short time before his death expressed regret that he had not been able to pay the balance.

In the summer or fall of 1892 he stated to his daughter, Mrs. Scothorn, that if he could sell his farm in Ohio he would pay the note out of the proceeds. He at no time repudiated the obligation. We quite agree with counsel for the defendant that upon this evidence there was nothing to submit to the jury, and that a verdict should have been directed peremptorily for one of the parties. The testimony of Flodene and Mrs. Scothorn, taken together, conclusively establishes the fact that the note was not given in consideration of the plaintiff pursuing, or agreeing to pursue, any particular line of conduct. There was no promise on the part of the plaintiff to do, or refrain from doing, anything. Her right to the money promised in the note was not made to depend upon an abandonment of her employment with Mayer Bros., and further abstention from like service. Mr. Ricketts made no condition, requirement, or request. He exacted no quid pro quo. He gave the note as a gratuity, and looked for nothing in return. So far as the evidence discloses, it was his purpose to place the plaintiff in a position of independence, where she could work or remain idle, as she might choose. The abandonment of Miss Scothorn of her position as bookkeeper was altogether voluntary. It was not an act done in fulfillment of any contract obligation assumed when she accepted the note. The instrument in suit, being given without any valuable consideration, was nothing more than a promise to make a gift in the future of the sum of money therein named. Ordinarily, such promises are not enforceable, even when put in the form of a promissory note. *Kirkpatrick v. Taylor*, 43 Ill. 207; *Phelps v. Phelps*, 28 Barb. 121. . . . But it has often been held that an action on a note given to a church, college, or other like institution, upon the faith of which money has been expended or obligations incurred, could not be successfully defended on the ground of a want of consideration. *Barnes v. Perine*, 12 N.Y. 18; *Philomath College v. Hartless*, 6 Or. 158; *Thompson v. Board*, 40 Ill. 379. . . . In this class of cases the note in suit is nearly always spoken of as a gift or donation, but the decision is generally put on the ground that the expenditure of money or assumption of liability by the donee on the faith of the promise constitutes a valuable and sufficient consideration. It seems to us that the true reason is the preclusion of the defendant, under the doctrine of estoppel, to deny the consideration. Such seems to be the view of the matter taken by the supreme court of Iowa in the case of Simpson Centenary *College v. Tuttle*, 71 Iowa 596,33 N.W. 74, where Rothrock, J., speaking for the court, said: "Where a note, however, is based on a promise to give for the support of the objects referred to, it may still be open to this defense [want of consideration], unless it shall appear that the donee has, prior to any revocation, entered into engagements, or made expenditures based on such promise, so that he must suffer loss or injury if the note is not paid. This is based on the equitable principle that, after allowing the donee to incur obligations on the faith that the note would be paid, the donor would be estopped from pleading want of consideration." And in the case of *Reimensnyder v. Gans*, 110 Pa. St. 17, 2 Atl. 425, which was an action on a note given as a donation to a charitable object, the court said: "The fact is that, as we may see from the case of *Ryers v. Trustees*, 33 Pa. St. 114, a contract of the kind here involved is enforceable rather by way of estoppel than on the ground of consideration in the original undertaking." It has, been held that a note given in expectation of the payee performing certain services, but without any contract binding him to serve, will not support an action. *Hulse v. Hulse*, 84 E.C.L. 709. But when the payee changes his position to his disadvantage in reliance on the promise, a right of action does arise. *McClure v. Wilson*, 43 Ill. 356; *Trustees v. Garvey*, 53 Ill. 401.

Under the circumstances of this case, is there an equitable estoppel which ought to preclude the defendant from alleging that the note in controversy is lacking in one of the essential elements of a valid contract? We think there is. An estoppel in pais is defined to be "a right arising from acts, admissions, or conduct which have induced a change of position in accordance with the real or apparent intention of the party against whom they are alleged." Mr. Pomeroy has formulated the following definition: "Equitable estoppel is the effect of the voluntary conduct of a party whereby he is absolutely precluded, both at law and in equity, from asserting rights which might, perhaps, have otherwise existed, either of property, of contract, or of remedy, as against another person who in good faith relied upon such conduct and has been led thereby to change his position for the worse, and who on his part acquires some corresponding right, either of property, of contract, or of remedy." 2 POM. EQ. JUR. 804. According to the undisputed proof, as shown by the record before us, the plaintiff was a working girl, holding a position in which she earned a salary of $10 per week. Her grandfather, desiring to put her in a position of independence, gave her the note, accompanying it with the remark that his other grandchildren did not work, and that she would not be obliged to work any longer. In effect, he suggested that she might abandon her employment, and rely in the future upon the bounty which he promised. He doubtless desired that she should give up her occupation, but, whether he did or not, it is entirely certain that he contemplated such action on her part as a reasonable and probable consequence of his gift. Having intentionally influenced the plaintiff to alter her position for the worse on the faith of the note being paid when due, it would be grossly inequitable to permit the maker, or his executor, to resist payment on the ground that the promise was given without consideration. The petition charges the elements of an equitable estoppel, and the evidence conclusively establishes them. . . . The judgment is right, and is affirmed.

NOTES & QUESTIONS

1. Could this case be argued by the plaintiff as a unilateral contract case? (*See* Chapter 3, section E. Unilateral Contracts.)

2. What is the difference between equitable estoppel and promissory estoppel? Was the preceding case genuinely an equitable estoppel case?

3. How would this case have turned out under the RESTATEMENT approach?

HOFFMAN v. RED OWL STORES, INC.
26 Wis. 2d 683, 133 N.W.2d 267 (1965)

Action by Joseph Hoffman (hereinafter "Hoffman") and wife, plaintiffs, against defendants Red Owl Stores, Inc. (hereinafter "Red Owl") and Edward Lukowitz.

The complaint alleged that Lukowitz, as agent for Red Owl, represented to and agreed with plaintiffs that Red Owl would build a store building in Chilton and stock it with merchandise for Hoffman to operate in return for which plaintiffs were to put up and invest a total sum of $18,000; that in reliance upon the above mentioned agreement and representations plaintiffs sold their bakery building and business and their grocery store and business; also in reliance on the agreement and representations Hoffman purchased the building site in Chilton and rented a residence for himself and his family in Chilton; plaintiffs' actions in reliance on the representations and agreement disrupted their personal and business life; plaintiffs lost substantial amounts of income and expended large sums of money as expenses. Plaintiffs demanded recovery of damages for the breach of defendants' representations and agreements.

The action was tried to a court and jury. The facts hereafter stated are taken from the evidence adduced at the trial. Where there was a conflict in the evidence the version favorable to plaintiffs has been accepted since the verdict rendered was in favor of plaintiffs.

Hoffman assisted by his wife operated a bakery at Wautoma from 1956 until sale of the building late in 1961. The building was owned in joint tenancy by him and his wife. Red Owl is a Minnesota corporation having its home office at Hopkins, Minnesota. It owns and operates a number of grocery supermarket stores and also extends franchises to agency stores which are owned by individuals, partnerships and corporations. Lukowitz resides at Green Bay and since September, 1960, has been divisional manager for Red Owl in a territory comprising Upper Michigan and most of Wisconsin in charge of 84 stores. Prior to September, 1960, he was district manager having charge of approximately 20 stores.

In November, 1959, Hoffman was desirous of expanding his operations by establishing a grocery store and contacted a Red Owl representative by the name of Jansen, now deceased. Numerous conversations were had in 1960 with the idea of establishing a Red Owl franchise store in Wautoma. In September, 1960, Lukowitz succeeded Jansen as Red Owl's representative in the negotiations. Hoffman mentioned that $18,000 was all the capital he had available to invest and he was repeatedly assured that this would be sufficient to set him up in business as a Red Owl store. About Christmastime, 1960, Hoffman thought it would be a good idea if he bought a small grocery store in Wautoma and operated it in order that he gain experience in the grocery business prior to operating a Red Owl store in some larger community. On February 6, 1961, on the advice of Lukowitz and Sykes, who had succeeded Lukowitz as Red Owl's district manager, Hoffman bought the inventory and fixtures of a small grocery store in Wautoma and leased the building in which it was operated.

After three months of operating this Wautoma store, the Red Owl representatives came in and took inventory and checked the operations and found the store was operating at a profit. Lukowitz advised Hoffman to sell the store to his manager, and assured him that Red Owl would find a larger store for him elsewhere. Acting on this advice and assurance, Hoffman sold the fixtures and inventory to his manager on June 6, 1961. Hoffman was reluctant to sell at that time because it meant losing the summer tourist business, but he sold on the assurance that he would be operating in a new location by fall and that he must sell this store if he wanted a bigger one. Before selling, Hoffman told the Red Owl representatives that he had $18,000 for "getting set up in business" and they assured him that there would be no problems in establishing him in a bigger operation. The makeup of the $18,000 was not discussed; it was understood plaintiff's father-in-law would furnish part of it. By June, 1961, the towns for the new grocery store had been narrowed down to two, Kewaunee and Chilton. In Kewaunee, Red Owl had an option on a building site. In Chilton, Red Owl had nothing under option, but it did select a site to which plaintiff obtained an option at Red Owl's suggestion. The option stipulated a purchase price of $6,000 with $1,000 to be paid on election to purchase and the balance to be paid within 30 days. On Lukowitz's assurance that everything was all set plaintiff paid $1,000 down on the lot on September 15th.

On September 27, 1961, plaintiff met at Chilton with Lukowitz and Mr. Reymund and Mr. Carlson from the home office who prepared a projected financial statement. Part of the funds plaintiffs were to supply as their investment in the venture were to be obtained by sale of their Wautoma bakery building.

On the basis of this meeting Lukowitz assured Hoffman: ". . . [E]verything is ready to go. Get your money together and we are set." Shortly after this meeting Lukowitz told plaintiffs that they would have to sell their bakery business and bakery building, and that their retaining this property was the only "hitch" in the entire plan. On November 6, 1961, plaintiffs sold their bakery building for $10,000. Hoffman was to retain the bakery equipment as he contemplated using it to operate a bakery in connection with his Red Owl store. After sale of the bakery Hoffman obtained employment on the night shift at an Appleton bakery.

The record contains different exhibits which were prepared in September and October, some of which were projections of the fiscal operation of the business and others were proposed building and floor plans. Red Owl was to procure some third party to buy the Chilton lot from Hoffman, construct the building, and then lease it to Hoffman. No final plans were ever made, nor were bids let or a construction contract entered. Some time prior to November 20, 1961, certain of the terms of the lease under which the building was to be rented by Hoffman were understood between him and Lukowitz. The lease was to be for 10 years with a rental approximating $550 a month calculated on the basis of 1 percent per month on the building cost, plus 6 percent of the land cost divided on a monthly basis. At the end of the 10-year term he was to have an option to renew the lease for an additional 10-year period or to buy the property at cost on an installment basis. There was no discussion as to what the installments would be or with respect to repairs and maintenance.

On November 22nd or 23rd, Lukowitz and plaintiffs met in Minneapolis with Red Owl's credit manager to confer on Hoffman's financial standing and on financing the agency. Another projected financial statement was there drawn up entitled, "Proposed Financing For An Agency Store." This showed Hoffman contributing $24,100 of cash capital of which only $4,600 was to be cash possessed by plaintiffs. Eight thousand was to be procured as a loan from a Chilton bank secured by a mortgage on the bakery fixtures, $7,500 was to be obtained on a 5 percent loan from the father-in-law, and $4,000 was to be obtained by sale of the lot to the lessor at a profit.

A week or two after the Minneapolis meeting Lukowitz showed Hoffman a telegram from the home office to the effect that if plaintiff could get another $2,000 for promotional purposes the deal could go through for $26,000. Hoffman stated he would have to find out if he could get another $2,000. He met with his father-in-law, who agreed to put $13,000 into the business provided he could come into the business as a partner. Lukowitz told Hoffman the partnership arrangement "sounds fine" and that Hoffman should not go into the partnership arrangement with the "front office." On January 16, 1962, the Red Owl credit manager teletyped Lukowitz that the father-in-law would have to sign an agreement that the $13,000 was either a gift or a loan subordinate to all general creditors and that he would prepare the agreement. On January 31, 1962, Lukowitz teletyped the home office that the father-in-law would sign one or other of the agreements. However, Hoffman testified that it was not until the final meeting some time between January 26th and February 2nd, 1962, that he was told that his father-in-law was expected to sign an agreement that the $13,000 he was advancing was to be an outright gift. No mention was then made by the Red Owl representatives of the alternative of the father-in-law signing a subordination agreement. At this meeting the Red Owl agents presented Hoffman with [a] projected financial statement.

. . .

Hoffman interpreted the . . . statement to require of plaintiffs a total of $34,000 cash made up of $13,000 gift from his father-in-law, $2,000 on mortgage, $8,000 on Chilton bank loan, $5,000 in cash from plaintiff, and $6,000 on the resale of the Chilton lot. Red Owl claims $18,000 is the total of the unborrowed or unencumbered cash, that is, $13,000 from the father-in-law and $5,000 cash from Hoffman himself. Hoffman informed Red Owl he could not go along with this proposal, and particularly objected to the requirement that his father-in-law sign an agreement that his $13,000 advancement was an absolute gift. This terminated the negotiations between the parties.

The case was submitted to the jury on a special verdict with the first two questions answered by the court. This verdict, as returned by the jury, was as follows:

> Question No. 1: Did the Red Owl Stores, Inc. and Joseph Hoffman on or about mid-May of 1961 initiate negotiations looking to the establishment of Joseph Hoffman as a franchise operator of a Red Owl Store in Chilton? Answer: Yes. (Answered by the Court.)

Question No. 2: Did the parties mutually agree on all of the details of the proposal so as to reach a final agreement thereon? Answer: No. (Answered by the Court.)

Question No. 3: Did the Red Owl Stores, Inc., in the course of said negotiations, make representations to Joseph Hoffman that if he fulfilled certain conditions that they would establish him as franchise operator of a Red Owl Store in Chilton? Answer: Yes.

Question No. 4: If you have answered Question No. 3 "Yes," then answer this question: Did Joseph Hoffman rely on said representations and was he induced to act thereon? Answer: Yes.

Question No. 5 : If you have answered Question No. 4 "Yes," then answer this question: Ought Joseph Hoffman, in the exercise of ordinary care, to have relied on said representations? Answer: Yes.

Question No. 6: If you have answered Question No. 3 "Yes" then answer this question: Did Joseph Hoffman fulfill all the conditions he was required to fulfill by the terms of the negotiations between the parties up to January 26, 1962? Answer: Yes.

Question No. 7: What sum of money will reasonably compensate the plaintiffs for such damages as they sustained by reason of:

(a) The sale of the Wautoma store fixtures and inventory?

Answer: $16,735.00.

(b) The sale of the bakery building?

Answer: $2,000.00.

(c) Taking up the option on the Chilton lot?

Answer: $1,000.00.

(d) Expenses of moving his family to Neenah?

Answer: $140.00.

(e) House rental in Chilton?

Answer: $125.00.

. . . On March 31, 1964, the circuit court entered the following order:

IT IS ORDERED in accordance with said decision on motions after verdict hereby incorporated herein by reference:

1. That the answer of the jury to Question No. 7(a) be and the same is hereby vacated and set aside and that a new trial be had on the sole issue of the damages for loss, if any, on the sale of the Wautoma store, fixtures and inventory.

2. That all other portions of the verdict of the jury be and hereby are approved and confirmed and all after verdict motions of the parties inconsistent with this order are hereby denied. . . .

CURRIE, Chief Justice:

The instant appeal and cross-appeal present these questions:

(1) Whether this court should recognize causes of action grounded on promissory estoppel as exemplified by § 90 of RESTATEMENT, 1 CONTRACTS?

(2) Do the facts in this case make out a cause of action for promissory estoppel?

(3) Are the jury's findings with respect to damages sustained by the evidence?

Recognition of a Cause of Action
Grounded on Promissory Estoppel.

Sec. 90 of RESTATEMENT, 1 CONTRACTS [1932], provides (at p. 110):

> A promise which the promisor should reasonably expect to induce action or forbearance of a definite and substantial character on the part of the promisee and which does induce such action of forbearance is binding if injustice can be avoided only by enforcement of the promise. . . .

Since 1933, the closest approach this court has made to adopting the rule of the RESTATEMENT occurred in the recent case of *Lazarus v. American Motors Corp.*, 21 Wis. 2d 76, 85, 123 N.W.2d 548, 553 (1963) wherein the court stated:

> We recognize that upon different facts it would be possible for a seller of steel to have altered his position so as to effectuate the equitable considerations inherent in § 90 of the RESTATEMENT.

While it was not necessary to the disposition of the Lazarus case to adopt the promissory estoppel rule of the RESTATEMENT, we are squarely faced in the instant case with that issue. Not only did the trial court frame the special verdict on the theory of § 90 of RESTATEMENT, 1 CONTRACTS, but no other possible theory has been presented to or discovered by this court which would permit plaintiffs to recover. Of other remedies considered that of an action for fraud and deceit seemed to be the most comparable. An action at law for fraud, however, cannot be predicated on unfulfilled promises unless the promisor possessed the present intent not to perform. *Suskey v. Davidoff* (1958), 2 Wis. 2d 503, 507, 87 N.W.2d 306, and cases cited, Here, there is no evidence that would support a finding that Lukowitz made any of the promises, upon which plaintiffs' complaint is predicated, in bad faith with any present intent that they would not be fulfilled by Red Owl.

Many courts of other jurisdictions have seen fit over the years to adopt the principle of promissory estoppel, and the tendency in that direction continues. As Mr. Justice McFADDIN, speaking in behalf of the Arkansas court, well stated, that the development of the law of promissory estoppel "is an attempt by the courts to keep remedies abreast of increased moral consciousness of honesty and fair representations in all business dealings." *Peoples National Bank of Little Rock v. Linebarger Construction Company* (1951), 219 Ark. 11, 17, 240 S.W.2d 12, 16. . . .

The RESTATEMENT avoids use of the term "promissory estoppel," and there has been criticism of it as an inaccurate term. *See* 1A Corbin, CONTRACTS, p. 232, *et seq.*, § 204. On the other hand, Williston advocated the use of this term or something equivalent. 1 Williston, CONTRACTS (1st ed.), p. 308, § 139. Use of the word "estoppel" to describe a doctrine upon which a party to a lawsuit may obtain affirmative relief offends the traditional concept that estoppel merely serves as a shield and cannot serve as a sword to create a cause of action. *See Utschig v. McClone* (1962), 16 Wis.

2d 506, 509, 114 N.W.2d 854. "Attractive nuisance" is also a much criticized term. *See* concurring opinion, *Flamingo v. City of Waukesha* (1952), 262 Wis. 219, 227, 55 N.W.2d 24. However, the latter term is still in almost universal use by the courts because of the lack of a better substitute. The same is also true of the wide use of the term "promissory estoppel." We have employed its use in this opinion not only because of its extensive use by other courts but also since a more accurate equivalent has not been devised.

Because we deem the doctrine of promissory estoppel, as stated in Section 90 of RESTATEMENT, 1 CONTRACTS, is one which supplies a needed tool which courts may employ in a proper case to prevent injustice, we endorse and adopt it.

Applicability of Doctrine to Facts of this Case.

The record here discloses a number of promises and assurances given to Hoffman by Lukowitz in behalf of Red Owl upon which plaintiffs relied and acted upon to their detriment.

Foremost were the promises that for the sum of $18,000 Red Owl would establish Hoffman in a store. After Hoffman had sold his grocery store and paid the $1,000 on the Chilton lot, the $18,000 figure was changed to $24,100. Then in November, 1961, Hoffman was assured that if the $24,100 figure were increased by $2,000 the deal would go through. Hoffman was induced to sell his grocery store fixtures and inventory in June, 1961, on the promise that he would be in his new store by fall. In November, plaintiffs sold their bakery building on the urging of defendants and on the assurance that this was the last step necessary to have the deal with Red Owl go through.

We determine that there was ample evidence to sustain the answers of the jury to the questions of the verdict with respect to the promissory representations made by Red Owl, Hoffman's reliance thereon in the exercise of ordinary care, and his fulfillment of the conditions required of him by the terms of the negotiations had with Red Owl.

There remains for consideration the question of law raised by defendants that agreement was never reached on essential factors necessary to establish a contract between Hoffman and Red Owl. Among these were the size, cost, design, and layout of the store building; and the terms of the lease with respect to rent, maintenance, renewal, and purchase options. This poses the question of whether the promise necessary to sustain a cause of action for promissory estoppel must embrace all essential details of a proposed transaction between promisor and promisee so as to be the equivalent of an offer that would result in a binding contract between the parties if the promisee were to accept the same.

Originally the doctrine of promissory estoppel was invoked as a substitute for consideration rendering a gratuitous promise enforceable as a contract. *See* Williston, CONTRACTS (1st ed.), p. 307, § 139. In other words, the acts of reliance by the promisee to his detriment provided a substitute for consideration. If promissory estoppel were to be limited to only those situations where the promise giving rise to the cause of action must be so definite with respect to all details that a contract would result were the promise supported by consideration, then the defendants' instant promises to Hoffman would not meet this test. However, § 90 of RESTATE-MENT, 1 CONTRACTS, does not impose the requirement that the promise giving rise to the cause of action must be so comprehensive in scope as to meet the requirements of an offer that would ripen into a contract if accepted by the promisee. Rather the conditions imposed are:

(1) Was the promise one which the promisor should reasonably expect to induce action or forbearance of a definite and substantial character on the part of the promisee?

(2) Did the promise induce such action or forbearance?

(3) Can injustice be avoided only by enforcement of the promise?

We deem it would be a mistake to regard an action grounded on promissory estoppel as the equivalent of a breach of contract action. As Dean Boyer points out, it is desirable that fluidity in the application of the concept be maintained. 98 University of Pennsylvania Law Review (1950), 459, at page 497. While the first two of the above listed three requirements of promissory estoppel present issues of fact which ordinarily will be resolved by a jury, the third requirement, that the remedy can only be invoked where necessary to avoid injustice, is one that involves a policy decision by the court. Such a policy decision necessarily embraces an element of discretion.

We conclude that injustice would result here if plaintiffs were not granted some relief because of the failure of defendants to keep their promises which induced plaintiffs to act to their detriment.

Damages.

Defendants attack all the items of damages awarded by the jury.

The bakery building at Wautoma was sold at defendants' instigation in order that Hoffman might have the net proceeds available as part of the cash capital he was to invest in the Chilton store venture. The evidence clearly establishes that it was sold at a loss of $2,000. Defendants contend that half of this loss was sustained by Mrs. Hoffman because title stood in joint tenancy. They point out that no dealings took place between her and defendants as all negotiations were had with her husband. Ordinarily only the promisee and not third persons are entitled to enforce the remedy of promissory estoppel against the promisor. However, if the promisor actually foresees, or has reason to foresee, action by a third person in reliance on the promise, it may be quite unjust to refuse to perform the promise. 1A Corbin, Contracts, p. 220, § 200. Here not only did defendants foresee that it would be necessary for Mrs. Hoffman to sell her joint interest in the bakery building, but defendants actually requested that this be done. We approve the jury's award of $2,000 damages for the loss incurred by both plaintiffs in this sale.

Defendants attack on two grounds the $1,000 awarded because of Hoffman's payment of that amount on the purchase price of the Chilton lot. The first is that this $1,000 had already been lost at the time the final negotiations with Red Owl fell through in January, 1962, because the remaining $5,000 of purchase price had been due on October 15, 1961. The record does not disclose that the lot owner had foreclosed Hoffman's interest in the lot for failure to pay this $5,000. The $1,000 was not paid for the option, but had been paid as part of the purchase price at the time Hoffman elected to exercise the option. This gave him an equity in the lot which could not be legally foreclosed without affording Hoffman an opportunity to pay the balance. The second ground of attack is that the lot may have had a fair market value of $6,000, and Hoffman should have paid the remaining $5,000 of purchase price. We determine that it would be unreasonable to require Hoffman to have invested an additional $5,000 in order to protect the $1,000 he had paid. Therefore, we find no merit to defendants' attack upon this item of damages.

We also determine it was reasonable for Hoffman to have paid $125 for one month's rent of a home in Chilton after defendants assured him everything would be set when plaintiff sold the bakery building. This was a proper item of damage.

Plaintiffs never moved to Chilton because defendants suggested that Hoffman get some experience by working in a Red Owl store in the Fox River Valley. Plaintiffs, therefore, moved to Neenah instead of Chilton. After moving, Hoffman worked at night in an Appleton bakery but held himself available for work in a Red Owl store. The $140 moving expense would not have been incurred if plaintiffs had not sold their bakery building in Wautoma in reliance upon defendants' promises. We consider the $140 moving expense to be a proper item of damage.

We turn now to the damage item with respect to which the trial court granted a new trial, i.e., that arising from the sale of the Wautoma grocery store fixtures and inventory for which the jury awarded $16,735. The trial court ruled that Hoffman could not recover for any loss of future profits for the summer months following the sale on June 6, 1961, but that damages would be limited to the difference between the sales price received and fair market value of the assets sold, giving consideration to any goodwill attaching thereto by reason of the transfer of a going business. There was no direct evidence presented as to what this fair market value was on June 6, 1961. The evidence did disclose that Hoffman paid $9,000 for the inventory, added $1,500 to it and sold it for $10,000 or a loss of $500. His 1961 federal income tax return showed that the grocery equipment had been purchased for $7,000 and sold for $7,955.96. Plaintiffs introduced evidence of the buyer that during the first eleven weeks of operation of the grocery store his gross sales were $44,000 and his profit was $6,000 or roughly 15 percent. On cross-examination he admitted that this was gross and not net profit. Plaintiffs contend that in a breach of contract action damages may include loss of profits. However, this is not a breach of contract action.

The only relevancy of evidence relating to profits would be with respect to proving the element of goodwill in establishing the fair market value of the grocery inventory and fixtures sold. Therefore, evidence of profits would be admissible to afford a foundation for expert opinion as to fair market value.

Where damages are awarded in promissory estoppel instead of specifically enforcing the promisor's promise, they should be only such as in the opinion of the court are necessary to prevent injustice. Mechanical or rule of thumb approaches to the damage problem should be avoided. In discussing remedies to be applied by courts in promissory estoppel we quote the following views of writers on the subject:

> Enforcement of a promise does not necessarily mean Specific Performance. It does not necessarily mean Damages for breach. Moreover the amount allowed as Damages may be determined by the plaintiff's expenditures or change of position in reliance as well as by the value to him of the promised performance. Restitution is also an 'enforcing' remedy, although it is often said to be based upon some kind of a rescission. In determining what justice requires, the court must remember all of its powers, derived

from equity, law merchant, and other sources, as well as the common law. Its decree should be molded accordingly.

1A Corbin, CONTRACTS, p. 221, § 200.

> The wrong is not primarily in depriving the plaintiff of the promised reward but in causing the plaintiff to change position to his detriment. It would follow that the damages should not exceed the loss caused by the change of position, which would never be more in amount, but might be less, than the promised reward.

Seavey, *Reliance on Gratuitous Promises or Other Conduct*, 64 HARVARD LAW REVIEW (1951), 913, 926.

> There likewise seems to be no positive legal requirement, and certainly no legal policy, which dictates the allowance of contract damages in every case where the defendant's duty is consensual.

Shattuck, *Gratuitous Promises — A New Writ?*, 35 MICHIGAN LAW REVIEW (1936), 908, 912.[1]

At the time Hoffman bought the equipment and inventory of the small grocery store at Wautoma he did so in order to gain experience in the grocery store business. At that time discussion had already been had with Red Owl representatives that Wautoma might be too small for a Red Owl operation and that a larger city might be more desirable. Thus Hoffman made this purchase more or less as a temporary experiment. Justice does not require that the damages awarded him, because of selling these assets at the behest of defendants, should exceed any actual loss sustained measured by the difference between the sales price and the fair market value.

Since the evidence does not sustain the large award of damages arising from the sale of the Wautoma grocery business, the trial court properly ordered a new trial on this issue.

Order affirmed. . . .

NOTES & QUESTIONS

1. As the Hoffmans' attorney, would you have advised the Hoffmans that they were acting reasonably?

2. Should the level of sophistication of the promisee, as it relates to their business intellect, make any difference to the determination of whether their actions were reasonable? *See Garwood Packaging, Inc. v. Allen & Co.*, 378 F.3d 698 (2004), for the proposition that a sophisticated business person does not act reasonably when he should have known better.

3. Notice the reference to the foreseeable reliance by a third party (Mrs. Hoffman).

---

[1] [3] For expression of the opposite view, that courts in promissory estoppel cases should treat them as ordinary breach of contract cases and allow the full amount of damages recoverable in the latter, *see* Note, 13 VANDERBILT LAW REVIEW (1960) 705.

a. Would Mrs. Hoffman been able to recover under the FIRST RESTATE-MENT § 90? The RESTATEMENT SECOND?

b. Could Mr. or Mrs. Hoffman recover for their mental suffering under the RESTATEMENT approach? (See the discussion of this aspect in the *Ravelo* case, which immediately follows.)

RAVELO v. COUNTY OF HAWAII
658 P.2d 883 (Haw. 1983)

NAKAMURA, Justice:

The question in this interlocutory appeal from the Circuit Court of the Third Circuit is whether the complaint filed by Plaintiffs-appellants Benjamin Ravelo and Marlene Ravelo (Mr. and Mrs. Ravelo) against Defendant-appellee County of Hawaii (the County) stated a cause of action upon which relief could be granted. . . .

The controversy stems from the rescission by the County Police Department of a prior acceptance of Benjamin Ravelo's application for employment. . . .

The dispositive allegations of the complaint are: (1) on December 13, 1978, the County Police Department informed Benjamin Ravelo by letter that his application for employment as a police officer had been accepted and he would be sworn in as a police recruit on January 2, 1979; (2) "in reliance" thereon, he resigned from his position as a police officer with the Honolulu Police Department and Mrs. Ravelo submitted a notice of termination to her employer; (3) in further anticipation of a residence change, Mr. and Mrs. Ravelo informed the private school where their children were enrolled that they were being removed from the school; (4) but on December 20, 1978, Benjamin Ravelo "was informed by the Hawaii County Police Department that he was not going to be hired after all"; and (5) Mr. and Mrs. Ravelo thereafter attempted to rescind the resignations submitted to their respective employers but "were informed that it was too late to get their jobs back."

Plaintiffs-appellants claimed the County's "wrongful breach of its agreement to hire Benjamin Ravelo" caused both economic loss and mental anguish and prayed for specific enforcement of such agreement and damages, including large sums for mental anguish and unstated sums for "loss of projected income and related benefits for the rest of the projected lives" of Mr. and Mrs. Ravelo.

After submitting an answer which averred a lack of sufficient knowledge to respond directly to the complaint's principal allegations but nonetheless raised several affirmative defenses, including the Statute of Frauds, Ravelo's breach of a precondition of employment, and his failure to exhaust administrative remedies, the County moved for the dismissal of the complaint or summary judgment. The primary arguments advanced in support of dismissal or summary determination were that the complaint stated no basis upon which relief could be granted for either a breach of contract or a tortious infliction of emotional distress and Ravelo neglected to pursue the appropriate remedy through an administrative appeal to the County Civil Service Commission.

The circuit court agreed that no grounds for relief were pleaded, and dismissed the complaint without prejudice. It adopted the County's reasoning that under applicable provisions of the civil service law and regulations, Ravelo was at best a probationary employee whose employment was terminable without cause at any time prior to the completion of a period of probationary service. Thus in the court's view, there was no possible basis upon which damages for either a contractual breach or an infliction of emotional distress could be predicated. . . .

The circuit court concluded the Ravelos' complaint did not articulate an enforceable claim sounding in contract because Benjamin Ravelo obviously did not attain membership in the County civil service. And as the lack of such status enabled the County to terminate any purported employment with impunity, the court could observe no cause of action for the negligent infliction of emotional distress. We cannot fault the circuit court's perception that the averments in the complaint could not sustain an action premised on a breach of a formal contract or tortious conduct.

Still, our position has been that "a complaint should not be dismissed for failure to state a claim unless it appears beyond doubt that the plaintiff can prove no set of facts in support of his claim which would entitle him to relief." *Midkiff v. Castle & Cooke, Inc.*, 45 Haw. 409, 414, 368 P.2d 887, 890 (1962) (quoting *Conley v. Gibson*, 355 U.S. 41, 45-46, 78 S. Ct. 99, 101-2, 2 L. Ed. 2d 80 (1957). . . .

The allegations recounted earlier state there was a promise of employment extended to Benjamin Ravelo. The Ravelos further maintain they relied on the County's word that Benjamin Ravelo would be sworn in as a police recruit several weeks hence in quitting their jobs and laying plans to move to the Big Island. The County, we believe, could have anticipated the assurance of employment at a definite time would induce a reaction of that nature. These circumstances, in our opinion, provide a basis upon which relief could be granted the Ravelos.

We rest our conclusion on promissory estoppel, the essence of which is detrimental reliance on a promise. *See* Henderson, *Promissory Estoppel and Traditional Contract Doctrine*, 78 YALE L.J. 343 (1969). In *Anthony v. Hilo Electric Light Co.*, 50 Haw. 453, 442 P.2d 64 (1968), we concluded the defendant power company was obligated to pay over part of the sums it received from the telephone company to the plaintiff who had applied for telephone service, along with electric service, on the defendant's promise that part of his cost for the installation of telephone service would be refunded when payments made by the telephone company pursuant to the utility companies' "joint pole" agreement were received. We found the promise "induced plaintiff to make a payment for telephone line which he might not have made otherwise" and cited RESTATEMENT OF CONTRACTS § 90 (1932) to support our conclusion that the promise was enforceable. . . . The RESTATEMENT provision then read:

§ 90. Promise Reasonably Inducing Definite And Substantial Action.

A promise which the promisor should reasonably expect to induce action or forbearance of a definite and substantial character on the part of the promisee and which does induce such action or forbearance is binding if injustice can be avoided only by enforcement of the promise.

Section 90, however, has been substantially revised by the American Law Institute since we adopted the section as authority for the enforcement of a promise on the basis of detrimental reliance thereon even though the reliance is not bargained for. It now provides:

§ 90. Promise Reasonably Inducing Action or Forbearance

(1) A promise which the promisor should reasonably expect to induce action or forbearance on the part of the promisee or a third person and which does induce such action or forbearance is binding if injustice can be avoided only by enforcement of the promise. The remedy granted for breach may be limited as justice requires.

(2) A charitable subscription or a marriage settlement is binding under Subsection (1) without proof that the promise induced action or forbearance.

Changes from the former § 90 are reflected in the deletion of the requirement that the action or forbearance induced be of "a definite and substantial character," the addition of third persons as possible beneficiaries of the doctrine, and a recognition of the possibility of partial enforcement.

In our estimation the revised section provides a sounder legal foundation for the application of promissory estoppel, and we deem it advisable that the current § 90 be followed hereafter. Hence, we expect that relief here, if appropriate, will extend to Mrs. Ravelo as well as Mr. Ravelo and that any relief granted will not place the Ravelos in a better position than performance of the promise to hire him as a police recruit would have.[2]

The order of the circuit court dismissing the complaint is reversed, and the case is remanded for further proceedings not inconsistent with this decision.

NOTES & QUESTIONS

1. If you were the trial judge and if Mr. and Mrs. Ravelo were to prevail in their suit, what relief would you award to them?

2. *Practice Point:* Why should you as an attorney worry about formal contracts if promises can still be enforced as quasi-contracts through promissory estoppel?

C. PROMISSORY ESTOPPEL IN THE COMMERCIAL BIDDING PROCESS

The construction industry, and other similar industries, presents a unique situation due to the bidding process and the presence and use of option contracts. The problem in the construction bidding process is determining the precise points within the interactions when the various parties become bound to each other. The primary disputes arise between contractors and subcontractors and focus on when the subcontractor is obligated to do the work described in their bid, and when a

---

[2] [4] We think the Reporter's discussion of partial enforcement particularly apt in this situation; it reads:

> *d.* Partial enforcement. A promise binding under this section is a contract, and full-scale enforcement by normal remedies is often appropriate. But the same factors which bear on whether any relief should be granted also bear on the character and extent of the remedy. In particular, relief may sometimes be limited to restitution or to damages or specific relief measured by the extent of the promisee's reliance rather than by the terms of the promise. *See* §§ 84, 89; compare RESTATEMENT (SECOND), TORTS § 549 on damages for fraud. Unless there is unjust enrichment of the promisor, damages should not put the promisee in a better position than performance of the promise would have put him. *See* §§ 344, 349. In the case of a promise to make a gift it would rarely be proper to award consequential damages which would place a greater burden on the promisor than performance would have imposed.

party is obligated to hire a contractor or subcontractor who submits a bid.

The determination of when parties become obligated to each other is important to the maintenance of the bidding process because the contractors must be able to rely on the bids, because without the ability to rely on the bids the entire process will deteriorate as the contractors could no longer proceed in the face of uncertainty. This type of situation demands consideration as the construction industry continues to grow exponentially. Therefore, a special use of RESTATEMENT (SECOND) § 90 has been applied to the construction industry. The general principles of promissory estoppel have been applied to enforce the promises made between the parties to the bidding process even though traditional contract elements have not been satisfied.

A line of cases in the construction industry led to the development of a special use of the reliance doctrine of § 90. Indeed, by the time of the adoption and publication of the RESTATEMENT (SECOND) OF CONTRACTS, there was a separate section for an option by operation of law under § 87(2) as follows:

> An offer which the offeror should reasonably expect to induce action or forbearance of a substantial character on the part of the offeree before acceptance and which does induce such action or forbearance is binding as an option contract to the extent necessary to avoid injustice.

However, § 87(2) is not limited in its application to construction cases. How does it differ from modern § 90? Consider, for example, the obligations of auctioneers and auction bidders. Is a party required to sell a painting to the highest bidder where the value of the item is significantly higher than the final bid? Is the highest bidder obligated to pay if the value is significantly lower than the final bid? (*See Kimmel v. DeGasperi*, 2000 U.S. Dist. LEXIS 4935, for a discussion of these issues).

To understand the relationship between contractors and subcontractors, consider the following excerpts from *The Construction Industry Bidding Cases: Application of Traditional Contract, Promissory Estoppel, and Other Theories to the Relations Between General Contractors and Subcontractors*, 13 J. MARSHALL L. REV. 565 (1980), by Michael L. Closen and Donald G. Weiland.

> The construction industry bidding cases involving disputes between general contractors and subcontractors have proved especially troublesome for the courts. The early decisions were largely unresponsive to the financial realities and needs of that industry, leaving it clouded with uncertainty and instability. Thus, neither the general contractor nor the subcontractor was legally bound until the bidding procedure culminated in the owner's or developer's selection of the general contractor to do the work on the overall project *and* in award of the job by the general contractor to the subcontractor. The subcontractor could withdraw at any time before it had been awarded the work by the general contractor, which meant that a general contractor might be placed in the financially precarious position of having based its bid on the overall project on a subcontractor's bid that was later withdrawn. On the other hand, until the work was awarded to a subcontractor, the general contractor was free to engage in the practice of bid shopping or to encourage bid chopping.

> Later decisions recognized that a reliance analysis based upon the contract theory of promissory estoppel fit the factual setting at the early

stage of many construction industry bidding cases. That is, the use of the subcontractor's bid by the general contractor in computing and submitting the bid on the prime contract was viewed to be reasonable detrimental reliance by the general contractor which prohibited the subcontractor from withdrawing its bid.

THE BIDDING PROCEDURE

On even fairly small construction projects where competitive bidding is employed, at least two sets of bids are ordinarily taken. One set of bids is submitted to the landowner or project developer by the general or prime contractors interested in undertaking the job. Usually, such bids include the cost estimates for the entire project, but a project could be divided into a number of large segments each to be awarded to a separate contractor. The other set of bids is submitted by the subcontractors and materialmen to the general contractors. Because general contractors do not actually perform the work, but instead coordinate and supervise its progress, subcontractors and materialmen (such as electrical, plumbing, carpentry, painting, landscaping, and so on) bid for the purpose of securing the specialty work on the project.

General Contractor Bids

. . . The process is generally initiated when an owner or developer, having decided to go forward with a project, invites or solicits bids. Blueprints and specifications for the project must be made available for examination by the subcontractors in order for them to prepare their bids. The common practice is to require written, sealed bids which must arrive on or before a specified time. The sealed bids are then opened and read (sometimes at an open meeting), and the owner or developer reviews the bids and investigates the bidders.

Because there is a time lag between the submission of bids and the award of the project to the successful general contractor, the owner or developer would prefer that the bids be irrevocable for a period of time. This situation allows him to open the bids and to consider and complete any final details (possibly including arrangements for financing). In government bidding situations, the governmental units involved usually have had the foresight to adopt legislation in the form of ordinances or statutes requiring that bids remain irrevocable for a specified time. The most widely used device in the private sector (as well as in government bidding) is the bid bond. Under the terms of a bid bond, a contractor posts a bond — usually ten percent of its bid — and guarantees that its bid will not be withdrawn for a specified period of time — frequently 30, 60, or 90 days from the date the bids are opened. The bond is forfeited in the event the bid is withdrawn during that time or the contractor refuses to abide by the timely award and proceed with performance on the project.

Subcontractor Bids

The other setting in which bids are solicited, submitted, and considered on a construction project involves the relationship between general contractors and subcontractors. Just as the owner or developer solicits bids for the overall project, general contractors (if they choose to use competitive bidding at all) solicit bids from subcontractors and materialmen for specialty work. A very significant fact is that the bidding process at this level is far less organized and sophisticated than the bidding procedure between the owner or developer and the general contractors. As a result, subcontractors frequently finalize their bids in the early morning hours under intense pressures, submitting them at the eleventh hour (by telephone or private messenger).

These bids are offers and are revocable, as a general rule, for there are ordinarily no ordinances or statutes requiring them to be kept open (even where a "naming" statute has been adopted), no bid bonds are required, and no consideration is paid in order to form option contracts to hold the bids open. Recently, the usual bidding process in one area of the country was described as follows:

> According to the normal bidding practices in the construction industry in the area, a contemplated project is generally listed or advertised in trade magazines and in the "Dodge Reports," a daily construction news service which lists proposed construction activity for various areas of the country. A subscriber to the "Dodge Reports" for a particular area may inspect the plans for a project in any Dodge plan room located in that area. An interested materials supplier checks the plans and specifications to determine if he can supply any of the required materials. He then submits a quotation by telephone, mail, or both, to the contractors interested in bidding on the project. It is in this manner that contractors usually obtain quotations from competing suppliers and subcontractors. These quotations are then used by the contractors to estimate their own costs in preparing their bids. Normally, the twenty-four hour period preceding the prime bid deadline is one of great activity, with the subcontractors and suppliers making the rounds of the contractors who are still preparing their bids. By this time the first quotations have generally become known and the quoted prices are often revised downward at the last minute, with the prime contractors revising their bids accordingly.

The contractor usually purchases the materials from the supplier upon whose prices he relied in preparing his bid; however, a contract to purchase the materials is not entered into until after the contractor has been awarded the contract and the project engineers have approved the materials, if such approval is needed. The supplier then prepares the shop drawings for the project after the successful bidder signs a letter of intent to purchase the materials.[3]

This description reflects practices throughout the country.

---

[3] [34] Janke Constr. Co. v. Vulcan Materials Co., 527 F.2d 772, 775-76 (7th Cir. 1976).

NOTES & QUESTIONS

1. How do the subcontractor bidding cases compare to ordinary auctions? Are they like auctions with reserve? Could they be structured like auctions without reserve?

2. Why is it that the informal and problem-ridden system of bidding in the construction industry has remained largely unchanged (as you will observe from the following cases spanning some 40 years)?

Notice the many problems that the bidding process presents, as evidenced by the following cases.

DRENNAN v. STAR PAVING COMPANY
333 P.2d 757 (Cal. 1958)

TRAYNOR, Justice:

Defendant appeals from a judgment for plaintiff in an action to recover damages caused by defendant's refusal to perform certain paving work according to a bid it submitted to plaintiff.

On July 28, 1955, plaintiff, a licensed general contractor, was preparing a bid on the "Monte Vista School Job" in the Lancaster school district. Bids had to be submitted before 8:00 p.m. Plaintiff testified that it was customary in that area for general contractors to receive the bids of subcontractors by telephone on the day set for bidding and to rely on them in computing their own bids. Thus on that day plaintiff's secretary, Mrs. Johnson, received by telephone between fifty and seventy-five subcontractors' bids for various parts of the school job. As each bid came in, she wrote it on a special form, which she brought into plaintiff's office. He then posted it on a master cost sheet setting forth the names and bids of all subcontractors. His own bid had to include the names of subcontractors who were to perform one-half of one per cent or more of the construction work, and he had also to provide a bidder's bond often per cent of his total bid of $317,385 as a guarantee that he would enter the contract if awarded the work.

Late in the afternoon, Mrs. Johnson had a telephone conversation with Kenneth R. Hoon, an estimator for defendant. He gave his name and telephone number and stated that he was bidding for defendant for the paving work at the Monte Vista School according to plans and specifications and that his bid was $7,131.60. At Mrs. Johnson's request he repeated his bid. Plaintiff listened to the bid over an extension telephone in his office and posted it on the master sheet after receiving the bid form from Mrs. Johnson. Defendant's was the lowest bid for the paving. Plaintiff computed his own bid accordingly and submitted it with the name of defendant as the subcontractor for the paving. When the bids were opened on July 28th, plaintiff's proved to be the lowest, and he was awarded the contract.

On his way to Los Angeles the next morning plaintiff stopped at defendant's office. The first person he met was defendant's construction engineer, Mr. Oppenheimer. Plaintiff testified:

I introduced myself and he immediately told me that they had made a mistake in their bid to me the night before, they couldn't do it for the price they had bid, and I told him I would expect him to carry through with their original bid because I had used it in compiling my bid and the job was being awarded them. And I would have to go and do the job according to my bid and I would expect them to do the same.

Defendant refused to do the paving work for less than $15,000. Plaintiff testified that he "got figures from other people" and after trying for several months to get as low a bid as possible engaged L&H Paving Company, a firm in Lancaster, to do the work for $10,948.60.

The trial court found on substantial evidence that defendant made a definite offer to do the paving on the Monte Vista job according to the plans and specifications for $7,131.60, and that plaintiff relied on defendant's bid in computing his own bid for the school job and naming defendant therein as the subcontractor for the paving work.

Accordingly, it entered judgment for plaintiff in the amount of $3,817.00 (the difference between defendant's bid and the cost of the paving to plaintiff) plus costs.

Defendant contends that there was no enforceable contract between the parties on the ground that it made a revocable offer and revoked it before plaintiff communicated his acceptance to defendant.

There is no evidence that defendant offered to make its bid irrevocable in exchange for plaintiff's use of its figures in computing his bid. Nor is there evidence that would warrant interpreting plaintiff's use of defendant's bid as the acceptance thereof, binding plaintiff, on condition he received the main contract, to award the subcontract to defendant. In sum, there was neither an option supported by consideration nor a bilateral contract binding on both parties.

Plaintiff contends, however, that he relied to his detriment on defendant's offer and that defendant must therefore answer in damages for its refusal to perform. Thus the question is squarely presented: Did plaintiff's reliance make defendant's offer irrevocable?

Section 90 of the RESTATEMENT OF CONTRACTS states: "A promise which the promisor should reasonably expect to induce action or forbearance of a definite and substantial character on the part of the promisee and which does induce such action or forbearance is binding if injustice can be avoided only by enforcement of the promise." This rule applies in this state. *Edmonds v. County of Los Angeles*, 40 Cal.2d 642, 255 P.2d 772.

Defendant's offer constituted a promise to perform on such conditions as were stated expressly or by implication therein or annexed thereto by operation of law. (*See* 1 Williston, CONTRACTS (3rd. ed.), § 24A, p. 56, § 61, p. 196.) Defendant had reason to expect that if its bid proved the lowest it would be used by plaintiff. It induced "action . . . of a definite and substantial character on the part of the promisee."

Had defendant's bid expressly stated or clearly implied that it was revocable at any time before acceptance we would treat it accordingly. It was silent on revocation, however, and we must therefore determine whether there are conditions to the right of revocation imposed by law or reasonably inferable in fact. In the analogous problem of an offer for a unilateral contract, the theory is now obsolete that the offer is revocable at any time before complete performance. Thus § 45 of the RESTATEMENT OF CONTRACTS provides: "If an offer for a unilateral contract is made, and part of the consideration requested in the offer is given or tendered by the offeree in response thereto, the offeror is bound by a contract, the duty of immediate performance of which is conditional on the full consideration being given or tendered within the time stated in the offer, or, if no time is stated therein, within a reasonable time." In explanation, comment b states that the "main offer includes as a subsidiary promise, necessarily implied, that if part of the requested performance is given, the offeror will not revoke his offer, and that if tender is made it will be accepted. Part performance or tender may thus furnish consideration for the subsidiary promise. Moreover, merely acting in justifiable reliance on an offer may in some cases serve as sufficient reason for making a promise binding (*see* § 90)."

Whether implied in fact or law, the subsidiary promise serves to preclude the injustice that would result if the offer could be revoked after the offeree had acted in detrimental reliance thereon. Reasonable reliance resulting in a foreseeable prejudicial change in position affords a compelling basis also for implying a subsidiary promise not to revoke an offer for a bilateral contract.

The absence of consideration is not fatal to the enforcement of such a promise. It is true that in the case of unilateral contracts the RESTATEMENT finds consideration for the implied subsidiary promise in the part performance of the bargained — for exchange, but its reference to section 90 makes clear that consideration for such a promise is not always necessary. The very purpose of section 90 is to make a promise binding even though there was no consideration "in the sense of something that is bargained for and given in exchange." (*See* 1 Corbin, CONTRACTS 634 *et seq.*) Reasonable reliance serves to hold the offeror in lieu of the consideration ordinarily required to make the offer binding. In a case involving similar facts the Supreme Court of South Dakota stated that "we believe that reason and justice demand that the doctrine (of § 90) be applied to the present facts. We cannot believe that by accepting this doctrine as controlling in the state of facts before us we will abolish the requirement of a consideration in contract cases, in any different sense than an ordinary estoppel abolishes some legal requirement in its application. We are of the opinion, therefore, that the defendants in executing the agreement (which was not supported by consideration) made a promise which they should have reasonably expected would induce the plaintiff to submit a bid based thereon to the Government, that such promise did induce this action, and that injustice can be avoided only by enforcement of the promise." *Northwestern Engineering Co. v. Ellerman*, 69 S.D. 397, 408, 10 N.W.2d 879, 884; see also, *Robert Gordon, Inc. v. Ingersoll-Rand Co.*, 7 Cir., 117 F.2d 654, 661; cf. *James Baird Co. v. Gimbel Bros.*, 2 Cir., 64 F.2d 344.

When plaintiff used defendant's offer in computing his own bid, he bound himself to perform in reliance on defendant's terms. Though defendant did not bargain for this use of its bid neither did defendant make it idly, indifferent to whether it would be used or not. On the contrary it is reasonable to suppose that defendant submitted its bid to obtain the subcontract. It was bound to realize the substantial possibility that its bid would be the lowest, and that it would be included by plaintiff in his bid. It was to its own interest that the contractor be awarded the general contract; the lower the subcontract bid, the lower the general contractor's bid was likely to be and the greater its chance of acceptance and hence the greater defendant's chance of getting the paving subcontract. Defendant had reason not only to expect plaintiff to rely on its bid but to want him to. Clearly defendant had a stake in plaintiff's reliance on its bid. Given this interest and the fact that plaintiff is bound by his own bid, it is only fair that plaintiff should have at least an opportunity to accept defendant's bid after the general contract has been awarded to him.

It bears noting that a general contractor is not free to delay acceptance after he has been awarded the general contract in the hope of getting a better price. Nor can he reopen bargaining with the subcontractor and at the same time claim a continuing right to accept the original offer. . . . In the present case plaintiff promptly informed defendant that plaintiff was being awarded the job and that the subcontract was being awarded to defendant.

Defendant contends, however, that its bid was the result of mistake and that it was therefore entitled to revoke it. It relies on the rescission cases of *M.F. Kemper Const. Co. v. City of Los Angeles*, 37 Cal. 2d 696, 235 P.2d 7, and *Brunzell Const. Co. v. G.J. Weisbrod, Inc.*, 134 Cal. App. 2d 278, 285 P.2d 989. . . . In those cases, however, the bidder's mistake was known or should have been known to the offeree, and the offeree could be placed in status quo. Of course, if plaintiff had reason to believe that defendant's bid was in error, he could not justifiably rely on it, and § 90 would afford no basis for enforcing it. *Robert Gordon, Inc. v. Ingersoll-Rand, Inc.*, 7 Cir., 117 F.2d 654, 660. Plaintiff, however, had no reason to know that defendant had made a mistake in submitting its bid, since there was usually a variance of 160 per cent between the highest and lowest bids for paving in the desert around Lancaster. He committed himself to performing the main contract in reliance on defendant's figures. Under these circumstances defendant's mistake, far from relieving it of its obligation, constitutes an additional reason for enforcing it, for it misled plaintiff as to the cost of doing the paving. Even had it been clearly understood that defendant's offer was revocable until accepted, it would not necessarily follow that defendant had no duty to exercise reasonable care in preparing its bid. It presented its bid with knowledge of the substantial possibility that it would be used by plaintiff; it could foresee the harm that would ensue from an erroneous underestimate of the cost. Moreover, it was motivated by its own business interest. Whether or not these considerations alone would justify recovery for negligence had the case been tried on that theory (*see Biakanja v. Irving*, 49 Cal. 2d 647, 650, 320 P.2d 16), they are persuasive that defendant's mistake should not defeat recovery under the rule of § 90 of the RESTATEMENT OF CONTRACTS. As between the subcontractor who made the bid and the general contractor who reasonably relied on it, the loss resulting from the mistake should fall on the party who caused it.

. . .

The judgment is affirmed.

NOTES & QUESTIONS

1. The preceding opinion has become a landmark decision. One court capsulized its holding this way: "Justice Traynor reasoned that the subcontractor's bid contained an implied subsidiary promise not to revoke the bid." *Pavel v. A.S. Johnson*, 342 Md. 143, 674 A.2d 521, 527 (1996).

2. When the general contractor prevails against the subcontractor, does the general's recovery protect its profit margin on the prime contract? If so, is that a full contract recovery? And if it is, should such a recovery be allowed in a promissory estoppel case?

DOUBLE AA BUILDERS, LTD. v. GRAND STATE CONSTRUCTION L.L.C.
114 P.3d 835 (Ariz. 2006)

GEMMILL, Judge:

Grand State Construction L.L.C., a subcontractor, appeals a judgment awarding damages to Double AA Builders, Ltd., a general contractor, on a promissory estoppel claim. Double AA cross-appeals the trial court's denial of attorneys' fees under Arizona Revised Statutes ("A.R.S.") § 12-341.01(A) (2003). We affirm the judgment in favor of the general contractor because the evidence is sufficient to support the trial court's implied findings of each element of promissory estoppel. We also conclude that § 12-341.01(A) is not applicable to a promise made enforceable by the doctrine of promissory estoppel and we therefore affirm the trial court's denial of attorneys' fees to the general contractor.

I.

In anticipation of submitting a bid for the construction of a Home Depot Store in Mesa, Double AA ("General Contractor") solicited bids from subcontractors for various portions of the work.

On December 18, 2001, Grand State ("Subcontractor") faxed a written but unsigned bid to General Contractor in the amount of $115,000 for installation of the Exterior Insulation Finish System ("EIFS") on the project. Subcontractor's proposal stated: "Our price is good for 30 days." General Contractor also received other bids from subcontractors for the EIFS work.

General Contractor relied upon several subcontractor bids, including Subcontractor's, in preparing its overall price for the project. Specifically, General Contractor used Subcontractor's price of $115,000 for the EIFS portion of the work in arriving at the total bid submitted to the owner.

On December 21, 2001, Home Depot advised General Contractor that General Contractor was the successful bidder for the project. On December 31, 2001, Home Depot forwarded a contract to General Contractor for the project.

On January 11, 2002, within the 30-day "price is good" period, General Contractor sent a subcontract for the EIFS work to Subcontractor to be signed and returned. Subcontractor advised General Contractor that it would not sign the subcontract or perform on the project. A letter from Subcontractor to General Contractor explained: "Upon reviewing your schedule for this upcoming project and our own inventory of presently scheduled work, we will not be able to enter into a contract with your company. From the time we received a contract from your office we signed four other contracts that were bid around the same time period."

General Contractor subsequently entered into a subcontract with a replacement subcontractor to install the EIFS at a cost of $131,449, which exceeded Subcontractor's quoted price by $16,449. General Contractor demanded that Subcontractor pay the difference between its bid and General Contractor's ultimate cost to perform the same work. After Subcontractor refused, General Contractor filed suit based upon promissory estoppel.

In accordance with superior court rules, an arbitrator initially heard the case. The arbitrator ruled in favor of Subcontractor. General Contractor appealed, seeking a trial *de novo* in superior court. After a one-day bench trial, the court ruled in favor of General Contractor and awarded $16,449 in damages but denied General Contractor's request for attorneys' fees. This appeal and cross-appeal followed.

II.

Because this case was tried to the court, we view the evidence in the light most favorable to upholding the trial court's decision. *See Federoff v. Pioneer Title & Trust Co.*, 166 Ariz. 383, 388, 803 P.2d 104, 109 (1990). Neither side requested that the court make specific findings of fact and conclusions of law pursuant to ARIZONA RULE OF CIVIL PROCEDURE52(a), and the court did not, *sua sponte*, make detailed findings. Under these circumstances, we must presume that the trial court found every fact necessary to support its judgment and we will affirm if any reasonable construction of the evidence justifies it. *See Garden Lakes Comty. Ass'n, Inc. v. Madigan*, 204 Ariz. 238, 240, P9, 62 P.3d 983, 985 (App. 2003); *In re CVR 1997 Irrevocable Trust*, 202 Ariz. 174, 177, P16, 42 P.3d 605, 608 (App. 2002).

We apply a *de novo* standard when reviewing issues of law and statutory interpretation. *See Jangula v. Ariz. Prop. and Cas. Ins. Guar. Fund*, 207 Ariz. 468, 470, P12, 88 P.3d 182, 184 (App. 2004); *Maycock v. Asilomar Dev., Inc.*, 207 Ariz. 495, 500, P24, 88 P.3d 565, 570 (App. 2004).

III.

We first address Subcontractor's position that the doctrine of promissory estoppel should not be applied in the context of subcontractors submitting bids to general contractors.

When a general contractor prepares an overall bid for a competitively-bid construction project, it receives bids and quotes from subcontractors for portions of the work. The general contractor uses the bids in preparing its overall price for the project. A subcontractor's refusal to honor its bid can be financially disastrous for the general contractor, because it will typically be bound by the bid price submitted to the owner.

Arizona has previously adopted § 90(1) of the RESTATEMENT (SECOND) OF CONTRACTS (1981), *see Chewning v. Palmer*, 133 Ariz. 136, 138, 650 P.2d 438, 440 (1982), which describes those promises that will be binding under the promissory estoppel doctrine:

A promise which the promisor should reasonably expect to induce action or forbearance on the part of the promisee or a third person and which does induce such action or forbearance is binding if injustice can be avoided only by enforcement of the promise. The remedy granted for breach may be limited as justice requires.

This doctrine "has been used to require the subcontractor to perform according to the terms of its bid to the contractor if the contractor receives the contract award, since the contractor has relied on the subcontractor's bid and must perform for a price based on that reliance." Thomas C. Horne, *Arizona Construction Law*

§ 202, at 97 (2d ed. 1994).

The leading case applying promissory estoppel in this context is *Drennan v. Star Paving Co.*, 51 Cal. 2d 409, 333 P.2d 757 (Cal. 1958). The *Drennan* general contractor was preparing a bid for a public school job. *Id.* at 758. Before submitting the bid, the general contractor received a telephoned bid from a subcontractor of $7,131.60 for paving work. *Id.* One day later, the subcontractor informed the general contractor that the bid contained a mistake and that it would not perform the work for less than $15,000. *Id.* at 758-59. The general contractor, however, had already included the subcontractor's bid in its price, and the owner had accepted the general contractor's bid. *Id.* at 759.

Eventually, the general contractor retained another subcontractor to perform the paving work at a cost of $10,948.60. *Id.* The California Supreme Court ruled that the general contractor was entitled to a judgment against the subcontractor for $3,817, the difference between the subcontractor's bid and the general contractor's cost to perform the same scope of work. *Id.* at 759, 761. The court explained:

> When [general contractor] used [subcontractor]'s offer in computing his own bid, he bound himself to perform in reliance on [subcontractor]'s terms. Though [subcontractor] did not bargain for this use of its bid neither did [subcontractor] make it idly, indifferent to whether it would be used or not. On the contrary it is reasonable to suppose that [subcontractor] submitted its bid to obtain the subcontract. It was bound to realize the substantial possibility that its bid would be the lowest, and that it would be included by [general contractor] in his bid. It was to its own interest that the contractor be awarded the general contract; the lower the subcontract bid, the lower the general contractor's bid was likely to be and the greater its chance of acceptance and hence the greater [subcontractor]'s chance of getting the paving subcontract. [Subcontractor] had reason not only to expect [general contractor] to rely on its bid but to want him to. Clearly [subcontractor] had a stake in [general contractor]'s reliance on its bid. Given this interest and the fact that [the general contractor] is bound by his own bid, it is only fair that [general contractor] should have at least an opportunity to accept [subcontractor]'s bid after the general contract has been awarded to him.

Id. at 760; *accord Alaska Bussell Elec. Co. v. Vern Hickel Constr. Co.*, 688 P.2d 576, 579-80 (Alaska 1984); *C.H. Leavell & Co. v. Grafe & Assocs., Inc.*, 90 Idaho 502, 414 P.2d 873, 878 (Idaho 1966); *Pavel Enters., Inc. v. A.S. Johnson Co. Inc.*, 342 Md. 143, 674 A.2d 521, 526 (Md. 1996); *Loranger Constr. Corp. v. E.F. Hauserman Co.*, 6 Mass. App. Ct. 152, 374 N.E.2d 306, 309-10 (Mass. App. Ct. 1978); *Constructors Supply Co. v. Bostrom Sheet Metal Works, Inc.*, 291 Minn. 113, 190 N.W.2d 71, 75-76 (Minn. 1971); *E.A. Coronis Assocs. v. M. Gordon Constr. Co.*, 90 N.J. Super. 69, 216 A.2d 246, 251 (N.J. Super. Ct. App. Div. 1966).

Arizona has long recognized and applied the promissory estoppel doctrine. *See Weiner v. Romley*, 94 Ariz. 40, 43, 381 P.2d 581, 584 (1963); *Waugh v. Lennard*, 69 Ariz. 214, 223-24, 211 P.2d 806, 812 (1949); *Higginbottom v. State*, 203 Ariz. 139, 144, P18, 51 P.3d 972, 977 (App. 2002). Furthermore, this court in *Tiffany Inc. v. W.M.K. Transit Mix, Inc.*, 16 Ariz. App. 415, 493 P.2d 1220 (1972), determined that the doctrine of promissory estoppel was applicable in a dispute involving a highway contractor and a sealcoat chip supplier, but barred recovery based on the statute of frauds. Before addressing the statute of frauds defense, the court explained why promissory estoppel would otherwise be applicable:

> In analyzing promissory estoppel in relation to the facts of this case viewed in the light most favorable to plaintiff, the party opposing the motion for summary judgment, we find that the elements of this theory are met. In viewing the facts in favor of plaintiff, the record shows that defendant promised to supply class C sealcoat chips at a price of $3.50 per ton. *Plaintiff relied to his detriment on this promise in that it subsequently used the quote to secure its successful bid from the Highway Department. Further, the defendant should reasonably have foreseen that plaintiff would rely on the quote and use it in its bid, if the quote were the lowest.* In a case involving a similar set of facts, the California Supreme Court in *Drennan v. Star Paving Company* also reached the conclusion that this was a proper case for promissory estoppel.

16 Ariz. App. at 420, 493 P.2d at 1225 (emphasis added) (citation omitted).

Subcontractor has set forth no persuasive reason not to apply the doctrine of promissory estoppel in the context of subcontractor bids to general contractors. We hold, therefore, that promissory estoppel may be applied in this context if the required elements are proven.

To prove promissory estoppel, a general contractor must show that the subcontractor made a promise and should have reasonably foreseen that the general contractor would rely on that promise and further that the general contractor did in fact rely on that promise. *See* RESTATEMENT (SECOND) OF CONTRACTS § 90(1); *Drennan*, 333 P.2d at 760; *see also Higginbottom*, 203 Ariz. at 144, P18, 51 P.3d at 977 (stating elements of promissory estoppel in different context). The general contractor must also show that he had a "justifiable right to rely" on the promise. *See Higginbottom*, 203 Ariz. at 144, P18, 51 P.3d at 977. If these elements are proven, the promise "is binding if injustice can be avoided only by enforcement of the promise." RESTATEMENT (SECOND) OF CONTRACTS § 90(1).

Subcontractor submitted a bid stating "our price is good for 30 days." This statement constituted a promise to perform at the stated price. Subcontractor admitted that it realized that if its bid was the lowest, General Contractor might rely on the bid in preparing its overall project price. General Contractor did in fact rely on this bid by incorporating it into its own proposal. Reviewing the evidence in the light most favorable to upholding the decision, we find that substantial evidence in the record supports the trial court's application of promissory estoppel to allow General Contractor to recover damages for Subcontractor's refusal to perform on its bid.

Subcontractor advances four specific arguments why the promissory estoppel doctrine should not be applied in this particular case: Subcontractor's bid was not a promise; General Contractor did not accept Subcontractor's bid in a timely manner; the statute of frauds precludes enforcement of Subcontractor's bid; and General Contractor failed to prove its damages with certainty. We address each of these arguments in turn.

A.

Subcontractor contends that its bid was not a promise, but rather an expression of intent or desire to perform the work. This claim is belied by the content of its communication. The faxed quotation included the job name, the scope of work, Subcontractor's price, and certain additional terms, including payment every thirty days. The quote also stated that the price "is good for 30 days." Moreover, Subcontractor's general manager acknowledged at trial that the reason Subcontractor submitted the bid was for Subcontractor to obtain the work covered by its bid if General Contractor were the successful bidder. The quote therefore constitutes an unequivocal commitment to perform certain work at a certain price.

Similar statements have been found to be promises. In *Tiffany*, for example, we explained that a representation that a party would supply class C sealcoat chips at a certain price if the plaintiff was awarded a highway contract constituted a promise. 16 Ariz. App. at 420, 493 P.2d at 1225. Similarly, the *Drennan* court found that the bid "constituted a promise to perform on such conditions as were stated expressly or by implication therein or annexed thereto by operation of law." 333 P.2d at 759.

Subcontractor contends that two Arizona cases defeat these arguments, but its reliance on these authorities is misplaced. In *School District No. 69 of Maricopa County v. Altherr*, 10 Ariz. App. 333, 458 P.2d 537 (1969), disapproved in part on other grounds by *Board of Trustees of Marana Elementary School, District No. 6 v. Wildermuth*, 16 Ariz. App. 171, 173, 492 P.2d 420, 422 (1972), the court held that no promise existed because the school district's board of trustees merely expressed their "intent" or "desire" to buy the school building. *Id.* at 340, 458 P.2d at 544. In contrast, Subcontractor proposed to perform a definite scope of work for a specific price.

The second case, *Johnson International, Inc. v. City of Phoenix*, 192 Ariz. 466, 967 P.2d 607 (App. 1998), is also distinguishable. The court refused to enforce a memorandum of understanding of the parties' intentions regarding a potential development agreement that included the following language: "This memorandum is not intended to be the final agreement or to include all of the material terms, which shall be subject to further negotiations, and it shall not be binding on either party." *Id.* at 468, 967 P.2d at 609. The court held that the memorandum could not, by itself, be a promise because its clear language precluded that interpretation. *Id.* at 474, 967 P.2d at 615. In contrast, Subcontractor's bid contained no such limitations.

The evidence at trial was sufficient to support the trial court's implied finding that Subcontractor's bid constituted a promise that could be enforced on the basis of promissory estoppel.

B.

Subcontractor also attempts to justify its refusal to perform on its bid by claiming that General Contractor failed to accept the bid promptly. The record, however, supports the implied finding of the court that General Contractor accepted the bid within a reasonable period of time in accordance with the terms of Subcontractor's proposal.

Subcontractor faxed its bid on December 18, 2001, and the bid stated that it was "good for 30 days." General Contractor mailed a subcontract to Subcontractor on January 11, 2002, twenty-four days later. Acceptance is generally complete upon mailing, unless the proposal stipulates that acceptance is not effective until received. *See generally Cohen v. First Nat'l Bank*, 22 Ariz. 394, 400, 198 P. 122, 124 (1921) (in a banking context, applying the rule that acceptance is generally complete upon mailing). Subcontractor placed no limitations on General Contractor's method of acceptance. Therefore, General Contractor accepted when it mailed the subcontract on the twenty-fourth day of the thirty-day period specified in Subcontractor's proposal.

Subcontractor contends that the leading case of *Drennan* does not support the application of promissory estoppel in this case because the general contractor in *Drennan* contacted the subcontractor one day after the latter submitted its bid. But *Drennan* does not establish an outer limit of time for acceptance of a bid nor does it curtail the ability of a bidder to define the time period for acceptance of its proposal. As the *Drennan* court explained, "Had defendant's bid expressly stated or clearly implied that it was revocable at any time before acceptance we would treat it accordingly." 333 P.2d at 759. Here, General Contractor accepted within a reasonable period of time because the acceptance was within the thirty-day commitment of Subcontractor.

Subcontractor also contends that enforcement of subcontract bids not immediately accepted will chill the bidding process. However, enforcing bids under the promissory estoppel doctrine may in fact enhance the effective functioning of the construction industry. As the Alaska Supreme Court explained: "If a contractor is set to deliver a set price to an owner, these [subcontractor] bids must be binding for a reasonable time. This operates to the benefit of the construction industry. Promissory estoppel, as applied in *Drennan* and adopted by this court, is a necessary element of this scheme." *Alaska Bussell*, 688 P.2d at 580.

*   *   *

D.

Subcontractor also challenges the award of damages on the ground that General Contractor failed to prove "with certainty" that it actually sustained damages in the amount awarded. The record, however, contains evidence sufficient to support the award. A vice president of General Contractor testified that General Contractor contracted with the replacement subcontractor for $131,449, which was $16,449 more than Subcontractor's quote.

Although Subcontractor claims that there was inconsistent evidence regarding these damages, the trial court's conclusion was a reasonable construction of the evidence. Our duty on review does not include re-weighing conflicting evidence or redetermining the preponderance of the evidence. *See In re Estate of Pouser*, 193 Ariz. 574, 579, P13, 975 P.2d 704, 709 (1999) (upholding the trial court's intent finding because it was supported by substantial evidence, even though conflicting evidence existed). We must give due regard to the trial court's opportunity to judge the credibility of the witnesses. Even though conflicting evidence may exist, we affirm the trial court's ruling because substantial evidence supports it. *See id.* at 580, 975 P.2d at 710.

For these reasons, we affirm the trial court's award of compensatory damages to General Contractor based on promissory estoppel.

IV.

General Contractor cross-appeals the trial court's denial of attorneys' fees, arguing that A.R.S. § 12-341.01(A) allows an award of fees in conjunction with a promise made enforceable by promissory estoppel. Subcontractor contends that § 12-341.01(A) is not applicable to a promissory estoppel claim.[4] The application of § 12-341.01(A) to this claim is a question of statutory interpretation that we review *de novo. See Jangula*, 207 Ariz. at 470, P12, 88 P.3d at 184.

Section 12-341.01(A) applies to actions that arise out of "express or implied" contracts. For the following reasons, we hold that a recovery based on promissory estoppel does not arise out of an express or implied contract within the meaning of § 12-341.01(A).

A promissory estoppel claim is not the same as a contract claim. Promissory estoppel provides an equitable remedy and is not a theory of contract liability. *See Chewning*, 133 Ariz. at 138, 650 P.2d at 440 (distinguishing "equitable remedy under the theory of promissory estoppel" from breach of contract); *State ex rel. Romley v. Gaines*, 205 Ariz. 138, 143, P15, 67 P.3d 734, 739 (App. 2003) (stating that promissory estoppel is not a theory of contract recovery); *Johnson Int'l, Inc. v. City of Phoenix*, 192 Ariz. 466, 474, 967 P.2d 607, 615 (App. 1998) (same). Although a promise made enforceable by promissory estoppel is similar to a binding contractual promise, a promissory estoppel claim does not arise out of a contract. *See Johnson Int'l, Inc.*, 192 Ariz. at 474, 967 P.2d at 615; *see also Kersten v. Cont'l Bank*, 129 Ariz. 44, 47, 628 P.2d 592, 595 (App. 1981) (stating that promissory estoppel may afford relief if "some element necessary to the creation of an enforceable contract, such as consideration, is not present").

Some authorities hold that a promise made enforceable by promissory estoppel constitutes an implied-in-law contract. *See Sam Gray Enters., Inc. v. United States*, 43 Fed. Cl. 596, 605 (Fed. Cl. 1999) (holding that promissory estoppel creates implied-in-law, as opposed to implied-in-fact, contract); *Schwartz v. United States*, 16 Cl. Ct. 182, 185 (Cl. Ct. 1989) (explaining that promissory estoppel operates in an equitable sense to bind the promisor to an implied-in-law contract); *Jablon v. United States*, 657 F.2d 1064, 1070 (9th Cir. 1981) (stating that promissory estoppel theory is not an "express or implied-in-fact contract" theory); *Del Hayes & Sons, Inc. v. Mitchell*, 304 Minn. 275, 230 N.W.2d 588, 593 (Minn. 1975) ("Promissory estoppel is the name applied to a contract implied in law where no contract exists in fact.")

Even if we consider General Contractor's recovery to be based on an implied-in-law contract, A.R.S. § 12-341.01(A) would not be applicable. In *Barmat v. John and Jane Doe Partners A-D*, 155 Ariz. 519, 747 P.2d 1218 (1987), our supreme court

---

[4] [2] The trial court provided no reason for denying the requested fees. Subcontractor's primary argument to the trial court was that § 12-341.01(A) did not, as a matter of law, support awarding fees in promissory estoppel cases. Alternatively, Subcontractor argued that the court should award a lesser amount of fees than General Contractor had requested. The record contains no argument that, assuming § 12-341.01(A) is applicable, the trial court should exercise its discretion to award no fees. Under these circumstances, we will address the legal question whether fees may be awarded under § 12-341.01(A) on a promissory estoppel theory.

held that attorneys' fees could be awarded under § 12-341.01(A) for claims arising out of express and implied-in-fact contracts but not for claims arising out of implied-in-law contracts. *Id.* at 523, 747 P.2d at 1222.

General Contractor cites no authority holding that promissory estoppel creates an implied-in-fact contract. And, as already noted, the doctrine applies to allow a promise to be enforced in certain instances even though no actual contract exists. We conclude, therefore, that even if a promise made enforceable by promissory estoppel could be considered a contractual obligation, it is based on a contract implied in law, not a contract implied in fact. Under *Barmat*, recoveries based on implied-in-law contracts do not qualify for awards of attorneys' fees under § 12-341.01(A). 155 Ariz. at 523, 747 P.2d 1222.

We affirm the judgment awarding damages to General Contractor based on the doctrine of promissory estoppel. We also affirm the trial court's denial of attorneys' fees to General Contractor, and for the same reasons we deny General Contractor's request for an award of attorneys' fees on appeal.

NOTES & QUESTIONS

1. *Practice Points*: What kind of advice would you expect attorneys representing general contractors to give to their clients in light of the reasoning of this case?

2. What if a contractor would have been selected to complete the entire job, but a subcontractor withdrew its bid, which the contractor used in compiling his bid, and the contractor was forced to withdraw his bid on the project, causing the contractor to lose the potential profits from the job? Would the contractor be able to recover the lost profits from the subcontractor who withdrew their bid? *See Gerson Electric Construction Co. v. Honeywell, Inc.*, 453 N.E.2d 726 (Ill. App. 1988)

3. Does allowing the contractor to sue for loss of potential profits go beyond the limits of contract, in opening the door to recovery in an amount that was not reasonably within the contemplation of the breaching party? What else could the contractor have done, without withdrawing his overall bid? See *Pavel v. Johnson*, 342 Md. 143, 674 A.2d 521 (1996), for a discussion of another measure of recovery.

PROBLEMS

1. At age 17 years, Freeda Freeberg began working on the assembly line at Acme Manufacturing Company, and 45 years later she had worked her way up to the position of office manager and assistant treasurer of the company, which had no employee retirement plan. At the annual meeting of the company's Board of Directors on December 27, 1990, the following resolution was unanimously adopted:

> In consideration of her many years of loyal and faithful service, Acme Manufacturing Company grants to Freeda Freeberg retirement pay of $2000 per month upon her retirement whenever in the future she should decide to leave Acme, such resolution being intended to fix the obligation of Acme and to assist in planning by Freeda Freeberg, who it is hoped will continue in active service to Acme for many years to come.

Freeda worked for Acme for one more year, and then retired in December of 1991. For the next 6 years, Acme paid her $2000 a month, until December of 1997 when a new treasurer joined the company and pointed out that there was no legal contract obligation to pay the $2000 monthly to Freeda. So, Acme stopped the payments. Freeda sues. Acme asserts that the payments to Freeda were gifts to her. What result? *See Feinberg v. Pfeiffer Co.*, 322 S.W.2d 163 (Mo. App. 1959).

2. Assume the same facts as above, except that Freeda had worked for the company for only 25 years at the time of the resolution granting her a retirement benefit of $2000 a month and that she was in good health at age 49 when the company discontinued the monthly payments. Would these facts change your conclusion about who should prevail? Finally, assume that after 25 years of service and 6 years of retirement, Freeda had developed cancer and was expected to live only 5 years. Would her health condition affect your conclusion?

3. *Estate of Timko v. Oral Roberts Evangelistic Association*, 215 N.W.2d 750 (Mich. App. 1974), recited the following facts in this first-impression charitable contribution case in Michigan:

> The decedent, Nicholas Timko, was a member of the board of trustees of the Oral Roberts Evangelistic Association. . . . In January of 1964 at a meeting of the board of trustees Mr. Timko proposed that the board buy a building in Detroit. . . . The minutes of the board of trustees' meeting relating to this proposal read in pertinent part as follows:

> Mr. Timko called attention to a building in Detroit, Michigan known as 7030 East Seven Mile Road, and stated that it was being offered for sale for $155,000, but that he thought he might be able to buy it for the Association for $145,000. Mr. Timko proposed that if arrangements could be made whereby the Association could purchase the building for $145,000 upon a down payment of $25,000 cash, $1,000 per month for five years, and the remaining balance at the end of five years, it would be his intention to make contributions to the Association which would match the deferred payments of the purchase price. It was thereupon moved . . . and unanimously carried that the Association purchase the said building at a purchase price of $145,000, $25,000 cash down payment, $120,000 to be paid by the Association at the rate of $1,000 per month for five years, and the remaining balance to be paid at the end of the five years, with interest on the unpaid balance of the purchase price at the rate of 6% per annum.

> After the trustees' meeting, the minutes were signed by all the members of the board including the decedent, Mr. Timko. Subsequently, on February 21, 1964, the building was purchased by the Association. Mr. Timko dealt with the owners of the property on behalf of the Association, arranged for a bank loan, attended to other closing details, and paid closing costs in excess of $5,000.

> On December 17, 1964, Mr. Timko wrote a letter to the president of the Association indicating that he expected to donate the full amount of the building sometime in February of 1965 and that this donation would "clear off all debts."

> After Mr. Timko paid the closing costs, he made no additional payments to the Association toward the purchase of the building. . . .

Mr. Timko died on January 2, 1969. The Association filed a claim against his estate for the amount of the unpaid balance on the purchase price of the building.

What should be the court's decision? If Timko's estate is liable, for how much?

4. Tonya Talker and Wade Walker both live in Chicago. One Monday, Talker said to Walker, "I will pay you $1,000 if you will walk across the Brooklyn Bridge by 5:00 p.m. New York time this Friday." That Monday evening, Walker bought a plane ticket on a discount airline to fly him roundtrip Wednesday to and from New York City for $225 on a non-refundable ticket. On Tuesday, Talker told Walker that the $1,000 offer was withdrawn. What advice would you give to Walker if it were still Tuesday, subsequent to the announced revocation by Talker? Should Walker go to New York and walk the bridge? Can Walker at least receive payment for the $225 if he does not go to New York? Would it matter to you if evidence would show that Talker had no intention of honoring the offer even at the time she made it?

DEFENSES TO CONTRACT FORMATION

We now return our attention primarily to traditional contract formation, and we ask the last question on the contract formation process, namely, whether any theory of defense against a contract can be asserted under the circumstances of a particular case. We will study several common law and statutory doctrines. Sometimes, the effect of the existence of the defense (such as illegality) will be to render a contract void. Sometimes the effect of the defense (such as duress) will be to render the contract violable. And, under the defense of the failure to satisfy the Statute of Frauds, the contract will be unenforceable. It is important to develop an understanding of both the substance of the various defenses and the effects of each on contracts.

CHAPTER 8

CONTRACT DEFENSES: CONSENT TO CONTRACT IMPAIRED BY INCAPACITY, DURESS, UNDUE INFLUENCE, FRAUD, MISTAKE, AND UNCONSCIONABILITY

In an action for the breach of a contract, the plaintiff must allege that all requirements for a valid contract are met and establish a prima facie case for breach of contract. In response, the defendant may raise defenses that focus on the mutual assent needed for a valid contract. If the defendant's consent to the contract was impaired in some way, the court may determine the contract unenforceable. These contract defenses include incapacity to contract caused by minority or mental incapacity; duress; undue influence; fraud; mistake; and unconscionability.

A. INCAPACITY

"No one can be bound by contract who has not legal capacity to incur at least voidable contractual duties. . . . A natural person who manifests assent to a transaction has full legal capacity to incur contractual duties thereby unless he is (a) under guardianship, or (b) an infant, or (c) mentally ill or defective, or (d) intoxicated." Restatement (Second) of Contracts §§ (1), (2). Thus, a person who lacks capacity cannot form the necessary intent required to manifest assent to a contract. *Id.* comment c.

1. Minors

Lack of capacity to contract defenses arise frequently in cases where a minor enters into a contract. The public policy concern for minors who enter contracts with adults is the fear that adults will take advantage of the minor. Today a contract between an adult and a minor is generally viewed not as void, but as voidable. Thus, if the minor chooses to perform and enforce the contract, the adult is liable. It is the adult who may not enforce the contract against the minor. The exception to this general rule is that an infant may be liable for contracts for "necessaries."

KESER v. CHAGNON
410 P.2d 637 (Colo. 1966)

McWilliams, Justice:

This writ of error concerns the purchase of an automobile by a minor and his efforts to thereafter avoid the contract of purchase. The salient facts are as follows:

> 1. on June 11, 1964 Chagnon bought a 1959 Edsel from Keser for the sum of $1025, payment therefor being in cash which Chagnon obtained by borrowing a portion of the purchase price from the Cash Credit Company on a signature note, with the balance of the money being obtained from the

Public Finance Corporation, the latter loan being secured by a chattel mortgage upon the automobile;

2. as of June 11, 1964 Chagnon was a minor of the age of twenty years, ten months and twenty days, although despite this fact Chagnon nonetheless falsely advised Keser that he was then over the age of twenty-one; and

3. on about September 25, 1964, when Chagnon was then of the age of twenty-one years, two months and four days, Chagnon formally advised Keser of his desire to disaffirm the contract theretofore entered into by the parties, and thereafter on October 5, 1964 Chagnon returned the Edsel to Keser.

Based on this sequence of events Chagnon brought an action against Keser wherein he sought to recover the $1025 which he had allegedly theretofore paid Keser for the Edsel. By answer Keser alleged, among other things, that he had suffered damage as the direct result of Chagnon's false representation as to his age.

A trial was had to the court, sitting without a jury, all of which culminated in a judgment in favor of Chagnon against Keser in the sum of $655.78. This particular sum was arrived at by the trial court in the following manner: the trial court found that Chagnon initially purchased the Edsel for the sum of $995 (not $1025) and that he was entitled to the return of his $995; and then by way of set-off the trial court subtracted from the $995 the sum of $339.22, this latter sum apparently representing the difference between the purchase price paid for the vehicle and the reasonable value of the Edsel on October 5, 1964, which was the date when the Edsel was returned to Keser. By writ of error Keser now seeks reversal of this judgment.

In this court Keser summarizes his argument as follows:

1. Chagnon's attempted disaffirmance was ineffective because though he returned the automobile, he nonetheless failed to also return the certificate of title thereto which was then and there in the possession of the Public Finance Corporation;

2. Chagnon in reality ratified the contract because he failed to disaffirm within a reasonable time after reaching his majority and for such length of time retained possession of the Edsel; and

3. in connection with Keser's set-off the trial court erred in its determination of Keser's damages resulting from Chagnon's false representation as to his age.

Before considering each of these several matters, it is deemed helpful to allude briefly to some of the general principles pertaining to the longstanding policy of the law to protect a minor from at least some of his childish foibles by affording him the right, under certain circumstances, to avoid his contract, not only during his minority but also within a reasonable time after reaching his majority. In *Mosko v. Forsythe*, 102 Colo. 115, 76 P.2d 1106 we held that when a minor elects to disaffirm and avoid his contract, the "contract" becomes invalid *ab initio* and that the parties thereto then revert to the same position as if the contract had never been made. In that case we went on to declare that when a minor thus sought to avoid his contract and had in his possession the specific property received by him in the transaction, he was in such circumstance required to return the same as a prerequisite to any avoidance.

In 43 C.J.S. *Infants* § 75 at page 171 it is said that a minor failing to disaffirm within a "reasonable time" after reaching his majority loses the right to do so and that just what constitutes a "reasonable time" is ordinarily a question of fact. As regards the necessity for restoration of consideration, in 43 C.J.S. at page 174 it is stated that the minor after disaffirming is "usually required. . . to return the consideration, if he can, or the part remaining in his possession or control."

Finally, we believe that *Doenges-Long Motors, Inc. v. Gillen*, 138 Colo. 31, 328 P.2d 1077 answers most of the matters sought to be raised here by Keser. In that case it was held that the right of an infant to disaffirm his contract is absolute and is not lost by reason of the fact that the infant induced the making of the contract by a deliberate misrepresentation of his age. However, in that case it was also held that even though an infant has the right to disaffirm his contract, if he falsely represents his age and as a result thereof obtains an automobile, he is at the same time answerable to the seller for his tort. In other words, though the seller is required to return to the infant that which he, the seller, received in exchange for the automobile, the seller is entitled to set-off against such sum any damage sustained by him as a result of the infant's false representation as to his age. And in this regard the measure of damage was declared to be the difference between the reasonable value of the automobile at the time of its sale and delivery and its reasonable value at the time of its return.

Proceeding, then, to a consideration of those matters which Keser now contends require a reversal of this case, it is first urged that Chagnon's attempted disaffirmance is ineffective because, although Chagnon did return the Edsel to Keser, he did not at the same time return the certificate of ownership thereto, which certificate was then in possession of the Public Finance Corporation. And needless to say, Public Finance Corporation was not about to voluntarily give up the certificate of title! This contention, however, is without merit. It is true that Mosko v. Forsythe, supra, holds that a prerequisite to the avoidance of an executed contract by a minor is that if he then has in his possession the property which he received in the transaction, he must return the same. All that is required in this regard, however, is that the disaffirming party return only those fruits of his contract which are then in his possession and if for any reason he cannot thus place the other party in status quo, he does not because of such inability lose his right to disaffirm. To hold otherwise would strike at the very root of the well-settled principle that, with certain exceptions which are not applicable to the instant controversy, he who deals with a minor does so at his own peril and with the attendant risk that the minor may at his election disaffirm the transaction because of his minority. *Weathers v. Owen*, 78 Cal. App. 505, 51 S.E.2d 584 presents a factual situation most analogous to the instant one. *See also Dawson v. Fox*, 64 A.2d 162, (D.C. Mun. App.); and *Freiburg-haus v. Herman*, 102 S.W.2d 743 (Mo. App.). In the instant case Chagnon returned to Keser all of the fruits of the transaction which were then in his possession or under his control, *i.e.* the Edsel. The fact that the Public Finance Corporation held the certificate of title and would not deliver it over to either Chagnon or Keser does not defeat Chagnon's right to disaffirm.

Keser's next contention that Chagnon upon attaining his majority ratified the contract by his failure to disaffirm within a reasonable time after becoming twenty-one and by his retention and use of the Edsel prior to its return to the seller is equally untenable. In this connection it is pointed out that Chagnon did not notify

Keser of his desire to disaffirm until 66 days after he became twenty-one and that he did not return the Edsel until 10 days after his notice to disaffirm, during all of which time Chagnon had the possession and use of the vehicle in question. As already noted, when an infant attains his majority he has a reasonable time within which he may thereafter disaffirm, a contract entered into during his minority. And this rule is not as strict where, as here, we are dealing with an executed contract. There is no hard and fast rule as to just what constitutes a "reasonable" time within which the infant may disaffirm. In *Fellows v. Cantrell*, 143 Colo. 126 352 P.2d 289 we held that the failure to disaffirm for a period of five years after a minor reached his majority, together with other acts recognizing the validity of the contract, constituted ratification. In *Merchants' Credit Union v. Ariyama*, 64 Utah 364, 230 P. 1017 disaffirmance four months after reaching majority was held to be within a reasonable time. Similarly, in *Haines v. Fitzgerald*, 108 Pa. Super. 290, 165 A. 52, three months was held to be a reasonable time within which to disaffirm; and in *Adamroski v. Curtis-Wright*, 300 Mass. 281, 15 N.E.2d 467 "nearly a year" was also held to be "reasonable." Suffice it to say, that under the circumstances disclosed by the record we are not prepared to hold that as a matter of law Chagnon ratified the contract either by his actions or by his alleged failure to disaffirm within a reasonable time after reaching his majority. In other words, there is competent evidence to support the conclusion of the trial court that Chagnon disaffirmed the contract within a reasonable time after reaching his majority and such finding of fact cannot be disturbed by us on review. Finally, error is predicated upon the trial court's finding in connection with Keser's set-off for the damage occasioned him by Chagnon's admitted false representation of his age. In this regard the trial court apparently found that the reasonable value of the Edsel when it was returned to Keser by Chagnon was $655.78, and accordingly went on to allow Keser a set-off in the amount of $339.22, this latter sum representing the difference between the purchase price, $995, and the value of the vehicle on the date it was returned. Finding, then, that Chagnon was entitled to the return of the $995 which he had theretofore paid Keser for the Edsel, the trial court then subtracted therefrom Keser's set-off in the amount of $339.22, and accordingly entered judgment for Chagnon against Keser in the sum of $655.78. Whether it was by accident or design we know not, but $655.78 is apparently the exact amount which Chagnon "owed" the Public Finance Corporation on his note with that company.

In this regard as concerns his setoff Keser complains that the trial court did not follow the rule regarding the measure of damages as laid down in *Doenges-Long v. Gillen, supra.* More particularly, Keser claims that there is no evidence which supports the trial court's finding that the value of the automobile on the date it was returned to Keser was $655.78. The evidence as to the value of the Edsel on the date Chagnon returned it to Keser was as follows:

1. Chagnon said the car was worth more when he returned it than when he bought it;

2. An expert called by Keser opined that the car was worth $245 and

3. Keser testified that if he had a clear title to the vehicle it had a reasonable value of $395.

Based on this evidence the trial court found that the reasonable value of the automobile on the date of its return to Keser was $655.78, which determination from the arithmetical standpoint, at least, permitted the trial court to then enter judgment in favor of Chagnon in an amount equal to the balance then due and owing the Public Finance Corporation. Without belaboring the point, it is apparent that in its determination of the reasonable value of the Edsel on the date of its return to Keser, the trial court was influenced by factors other than the evidence before it as to such value. The judgment is reversed and the cause remanded with direction that the trial court determine Keser's set-off in accord with the rule in Doenges-Long v. Gillen, supra, and once this set-off has been thus determined, to then enter judgment for Chagnon in an amount equal to the difference between $995 and the amount of such set-off.

NOTES & QUESTIONS

1. The age of majority has shifted over time. Many states for many years considered 21 the age of majority, but currently 18 is viewed as the age of capacity. Various states find that men and women reach the age of majority when they marry. *See* RESTATEMENT (SECOND) OF CONTRACTS § 14, comment (a).

2. The *Keser* court found "a prerequisite to the avoidance of an executed contract by a minor is that if he then has in his possession the property which he received in the transaction, he must return the same. All that is required in this regard, however, is that the disaffirming party return only those fruits of his contract which are then in his possession and if for any reason he cannot thus place the other party in status quo, he does not because of such inability lose his right to disaffirm."

What are the policy considerations underlying the minor's obligation to make restitution? To what extent must the infant make the restitution? *See Porter v. Wilson*, 209 A.2d 730 (N.H. 1965).

3. A minor may, by his acts or words, ratify his contract after reaching the age of majority. Within a reasonable time of reaching majority, the minor may choose to ratify or to disaffirm the obligations under the contract. The *Keser* court found that upon reaching majority, the minor had not ratified the contract, but had acted within a reasonable time to disaffirm the contract, noting a range of reasonable time elapsed in similar cases.

But can a minor's parent affirm or ratify the minor's contract? A minor signed a contract with defendant that permitted the minor to use defendant's recreational skydiving facilities, including use of an airplane to transport sky divers to the jumping site. The contract also contained a covenant not to sue and a clause exempting defendant from all liability. The court found the plaintiff's mother had ratified the terms of the contract. Plaintiff had reached majority when he was injured in a plane crash at the skydiving facility. To avoid the contract's covenant not to sue, the plaintiff attempted to disaffirm the contract based upon his minority at the time of the contract. Can the mother affirm the infant's contract? What facts show that the minor ratified the contract? *See Jones v. Dressel*, 623 P.2d 370 (Colo. 1981).

4. When Chagnon purchased the car, he "was a minor of the age of twenty years, ten months and twenty days, although despite this fact Chagnon nonetheless falsely advised Keser that he was then over the age of twenty-one." Should this false statement have prevented Chagnon from disaffirming the contract? *See Gillis v. Whitley's Discount Auto Sales*, 319 S.E.2d 661 (N.C. Ct. App. 1984).

WEBSTER STREET PARTNERSHIP, LTD. v. SHERIDAN
220 Neb. 9, 368 N.W.2d 439 (1985)

KRIVOSHA, Chief Justice:

Webster Street Partnership, Ltd. (Webster Street), appeals from an order of the district court for Douglas County, Nebraska, which modified an earlier judgment entered by the municipal court of the city of Omaha, Douglas County, Nebraska. The municipal court entered judgment in favor of Webster Street and against the appellees, Matthew Sheridan and Pat Wilwerding, in the amount of $630.94. On appeal the district court found that Webster Street was entitled to a judgment in the amount of $146.75 and that Sheridan and Wilwerding were entitled to a credit in the amount of $150. The district court therefore entered judgment in favor of Sheridan and Wilwerding and against Webster Street in the amount of $3.25. It is from this $3.25 judgment that appeal is taken to this court.

Webster Street is a partnership owning real estate in Omaha, Nebraska. On September 18, 1982, Webster Street, through one of its agents, Norman Sargent, entered into a written lease with Sheridan and Wilwerding for a second floor apartment at 3007 Webster Street. The lease provided that Sheridan and Wilwerding would pay to Webster Street by way of monthly rental the sum of $250 due on the first day of each month until August 15, 1983. The lease also required the payment of a security deposit in the amount of $150 and a payment of $20 per month for utilities during the months of December, January, February, and March. Liquidated damages in the amount of $5 per day for each day the rent was late were also provided for by the lease.

The evidence conclusively establishes that at the time the lease was executed both tenants were minors and, further, that Webster Street knew that fact. At the time the lease was entered into, Sheridan was 18 and did not become 19 until November 5, 1982. Wilwerding was 17 at the time the lease was executed and never gained his majority during any time relevant to this case.

The tenants paid the $150 security deposit, $100 rent for the remaining portion of September 1982, and $250 rent for October 1982. They did not pay the rent for the month of November 1982, and on November 5 Sargent advised Wilwerding that unless the rent was paid immediately, both boys would be required to vacate the premises. The tenants both testified that, being unable to pay the rent, they moved from the premises on November 12. In fact, a dispute exists as to when the two tenants relinquished possession of the premises, but in view of our decision that dispute is not of any relevance.

In a letter dated January 7, 1983, Webster Street's attorney made written demand upon the tenants for damages in the amount of $630.94. On January 12, 1983, the tenants' attorney denied any liability, refused to pay any portion of the amount demanded, stated that neither tenant was of legal age at the time the lease was executed, and demanded return of $150 security deposit.

Webster Street thereafter commenced suit against the tenants and sought judgment in the amount of $630.94, which was calculated as follows:

Rent due Nov.	$250.00
Rent due Dec.	250.00
Dec. utility allowance	20.00

Garage rental	40.00
Clean up and repair	
Broken window, de-	
grease	
kitchen stove, sham-	
poo	
carpet, etc.	46.79
Advertising	24.15
Re-rental fee	150.00
	$780.94
Less security deposit	150.00
	$630.94

To this petition the tenants filed an answer alleging that they were minors at the time they signed the lease, that the lease was therefore voidable, and that the rental property did not constitute a necessary for which they were otherwise liable. In addition, Sheridan cross-petitioned for the return of the security deposit, and Wilwerding filed a cross-petition seeking the return of all moneys paid to Webster Street. Following trial, the municipal court of the city of Omaha found in favor of Webster Street and against both tenants in the amount of $630.94.

The tenants appealed to the district court for Douglas County. The district court found that the tenants had vacated the premises on November 12, 1982, and therefore were only liable for the 12 days in which they actually occupied the apartment and did not pay rent. The district court also permitted Webster Street to recover $46.79 for cleanup and repairs. The tenants, however, were given credit for their $150 security deposit, resulting in an order that Webster Street was indebted to the tenants in the amount of $3.25.

Webster Street then perfected an appeal to this court assigning but one error in terms which provide little assistance to the court in considering the appeal. The assignment of error, in pertinent part, reads as follows: "The District Court . . . abused [its] discretion and committed errors of law in improperly modifying the judgment of the Municipal Court. . . ." It appears, in fact, to be Webster Street's position that the district court erred in failing to find that Sheridan had ratified the lease within a reasonable time after obtaining majority, and was therefore responsible for the lease, and that the minors had become emancipated and were therefore liable, even though Wilwerding had not reached majority. Webster Street is simply wrong in both matters.

As a general rule, an infant does not have the capacity to bind himself absolutely by contract. . . . The right of the infant to avoid his contract is one conferred by law for his protection against his own improvidence and the designs of others. . . . The policy of the law is to discourage adults from contracting with an infant; they cannot complain if, as a consequence of violating that rule, they are unable to enforce their contracts. As stated in *Curtice Co. v. Kent*, 89 Neb. 496, 500, 131 N.W. 944, 945 (1911): "The result seems hardly just to the [adult], but persons dealing with infants do so at their peril. The law is plain as to their disability to contract, and safety lies in refusing to transact business with them."

However, the privilege of infancy will not enable an infant to escape liability in all cases and under all circumstances. For example, it is well established that an infant is liable for the value of necessaries furnished him. . . . . An infant's liability for necessaries is based not upon his actual contract to pay for them but upon a contract implied by law, or, in other words, a quasi-contract. . . .

Just what are the necessaries, however, has no exact definition. The term is flexible and varies according to the facts of each individual case. In *Cobbey v. Buchanan*, 48 Neb. 391, 397, 67 N.W. 176, 178 (1896), we said:

> The meaning of the term 'necessaries' cannot be defined by a general rule applicable to all cases; the question is a mixed one of law and fact, to be determined in each case from the particular facts and circumstances in such case.

A number of factors must be considered before a court can conclude whether a particular product or service is a necessary. As stated in *Schoenung v. Gallet*, 206 Wis. 52, 54, 238 N.W. 852, 853 (1931):

> The term "necessaries," as used in the law relating to the liability of infants therefor, is a relative term, somewhat flexible, except when applied to such things as are obviously requisite for the maintenance of existence, and depends on the social position and situation in life of infant, as well as upon his own fortune and that of his parents. The particular infant must have an actual need for the articles furnished; not for mere ornament or pleasure. The articles must be useful and suitable, but they are not necessaries merely because useful or beneficial. Concerning the general character of the things furnished, to be necessaries the articles must supply the infant's personal needs, either those of his body or those of his mind. However, the term "necessaries" is not confined to merely such things as are required for a bare subsistence. There is no positive rule by means of which it may be determined what are or what are not necessaries, for what may be considered necessary for one infant may not be necessaries for another infant whose state is different as to rank, social position, fortune, health, or other circumstances, the question being one to be determined from the particular facts and circumstances of each case.

(Citation omitted.) This appears to be the law as it is generally followed throughout the country.

In *Ballinger v. Craig*, 95 Ohio App. 545, 121 N.E.2d 66 (1953), the defendants were husband and wife and were 19 years of age at the time they purchased a house trailer. Both were employed. However, prior to the purchase of the trailer, the defendants were living with the parents of the husband. The Court of Appeals for the State of Ohio held that under the facts presented the trailer was not a necessary. The court stated:

> To enable an infant to contract for articles as necessaries, he must have been in actual need of them, and obliged to procure them for himself. They are not necessaries as to him, however necessary they may be in their nature, if he was already supplied with sufficient articles of the kind, or if he had a parent or guardian who was able and willing to supply them. The burden of proof is on the plaintiff to show that the infant was destitute of the articles, and had no way of procuring them except by his own contract.

(Citation omitted.) *Id.* at 547, 121 N.E.2d at 67. Under Ohio law the marriage of the parties did not result in their obtaining majority.

In 42 AM. JUR. 2D *Infants* § 67 at 68-69 (1969), the author notes:

> Thus, articles are not necessaries for an infant if he has a parent or guardian who is able and willing to supply them, and an infant residing with and being supported by his parent according to his station in life is not absolutely liable for things which under other circumstances would be considered necessaries.

The undisputed testimony is that both tenants were living away from home, apparently with the understanding that they could return home at any time. Sheridan testified:

> Q. During the time that you were living at 3007 Webster, did you at any time, feel free to go home or anything like that?
>
> A. Well, I had a feeling I could, but I just wanted to see if I could make it on my own.
>
> Q. Had you been driven from your home?
>
> A. No.
>
> Q. You didn't have to go?
>
> A. No.
>
> Q. You went freely?
>
> A. Yes.
>
> Q. Then, after you moved out and went to 3417 for a week or so, you were again to return home, is that correct?
>
> A. Yes, sir.

It would therefore appear that in the present case neither Sheridan nor Wilwerding was in need of shelter but, rather, had chosen to voluntarily leave home, with the understanding that they could return whenever they desired. One may at first blush believe that such a rule is unfair. Yet, on further consideration, the wisdom of the rule is apparent. If, indeed, landlords may not contract with minors, except at their peril, they may refuse to do so. In that event, minors who voluntarily leave home but who are free to return will be compelled to return to their parents' home — a result which is desirable. We therefore find that both the municipal court and the district court erred in finding that the apartment, under the facts in this case, was a necessary.

Having therefore concluded that the apartment was not a necessary, the question of whether Sheridan and Wilwerding were emancipated is of no significance. The effect of emancipation is only relevant with regard to necessaries. If the minors were not emancipated, then their parents would be liable for necessaries provided to the minors.

As we recently noted in *Accent Service Co., Inc. v. Ebsen*, 209 Neb. 94, 96, 306 N.W.2d 575, 576 (1981):

> In general, even in the absence of statute, parents are under a legal as well as a moral obligation to support, maintain, and care for their children, the basis of such a duty resting not only upon the fact of the parent-child relationship, but also upon the interest of the state as parens patriae of

children and of the community at large in preventing them from becoming a public burden. However, various voluntary acts of a child, such as marriage or enlistment in military service, have been held to terminate the parent's obligation of support, the issue generally being considered by the courts in terms of whether an emancipation of the child has been effectuated. In those cases involving the issue of whether a parent is obligated to support an unmarried minor child who has voluntarily left home without the consent of the parent, the courts, in actions to compel support from the parent, have uniformly held that such conduct on the part of the child terminated the support obligation. . . .

If, on the other hand, it was determined that the minors were emancipated and the apartment was a necessary, then the minors would be liable. But where, as here, we determine that the apartment was not a necessary, then neither the parents nor the infants are liable and the question of emancipation is of no moment. Because the rental of the apartment was not a necessary, the minors had the right to avoid the contract, either during their minority or within a reasonable time after reaching their majority. . . . Disaffirmance by an infant completely puts an end to the contract's existence, both as to him and as to the adult with whom he contracted. . . .

Because the parties then stand as if no contract had ever existed, the infant can recover payments made to the adult, and the adult is entitled to the return of whatever was received by the infant. . . .

The record shows that Pat Wilwerding clearly disaffirmed the contract during his minority. Moreover, the record supports the view that when the agent for Webster Street ordered the minors out for failure to pay rent and they vacated the premises, Sheridan likewise disaffirmed the contract. The record indicates that Sheridan reached majority on November 5. To suggest that a lapse of 7 days was not disaffirmance within a reasonable time would be foolish. Once disaffirmed, the contract became void; therefore, no contract existed between the parties, and the minors were entitled to recover all of the moneys which they paid and to be relieved of any further obligation under the contract. The judgment of the district court for Douglas County, Nebraska, is therefore reversed and the cause remanded with directions to vacate the judgment in favor of Webster Street and to enter a judgment in favor of Matthew Sheridan and Pat Wilwerding in the amount of $500, representing September rent in the amount of $100, October rent in the amount of $250, and the security deposit in the amount of $150.

REVERSED AND REMANDED WITH DIRECTIONS.

NOTES & QUESTIONS

1. What are necessaries for one minor may not be necessaries for another. When might a car be a necessary? A minor purchases a car, but later seeks to disaffirm the contract based on infancy. Under what particular circumstances might a court find a car to be a necessary? *See Star Chevrolet Co. v. Green*, 473 So. 2d 157 (Miss. 1985); *Warwick Municipal Employees Credit Union v. McCallister*, 293 A.2d 516 (R.I. 1972); *Rose v. Sheehan Buick, Inc.*, 204 So.2d 903 (Fla. Dist. Ct. App. 1967).

2. When would a professional education be a necessary?

Consider Connelly, a minor enrolled in the plaintiff's correspondence school. Under the enrollment contract, Connelly was to make monthly payments until the entire enrollment fee was paid. Connelly made the first payment, but then stopped paying. Plaintiff school filed suit to recover the balance of the enrollment fee plus costs. In defense, Connelly pleaded the defense of infancy. The court concluded that a proper education is a necessary; however, a professional school education is typically not a necessary. Further, the court held that plaintiff had failed to demonstrate that its correspondence school was a necessary; thus, the court denied plaintiff recovery on the contract. *See International Text-Book Co. v. Connelly*, 99 N.E. 722 (N.Y. 1912) ("A proper education is a necessary, so that a contract by an infant therefor is binding, but what is a proper education will depend on circumstances, and, while a common school education is a necessary, a classical or professional education is not a necessary, in the absence of special circumstances.").

2.   Mental Infirmity

Public policy supports the need to protect minors from adults who would take advantage of their youth and inexperience in contracting with them. Similarly, courts protect the mentally ill or mentally impaired. Mental incapacity is difficult to determine and may shift over time as a person achieves and then loses mental capacity to contract. When a court declares a person mentally incompetent, a guardian will be appointed to handle all legal matters, including contracts. Thus, any contracts the court declared incompetent enters are void, not simply voidable.

When no adjudication of incompetency has been issued, the court is left to determine a party's mental incapacity: was the party capable of understanding the nature and consequences of a transaction? Did the other party know or have reason to know of the party's impairment? Consider these questions as you read the following cases involving parties suffering from mental illnesses that may permit them cognitive understanding of a contract, but rob them of judgment.

ORTELERE v. TEACHERS' RETIREMENT BOARD OF THE CITY OF NEW YORK
25 N.Y.2d 196, 303 N.Y.S.2d 362, 250 N.E.2d 460 (1969)

BREITEL, Judge:

This appeal involves the revocability of an election of benefits under a public employees' retirement system and suggests the need for a renewed examination of the kinds of mental incompetency which may render voidable the exercise of contractual rights. The particular issue arises on the evidently unwise and foolhardy selection of benefits by a 60-year-old teacher, on leave for mental illness and suffering from cerebral arteriosclerosis, after service as a public schoolteacher and participation in a public retirement system for over 40 years. The teacher died a little less than two months after making her election of maximum benefits, payable to her during her life, thus causing the entire reserve to fall in. She left surviving her husband of 38 years of marriage and two grown children.

There is no doubt that any retirement system depends for its soundness on an actuarial experience based on the purely prospective selections of benefits and mortality rates among the covered group, and that retrospective or adverse selection after the fact would be destructive of a sound system. It is also true that members of retirement systems are free to make choices which to others may seem unwise or foolhardy. The issue here is narrower than any suggested by these basic principles. It is whether an otherwise irrevocable election may be avoided for incapacity because of known mental illness which resulted in the election when, except in the barest actuarial sense, the system would sustain no unfavorable consequences.

The husband and executor of Grace W. Ortelere, the deceased New York City schoolteacher, sues to set aside her application for retirement without option, in the event of her death. It is alleged that Mrs. Ortelere, on February 11, 1965, two months before her death from natural causes, was not mentally competent to execute a retirement application. By this application, effective the next day, she elected the maximum retirement allowance. . . . She thus revoked her earlier election of benefits under which she named her husband a beneficiary of the unexhausted reserve upon her death. Selection of the maximum allowance extinguished all interests upon her death.

Following a nonjury trial in Supreme Court, it was held that Grace Ortelere had been mentally incompetent at the time of her February 11 application, thus rendering it "null and void and of no legal effect". The Appellate Division, by a divided court, reversed the judgment of the Supreme Court and held that, as a matter of law, there was insufficient proof of mental incompetency as to this transaction. . . .

Mrs. Ortelere's mental illness, indeed, psychosis, is undisputed. It is not seriously disputable, however, that she had complete cognitive judgment or awareness when she made her selection. A modern understanding of mental illness, however, suggests that incapacity to contract or exercise contractual rights may exist, because of volitional and affective impediments or disruptions in the personality, despite the intellectual or cognitive ability to understand. It will be recognized as the civil law parallel to the question of criminal responsibility which has been the recent concern of so many and has resulted in statutory and decisional changes in the criminal law. . . .

Mrs. Ortelere, an elementary school teacher since 1924, suffered a "nervous breakdown" in March, 1964 and went on a leave of absence expiring February 5, 1965. She was then 60 years old and had been happily married for 38 years. On July 1, 1964 she came under the care of Dr. D'Angelo, a psychiatrist, who diagnosed her breakdown as involutional psychosis, melancholia type. Dr. D'Angelo prescribed, and for about six weeks decedent underwent, tranquilizer and shock therapy. Although moderately successful, the therapy was not continued since it was suspected that she also suffered from cerebral arteriosclerosis, an ailment later confirmed. However, the psychiatrist continued to see her at monthly intervals until March, 1965. On March 28, 1965 she was hospitalized after collapsing at home from an aneurysm. She died to days later; the cause of death was "Cerebral thrombosis due to H(ypertensive) H(eart) D(isease)."

As a teacher she had been a member of the Teachers' Retirement System of the City of New York. . . . This entitled her to certain annuity and pension rights, pre-retirement death benefits, and empowered her to exercise various options concerning the payment of her retirement allowance.

Some years before, on June 28, 1958, she had executed a "Selection of Benefits under Option One" naming her husband as beneficiary of the unexhausted reserve.

Under this option upon retirement her allowance would be less by way of periodic retirement allowances, but if she died before receipt of her full reserve the balance of the reserve would be payable to her husband. On June 16, 1960, two years later, she had designated her husband as beneficiary of her service death benefits in the event of her death prior to retirement.

Then on February 11, 1965, when her leave of absence had just expired and she was still under treatment, she executed a retirement application, the one here involved, selecting the maximum retirement allowance payable during her lifetime with nothing payable on or after death. She also, at this time, borrowed from the system the maximum cash withdrawal permitted, namely, $8,760. Three days earlier she had written the board, stating that she intended to retire on February 12 or 15 or as soon as she received "the information I need in order to decide whether to take an option or maximum allowance." She then listed eight specific questions, reflecting great understanding of the retirement system, concerning the various alternatives available. An extremely detailed reply was sent, by letter of February 15, 1965, although by that date it was technically impossible for her to change her selection. However, the board's chief clerk, before whom Mrs. Ortelere executed the application, testified that the questions were "answered verbally by me on February 11th." Her retirement reserve totalled $62,165 (after deducting the $8,760 withdrawal), and the difference between electing the maximum retirement allowance (no option) and the allowance under "option one" was $901 per year or $75 per month. That is, had the teacher selected "option one" she would have received an annual allowance of $4,494 or $375 per month, while if no option had been selected she would have received an annual allowance of $5,395 or $450 per month. Had she not withdrawn the cash the annual figures would be $5,247 and $6,148 respectively.

Following her taking a leave of absence for her condition, Mrs. Ortelere had become very depressed and was unable to care for herself. As a result her husband gave up his electrician's job, in which he earned $222 per week, to stay home and take care of her on a full-time basis. She left their home only when he accompanied her. Although he took her to the Retirement Board on February 11, 1965, he did not know why she went, and did not question her for fear "she'd start crying hysterically that I was scolding her. That's the way she was. And I wouldn't upset her."

The Orteleres were in quite modest circumstances. They owned their own home, valued at $20,000, and had $8,000 in a savings account. They also owned some farm land worth about $5,000. Under these circumstances, as revealed in this record, retirement for both of the Orteleres or the survivor of them had to be provided, as a practical matter, largely out of Mrs. Ortelere's retirement benefits.

According to Dr. D'Angelo, the psychiatrist who treated her, Mrs. Ortelere never improved enough to "warrant my sending her back (to teaching)." A physician for the Board of Education examined her on February 2, 1965 to determine her fitness to return to teaching. Although not a psychiatrist but rather a specialist in internal medicine, this physician 'judged that she had apparently recovered from the depression' and that she appeared rational. However, before allowing her to return to teaching, a report was requested from Dr. D'Angelo concerning her condition. It is notable that the Medical Division of the Board of Education on February 24, 1965 requested that Mrs. Ortelere report to the board's "panel psychiatrist" on March 11, 1965. Dr. D'Angelo stated "(a)t no time since she was under my care was she ever mentally competent"; that '(m)entally she couldn't make a decision of any kind, actually, of any kind, small or large.' He also described how involutional melancholia affects the judgment process:

> They can't think rationally, no matter what the situation is. They will even tell you, "I used to be able to think of anything and make any decision. Now," they say, "even getting up, I don't know whether I should get up or whether I should stay in bed." Or, "I don't even know how to make a slice of toast any more." Everything is impossible to decide, and everything is too great an effort to even think of doing. They just don't have the effort, actually, because their nervous breakdown drains them of all their physical energies.

While the psychiatrist used terms referring to "rationality", it is quite evident that Mrs. Ortelere's psychopathology did not lend itself to a classification under the legal test of irrationality. It is undoubtedly, for this reason, that the Appellate Division was unable to accept his testimony and the trial court's finding of irrationality in the light of the prevailing rules as they have been formulated.

The well-established rule is that contracts of a mentally incompetent person who has not been adjudicated insane are voidable. Even where the contract has been partly or fully performed it will still be avoided upon restoration of the status quo. . . .

Traditionally, in this State and elsewhere, contractual mental capacity has been measured by what is largely a cognitive test. . . . Under this standard the "inquiry" is whether the mind was "so affected as to render him wholly and absolutely incompetent to comprehend and understand the nature of the transaction". . . . A requirement that the party also be able to make a rational judgment concerning the particular transaction qualified the cognitive test. . . . Conversely, it is also well recognized that contractual ability would be affected by insane delusions intimately related to the particular transaction. . . .

These traditional standards governing competency to contract were formulated when psychiatric knowledge was quite primitive. They fail to account for one who by reason of mental illness is unable to control his conduct even though his cognitive ability seems unimpaired. When these standards were evolving it was thought that all the mental faculties were simultaneously affected by mental illness. . . . This is no longer the prevailing view. . . .

Of course, the greatest movement in revamping legal notions of mental responsibility has occurred in the criminal law. The nineteenth century cognitive test embraced in the M'Naghten rules has long been criticized and changed by statute and decision in many jurisdictions. . . .

While the policy considerations for the criminal law and the civil law are different, both share in common the premise that policy considerations must be based on a sound understanding of the human mind and, therefore, its illnesses. Hence, because the cognitive rules are, for the most part, too restrictive and rest on a false factual basis they must be re-examined. Once it is understood that, accepting plaintiff's proof, Mrs. Ortelere was psychotic and because of that psychosis could have been incapable of making a voluntary selection of her retirement system benefits, there is an issue that a modern jurisprudence should not exclude, merely because her mind could pass a 'cognition' test based on nineteenth century psychology.

There has also been some movement on the civil law side to achieve a modern posture. For the most part, the movement has been glacial and has been disguised under traditional formulations. Various devices have been used to avoid unacceptable results under the old rules by finding unfairness or overreaching in order to avoid transactions.

. . .

In this State there has been at least one candid approach. In *Faber v. Sweet Style Mfg. Corp.*, 40 Misc. 2d 212, at p. 216, 242 N.Y.S.2d 763, at p. 768, Mr. Justice MEYER wrote: "(i)ncompetence to contract also exists when a contract is entered into under the compulsion of a mental disease or disorder but for which the contract would not have been made." . . . This is the first known time a court has recognized that the traditional standards of incompetency for contractual capacity are inadequate in light of contemporary psychiatric learning and applied modern standards. Prior to this, courts applied the cognitive standard giving great weight to objective evidence of rationality.

. . .

It is quite significant that RESTATEMENT (SECOND) OF CONTRACTS, states the modern rule on competency to contract. This is in evident recognition, and the Reporter's Notes support this inference, that, regardless of how the cases formulated their reasoning, the old cognitive test no longer explains the results. Thus, the new RESTATEMENT section reads:

> (1) A person incurs only voidable contractual duties by entering into a transaction if by reason of mental illness or defect . . . (b) he is unable to act in a reasonable manner in relation to the transaction and the other party has reason to know of his condition. (RESTATEMENT (SECOND) OF CONTRACTS . . .).

The avoidance of duties under an agreement entered into by those who have done so by reason of mental illness, but who have understanding, depends on balancing competing policy considerations. There must be stability in contractual relations and protection of the expectations of parties who bargain in good faith. On the other hand, it is also desirable to protect persons who may understand the nature of the transaction but who, due to mental illness, cannot control their conduct. Hence, there should be relief only if the other party knew or was put on notice as to the contractor's mental illness. Thus, the RESTATEMENT provision for avoidance contemplates that "the other party has reason to know" of the mental illness (*Id.*).

When, however, the other party is without knowledge of the contractor's mental illness and the agreement is made on fair terms, the proposed RESTATEMENT rule is:

> The power of avoidance under subsection (1) terminates to the extent that the contract has been so performed in whole or in part or the circumstances have so changed that avoidance would be inequitable. In such a case a court may grant relief on such equitable terms as the situation requires. (RESTATEMENT (SECOND) OF CONTRACTS, *supra*, § 18C, subd. (2).)

The system was, or should have been, fully aware of Mrs. Ortelere's condition. They, or the Board of Education, knew of her leave of absence for medical reasons and the resort to staff psychiatrists by the Board of Education. Hence, the other of the conditions for avoidance is satisfied.

Lastly, there are no significant changes of position by the system other than those that flow from the barest actuarial consequences of benefit selection.

Nor should one ignore that in the relationship between retirement system and member, and especially in a public system, there is not involved a commercial, let alone an ordinary commercial, transaction. Instead the nature of the system and its announced goal is the protection of its members and those in whom its members have an interest. It is not a sound scheme which would permit 40 years of contribution and participation in the system to be nullified by a one-instant act committed by one known to be mentally ill. This is especially true if there would be no substantial harm to the system if the act were avoided. On the record none may gainsay that her selection of a "no option" retirement while under psychiatric care, ill with cerebral arteriosclerosis, aged 60, and with a family in which she had always manifested concern, was so unwise and foolhardy that a factfinder might conclude that it was explainable only as a product of psychosis.

On this analysis it is not difficult to see that plaintiff's evidence was sufficient to sustain a finding that, when she acted as she did on February 11, 1965, she did so solely as a result of serious mental illness, namely, psychosis. Of course, nothing less serious than medically classified psychosis should suffice or else few contracts would be invulnerable to some kind of psychological attack. Mrs. Ortelere's psychiatrist testified quite flatly that as an involutional melancholiac in depression she was incapable of making a voluntary "rational" decision. Of course, as noted earlier, the trial court's finding and perhaps some of the testimony attempted to fit into the rubrics of the traditional rules. For that reason rather than reinstatement of the judgment at Trial Term there should be a new trial under the proper standards frankly considered and applied.

Accordingly, the order of the Appellate Division should be reversed, without costs, and the action remanded to Special Term for a new trial.

JASEN, Judge (dissenting):

Where there has been no previous adjudication of incompetency, the burden of proving mental incompetence is upon the party alleging it. I agree with the majority at the Appellate Division that the plaintiff, the husband of the decedent, failed to sustain the burden incumbent upon him of proving deceased's incompetence.

The evidence conclusively establishes that the decedent, at the time she made her application to retire, understood not only that she was retiring, but also that she had selected the maximum payment during her lifetime.

Indeed, the letter written by the deceased to the Teachers' Retirement System prior to her retirement demonstrates her full mental capacity to understand and to decide whether to take an option or the maximum allowance. The full text of the letter reads as follows:

> February 8, 1965
>
> Gentlemen:
>
> I would like to retire on Feb. 12 or Feb. 15. In other words, just as soon as possible after I receive the information I need in order to decide whether

to take an option or maximum allowance. Following are the questions I would like to have answered:

1. What is my "average" five-year salary?

2. What is my maximum allowance?

3. I am 60 years old. If I select option four-a with a beneficiary (female) 27 years younger, what is my allowance?

4. If I select four-a on the pension part only, and take the maximum annuity, what is my allowance?

5. If I take a loan of 89% of my year's salary before retirement, what would my maximum allowance be?

6. If I take a loan of $5,000 before retiring, and select option four-a on both the pension and annuity, what would my allowance be?

7. What is my total service credit? I have been on a leave without pay since Oct. 26, 1964.

8. What is the "factor" used for calculating option four-a with the above beneficiary?

Thank you for your promptness in making the necessary calculations. I will come to your office on Thursday afternoon of this week.

It seems clear that this detailed, explicit and extremely pertinent list of queries reveals a mind fully in command of the salient features of the Teachers' Retirement System. Certainly, it cannot be said that the decedent could possess sufficient capacity to compose a letter indicating such a comprehensive understanding of the retirement system, and yet lack the capacity to understand the answers.

As I read the record, the evidence establishes that the decedent's election to receive maximum payments was predicated on the need for a higher income to support two retired persons — her husband and herself. Since the only source of income available to decedent and her husband was decedent's retirement pay, the additional payment of $75 per month which she would receive by electing the maximal payment was a necessity. Indeed, the additional payments represented an increase of 20% over the benefits payable under option 1. Under these circumstances, an election of maximal income during decedent's lifetime was not only a rational, but a necessary decision.

Further indication of decedent's knowledge of the financial needs of her family is evidenced by the fact that she took a loan for the maximum amount ($8,760) permitted by the retirement system at the time she made application for retirement.

Moreover, there is nothing in the record to indicate that the decedent had any warning, premonition, knowledge or indication at the time of retirement that her life expectancy was, in any way, reduced by her condition. Decedent's election of the maximum retirement benefits, therefore, was not so contrary to her best interests so as to create an inference of her mental incompetence.

Indeed, concerning election of options under a retirement system, it has been held: "Even where no previous election has been made, the court must make the election for an incompetent which would be in accordance with what would have been his manifest and reasonable choice if he were sane, and, in the absence of convincing evidence that the incompetent would have made a different selection, it is presumed that he would have chosen the option yielding the largest returns in his lifetime.". . .

Nor can I agree with the majority's view that the traditional rules governing competency to contract "are, for the most part, too restrictive and rest on a false factual basis."

The issue confronting the courts concerning mental capacity to contract is under what circumstances and conditions should a party be relieved of contractual obligations freely entered. This is peculiarly a legal decision, although, of course, available medical knowledge forms a datum which influences the legal choice. It is common knowledge that the present state of psychiatric knowledge is inadequate to provide a fixed rule for each and every type of mental disorder. Thus, the generally accepted rules which have evolved to determine mental responsibility are general enough in application to encompass all types of mental disorders, and phrased in a manner which can be understood and practically applied by juries composed of laymen.

The generally accepted test of mental competency to contract which has thus evolved is whether the party attempting to avoid the contract was capable of understanding and appreciating the nature and consequences of the particular act or transaction which he challenges. . . . This rule represents a balance struck between policies to protect the security of transactions between individuals and freedom of contract on the one hand, and protection of those mentally handicapped on the other hand. In my opinion, this rule has proven workable in practice and fair in result. A broad range of evidence including psychiatric testimony is admissible under the existing rules to establish a party's condition. . . . In the final analysis, the lay jury will infer the state of the party's mind from his observed behavior as indicated by the evidence presented at trial. Each juror instinctively judges what is normal and what is abnormal conduct from his own experience, and the generally accepted test harmonizes the competing policy considerations with human experience to achieve the fairest result in the greatest number of cases.

As in every situation where the law must draw a line between liability and nonliability, between responsibility and nonresponsibility, there will be borderline cases, and injustices may occur by deciding erroneously that an individual belongs on one side of the line or the other. To minimize the chances of such injustices occurring, the line should be drawn as clearly as possible.

The Appellate Division correctly found that the deceased was capable of understanding the nature and effect of her retirement benefits, and exercised rational judgment in electing to receive the maximum allowance during her lifetime. I fear that the majority's refinement of the generally accepted rules will prove unworkable in practice, and make many contracts vulnerable to psychological attack. Any benefit to those who understand what they are doing, but are unable to exercise self-discipline, will be outweighed by frivolous claims which will burden our courts and undermine the security of contracts. The reasonable expectations of those who innocently deal with persons who appear rational and who understand what they are doing should be protected.

Accordingly, I would affirm the order appealed from.

Order reversed, without costs, and a new trial granted.

FABER v. SWEET STYLE MANUFACTURING CORPORATION
40 Misc. 2d 212, 242 N.Y.S.2d 763 (1963)

BERNARD S. MEYER, Justice:

The relationship of psychiatry to the criminal law has been the subject of study and recommendation by the Temporary Commission on Revision of the Penal Law and Criminal Code. . . . This court had reason to touch upon the relationship of psychiatry to matrimonial law in *Anonymous v. Anonymous*, 37 Misc. 2d 773, 236 N.Y.S.2d 288. The instant case presents yet a third aspect of the same basic problem: that involving the law of contract.

Plaintiff herein seeks rescission of a contract for the purchase of vacant land in Long Beach on the ground that he was not at the time the contract was entered into of sufficient mental competence. Defendant counterclaims for specific performance.

The evidence demonstrates that from April until July 1961, plaintiff was in the depressed phase of a manic-depressive psychosis and that from August until the end of October he was in the manic stage. Though under care of Dr. Levine, a psychiatrist, beginning June 8th for his depression, he cancelled his August 8th appointment and refused to see the Doctor further. Previously frugal and cautious, he became more expansive beginning in August, began to drive at high speeds, to take his wife out to dinner, to be sexually more active and to discuss his prowess with others. In a short period of time, he purchased three expensive cars for himself, his son and his daughter, began to discuss converting his Long Beach bathhouse and garage property into a twelve story cooperative and put up a sign to that effect, and to discuss the purchase of land in Brentwood for the erection of houses. In September, against the advice of his lawyer, he contracted for land at White Lake in the Catskills costing $11,500 and gave a $500 deposit on acreage, the price of which was $41,000 and talked about erecting a 400 room hotel with marina and golf course on the land.

On September 16, 1961, he discussed with Mr. Kass, defendant's president, the purchase of the property involved in this litigation for the erection of a discount drug store and merchandise mart. During the following week Kass advised plaintiff that defendant would sell. On the morning of Saturday, September 23, plaintiff and Kass met at the office of defendant's real estate broker. Kass asked $55,000, plaintiff offered $50,000; when the broker agreed to take $1,500 commission, Kass offered to sell for $51,500 and plaintiff accepted. It was agreed the parties would meet for contract that afternoon. Kass obtained the services of attorney Nathan Suskin who drew the contract prior to the 2 P.M. conference. Plaintiff returned to that conference with his lawyer (who is also his brother-in-law) who approved the contract as to form but asked plaintiff how he would finance it and also demanded that the contract include as a condition that a nearby vacant property would be occupied by Bohack. No mention was made of plaintiff's illness. When Suskin refused to consider such a condition, plaintiff's lawyer withdrew. The contract was signed in the absence of plaintiff's lawyer and the $5,150 deposit paid by check on plaintiff's checking account in a Rockaway bank.

On the following Monday morning, plaintiff transferred funds from his Long Beach bank account to cover the check. On the same day, he went to Jamaica and arranged with a title abstract company for the necessary search and policy, giving correct details concerning the property, price and his brother-in-law's address and phone number and asking that search be completed within one week. Between September 23rd when the contract was signed and October 8th when plaintiff was sent to a mental institution, he persuaded Leonard Cohen, a former employee, to join in the building enterprise promising him a salary of $150 a week and a Lincoln Continental when the project was complete, caused a sign to be erected on the premises stating that "Faber Drug Company" and a "merchandise mart" were coming soon, hired an architect, initiated a mortgage application giving correct details as to price and property dimensions, hired laborers to begin digging (though title was not to close until October 20th), filed plans with city officials and when told by them that State Labor Department approval was required, insisted on driving to Albany with the architect and Leonard Cohen to obtain the necessary approval.

On September 25th plaintiff saw Dr. Levine as a result of plaintiff's complaint that his wife needed help, that she was stopping him from doing what he wanted to. He was seen again on September 26th and 28th, October 2nd and October 8th, and hospitalized on October 8th after he had purchased a hunting gun. Dr. Levine, Dr. Sutton, who appeared for defendant, and the hospital all agree in a diagnosis of manic-depressive psychosis. Dr. Levine testified that on September 23rd plaintiff was incapable of reasoned judgment; the hospital record shows that on October 9th, Dr. Krinsky found plaintiff's knowledge good, his memory and comprehension fair, his insight lacking and his judgment defective. Dr. Sutton's opinion, based on the hospital record and testimony of plaintiff's wife and Dr. Levine, was that plaintiff was subject to mood swings, but that there was no abnormality in his thinking, that his judgment on September 23rd was intact.

The contract of a mental incompetent is voidable at the election of the incompetent, . . . and if the other party can be restored to status quo rescission will be decreed upon a showing of incompetence without more. . . . If the status quo cannot be restored and the other party to the contract was ignorant of the incompetence and the transaction was fair and reasonable, rescission will, however, be denied notwithstanding incompetence. . . . The burden of proving incompetence is upon the party alleging it, but once incompetence has been shown, the burden of proving lack of knowledge and fairness is upon the party asking that the transaction be enforced. . . . In the instant case the contract concerns vacant land and is executory and though plaintiff caused some digging to be done on the premises, the proof shows that the land has been levelled again. Clearly, the status quo can be restored and plaintiff is, therefore, entitled to rescission if the condition described meets the legal test of incompetence.

The standards by which competence to contract is measured were, apparently, developed without relation to the effects of particular mental diseases or disorders and prior to recognition of manic-depressive psychosis as a distinct form of mental illness. . . . Primarily they are concerned with capacity to understand: . . . "so deprived of his mental faculties as to be wholly, absolutely, and completely unable to understand or comprehend the nature of the transaction;" *Paine v. Aldrich*, 133 N.Y. 544, 546, 30 N.E. 725 — "such mental capacity at the time of the execution of the deed that he could collect in his mind without prompting all the elements of the transaction, and retain them for a sufficient length of time to perceive their obvious relations to each other, and to form a rational judgment in regard to them;" *Matter of Delinousha v. National Biscuit Co.*, 248 N.Y. 93, 95, 161 N.E. 431, 432 — "A contract may be avoided only if a party is so affected as to be unable to see things in their true relations and to form correct conclusions in regard thereto." . . . If cognitive capacity is the sole criterion used, the manic must be held competent, . . . for manic-depressive psychosis affects motivation rather than ability to understand.

The law does, however, recognize stages of incompetence other than total lack of understanding. Thus it will invalidate a transaction when a contracting party is suffering from delusions if there is "some such connection between the insane delusions and the making of the deed as will compel the inference that the insanity induced the grantor to perform an act the purport and effect of which he could not understand, and which he would not have performed if thoroughly sane". . . . Moreover, it holds that understanding of the physical nature and consequences of an act of suicide does not render the suicide voluntary within the meaning of a life insurance contract if the insured "acted under the control of an insane impulse caused by disease, and derangement of his intellect, which deprived him of the capacity of governing his own conduct in accordance with reason." . . . Finally, *Paine v. Aldrich, supra*, and the Delinousha case consider not only ability to understand but also capacity to form "'rational judgment' or 'correct conclusions.'" Thus, capacity to understand is not, in fact, the sole criterion. Incompetence to contract also exists when a contract is entered into under the compulsion of a mental disease or disorder but for which the contract would not have been made.

Whether under the latter test a manic will be held incompetent to enter into a particular contract will depend upon an evaluation of (1) testimony of the claimed incompetent, (2) testimony of psychiatrists, and (3) the behavior of the claimed incompetent as detailed in the testimony of others . . . including whether by usual business standards the transaction is normal or fair. . . .Testimony of the claimed incompetent often is not available, and in any event is subject to the weakness of his mental disorder, on the one hand, and of his self interest on the other. The psychiatrist in presenting his opinion is, in final analysis, evaluating factual information rather than medical data, and is working largely with the same evidence presented to the court by the other witnesses in the action. . . . Moreover, in the great majority of cases psychiatrists of equal qualification and experience will reach diametrically opposed conclusions on the same behavioral evidence. The courts have, therefore, tended to give less weight to expert testimony than to objective behavioral evidence. . . .

In the instant case, plaintiff did not testify at the trial, but his examination before trial was read into the record. It shows that he understood the transaction in which he was engaged, but throws no light on his motivation. Plaintiff introduced no evidence concerning the rationality or fairness of the transaction (in the apparent belief that *Merritt v. Merritt, supra*, applied and that such proof, therefore, was not part of his case) so the court has no basis for comparison in that respect. Plaintiff's evidence concerning the location of the property and the nature of the business he proposed to carry on there fell short of establishing irrationality, nor can it be said that the making of an all cash contract was abnormal, even if the two earlier White Lake dealings are considered, in view of the testimony of plaintiff and his wife that the Long Beach bathhouse property was worth $200,000 and that it was free and clear. But the rapidity with which plaintiff moved to obtain an architect and plans, hire laborers, begin digging on the property, and his journey to Albany to obtain building approval, all prior to title closing, are abnormal acts. Viewing those acts in the context of his actions, detailed above, with respect to the White Lake properties, his plans with respect to the Brentwood property and the conversion of his bathhouse premises, and his complaint to Dr. Levine on September 25th that his wife was in need of help because she was trying to hold him back, the court is convinced that the contract in question was entered into under the compulsion of plaintiff's psychosis. That conclusion is contrary to the opinion expressed by Dr. Sutton, but the court concludes that Doctors Levine and Krinsky as treating physicians had the better basis for the opinions they expressed. In any event their opinions are but confirmatory of the conclusion reached by the court on the basis of the evidence above detailed.

Defendant argues, however, that the contract was ratified by the acts of plaintiff's attorney in forwarding a title objection sheet to defendant's attorney and in postponing the closing and by plaintiff himself. Ratification requires conscious action on the part of the party to be charged. Plaintiff was still in the mental hospital when the objection sheet was sent and the closing date postponed and these acts have not been shown to have been carried out with his knowledge or by his direction. As for his own action it was merely to answer, in reply to an inquiry from defendant's president as to when he was going to take title, that he did not know, it was up to his attorney. The contract with defendant had been signed on September 23rd, plaintiff had been sent to the hospital on October 8th and remained there until November 11th, having a series of electro-shock treatments while there, and the complaint in this action was verified November 20th. The conversation with defendant's president could not have occurred until after November 11th and must have occurred several days prior to November 20th. An answer as equivocal in nature and made under the circumstances as the one under consideration cannot in any fair sense be characterized as an exercise of plaintiff's right of election to "hold on to the bargain if it is good, and let it go if it is bad.". . .

Accordingly, defendant's motions at the end of plaintiff's case and of the whole case, on which decision was reserved, are now denied, and judgment will be entered declaring the contract rescinded and dismissing the counterclaim. The foregoing constitutes the decision of the court pursuant to Civil Practice Act § 440.

NOTES & QUESTIONS

1. RESTATEMENT (SECOND) OF CONTRACTS § 13 states: "A person has no capacity to incur contractual duties if his property is under guardianship by reason of an adjudication of mental illness or defect."

Comment:

a. Rationale. The reason for appointing a guardian of property is to preserve the property from being squandered or improvidently used. The guardianship proceedings are treated as giving public notice of the ward's incapacity and establish his status with respect to transactions during guardianship even though the other party to a particular transaction may have no knowledge or reason to know of the guardianship: the guardian is not required to give personal notice to all persons who may deal with the ward. The control of the ward's property is vested in the guardian, subject to court supervision; that control and supervision are not to be impaired or avoided by proof that the ward has regained his reason or has had a lucid interval, unless the guardianship is terminated or abandoned.

Thus, one adjudicated incompetent cannot enter into an enforceable contract, even during a lucid moment.

2. Can a party who contracts with one adjudicated incompetent ever recover?

Consider the plaintiff who rendered services for her incompetent great-aunt during the last years of the great-aunt's life. Plaintiff brought suit for payment of the services she has supplied. The administrator of the great-aunt's estate defended on the grounds that no valid agreement could have been reached because of the great-aunt's incompetency. The court held the plaintiff's services were "necessary" and although the great-aunt could not have entered into an express agreement because of her incompetency, the plaintiff could recover under a theory of implied in law contract. The plaintiff also had to overcome the presumption that services supplied to a family member would be performed gratuitously. *See Monteroso v. Schulte*, 239 N.W. 260 (Mich. 1931).

3. Can intoxication at the time of making a contract render the contract voidable? What evidence would be sufficient to show the intoxication rendered the party incompetent to contract?

Williamson signed a deed transferring her home to the Matthews for $1800. Later Williamson sought an injunction to cancel the deed and set aside the sale of the property. She contended that her capacity to contract was impaired by her history of drinking. Specifically, her doctor testified that she "showed signs of an early organic brain syndrome due to her excessive drinking . . . that he thought some of her brain cells were destroyed, and that her ability to transact business had been impaired." Further, the court had evidence of her drinking the day of the contract and that she told her attorney she wanted to undo the transaction only hours after it had been completed. *See Williamson v. Matthews*, 379 So. 2d 1245 (Ala. 1980).

4. One who contracts with an incompetent person may seek to enforce the contract by arguing that the parties cannot be restored to their original positions. In general, an "instrument obtained from an incompetent person by one who was ignorant of the incompetency, and who acted in good faith, and gave fair consideration, will not be set aside unless the parties can be restored to their original positions. This rule is not without exceptions however." *McElroy v. Security Nat'l Bank of Kansas City, Kan*, 215 F. Supp. 775 (D. Kan. 1963).

Edmonds entered into two contracts with Chandler for the lease of Chandler's farm to operate a stone quarry. Later Chandler was adjudicated incompetent. The court rescinded the contracts. Edmonds argued that rescission was not the proper remedy because he could not be restored to status quo. However, the court held that "the restoration demanded is not literal, but such as is reasonably possible and demanded by the equities of the case." *See Edmunds v. Chandler*, 127 S.E.2d 73 (Va. 1962).

For the tale of a traveling theater troupe and an incompetent party who did not have to restore the other party to status quo, *see Tubbs v. Hilliard*, 89 P.2d 535 (Colo. 1939).

B. DURESS, UNDUE INFLUENCE, FRAUD

In the three defenses of duress, undue influence, and fraud, the court looks at the circumstances surrounding the contract formation to determine if the court should refuse to enforce the contract based on this conduct. Duress occurs when a party physically compels or "makes an improper threat that induces a party who has no reasonable alternative but to manifest assent." RESTATEMENT (SECOND) OF CONTRACTS §§ 174, 175, 176. Undue influence arises when a party applies unfair persuasion in the context of a confidential relationship or domination over the other party. *See* RESTATEMENT (SECOND) OF CONTRACTS § 177. Fraud or misrepresentation is "an assertion that is not in accord with the facts" made by a party which induces the other party's assent to a contract. *See* RESTATEMENT (SECOND) OF CONTRACTS § 159.

1. Duress

In addressing the defense of duress, a court determines if the physical compulsion or improper threat robbed the other party of his or her ability to freely assent to the contract. Physical compulsion makes a party's assent ineffective and the contract entered is void. *See* RESTATEMENT (SECOND) OF CONTRACTS § 174. In the absence of physical compulsion, but in the presence of improper threats, the contract is made voidable at the victim's choice. *See* RESTATEMENT (SECOND) OF CONTRACTS § 175. Like a minor, however, the victim of improper threats may later be deemed to have ratified the contract made by her conduct or words of acceptance after the threat no longer exists.

ECKSTEIN v. ECKSTEIN
38 Md. App. 506, 379 A.2d 757 (1978)

LISS, Judge:

Judith Eckstein, appellant (hereinafter "wife"), and Donald Eckstein, appellee (hereinafter "husband"), were married in Maryland on May 25, 1968. The wife had one daughter from a previous marriage, Kimberly, who was adopted by the husband after their marriage; and a second daughter, Donna, was born to the Ecksteins. At the time of the separation between the parties the children were eight and six years old respectively. The wife had a history of mental disturbances, and in September of 1973, she sought professional help from a psychiatrist, Dr. Gultken Ovacik. During the course of her sessions with Dr. Ovacik, in January of 1974, the wife was committed to the Prince George's Hospital Psychiatric Ward for treatment, where she remained confined for a period of 46 days. Dr. Ovacik, who continued to see her at the hospital, testified that her last visit with him during that period was April 3,1974, at which time she advised him that she was not going to see him again because her husband objected to her seeing a psychiatrist. She did not see him again until July 21, 1975. The doctor testified that he found the wife to be suffering from a reactive depression when he saw her in April of 1974 and that the condition had not changed when he saw her in July of 1975. Her history indicated that she had attempted suicide four or five times and that she was hospitalized on at least three occasions as a result of these attempts. Dr. Ovacik indicated that in his opinion she was suffering from the reactive depression well before he first saw her in September of 1973.

The marriage was hardly an idyll of matrimonial bliss, and the parties separated temporarily on a number of occasions. During one of these separations in 1971, the husband had his lawyer, a Mr. Leitch, prepare a separation and property settlement agreement; and on April 13, 1971, the husband took the wife who had no counsel and was not given an opportunity to consult counsel to his lawyer's office. The wife signed the agreement, and later that afternoon, she took an overdose of prescribed drugs and was hospitalized. The husband communicated with her by phone while she was in the hospital, and a reconciliation ensued. Several other separations had occurred between the parties and during one such period (in November of 1970), the wife employed an attorney who prepared a separation agreement more favorable to her than the one she ultimately signed but which her husband refused to sign.

On the evening of February 1, 1975, the wife left the marital abode in the parties' jointly owned 1973 Volkswagen van with only the clothes on her back. She had no funds and the husband promptly closed the couple's joint bank account. The wife consulted Legal Aid but was advised that she did not qualify for their assistance. Shortly after the wife left her husband, he discovered her whereabouts and the location of the van and with the assistance of the wife's stepfather seized and secreted the van The husband refused the wife's request to visit or communicate with her children and refused to give her her clothing. He told her that she could see her children and take her clothes only if she signed a separation agreement prepared by Mr. Leitch, his attorney. Subsequent events disclosed that the agreement was almost an exact duplicate of the one she signed in 1971 after which she attempted suicide.

On February 10, 1975, she was directed by her husband to go to Mr. Leitch's office; she had no money to employ counsel. At Mr. Leitch's office she was advised that her husband was in the suite but would not talk to her in person. A copy of the separation agreement was given to her to read. She asked several questions of Mr. Leitch who testified that he did not recollect what the questions were but that he refused to give her any advice because he was representing her husband. He asked her if she wanted to talk to her husband and put him on an inter-office phone to discuss the matter with her. The husband also admitted that the wife asked several questions about the agreement but stated that he could not remember what the inquiries were and he did not answer them. The wife testified that her husband told her that if she did not sign the agreement he would get her for desertion, that she would never see her children again, and that she would get nothing neither her clothes nor the van unless she signed the agreement as written. No changes were made in the document, and the wife signed the agreement in Mr. Leitch's office. Immediately after signing, her clothes were surrendered to her and she was given the keys to the Volkswagen van.

The separation agreement provided that the wife give custody of the children to her husband. . . . She agreed to deed to her husband her interest in the jointly owned home of the parties. She agreed to assign to her husband her interest in a jointly owned new 1975 Chevrolet van; she received the Volkswagen. She waived alimony, support, maintenance, court costs, attorney's fees, and any right of inheritance in her husband's estate. She was to receive one-half of the income tax refunds due the parties, of which her share would be approximately $1,000. She was paid $1100 at the time of the execution of the agreement. The husband agreed to retain the wife on his health insurance policy until they were divorced. The wife was to receive any of their furniture which she desired. . . .

On February 10, 1976, the husband filed a bill of complaint in the Circuit Court for Prince George's County in which he prayed the court to grant him a divorce a vinculo matrimonii on the ground of voluntary separation and to require specific performance of the third and fourth paragraphs of the property settlement agreement executed by the parties on February 10, 1975. These paragraphs concerned the exchange of the titles to the two vans owned by the parties.

The wife filed an answer in which she prayed that the court grant the divorce but alleged lack of mental capacity on her part and coercion, duress, fraud, breach of contract, lack of consideration and gross overreaching on the part of the husband in securing the execution of the agreement, and requested that the court set aside the property settlement between the parties. She also sought custody of the minor children and counsel fees. The trial court, with the approval of both parties, treated the answer filed by the wife as a cross-bill of complaint seeking affirmative relief. At the conclusion of two days of testimony, the trial court granted the husband's prayer for a divorce a vinculo; granted him custody of the minor children, with visitation rights to the wife; and upheld the validity of the separation and property agreement. All the prayers for relief of the wife were denied, and her cross-bill of complaint was dismissed.

Appellant in this appeal has raised no issue as to the trial court's granting of the divorce a vinculo matrimonii or the awarding of custody of the minor children of the parties to the husband. The issue . . . to be considered by us . . . [is]:

> 1) Did the trial court err in refusing to set aside the separation agreement between the parties on the grounds of duress? . . .
>
> A separation agreement, being a contract between the parties, is subject to the same general rules governing other contracts. . . .
>
> Separation agreements not disclosing any injustice or inequity on their face are presumptively valid; and the burden is on the party challenging the agreement to show that its execution resulted from coercion, fraud, or mistake. . . .

Appellant contends that the separation agreement which she signed was on its face unjust and inequitable. Her principal complaint concerns the value of the jointly owned home which she conveyed to her husband for $1100. . . . The wife also alleged an interest in certain secret personal bank accounts held by the husband in his name in trust for himself and the children of the parties, but these accounts have no relevance in this case. In *Bell, supra*, we held that the relinquishment by a wife of her interest in jointly owned real estate worth $210,000 for approximately $45,000 in property and cash was not sufficient to make a settlement agreement between the husband and wife inequitable and unjust on its face. There, we distinguished the facts in *Bell* from *Eaton v. Eaton*, 34 Md. App. 157, 366 A.2d 121 (1976), where we set aside an agreement in which the wife surrendered her interest in property worth a quarter million dollars for $4300. We cannot say that this agreement on its face is so inequitable and unjust that we are required to set it aside. The appellant, therefore, was left in the position that in order to prevail before the trial court, she had to assume the burden of proving that the agreement which she executed was not made in the exercise of her own free will but was exacted from her by duress.

In order to establish duress, there must be a wrongful act which deprives an individual of the exercise of his free will. *Central Bank v. Copeland*, 18 Md. 305 (1862); RESTATEMENT (SECOND) OF CONTRACTS, §§ 316-318 (Tent. Draft No. 12, 1977); 13 WILLISTON ON CONTRACTS, §§ 1606-1607 (3 ed. W. Jaeger ed. 1970). In *Central Bank, supra,* the Court stated the rule as follows:

> The element of obligation upon which a contract may be enforced springs primarily from the unrestrained mutual assent of the contracting parties, and where the assent of one to a contract is constrained and involuntary, he will not be held obligated or bound by it. A contract, the execution of which is induced by fraud, is void, and a stronger character cannot reasonably be assigned to one, the execution of which is obtained by duress. Artifice and force differ only as modes of obtaining the assent of a contracting party, and a contract to which one assents through imposition or overpowering intimidation, will be declared void, on an appeal to either a court of law or equity to enforce it. The question, whether one executes a contract or deed with a mind and will sufficiently free to make the act binding, is often difficulty to determine, but for that purpose a court of equity, unrestrained by the more technical rules which govern courts of law in that respect, will consider all the circumstances from which rational inferences may be drawn, and will refuse its aid against one who, although apparently acting voluntarily, yet, in fact, appears to have executed a contract, with a mind so subdued by harshness, cruelty, extreme distress, or apprehensions short of legal duress, as to overpower and control the will.

Id. at 317-18. (Citations omitted).

The RESTATEMENT (SECOND) OF CONTRACTS, *supra,* § 318(2), speaks of the circumstances under which a threat is improper and may amount to duress:

> A threat is improper if the resulting exchange is not on fair terms, and
>
> (a)   the threatened act would harm the recipient and would not significantly benefit the party making the threat, or
>
> (b)   the effectiveness of the threat in inducing the manifestation of assent is significantly increased by prior unfair dealing by the party making the threat, or
>
> (c)   what is threatened is otherwise a use of power for illegitimate ends.

The comment in the RESTATEMENT on this section indicates that clause (b) is concerned with cases in which the party making the threat has by unfair dealing achieved an advantage over the recipient which makes the threat unusually effective. Typical examples involve manipulative conduct during the bargaining stage that leaves one person at the mercy of another. Clause (c) is concerned with other cases in which the threatened act involves the use of power for illegitimate ends. Illustration 15 postulates the following situation:

> A operates a fur storage concession for customers of B's store. A becomes bankrupt and fails to pay C $1,000 for charges for storing furs of B's customers. C makes a threat to B not to deliver the furs to B's customers unless B makes a contract to pay C the $1,000 plus $2,000 that A owes C for storage of other furs. B, afraid of offending its customers and having no reasonable alternative, makes the contract. If the court con-

cludes that C's threat to B is a use for illegitimate ends of its power as against B to retain the furs for the $1,000 owed for the storage of furs for B's customers, C's threat is improper and the contract is voidable by B.

13 WILLISTON ON CONTRACTS, *supra*, § 1603, summarizes the manner in which duress may be exercised and gives as one of the methods "any . . . wrongful acts that compel a person to manifest apparent assent to a transaction without his volition or cause such fear as to preclude him from exercising free will and judgment in entering into a transaction." *Id.* at 663. While the determination of duress is dependent upon the circumstances of each individual case, Williston states that the cases indicate that three elements are common to all situations where duress has been found to exist: "1) that one side involuntarily accepted the terms of another; 2) that circumstances permitted no other alternative; and 3) that the circumstances were the result of the coercive acts of the opposite party." . . .

Any agreement, contract, or deed obtained by oppressing a person by threats regarding the safety or liberty of himself, or his property, or a member of his family so as to deprive him of the free exercise of his will and prevent the mutuality of assent required for a valid contract may be avoided on the ground of duress. . . .

Nor must the acts or threats which constitute duress be unlawful in order to affect the validity of the agreement. *Fowler v. Mumford*, 48 Del. 282, 9 Terry 282, 102 A.2d 535 (1954) stated:

> It is true that under the modern view, acts or threats cannot constitute duress unless they are wrongful; but an act may be wrongful though lawful. Acts that are wrongful in a moral sense, though not criminal or tortious or in violation of contractual duty, may also constitute duress under the doctrine sought to be invoked by the defendant.

102 A.2d at 538. *See* RESTATEMENT OF CONTRACTS, § 492(g).

In *Bell*, *supra*, Judge Thompson, quoting *Link v. Link*, 278 N.C. 181, 179 S.E.2d 697 (1971), pointed out the direction which the law of duress has taken in the more recent decisions:

> The law with reference to duress has, however, undergone an evolution favorable to the victim of oppressive action or threats. The weight of modern authority supports the rule, which we here adopt, that the act done or threatened may be wrongful even though not unlawful, per se; and that the threat to institute legal proceedings, criminal or civil, which might be justifiable, per se, becomes wrongful, within the meaning of this rule, if made with the corrupt intent to coerce a transaction grossly unfair to the victim and not related to the subject of such proceedings.

179 S.E.2d at 705.

It becomes our responsibility at this point to review the facts as established at the lengthy hearing before the trial court and to review the law of the case. We are, of course, aware of the strictures of Maryland Rule 1086, which cautions that the judgment of the lower court shall not be set aside on the evidence unless clearly erroneous. We are also bound by the oft enunciated principle that the credibility of witnesses is primarily for the trier of the facts, and the appellate courts of Maryland will only overrule the findings of fact of a trial judge when they are clearly erroneous. . . .

We believe, however, that the appellant did, in fact, meet her burden of establishing that the separation agreement executed by her was signed under such circumstances as to preclude a finding that her actions were the product of her own free will. We further find that the facts which established the duress exercised by the husband on the wife in this case are not only found in the testimony of the wife and her witnesses but are in many instances corroborated by the husband and his witnesses. It is, we think, particularly significant that Mr. Leitch, appellee's attorney, confirmed the appellant's story concerning the withholding of her property from her until after she signed the agreement. Significant also is the fact that the husband never denied the wife's statement as to his threat that she would be denied communication and visitation with her children and would not get her clothes and van unless she signed the agreement. . . .

Initially, it is clear that the wife had a long history of depressive behavior which indicated mental and emotional instability. Whether or not the trial court chose to accept the opinion of her psychiatrist regarding her mental capacity at the time of the execution of the agreement (which, incidentally, it did not) is unimportant. What is obvious, however, is that the psychiatrist's undisputed testimony concerning her medical history and hospital confinements was sufficient to establish that the wife had a severe mental and emotional problem both before and after the execution of the agreement.

The testimony discloses that the wife was entirely without funds and without counsel at the time of the signing of the agreement. . . . The husband had denied the wife access to the funds in their joint checking account and gave her no money from the date of the separation until the date of the execution of the agreement. The wife was unemployed. The record indicates that the wife attempted to get legal assistance from Legal Aid and the Public Defender's office but was denied assistance because she was found to be ineligible for their services. The record further indicates that when the wife left the husband she took only the clothes that she was wearing and that when she later called and asked her husband for the clothes, he refused to give them to her until she signed the agreement prepared by his lawyer. He also refused to give her the jointly owned Volkswagen van or to permit her to see the children or even to communicate with them until after she signed the agreement. When asked why he would not give her her clothes and the Volkswagen, his answer was, "Why should I?" He admitted that his frame of mind at that time was one of being "mad" and "hurt."

The circumstances surrounding the signing of the agreement were bizarre, to say the least: We have already described what occurred between the husband and wife prior to her going to the office of her husband's attorney. When she arrived at Mr. Leitch's office, the agreement was in the process of being typed; the deed transferring her interest in the home had already been prepared. The wife raised several questions concerning the agreement, but neither the attorney nor the husband would answer them. The latter both admitted in their testimony that she raised some such questions, but, neither could remember what they were. When she told her husband that she would not sign the agreement, which was identical with the one she repudiated in 1971, he repeated his threats that she would get nothing neither her van, nor her clothes, nor the right to see or communicate with her children. No changes at all were made in the agreement as prepared by Mr. Leitch.

It is significant, we believe, that when under the circumstances she capitulated and signed the agreement, Mr. Leitch immediately delivered to her, in cash, the

$1100 she was to receive for her interest in the property, and her clothes and the van were surrendered to her. These facts indicate to us a strong determination by the husband and his lawyer to pressure the wife into then and there executing the agreement.

The trial judge said that he was not "convinced that the contract should be set aside because of any inequity, or any coercion or undue influence or because of a breach of any fiduciary relationship or marital relationship existing between the parties." He did not, however, state the facts which brought him to this conclusion. He refused to set aside the separation agreement. We believe this was error.

We conclude that it was irregular for the husband and his counsel to prepare a complicated legal document and deeds conveying to the husband her interest in jointly held property without at least offering her an opportunity to have her questions answered by her own legal advisor. It was, we believe, improper to submit the documents to her on a take it or leave it basis and to coerce her signature by withholding her property and threatening to prevent her from seeing or communicating with her children. We might well have reached that conclusion even if the evidence was clear that the wife was a competent, stable, knowledgeable woman; but when, as here, it is obvious that the husband and his lawyer were dealing with an emotionally and mentally unstable individual, we think that the conclusion that the execution of the agreement was obtained by duress is inescapable. With no funds, no lawyer, no clothes, no transportation, and no viable alternative, it is not surprising that the wife capitulated and signed the agreement. We cannot accept that action, under all the circumstances, as one taken by her of her own free will.

THAT PORTION OF DECREE INCORPORATING THE SEPARATION AGREEMENT BETWEEN THE PARTIES VACATED; ALL OTHER PORTIONS OF DECREE AFFIRMED; CASE REMANDED FOR FURTHER PROCEEDINGS. COSTS TO BE PAID BY APPELLEE.

NOTE

Compare Eckstein to *Kaplan v. Kaplan*, 182 N.E.2d 706 (Ill. 1962) (citations omitted):

Plaintiff, Leonard Kaplan, filed a complaint in the superior court of Cook County praying, on the grounds of duress and lack of consideration, for either the rescission or reformation of a property settlement agreement he had entered into with his wife, Elaine Kaplan, prior to their divorce, and of a trust agreement, designed to secure his covenants in the property settlement agreement. . . .

[P]laintiff [alleged he] had received no consideration for entering into the agreements, and that they had been entered into by him as the result of duress applied upon him by Elaine Kaplan. Specifically, it was alleged that during the pendency of the separate maintenance action private detectives employed by Elaine Kaplan or her attorneys forcibly broke into an apartment and took photographs of plaintiff and another woman, and that although there had never been immoral or improper behavior between plaintiff and the woman, the circumstances of the occurrence and the photographs were intended to cause great embarrassment to plaintiff and the other woman. Continuing, it was alleged that Elaine Kaplan thereafter expressly threatened to publicize the photographs by suing the other woman for alienation of affections, "by publicizing the said occurrence and photographs, and by other means calculated to cause great embarrassment to Leonard Kaplan, to the said woman in whose apartment he had been photographed, and to the family of said woman, all without cause." Immediately following, it was alleged that "in order to avoid the said embarrassment to himself and to the said woman, and under duress as aforesaid," plaintiff agreed to sign the two agreements previously described. How closely the execution of the agreements followed the alleged photographing and alleged threats of publication in point of time does not appear.

Plaintiff contends here that the allegations of his complaint are sufficient to entitle him to equitable relief on the grounds of duress. . . .

. . . [T]he issue to be determined here is whether the alleged duress of which the plaintiff complains is such as would render the contract voidable at law and entitle him to equitable relief.

Duress has been defined as a condition where one is induced by a wrongful act or threat of another to make a contract under circumstances which deprive him of the exercise of his free will, and it may be conceded that a contract executed under duress is voidable. Acts or threats cannot constitute duress unless they are wrongful; however, the rule is not limited to acts that are criminal, tortious or in violation of a contractual duty, but extends to acts that are wrongful in a moral sense. At common law duress meant only duress of the person, that is a threat to life, limb or liberty, and the threat must have been of a nature as to create such fear as would impel a person of ordinary courage to yield to it. Under modern views and developments, however, duress is no longer confined to situations involving threats of personal injury or imprisonment, and the standard of whether a man of ordinary courage would yield to the threat has been supplanted by a test which inquires whether the threat has left the individual bereft of the quality of mind essential to the making of a contract. Any wrongful threat which actually puts the victim in such fear as to act against his will constitutes duress and, according to some authorities, a threat of personal or family disgrace may be of such gravity as to deprive the person threatened of the mental capacity necessary to execute a valid contract.

* * *

. . . the allegations fall short of establishing grounds upon which to lay a claim of legal duress. The first allegation of the complaint is that Elaine Kaplan threatened to publicize the photographs by suing the woman in whose apartment they had been taken for alienation of affections. This allegation clearly presents no basis for a claim of duress inasmuch as it is well established that it is not duress to institute or threaten to institute civil suits, or for a person to declare that he intends to use the courts to insist upon what he believes to be his legal rights, at least where the threatened action is made in the honest belief that a good cause of action exists, and does not involve some actual or threatened abuse of process. . . . The allegations of the complaint in the present case make it appear that Elaine Kaplan would have the honest belief, if not the right, that she had a cause of action for alienation of affections. Any use of the photographs in such a proceeding, or personal embarrassment suffered by plaintiff or his woman friend as a result, would be no more than incidents of the suit.

. . . Elaine Kaplan by the allegations of the complaint . . . threatened to publicize the photographs and occurrence by other means calculated to cause great embarrassment to plaintiff, the other woman, and the latter's family. Even if we assume, without deciding, that the threat of an outraged and humiliated wife to publicize the affair of her husband is wrongful in a moral sense, it is our opinion that this allegation is not sufficient to entitle plaintiff to the relief he seeks. . . . We have said before that duress is not shown by subjecting one to annoyance or vexation and it is our belief that a threat of personal embarrassment does not rise above annoyance and vexation. In looking to the circumstances under which the agreements were executed, we cannot help but note the recital that the settlement agreement was executed "freely and voluntarily" by plaintiff, and that he did so with the "benefit of investigation, advice and recommendation" of legal counsel.

* * *

GOLDEN v. McDERMOTT, WILL & EMERY
702 N.E.2d 581 (Ill. 1998)

Justice COUSINS delivered the opinion of the court:

Bruce Golden, the appellant, filed suit against the appellees, law firm McDermott, Will & Emery, as well as certain partners in their individual capacities. Golden alleged that the appellees breached the partnership agreement by expelling him in contravention of specified procedures, breached their fiduciary duty as co-partners and committed fraud in misrepresenting and withholding information from him while his severance agreement was being negotiated, and breached the severance agreement by not paying him the full amount due under it.

. . . Golden appeals, claiming that the trial court erred in granting the motion to dismiss his complaint. The plaintiff's complaint alleged, *inter alia*, (1) breach of contract, (2) breach of fiduciary duty, and (3) duress. . . . We affirm.

BACKGROUND

The appellant, Bruce Golden, is a securities lawyer who worked for the appellee law firm McDermott, Will & Emery (MWE) for 21 years. He joined the firm in 1970, was made an income partner in 1976 and was made a capital partner in 1981. Among the clients he brought to MWE were a public real estate syndicator known as Avanti Associates (Avanti), and its promoter, Timothy Sasak.

In 1989, a class action suit (the Avanti suit) was brought against Sasak and Avanti for, among other things, violation of securities laws in the sale of its partnership assets. MWE was also named as a defendant. The plaintiffs sought to recover $120 million from MWE. Golden alleges that shortly prior to the Avanti suit, MWE obtained a malpractice insurance policy with Attorney's Liability Assurance Society, Ltd. (ALAS). The claims from the Avanti suit were the first that ALAS had to pay out for MWE, and ALAS said that those claims were the largest it had ever been required to cover for any firm.

Golden also alleges that ALAS was hesitant to renew MWE's insurance policy as a result of the Avanti suit and that MWE had talks with ALAS in order to save its coverage. ALAS, he alleges, wanted him removed from the firm, and MWE acceded. MWE postponed his termination, Golden claims, because it needed his cooperation in the Avanti litigation.

Golden further alleges that from the time of the Avanti suit MWE began to limit his participation in partnership business and reduced his partnership interest. In particular, he alleges the following: (1) around the beginning of 1990, he was told that John McDermott, a partner of MWE and a named defendant in this suit, had directed that he not be given any more work for United Airlines, a major MWE client for which Golden had been doing much work; (2) from that time he was not given any "meaningful assignments" with United or any other MWE client; (3) John McDermott told him that he should not bring in any new business and McDermott also took over his contact list, purportedly in order to ease his workload; and (4) late in 1990, partner Robert McDermott suggested that he look into non-legal careers.

In January 1991, the firm reduced Golden's partnership units by a third. Golden's compensation was based upon these units, as was the amount he would receive in a severance package.

The Avanti litigation settled on July 18, 1991. The next day, partners Stanley Meadows and James Roche, also defendants in this action, informed Golden that he was being fired but that the firm would give him the opportunity to resign first. At that meeting Golden was told that the reason for his firing was "lack of production," although he says that Meadows later informed him in confidence that pressure from ALAS was the real reason.

Over the next few months Golden and the firm worked out a severance agreement to settle his accounts. The severance agreement contained the following release clause: "Golden . . . releases . . . the Firm . . . from any and all claims . . . whether now known or unknown . . . including, but not limited to, any and all claims . . . relating to or arising out of Golden's partnership, tenure or separation from the firm . . . provided, however, that this release and discharge shall not bar Golden from bringing any action to . . . enforce this agreement."

In consideration for the release, MWE gave Golden a one-time payment of $225,000 minus the amount of his draw subsequent to October 31, 1991. Golden claims that MWE deducted more than this amount from the $225,000, although he did not specify the amount of the excess deduction. At Golden's behest, a provision was also included in the agreement that would allow him to sue ALAS for getting him fired. Golden claims that in the negotiations MWE falsely told him that his severance payment was the largest given to any terminated partner and was the same amount that he would have gotten had he resigned voluntarily. He also claims that MWE concealed the fact that no vote had been taken on his expulsion, as was mandated by the partnership agreement. Around the time that Golden signed the severance agreement, he was having personal problems. He had just lost a lawsuit concerning a major defect in a house he had bought. His wife's employer had died, and, as a result, she also was out of work. Golden sought counseling. He says that the mental health professional reported that the termination had left Golden "paranoid," "fragmented," having "major depression, recurrent" and as "dysfunctional" with "chaos reigning supreme."

On November 7, 1991, Meadows told Golden that the management committee had not taken a vote on his expulsion. He told Golden that he would have difficulty finding new legal employment, because ALAS had "blacklisted" him. Golden says that Meadows also told him at some time during negotiations that "he was personally embarrassed by [the proposed settlement agreement's] burdensome language, and that no other partner had ever been asked to sign such a harsh document."

Golden took out a lease on an office at what he claims to be a grossly inflated rent. He says that he took an "of counsel" position with another law firm but received no compensation for it. In February of 1992, MWE tendered, and Golden accepted, payment of money due under the severance agreement.

In December 1995, Golden filed suit against ALAS. He alleges that he learned facts in discovery that led him, on December 30, 1996, to file the instant action against MWE and some of its partners. In February of 1997, MWE partner James Roche was deposed in the ALAS case. Golden alleges that many facts important to his case came to light only as of the time of this deposition.

Golden's complaint alleged, *inter alia*, that MWE breached the severance agreement by not paying him the full amount due under it; that MWE violated the partnership agreement by not following the termination procedure outlined therein; and that the defendant partners violated their fiduciary duty to him as co-partners and committed fraud on him. He asked for damages, as well as a dissolution and accounting of the firm.

Golden argued that the release that he signed was voidable because it was signed under moral and economic duress, and because the defendants withheld and misrepresented facts to him in negotiations, in violation of their fiduciary duty. . . .

The trial court agreed with the defendants and dismissed the complaint. It held that the claim for the breach of the severance agreement was not adequately pled, that the claim for breach of the partnership agreement was barred by the release, and that the other claims were barred by the statute of limitations.

ANALYSIS

*   *   *

On the issue of duress, we agree with the trial court that Golden's allegations were insufficient to make out a claim. Golden alleges three closely related types of duress. First he claims that MWE coerced him by threatening to fire him. Then he says that it practiced economic duress (also known as "business compulsion") by taking unfair advantage of his financial and personal difficulties. Finally he alleges moral duress. Although there are several proposed definitions of duress, the supreme court has defined it as "a condition where one is induced by a wrongful act or threat of another to make a contract under circumstances which deprive him of the exercise of his free will." *Kaplan v. Kaplan*, 182 N.E.2d 706 (Ill. 1962). MWE contends that the pressure it applied to Golden did not constitute duress, because it was not wrongful.

MWE argues that it had a right to expel Golden without cause and that it cannot be duress for it to threaten to do what it has a legal right to do. Illinois cases support MWE's position, *e.g.*, *Butler v. Metz, Train, Olson & Youngren, Inc.*, 379 N.E.2d 1255 (Ill. App. 978). But while it is true that one must threaten "wrongful" action in order to be guilty of duress, the landmark supreme court case on duress, *Kaplan v. Kaplan*, 182 N.E.2d 706 (Ill. 1962), says that the meaning of "wrongful" is "not limited to acts that are criminal, tortious or in violation of a contractual duty, but extends to acts that are wrongful in a moral sense." *Kaplan*, 25 Ill. 2d at 186, 182 N.E.2d 706. So even though an employee may be terminable at will, it is not impossible for the threat of discharge to constitute duress. *Laemmar v. J. Walter Thompson Co.*, 435 F.2d 680, 682 (7th Cir. 1970); *Mitchell v. C.C. Sanitation Co.*, 430 S.W.2d 933 (Tex. Civ. App. 1968); *see also* Annotation, *What Constitutes Duress by Employer or Former Employer Vitiating Employee's Release of Employer from Claims Arising out of Employment*, 30 A.L.R. 4th 294 (1984).

On the other hand, it is not wrongful, and does not constitute duress for an employer to give an employee who is about to be fired the option to resign. *Enslen v. Village of Lombard*, 470 N.E.2d 1188 (Ill. App. 1984). "It would be a dangerous doctrine to hold that to offer an employee a choice of resigning or accepting a discharge would amount to such compulsion that the employee could avoid his resignation for duress." *Fox v. Piercey*, 227 P.2d 763, 767 (Utah 1951).

Golden cites *Oglesby v. Coca-Cola Bottling Co.*, 620 F. Supp. 1336 (N.D. Ill. 1985), a case under the Age Discrimination in Employment Act of 1967 (29 U.S.C. §§ 629–634 (1994)) that seems contrary to this principle. *See also Massi v. Blue Cross & Blue Shield Mutual*, 765 F. Supp. 904 (N.D. Ohio 1991). In our view, *Oglesby* is distinguishable. *Oglesby* held that a "resign or be fired" choice could be duress. *Oglesby*, 620 F. Supp. at 1342. In that case, however, a condition of resignation was the signing of a release that the employee was not given an adequate opportunity to read, much less negotiate. The plaintiff did not have a chance to get legal advice concerning his dilemma. He was forced to choose on the spot between termination or resignation coupled with a mysterious agreement. *Oglesby*, 620 F. Supp. at 1342. So, even if the choice of "resign or be fired" can constitute duress, the choice was not sufficient to constitute duress under the facts as alleged here.

Golden next alleges economic duress or business compulsion. Economic duress occurs where "undue or unjust advantage has been taken of a person's economic necessity or distress to coerce him into making the agreement." 12 Ill. L. & Prac. Contracts § 142 (1983). These dire circumstances must be such as to overbear the will of the plaintiff. *Higgins v. Brunswick Corp.*, 395 N.E.2d 81 (Ill. App. 1979). Whether the circumstances did in fact overbear the plaintiff's will is ordinarily a question of fact. *Slade v. Slade*, 33 N.E.2d 951 (Ill. App. 1941).

However, it is not enough for economic duress that the plaintiff be in great financial or personal difficulty. The defendant must have been in some way responsible for that difficulty. " '[A] duress claim of this nature must be based on the acts or conduct of the other party and not merely on the necessities of the purported victim.' " *Alexander v. Standard Oil Co.*, 423 N.E.2d 578, 583 (Ill. App. 1981) (quoting *Chouinard v. Chouinard*, 568 F.2d 430, 434 (5th Cir.1978)); *see also Higgins*, 395 N.E.2d 81.

Assuming, under the facts as alleged, that MWE and the defendant partners were partially responsible for some of Golden's troubles, they still were not responsible for the death of his wife's employer, the loss of her job, or the loss of the lawsuit concerning Golden's house. In our view, the claim of duress lacked this necessary element of responsibility on the part of defendants for the plaintiff's circumstances. *See Alexander*, 423 N.E.2d 578.

Finally, Golden alleges moral duress. Moral duress is quite similar to economic duress. It "consists in imposition, oppression, undue influence, or the taking of undue advantage of the business or financial stress or extreme necessities or weaknesses of another." *People ex rel. Buell v. Bell*, 155 N.E.2d 104 (Ill. App. 1959). "[R]elief is granted in such cases on the basis that the party benefiting thereby has received money, property, or other advantage which in equity and good conscience he should not be permitted to retain." *People ex rel. Buell*, 155 N.E.2d 104.

As the trial judge observed, there are only a few Illinois cases on moral duress. Reported Illinois opinions have only found moral duress in extreme circumstances, such as those in *People ex rel. Buell v. Bell*, 155 N.E.2d 104 (1959). *See also In re Petition of Huebert*, 270 N.E.2d 464 (Ill. App. 1971); *Pittman v. Lageschulte*, 195 N.E.2d 394 (Ill. App. 1964). In *People ex rel. Buell*, an unwed mother was pressured into giving up her child for adoption. She was wrongfully told that if she did not give up the child she would not be able to keep her other children. She was weak and in poor condition when she signed the agreement, which she did not read and was not read to her.

In our view, these cases are inapposite. Golden was a legally sophisticated attorney who negotiated the severance agreement over the course of several months. Given the dissimilarity of these facts to the above cases, we hold that Golden has not established a claim for moral duress.

Even if the severance agreement were voidable because of duress or a breach of fiduciary duty, we believe that Golden ratified the agreement by his subsequent conduct. "It is well established that the retention of the consideration by one sui juris, with knowledge of the facts will amount to a ratification of a release executed by him in settlement of a claim, where the retention is for an unreasonable time under the circumstances of the case." 66 AM. JUR. 2D *Release* § 27 (1973). . . . .

For the foregoing reasons, the judgment of the trial court is affirmed.

Affirmed.

GORDON P.J., and WOLFSON J., concur.

NOTES

What settings will warrant a valid defense of economic duress? Consider these examples:

1. Centric signed a construction contract with Morrison-Knudsen. Despite constant problems, Centric completed the contract and Morrison-Knudsen paid the full contract price. However, due to numerous problems, Centric experienced cost overruns, and the parties entered into negotiations in an attempt to remedy the situation. Morrison-Knudsen allegedly knew of Centric's possible bankruptcy and presented a "take it or leave it" offer, which Centric accepted. The court found that economic duress was present in this case because Morrison-Knudsen used Centric's "precarious economic position in order to obtain favorable settlement." *See Centric Corporation v. Morrison-Knudsen Co.*, 731 P.2d 411 (Okla. 1986). Loral, the principal contractor, was granted a contract by the Navy to produce radar sets.

2. Loral awarded Austin a subcontract to supply various gears needed to produce the radar sets. Subsequently, Loral was granted a second contract with the Navy to produce radar sets. Again, Loral offered Austin a contract to produce some of the gears needed to produce the radar sets under the second contract.

Demanding to produce all the gear parts for the second contract, Austin notified Loral the next day that Austin would cease delivery of the gear parts under the first contract unless Loral agreed to a significant increase in price. Loral consented to Austin's demand. The court found that Austin had engaged in economic duress since Loral faced significant liquidated damages for later deliveries of the radar sets, Austin's production of the gear parts was essential to the delivery of the radar sets, and a substitute producer of the gear parts could not be found. *See Austin Instrument Inc. v. Loral Corp.*, 272 N.E.2d 533 (N.Y. 1971).

2.   Undue Influence

Undue influence may not rise to the level of a threat. Close friends and family members may try to pressure or "over-persuade" a person. Outside forces may also play a role in leaving a party especially vulnerable to undue influence. Consider how the *Odorizzi* court fashioned a set of guidelines to express the concept of "overpersuasion."

ODORIZZI v. BLOOMFIELD SCHOOL DISTRICT
246 Cal. App. 2d 123, 54 Cal. Rptr. 533 (1966)

FLEMING, Justice:

Appeal from a judgment dismissing plaintiff's amended complaint on demurrer. Plaintiff Donald Odorizzi was employed during 1964 as an elementary school teacher by defendant Bloomfield School District and was under contract with the District to continue to teach school the following year as a permanent employee. On June 10 he was arrested on criminal charges of homosexual activity, and on June 11 he signed and delivered to his superiors his written resignation as a teacher, a resignation which the District accepted on June 13. In July the criminal charges against Odorizzi were dismissed under Penal Code, section 995, and in September he sought to resume his employment with the District. On the District's refusal to reinstate him he filed suit for declaratory and other relief.

Odorizzi's amended complaint asserts his resignation was invalid because obtained through duress, fraud, mistake, and undue influence and given at a time when he lacked capacity to make a valid contract. Specifically, Odorizzi declares he was under such severe mental and emotional strain at the time he signed his resignation, having just completed the process of arrest, questioning by the police, booking, and release on bail, and having gone for forty hours without sleep, that he was incapable of rational thought or action. While he was in this condition and unable to think clearly, the superintendent of the District and the principal of his school came to his apartment. They said they were trying to help him and had his best interests at heart, that he should take their advice and immediately resign his position with the District, that there was no time to consult an attorney, that if he did not resign immediately the District would suspend and dismiss him from his position and publicize the proceedings, his "aforedescribed arrest" and cause him "to suffer extreme embarrassment and humiliation"; but that if he resigned at once the incident would not be publicized and would not jeopardize his chances of securing employment as a teacher elsewhere. Odorizzi pleads that because of his faith and confidence in their representations they were able to substitute their will and judgment in place of his own and thus obtain his signature to his purported resignation. A demurrer to his amended complaint was sustained without leave to amend.

By his complaint plaintiff in effect seeks to rescind his resignation pursuant to Civil Code, § 1689, on the ground that his consent had not been real or free within the meaning of Civil Code, § 1567, but had been obtained through duress, menace, fraud, undue influence, or mistake. A pleading under these sections is sufficient if, stripped of its conclusions, it sets forth sufficient facts to justify legal relief. . . . In our view the facts in the amended complaint are insufficient to state a cause of action for duress, menace, fraud, or mistake, but they do set out sufficient elements to justify rescission of a consent because of undue influence. We summarize our conclusions on each of these points.

1. No duress or menace has been pleaded. Duress consists in unlawful confinement of another's person, or relatives, or property, which causes him to consent to a transaction through fear. . . . Duress is often used interchangeably with menace . . . but in California menace is technically a threat of duress or a threat of injury to the person, property, or character of another. . . . We agree with respondent's contention that neither duress nor menace was involved in this case, because the action or threat in duress or menace must be unlawful, and a threat to take legal action is not unlawful unless the party making the threat knows the falsity of his claim. . . . The amended complaint shows in substance that the school representatives announced their intention to initiate suspension and dismissal proceedings under Education Code, §§ 13403, 13408 *et seq.* at a time when the filing of such proceedings was not only their legal right but their positive duty as school officials. . . . Although the filing of such proceedings might be extremely damaging to plaintiff's reputation, the injury would remain incidental so long as the school officials acted in good faith in the performance of their duties. . . . Neither duress nor menace was present as a ground for rescission.

2. Nor do we find a cause of action for fraud, either actual or constructive. . . . Actual fraud involves conscious misrepresentation, or concealment, or non-disclosure of a material fact which induces the innocent party to enter the contract. . . . A complaint for fraud must plead misrepresentation, knowledge of falsity, intent to induce reliance, justifiable reliance, and resulting damage. . . . While the amended complaint charged misrepresentation, it failed to assert the elements of knowledge of falsity, intent to induce reliance, and justifiable reliance. A cause of action for actual fraud was therefore not stated. . . .

Constructive fraud arises on a breach of duty by one in a confidential or fiduciary relationship to another which induces justifiable reliance by the latter to his prejudice. . . . Plaintiff has attempted to bring himself within this category, for the amended complaint asserts the existence of a confidential relationship between the school superintendent and principal as agents of the defendant, and the plaintiff. Such a confidential relationship may exist whenever a person with justification places trust and confidence in the integrity and fidelity of another. . . . Plaintiff, however, sets forth no facts to support his conclusion of a confidential relationship between the representatives of the school district and himself, other than that the parties bore the relationship of employer and employee to each other. Under prevailing judicial opinion no presumption of a confidential relationship arises from the bare fact that parties to a contract are employer and employee; rather, additional ties must be brought out in order to create the presumption of a confidential relationship between the two. . . . The absence of a confidential relationship between employer and employee is especially apparent where, as here, the parties were negotiating to bring about a termination of their relationship. In such a situation each party is expected to look after his own interests, and a lack of confidentiality is implicit in the subject matter of their dealings. We think the allegations of constructive fraud were inadequate.

3. As to mistake, the amended complaint fails to disclose any facts which would suggest that consent had been obtained through a mistake of fact or of law. The material facts of the transaction were known to both parties. Neither party was laboring under any misapprehension of law of which the other took advantage. The discussion between plaintiff and the school district representatives principally attempted to evaluate the probable consequences of plaintiff's predicament and to predict the future course of events. The fact that their speculations did not forecast the exact pattern which events subsequently took does not provide the basis for a claim that they were acting under some sort of mistake. The doctrine of mistake customarily involves such errors as the nature of the transaction, the identity of the parties, the identity of the things to which the contract relates, or the occurrence of collateral happenings. (RESTATEMENT, CONTRACTS, § 502, comment e.) Errors of this nature were not present in the case at bench.

4. However, the pleading does set out a claim that plaintiff's consent to the transaction had been obtained through the use of undue influence.

Undue influence, in the sense we are concerned with here, is a shorthand legal phrase used to describe persuasion which tends to be coercive in nature, persuasion which overcomes the will without convincing the judgment. . . . The hallmark of such persuasion is high pressure, a pressure which works on mental, moral, or emotional weakness to such an extent that it approaches the boundaries of coercion. In this sense, undue influence has been called overpersuasion. . . . Misrepresentations of law or fact are not essential to the charge, for a person's will may be overborne without misrepresentation. By statutory definition undue influence includes "taking an unfair advantage of another's weakness of mind; or . . . taking a grossly oppressive and unfair advantage of another's necessities or distress." . . . While most reported cases of undue influence involve persons who bear a confidential relationship to one another, a confidential or authoritative relationship between the parties need not be present when the undue influence involves unfair advantage taken of another's weakness or distress. . . .

We paraphrase the summary of undue influence given the jury by Sir James P. Wilde in *Hall v. Hall*, L.R. 1, P&D 481, 482 (1868):

To make a good contract a man must be a free agent. Pressure of whatever sort which overpowers the will without convincing the judgment is a species of restraint under which no valid contract can be made. Importunity or threats, if carried to the degree in which the free play of a man's will is overborne, constitute undue influence, although no force is used or threatened. A party may be led but not driven, and his acts must be the offspring of his own volition and not the record of someone else's.

In essence undue influence involves the use of excessive pressure to persuade one vulnerable to such pressure, pressure applied by a dominant subject to a servient object. In combination, the elements of undue susceptibility in the servient person and excessive pressure by the dominating person make the latter's influence undue, for it results in the apparent will of the servient person being in fact the will of the dominant person.

Undue susceptibility may consist of total weakness of mind which leaves a person entirely without understanding; . . . or, a lesser weakness which destroys the capacity of a person to make a contract even though he is not totally incapacitated; . . . or, the first element in our equation, a still lesser weakness which provides sufficient grounds to rescind a contract for undue influence. . . . Such lesser weakness need not be long-lasting nor wholly incapacitating, but may be merely a lack of full vigor due to age . . . physical condition . . . emotional anguish . . . or a combination of such factors. The reported cases have usually involved elderly, sick, senile persons alleged to have executed wills or deeds under pressure. . . . In some of its aspects this lesser weakness could perhaps be called weakness of spirit. But whatever name we give it, this first element of undue influence resolves itself into a lessened capacity of the object to make a free contract.

In the present case plaintiff has pleaded that such weakness at the time he signed his resignation prevented him from freely and competently applying his judgment to the problem before him. Plaintiff declares he was under severe mental and emotional strain at the time because he had just completed the process of arrest, questioning, booking, and release on bail and had been without sleep for forty hours. It is possible that exhaustion and emotional turmoil may wholly incapacitate a person from exercising his judgment. As an abstract question of pleading, plaintiff has pleaded that possibility and sufficient allegations to state a case for rescission.

Undue influence in its second aspect involves an application of excessive strength by a dominant subject against a servient object. Judicial consideration of this second element in undue influence has been relatively rare, for there are few cases denying persons who persuade but do not misrepresent the benefit of their bargain. Yet logically, the same legal consequences should apply to the results of excessive strength as to the results of undue weakness. Whether from weakness on one side, or strength on the other, or a combination of the two, undue influence occurs whenever there results "that kind of influence or supremacy of one mind over another by which that other is prevented from acting according to his own wish or judgment, and whereby the will of the person is over-borne and he is induced to do or forbear to do an act which he would not do, or would do, if left to act freely." . . . Undue influence involves a type of mismatch which our statute calls unfair advantage. . . . Whether a person of subnormal capacities has been subjected to ordinary force or a person of normal capacities subjected to extraordinary force, the match is equally out of balance. If will has been overcome against judgment, consent may be rescinded.

The difficulty, of course, lies in determining when the forces of persuasion have overflowed their normal banks and become oppressive flood waters. There are second thoughts to every bargain, and hindsight is still better than foresight. Undue influence cannot be used as a pretext to avoid bad bargains or escape from bargains which refuse to come up to expectations. A woman who buys a dress on impulse, which on critical inspection by her best friend turns out to be less fashionable than she had thought, is not legally entitled to set aside the sale on the ground that the saleswoman used all her wiles to close the sale. A man who buys a tract of desert land in the expectation that it is in the immediate path of the city's growth and will become another Palm Springs, an expectation cultivated in glowing terms by the seller, cannot rescind his bargain when things turn out differently. If we are temporarily persuaded against our better judgment to do something about which we later have second thoughts, we must abide the consequences of the risks inherent in managing our own affairs. . . . However, overpersuasion is generally accompanied by certain characteristics which tend to create a pattern. The pattern usually involves several of the following elements: (1) discussion of the transaction at an unusual or inappropriate time, (2) consummation of the transaction in an unusual place, (3) insistent demand that the business be finished at once, (4) extreme emphasis on untoward consequences of delay, (5) the use of multiple persuaders by the dominant side against a single servient party, (6) absence of third-party advisers to the servient party, (7) statements that there is no time to consult financial advisers or attorneys. If a number of these elements are simultaneously present, the persuasion may be characterized as excessive. The cases are illustrative:

Moore v. Moore, 56 Cal. 89, 93, and 81 Cal. 195, 22 P. 589, 874. The pregnant wife of a man who had been shot to death on October 30 and buried on November 1 was approached by four members of her husband's family on November 2 or 3 and persuaded to deed her entire interest in her husband's estate to his children by a prior marriage. In finding the use of undue influence on Mrs. Moore, the court commented:

> It was the second day after her late husband's funeral. It was at a time when she would naturally feel averse to transacting any business, and she might reasonably presume that her late husband's brothers would not apply to her at such a time to transact any important business, unless it was of a nature that would admit of no delay. And as it would admit of delay, the only reason which we can discover for their unseemly haste is, that they thought that she would be more likely to comply with their wishes then than at some future time, after she had recovered from the shock which she had then so recently experienced. If for that reason they selected that time for the accomplishment of their purpose, it seems to us that they not only took, but that they designed to take, an unfair advantage of her weakness of mind. If they did not, they probably can explain why they selected that inappropriate time for the transaction of business which might have been delayed for weeks without injury to any one. In the absence of any explanation, it appears to us that the time was selected with reference to just that condition of mind which she alleges that she was then in.

> Taking an unfair advantage of another's weakness of mind is undue influence, and the law will not permit the retention of an advantage thus obtained. . . .

Weger v. Rocha, 138 Cal. App. 109, 32 P.2d 417. Plaintiff, while confined in a cast in a hospital, gave a release of claims for personal injuries for a relatively small sum to an agent who spent two hours persuading her to sign. At the time of signing plaintiff was in a highly nervous and hysterical condition and suffering much pain, and she signed the release in order to terminate the interview. The court held that the release had been secured by the use of undue influence.

Fyan v. McNutt, 266 Mich. 406, 254 N.W. 146 (1934). At issue was the validity of an agreement by Mrs. McNutt to pay Fyan, a real estate broker, a five-percent commission on all moneys received from the condemnation of Mrs. McNutt's land. Earlier, Fyan had secured an option from Mrs. McNutt to purchase her land for his own account and offer it for sale as part of a larger parcel to Wayne County for an airport site. On July 25 Fyan learned from the newspapers that the county would probably start condemnation proceedings rather than obtain an airport site by purchase. Fyan, with four others, arrived at Mrs. McNutt's house at 1 a.m. on July 26 with the commission agreement he wanted her to sign. Mrs. McNutt protested being awakened at that hour and was reluctant to sign, but Fyan told her he had to have the paper in Detroit by morning, that the whole airport proposition would fall through if she did not sign then and there, that there wasn't time to wait until morning to get outside advice. In holding the agreement invalid the Michigan Supreme Court said:

> The late hour of the night at which her signature was secured over her protest and plea that she be given until the next day to consider her action, the urge of the moment, the cooperation of the others present in their desire to obtain a good price for their farm lands, the plaintiff's anxiety over the seeming weakness of his original option, all combined to produce a situation in which, to say the least, it is doubtful that the defendant had an opportunity to exercise her own free will. . . . A valid contract can be entered into only when there is a meeting of the minds of the parties under circumstances conducive to a free and voluntary execution of the agreement contemplated. It must be conceived in good faith and come into existence under circumstances that do not deprive the parties of the exercise of their own free will.

The difference between legitimate persuasion and excessive pressure, like the difference between seduction and rape, rests to a considerable extent in the manner in which the parties go about their business. For example, if a day or two after Odorizzi's release on bail the superintendent of the school district had called him into his office during business hours and directed his attention to those provisions of the Education Code compelling his leave of absence and authorizing his suspension on the filing of written charges, had told him that the District contemplated filing written charges against him, had pointed out the alternative of resignation available to him, had informed him he was free to consult counsel or any adviser he wished and to consider the matter overnight and return with his decision the next day, it is extremely unlikely that any complaint about the use of excessive pressure could ever have been made against the school district.

But, according to the allegations of the complaint, this is not the way it happened, and if it had happened that way, plaintiff would never have resigned. Rather, the representatives of the school board undertook to achieve their objective by overpersuasion and imposition to secure plaintiff's signature but not his consent to his resignation through a high-pressure carrot-and-stick technique — under which they assured plaintiff they were trying to assist him, he should rely on their advice, there wasn't time to consult an attorney, if he didn't resign at once the school district would suspend and dismiss him from his position and publicize the proceedings, but if he did resign the incident wouldn't jeopardize his chances of securing a teaching post elsewhere.

Plaintiff has thus pleaded both subjective and objective elements entering the undue influence equation and stated sufficient facts to put in issue the question whether his free will had been overborne by defendant's agents at a time when he was unable to function in a normal manner. It was sufficient to pose '. . . the ultimate question . . . whether a free and competent judgment was merely influenced, or whether a mind was so dominated as to prevent the exercise of an independent judgment.' . . . The question cannot be resolved by an analysis of pleading but requires a finding of fact.

We express no opinion on the merits of plaintiff's case, or the propriety of his continuing to teach school . . . or the timeliness of his rescission. . . . We do hold that his pleading, liberally construed, states a cause of action for rescission of a transaction to which his apparent consent had been obtained through the use of undue influence.

The judgment is reversed.

NOTE

1. Persuasion is the primary characteristic of undue influence. The RESTATEMENT (SECOND) OF CONTRACTS § 177 provides:

> (1) Undue influence is unfair persuasion of a party who is under the domination of the person exercising the persuasion or who by virtue of the relation between them is justified in assuming that that person will not act in a manner inconsistent with his welfare.

> (2) If a party's manifestation of assent is induced by undue influence by the other party, the contract is voidable by the victim.

Comment:

> *a. Required domination or relation.* The rule stated in this Section protects a person only if he is under the domination of another or is justified, by virtue of his relation with another in assuming that the other will not act inconsistently with his welfare. Relations that often fall within the rule include those of parent and child, husband and wife, clergyman and parishioner, and physician and patient. In each case it is a question of fact whether the relation is such as to give undue weight to the other's attempts at persuasion. The required relation may be found in situations other than those enumerated. However, the mere fact that a party is weak, infirm or aged does not of itself suffice, although it may be a factor in determining whether the required relation existed.

2. Rodgers suffered from various illnesses common to a 75-year-old individual and lived with her invalid son.

Rodgers hired McCollough to perform various chores on a daily basis including cooking, cleaning and chauffeuring. While McCollough worked for Rogers, Rogers was hospitalized with severe hypertension and a mild stroke. A few months after the hospitalization, Rodgers set up a joint savings account with McCollough. McCollough began making withdrawals during Rodgers' lifetime and eventually withdrew all the funds upon Rodgers' death. Do you think McCollough's conduct illustrated undue influence? What was the nature of the relationship? *See McCollough v. Rodgers,* 431 So. 2d 1246 (Ala. 1983).

3. Misrepresentation and Fraud

A misrepresentation is a false assertion of the facts and is demonstrated by written or spoken words, concealment or nondisclosure. Misrepresentation may be innocent or intentional. *See* RESTATEMENT (SECOND) OF CONTRACTS § 159 comment (a); §§ 160, 161.

A misrepresentation reaches the level of fraud when a party acts intentionally to mislead another party with an assertion and the asserting party knows or doubts the truth of the assertion. *See* RESTATEMENT (SECOND) OF CONTRACTS § 162.

Fraud at its worst or most serious is "fraud in the factum." This type of fraud occurs when a victim enters into a contract without understanding the import of the document being signed. Rather than understanding she is signing an important contract, the party thinks she is signing a letter to a relative. Much fraud, however, is "fraud in the inducement." Fraud in the inducement arises when one party makes an intentionally false material statement to another party and the statement causes that party to assent to the contract.

BARRER v. WOMEN'S NATIONAL BANK
761 F.2d 752, 245 U.S. App. D.C. 349 (1985)

HARRY T. EDWARDS, Circuit Judge:

The appellant, Lester A. Barrer, brought this action against Women's National Bank ("the Bank" or "WNB") for damages he allegedly sustained as the result of the Bank's eleventh hour decision to rescind a loan agreement. WNB defended and moved for summary judgment on the ground that Barrer had made innocent material misrepresentations in his loan application that justified the Bank's avoidance of the contract. The magistrate found that Barrer had made five material representations to the Bank that were not in accord with the facts and, on that basis, granted WNB's motion for summary judgment. We find that the magistrate failed to apply the correct legal test for determining when an innocent material misrepresentation permits the rescission of a contract, and that there are material issues of fact that make summary judgment inappropriate. Accordingly, we reverse and remand for further proceedings consistent with this opinion.

I. BACKGROUND

A. Factual Background

On June 24, 1981, Lester Barrer's personal home was sold at a tax sale by the Internal Revenue Service ("IRS") because of his inability to pay certain employment taxes. The taxes were owed by Barrer's closely-held corporation, Today News Service, Inc., and had been asserted against him personally as a 100 percent penalty pursuant to 26 U.S.C. § 6672 (1982). At the tax sale, Barrer's home was purchased by Edward L. Curtis, Jr., for $16,326, subject to the underlying mortgage. The Internal Revenue Code provides for the redemption of real property within 120 days of a tax sale upon payment to the purchaser of the purchase price plus interest. . . . Barrer accordingly was advised by the IRS that he could redeem his home by delivering $17,400, in cash or its equivalent, to the IRS or to Curtis on or before October 22, 1981.

On October 20, 1981, Barrer went to WNB to discuss a personal loan for the redemption amount. Apparently, on the previous day, Barrer had approached one other bank about the possibility of a loan; however, he had been advised by the President of that bank that it would not be possible to process an application for a loan in the amount sought by Barrer in such a short period of time. . . . Barrer indicated in his deposition statement that he waited until the last minute to seek a bank loan because he had been involved in serious negotiations over the sale of his business and had expected to close on the sale before October 20, 1981, and that he had intended to use the proceeds from that sale to redeem his house. . . .

At WNB, Barrer spoke with Emily Womack, the President of the Bank, with whom he had a professional acquaintance. Barrer's corporation published the Women Today Newsletter, a periodical to which the Bank subscribed and which, according to Barrer's deposition statement, had published an article on the Bank. . . . Barrer's corporation also maintained an account with the Bank. Womack gave Barrer a loan application form, which he completed and returned to her the next day, October 21, along with certain supporting documents, including those concerning the tax sale and his efforts to sell the business.

Barrer evidently explained to Womack that he had experienced severe financial difficulties since his wife and long-time professional collaborator died of cancer in 1978. . . . At his deposition, Barrer testified that he told Womack that, for a period after his wife died, he lost his motivation to work and that the business they had jointly owned and managed suffered serious economic reverses as a consequence. . . . Those reverses led to Today News Service, Inc.'s inability to pay its employment taxes and ultimately to the tax sale of Barrer's home. Womack sympathized with Barrer's plight and expressed to one of her bank officers the hope that they could help him. . . .

On October 21, Barrer and Womack reviewed his loan application line by line. With reference to his home mortgage, Barrer told her that his house was worth approximately $130,000 and that Columbia First Federal Savings and Loan Association ("Columbia") held a $65,000 mortgage on it. When asked whether his mortgage payments were up-to-date, Barrer recalls replying that he "thought" he was two months behind. . . . By contrast, Womack testified that Barrer said he was current. . . . In fact, Barrer was six months behind. Barrer explained that he thought his obligation to pay his mortgage ceased at the time of the tax sale and that he did not realize that he was responsible for more than the two months' mortgage payments that had been due before the sale. . . .

Because Barrer's mortgage payments were in arrears, Columbia had begun foreclosure proceedings — also a fact that Barrer did not disclose to Womack. In his deposition statement, Barrer accounted for this failure by stating that on October 21, 1981, he did not know that Columbia had initiated foreclosure proceedings. . . .

On the liability side of the loan application, Barrer revealed that he had borrowed $40,000 from friends and relatives. Barrer testified that he explained to Womack that he had borrowed this sum to ease the financial difficulties he had encountered since his wife's death. . . .

Barrer also disclosed the $38,000 tax liability which was the cause of the tax sale. He did not indicate, however, a contingent liability for an additional $11,000 in employment taxes owed by his corporation which had not, at that time, been asserted against him personally under 26 U.S.C. § 6672. Barrer seems to argue both that this $11,000 was included in the $38,000 figure, and that because the $11,000 tax liability had not been assessed against him personally it was not a contingent liability that he was obligated to reveal. . . .

Nor did Barrer list as a contingent liability a $5,300 debt owed by his wife's estate to IBM. The Bank argues that this debt should have been revealed because Barrer had demonstrated, by requesting the probate court to charge the obligation to him, that he thought himself responsible for the debt. Barrer contends that because the probate court ultimately ruled that the obligation belonged to the estate, his failure to list the amount on the loan application was not a misrepresentation.

Finally, Barrer did not indicate on the loan application that he had approximately $1,500 in unsatisfied judgments pending against him. However, he answered in the affirmative to a specific question on the application form which inquired whether he was "a defendant in any suits or legal actions." . . . Barrer also stated at his deposition that he told Womack that he owed small amounts arising out of these lawsuits. He said that he explained to her that these debts involved disputes over medical bills and that he expected his major medical insurance to cover most of them. . . .

After Barrer and Womack finished discussing the content of the completed loan application form and Barrer's financial situation, Womack indicated that, in order for the Bank to grant the loan, the IRS would have to agree to subordinate its claim with respect to Barrer's house to that of WNB. On October 22, 1981, the last redemption day, Barrer obtained the subordination agreement from the IRS and delivered it to the Bank. Barrer then executed a collateral note for $17,400, payable in 90 days at 15 percent interest, which gave the Bank the right to a security interest in his house. . . . The Bank's Vice President, Emma Carrera, gave Barrer a cashier's check, payable to him, for the loan amount. Prior to granting the loan, neither Womack nor Carrera obtained a credit report on Barrer and neither officer phoned Columbia about the status of his mortgage.

That afternoon, Barrer delivered the endorsed check to the IRS in accordance with the required redemption procedure and returned home, believing that his home had been saved.

In the meantime, the tax sale purchaser, Curtis, phoned WNB and spoke with Carrera. According to her deposition, their conversation was as follows:

> He stated that he had some information that he thought would be of interest to me on the loan that the bank had made to Mr. Barrer. I told him at that time that I could not discuss any loan with him in regards to who it was or what it was for. He said he didn't want me to do any discussing, but he just wanted to tell me some facts.

> He then told me he was the purchaser of the property at the tax sale. He couldn't believe that a bank would make a loan to a man who was in the credit position that he was in; that there were liens and judgments and so forth against him and at that time, I signalled for my secretary to bring me the file on Mr. Barrer.

> I quickly looked through the file and found there wasn't a credit report in the file. At that time I told her to pull a credit report on him, which she

did, and brought it to me within just a couple of minutes.

In the meantime, Mr. Curtis was continuing to talk. He had mentioned something about some kind of code that says that a person who buys a property at a tax sale cannot interfere with the owner's right to redeem, but that he didn't feel he was doing that just by informing the bank of Mr. Barrer's situation. He put me on a conference call with a gentleman who identified himself as an official of the mortgage company [Columbia] that held the mortgage on Mr. Barrer's property. He [Mr. Ford] asked me at that time who, in his organization, had given us a credit report.

. . . I . . . answer[ed] him . . . that it was my understanding that all of the savings and loan associations required a written request for credit rating [sic] on any of the mortgages that they held and it had always been, to my knowledge, their policies not to give a reference by phone.

[Mr. Ford] said at that point he thought it was important that we know that Mr. Barrer's mortgage was six months in arrears and they were prepared to go to foreclosure on the property. He excused himself and Mr. Curtis stayed on the line.

[Mr. Curtis] said that he had knowledge that IRS had not made an agreement with Mr. Barrer to repay the balance of the taxes; that they were ready to go back to another tax sale as soon as this $17,400 was paid. . . .

Based on the information furnished by Curtis, Ford, and the credit report, the Bank decided to stop payment on the cashier's check. The Bank's counsel called Barrer later that day to inform him that the check would not be honored. . . . When Curtis, to whom the IRS had turned over the check, presented it for payment the Bank refused to cash it. Barrer, therefore, did not effect the redemption of his home within the statutory period and Curtis became the owner.

B. Procedural History

Barrer filed suit against the Bank in District Court to recover damages to compensate him for the loss of $94,000 equity in his home — the difference between the market value of the house and the balance due on the mortgage — that he allegedly suffered as a result of the Bank's rescission of the loan agreement. Barrer also claimed punitive damages for the embarrassment he endured and the rent he has been required to pay Curtis in order to remain in his home.

The case was referred to a magistrate for pretrial proceedings. On the Bank's motion for summary judgment, the magistrate found that Barrer did not disclose the following five material facts to the Bank: (1) that he was six months delinquent in mortgage payments, (2) that Columbia had begun foreclosure procedures, (3) that Barrer had at least an $11,000 contingent liability to the I S in addition to his $38,000 actual liability, (4) that he had a contingent liability to IBM of approximately $5,000, and (5) that he had approximately $1,500 in unsatisfied judgments pending against him. The magistrate purported to rely on the law of innocent material misrepresentation to hold that these disclosure omissions justified WNB's rescission of the loan contract. On that basis, he granted summary judgment in favor of the Bank. This appeal followed.

II. ANALYSIS

A. Standards for Summary Judgment

A motion for summary judgment may be granted only where the record makes clear "that there is no genuine issue as to any material fact and that the moving party is entitled to a judgment as a matter of law." . . . The burden of demonstrating the absence of any genuine issue of material fact is on the movant. . . . In assessing a motion for summary judgment, the court must view all inferences to be drawn from the evidence in the light most favorable to the party opposing the motion. . . . All doubts as to the existence of a material dispute must be resolved against summary judgment. . . . If conflict appears as to a material fact, summary judgment is not proper, "unless the evidence on one or the other hand is too incredible to be accepted by reasonable minds or is without legal probative force even if true." . . .

As we demonstrate below, the magistrate failed both to apply the correct legal test for determining whether an "innocent" misrepresentation justifies the rescission of a contract and to recognize that with regard to each of the five alleged misrepresentations there exist legally probative, material issues of fact in dispute. . . . Thus, the award of summary judgment in favor of the Bank was erroneous and must be reversed.

B. Elements of Innocent Material Misrepresentation

It is well established that misrepresentation of material facts may be the basis for the rescission of a contract, even where the misrepresentations are made innocently, without knowledge of their falsity and without fraudulent intent. . . . The rationale supporting this rule, which has its origins in equity, . . . is that, as between two innocent parties, the party making the representation should bear the loss. . . . Stated another way, the rule is based on the view that "one who has made a false statement ought not to benefit at the expense of another who has been prejudiced by relying on the statement." . . . This rule may be employed "actively," as in a suit at equity or law for rescission and restitution, or "passively," as a defense to a suit for breach of contract.

It is generally understood that four conditions must be met before a contract may be avoided for innocent misrepresentation. The recipient of the alleged misrepresentation must demonstrate that the maker made an assertion: (1) that was not in accord with the facts, (2) that was material, and (3) that was relied upon (4) justifiably by the recipient in manifesting his assent to the agreement. . . . District of Columbia law adds a fifth condition, i.e., that the recipient relied to his detriment. . . .

Unfortunately, the applicable precedent does not elaborate on the meaning of these conditions. In trying to give them content, we have found that the RESTATEMENT (SECOND) OF CONTRACTS ("RESTATEMENT (SECOND)") . . . provides helpful guidance concerning the first four conditions.

* * *

1. Misrepresentation

§ 159 of the RESTATEMENT (SECOND) defines a misrepresentation as "an assertion that is not in accord with the facts." . . . Comment c explains that an "assertion must relate to something that is a fact at the time the assertion is made in order to be a misrepresentation. Such facts include past events as well as present circumstances but do not include future events." Comment d observes that a person's state of mind is a fact and that an assertion of one's opinion constitutes a misrepresentation if the state of mind is other than as asserted.

According to § 161, the only non-disclosures that may be considered assertions of fact for purposes of misrepresentation analysis[1] are non-disclosures of facts known to the maker where the maker knows that disclosure: (a) is necessary to prevent a previous assertion from being a misrepresentation or from being fraudulent or material, (b) would correct a mistake of the other party as to a basic assumption on which that party is making the contract, if non-disclosure amounts to a failure to act in good faith and in accordance with reasonable standards of fair dealing, or (c) would correct a mistake of the other party as to the contents or effect of a writing. The section also provides that where the other person is entitled to know the non-disclosed facts because a relation of trust and confidence exists between the parties, non-disclosure is equivalent to an assertion of facts.

2. Materiality

In § 162, comment c, the RESTATEMENT (SECOND) explains that a misrepresentation is material "if it would be likely to induce a reasonable person to manifest his assent." The court in Cousineau v. Walker elaborated on the materiality requirement, noting that it is a mixed question of law and fact that asks whether the assertion is one to which a reasonable person might be expected to attach importance in making a choice of action. . . . A material fact is one that could reasonably be expected to influence a person's judgment or conduct concerning a transaction. . . .

The justification for the materiality requirement is that it is believed to encourage stability in contract relations. It prevents parties who become disappointed at the outcome of their bargain from seizing upon any insignificant discrepancy to void the contract. . . .

3. Reliance

§ 167 requires that the misrepresentation be causally related to the recipient's decision to agree to the contract — that it have been an inducement to agree. Inducement, as comment a explains, is shown through actual reliance. Comment a goes on to state that this reliance need not, however, be the sole or predominant factor influencing the recipient's decision. Comment b indicates that circumstantial evidence is often important in determining whether there was actual reliance. . . .

---

[1] [34] The RESTATEMENT (SECOND) distinguishes between nondisclosures, § 161 and comment a, and actions that are equivalent to assertions (concealment), § 160.

4. Justifiability of Reliance

§ 172 of the RESTATEMENT (SECOND) provides that a recipient's fault in not knowing or discovering the facts before making the contract does not make his reliance unjustified unless it amounts to a failure to act in good faith and in accordance with reasonable standards of fair dealing. . . .

While § 169 suggests that reliance on an assertion of opinion often is not justified, section 168(2) and the accompanying comment d make clear that in some situations the recipient may reasonably understand a statement of opinion to be more than an assertion as to the maker's state of mind. Where circumstances justify it, a statement of opinion may also be reasonably understood as carrying with it an assertion that the maker knows facts sufficient to justify him in forming it. . . .

5. Detriment

Because the RESTATEMENT (SECOND) does not require a showing of detriment for rescission, it does not define it.[2] We think that, in the innocent material misrepresentation context, a recipient is appropriately considered to have relied to his detriment where he receives something that is less valuable or different in some significant respect from that which he reasonably expected. . . .

C. Application of Legal Standards

Application of the foregoing principles to the facts of this case requires that the case be remanded for trial. The magistrate tested Barrer's alleged misrepresentations against only two of the five elements necessary for rescission — he asked only if the representations were in accord with the facts and if they were material. In making this inquiry, the magistrate failed to consider the legal distinctions between assertions of fact and nondisclosure and between assertions of fact and statements of opinion. He neglected to investigate whether the Bank actually relied on the representations in deciding to make the loan; whether that reliance, if it existed, was justifiable; and whether the Bank relied to its detriment. Furthermore, the magistrate incorrectly concluded that there were no legally probative, material issues of fact in dispute.

1. Elements the Magistrate Failed to Consider

Initially, assuming for a moment that Barrer actually "misrepresented" certain facts, the materiality of the representations is hardly obvious. After deciding which representations meet the legal definition of misrepresentation, the trial court must determine with regard to each individual misrepresentation whether it was "likely to induce a reasonable [bank] to manifest [its] assent"[3] to the loan agreement. If no single misrepresentation is found to be material, the court may consider, after ascertaining the assertions upon which WNB justifiably relied, whether those assertions are material when taken together.

---

[2] [41] *See* § 164, comment c ("In general, the recipient of a misrepresentation need not show that he has actually been harmed by relying on it in order to avoid the contract.").

[3] [43] RESTATEMENT (SECOND), . . . § 162 comment c.

All five alleged "misrepresentations" also raise serious factual questions as to whether the Bank actually and justifiably relied on them. Womack's expressed sympathy for Barrer combined with the fact that the loan was issued in a very short time, without either a credit check, which was obtainable in minutes, or an inquiry into the status of Barrer's mortgage, and the fact that the loan was withdrawn only when the Bank was placed in an embarrassing position by the tax sale purchaser — all these circumstances could suggest that the Bank was not very interested in the particulars of Barrer's financial condition. Indeed, it was clear from the loan application that Barrer did admit that he was experiencing financial difficulties, yet WNB chose to make no further inquiry into the details of these problems. These facts could be construed to show that Womack's sympathy for Barrer's predicament was the real inducement for the loan. If the trial court finds that the Bank actually relied on Barrer's alleged "misrepresentations," it nonetheless must proceed to decide whether that reliance was justified.

The trial court must also determine whether the Bank's reliance on Barrer's alleged "misrepresentations" caused it any detriment. Did WNB receive as its benefit of the bargain something less valuable or significantly different from what it reasonably expected? In addition, the trial court should consider whether the subordination agreement, in combination with the right to a security interest in Barrer's house granted by the collateral note, fully satisfied the Bank's expectations.

The magistrate also made individual errors with respect to the five representations. These errors are outlined below.

2. Delinquency in Mortgage Payments

Barrer and Womack disagree over whether he told her that he "thought" he was two months behind in his mortgage payments or whether he said that he was current. Because this case is before us on appeal from the magistrate's grant of summary judgment for the Bank, we must accept Barrer's statement of the facts. The Bank argues that even if Barrer's version is accepted, a misrepresentation still occurred because Barrer was actually six months behind. The Bank's position is not necessarily correct.

Barrer's statement that he "thought" he was in arrears by two months initially raises the factual question whether he made any misrepresentation. On the surface, the fact asserted by Barrer was his state of mind — what he thought. No finding was made below that Barrer's state of mind was other than what he declared. On remand, before it may determine that this statement constituted a misrepresentation, the court must find either that Barrer misstated his thoughts, in accordance with the rule laid out in section 159, comment d of the RESTATEMENT (SECOND), . . . or that Barrer's statement could reasonably have been understood as carrying with it an assertion that Barrer knew sufficient facts that justified him in forming his opinion, in accordance with § 168(2). . . .

When evaluating the materiality of this particular representation, the court should keep in mind the concession made by WNB's counsel at oral argument-that by itself this representation might not be sufficient to justify summary judgment.

3. Failure to Disclose Mortgage Foreclosure Proceedings

Although the Bank evidently did not ask Barrer directly whether his mortgage was being foreclosed upon, it contends that he had an obligation to volunteer that % information and that his failure to do so is tantamount to a misrepresentation. Barrer argues that he had no duty to reveal the existence of the foreclosure proceedings because he did not know about them. The Bank maintains that he must have known, because before Barrer applied for the loan his teen-age daughter signed for a certified letter from Columbia notifying him of the foreclosure.

The magistrate erred in finding on summary judgment that this non-disclosure is equivalent to a misrepresentation. The RESTATEMENT (SECOND) provides that a non-disclosure may be considered an assertion of fact for purposes of misrepresentation analysis only if the non-disclosed fact is known . . . to the maker and if certain other conditions are met. Because there exists a material issue of fact as to whether Barrer knew that Columbia had begun to foreclose, summary judgment was inappropriate.

4. $11,000 Contingent Liability

The magistrate also erred in finding on summary judgment that Barrer's alleged failure to list as a personal contingent liability an $11,000 tax debt owed to the IRS by his corporation constituted a misrepresentation. First, summary judgment is precluded by the existence of a factual dispute over whether this $11,000 was included in the $38,000 tax liability that Barrer did list. Barrer seems to contend that at least some of this amount was included in the $38,000 figure; . . . the Bank seems to dispute this contention. Second, there is a mixed question of law and fact as to whether the IRS had, at the time of the loan application, taken any action to assert the $11,000 tax debt owed by Today News Service, Inc., against Barrer personally and, if not, whether the corporation's liability may be considered Barrer's contingent liability. If the $11,000 tax debt could not at that time have been considered Barrer's liability, his failure to list such a debt was not a misrepresentation?[4]

5. $5,300 Debt Owed to IBM

The magistrate found that Barrer's failure to reveal as a personal liability a $5,300 debt owed to IBM for equipment purchased by his wife was a misrepresentation. We disagree as a matter of law. Although Barrer asked the probate court handling his wife's estate to charge him with the debt, the court refused, ruling that the debt was hers alone. Contrary to the Bank's protestations, it makes no difference to the determination whether a misrepresentation occurred that Barrer asked the probate court to charge him with the debt before, and the court refused after, Barrer submitted the loan application. A misrepresentation is "an assertion that is not in accord with the facts."[5] The fact is that a court decided that this debt never legally belonged to Barrer. Barrer's thoughts or wishes on the matter are irrelevant. He made no legal misrepresentation to the Bank on this subject.

---

[4] [48] According to the RESTATEMENT (SECOND), a misrepresentation includes past and present events, but not future ones. See § 159 comment c. . . .

[5] [49] RESTATEMENT (SECOND), . . . § 159.

6. $1,500 in Judgments

Finally, the magistrate determined that Barrer's failure to list $1,500 in judgments that were outstanding against him constituted a misrepresentation. This issue should not have been resolved on summary judgment. Barrer disclosed on the loan application that he was a defendant in some lawsuits. . . . Furthermore, in his deposition he stated that he had informed Womack that he owed some small judgments arising out of these suits and that he expected his health insurance to cover most of them. . . . Accepting Barrer's version of the facts, as we must in reviewing a grant of summary judgment, he revealed both his defendant status and the existence of judgments against him. It is true that he did not list them on the application form. Because, however, Barrer contends that he adequately disclosed these debts in connection with the question concerning lawsuits and in his discussion with Womack, there exists a dispute over whether he actually revealed these debts; consequently the magistrate should not have resolved this issue on summary judgment. On remand, two factual questions must be decided. First, what information concerning these judgments did Barrer give to Womack? Second, was that information sufficient to give the Bank notice of them? . . . If it was sufficient, then Barrer made no misrepresentation.

III. CONCLUSION

The magistrate both failed to utilize the correct legal test for determining when an innocent material misrepresentation permits the rescission of a contract and to recognize that this case presents disputed material issues of fact that render summary judgment inappropriate. . . . We reverse and remand for further proceedings consistent with this opinion.

DE JOSEPH v. ZAMBELLI
392 Pa. 24, 139 A.2d 644 (1958)

The Opinion Sur Findings of Fact and Conclusions of Law of President Judge Dannehower follows:

This is an action in equity by a purchaser of real estate seeking a rescission and cancellation of a deed, and the recovery of the purchase price, $18,000, together with *costs* and expenses incidental thereto, from the defendant vendors, on the grounds of false and fraudulent representations inducing the sale.

The complaint avers that defendants falsely represented that the recently white-washed joists in the basement were 'as good as new', when they were badly infested with termites; that the roof was new and didn't leak, and that the basement was water-tight, all of which representations were false, known to be untrue by the vendors and were relied upon by the purchaser to his damage and loss.

Defendants filed a responsive answer denying that any misrepresentations or representations were made, or that plaintiff was fraudulently induced to purchase the dwelling. It was averred that the real estate was purchased 'as is' and for their defense the vendors rely upon the doctrine of caveat emptor.

A hearing was held and from the evidence and exhibits there are made the following:

Findings of Fact

1. On February 25, 1955, the plaintiff, Paul DeJoseph, entered into a written agreement sale with the defendants, Pietro Zambelli and Concetta Zambelli, for the purchase of the latter's dwelling house at 26 Madison Avenue, Belmont Hills, Montgomery County, Pennsylvania, for a total consideration of $18,000. Upon signing the agreement the plaintiff made a down payment of $1,800.

2. On May 25, 1955, the plaintiff completed settlement and paid the balance of $16,200 due on the contract. On May 26, 1955, the plaintiff and his wife, Lillian De-Joseph, entered the premises and found the kitchen floor to be literally covered with termites, looking like flying ants. They never actually lived in the house, and on June 14, 1955, served notice on the defendants of their election to rescind the sale and to recover the purchase price.

3. The subject premises were purchased by the defendants in April, 1950, for $7,500. The dwelling was repaired and completely remodeled and the second floor was made into an apartment. The partitions dividing the rooms on the first floor were removed and the floor plan was altered, the interior was replastered and painted, and a new floor was laid on the old subfloor. The roof was replaced in 1950 and a brick veneer was placed on the exterior siding. No repairs were made to the joists in the basement. In 1953 the defendants put the property up for sale.

4. The plaintiff first became interested in the premises on Labor Day of 1954, which had been advertised for sale. The defendants offered to sell the property for $18,500. In the middle of February, 1955, the plaintiff again visited the premises and offered the defendants $18,000. The offer was accepted and on February 25, 1955, the agreement of sale was executed.

5. Sometime in February, 1955, prior to the execution of the agreement of sale, the plaintiff and his wife inspected the premises, accompanied by the defendants. They were shown the first floor and the basement. The basement had been recently painted or whitewashed. When the plaintiff inquired about the joists in the basement he was told by the defendant, Pietro Zambelli, that "they are as good as new". Some of the joists were obscured by shelves which were filled with jars and articles of clothing. The plaintiff also asked about the roof and was told by Pietro Zambelli that it had been replaced four years ago and did not leak.

6. The plaintiff did not return to the premises until May 26, 1955, the day after final settlement. Two or three days thereafter an inspection of the basement disclosed that the joists had been completely ravaged by termites and provided inadequate support for the floor above. At this time the plaintiff also discovered that water had been leaking through the roof into the bedroom on the second floor. Evidence of leakage was also revealed in the vestibule of the first floor and behind the steps in the basement.

7. The inspection made of the basement further revealed that paint or whitewash had been applied to the joists in a heavy layer and that strips of wood were used to cover some of the more severe termite damage. The termite condition which was not visible to the naked eye, could not be treated until the joists were replaced. The joists were easily penetrated with a pointed instrument and some would disintegrate and crumble when touched with the bare hand. Though most of the termite damage occurred in the basement, other parts of the dwelling, mainly the doorway to the living room on the first floor and parts of the second floor

apartment were also affected to some degree.

8. On October 1, 1956, the premises were inspected by the Township Superintendent of Building Regulations and the first floor was declared to be unsafe and dangerous for human occupancy. The prohibition, however, did not apply to the second floor apartment.

9. The plaintiff went through the dwelling for the first time in February, 1955, but made no further inspections until after settlement. The defendants were aware that the dwelling was infested by termites as early as May 1952, and also knew at that time of water leakage in the second floor apartment.

10. The second floor apartment had been leased by defendants to Anthony and Rosa Casavecchia from April 1952, to June 1955. Within a month after entering into possession they began noticing termites coming from around the doorway of the porch, from the kitchen floor and from a crack in one of the window sills. The termites got into the tenants' food and clothing and could be seen crawling on the floor and on the porch outside. In the Spring of 1953, the defendant, Pietro Zambelli, instructed the tenants to gather the termites with a vacuum cleaner and also offered a liquid insecticide for their extermination. The termite condition persisted up until the time the property was sold, and during this time the defendants continued in their efforts to arrest and exterminate them.

11. Since July 15, 1955, the second floor apartment has been leased by the plaintiff and the rentals received have been placed in trust for the defendants. The plaintiff has also paid interest on the mortgage, the fuel and electric bills, water rent, and taxes for the maintenance of the subject premises.

This case involves an action by a vendee of real property to rescind the contract of purchase on the grounds of fraud and misrepresentation, and to require the vendor to return the purchase money and restore the vendee to status quo. The defense is a general denial and caveat emptor.

The evidence discloses that the defendants vendors had knowledge of the existence of termites in their premises as early as May, 1952, and that they persisted in attempts to check and abate them until May, 1955, when the property was sold to the plaintiff. This is established clearly by the testimony of the tenants in the second floor apartment who were disinterested parties to the controversy.

It was further disclosed that the basement had been given a heavy application of paint or whitewash shortly before the plaintiff first inspected the premises in February, 1955. According to the description of one witness, the basement looked like a "white sepulcher". In addition, the joists were partially obscured by shelves laden with jars and articles of clothing, and in some areas, strips of wood had been attached with the apparent purpose of concealing the more obvious termite damage. As a result of this deception and concealment the latent defects in the joists could not be detected and were not susceptible of discovery except by expert investigation.

The inference is inescapable that the defendants knew that the dwelling was infested with termites and were aware of the serious deterioration of the joists when the property was offered for sale to the plaintiff. The reply to the plaintiff's inquiry that the joists were "as good as new" was therefore a false, material and erroneous statement of fact. It does not occur to us that the plaintiff, with the exercise of ordinary diligence, could have ascertained the falsity of the defendants' representation.

As to the condition of the roof and the basement, the evidence was only slight and of little significance. Hence, whether or not the case commends itself to equitable relief must depend upon the misrepresentations concerning the joists and the latent termite condition.

Where a party is induced to enter into a transaction with another by means of the latter's fraud or material misrepresentation, such a transaction can be avoided by the innocent party. Fraud arises where the misrepresentation is knowingly false, where there is a concealment calculated to deceived, or where there is a non-privileged failure to disclose. Fraud renders a transaction voidable even where the misrepresentation is not material; on the other hand, a misrepresentation made innocently is not actionable unless it is material, and in such case there must be a right to reliance. A misrepresentation is material when it is of such a character, that if it had not been made the transaction would not have been entered into. *See* RESTATEMENT OF CONTRACTS, 470, 471, 476.

Applying the above principles to the case at bar, we are of the opinion that the defendants are guilty of fraud in the purposeful concealment of the termite condition in the premises, and in misrepresenting to the plaintiff that the joists in the basement were "as good as new". This being true we must conclude that the plaintiff is entitled to avoid the transaction and be returned to status quo. Even in the absence of fraud, we believe the misrepresentation to be actionable, for had the plaintiff known the truth of the ravaged condition of the joists, it is unlikely that he would have entered into the contract. In other words, the misrepresentation was material, and under the circumstances of the case the plaintiff was entitled to rely upon it.

The evidence in the case amply supports a finding of fraud. The artifice employed by the defendants in concealing the termite condition was undoubtedly calculated to deceive and mislead the plaintiff. Because of the heavy layer of paint or whitewash, the strips of wood attached to the joists, and the laden shelves, it was virtually impossible for the plaintiff to detect by a reasonable inspection the presence of termites or the ravaged and spoiled condition of the wood. In view of these facts, and the age and relationship of the parties, we are constrained to find that the equities in the case lie with the plaintiff and that he should be entitled to the relief prayed for.

In the case of *Lake v. Thompson*, 366 Pa. 352, 358, 77 A.2d 364, the lower court was reversed and the appellant was allowed to rescind a contract for the purchase of a dwelling where the seller falsely represented that the heater, plumbing and wiring were in good condition; that a 60 foot lot off the property could be sold; that a 60 foot frontage was required by ordinance; that a ramshackle house next door was condemned and would be demolished; that an unsightly water tank in the kitchen could be removed; and that the cellar was dry and in good condition.

In *LaCourse v. Kiesel*, 366 Pa. 385, 77 A.2d 877, the plaintiffs were induced to buy certain real property advertised in an auctioneer's handbill as "splendid for apartments", where, in fact, restrictions prohibited the use of the property other than as a single residence. The court in allowing a rescission, held that the representation in the handbill was material and was relied upon by the purchaser. At page 390 of 366 Pa., at page 880 of 77 A.2d, the Court stated:

A material misrepresentation of an existing fact confers on the party who relies on it the right to rescind whether the defendants here actually knew the truth or not, especially where, as here, they had means of knowledge from which they were bound to ascertain the truth before making the representation.

In *Berger v. Pittsburgh Auto Equipment Co.*, 387 Pa. 61, 62, 127 A.2d 334, it was decided that a representation that a warehouse floor would support weights of 300 pounds and upwards per square foot, subsequently found to be incapable of withstanding even the minimum of 125 pounds as required by the building code, was material and constituted grounds for cancellation of a contract to lease.

A consideration of the evidence in this case leads to the just conclusion that plaintiff has shown by the preponderance of credible testimony the elements necessary to sustain this action for rescission of a sale of a house and lot, namely, that a representation was made as to a statement of fact; that it was untrue and known to be untrue by the party making it; that it was made for the purpose of inducing the other party to act upon it; that the latter was in fact induced to act upon it and that he did so act to his injury. Furthermore, it is not necessary for a plaintiff to prove all the fraudulent misrepresentations he alleges, but may prevail if he proves any which in fact served as inducing causes.

Conclusions of Law

1. Equity has jurisdiction.

2. The statement by the defendants that the joists were "as good as new" was a material misrepresentation of a material fact, relied upon by plaintiff, which induced him to purchase defendants' dwelling.

3. The coats of white paint or whitewash applied to the joists and boards used to cover some of the decayed rafters, and clothing, shelving, etc., in the basement concealed the termite infested joists and showed an intent to conceal and deceive.

4. Plaintiff is entitled to rescind the contract and deed and the return of his purchase money and expenses and costs incurred by the fraudulent representations.

5. The doctrine of caveat emptor is inapplicable because defendants committed the frauds of concealment and material misrepresentations and thereby prevented detection of termite damage.

6. Costs of this proceeding should be paid by defendants. . . .

PER CURIAM.

A Chancellor who saw and heard all the witnesses decreed a rescission of a contract of purchase and a recovery of the purchase price on the ground of fraud and misrepresentation.

In *Howarth v. Miller*, 382 Pa. 419, at page 424, 115 A.2d 222, at page 224, the Court, quoting from *Peters v. Machikas*, 378 Pa. 52, 56, 105 A.2d 708, said: "Findings of fact [which are genuine findings of fact] made by a Chancellor who saw and heard the witnesses, when confirmed by the Court en banc, will not be reversed on appeal if they are supported by adequate evidence.". . .

In the instant case the Chancellor's findings of fact were supported by adequate evidence and were affirmed by the Court en banc and justified his conclusions of law.

The decree is affirmed on the opinion sur findings of fact and conclusions of law of the Chancellor, President Judge Dannehower. Costs to be paid by appellants.

NOTES & QUESTIONS

1. The RESTATEMENT (SECOND) OF CONTRACTS provides that a misrepresentation is material "if it would be likely to induce a reasonable person to manifest his assent." § 162. Thus, a material fact is one that could reasonably be expected to influence a person's judgment or conduct concerning a transaction. Consider this contract: Gibson went to purchase a television and the store salesman told him the purchase price was $189. Gibson agreed to purchase the television at that price, but later learned he had paid $289. Store personnel refused to take back the television. Gibson filed suit to avoid the contract based on fraud or misrepresentation. Can Gibson recover the contract price on the grounds that the salesman's misrepresentation was a material fact? See *Hollywood Credit Clothing Co. v. Gibson*, 188 A.2d 348 (D.C. 1963).

2. The RESTATEMENT (SECOND) OF CONTRACTS § 161 describes non-disclosure and its relationship to misrepresentation.

A person's non-disclosure of a fact known to him is equivalent to an assertion that the fact does not exist in the following cases only:

(a) where he knows that disclosure of the fact is necessary to prevent some previous assertion from being a misrepresentation or from being fraudulent or material.

(b) where he knows that disclosure of the fact would correct a mistake of the other party as to a basic assumption on which that party is making the contract and if non-disclosure of the fact amounts to a failure to act in good faith and in accordance with reasonable standards of fair dealing.

(c) where he knows that disclosure of the fact would correct a mistake of the other party as to the contents or effect of a writing, evidencing or embodying an agreement in whole or in part.

(d) where the other person is entitled to know the fact because of a relation of trust and confidence between them.

The Russes entered into a contract with Brown for the sale of land. During contract negotiations, the parties spoke about water and ditch rights related to the property. Brown never referred to a dispute existing over the water and ditch rights, although the court found such a contest did exist. Once he learned of this dispute over the water and ditch rights, the Russes sought to rescind the contract. The court concluded that Brown had a duty to disclose predicated on the concept that "a vendor may not be required to make representations to purchasers regarding his property, but once he undertakes to do so, he must fully disclose." What is the proper remedy for this non-disclosure? See *Russ v. Brown*, 529 P.2d 765 (Idaho 1974). See also *Faulkner Drilling Co. v. Gross*, 943 S.W.2d 634 (Ky. App. 1997) (finding fraud in the inducement of the contract that entitled party to rescission).

C. MISTAKE

Where a party has an erroneous belief regarding a contract, a mistake has resulted. "A mistake is a belief that is not in accord with the facts." *See* RESTATEMENT (SECOND) OF CONTRACTS § 151. A mistake may take two forms: mutual or unilateral. The remedies that accompany a mistake include rescission and reformation.

DINGEMAN v. REFFITT
393 N.W.2d 632 (Mich. App. 1986)

PER CURIAM.

Plaintiffs appeal as of right from an order granting defendant's motion for summary judgment.

Plaintiffs were the owners of two parcels of lakefront property located in Antrim County on the east and west sides of West Torch Lake Drive. In 1973, plaintiffs contemplated developing the east parcel of property and contacted the local health department for a land evaluation concerning the installation of septic tanks on the property. Pursuant to plaintiffs' request, Walter Franczek of the Department of Health examined the east parcel and concluded that, due to the composition of the soil, serious problems existed for residential development of the property at least with regard to on-site sewage disposal systems. In 1978, plaintiffs received a letter from Franczek in which he stated that any application to install on-site sewage disposal systems on the east parcel would be denied.

In the summer of 1979, plaintiffs commissioned a second set of tests to be done. The tests resulted in a similar conclusion that the east parcel site would not permit on-site sewage disposal. In 1978, plaintiffs hired Art Lennox of Lennox Engineering to inspect the west parcel for an opinion on its suitability for on-site sewage disposal. After examining the parcel, Lennox advised plaintiffs that the west parcel was suitable for an on-site sewage disposal permit. Lennox also informed plaintiffs that the only practical method of providing sewage disposal for the east parcel would be to install an expensive pump disposal system to pump sewage from the east parcel to a drain field on the west parcel.

On April 22, 1980, plaintiffs listed the property with Schmidt Real Estate, Inc. The listing agreement stated:

> Prime Torch Lake frontage. However, Antrim County Health Department will not issue septic permit due to heavy clay soils. Development may be possible with drain field constructed on property located to west of road or with central sewer system.

In the summer of 1980, defendant received a brochure from Schmidt Realty describing the property as follows:

> 34. 600 FEET ON TORCH LAKE: 600' on lake and over 1200' deep. Located along West Torch Lake Drive. Heavy soils will not permit septic permits except possible drain field located on west side of road. $75,000.00.

On August 9, 1980, plaintiffs and defendant executed a land contract for the purchase of the property for $75,000. In the summer of 1983, defendant commenced construction of a home on the east parcel with the intent of installing a disposal system on the property which would pump the sewage to a drain field on the west parcel. While transporting trees on the east parcel in July, 1983, defendant found an area of sand and gravel that he thought might be appropriate for an on-site septic system. He immediately applied for and was granted a permit for an on-site sewage disposal system on the east parcel. The permit was issued on August 1, 1983.

After learning of the issuance of the permit for the east parcel, plaintiffs commenced the instant action, seeking reformation or rescission of the land contract on the ground that there had been a mutual mistake in the formation of the contract. At a hearing held on August 20, 1984, and in a corresponding order dated October 15, 1984, the trial court granted defendant's motion for summary judgment. . . . A motion for summary judgment on the ground that there is no genuine issue as to any material fact tests whether there is factual support for a claim. When passing upon a motion based on rule 117.2(3), the court must consider the pleadings, affidavits, depositions, admissions and other documentary evidence available to it. *Longley v. Blue Cross & Blue Shield of Michigan*, 136 Mich. App. 336, 356 N.W.2d 20 (1984).

Plaintiffs argue that there are two mutual mistakes of fact: (1) that the soil characteristics of the east parcel precluded an on-site sewage system, and (2) that the Antrim County Department of Health would never issue a sewage permit. Based upon these alleged mutual mistakes, plaintiffs seek rescission of the contract or, in the alternative, reformation of the land contract to reflect the fair market value of the property.

A contract may be rescinded because of a mutual mistake of the parties, however, this equitable remedy is granted only in the sound discretion of the trial court. *Lenawee County Bd. of Health v. Messerly*, 417 Mich. 17, 26, 331 N.W.2d 203 (1982). *Harris v. Axline*, 323 Mich. 585, 36 N.W.2d 154 (1949). The determination of whether plaintiffs are entitled to rescission involves a bifurcated inquiry: (1) was there a mistaken belief entertained by one or both of the parties to a contract? and (2) if so, what is the legal significance of the mistaken belief?

" 'A contractual mistake 'is a belief that is not in accord with the facts'. 1 RESTATEMENT (SECOND) OF CONTRACTS § 151, p. 383. The erroneous belief of one or both of the parties must relate to a fact in existence at the time the contract is executed. That is to say, the belief which is found to be in error may not be, in substance, a prediction as to a future occurrence or non-occurrence." *Lenawee County, supra*, 417 Mich. at p. 24, 331 N.W.2d 203. (Citations omitted.)

At the time the parties executed the land contract, they believed that the health department would not issue a permit for an on-site septic tank because of the heavy clay composition of the soil on the east parcel. This belief proved to be erroneous because, after purchasing the property, defendant discovered a sand and gravel area on the east parcel which proved suitable for an on-site septic tank. As a result, he was issued the permit which plaintiffs unsuccessfully sought. Contrary to the parties' belief, the east parcel was perkable. Thus, when the parties entered into the land contract they were laboring under a mutual mistake of fact, and we must determine the legal significance of that mistaken belief.

In *Lenawee County, supra*, pp. 26-28, 331 N.W.2d 203, the Supreme Court criticized its prior decisions which distinguished mistakes affecting the essence of consideration[6] from those which go to the quality or the nature of the thing

---

[6] [1] A&M Land Development Co. v. Miller, 354 Mich. 681, 94 N.W.2d 197 (1959).

bargained for.[7] Noting that such distinctions do not provide a satisfactory analysis of the nature of the mistake sufficient to invalidate a contact, the Supreme Court held that a case-by-case analysis is the better approach. *Lenawee County, supra*, p. 29, 331 N.W.2d 203. Under this approach, rescission is appropriate where "the mistaken belief relates to a basic assumption of the parties upon which the contract is made, and which materially affects the agreed performances of the parties." *Id.* Rescission is not available, however, to relieve a party who has assumed the risk of loss in connection with the mistake. *Lenawee County, supra*, p. 30, 331 N.W.2d 203.

In this case, the parties erroneously assumed that the east parcel was not suitable for on-site sewage disposal. Unlike *Lenawee County*, however, the erroneous assumption does not materially affect the agreed performances of the parties. In *Lenawee County*, the parties to the land contract believed the land was suitable for human habitation and could be utilized to generate rental income. Their erroneous assumptions precluded the vendees' intended use of the land. In this case, defendant bought the land with the intent of building a home on the east parcel even though he would have to bear the cost of installing an expensive system to pump the sewage to the west parcel.[8]

Even if we were to determine that the mutual mistake related to a basic assumption and materially affected the agreed performance of the parties, we do not believe rescission of the contract would be appropriate. In cases of mistake by two equally innocent parties, this Court, in the exercise of its equitable powers, must determine which blameless party should assume the loss resulting from the misapprehension they shared. *Lenawee County, supra*, p. 31, 331 N.W.2d 203. We do so by examining our notions of what is reasonable and just under all the circumstances.

In this case, equity suggests that the sellers should assume the loss of the mistake. Guided by the standard announced in 1 RESTATEMENT (SECOND) OF CONTRACTS, § 154, pp. 402-406,[9] we look to whether the parties have agreed to the allocation of the risk between themselves. The "as is" clause incorporated into the contract[10] is a persuasive indication that the parties intended that defendant would bear both the risks and the benefits of the present condition of the property.

---

[7] [2] Sherwood v. Walker, 66 Mich. 568, 33 N.W. 919 (1887).

[8] [3] Plaintiffs argue that they never would have sold the land had the east parcel been "capable of any sewage system or supporting a residence". We find this argument without merit as it is clear from the record that plaintiffs could have built a home on the east parcel and pumped the sewage to the west parcel, albeit at some expense.

[9] [4] Section 154, which was cited with approval in Lenawee County, *supra*, 417 Mich. at p. 30, fn. 12, 331 N.W.2d 203, reads as follows:

§ 154. When a Party Bears the Risk of a Mistake

A party bears the risk of a mistake when

(a) the risk is allocated to him by agreement of the parties, or

(b) he is aware, at the time the contract is made, that he has only limited knowledge with respect to the facts to which the mistake relates but treats his limited knowledge as sufficient, or

(c) the risk is allocated to him by the court on the ground that it is reasonable in the circumstances to do so."

[10] [5] The land contract contained the following provision:

(m) Purchaser accepts the property as is, and with knowledge that Seller has been informed by District Health Department No. 3 that the soil character is such that any applications to install an on-site sewage disposal system will be denied."

Plaintiffs alternatively sought reformation of the land contract. The burden of proof is upon the party seeking reformation to present clear and convincing evidence that the contract should be reformed in order to carry out the true agreement of the parties. *E.R. Brenner Co. v. Brooker Engineering Co.*, 301 Mich. 719, 724, 4 N.W.2d 71 (1942). In order to decree the reformation of a written instrument on the ground of mistake, the mistake must be mutual and common to both parties to the instrument. *Stevenson v. Aalto*, 333 Mich. 582, 589, 53 N.W.2d 382 (1952). If the asserted mutual mistake is with respect to an extrinsic fact, reformation is not allowed, even though the fact is one which would have caused the parties to make a different contract, because courts cannot make a new contract for the parties. *Brenner, supra,* 301 Mich. 724, 4 N.W.2d 71; *Marshall v. Marshall,* 135 Mich. App. 702, 710-711, n. 3, 355 N.W.2d 661 (1984).

In this case, there was no mistake as to the instrument actually entered into. The mutual mistake is not of an intrinsic fact. The land contract reflects the agreement of the parties and, thus, is incapable of reformation. . . .

From our careful review of the record, we conclude that there were no material issues of fact to be resolved, and therefore, summary judgment was not prematurely granted.

Affirmed.

NOTES & QUESTIONS

1. The *Dingeman* court found that rescission was appropriate where "the mistaken belief relates to a basic assumption of the parties upon which the contract is made, and which materially affects the agreed performances of the parties." The mistake in *Dingeman* did not justify rescission.

2. In *Wood v. Boynton*, 25 N.W. 42 (Wis. 1885), Wood found an attractive stone, but was ignorant of the stone's nature or value. Wood took the stone to a jeweler, Boynton, who also knew neither the nature nor value of the stone. Boynton purchased the stone from Wood for one dollar. Later, the stone was found to be an uncut diamond worth approximately $700. Wood returned the one dollar to Boynton and asked for the stone back. When Boynton refused, Wood sued to recover the stone, arguing that the contract should be rescinded on the grounds of mistake. The court upheld the contract concluding that "there is no pretense as to any mistake as to the identity of the thing sold" and "the value of the property sold as compared with the price paid is no ground for a rescission of a sale." Was there a mistake as to a basic assumption of the parties upon which the contract was made which materially affected the performance of the parties?

3. The *Dingeman* court denied both rescission and reformation of the contract. Under what circumstances is each remedy appropriate?

In *Omaha Door Co. v. Mexican Food Manufacturers of Omaha, Inc.*, 439 N.W.2d 776 (Neb. 1989), Omaha and Mexican entered into a written lease for rental of a piece of realty. The lease included an amortization schedule requiring repayment of a loan taken out to remodel and improve the property before it would be suitable for occupation. The parties agreed the amount of the loan would be $25,000. But through a scrivener's mistake, the amount was entered into the contract as $15,000. In granting reformation of the lease, the court concluded that reformation may be warranted if an incorrect term is inserted by mistake, the mistake is mutual, and the mistake is contrary to the parties' intentions.

WIL-FRED'S INC. v. METROPOLITAN SANITARY DISTRICT OF GREATER CHICAGO
57 Ill. App. 3d 16, 14 Ill. Dec. 667, 372 N.E.2d 946 (1978)

PERLIN, Justice:

In response to an advertisement published by the Metropolitan Sanitary District of Greater Chicago (hereinafter Sanitary District) inviting bids for rehabilitation work at one of its water reclamation plants, Wil-Fred's Inc. submitted a sealed bid and, as a security deposit to insure its performance, a $100,000 certified check. After the bids were opened, Wil-Fred's, the low bidder, attempted to withdraw. The Sanitary District rejected the request and stated that the contract would be awarded to Wil-Fred's in due course. Prior to this award, Wil-Fred's filed a complaint for preliminary injunction and rescission. After hearing testimony and the arguments of counsel, the trial court granted rescission and ordered the Sanitary District to return the $100,000 bid deposit to Wil-Fred's. The Sanitary District seeks to reverse this judgment order.

The Sanitary District's advertisement was published on November 26, 1975, and it announced that bids on contract 75-1 13-2D for the rehabilitation of sand drying beds at the District's West-Southwest plant in Stickney, Illinois, would be accepted up to January 6, 1976. This announcement specified that the work to be performed required the contractor to remove 67,500 linear feet of clay pipe and 53,200 cubic yards of gravel from the beds and to replace these items with plastic pipe and fresh filter material. Although plastic pipes were called for, the specifications declared that "all pipes . . . must be able . . . to withstand standard construction equipment."

The advertisement further stated that "[t]he cost estimate of the work under Contract 75-113-2D, as determined by the Engineering Department of the. . . Sanitary District . . . is $1,257,000."

A proposal form furnished to Wil-Fred's provided:

> The undersigned hereby certifies that he has examined the contract documents . . . and has examined the site of the work. . . .

> The undersigned has also examined the Advertisement, the 'bidding requirements,' has made the examinations and investigation therein required. . . .

> The undersigned hereby accepts the invitation of the Sanitary District to submit a proposal on said work with the understanding that this proposal will not be cancelled or withdrawn.

> It is understood that in the event the undersigned is awarded a contract for the work herein mentioned, and shall fail or refuse to execute the same and furnish the specified bond within thirteen (13) days after receiving notice of the award of said contract, then the sum of One Hundred Thousand Dollars ($100,000), deposited herewith, shall be retained by the Sanitary District as liquidated damages and not as a penalty, it being understood that said sum is the fair measure of the amount of damages that said Sanitary District will sustain in such event.

On December 22, 1975, the Sanitary District issued an addendum that changed the type of sand filter material which was to be supplied by the contractor. During the bidding period the District's engineering department discovered that the material originally specified in the advertisement was available only out of state and consequently was extremely expensive. This addendum changed the filter material to a less expensive type that could be obtained locally.

On January 6, 1976, Wil-Fred's submitted the low bid of $882,600 which was accompanied by the $100,000 bid deposit and the aforementioned proposal form signed on behalf of the company by Wil-Fred's vice president. Eight other companies submitted bids on January 6. The next lowest bid was $1,118,375, and it was made by Greco Contractors, Inc.

On January 8, 1976, Wil-Fred's sent the Sanitary District a telegram which stated that it was withdrawing its bid and requested return of its bid deposit. This telegram was confirmed by a subsequent letter mailed the same day.

On January 12, 1976, Wil-Fred's, at the request of the Sanitary District, sent a letter setting forth the circumstances that caused the company to withdraw its bid. The letter stated that upon learning the amount by which it was the low bidder, Wil-Fred's asked its excavating subcontractor, Ciaglo Excavating Company, to review its figures; that excavation was the only subcontracted trade in Wil-Fred's bid; that the following day Ciaglo informed Wil-Fred's that there had been a substantial error in its bid, and therefore it would have to withdraw its quotation since performing the work at the stated price would force the subcontractor into bankruptcy; that Wil-Fred's then checked with other excavation contractors and confirmed that Ciaglo's bid was in error; that Wil-Fred's had used Ciaglo as an excavating subcontractor on many other projects in the past, and Ciaglo had always honored its previous quotations; that Ciaglo had always performed its work in a skillful fashion; that because of these facts WilFred's acted reasonably in utilizing Ciaglo's quoted price in formulating its own bid; and that with the withdrawal of Ciaglo's quotation Wil-Fred's could not perform the work for $882,600.

On February 2, 1976, Wil-Fred's received a letter from Thomas W. Moore, the Sanitary District's purchasing agent. Moore's letter stated that in his opinion the reasons cited in Wil-Fred's letter of January 12 did not justify withdrawal of the bid. For this reason Moore said that he would recommend to the Sanitary District's general superintendent that the contract be awarded to Wil-Fred's at the original bid price.

At a February 20 meeting between representatives of the Sanitary District and Wil-Fred's, the company was informed that the District's board of trustees had rejected its withdrawal request, and that it would be awarded the contract.

In response to this information, Wil-Fred's filed its complaint for preliminary injunction and rescission on February 26, 1976. The complaint alleged that the company would be irreparably injured if required to perform the contract at such an unconscionably low price or if forced to forfeit the $100,000 bid deposit. The hearing on this complaint commenced on March 10, 1976. At the hearing William Luxion, president of Wil-Fred's, testified that the company had been in business for 18 years; that Wil-Fred's did 13 to 14 million dollars worth of business in 1975; that 95% of the company's work was done on a competitive bid basis; that Wil-Fred's never had withdrawn a competitive bid in the past; and that he personally examined the company's bid prior to its submission. Luxion further stated that he told

Wil-Fred's chief estimator to review the company's quotation immediately after he was notified on January 6 that Wil-Fred's bid was more than $235,000 below the next lowest bid. At this time he also requested that Ciaglo Company review its figures.

The reexamination by the chief estimator revealed that there was no material error in the portion of the bid covering work to be done by Wil-Fred's. However, the president of Ciaglo contacted Luxion on January 8 and stated that his bid was too low on account of an error and that, because of this, he was withdrawing his quotation. Upon receiving this information, Luxion sent the Sanitary District the telegram and letter in which he informed the District of this error, withdrew Wil-Fred's bid and requested a return of the company's bid deposit.

Lastly, Luxion testified that a loss of the $100,000 security deposit would result in the company's loss of bonding capacity in the amount of two to three million dollars; that Wil-Fred's decided not to attempt to force Ciaglo to honor its subcontract because the company felt that Ciaglo was not financially capable of sustaining a $150,000 loss; and that he was aware of the Sanitary District's cost estimate before Wil-Fred's submitted its bid. However, Luxion stated that he took the addendum changing the filter material into account when calculating the price of the bid and concluded that this alteration would result in a cost savings of over $200,000.

Dennis Ciaglo, president of Ciaglo Excavating, Inc., also testified on behalf of WilFred's and stated that prior to January 6, 1976, his company submitted a quote of $205,000 for the removal of the existing material in the sand beds, for digging trenches for the new pipe and for spreading the new filter materials. Ciaglo further stated that a representative of Wil-Fred's called him on January 6 and asked him to review his price quotation. During his examination the witness discovered that he underestimated his projected costs by $150,000. Ciaglo said that this error was caused by his assumption that heavy equipment could be driven into the beds to spread the granular fill. Although he was aware that plastic pipes were to be used in the beds, Ciaglo still presumed that heavy equipment could be employed because the specifications called for the utilization of standard construction equipment. Ciaglo first learned that the plastic pipes would not support heavy equipment when, as part of his review of the price quote, he contacted the pipe manufacturer.

Ciaglo testified additionally that his company probably would have to file for bankruptcy if forced to take a $150,000 loss; that Ciaglo Excavating Co. had never before withdrawn a price quotation given to Wil-Fred's or any other company; and that in his opinion the change in the filter material called for by the second addendum would cause a $300,000 reduction in "the cost of the material for the bids. . . ."

Only one witness testified for the Sanitary District. Leslie Dombai, a registered structural engineer for the District, stated that the Sanitary District's cost estimate was based directly upon the expense of the material specified in the advertisement, and he confirmed that the filter material was changed because the type initially called for was expensive and was not available locally. However, Dombai claimed that this substitution increased the District's original cost estimate by $40,000.

By bidding on the Sanitary District's rehabilitation project, Wil-Fred's made a binding commitment. Its bid was in the nature of an option to the District based upon valuable consideration: the assurance that the award would be made to the lowest bidder. The option was both an offer to do the work and a unilateral agreement to enter into a contract to do so. When the offer was accepted, a bilateral contract arose which was mutually binding on Wil-Fred's and the Sanitary District. . . . When Wil-Fred's attempted to withdraw its bid, it became subject to the condition incorporated in the proposal form furnished by the Sanitary District. Under this condition, the company's bid deposit was forfeited when it refused to execute the contract within the specified time period.

The principal issue, therefore, is whether Wil-Fred's can obtain rescission of its contract with the Sanitary District because of its unilateral mistake.

Wil-Fred's argues that the mistake was material to the contract; that this error was directly caused by the Sanitary District's misleading specifications; that the Sanitary District did not alter its position in reliance upon the erroneous bid because the company promptly notified the District of the mistake; and that under these circumstances it would be unconscionable to enforce the contract or to allow the Sanitary District to retain the security deposit.

As a general rule, it is often said that relief will not be granted if but one party to a contract has made a mistake. . . . However, Professor Williston in his treatise on contracts indicates that unilateral mistake may afford ground for rescission where there is a material mistake and such mistake is so palpable that the party not in error will be put on notice of its existence. 13 WILLISTON ON CONTRACTS § 1578 (3d ed. Jaeger 1970).

In Illinois the conditions generally required for rescission are: that the mistake relate to a material feature of the contract; that it occurred notwithstanding the exercise of reasonable care; that it is of such grave consequence that enforcement of the contract would be unconscionable; and that the other party can be placed in status quo. . . . Evidence of these conditions must be clear and positive. . . .

If Ciaglo's misestimation was established by competent evidence, it is apparent that the error was material. This determination is based on the fact that the $150,000 mistake represents approximately 17% Of Wil-Fred's bid. *See Department of Public Works and Buildings v. South East National Bank.*

However, the Sanitary District contends that Wil-Fred's failed to support its claim of materiality with clear and positive evidence. The District points out that neither of the plaintiff's two witnesses described the proper method for spreading the new filter material on the plastic pipes, and it argues that because of this omission Wil-Fred's failed to introduce sufficient evidence to substantiate Dennis Ciaglo's conclusion that the correct procedure would have cost $150,000 more than the system he had planned to use.

We do not find this argument persuasive. It is manifest from the trial court's judgment order that the trier of fact decided that Ciaglo's mistake related to a material feature of the rehabilitation contract and that this condition was supported by clear and positive evidence. After carefully examining the record, we are in agreement with this finding.

Dennis Ciaglo testified that he gave Wil-Fred's a price quotation of $205,000 for his work allotment, and he indicated that the amount of this bid was based directly upon his incorrect assumption that heavy trucks could be driven into the sand drying beds and onto the plastic pipes. This testimony is corroborated by the subcontractor's price estimate sheet which was introduced into evidence by the Sanitary District.

It is true, nevertheless, that plaintiff's witnesses failed to describe the correct spreading method, and that Ciaglo made only a conclusionary statement to the effect that employment of the proper procedure would have increased his original quotation by $150,000. However, the District did not cross-examine the subcontractor concerning this matter, and it failed to produce any evidence, testimonial or otherwise, that contravened his statement. Consequently, Ciaglo's conclusion stands uncontradicted.

Furthermore, it is our opinion that the accuracy of the estimated error is supported by the fact that Ciaglo had eight years experience in the excavating business and by the fact that he confirmed this figure by checking with other contractors who had submitted bids on the same portion of the project. Under these particular circumstances we feel that Wil-Fred's produced sufficient evidence to sustain its claim of a $150,000 error.

In addition to satisfying the first condition for rescission, Wil-Fred's has decidedly fulfilled two of the three remaining requirements. The consequences of Ciaglo's error were grave. Since the subcontractor was not capable of sustaining a $150,000 loss, Wil-Fred's stood to lose the same amount if it performed the contract for $882,600. Wil-Fred's will forfeit $100,000 if the contract is enforced. A loss of $100,000 will decrease the plaintiff's bonding capacity by two to three million dollars. It is evident, therefore, that either deprivation will constitute substantial hardship. The Sanitary District was not damaged seriously by the withdrawal of the bid. When the subcontractor's mistake was discovered 48 hours after the bid opening, Wil-Fred's promptly notified the District by telegram and declared its intention to withdraw. The rehabilitation contract had not been awarded at this time. Accordingly, the District suffered no change in position since it was able, with no great loss other than the windfall resulting from Ciaglo's error, to award the contract to the next lowest bidder, Department of Public Works.

The central question, therefore, is whether the error occurred despite the use of reasonable care. The Sanitary District asserts that the mistake itself evidences Wil-Fred's failure to use ordinary care in the preparation of its bid and argues that rescission is not warranted under such circumstances. We cannot agree with this contention. Wil-Fred's unquestionably exercised due care when it selected Ciaglo Excavating Company as its subcontractor. Ciaglo Excavating Company had been in business for five years; its president had eight years experience in the excavating field; the company had worked for Wil-Fred's on 12 previous occasions; it had never failed to honor a prior quotation; and it had always performed its assignments in a highly skilled manner. Also, Dennis Ciaglo testified that prior to submitting his bid to Wil-Fred's, he inspected the jobsite and carefully examined the specifications with plaintiff's estimators. Taking into account the experience and preparations of the subcontractor, the prior business dealings between the two companies and the high quality of Ciaglo Excavating Company's past performance, we conclude that Wil-Fred's was justified in relying on the subcontractor's quotation in formulating its own bid.

Similarly, we feel that Wil-Fred's exercised reasonable care in the preparation of its portion of the total bid. The plaintiff made two separate reviews of its price quotation. The first was conducted prior to the bid's submission, and it took into account the addendum that substituted a cheaper filter material for the type originally called for by the specifications. The second examination was made immediately after Wil-Fred's president learned that his company's bid was the lowest quotation. It revealed that plaintiff had not erred in estimating expenses for its part of the rehabilitation project.

Additionally, the Sanitary District's engineer stated that the District's estimate was based directly upon the cost of the material specified in the advertisement, and he admitted that the initial type of filter material was very expensive because it was not available locally. In view of this testimony we must conclude that the large discrepancy would not necessarily have alerted Wil-Fred's president to the fact that there was a substantial error in his company's bid.

The question of due care is a factual question to be determined by the trial court, and such determination will not be disturbed unless it is against the manifest weight of the evidence. . . . For the aforementioned reasons we feel that the record supports the trial court's finding of due care on the part of Wil-Fred's.

The Sanitary District asserts that even if due care was exercised by Wil-Fred's, Illinois courts have granted relief only in cases where the bid has contained a clerical or mathematical error. Defendant argues that the trial court's grant of rescission should not be upheld because Ciaglo's mistake was not a factual error but an error in business judgment.

Regarding the District's argument, it is the opinion of this court that Ciaglo's error amounts to a mixed mistake of judgment and fact. Ciaglo's belief that the plastic pipes would support heavy trucks was judgmental in nature and in this narrow sense his mistake was one of business judgment. However, his belief was predicated on a misunderstanding of the actual facts occasioned, at least in part, by his reliance on the Sanitary District's misleading specifications which stated that all pipes had to be able to withstand standard construction equipment.

Generally, relief is refused for errors in judgment and allowed for clerical or mathematical mistakes. . . . Nonetheless, we believe, in fairness to the individual bidder, that the facts surrounding the error, not the label, i.e., "mistake of fact" or "mistake of judgment," should determine whether relief is granted. . . .

The testimonial evidence reveals that Wil-Fred's acted in good faith and that Ciaglo's error occurred notwithstanding the exercise of reasonable care. Furthermore, it was established that Wil-Fred's quotation was $235,775 lower than the next lowest bid. It is apparent that such a sizable discrepancy should have placed the Sanitary District on notice that plaintiff's bid contained a material error. . . . Accordingly equity will not allow the District to take advantage of Wil-Fred's low offer.

We are aware of the importance of maintaining the competitive bidding system which is used in the letting of municipal construction contracts. Consequently we do not mean to imply by affirming the trial court's order that a bidder who has submitted the lowest quotation on a municipal contract may cavalierly disregard the contract's irrevocability clause and seek rescission. Allowing such action would be unfair to the other bidders and would result in the destruction of the system's integrity. However, we are certain that the courts of this state are capable of preventing such a result by refusing to grant rescission where, unlike the present circumstances, the facts do not justify relieving the lowest bidder from his bid. *See*

Calnan Co. v. Talsma Builders, Inc. (1977), 67 Ill. 2d 213, 10 Ill. Dec. 242, 367 N.E.2d 695, in which our supreme court, although not dealing with a municipal construction contract, recently denied rescission of a plumbing subcontract where the subcontractor failed to include the cost of the entire water supply system in its bid, a concededly material feature of the subcontract. The supreme court held that the subcontractor had not exercised reasonable care by failing to utilize its own bid preparation review system and by not discovering its error until four months after acceptance of its bid. The court also found that the general contractor could not be placed in statu quo since work had begun and the general contractor had no options; it either had to account for the error ($31,000) or had to negotiate another subcontract, at a greater cost with lack of continuity in work.

We note but do not consider the Sanitary District's other arguments which we find to be without merit.

For the above stated reasons, the trial court's order granting rescission and the return of Wil-Fred's security deposit is affirmed.

Affirmed.

STAMOS, P. J., and PUSATERI, J., concur.

NOTES & QUESTIONS

1. In general, relief in the form of rescission will be denied when only one party to the contract is mistaken. Yet a unilateral mistake can sometimes form the basis for rescission. The *Wil-Fred* court granted rescission of the contractor's bid even though the mistake was the bidder's mistake alone.

2. There are times when a bid is just "too good to be true." *See Ex parte Perusini Construction Co.*, 7 So. 2d 576 (Ala. 1942), *cited in,* 27 WILLISTON ON CONTRACTS § 70:117 (2006):

> If one of the parties, through mistake, names a consideration that is all out of proportion to the value of the subject of the negotiation and the other party, realizing that a mistake must have been committed, takes advantage of it and refuses to let the mistake be corrected hen discovered, [no one can] under these conditions claim enforceable contract.

D.   UNCONSCIONABILITY

The unconscionable contract is one that "no man in his senses and not under delusion would make on the one hand, and as no honest and fair man would accept on the other." *Hume v. United States*, 132 U.S. 406 (1889). This definition has been refined by the common law and the Uniform Commercial Code to test if contracts made for the sales of services and goods are unconscionable. The RESTATEMENT (SECOND) OF CONTRACTS § 208 (cmts. c, d), finds unconscionability where there is a gross disparity of consideration, substantial inequality of bargaining power, or overall oppression in the contract process. Courts have developed a two-pronged approach by defining substantive and procedural unconscionability. Procedural unconscionability occurs during the process of contract formation, while substantive unconscionability addresses the term of the contract itself.

WILLIAMS v. WALKER-THOMAS FURNITURE COMPANY
350 F.2d 445, 121 U.S. App. D.C. 315 (D.C. Cir. 1965)

J. SKELLY WRIGHT, Circuit Judge:

Appellee, Walker-Thomas Furniture Company, operates a retail furniture store in the District of Columbia. During the period from 1957 to 1962 each appellant in these cases purchased a number of household items from Walker-Thomas, for which payment was to be made in installments. The terms of each purchase were contained in a printed form contract which set forth the value of the purchased item and purported to lease the item to appellant for a stipulated monthly rent payment. The contract then provided, in substance, that title would remain in Walker-Thomas until the total of all the monthly payments made equaled the stated value of the item, at which time appellants could take title. In the event of a default in the payment of any monthly installment, Walker-Thomas could repossess the item.

The contract further provided that "the amount of each periodical installment payment to be made by (purchaser) to the Company under this present lease shall be inclusive of and not in addition to the amount of each installment payment to be made by (purchaser) under such prior leases, bills or accounts; and all payments now and hereafter made by (purchaser) shall be credited pro rata on all outstanding leases, bills and accounts due the Company by (purchaser) at the time each such payment is made." The effect of this rather obscure provision was to keep a balance due on every item purchased until the balance due on all items, whenever purchased, was liquidated. As a result, the debt incurred at the time of purchase of each item was secured by the right to repossess all the items previously purchased by the same purchaser, and each new item purchased automatically became subject to a security interest arising out of the previous dealings.

On May 12, 1962, appellant Thorne purchased an item described as a Daveno, three tables, and two lamps, having total stated value of $391.10. Shortly thereafter, he defaulted on his monthly payments and appellee sought to replevy all the items purchased since the first transaction in 1958. Similarly, on April 17, 1962, appellant Williams bought a stereo set of stated value of $514.95. . . . She too defaulted shortly thereafter, and appellee sought to replevy all the items purchased since December, 1957. The Court of General Sessions granted judgment for appellee. The District of Columbia Court of Appeals affirmed, and we granted appellants' motion for leave to appeal to this court.

Appellants' principal contention, rejected by both the trial and the appellate courts below, is that these contracts, or at least some of them, are unconscionable and, hence, not enforceable. In its opinion in *Williams v. Walker-Thomas Furniture Company*, 198 A.2d 914, 916 (1964), the District of Columbia Court of Appeals explained its rejection of this contention as follows:

> Appellant's second argument presents a more serious question. The record reveals that prior to the last purchase appellant had reduced the balance in her account to $164. The last purchase, a stereo set, raised the balance due to $678. Significantly, at the time of this and the preceding purchases, appellee was aware of appellant's financial position. The reverse side of the stereo contract listed the name of appellant's social worker and her $218 monthly stipend from the government. Nevertheless, with full

knowledge that appellant had to feed, clothe and support both herself and seven children on this amount, appellee sold her a $514 stereo set.

We cannot condemn too strongly appellee's conduct. It raises serious questions of sharp practice and irresponsible business dealings. A review of the legislation in the District of Columbia affecting retail sales and the pertinent decisions of the highest court in this jurisdiction disclose, however, no ground upon which this court can declare the contracts in question contrary to public policy. We note that were the Maryland Retail Installment Sales Act, Art. 83 §§ 128-153, or its equivalent, in force in the District of Columbia, we could grant appellant appropriate relief. We think Congress should consider corrective legislation to protect the public from such exploitive contracts as were utilized in the case at bar.

We do not agree that the court lacked the power to refuse enforcement to contracts found to be unconscionable. In other jurisdictions, it has been held as a matter of common law that unconscionable contracts are not enforceable. . . . While no decision of this court so holding has been found, the notion that an unconscionable bargain should not be given full enforcement is by no means novel. In *Scott v. United States*, 79 U.S. (12 Wall.) 443, 445, 20 L. Ed. 438 (1870), the Supreme Court stated: "If a contract be unreasonable and unconscionable, but not void for fraud, a court of law will give to the party who sues for its breach damages, not according to its letter, but only such as he is equitably entitled to." . . .

Since we have never adopted or rejected such a rule, . . . the question here presented is actually one of first impression.

Congress has recently enacted the Uniform Commercial Code, which specifically provides that the court may refuse to enforce a contract which it finds to be unconscionable at the time it was made. . . . The enactment of this section, which occurred subsequent to the contracts here in suit, does not mean that the common law of the District of Columbia was otherwise at the time of enactment, nor does it preclude the court from adopting a similar rule in the exercise of its powers to develop the common law for the District of Columbia. In fact, in view of the absence of prior authority on the point, we consider the congressional adoption of § 2-302 persuasive authority for following the rationale of the cases from which the section is explicitly derived. Accordingly, we hold that where the element of unconscionability is present at the time a contract is made, the contract should not be enforced.

Unconscionability has generally been recognized to include an absence of meaningful choice on the part of one of the parties together with contract terms which are unreasonably favorable to the other party. . . . Whether a meaningful choice is present in a particular case can only be determined by consideration of all the circumstances surrounding the transaction. In many cases the meaningfulness of the choice is negated by a gross inequality of bargaining power. . . . The manner in which the contract was entered is also relevant to this consideration. Did each party to the contract, considering his obvious education or lack of it, have a reasonable opportunity to understand the terms of the contract, or were the important terms hidden in a maze of fine print and minimized by deceptive sales practices? Ordinarily, one who signs an agreement without full knowledge of its terms might be held to assume the risk that he has entered a one-sided bargain. . . . But when a party of little bargaining power, and hence little real choice, signs a commercially unreasonable contract with little or no knowledge of its terms, it is hardly likely that his consent, or even an objective manifestation of his consent, was ever given to all the terms. In such a case the usual rule that the terms of the agreement are not to be questioned should be abandoned and the court should consider whether the terms of the contract are so unfair that enforcement should be withheld. . . .

In determining reasonableness or fairness, the primary concern must be with the terms of the contract considered in light of the circumstances existing when the contract was made. The test is not simple, nor can it be mechanically applied. The terms are to be considered 'in the light of the general commercial background and the commercial needs of the particular trade or case.' . . . Corbin suggests the test as being whether the terms are "so extreme as to appear unconscionable according to the mores and business practices of the time and place.' . . . We think this formulation correctly states the test to be applied in those cases where no meaningful choice was exercised upon entering the contract.

Because the trial court and the appellate court did not feel that enforcement could be refused, no findings were made on the possible unconscionability of the contracts in these cases. Since the record is not sufficient for our deciding the issue as a matter of law, the cases must be remanded to the trial court for further proceedings.

So ordered.

DANAHER, Circuit Judge (dissenting):

The District of Columbia Court of Appeals obviously was as unhappy about the situation here presented as any of us can possibly be. Its opinion in the Williams case, quoted in the majority text, concludes: "We think Congress should consider corrective legislation to protect the public from such exploitive contracts as were utilized in the case at bar."

My view is thus summed up by an able court which made no finding that there had actually been sharp practice. Rather the appellant seems to have known precisely where she stood.

There are many aspects of public policy here involved. What is a luxury to some may seem an outright necessity to others. Is public oversight to be required of the expenditures of relief funds? A washing machine, e.g., in the hands of a relief client might become a fruitful source of income. Many relief clients may well need credit, and certain business establishments will take long chances on the sale of items, expecting their pricing policies will afford a degree of protection commensurate with the risk. Perhaps a remedy when necessary will be found within the provisions of the "Loan Shark" law, D.C. Code §§ 26-601 et seq. (1961).

I mention such matters only to emphasize the desirability of a cautious approach to any such problem, particularly since the law for so long has allowed parties such great latitude in making their own contracts. I dare say there must annually be thousands upon thousands of installment credit transactions in this jurisdiction, and one can only speculate as to the effect the decision in these cases will have. . . .

I join the District of Columbia Court of Appeals in its disposition of the issues.

FOTOMAT CORPORATION OF FLORIDA v. CHANDA
464 So. 2d 626 (Fla. App. 1985)

ORFINGER, Judge:

The defendant appeals from a final judgment awarding damages of $9,500 to plaintiff, resulting from the loss of film which plaintiff had delivered to defendant for processing. We reverse.

Plaintiff Chanda, a medical doctor, after reading a magazine article indicating that the deterioration of movie film could be avoided by transferring the images on the film to videotape, and having read a flyer distributed by defendant which advertised the availability of such service, delivered 28 rolls of already developed Super-8 movie film to one of defendant's outlets in Melbourne, Florida in April of 1980. Defendant's clerk prepared an order form which contained information necessary to identify the customer, type of film and type of videocassette ordered, and other matters incidental to the transaction, and which also contained in a conspicuous place on the sheet and in bold type, the following language:

IMPORTANT

THE WARRANTY BELOW GIVES YOU SPECIFIC LEGAL RIGHTS AND LIMITATIONS. PLEASE READ IT CAREFULLY.

By depositing film or other material with Fotomat, customer acknowledges and agrees that Fotomat's liability for any loss, damage, or delay to film during the processing service will be limited to the replacement cost of a non-exposed roll of film and/or a blank cassette of similar size. Except for such replacement, Fotomat shall not be liable for any other loss or damage, direct, consequential, or incidental, arising out of customer's use of Fotomat's service.

X

Customer Signature

Dr. Chanda read this clause, asked the clerk about it, and then signed it.

The film was lost and never made its way back to the plaintiff. Despite every effort on the part of defendant to locate it, it was never found nor could anyone account for its disappearance. Dr. Chanda testified that the film was of great sentimental value to him and to his family because it contained depictions of his honeymoon, the graduation ceremony at his medical school, movies of his son's birth and early life, and many memorable vacations which he and his wife had taken. In proving his damages, he was permitted to testify, over objection, on how much time and expense would be involved in duplicating so much of the lost film as was capable of duplication. This claim included travel expenses, lodging, meals, child care for his two children at home, and the overhead expense he would incur in his medical practice while he was away.

At an in-camera hearing prior to the commencement of the jury trial, the court determined that the limitation of liability clause was unconscionable at the time it was made. *See* § 672.302, Florida Statutes (1981). At the conclusion of the evidentiary portion of the trial, the court instructed the jury to disregard the loss limitation provision of the agreement in arriving at their verdict. Defendant contends that the trial court erred in permitting evidence as to plaintiff's consequential damages, and in its ruling that the limitation of liability clause was invalid as unconscionable. Because we agree that the court erred in holding the limitation of liability provision to be invalid, we need not discuss the damage issue.

Florida has adopted the Uniform Commercial Code in dealing with commercial transactions. § 672.2-302 of the Florida Statutes (1979) states:

> (1) If the court as a matter of law finds the contract or any clause of the contract to have been unconscionable at the time it was made the court may refuse to enforce the contract, or it may enforce the remainder of the contract without the unconscionable clause, or it may so limit the application of any unconscionable clause as to avoid any unconscionable result.

> (2) When it is claimed or appears to the court that the contract or any clause thereof may be unconscionable the parties shall be afforded a reasonable opportunity to present evidence as to its commercial setting, purpose and effect to aid the court in making the determination.

The code does not attempt to define "unconscionability."[11] Consequently, those courts which have dealt with the problem have often looked to the common law of their respective jurisdictions because, in most, this code provision is, in reality, a codification of the common law rules. In the seminal case of *Williams v. Walker-Thomas Furniture Company*, 350 F.2d 445 (C.A.D.C. 1965), the court was faced with a contract entered into before the adoption by Congress of the Uniform Commercial Code for the District of Columbia, but decided after its adoption. First determining that the code provision followed the common law of the District, the court discussed unconscionability in terms of its elements:

> Unconscionability has generally been recognized to include an absence of meaningful choice on the part of one of the parties together with contract terms which are unreasonably favorable to the other party. Whether a meaningful choice is present in a particular case can only be determined by consideration of all the circumstances surrounding the transaction. In many cases the meaningfulness of the choice is negated by a gross inequality of bargaining power. The manner in which the contract was entered is also relevant to this consideration. Did each party to the contract, considering his obvious education or lack of it, have a reasonable opportunity to understand the terms of the contract, or were the important terms hidden in a maze of fine print and minimized by deceptive sales practices? Ordinarily, one who signs an agreement without full knowledge of its terms might be held to assume the risk that he has entered a one-sided bargain. But when a party of little bargaining power, and hence little real choice, signs a commercially unreasonable contract with little or no knowledge of its terms, it is hardly likely that his consent, or even an

---

[11] [1] Text writers have pointed up the lack of clear definition of the term. In 15 S. Williston, A Treatise on the Law of Contracts, § 1763A (3d ed. 1972) it is referred to as "so vague, that neither the courts, practicing attorneys, nor contract draftsmen can determine with any degree of certainty . . ." when it will apply in any given situation. The same section refers to it as "an amorphous concept obviously designed to establish a broad business ethic." *See also*, Restatement (Second) of Contracts § 208 (1979). In *Steinhardt v. Rudolph*, 422 So. 2d 884, 890 (Fla. 3d D.C.A. 1982), *review denied*, 434 So. 2d 889 (Fla. 1983), the court points out that the Restatement "does not even attempt to define unconscionability in a black letter rule of law, whether in procedural-substantive terms or otherwise, because the legal concept involved here is so flexible and chameleon-like."

objective manifestation of his consent, was ever given to all the terms. In such a case the usual rule that the terms of the agreement are not to be questioned should be abandoned and the court should consider whether the terms of the contract are so unfair that enforcement should be withheld.

(Footnotes omitted). *Id.* at 449-450.

Florida has long recognized the principle that the courts are not concerned with the wisdom or folly of contracts, *Duvall v. Walton,* 107 Fla. 60, 144 So. 318 (1932), but where it is perfectly plain to the court that one party has overreached the other and has gained an unjust and undeserved advantage which it would be inequitable to permit him to enforce, a court will grant relief even though the victimized parties owe their predicament largely to their own stupidity. *Peacock Hotel, Inc. v. Shipman,* 103 Fla. 633, 138 So. 44 (1931). Decisions in Florida since the adoption of the Uniform Commercial Code appear to follow the principles espoused in the earlier cases.

In *Kohl v. Bay Colony Club Condominium, Inc.*, 398 So.2d 865 (Fla. 4th D.C.A.), *review denied,* 408 So.2d 1094 (Fla. 1981), the court reviewed the authorities on the subject and concluded that: The authorities appear to be virtually unanimous in declaring (or assuming) that two elements must coalesce before a case for unconscionability is made out. The first is referred to as substantive unconscionability and the other procedural unconscionability.

*   *   *

A case is made out for substantive unconscionability by alleging and proving that the terms of the contract are unreasonable and unfair.

*   *   *

Procedural unconscionability, on the other hand, speaks to the individualized circumstances surrounding each contracting party at the time the contract was entered into. This is thoughtfully discussed by the court in *Johnson v. Mobil Oil Corp.*, 415 F. Supp. 264, 268 (E.D. Mich. 1967): The various factors considered by the courts in deciding questions of unconscionability have been divided by the commentators into "procedural" and "substantive" categories. *See J. White & R. Summers, supra,* at 118-30. Under the "procedural" rubric come those factors bearing upon what in the *Weaver* case was called the "real and voluntary meeting of the minds" of the contracting parties: age, education, intelligence, business acumen and experience, relative bargaining power, who drafted the contract, whether the terms were explained to the weaker party, whether alterations in the printed terms were possible, whether there were alternative sources of supply for the goods in question. The "substantive" heading embraces the contractual terms themselves, and requires a determination whether they are commercially reasonable. According to *J. White & R. Summers, supra,* at 128:

> Most courts take a "balancing approach" to the unconscionability question, and to tip the scales in favor of unconscionability, most courts seem to require a certain quantum of procedural plus a certain quantum of substantive unconscionability.

Id. at 867-68. *See also, Bennett v. Behring Corp.*, 466 F. Supp. 689, 696 (S.D. Fla. 1979).

This court has approved the "procedural-substantive" analysis in determining the question of unconscionability, and has approved *Kohl*. *State v. De Anza Corporation*, 416 So.2d 1173 (Fla. 5th DCA), *review denied*, 424 So.2d 763 (Fla.1982). Although rejecting the notion that the *Kohl* analysis is a rule of law, the court in *Steinhardt v. Rudolph*, 422 So.2d 884 (Fla. 3d D.C.A. 1982), *review denied*, 434 So.2d 889 (Fla. 1983), found it "generally helpful" and applied it to the facts of that case. The *Steinhardt* court nevertheless recognized the long standing principle of law that: All of this does not mean, however, that a court will relieve a party of his obligations under a contract because he has made a bad bargain containing contractual terms which are unreasonable or impose an onerous hardship on him. Indeed, the entire law of contracts, as well as the commercial value of contractual arrangements, would be substantially undermined if parties could back out of their contractual undertakings on that basis.

> People should be entitled to contract on their own terms without the indulgence of paternalism by courts in the alleviation of one side or another from the effects of a bad bargain. Also, they should be permitted to enter into contracts that actually may be unreasonable or which may lead to hardship on one side. It is only where it turns out that one side or the other is to be penalized by the enforcement of the terms *of a contract so unconscionable that no decent, fairminded person would view the ensuing result without being possessed of a profound sense of injustice*, that equity will deny the use of its good offices in the enforcement of such unconscionability.

(Citations omitted). (Emphasis added). *Id.* at 890.

Applying the substantive prong of the test here, it cannot be said, as a matter of law, that the limitation clause here was unreasonable, when viewed in its commercial setting and when considering its purpose and effect. The charge for the processing service here was $31.00. The videocassette was priced at $18.95, and there was an additional $2.00 charge for an item not identified. There was unrebutted defense testimony that the limitation of liability provision was standard in the industry because, although loss and damage of film was relatively low in view of the tremendous volume of work done, no film processor would expose itself to liability for the unknown content of film without having to so greatly increase the cost to the public as to price the service out of the market. This is clearly a commercially reasonable consideration. As one court has aptly put it,

> To put the company . . . in that type of situation in which it rides every tiger that a person with a camera can imagine and carry out seems to be unconscionable. That is not to say that this limitation of liability is a perfect one, but it seems a fairly reasonable one. *Aetna Casualty & Surety Co. v. Eastman Kodak Co.*, District of Columbia Superior Court, 10 U.C.C. Rep. Serv. 53 (1972).

Other courts have examined similar limitation clauses in film transactions and have refused to declare these provisions unconscionable. In a commercial film transaction, the court in *Posttape Associates v. Eastman Kodak Co.*, 450 F. Supp. 407 (E.D. Pa. 1978) considered a clause similar to the one here, and commented:

> It is the "unknown or undeterminable risks" which justify the utilization of a limitation in the film industry. Not only are the risks difficult to access because of the latent nature of any film defect, but also because usually the

seller is not aware of the scope of the commercial film maker's undertaking. *Id.* at 412.

The same principle has been applied in cases where the work was non-commercial, as where an amateur photographer leaves his vacation films with a photo supply shop for processing. *Carr v. Hoosier Photo Supplies, Inc.,* 441 N.E.2d 450 (Ind. 1982).

The reasonableness of the clause is demonstrated by the huge loss claimed by Dr. Chanda, compared to the cost of the service. Without a doubt the film had peculiar value to the plaintiff. Some of it was irreplaceable and all of it was of great sentimental value, but that unknown "tiger" is the very reason for the inclusion of the limitation of liability provision in the transaction. There is no way the processor can conceive of the risk it takes in accepting film for processing absent an explicit agreement to accept such risk. When the customer is made aware of the provision for limitation of liability and nevertheless proceeds with the transaction he has assented to an agreement for which there is a commercial need, if the cost of the service is to be made reasonable.

Neither can we perceive that plaintiff satisfied the procedural prong of the test. The evidence reflects that Dr. Chanda saw and read the clause in question, asked a question about it and was apparently satisfied with the answer because he signed it. He had previously suffered the loss of film at a different place of business, and it had been replaced by new film. He was a doctor, well educated, experienced in business transactions, and well aware of what he was signing. While he was given no opportunity to negotiate the terms of this agreement, he did not attempt to determine if anyone else could provide this service. Thus the evidence falls short of showing procedural unconscionability. If, as indicated by the official comment to § 2-302 of the Uniform Commercial Code, the principle involved in the section "is one of the prevention of oppression and unfair surprise . . . and not of disturbance of allocation of risks because of superior bargaining power," no such oppression or unfair surprise is shown here.

Appellee's reliance on *Mieske v. Bartell Drug Co.,* 92 Wash. 2d 40, 593 P.2d 1308 (1979) is misplaced. Although the scenario in that case is much like the one here, there is one very salient and important distinction. In *Mieske,* the plaintiff's wife, who brought the already developed film to the drug store for splicing and placing onto larger reels, was given a receipt for the film which contained a brief limitation of liability clause. It was not called to her attention nor discussed, she was not aware of it, and she had had no prior experience with or knowledge of any custom of the trade to include such provision in film transactions. The clerk who accepted the film did not recall discussing the clause with her, nor was he even sure what it meant. The court found that:

> As to course of dealings, the record is clear that Mrs. Mieske and the Bartell manager never discussed the exclusionary clause. Mrs. Mieske had never read it, she viewed the numbered slip as merely a receipt. The manager was not "too clear on what it said." There was no showing what was the language on any other receipt given in prior dealings between the parties. In summary, defendants' proof fell short of that required by the express language of [the statute].

Id. at 1313.

It is clear from the record here that the trial court refused to consider and apply the procedural/substantive test to determine the issue of unconscionability. Neither was any other objective analysis applied, but instead, the court appeared to view the unfairness of the agreement in retrospect, because of the result. The contract should have been reviewed in the light of the circumstances that existed when it was made. The judgment for plaintiff is reversed, and the cause is remanded to the trial court with directions to enter judgment for plaintiff for the cost of 28 rolls of unexposed Super-8 movie film.

REVERSED AND REMANDED.

NOTES & QUESTIONS

1. In an effort to resolve marital problems, Robert signed a separation agreement drafted by his wife Kathleen's attorney. The agreement was fully drafted and ready to sign when Robert arrived at the meeting, unaccompanied by counsel. No discussion of the terms of the agreement took place. Under this agreement, Robert retained property valued at $1100, while Kathleen received property valued at $131,000. After learning of Kathleen's adultery, Robert sought to set aside the separation agreement on the grounds of unconscionability. How would the substantive and procedural prongs of unconscionability be analyzed? *See Williams v. Williams*, 508 A.2d 985 (Md. 1986).

2. Would the presence of an attorney with Robert when he signed the separation agreement have changed the unconscionability analysis? Why or why not? *See Resource Management Co. v. Western Ranch and Livestock, Co.*, 706 P.2d 1028 (Utah 1985) (". . . we note that numerous courts have considered the presence and advice of counsel to constitute circumstantial, if not conclusive, evidence that a contract is not unconscionable. . . .").

3. How can courts distinguish between an unconscionable contract and a contract a party voluntarily entered into that turned out to be a bad bargain? Courts generally will not intervene in a contract that is made unwisely when the parties to the contract had alternatives, some experience and adequate information about the contract. Consider the following facts and determine whether it was a bad bargain or an unconscionable contract:

Plaintiff leased a store in a shopping center from the defendant. Under the terms of the lease, plaintiff was required to pay defendant a fixed minimum annual rent, plus a percentage of the plaintiff's gross sales. Additionally, the lease terms required plaintiff to "keep the entire demised premises open for business during business hours. . ." for the entire twenty-five years of the lease's term. Unfortunately, the plaintiff's store sustained losses of $1,262,000. Plaintiff sought to have the term requiring that it remain open for the entire twenty-five years of the lease declared unconscionable. What decision should the judge reach and why? *See J.J. Newberry Co. v. Mixon*, 440 F. Supp. 20 (E.D. Mo. 1977).

CHAPTER 9

IMPACT OF EXTERNAL LAW:
ILLEGALITY AND PUBLIC POLICY

A. OVERVIEW

Like all other law, "contract law" does not exist in a void. To the contrary, public policies in other areas of law inform contract enforceability. Thus, for example, a contract to hire a hit man is unenforceable even though a bargained-for exchange may have occurred, complete with offer, acceptance and consideration. While such determinations inhibit a party's freedom to contract, and may adversely affect predictability of economic relations, they serve other vital public interests. As you read the following cases, ask yourself what other areas of law are being considered in deciding whether an enforceable contract has been formed. Is the sacrifice of potential contract predictability warranted in these cases? In what instances should the contracting parties' intentions be ignored?

B. ILLEGALITY AND ITS EXCEPTIONS

One of the grayest areas of contract law is the subject of illegality. In the abstract, the principle itself is simple — a contract that is illegal is void. Moreover, where such an illegal contract exists, the courts will leave the parties where the courts find them. But what do these propositions actually mean when applied to real cases?

As you read the next series of cases, ask yourself whether the subject matter of the contract, or one or more of its terms, is illegal. On what basis does the court decide there is illegality? Is a statute or ordinance violated? Or is public policy evidenced in some other form? If no illegality is found, is it due to the absence of an illegal purpose, or to avoid the possibly harsh consequences of an illegality ruling? Do you agree with the courts' decisions? Why or why not?

A.Z. vs. B.Z.
725 N.E.2d 1051 (Mass. 2000)

COWIN, Judge:

We transferred this case to this court on our own motion to consider for the first time the effect of a consent form between a married couple and an *in vitro* fertilization (IVF) clinic (clinic) concerning disposition of frozen preembryos. B.Z., the former wife (wife) of A.Z. (husband), appeals from a judgment of the Probate and Family Court that included, inter alia, a permanent injunction in favor of the husband, prohibiting the wife from "utilizing" the frozen preembryos held in cryopreservation at the clinic. . . . The wife appeals only from the issuance of the permanent injunction. . . [The husband and wife underwent successful IVF treatment. During such treatment more pre-embryos were formed than were necessary and two vials were frozen for possible future implantation.]

In the spring of 1995, before the couple separated, the wife desired more children and had one of the remaining vials of preembryos thawed and one preembryo was implanted. She did so without informing her husband. [Ultimately no pregnancy resulted.] The husband learned of this when he received a notice from his insurance company regarding the procedure. During this period relations between the husband and wife deteriorated. . . .

At the time of the divorce, one vial containing four frozen preembryos remained in storage at the clinic. Using one or more of these preembryos, it is possible that the wife could conceive; the likelihood of conception depends, inter alia, on the condition of the preembryos, which cannot be ascertained until the preembryos are thawed. The husband filed a motion to obtain a permanent injunction, prohibiting the wife from "using" the remaining vial of frozen preembryos.

In order to participate in fertility treatment, including . . . IVF, the clinic required egg and sperm donors (donors) to sign certain consent forms for the relevant procedures. Each time before removal of the eggs from the wife, the clinic required the husband and wife in this case to sign a preprinted consent form concerning ultimate disposition of the frozen preembryos. The wife signed a number of forms on which the husband's signature was not required. The only forms that both the husband and the wife were required to sign were those entitled "Consent Form for Freezing (Cyropreservation) of Embryos" (consent form), one of which is the form at issue here.

Each consent form explains the general nature of the IVF procedure and outlines the freezing process, including the financial cost and the potential benefits and risks of that process. The consent form also requires the donors to decide the disposition of the frozen preembryos on certain listed contingencies: "wife or donor" reaching normal menopause or age forty-five years; preembryos no longer being healthy; "one of us dying;" "should we become separated"; "should we both die." Under each contingency the consent form provides the following as options for disposition of the preembryos: "donated or destroyed — choose one or both." A blank line beneath these choices permits the donors to write in additional alternatives not listed as options on the form, and the form notifies the donors that they may do so. The consent form also informs the donors that they may change their minds as to any disposition, provided that both donors convey that fact in writing to the clinic. . . .

Every time before eggs were retrieved from the wife and combined with sperm from the husband, they each signed a consent form. The husband was present when the first form was completed by the wife in October, 1988. They both signed that consent form after it was finished. The form, as filled out by the wife, stated, inter alia, that if they "should become separated, [they] both agree[d] to have the embryo(s) . . . return[ed] to [the] wife for implant." The husband and wife thereafter underwent six additional egg retrievals for freezing and signed six additional consent forms, one each in June, 1989, and February, 1989, two forms in December, 1989, and one each in August, 1990, and August, 1991. The August, 1991, consent form governs the vial of frozen preembryos now stored at the clinic.

Each time after signing the first consent form in October, 1988, the husband always signed a blank consent form. Sometimes a consent form was signed by the husband while he and his wife were traveling to the IVF clinic; other forms were signed before the two went to the IVF clinic. Each time, after the husband signed the form, the wife filled in the disposition and other information, and then signed the form herself. All the words she wrote in the later forms were substantially similar to the words she inserted in the first October, 1988, form. In each instance the wife specified in the option for "should we become separated," that the preembryos were to be returned to the wife for implantation.

The probate judge concluded that, while donors are generally free to agree as to the ultimate disposition of frozen preembryos, the agreement at issue was unenforceable because of a "change in circumstances" occurring during the four years after the husband and wife signed the last, and governing, consent form in 1991: the birth of the twins as a result of the IVF procedure, the wife's obtaining a protective order against the husband, the husband's filing for a divorce, and the wife's then seeking "to thaw the preembryos for implantation in the hopes of having additional children." The probate judge concluded that "no agreement should be enforced in equity when intervening events have changed the circumstances such that the agreement which was originally signed did not contemplate the actual situation now facing the parties." In the absence of a binding agreement, the judge determined that the "best solution" was to balance the wife's interest in procreation against the husband's interest in avoiding procreation. Based on his findings, the judge determined that the husband's interest in avoiding procreation outweighed the wife's interest in having additional children and granted the permanent injunction in favor of the husband. . . .

This is the first reported case involving the disposition of frozen preembryos in which a consent form signed between the donors on the one hand and the clinic on the other provided that, on the donors' separation, the preembryos were to be given to one of the donors for implantation. In view of the purpose of the form (drafted by and to give assistance to the clinic) and the circumstances of execution, we are dubious at best that it represents the intent of the husband and the wife regarding disposition of the preembryos in the case of a dispute between them. In any event, for several independent reasons, we conclude that the form should not be enforced in the circumstances of this case.

First, the consent form's primary purpose is to explain to the donors the benefits and risks of freezing, and to record the donors' desires for disposition of the frozen preembryos at the time the form is executed in order to provide the clinic with guidance if the donors (as a unit) no longer wish to use the frozen preembryos. The form does not state, and the record does not indicate, that the husband and wife intended the consent form to act as a binding agreement between them should they later disagree as to the disposition. Rather, it appears that it was intended only to define the donors' relationship as a unit with the clinic.

Second, the consent form does not contain a duration provision. The wife sought to enforce this particular form four years after it was signed by the husband in significantly changed circumstances and over the husband's objection. In the absence of any evidence that the donors agreed on the time period during which the consent form was to govern their conduct, we cannot assume that the donors intended the consent form to govern the disposition of the frozen preembryos four years after it was executed, especially in light of the fundamental change in their relationship (i.e., divorce).

Third, the form uses the term "should we become separated" in referring to the disposition of the frozen preembryos without defining "become separated." Because this dispute arose in the context of a divorce, we cannot conclude that the consent form was intended to govern in these circumstances. Separation and divorce have distinct legal meanings. Legal changes occur by operation of law when a couple divorces that do not occur when a couple separates. Because divorce legally ends a couple's marriage, we shall not assume, in the absence of any evidence to the contrary, that an agreement on this issue providing for separation was meant to govern in the event of a divorce.

The donors' conduct in connection with the execution of the consent forms also creates doubt whether the consent form at issue here represents the clear intentions of both donors. . . . [A]lthough the wife used language in each subsequent form similar to the language used in the first form that she and her husband signed together, the consent form at issue here was signed in blank by the husband, before the wife filled in the language indicating that she would use the preembryos for implantation on separation. We therefore cannot conclude that the consent form represents the true intention of the husband for the disposition of the preembryos.

Finally, the consent form is not a separation agreement that is binding on the couple in a divorce proceeding . . . The consent form does not contain provisions for custody, support, and maintenance, in the event that the wife conceives and gives birth to a child. . . .

With this said, we conclude that, even had the husband and the wife entered into an unambiguous agreement between themselves regarding the disposition of the frozen preembryos, we would not enforce an agreement that would compel one donor to become a parent against his or her will. As a matter of public policy, we conclude that forced procreation is not an area amenable to judicial enforcement. . . .While courts are hesitant to invalidate contracts on these public policy grounds, the public interest in freedom of contract is sometimes outweighed by other public policy considerations. . . . To determine public policy, we look to the expressions of the Legislature and to those of this court. *Capazzoli v. Holzwasser*, 397 Mass. 158, 160, 490 N.E.2d 420 (1986).

The Legislature has already determined by statute that individuals should not be bound by certain agreements binding them to enter or not enter into familial relationships. In G.L. c. 207, § 47A, the Legislature abolished the cause of action for the breach of a promise to marry. In G.L. c. 210, § 2, the Legislature provided that no mother may agree to surrender her child "sooner than the fourth calendar day after the date of birth of the child to be adopted" regardless of any prior agreement.

Similarly, this court has expressed its hesitancy to become involved in intimate questions inherent in the marriage relationship. *Doe v. Doe* 365 Mass. 556, 563, 314 N.E.2d 128 (1974). "Except in cases involving divorce or separation, our law has not in general undertaken to resolve the many delicate questions inherent in the marriage relationship. We would not order either a husband or a wife to do what is necessary to conceive a child or to prevent conception, any more than we would order either party to do what is necessary to make the other happy." *Id.*

In our decisions, we have also indicated a reluctance to enforce prior agreements that bind individuals to future family relationships. [n25] In *R.R. v.*

M.H., 426 Mass. 501, 689 N.E.2d 790 (1998), we held that a surrogacy agreement in which the surrogate mother agreed to give up the child on its birth is unenforceable unless the agreement contained, inter alia, a "reasonable" waiting period during which the mother could change her mind. *Id.* at 510. In *Capazzoli v. Holzwasser, supra*, we determined, as an expression of public policy, that a contract requiring an individual to abandon a marriage is unenforceable. And, in the same spirit, we stated in *Gleason v. Mann*, 312 Mass. 420, 425, 45 N.E.2d 280 (1942), that agreements providing for a general restraint against marriage are unenforceable.

We glean from these statutes and judicial decisions that prior agreements to enter into familial relationships (marriage or parenthood) should not be enforced against individuals who subsequently reconsider their decisions. This enhances the "freedom of personal choice in matters of marriage and family life." *Moore v. East Cleveland*, 431 U.S. 494, 499, 97 S. Ct. 1932, 52 L. Ed. 2d 531 (1977), quoting *Cleveland Bd. of Educ. v. LaFleur*, 414 U.S. 632, 639–640, 94 S. Ct. 791, 39 L. Ed. 2d 52 (1974).

We derive from existing State laws and judicial precedent a public policy in this Commonwealth that individuals shall not be compelled to enter into intimate family relationships, and that the law shall not be used as a mechanism for forcing such relationships when they are not desired. This policy is grounded in the notion that respect for liberty and privacy requires that individuals be accorded the freedom to decide whether to enter into a family relationship. *See Commonwealth v. Stowell*, 389 Mass. 171, 173, 449 N.E.2d 357 (1983). "There are 'personal rights of such delicate and intimate character that direct enforcement of them by any process of the court should never be attempted.' " *Doe v. Doe, supra* at 559, quoting *Kenyon v. Chicopee*, 320 Mass. 528, 534, 70 N.E.2d 241 (1946).

In this case, we are asked to decide whether the law of the Commonwealth may compel an individual to become a parent over his or her contemporaneous objection. The husband signed this consent form in 1991. Enforcing the form against him would require him to becoe a parent over his present objection to such an undertaking. We decline to do so.

NOTES & QUESTIONS

1. Did the court find the consent to implantation agreement illegal or merely unenforceable?

2. What are the competing public policies that the court is balancing in this case?

3. Assume extrinsic evidence demonstrates clearly that the parties contemplated the wife would be allowed to implant the embryos in the event of a divorce and that the husband would have no obligation of support for any resulting offspring. Would the contract still be against public policy? *See Kass v. Kass*, 91 N.Y.2d 554 (N.Y. Ct. App. 1998).

4. *Practice Points:* Procreation agreements, whether involving surrogacy, or in vitro fertilization, remain highly contested, even when such agreements are in writing. Family law-based agreements invoke serious public policy implications and should address changed circumstances in clear, concise terms. Although reluctance to put oral promises in writing in these situations largely stems from fear that the other party will think his or her honesty is being questioned,

sometimes this issue can be avoided if the agreement is contained in a less formal document, such as a letter agreement signed by both parties.

McCONNELL v. COMMONWEALTH PICTURES CORPORATION
7 N.Y.2d 465, 166 N.E.2d 494 (1960)

DESMOND, Chief Judge:

. . . Plaintiff sues for an accounting. Defendant had agreed in writing that, if plaintiff should succeed in negotiating a contract with a motion-picture producer whereby defendant would get the distribution rights for certain motion pictures, defendant would pay plaintiff $10,000 on execution of the contract between defendant and the producer, and would thereafter pay plaintiff a stated percentage of defendant's gross receipts from distribution of the pictures. Plaintiff negotiated the distribution rights for defendant and defendant paid plaintiff the promised $10,000 but later refused to pay him the commissions or to give him an accounting of profits.

Defendant's answer contains, besides certain denials and counterclaims not now before us, two affirmative defenses the sufficiency of which we must decide. In these defenses it is asserted that plaintiff, without the knowledge of defendant or of the producer, procured the distribution rights by bribing a representative of the producer and that plaintiff agreed to pay and did pay to that representative as a bribe the $10,000 which defendant paid plaintiff. The courts below (despite a strong dissent in the Appellate Division) held that the defenses were insufficient to defeat plaintiff's suit. Special Term's opinion said that, since the agreement sued upon between plaintiff and defendant was not in itself illegal, plaintiff's right to be paid for performing it could not be defeated by a showing that he had misconducted himself in carrying it out. The court found a substantial difference between this and the performance of an illegal contract. We take a different view. Proper and consistent application of a prime and long-settled public policy closes the doors of our courts to those who sue to collect the rewards of corruption.

New York's policy has been frequently and emphatically announced in the decisions. "It is the settled law of this State (and probably of every other State) that a party to an illegal contract cannot ask a court of law to help him carry out his illegal object, nor can such a person plead or prove in any court a case in which he, as a basis for his claim, must show forth his illegal purpose", *Stone v. Freeman*, 298 N.Y. 268, 27 1, 82 N.E.2d 571, 572, 8 A.L.R.2d 304, citing the leading cases. The money plaintiff sues for was the fruit of an admitted crime and "(no court should be required to serve as paymaster of the wages of crime". *Stone v. Freeman, supra*, 298 N.Y. at page 271, 82 N.E.2d at page 572. And it makes no difference that defendant has no title to the money since the court's concern "is not with the position of the defendant" but with the question of whether "a recovery by the plaintiff should be denied for the sake of public interests", a question which is one "of public policy in the administration of the law". *Flegenheimer v. Brogan*, 284 N.Y. 268, 272, 30 N.E.2d 591, 592, 132 A.L.R. 613. That public policy is the one described in *Riggs v. Palmer*, 115 N.Y. 506, 511–512, 22 N.E. 188, 190, 5 A.L.R. 340: "No one shall be permitted to profit by his own fraud, or to take advantage of his own wrong, or to found any claim upon his own iniquity, or to acquire property by his own crime. These maxims are dictated by public policy, have their foundation in universal law administered in all civilized countries, and have nowhere been superseded by statutes" (*Carr v. Hoy*, 2 N.Y.2d 185, 187, 158 N.Y.S.2d 572, 574–575).

We must either repudiate those statements of public policy or uphold these challenged defenses. It is true that some of the leading decisions . . . were in suits on intrinsically illegal contracts but the rule fails of its purpose unless it covers a case like the one at bar. Here, as in *Stone v. Freeman* and *Carr v. Hoy* (*supra*), the money sued for was (assuming the truth of the defenses) "the fruit of an admitted crime". To allow this plaintiff to collect his commissions would be to let him "profit by his own fraud, or to take advantage of his own wrong, or to found (a) claim upon his own iniquity, or to acquire property by his own crime" (*Riggs v. Palmer*, 115 N.Y. 506, 511, 22 N.E. 188, 190, 5 A.L.R. 340). The issue is not whether the acts alleged in the defenses would constitute the crime of commercial bribery under section 439 of the Penal Law, Consol.Laws, c. 40, although it appears that they would. "A seller cannot recover the price of goods sold where he has paid a commission to an agent of the purchaser (*Sirkin v. Fourteenth Street Store*, 124 App. Div. 384, 108 N.Y.S. 830); neither could the agent recover the commission, even at common law and before the enactment of section 384-r of the Penal Law (now section 439)" (Judge Crane in *Reiner v. North American Newspaper Alliance*, 259 N.Y. 250, 261, 181 N.E. 561, 565, 83 A.L.R. 23). . . .

We are not working here with narrow questions of technical law. We are applying fundamental concepts of morality and fair dealing not to be weakened by exceptions. So far as precedent is necessary, we can rely on *Sirkin v. Fourteenth Street Store*, 124 App. Div. 384, 108 N.Y.S. 830, *supra*. . . . *Sirkin* is the case closest to ours and shows that, whatever be the law in other jurisdictions, we in New York deny awards for the corrupt performance of contracts even though in essence the contracts are not illegal. Sirkin had sued for the price of goods sold and delivered to defendant. Held to be good was a defense which charged that plaintiff seller had paid a secret commission to an agent of defendant purchaser. There cannot be any difference in principle between that situation and the present one where plaintiff (it is alleged) contracted to buy motion-picture rights for defendant but performed his covenant only by bribing the seller's agent. . . .

It is argued that a reversal here means that the doing of any small illegality in the performance of an otherwise lawful contract will deprive the doer of all rights, with the result that the other party will get a windfall and there will be great injustice. Our ruling does not go as far as that. It is not every minor wrongdoing in the course of contract performance that will insulate the other party from liability for work done or goods furnished. There must at least be a direct connection between the illegal transaction and the obligation sued upon. Connection is a matter of degree. Some illegalities are merely incidental to the contract sued on. . . . We cannot now, any more than in our past decisions, announce what will be the results of all the kinds of corruption, minor and major, essential and peripheral. All we are doing here is labeling the conduct described in these defenses as gross corruption depriving plaintiff of all right of access to the courts of New York State. Consistent with public morality and settled public policy, we hold that a party will be denied recovery even on a contract valid on its face, if it appears that he has resorted to gravely immoral and illegal conduct in accomplishing its performance.

Perhaps this application of the principle represents a distinct step beyond *Sirkin* and *Reiner* (*supra*) in the sense that we are here barring recovery under a contract which in itself is entirely legal. But if this be an extension, public policy supports it. We point out that our holding is limited to cases in which the illegal performance of a contract originally valid takes the form of commercial bribery or similar conduct and in which the illegality is central to or a dominant part of the plaintiff's whole course of conduct in performance of the contract. . . .

FROESSEL, Judge (dissenting):

Plaintiff sues for an accounting and related relief under a clearly lawful contract, whereby defendant agreed to make certain payments in connection with plaintiff's negotiation, on behalf of defendant, of an agreement with Universal Pictures Company, Inc., for distribution rights with respect to 40 western feature films and 4 serial motion pictures. The payments agreed upon were $10,000 upon the execution of a contract with Universal, and 20% of all the gross receipts received by defendant from the distribution of said pictures after defendant had recouped the amount of $100,000 from 60% of the gross receipts. Upon negotiation of the distribution rights, defendant paid plaintiff said sum of $10,000, but thereafter declined upon demand to pay plaintiff any further moneys.

Two defenses set forth in the answer were stricken below. The first defense alleged that plaintiff secured the Universal contract as a result of influencing an agent of Universal and United World Films, Inc., to cause United to execute the contract with defendant, for which he paid the agent $10,000, in claimed violation of § 439 of the Penal Law. The second defense reiterated the allegations of the first, and alleged that the enforcement of the contract would be contrary to public policy. These allegations are denied, except of course as they are deemed admitted as a matter of law by challenging their legal sufficiency. It is to be noted that defendant does not charge that its own agent was bribed or that its contract with plaintiff contemplates any illegal act. Moreover, neither the answer nor the affidavit in opposition suggests that Universal or United has in anywise questioned the distribution contract or that defendant has not enjoyed the full fruits thereof.

The narrow question before us as framed by Special Term is "whether the unlawful acts imputed to the plaintiff in performance are fatal to recovery under a lawful contract." We agree with the courts below "that recovery for services under a valid agreement may be had, notwithstanding that the plaintiff has in the course of their rendition committed illegal acts." This was implicit in our holding in *Chesebrough v. Conover*, 140 N.Y. 382, 35 N.E. 633, and it was so squarely held in *Dunham v. Hastings Pavement Co.*, 56 App. Div. 244, at pages 251, 252, 67 N.Y.S. 632, at page 637, where the court correctly stated the applicable rule of law as follows: "If the contract contemplated legal service, and that alone, we do not think that it would be rendered illegal by the fact that the plaintiff did illegal acts in its performance. The question is and continues, was the contract in fact for the performance of illegal service? If it was not, then it is valid and can be enforced." . . .

This is not a case where the contract sued upon is intrinsically illegal (cf. *Stone v. Freeman*, 298 N.Y. 268, 82 N.E.2d 571, 8 A.L.R.2d 304; *Reiner v. North American Newspaper Alliance*, 259 N.Y. 250, 181 N.E. 561, 83 A.L.R. 23); or was procured by the commission of a crime (*Sirkin v. Fourteenth Street Store*, 124 App. Div. 384, 108 N.Y.S. 830); or where a beneficiary under a will murdered his ancestor in order to obtain the speedy enjoyment of his property) *Riggs v. Palmer*, 115 N.Y. 506, 22 N.E. 188,5 A.L.R. 340). In the *Sirkin* case, so heavily relied upon by the majority, the plaintiff obtained the very contract he was seeking to enforce by paying secret commissions to defendant's own purchasing agent. In *Merchants' Line v. Baltimore & Ohio R. Co.*, 222 N.Y. 344, 347, 118 N.E. 788, we pointed out that in *Sirkin* "the plaintiff reached and bribed the man who made *the contract under which he was seeking to recover*" (emphasis supplied). In *Morgan Munitions Supply Co. v. Studebaker Corp.*, 226 N.Y. 94,99, 123 N.E. 146, 147, we likewise cited the *Sirkin* case for the proposition that "a contract *procured by* the commission of a crime is unenforceable even if executed" (emphasis supplied).

In the instant case, the contract which plaintiff is seeking to enforce is perfectly valid, and it was not intended or even contemplated that plaintiff would perform the contract by illegal or corrupt means. Having received and retained the full benefits of plaintiff's performance, defendant now seeks to "inject into" its contract with plaintiff, "which was fair and legal in itself, the illegal feature of the other independent transaction." *Messersmith v. American Fidelity Co.*, 187 App. Div. 35, 37, 175 N.Y.S. 169, 170, *affirmed* 232 N.Y. 161, 133 N.E. 432, 19 A.L.R. 876. This court is now adopting a rule that a party may retain the benefits of, but escape his obligations under, a wholly lawful contract if the other party commits some illegal act not contemplated nor necessary under the contract. By way of a single illustration, an owner may thus avoid paying his contractor for the cost of erecting a building because the contractor gave an inspector a sum of money to expedite an inspection.

The majority opinion seeks to distinguish between "major" and "minor" illegality and "direct" and "peripheral" corruption. It decides this case on the ground that the manner in which plaintiff performed his admittedly valid contract with defendant was "gravely immoral and illegal." Such distinctions are neither workable nor sanctioned by authority. If a contract was lawfully made, and did not contemplate wrongdoing, it is enforcible; if, on the other hand, it was procured by the commission of a crime, or was in fact for the performance of illegal services, it is not enforcible. These are the criteria distinguishing enforcible from unenforcible contracts — not "nice" distinctions between degrees of illegality and immorality in the performance of lawful contracts, or whether the illegal act of performance was "directly" or "peripherally" related to the main contract.

Moreover, a reversal here would be contrary to the spirit, if not the letter, of our holding in *Southwestern Shipping Corp. v. National City Bank*, 6 N.Y.2d 454, 190 N.Y.S.2d 352. The broad proposition for which that case stands is that a party unconnected with an illegal agreement should not be permitted to reap a windfall by pleading the illegality of that agreement, to which he was a stranger. There, the contract between the plaintiff and the bank was entirely lawful, and the bank attempted to avoid the consequences of its breach of contract and negligence by asserting the illegality of a different contract between plaintiff and a third party. Here, the contract between plaintiff and defendant was perfectly legal, and defendant is seeking to avoid its obligations under the contract of which it has reaped the benefits for some 12 years by asserting the illegality of a different and subsequent agreement between plaintiff and a third party. This it should not be permitted to do. . . .

Van Voorhis, Judge (dissenting):

Public morals and fair dealing are likely to be advanced by limiting rather than by enlarging the rule that is being extended to the facts of this case. This rule is grounded on considerations of public policy. Courts will not intervene between thieves to compel them to divide the spoils. But in a situation like the present, it seems to me that the effect of this decision will not be to restrain the corrupt influencing of agents, employees or servants but to encourage misappropriation of funds and breaches of faith between persons who do not stand in corrupt relationships with one another. The public interest is not served best by decisions which put a premium on taking unconscionable advantage of such situations, or which drive the enforcement of obligations of this kind underground. I concur in the dissenting opinion by Judge FROESSEL.

NOTES & QUESTIONS

1. On what basis did the court determine that plaintiff's bribery was "central to or a dominant part of [his] whole course of conduct in performance of the contract"?

2. Would the result in *McConnell* have changed if the defendant had been aware of plaintiff's intended bribery before signing the agreement?

3. How would you respond to the criticism raised by the dissent? Do you agree with them?

GODLEY v. THE UNITED STATES
5 F.3d 1473 (Fed. Cir. 1993)

RADER, Circuit Judge:

William C. Godley sued the United States Postal Service in the United States Court of Federal Claims for breach of contract. . . .

Mr. Godley owned an interest in a tract of land in Mecklenburg County, North Carolina. When the Postal Service advertised its need for a postal facility, Mr. Godley offered to build one on his land. Mr. Godley made this offer to Charles D. Paramore, the Postal Service agent responsible for this project. Mr. Godley offered to build a postal facility and to provide a ten-year lease with an option to buy after the first year. The Postal Service accepted Mr. Godley's offer in February 1989.

On September 5, 1989, Mr. Paramore was indicted for conspiracy and bribery. The charges stemmed from his involvement with Postal Service projects. On November 22, 1989, Mr. Paramore pled guilty to several counts of conspiracy and bribery. *United States v. Paramore*, No. 91-6630, 1992 U.S. App. LEXIS 13606 (4th Cir. June 10, 1992). The bribery and conspiracy charges involved a subcontractor, not Mr. Godley. Mr. Godley allegedly lacked any knowledge of the illegal activities.

In October 1989, the facility was complete and the Postal Service took possession. Mr. Godley and the Postal Service entered a final lease agreement on December 5, 1989. On March 27, 1990, however, the Postal Service informed Mr. Godley that the contract was not valid because it was tainted by Mr. Paramore's illegal conduct. The Postal Service offered instead to renegotiate. The Postal Service stopped paying the lease amount in the contract.

On May 17, 1990, Mr. Godley filed claims against the Postal Service under the Contract Disputes Act of 1978, 41 U.S.C. §§ 601-613 (1988). Mr. Godley claimed that the Postal Service breached the contract. As damages, Mr. Godley sought the payments required by the original lease. In addition, Mr. Godley sought compensation for changes in the contract. On June 21, 1990, the Postal Service began paying a reduced lease rate. In November 1990, the contracting officer for the Postal Service denied Mr. Godley's claims.

In the Court of Federal Claims, Mr. Godley claimed that the contract was valid and sought to enforce the lease. The Postal Service answered that the contract was void ab initio due to the alleged taint from Mr. Paramore's illegal actions and alleged fraud on the part of Mr. Godley. . . .

In general, a Government contract tainted by fraud or wrongdoing is void ab initio. *J.E.T.S., Inc. v. United States*, 838 F.2d 1196, 1200 (Fed. Cir.), *cert. denied* 486 U.S. 1057 (1988). This general rule protects the integrity of the federal contracting process and safeguards the public from undetectable threats to the public fisc. *United States v. Mississippi Valley Generating Co.*, 364 U.S. 520, 565, 81 S. Ct. 294, 5 L. Ed. 2d 268 (1961). The Supreme Court explained:

> It is this inherent difficulty in detecting corruption which requires that contracts made in violation of [a conflict of interest statute] be held unenforceable, even though the party seeking enforcement ostensibly appears entirely innocent.

Id.

In Mississippi Valley, the contract sought construction and operation of a steam power plant near Memphis, Tennessee, to take pressure off the Tennessee Valley Authority. Mr. Adophe H. Wenzell acted as a Government agent to negotiate the contract. Mr. Wenzell was also Vice President and Director of First Boston Corporation, the financial institution eventually chosen to finance the project. Although First Boston declined to accept a fee for the project, the Court held that Mr. Wenzell's conflict of interest rendered the contract unenforceable:

> The negotiations in which [Wenzell] participated were the very foundation upon which the final contract was based . . . . If the [Mississippi Valley Generating Company] and the Government had not agreed on the cost of construction and on the cost of money, no contract would have been made.

Id. at 553.

As the Court explicitly stated, in Mississippi Valley the taint of illegality clearly infected the contract itself. Moreover, the contractor was not innocent of the fraud. The Court noted that the Mississippi Valley Generating Company "recognized Wenzell's conflict of interest almost from the outset of the negotiations." *Id.* at 565, n.19. Nonetheless the company took no action to diffuse the conflict. *Id.*

Thus, Mississippi Valley does not present a situation where a completely innocent contractor entered a contract with the Government which, despite illegal conduct by a Government agent associated with the contract, was nonetheless wholly untainted by fraud. Rather, in Mississippi Valley, the contractor, with knowledge, implicitly condoned the illegal conflict of interest. Moreover the illegality permeated the contract. Without Mr. Wenzell's illegal participation, the Court noted, "no contract would have been made." *Mississippi Valley*, 364 U.S. at 553.

Thus, as stated above, the general rule is that a Government contract tainted by fraud or wrongdoing is void ab initio. *J.E.T.S.*, 838 F.2d at 1200; *Mississippi Valley*, 364 U.S. at 564. A contract without the taint of fraud or wrongdoing, however, does not fall within this rule. Illegal acts by a Government contracting agent do not alone taint a contract and invoke the void ab initio rule. Rather, the record must show some causal link between the illegality and the contract provisions. Determining whether illegality taints a contract involves questions of fact.

On this record, this court cannot determine whether Mr. Paramore's illegal conduct tainted the contract. Specifically, this court cannot on this record determine whether Mr. Paramore's illegal conduct caused any unfavorable contract terms. Moreover, the existence of genuine and material factual disputes and inferences in favor of the Postal Service precludes summary judgment in favor of Mr. Godley. . .

Consistent with this opinion, this court vacates the decision of the Court of Federal Claims and remands for determination of material issues of disputed fact.

NOTES & QUESTIONS

1. Assume that on remand evidence indicates that Godley was unaware of Paramore's fraud but indirectly benefited through lower fees for sub-contractors under the agreement. Should the government be able to avoid enforcement of the contract on the grounds of illegality?

2. In the *Godley* case, it is the party allegedly involved in the illegal conduct which seeks to use its own illegality to avoid enforcement. What limits, if any, did the court place on the offensive use of an illegality defense? What limits, if any, should there be?

HOMAMI v. IRANZADI
211 Cal. App. 3d 1104, 160 Cal. Rptr. 6 (1989)

BRAUER, Associate Justice:

Ahmad Homami sued Mansoor Iranzadi to collect the balance due on a promissory note. Iranzadi claimed he had paid down the principal balance by approximately $40,000. Homami acknowledged receiving that amount but claimed the payments represented interest only. The note expressly provided: "This note shall bear no interest." But Homami testified at trial that the parties nonetheless had an oral agreement for the payment of 12 percent interest per annum. According to Homami the no interest provision on the note was only so that he could avoid reporting the income for state and federal income tax purposes.

The trial court granted judgment in favor of Homami. . . .

Homami and Iranzadi were brothers-in-law. At the time of this transaction, they had been involved in various business dealings together both in Iran and in the United States.

On January 9, 1984, Homami wrote a check for $250,000 to California Land Title in order to fund a real estate transaction on behalf of Iranzadi. . . .

On March 18, 1985, Homami and Iranzadi signed a document entitled "Modification Agreement" for each of the promissory notes. The modification agreements were identical except for their reference to the respective notes and deeds of trust. Each provided for the following modification of terms:

1. The note shall be all due and payable on or before September 22, 1985.

2. The note shall bear no interest until June 22, 1985.

3. On June 22, 1985, interest shall commence at the rate of eighteen percent per annum; said interest shall be payable monthly commencing on July 22, 1985 and continue monthly thereafter until the maturity date expressed herein. . . .

At trial Homami testified that he and Iranzadi had orally agreed on an interest rate of 12 percent, and had also agreed that Iranzadi would not report interest paid and Homami would not have to report receiving the income. He testified that this arrangement was discussed and reiterated at a family meeting March 15, 1985. And he specifically stated that the reason the loan documents did not reflect any interest was so that he could avoid reporting income to the IRS.

Iranzadi, on the other hand, claimed that he and Homami had never discussed interest on the loan. He testified that in family dealings interest was never charged and that he had often loaned money to Homami without interest. . . .

The trial court found that the payments made by Iranzadi to Homami totalling $39,324.68 represented interest only, and no principal reduction. Therefore Iranzadi still owed Homami that amount on the loan. The court rendered judgment in favor of Homami for $39,324.68 plus interest at 18 percent from June 30, 1986, the close of escrow, plus attorneys fees and costs. . . .

The Civil Code provides a starting place. A contract must have a lawful object. (Civ. Code, § 1550.) Any contract which has as its object the violation of an express provision of law is unlawful. (Civ. Code, § 1667, subd. (1).) The object of a contract is the thing which it is agreed, on the part of the party receiving the consideration, to do or not to do. (Civ. Code, § 1595.) The object must be lawful when the contract is made. (Civ. Code, § 1596.) And that part of the contract which is unlawful is void. (Civ. Code, § 1599.)

Courts have interpreted these statutes liberally. "The general principle is well established that a contract founded on an illegal consideration, or which is made for the purpose of furthering any matter or thing prohibited by statute, or to aid or assist any party therein, is void. This rule applies to every contract which is founded on a transaction malum in se, or which is prohibited by a statute on the ground of public policy." (*C.I.T. Corp. v. Breckenridge* (1944) 63 Cal. App. 2d 198, 200, 146 P.2d 271.)

It makes no difference whether the contract has been partially or wholly performed. Rather, the test is "whether the plaintiff requires the aid of the illegal transaction to establish his case. If the plaintiff cannot open his case without showing that he has broken the law, the court will not assist him, whatever his claim in justice may be upon the defendant." (*C.I.T. Corp. v. Breckenridge, supra*, 63 Cal. App. 2d 198, 200, 146 P.2d 271.)

Nor does it matter that the illegality has not been pleaded. "[I]f the question of illegality develops during the course of a trial, a court must consider it whether pleaded or not. . . . 'Whenever the evidence discloses the relations of the parties to the transaction to be illegal and against public policy, it becomes the duty of the court to refuse to entertain the action.' " (*Russell v. Soldinger* (1976) 59 Cal. App. 3d 633, 642, 131 Cal. Rptr. 145.)

Cases which have applied these principles fall into several broad categories. A common situation involves the unlicensed contractor, or other unlicensed professional, who seeks to collect money for services rendered. Courts have routinely refused to grant relief in such cases on the ground that the failure to comply with licensing requirements violates a law designed to protect and benefit the public. Therefore a party who has violated the law and entered into an agreement to perform services while unlicensed cannot obtain the aid of courts to enforce the agreement. (*Loving & Evans v. Blick* (1949) 33 Cal. 2d 603, 607, 204 P.2d 23. . . .)

In another factual context, courts have refused to grant relief to parties seeking to collect monies arising from illegal gambling activities. (*Lee On v. Long* (1951) 37 Cal. 2d 499, 234 P.2d 9. . . .)

A third group of cases closer to our facts involves plaintiffs who have attempted to circumvent federal law. Generally these cases arise where nonveterans seek to obtain government benefits and entitlements available to veterans only, either by setting up a strawman veteran or otherwise by falsifying documents.

For example, in *May v. Herron* (1954) 127 Cal. App. 2d 707, 274 P.2d 484, the Newmans transferred property to a veteran for the sole purpose of obtaining a Veteran's Priority under Federal Priorities Regulation No. 33. That regulation provided that veterans who wished to build houses for their own occupancy would receive preferential treatment in obtaining construction materials. The Newmans had been advised to obtain the illegal veteran's priority by their building contractor, who then entered into a contract with the veteran to build a house which he knew the Newmans intended to occupy. When the builder sued to recover a balance due on the construction contract, the court refused to come to his aid, finding that he had "initiated, suggested and directed a conspiracy to violate and circumvent a federal regulation which had the force of law." . . . The court concluded in this vein: "To permit a recovery here on any theory would permit plaintiff to benefit from his willful and deliberate flouting of a law designed to promote the general public welfare." . . .

We do not perceive any meaningful difference between the unlawful agreements described in the above example[] and the tax evasion scheme perpetrated by Homami and Iranzadi in our case. Here Homami entered into a written agreement which specifically provided that he would be paid no interest. The purpose of the provision was to enable him to avoid compliance with state and federal income tax regulations. He then secretly collected interest income which he had no intention of reporting. And when a dispute developed, he sought the aid of the court to enforce the secret agreement so that he could keep the money he had collected.

Homami has taken the position that he was not seeking enforcement of the side agreement to pay 12 percent interest; rather he was simply suing to collect the principal balance due on the promissory note plus interest at 18 percent as per the written modification agreement. He points out that neither the promissory notes nor the modification agreements are facially illegal. And he claims that the issue of the $39,324.68 paid was first raised as a defense and was not necessary to pleading or proving his case on the written documents.

First, even though a written contract is legal on its face, evidence may be introduced to establish its illegal character. (*May v. Herron, supra,* 127 Cal. App. 2d 707, 710–771, 274 P.2d 484.) And if the substance of the transaction is illegal, it matters not when or how the illegality is raised in the course of the lawsuit. Whether the evidence comes from one side or the other, the disclosure is fatal to the case. . . . The fact is that Homami, in order to state his claim to the funds held out of the escrow proceeds, was obliged to testify and did testify that he collected interest secretly in order to circumvent income tax laws. As the cases have repeatedly pointed out, "the test . . . is whether the plaintiff can establish his case otherwise than through the medium of an illegal transaction to which he himself was a party." (*Schur v. Johnson* (1934) 2 Cal. App. 2d 680, 683–684, 38 P.2d 844.) It is clear that Homami could not do so.

Finally Homami points out that the parties are in pari delicto; therefore, he argues, Iranzadi should not be allowed to reap an unexpected benefit from the transaction. His complaint is a familiar cry of plaintiffs who find that they have been wronged by their companions in illegal ventures. . . . Such a plea is always unavailing for this reason: the rule that courts will not enforce illegal agreements is not applied in order to correct injustice between the parties, "but from regard for a higher interest — that of the public, whose welfare demands that certain transactions be discouraged." (*Haruko Takeuchi v. Schmuck* (1929) 206 Cal. 782, 786–787, 276 P. 345.) Even though a defendant may be left in possession of some benefit he should in good conscience turn over to plaintiff, that consideration is outweighed by the importance of deterring illegal conduct. "Knowing that they will receive no help from the courts and must trust completely to each other's good faith, the parties are less likely to enter an illegal arrangement in the first place." (*Harrison v. Butte Steel Buildings, Inc., supra,* 150 Cal. App. 2d 296, 301, 310 P.2d 126.)

Because his agreement violated the law, Homami is not entitled to the $39,624.86 he collected as unreported interest. That amount is to be credited to Iranzadi from the escrow proceeds. Distribution of the balance of the funds held in the trust account is to be determined by the court on remand. Judgment in favor of plaintiff Homami is reversed and the matter is remanded to the trial court for further proceedings. . . .

NOTES & QUESTIONS

1. What is the holding in this case? The contract seems to have been illegal and void, but the court will assess the interests of the parties and attempt to settle on a fair financial accounting between them. Does this make sound legal policy?

2. If only one party had the illegal tax scheme as his purpose but the other did not, should the contract be considered illegal in its entirety or should only the interest provisions be illegal? Which decision meets the public policy concerns of reducing fraud and other illegal conduct? Should the court's decision have been different? Why or why not?

GATES v. RIVERS CONSTRUCTION CO., INC.
515 P.2d 1020 (Alaska 1973)

BOOCHEVER, Justice:

A contract of employment was entered into in Alaska by a Canadian alien. The trial court held it to be in violation of the immigration and nationality laws of the United States, and held that the alien was barred by the illegality of the contract from securing recovery of sums allegedly due. This appeal has been taken from that decision.

In late February or early March of 1969, John G. Gates traveled from his home in Alberta, Canada, to Fairbanks, Alaska. His expenses were paid by Guy Rivers, acting on behalf of Rivers Construction Co. and General Construction Co., Inc. Gates entered into discussions with Rivers and, as a result, agreed to engage in public relations work in order to obtain construction contracts for the two companies. The work was to be performed in Alaska, and Gates was to receive a salary of $1,400 or $1,600 per month, commencing immediately; the funds were to be placed in trust for him in a bank in Alaska and were to be paid to him when, and only when, he obtained a visa to remain in the United States as a landed alien or permanent resident. The arrangement to withhold his salary was made for the reason that both Gates and Rivers believed that Gates could not lawfully remain in Alaska and perform services for a salary without first having received certification of permanent resident status.

Gates' employment was terminated by the companies on December 4, 1970. He became a landed alien or "permanent resident" on December 11, 1970. In February of 1971 he filed suit against the two corporations alleging that no payment of the salary which was to have been held in trust for him had been made. The companies answered admitting that services were performed and denying other allegations of the complaint.

At the conclusion of appellant's case in the court below, the companies moved to dismiss on the grounds that the contract of employment was in violation of the immigration laws. § 1182(a)(14) of 8 United States Code provides in part:

(a) Except as otherwise provided in this chapter, the following classes of aliens shall be ineligible to receive visas and shall be excluded from admission into the United States:

*   *   *

(14) Aliens seeking to enter the United States, for the purpose of performing skilled or unskilled labor, unless the Secretary of Labor has determined and certified to the Secretary of State and to the Attorney General that (A) there are not sufficient workers in the United States who are able, willing, qualified, and available at the time of application for a visa and admission to the United States and at the place to which the alien is destined to perform such skilled or unskilled labor, and (B) the employment of such aliens will not adversely affect the wages and working conditions of the workers in the United States similarly employed. . . .

The court granted the motion to dismiss, concluding that the contract of employment was "in violation of law, and as such, is a contract contrary to public policy, is void, and is unenforceable." . . .

Generally, a party to an illegal contract cannot recover damages for its breach. But as in the case of many such simplifications, the exceptions and qualifications to the general rule are numerous and complex. Thus, when a statute imposes sanctions but does not specifically declare a contract to be invalid, it is necessary to ascertain whether the legislature intended to make unenforceable contracts entered into in violation of the statute.

> Among the factors taken into consideration by the courts are the language of the statute; its nature, object, and purpose; and its subject matter and reach; the wrong or evil which the statute seeks to remedy or prevent; the nature of the prohibited act as malum in se or malum prohibitum; the class of persons sought to be controlled; the legislative history; the effect of holding contracts in violation of the statute void; and the later repeal of the statute by a new act which specifically provides that a contract in contravention thereof should be void. If, from all these factors, it is manifest that the statute was not intended to render the prohibited act void, the courts will construe the statute accordingly (footnotes omitted). [Annotation, 55 A.L.R. 2d 488–90.]

Applying these considerations to this case, it is clear that the contract involved here should be enforced. First, it is apparent that the statute itself does not specifically declare the labor or service contracts of aliens seeking to enter the United States for the purpose of performing such labor or services to be void. The statute only specifies that aliens who enter this country for such purpose, without having received the necessary certification, "shall be ineligible to receive visas and shall be excluded from admission into the United States."

Second, that the appellee, who knowingly participated in an illegal transaction, should be permitted to profit thereby at the expense of the appellant is a harsh and undesirable consequence of the doctrine that illegal contracts are not to be enforced.[1] This result, so contrary to general considerations of equity and fairness, should be countenanced only when clearly demonstrated to have been intended by the legislature. Third, since the purpose of this section would appear to be the safeguarding of American labor from unwanted competition, the appellant's contract should be enforced because such an objective would not be furthered by permitting employers knowingly to employ excludable aliens and then, with impunity, to refuse to pay them for their services. Indeed, to so hold could well have the opposite effect from the one intended, by encouraging employers to enter into the very type of contracts sought to be prevented.

We find no such clear command indicated by the language or general purposes to be accomplished by the statute in question. Our conclusion in that regard is further bolstered by the fact that the predecessor to the present statute expressly made such contracts void and of no effect:

> All contracts or agreements, express or implied, parol, or special, which may hereafter be made by and between any person, company, partnership, or corporation, and any foreigner or foreigners, alien or aliens, to perform labor or service or having reference to the performance of labor or service by any person in the United States, its Territories, or the District of Columbia previous to the migration or importation of the person or persons

---

[1] [4] Lord Mansfield said, with a very proper sensibility of the injustice of such a plea, and of the policy which permits it to be insisted upon, "The objection, that a contract is immoral or illegal as between plaintiff and defendant, sounds at all times very ill in the mouth of a defendant. It is not for his sake, however, that the objection is ever allowed, but it is founded on general principles of policy, which the defendant has the advantage of, contrary to the real justice as between him and the plaintiff." Harris v. Runnels, 53 U.S. (12 How.) 79, 86, 13 L. Ed. 901, 904 (1851)

whose labor or service is contracted for into the United States, *shall be utterly void and of no effect* (emphasis added).[2]

That provision was repealed by the Immigration and Nationality Act of 1952 and was replaced with what is now 8 U.S.C. § 1182(a)(14), which does not make such contracts void, but merely provides, as a deterrent, for ineligibility to receive visas and for exclusion from admission into the United States. The repeal of the former section coupled with the new enactment evinces an intent on the part of Congress that such contracts are no longer to be "void and of no effect." Apparently, Congress determined that the exclusion of certain aliens from admission to the United States was a more satisfactory sanction than rendering their contracts void and thus unjustifiably enriching employers of such alien laborers.

There are no cases construing § 1182(a)(14) with reference to this issue. Cases interpreting the former § 141 are obviously of little value in view of the material changes in its provisions. Even under the former section, however, one court permitted an alien who had entered the United States illegally to recover for services rendered under a contract which, as here, was entered into after the alien had entered the United States.[3] The court stated:

> An examination of this enactment reveals that the contracts or agreements that are denounced and rendered unenforcible (sic) are only those made "previous" to the migration or importation into the United States of the person or persons whose labor or service is contracted for. It does not declare void or in any manner vitiate contracts or agreements made after their entry into the United States, even though such entry and continued presence is unlawful. The sole penalties prescribed for unlawful entry are deportation or fine and imprisonment; no civil rights or right to sue or seek redress in judicial tribunals is denied to an alien here under the circumstances mentioned, and I do not see how it can be read into the statute without violating basic rules of statutory construction.[4]

A leading and often cited case from another era, although involving a different factual background, is also pertinent. *Harris v. Runnels*[5] involved the sale of slaves brought into Mississippi in violation of that state's statute prohibiting the importation of slaves without a certificate indicating that they had not been guilty of a felony. The statute imposed a fine on the buyer and seller for each slave sold without compliance with the statute. The plaintiff sued the defendant for payment for the slaves.

The court explained that the defendant buyer stood *in pari delicto* with the seller "with this difference between them, that he is now seeking to add to his breach of the law the injustice of retaining the negroes without paying for them."[6] It concluded that such a result could not have been intended by the legislature under the terms of the statute construed. Further support for the decision was found in the subsequent repeal of the Mississippi statute, and a new enactment specifically

---

[2] [6] Act of Feb. 26, 1885, ch. 164,'s 2,23 Stat. 332 (formerly 8 U.S.C. § 141) (repealed 1952).

[3] [8] Dezsofi v. Jacoby, 178 Misc. 851, 36 N.Y.S. 2d 672 (Sup. Ct. N.Y. 1942).

[4] [9] *Id.* at 675.

[5] [10] 53 U.S. (12 How.) 79, 13 L. Ed. 901 (1851).

[6] [11] *id.* at 85–86, 13 L. Ed. at 904.

providing that contracts in contravention of its provisions would be void. The court stated that:

> There could not be, . . . a stronger circumstance to show, that under the first statute in order, contracts in violation of it were not meant to be irrecoverable by suit.[7]

Because a subsequent harsher statute is at best a contemporary legislative interpretation of the former statute, the rationale for enforcing the contract is all the more compelling here, where the legislature which enacted the law being construed by us has expressly abrogated the harsher enactment. For the reasons set forth above, we therefore conclude that it was error to enter a judgment of dismissal, and the case is remanded for completion of the trial.

Reversed and remanded.

NOTES & QUESTIONS

1. Are there degrees of illegality? Are there degrees of "voidness"?

2. Assume that Rivers Construction hired Gates without knowledge of his status as an alien, and that his services were terminated upon learning of his immigration status. What impact, if any, would this have on the court's illegality decision?

3. The focus of this chapter is on illegality at the time the parties enter into a contract, as opposed to what is known as subsequent illegality (illegality that arises after the parties have entered into a contract). In the former situation, a valid contract never came into existence. In the latter circumstances, a valid contract is rendered void by a change in the law. That is the conceptual difference. Is there any practical difference?

TOMM'S REDEMPTION, INC v. JAE PARK, d/b/a ROYAL BILLIARDS
333 Ill. App. 3d 1003, 777 N.E.2d 522 (Ill. App. 2002)

WOLFSON, Justice:

This case poses the question of how long a party to an illicit contract can wait before asking a court to declare the contract void and unenforceable.

Defendant Jae Park, d/b/a Royal Billiards, appeals from a circuit court judgment granting a motion by plaintiff Tomm's Redemption, Inc., to dismiss defendant's petition to vacate a default judgment. The default judgment was entered on plaintiff's lawsuit against defendant for breach of contract. Defendant contends on appeal the court erred in granting plaintiff's motion. He gives two reasons: the default judgment was void because it was based on an illegal gambling contract, and plaintiff fraudulently concealed from the court the illegal nature of the contract.

We reverse the trial court's judgment and remand for further proceedings.

Plaintiff filed a complaint on August 4, 1999, alleging defendant entered into a contract with plaintiff on February 2, 1999. The contract specified plaintiff would

---

[7] [12] *Id.* at 87, 13 L. Ed. at 904.

provide, maintain, and service coin operated devices on the business premises of defendant for five years from the date of installation of the machines. Defendant terminated the contract in July 1999, 235 weeks before the contract was to expire. In the event of breach, the contract required defendant to pay liquidated damages of $ 500 for each remaining week of the contract plus costs and reasonable attorney fees. Plaintiff alleged defendant refused to pay liquidated damages in the amount of $ 117,500.

Defendant was personally served with process on September 16, 1999. Plaintiff filed a motion for default judgment on December 3, 1999, alleging defendant failed to file his appearance or respond to the complaint and requesting damages in the amount of $ 118,100. The circuit court entered an order for default judgment in that amount the same day. . . .

[Eventually plaintiff obtained a levy against defendant's homestead.] Defendant filed an "Emergency Petition to Vacate Void Judgment and Set Aside Judicial Levy Sale," on October 4, 2001, the day his right of redemption regarding the judicial levy sale was due to expire. Defendant's petition and attached affidavit alleged:

> "2. This contract is part of an agreement between the Plaintiff and the Defendant for the supply of video gambling machines so that the customers of Royal Billiards could engage in gambling transactions.
>
> 3. The customers of Royal Billiards would play the video gambling machines and be paid money for their winnings.
>
> 4. Periodically, the Plaintiff's representatives would come to the Defendant's pool hall and empty the money from the gambling machines after checking the machines [sic] registers for the amounts won and lost.
>
> 5. The money in the machines would be divided 40% to the Plaintiff and 60% to the Defendant, after all adjustments were made for the winnings that were paid out to the players.
>
> 6. The Defendant has in his control, evidence that the machines in this case were used for illegal gambling, including but not limited to a stack of weekly records showing: the total amount taken in; the total amount paid out as winnings; the net profit; and the split of the net profit. Each of these records are [sic] initialed by a collector of the Plaintiff's company.

* * *

> 9. The contract is an agreement between the parties to engage in gambling transactions using said vending machines."
>
> In short, defendant alleged he willingly entered into an illegal contract for profit.

Defendant's affidavit also stated he asked plaintiff to remove the machines because he no longer wanted them in his establishment. Defendant requested that the court vacate the default judgment and the resulting levy sale of his home as void because the judgment was entered on an illegal gambling contract. . . .

Although the contract stated nothing on its face about machines used for gambling, defendant contends the "coin operated machines" mentioned in the contract were actually video gambling machines used in furtherance of an illegal gambling contract. In support of his position, defendant cites section 28-7 of the Gambling Act, which states that all contracts "where the whole or any part of the consideration thereof is for any money or thing of value, won or obtained in violation of any Section of this Article are null and void." 720 ILCS 5/28-7(a) (West 2000). Furthermore, any obligation void under the Gambling Act may be set aside and vacated by any court of competent jurisdiction, upon a complaint filed for that purpose. 720 ILCS 5/28-7(b) (West 2000).

Defendant also relies on decisions holding contracts made in furtherance of gambling are null and void. *See Hall v. Montaleone*, 38 Ill. App. 3d 591, 592, 348 N.E.2d 196 (1976) (gambling contracts are absolutely void and unenforceable, by reason of public policy); *Brelsford v. Stoll*, 304 Ill. App. 222, 226, 26 N.E.2d 159 (1940) ("alleged contract was illegal and void from its inception as contravening the provisions of the gaming statutes of Illinois and against public policy and was therefore unenforceable"); *Schneider v. Turner*, 130 Ill. 28, 39, 22 N.E. 497 (1889) ("[n]othing is more clearly and firmly established by the common law, than that all gambling contracts are void") *Mallett v. Butcher*, 41 Ill. 382, 384 (1866) (all contracts having their origin in gaming are void, not voidable, and it is immaterial when or how the fact is made patent to the court) Defendant relies on *Schneider*, 130 Ill. at 39, in contending that illegal gambling contracts are void whether the agreement is expressed on the face of the contract or simply exists by secret understanding.

Plaintiff responds that the court's judgment was not void, as defendant contends, because the contract on which the judgment was based is a legal contract for the lease of coin operated machines. Nothing is stated in the contract regarding gambling. . . .

It is clear to us that the facts in defendant's affidavit, taken as true for purposes of the section 2-615 motion, establish that this was a gambling contract. The plaintiff and the defendant were to split the proceeds 60-40 after deducting the winnings of the players. That is gambling, pure and simple. We conclude the trial court erred when it held defendant did not demonstrate in his affidavit that this was a gambling contract. . . .

Defendant is entitled to a hearing on his factual allegations. At that hearing the trial court is to consider whether defendant has proved this was a void gambling contract and, if so, whether this defendant, as a willing participant in the unlawful enterprise, is entitled to seek relief in the courts. *See Brelsford*, 304 Ill. App. at 227 (When a contract is illegal, courts of equity will neither compel the execution of the agreement nor set it aside after it has been executed, "because to give relief in such a case would injure and counteract public morals"). Also *see In re Marriage of Steinberg*, 302 Ill. App. 3d 845, 857, 706 N.E.2d 895, 236 Ill. Dec. 21 (1998), where this court held a contract for splitting contingency fees was void as against public policy, but where both parties to the contract are equally at fault we will not aid either one, but will leave them where we find them.

NOTES & QUESTIONS

1. The parol evidence rule, discussed more completely in Chapter 12, prevents parties from introducing extrinsic evidence regarding the meaning of clear terms in a contract. What consideration, if any, did the court give to this rule in *Tomm's Redemption*?

2. If the contract is found void *ab initio* must defendant return the leased equipment? Must he pay the agreed lease rate?

3. If a contract is found illegal, who bears the greatest burden of loss? The one who provides the illegal services or the one who agrees to pay for such services? Who should bear the burden?

CARROLL v. BEARDON
381 P.2d 295 (Mont. 1963)

JOHN C. HARRISON, Justice:

This is an appeal from a judgment of the district court of the ninth judicial district, County of Toole, in favor of plaintiff-respondent and against defendant-appellant.

This matter was submitted to the district court on depositions of the parties involved and judgment rendered after findings of fact and conclusions of law.

On March 15, 1960, Edna Carroll, hereinafter referred to as the respondent, and Agnes Beardon, hereinafter referred to as the appellant, executed instruments in writing, one a warranty deed from respondent to appellant, and a note and mortgage back from appellant to respondent for the sale of a building and acreage in the amount of $42,000. A down payment of $8,000 was made at the time of the sale, and the note and mortgage provided that the appellant would pay to respondent monthly, the sum of $1,000 for the months of January through June and $2,000 for the months of July through December. The appellant paid one monthly payment. In September 1960, a mortgage foreclosure action was instituted by the respondent setting forth the above facts, showing a sum due in the amount of $41,805.53 for the building, personal property and 50 acres of land located in Toole County.

So far the facts in the case set forth an ordinary real estate transaction with a default by the purchaser, and it is not until the appellant's answer is read that the court finds itself trying to settle a dispute of two madams over a house of prostitution. The appellant alleges by way of her answer that although she secured the deed for the property, gave the note and mortgage, and entered into possession, that the mortgage is absolutely void as contrary to express law, and public policy; that the alleged mortgage was entered into in furtherance of prostitution in violation of the laws of the State of Montana and intended by respondent Carroll and the appellant Beardon so to be, and was entered into by the parties hereto with the knowledge, intent and purpose on their part that the said property would be used for the purpose of prostitution in violation of the laws of the State of Montana; and that prior to, and on the date of the consummation of this illegal transaction, prostitution was the only activity at the so-called Hillside Ranch.

While neither counsel had the effrontery to parade these indignant madams before the court, their depositions speak for them, and are most enlightening. Both admit that they are madams, in the limited sense of the word, and have operated this valuable piece of property, known as the Hillside Ranch as a house of prostitution, the respondent some four years prior to the sale, and the appellant since that date. Both admit to the sale of liquor without a state license, but the respondent deposed she had a federal license, leaving the court to wonder whether she is a strong central government supporter, or a more careful business woman. The appellant's position concerning these lawful taxes seem to be that her payments going from $1,000 per month to $2,000 per month during the harvest months and the Christmas season, that she could not afford the luxury of taxation.

Counsel on both sides of the case dig deep in legal lore to convince the court of the righteousness of their client's cause; the respondent with the citation of *Sampson v. Townsend* (1873), 25 La. Ann. 78, which was soon after the Civil War when Louisiana was still occupied by Federal troops; and the appellant not to be outdone, relies on *Pearce v. Brooks* (1866), LR 1 Exch. 213, 6 Eng. Rul. Cas. 326, an 1866 English case, and then perhaps because his client's place of business is some 50 miles from the Canadian border, and to give the case a good neighborly aroma, he cites and argues the merits of a case from our neighboring province of Alberta, *Rose v. Donaldson*, (Alta. 1931) 3 WWR 480.

To the findings of the district court, the appellant's three specifications of error direct themselves to an alleged abuse of discretion of the court as to the law and the evidence.

Many courts refuse to aid either party to contracts where the transaction is illegal. *E.P. Wilbur Trust Co. v. Fahrendorf,* 64 S.D. 124,2 65 N.W. 1. . . .

A review of the evidence put before the court in this case tempts this court to dismiss the appeal, however, there are many decisions to the effect that where the sale is of property that may or may not be used for an illegal purpose, that it is no defense that the seller knew the purpose of the buyer, without 'further evidence implicating the seller. *See State of New Mexico v. Capital Bank*, 32 N.M. 369, 257 P. 993. . . .

In the absence of active participation, the defense of illegality is ordinarily not available to the party who has breached the contract, where the fault and illegality are unilateral on her side of the transaction. *See Augir v. Ryan*, 63 Minn. 373, 65 N.W. 640.

. . .

The bare knowledge of the purpose for which the property is sold is not enough to raise the valid defense of illegality. *Anheuser-Busch Brg. Ass'n v. Mason*, 44 Minn. 318, 46 N.W. 558, 9 L.R.A. 506 . . . ; RESTATEMENT, CONTRACTS, § 602(1).

It is also important to consider the fact that the defendant has had the benefit of this contract for several years. Her status naturally does not appeal to the favor of this court, and in order to sustain such a defense a party who has reaped its benefits must show more active participation by the seller than has been shown here.

As pointed out in the brief of respondent, this same question, raising the illegality of the sale of gambling equipment was before the Supreme Court of Wyoming in the case of *Fuchs v. Goe*, 62 Wyo. 134, 163 P.2d 783, 166 A.L.R. 1329. The appellant's answer is amazingly similar to the answer in the *Fuchs* case, excepting where of necessity the words must be changed from gambling to prostitution. Under the circumstances of this case we feel the holding in the *Fuchs* case, *supra*, should prevail here. In the *Fuchs* case, as in this case, after the sale of the property, the seller had no connection with the business. The court, quoting from 32 Am. Jur. 68–69, § 49, in the *Fuchs* case in this connection stated:

. . . in order to defeat a recovery for rent by the lessor it must be shown that he participated in some degree, however slight, in the wrongful purpose and intended the property be so used, and that mere indifference on his part as to the intended use of the premises is not sufficient to bar his recovery. Mere knowledge on the lessor's part that the lessee will use the premises for an unlawful purpose does not make the lessor a participant in that purpose; for mere knowledge that the lessee may or will use the premises for an unlawful purpose is not of itself sufficient to show that the lessor intended that they must or shall be so used. . . .

Finding ample evidence in the record to sustain the trial court's findings and conclusions, the judgment appealed from is affirmed.

ADAIR, Justice (concurring in part and dissenting in part).

I concur in the result, but not in all that is said in the above opinion. This is a case of the pot calling the kettle black. However, the calling of names will not pay the promissory note nor discharge nor invalidate the mortgage upon which this action was brought. Each party to the contract is required to keep her promises and to perform her obligations thereunder. Refusal and failure to keep her promises or to perform her obligations subject the defaulting defendant, Agnes Beardon, to the penalties that attach upon the breach of her contract. These penalties were lawfully invoked and judgment for the plaintiff, Edna Carroll, rightfully given and entered.

NOTES & QUESTIONS

1. If the defendant-purchaser of the business were to prevail upon her defense, what would be its practical effect in this case?

2. What is the consequence of the court's leaving parties to illegal contracts where those parties are found? Is it not effectively to find for, or to side with, the defendant?

3. Assume that as opposed to serving as a house of prostitution, the property at issue was being used to manufacture illegal narcotics and that both parties were aware of its intended use. In fact, the seller made oral representations regarding the property's fitness for its intended use. Would you enforce a subsequent suit for payment by the seller? Why or why not?

4. If no payment is required on the grounds of illegality, is the defendant allowed to retain possession of the property? Does this support the State's public policy against illegal drug manufacture, use and distribution?

DANZIG v. DANZIG
79 Wash. App. 612, 904 P.2d 312 (1995)

MUNSON, Judge:

Steven Danzig appeals the dismissal of his contract claim against Jeffrey Danzig, . . . and Jeffrey's law firm on a C.R. 12(b)(6) motion. . . .

In his complaint, Steven states he is not a lawyer and that Jeffrey is a lawyer, licensed in the State of Washington. Steven alleges Jeffrey approached him in January 1992 with a business proposition: for every client Steven steered into Jeffrey's office,

Steven would receive one-third of any fee received. Steven states he accepted the offer and directed clients to Jeffrey. In each case, Jeffrey directed him to submit a billing statement making it appear as though he was billing for his time at an hourly rate. The total amount of the bill never deviated appreciably from one-third of the total fee. In each case, he was paid by Jeffrey. Steven maintains he directed a client to Jeffrey in March 1993; Jeffrey breached the agreement and refused to pay him. Steven states the one-third of the fee due him is about $89,000.

The trial court found the alleged contract was illegal and unenforceable under Washington law and dismissed Steven's claim with prejudice. Even though it dismissed Steven's claim, the trial court was concerned with the propriety of Jeffrey's fee and ordered him to pay $89,000 into the court registry pending an investigation of the fee. Jeffrey moved for reconsideration, but the motion was denied. The trial court did, however, stay its order compelling Jeffrey to pay, pending this appeal. . . .

As a general rule, contracts which are illegal or against public policy will not be enforced by the courts. *See Golberg v. Sanglier*, 96 Wash. 2d 874 (1982). That rule, however, is subject to an exception where a court determines the parties are not in pari delicto, that IS, they are not equally culpable. In those cases, a court may choose to enforce a contract despite the fact it is illegal or against public policy. As the court noted in *Golberg*, "in pari delicto" is only a label, and the decision to enforce a contract contrary to public policy requires more than just a weighing of fault and requires consideration of public policy. . . . As the court stated in *Tri-Q, Inc. v. Sta-Hi Corp.*, 63 Cal. 2d 199, 404 P.2d 486,498 (1965):

Where, by applying the [general] rule, the public cannot be protected because the transaction has been completed, where no serious moral turpitude is involved, where the defendant is the one guilty of the greatest moral fault, and where to apply the rule will be to permit the defendant to be unjustly enriched at the expense of the plaintiff, the rule should not be applied.

Under the alleged contract, Steven was to serve as a "runner" who solicited clients for Jeffrey. Such a contract would be illegal, as to the lawyer, under R.C.W. 9.12.010, Washington's barratry statute. In part, the statute provides that "every person, being an attorney or counselor at law, who shall personally, or through the agency of another, solicit employment as such attorney, in any suit pending or prospective . . . shall be guilty of a misdemeanor. . . ." R.C.W. 9.12.010. The alleged agreement is also in violation of R.F.C. 7.2(c) which states a "lawyer shall not give anything of value to a person for recommending the lawyer's services. . . ." Agreements which violate the Rules of Professional Conduct are contrary to public policy. . . .

Although Jeffrey argues R.C.W. 9.12.010 criminalizes Steven's conduct, we would disagree. He cites to cases from other jurisdictions in which courts have refused to provide a remedy for breach of a contract to procure clients for an attorney. *See Van Bergh v. Simons*, 286 F.2d 325 (2d Cir.1961); *Landi v. Arkules*, 172 Ariz. 126, 835 P.2d 458 (App. 1992); *Plumlee v. Paddock*, 832 S.W.2d 757 (Tex. Ct. App. 1992). The statutes at issue in those cases criminalized the conduct of the runner as well as that of the attorney. In contrast, the relevant language of R.C.W. 9.12.010 clearly only addresses the conduct of attorneys. Likewise, the Rules of Professional Conduct apply only to those admitted to practice law in the State of

Washington. In both cases, the prohibitions apply only to Jeffrey's conduct, not Steven's.

Jeffrey argues that Steven's admission in his complaint that he submitted billing statements falsely detailing hours worked is evidence of moral fault. Jeffrey maintains a reasonable person should have deduced the alleged contract was improper. While Steven's statement may be evidence of moral fault on his part, he may yet be able to prove facts in support of his claim which entitle him to relief.

If a promisee is excusably ignorant of facts or of legislation of a minor character, of which the promisor is not excusably ignorant and in the absence of which the promise would be enforceable, the promisee has a claim for damages for its breach but cannot recover damages for anything he has done after he learns of the facts or legislation.

RESTATEMENT (SECOND) OF CONTRACTS § 180 (1979). Further, "[s]uch ignorance is more likely to be excusable where the legislation is of a local, specialized or technical nature and where the other party may be assumed to have knowledge as to such matters." RESTATEMENT (SECOND) OF CONTRACTS § 180 comment a (1979). Both R.C.W. 9.12.010 and R.P.C. 7.2(c) are specialized in that they address only the conduct of members of the legal profession. As an attorney, Jeffrey may be assumed to have knowledge of such matters.

Here, the conduct proscribed by R.C.W. 9.12.010 and R.P.C. 7.2(c) has already occurred. Refusing to enforce the sole remaining task under the alleged contract, payment of money, would not further protect the public. Jeffrey argues public policy would best be served by sending a message to potential runners that their efforts will not be rewarded. Knowing that disclosure of their unethical acts would almost certainly lead to disciplinary proceedings would serve a strong disincentive to attorneys considering an agreement like that at issue here. These issues cannot be resolved on a C.R. 12(b)(6) motion. . . .

Taken as true, the allegations in Steven's complaint state a claim upon which relief may be granted. The trial court erred in granting the C.R. 12(b)(6) motion to dismiss. Whether Steven can support those allegations in further proceedings remains to be seen.

We reverse that portion of the trial court's order dismissing Steven's claim and remand for further proceedings. . . .

THOMPSON, Chief Judge, dissenting: . . .

As the majority recognizes, contracts which are illegal or which are connected with an illegal act are against public policy and are unenforceable. . . . Contracts may also be unenforceable as against public policy independent of any statute prohibiting their subject matter. . . . *Wright v. Corbin*, 190 Wash. 260, 267, 67 P.2d 868 (1937) (contracts "obnoxious to the pure administration of justice, or . . . injurious to the interest of the public" can be declared illegal because against public policy).

The contract between Steven and Jeffrey should not be enforced because it is contrary to R.P.C. 7.2(c). It is contrary to R.C.W. 9.12.010. Further, it is contrary to the general public policy of this state which disapproves of the brokerage of lawyer services. *See Goodier v. Hamilton*, 172 Wash. 60, 19 P.2d 392 (1933) (layperson's contract with insurance agent to locate attorney who would secure a certificate from state board of public works void as against public policy).

The policy behind the nonenforcement of illegal contracts and contracts against public policy is to protect the public, not to protect or punish either party to the contract. Accordingly, courts generally leave the parties as they find them. That is just where Steven and Jeffrey should be left. While application of the doctrine of "*in pari delicto*" is appropriate in exceptional cases such as Golberg, [*supra*,] its application here is misplaced. Steven is not only presumed to know the law which made Jeffrey's actions illegal, his own acts in aiding and abetting Jeffrey in those illegal acts should not be rewarded. Further, by his own assertion, Steven completed and submitted hourly time sheets for services he never performed.

It is with some hesitation that I reach this conclusion, which enables a lawyer, who himself violates the law and the Rules of Professional Conduct, to urge his own violation as a defense to a suit for monies owing. However, we cannot allow use of our courts to enforce such illegal contracts and thereby infer approval of the brokering of legal services. Further, there is little doubt that any inequity generated by a decision not to allow Steven to enforce the contract will be remedied in subsequent litigation and hearings between the offending lawyer and others who are not parties to this litigation.

NOTES AND QUESTIONS

1. Which result would more effectively serve sound public policy — the decision of the majority or the one proposed by the dissent?

2. Do you really believe that Steven was unaware of the illegal nature of his arrangement with Jeffrey? Must a party be "innocent" or merely "less guilty" than another to avoid application of the illegality bar to contract enforcement?

3. What does the dissenting judge mean about subsequent remedies to disgorge the $89,000 windfall from Jeffrey? Who would have standing to do so, and on what grounds?

4. Lawyers can and do advertise their professional services in various forms — business cards, telephone directories, print advertising, and television commercials. What is wrong with lawyers utilizing agents or runners in soliciting clients, and what is wrong with paying those agents or runners a fee or commission for doing so?

HEWITT v. HEWITT
77 Ill. 2d 49, 394 N.E.2d 1204 (1 979)

UNDERWOOD, Justice:

The issue in this case is whether plaintiff Victoria Hewitt, whose complaint alleges she lived with defendant Robert Hewitt from 1960 to 1975 in an unmarried, family-like relationship to which three children have been born, may recover from him "an equal share of the profits and properties accumulated by the parties" during that period. . . .

Plaintiff . . . filed an amended complaint alleging the following bases for her claim: (1) that because defendant promised he would "share his life, his future, his earnings and his property" with her and all of defendant's property resulted from the parties' joint endeavors, plaintiff is entitled in equity to a one-half share; (2)

that the conduct of the parties evinced an implied contract entitling plaintiff to one-half the property accumulated during their "family relationship"; (3) that because defendant fraudulently assured plaintiff she was his wife in order to secure her services, although he knew they were not legally married, defendant's property should be impressed with a trust for plaintiff's benefit; (4) that because plaintiff has relied to her detriment on defendant's promises and devoted her entire life to him, defendant has been unjustly enriched.

The factual background alleged or testified to is that in June 1960, when she and defendant were students at Grinnell College in Iowa, plaintiff became pregnant; that defendant thereafter told her that they were husband and wife and would live as such, no formal ceremony being necessary, and that he would "share his life, his future, his earnings and his property" with her; that the parties immediately announced to their respective parents that they were married and thereafter held themselves out as husband and wife; that in reliance on defendant's promises she devoted her efforts to his professional education and his establishment in the practice of pedodontia, obtaining financial assistance from her parents for this purpose; that she assisted defendant in his career with her own special skills and although she was given payroll checks for these services she placed them in a common fund; that defendant, who was without funds at the time of the marriage, as a result of her efforts now earns over $80,000 a year and has accumulated large amounts of property, owned either jointly with her or separately; that she has given him every assistance a wife and mother could give, including social activities designed to enhance his social and professional reputation.

The . . . complaint was . . . dismissed, the trial court finding that Illinois law and public policy require such claims to be based on a valid marriage. The appellate court reversed, stating that because the parties had outwardly lived a conventional married life, plaintiff's conduct had not "so affronted public policy that she should be denied any and all relief" (62 Ill. App. 3d 861, 869, . . .) and that plaintiff's complaint stated a cause of action on an express oral contract. We granted leave to appeal. Defendant apparently does not contest his obligation to support the children, and that question is not before us.

The appellate court, in reversing, gave considerable weight to the fact that the parties had held themselves out as husband and wife for over 15 years. The court noted that they lived "a most conventional, respectable and ordinary family life" . . . that did not openly flout accepted standards, the "single flaw" being the lack of a valid marriage. Indeed the appellate court went so far as to say that the parties had "lived within the legitimate boundaries of a marriage and family relationship of a most conventional sort," . . . an assertion which that court cannot have intended to be taken literally. Noting that the Illinois Marriage and Dissolution of Marriage Act (Ill. Rev. Stat. 1977, ch. 40, par. 101 *et. seq.*) does not prohibit nonmarital cohabitation and that the Criminal Code of 1961 (Ill. Rev. Stat. 1977, ch. 38, par. 11-8(a)) makes fornication an offense only if the behavior is open and notorious, the appellate court concluded that plaintiff should not be denied relief on public policy grounds.

In finding that plaintiff's complaint stated a cause of action on an express oral contract, the appellate court adopted the reasoning of the California Supreme Court in the widely publicized case of *Marvin v. Marvin* (1976), 18 Cal. 3d 660, 557 P.2d 106, quoting extensively therefrom. In *Marvin*, Michelle Triola and defendant Lee Marvin lived together for 7 years pursuant to an alleged oral agreement that while "the parties lived together they would combine their efforts and earnings and would share equally any and all property accumulated as a result of their efforts whether individual or combined." . . . In her complaint she alleged that, in reliance on this agreement, she gave up her career as a singer to devote herself full time to defendant as "companion, homemaker, housekeeper and cook." . . . In resolving her claim for one-half the property accumulated in defendant's name during that period the California court held that "The courts should enforce express contracts between nonmarital partners except to the extent that the contract is explicitly founded on the consideration of meretricious sexual services" and that "In the absence of an express contract, the courts should inquire into the conduct of the parties to determine whether that conduct demonstrates an implied contract, agreement of partnership or joint venture, or some other tacit understanding between the parties. The courts may also employ the doctrine of quantum meruit, or equitable remedies such as constructive or resulting trusts, when warranted by the facts of the case." . . . The court reached its conclusions because:

> In summary, we believe that the prevalence of nonmarital relationships in modern society and the social acceptance of them, marks this as a time when our courts should by no means apply the doctrine of the unlawfulness of the so-called meretricious relationship to the instant case. . . .

> The mores of the society have indeed changed so radically in regard to cohabitation that we cannot impose a standard based on alleged moral considerations that have apparently been so widely abandoned by so many. . . .

It is apparent that the *Marvin* court adopted a pure contract theory, under which, if the intent of the parties and the terms of their agreement are proved, the pseudo-conventional family relationship which impressed the appellate court here is irrelevant; recovery may be had unless the implicit sexual relationship is made the explicit consideration for the agreement. In contrast, the appellate court here, as we understand its opinion, would apply contract principles only in a setting where the relationship of the parties outwardly resembled that of a traditional family. It seems apparent that the plaintiff in Marvin would not have been entitled to recover in our appellate court because of the absence of that outwardly appearing conventional family relationship.

The issue of whether property rights accrue to unmarried cohabitants cannot, however, be regarded realistically as merely a problem in the law of express contracts. Plaintiff argues that because her action is founded on an express contract, her recovery would in no way imply that unmarried cohabitants acquire property rights merely by cohabitation and subsequent separation. However, the Marvin court expressly recognized and the appellate court here seems to agree that if common law principles of express contract govern express agreements between unmarried cohabitants, common law principles of implied contract, equitable relief and constructive trust must govern the parties' relations in the absence of such an agreement. . . . In all probability the latter case will be much the more common, since it is unlikely that most couples who live together will enter into express agreements regulating their property rights. . . . The increasing incidence of nonmarital cohabitation referred to in Marvin and the variety of legal remedies therein sanctioned seem certain to result in substantial amounts of litigation, in which, whatever the allegations regarding an oral contract, the proof will necessarily involve details of the parties' living arrangements.

Apart, however, from the appellate court's reliance upon Marvin to reach what appears to us to be a significantly different result, we believe there is a more fundamental problem. We are aware, of course, of the increasing judicial attention given the individual claims of unmarried cohabitants to jointly accumulated property, and the fact that the majority of courts considering the question have recognized an equitable or contractual basis for implementing the reasonable expectations of the parties unless sexual services were the explicit consideration. (*See* cases collected in Annot., 31 A.L.R. 2d 1255 (1953) and A.L.R. 2d Later Case Service supplementing vols. 25 to 31.) The issue of unmarried cohabitants' mutual property rights, however, as we earlier noted, cannot appropriately be character-ized solely in terms of contract law, nor is it limited to considerations of equity or fairness as between the parties to such relationships. There are major public policy questions involved in determining whether, under what circumstances, and to what extent it is desirable to accord some type of legal status to claims arising from such relationships. Of substantially greater importance than the rights of the immediate parties is the impact of such recognition upon our society and the institution of marriage. Will the fact that legal rights closely resembling those arising from conventional marriages can be acquired by those who deliberately choose to enter into what have heretofore been commonly referred to as "illicit" or "meretricious" relationships encourage formation of such relationships and weaken marriage as the foundation of our family-based society? In the event of death shall the survivor have the status of a surviving spouse for purposes of inheritance, wrongful death actions, workmen's compensation, etc.? And still more importantly: what of the children born of such relationships? What are their support and inheritance rights and by what standards are custody questions resolved? What of the sociological and psychological effects upon them of that type of environment? Does not the recognition of legally enforceable property and custody rights emanating from nonmarital cohabitation in practical effect equate with the legalization of common law marriage at least in the circumstances of this case? And, in summary, have the increasing numbers of unmarried cohabitants and changing mores of our society . . . reached the point at which the general welfare of the citizens of this State is best served by a return to something resembling the judicially created common law marriage our legislature outlawed in 1905?

Illinois' public policy regarding agreements such as the one alleged here was implemented long ago in *Wallace v. Rappleye* (1882), 103 Ill. 229, 249, where this court said: "An agreement in consideration of future illicit cohabitation between the plaintiffs is void." This is the traditional rule, in force until recent years in all jurisdictions. . . . § 589 of the RESTATEMENT OF CONTRACTS (1932) states, "A bargain in whole or in part for or in consideration of illicit sexual intercourse or of a promise thereof is illegal." . . .

It is true, of course, that cohabitation by the parties may not prevent them from forming valid contracts about independent matters, for which it is said the sexual relations do not form part of the consideration. (RESTATEMENT OF CONTRACTS §§ 589, 597 (1932); 6A Corbin, CONTRACTS § 1476 (1962).) Those courts which allow recovery generally have relied on this principle to reduce the scope of the rule of illegality. Thus, California courts long prior to Marvin held that an express agreement to pool earnings is supported by independent consideration and is not invalidated by cohabitation of the parties, the agreements being regarded as simultaneous but separate. (*See, e.g., Trutalli v. Meraviglia* (1932), 215 Cal. 698, 12 P.2d 430; *see also* Annot., 31 A.L.R. 2d 1255 (1953), and cases cited therein.) More recently, several courts have reasoned that the rendition of housekeeping and homemaking services such as plaintiff alleges here could be regarded as the consideration for a separate contract between the parties, severable from the illegal contract founded on sexual relations. (*Kozlowski v. Kozlowski* (1979), 80 N.J. 378, 403 A.2d 902. . . .

The real thrust of plaintiff's argument here is that we should abandon the rule of illegality because of certain changes in societal norms and attitudes. It is urged that social mores have changed radically in recent years, rendering this principle of law archaic. It is said that because there are so many unmarried cohabitants today the courts must confer a legal status on such relationships. This, of course, is the rationale underlying some of the decisions and commentaries. . . . If this is to be the result, however, it would seem more candid to acknowledge the return of varying forms of common law marriage than to continue displaying the naivete we believe involved in the assertion that there are involved in these relationships contracts separate and independent from the sexual activity, and the assumption that those contracts would have been entered into or would continue without that activity.

Even if we were to assume some modification of the rule of illegality is appropriate, we return to the fundamental question earlier alluded to: If resolution of this issue rests ultimately on grounds of public policy, by what body should that policy be determined? Marvin, viewing the issue as governed solely by contract law, found judicial policy-making appropriate. Its decision was facilitated by California precedent and that State's no-fault divorce law. In our view, however, the situation alleged here was not the kind of arm's length bargain envisioned by traditional contract principles, but an intimate arrangement of a fundamentally different kind. The issue, realistically, is whether it is appropriate for this court to grant a legal status to a private arrangement substituting for the institution of marriage sanctioned by the State. The question whether change is needed in the law governing the rights of parties in this delicate area of marriage-like relationships involves evaluations of sociological data and alternatives we believe best suited to the superior investigative and fact-finding facilities of the legislative branch in the exercise of its traditional authority to declare public policy in the domestic relations field. . . . That belief is reinforced by the fact that judicial recognition of mutual property rights between unmarried cohabitants would, in our opinion, clearly violate the policy of our recently enacted Illinois Marriage and Dissolution of Marriage Act. Although the Act does not specifically address the subject of nonmarital cohabitation, we think the legislative policy quite evident from the statutory scheme.

The Act provides:

> This Act shall be liberally construed and applied to promote its underlying purposes, which are to:
>
> (1) provide adequate procedures for the solemnization and registration of marriage;
>
> (2) strengthen and preserve the integrity of marriage and safeguard family relationships.

(Ill. Rev. Stat. 1977, ch. 40, par. 102.)

We cannot confidently say that judicial recognition of property rights between unmarried cohabitants will not make that alternative to marriage more attractive by allowing the parties to engage in such relationships with greater security. As one commentator has noted, it may make this alternative especially attractive to persons who seek a property arrangement that the law does not permit to marital partners. (Comment, 90 HARV. L. REV. 1708, 1713 (1977).) This court, for example, has held void agreements releasing husbands from their obligation to support their wives. (*Vock v. Vock* (1937), 365 Ill. 432, 6 N.E.2d 843. . . .) In thus potentially enhancing the attractiveness of a private arrangement over marriage, we believe that the appellate court decision in this case contravenes the Act's policy of strengthening and preserving the integrity of marriage.

The Act also provides: "Common law marriages contracted in this State after June 30, 1905 are invalid." (Ill. Rev. Stat. 1977, ch. 40, par. 214.) The doctrine of common law marriage was a judicially sanctioned alternative to formal marriage designed to apply to cases like the one before us. . . .

While the appellate court denied that its decision here served to rehabilitate the doctrine of common law marriage, we are not persuaded. Plaintiff's allegations disclose a relationship that clearly would have constituted a valid common law marriage in this State prior to 1905. The parties expressly manifested their present intent to be husband and wife; immediately thereafter they assumed the marital status; and for many years they consistently held themselves out to their relatives and the public at large as husband and wife. Revealingly, the appellate court relied on the fact that the parties were, to the public, husband and wife in determining that the parties' living arrangement did not flout Illinois public policy. It is of course true, as plaintiff argues, that unlike a common law spouse she would not have full marital rights in that she could not, for example, claim her statutory one-third share of defendant's property on his death. The distinction appears unimpressive, however, if she can claim one-half of his property on a theory of express or implied contract.

Further, in enacting the Illinois Marriage and Dissolution of Marriage Act, our legislature considered and rejected the "no-fault" divorce concept that has been adopted in many other jurisdictions, including California. . . . Illinois appears to be one of three States retaining fault grounds for dissolution of marriage. (Ill. Rev. Stat. 1977, ch. 40, par. 401; Comment, *Hewitt v. Hewitt, Contract Cohabitation and Equitable Expectations Relief for Meretricious Spouses*, 12 JOHN MARSHALL JOURNAL OF PRACTICE AND PROCEDURE 435, 452-53 (1979).) Certainly a significantly stronger promarriage policy is manifest in that action, which appears to us to reaffirm the traditional doctrine that marriage is a civil contract between three parties — the husband, the wife and the State. . . . The policy of the Act gives the State a strong continuing interest in the institution of marriage and prevents the marriage relation from becoming in effect a private contract terminable at will. This seems to us another indication that public policy disfavors private contractual alternatives to marriage.

Lastly, in enacting the Illinois Marriage and Dissolution of Marriage Act, the legislature adopted for the first time the civil law concept of the putative spouse. The Act provides that an unmarried person may acquire the rights of a legal spouse only if he goes through a marriage ceremony and cohabits with another in the good-faith belief that he is validly married. When he learns that the marriage is not valid his status as a putative spouse terminates; common law marriages are expressly excluded. (Ill. Rev. Stat. 1977, ch. 40, par. 305.) The legislature thus extended legal recognition to a class of nonmarital relationships, but only to the extent of a party's good-faith belief in the existence of a valid marriage. Moreover, during the legislature's deliberations on the Act Marvin was decided and received wide publicity. (*See* Note, 12 J. Mar. J. Prac. & Proc. 435, 450 (1979).) These circumstances in our opinion constitute a recent and unmistakable legislative judgment disfavoring the grant of mutual property rights to knowingly unmarried cohabitants. . . .

Actually, however, the legislative judgment is in accord with the history of common law marriage in this country. "Despite its judicial acceptance in many states, the doctrine of common-law marriage is generally frowned on in this country, even in some of the states that have accepted it." (52 Am. Jur. 2d 902 *Marriage* § 46 (1970)) Its origins, early history and problems are detailed in *In re Estate of Soeder* (1966), 7 Ohio App. 2d 271, 220 N.E.2d 547, where that court noted that some 30 states did not authorize common law marriage. . . . "It tends to weaken the public estimate of the sanctity of the marriage relation. It puts in doubt the certainty of the rights of inheritance. It opens the door to false pretenses of marriage and the imposition on estates of suppositious heirs." 7 Ohio App. 2d 271, 290, 220 N.E.2d 547, 561.

In our judgment the fault in the appellate court holding in this case is that its practical effect is the reinstatement of common law marriage, as we earlier indicated, for there is no doubt that the alleged facts would, if proved, establish such a marriage under our pre-1905 law. . . .

We do not intend to suggest that plaintiff's claims are totally devoid of merit. Rather, we believe that our statement in *Mogged v. Mogged* (1973), 55 Ill. 2d 221, 225, 302 N.E.2d 293, 295, made in deciding whether to abolish a judicially created defense to divorce, is appropriate here:

> Whether or not the defense of recrimination should be abolished or modified in Illinois is a question involving complex public-policy considerations as to which compelling arguments may be made on both sides. For the reasons stated hereafter, we believe that these questions are appropriately within the province of the legislature, and that, if there is to be a change in the law of this State on this matter, it is for the legislature and not the courts to bring about that change.

We accordingly hold that plaintiff's claims are unenforceable for the reason that they contravene the public policy, implicit in the statutory scheme of the Illinois Marriage and Dissolution of Marriage Act, disfavoring the grant of mutually enforceable property rights to knowingly unmarried cohabitants. The judgment of the appellate court is reversed and the judgment of the circuit court of Champaign County is affirmed. . . .

NOTES & QUESTIONS

1. Were the parties in *Hewitt in pari delicto?* Was the outcome of *Hewitt* the fair and just result?

2. In *Watts v. Watts*, 405 N.W.2d 303 (Wis. 1987), the court criticized the *Hewitt* court's "unsupportable inferential leap when it found that cohabitation agreements run contrary to statutory policy." The court distinguished Illinois law from Wisconsin law on the grounds that Wisconsin has abolished "fault" divorce. It

further rejected the argument that agreements between cohabitants are necessarily against public policy:

> Courts have generally refused to enforce contracts for which the sole consideration is sexual relations, sometimes referred to as "meretricious" relationships. *See In re Estate of Steffes*, 95 Wis. 2d 490, 514, 290 N.W.2d 697 (1980), *citing* RESTATEMENT OF CONTRACTS § 589 (1932). Courts distinguish, however, between contracts that are explicitly and inseparably founded on sexual services and those that are not. This court, and numerous other courts, have concluded that "a bargain between two people is not illegal merely because there is an illicit relationship between the two so long as the bargain is independent of the illicit relationship and the illicit relationship does not constitute any part of the consideration bargained for and is not a condition of the bargain.". . .

> While not condoning the illicit sexual relationship of the parties, many courts have recognized that the result of a court's refusal to enforce contract and property rights between unmarried cohabitants is that one party keeps all or most of the assets accumulated during the relationship, while the other party, no more or less "guilty, " is deprived of property which he or she has helped to accumulate. *See e.g., Glasgo v. Glasgo*, 410 N.E.2d 1325, 1330 Ind. App. 1980); *Latham v. Latham*, 274 Or. 421, 426, 547 P.2d 144 (1976); *Marvin v. Marvin, supra*, 18 Cal. 3d at 682, 134 Cal. Rptr. at 830, 557 P.2d at 121; *West v. Knowles*, 50 Wash. 2d 311, 315–16, 311 P.2d 689 (1957). . . .

> [T]he plaintiff alleges that she performed housekeeping, childbearing, childrearing, and other services related to the maintenance of the parties' home, in addition to various services for the defendant's business and her own business, for which she received no compensation. Courts have recognized that money, property, or services (including housekeeping or childrearing) may constitute adequate consideration independent of the parties' sexual relationship to support an agreement to share or transfer property. *See Tyranski, supra*, 44 Mich. App. at 574, 205 N.W.2d at 597; *Carlson v. Olson*, 256 N.W.2d 249, 253–254 (1977); *Carroll v. Lee*, 148 Ariz. 10, 14, 712 P.2d 923, 927 (1986); *Steffes, supra*, 95 Wis. 2d at 501, 290 N.W.2d 697.[8]

> According to the plaintiff's complaint, the parties cohabited for more than twelve years, held joint bank accounts, made joint purchases, filed joint income tax returns, and were listed as husband and wife on other legal documents. Courts have held that such a relationship and "joint acts of a financial nature can give rise to an inference that the parties intended to share equally." *Beal v. Beal*, 282 Or. 115, 122, 577 P.2d 507, 510 (1978). The joint ownership of property and the filing of joint income tax returns strongly implies that the parties intended their relationship to be in the nature of a joint enterprise, financially as well as personally. *See Beal*, 282

---

[8] Until recently, the prevailing view was that services performed in the context of a "family or marriage relationship" were presumed gratuitous. However, that presumption was rebuttable. See Steffes, 95 Wis. 2d at 501, 290 N.W.2d at 703–704. In Steffes, we held the presumption to be irrelevant where the plaintiff can show either an express or implied agreement to pay for those services, even where the plaintiff has rendered them "with a sense of affection, devotion and duty." . . .

Or. at 122, 577 P.2d at 510; *Warden v. Warden, supra*, 36 Wash. App. at 696–97, 676 P.2d at 1038.

Having reviewed the complaint and surveyed the law in this and other jurisdictions, we hold that the Family Code does not preclude an unmarried cohabitant from asserting contract and property claims against the other party to the cohabitation. We further conclude that public policy does not necessarily preclude an unmarried cohabitant from asserting a contract claim against the other party to the cohabitation so long as the claim exists independently of the sexual relationship and is supported by separate consideration. Accordingly, we conclude that the plaintiff in this case has pleaded the facts necessary to state a claim for damages resulting from the defendant's breach of an express or an implied in fact contract to share with the plaintiff the property accumulated through the efforts of both parties during their relationship. Once again, we do not judge the merits of the plaintiff's claim; we merely hold that she be given her day in court to prove her claim.

What was the separate consideration for plaintiff's housekeeping and child-rearing activities?

3. *Practice Points:* To help assure that their intentions are honored, should unmarried cohabitants formalize their oral agreements regarding property division in a writing sufficiently clear to demonstrate their intent?

4. *Drafting Exercise*: Draft a contract that would support *Hewitt's* property division claims.

5. Could Ms. Hewitt have prevailed upon a claim for *quantum meruit*? In *Watts v. Watts, supra*, the court also addressed the availability of relief under claims of unjust enrichment:

Unlike claims for breach of an express or implied in fact contract, a claim of unjust enrichment does not arise out of an agreement entered into by the parties. Rather, an action for recovery based upon unjust enrichment is grounded on the moral principle that one who has received a benefit has a duty to make restitution where retaining such a benefit would be unjust. *Puttkammer v. Minth*, 83 Wis. 2d 686, 689, 266 N.W.2d 361, 363 (1978).

Because no express or implied in fact agreement exists between the parties, recovery based upon unjust enrichment is sometimes referred to as "quasi contract, " or contract "implied in law" rather than "implied in fact." Quasi contracts are obligations created by law to prevent injustice. *Shulse v. City of Mayville*, 223 Wis. 624, 632, 271 N.W. 643 (1937).

In Wisconsin, an action for unjust enrichment, or quasi contract, is based upon proof of three elements: (1) a benefit conferred on the defendant by the plaintiff, (2) appreciation or knowledge by the defendant of the benefit, and (3) acceptance or retention of the benefit by the defendant under circumstances making it inequitable for the defendant to retain the benefit. *Puttkammer, supra*, 83 Wis. 2d at 689, 266 N.W.2d 361; Wis. J.I. Civil No. 3028 (1981). The plaintiff has cited no cases directly supporting actions in unjust enrichment by unmarried cohabitants, and the defendant provides no authority against it. This court has previously extended such relief to a party to a cohabitation in *Estate of Fox*, 178 Wis. 369, 190 N.W. 90, 31

A.L.R. 420 (1922). In *Fox*, the plaintiff was a woman who had believed in good faith that she was married to the decedent, when in fact she was not. The court found that the decedent "husband" had "by fraudulent representations induced the plaintiff to enter into the illicit relationship." . . . *Fox*, *supra*, 178 Wis. at 372, 190 N.W. 90. Under those circumstances, the court reasoned that it was "just and logical" to infer "from the nature of the transaction" that "the supposed husband [can be] held to have assumed to pay [for services rendered by his 'spouse'] because in point of law and equity it is just that he should pay."

In *Fox*, the court expressly refused to consider whether the same result would necessarily follow in other circumstances. Thus, *Fox* does not supply explicit support for the plaintiff's position here where she does not claim that she thought the parties were actually married.

The *Steffes* case, however, does provide additional support for the plaintiff's position. Although *Steffes* involved a claim for recovery in contract by an unmarried cohabitant for the value of services she performed for the decedent, the same equitable principles that governed that case would appear to apply in a case where the plaintiff is seeking recovery based upon unjust enrichment. In *Steffes*, the court cited with approval a statement by the trial judge that "[t]he question I have in mind is why should the estate be enriched when that man was just as much a part of the illicit relationship as she was and not let her have her fair dues. I don't understand that law that would interpret unjust enrichment that way and deprive one and let the other benefit and do it on the basis that there was an illicit relationship but not equally held against the both." . . .

As part of his general argument, the defendant claims that the court should leave the parties to an illicit relationship such as the one in this case essentially as they are found, providing no relief at all to either party. For support, the defendant relies heavily on *Hewitt v. Hewitt*, *supra*, and the dissent in Steffes, to argue that courts should provide no relief whatsoever to unmarried cohabitants until the legislature provides specifically for it. *See Steffes*, *supra*, 95 Wis. 2d at 521–22, 290 N.W.2d 697 (Coffey, J., dissenting).

As we have discussed previously, allowing no relief at all to one party in a so-called "illicit" relationship effectively provides total relief to the other, by leaving that party owner of all the assets acquired through the efforts of both. Yet it cannot seriously be argued that the party retaining all the assets is less "guilty" than the other. Such a result is contrary to the principles of equity. Many courts have held, and we now so hold, that unmarried cohabitants may raise claims based upon unjust enrichment following the termination of their relationships where one of the parties attempts to retain an unreasonable amount of the property acquired through the efforts of both. In this case, the plaintiff alleges that she contributed both property and services to the parties' relationship. She claims that because of these contributions the parties' assets increased, but that she was never compensated for her contributions. She further alleges that the defendant, knowing that the plaintiff expected to share in the property accumulated, "accepted the services rendered to him by the plaintiff" and that it would be unfair under the circumstances to allow him to retain everything while she receives nothing. We conclude that the facts alleged are sufficient to state a claim for recovery based upon unjust enrichment.

Do you agree?

6. Which case, *Hewitt* or *Watts*, establishes more sound family law policy? More sound contract law policy?

7. Should it make a difference whether the parties to one of these cohabitation agreements are same-sex partners? *See, for example, Whorton v. Dillingham*, 202 Cal. App. 3d 447, 248 Cal. Rptr. 405 (1988).

8. In addition to refusing to enforce contracts which contain objects or provision that violate public policy, courts also often decline to enforce contractual provisions which seek to limit evidentiary proofs to exculpate parties from liability on grounds of public policy. Thus, for example, in *Garden State Plaza Corp. v. S.S. Kresge Company*, 189 A.2d 448 (N.J. App. Div. 1963), the court considered the legality of the following provisions in a case involving a disputed lease for space in a shopping center:

> There are no oral agreements between the parties hereto affecting this lease, and this lease supersedes and cancels any and all previous negotiations, arrangements, agreements and understandings, if any, between the parties hereto with respect to the subject matter thereof, and none thereof shall be used to interpret or construe this lease.

In analyzing the enforceability of this clause, the court rejected the exclusionary effect of such clauses on the court's ability to interpret submitted contract claims. It stated:

> Short of the last clause, the stipulation is to all intents and purposes the equivalent of the parol evidence rule, and . . . does not militate against the conclusions arrived at earlier in this opinion [regarding the court's ability to rely on extrinsic evidence to determine the meaning of the disputed terms of the lease.] The last clause, however, if given effect, would obviously forbid using any of the materials of negotiation in construing the lease. In so doing it would seriously impair a basic adjudicatory tool with which courts attempt to do justice when called upon to construe a contract over the meaning of which its signatories argue different choices.

> So-called "contracts to alter or waive the rules of evidence" have been discussed in a wide range of settings. 1 Wigmore, Evidence (1940), § 7a, p. 213 *et seq.*; 6 Williston, Contracts (1938), § 1722, p. 4862; Note, 46 Harv. L. Rev. 138 (1932). Most of the cases have involved stipulations in insurance policies, which, though couched in terms of prerequisites of proof to establish entitling conditions or events, and frequently invalidated on purported principles of preclusion of ousting the court of jurisdiction or tampering with rules of evidence, are seen to rest more fundamentally on concepts of public policy hostile to harsh or unfair restrictions against recovery on such policies. . . . In one typical such case, *American Ben. Life Ass'n v. Hall*, 96 Ind. App. 498, 185 N.E. 344 (App. Ct. 1933), invalidating a stipulation that "total disability" could be evidenced only by proof of actual continuous confinement in a dwelling or hospital for at least two weeks and the necessary attendance of a doctor at least every three days,

the court said, in language frequently cited and quoted (at p. 345 of 185 N.E.):

* * *

Courts for centuries have been gradually working to establish what evidence may be admissible under certain circumstances. For years the rule has been that any evidence relative to the issues and competent under the general rules of evidence is admissible in an action on an insurance policy. 14 R.C.L. 1438; 33 C.J. § 835.

If it were otherwise, there could be no settled rule of evidence and every contract would of necessity have to provide what rules of evidence could be used in any suit on such contract. It is far better for the courts to make the rules of evidence for all cases, as it is only by such method that any uniformity can be attained and any degree of certainty assured.

It may well be questioned, however, whether the underlying philosophy of the holding is not really more one of abhorrence at the substantive unfairness of contractual conditions for recovery than at contracting for rules of evidence.

A significant approach in a case analogous to the instant problem may be found in *Swift & Co. v. Hocking Valley R. Co.*, 243 U.S. 281, 37 S. Ct. 287, 61 L. Ed. 722 (1917). It illustrates the limits the courts will impose on recognition of unwarranted stipulations by parties in respect of the adjudicatory function. In that case it was material whether, for purposes of the right of a carrier to impose a demurrage charge on railroad cars, the track upon which they laid over was a private track of the shipper. The character of the track depended upon construction of a written agreement between the parties, but it was stipulated between them for purposes of the appeal that the track was private. The Supreme Court (*per* Brandeis, J.) held the stipulation void as contrary to the true fact, seemingly on its own motion. It said (at p. 289 of 37 S. Ct.):

The construction and effect of a written instrument is a question of law. *Dillon v. Barnard*, 22 L. Ed. 673, 676, 21 Wall. 430, 437. Clearly the track in question was not a private track of the shipper, but a track of the carrier, — like the spur passed upon in *National Ref. Co. v. St. Louis, I.M. & S.R. Co.* 150 C.C.A. 361, 237 Fed. 347, affirming [D.C.] 226 Fed. 357.

If the stipulation is to be treated as an agreement concerning the legal effect of admitted facts, it is obviously inoperative; since the court cannot be controlled by agreement of counsel on a subsidiary question of law. See cases cited in the margin. If the stipulation is to be treated as an attempt to agree "for the purpose only of reviewing the judgment" below, that what are the facts shall be assumed not to be facts, a moot or fictitious case is presented. "The duty of this court, as of every judicial tribunal, is limited to determining rights of persons or of property, which are actually controverted in the particular case before it.. . . No stipulation of parties or counsel, whether in the case before the court or in any other case, can enlarge the power, or affect the duty, of the court in this regard."

Cf. Wheeler v. Barnes, 100 Conn. 57, 122 A. 912, 914 (Sup. Ct. Err. 1923).

In his discussion of contracts to alter general rules of evidence Wigmore lists four categories. The third is applicable here:

> (C). It may *exclude*, for the *other party*, evidence which the usual law would *admit; e.g.*, if a vendor should stipulate that no person not an expert should testify to the sold article's failure to equal sample; but no actual instance of this variety appears in the cases.

1 Wigmore, op. cit., *supra*, at p. 214 (emphasis by author).

The author states that there are "apparently not" any "reasons of policy" which would mark any of the listed categories as objectionable, excepting possibly the fourth, which would admit for the stipulating party evidence ordinarily inadmissible in law. A converse approach, however, is taken by the writer of the HARVARD LAW REVIEW note cited above. He says:

> But if the parties resort to a judicial determination of their disputes, a contract to deprive the court of relevant testimony, or to restrict its judgment to a finding based upon incomplete facts, stands on a different ground than one admitting evidence that would otherwise have been barred by an exclusionary rule. One contract is an impediment to ascertaining the facts, the other aids in the final determination of the true situation. Differentiation upon this basis provides a desirable flexibility in dealing with the exclusionary rules of proof, yet safeguards the litigants by assuring a complete and adequate determination of the issues.

(46 HARV. L. REV., at pp. 142, 143.)

We find the foregoing reasoning sound and persuasive as applied to the situation here presented. While plaintiff invokes the jurisdiction of the court to construe and enforce its contract, it would have us do so wearing judicial blinders. We are requested to conform to a private agreement mandating our performance of a judicial function in a manner which, under our precedents, is not the path to justice in arriving at the binding meaning of a contract. It would be wrong for us to do so. Confining our holding strictly to the situation before us, we hold that the relied upon portion of section 17.23 of the lease is void as against public policy. It consequently does not bar the admission of the proofs discussed above.

Reversed and remanded for a new trial conforming to this opinion.

9. Contracts contain a wide array of exclusionary clauses, including definitions that limit the evidence used to establish the fair market value of an object, integration clauses that prohibit consideration of extra-contractual evidence, and even choice of law and choice of forum clauses that may restrict a court's determination of applicable law. Where does the court in *Garden State Plaza* draw the line in deciding the enforceability of these provisions?

10. Clauses which allow seller to avoid liability for intentional or reckless conduct are also generally held void as against public policy where such clauses "contravene long established common law rules" of liability and other factors of unconscionability arise. *See, e.g., McCutcheon v. United Homes Corp.*, 486 P.2d 1093 (Wash. 1971). Similar to the other public policy grounds examined in this Chapter, these clauses raise difficult issues about the balance to be struck between contractual

freedom, and the public interest in striking clauses that insulate parties from their own negligence or willful conduct.

PROBLEMS

1. Joe runs a successful import/export company. He enters into a three-year contract with Herbs Incorporated to import a new herbal treatment for weight loss. One year into the contract the Federal Drug Administration outlaws the sale of the herbal treatment. Joe refuses to pay for the most recent shipment, made just before the law was changed. Would a claim of illegality in Herbs Incorporated's suit for breach be successful? Who should bear the burden of loss when the law or public policy changes?

2. Gary Gambler enters into an agreement with Wally Website to create a website under the domain name Pokerpalace.com which will permit on-line gambling through use of credit card charges. Gary agrees to compensate Wally for his design services by paying him 20% of all proceeds earned from the website. Gary earns $1,000, 000 net profits in the first six months of operation of the website but refuses to pay Wally. Wally has hired you to represent him in his breach of contract suit. What are his chances of success? What is the strongest argument you can make to counter Gary's anticipated illegality defense?

3. WorldCom, prior to its bankruptcy, entered into office leases. When it came time for renewal of the leases, WorldCom directed 485 Properties, a licensed real estate broker, to deal with its own its leasing agent, WorkPlace U.S.A., Inc. Workplace is not licensed under Georgia law to serve as a real estate broker. Workplace later refuses to pay the agreed-upon brokerage free. What result? *See Amend v. 485 Properties, LLC*, 401 F.3d 1255 (11th Cir. 2005).

4. Blake, a devoted Internet blogger, writes on his weekly blog, "I will bet $100 that Star Wars: Episode 8 is the largest grossing movie in the Star Wars pantheon." Bonita writes back "I'll take that bet." Star Wars: Episode 8 tanks at the box office. Bonita demands that Blake "pay up." Blake refuses. Bonita sues him for breach of contract. What result?

C. RESTRICTIVE EMPLOYMENT COVENANTS

A post-term restrictive covenant in an employment setting is a contractual provision which is part of the employment relationship and which restricts the employee's competition with the employer after the employment ends. Such covenants typically limit the time, geographic territory, and subject matter activity in which the former employee may engage. By way of example, a restrictive covenant for a veterinarian might prohibit the veterinarian from practicing veterinary medicine on small animals within a 50-mile radius of the small animal clinic at which the veterinarian worked for a period of two years after the employment ended.

Because each working individual's occupation is critical to his/her livelihood and enjoyment of life, the law will scrutinize closely the attempt by an employer to limit one's employment mobility and competition by means of a post-term restrictive covenant. Public policy demands that there be both a legitimate business interest warranting protection by means of a restrictive covenant and that the restrictive covenant be reasonable in its terms in order for a court to enforce it. As you read the following cases, consider how the court should treat an unreasonable restriction. Should it strike the clause in its entirety or read the clause to reach only so far as the law allows? To what extent should contract law be allowed to interfere with the parties' clearly expressed intentions?

KARPINSKI v. INGRASCI
28 N.Y. 2d 45, 268 N.E.2d 751 (1971)

FULD, Chief Judge:

This appeal requires us to determine whether a covenant by a professional man not to compete with his employer is enforceable and, if it is, to what extent.

The plaintiff, Dr. Karpinski, an oral surgeon, had been carrying on his practice alone in Auburn — in Cayuga County — for many years. In 1953, he decided to expand and, since nearly all of an oral surgeon's business stems from referrals, he embarked upon a plan to "cultivate connections" among dentists in the four nearby Counties of Tompkins, Seneca, Cortland and Ontario. The plan was successful, and by 1962 twenty per cent of his practice consisted of treating patients referred to him by dentists located in those counties. In that year, after a number of those dentists had told him that some of their patients found it difficult to travel from their homes to Auburn, the plaintiff decided to open a second office in centrally-located Ithaca. He began looking for an assistant and, in the course of his search, met the defendant, Dr. Ingrasci, who was just completing his training in oral surgery at the Buffalo General Hospital and was desirous of entering private practice. Dr. Ingrasci manifested an interest in becoming associated with Dr. Karpinski and, after a number of discussions, they reached an understanding; the defendant was to live in Ithaca, a locale with which he had no prior familiarity, and there work as an employee of the plaintiff.

A contract, reflecting the agreement, was signed by the defendant in June, 1962. It was for three years and, shortly after its execution, the defendant started working in the office which the plaintiff rented and fully equipped at his own expense. The provision of the contract with which we are concerned is a covenant by the defendant not to compete with the plaintiff. More particularly, it recited that the defendant

> promises and covenants that while this agreement is in effect and forever thereafter, he will never practice dentistry and/or Oral Surgery in Cayuga, Cortland, Seneca, Tompkins or Ontario counties except: (a) In association with the (plaintiff) or (b) If the (plaintiff) terminates the agreement and employs another oral surgeon.

In addition, the defendant agreed, "in consideration of the . . . terms of employment, and of the experience gained while working with" the plaintiff, to execute a $40, 000 promissory note to the plaintiff, to become payable if the defendant left the plaintiff and practiced "dentistry and/or Oral Surgery" in the five enumerated counties.[9] When the contract expired, the two men engaged in extended discussions as to the nature of their continued association — as employer and employee or as partners. Unable to reach an accord, the defendant, in

---

[9] [1] Either party was privileged to terminate the agreement on 60 days' notice within the three-year period and, if the plaintiff were to do so, the contract recited, the defendant was released from the restrictive covenant and the note.

February, 1968, left the plaintiff's employ and opened his own office for the practice of oral surgery in Ithaca a week later. The dentists in the area thereupon began referring their patients to the defendant rather than to the plaintiff, and in two months the latter's practice from the Ithaca area dwindled to almost nothing and he closed the office in that city. In point of fact, the record discloses that about 90% of the defendant's present practice comes from referrals from dentists in the counties specified in the restrictive covenant, the very same dentists who had been referring patients to the plaintiff's Ithaca office when the defendant was working there.[10]

The plaintiff, alleging a breach of the restrictive covenant, seeks not only an injunction to enforce it but also a judgment of $40, 000 on the note. The Supreme Court, after a nonjury trial, decided in favor of the plaintiff and granted him both an injunction and damages as requested. On appeal, however, the Appellate Division reversed the resulting judgment and dismissed the complaint; it was that court's view that the covenant was void and unenforceable on the ground that its restriction against the practice of both dentistry *and* oral surgery was impermissibly broad.

There can be no doubt that the defendant violated the terms of the covenant when he opened his own office in Ithaca. But the mere fact of breach does not, in and of itself, resolve the case. Since there are "powerful considerations of public policy which militate against sanctioning the loss of a man's livelihood, " the courts will subject a covenant by an employee not to compete with his former employer to an "overriding limitation of reasonableness." (*Purchasing Assoc. v. Weitz*, 13 N.Y. 2d 267, 272, 246 N.Y.S. 2d 600, 603, 196 N.E.2d 245. . . .) Such covenants by physicians are, if reasonable in scope, generally given effect. (*See Millet v. Slocum*, 5 N.Y. 2d 734, 177 N.Y.S. 2d 716, 152 N.E.2d 672. . . .) "It is a firmly established doctrine," it has been noted, "that a member of one of the learned professions, upon becoming assistant to another member thereof, may, upon a sufficient consideration, bind himself not to engage in the practice of his profession upon the termination of his contract of employment, within a reasonable territorial extent, as such an agreement is not in restraint of trade or against public policy" (Ann., *Restriction on Practice of Physician*, 58 A.L.R. 156, 162).

Each case must, of course, depend, to a great extent, upon its own facts. It may well be that, in some instances, a restriction not to conduct a profession or a business in two counties or even in one, may exceed permissible limits. But, in the case before us, having in mind the character and size of the counties involved, the area restriction imposed is manifestly reasonable. The five small rural counties which it encompasses comprise the very area from which the plaintiff obtained his patients and in which the defendant would be in direct competition with him. Thus, the covenant's coverage coincides precisely with "the territory over which the practice extends, " and this is proper and permissible. . . . In brief, the plaintiff made no attempt to extend his influence beyond the area from which he drew his patients, the defendant being perfectly free to practice as he chooses outside the five specified counties.

Nor may the covenant be declared invalid because it is unlimited as to time, forever restricting the defendant from competing with the plaintiff. It is settled that such a covenant will not be stricken merely because it "contains no time limit or is

---

[10] [2] There are two other oral surgeons, in addition to the plaintiff and the defendant, serving the Ithaca area.

expressly made unlimited as to time." (. . . *Foster v. White*, 248 App. Div. 451, 456, 290 N.Y.S. 394, 399, *aff'd*, 273 N.Y. 596, 7 N.E.2d 710 . . . .) "According to the weight of authority as applied to contracts by physicians, surgeons and others of kindred profession, " the court wrote in Foster "relief for violation of these contracts will not be denied merely because the agreement is unlimited as to time, where as to area the restraint is limited and reasonable." In the present case, the defendant opened an office in Ithaca, in competition with the plaintiff, just one week after his employment had come to an end. Under the circumstances presented, we thoroughly agree with the trial judge that it is clear that nearly all of the defendant's practice was, and would be, directly attributable to his association with his former employer.

This brings us to the most troublesome part of the restriction imposed upon the defendant. By the terms of the contract, he agreed not to practice "dentistry and/or Oral Surgery" in competition with the plaintiff. Since the plaintiff practices only "oral surgery, " and it was for the practice of that limited type of "dentistry" that he had employed the defendant, the Appellate Division concluded that the plaintiff went beyond permissible limits when he obtained from the defendant the covenant that he would not engage in any "dentistry" whatsoever.[11] The restriction, *as formulated*, is, as the Appellate Division concluded, too broad; it is not reasonable for a man to be excluded from a profession for which he has been trained when he does not compete with his former employer by a practicing it.

The plaintiff seeks to justify the breadth of the covenant by urging that, if it had restricted only the defendant's practice of oral surgery and permitted him to practice "dentistry" — that is, to hold himself out as a dentist generally — the defendant would have been permitted, under the Education Law (§ 6601, subd. 3), to do all the work which an oral surgeon could. We have no sympathy with this argument; the plaintiff was not privileged to prevent the defendant from working in an area of dentistry in which he would not be in competition with him. The plaintiff would have all the protection he needs if the restriction were to be limited to the practice of oral surgery, and this poses the question as to the court's power to "sever" the impermissible from the valid and uphold the covenant to the extent that it is reasonable.

Although we have found no decision in New York directly in point, cases in this court support the existence of such a power. (*See, e.g., Purchasing Assoc. v. Weitz*, 13 N.Y. 2d 267, 272, 246 N.Y.S. 2d 600 . . . .) Moreover, a number of out-of-state decisions, and they are supported by authoritative texts and commentators, explicitly recognize the court's power of severance and divisibility in order to sustain the covenant insofar as it is reasonable.[12] As Professor Blake put it (73 HARV. L. REV. at pp. 674–675), "If in balancing the equities the court decides that his (the employee's) activity would fit within the scope of a reasonable prohibition, it is apt to make use of the tool of severance, paring an unreasonable restraint down to appropriate size and enforcing it." In short, to cull from the Washington Supreme

---

[11] [3] Some of the things a dentist may do, which a practitioner who limits himself to oral surgery is ethically prevented from doing include the filling of teeth, placing crowns on teeth, doing reconstruction work of the mouth, dentures, prophylaxis or straightening of the teeth.

[12] [4] *See, e.g.*, John Roane, Inc. v. Tweed, 33 Del. Ch. 4, 17, 89 A.2d 548; New England Tree Expert Co. v. Russell, 306 Mass. 504, 509, 28 N.E.2d 997. . . . Some of these authorities would only sever by applying the so-called "blue pencil" rule — that is, dividing the contract only when it is grammatically severable. Even this limited approach, however, would be sufficient in the case before us.

Court's opinion in *Wood v. May*, 73 Wash. 2d 307, 314, 438 P.2d 587, 591, "we find it just and equitable to protect appellant (employer) by injunction to the extent necessary to accomplish the basic purpose of the contract insofar as such contract is reasonable." Accordingly, since his practice is solely as an oral surgeon, the plaintiff gains all the injunctive protection to which he is entitled if effect be given only to that part of the covenant which prohibits the defendant from practicing oral surgery.

The question arises, however, whether injunctive relief is precluded by the fact that the defendant's promissory note for $40, 000 was to become payable if he breached the agreement not to compete. We believe not. The mere inclusion in a covenant of a liquidated damages provision does not automatically bar the grant of an injunction. . . . As this court wrote in the *Diamond Match Co.* case (106 N.Y. at p. 486, 13 N.E. at p. 424), "It is a question of intention, to be deduced from the whole instrument and the circumstances; and if it appear that the performance of the covenant was intended, and not merely the payment of damages in case of a breach, the covenant will be enforced." The covenant under consideration in this case may not reasonably be read to render "the liquidated damages provision . . . the sole remedy." (*Rubinstein v. Rubinstein*, 23 N.Y. 2d 293, 298, 296 N.Y.S. 2d 354, 358, 244 N.E.2d 49, 51, *supra*.) On the other hand, it would be grossly unfair to grant the plaintiff, in addition to an injunction, the full amount of damages ($40, 000) which the parties apparently contemplated for a total breach of the covenant, since the injunction will halt any further violation. The proper approach is that taken in *Wirth* (265 N.Y. 214, 192 N.E. 297, supra). The court, there faced with a similar situation, granted the injunction sought and, instead of awarding the amount of liquidated damages specified, remitted the matter for determination of the actual damages suffered during the period of the breach.

The hardship necessarily imposed on the defendant must be borne by him in view of the plaintiff's rightful interest in protecting the valuable practice of oral surgery which he built up over the course of many years. The defendant is, of course, privileged to practice "dentistry" generally in Ithaca or continue to practice "oral surgery" anywhere in the United States outside of the five small rural counties enumerated. The covenant, part of a contract carefully negotiated with no indication of fraud or overbearing on either side, must be enforced, insofar as it reasonably and validly may, according to its terms. In sum, then, the plaintiff is entitled to an injunction barring the defendant from practicing oral surgery in the five specified counties and to damages actually suffered by him in the period during which the defendant conducted such a practice in Ithaca after leaving the plaintiff's employ. . . .

NOTES & QUESTIONS

1. Footnote 2 indicates that there were two other oral surgeons within the geographic area of restriction for Dr. Ingrasci. If there had been no other oral surgeons servicing the affected counties, should the court's decision have been different?

2. Under the covenant in this case, during the term of his employment could Dr. Ingrasci have practiced dentistry for another dental clinic on days when he was not working for Dr. Karpinski (a so-called "moonlighting" restriction)? Could Karpinski have restricted Ingrasci's work at other non-dental related positions

during the term of the employment, such as a bartender?

3. What does "forever" mean in the preceding case?

4. Is there an inherent inconsistency in the remedies granted by the court? That is, the equitable relief of injunction is an extraordinary remedy granted only in circumstances in which monetary relief would be insufficient to satisfy the plaintiff. So how can the plaintiff obtain both remedies here?

5. Restrictive covenants in the medical field raise strong public interest issues. What is the public interest in connection with the enforcement of the restrictive covenant?

6. Assume that if the restrictive covenant in *Ingrasi* is enforced, there are only two oral surgeons in the City of Ithaca. What impact, if any, would this fact have on the reasonableness of the restrictive covenant? *See, e.g., The Community Hospital Group, Inc. v. More*, 869 A.2d 884 (N.J. 2005).

HOPPER v. ALL PET ANIMAL CLINIC, INC.
861 P.2d 531 (Wyo. 1993)

Taylor, Justice:

These consolidated appeals test the enforceability of a covenant not to compete which was included in an employment contract. . . . Following her graduation from Colorado State University, Dr. Glenna Hopper (Dr. Hopper) began working part-time as a veterinarian at the All Pet Animal Clinic, Inc.(All Pet) in July of 1988. All Pet specialized in the care of small animals; mostly domesticated dogs and cats, and those exotic animals maintained as household pets. Dr. Hopper practiced under the guidance and direction of the President of All Pet, Dr. Robert Bruce Johnson (Dr. Johnson).

Dr. Johnson, on behalf of All Pet, offered Dr. Hopper full-time employment in February of 1989. The oral offer included a specified salary and potential for bonus earnings as well as other terms of employment. According to Dr. Johnson, he conditioned the offer on Dr. Hopper's acceptance of a covenant not to compete, the specific details of which were not discussed at the time. Dr. Hopper commenced full-time employment with All Pet under the oral agreement in March of 1989 and relocated to Laramie, discontinuing her commute from her former residence in Colorado.

A written Employment Agreement incorporating the terms of the oral agreement was finally executed by the parties on December 11, 1989. Ancillary to the provisions for employment, the agreement detailed the terms of a covenant not to compete:

> 12. This agreement may be terminated by either party upon 30 days' notice to the other party. Upon termination, Dr. Hopper agrees that she will not practice small animal medicine for a period of three years from the date of termination within 5 miles of the corporate limits of the City of Laramie, Wyoming. Dr. Hopper agrees that the duration and geographic scope of that limitation is reasonable.

The agreement was antedated to be effective to March 3, 1989.

The parties executed an Addendum To Agreement on June 1, 1990. The addendum provided that All Pet and a newly acquired corporate entity, Alpine Animal Hospital, Inc. (Alpine), also located in Laramie, would share in Dr. Hopper's professional services. As the President of All Pet and Alpine, Dr. Johnson agreed, in the addendum, to raise Dr. Hopper's salary. The bonus provision of the original agreement was eliminated. Except as modified, the other terms of the March 3, 1989 employment agreement, including the covenant not to compete, were reaffirmed and Dr. Hopper continued her employment.

One year later, reacting to a rumor that Dr. Hopper was investigating the purchase of a veterinary practice in Laramie, Dr. Johnson asked his attorney to prepare a letter which was presented to Dr. Hopper. The letter, dated June 17, 1991, stated:

> I have learned that you are considering leaving us to take over the small animal part of Dr. Meeboer's practice in Laramie.
>
> When we negotiated the terms of your employment, we agreed that you could leave upon 30 days' notice, but that you would not practice small animal medicine within five miles of Laramie for a three-year period. We do not have any non-competition agreement for large-animal medicine, which therefore does not enter into the picture.
>
> I am willing to release you from the non-competition agreement in return for a cash buy-out. I have worked back from the proportion of the income of All-Pet and Alpine which you contribute and have decided that a reasonable figure would be $40, 000.00, to compensate the practice for the loss of business which will happen if you practice small-animal medicine elsewhere in Laramie.
>
> If you are willing to approach the problem in the way I suggest, please let me know and I will have the appropriate paperwork taken care of.
>
> Sincerely,
>
> [Signed]
>
> R. Bruce Johnson,
>
> D.V.M.

Dr. Hopper responded to the letter by denying that she was going to purchase Dr. Meeboer's practice. Dr. Hopper told Dr. Johnson that the Employment Agreement was not worth the paper it was written on and that she could do anything she wanted to do. Dr. Johnson terminated Dr. Hopper's employment and informed her to consider the 30-day notice as having been given. An unsigned, handwritten note from Dr. Johnson to Dr. Hopper, dated June 18, 1991, affirmed the termination and notice providing, in part:

> Per your request to abide by your employment agreement with All Pet and Alpine as regards termination:
>
> Be advised that your last day of employment is July 18, 1991 for reasons that we are both aware of and have discussed previously.

Subsequently, Dr. Hopper purchased Gem City Veterinary Clinic (Gem City), the practice of Dr. Melanie Manning. Beginning on July 15, 1991, Dr. Hopper operated Gem City, in violation of the covenant not to compete, within the City of Laramie and with a practice including large and small animals. Under Dr. Hopper's guidance, Gem City's client list grew from 368 at the time she purchased the practice to approximately 950 at the time of trial. A comparison of client lists disclosed that 187 clients served by Dr. Hopper at Gem City were also clients of All Pet or Alpine. Some of these shared clients received permissible large animal services from Dr. Hopper. Overall, the small animal work contributed from fifty-one to fifty-two percent of Dr. Hopper's gross income at Gem City.

All Pet and Alpine filed a complaint against Dr. Hopper on November 15, 1991 seeking injunctive relief and damages for breach of the covenant not to compete contained in the Employment Agreement. Notably, All Pet and Alpine did not seek a temporary injunction to restrict Dr. Hopper's practice and possibly mitigate damages during the pendency of the proceeding. Trial was conducted on September 28, 1992.

The district court, in its Findings of Fact, Conclusions of Law and Judgment, determined that the covenant not to compete was enforceable as a matter of law and contained reasonable durational and geographic limits necessary to protect All Pet's and Alpine's special interests. . . .

The common law policy against contracts in restraint of trade is one of the oldest and most firmly established. RESTATEMENT (SECOND) OF CONTRACTS §§ 185–188 (1981) (Introductory Note at 35). *See Dutch Maid Bakeries v. Schleicher*, 58 Wyo. 374, 131 P.2d 630, 634 (1942). The traditional disfavor of such restraints means covenants not to compete are construed against the party seeking to enforce them. *Commercial Bankers Life Ins. Co. of America v. Smith*, 516 N.E.2d 110, 112 (Ind. App. 1987). The initial burden is on the employer to prove the covenant is reasonable and has a fair relation to, and is necessary for, the business interests for which protection is sought. *Tench v. Weaver*, 374 P.2d 27, 29 (Wyo. 1962).

Two principles, the freedom to contract and the freedom to work, conflict when courts test the enforceability of covenants not to compete. *Ridley v. Krout*, 63 Wyo. 252, 180 P.2d 124, 128 (1947). There is general recognition that while an employer may seek protection from improper and unfair competition of a former employee, the employer is not entitled to protection against ordinary competition. . . . The enforceability of a covenant not to compete depends upon a finding that the proper balance exists between the competing interests of the employer and the employee. *See* RESTATEMENT (SECOND) OF AGENCY § 393 comment e (1958) (noting that without a covenant not to compete, an agent, employee, can compete with a principal despite past employment and can begin preparations for future competition, such as purchasing a competitive business, before leaving present employment).

Wyoming adopted a rule of reason inquiry from the RESTATEMENT OF CONTRACTS testing the validity of a covenant not to compete. *Dutch Maid Bakeries*, 131 P.2d at 634 (citing RESTATEMENT OF CONTRACTS §§ 513–515 (1932)); *Ridley*, 180 P.2d at 127. The present formulation of the rule of reason is contained in RESTATEMENT (SECOND) OF CONTRACTS, *supra*, § 188:

    (1) A promise to refrain from competition that imposes a restraint that is ancillary to an otherwise valid transaction or relationship is unreasonably in restraint of trade if

(a) the restraint is greater than is needed to protect the promisee's legitimate interest, or

(b) the promisee's need is outweighed by the hardship to the promisor and the likely injury to the public.

(2) Promises imposing restraints that are ancillary to a valid transaction or relationship include the following:

(a) a promise by the seller of a business not to compete with the buyer in such a way as to injure the value of the business sold;

(b) a promise by an employee or other agent not to compete with his employer or other principal;

(c) a promise by a partner not to compete with the partnership. . . .

An often quoted reformulation of the rule of reason inquiry states that "[a] restraint is reasonable only if it (1) is no greater than is required for the protection of the employer, (2) does not impose undue hardship on the employee, and (3) is not injurious to the public." Harlan M. Blake, Employee Agreements Not to Compete, 73 HARV. L. REV. 625, 648–49 (1960).

A valid and enforceable covenant not to compete requires a showing that the covenant is: (1) in writing; (2) part of a contract of employment; (3) based on reasonable consideration; (4) reasonable in durational and geographical limitations; and (5) not against public policy. *A.E.P. Industries, Inc. v. McClure*, 308 N.C. 393, 302 S.E.2d 754, 760 (1983). . . . The reasonableness of a covenant not to compete is assessed based upon the facts of the particular case and a review of all of the circumstances.

. . .

While many factors may be considered by the court in evaluating reasonableness as a matter of law, a useful enumeration is contained in *Philip G. Johnson & Co. v. Salmen*, 211 Neb. 123, 317 N.W.2d 900, 904 (1982):

> The considerations to be balanced are the degree of inequality in bargaining power; the risk of the covenantee losing customers; the extent of respective participation by the parties in securing and retaining customers; the good faith of the covenantee; the existence of sources or general knowledge pertaining to the identity of customers; the nature and extent of the business position held by the covenantor; the covenantor's training, health, education, and needs of his family; the current conditions of employment; the necessity of the covenantor changing his calling or residence; and the correspondence of the restraint with the need for protecting the legitimate interests of the covenantee.

Wyoming has previously recognized that the legitimate interests of the employer, covenantee, which may be protected from competition include: (a) the employer's trade secrets which have been communicated to the employee during the course of employment; (b) confidential information communicated by the employer to the employee, but not involving trade secrets, such as information on a unique business method; and (c) special influence by the employee obtained during the course of employment over the employer's customers. . . .

The enforceability of a covenant not to compete using the rule of reason analysis depends upon a determination, as a matter of law, that the promise not to compete is ancillary to the existence of an otherwise valid transaction or relationship. RESTATEMENT (SECOND) OF CONTRACTS, *supra*, § 187. If, for example, the contract of employment containing the covenant not to compete fails for lack of consideration, adhesion or other contractual excuse, the covenant is without effect. *Reddy v. Community Health Foundation of Man*, 171 W. Va. 368, 298 S.E.2d 906, 915 (1982). The covenant is also without effect because it is not ancillary when it is made in a promise subsequent to the transaction or relationship. RESTATEMENT (SECOND) OF CONTRACTS, *supra*, § 187 comment b.

When Dr. Johnson made the oral promise of employment to Dr. Hopper, the specific terms of the covenant were not discussed. Dr. Johnson testified that no terms for a geographic radius or time restriction on competition were stated during formation of the oral contract of employment. Without terms and without a writing, Wyo. Stat § 1-23-105, a promise not to compete at this time failed as ancillary to the creation of the relationship.

The written Employment Agreement Dr. Hopper signed does contain a covenant not to compete which is ancillary to the previously agreed provisions for employment memorialized from the oral contract. RESTATEMENT (SECOND) OF CONTRACTS, *supra*, § 187 comment b recognizes that in an ongoing transaction or relationship, a promise not to compete may be made before the termination of the relationship and still be ancillary as long as it is supported by consideration and meets other requirements for enforceability. It is necessary to analyze whether Dr. Hopper's promise not to compete, made after the creation of the relationship while executing the written Employment Agreement, was supported by consideration. . . .

Wyoming has never determined whether a promise not to compete made during the employment relationship is supported merely by the consideration of continued employment or must be supported by separate contemporaneous consideration.

Authorities from other jurisdictions are not in agreement on whether continued employment provides sufficient consideration or whether separate consideration is required to create an ancillary covenant not to compete made during the existence of the relationship. *See* Howard A. Specter & Matthew W. Finkin, INDIVIDUAL EMPLOYMENT LAW AND LITIGATION § 8.02 (1989) (collecting cases). We believe strong public policy favors separate consideration.

> The better view, even in the at-will relationship, is to require additional consideration to support a restrictive covenant entered into during the term of the employment. This view recognizes the increasing criticism of the at-will relationship, the usually unequal bargaining power of the parties, and the reality that the employee rarely "bargains for" continued employment in exchange for a potentially onerous restraint on the ability to earn a living.

Id. § 8.02 at 450.

The separate consideration necessary to support an ancillary promise not to compete made after creation of the employment relationship would include promotion, pay raise, special training, employment benefits or other advantages for the employee.

The written Employment Agreement Dr. Hopper signed contains no evidence of separate consideration, such as a pay raise or other benefit, in exchange for the covenant not to compete. Standing alone, the covenant not to compete contained in the Employment Agreement failed due to lack of separate consideration. RESTATEMENT (SECOND) OF CONTRACTS, *supra*, § 187. However, on June 1, 1990, the parties executed the Addendum to Agreement. In that agreement, Dr. Hopper accepted a pay raise of $550.00 per month. This agreement restates, by incorporation, the terms of the covenant not to compete. We hold that the Addendum to Agreement, with its pay raise, represented sufficient separate consideration supporting the reaffirmation of the covenant not to compete. Therefore, the district court's findings that the covenant was ancillary to an employment contract and that consideration was received in exchange for the covenant are not clearly erroneous.

The contract permitted either Dr. Hopper or her corporate employers to terminate her employment with notice. The agreement did not state a length of employment and it permitted termination at will. Without more, the terms present the potential for an unreasonable restraint of trade. For example, if an employer hired an employee at will, obtained a covenant not to compete, and then terminated the employee, without cause, to arbitrarily restrict competition, we believe such conduct would constitute bad faith. Simple justice requires that a termination by the employer of an at will employee be in good faith if a covenant not to compete is to be enforced.

Under the present facts, we cannot say that the termination of Dr. Hopper occurred in bad faith. Trial testimony presented evidence of increasing tension prior to termination in the professional relationship between Dr. Johnson and Dr. Hopper. This tension, however, did not appear to result in the termination. The notice of termination was given after Dr. Hopper was confronted about her negotiations to purchase a competitive practice and after Dr. Hopper had termed the employment contract worthless. We cannot find in these facts a bad faith termination which would provide a reason to depart from the district court's finding that the contract of employment was valid. With the determination that as a matter of law the covenant is ancillary to a valid employment relationship, we turn to the rule of reason inquiry.

Employers are entitled to protect their business from the detrimental impact of competition by employees who, but for their employment, would not have had the ability to gain a special influence over clients or customers. *Beckman v. Cox Broadcasting Corp.*, 250 Ga. 127, 296 S.E.2d 566 (1982) illustrates the principle in the broadcast industry where the clients are the viewers of a particular station. Beckman was a television weather forecaster whose contributions to the "Action News Team" had been extensively promoted by Cox during his employment. The promotion and Beckman's personality succeeded in attracting viewers to watch the television station. When his contract with Cox expired, Beckman accepted employment with a competitive television station in the same city and sought a declaratory judgment to determine the validity of a restrictive covenant which prevented him from appearing on television for six months within a radius of thirty-five miles of Cox's station offices.

The Supreme Court of Georgia agreed that Beckman was entitled to take to a new employer his assets as an employee which he had contributed to his former employer. "It is true that an employee's aptitude, skill, dexterity, manual and mental ability and other subjective knowledge obtained in the course of employment are not property of the employer which the employer can, in absence of a contractual right, prohibit the employee from taking with him at the termination of employment." The covenant permitted Cox to recover from the loss of Beckman's services by implementing a transition plan while still permitting Beckman to work as a meteorologist, but not to the extent of appearing on air with a competitive television station. The Beckman court determined that the business interests of Cox required protection which enforcement of the reasonable terms of the covenant provided.

The special interests of All Pet and Alpine identified by the district court as findings of fact are not clearly erroneous. Dr. Hopper moved to Laramie upon completion of her degree prior to any significant professional contact with the community. Her introduction to All Pet's and Alpine's clients, client files, pricing policies, and practice development techniques provided information which exceeded the skills she brought to her employment. While she was a licensed and trained veterinarian when she accepted employment, the additional exposure to clients and knowledge of clinic operations her employers shared with her had a monetary value for which the employers are entitled to reasonable protection from irreparable harm. The proven loss of 187 of All Pet's and Alpine's clients to Dr. Hopper's new practice sufficiently demonstrated actual harm from unfair competition.

The reasonableness, in a given fact situation, of the limitations placed on a former employee by a covenant not to compete are determinations made by the court as a matter of law. *See, e.g., Jarrett v. Hamilton*, 179 Ga. App. 422, 346 S.E.2d 875, 876 (1986). Therefore, the district court's conclusions of law about the reasonableness of the type of activity, geographic, and durational limits contained in the covenant are subject to de novo review.

All parties to this litigation devoted extensive research to evaluations of the reasonableness of various covenants not to compete from different authorities. However, we find precedent from our own or from other jurisdictions to be of limited value in considering the reasonableness of limits contained in a specific covenant not to compete. For example, in *Cukjati*, 772 S.W.2d at 216, 218, the Court of Appeals of Texas held a covenant not to compete was unreasonable because it limited a veterinarian from practicing within twelve miles of his former employer's clinic in North Irving, a community within the Dallas-Fort Worth metropolitan area. Because evidence from that proceeding disclosed that Dallas area residents are unlikely to travel more than a few miles for pet care, the court found the restriction unreasonable. The number of veterinarians and the demands upon their services obviously varies between Laramie, Wyoming and metropolitan Dallas, Texas, creating a different usage pattern. We believe the reasonableness of individual limitations contained in a specific covenant not to compete must be assessed based upon the facts of that proceeding.

Useful legal principles do emerge from a survey of relevant authorities and may certainly be applied to decisions about the reasonableness of the type of activity, geographic, and durational limitations. Testing the reasonableness of the type of activity limitation provides an opportunity for the court to consider the broader public policy implications of a covenant not to compete. The decision of the Court of Appeals of Ohio in *Williams v. Hobbs*, 9 Ohio App. 3d 331, 460 N.E.2d 287, 9 O.B.R. 599 (1983) explains. The Williams court determined that enforcing a covenant not to compete restricting a radiologist's uncommon specialty practice would violate public policy because the community would be deprived of a unique skill. In addition, the court held the type of activity limitation was unreasonable because it created an undue hardship on the physician where there were only a limited number of osteopathic hospitals available to practice his specialty.

The Court of Appeals of Arkansas, in an en banc opinion, used a similar analysis in reviewing a covenant not to compete which restricted an orthopedic surgeon from practicing medicine within a radius of thirty miles from the offices of his former partners. *Duffner*, 718 S.W.2d at 113–14. The court held that the covenant interfered with the public's right to choose an orthopedic surgeon and that enforcement of the covenant created an unreasonable restraint of trade. In determining that no business interests of the partnership were lost, the court noted that while the surgeon provided normal postoperative care for those patients he had operated on while associated with the partnership, he had not "appropriated" any of the partnership's "stock of patients" when he moved to another office.

Enforcement of the practice restrictions Dr. Hopper accepted as part of her covenant not to compete does not create an unreasonable restraint of trade. While the specific terms of the covenant failed to define the practice of small animal medicine, the parties' trade usage provided a conforming standard of domesticated dogs and cats along with exotic animals maintained as household pets. As a veterinarian licensed to practice in Wyoming, Dr. Hopper was therefore permitted to earn a living in her chosen profession without relocating by practicing large animal medicine, a significant area of practice in this state. The restriction on the type of activity contained in the covenant was sufficiently limited to avoid undue hardship to Dr. Hopper while protecting the special interests of All Pet and Alpine. . . .

Reasonable geographic restraints are generally limited to the area in which the former employee actually worked or from which clients were drawn. *Commercial Bankers Life Ins. Co. of America*, 516 N.E.2d at 114–15; *Brewer v. Tracy*, 198 Neb. 503, 253 N.W.2d 3 19, 322 (1977). When the business serves a limited geographic area, as opposed to statewide or nationwide, courts have upheld geographic limits which are coextensive with the area in which the employer conducts business. *Torrence v. Hewitt Associates*, 143 Ill. App. 3d 520, 97 Ill. Dec. 592, 596, 493 N.E.2d 74, 78 (1986). A broad geographic restriction may be reasonable when it is coupled with a specific activity restriction within an industry or business which has an inherently limited client base. *System Concepts, Inc. v. Dixon*, 669 P.2d 421, 427 (Utah 1983).

The geographical limit contained in the covenant not to compete restricts Dr. Hopper from practicing within a five mile radius of the corporate limits of Laramie. As a matter of law, this limit is reasonable in this circumstance. The evidence presented at trial indicated that the clients of All Pet and Alpine were located throughout the county. Despite Wyoming's rural character, the five mile restriction effectively limited unfair competition without presenting an undue hardship. Dr. Hopper could, for example, have opened a practice at other locations within the county.

A durational limitation should be reasonably related to the legitimate interest which the employer is seeking to protect. RESTATEMENT (SECOND) OF CONTRACTS, *supra*, § 188 comment b.

In determining whether a restraint extends for a longer period of time than necessary to protect the employer, the court must determine how much time is needed for the risk of injury to be reasonably moderated. When the restraint is for the purpose of protecting customer relationships, its duration is reasonable only if it is no longer than necessary for the employer to put a new [individual] on the job and for the new employee to have a reasonable opportunity to demonstrate his [or her] effectiveness to the customers. If a restraint on this ground is justifiable at all, it seems that a period of several months would usually be reasonable. If the selling or servicing relationship is relatively complex, a longer period may be called for. Courts seldom criticize restraints of six months or a year on the grounds of duration as such, and even longer restraints are often enforced.

Blake, 73 HARV. L. REV. at 677 (footnote omitted). *See Amex Distributing Co., Inc. v. Mascari,* 150 Ariz. 510, 724 P.2d 596, 604–05 (1986) (quoting *Blake* and applying rule in determining that a three year duration of a covenant not to compete was unreasonable).

The evidence at trial focused on the durational requirement in attempting to establish the three year term as being necessary to diffuse the potential loss of clients from All Pet and Alpine to Dr. Hopper. Dr. Charles Sink, a licensed veterinarian, testified as an expert on behalf of All Pet and Alpine and indicated that in Wyoming, his experience correlated with national studies that disclosed about 70% of clients visit a clinic more than once per year. The remaining 30% of the clients use the clinic at least one time per year. Dr. Johnson estimated that at All Pet and Alpine, the average client seeks veterinarian services one and one-half times a year. Apart from this data about average client visits, other support for the three year durational requirement was derived from opinion testimony. Dr. Johnson admitted that influence over a client disappears in an unspecified "short period of time, " but expressed a view that three years was "safe." He also agreed that the number of clients possibly transferring from All Pet or Alpine to Dr. Hopper would be greatest in the first year and diminish in the second year.

We are unable to find a reasonable relationship between the three year durational requirement and the protection of All Pet's and Alpine's special interests. Therefore, enforcement of the entire durational term contained in the covenant not to compete violates public policy as an unreasonable restraint of trade. RESTATEMENT (SECOND) OF CONTRACTS, *supra,* § 188. Based on figures of client visits, a replacement veterinarian at All Pet and Alpine would be able to effectively demonstrate his or her own professionalism to virtually all of the clinics' clients within a one year durational limit. Since no credible evidence was presented supporting the need for multiple visits to establish special influence over clients, a one year limit is sufficient to moderate the risk of injury to All Pet and Alpine from unfair competition by Dr. Hopper. . . .

Under the formulation of the rule of reason inquiry adopted by Wyoming from the first RESTATEMENT OF CONTRACTS, the unreasonableness of any non-divisible term of a covenant not to compete made the entire covenant unenforceable. RESTATEMENT OF CONTRACTS, *supra,* § 518. It is perhaps due to the arbitrary nature of this rule that no previous decision of this court has permitted enforcement of a covenant not to compete. *Tench,* 374 P.2d at 29; *Ridley,* 180 P.2d at 133; *Dutch Maid Bakeries,* 131 P.2d at 636. The conceptual difficulty of the position taken in the former RESTATEMENT OF CONTRACTS, *supra,* § 518 leads to strong criticism by noted authors and the rejection of this so-called "blue pencil rule" by many courts.

In very many cases the courts have held the whole contract to be illegal and void where the restraint imposed was in excess of what was reasonable and the terms of the agreement indicated no line of division that could be marked with a "blue pencil." *In the best considered modern cases, however, the court has decreed enforcement as against a defendant whose breach has occurred within an area in which restriction would clearly be reasonable, even though the terms of the agreement imposed a larger and unreasonable restraint.* Thus, the seller of a purely local business who promised not to open a competing store anywhere in America has been prevented by injunction from running such a store within the same block as the one that he sold. In some cases it may be difficult to determine what is the exact limiting boundary of reasonable restriction; but often such a determination is not necessary. The question usually is whether a restriction against what the defendant has in fact done or is threatening would be a reasonable and valid restriction. The plaintiff should always be permitted to show the actual extent of the good will that is involved and that the defendant has committed a breach within that extent. If a restriction otherwise reasonable has no time limit, it is quite possible for the court to grant injunctive relief for a specific and reasonable time.

Arthur L. Corbin, CORBIN ON CONTRACTS § 1390 at 69–73 (1962) (footnotes omitted and emphasis added).

RESTATEMENT (SECOND) OF CONTRACTS, *supra*, § 184, which we now adopt, accepts the Corbin view permitting enforcement of a narrower term which is reasonable in a covenant not to compete:

> (1) If less than all of an agreement is unenforceable under the rule stated in § 178 [dealing with restraints in violation of public policy in general], a court may nevertheless enforce the rest of the agreement in favor of a party who did not engage in serious misconduct if the performance as to which the agreement is unenforceable is not an essential part of the agreed exchange.

> (2) A court may treat only part of a term as unenforceable under the rule stated in Subsection (1) if the party who seeks to enforce the term obtained it in good faith and in accordance with reasonable standards of fair dealing.

The position adopted in RESTATEMENT (SECOND) OF CONTRACTS, *supra*, § 184 does not permit the court to add to the terms of the covenant.

> Sometimes a term is unenforceable on grounds of public policy because it is too broad, even though a narrower term would be enforceable. In such a situation, under Subsection (2), the court may refuse to enforce only part of the term, while enforcing the other part of the term as well as the rest of the agreement. The court's power in such a case is not a power of reformation, however, and it will not, in the course of determining what part of the term to enforce, add to the scope of the term in any way.

Id. at § 184 comment b.

We believe the ability to narrow the term of a covenant not to compete and enforce a reasonable restraint permits public policy to be served in the most effective manner. . . . When the employer-employee relationship terminates, a reasonable covenant not to compete then avoids unfair competition by the employee against the former employer and the specter, which no court would enforce, of specific performance of the employment agreement. When the parties agree to terms of a covenant, one of which is too broad, the court is permitted to enforce a narrower term which effectuates these public policy goals without arbitrarily invalidating the entire agreement between the parties and creating an uncertain business environment. In those instances where a truly unreasonable covenant operates as a restraint of trade, it will not be enforced. . . .

Enforcement of a one year durational term, along with the other terms of the covenant not to compete, is reasonable in light of the circumstances of this case. Public policy is fairly served by this restraint on unfair competition by Dr. Hopper. All Pet and Alpine established irreparable harm from the loss of clients to unfair competition which entitled them to injunctive relief. While the terms of the covenant, as enforced, restrict Dr. Hopper's practice for a limited time, she will suffer no undue hardship from compliance with her bargained for promise. We, therefore, affirm the district court's conclusions of law that the type of activity and geographic limitations contained in the covenant not to compete were reasonable and enforceable as a matter of law. Because we hold that the covenant's three year durational term imposed a partially unreasonable restraint of trade, we remand for a modification of the judgment to enjoin Dr. Hopper from unfair competition for a duration of one year from the date of termination.

CARDINE, Justice, dissenting:

Glenna Hopper has beaten the system. Just prior to being terminated, Dr. Hopper informed Dr. Johnson that "the [covenant] isn't worth the paper it's written on." And she was right. Upon termination, she went into the veterinary business in violation of her covenant not to compete. From July 15, 1991, until October 6, 1992, Dr. Hopper practiced small animal medicine in violation of her solemn promise in her employment agreement not to compete. Whether she continued to practice small animal veterinary medicine after October 6, 1992, in violation of the covenant is not disclosed by the record on appeal.

The court has now decided as a matter of law that a one-year non-competition restriction is reasonable, and a longer period is unreasonable. This pronouncement establishes for the future the period during which competition can be restricted. In this case, appellant may have continued violating the covenant during her appeal — or she may have complied. We do not know. The trial court, on remand, should determine this question, and appellant ought to at least satisfy the one-year non-compete now imposed by this court.

I would hold, therefore, that the covenant was supported by consideration from the beginning and was lawful and enforceable, and I would require that appellant be enjoined from that part of the practice of veterinary medicine specified in the covenant not to compete from the date the trial court, on remand, enters its modified judgment for at least the one-year period which this court now finds reasonable.

NOTES & QUESTIONS

1. Are you troubled by the facts that: (1) at the time of the initial oral agreement of full-time employment that terms of the covenant not to compete were "not discussed at the time" and (2) the written contract was antedated from December

11 to March 3? What role, if any, should these factors play in determining the reasonableness of the restrictive covenant?

2. Notice the statement in the restrictive covenant to the effect that "Dr. Hopper agrees that the duration and geographic scope of that limitation is reasonable." Do you believe this provision would help the employer in enforcing the covenant, or does such a provision almost have the opposite effect?

3. What is the rationale for enforcing restrictive covenants? What interests of the employer are being protected?

4. In *The Community Hospital Group, Inc. v. More*, 869 A.2d 884 (N.J. 2005), the court described the following interests of the hospital employer in connection with a one-year restrictive covenant for a neurosurgeon:

> In this case, the evidence established that JFK made a substantial investment in Dr. More by giving him the opportunity to accumulate knowledge and hone his skills as a neurosurgeon. Indeed, Dr. More acknowledges that it "takes years of education, practical experience and accumulated skills and knowledge, as well as an innate talent, for a doctor to reach [his] level of practice." Further, Dr. More admitted he removed patient and patient referral lists from JFK between the time of his resignation and his eventual departure from JFK. It was also undisputed that many of the patients Dr. More treated after joining NAPA and Somerset were once patients of JFK or were referred to Dr. More from one of JFK's referral sources. Further, in addition to training Dr. More, JFK paid for his attendance at seminars and other events, and paid for his malpractice insurance as well. In short, we agree with the Appellate Division's conclusion that JFK established that it had several legitimate protectable interests in enforcement of the restriction.

What are the countervailing interests of the doctor? Of the public?

4. Assume that Dr. Hopper learned trade secret surgical techniques which Dr. Johnson disclosed only on Dr. Hopper's oral promise that she would not disclose or use these techniques except in her work at The All Pet Animal Clinic. This oral promise is later included in the written agreements. No period of time for ending the obligation of confidentiality has been included. What impact, if any, would this trade secret have upon the reasonableness of the restrictive covenant? How long should such a promise of confidentiality last?

5. What are the adverse consequences, if any, of allowing courts to "blue pencil" an otherwise unenforceable restrictive covenant? Should a restrictive covenant always be blue penciled?

6. *Practice Points:* The plaintiff-employer filed its suit for injunction and damages some 120 days after the former employee began to compete. Then, as the opinion emphasizes, the trial did not occur for about 10 months, during which time the employer "did not seek a temporary injunction to restrict Dr. Hopper's practice and possibly mitigate damages." Such tardiness and delay would certainly seem to suggest that there was neither urgency nor irreparable harm in the case.

7. *Drafting Exercise:* Craft a restrictive covenant for Dr. Hopper that would both limit Dr. Hopper's ability to compete on termination of her employment contract as well as prohibit her use of Dr. Johnson's trade secret surgical techniques. Your

client wants the restriction to be as broad as possible and still be enforceable.

LIAUTAUD AND JIMMY JOHN'S INCORPORATED v. MICHAEL LIAUTAUD
221 F.3d 981 (7th Cir. 2000)

RIPPLE, Circuit Judge:

Jim Liautaud, upon request, provided his cousin, Michael Liautaud, with the secrets behind his successful sandwich shop business. To protect himself, he proffered to Michael a noncompetition agreement, which prevented Michael from expanding his new business beyond the Madison, Wisconsin, market. Michael agreed to the terms of the agreement; however, he later violated it by expanding his business into other parts of Wisconsin. This lawsuit followed.

Jurisdiction in this suit is based on diversity of citizenship under 28 U.S.C. § 1332. The amount in controversy exceeds $ 50, 000, and the parties are of diverse citizenship. The parties do not dispute that the applicable law is Illinois state law. The district court granted summary judgment for Michael and, for the reasons set forth in this opinion, we affirm the judgment of the district court.

Jim Liautaud owns and operates a chain of gourmet submarine sandwich shops in Illinois called Jimmy John's, Inc. He claims that the secret behind the success of his shops is a combination of his style of preparing the sandwiches and of his business strategies.

In 1988, Jim's cousin, Michael, approached Jim about opening his own submarine sandwich shop in Madison, Wisconsin. Jim agreed to provide Michael with his "secrets of success" so that Michael could open Big Mike's Super Subs. Pursuant to his offer to help, Jim sent Michael a letter outlining the agreement between the cousins. The letter states as follows:

> I want to confirm at this time exactly what we agreed on so that it is clear and understood by both parties.

> The agreement:

> 1. Mike will open up a sub shop in Madison using Jimmy John's products and systems.

> 2. Mike can open up as many shops [as] he would like in Madison only.

> 3. If you want to expand the sub/club business beyond Madison you will do so using Jimmy John's sub shops as a partner or franchisee. This is subject to 100% agreement on both parties. If you don't use Jimmy John's Inc. you will not expand the sub/club business beyond Madison.

> 4. You will not disclose to any one: recipes, products or systems that are given to you. (Except your managers who run your store).

I believe thats [sic] what we agreed on. If I have made any misrepresentations of our agreement please correct them in the margin of this letter and return a copy to me. If I don't receive a copy I'll assume this letter to be the agreement. R.1, Ex.A. Michael returned the letter to Jim and, in handwriting at the bottom, wrote: "Jimmy, If I agree on all items stated above, you must agree that you (Jimmy Johns Inc.) won't enter the Madison WI market." *id.*

Jim then helped Michael open a sandwich shop in Madison. In 1991, Michael opened a sandwich shop outside Madison, in LaCrosse, Wisconsin, in violation of the cousins' agreement. Although the cousins attempted to reach a franchise agreement, it never materialized. Jim thereafter filed this action against Michael to enforce the terms of their agreement and for unjust enrichment.

The district court held that the "agreement" between the cousins constituted a "classic noncompetition covenant." [T]he court found that the covenant was unreasonable because it was overly restrictive and, thus, that it was void as against public policy. . . .

Under Illinois law, "[a] 'naked' promise by one merchant not to compete against another merchant is against public policy because it injures the public and the promisor, while at the same time it serves no *protectible* interest of the promisee." *Abel v. Fox*, 274 Ill. App. 3d 811, 211 Ill. Dec. 129, 654 N.E.2d 591, 596 (Ill. App. Ct. 1995). In order for a noncompetition agreement to be valid, therefore, it must be ancillary to a valid transaction, such that the covenant not to compete is subordinate to the main purpose of the transaction. *See* 654 N.E.2d at 593. Although noncompetition agreements typically stem from an employment relationship or from the sale of a business, another valid transaction may support a covenant not to compete. The Supreme Court of Illinois has stated that a valid restraint on trade may be based on a purchase or sale of a business or "any other analogous circumstance giving one party a just right to be protected against competition from the other." *More v. Bennett*, 140 Ill. 69, 29 N.E. 888, 891 (Ill. 1892).

Although Jim urges that we characterize the transaction as a franchise agreement, we believe that the arrangement is more accurately characterized as a gift. "A gift is a voluntary gratuitous transfer of property from donor to donee where the donor manifests an intent to make such a gift and absolutely and irrevocably delivers the property to the donee." *In re Estate of Poliquin*, 247 Ill. App. 3d 112, 186 Ill. Dec. 801, 617 N.E.2d 40, 42 (Ill. App. Ct. 1993). We believe that there is no question that Jim intended to provide Michael with the gift of the "secrets of his success." Also, the parties do not dispute that Jim delivered his gift to Michael and that Michael accepted Jim's gift. Thus, the parties entered a valid gift relationship. The donor in a gift relationship, when the gift is trade secrets, is providing the donee with valuable advice for free. The donor may wish to protect both his generosity and his business interests from exploitation; therefore, he may desire to impose a covenant not to compete on his donee. *See More*, 29 N.E. at 891. Here, the covenant not to compete was ancillary to the gift transaction between Jim and Michael: The gift from Jim to Michael was the essential element of the transaction, and the noncompetition agreement was subordinate to the main purpose of that transaction. Thus, because the gift relationship is a valid relationship or transaction and the noncompetition agreement is subordinate to that relationship, the noncompetition agreement meets the first requirement that it be ancillary to a valid relationship or transaction.

The next question is whether the scope of the noncompetition agreement is reasonable, a determination which is based on the facts and circumstances of the particular case. *See Eichmann v. National Hosp. & Health Care Servs., Inc.*, 308 Ill. App. 3d 337, 241 Ill. Dec. 738, 719 N.E.2d 1141, 1143 (Ill. App. Ct. 1999); *Lawrence & Allen*, 685 N.E.2d at 441; *Weitekamp v. Lane*, 250 Ill. App. 3d 1017, 189 Ill. Dec. 486, 620 N.E.2d 454, 462 (Ill. App. Ct. 1993). For this restrictive covenant to be reasonable, its terms (1) must not be greater than necessary to protect Jim,

(2) must not be oppressive to Michael, and (3) must not be injurious to the general public. *See Decker, Berta & Co. v. Berta*, 225 Ill. App. 3d 24, 167 Ill. Dec. 190, 587 N.E.2d 72, 76 (Ill. App. Ct. 1992); *see also Lawrence & Allen*, 685 N.E.2d at 441; *Abel*, 654 N.E.2d at 593; *Weitekamp*, 620 N.E.2d at 462; *Howard Johnson & Co. v. Feinstein*, 241 Ill. App. 3d 828, 182 Ill. Dec. 396, 609 N.E.2d 930, 934 (Ill. App. Ct. 1993); *accord Applied Micro*, 941 F. Supp. at 753.

Jim asserts first that, given the nature of his business and the trade secrets involved, the restraint on Michael's expansion was necessary to protect his business interests. He explains that his trade secrets are the fundamental elements of his business success and that providing Michael with access to these secrets, without compensation for Jim, is fundamentally unfair. Next, Jim argues that the restrictions were not oppressive to Michael because (1) he provided the trade secrets to Michael for free, (2) Michael could expand outside Madison in any business other than the submarine sandwich business, and (3) Michael could expand his submarine sandwich business outside Madison, as long as he used Jimmy John's, Inc. as a partner. Finally, Jim asserts that not enforcing the covenant would be injurious to the public because it would restrict the freedom of parties to contract.

Conversely, Michael submits that the noncompetition agreement was unreasonable. According to Michael, Jim does not have a legitimate business interest in preventing Michael from establishing submarine sandwich shops where Jim is not located. Also, the geographical restriction is not reasonable, Michael claims, because the restriction prevents Michael from expanding anywhere in the world besides Madison, Wisconsin.

In our view, under Illinois common law principles, the covenant here is overly broad because there is an unnecessarily stringent geographic restriction on the promisor, Michael, and no temporal restriction whatsoever. These restrictions are not necessary to protect Jim's business interest, are oppressive to Michael, and are injurious to the public. Generally, in a covenant not to compete, the agreement restricts competition within a certain town or city or within a defined radius from the promisee's own business. *See, e.g., Prairie Eye Ctr.*, 713 N.E.2d at 612 (upholding an agreement which restricted the promisor from competing within specified cities as well as within a 10-mile radius from certain other cities); *Gillespie*, 622 N.E.2d at 1270 (enforcing a 50-mile radius restriction on competition with a medical practice); *Weitekamp*, 620 N.E.2d at 462 (allowing an agreement with a 300-mile radius limit); *Decker, Berta & Co.*, 587 N.E.2d at 76 (sanctioning a covenant with a 35-mile radius restriction). Although a lack of geographic limits is not per se unreasonable, the complete bar on competition needs to be reasonably related to the promisee's interest in protecting his own business. *See Eichmann*, 719 N.E.2d at 1147; *Lawrence & Allen*, 685 N.E.2d at 441.

Here, Michael is prevented from expanding anywhere in the world outside of Madison. Although this may seem to be an exaggeration of what the parties expected in reality, we can only read the plain language of the agreement, and in its terms the covenant not to compete does not contain any geographic limitations. Jim's articulated legitimate business interest, protection of his trade secrets, does not show why Michael should not be able to expand to locations other than Madison, even when Jim is not in those locations. Jim has not indicated that he plans to expand into the markets where Michael is located. Also, Michael has not suggested that he plans to expand to places where Jim already is located. Generally, courts will uphold a restriction on competition that is coextensive with the area where the promisee is doing business. *See Lawrence & Allen*, 685 N.E.2d at 442. Jim has not demonstrated why expansion by Michael in cities and states where Jim is not located would injure Jim.

Moreover, the agreement is oppressive to Michael because it restricts him from expanding his sandwich business, regardless of whether he continues to use Jim's trade secrets. According to the terms of the agreement, Michael could not open *any* kind of sandwich shop outside Madison without Jim's approval. Finally, the complete ban on expansion is injurious to the public because it completely restricts competition. Although it seems "fair" that Jim should receive some compensation for Michael's use of Jim's trade secrets, this noncompetition agreement, without any geographic limitations, is not the reasonable means of accomplishing that end.

The agreement also fails to provide any limits on time. Instead, the agreement, as written, merely states that Michael may not expand his business. Read literally, this means that Michael may not expand his business beyond Madison for the rest of his life. Illinois courts generally have refused to enforce noncompetition agreements that do not limit the duration of the restriction. *See Eichmann*, 719 N.E.2d at 1148; *but see Storer v. Brock*, 351 Ill. 643, 184 N.E. 868 (Ill. 1933) (allowing an activity restriction for all time within Chicago on retired physician because physician received valuable consideration for contract and could practice anywhere outside the city). The length of time for the restriction must be reasonably related to the needs of the promisee's business. *See Eichmann*, 719 N.E.2d at 1148; *Lawrence & Allen*, 685 N.E.2d at 442. For example, in a business where client development takes over a year, a restriction on competition for one to two years is reasonable because of the time it takes to cultivate a client. *See, e.g., Prairie Eye Ctr.*, 713 N.E.2d at 612 (upholding a two-year restriction because of the time needed to cultivate patients); *Gillespie*, 622 N.E.2d at 1270 (enforcing a two-year restriction on competition with a medical practice).

Jim has not produced any reason for perpetually restricting Michael's ability to expand beyond Madison. Even though it may take time to establish a sandwich shop business and to attract a sufficient customer base to make the venture profitable, the time to accomplish this is not in perpetuity. Jim has not shown that he needs to prevent Michael from ever expanding beyond Madison in order to protect his business interests. Also, as stated above, under the agreement, Michael is prevented from ever expanding his shops, even if he develops his own recipes and business strategies. Finally, this infinite agreement injures the public because it stifles competition. We conclude that, in light of the severe and unnecessary restrictions on Michael, this covenant not to compete is unreasonable and is, therefore, void as against public policy.

NOTES & QUESTIONS

1. Trade secrets are generally considered valuable business assets and can be protected through confidentiality agreements and other methods designed to protect their secrecy. Trade secrets remain protectable under state statutes and common law only so long as they remain secret, including being protected by adequate confidentiality agreements. One of the most famous trade secrets which has been protected for over 100 years is the formula for Coca Cola. If trade secrets can last so long, what would qualify as a reasonable time period for a restrictive covenant for Michael's use of Jimmy's trade secrets? What evidence would you

need to determine an appropriate time period?

2. Compare the court's treatment of the restrictive covenant in *Jimmy John's* with that of *Hopper*. Which approach to the issue of blue penciling is better adapted to assuring the parties' contract intentions are carried out?

3. *Practice Points:* Because restrictive covenants are generally disfavored, as the court demonstrated in *Jimmy John's*, any ambiguity will generally be construed against their enforcement, particularly for courts that do not allow blue penciling. Restrictive covenants should always be drafted as narrowly as possible to achieve their goals.

4. *Drafting Exercise:* Draft an enforceable restrictive covenant for Jimmy which will protect his trade secret against unauthorized use by Michael in territories beyond Madison.

PROBLEMS

1. Tom Tapper went to the Martha Murphy Dance Studio in the State of Marshall because Tapper had decided he wanted a career in dance. He wrote a check for $10,000 for 100 dance lessons upon an oral contract, such lessons to begin one week later. The studio promptly signed and deposited the check in its account. But alas, four days later, Tapper, who was 89 years old, concluded that perhaps his decision had been made too hastily. So, before ever taking a dance lesson, Tapper demanded the return of his money from Martha Murphy Studio. The Studio refused. The State of Marshall had enacted a statute which provides, in relevant part, as follows:

> Every contract for social and sports entertainments, including acting lessons, dance lessons, music and voice lessons, and sports lessons, of a price of $500 or more shall be in writing, which writing shall itemize the fees, including interest and other charges, and shall provide the consumer with a 3 day period within which to cancel and obtain a full refund of all amounts paid.

The Studio asserted the illegality of the contract with Tapper and argued that it should retain the $10,000. Tapper sued. Who should win? Why?

2. Linda Landowner held title to a piece of residential property in the City of Smalltown. She submitted an application along with supporting documents and the $475 application fee to the city zoning board to obtain a zoning change to allow her to operate an adult bookstore on the premises. The board rejected her request and returned the documents and $475 fee. Sly Scammer, an acquaintance of Landowner, told her that he could obtain the zoning variance for the price of $5475. She paid Scammer, who is not an attorney or other professional, that amount and provided him with her supporting documents. He agreed to obtain the variance. When Scammer did not succeed in securing the zoning change and after he refused to return the $5475, Landowner sued him. In part, Scammer defended by claiming he had paid $3475 to a third party in the attempt to effect the zoning variance. Should Landowner recover her money? *See Sinar v. LeRoy*, 270 P.2d 800 (Wash. 1954).

3. Greta Greene was employed as a sales agent for Ball-Mart Incorporated, a large sporting goods distributor, and Walter White was employed as a purchasing agent for Marshall Shields Incorporated, an even larger upscale national depart-

ment store chain. Greene was paid a 10% commission by Ball-Mart on sales of $1 million or more, so Greene offered White a 5% payment if White would order $5 million worth of golf balls and tennis balls from Ball-Mart for Marshall Shields. White placed the order, and Ball-Mart promptly delivered the balls to Marshall Shields. But, before Marshall Shields paid the purchase price, it discovered that its agent had been bribed. Marshall Shields refused to pay for the balls or to return them. Ball-Mart sues. What result?

4. Under the same facts as above, would your conclusion change if the executive offices of Marshall Shields knew that White and several of its other purchasing agents regularly accepted kickbacks from sales agents like Greene?

5. Neil Numbers of Smalltown, Alaska, went off to the state university to study to become a certified public accountant. He succeeded in earning a degree and passing the CPA examination. Sam Slick, the only CPA in Smalltown, learned of this and became concerned that Numbers might return to Smalltown to practice accountancy. Slick sent a letter and a $5000 check to Numbers, offering the $5000 as payment if Numbers would agree not to return to Smalltown to practice accountancy for a period of two years. Since Numbers had no intention of returning to Smalltown anyway, he promptly accepted the offer and endorsed and cashed the check.

Numbers got a job in Chicago with Big Three Accounting Firm, which included a term in his employment contract that barred Numbers from engaging in any other gainful employment of any kind whatsoever during the term of his employment with Big Three. However, Numbers wanted to become a part-time adjunct professor of accounting.

Is the in-term restriction of Big Three enforceable to prevent Numbers from teaching part-time? Would it matter whether Numbers was employed at-will or on a year-to-year contract with Big Three? If Numbers decided to leave Big Three, could he return to Smalltown to practice accountancy within the two-year time restriction imposed by Slick? If so, can Slick at least recover the $5000?

CHAPTER 10

STATUTE OF FRAUDS

A. OVERVIEW

A defense to contract enforcement, although not necessarily to actual contract formation, is the failure of the parties to comply with the Statute of Frauds.

As the phrase *Statute of Frauds* suggests, this defense is fundamentally statutory. Each state has adopted its own version of the statute, and there are relatively minor variations from place to place. However, a survey of the case law interpreting the various statutes reveals that the differences among jurisdictions, and even within a single jurisdiction, are more pronounced.

The Statute of Frauds represents one more feature of United States law adopted from the British. Parliament enacted the statute in 1676.

The modern Statute of Frauds provides that certain kinds of contracts will be enforced only if they are evidenced by a writing which sets out the material terms with reasonable certainty and which is signed by the party to be charged with the contract.

Generally, the Statute of Frauds applies to several kinds of contracts:

(1) Contracts for the sale of goods having a price of $500 or more;

(2) Contracts for the sale of any interest in real estate;

(3) Contracts which cannot be completely performed within one year from the time they are made;

(4) Contracts by which one party undertakes the obligation of another party (a surety contract); and

(5) Other contracts specified by particular statutes.

The underlying purpose of the Statute of Frauds is to prevent fraud. That is, the requirement of a writing to evidence a contract should deter fraud where an unscrupulous party would otherwise falsely testify to the existence of an entirely oral contract. Parliament and the state legislatures abhorred the prospect that their courts would come to the aid of perjurers and enforce contracts which did not really exist. The writing requirement of the Statute of Frauds also provides an opportunity for the contracting parties to reflect and consider the importance of their commitment. Further, the writing requirement provides guidance as to which contracts must be in writing and which contracts are unenforceable without a written record. Consider these goals of the Statute of Frauds as you read the following case.

McINERNEY v. CHARTER GOLF, INC.
680 N.E.2d 1347 (Ill. 1997)

Justice HEIPLE delivered the opinion of the court:

Is an employee's promise to forgo another job opportunity in exchange for a guarantee of lifetime employment sufficient consideration to modify an existing employment-at-will relationship? If "yes," must such an agreement be in writing to satisfy the requirements of the statute of frauds? These questions, among others, must be answered in plaintiff Dennis McInerney's appeal from an order of the appellate court affirming a grant of summary judgment in favor of the defendant, Charter Golf, Inc. . . .

From 1988 through 1992, Dennis McInerney worked as a sales representative for Charter Golf, Inc., a company which manufactures and sells golf apparel and supplies. Initially, McInerney's territory included Illinois but was later expanded to include Indiana and Wisconsin. In 1989, McInerney allegedly was offered a position as an exclusive sales representative for Hickey-Freeman, an elite clothier which manufactured a competing line of golf apparel. Hickey-Freeman purportedly offered McInerney an 8% commission.

Intending to inform Charter Golf of his decision to accept the Hickey-Freeman offer of employment, McInerney called Jerry Montiel, Charter Golf's president. Montiel wanted McInerney to continue to work for Charter Golf and urged McInerney to turn down the Hickey-Freeman offer. Montiel promised to guarantee McInerney a 10% commission on sales in Illinois and Wisconsin "for the remainder of his life, " in a position where he would be subject to discharge only for dishonesty or disability. McInerney allegedly accepted Charter Golf's offer and, in exchange for the guarantee of lifetime employment, gave up the Hickey-Freeman offer. McInerney then continued to work for Charter Golf.

In 1992, the relationship between Charter Golf and McInerney soured: Charter Golf fired McInerney. McInerney then filed a complaint in the circuit court of Cook County, alleging breach of contract. The trial court granted Charter Golf's motion for summary judgment after concluding that the alleged oral contract was unenforceable under the statute of frauds because the contract amounted to an agreement which could not be performed within a year from its making. The appellate court affirmed, but on a wholly different ground. . . . The appellate court held that the putative contract between McInerney and Charter Golf suffered from a more fundamental flaw, namely, that no contract for lifetime employment even existed because a promise to forbear another job opportunity was insufficient consideration to convert an existing employment-at-will relationship into a contract for lifetime employment. . . .

Employment contracts in Illinois are presumed to be at-will and are terminable by either party; this rule, of course, is one of construction which may be overcome by showing that the parties agreed otherwise. *Duldulao v. St. Mary of Nazareth Hospital Center*, 115 Ill. 2d 482, 489, 106 Ill. Dec. 8, 505 N.E.2d 314 (1987). As with any contract, the terms of an employment contract must be clear and definite. . . .

Although the rules of contract law are well-established and straightforward, a conflict has emerged in the appellate court decisions on the subject of consideration in the context of a lifetime employment contract. Several decisions have held that a promise of lifetime employment, which by its terms purports to alter an employment-at-will contract, must be supported by "additional" consideration beyond the standard employment duties. Heuvelman, 23 Ill. App. 2d at 235–36, 161 N.E.2d 875; *Koch v. Illinois Power Co.*, 175 Ill. App. 3d 248, 252, 124 Ill. Dec. 461, 529 N.E.2d 281 (1988); *Ladesic*, 140 Ill. App. 3d at 492–93, 95 Ill. Dec. 12, 488 N.E.2d 1355. These cases have held that an employee's rejecting an outside job offer in exchange for a promised guarantee of lifetime employment is not sufficient consideration to alter an employment-at-will relationship. The premise underlying these cases is that the employee simply weighs the benefits of the two positions, and by accepting one offer the employee necessarily rejects the other. As such, these cases have reasoned that the employee has not given up anything of value, and thus there is no consideration to support the promise of lifetime employment.

One case, however, has taken issue with this analysis. In *Martin v. Federal Life Insurance Co.*, the appellate court held that an enforceable contract for lifetime employment was formed when an employee relinquished a job offer in exchange for a promise of permanent employment from his current employer. *Martin v. Federal Life Insurance Co.*, 109 Ill. App. 3d 596, 601, 65 Ill. Dec. 143, 440 N.E.2d 998 (1982). The *Martin* court recognized that there was consideration in an exchange of promises: the employer promised to give up his right to terminate the employee at-will, and in exchange the employee agreed to continue working for his current employer and to forgo a lucrative opportunity with a competitor. *Martin*, 109 Ill. App. 3d at 601, 65 Ill. Dec. 143, 440 N.E.2d 998.

What is consideration? Under the prevailing view, embodied in the RESTATEMENT (SECOND) OF CONTRACTS, consideration is the bargained-for exchange of promises or performances, and may consist of a promise, an act or a forbearance. RESTATEMENT (SECOND) OF CONTRACTS § 71 (1981). Thus, a promise for a promise is, without more, enforceable. RESTATEMENT (SECOND) OF CONTRACTS § 79, Comment a, at 200 (1981). In past cases, this court has recognized this basic precept, i.e., mutual assent and an exchange of promises provides consideration to support the formation of a contract. *See, e.g., Patton v. Carbondale Clinic*, 161 Ill. 2d 357, 372, 204 Ill. Dec. 203, 641 N.E.2d 427 (1994); *Steinberg v. Chicago Medical School*, 69 Ill. 2d 320, 13 Ill. Dec. 699, 371 N.E.2d 634 (1977) (holding that any act or promise which is of benefit to one party or disadvantage to the other is sufficient "consideration" to support a contract).

While this court has never directly addressed the specific requirements to establish a permanent employment contract, it has held more generally that the employment relationship is governed by the law of contract. Existence of an employment contract, express or implied, is essential to the employer-employee relationship. *A.J. Johnson Paving Co. v. Industrial Comm'n*, 82 Ill. 2d 341, 350, 45 Ill. Dec. 126, 412 N.E.2d 477 (1980). As with any contract, it is not possible for a contract of employment to exist without consent of the parties. *M&M Electric Co. v. Industrial Comm'n*, 57 Ill. 2d 113, 119, 311 N.E.2d 161 (1974). Indeed, this court held in *Duldulao*, 115 Ill. 2d at 490, 106 Ill. Dec. 8, 505 N.E.2d 314, that an employee handbook or other policy statement creates enforceable contractual rights governed by the traditional requirements for contract formation.

In the instant case, Charter Golf argues that an employee's promise to forgo another employment offer in exchange for an employer's promise of lifetime employment is not sufficient consideration. But why not? The defendant has failed to articulate any principled reason why this court should depart from traditional notions of contract law in deciding this case. While we recognize that some cases have indeed held that such an exchange is "inadequate" or "insufficient" consideration to modify an employment-at-will relationship, we believe that those cases have confused the conceptual element of consideration with more practical problems of proof. As we discussed above, this court has held that a promise for a promise constitutes consideration to support the existence of a contract. To hold otherwise in the instant case would ignore the economic realities underlying the case. Here McInerney gave up a lucrative job offer in exchange for a guarantee of lifetime employment; and in exchange for giving up its right to terminate McInerney at will, Charter Golf retained a valued employee. Clearly both parties exchanged bargained-for benefits in what appears to be a near textbook illustration of consideration.

Of course, not every relinquishment of a job offer will necessarily constitute consideration to support a contract. On the related issue of mutuality of obligation, Charter Golf complains that McInerney's promise to continue working was somehow illusory, because it alleges that McInerney had the power to terminate the employment relationship at his discretion while it lacked any corresponding right. The court's decision in *Armstrong Paint & Varnish Works v. Continental Can Co.*, 301 Ill. 102, 108, 133 N.E. 71 1 (1922), teaches that "where there is any other consideration for the contract mutuality of obligation is not essential." Charter Golf's argument on this point fails because McInerney continued working for Charter Golf and relinquished his right to accept another job opportunity. When, as here, the employee relinquishes something of value in a bargained-for exchange for the employer's guarantee of permanent employment, a contract is formed.

So there is a contract, but should we enforce it? Charter Golf argues that the oral contract at issue in this case violates the statute of frauds and is unenforceable because it is not capable of being performed within one year of its making. By statute in Illinois, "[n]o action shall be brought. . . upon any agreement that is not to be performed within the space of one year from the making thereof, unless . . . in writing and signed by the party to be charged." 740 ILCS 80/1 (West 1994). Our statute tracks the language of the original English Statute of Frauds and Perjuries. 29 Charles II ch. 3 (1676). The English statute enacted by Parliament had as its stated purpose the prohibition of those "many fraudulent practices, which are commonly endeavored to be upheld by perjury and subordination of perjury." 29 Charles II ch. 3, introductory clause (1676). Illinois' statute of frauds seeks to do the same by barring actions based upon nothing more than loose verbal statements.

The period of one year, although arbitrary, recognizes that with the passage of time evidence becomes stale and memories fade. The statute proceeds from the legislature's sound conclusion that while the technical elements of a contract may exist, certain contracts should not be enforced absent a writing. It functions more as an evidentiary safeguard than as a substantive rule of contract. As such, the statute exists to protect not just the parties to a contract, but also — perhaps more importantly — to protect the fact finder from charlatans, perjurers and the problems of proof accompanying oral contracts.

There are, of course, exceptions to the statute of frauds' writing requirement which permit the enforcement of certain oral contracts required by the statute to be in writing.

One such exception is the judicially created exclusion for contracts of uncertain duration. In an effort to significantly narrow the application of the statute, many courts have construed the words "not to be performed" to mean "not capable of being performed" within one year. *See* RESTATEMENT (SECOND) OF CONTRACTS § 130 (1981). These cases hold that if performance is possible by its terms within one year, the contract is not within the statute regardless of how unlikely it is that it will actually be performed within one year. Under this interpretation, the actual course of subsequent events and the expectations of the parties are entirely irrelevant. RESTATEMENT (SECOND) OF CONTRACTS § 130, Comment a (1981). A contract for lifetime employment would then be excluded from the operation of the statute because the employee could, in theory, die within one year, and thus the contract would be "capable of being performed."[1]

We find such an interpretation hollow and unpersuasive. A "lifetime" employment contract is, in essence, a permanent employment contract. Inherently, it anticipates a relationship of long duration — certainly longer than one year. In the context of an employment-for-life contract, we believe that the better view is to treat the contract as one "not to be performed within the space of one year from the making thereof." To hold otherwise would eviscerate the policy underlying the statute of frauds and would invite confusion, uncertainty and outright fraud. Accordingly, we hold that a writing is required for the fair enforcement of lifetime employment contracts.

The plaintiff argues that the statute of frauds' writing requirement is nonetheless excused because he performed, either fully or partially, according to the terms of the oral contract. Illinois courts have held that a party who has fully performed an oral contract within the one-year provision may nonetheless have the contract enforced. Full or complete performance of the instant contract, by its terms, would have required the plaintiff to work until his death, but our plaintiff lives.

A party's partial performance generally does not bar application of the statute of frauds, unless it would otherwise be "impossible or impractical to place the parties in status quo or restore or compensate" the performing party for the value of his performance. *Mapes v. Kalva Corp.*, 68 Ill. App. 3d 362, 368, 24 Ill. Dec. 944, 386 N.E.2d 148 (1979). . . . This so-called exception resembles the doctrines of restitution, estoppel and fraud, and exists to avoid a "virtual fraud" from being perpetrated on the performing party. *Barrett v. Geisinger*, 148 Ill. 98, 35 N.E. 354 (1893); *see also* RESTATEMENT (SECOND) OF CONTRACTS § 130, Comment e (1981). In any event, our plaintiff has been fully compensated for the work that he performed. Accordingly, part performance — on these facts — will not take the case out of the statute of frauds.

---

[1] In attempting to rein in this exception to the statute of frauds, some courts have made a distinction — at times quite attenuated — between death as full performance and death operating to terminate or excuse the contract. . . . Under this view, an oral contract for employment for a stated period longer than one year will not be enforced because, although the employee could die within one year of the making of the contact, these courts elect to treat that contingency as an excuse or termination of the contract and not as performance. This distinction, while perhaps logical in other contexts, is meaningless in our case where the complete performance contemplated by the parties, i.e., employment for life, is identical to the event giving rise to termination or excuse. Under the terms of the oral contract alleged in this case, the employee's death would have resulted in full performance.

Finally, the plaintiff argues that the defendant should be estopped from asserting the defense of statute of frauds. Traditionally, a party's reliance estopped the other party from asserting the statute only under the doctrine of equitable estoppel. *Ozier v. Haines*, 411 Ill. 160, 163–65, 103 N.E.2d 485 (1952); *Sinclair v. Sullivan Chevrolet Co.*, 45 Ill. App. 2d 10, 17–19, 195 N.E.2d 250 (1964), aff'd, 31 Ill. 2d 507, 202 N.E.2d 516 (1964). Equitable estoppel is available if one party has relied upon another party's misrepresentation or concealment of a material fact. Absent such misrepresentation or fraud, the defense is not available. *Ozier*, 41 1 Ill. at 165, 103 N.E.2d 485. . . . No misrepresentation has been alleged here.

Rather, the plaintiff complains that he relied upon the oral promises of his employer and makes much of the injustice done him — indeed, too much. While agreeing to work for an employer and giving up other employment opportunities can clearly be described as reliance on the employer's oral promises concerning the terms of employment, promissory estoppel does not bar the application of the statute of frauds § 16 (rejecting, at least implicitly, the suggestion that promissory estoppel bars the application of the statute of frauds). In the context of an employment relationship, reasonable reliance is insufficient to bar the application of the statute of frauds. Some authorities — reflected in the view of the SECOND RESTATEMENT — have used promissory estoppel to bar the application of the statute of frauds in a narrow class of cases in which a performing party would otherwise be without an adequate remedy and there is some element of unjust enrichment. RESTATEMENT (SECOND) OF CONTRACTS § 139, Comment c, at 355–56 (1981). We do not believe that this case is one which requires us to adopt such a rule. As we have observed, McInerney has been compensated for his services, and the sole injustice of which he complains is his employer's failure to honor its promise of lifetime employment. Our plaintiff, however, is a salesman — a sophisticated man of commerce — and arguably should have realized that his employer's oral promise was unenforceable under the statute of frauds and that his reliance on that promise was misplaced. Our parties entered into this disputed oral contract freely and without any hint of coercion, fraud or misrepresentation, and thus we adhere to the rule of Ozier and Sinclair and hold that the statute of frauds operates even where there has been reliance on a promise.

In sum, though an employee's promise to forgo another job opportunity in exchange for a guarantee of lifetime employment is consideration to support the formation of a contract, the statute of frauds requires that contracts for lifetime employment be in writing. Accordingly, we affirm the judgment of the appellate court. *See Ozier*, 41 1 Ill. 160, 103 N.E.2d 485; *Sinclair*, 31 Ill. 2d 507, 202 N.E.2d.

Justice NICKELS, dissenting [joined by Justice McMORROW and MILLER]:

I agree with the majority's conclusion that plaintiff's promise to forgo another job opportunity is sufficient consideration in return for defendant's promise of lifetime employment to plaintiff. However, I disagree with the majority's holding that the employment contract in the case at bar must be in writing because it falls within the requirements of the statute of frauds.

The writing requirement applies to "any agreement that is not to be performed within the space of one year from the making thereof." 740 ILCS 80/1 (West 1994). Commenting on this language, the RESTATEMENT (SECOND) OF CONTRACTS observes:

> [T]he enforceability of a contract under the one-year provision does not turn on the actual course of subsequent events, nor on the expectations of

the parties as to the probabilities. Contracts of uncertain duration are simply excluded; the provision covers only those contracts whose performance cannot possibly be completed within a year.

RESTATEMENT (SECOND) OF CONTRACTS § 130, Comment a, at 328 (1981).

A contract of employment for life is necessarily one of uncertain duration. Since the employee's life may end within one year, and, as the majority acknowledges, the contract would be fully performed upon the employee's death . . . the contract is not subject to the statute of frauds' one-year provision. *See* RESTATEMENT (SECOND) OF CONTRACTS § 130, Illustration 2, at 328 (1981); *see also* 72 AM. JUR. 2D *Statute of Frauds* § 14, at 578 (1974) ('The rule generally accepted by the authorities is that an agreement or promise the performance or duration of which is contingent on the duration of human life is not within the statute"); J. Calamari & J. Perillo, THE LAW OF CONTRACTS § 19–20 (3d ed. 1987) ("if A promises . . . to employ X for life, the promise is not within the Statute because it is not for a fixed term and the contract by its terms is conditioned upon the continued life of X and the condition may cease to exist within a year because X may die within a year"). It is irrelevant whether the parties anticipate that the employee will live for more than a year or whether the employee actually does so.

The majority acknowledges that "many courts" subscribe to this view. More accurately, the RESTATEMENT rule represents "the prevailing interpretation" of the statute of frauds' one-year provision. RESTATEMENT (SECOND) OF CONTRACTS § 130, Comment a, at 328 (1981). Only a "distinct minority" of cases have ascribed significance to whether the parties expected that a contract would take more than a year to perform. J. Calamari & J. Perillo, THE LAW OF CONTRACTS § 19-18, at 808 (3d ed. 1987). According to WILLISTON ON CONTRACTS:

It is well settled that the oral contracts invalidated by the Statute because not to be performed within a year include only those which cannot be performed within that period. A promise which is not likely to be performed within a year, and which in fact is not performed within a year, is not within the Statute if at the time the contract is made there is a possibility in law and in fact that full performance such as the parties intended may be completed before the expiration of a year. In the leading case on this section of the Statute the Supreme Court of the United States said: "The parties may well have expected that the contract would continue in force for more than one year; it may have been very improbable that it would not do so; and it did in fact continue in force for a much longer time. But they made no stipulation which in terms, or by reasonable inference, required that result. The question is not what the probable, or expected, or actual performance of the contract was; but whether the contract, according to the reasonable interpretation of its terms, required that it should not be performed within the year".

3 W. Jaeger, WILLISTON ON CONTRACTS § 495 at 575–79 (3d ed. 1960), quoting *Warner v. Texas & Pacific Ry. Co.*, 164 U.S. 418, 434, 17 S. Ct. 147, 153, 41 L. Ed. 495, 504 (1896).

Although the majority brands this interpretation "hollow and unpersuasive" . . . it has a sound basis in the plain language of the statute. Corbin notes:

[Courts] have observed the exact words of [the one-year] provision and have interpreted them literally and very narrowly. The words are "agreement that is not to be performed." They are not "agreement that is not in fact performed" or "agreement that may not be performed" or "agreement that is not at all likely to be performed." To fall within the words of the provision, therefore, the agreement must be one of which it can truly be said at the very moment that it is made, 'This agreement is not to be performed within one year'; in general, the cases indicate that there must not be the slightest possibility that it can be fully performed within one year.

2 A. Corbin, CORBIN ON CONTRACTS § 444, at 535 (1950). *See also* 3 W. Jaeger, WILLISTON ON CONTRACTS § 495, at 585 n.7 (3d ed. 1960) (criticizing *Marshall v. Lowd*, 154 Me. 296, 147 A.2d 667 (1958)).

It is well established that where the words of a statutory provision are unambiguous, there is no need to resort to external aids of interpretation in order to glean the legislature's purpose. *People v. Hicks*, 164 Ill. 2d 218, 222, 207 Ill. Dec. 295, 647 N.E.2d 257 (1995). Although the statutory language at issue in this case is clear and unambiguous, the majority improperly relies upon policies identified in the introductory clause to the original English statute of frauds (176 Ill. 2d at 489, 223 Ill. Dec. at 914–915, 680 N.E.2d at 1350–1351) in order to significantly expand the scope of the one-year provision. Even assuming, arguendo, that it is proper to look beyond the language of the statute in order to determine its meaning, I do not find the majority's policy analysis to be persuasive justification for the broad construction it gives the statute.

The majority notes the dangers of stale evidence and faded memories. . . . But the one-year provision does not effectively guard against these dangers because "[t]here is no necessary relationship between the time of the making of the contract, the time within which its performance is required and the time when it might come to court to be proven." J. Calamari & J. Perillo, THE LAW OF CONTRACTS § 19-17, at 807 (3d ed. 1987), quoting *D&N Boening, Inc. v. Kirsch Beverages, Inc.*, 63 N.Y.2d 449, 454, 483 N.Y.S.2d 164, 165, 472 N.E.2d 992, 993 (1984); *see also* E. Farnsworth, CONTRACTS § 6.4, at 391 (1982).

Courts have tended to give the one-year provision a narrow construction precisely because of the lack of a discernable rationale for it. J. Calamari & J. Perillo, THE LAW OF CONTRACTS § 19-17, at 807 (3d ed. 1987); *see also* RESTATEMENT (SECOND) OF CONTRACTS § 130, comment a, at 328 (1981) ("The design was said to be not to trust to the memory of witnesses for a longer time than one year, but the statutory language was not appropriate to carry out that purpose. The result has been a tendency to construction narrowing the application of the statute"). I am inclined to do likewise. Since the one-year provision is so poorly suited to the aims it was ostensibly designed to accomplish, I see no compelling reason to expand the provision's scope beyond the class of contracts to which it applies by its terms. The narrow and literal interpretation that most courts have given to the language of the one-year provision is entirely appropriate under these circumstances.

Lacking any reasoned basis for its holding, the majority resorts to nearly tautological wordplay, declaring that because a "lifetime" employment contract is essentially a "permanent" employment contract, it inherently anticipates a relationship of long duration. . . . Merely labelling a lifetime employment contract "permanent" should not change the result that the statute of frauds is inapplicable. *See* 2 A. Corbin, CORBIN ON CONTRACTS § 446, at 549–50 (1950) ("A contract for 'permanent' employment is not within the one-year clause for the reason that such a contract will be fully performed, according to its terms, upon the death of the employee. The word 'permanent' has, in this connection, no more extended meaning than 'for life' "); 3 W. Jaeger, WILLISTON ON CONTRACTS § 495, at 582 (3d ed. 1960) ("A promise of permanent personal performance is on a fair interpretation a promise of performance for life, and therefore not within the Statute"). The parties in this case allegedly agreed to plaintiff's employment for life. But with suitable modesty befitting mere mortals, the parties did not stipulate how long plaintiff's life should be. They left that matter — and hence the duration of the contract — to a higher power (I do not refer to this court).

The majority also suggests that its holding is necessary to avoid confusion and uncertainty. . . . I fail to see how the generally accepted rule that lifetime employment contracts need not be in writing is any more confusing or uncertain than the contrary rule adopted by the majority. Indeed, the majority's reasoning is likely to cause greater confusion and uncertainty. A lifetime employment contract is only one example of a broader general category of contracts of uncertain duration. While the majority has declared that lifetime employment contracts anticipate a relationship of longer than one year, the decision in this case supplies no guidance as to other types of contracts that do not, by their terms, set forth a specific time frame for performance. Contracting parties can no longer simply look to the actual terms of their agreement to ascertain whether it must be in writing. Instead, they are left to guess whether the type of contract they have entered into will be viewed by a court as inherently anticipating a relationship of more than one year.

In summary, the majority's holding: (1) is contrary to the relevant statutory language and the great weight of authority; (2) finds no justification in the policy considerations ostensibly underlying the statute of frauds; and (3) is likely to increase, rather than reduce, uncertainty regarding the application of the one-year provision. I would hold that the statute of frauds does not require the contract in this case to be in writing, and I would reverse the judgments of the courts below. Accordingly, I respectfully dissent.

B.   COMPLIANCE WITH THE STATUTE OF FRAUDS

To satisfy the Statute, there must be written evidence of the existence of a contract. Thus, the contract itself need not be written. The written evidence may be multiple writings that suggest they can and should be read together and may have been created contemporaneously with the negotiation and formation of the alleged contract or after its formation.

The important or material terms of the contract (such as its parties, subject matter, duration, price, and other provisions significant in the particular setting) must be set out with a reasonable degree of specificity. What is sufficiently certain to be legally reasonable in clarity raises a somewhat elusive requirement.

Additionally, the required writing must be signed by the party to be charged. In other words, the party who seeks to deny the contract and who is to be held bound to the deal must have signed the writing. Hence, not all of the parties must have signed. And the signature need not be a handwritten name, but can be a stamp, a mark, or a nickname. Further, the test of a signature for Statute of Frauds purposes is whether the party's name was affixed for the purpose of authenticating the document. The test is *not* whether the party displayed contractual intent by signing the document. For instance, letterhead stationery with the party's name identified could satisfy the signature test.

EAST PIEDMONT 120 ASSOCIATES, L.P. v. SHEPPARD
434 S.E.2d 101 (Ga. App. 1993)

COOPER, Judge:

Appellants sued Ray and Clara Joy Sheppard for fraud and breach of an alleged oral agreement to form a joint venture to develop Mrs. Sheppard's land into a shopping center. On appeal, appellants challenge an order of the trial court granting summary judgment for Mrs. Sheppard ("appellee") and declaring her real property free from any claim of lien.

Viewing the facts in a light most favorable to appellants as nonmovants on a motion for summary judgment, it appears that Asa G. Candler V, Asa G. Candler VI, Richard B. Candler and William R. Candler, all doing business as the Candler Development Company ("appellants"), were engaged in the business of locating and developing sites for shopping centers with Publix Super Markets as anchor tenants. After a number of meetings with Ray Sheppard, appellants entered into an oral joint venture agreement with him on August 2, 1991. Pursuant to this oral agreement, Ray Sheppard was to contribute a particular parcel of land to the joint venture and appellants would contribute their expertise, services and relationship with Publix. The specific terms of the agreement were not addressed at that time, but the intent to create the joint venture was memorialized in a Letter of Intent executed by appellants and Ray Sheppard that same day. At some point, appellants learned that the land was in fact owned by appellee rather than Ray Sheppard. Based on Ray Sheppard's actions and declarations, however, they assumed the land was in appellee's name for tax purposes only and that Ray Sheppard had complete authority to manage, control and dispose of it. After the alleged oral agreement was made, appellants secured approval of the site by Publix, engaged an architect to prepare a site plan and conducted engineering studies. In January 1992, appellants' attorney drafted a proposed written joint venture agreement that purportedly reflected negotiations with Ray Sheppard. When the written document was presented to appellee, however, she found it unacceptable, primarily because it did not provide for any payment up front for the contribution of her land. Appellants then offered to purchase the property, but appellee rejected this offer as well because it did not give her the immediate cash she needed. After the Sheppards notified appellants that they intended to pursue other options for appellee's $1.6 million parcel of land, appellants brought this action, seeking damages as well as an equitable lien on the land. In their sole enumeration of error, appellants contend the trial court erred in ruling that there was no issue of fact as to whether there was a joint venture agreement binding on appellee and her land.

Essentially, appellants seek to enforce Ray Sheppard's oral promise to convey an interest in land, and to bind appellee by that promise on the theory that Ray Sheppard had authority to act as her agent. However, oral promises to convey interests in land are unenforceable under the Statute of Frauds. O.C.G.A. § 135-30(4). Although partnership or joint venture agreements need not be in writing as a general matter, *see Vitner v. Funk*, 182 Ga. App. 39(2), 354 S.E.2d 666 (1987), the fact that promises covered by the Statute of Frauds are made in the context of a partnership or joint venture agreement does not render the statute inapplicable. . . . *See id*; *Shivers v. Barton & Ludwig, Inc.*, 164 Ga. App. 490, 296 S.E.2d 749 (1982). . . .

The evidentiary and cautionary purposes of the statute — to prevent fraud and perjury on the one hand and to ensure that parties are aware of the serious consequences of their actions on the other — are implicated when a promise to convey an interest in land is made in the context of a partnership or joint venture agreement just as they are when such a promise is made in any other context.

Furthermore, the fact that Ray Sheppard was appellee's husband did not negate the need for a written authorization to convey or promise to convey any interest in appellee's land. *See Deal v. Dickson*, 232 Ga. 885(1), 209 S.E.2d 214 (1974). It is undisputed that Ray Sheppard had no written authorization and that appellants never asked for one. Accordingly, the trial court properly ruled that agency could not be established as a matter of law and that appellee's property was free from any claim of lien, and thus properly granted summary judgment as to appellee and her land.

NOTES & QUESTIONS

1. *Practice Points:* The holding of this case about the Statute of Frauds is valuable. If the subject matter falls within the coverage of the Statute, even though the transaction is part of a larger or tiered transaction, it remains subject to the Statute's requirements. For example, if goods (of a price of $500 or more) or realty are to be sold at auction, the Statute of Frauds applies.

CENTRAL ILLINOIS LIGHT CO.
v. CONSOLIDATED COAL CO.
349 F.3d 488 (7th Cir. 2003)

Posner, Circuit Judge:

The district judge granted summary judgment for the defendant, Consolidation Coal Company, in this diversity breach of contract suit brought by Central Illinois Light Company (CILCO). 235 F. Supp. 2d 916 (C.D. Ill. 2002). The judge's ground was that CILCO had failed to comply with the Uniform Commercial Code's statute of frauds (codified in Illinois as 810 ILCS, ch. 5). Consolidation had been selling coal to CILCO for several years under one-year contracts. Between September 2000 and June 2001 the parties engaged in protracted negotiations for a contract to succeed their 2000 contract, which was due to expire on the last day of that year. CILCO contends that in December, in the course of the negotiations, it made an oral contract with Consolidation to buy from the latter 1.5 million tons of coal in 2001 and 2002 at a total price of $34 million.

The negotiations involved the exchange of many documents, but documents that *merely* evidence negotiations do not satisfy the statute of frauds. *Lee v. Voyles*, 898 F.2d 76, 78–79 (7th Cir. 1990) (interpreting Illinois UCC law); *General Trading Int'l, Inc. v. Wal-Mart Stores, Inc.*, 320 F.3d 831, 836 (8th Cir. 2003); *Dutchess Development Co. v. Jo-Jam Estates, Inc.*, 134 A.D.2d 478, 521 N.Y.S.2d 262, 263 (App. Div. 1987); *Howard Construction Co. v. Jeff-Cole Quarries, Inc.*, 669 S.W.2d

221, 227–28 (Mo. App. 1983). There has to be "some writing sufficient to indicate that a contract for sale has been made, " provided it has been signed by the party (or the party's agent) against whom the contract is sought to be enforced. U.C.C. § 2-201(1).

It is true that the contracting parties in this case are "merchants," defined as those "who deal in goods of the kind" involved in the transaction at issue or who hold themselves out "as having knowledge or skill peculiar to the practices or goods involved in the transaction." U.C.C. § 2-104(1). (As White and Summers explain, "the first phrase captures the jeweler, the hardware store owner, the haberdasher, and others selling from inventory. . . [while] the second description, having to do with occupation, knowledge, and skill, includes electricians, plumbers, carpenters, boat builders, and the like." 1 James J. White & Robert S. Summers, Uniform Commercial Code § 9-7, p. 513 (4th ed. 1995).) In a contract between merchants, the requirement of a signature is relaxed; it is enough "if within a reasonable time" of the making of the alleged contract "a writing in confirmation of the contract and sufficient against the sender is received and the party receiving it has reason to know its contents, " unless he objects in writing within ten days. U.C.C. § 2-201(2). But signature, as we'll see, is not a serious issue in this case.

A further qualification — one that *is* potentially important to this case — is that a signed document is not necessarily disqualified because it preceded the making of the contract. *Monetti, S.P.A. v. Anchor Hocking Corp.*, 931 F.2d 1178, 1182–83 (7th Cir. 1991). The clearest case would be one in which the party sought to be held to the contract (that is, the party asserting the statute of frauds defense) had made a written offer which the offeree had accepted in writing explicitly stating that he was accepting all the terms in the offer. The statute of frauds defense would fail even though the only writing signed by the party sought to be held to the contract had preceded the making of the contract, which would have occurred only on acceptance. *Huntington Beach Union High School District v. Continental Information Systems Corp.*, 621 F.2d 353, 356 (9th Cir. 1980). But that case is to be distinguished not only from one in which the acceptance is oral, so that there is no written confirmation of the existence of a contract (we thus disagree with the suggestion in *Farrow v. Cahill*, 663 F.2d 201, 206-10, 214 U.S. App. D.C. 24 (D.C. Cir. 1980), that a written offer can be the confirmation that satisfies the statute of frauds even when the acceptance is oral), but also, and more directly pertinent to this case, from a case involving "notes made in preparation for a negotiating session, . . . lest a breakdown of contract negotiations become the launching pad for a suit on an alleged oral contract." *Monetti, S.P.A. v. Anchor Hocking Corp.*, *supra*, 931 F.2d at 1182.

The critical point — issues of signature, promptness, and temporal sequence to one side — is that the documentation presented by the party seeking to demonstrate compliance with the statute of frauds must "indicate" or "confirm" the existence of a contract. CILCO seems to think that it is enough that the documentation is consistent with the existence of a contract — that it does not negate the contract's existence — but that can't be right. The writing must, remember, be "sufficient to indicate" that there *is* a contract. *Howard Construction Co. v. Jeff-Cole Quarries, Inc.*, *supra*, 669 S.W.2d at 227–28. Its existence must, at the very least, be more probable than not. *See* 1 White & Summers, *supra* § 2-4, pp. 64–65. Otherwise the statute of frauds would have no application to a case in which the parties had exchanged documents in the course of negotiations; and that is not the law. *E.g., Monetti, S.P.A. v. Anchor Hocking Corp.*, supra, 931 F.2d at 1180, 1182–83; *Howard Construction Co. v. Jeff-Cole Quarries, Inc.*, supra, 669 S.W.2d at 227–28; *BDT Products, Inc. v. Lexmark Int'l, Inc.*, 274 F. Supp. 2d 880, 889 (E.D. Ky. 2003). A mere written offer, without written proof of acceptance, would then satisfy the statute of frauds, and that is not correct either. *Monetti, S.P.A. v. Anchor Hocking Corp.*, supra, 931 F.2d at 1182; *R.S. Bennett & Co. v. Economy Mechanical Industries, Inc.*, 606 F.2d 182, 184–86 (7th Cir. 1979) (interpreting Illinois U.C.C. law). The documentation must enable an inference to be drawn that there *was* a contract, though once that has been established the parties are free to present oral evidence of the contract's terms, *Guel v. Bullock*, 127 Ill. App. 3d 36, 82 Ill. Dec. 264, 468 N.E.2d 811, 814–15 (Ill. App. 1984); *Impossible Electronics Techniques, Inc. v. Wackenhut Protective Systems, Inc.*, 669 F.2d 1026, 1034 (5th Cir. 1982) — all but the quantity term, which must be stated in the writing that establishes compliance with the statute of frauds. U.C.C. § 2-201(1).

The principal document on which CILCO relies to show that an oral contract for the sale to it of 1.5 million tons of coal was indeed made in December of 2000 is an internal Consolidation document created that month entitled "Coal Sales Invoicing System Order Print." The document has the form of an invoice and contains most of the detail that an invoice for a two-year sale of 1.5 million tons of coal would be expected to contain, except the price for the second year's shipments. The document states that it was created by Debbie Womack and "released to system by" Beverly Wilson. Neither of these individuals is otherwise identified. The district judge thought that without further identification of them it could not be said that the document had been signed by an agent of Consolidation. That was not a realistic assessment. It is obvious that the people who prepare internal documents of this sort are employees, and hence agents, of Consolidation. The judge was right that oral testimony cannot be used to supply the information required for compliance with the statute of frauds. *Monetti, S.P.A. v. Anchor Hocking Corp.*, supra, 931 F.2d at 1181; *Bazak Int'l Corp. v. Mast Industries, Inc.*, 73 N.Y.2d 113, 538 N.Y.S.2d 503, 535 N.E.2d 633, 635 (N.Y. 1989). That would be bootstrapping. But what is obvious, like what is admitted, U.C.C. § 2-201(3)(b); *URSA Farmers Cooperative Co. v. Trent*, 58 Ill. App. 3d 930, 16 Ill. Dec. 348, 374 N.E.2d 1123, 1125 (Ill. App. 1978); *DF Activities Corp. v. Brown*, 851 F.2d 920, 923–24 (7th Cir. 1988) (interpreting Illinois U.C.C. law), need not be documented. The purpose of the statute of frauds is to protect against the uncertainty of oral testimony, and if there is no possible uncertainty there is no work for the statute to do.

The problem with the invoice is not that it wasn't signed by an agent, for it is obvious as we have said that Womack and Wilson were agents of Consolidation. The absence of a handwritten signature is not a problem either. *Weston v. Myers*, 33 Ill. 424 (1864); *Just Pants v. Wagner*, 247 Ill. App. 3d 166, 187 Ill. Dec. 38, 617 N.E.2d 246, 250–51 (Ill. App. 1993); *Cloud Corp. v. Hasbro, Inc.*, 314 F.3d 289, 295–96 (7th Cir. 2002) (interpreting Illinois U.C.C. law); *Barber & Ross Co. v. Lifetime Doors, Inc.*, 810 F.2d 1276, 1280 (4th Cir. 1987). But all the invoice shows is that Consolidation prepared an invoice consistent with what it hoped would be a contract. The invoice was never sent — which, if anything, is evidence that there was no contract, at least no contract containing terms consistent with the invoice.

The invoice loses all possible significance, moreover, when placed in its documentary context. Beginning in September 2000, three months before the invoice was created, and continuing until the end of May of the following year, the parties exchanged at least eleven drafts of a possible contract, with many different terms, though the quantity remained at or close to 1.5 million tons over two years. Negotiations collapsed in June when Consolidation, having encountered production difficulties at its mine, told CILCO it would contract to sell it only 600, 000 tons. (CILCO regards that statement as a repudiation, and hence breach, of the oral contract made the previous December.) Against this background it is apparent that the invoice was wishful thinking rather than evidence of an oral contract.

It is true, as CILCO points out, that a binding contract, oral or otherwise, can come into being before all the details of the parties' contractual relationship are worked out. *Quake Construction, Inc. v. American Airlines, Inc.*, 141 Ill. 2d 281, 152 Ill. Dec. 308, 565 N.E.2d 990, 993–94 (Ill. 1990); *Dawson v. General Motors Corp.*, 977 F.2d 369, 374 (7th Cir. 1992) (Illinois law); E. Allan Farnsworth, "Precontractual Liability and Preliminary Agreements: Fair Dealing and Failed Negotiations, " 87 COLUM. L. REV. 217, 253–63 (1987). This is especially likely when the business relationship is complex and the parties have come to trust each other through previous dealings (and there were previous dealings here). It may then be in the parties' mutual interest to exchange binding commitments on the essentials of their deal so that they have at least a rough idea of where they stand and can make their plans accordingly, and to commit to negotiate in good faith, the details of the deal at a later date: in effect to agree to agree. Duties to bargain in good faith are not empty, as we know from labor law; and they can be voluntarily assumed and enforced. But no document indicates that our two parties agreed, whether in an oral contract made in December 2000 or at any other time, to agree. On the contrary, CILCO itself — oddly — points to an email from Consolidation in February 2001, two months after the invoice and the so-called oral contract, in which Consolidation's salesman described a draft from CILCO as a great "starting point." And in another email, sent the same day between the same individuals, the salesman said, "OK, let's try again."

The question is not how close the parties were to agreement, but whether there was an agreement. It could, as we have said, have been an agreement to agree, but no document indicates that. The reference to "starting point" could mean merely the starting point of the process of drafting the formal written contract confirming an oral contract, but there is no documentary evidence for this interpretation. CILCO seems to think that if writings establish price and quantity, there *must* be a contract — as if the statute of frauds displaced the requirement of agreement. Often price + quantity = contract. When the parties are dealing in standard goods, what more is needed? But coal comes in many varieties; size, plus ash and sulfur content, require attention, as do the adoption and wording of clauses covering taxes, environmental costs (who bears the costs of new regulations?), delays in shipment, and so on. These items, which may be more important in the case of coal than base price is, are what these parties could not agree on.

In principle, of course, and often in practice, the question whether the statute of frauds has been satisfied is separable from the question whether there was a contract. There could be an oral contract that, were it not for the statute of frauds, would be provable by oral testimony; or the statute of frauds might be satisfied yet a full trial show that really there was no contract — that the document evidencing it was contradicted by more persuasive evidence, oral or written. But in this case the questions have tended to merge, with the parties in the briefs and at argument frequently sliding from the question of compliance with the statute of frauds to the question whether there was a contract. A telling piece of evidence against the inference that there was, much emphasized by Consolidation, is the statement by its salesman at his deposition that in early 2001 (after the famous invoice) CILCO was still "out looking at alternative fuels and trying to determine whether or not they could get coal in there from someone else cheaper" than from Consolidation. CILCO argues that this is not admissible evidence because how could Consolidation's salesman know what CILCO was doing? But that is a poor argument because it's the business of a salesman to know what alternatives his customer is exploring; that is something that is within a salesman's personal knowledge, rather than being hearsay. *See Kansas City Power & Light Co. v. Ford Motor Credit Co.*, 995 F.2d 1422, 1432 (8th Cir. 1993). CILCO denies that the salesman's testimony is accurate but has offered no contrary evidence (denials in pleadings and briefs are not evidence), and so it stands uncontradicted for purposes of summary judgment. It is further evidence that months after the invoice CILCO did not consider itself bound to any contract with Consolidation.

AFFIRMED.

NOTES & QUESTIONS

1. Consider how other technological advances are creating complications under the Statute of Frauds, such as computerization and the arrival of electronic communications and digital signatures. If an oral contract negotiation and agreement were recorded on videotape, would the tape satisfy the Statute? Should it? With every technological advance there are legal implications. For a discussion of some of the problems associated with electronic transactions under the new digital signature laws, *see* Michael L. Closen & R. Jason Richards, *Notaries Public — Lost in Cyberspace, Or Key Business Professionals of the Future?*, 15 J. MARSHALL J. COMPUTER & INFO. L. 703 (1997).

2. *Practice Points*: What advice would you give a commercial client with a fax machine, in light of the issue raised in the preceding case? *See Parma Tile Mosaic & Marble Co. v. Estate of Short*, 87 N.Y.2d 524, 663 N.E.2d 663 (1996), for a discussion of the use of a fax machine as it relates to the Statute of Frauds.

DeROSIS v. KAUFMAN
641 N.Y.S.2d 831 (A.D. 1996)

WALLACH, Justice:

On this appeal we are required to determine whether a series of writings, executed and delivered by defendant to plaintiff at various times over a four-year period, are sufficient to overcome the defense of the Statute of Frauds. Framing the issue as entirely one of law, both parties moved for summary judgment. The [trial] court granted plaintiff's cross motion and directed judgment in his favor.

In our view, the writings proffered by plaintiff are woefully insufficient to establish that defendant became a guarantor of repayment to plaintiff of a $75,000 "loan" allegedly made by plaintiff to one Michael Goldberg. There is no dispute that such a promise, to be enforceable, must be in writing (General Obligations Law § 5-701[a][2]).

Plaintiff places major reliance upon two memoranda which defendant signed and delivered to him on July 28, 1993. The first reads:

> I owe Louis De Rosis $75000
>
> [signed] Bernard Kaufman
>
> 7/28/93

The second reads:

> As of 7/28/93 my obligation to pay Louis De Rosis for his prior investment in Schact Fish Co. is $*75000*
>
> [Therefore] I owe Louis De Rosis *75000*
>
> [signed] Bernard Kaufman

It may be noted that these two documents are somewhat self-contradictory: the first suggests a direct debtor-creditor relationship; the second, although repeating the status, is adopted in plaintiff's complaint as a "guarantee." Yet that word or concept never appears in the second instrument. There is a reference to plaintiff's prior investment in Schact Fish Co., but this writing is as consistent with a purchase by defendant of an equity "investment" in Schact Fish, held by plaintiff, as with anything else. There is nothing in the writing to tie the alleged primary obligor, Goldberg, to Schact Fish Co. Thus, missing from this pair of memoranda is any reference to (1) a loan (2) from plaintiff to Goldberg (3) which defendant is undertaking to guarantee.

A third (earlier) writing, which also fails to advance plaintiff's case, reads as follows:

> I owe Louis De Rosis $150000 and $25000 for a total of $175000
>
> [signed] Bernard Kaufman
>
> 6/6/89.
>
> Returnable and payable by July 1, 1989

Clearly, this June 1989 writing does nothing to supply any of the elements of guaranty missing from the August 1993 writing. However, it is urged in the dissent that light can be found in the circumstance that about five months earlier, on January 14, 1989, "Mike Goldberg" signed a six-month promissory note in the sum of $25,000 to the order of plaintiff. Beneath Mr. Goldberg's signature is identified an entirely different entity, "Seafood Acquisition Group." Rather than appearing as a *guarantor* on this instrument, defendant signed simply as a *witness* to Mr. Goldberg's signature. And nothing therein enables us to say that the $25,000 referred to in this note is a component of the $75,000 referred to in the paper signed and delivered four and a half years later. We *can* say that "Seafood Acquisition Group" is not the same as "Schact Fish Co., " and Mr. Goldberg's connection to that latter entity remains pure conjecture.

What these bits of paper bearing defendant's signature resemble, if anything, is the type of I.O.U. sometimes accepted by casinos in exchange for a stack of chips. Damon Runyon would have called them "markers"; his story about one ended up as a movie in which Hollywood's then most valuable property[2] was delivered as security for repayment of same. But even if these writings might do "nicely, nicely, thank you" in the world of GUYS AND DOLLS, they cannot overcome the barrier of the statute in an ordinary commercial setting so as to create a guaranty to make good the default of another.

As we recently held in *Allied Sheet Metal Works v. Saunders*, 206 A.D.2d 166, 168, 619 N.Y.S.2d 260, "To be considered a sufficient memorandum within the ambit of the Statute of Frauds, a writing 'must designate the parties, identify and describe the subject matter and state *all* the essential or material terms of the contract' " (emphasis added). This has been settled law in this state for over a century (*see Mentz v. Newwitter*, 122 N.Y. 491, 497, 25 N.E. 1044 . . .). While it is true that an agreement may be pieced together from separate writings, those writings must be "connected with one another either expressly or by the internal evidence of subject matter and occasion" (*Marks v. Cowdin*, 226 N.Y. 138, 145, 123 N.E. 139 [Cardozo, J.]). The documents offered here meet neither test.

In a futile attempt to remedy the manifest deficiencies of the writings, plaintiff submitted an affidavit setting forth his version of the guaranty scenario. . . .

Plaintiff's affidavit must be disregarded as a matter of law. The court of Appeals was unanimous on this point in *Bazak Intl. Corp. v. Mast Indus.*, 73 N.Y.2d 113, 117–118, 538 N.Y.S.2d 503, 535 N.E.2d 633:

> Although a court ordinarily might take plaintiff's affidavits into account on a dismissal motion, . . . different considerations apply where the basis for the dismissal motion is a Statute of Frauds defense. Parol evidence, even in affidavit form, is immaterial to the threshold issue whether the documents are sufficient on their face to satisfy the Statute of Frauds. Consideration of parol evidence in assessing the adequacy of a writing for Statute of Frauds purposes would otherwise undermine the very reason for a Statute of Frauds in the first instance. That issue must be determined from the documents themselves, as a matter of law (*see Scheck v. Francis*, 26 N.Y.2d 466, 472, 311 N.Y.S.2d 841, 260 N.E.2d 493).

In sum, because the writings do not conform at all to plaintiff's version of the oral contract of guaranty, and, indeed, tend to contradict it . . . the complaint must be dismissed.

Accordingly, the order, Supreme Court, New York County . . . entered July 7, 1995, which denied defendant's motion to dismiss the complaint upon a Statute of Frauds defense, and which granted plaintiff's cross motion for summary judgment in the amount of $75,000, plus interest, costs and disbursements, should be reversed, to the extent appealed from, on the law, the cross motion denied, the judgment in favor of plaintiff vacated, and defendant's motion for summary judgment dismissing the complaint granted, without costs. The Clerk is directed to enter judgment accordingly. . . .

Tom, Justice (dissenting, with Kaufman).

This action arises out of certain business loans made by plaintiff to Michael Goldberg, which loans were allegedly induced and guaranteed by defendant.

---

[2] Shirley Temple, in *Little Miss Marker* (Twentieth Century Fox 1934).

General Obligations Law § 5-701(a)(2) (the "Statute of Frauds") states:

> Every agreement, promise or undertaking is void, unless it or some note or memorandum thereof be in writing, and subscribed by the party to be charged therewith, or by his lawful agent, if such agreement, promise or undertaking . . . [i]s a special promise to answer for the debt, default or miscarriage of another person. . . .

The Statute of Frauds' purpose is "to avoid fraud by preventing the enforcement of contracts that were never in fact made. Generally the statute is satisfied by some note or memorandum signed by the party to be charged that is adequate to establish an agreement when considered in light of the admitted facts and surrounding circumstances" (*Henry L. Fox Co., Inc. v. William Kaufman Org., Ltd.*, 74 N.Y.2d 136, 140, 544 N.Y.S.2d 565, 542 N.E.2d 1082). . . .

It is also well-settled that the agreement may be furnished by piecing together related writings (*Henry L. Fox Co., Inc. v. William Kaufman Org., Ltd., supra*, at 139, 544 N.Y.S.2d 565, 542 N.E.2d 1082; *Crabtree v. Elizabeth Arden Sales Corp.*, 305 N.Y. 48, 110 N.E.2d 551). In order to be considered a sufficient memorandum within the parameters of the Statute of Frauds, the writings must designate, with reasonable certainty, the parties involved, the subject matter of the agreement, and all of the essential or material terms of the contract (*Allied Sheet Metal Works, Inc. v. Kerby Saunders, Inc.*, 206 A.D.2d 166, 168, 619 N.Y.S.2d 260. . .).

In the matter at bar, the following memoranda are submitted as evidence of the agreement:

> I owe Lewis De Rosis $75000
>
> Bernard Kaufman [signed]
>
> 7/28/93
>
> As of 7/28/93 my obligation to pay Louis De Rosis for his prior investment in Schact Fish Co. is $75000
>
> I owe Louis De Rosis 75000
>
> Bernard Kaufman [signed]
>
> I owe Louis De Rosis $150000 and $25000 for a total of $175000
>
> Bernard Kaufman [signed]
>
> 6/6/89
>
> Returnable and payable by July 1, 1989.

A fourth writing is in the form of a Promissory Note, dated January 14, 1989, indicating a debt of $25,000 owed to plaintiff by Mike Goldberg, who signed above the corporate name Seafood Acquisition Group. Defendant witnessed the signing of the Note, the payment of which was due on June 15, 1989, or at approximately the same time that defendant signed the first of his memoranda which indicated that he had assumed a $25,000 debt to plaintiff.

There is no dispute that defendant Bernard Kaufman's signature is affixed to all three writings, which specify the party charged with the obligation (defendant), the amount of the obligation (first $175,000 in June 1989 and, later, presumably after some payments, $75,000 in 1993), the date the promise was made (July 28, 1993) and the underlying obligation (investment in Schact Fish Co.) which was guaranteed. Since the foregoing represent all of the material terms of the contract, the Statute of Frauds is satisfied.

Defendant's arguments to the contrary are meritless. While defendant avers that the memoranda "made no mention of any guarantee of any third party's obligation, " one of the July 1993 notes specifically states that defendant's obligation to pay plaintiff arises from plaintiff's "prior investment in Schact Fish Co."

Similarly unfounded is defendant's contention that the obligor of the loan, Goldberg, is not mentioned or identified. As is clear from one of the writings, Goldberg's company is identified (Schact Fish Co.) as being the recipient of the loan. In addition, the fact that the later, 1993 memoranda indicate that defendant owed plaintiff $75,000, whereas one earlier memorandum indicates a much larger amount is irrelevant as other, earlier obligations may have been satisfied.

Lastly, and despite defendant's protestations to the contrary, the memoranda do not run afoul of the Statute of Frauds because they do not indicate consideration running to the defendant because . . . "[w]hen a party promises to answer for the debt of another . . . the promise, if it is to be enforceable under the statute, must *either be evidenced in writing or* plaintiff must prove it is supported by a new consideration moving to the promisor. . ." (emphasis added) (*Martin Roofing, Inc. v. Goldstein, supra*, at 265, 469 N.Y.S.2d 595, 457 N.E.2d 700).

Accordingly, since the promise is evidenced in writing, and since reasonable certainty, and not absolute certainty, is required to satisfy the Statute of Frauds in order to avoid the cancellation of an otherwise viable contract, . . . I vote to affirm the [trial] court.

NOTES & QUESTIONS

1. As the result of the decision, if Kaufman really did owe De Rosis $75,000, will that obligation be enforceable?

2. Which is the more persuasive view of this case — the majority opinion or the dissent?

FISCHER v. MANN
514 N.E.2d 566 (Ill. App. 1987)

Justice INGLIS:

This is an appeal from an order of the trial court granting a motion by defendants, Lois Mann and F Fred Mann, to dismiss the first amended complaint (complaint) of plaintiff, Joyce A. Fischer, concerning a purported rental agreement. The agreement was found to be unenforceable pursuant to section 2 of "An Act to revise the law in relation to frauds and perjuries" (Statute of Frauds) (Ill. Rev. Stat. 1985, ch. 59, par. 2.).

The complaint alleges that on May 23, 1986, plaintiff filled out a standard form captioned "Application for Rental" for the premises described as 4236 Lori Drive, located in Rockford, Illinois. The application was addressed to F. Fred and Lois Mann. A copy of the application is attached to the complaint. The term originally stated on the application was from August 1, 1986, to August 1, 1988. The parties agree that at some time between May 23, 1986, and July 28, 1986, one of defendants altered the application to change August 1, 1986, to read August 9, 1986.

. . .

The application contained the following final clause:

> I have deposited on account, $500, which is to be forfeited if lease is not signed and balance of first month's rent paid within 3 days after notice of acceptance is mailed to me at address given below. Deposit to be refunded if references are not satisfactory or application rejected.

The above language of the application was followed by plaintiff's signature and address. Defendants did not sign the application.

Plaintiff tendered a $500 check to defendants. The check was attached to the complaint as an exhibit. The check was payable to Lois Mann and endorsed by her. Contrary to the allegations of the complaint, the signature of F. Fred Mann does not appear on the check. The check was subsequently deposited in a bank account.

Additional allegations of the complaint are as follows:

> 7. On several occasions between May 23, 1986 at [sic] July 28, 1986, Defendants made oral statements to Plaintiff and engaged in conduct which unequivocally indicated that Plaintiff's offer to rent the above-described premises had been accepted by Defendants.

> 8. Sometime between May 23, 1986 and July 28, 1986, Plaintiff was informed by Defendants that, due to some problems with a home they were purchasing, Plaintiff could not take possession of the above-described premises until August 9, 1986. Accordingly, one of the Defendants altered the August 1st possession date on Exhibit 1 to read 'August 9, 1986.'

> 9. By altering the date on the application, Defendants clearly indicated not only their acceptance of Plaintiff's offer but their adoption of the application as a writing evidencing the agreement of the parties.

> 10. On or about July 28, 1986, Defendant LOIS MANN wrote Plaintiff a letter informing her that possession could not be turned over to her on or about August 9, 1986, and that Defendants did not intend to yield possession to Plaintiff at anytime thereafter.

We note that the alleged July 28, 1986, letter is not attached to the complaint.

The application was never accepted in writing, the lease was never prepared, the balance of the first month's rental was never tendered, and the premises were never delivered to plaintiff. These facts all appear as agreed from the parties' statements of facts.

Plaintiff subsequently filed a complaint for money damages, and defendants filed a motion to dismiss based on the Statute of Frauds. Defendants' motion was granted.

. . .

Plaintiff raises two issues on appeal: (1) whether the application and check constitute a sufficient writing under the Statute of Frauds; and (2) whether plaintiff has alleged sufficient facts to estop defendants from asserting the Statute of Frauds as a defense.

Plaintiff admits in her brief that the facts bring the complaint within the Statute of Frauds, which provides:

> No action shall be brought to charge any person upon any contract for the sale of lands, tenements or hereditaments or any interest in or concerning them, for a longer term than one year, unless such contract or some memorandum or note thereof shall be in writing, and signed by the party to be charged therewith, or some other person thereunto by him lawfully authorized in writing, signed by such party.

Ill. Rev. Stat. 1985, ch. 59, par. 2.

The Statute of Frauds clearly applies to a lease for a term of more than one year. (Ill. Rev. Stat. 1985, ch. 59, par. 2; *see also Daehler v. Oggoian* (1979), 72 Ill. App. 3d 360, 28 Ill. Dec. 250, 390 N.E.2d 417.) The court in *Daehler* discussed the Statute of Frauds in relationship to leases as follows:

> In order to satisfy the Statute of Frauds, a lease for a term of more than one year or a memorandum thereof must be in writing and contain the names of the parties, a description of the property sufficient enough to identify the property, the amount of rent, and the term of the lease. The writing must also have been signed by the party to be charged, or by some other person authorized by him in writing. [Citations.] It is not necessary that a lease or a memorandum thereof be in one writing, as it may be gathered from several writings taken together, including letters between the parties. [Citations.] However, to establish a lease or memorandum thereof from more than one writing, only one of which has been signed, the signed writing "must refer expressly to the other writing, or the several writings must be so connected, either physically or otherwise, as to show by internal evidence that they relate to the same contract." [Citation.] . . .

Plaintiff first contends that the application and check satisfy the writing requirement of the Statute of Frauds. Plaintiff argues that these two documents, when taken together, constitute a memorandum or note of the alleged contract which has been signed by the party to be charged. Plaintiff further argues that the signature of Lois Mann on the $500 check fulfills the requirement of a signature of the party being charged and supports the allegation that *defendants* endorsed the check. We disagree.

No amount of allegation or argument can overcome the check itself which bears only the signature of Lois Mann and not the signature of F. Fred Mann, one of the parties being charged. The court notes the absence of any allegation of authority or agency for Lois Mann to act for F. Fred Mann. The record is also silent as to any allegation of their relationship, if any. One of the necessary parties to be charged has not signed, and, therefore, plaintiff fails to meet the signature requirement of the Statute of Frauds.

Furthermore, we disagree with plaintiff's contention that the application and the check, when taken together, constitute a sufficient writing. The check has the notation "for security deposit" on the lower left-hand corner. Plaintiff argues that "[t]he check is specifically refferrable [sic] to that portion of the application regarding a $500 deposit." Following Daehler, this court's inquiry is necessarily directed to whether the check expressly refers to the application or whether the check and application are so connected as to show by internal evidence that they relate to the same contract.

Plaintiff argues that the facts as alleged in the complaint and disclosed by the application and check demonstrate a striking similarity to this court's decision in *Jones v. Olsen* (1980), 80 Ill. App. 3d 1016, 36 Ill. Dec. 245, 400 N.E.2d 665, appeal denied (1980), 81 Ill. 2d 584. In *Jones*, the plaintiff delivered to defendants a $12,000 check payable to defendants pursuant to an unsigned sales contract. . . . The check stated on its face that it was earnest money for the purchase of property known as 029 Lakeview, Mundelein. . . . Defendants both endorsed and negotiated the check, but never signed the form sales contract. . . . The contract provided that $12,000 earnest money, in the form of a check payable to defendant sellers, be deposited by sellers on acceptance of the contract, and the contract was to be void if not accepted by a certain date. . . . The sale was not consummated, and the $12,000 was not returned. . . .

The trial court held that the contract violated the Statute of Frauds for lack of signature. . . . We reversed, pointing out that "the form contract specifically calls for the purchaser of 029 Lakeview, Mundelein, to deliver to the 'Owner of Record' a $12,000 check as an earnest money deposit, to be deposited by seller on acceptance of the contract, " and it further provided "that the earnest money shall be returned and the contract rendered void if not accepted on or before February 28, 1978." . . . This court held that the form contract and check were sufficiently connected as to allow them to be read together as they "refer to the same common address in the same municipality; the earnest money check is for the same amount as the earnest money specified in the contract; the check and the contract are dated with the same date; and defendants endorsed and cashed the check prior to February 28, 1978, as required by the contract."

Plaintiff argues that the documents in the instant action are identical in their relevance to those discussed in the Jones case. We disagree.

The case before this court differs in many ways. First, in Jones, the plaintiff's check was not returned when the sale failed to take place. . . . In the present case, there is no allegation that the $500 was not returned. In fact, plaintiff concedes in her brief that it was returned. Second, in Jones, the check was payable to and signed by both defendants. . . . In our case, the check was payable to and signed by only one defendant. Third, in Jones, the check stated on its face it was earnest money for the purchase of 029 Lakeview, Mundelein. . . . In our case, the check only states that it is "for security deposit, " and there is no internal reference to either the application, any specific property, or any specific agreement. Fourth, in Jones, the sales contract stated that the check was an earnest money deposit, to be deposited by defendant on *acceptance of the contract*. . . . The Jones contract further provided that the earnest money was to be returned and the contract rendered void *if not accepted* on or before February 28, 1978. . . . The fact that "defendants endorsed and cashed the check prior to February 28, 1978, *as required by the contract*" was a factor in the Jones court ruling that the Statute of Frauds requirements had been met. (Emphasis added.) . . . In our case, the only internal evidence alleged to indicate acceptance is the alteration of the term from August 1, 1986 to August 9, 1986. Finally, unlike a contract to sell or a lease, an application to rent is simply that, an application to enter into a lease. Unlike the contract to sell in Jones, the application in the present case contains no provision for deposit on acceptance. In fact, the application contains a clear statement that the deposit of

$500 will be refunded if references are not satisfactory or if the application is rejected. Because of these significant differences, we find that Jones does not control this case.

In reading the application and check together, we find that the trial court was correct in its ruling and that the requirements of the Statute of Frauds have not been met.

Plaintiff next contends that defendants should be estopped from asserting the Statute of Frauds since they agreed to lease the premises to her for two years and failed to provide a written lease. Plaintiff argues that defendants are attempting to take advantage of their own inequitable conduct and that she relied to her detriment on defendants' representation that the premises could be occupied by her in accordance with the application.

It is a fundamental principle that no person shall be permitted to take advantage of his own wrong. (*Loeb v. Gendel* (1961), 23 Ill. 2d 502, 505, 179 N.E.2d 7) Illinois courts have long recognized the inequity of allowing a party to utilize the Statute of Frauds to work an injustice or fraud and have refused in such cases to permit its assertion as a defense. (*Id.*)

Plaintiff argues that defendants should be estopped from asserting the Statute of Frauds since they represented to her that she could take possession of the premises in August 1986. However, in *Ceres Illinois, Inc. v. Illinois Scrap Processing, Inc.* (1984), 130 Ill. App. 3d 798, 805, 86 Ill. Dec. 48, 474 N.E.2d 1245, aff'd (1986), 114 Ill. 2d 133, 102 Ill. Dec. 379, the defendant similarly argued that the plaintiff, by its conduct, led the defendant to believe that it could take possession of certain land for a 15-year lease. That court held that since the defendant knew that a written agreement regarding the premises was being negotiated, it could not rely on the fact that plaintiff had allowed it to occupy the land on an oral license. . . . The court refused to estop the assertion of the Statute of Frauds because both parties had equal access to information regarding the negotiations. . . .

We agree with plaintiff that *Ceres Illinois, Inc.* is distinguishable in that plaintiff in the present case was not privy to any special knowledge regarding the availability of the premises. However, that court further stated that "[i]n order to invoke the doctrine of equitable estoppel, the guilty party must exhibit words or conduct amounting to a misrepresentation or concealment of a material fact." . . . In the instant case, there are no allegations in the complaint of misrepresentation or concealment of material facts despite the court's having given plaintiff the opportunity to amend. Plaintiff did allege that, as a result of defendants' failure to yield the premises, she was required to seek temporary housing and incurred additional expenses. However, "[a] party's decision to make expenditures and to change its position in reliance on an oral promise is an insufficient basis for equitable estoppel in the absence of fraud or misrepresentation." 130 Ill. App. 3d 798, 805, 86 Ill. Dec. 48, 474 N.E.2d 1245.

We also note that the supreme court in *Ozier v. Haines* (1952), 411 Ill. 160, 163, 103 N.E.2d 485, held that the breach of a promise which the law does not regard as binding is not a fraud and does not justify the application of the doctrine of estoppel.

Affirmed.

NOTES & QUESTIONS

1. What factors about or features of multiple writings would suggest that such writings should be read together (other than the most obvious feature of express incorporation by reference)?

2. *Drafting Point:* In preparing an important multiple page document, do not rely upon staples, paper clips, and the like to hold pages together. What drafting techniques can be employed to help assure that all of the pages will be accepted as part of a single document?

C. EXCEPTIONS TO THE STATUTE OF FRAUDS

Because the purpose of the Statute of Frauds is to avoid fraudulent enforcement of a non-existent contract, then proof equal to or better than written evidence of the contract would seem to satisfy the Statute's purpose. For this reason, the courts long ago accepted the parties' conduct as just as persuasive as written evidence and created a narrow field of exceptions to compliance with the Statute of Frauds. These exceptions operate to bar the assertion of the Statute of Frauds as a defense.

SIEMENS v. GRIFFITH
2001 ML 1409 (Mont. Dist. 2001)

This matter comes before the Court upon the Plaintiffs' motion for summary judgment. The parties have fully briefed the motion and waived oral argument and the matter is deemed submitted and ready for ruling.

The Plaintiffs' complaint alleges breach of a stock sales agreement. The Defendant answered the complaint alleging the following affirmative defenses:

(1) The complaint fails to state a claim,

(2) Plaintiffs' own actions are the cause of their own damage,

(3) Plaintiffs claims are barred by their own breach, and

(4) The claims are barred by the doctrine of estoppel.

The Plaintiffs' argue in their pending motion for summary judgment that the Defendant's own answers to Plaintiffs' first discovery requests reveal that a $ 50,000 debt under the terms of the stock sales agreement exists, and that the Defendant failed to pay the debt after receipt of appropriate notice. The Plaintiffs argue that the affirmative defenses raised by the Defendant do not raise material issues of fact, and therefore summary judgment is appropriate.

Specifically, the Plaintiffs allege that Defendant made the following admission to Plaintiffs' first discovery requests:

[1] The Defendant admitted that he entered into a stock sale agreements with Plaintiffs. *Request for Admission No. 1, Defendant's Response to Plaintiff's First Discovery Requests.*

[2] The Defendant admitted that pursuant to the terms of the stock sale agreement that he agreed to pay $ 150,000 for all shares of common stock. *Request for Admission No. 2, Defendant's Response to Plaintiff's First Discovery Requests.*

[3] The Defendant admitted that $ 100,000 was paid at the time of closing on the stock sale agreement. *Request for Admission No. 3, Defendant's Response to Plaintiff's First Discovery Requests.*

[4] The Defendant admits that he failed to make the payment of the remaining $50,000 due on April 15, 2000 under the terms of the stock sales agreement. *Request for Admission No. 8, Defendant's Response to Plaintiff's First Discovery Requests.*

[5] The Defendant admits that he received a notice of default informing him that he had until May 17, 2000 to cure default. *Request for Admission No. 9, Defendant's Response to Plaintiff's First Discovery Requests.*

[6] The Defendant admits that he failed to cure the default. *Requests for Admission No. 10, Defendant's Response to Plaintiff's First Discovery Requests.*

The Defendant has responded to the motion by arguing that Plaintiffs made "serious misrepresentations" with regard to the existing inventory, and "failed to disclose" the extent of the existing debt on the business. The Defendant argues that Plaintiffs breached the contract and breached the implied covenant of good faith and fair dealing by failing to provide accurate and complete financial statements. The Defendant also alleges that he is entitled to an "offset" on monies claimed by the Plaintiffs.

The Defendant has not pled misrepresentation, fraud, or breach of the implied covenant of good faith and fair dealing in his answer, and the Court will not address claims asserted now that Defendant has never pled. However, the Defendant has pled the affirmative defense of estoppel.

D. EQUITABLE ESTOPPEL

In order to prove equitable estoppel, the party claiming it must establish the following six elements by clear and convincing evidence:

[1] The existence of conduct, acts, language, or silence amounting to a representation or concealment of material facts;

[2] The party estopped must have knowledge of these facts at the time of the representation or concealment, or the circumstances must be such that knowledge is necessarily imputed to that party;

[3] The truth concerning these facts must be unknown to the other party at the time it was acted upon;

[4] The conduct must be done with the intention or expectation that it will be acted upon by the other party, or have occurred under circumstances showing it to be both natural and probable that it will be acted upon;

[5] The conduct must be relied upon by the other party and lead that party to act; and

[6] The other party must in fact act upon the conduct in such a manner as to change its position for the worse.

Selley v. Liberty Northwest Ins. Corp. 299 Mont. 127, 998 P.2d 156 (2000). Equitable estoppel is not a favored doctrine, and thus the requirement that it be proved by "clear and convincing" evidence. *Ducham v. Tuma* 265 Mont. 436, 877 P.2d 1002 (1994).

In the Plaintiffs' reply brief, they argue that the parol evidence rule bars Defendant's affirmative defenses. The Plaintiffs cite *Sherrodd, Inc. v. Morrison-Knudsen Company* 249 Mont. 282, 815 P.2d 1135 (1991) for the argument that the parol evidence rule bars evidence of allegations of oral promises that contradict the terms of an express written contract. The *Sherrodd* case does not reveal that an affirmative defense of estoppel was alleged.

A review of the Montana Supreme Court case of *Farm Credit Bank of Spokane v. District Court* 267 Mont. 1, 881 P.2d 594 (1994) reveals that where there is an affirmative defense of equitable estoppel alleged, the admission of testimony regarding verbal representations does not violate the parol evidence rule, even though the verbal representations were not included within the parties' written agreement.

The specific issue raised in *Farm Credit Bank of Spokane* was whether unilateral representations allegedly made by a lender and upon which a borrower relied to his detriment provides a basis for an affirmative defense of equitable estoppel to a foreclosure action, when the representations were verbal and not included in a written agreement. The Supreme Court held the following:

> On appeal, the FCB contends that the only evidence in support of the Graveleys' equitable estoppel defense is the Graveleys' testimony regarding Valerie Warehime's oral representation, and that since those representations are superseded by the written terms of the parties' loan documents, that evidence is barred by Montana's parol evidence rule found at § 28-2-905, M.C.A. The FCB cites this Court's decision in *Sherrodd, Inc. v. Morrison-Knudsen Company* (1991), 249 Mont. 282, 815 P.2d 1135, for the proposition that oral negotiations which contradict the terms of the written contract are not admissible and that on this basis the District Court's order denying summary judgment should be reversed.

> The Graveleys respond that reliance on the statute of frauds in this case is not applicable because it is a legal theory and the issues raised by the counterclaim and affirmative defense are equitable issues. The Graveleys further assert that neither *Sherrodd*, nor any other authorities cited by the FCB, are on point because none of them involve the issue of equitable estoppel. Finally, the Graveleys contend that to the extent that § 28-2-905 (2), M.C.A., which sets forth the parol evidence rule is applicable, we should consider the defense of equitable estoppel analogous to the exception for evidence of fraud which is made in § 28-2-905 (2), M.C.A.

> We conclude that the Graveleys' arguments are more persuasive, and therefore, affirm the District Court's conclusion that there was evidence to support the defense of equitable estoppel, but reverse that part of the District Court's order which held that the resolution of the estoppel issue must necessarily decide the affirmative defense based on the Agricultural Credit Act as a matter of law.

> First, our decision in *Sherrodd* is not on point. In that action, a subcontractor brought a claim for damages based on oral representations by the defendant general contractor which this Court held were contrary to

the express terms of the contract, and therefore, superseded by the contract pursuant to § 28-2-904, M.C.A. *That case neither involved an equitable claim for foreclosure, nor the defense of equitable estoppel.* Therefore, we conclude that our decision in *Sherrodd* does not apply to this case.

Second, it is well recognized that courts of equity will consider the statute of frauds differently than courts of law. For example, it is stated that:

The purpose and intent of the statute of frauds is to prevent fraud, and not to aid in its perpetration, and the courts, *particularly courts of equity*, will, so far as possible, refuse to allow it to be used as a shield or cloak to protect fraud, or as an instrument whereby to perpetrate a fraud, or as a vehicle or means of culpable wrong, injustice or oppression.

73 AM. JUR. 2D *Statute of Frauds*, § 562 (1974).

In particular, courts have been reluctant to apply the statute of frauds to bar a claim of equitable estoppel:

Closely allied to the principles of protection against the assertion of the statute of frauds to accomplish a fraud upon the party who has acted in reliance upon an oral contract or the assertion of the statute as a shield to protect fraud is the doctrine of estoppel to assert the statute. It is universally conceded that the doctrine of equitable estoppel may be invoked to preclude a party to a contract from asserting the unenforceability of a contract by reason of the fact that it is not in writing as required by the statute of frauds. As is often said, the statute of frauds may be rendered inoperative by an estoppel in pais. Where one has acted to his detriment solely in reliance on an oral agreement, an estoppel may be raised to defeat the defense of the statute of frauds. This is based upon the principle established in equity, and applying in every transaction where the statute is invoked, that the statute of frauds, having been enacted for the purpose of preventing fraud, shall not be made the instrument of shielding, protecting, or aiding the party who relies upon it in the perpetration of fraud or in the consummation of a fraudulent scheme. It is called into operation to defeat what would be an unconscionable use of the statute, and guards against the utilization of the statute, and guards against the utilization of the statute as a means for defrauding innocent persons who have been induced or permitted to change their position in reliance upon oral agreements within its operation.

73 AM. JUR. 2D *Statute of Frauds*, § 565 (1974).

Our prior decisions are consistent with these equitable principles. In *Fiers v. Jacobson (1949)*, 123 Mont. 242, 211 P.2d 968, the plaintiff sought to enforce a provision in his lease agreement which gave him the option to purchase the property he was leasing. However, the defendant sold the land while the agreement was in effect, and when sued by the plaintiff, claimed that the plaintiff was estopped from enforcing the option because he had repeatedly told the defendant that he had no intention of exercising it. The plaintiff in that case, as does the defendant in this case, sought to prohibit evidence of the oral representations based on the parol evidence rule.

In *Fiers*, this Court concluded that the evidence of the plaintiff's oral statements were insufficient to establish estoppel, however, refused to disregard that evidence based on the parol evidence rule. . .

See Farm Credit Bank of Spokane v. District Court, 267 Mont. at 25, 26, and 27.

The Farm Credit Bank case reveals that if an affirmative defense of estoppel is alleged, and the Defendant raises material issues of fact with regard to the defense, then a denial of summary judgment is appropriate.

In this case, the Defendant's affidavit clearly attests to the following alleged facts:

[1] That during negotiations to the stock sales agreement, the Plaintiffs provided Defendant's son with data concerning the business, such as the business plan.

[2] That after the deal was closed, that the Defendant and his son discovered that Plaintiffs made "serious misrepresentations."

[3] Specifically, the Plaintiffs overstated the value of the inventory for the business, they failed to accurately disclose the extent of existing liabilities, they inflated figures on annual profits, and they made "wildly distorted claims regarding projected income."

[4] The Plaintiffs informed Defendant and his son that they could "rely" on the figures given to them.

Although the doctrine of equitable estoppel is not favored, and the Defendant will ultimately be required to prove it by "clear and convincing" evidence, his burden as an opposing party on a motion for summary judgment is not as heavy. The Defendant must simply present evidence of a "material and substantial nature raising genuine issue of material fact." *Estate of Nielsen v. Pardis* (1994), 265 Mont. 470, 878 P.2d 234.

The Defendant has raised material issues of fact with regard to his affirmative defense of estoppel, which precludes summary ruling in Plaintiffs favor at this time.

IT IS THEREFORE ORDERED that Plaintiff's Motion for Summary Judgment is hereby DENIED.

NOTES & QUESTIONS

1. Although the defendant has survived the plaintiff's motion for summary judgment, what obstacles does the defendant now face in order to prevail in this case?

2. What conduct of each party to an oral real estate sale could indicate conclusively that they must have had a contract?

3. Consider the RESTATEMENT (SECOND) OF CONTRACTS treatment of the Statute of Frauds and determine what, if any, differences exist between the Montana approach and the RESTATEMENT approach.

§ 139. Enforcement By Virtue Of Action In Reliance

(1) A promise which the promisor should reasonably expect to induce action or forbearance on the part of the promisee or a third person and which does induce the action or forbearance is enforceable notwithstanding the Statute of Frauds if injustice can be avoided only by enforcement of the promise. The remedy granted for breach is to be limited as justice requires.

(2) In determining whether injustice can be avoided only by enforcement of the promise, the following circumstances are significant:

(a) the availability and adequacy of other remedies, particularly cancellation and restitution;

(b) the definite and substantial character of the action or forbearance in relation to the remedy sought;

(c) the extent to which the action or forbearance corroborates evidence of the making and terms of the promise, or the making and terms are otherwise established by clear and convincing evidence;

(d) the reasonableness of the action or forbearance;

(e) the extent to which the action or forbearance was foreseeable by the promisor.

4. *Practice Points:* Note that in the preceding case, the defendant had not pled misrepresentation, fraud or breach of covenant of good faith and fair dealing, but asserted those issues during on appeal. Was it proper for the appellate court not to address these claims on appeal?

SKAGGS v. DIAL
861 S.W.2d 188 (Mo. App. 1993)

BRECKENRIDGE, Judge:

This appeal concerns an action seeking specific performance of an oral contract to purchase residential real estate. Joe David Dial and Sharon Lorraine Dial, husband and wife, appeal from the trial court's judgment vesting fee simple title to the real estate at issue in Clara B. Skaggs. This suit originated in a seven count petition. In Counts I, II and III against the Dials, Skaggs requested the court to quiet title in her favor, grant a declaratory judgment and decree specific performance, respectively. Skaggs requested recovery against the Dials and [their daughter] Audra Jo Stith in Counts IV, V, VI and VII for ejectment, slander of title, conversion of chattels and trespass to realty, respectively. The trial court ordered that the oral contract be specifically performed and that the Dials, after satisfying all liens on the property, execute a deed conveying the property to Skaggs so that Skaggs is vested with fee simple title to the property. The trial court found the Dials and Stith guilty of ejectment, conversion and trespass, for which the court awarded damages in the amount of $8,700 and punitive damages in the amount of $20. The trial court also awarded Skaggs $400 a month, the monthly rental value of the property, until she is restored to possession of the property, and $4,500 for attorney's fees. . . .

At issue in the instant case is title to the residence and lot located at 1018 N.E. 44th Terrace (the property) in Kansas City, Clay County, Missouri. In July of 1969,

Skaggs entered into an oral agreement with the Dials to purchase the property. Skaggs had known the Dials for a number of years because Skaggs' brother was Sharon Dial's step-father. Skaggs orally agreed to pay the Dials $1,000 as a down payment for the equity in the property and to, thereafter, make payments to pay off the $11,650 mortgage. Title to the property remained in the Dials' name even after Skaggs agreed to purchase the property so that the financing could continue through a GI loan. Sharon Dial told Skaggs that if the property was placed in Skaggs' name, the mortgage payment would be higher.

Skaggs began residing on the property shortly after she agreed to purchase it. Skaggs made mortgage payments on the property from 1969 through 1988. Exhibits admitted at trial indicated that the checks for the mortgage payments were made out to the mortgage company, not to the Dials. The exhibits also showed that correspondence from the mortgage company, as well as annual statements, payment books, and interest statements for income tax purposes, were addressed to Joe Dial in care of Skaggs at the street address of the property. Skaggs paid the taxes and maintained insurance on the property. Skaggs also paid all bills associated with the property and the utilities were in her name.

Skaggs introduced evidence at trial that, since 1969, she had paid for $11,000 of improvements to the property. The improvements made by Skaggs to the house included the addition of aluminum siding, a porch, a shower, and a new roof, the installation of carpet, paneling and kitchen cabinets, and various plumbing improvements. Skaggs also installed a fence in the front yard and planted trees and flowers on the property.

Prior to the addition of aluminum siding to the house, Skaggs attempted to secure a bank loan to pay for the siding. The bank required proof that Skaggs was buying the house so the Dials signed a notarized statement, dated July 31, 1973, which read as follows:

> This is to certify that Mrs. Clara B. Skaggs is buying our home. On July 10, 1969, we received $1000 as down payment on Block, Lot 11, Kansas City North, Missouri. She has been making the house payments to Don J. MacMurray Company, who carried the mortgage in our name until the property is paid for.

> She is to make any and all improvements on this property.

On April 26, 1977, unbeknownst to Skaggs, the Dials borrowed $19,424.26 from Homemakers Financial Service. The Dials executed a deed of trust with the property serving as security for the loan. The Dials borrowed $25,000 from GECC Financial Services on July 31, 1988 and again, without Skaggs' knowledge, used the property as security for the loan.

In the winter of 1989, Skaggs allowed the Dials to move in with her because of the difficulty they encountered in traveling back and forth through the snow to the farm where they resided in Cameron, Missouri. On May 3, 1989, the Dials borrowed $66,446.43 from Ford Consumer Finance Company by placing a $66,000 mortgage on the property which also resulted in the GI loan being paid off. The Dials told Skaggs to stop making mortgage payment because the mortgage had been completely paid off. Although the Dials informed Skaggs that the mortgage was completely paid off, they did not transfer title to her.

In January of 1989, the Dials' daughter, Audra Jo Stith, also moved into the house. Although the Dials and Stith moved out sometime during 1989, they moved back in again during the winter of 1990. In early 1991, the Dials and Stith denied Skaggs access to her house after Skaggs requested that they move out of the house. Skaggs was forced to live in the garage of the house, which Skaggs had made into a small apartment prior to the time the Dials and Stith moved into the house. The Dials changed the locks on the front door and Stith nailed shut the door from the garage to the house. Without Skaggs' permission, the Dials moved Skaggs' furniture out of the house onto the back porch, cut vegetation and trees down on the property, and removed the fence in the front yard.

The Dials filed a petition for bankruptcy on July 10, 1991. . . .

An oral agreement for the sale of real property falls squarely within the Statute of Frauds, § 432.010, RSMo 1986, and will not be enforced at law. *Straatmann v. Straatmann*, 809 S.W.2d 95, 98 (Mo. App. 1991). Equity will decree specific performance of such a contract, however, if a party has acted to such a degree upon the contract that denying the party the benefit of the agreement would be unjust. The eight elements of proof required for specific performance of a oral contract to convey real property were originally set forth in *Walker v. Bohannan*, 243 Mo. 119, 146 S.W. 1024, 1028–29 (1912), and are as follows:

> (1) The alleged oral contract must be clear, explicit, and definite; (2) it must be proven as pleaded; (3) such contract cannot be established by conversations either too ancient on the one hand, or too loose or casual upon the other; (4) the alleged oral contract must itself be fair, and not unconscionable; (5) the proof of the contract as pleaded must be such as to leave no reasonable doubt in the mind of the chancellor that the contract as alleged was in fact made, and that the full performance, so far as lies in the hands of the parties to perform, has been had; (6) and the work constituting performance must be such as is referable solely to the contract as sought to be enforced and not such as might be reasonably referable to some other and different contract; (7) the contract must be one based upon an adequate and legal consideration, so that its performance upon the one hand, but not upon the other, would bespeak an unconscionable advantage and wrong, demanding in good conscience relief in equity; (8) proof of mere disposition to devise by will or convey by deed by way of gift, or as a reward for services, is not sufficient, but there must be shown a real contract to devise by will or convey by deed made before the acts of performance relied upon were had.

Specific performance is granted sparingly and only when the terms of the oral agreement are proved by clear and convincing evidence. *Gegg v. Kiefer*, 655 S.W.2d 834, 837 (Mo. App. 1983). The court cannot create a contract for the parties nor can the court decree specific performance if the agreement sought to be enforced is indefinite. *Quality Wig Co., Inc. v. J.C. Nichols Co.*, 728 S.W.2d 611, 617 (Mo. App. 1987).

The Dials argue that Skaggs failed to prove that the oral contract for the purchase of the property was "clear, explicit and definite, " which is the first element of the eight part test. The Dials argue that Skaggs failed to present evidence proving the total purchase price of the property or the period of time in which she was to complete payment. The Dials contend that Skaggs was a tenant who was using the property and paying rent for doing so.

The trial court found that Skaggs entered into "a clear, explicit and definite oral contract" with the Dials to purchase the property at issue in this case. The evidence, when considered in the light most favorable to the judgment, overwhelmingly supports the trial court's judgment.

Skaggs introduced evidence at trial showing that the terms of the agreement were that Skaggs would pay the Dials $1000 for their equity in the property and, thereafter, would make the mortgage payments directly to the mortgage company. At trial, Skaggs presented her canceled check for $1,000 to the Dials, on the face of which is the notation "$1000. Equity on 1018 E. 44 Terr. No." Skaggs also admitted into evidence receipts from the various mortgage companies that serviced the mortgage on the property from 1969 to 1988 and numerous cancelled checks made out to those mortgage companies. In addition, Skaggs introduced at trial the notarized statement signed by both Sharon and Joe Dial which specifically stated that Skaggs was buying their home and set forth the payment terms of their agreement. . . .

The responsibilities assumed by Skaggs do not support the Dials' argument that Skaggs was merely a rent-paying tenant. Paying mortgage payments directly to the mortgage company and making large-scale improvements to the property are not the usual responsibilities of a tenant. There was also testimony at trial that Skaggs paid the taxes on the property which is not generally the responsibility of a tenant.

The essential elements of an agreement to convey real property are: 1) the parties; 2) the subject matter; 3) the promises on both sides; 4) the price; and 5) the consideration. *Kemp Const, v. Landmark Bancshares*, 784 S.W.2d 306, 308 (Mo. App. 1990). Skaggs proved these elements by "clear, explicit, and definite" evidence. Skaggs proved that she contracted with the Dials to purchase their Kansas City property for $1,000 plus payment of the mortgage on the property, which at the time of the agreement was $11, 650. Such proof establishes the essential elements of an agreement to convey real property in a manner which is "clear, explicit and definite."

The trial court correctly found that Skaggs proved the terms of the oral contract between Skaggs and the Dials clearly, explicitly and definitely. The trial court's judgment granting Skaggs specific performance and vesting fee simple title to the property in Skaggs is supported by substantial evidence.

The judgment is affirmed.

NOTES & QUESTIONS

1. Do you have any doubt that there was a contract for the purchase of the realty by Skaggs? If not, should the law insist upon what is then a mere technicality that there be a written document to evidence the contract of sale?

2. Consider the notarized document signed by the Dials and used to show that Skaggs had purchased the house. Why is it important in this case to note that the document was notarized? Some notarizations involve only the identification by the notary of the signers of documents. Other notarizations also involve the swearing of the signers under oath as to the truth of the contents of signed documents.

3. Although contracts are not required by law to be notarized, sometimes the parties will insist upon notarization, or one of the parties will simply unilaterally have his/her signature notarized. Should parties be encouraged to obtain notarizations of their signatures on contracts? Are there disadvantages of this practice? *See* Michael L. Closen et al., Notary Law and Practice: Cases and Materials 135-46 (1997).

4. If Skaggs had lived in the house and made payments of less than $100 per month for almost 20 years, but had not made any permanent improvements, should Skaggs win the lawsuit?

5. The Uniform Electronic Transactions Act (U.E.T.A.) permits the contracting parties to agree to make electronic signatures contained in a record (such as emails) sufficient to operate as a signed writing in satisfaction of the Statute of Frauds. The parties must make a separate agreement regarding the electronic signatures. To date, 46 states and the District of Columbia have enacted some variation of the Uniform Act, and thus allow parties to substitute electronic signatures for paper and pen signatures. Consider what effect this recent legislation regarding electronic signatures may have on the Statute of Frauds and its underlying purpose.

REMILONG v. CROLLA
576 P.2d 461 (Wyo. 1978)

Guthrie, Chief Justice:

Appellants prosecute this appeal from a judgment ordering them to remove certain trailers and mobile homes from lands which they own and permanently enjoining them and their successors or assigns from placing, or allowing the placement of, any such trailers or mobile homes upon these lands.

Appellants Remilongs were the original owners of the lands now owned and occupied by appellees Crollas and sold them the tract which they now own and where their home is located, but appellants retained a portion thereof, being an adjoining tract to which this injunctive action was applied. The tract which the Remilongs retained contains 2.9 acres. The adjoining tract sold to the Crollas is one containing approximately .88 acres upon which is located a house which Remilongs sold to Crollas for the sum of $50,000. Crollas assert that a condition of the purchase was that Remilongs would remove all the trailers or mobile homes from the tract which they retained and claim that the fact they have now moved trailers thereon greatly diminishes the value of the lands purchased and that these lands were purchased in reliance upon such promise and agreement. Additionally, they claim damages in the sum of $10,000. This judgment is based upon findings of fact and conclusions of law, which are as follows:

FINDINGS OF FACT

1. During late winter or early spring of 1974, Plaintiffs and Defendants entered into an oral agreement whereby Defendants would sell to Plaintiffs a certain parcel of property adjoining property owned by Defendants.

2. Defendants promised and it was a condition of said agreement that Defendants would remove all trailers or mobile homes then existing on their remaining property and that they would never again permit or suffer

the placement of trailers or mobile homes on said property.

3. Pursuant to said agreement and prior to the consummation of the sale referred to, Defendants procured the removal from their property of all trailers and mobile homes.

4. On May *28*, 1974, Plaintiffs, acting in reliance upon the aforesaid promise or representation, purchased said property.

5. Since the time of said purchase Defendants have placed and have allowed the placement of trailers and mobile homes upon their property adjacent to the property purchased by the Plaintiffs.

6. That the placement and presence of said trailers on the property adjacent to Plaintiffs injures Plaintiffs by causing a diminution in the value of their adjoining property.

Based on the foregoing Findings of Fact, the Court makes the following Conclusions of Law:

CONCLUSIONS OF LAW

1. The parties' oral contract was a valid and binding contract, a condition or term of which was that Defendants would remove any trailers or mobile homes on their property and never allow said structures to be placed on their property again.

2. That said promise was in the nature of a restrictive covenant, running with the land, restricting the use of Defendants' land.

3. It would be an unjust and unconscionable result and a breach of contract and a breach of a restrictive covenant if Defendants were allowed to place or allow the placement of trailers upon their aforesaid property.

4. That a mandatory injunction should issue requiring Defendants to remove all trailers or mobile homes from their property and that a permanent injunction issue enjoining the Defendants, or their successors and assigns, from placing trailers on said property."

This matter presents two questions upon which our decision must be based, i.e., does an oral contract creating a restrictive covenant come within the statute of frauds? If such agreement is within the prohibition of the statute of frauds, may the effect thereof be avoided by the application of an equitable or promissory estoppel?

It is apparent that if the answer to the first question is in the negative, this judgment should be summarily affirmed. We do not find that this may be so answered, however.

Appellees concede an existent conflict of judicial opinion in this area, and cite authority sustaining their position that such an agreement does not come within the statute. However, in our view, and after examining such authorities, it appears that these opinions are "result oriented" and that the logic upon which they are based is at least questionable. It may be suggested that these opinions ignore certain realities as to the possible effect of such restrictions upon the use, enjoyment, and value of the lands to which they are attached and that the courts may have been more interested in relieving what appeared to be onerous situations than in a proper application of the law. It is probable that the dangers of this apparent approach were in the mind of the court when it said in *Crosby v. Strahan's Estate*, 78 Wyo. 302, 324 P.2d 492, 496:

> . . . The tendency has been to restrict rather than enlarge and multiply the cases of exceptions to the statute, and the courts should not be tempted to turn aside from its plain provisions merely because of the hardship of the particular case.

49 Am. Jur. *Statute of Frauds* § 533, pp. 832, 833.

There is no reason now to disregard this caveat.

Appellants assert that the oral agreement which the court found to exist is within the prohibition of two subsections of the Statute of Frauds, § 16-1-101, W.S. 1977:

> (i) Every agreement that by its terms is not to be performed within one (1) year from the making thereof; . . .

> (v) Every agreement or contract for the sale of real estate, or the lease thereof, for more than one (1) year.

Although there may be some apparent application of the first subsection of this statute, we shall not explore or discuss this because of the abundant authority which brings such an agreement within the fifth paragraph of the statute.

This court has not heretofore considered the question of whether a restrictive covenant is within the statute of frauds, although an easement for an irrigation ditch has been held to be an interest in real estate within the statute, *Linck v. Brown*, 55 Wyo. 100, 96 P.2d 909, 911. An agreement restricting the use of land is described in many cases and considered to be a negative easement, *Huggins v. Castle Estates, Inc.*, 36 N.Y.2d 427, 369 N.Y.S.2d 80, 330 N.E.2d 48. . . . When its establishment is sought in equity it has been treated or described as an equitable estate or interest in land, *Turner v. Brocato*, 206 Md. 336, 111 A.2d 855, 861. . . . However, it is not necessary herein to categorize the nature of the interest created by a restrictive covenant because its real effect upon the use, enjoyment and value of the property to which it may be attached is obvious. A statement appearing in *Wiley v. Dunn*, 358 Ill. 97, 192 N.E. 661, 663, is most applicable in this case:

> . . . The policy of the law requires that everything which affects the title to real estate shall be in writing, and that nothing shall be left to the frailty of human memory or as a temptation to perjury. . . .

This view is consistent with *Crosby v. Strahan's Estate, supra,* and only serves to implement and strengthen that holding. It may be more desirable, instead of categorizing such restrictive covenant as an equitable interest, equitable servitude, or a negative easement, to frankly recognize that such covenant does affect the title, use, and estate, and recognize it independently for what it is. At best, it could probably be classified as creating a type of equitable ownership or servitude. It would appear of particular importance that such restrictive covenants be classified as interests in land without reference to particular terminology because of their increasing importance and use in our modern-day society. We would then hold that this asserted agreement creating a restrictive covenant upon appellants' land was within the prohibition of the statute of frauds. . . This does not, however, dispose of this case.

In defense of their judgment, appellees raise another proposition, i.e., if the statute of frauds does apply to this case appellants should not be allowed to rely upon it because of fraud or equitable or promissory estoppel, and the trial court apparently recognized that in its findings.

This case poses the direct question of whether equitable, or particularly promissory, estoppel may be used to defeat the statute of frauds and result in the creation of a restrictive covenant, a negative covenant, or equitable servitude upon the lands of the Remilongs. In *Crosby v. Strahan's Estate, supra,* this court examined and cited with approval authorities which expressed the view that the statute of frauds was an expression of "fixed legislative policy of the state" and that it was "absolutely necessary to preserve the title to real property from the chances, the uncertainty, and the fraud attending the admission of parol testimony." It further enunciated the caveat that the court should not be tempted to turn aside from its plain provisions merely because of the hardship of a particular case.

Since this is the first case before us involving the avoidance of the statute of frauds to effect the creation of such restrictive covenants, and realizing their increased use, their importance and necessity to present-day society, and the potential number of land titles which could conceivably be affected, this question must be approached with the greatest of caution.

Many authorities, in applying the principle of promissory estoppel, to avoid the provisions of this statute suggest that the purpose of the statute is to prevent suborned perjury in apparent recognition that this was at least one purpose which the statute of frauds no longer subserved. England partially repealed the statute of frauds because this necessity had been removed. *See* 68 HARV. L. REV. 383 (1954). It is for this reason your writer finds helpful the application of the rules set out in many cases which involve the application of estoppel in cases which arise other than under paragraph 5 of our statute.

Some courts have met this problem squarely and held they would not by adoption of the doctrine of promissory estoppel avoid the legislative action embraced in the statute of frauds, *Tanenbaum v. Biscayne Osteopathic Hospital, Inc., Fla.,* 190 So. 2d 777, 779. If a contract is clearly within the statute, to apply this doctrine of promissory estoppel is to repeal the statute, *Sinclair v. Sullivan Chevrolet Company,* 45 Ill. App. 2d 10, 195 N.E.2d 250, 253, *affirmed* 31 Ill. 2d 507, 202 N.E.2d 516. The rule has been recognized that the defense of the statute cannot be raised unless there is a misrepresentation that the requirements of the statute had been complied with or there had been a promise to make a written memorandum, *21 Turtle Creek Square, Ltd. v. New York State Teachers' Retirement System,* 5th Cir., 432 F.2d 64, 65, *certiorari denied* 401 U.S. 955, 91 S. Ct. 975, 28 L. Ed. 2d 239.

Although this court has recognized the almost universal rule that restrictions upon the use of lands are not favored, we have also recognized that equity does have a role to play in limited circumstances. . . . We speak of limited circumstances because the declared legislative policy encompassed in the statute of frauds should be departed from only when such action is necessary to "avoid the fraud, and accomplish what justice and good conscience demand," *Metcalf v. Hart, supra,* 27 P. at 913. . . . To accomplish the purposes of the statute of frauds, it may be necessary for a court to uphold oral agreements, *Tucker v. Owen,* 4 Cir., 94 F.2d 49, 52.

In light of the fact that appellees could easily have avoided this problem by plating all commitments in writing, they bear a heavy burden to show why the court should come to their rescue, but they have sustained such burden in this case. The trial court's findings that the appellants' promise to remove all the trailers from the remaining property and not permit the further placement of trailers thereon, that the appellants took affirmative action in removing all such trailers at that time, and that the appellees relied thereon, were sustained by the evidence. This is sufficient to apply the doctrine of promissory estoppel, *Hanna State & Savings Bank v. Matson*, 53 Wyo. 1, 77 P.2d 621, 625, wherein this court cites § 90, RESTATEMENT OF CONTRACTS. . . .

We have no problem with the fact that appellees relied on a mere promise, as in *Johnson v. Soulis*, Wyo. 542 P.2d 867, 872–873, we considered allegations of fraud which were founded on promises of future action, and there is no need to repeat our discussion here.

For the reasons stated above, the judgment is affirmed.

NOTES & QUESTIONS

1. How do the doctrines of equitable estoppel (i.e., substantial partial performance) and promissory estoppel differ?

2. *Practice Points:* In a portion of the opinion not included here, the court notes a statute requiring that judgments which affect real estate titles be filed in the county where the property is situated. The Crollas would certainly want to file something to put subsequent purchasers of the adjacent parcel on notice of the restrictive covenant.

PROBLEMS

1. On Monday, Dan Daniels orally contracted to sell his vacant lot to Paula Paulsen, who lived right next door to that vacant land. They agreed to a purchase price of $25,000 cash, which Paula said she had available in her bank.

Alas, on Wednesday, Dan sent a telegram to Paula in these words: "Sorry, I cannot honor my contract with you to sell the vacant land at 123 Main Street, Peoria, for $25,000. Signed: Dan Daniels." What really happened is that Dan received an offer of $35,000 for the lot on Tuesday. Can Dan avoid the contract with Paula? Will it matter whether Dan quickly conveys the title to the new purchaser for $35,000?

2. John and Sue agreed that John would spend $50 on lottery tickets in the $20 million drawing in the State of Marshall on the next Saturday if Sue would drive the hour to get there, and the hour back, in order to enter "quick pick" numbers for their joint tickets. They agreed they would divide the proceeds equally if they won. John contributed the $50; Sue drove to Marshall and purchased the tickets; and she returned and handed the tickets to John for safekeeping. A few days later, on that Saturday, one of the tickets Sue bought with John's money won the $20 million drawing. Incidentally, the $20 million prize was to be paid annually over a 20-year term. But John had the ticket and refused to share the proceeds with Sue, and he asserted the failure to satisfy the Statute of Frauds when she sued him. Who should prevail?

3. An authorized agent of Ace Auto Sales enticed Frank Flam, an experienced use car sales manager working at a competitor's automobile sales facility, to leave his position there in order to come to work as sales manager at Ace. The agent had orally offered Frank "lifetime employment," which Frank had accepted. No writing was executed, and after three days on the job, Frank was terminated for no apparent reason. When Frank sued Ace Auto Sales, the defense asserted was the failure to comply with the Statute of Frauds. Will the defense prevail? If Frank were to win, what should be his remedy? Would the court enforce an uneconomical arrangement?

PART II
HONORING CONTRACT OBLIGATIONS

SECTION E

OVERVIEW

Once an otherwise binding contract exists (because the requirements of offer, acceptance and consideration have been met), there are numerous, sometimes conflicting, policies that affect its legal enforceability. You have already discovered that sometimes agreements will be held unenforceable because of the incapacity of one of the parties (caused by a mental defect, intoxication or age below majority) or because of inequitable conduct by one of the parties (such as fraud or duress). In the following chapters, you will discover that there are other reasons why an agreement may not be legally enforceable, including when supervening events make the bargained-for performance impossible or impractical.

Courts, scholars and commentators have struggled to explain why contracts should be binding. Moral obligation, commercial predictability, and economic desirability are among the justifications offered for requiring parties to honor their contractual obligations. But you will discover in the following chapters that contracts are not always enforced. To the contrary, there may be conflicting policies under family, criminal, and Constitutional law (among others) that are given precedence over contract enforcement policies. Even where a contract is held otherwise enforceable, courts provide remedies that reflect economic allocation concerns. Thus, breaches of contract are actually encouraged in certain situations.

Contract law reflects (at least in part) society's choices regarding economic policy. But at the heart of every contract dispute is a private agreement between two parties. Before courts can decide the extent to which any contractual obligation will be enforced, they must start with the fundamental question — what was the scope of performances that were bargained for between the parties? Although on its face, the question seems obvious, determining the intention of the parties is a complicated process. What principles should be used in determining what the express terms of the contract mean with regard to performance obligations? What role should extrinsic evidence play in determining the parties' intention? What if events occur which are not addressed in the contract? How can the court determine the parties' intention, when the parties never even considered the matter? More importantly, perhaps, when, if ever, should a court rewrite a party's agreement to cover such unforeseen circumstances?

Once a court has determined the terms of the contract, it must still determine whether one of the parties has failed to honor its obligations. If less than the full performance has been given by a party, should that failure result in compensation to the non-breaching party? What steps should a party take if she has reason to believe the other party has breached his obligations? What if one of the parties to the contract has already given notice of her intention not to perform her obligations? Must the non-breaching wait until the time of performance before she can seek relief? You will discover that courts often struggle to strike a balance between contract predictability and the economic realities of the marketplace. As a result of that struggle, sometimes parties will be held to terms they never expressly agreed to.

Finally, even though modern contract law generally supports the predictable enforcement of contractual obligations, you will discover that remedies for breach of contract do not always provide the disappointed party with the full value of his bargained-for performance. Although courts sometimes order specific performance of a party's contractual obligations, more often they provide monetary compensation. The amount of such compensation often reflects the competing policies underlying the legal enforcement of contractual obligations. On one hand, the non-breaching party should receive adequate compensation to ensure that parties will honor their obligations. On the other hand, maximization of resources requires that such compensation should permit, and perhaps even encourage, economically rational breaches. In striking the appropriate balance between predictability of enforcement and efficient use of resources, courts must make a variety of choices among competing considerations. How should the court value the expectations of the parties to assure adequate compensation for breach? Should a party recover for the money he spent in reliance on the contract? Should he recover for the consequential damages he suffers as a result of the other party's failure to perform under the contract? Should he be required to pay a "penalty" for any breach, regardless of the reason for failing to perform as promised? As you read the cases that follow, ask yourself what policy the court is upholding, and whether the relief granted is the right one under the circumstances.

CHAPTER 11

LEGAL ISSUES AND BUSINESS POLICY

A. INTRODUCTION

Business runs on contractual relationships. Employment, supply, construction, finance, research and development, distribution, sales and purchase — all of the fundamental commercial relationships required to fuel the economy are governed by contracts. Consequently, the enforceability of contractual relationships, and more precisely the legal liabilities imposed for failing to honor contractual obligations, can be seen as a direct reflection of a country's economic and industrial public policies.

If contract law reflects (at least in part) a society's choices regarding economic policy, then one strong policy behind requiring parties to "honor their promises" (particularly in a commercial setting) will be the need for predictability of enforcement of those obligations. Only when commercial parties can rely on each other's promises (because they are legally enforceable), can they develop the commercial relationships required to sustain a modern, industrial and commercial economy. Predictability, however, is often tempered with other public policy concerns — including prevention of perjury, protection of those who may be suffering from capability problems, and avoidance of contracts which violate other, non-contract-based, public policies.

Even though modern contract law generally supports the predictable enforcement of commercial obligations, you will discover in the following chapters that enforcement does not always mean that the non-breaching party receives the performance it bargained for. To the contrary, much of the history of the enforcement of contractual obligations concerns the courts' struggles in ascertaining an appropriate monetary approximation of the value of the breaching party's bargained-for performance. Too little relief can encourage breach and seriously reduce the incentive for parties to honor their contractual obligations. Too much relief creates a windfall for the non-breaching party — a benefit he or she never bargained for. Such windfall may also serve to penalize the breaching party beyond the level of readily predictable economic harm. This "*supra*" penalty may ultimately have an adverse impact on the market because it may cause parties to honor obligations in settings where it would be economically more desirable for the contract to be breached.

For example, assume that Factory Owner A manufactures homemade lemonade from "the freshest lemons." In order to assure a steady supply of fresh lemons, Factory Owner A enters into a supply agreement with Lemon Grower B. Under the agreement, Lemon Grower B agrees to sell to Factory Owner A "1,000 bushels of lemons on or before May 2, 2008 at a price of $0.50 per bushel." Because of an unseasonably short growing season (and an unexpected scarcity of lemons), the market price for lemons rises to $1 per bushel. Lemon Grower B has enough lemons to fill the contract with Factory Owner A. Lemon Grower B must choose between selling 1,000 bushels of lemons to Factory Owner A under the contract price of $500, or breaching the contract to sell the lemons at the market price of $1,000. If contractual obligations were not enforceable, Lemon Grower B would always breach her agreement with Factory Owner A because $1,000 provides a larger profit than $500. If, however, contractual obligations are enforced, Lemon Grower B may still breach her obligations if: (1) she can readily predict the damages she will owe to Factory Owner A for her breach; and (2) such damages do not *equal or exceed* $1,000. So long as both parties receive the monetary equivalent of their bargained-for exchange (and no more), breach in this instance may be an economically viable option which should be available to assure the maximization of resources. Such option is only feasible if both the enforcement of obligations, and the amount of damages awarded for breach, are predictable.

Although predictable enforcement of contractual obligations is a necessary complement for a commercial society, such predictability may give way to other competing policies. As you have already seen, courts often choose not to create an enforceable legal obligation in situations where the bargaining process has been corrupted or tainted in some way. Thus, "contracts" created as a result of fraud, over-reaching, or some other form of unconscionable conduct, are often found legally unenforceable. Similarly, courts may choose not to require parties to honor their contractual obligations because such enforcement is contrary to other non-contract related policies. The scope of these policies will become apparent as you learn more about the general principles courts have applied in interpreting the scope of a party's contractual obligations, in determining whether a party has properly performed those obligations, and, if not, in establishing the type of relief under contract law, if any, that the non-breaching party should receive.

B. A PHILOSOPHY OF CONTRACT ENFORCEMENT

Theories regarding the philosophical foundations for contract law — or more precisely, theories explaining why contractual obligations should be enforceable — have been hotly debated and have changed over time. In Chapter One, you have already learned that, over time, courts and scholars have suggested several reasons for requiring parties to honor their contractual obligations. In the following excerpt, Dennis Patterson examines Professor James Gordley's attempt in *The Philosophical Origins of Modern Contract Doctrine* (1991) to impose a philosophical construct on the question of why contracts are legally binding. As you read the excerpt, consider whether you agree with Professor Patterson's criticisms.

Dennis M. Patterson,
The Philosophical Origins of Modern Contract Doctrine:
An Open Letter to Professor James Gordley
1991 Wis. L. Rev. 1432 (1991)

Throughout your book you refer to the need "to explain why contracts are binding." You think that in order to answer this question, we need a "theory" of contract. The theory of contract that provides an answer to your question will be the "correct" theory. As you know, there are many answers to the question "Why do promises bind?" To take just one group with several answers, economists believe that promises are binding because, among other reasons, it is in the interest of all concerned that they be so viewed (rule-utilitarianism). You are unsatisfied with the answers to your question given by modern theorists. But should we go back to Aristotle? You claim not to be able to see how a theory of the normative foundations of contract could be possible "without using these older [Aristotelian] concepts." And why is that? Because "[t]hese difficulties cannot be resolved by a Kantian or a utilitarian approach. They seem to be inherent in any theory that seeks the ultimate source of law or morality in human choice." As you make clear, Kant gets hoisted on the petard of his own universalizations when he simultaneously urges us to see contracts as binding because to will otherwise would be to will violation of promises as universal law, yet he insists that not all promises (e.g., promises to make a gift) should be treated the same way.

I have a solution to the problem of the unsatisfactory quality of the answers you are getting to your question "What is the correct theory of contract?": *Stop asking the question.* The reason I urge you to stop asking the question is that the question asks for something that is quite unintelligible. Time and again you demand that theorists "explain" why contracts are binding, but you never tell the reader what it is you mean by "explanation." I take it the answer has something to do with a "correct theory of contracts" but I am uncertain. What I am most unclear about is what a "correct" theory of contract would look like. In fact, it is entirely unclear to me what a "correct" theory of anything would look like.

It seems to me that the most one can mean by a "correct" theory is that, for whatever reason, it commands the assent of the relevant practitioners of the enterprise who use it to carry on their day-to-day activities (e.g., advancing claims to truth, knowledge, correct judgment). "Correct" is nothing more than a synonym for a complex and coordinated set of intersubjective practices, which practices are the concrete expression of the self-understanding of those who partake of the practice in question (in this case contract law). I suppose I would want to put it this way: the mistake you make is to think of contract as a "thing" about which we can have "right" or "wrong" theories. Perhaps it is better to think of contract law not as a thing but more akin to an ongoing, self-transforming cultural activity. Two thousand years of philosophy has failed to yield anything like a plausible account of what it would mean to provide a "correct" account of the "thing" called contract. Instead of continuing to ask for such an account, we might be better off dropping the question.

NOTES & QUESTIONS

1. If you had to explain in one sentence why a contract should be enforced, what would your answer be?

2. If contracts were not enforceable, what impact would this have on the way businesses govern themselves? Could a modern society exist if contractual obligations were not binding?

3. As you learned in Chapter One, scholars have proposed several bases for enforcing promises, including: that the parties, by their actions, have consented to be bound (the consent theory); that the willing exercise of the freedom to contract should be enforced to promote individual liberty (the will theory); that promises are sacred as a moral issue (the promise theory); and that a party's reasonable reliance on a promise should be protected to avoid injustice (the reliance theory).

Which theory would you use to respond to Professor Gordley's question "why do promises bind?" (examined in the above article)? Why?

4. Although the introduction to this Chapter indicates that economic predictability underscores modern contract law, as the Patterson excerpt above indicates, there is no one legal philosophy or public policy that fully explains the reasons why contractual obligations are enforced. The "classical" view of contract law considered legal obligations to arise primarily as a result of the consent and agreement of individual parties (as opposed to society's dictates). Contracts were bound up with notions of liberty and individual free will (including the freedom to bind oneself voluntarily). Under this classical view, enforceable obligations required clear language, and mutual obligations, and performance was rarely excused. These obligations reflected a "laissez-faire" economic policy that often denied the government's power to "interfere" with contract "rights."

Subsequent scholars criticized this "classical" approach and found other goals and purposes for contract law. In a notable work, examining the "dissolution" of the "classical theory of contract," Grant Gilmore contended that "contract" was being reabsorbed into the mainstream of "tort." He stated:

> We have had more than one occasion to notice the insistence of the classical theorists on the sharp differentiation between contract and tort — the refusal to admit any liability in "contract" until the formal requisites of offer, acceptance and consideration had been satisfied, the dogma that only "bargained-for" detriment or benefit could count as consideration, and notably, the limitations on damage recovery. Classical contract theory might well be described as an attempt to stake out an enclave within the general domain of tort. The dykes which were set up to protect the enclave have, it is clear enough, been crumbling at a progressively rapid rate. With the growth of the ideas of quasi-contract and unjust enrichment, classical consideration theory was breached on the benefit side. With the growth of the promissory estoppel idea, it was breached on the detriment side. We are fast approaching the point where, to prevent unjust enrichment, any benefit received by a defendant must be paid for unless it was clearly meant as a gift; where any detriment reasonably incurred by a plaintiff in reliance on a defendant's assurances must be recompensed. When that point is reached, there is really no longer any viable distinction between liability in contract and liability in tort. We may take the fact that damages in contract have become indistinguishable from damages in tort as obscurely reflecting an instinctive, almost unconscious realization that the two fields, which had been artificially set apart, are gradually merging and becoming one.

Grant Gilmore, The Death of Contract 87 (1974).

5. The theory examined by Gilmore has often been referred to as "contorts." *Sullivan v. O'Connor* below represents a "contorts" case.

6. Contract enforcement has been justified on the basis of the sanctity of promises — that "there is something inherently despicable about not keeping a promise, and that a properly organized society should not tolerate this." Morris R. Cohen, *The Basis of Contract*, 46 Harv. L. Rev. 553 (1933). Enforcement has also been justified on the basis of injurious reliance. Closely related to the "sanctity of promises" view, this "reliance" theory basically imposes contractual liability when there has been an explicit promise, reliance on that promise by another who has

suffered harm as a result of that reliance and who, as a result of that reliance, is entitled to have her loss "made good" by the one responsible. These theories have lead to intense debates in the literature regarding the role of moral imperatives in enforcing contractual obligations. *See* Charles F. Fried, CONTRACT AS PROMISE: A THEORY OF CONTRACTUAL OBLIGATION (1981).

7. Modern enforcement doctrines, exemplified by the Uniform Commercial Code, have emphasized society's perceived need to protect certain parties from overreaching or imbalances in economic or bargaining power. Others have suggested that consent and promise are less important in explaining the enforceability of contractual obligations. Instead, certain long-term contractual relationships (such as employment and long-term supply contracts) rely upon "relational" needs, which may not be completely satisfied by the promise and consent requirements of "classical" contract law. *See* Ian R. Macneil, *Contracts: Adjustment of Long-Term Economic Relations Under Classical, Neoclassical, and Relational Contract Law,* 72 NW. U. L. REV. 854 (1978).

8. Even where consent is considered the foundation of contractual enforcement, theories regarding the nature of such consent differ. The libertarian liberal consent theory, summarized by Professor Randy Barnett, views consent as follows:

> A consent theory of contract requires that an enforceable contract satisfy at least two conditions. First, the subject of a contract must be a morally cognizable right possessed by the transferor that is interpersonally transferable, or "alienable." Second, the possessor of the alienable right must manifest his intention to be legally bound to transfer the right — that is, he must consent.

Randy E. Barnett, *Squaring Undisclosed Agency Law with Contract Theory,* 75 CAL. L. REV. 1969, 1972 (1987).

In contrast, Richard Posner, with his law and economic theory, views as consensual those principles which serve a wealth maximization role. Thus, Posner views contract law as fulfilling a social policy choice, based upon an assumption that "wealth-maximization" is what most people would choose, if they could bargain over every social interaction. Richard A. Posner, *Utilitarianism, Economics, and Legal Theory,* 8 J. LEGAL STUD. 103 (1979). *See also* Alan Schwartz & Robert E. Scott, *Contract Theory and the Limits of Contract Law,* 113 YALE L.J. 541, 547 (2003).

More recently, the relationship between objective and subjective norms has come under scrutiny as promise and utilitarian efficiency goals of contract are being re-examined in light of growing evidence of more individualized considerations. Some scholars claim that contract law has become more dynamic as social considerations, and the process of contract formation and performance, are understood in greater detail. In describing these new developments, Professor Eisenberg has stated:

> [W]here classical contract law was largely static, modern contact law is in large part dynamic. So, for example, static rules of interpretation have been replaced by dynamic rules that take into account events before and after the moment of contract formation; the static legal-duty rule has withered almost completely away, to be largely replaced by a dynamic modification regime that takes into account the value of ongoing reciprocity; a static review of liquidated damages provisions is giving way to a

dynamic review that takes account of the actual loss; and static offer-and-acceptance rules have been replaced by dynamic rules, such as the duty to negotiate in good faith. More generally, as I have shown elsewhere, modern contract law has in various ways come to grips with the universe of chance in which contracting actually occurs.

The paradigm at the center of classical contract law was a snapshot taken at the moment a bargain was made. In contrast, modern contract law recognizes that contract is a process, so that the picture we see at the time of contract formation, however important, is only one of a series of frames. Unless contract law responds to the whole moving picture, it cannot capture the reality of contract.

Melvin Aron Eisenberg, *The Emergence of Dynamic Contract Law,* 88 CAL. L. REV. 1743, 1751 (2000).

9. Increasingly in the Digital Age, contract law has been called upon to face new challenges of authenticity and predictability as economic and other obligations are derived from digital communications, or performance impacted by changes in technology. As the global digital marketplace has grown with the advent of the Internet and other digital forms of communication and performance, contract law is increasingly being called upon to serve as a private enforcement device for rights whose protection cannot readily be secured through statutory means. Thus, for example, concerns over the rise of domain names which improperly included another's trademark (such as cocacola.com, registered and used by someone *not* authorized by the lawful holder of the COCA-COLA trademark, referred to commonly as a "cybersquatter") were ultimately resolved internationally through a private contractual solution. The agreed-upon domain name registration agreement for all domain names registered under the .com top-level generic domain included a clause obligating any domain name registrant to agree to submit to arbitration under a "Uniform Dispute Resolution Policy" (UDRP) before specified international tribunals. In essence, international protection of trademarks in cyberspace in the case of cybersquatting was resolved through private contractual obligations. These changing demands on contract law have placed new stresses on the formal roles of consent and textualization.

10. Contracts have further become even more closely intertwined with digital developments in the use of diverse forms of licensing which seek to either protect or free information. Thus, for example, many computer software programs are currently distributed as "open source" goods, which require, for example, that any one who modifies or changes such a program "must cause any work that [he or she] distribute or publish, that in whole or in part contains or is derived from the Program or any part thereof, to be licensed as a whole at no charge to all third parties under the terms of this License." (§ 2(b) General Public License, *http://www.opensource.org/licenses.*) Similarly, under another standard distribution license designed for the challenges of digital information distribution, the Creative Commons license allows owners of copyrighted works to establish standard licensing terms that permit others to use the works in question on a royalty-free basis, so long as requirements of credit and free distribution are met. Creative Commons, *http://www.creativecommons.org.*

11. While the above-described standard form agreements are generally seen as improving the ability of the general public to gain access to otherwise protected

information and technology, other digital form standard licenses, referred to as Digital Rights Management, may also be used to impose stricter distribution and use requirements for copyrighted works, including limitations on the ability of end users to copy or distribute further copies of the work in question. *See, e.g.*, 17 U.S.C. § 1201 *et seq.* These new types of digital agreements will continue to impact the nature of contract law and policy in the future.

12. For an excellent selection of articles regarding the philosophical debates that have informed contract law, *see* A CONTRACTS ANTHOLOGY (Peter Lizner ed., 2d ed. 1995); *Symposium: Cyberspace, Propertization and Contract in the Information Culture*, 54 CLEVE. L. REV. 1, *et seq.* (2006); Jeffrey M. Lipshaw, *Duty and Consequence: A Non-conflating Theory of Promise and Contract*, 36 CUMB. L. REV. 321 (2005).

C. THE RELATIONSHIP OF CONTRACT LAW TO SOCIAL POLICY

Although the philosophical and theoretical basis for enforcing contractual obligations may vary from decade to decade, and from scholar to scholar, the general acceptance that certain categories of obligations are enforceable is not subject to reasonable debate.

Nevertheless, certain social situations arise in which potential contractual obligations will not be found to result in legally binding obligations. Thus, for instance, despite a general consensus that individual voluntary consent serves to create binding obligations, a promise to meet a party for a social engagement which is later broken does not generally give rise to legal liability.

Similarly, despite the strong emphasis in U.S. law on the duty to honor contractual obligations, in the cases you will read in this chapter you will discover that contract law principles sometimes give way to other public policies. In each of the cases that you read below, you should consider what conflicting policies are at work and whether you would strike the same balance between the predictable enforcement of contractual obligations and the "competing" policy.

SULLIVAN v. O'CONNOR
363 Mass. 579, 296 N.E.2d 183 (1973)

KAPLAN, Justice:

. . . [T]he plaintiff alleged that she, as patient, entered into a contract with the defendant, a surgeon, wherein the defendant promised to perform plastic surgery on her nose and thereby to enhance her beauty and improve her appearance; that he performed the surgery but failed to achieve the promised result; rather the result of the surgery was to disfigure and deform her nose, to cause her pain in body and mind, and to subject her to other damage and expense. The second count, based on the same transaction, was in the conventional form for malpractice, charging that the defendant had been guilty of negligence in performing the surgery. . . .

The jury returned a verdict for the plaintiff on the contract count, and for the defendant on the negligence count. . . .

The plaintiff was a professional entertainer, and this was known to the defendant. . . . [T]he plaintiff's nose had been straight, but long and prominent; the defendant undertook by two operations to reduce its prominence and somewhat to shorten it, thus making it more pleasing in relation to the plaintiff's other features. Actually the plaintiff was obliged to undergo three operations, and her appearance was worsened. Her nose now had a concave line to about the midpoint, at which it became bulbous; viewed frontally, the nose from bridge to midpoint was flattened and broadened, and the two sides of the tip had lost symmetry. This configuration evidently could not be improved by further surgery. The plaintiff did not demonstrate, however, that her change of appearance had resulted in loss of employment. Payments by the plaintiff covering the defendant's fee and hospital expenses were stipulated at $622.65.

The judge instructed the jury, first, that the plaintiff was entitled to recover her out-of-pocket expenses incident to the operations. Second, she could recover the damages flowing directly, naturally, proximately, and foreseeably from the defendant's breach of promise. These would comprehend damages for any disfigurement of the plaintiff's nose — that is, any change of appearance for the worse — including the effects of the consciousness of such disfigurement on the plaintiff's mind, and in this connection the jury should consider the nature of the plaintiff's profession. Also consequent upon the defendant's breach, and compensable, were the pain and suffering involved in the third operation, but not in the first two. As there was no proof that any loss of earnings by the plaintiff resulted from the breach, that element should not enter into the calculation of damages.

By his exceptions the defendant contends that the judge erred in allowing the jury to take into account anything but the plaintiff's out-of-pocket expenses (presumably at the stipulated amount). . . .

It has been suggested on occasion that agreements between patients and physicians by which the physician undertakes to effect a cure or to bring about a given result should be declared unenforceable on grounds of public policy. But there are many decisions recognizing and enforcing such contracts. . . . These causes of action are, however, considered a little suspect, and thus we find courts straining sometimes to read the pleadings as sounding only in tort for negligence, and not in contract for breach of promise, despite sedulous efforts by the pleaders to pursue the latter theory.

. . .

It is not hard to see why the courts should be unenthusiastic or skeptical about the contract theory. Considering the uncertainties of medical science and the variations in the physical and psychological conditions of individual patients, doctors can seldom in good faith promise specific results. Therefore it is unlikely that physicians of even average integrity will in fact make such promises. Statements of opinion by the physician with some optimistic coloring are a different thing, and may indeed have therapeutic value. But patients may transform such statements into firm promises in their own minds, especially when they have been disappointed in the event, and testify in that sense to sympathetic juries. If actions for breach of promise can be readily maintained, doctors, so it is said, will be frightened into practising 'defensive medicine.' On the other hand, if these actions were outlawed, leaving only the possibility of suits for malpractice, there is fear that the public might be exposed to the enticements of charlatans, and confidence in the profession might ultimately be shaken. *See* Miller, *The Contractual Liability of Physicians and Surgeons*, 1953 Wash. L.Q. 413, 416–423. The law has taken the middle of the road position of allowing actions based on alleged contract, but insisting on clear proof. . . .

If an action on the basis of contract is allowed, we have next the question of the measure of damages to be applied where liability is found. Some cases have taken the simple view that the promise by the physician is to be treated like an ordinary commercial promise, and accordingly that the successful plaintiff is entitled to a standard measure of recovery for breach of contract — "compensatory" ("expectancy") damages, an amount intended to put the plaintiff in the position he would be in if the contract had been performed, or, presumably, at the plaintiff's election, "restitution" damages, an amount corresponding to any benefit conferred by the plaintiff upon the defendant in the performance of the contract disrupted by the defendant's breach. RESTATEMENT OF CONTRACTS § 329 and comment a, §§ 347, 384(1). Thus in *Hawkins v. McGee*, 84 N.H. 114, 146A. 641, the defendant doctor was taken to have promised the plaintiff to convert his damaged hand by means of an operation into a good or perfect hand, but the doctor so operated as to damage the hand still further. The court, following the usual expectancy formula, would have asked the jury to estimate and award to the plaintiff the difference between the value of a good or perfect hand, as promised, and the value of the hand after the operation. (The same formula would apply, although the dollar result would be less, if the operation had neither worsened nor improved the condition of the hand.) If the plaintiff had not yet paid the doctor his fee, that amount would be deducted from the recovery. There could be no recovery for the pain and suffering of the operation, since that detriment would have been incurred even if the operation had been successful; one can say that this detriment was not 'caused' by the breach. But where the plaintiff by reason of the operation was put to more pain that he would have had to endure, had the doctor performed as promised, he should be compensated for that difference as a proper part of his expectancy recovery. . . .

For breach of the patient-physician agreements under consideration, a recovery limited to restitution seems plainly too meager, if the agreements are to be enforced at all. On the other hand, an expectancy recovery may well be excessive. The factors, already mentioned, which have made the cause of action somewhat suspect, also suggest moderation as to the breadth of the recovery that should be permitted. Where, as in the case at bar and in a number of the reported cases, the doctor has been absolved of negligence by the trier, an expectancy measure may be thought harsh. We should recall here that the fee paid by the patient to the doctor for the alleged promise would usually be quite disproportionate to the putative expectancy recovery. To attempt, moreover, to put a value on the condition that would or might have resulted, had the treatment succeeded as promised, may sometimes put an exceptional strain on the imagination of the fact finder. As a general consideration, Fuller and Perdue [*The Reliance Interest in Contract Damages*, 46 YALE L.J. 52, 373] argue that the reasons for granting damages for broken promises to the extent of the expectancy are at their strongest when the promises are made in a business context, when they have to do with the production or distribution of goods or the allocation of functions in the market place; they become weaker as the context shifts from a commercial to a noncommercial field.

There is much to be said, then, for applying a reliance measure to the present facts, and we have only to add that our cases are not unreceptive to the use of that formula in special situations. We have, however, had no previous occasion to apply it to patient-physician cases. . . .

The question of recovery on a reliance basis for pain and suffering or mental distress requires further attention. We find expressions in the decisions that pain and suffering (or the like) are simply not compensable in actions for breach of contract. The defendant seemingly espouses this proposition in the present case. True, if the buyer under a contract for the purchase of a lot of merchandise, in suing for the seller's breach, should claim damages for mental anguish caused by his disappointment in the transaction, he would not succeed; he would be told, perhaps, that the asserted psychological injury was not fairly foreseeable by the defendant as a probable consequence of the breach of such a business contract. *See* RESTATEMENT OF CONTRACTS, § 341, and comment a. But there is no general rule barring such items of damage in actions for breach of contract. It is all a question of the subject matter and background of the contract, and when the contract calls for an operation on the person of the plaintiff, psychological as well as physical injury may be expected to figure somewhere in the recovery, depending on the particular circumstances. . . . Suffering or distress resulting from the breach going beyond that which was envisaged by the treatment as agreed, should be compensable on the same ground as the worsening of the patient's condition because of the breach. Indeed it can be argued that the very suffering or distress "contracted for" — that which would have been incurred if the treatment achieved the promised result — should also be compensable. . . . For that suffering is "wasted" if the treatment fails. Otherwise stated, compensation for this waste is arguably required in order to complete the restoration of the status quo ante.

In the light of the foregoing discussion, . . . the plaintiff was not confined to the recovery of her out-of-pocket expenditures; she was entitled to recover also for the worsening of her condition, and for the pain and suffering and mental distress involved in the third operation. These items were compensable on either an expectancy or a reliance view. We might have been required to elect between the two views if the pain and suffering connected with the first two operations contemplated by the agreement, or the whole difference in value between the present and the promised conditions, were being claimed as elements of damage. But the plaintiff waives her possible claim to the former element, and to so much of the latter as represents the difference in value between the promised condition and the condition before the operations.

NOTES & QUESTIONS

1. *Sullivan v. O'Connor* is representative of a line of cases that appears to combine contract principles with tort principles of recovery (for emotional harm or pain and suffering). This combination has been referred to as "contorts."

2. Both contract and tort law provide compensatory damages in order to "make the injured party whole." Tort law routinely provides relief for emotional distress, and pain and suffering. Contract law typically does not. Is there any reason why contract law should not usually provide relief for "emotional" harm? *See* RESTATEMENT (SECOND) OF CONTRACTS § 353.

3. *Sullivan v. O'Connor* suggests that there are three distinct "interests" for which recovery under contract law may be sought. The non-breaching party may be compensated for its lost expectancy interest by putting that party in as good a position as if the contract had been fully performed. Alternatively, the court may compensate the non-breaching party for the costs incurred in reliance on the contract (to put the party in at least as good a position as it was before the contract existed). Finally, the court may require restitution by the breaching party of any benefits it has received under the contract (to avoid unjust enrichment). In *Sullivan*, what interest would be compensated if the court had ordered the following relief?

(A) The doctors' fees paid before the breach.

(B) The estimated lost future income due to the plaintiff's reduced physical attractiveness.

(C) The plaintiff's pain and suffering for the two required operations prior to breach.

PROBLEM

Social situations often give rise to exchanges of promises which may result in contractual obligations. Would you enforce the contract in the following situation? What competing policies are you balancing in order to reach your decision?

Tom has called Carla ten times to ask her out on a date. After the tenth time, Carla reluctantly agrees to meet Tom that Friday night at 7:00, in front of the local theatre. Tom spends $120 for two tickets to the theatre, buys a bouquet of roses for Carla for $80 and rents a car (since his car is currently in the garage being repaired) for $100. Friday morning, a former boyfriend calls Carla and invites her to dinner. Carla does not try to reach Tom to cancel their date, even though she decides to go out with her former beau instead of Tom. Angry at being stood up, Tom sues Carla for breach of contract.

Technology and the Internet have changed much social interaction. Would your answer to the previous problem be different if the Tom had e-mailed Carla who had agreed by return e-mail to go out with Tom? Would it be different if all exchanges had taken place in an Internet chat room? Through text messaging? In reading the next case, ask yourself how technology is impacting contract law application, particularly in social situations.

ANTHONY v. YAHOO! INC
421 F. Supp. 2d 1257 (N.D. Cal. 2006)

WHYTE, United States District Judge:

Robert Anthony ("Anthony") has sued Yahoo! Inc. ("Yahoo!") for (1) breach of contract . . . Anthony alleges that Yahoo! offers two on-line dating services: Yahoo! Personals and Yahoo! Premier. First Amended Complaint ("FAC") p. 13. The former is "for dates and fun," while the latter caters to people looking for "loving, lasting relationships." *Id.* at PP 14–16. Yahoo! represents that both services "will help the subscriber find better first dates and more second dates." *Id.* at p. 17. Yahoo! advises users to be truthful and reserves the right to remove deceptive profiles, thus "giv[ing] all subscribers and potential subscribers a sense of confidence in the authenticity of the images displayed on [its] website [.]" *Id.* at p. 18. However, Anthony claims, Yahoo! "deliberately and intentionally originates, creates, and perpetuates false and/or non-existent profiles on its site" to trick people like Anthony into joining the service and renewing their memberships. *Id.* at pp. 19–20. In addition, Anthony asserts, when a subscription nears its end date, Yahoo! sends the subscriber a fake profile, heralding it as a "potential new match.' " *Id.* at p. 24. Anthony provides twenty-three examples of these "false and/ or non-existent profiles, "which include (1) "[u]sing recurrent phrases for multiple images with such unique dictation and vernacular that such a random occurrence would not be possible" and (2) "[i]dentical images [with] multiple 'identities.' " *Id.* at p. 28. Finally, Anthony alleges that Yahoo! continues to circulate profiles of "actual, legitimate former subscribers whose subscriptions had expired," thus giving the misleading impression that these individuals are still available for dates. *Id.* at p. 33. Anthony claims to represent two nationwide subclasses: (1) current members of Yahoo!'s dating services and (2) former members who subscribed after January 1, 2001. *Id.* at p. 9. . . .

Anthony alleges that subscribers must agree to Yahoo!'s Terms of Service, Personals Additional Terms of Service, and Personals Guidelines. FAC p. 35. He asserts that (1) "Yahoo! entered into a valid, fully integrated contract . . . representing its online dating services as genuine," (2)" [a]ll parties to the contract understood the nature of the contract was intended to provide each paying subscriber with access to a legitimate and genuine online dating service," and (3) Yahoo! "breached the aforementioned contract by . . . creating and forwarding false and/or nonexistent profiles [.]" *Id.* at pp. 36–37. "[T]he elements of [a breach of contract] cause of action are the existence of the contract, performance by the plaintiff or excuse for nonperformance, breach by the defendant and damages." *First Comm. Mortgage Co. v. Reece*, 89 Cal. App. 4th 731, 745, 108 Cal. Rptr. 2d 23 (2001). Courts may dismiss breach of contract claims when the agreement is not reasonably susceptible to any meaning that could support the plaintiff's legal theories. *See Martinez v. Socoma Companies, Inc.*, 11 Cal. 3d 394, 397, 113 Cal. Rptr. 585, 521 P.2d 841 (1974).

Anthony cannot identify any contractual term that requires Yahoo! not to create or forward false profiles. First, he asserts that Yahoo! breached its Personals Guidelines, which provide that "Yahoo! Personals gives Yahoo! users a way to find and interact with other people who may share their interests and goals. Just like a real community, different people may have different opinions and personalities in Yahoo! Personals." Opp. Mot. Dism. at 8:12–15 (*quoting* Yahoo! Personals Guidelines, FAC Ex. A, at 16). He argues that Yahoo! violated this clause by creating and forwarding profiles "that do not represent other people who may share their interests and goals and are not part of a real community.' " *Id.* at 8:16–18. However, the language upon which Anthony relies merely describes Yahoo!'s dating service and does not commit Yahoo! to performing or not performing any particular action. *See, e.g.*, RESTATEMENT (SECOND) OF CONTRACTS § 2 ("[a] promise is a manifestation of intention to act or refrain from acting in a specified way, so made as to justify a promisee in understanding that a commitment has been made"). Anthony cannot predicate a breach of contract claim upon it.

Second, Anthony asserts that Yahoo! breached its Terms of Service by allegedly sending expired profiles to existing subscribers. He alleges that many individuals whose expired profiles Yahoo! forwarded had "specifically directed" Yahoo! to remove their profiles. FAC p. 33. According to Anthony, Yahoo!'s conduct violates a provision of the Personals Terms of Service that grants Yahoo! a broad license:

> [W]ith respect to Content you submit or make available for inclusion on publicly accessible areas of the Service, you grant Yahoo! the following world-wide, royalty free and non-exclusive license(s), as applicable:
>
> • With respect to Content you submit or make available for inclusion on publicly accessible areas of Yahoo! Groups, the license to use, distribute, reproduce, modify, adapt, publicly perform and publicly display such Content on the Service. . . . *This license exists only for as long as you elect to continue to include such Content on the Service and will terminate at the time you remove or Yahoo! removes such Content from the Service.*
>
> • With respect to photos, graphics, audio or video you submit or make available for inclusion on publicly accessible area[s] of the Service other than Yahoo! Groups, the license to use, distribute, reproduce, modify, adapt, publicly perform and publicly display such Content on the Service. . . . *This license exists only for as long as you elect to continue to include such Content on the Service and will terminate at the time you remove or Yahoo! removes such Content from the Service.*

Opp. Mot. Dism. at 8:23–9:14 (quoting Yahoo! Personals Terms of Service, FAC Ex. A, at p. 8) (emphasis supplied by Anthony).

Anthony argues that "[u]pon being directed by a subscriber to remove a profile, YAHOO is contractually bound to do such that its failure not to do so constitutes a breach of its contractual obligations [.]" *Id.* at 9:14-18. However, the license provision does not specifically require Yahoo! to remove profiles. . . .

Finally, Anthony asserts that "if the Court determines that no express provision of the contract was violated by [Yahoo!'s] conduct, [Anthony] may still nonetheless maintain an action . . . for breach of the [implied] covenant of good faith and fair dealing." Opp. Mot. Dism. at 11:16-18. He then requests leave to amend such a theory. The court permits him to do so.

NOTES & QUESTIONS

1. What impact, if any, did the technological nature of the social interaction at issue have on the court's deliberations?

2. Do you think the provision of false profiles was anticipated by Anthony at the time that he became a subscriber? Should it have been?

3. What competing policies do you think are at play in the enforceability of social dating obligations on the Internet?

4. The court allowed Anthony to amend his complaint to allege a breach of Yahoo's implied covenant of good faith and fair dealing. Would you grant relief on this claim? Why or why not?

5. *Practice Point:* Many Internet websites contain End User Agreements and Terms of Service Agreements that clarify the rights and obligations of the service provider. Among typical issues addressed by such agreements are privacy rights, license terms for use of end user submitted materials, and service provider liability

limits. These agreements are usually in a standard form and are considered agreed to upon use of the website, regardless of whether a party has read the agreement or not.

PEOPLE v. STARKS
106 Ill. 2d 441, 478 N.E.2d 350 (1985)

CLARK, Chief Justice:

The defendant, Ronnie L. Starks, was indicted for the armed robbery (Ill. Rev. Stat. 1981, ch. 38, par. 18-2) of the Libertyville Federal Savings and Loan Association branch in Gurnee, Illinois. A jury in Lake County convicted him and he was sentenced to 11 years' imprisonment. The defendant filed a motion for a new trial which was denied. On defendant's appeal, the appellate court affirmed the circuit court. (122 Ill. App. 3d 228, 460 N.E.2d 1181.) The defendant then petitioned this court for leave to appeal, and we granted the defendant's petition. . . .

The defendant's attorney filed a motion for a new trial. . . . The motion . . . alleged that the defendant had submitted himself to a polygraph examination based upon a representation by the Lake County State's Attorney's office that the charge would be dismissed if the defendant passed the test. The motion further alleged that the defendant passed the test, but that the State's Attorney's office reneged on its part of the agreement. . . .

Starks contends that a Lake County assistant State's Attorney agreed to dismiss the charge against him if he would submit to and pass a polygraph examination conducted by Libertyville police lieutenant Danny McCormick. Pursuant to the agreement, Starks was transported from the Lake County jail on March 30, 1982, to the Libertyville police department, where the polygraph examination was conducted. Starks further contends that McCormick specifically questioned him as to his involvement in the January 15, 1982, armed robbery and that McCormick found him to be truthful in his denial of any knowledge of or involvement in the robbery. . . .

We agree with the appellate court's interpretation of our holding in *People v. Baynes* (1981), 88 Ill. 2d 225, 430 N.E.2d 1070. In Baynes, this court held that polygraph evidence is not admissible, even if the parties stipulated to the results, to prove the guilt or innocence of the defendant.

The case at bar, however, does not involve the admissibility of polygraph evidence to prove guilt or innocence. In this case the issue is whether an agreement between the State and a defendant, which required the State to dismiss its case against the defendant if the defendant took and passed a polygraph examination, is enforceable. . . .

The State's Attorney is an elected representative of the People; he has been given the responsibility of evaluating evidence and determining what offense, if any, can and should properly be charged. Prosecutors have traditionally been afforded a broad range of discretion within which to perform their public duties. The prosecution must honor the terms of agreements it makes with defendants. To dispute the validity of this precept would surely result in the total nullification of the bargaining system between the prosecution and the defense. Therefore, this court believes that if the prosecution did make an agreement with the defendant, it must abide by its agreement in this case. . . .

The record in the case at bar is unclear as to the exact terms of the agreement. Therefore, we do not know what Starks agreed to do had he not passed the polygraph examination. Assuming, arguendo, that Starks did not agree to do anything if he did not pass the polygraph examination, we do not agree with the State's contention that the bargained offer to Starks was a "gift-type" bargain which lacked the consideration to make it binding. Such a contention is without merit because there would be consideration given by both parties in the alleged agreement in the case at bar. By submitting himself to the polygraph examination, the defendant surrendered his fifth amendment privilege against self-incrimination. When a prosecutor enters into an agreement of this kind he has doubts about a defendant's guilt. If the defendant fails the polygraph examination, such doubts may be removed and a faltering investigation can be revitalized. A prosecutor is less likely to agree to concessions after a defendant's failure of a polygraph examination. He also knows that if the defendant fails the polygraph examination and then takes the stand at trial the defendant may wilt under the pressure of intense cross-examination. Additionally, there is no way of assuring that the test results will not come to the judge's attention; therefore, a defendant may be compelled, as a practical matter, to elect a jury trial. The test results may also strengthen a judgment of conviction resulting in imposition of a longer sentence or delay in parole.

In *Butler v. State*, the defendant was charged with rape. After indictment, Butler and the prosecutor reached an agreement that the charges would be dismissed if the polygraph results indicated that Butler was telling the truth. However, if the results were unfavorable to Butler the test would be admissible in his rape trial. The polygraph examiner concluded that the defendant was telling the truth when he denied participation in the rape. An order of nolle prosequi was entered. Nevertheless, the State initiated prosecution. The defendant was indicted and convicted. His motion to quash on the basis of the agreement was denied.

In holding that the State was bound to abide by the agreement, the Butler court questioned the "wisdom" of entering into such agreements. The court concluded that the State has the right to "choose its procedures and weapons of prosecution"; however, the State also has the duty to abide by an agreement it makes with a defendant.

We believe that in the case at bar if the State made an agreement with the defendant, it is bound to abide by that agreement. . . .

WARD, Justice, dissenting:

I join in the dissent of Justice Miller, who correctly observes that the defendant was not disadvantaged in any way by taking the polygraphic examination.

Of course, there are circumstances in which the prosecution should be and is bound to fulfill promises to an accused. Plea bargaining . . . is a familiar example of the binding promise. There are circumstances, too, where it would be a disservice to the public interest and justice to enforce the terms of a statement made to an accused. The required balancing of considerations was described in *United States v. Pascal* (N.D. Ill. 1979), 496 F. Supp. 313, which involved a promise made by agents that any cooperation by the defendant would be made known to the United States Attorney. The court observed: "Case law also dictates that when the 'totality of circumstances' surrounding the government misconduct is such as to offend basic tenets of fair play and justice, dismissal of the indictment with prejudice is proper." The court went on to say:

> This court recognizes that dismissal of an indictment with prejudice is not a step to be taken lightly. Nor is this court unaware that its supervisory power is limited and should be exercised rarely and with extreme caution. As pointed out by the government in its response to the defendant's brief, "the basis of this restraint is the public interest in enforcement of our criminal laws, an interest which should not be forfeited on less than compelling evidence of prejudice and inability to receive a fair trial."

496 F. Supp. 313, 319–20.

The majority paints with too broad a brush when it says that the prosecution must honor the terms of all agreements made with defendants.

The majority, following the mistaken analysis of the defendant, talks in terms of legal consideration as if contract law were involved. (Even in *People v. Reagan* (1975), 395 Mich. 306, 314, 235 N.W.2d 581, 585, on which the majority principally relies, the court pointed out that a contract law analysis is incorrect, saying "[t]he standards of commerce do not govern, and should not govern, the administration of criminal justice.") The majority then goes on to say under this contract analysis that the defendant surrendered his fifth amendment privilege against self-incrimination. This, of course, is illusory. Results of a polygraphic examination are inadmissible even though the parties might wish to stipulate to the results being received in evidence. The defendant here gave up nothing; he did not risk self-incrimination in submitting to a test, the results of which could not be introduced in evidence. In no way did the defendant impair his "not guilty" position, and in no way did his taking the test improve the prosecution's opportunities for conviction. The taking of the polygraph examination was of no more legal effect than if he had agreed to a spiritualistic seance, or to having tea leaves read or to having a coin flipped on the question of whether he robbed the bank. The dissenting opinion in *People v. Reagan* acutely noted that under the resembling circumstances there:

> The defendant having given up nothing has lost nothing. The worst that could have happened to him was to remain in the same legal posture. . . . Defendant risked nothing in this one-sided "agreement" — and indeed had nothing to lose by taking the polygraph test. It is the people of Michigan who instead are cast in the role of "losers."

People v. Reagan (1975), 395 Mich. 306, 325, 235 N.W.2d 581, 590.

NOTES & QUESTIONS

1. What are the competing policies the court is balancing to determine enforceability of the "polygraph agreement"?

2. If the agreement is not enforced, what are the consequences for the criminal justice system?

3. What balance would you strike in this case? Should principles of contract law or constitutional criminal procedure control the outcome?

4. *Drafting Exercise:* Draft a polygraph agreement that would assure that the charges would be dropped only if the defendant were testifying truthfully.

5. *Practice Points:* There is an old saying: "An oral contract isn't worth the paper it is written on." Protect your clients by being certain any oral promises are memorialized. Such memorialization may not avoid future disputes over the meaning or affect of the promise, but it should reduce them.

COHEN v. COWLES MEDIA COMPANY
501 U.S. 663, 111 S. Ct. 2513 (1991)

Justice WHITE delivered the opinion of the Court:

The question before us is whether the First Amendment prohibits a plaintiff from recovering damages, under state promissory estoppel law, for a newspaper's breach of a promise of confidentiality given to the plaintiff in exchange for information. We hold that it does not.

During the closing days of the 1982 Minnesota gubernatorial race, Dan Cohen, an active Republican associated with Wheelock Whitney's Independent-Republican gubernatorial campaign, approached reporters from the St. Paul Pioneer Press Dispatch (Pioneer Press) and the Minneapolis Star and Tribune (Star Tribune) and offered to provide documents relating to a candidate in the upcoming election. Cohen made clear to the reporters that he would provide the information only if he was given a promise of confidentiality. Reporters from both papers promised to keep Cohen's identity anonymous and Cohen turned over copies of two public court records concerning Marlene Johnson, the Democratic-Farmer-Labor candidate for Lieutenant Governor. The first record indicated that Johnson had been charged in 1969 with three counts of unlawful assembly, and the second that she had been convicted in 1970 of petit theft. Both newspapers interviewed Johnson for her explanation and one reporter tracked down the person who had found the records for Cohen. As it turned out, the unlawful assembly charges arose out of Johnson's participation in a protest of an alleged failure to hire minority workers on municipal construction projects, and the charges were eventually dismissed. The petit theft conviction was for leaving a store without paying for $6 worth of sewing materials. The incident apparently occurred at a time during which Johnson was emotionally distraught, and the conviction was later vacated.

After consultation and debate, the editorial staffs of the two newspapers independently decided to publish Cohen's name as part of their stories concerning Johnson. In their stories, both papers identified Cohen as the source of the court records, indicated his connection to the Whitney campaign, and included denials by Whitney campaign officials of any role in the matter. The same day the stories appeared, Cohen was fired by his employer.

Cohen sued respondents, the publishers of the Pioneer Press and Star Tribune, in Minnesota state court, alleging fraudulent misrepresentation and breach of contract. The trial court rejected respondents' argument that the First Amendment barred Cohen's lawsuit. A jury returned a verdict in Cohen's favor, awarding him $200,000 in compensatory damages and $500,000 in punitive damages. The Minnesota Court of Appeals, in a split decision, reversed the award of punitive damages after concluding that Cohen had failed to establish a fraud claim, the only claim which would support such an award. 445 N.W.2d 248, 260 (1989). However, the court upheld the finding of liability for breach of contract and the $200,000 compensatory damages award. *Id.* at 262.

A divided Minnesota Supreme Court reversed the compensatory damages award. 457 N.W.2d 199 (1990). After affirming the Court of Appeals' determination that Cohen had not established a claim for fraudulent misrepresentation, the court considered his breach-of-contract claim and concluded that "a contract cause of action is inappropriate for these particular circumstances." The court then went on to address the question whether Cohen could establish a cause of action under Minnesota law on a promissory estoppel theory. Apparently, a promissory estoppel theory was never tried to the jury, nor briefed nor argued by the parties; it first arose during oral argument in the Minnesota Supreme Court when one of the justices asked a question about equitable estoppel.

In addressing the promissory estoppel question, the court decided that the most problematic element in establishing such a cause of action here was whether injustice could be avoided only by enforcing the promise of confidentiality made to Cohen. The court stated: "Under a promissory estoppel analysis there can be no neutrality towards the First Amendment. In deciding whether it would be unjust not to enforce the promise, the court must necessarily weigh the same considerations that are weighed for whether the First Amendment has been violated. The court must balance the constitutional rights of a free press against the common law interest in protecting a promise of anonymity." 457 N.W.2d at 205. After a brief discussion, the court concluded that "in this case enforcement of the promise of confidentiality under a promissory estoppel theory would violate defendants' First Amendment rights."

We granted certiorari to consider the First Amendment implications of this case.

. . .

Respondents rely on the proposition that "if a newspaper lawfully obtains truthful information about a matter of public significance then state officials may not constitutionally punish publication of the information, absent a need to further a state interest of the highest order." That proposition is unexceptionable, and it has been applied in various cases that have found insufficient the asserted state interests in preventing publication of truthful, lawfully obtained information. *See, e.g., Florida Star v. B.J.F.*, 491 U.S. 524, 109 S. Ct. 2603, 105 L. Ed. 2d 443 (1989); *Smith v. Daily Mail, supra; Landmark Communications, Inc. v. Virginia*, 435 U.S. 829, 98 S. Ct. 1535, 56 L. Ed. 2d 1 (1978).

This case, however, is not controlled by this line of cases but, rather, by the equally well-established line of decisions holding that generally applicable laws do not offend the First Amendment simply because their enforcement against the press has incidental effects on its ability to gather and report the news. As the cases relied on by respondents recognize, the truthful information sought to be published must have been lawfully acquired. The press may not with impunity break and enter an office or dwelling to gather news. Neither does the First Amendment relieve a newspaper reporter of the obligation shared by all citizens to respond to a grand jury subpoena and answer questions relevant to a criminal investigation, even though the reporter might be required to reveal a confidential source. *Branzburg v. Hayes*, 408 U.S. 665, 92 S. Ct. 2646, 33 L. Ed. 2d 626 (1972). The press, like others interested in publishing, may not publish copyrighted material without obeying the copyright laws. *See Zacchini v. Scripps-Howard Broadcasting Co.*, 433 U.S. 562, 576–579, 97 S. Ct. 2849, 2857–2859, 53 L. Ed. 2d

965 (1977). . . . It is, therefore, beyond dispute that "[t]he publisher of a newspaper has no special immunity from the application of general laws. He has no special privilege to invade the rights and liberties of others." *Associated Press v. NLRB, supra,*, 301 U.S. at 132–133, 57 S. Ct. at 655–656. Accordingly, enforcement of such general laws against the press is not subject to stricter scrutiny than would be applied to enforcement against other persons or organizations.

There can be little doubt that the Minnesota doctrine of promissory estoppel is a law of general applicability. It does not target or single out the press. Rather, insofar as we are advised, the doctrine is generally applicable to the daily transactions of all the citizens of Minnesota. The First Amendment does not forbid its application to the press.

Justice BLACKMUN suggests that applying Minnesota promissory estoppel doctrine in this case will "punish" respondents for publishing truthful information that was lawfully obtained. This is not strictly accurate because compensatory damages are not a form of punishment . . . . If the contract between the parties in this case had contained a liquidated damages provision, it would be perfectly clear that the payment to petitioner would represent a cost of acquiring newsworthy material to be published at a profit, rather than a punishment imposed by the State. The payment of compensatory damages in this case is constitutionally indistinguishable from a generous bonus paid to a confidential news source. In any event, as indicated above, the characterization of the payment makes no difference for First Amendment purposes when the law being applied is a general law and does not single out the press. . . .

Respondents and amici argue that permitting Cohen to maintain a cause of action for promissory estoppel will inhibit truthful reporting because news organizations will have legal incentives not to disclose a confidential source's identity even when that person's identity is itself newsworthy. But if this is the case, it is no more than the incidental, and constitutionally insignificant, consequence of applying to the press a generally applicable law that requires those who make certain kinds of promises to keep them. Although we conclude that the First Amendment does not confer on the press a constitutional right to disregard promises that would otherwise be enforced under state law, we reject Cohen's request that in reversing the Minnesota Supreme Court's judgment we reinstate the jury verdict awarding him $200,000 in compensatory damages. The Minnesota Supreme Court's incorrect conclusion that the First Amendment barred Cohen's claim may well have truncated its consideration of whether a promissory estoppel claim had otherwise been established under Minnesota law and whether Cohen's jury verdict could be upheld on a promissory estoppel basis. Or perhaps the State Constitution may be construed to shield the press from a promissory estoppel cause of action such as this one. These are matters for the Minnesota Supreme Court to address and resolve in the first instance on remand. Accordingly, the judgment of the Minnesota Supreme Court is reversed, and the case is remanded for further proceedings not inconsistent with this opinion.

*   *   *

Justice SOUTER, with whom Justice MARSHALL, Justice BLACKMUN, and Justice O'CONNOR join, dissenting:

. . . Because I do not believe the fact of general applicability to be dispositive, I find it necessary to articulate, measure, and compare the competing interests involved in any given case to determine the legitimacy of burdening constitutional interests, and such has been the Court's recent practice in publication cases. *See Hustler Magazine, Inc. v. Falwell*, 485 U.S. 46, 108 S. Ct. 876, 99 L. Ed. 2d 41 (1988); *Zacchini v. Scripps-Howard Broadcasting Co.*, 433 U.S. 562, 97 S. Ct. 2849, 53 L. Ed. 2d 965 (1977).

Nor can I accept the majority's position that we may dispense with balancing because the burden on publication is in a sense "self-imposed" by the newspaper's voluntary promise of confidentiality. This suggests both the possibility of waiver, the requirements for which have not been met here, *see, e.g., Curtis Publishing Co. v. Butts*, 388 U.S. 130, 145, 87 S. Ct. 1975, 1986, 18 L. Ed. 2d 1094 (1967), as well as a conception of First Amendment rights as those of the speaker alone, with a value that may be measured without reference to the importance of the information to public discourse. But freedom of the press is ultimately founded on the value of enhancing such discourse for the sake of a citizenry better informed and thus more prudently self-governed. "[T]he First Amendment goes beyond protection of the press and the self-expression of individuals to prohibit government from limiting the stock of information from which members of the public may draw." In this context, "[i]t is the right of the [public], not the right of the [media], which is paramount," for "[w]ithout the information provided by the press most of us and many of our representatives would be unable to vote intelligently or to register opinions on the administration of government generally."

The importance of this public interest is integral to the balance that should be struck in this case. There can be no doubt that the fact of Cohen's identity expanded the universe of information relevant to the choice faced by Minnesota voters in that State's 1982 gubernatorial election, the publication of which was thus of the sort quintessentially subject to strict First Amendment protection. The propriety of his leak to respondents could be taken to reflect on his character, which in turn could be taken to reflect on the character of the candidate who had retained him as an adviser. An election could turn on just such a factor; if it should, I am ready to assume that it would be to the greater public good, at least over the long run.

This is not to say that the breach of such a promise of confidentiality could never give rise to liability. One can conceive of situations in which the injured party is a private individual, whose identity is of less public concern than that of petitioner; liability there might not be constitutionally prohibited. Nor do I mean to imply that the circumstances of acquisition are irrelevant to the balance, although they may go only to what balances against, and not to diminish, the First Amendment value of any particular piece of information.

Because I believe the State's interest in enforcing a newspaper's promise of confidentiality insufficient to outweigh the interest in unfettered publication of the information revealed in this case, I respectfully dissent.

NOTES & QUESTIONS

1. The Minnesota Supreme Court decision discussing promissory estoppel is located in Chapter One.

2. If promises of confidentiality are not enforceable in the context of news-gathering activities, what impact could this result have on future investigative reporting?

3. Whose decision do you agree with — the majority's or the dissent's? Why?

4. *Drafting Exercise:* Draft guidelines investigative reporters must follow when dealing with confidential sources.

TEXACO, INC. v. PENNZOIL CO.
729 S.W.2d 768 (Tex. 1987)

WARREN, Justice:

This is an appeal from a judgment awarding Pennzoil damages for Texaco's tortious interference with a contract between Pennzoil and the "Getty entities" (Getty Oil Company, the Sarah C. Getty Trust, and the J. Paul Getty Museum). . . .

The main questions for our determination are: (1) whether the evidence supports the jury's finding that there was a binding contract between the Getty entities and Pennzoil, and that Texaco knowingly induced a breach of such contract. . . .

Though many facts are disputed, the parties' main conflicts are over the inferences to be drawn from, and the legal significance of, these facts. There is evidence that for several months in late 1983, Pennzoil had followed with interest the well-publicized dissension between the board of directors of Getty Oil Company and Gordon Getty, who was a director of Getty Oil and also the owner, as trustee, of approximately 40.2% of the outstanding shares of Getty Oil. On December 28, 1983, Pennzoil announced an unsolicited, public tender offer for 16 million shares of Getty Oil at $100 each.

Soon afterwards, Pennzoil contacted both Gordon Getty and a representative of the J. Paul Getty Museum, which held approximately 11.8% of the shares of Getty Oil, to discuss the tender offer and the possible purchase of Getty Oil. In the first two days of January 1984, a "Memorandum of Agreement" was drafted to reflect the terms that had been reached in conversations between representatives of Pennzoil, Gordon Getty, and the Museum.

Under the plan set out in the Memorandum of Agreement, Pennzoil and the Trust (with Gordon Getty as trustee) were to become partners on a 3/7ths to 4/7ths basis respectively, in owning and operating Getty Oil. Gordon Getty was to become chairman of the board, and Hugh Liedtke, the chief executive officer of Pennzoil, was to become chief executive officer of the new company.

The Memorandum of Agreement further provided that the [Getty] Museum was to receive $110 per share for its 11.8% ownership, and that all other outstanding public shares were to be cashed in by the company at $110 per share. Pennzoil was given an option to buy an additional 8 million shares to achieve the desired ownership ratio. The plan also provided that Pennzoil and the Trust were to try in good faith to agree upon a plan to restructure Getty Oil within a year, but if they could not reach an agreement, the assets of Getty Oil were to be divided between them, 3/7ths to Pennzoil and 4/7ths to the Trust.

The Memorandum of Agreement stated that it was subject to approval of the board of Getty Oil, and it was to expire by its own terms if not approved at the board meeting that was to begin on January 2. Pennzoil's CEO, Liedtke, and Gordon Getty, for the Trust, signed the Memorandum of Agreement before the

Getty Oil board meeting on January 2, and Harold Williams, the president of the Museum, signed it shortly after the board meeting began. Thus, before it was submitted to the Getty Oil board, the Memorandum of Agreement had been executed by parties who together controlled a majority of the outstanding shares of Getty Oil.

The Memorandum of Agreement was then presented to the Getty Oil board, which had previously held discussions on how the company should respond to Pennzoil's public tender offer. A self-tender by the company to shareholders at $110 per share had been proposed to defeat Pennzoil's tender offer at $100 per share, but no consensus was reached.

The board voted to reject recommending Pennzoil's tender offer to Getty's shareholders, then later also rejected the Memorandum of Agreement price of $110 per share as too low. . . .

That evening, the lawyers and public relations staff of Getty Oil and the Museum drafted a press release describing the transaction between Pennzoil and the Getty entities. The press release, announcing an agreement in principle on the terms of the Memorandum of Agreement but with a price of $110 plus a $5 stub, was issued on Getty Oil letterhead the next morning, January 4, and later that day, Pennzoil issued an identical press release.

. . . [O]n January 4, Pennzoil's lawyers were working on a draft of a formal "transaction agreement" that described the transaction in more detail than the outline of terms contained in the Memorandum of Agreement and press release.

On January 5, the Wall Street Journal reported on an agreement reached between Pennzoil and the Getty entities, describing essentially the terms contained in the Memorandum of Agreement. The Pennzoil board met to ratify the actions of its officers in negotiating an agreement with the Getty entities, and Pennzoil's attorneys periodically attempted to contact the other parties' advisors and attorneys to continue work on the transaction agreement.

The board of Texaco also met on January 5, authorizing its officers to make an offer for 100% of Getty Oil and to take any necessary action in connection therewith. Texaco first . . . arranged a meeting to discuss the sale of the Museum's shares of Getty Oil to Texaco. Lipton [the Museum's lawyer] instructed his associate, on her way to the meeting in progress of the lawyers drafting merger documents for the Pennzoil/Getty transaction, to not attend that meeting, because he needed her at his meeting with Texaco. At the meeting with Texaco, the Museum outlined various issues it wanted resolved in any transaction with Texaco, and then agreed to sell its 11.8% ownership in Getty Oil.

That evening, Texaco met with Gordon Getty to discuss the sale of the Trust's shares. He was informed that the Museum had agreed to sell its shares to Texaco. Gordon Getty's advisors had previously warned him that the Trust shares might be "locked out" in a minority position if Texaco bought, in addition to the Museum's shares, enough of the public shares to achieve over 50% ownership of the company. Gordon Getty accepted Texaco's offer of $125 per share and signed a letter of his intent to sell his stock to Texaco. . . .

At noon on January 6, Getty Oil held a telephone board meeting to discuss the Texaco offer. The board voted to withdraw its previous counter-proposal to Pennzoil and unanimously voted to accept Texaco's offer. Texaco immediately issued a press release announcing that Getty Oil and Texaco would merge.

Soon after the Texaco press release appeared, Pennzoil telexed the Getty entities, demanding that they honor their agreement with Pennzoil. Later that day, prompted by the telex, Getty Oil filed a suit in Delaware for declaratory judgment that it was not bound to any contract with Pennzoil. . . .

Texaco contends that under controlling principles of New York law, there was insufficient evidence to support the jury's finding that at the end of the Getty Oil board meeting on January 3, the Getty entities intended to bind themselves to an agreement with Pennzoil.

Under New York law, if parties do not intend to be bound to an agreement until it is reduced to writing and signed by both parties, then there is no contract until that event occurs. If there is no understanding that a signed writing is necessary before the parties will be bound, and the parties have agreed upon all substantial terms, then an informal agreement can be binding, even though the parties contemplate evidencing their agreement in a formal document later.

If the parties do intend to contract orally, the mere intention to commit the agreement to writing does not prevent contract formation before execution of that writing, and even a failure to reduce their promises to writing is immaterial to whether they are bound.

However, if either party communicates the intent not to be bound before a final formal document is executed, then no oral expression of agreement to specific terms will constitute a binding contract. . . .

Several factors have been articulated to help determine whether the parties intended to be bound only by a formal, signed writing: (1) whether a party expressly reserved the right to be bound only when a written agreement is signed; (2) whether there was any partial performance by one party that the party disclaiming the contract accepted; (3) whether all essential terms of the alleged contract had been agreed upon; and (4) whether the complexity or magnitude of the transaction was such that a formal, executed writing would normally be expected.

Evaluating the first factor, Texaco contends that the evidence of expressed intent not to be bound establishes conclusively that there was no contract at the time of Texaco's alleged inducement of breach. Texaco argues that this expressed intent is contained in (1) the press releases issued by the Getty entities and Pennzoil, which stated that "the transaction is subject to execution of a definitive merger agreement"; (2) the phrasing of drafts of the transaction agreement, which Texaco alleges "carefully stated that the parties' obligations would become binding only 'after the execution and delivery of this Agreement' "; and (3) the deliberate reference by the press releases to the parties' understanding as an "agreement in principle."

In its brief, Texaco asserts that, as a matter of black letter New York law, the "subject to" language in the press release established that the parties were not then bound and intended to be bound only after signing a definitive agreement . . . . Although the intent to formalize an agreement is some evidence of an intent not to be bound before signing such a writing, it is not conclusive. The issue of when the parties intended to be bound is a fact question to be decided from the parties' acts and communications. The press release issued first by Getty, then by Pennzoil, on January 4, 1984, stated:

> Getty Oil Company, The J. Paul Getty Museum and Gordon Getty, as Trustee of the Sarah C. Getty Trust, announced today that they have agreed in principle with Pennzoil Company to a merger of Getty Oil and a newly formed entity owned by Pennzoil and the Trustee. In connection with the transaction, the shareholders of Getty Oil . . . will receive $110 per share cash plus the right to receive a deferred cash consideration in a formula amount. The deferred consideration will be equal to a pro rata share of the . . . proceeds, in excess of $1 billion, . . . of ERC Corporation, . . . and will be paid upon the disposition. In any event, under the formula, each shareholder will receive at least $5 per share within five years. Prior to the merger, Pennzoil will contribute approximately $2.6 billion in cash and the Trustee and Pennzoil will contribute the Getty Oil shares owned by them to the new entity. Upon execution of a definitive merger agreement, the . . . tender offer by a Pennzoil subsidiary for shares of Getty Oil stock will be withdrawn. The agreement in principle also provides that Getty Oil will grant to Pennzoil an option to purchase eight million treasury shares for $110 per share. The transaction is subject to execution of a definitive merger agreement, approval by the stockholders of Getty Oil and completion of various governmental filing and waiting period requirements. Following consummation of the merger, the Trust will own 4/7ths of the . . . stock of Getty Oil and Pennzoil will own 3/7ths. The Trust and Pennzoil have also agreed in principle that following consummation of the merger they will endeavor in good faith to agree upon a plan for restructuring Getty Oil [within a year] and that if they are unable to reach such an agreement then they will cause a division of assets of the company.

Any intent of the parties not to be bound before signing a formal document is not so clearly expressed in the press release to establish, as a matter of law, that there was no contract at that time. The press release does refer to an agreement "in principle" and states that the "transaction" is subject to execution of a definitive merger agreement. But the release as a whole is worded in indicative terms, not in subjunctive or hypothetical ones. The press release describes what shareholders will receive, what Pennzoil will contribute, that Pennzoil will be granted an option, etc. . . .

Texaco states that the use of the term "agreement in principle" in the press release was a conscious and deliberate choice of words to convey that there was not yet any binding agreement. Texaco refers to defense testimony that lawyers for Getty Oil and the Museum changed the initial wording of the press release from "agreement" to "agreement in principle" because they understood and intended that phrase to mean that there was no binding contract with Pennzoil. . . .

Pennzoil and Texaco presented conflicting evidence at trial on the common business usage and understanding of the term "agreement in principle." Texaco's witnesses testified that the term is used to convey an invitation to bid or that there is no binding contract. Pennzoil's witnesses testified that when business people use "agreement in principle," it means that the parties have reached a meeting of the minds with only details left to be resolved. There was testimony by Sidney Petersen, Getty Oil's chief executive officer, that an "agreement in principle" requires the parties to proceed to try to implement the details of the agreement in good faith, and that that was the case with the agreement in principle with Pennzoil.

The record as a whole demonstrates that there was legally and factually sufficient evidence to support the jury's finding in Special Issue No. 1 that the Trust, the Museum, and the Company intended to bind themselves to an agreement with Pennzoil at the end of the Getty Oil board meeting on January 3,1984.

NOTES & QUESTIONS

1. Agreements in principle have been referred to as "agreements to agree in the future." Should such "agreements" be enforceable? What limitations would you place on their enforceability as a matter of public policy?

2. *Practice Points:* Many different terms may be used to refer to "preliminary agreements," including "Agreement in Principle" and "Memorandum of Understanding." If the intention of the parties is not to be bound until a formal written agreement has been executed, this reservation should be expressly stated. Without such express reservation, use of such terms may be considered evidence of an intention to be bound without the need for a "formal" written document.

REDGRAVE v. BOSTON SYMPHONY ORCHESTRA, INC.
855 F.2d 888 (1st Cir. 1988)

Coffin, Circuit Judge:

. . . In March 1982, the Boston Symphony Orchestra (BSO) engaged Vanessa Redgrave to narrate Stravinsky's "Oedipus Rex" in a series of concerts in Boston and New York. Following announcement of the engagement, the BSO received calls from its subscribers and from community members protesting the engagement because of Redgrave's political support for the Palestine Liberation Organization and because of her views regarding the state of Israel. On or about April 1, 1982, the BSO cancelled its contract with Redgrave and its performances of "Oedipus Rex."

Redgrave sued the BSO for breach of contract. . . . The BSO argued at trial that the contract rightfully was cancelled because the cancellation was the result of "a cause or causes beyond the reasonable control" of the BSO. In response to the civil rights claim, BSO agents testified that they had not cancelled the performances in order to punish Redgrave for her past speech or repress her future speech, but because it was felt that potential disruptions, given the community reaction, would implicate the physical safety of the audience and players and would detract from the artistic qualities of the production.

Following a sixteen-day trial, the jury found that the BSO wrongfully had breached its contract with Redgrave. On that basis, the district court awarded Redgrave her stipulated performance fee of $27,500. The jury also found that the BSO's cancellation had damaged Redgrave's career by causing loss of future professional opportunities, and awarded Redgrave $100,000 in consequential damages. The district court found that the question whether there was sufficient evidence to support a finding of $100,000 in consequential damages was a "close and debatable" one, but concluded that there was sufficient evidence to support the award. Nevertheless, the district court overturned the grant of consequential damages, finding that a First Amendment right of freedom of speech was implicated by the theory of consequential damages advanced by Redgrave and that

Redgrave had not met the strict standards required by the First Amendment for recovery of damages. . . .

In response to special interrogatories, the jury found that the BSO's cancellation of the "Oedipus Rex" concerts caused consequential harm to Redgrave's professional career and that this harm was a foreseeable consequence within the contemplation of the parties at the time they entered the contract. 602 F. Supp. at 1204. A threshold question is whether Massachusetts contract law allows the award of such consequential damages for harm to a claimant's professional career.

Redgrave's consequential damages claim is based on the proposition that a significant number of movie and theater offers that she would ordinarily have received in the years 1982 and following were in fact not offered to her as a result of the BSO's cancellation in April 1982. The BSO characterizes this claim as one for damage to Redgrave's reputation,[1] and argues that the recent Massachusetts state court decisions in *McCone v. New England Telephone & Telegraph Co.*, 393 Mass. 231, 471 N.E.2d 47 (1984), and *Daley v. Town of West Brookfield*, 19 Mass. App. Ct. 1019, 476 N.E.2d 980 (1985), establish that Massachusetts law does not permit plaintiffs in breach of contract actions to recover consequential damages for harm to reputation.

In *McCone v. New England Telephone & Telegraph Co.*, plaintiffs alleged that their employer's breach of an implied covenant of good faith had caused them loss of salary increases, loss of pension benefits, and "damage to their professional reputations, disruption of their personal lives, and great pain of body and mind." The Massachusetts Supreme Judicial Court held that the claims for damages to reputation and other emotional injury could not be sustained in the suit because "these additional damages are not contract damages." In *Daley v. Town of West Brookfield*, a Massachusetts appellate court observed that "[d]amages for injury to reputation are usually not available in contract actions," noting that the rationale most often given is that "such damages are remote and not within the contemplation of the parties." . . .

In cases that have analyzed the reasons for disallowing a contract claim for reputation damages, courts have identified two determinative factors. First, courts have observed that attempting to calculate damages for injury to reputation is "unduly speculative." In many cases, the courts have viewed the claims for damages to reputation as analogous to claims for physical or emotional distress and have noted the difficulty in ascertaining such damages for contract purposes. . . .

The second factor that courts identify is that damages for injury to reputation "cannot reasonably be presumed to have been within the contemplation of the parties when they entered into the contract." These courts state that the basic rule of *Hadley v. Baxendale*, 9 Ex. 341, 156 Eng. Rep. 145 (1854), which requires that contract damages be of the kind that arise naturally from the breach of a contract or be of a kind that reasonably may have been in the contemplation of the parties when they entered the contract, cannot possibly be met in a claim for general damages to reputation occurring as the result of a breach of contract. . . .

---

[1] [3] The BSO notes that Redgrave contended that "the cancellation, as communicated to other employers through the news media, harmed Vanessa Redgrave because it carried with it the message 'that Vanessa Redgrave was unemployable,' a claim for damage to Redgrave's reputation."

The jury was given appropriate instructions to help it determine whether Redgrave had suffered consequential damages through loss of future professional opportunities. They were told to find that the BSO's cancellation was a proximate cause of harm to Redgrave's professional career only if they determined that "harm would not have occurred but for the cancellation and that the harm was a natural and probable consequence of the cancellation." In addition, they were told that damages should be allowed for consequential harm "only if the harm was a foreseeable consequence within the contemplation of the parties to the contract when it was made." In response to special interrogatories, the jury found that the BSO's cancellation caused consequential harm to Redgrave's career and that the harm was a foreseeable consequence within the contemplation of the parties.

NOTES & QUESTIONS

1. If Redgrave had fully performed, she would have been entitled to $27,500. What policy supports requiring BSO to pay more than the contract amount in damages?

2. Would you allow Redgrave to recover consequential damages for the following "harms":

(a) $30,000 for an existing contract to perform with the Chicago Symphony which was canceled as a result of her being fired by the BSO?

(b) $75,000 for a completely negotiated (but unsigned) agreement to appear in a made-for-TV movie canceled after BSO fired her?

(c) $500,000 for a theatrical release under preliminary negotiations?

(d) $100,000 for harm to her reputation for being fired?

If you would allow recovery, what business policy are you establishing in connection with the duty to honor contractual obligations?

3. *Practice Points:* Consequential damages are often difficult to predict. Consequently, you may want to insert specific provisions in any contract you draft expressly eliminating a party's liability for consequential damages. Alternatively, you may want to limit such liability through liquidated damage or limitation of liability clauses.

4. *Drafting Exercise:* Draft the employment agreement hiring Ms. Redgrave to perform with the BSO. Assume for purposes of this exercise that the parties have agreed in negotiations that Ms. Redgrave may only be fired for cause.

PROBLEMS

1. The plaintiff enters into a contract to hire a band for her wedding reception. She pays a $50 down payment. The total contract price for the band is $200. She hires caterers for food and drink, pays for decorations and rents a banquet room, spending $5,000 (excluding the cost of the band). The band fails to show up. Plaintiff sues for breach of contract and seeks $10,000 in damages (including $5,000 in emotional damages). You are the judge. What relief would you grant?

2. *Drafting Exercise:* Draft the contract for the band. What clauses would you include to limit liability for the ruined reception?

3. Section 3085 of the present California Family code provides: "Only marriage between a man and a woman is valid or recognized in California." A same-sex couple who have been living together for ten years and who hold themselves out to the world as spouses have broken up. One has sued the other for "alimony" based on an oral promise of support. Assuming the parties do not contest the nature of the oral promise of future support, what competing public policies would the court be required to balance? *See generally Lockyer v. City & County of San Francisco,* 95 P.3d 459 (Cal. 2004).

SECTION F

THE MEANING OF CONTRACTS

Before a court can enforce the contractual obligations between the parties, it must determine the precise terms of the agreement between them. On a fundamental level, the court must decide what document(s) and what oral discussions form the actual contract between the parties. To reach this determination, the court must decide to what extent, if any, it will consider extrinsic evidence such as prior negotiations or customs in the industry to determine the parties' intent. How should any gaps be filled, if at all?

Once the court determines the scope of the parties' mutual obligations, it must interpret those obligations to decide what performances have been bargained for between the parties. What if the parties disagree as to the meaning of a particular term or phrase? Whose interpretation should govern?

Even where parties agree regarding their intentions under a contract, intervening events may occur which make the original bargain less desirable for one of the parties. Should the disadvantaged party be excused from performing the bargain? What if one party has rented a concert hall for a symphony and the hall burns down before the concert? Must the renter pay rent on the now non-existent hall?

As you will discover in the following cases, the answers to these questions have changed over time.

CHAPTER 12

INTERPRETATION OF AGREEMENTS

A. INTRODUCTION

Assuming that an enforceable contractual obligation exists with no bar to enforcement (such as violation of the Statute of Frauds or public policy), before courts can enforce the contractual obligations between the parties, the scope of those obligations must be determined — in other words, the contract must be interpreted and the duties, obligations, performances and responsibilities which each party has agreed to undertake (the scope of the "bargained-for exchange") must be determined. You have already seen cases where courts interpret the terms of a purported offer or acceptance to determine if one party has made a manifestation of an intention to be bound, which has been properly accepted by another. (*See* Chapters Two and Three.) Just as courts have relied upon the intention of the parties in determining whether an agreement exists, courts similarly rely on the intention of the parties to determine the scope of the agreement to be enforced.

In interpreting contracts, the first question a court must ask itself is, quite simply, what are the terms of the agreement? Where the agreement is an oral one, courts will be forced to rely strictly on circumstantial evidence regarding the terms of the agreement. Such evidence may include testimony by the parties, and proof of the course of dealing or trade between them. Where the agreement at issue is at least partly in written form, courts are faced with difficult choices regarding the weight to give this written evidence. Should the written document be considered the sole evidence of the parties' intent? Under what circumstances, if any, should parties be allowed to go behind the written document and prove an agreement different from that derived from the "four corners" of the written document? These questions have been the subject of heated debate. The history of the development of contract law in the area of interpretation of terms is a history of the evolution from a purely subjective view ("the meeting of the minds"), to a purely objective view (strict reliance on the written word) to a mixed objective view, and from reliance on written documentation to a recognition that there are numerous situations where extrinsic (extra-contractual) evidence may be considered in determining the intention of the parties.

As you read the cases in this chapter, ask yourself whether each court's decision reflects the true intention of the parties or is based on a legal construct of their intention. If it is based on a legal construct, what impact does this construct have on the predictability of contractual obligations? Where there is a dispute regarding the meaning of contractual obligations, whose interpretation should apply? Is strict reliance on the written documents embodying an agreement appropriate? Should extra-contractual evidence always be allowed or should it only be allowed in certain situations? If only in certain situations, which ones? As you explore the answers to these questions, consider what impact each court's decision may have on the predictability of contractual enforcement, and whether there are competing policies that, under certain circumstances, take precedence over predictability concerns.

B. INTEGRATION: DETERMINING THE SCOPE OF THE AGREEMENT

Company A has decided to build a shopping center on pristine farmland owned by Rancher B. After lengthy negotiations, the parties agree on a price, on the amount of land to be bought by Company A, the financing terms, the closing date, and all other terms and conditions that affect the purchase of the land. Rancher B is concerned that the natural beauty of the land not be destroyed by Company A's shopping center. He is particularly concerned that a grove of rare fruit trees native to the land remain extant. Company A's representatives agree that they will not "remove, cut down, destroy or in any way harm the fruit trees currently standing on the property." The parties execute a written contract which contains all of the terms and conditions regarding the purchase of Rancher B's land. The contract, however, contains no reference to the fruit trees. After consummation of the sale, in the process of building the shopping center, all the fruit trees are destroyed. Rancher B sues for breach of contract. Company A admits that it made the oral promise but contends that the written contract is a fully integrated document, containing all of the terms relating to its purchase of the ranch. Consequently, the oral "promise" is no longer enforceable, because the written contract embodies all of the terms which were finally agreed upon by the parties. The first issue that the court is faced with in deciding what relief, if any, to grant Rancher B is whether the parol evidence rule precludes consideration of the oral terms.

Despite its misnomer, the parol evidence rule is not a rule of "evidence," but one of substantive law. Simply stated, the rule basically provides that where parties have reduced their final agreement to a writing, the writing cannot be varied or contradicted by prior or contemporaneous understandings or documentation.

Thus, the critical issue to be decided is whether the written contract embodies the final agreement of the parties regarding the subject at hand.

MITCHELL v. LATH
160 N.E. 646 (N.Y. 1928)

ANDREWS, Judge:

In the fall of 1923 the Laths owned a farm. This they wished to sell. Across the road, on land belonging to Lieutenant Governor Lunn, they had an icehouse which they might remove. Mrs. Mitchell looked over the land with a view to its purchase. She found the icehouse objectionable. Thereupon "the defendants orally promised and agreed, for and in consideration of the purchase of their farm by the plaintiff, to remove the said icehouse in the spring of 1924." Relying upon this promise, [Mrs. Mitchell] made a written contract to buy the property for $8,400, for cash and mortgage and containing various provisions usual in such papers. Later receiving a deed, she entered into possession, and has spent considerable sums in improving the property for use as a summer residence. The defendants have not fulfilled their promise as to the icehouse, and do not intend to do so. We are not dealing, however, with their moral delinquencies. The question before us is whether their oral agreement [to remove the icehouse] may be enforced in a court of equity.

[The response to this question] requires a discussion of the parol evidence rule — a rule of law which defines the limits of the contract to be construed. It is more than a rule of evidence, and oral testimony, even if admitted, will not control the written contract, unless admitted without objection. It applies, however, to attempts to modify such a contract by parol. It does not affect a parol collateral contract distinct from and independent of the written agreement. It is, at times, troublesome to draw the line. Williston, in his work on Contracts (section 637) points out the difficulty. "Two entirely distinct contracts," he says, "each for a separate consideration, may be made at the same time, and will be distinct legally. Where, however, one agreement is entered into wholly or partly in consideration of the simultaneous agreement to enter into another, the transactions are necessarily bound together. . . . Then if one of the agreements is oral and the other in writing, the problem arises whether the bond is sufficiently close to prevent proof of the oral agreement." That is the situation here. It is claimed that the defendants are called upon to do more than is required by their written contract in connection with the sale as to which it deals. . . .

Under our decisions before such an oral agreement as the present is received to vary the written contract, at least three conditions must exist: (1) The agreement must in form be a collateral one; (2) it must not contradict express or implied provisions of the written contract; (3) it must be one that parties would not ordinarily be expected to embody in the writing, or, put in another way, an inspection of the written contract, read in the light of surrounding circumstances, must not indicate that the writing appears "to contain the engagements of the parties, and to define the object and measure the extent of such engagement." Or, again, it must not be so clearly connected with the principal transaction as to be part and parcel of it. . . .

The respondent does not satisfy the third of these requirements. . . . We have a written contract for the purchase and sale of land. The buyer is to pay $8,400 in the way described. She is also to pay her portion of any rents, interest on mortgages, insurance premiums, and water meter charges. . . . On their part, the sellers are to give a full covenant deed of the premises as described, . . . they sell the personal property on the farm and represent they own it; they agree that all amounts paid them on the contract and the expense of examining the title shall be a lien on the property. . . . Are they to do more? Or is such a claim inconsistent with these precise provisions? . . . [A]n inspection of this contract shows a full and complete agreement, setting forth in detail the obligations of each party. On reading it, one would conclude that the reciprocal obligations of the parties were fully detailed. Nor would his opinion alter if he knew the surrounding circumstances. The presence of the icehouse, even the knowledge that Mrs. Mitchell thought it objectionable, would not lead to the belief that a separate agreement existed with regard to it. Were such an agreement made it would seem most natural that the inquirer should find it in the contract. Collateral in form it is found to be, but it is closely related to the subject dealt within the written agreement — so closely that we hold it may not be proved.

LEHMAN, J. (dissenting).

I accept the general rule as formulated by Judge ANDREWS. I differ with him only as to its application to the facts shown in the record. The plaintiff contracted to purchase land from the defendants for an agreed price. A formal written agreement was made between the sellers and the plaintiff's husband. It is on its face a complete contract for the conveyance of the land. It describes the property to be conveyed. It sets forth the purchase price to be paid. All the conditions and terms of the conveyance to be made are clearly stated. I concede at the outset that parol evidence to show additional conditions and terms of the conveyance would be inadmissible. There is a conclusive presumption that the parties intended to integrate in that written contract every agreement relating to the nature or extent of the property to be conveyed, the contents of the deed to be delivered, the consideration to be paid as a condition precedent to the delivery of the deeds, and indeed all the rights of the parties in connection with the land. The conveyance of that land was the subject-matter of the written contract, and the contract completely covers that subject. . . .

The fact that in this case the parol agreement is established by the overwhelming weight of evidence is, of course, not a factor which may be considered in determining the competency or legal effect of the evidence. Hardship in the particular case would not justify the court in disregarding or emasculating the general rule. It merely accentuates the outlines of our problem. The assumption that the parol agreement was made is no longer obscured by any doubts. The problem, then, is clearly whether the parties are presumed to have intended to render that parol agreement legally ineffective and nonexistent by failure to embody it in the writing. Though we are driven to say that nothing in the written contract which fixed the terms and conditions of the stipulated conveyance suggests the existence of any further parol agreement, an inspection of the contract, though it is complete on its face in regard to the subject of the conveyance, does not, I think, show that it was intended to embody negotiations or agreements, if any, in regard to a matter so loosely bound to the conveyance as the removal of an ice-house from land not conveyed.

The rule of integration undoubtedly frequently prevents the assertion of fraudulent claims. Parties who take the precaution of embodying their oral agreements in a writing should be protected against the assertion that other terms of the same agreement were not integrated in the writing. The limits of the integration are determined by the writing, read in the light of the surrounding circumstances. A written contract, however complete, yet covers only a limited field. I do not think that in the written contract for the conveyance of land here under consideration we can find an intention to cover a field so broad as to include prior agreements, if any such were made, to do other acts on other property after the stipulated conveyance was made.

In each case where such a problem is presented, varying factors enter into its solution. Citation of authority in this or other jurisdictions is useless, at least without minute analysis of the facts. The analysis I have made of the decisions in this state leads me to the view that the decision of the courts below is in accordance with our own authorities and should be affirmed.

NOTES & QUESTIONS

1. The majority in *Mitchell v. Lath* found the oral agreement to be collateral to the written purchase agreement because the defendants induced the plaintiff to agree to purchase the land that was the subject of the written agreement by the oral promise to remove the icehouse. The "collateral" nature of the agreement, however, may not be sufficient to avoid the application of the parol evidence rule to

bar the admission of extra-contractual evidence. As Judge Lehman in his dissent in *Mitchell v. Lath* warned:

> The parol agreement which the court below found the parties had made was collateral to, yet connected with, the agreement of purchase and sale. It has been found that the defendants induced the plaintiff to agree to purchase the land by a promise to remove an icehouse from land not covered by the agreement of purchase and sale. No independent consideration passed to the defendants for the parol promise. To that extent the written contract and the alleged oral contract are bound together. The same bond usually exists wherever attempt is made to prove a parol agreement which is collateral to a written agreement.

Mitchell v. Lath, 247 N.Y. 377, 385 (N.Y. 1928).

Do you agree with this analysis? If the written contract and the alleged oral agreement are always related, how do you determine whether the bond is sufficiently close to prevent proof of the oral agreement?

2. The RESTATEMENT (SECOND) OF CONTRACTS defines an "integrated" agreement as "a writing or writings constituting a final expression of one or more terms of an agreement." RESTATEMENT (SECOND) OF CONTRACTS § 209(1). Agreements may be either partially or fully integrated. *Id.* § 210. Under the RESTATEMENT (SECOND):

> (1) A binding integrated agreement discharges prior agreements to the extent that it is inconsistent with them.

> (2) A binding completely integrated agreement discharges prior agreements to the extent that they are within its scope.

Thus, under the RESTATEMENT (SECOND), integrated agreements supersede inconsistent terms of prior agreements. The RESTATEMENT further provides that "a writing cannot of itself prove its own completeness, and wide latitude must be allowed for inquiry into circumstances bearing on the intention of the parties." RESTATEMENT (SECOND) OF CONTRACTS § 210, cmt. b. If the majority in *Mitchell v. Lath* had applied the principles set forth in the RESTATEMENT (SECOND), would it have reached the same result?

3. Does the obligation in *Mitchell v. Lath* to remove the icehouse contradict any express or implied provisions of the written contract? Is it the type of agreement you would ordinarily expect to be embodied in the written agreement? What evidence would you consider in deciding this question?

4. Assume the written agreement in *Mitchell v. Lath* stated that it contained all pertinent provisions related to the purchase of the land. What impact, if any, should this statement have upon the application of the parol evidence rule?

5. What impact does the integration rule set forth in *Mitchell v. Lath* have upon the successful assertion of fraudulent claims based on oral conditions or obligations? Judge Lehman feared that this rule of interpretation would severely curtail such evidence. He stated:

> The rule of integration undoubtedly frequently prevents the assertion of fraudulent claims. Parties who take the precaution of embodying their oral agreements in a writing should be protected against the assertion that other terms of the same agreement were not integrated in the writing. The

limits of the integration are determined by the writing, read in the light of the surrounding circumstances. A written contract, however complete, yet covers only a limited field. I do not think that in the written contract for the conveyance of land here under consideration we can find an intention to cover a field so broad as to include prior agreements, if any such were made, to do other acts on other property after the stipulated conveyance was made.

Id. at 247 N.Y. 377 (N.Y. 1928).

Do you agree with his conclusion?

6. Both the majority and dissent agreed that Mitchell had proven the existence of the oral agreement to remove the icehouse. Consequently, refusal to enforce the oral agreement appears directly contrary to the parties' intention and denies Ms. Mitchell the full benefit of her bargain. What role, if any, should the hardship to the parties and the lack of disagreement about the existence of a previous "oral" understanding play in deciding whether to enforce the oral agreement?

MASTERSON v. SINE
436 P.2d 561 (Cal. 1968)

TRAYNOR, Chief Justice:

Dallas Masterson and his wife Rebecca owned a ranch as tenants in common. On February 25, 1958, they conveyed it to Medora and Lu Sine by a grant deed "Reserving unto the Grantors herein an option to purchase the above described property on or before February 25, 1968" for the "same consideration as being paid heretofore plus [the] depreciation value of any improvements Grantees may add to the property from and after two and a half years from this date." Medora is Dallas' sister and Lu's wife. Since the conveyance Dallas has been adjudged bankrupt. His trustee in bankruptcy and Rebecca brought this declaratory relief action to establish their right to enforce the option.

The court determined that the parol evidence rule precluded admission of extrinsic evidence offered by defendants to show that the parties wanted the property kept in the Masterson family and that the option was therefore personal to the grantors and could not be exercised by the trustee in bankruptcy. . . .

Defendants contend that the option provision is too uncertain to be enforced and that extrinsic evidence as to its meaning should not have been admitted. The trial court properly refused to frustrate the obviously declared intention of the grantors to reserve an option to repurchase by an overly meticulous insistence on completeness and clarity of written expression. . . . It properly admitted extrinsic evidence to explain the language of the deed. . . .

When the parties to a written contract have agreed to it as an "integration" — a complete and final embodiment of the terms of an agreement — parol evidence cannot be used to add to or vary its terms. *See* 3 Corbin, CONTRACTS (1960) § 573, p. 357; RESTATEMENT, CONTRACTS (1932) § 228 (and com. a). When only part of the agreement is integrated, the same rule applies to that part, but parol evidence may be used to prove elements of the agreement not reduced to writing.

The crucial issue in determining whether there has been an integration is whether the parties intended their writing to serve as the exclusive embodiment of their agreement. The instrument itself may help to resolve that issue. It may state, for example, that "there are no previous understandings or agreements not contained in the writing," and thus express the parties' "intention to nullify antecedent understandings or agreements." (*See* 3 Corbin, Contracts (1960) § 578, p. 411.) Any such collateral agreement itself must be examined, however, to determine whether the parties intended the subjects of negotiation it deals with to be included in, excluded from, or otherwise affected by the writing. Circumstances at the time of the writing may also aid in the determination of such integration. (*See* 3 Corbin, Contracts (1960) §§ 582–584; *contra*, 4 Williston, Contracts (3d ed. 1961) § 633, pp. 1014–1016.)

California cases have stated that whether there was an integration is to be determined solely from the face of the instrument, and that the question for the court is whether it "appears to be a complete . . . agreement . . . ." The requirement that the writing must appear incomplete on its face has been repudiated in many cases where parol evidence was admitted "to prove the existence of a separate oral agreement as to any matter on which the document is silent and which is not inconsistent with its terms" — even though the instrument appeared to state a complete agreement. Even under the rule that the writing alone is to be consulted, it was found necessary to examine the alleged collateral agreement before concluding that proof of it was precluded by the writing alone. (*See* 3 Corbin, Contracts (1960) § 582, pp. 444–446.) It is therefore evident that "The conception of a writing as wholly and intrinsically self-determinative of the parties' intent to make it a sole memorial of one or seven or twenty-seven subjects of negotiation is an impossible one." (9 Wigmore, Evidence (3d ed. 1940) § 2431, p. 103.) For example, a promissory note given by a debtor to his creditor may integrate all their present contractual rights and obligations, or it may be only a minor part of an underlying executory contract that would never be discovered by examining the face of the note.

In formulating the rule governing parol evidence, several policies must be accommodated. One policy is based on the assumption that written evidence is more accurate than human memory. This policy, however, can be adequately served by excluding parol evidence of agreements that directly contradict the writing. Another policy is based on the fear that fraud or unintentional invention by witnesses interested in the outcome of the litigation will mislead the finder of facts. (*Mitchell v. Lath* (1928) 247 N.Y. 377, 388, 160 N.E. 646, 68 A.L.R. 239 (dissenting opinion by Lehman, J.). McCormick has suggested that the party urging the spoken as against the written word is most often the economic underdog, threatened by severe hardship if the writing is enforced. In his view the parol evidence rule arose to allow the court to control the tendency of the jury to find through sympathy and without a dispassionate assessment of the probability of fraud or faulty memory that the parties made an oral agreement collateral to the written contract, or that preliminary tentative agreements were not abandoned when omitted from the writing. (*See* McCormick, Evidence (1954) § 210.) He recognizes, however, that if this theory were adopted in disregard of all other considerations, it would lead to the exclusion of testimony concerning oral agreements whenever there is a writing and thereby often defeat the true intent of the parties. (*See* McCormick, op. cit. *supra*, § 216, p. 441.)

Evidence of oral collateral agreements should be excluded only when the fact finder is likely to be misled. The rule must therefore be based on the credibility of the evidence. One such standard, adopted by section 240(1)(b) of the RESTATEMENT OF CONTRACTS, permits proof of a collateral agreement if it "is such an agreement as might naturally be made as a separate agreement by parties situated as were the parties to the written contract." The draftsmen of the Uniform Commercial Code would exclude the evidence in still fewer instances: "If the additional terms are such that, if agreed upon, they would certainly have been included in the document in the view of the court, then evidence of their alleged making must be kept from the trier of fact." (Com. 3, § 2-202.)[1]

The option clause in the deed in the present case does not explicitly provide that it contains the complete agreement, and the deed is silent on the question of assignability. Moreover, the difficulty of accommodating the formalized structure of a deed to the insertion of collateral agreements makes it less likely that all the terms of such an agreement were included.[2] The statement of the reservation of the option might well have been placed in the recorded deed solely to preserve the grantors' rights against any possible future purchasers and this function could well be served without any mention of the parties' agreement that the option was personal. There is nothing in the record to indicate that the parties to this family transaction, through experience in land transactions or otherwise, had any warning of the disadvantages of failing to put the whole agreement in the deed. This case is one, therefore, in which it can be said that a collateral agreement such as that alleged "might naturally be made as a separate agreement." *A fortiori*, the case is not one in which the parties "would certainly" have included the collateral agreement in the deed.

In the present case defendants offered evidence that the parties agreed that the option was not assignable in order to keep the property in the Masterson family. The trial court erred in excluding that evidence.

The judgment is reversed.

BURKE, Justice:

I dissent.

. . . This new rule [adopted by the majority], not hitherto recognized in California, provides that proof of a claimed collateral oral agreement is admissible if it is such an agreement as might naturally have been made a separate agreement by the parties under the particular circumstances. I submit that this approach opens the door to uncertainty and confusion. Who can know what its limits are? Certainly I do not. For example, in its application to this case who could be

---

[1] Corbin suggests that, even in situations where the court concludes that it would not have been natural for the parties to make the alleged collateral oral agreement, parol evidence of such an agreement should nevertheless be permitted if the court is convinced that the unnatural actually happened in the case being adjudicated. (3 CORBIN, CONTRACTS, § 485, pp. 478, 480; cf. Murray, The Parol Evidence Rule: A Clarification (1966) 4 Duquesne L. Rev. 337, 341–342.) This suggestion may be based on a belief that judges are not likely to be misled by their sympathies. If the court believes that the parties intended a collateral agreement to be effective, there is no reason to keep the evidence from the jury.

[2] See Goble v. Dotson (1962) 203 Cal. App. 2d 272, 21 Cal. Rptr. 769, where the deed given by a real estate developer to the plaintiffs contained a condition that grantees would not build a pier or boathouse. Despite this reference in the deed to the subject of berthing for boats, the court allowed plaintiffs to prove by parol evidence that the condition was agreed to in return for the developer's oral promise that plaintiffs were to have the use of two boat spaces nearby.

expected to divine as 'natural' a separate oral agreement between the parties that the assignment, absolute and unrestricted on its face, was intended by the parties to be limited to the Masterson family?

Or, assume that one gives to his relative a promissory note and that the payee of the note goes bankrupt. By operation of law the note becomes an asset of the bankruptcy. The trustee attempts to enforce it. Would the relatives be permitted to testify that by a separate oral agreement made at the time of the execution of the note it was understood that should the payee fail in his business the maker would be excused from payment of the note, or that, as here, it was intended that the benefits of the note would be personal to the payee? I doubt that trial judges should be burdened with the task of conjuring whether it would have been "natural" under those circumstances for such a separate agreement to have been made by the parties. Yet, under the application of the proposed rule, this is the task the trial judge would have, and in essence the situation presented in the instant case is no different. . . .

Comment hardly seems necessary on the convenience to a bankrupt of such a device to defeat his creditors. He need only produce parol testimony that any options (or other property, for that matter) which he holds are subject to an oral "collateral agreement" with family members (or with friends) that the property is nontransferable "in order to keep the property in the family" or in the friendly group. In the present case the value of the ranch which the bankrupt and his wife held an option to purchase has doubtless increased substantially during the years since they acquired the option. The initiation of this litigation by the trustee in bankruptcy to establish his right to enforce the option indicates his belief that there is substantial value to be gained for the creditors from this asset of the bankrupt. Yet the majority opinion permits defeat of the trustee and of the creditors through the device of an asserted collateral oral agreement that the option was "personal" to the bankrupt and nonassignable "in order to keep the property in the family"! . . .

These are only a few of the confusions and inconsistencies which will arise to plague property owners and, incidentally, attorneys and title companies, who seek to counsel and protect them.

I would hold that the trial court ruled correctly on the proffered parol evidence, and would affirm the judgment.

NOTES & QUESTIONS

1. If you were deciding the case, which position would you support — the majority's or the dissent's? Why?

2. How do you overcome the problem of fraud or perjury outlined by the dissent if you decide to permit testimony regarding the previous oral "agreement"?

3. In *Brown v. Oliver,* 256 P. 1008 (Kan. 1927), plaintiff purchased land from defendant on which stood a hotel operated by a tenant. The court found plaintiff had established through "ample oral evidence" that the sale included the hotel furniture owned by defendant. The written real estate purchase agreement made no reference to any item of personal property, and contained nothing to indicate the parties were dealing with respect to any subject except land and matters incidental to the land described. The court found that the oral agreement for the

sale of the personal property did not contradict the written contract since the written instrument "did not by itself conclusively establish whether the parties intended it should exclude every subject of sale except real estate." Consequently, the court could properly consider parol evidence regarding the collateral sale agreement. Would you uphold this determination?

LEE v. SEAGRAM
552 F.2d 447 (2d Cir. 1977)

GURFEIN, Circuit Judge:

This is an appeal by defendant Joseph E. Seagram & Sons, Inc. ("Seagram") from a judgment entered by the District Court, Hon. Charles H. Tenney, upon the verdict of a jury in the amount of $407,850 in favor of the plaintiffs on a claim asserting common law breach of an oral contract. . . .

The jury could have found the following. The Lees owned a 50% interest in Capitol City Liquor Company, Inc. ("Capitol City"), a wholesale liquor distributorship located in Washington, D.C. The other 50% was owned by Harold Lee's brother, Henry D. Lee, and his nephew, Arthur Lee. Seagram is a distiller of alcoholic beverages. Capitol City carried numerous Seagram brands and a large portion of its sales were generated by Seagram lines.

The Lees and the other owners of Capitol City wanted to sell their respective interests in the business and, in May 1970, Harold Lee, the father, discussed the possible sale of Capitol City with Jack Yogman ("Yogman"), then Executive Vice President of Seagram (and now President), whom he had known for many years. Lee offered to sell Capitol City to Seagram but conditioned the offer on Seagram's agreement to relocate Harold and his sons, the 50% owners of Capitol City, in a new distributorship of their own in a different city.

About a month later, another officer of Seagram, John Barth, an assistant to Yogman, visited the Lees and their co-owners in Washington and began negotiations for the purchase of the assets of Capitol City by Seagram on behalf of a new distributor, one Carter, who would take it over after the purchase. The purchase of the assets of Capitol City was consummated on September 30, 1970 pursuant to a written agreement. The promise to relocate the father and sons thereafter was not reduced to writing. Harold Lee had served the Seagram organization for thirty-six years in positions of responsibility before he acquired the half interest in the Capitol City distributorship. From 1958 to 1962, he was chief executive officer of Calvert Distillers Company, a wholly-owned subsidiary. During this long period he enjoyed the friendship and confidence of the principals of Seagram.

In 1958, Harold Lee had purchased from Seagram its holdings of Capitol City stock in order to introduce his sons into the liquor distribution business, and also to satisfy Seagram's desire to have a strong and friendly distributor for Seagram products in Washington, D.C. Harold Lee and Yogman had known each other for 13 years.

The plaintiffs claimed a breach of the oral agreement to relocate Harold Lee's sons, alleging that Seagram had had opportunities to procure another distributorship for the Lees but had refused to do so. The Lees brought this action on January 18, 1972, fifteen months after the sale of the Capitol City distributorship to Seagram. They contended that they had performed their obligation by agreeing to the sale by Capitol City of its assets to Seagram, but that Seagram had failed to perform its obligation under the separate oral contract between the Lees and Seagram. The agreement which the trial court permitted the jury to find was "an oral agreement with defendant which provided that if they agreed to sell their interest in Capitol City, defendant in return, within a reasonable time, would provide the plaintiffs a Seagram distributorship whose price would require roughly an amount equal to the capital obtained by the plaintiffs for the sale of their interest in Capitol City, and which distributorship would be in a location acceptable to plaintiffs." No specific exception was taken to this portion of the charge. By its verdict for the plaintiffs, we must assume as Seagram notes in its brief that this is the agreement which the jury found was made before the sale of Capitol City was agreed upon.

Appellant urges several grounds for reversal. It contends that, as a matter of law, (1) plaintiffs' proof of the alleged oral agreement is barred by the parol evidence rule; and (2) the oral agreement is too vague and indefinite to be enforceable. . . .

Judge Tenney, in a careful analysis of the application of the parol evidence rule, decided that the rule did not bar proof of the oral agreement. . . .

The District Court, in its denial of the defendant's motion for summary judgment, treated the issue as whether the written agreement for the sale of assets was an "integrated" agreement not only of all the mutual agreements concerning the sale of Capitol City assets, but also of all the mutual agreements of the parties. Finding the language of the sales agreement "somewhat ambiguous," the court decided that the determination of whether the parol evidence rule applies must await the taking of evidence on the issue of whether the sales agreement was intended to be a complete and accurate integration of all of the mutual promises of the parties.

Seagram did not avail itself of this invitation. It failed to call as witnesses any of the three persons who negotiated the sales agreement on behalf of Seagram regarding the intention of the parties to integrate all mutual promises or regarding the failure of the written agreement to contain an integration clause.

Appellant contends that, as a matter of law, the oral agreement was "part and parcel" of the subject-matter of the sales contract and that failure to include it in the written contract barred proof of its existence. *Mitchell v. Lath*, 247 N.Y. 377, 380, 160 N.E. 646 (1928). The position of appellant, fairly stated, is that the oral agreement was either an inducing cause for the sale or was a part of the consideration for the sale, and in either case, should have been contained in the written contract. In either case, it argues that the parol evidence rule bars its admission.

Appellees maintain, on the other hand, that the oral agreement was a collateral agreement and that, since it is not contradictory of any of the terms of the sales agreement, proof of it is not barred by the parol evidence rule. Because the case comes to us after a jury verdict we must assume that there actually was an oral contract, such as the court instructed the jury it could find. The question is whether the strong policy for avoiding fraudulent claims through application of the parol evidence rule nevertheless mandates reversal on the ground that the jury should not have been permitted to hear the evidence. *See Fogelson v. Rackfay*

Constr. Co., 300 N.Y. 334 at 337-38, 90 N.E.2d 881 (1950).

The District Court stated the cardinal issue to be whether the parties "intended" the written agreement for the sale of assets to be the complete and accurate integration of all the mutual promises of the parties. If the written contract was not a complete integration, the court held, then the parol evidence rule has no application. We assume that the District Court determined intention by objective standards. The parol evidence rule is a rule of substantive law. . . .

Certain oral collateral agreements, even though made contemporaneously, are not within the prohibition of the parol evidence rule "because [if] they are separate, independent, and complete contracts, although relating to the same subject. . . . [t]hey are allowed to be proved by parol, because they were made by parol, and no part thereof committed to writing." *Thomas v. Scutt*, 127 N.Y. 133, 140-41, 27 N.E. 961, 963 (1891).

Although there is New York authority which in general terms supports defendant's thesis that an oral contract inducing a written one or varying the consideration may be barred, the overarching question is whether, in the context of the particular setting, the oral agreement was one which the parties would ordinarily be expected to embody in the writing. *See* RESTATEMENT OF CONTRACTS § 240. For example, integration is most easily inferred in the case of real estate contracts for the sale of land, e.g., *Mitchell v. Lath, supra*, 247 N.Y. 377, 160 N.E. 646, or leases. In more complex situations, in which customary business practice may be more varied, an oral agreement can be treated as separate and independent of the written agreement even though the written contract contains a strong integration clause.

Thus, as we see it, the issue is whether the oral promise to the plaintiffs, as individuals, would be an expectable term of the contract for the sale of assets by a corporation in which plaintiffs have only a 50% interest, considering as well the history of their relationship to Seagram.

Here, there are several reasons why it would not be expected that the oral agreement to give Harold Lee's sons another distributorship would be integrated into the sales contract. In the usual case, there is an identity of parties in both the claimed integrated instrument and in the oral agreement asserted. Here, although it would have been physically possible to insert a provision dealing with only the shareholders of a 50% interest, the transaction itself was a corporate sale of assets. Collateral agreements which survive the closing of a corporate deal, such as employment agreements for particular shareholders of the seller or consulting agreements, are often set forth in separate agreements. . . . It was expectable that such an agreement as one to obtain a new distributorship for certain persons, some of whom were not even parties to the contract, would not necessarily be integrated into an instrument for the sale of corporate assets. As with an oral condition precedent to the legal effectiveness of an otherwise integrated written contract, which is not barred by the parol evidence rule if it is not directly contradictory of its terms, *Hicks v. Bush*, 10 N.Y.2d 488, 225 N.Y.S.2d 34, 180 N.E.2d 425 (1962); cf. 3 CORBIN ON CONTRACTS § 589, "it is certainly not improbable that parties contracting in these circumstances would make the asserted oral agreement. . . ." 10 N.Y.2d at 493, 225 N.Y.S.2d at 39, 180 N.E.2d at 428. Similarly, it is significant that there was a close relationship of confidence and friendship over many years between two old men, Harold Lee and Yogman, whose authority to bind Seagram has not been questioned. It would not be surprising that a handshake for the benefit of Harold's sons would have been thought sufficient. In point, as well, is the circumstance that the negotiations concerning the provisions of the sales agreement were not conducted by Yogman but by three other Seagram representatives, headed by John Barth. The two transactions may not have been integrated in their minds when the contract was drafted.

Finally, the written agreement does not contain the contain the integration clause, even though a good part of it (relating to warranties and negative covenants) is boiler-plate. The omission may, of course, have been caused by mutual trust and confidence, but in any event, there is no such strong presumption of exclusion because of the existence of a detailed integration clause.

Nor do we see any contradiction of the terms of the sales agreement. *Mitchell v. Lath, supra,* 247 N.Y. at 381, 160 N.E. 646; 3 CORBIN ON CONTRACTS § 573, at 357. The written agreement dealt with the sale of corporate assets, the oral agreement with the relocation of the Lees. Thus, the oral agreement does not vary or contradict the money consideration recited in the contract as flowing to the selling corporation. That is the only consideration recited, and it is still the only consideration to the corporation.[3]

We affirm Judge Tenney's reception in evidence of the oral agreement and his denial of the motion under Rule 50(b) with respect to the parol evidence rule.

Appellant contends, however, that the jury verdict cannot stand because the oral agreement was so vague and indefinite as to be unenforceable. First, appellant argues that the failure to specify purchase price, profitability or sales volume of the distributorship to be provided, is fatal to the contract's validity. The contention is that, because the oral agreement lacks essential terms, the courts cannot determine the rights and obligations of the parties. *See* 1 CORBIN ON CONTRACTS § 95, at 394. Second, appellant contends that the agreement is unenforceable because there were no specific limits to plaintiffs' discretion in deciding whether to accept or reject a particular distributorship; and hence the agreement was illusory.

The alleged agreement, as the jury was permitted to find, was to provide the Lees with a liquor distributorship of approximately half the value and profit potential of Capitol City, within a reasonable time. The distributorship would be "in a location acceptable to plaintiffs," and the price would require roughly an amount equal to the plaintiffs' previous investment in Capitol City. The performance by plaintiffs in agreeing to the sale of Capitol City caused the counter-performance of the oral promise to mature.

Once the nature of the agreement found by the jury is recognized, it becomes clear that appellant's contentions are without merit. As for the alleged lack of essential terms, there was evidence credited by the jury, which did establish the purchase price, profitability and sales volume of the distributorship with reasonable specificity. In addition to the direct testimony of the Lees, there was evidence that distributorships were valued, as a rule of thumb, at book value plus three times the previous year's net profit after taxes. Between this industry

---

[3] [5] Cf. Mitchell v. Lath, 247 N.Y. 377, 380–81, 160 N.E. 646, 647 (1928) (to escape the parol evidence rule, the oral agreement "must not contradict express or implied provisions of the written contract."). The parties do not contend, and we would be unwilling to hold, that the oral agreement was not "in form a collateral one."

standard and the reference to the Capitol City transaction, there was extrinsic evidence to render the parties' obligations reasonably definite. Professor Corbin has observed that a court should be slow to deny enforcement "if it is convinced that the parties themselves meant to make a 'contract' and to bind themselves to render a future performance. Many a gap in terms can be filled, and should be, with a result that is consistent with what the parties said and that is more just to both of them than would be a refusal of enforcement." CORBIN ON CONTRACTS § 97, at 425–26. . . .

As for the alleged unbridled discretion which the oral agreement conferred on the plaintiffs, we similarly conclude that there is no fatal defect. We note at the outset that the requirement that the new distributorship be "acceptable" to the Lees did not render the agreement illusory in the sense that it is not supported by consideration; the Lee's part of the bargain was to join in the sale of Capitol City's assets and assignment of its franchise, which they had already performed. More importantly, we do not agree that the Lees had "unbridled" discretion. New York courts would in all events impose an obligation of good faith on the Lees' exercise of discretion, *see e.g., Wood v. Lucy, Lady Duff-Gordon*, 222 N.Y. 88, 118 N.E. 214 (1917), and there was also extrinsic evidence of what would constitute an "acceptable distributorship," and hence constitute reasonable performance by Seagram. Seagram appears to contend that if it had tendered reasonable performance, by offering an acceptable distributorship to the Lees, that the Lees nevertheless could have found it not "acceptable." This is not correct. It is true that Seagram could not have forced the Lees to take a distributorship, because they had not promised to do so. But Seagram's tender of reasonable performance would discharge its obligations under the oral agreement, whether or not the Lees "accepted." *See* 15 WILLISTON ON CONTRACTS §§ 1808–10 (3d ed. 1972). The Lees could not prevent Seagram from fulfilling its obligations by unreasonably refusing an acceptable distributorship. Since the obligations of the parties under the contract therefore were ascertainable, it was not void for indefiniteness.

Affirmed.

NOTES & QUESTIONS

1. The court found that no integration clause was contained in the written contract. Is the absence of such a clause dispositive of the issue of whether the written contract is a fully integrated one? Should it be?

2. Was there any doubt in your mind about what the outcome of the above case would be after it became apparent that the defense did not deny the existence of the oral agreement? Consider the *Maddox* case below as well (88 F.3d 592 (8th Cir. 1996)).

3. In determining whether an agreement is a fully integrated one, the court in *Lee v. Seagram* suggested that the court must consider the written document "in light of the surrounding circumstances." Does this always require the court to consider extra-contractual evidence?

4. Section 214 of the RESTATEMENT (SECOND) OF CONTRACTS provides that "[a]greements and negotiations prior to or contemporaneous with the adoption of a writing are admissible in evidence to establish that the writing is or is not an integrated agreement [and] that the integrated agreement, if any, is completely or

partially integrated." Similarly § 2-202 of the Uniform Commercial Code provides that "evidence of consistent additional terms" may be considered "unless the court finds the writing to have been intended also as a complete and exclusive statement of the terms of the agreement." This view toward considering facts outside the four corners of the written agreement to determine integration is in direct contrast to the narrow rule cited by Judge Traynor in *Masterson v. Sine* (see above) that integration should be "determined solely from the face of the instrument." Which rule did the court in *Lee* follow? Which one would you follow if you were the judge?

5. *Practice Points:* "Handshake deals" such as the one described in *Lee* are fairly common among parties of long-standing relationships. Certain industries (such as the entertainment industry) are also known for operating on the basis of "handshake deals." Such handshake deals can become the basis for bitter disputes later. Although "papering the deal" may seem intrusive to the client (an unnecessary step designed to generate additional fees), the creation of written documents to formalize such oral agreements may avoid future disputes about the terms of such agreements.

6. *Practice Points:* Although the defendant objected to the admission of parol evidence during testimony in the case, the defendant did not object to the tender of the jury instruction describing the oral contract. That was a serious mistake of legal strategy. The court could probably have treated that omission as a waiver of the issue on review.

7. *Drafting Exercise:* Prepare a written document formalizing the "hand-shake" agreement between the parties in *Lee.* What terms could you include to reduce the problem of having the agreement excluded as a prior collateral agreement?

C.L. MADDOX, INC. v. THE BENHAM GROUP, INC.
88 F.3d 592 (8th Cir. 1996)

Magill, Circuit Judge:

. . . The dispute between the parties has its origins in the extensive and expensive remodeling of a coal processing system at an electrical power plant in Joppa, Illinois. The owner of the plant, Electric Energy, Inc. (EEI), contracted with Maddox to serve as the general contractor for the project. Maddox subcontracted with Benham to perform the engineering work and with Dynalogic Engineering, Inc. (Dynalogic) to provide the necessary computer hardware and software.

The project did not go well, and Maddox was forced to sue Benham and Dynalogic for breach of contract. . . .

The project began in March 1990, when EEI started soliciting bids. Jack Craig, a marketing agent for both Maddox and Benham, responded to the solicitation. In April and May of 1990, Maddox submitted several preliminary design/build[4] proposals to EEI. Each proposal increased in cost and complexity to meet changing requests made by EEI. The proposals were the combined product of

---

[4] [2] Under a design/build contract, the contractor agrees to both design and build the project. This differs significantly from traditional construction arrangements in which an architect/engineer first designs the project and prospective contractors then submit bids on the basis of the designer's drawings and specifications.

Craig, Mike Dover (Maddox's project manager), and Benham personnel. EEI reviewed the proposals and approved the design concept.

To assist it in preparing its formal proposal, Maddox entered into an oral agreement with Benham on June 1, 1990, under which Benham would complete the drawings and specifications necessary for the bid and provide Maddox with equipment lists and with quantity information. Benham was to receive $58,200 for this work. The terms of this oral contract were memorialized by Clete Schierman, Benham's project manager, who had prepared a chronology of the project and noted that, on June 1,

EEI approves $58,200 for TBG [Benham] to begin in-depth study of equipment layouts, equipment sizing and to supply necessary information and assistance for CLM [Maddox] to prepare a final construction cost (lump sum) for the project. TBG [Benham] is to develop a final lump sum engineering cost.

Maddox relied heavily on the estimates provided by Benham. Curt Maddox, president of Maddox, Inc., testified that the only way Maddox would have bid on the project was to rely on the estimates of Benham because Benham possessed all of the design information. Dover testified that in preparing the bid, he had to rely on the material quantity estimates provided by Benham. On the basis of this information, Maddox submitted a formal proposal on July 5, and EEI issued a letter of intent to Maddox. The final contract, signed on September 28, was for a fixed price of $10,326,881.

In mid-September of 1990, Maddox and Benham entered into a written subcontract for much of the design work on the project. This contract was retroactively dated "as of June 1, 1990," and it provided that Benham would perform its design work by January 2, 1991. Article 2 of the agreement described the "Basic Services" that Benham was to perform for a fixed price of $616,050. Under ¶ 2.1.6 of Article 2, Benham agreed that it would keep Maddox "informed of the progress and quality of the Work, and shall endeavor to guard [Maddox] against defects and deficiencies in the Work of [Maddox] [sic]." The Basic Services further included the preparation of construction drawings, but did not include the compilation or preparation of bidding information. Rather, ¶ 3.4 of the contract provided that Maddox "shall furnish all cost estimating services required for the Project." The contract contained a strict integration clause, providing that all prior agreements were superseded. Subcontract ¶ 7.5.1. . . .

From the start of the project, Maddox experienced problems with Benham. Benham was late in producing drawings; the drawings actually produced were often insufficient; and Benham underestimated the amount of work actually required to complete the final design. Dover testified that there were delays in getting drawings for the fabrication work. Jack Jenkins, Maddox's electrical supervisor, testified that prints for the electrical components of the project were not available, requiring that he lay much of the wiring for the project without plans, entailing a greater cost.

Benham countered that not all of the delay problems were Benham's fault. On cross-examination, Dover conceded that some of the delays in drawings were caused by EEI's continued alteration of the project. Other delays were caused by Maddox, which often failed to timely submit to Benham vendor-prepared drawings after purchasing equipment. Further, Maddox was not always timely in its approval of Benham's drawings, which only further delayed the submission of the drawings to EEI.

. . . Initially, Benham argues that Maddox should not have been able to present evidence of an oral agreement to supply bidding information to Maddox, because evidence of the oral agreement should have been precluded by the parol evidence rule. . . .

. . . The parol evidence rule prohibits evidence of prior or contemporaneous oral agreements which vary, add to, or contradict the terms of an unambiguous and complete contract absent fraud, common mistake, or erroneous admission. However, evidence of an oral agreement that is an independent and separate agreement will not be barred by the parol evidence rule, provided that the oral agreement is not inherently in conflict with the written agreement.

Given the integration clause found in Subcontract ¶ 7.5.1, it is evident that the parties intended the subcontract to be a complete expression of their intentions. However, we conclude that evidence of the prior oral agreement was admissible at trial, because the oral agreement was a wholly separate and independent contract that did not inherently conflict with the written agreement.

We begin by looking at the underlying substance of the transaction. Although the written contract was predated to June 1, it was only signed in mid-September. By this time, the oral contract for bidding services had already been entered into, executed, and paid for. Thus, the oral agreement can be characterized as a separate agreement, a stand-alone contract that was bargained and paid for by Maddox. . . .

Benham points to three facts in arguing that the oral contract was not a separate contract but was, instead, subsumed by the written contract. First, although the written contract was not signed until mid-September, it was predated to June 1, 1990, before the oral contract was entered into and executed. Second, Schierman testified that the compensation for the written contract, set at $616,050, included the $57,400 paid for the preliminary bidding work. This could indicate that the two agreements were in fact parts of one contract. Finally, the integration clause stated that the written contract "represents the entire agreement between [the parties] and supersedes . . . prior negotiations, representations or agreements." Subcontract ¶ 7.5.1. . . .

We disagree with Benham. Where the parties bargain for a contract, payment on that contract is made, and the contract is fully performed, we have little difficulty in concluding that the parties intended this interaction to constitute a separate contract. Benham would impermissibly elevate form over substance, which we are not willing to do.

Nor does the substance of the oral agreement inherently contradict the written agreement. Although ¶ 3.4 of the written contract provided that Maddox "shall furnish all cost estimating services required for the Project," this contract was titled "Agreement-Final Design." As this contract was signed two months after Maddox's bid was prepared and accepted, it is reasonable to assume that the parties might adopt a different arrangement for preliminary engineering services, such as preparing an initial bid for the project. Thus, there is no inherent contradiction here.

Because the oral agreement represents a wholly separate agreement from the written contract and does not inherently contradict the September agreement, the parol evidence rule is not applicable in this case. Evidence of the oral agreement was properly before the jury.

NOTES & QUESTIONS

1. Assume the contract in *C.L. Maddox* had been signed on June 1, 1990. Would the result have been the same? What if the contract did not contain an entirety or integration clause? Would that change the result? Should it?

2. "Entirety clauses" are often referred to a "boilerplate" provisions. "Boilerplate" provisions are standard terms in written documents that cover such diverse topics as entirety of contracts, severability of clauses, choice of law, arbitration, force majeure and Acts of God that excuse performance, and waiver. Such terms are included in many contracts with little or no negotiation or discussion. But they are meaningful terms, at least as a general rule.

3. Since entirety clauses are rarely negotiated, what impact, if any, should the lack of negotiation have on the enforcement of such an entirety clause? For example, in the problem regarding Rancher B's efforts to sell his land and yet protect his fruit trees that appeared at the beginning of this chapter, what impact, if any, would the following provision in the written sales contract have on the court's decision to permit parol evidence of the fruit tree protection agreement?

> This agreement represents the entire understanding of the parties regarding the subject matter hereof.

Could the court consider parol evidence in deciding whether the fruit tree protection agreement fell within the scope of the "subject matter of the agreement" of the land purchase agreement?

4. What if the entirety clause stated the following?

> There are no prior or contemporaneous understandings or agreements regarding the sale of Rancher B's land.

Would the presence of this clause preclude consideration of the fruit tree protection agreement?

5. Assume that the written sales contract for Rancher B's land includes a standard entirety clause. Rancher B testifies truthfully that Company A had, at the time the written document was signed, orally agreed that the entirety clause did not include the fruit tree agreement. Is evidence of this oral agreement barred?

6. *Drafting Exercise:* You represent the buyer of the Ranch. Draft a contract that would clearly preclude consideration of the oral fruit tree agreement.

7. Is the existence of an entirety clause always dispositive of the integration issue? *Compare KFC v. Darsam Corp.*, 543 F. Supp. 222 (W.D. Ky. 1982) (entirety clause is treated as dispositive of integration issue), *with Franklin v. White*, 493 N.E.2d 161 (Ind. 1986) (court treats merger clause as "only some evidence of the parties' intention").

8. *Practice Points:* Boilerplate clauses should never be included without thinking about the potential consequences of such clauses. If there have been oral under-

standings between the parties, the presence of boilerplate merger, entirety and/or severability clauses could preclude your client from enforcing her rights. Never accept "boilerplate" or "standard" provisions without analyzing their impact on the deal.

9. In *Mitchell v. Lath*, which you read earlier, the court found that the agreement regarding the removal of the icehouse was the type of agreement that would "naturally" have been included in the contract. Consequently, it was a collateral agreement which did not "survive" the written, final integration. Courts have applied different "tests" for determining whether a particular "term" might naturally be included. The RESTATEMENT (SECOND) OF CONTRACTS provides that an agreement is not completely integrated if the writing "omits a consistent additional agreed term which . . . might naturally be omitted from the writing." RESTATEMENT (SECOND) OF CONTRACTS § 216(2). Such omission is readily understandable under the RESTATEMENT (SECOND) if the written document is a standardized form or in other situations where non-standards terms might naturally be omitted. The U.C.C. also takes an open view of the introduction of evidence of consistent, additional terms. The Comment to § 2-202 provides that only if the additional consistent term "would certainly have been included in the document" should such evidence be excluded. Which of these tests might permit the greater introduction of parol evidence? Which of these tests more closely resembles the one applied by the court in *C.L. Maddox?*

10. Conflict in treatment regarding the ability to consider "parol evidence" in deciding whether a written document constitutes a fully integrated agreement depends largely on whether the court follows the approach of Professor Williston or Professor Corbin. The following extract contains a helpful "recap" of the major conflict between these two approaches.

John D. Calamari & Joseph M. Perillo,
A Plea for a Uniform Parol Evidence Rule and Principles of Contract Interpretation
421 IND. L.J. 333 (1967)

The parol evidence rule comes into play only when the last expression is in writing. Professor Corbin states the rule as follows: "When two parties have made a contract and have expressed it in a writing to which they have both assented as the complete and accurate integration of that contract, evidence, whether parol or otherwise, of antecedent understandings and negotiations will not be admitted for the purpose of varying or contradicting the writing." Professor Williston's formulation is not to the contrary: "Briefly stated," he writes, "this rule requires, in the absence of fraud, duress, mutual mistake, or something of the kind, the exclusion of extrinsic evidence, oral or written, where the parties have reduced their agreement to an integrated writing." Both agree that this, too, is a rule of substantive law that also operates as an exclusionary rule of evidence merely because prior understandings are irrelevant to the process of determining the content of the final contract. . . .

While it is unanimously agreed that the parol evidence rule applies to prior expressions, and has no application to an agreement made subsequent to the writing, there is no unanimity as to expressions contemporaneous with the writing. Williston and the RESTATEMENT take the position that contemporaneous expression should be treated the same as prior expressions except that contemporaneous writings should be deemed to be a part of the integration. Corbin appears to argue that expressions are either prior or subsequent to the writing and that therefore the word "contemporaneous" merely clouds the issue. Everyone agrees that the parol evidence rule does not apply to a separate agreement; that is, an agreement that has a separate consideration.

Apparent agreement by Professors Williston and Corbin, except as noted, on the rules stated above conceals real conflict. The battleground upon which they express disagreement is a major one: the concept of total integration. This, of course, is the area in which most of the cases arise. Both assert that the existence of a total integration depends on the intention of the parties. Williston dos so primarily in a section entitled, "Integration Depends Upon Intent." Corbin's emphasis on intent runs throughout his entire discussion of the rule. It appears, however, that in this context they use the term "intent" in ways that are remarkably dissimilar. A typical fact situation will illustrate this. A agrees to sell and B agrees to purchase Blackacre for $10,000. The contract is in writing and in all respects appears complete on its face. Prior to the signing of the contract A, in order to induce B's assent, orally promises him in the presence of a number of reputable witnesses that if B will sign the contract, A will remove an unsightly shack on A's land across the road from Blackacre. May this promise be proved and enforced? This depends upon whether the writing is a total integration.

Williston argues that if the intention to have a total integration were to be determined by the ordinary process of determining intention, the parol evidence rule would be emasculated. He points out that the mere existence of the collateral oral agreement would conclusively indicate that the parties intended only a partial integration and that the only question that would be presented is whether the alleged prior or contemporaneous agreement was actually made. This would be a question of fact for the jury, thus eliminating the special protection which the trial judge should afford the writing.

Williston, therefore, suggests that the issue of partial or total integration should be determined according to the following rules.

(1) If the writing expressly declares that it contains the entire agreement of the parties (what is sometimes referred to as a merger clause), the declaration conclusively establishes that the integration is total unless the document is obviously incomplete or the merger clause was included as a result of fraud or mistake or any other reason exists that is sufficient to set aside a contract. As previously indicated, even a merger clause does not prevent enforcement of a separate agreement supported by a distinct consideration.

(2) In the absence of a merger clause, the determination is made by looking to the writing. Consistent additional terms may be proved if the writing is obviously incomplete on its face or if it is apparently complete but, as in the case of deeds, bonds, bills and notes, expresses the undertaking of only one of the parties.

(3) Where the writing appears to be a complete instrument expressing the rights and obligations of both parties, it is deemed a total integration unless the alleged additional terms were such as might naturally be made as a separate agreement by parties situated as were the parties to the written contract.

Thus in the hypothetical case given, Williston's view is that the collateral promise to remove the unsightly shack could not be enforced.

Professor Corbin takes a contrary view as to the proper result in our hypothetical case: It can never be determined by mere interpretation of the words of a writing whether it is an "integration" of anything, whether it is "the final and complete expression of the agreement" or is a mere partial expression of the agreement." Elsewhere, he states: "Since the very existence of an 'integration' . . . is dependent on what the parties thereto say and do (necessarily extrinsic to the paper instrument), at the time they draw that instrument 'in usual form,' are we to continue like a flock of sheep to beg the question at issue, even when its result is to 'make a contract for the parties,' one that is vitally different from the one they made themselves?" When Professor Corbin speaks of the intent of the parties he emphatically means their actual expressed intent.

Thus, two schools of thought are on the scene, one determined to seek out the intent of the parties, the other speaking of intent but refusing to consider evidence of what the intent actually was.

PROBLEMS

1. From 1978 through 1982, the plaintiff, a sole proprietorship, was granted a dealership for recreational boats under a written contract which was renewed each year. Paragraphs 2 and 3 of the agreement provided in pertinent part:

2. COAST CATAMARAN CORP. ("Hobie Cat") hereby appoints:
Kinn Motors Marine
650 E. Wisconsin Ave.
Oconomowoc, Wis 53066

. . . ("Dealer") as a non-exclusive Authorized Retail Dealer of Hobie catamarans and catamaran parts and accessories (the "Products"). Dealer's territory for the resale of the products shall be Oconomowoc/Milwaukee Metro Area.

3. Dealer agrees that he will maintain the above retail outlet in the territory and understands that Hobie Cat will only ship to the above location address. Because of the importance of the Dealer's location to Hobie Cat, so long as this Agreement is in effect, Dealer cannot cease promoting and reselling the Products at the above location nor add additional locations without the prior written consent of Hobie Cat.

The contract also contained an integration clause which stated: "This Agreement embodies the entire agreement and understanding between the parties and supersedes all prior agreements." Kinn alleges that the term "non-exclusive" in the contract meant that Coast could appoint another dealer in his territory but only if Kinn's sales fell below a specified minimum. Coast admits that discussions about minimum sales were had but claims that any agreement regarding such minimum sales is superseded by the written document. What result? *See Kinn v. Coast Catamaran Corporation*, 582 F. Supp. 682 (E.D. Wisc. 1984).

2. The plaintiff agreed to sell defendant a certain quantity of logs. This agreement was set forth in a written document which contained no warranties regarding the quality of the logs to be sold. The defendant subsequently failed to pay for the delivered logs. He claimed that the quality was below that warranted by the plaintiff at the time of the sale. The plaintiff claims the written sales agreement is a complete and fully integrated agreement, and that evidence of any oral

representations should not be admitted. *See Thompson v. Libbey*, 34 Minn. 374, 26 N.W. 1 (1885).

3. Dave is the president and sole shareholder of Dave's Drug Company. Dave has agreed to sell the company, including all stock, assets and inventory, to Carla Co. The written agreement between the parties contains all the necessary terms for completing the stock and asset purchase. During the negotiations, Dave told Carla, the president of Carla Co., that he would agree not to work for any competitor for a period of one year after the sale of the company. This noncompetition agreement did not appear in the written contract between the parties. Six months after the sale, Dave has started a new company which directly competes with both Carla Co. and Dave's Drug Company. Carla Co. has sued Dave for breach of contract. Can Carla Co. introduce evidence of the oral agreement?

4. You represent Carla Co. Your client does not want the non-competition agreement with Dave included in the main written document. What can you do to assure that the non-competition agreement is enforceable?

C. INTERPRETING THE PARTIES' WORDS

Once the court determines the scope of the agreement (whether it is fully integrated, and if not, what additional documents or oral agreements must be included to complete the fully integrated agreement), it must still interpret the parties' intention. The same issues regarding the reliance on extrinsic evidence that the court faces in determining integration must be considered in determining the parties' reasonable expectations. However, unlike integration, the issue of interpretation often turns on the parol evidence rule and the extent to which the court must rely exclusively on the written word. In its early common law form, the parol evidence rule required exclusive reliance on the written agreement for determining the parties' intent where the written agreement is "complete on its face." The question of "completeness" turns primarily upon two issues — whether the document represents the fully integrated agreement between the parties, and if so, whether it is "clear on its face" or contains an ambiguity for which extrinsic (extra-contractual) evidence is required to determine the proper meaning. As the following cases demonstrate, the question of ambiguity is not easily determined. Moreover, simply engaging in an inquiry regarding ambiguity could lead to the problems of perjury that the parol evidence rule was initially designed to combat.

Company A has accidentally developed a new formula which appears to promote the rapid growth of wheat. Company A specializes in the manufacture and distribution of organic fertilizer. It has limited manufacturing facilities. In order to fully exploit its new formula, Company A enters into a joint research and development agreement with Big Time. The written agreement provides that Big Time will "do all acts necessary to refine The Formula so that it can easily be manufactured and commercialized." The agreement further provides that Big Time "will aid Company A in promoting, advertising and distributing any commercially viable product(s) that are derived from The Formula" and that the two will "share as equal partners in all proceeds derived from the commercialization of The Formula." For six months Big Time works steadily to develop a marketable plant growth liquid from Company A's formula. Finding that the formula will not work in liquid form, Big Time abandons its efforts. Company A sues for breach of contract.

Big Time claims that all discussions regarding commercialization of The Formula involved the creation of a liquid product. Big Time also wants to introduce evidence that in joint research and development agreements in the fertilizer industry, if solid fertilizer is expected to be developed, this fact is specifically stated in the agreement.

The first issue the court must face in deciding what relief, if any, to award to Company A is whether the written document constitutes the fully integrated agreement between the parties. Assuming the court finds that the written document does constitute the fully integrated agreement, it must then decide whether the parol evidence rule precludes consideration of the oral discussions between the parties and the industry meaning of the term "commercialize." As the following cases demonstrate, the answer to this question may depend on whether the parties' intent is unambiguously expressed in the written document.

E.I. DU PONT DE NEMOURS POWDER CO.
v. SCHLOTTMAN
218 F. 353 (2d Cir. 1914)

Ward, Circuit Judge:.

In July, 1908, Charles Grubb was negotiating for the sale of the Pittsburgh Fuse Company to the DuPont Company. On July 20, prior to the execution of a written agreement between the two, T.C. DuPont, the President of the DuPont Company, sent the following letter to Grubb:

> Mr. Chas. G. Grubb, Building — Dear Sir: Should the deal now under discussion for the Pittsburgh Fuse Mfg. Co. go through, and after we have had the property a year, it is understood that if in my judgment the property has for any reason been worth $175,000 to our company, and we manufactured double tape fuse at $2 per thousand with powder at $3.60 per keg, we are to pay you $25,000 in either bonds, preferred or common stock of our company as we may elect.

> Yours truly,

> T.C. Du Pont, President.

On July 24th the deal referred to in the letter went through in a formal agreement under which the Du Pont Company agreed to pay Grubb $75,000 of its preferred and $75,000 of its common stock for the whole capital stock of the Pittsburgh Fuse Company. Grubb delivered the Fuse Company's stock but, after operating the plant for about six months, DuPont sold the Fuse Company to other parties, who dismantled it.

Grubb's assignor sued DuPont for breach of contract, alleging that DuPont's sale of the Fuse Company breached its implied promise to operate the plant for a year (and pay additional compensation if the plant met the manufacturing requirements of the July 20th letter). The complaint treats the letter and the formal agreement as one contract, alleges that the defendant by selling the plant of the Fuse Company wrongfully prevented the test agreed upon, and claims damages for the difference between the fair and reasonable value of the Fuse Company's capital stock alleged to be $175,000 and the market value of the defendant's stock actually received, alleged to be $120,000. [DuPont contended that in the absence of an express agreement to operate the plant for a year, no such promise could be implied. The court disagreed:]

The letter does not contain any express promise to operate the plant for one year, and the question is whether such a promise is to be implied. We think the court below rightly held that it was. The seller evidently thought the plant worth $175,000 in the defendant's securities, and the buyer was willing to pay the additional $25,000 if such value was demonstrated in the way provided. The letter implies a promise on the Du Pont Company's part to operate the plant for a year, and that promise must be taken as part of the consideration for which Grubb sold the capital stock. The authorities support this conclusion. Allen, J., said in *Booth v. Cleveland Mill Co.*, 74 N.Y. 15, 21:

There is no particular formula of words, or technical phraseology, necessary to the creation of an express obligation to do, or forbear to do, a particular thing or perform a specified act. . . . It is a cardinal principle that every agreement or covenant must be interpreted according to its peculiar terms, and so as to carry out the intent of the parties. . . .

GIANNI v. R. RUSSEL & CO., INC.
126 A. 791 (Pa. 1924)

Schaffer, Justice:

Plaintiff had been a tenant of a room in an office building in Pittsburgh wherein he conducted a store, selling tobacco, fruit, candy and soft drinks. Defendant acquired the entire property in which the storeroom was located, and its agent negotiated with plaintiff for a further leasing of the room. A lease for three years was signed. It contained a provision that the lessee should "use the premises only for the sale of fruit, candy, soda water," etc., with the further stipulation that "it is expressly understood that the tenant is not allowed to sell tobacco in any form, under penalty of instant forfeiture of this lease." The document was prepared following a discussion about renting the room between the parties and after an agreement to lease had been reached. It was signed after it had been left in plaintiff's hands and admittedly had been read over to him by two persons, one of whom was his daughter.

Plaintiff sets up that in the course of his dealings with defendant's agent it was agreed that, in consideration of his promises not to sell tobacco and to pay an increased rent, and for entering into the agreement as a whole, he should have the exclusive right to sell soft drinks in the building. No such stipulation is contained in the written lease. Shortly after it was signed defendant demised the adjoining room in the building to a drug company without restricting the latter's right to sell soda water and soft drinks. Alleging that this was in violation of the contract which defendant had made with him, and that the sale of these beverages by the drug company had greatly reduced his receipts and profits, plaintiff brought this action for damages for breach of the alleged oral contract, and was permitted to recover. Defendant has appealed. . . .

Appellee's counsel argues this is not a case in which an endeavor is being made to reform a written instrument because of something omitted as a result of fraud, accident, or mistake, but is one involving the breach of an independent oral agreement which does not belong in the writing at all and is not germane to its provisions. We are unable to reach this conclusion.

> Where parties, without any fraud or mistake, have deliberately put their engagements in writing, the law declares the writing to be not only the best, but the only evidence of their agreement.
>
> *Martin v. Berens*, 67 Pa. 459, 463.

> All preliminary negotiations, conversations and verbal agreements are merged in and superseded by the subsequent written contract, . . . and unless fraud, accident, or mistake be averred, the writing constitutes the agreement between the parties, and its terms cannot be added to nor subtracted from by parol evidence.

Union Storage Co. v. Speck, 194 Pa. 126, 133, 45 A.48, 49.

. . . In cases of this kind, where the cause of action rests entirely on an alleged oral understanding concerning a subject which is dealt with in a written contract it is presumed that the writing was intended to set forth the entire agreement as to that particular subject.

> In deciding upon this intent [as to whether a certain subject was intended to be embodied by the writing], the chief and most satisfactory index . . . is found in the circumstance whether or not the particular element of the alleged extrinsic negotiation is dealt with at all in the writing. If it is mentioned, covered, or dealt with in the writing, then presumably the writing was meant to represent all of the transaction on that element, if it is not, then probably the writing was not intended to embody that element of the negotiation.

WIGMORE ON EVIDENCE (2d Ed.) vol. 5, p. 309.

As the written lease is the complete contract of the parties, and since it embraces the field of the alleged oral contract, evidence of the latter is inadmissible under the parol evidence rule. . . .

We have stated on several occasions recently that we propose to stand for the integrity of written contracts.

The judgment of the court below is reversed, and is here entered for defendant.

NOTES & QUESTIONS

1. Would you have reached a different decision in *Gianni* if a disinterested third party was willing to testify that two days before the lease was executed the witness heard the defendant say that plaintiff would have the exclusive right to sell soda water and soft drinks?

2. In supporting its view on the reliability of the written contract, the court in *Gianni* relied on both evidentiary, as well as contract, principles. The court quoted the following from WIGMORE ON EVIDENCE:

> In deciding upon this intent [as to whether a certain subject was intended to be embodied by the writing], the chief and most satisfactory index . . . is found in the circumstance whether or not the particular element of the alleged extrinsic negotiation is dealt with at all in the

writing. If it is mentioned, covered, or dealt with in the writing, then presumably the writing was meant to represent all of the transaction on that element, if it is not, then probably the writing was not intended to embody that element of the negotiation.

5 Wigmore on Evidence309 (2d ed.). Despite this reliance on evidentiary principles, the parol evidence rule is *not* an evidentiary rule, but one of substantive law. The policy behind the rule, however, is based on some of the same concerns — the desire to avoid perjured testimony.

3. The parol evidence rule is not limited strictly to oral agreements or negotiations. It includes consideration of such diverse extrinsic evidence as letters, memoranda, preliminary drafts, telegrams and evidence regarding industry customs and courses of dealing.

4. Is there any ambiguity in the written lease agreement in *Gianni* that would permit consideration of the purported oral agreement between the parties?

5. *Drafting Exercise:* You represent the plaintiff in *Gianni* who tells you about the written lease agreement, and the oral understanding between the parties. He does not want to offend the owner of the building by suggesting that he does not believe the owner will keep his word. What advice would you give your client? How would you draft a provision that protected your client's interest and did not anger the owner of the building?

6. How do you reconcile the court's treatment of the letter in *DuPont* with the oral conversations in *Gianni?* Which decision do you believe more accurately reflects the parties' intentions?

7. In the supplement to his treatise, Corbin offered a number of general principles as an introduction to the study of the parol evidence rule, including:

1. The primary and ultimate purpose of interpretation is to determine and make effective the Intention of the Contracting Parties.

2. No contract should ever be interpreted and enforced with a meaning that neither party gave it. . . .

4. No party to a contract should ever be bound by an interpretation that is determined exclusively by the linguistic education and experience of the judge. . . .

6. When a court enforces a contract in accordance with an interpretation that seems "plain and clear" to the court and excludes relevant convincing evidence that the parties intended a different interpretation, it is "making a contract for the parties," one that they did not make.

3 Corbin on Contracts § 572B (Supp. 1971) (capitalization in original). Are there other policies that support *not* considering extrinsic evidence in all cases to determine the presence of an ambiguity?

GRACE AND NINO, INC. v. ORLANDO
41 Mass. App. 111 (1996)

Gillerman, Justice:

After the defendants settled and collected $300,000 on account of the plaintiff's claim against an insurer, they disbursed the settlement proceeds to the plaintiff retaining, however, $49,980 as their fee for legal services rendered. The plaintiff had engaged the defendants under a contingent fee agreement signed by the plaintiff and the defendants.[5] The plaintiff claimed that under the agreement the defendants had the right to retain a fee of only $10,000, and it sought the recovery of $39,980 and interest.

At the close of the plaintiff's case, and at the close of all the evidence, the plaintiff moved for a directed verdict. The motions were denied. Both motions were grounded on the claim that the written contingent fee agreement must be construed against the defendants, and when so construed, the defendants would be entitled to a fee of $10,000. Following the answers of the jury to special questions, a final judgment was entered awarding the defendants $49,980 as their fee. . . .

The material facts are not in dispute. The plaintiff's claim was settled more than thirty days after the date of the fee agreement but prior to the commencement of any action. The defendants argue that the fee agreement was a "partially integrated contract" because there was no provision in the contingent fee agreement for the calculation of the fee in the event the case was settled after thirty days and before suit was brought. For that reason, argue the defendants, the judge was correct in admitting parol evidence of an antecedent oral agreement (establishing the fee at 16.66 percent of any settlement of the claim following the initial thirty-day period and prior to suit) which did not vary or contradict the terms of the written contingent fee agreement. . . .

The interpretive issue is whether, in paragraph (2) of the agreement . . . the clause "within thirty (30) days of this date" is a condition to a settlement that reduces the fee to $10,000, or merely a reference to the attorneys' expectation that

---

[5] [2] The following is the fee agreement signed by the parties: "Anthony Ciaramitaro, individually and as president for the Grace & Nino, Inc. of 28 Dale Avenue, Gloucester, MA 01930 retains the Attorneys Orlando & White of One Western Avenue, Gloucester, MA 01930, to perform the legal services mentioned in paragraph (1) below. The Attorneys agree to perform the legal services faithfully and with due diligence.

(1) The claim, controversy, and other matters with reference to which the services are to be performed are: damages sustained as a result of the loss of the F/V MARY GRACE on or about June 4, 1984.

(2) Client agrees that if suit is filed in this matter payment for services will be on a contingent fee basis as outlined below. In the event that the case is settled within thirty (30) days of this date prior to the institution of a suit the client agrees to pay the attorneys $10,000.00.

(3) The contingency upon which compensation is to be paid is that in the event there is any recovery by way of settlement or trial favorable to the Client on the claim or controversy under paragraph (1) of this agreement the Client shall be liable to the Attorneys for compensation as set forth in paragraph (5) below.

(4) The Client is not to be liable to pay compensation otherwise than from amounts collected for the Client by the Attorneys, except that the Client, as required by Rule 3:05 of the Supreme Judicial Court of Massachusetts, is in any event to be liable to the Attorneys for their reasonable expenses and disbursements.

(5) Reasonable compensation on the foregoing contingency is to be paid by the Client to the Attorneys, but such compensation is not to exceed: (a) 16.66% of the first $300,000.00 recovered; and (b) 40% of that sum which exceeds $300,000.00.

This agreement and its performance are subject to Rule 3:05 of the Supreme Judicial Court of Massachusetts.

suit would be brought within thirty days if the case was not settled by that time.[6] The choice between the two interpretations is sufficiently close that the resulting muddle may properly be regarded precisely as the kind of "obscurity" to which the court referred *In the Matter of Kerlinsky*, 406 Mass. 67, 73 n.5, 546 N.E.2d 150 (1989) (where the agreement is subject to Rule 3:05, the guiding principle is that "any obscurities in the agreement will be taken against the attorney who drafted it"). This is based on the obligation of the attorney who drafts such an agreement to "see[] that all its parts were completed with clarity." Here the defendants failed to perform that obligation, and we must take the "obscurities" of the agreement against the defendant.[7]

This construction is consistent with the plain meaning of the first sentence of the same paragraph: "Client agrees that if suit is filed in this matter payment for services will be on a contingent fee basis as outlined below." The contingent fee basis referred to in this last quoted clause and "outlined below" was 16.66% of the first $300,000, and 40% of any excess.

So construed, the agreement must be taken to mean that the agreed fee was $10,000 if the case was settled prior to suit, and the defendants are obliged to return $39,980 to the plaintiff.

STEUART v. McCHESNEY
444 A.2d 659 (Pa. 1982)

FLAHERTY, Justice:

On June 8, 1968, the appellant, Lepha I. Steuart, and her husband, James A. Steuart (now deceased), executed an agreement granting to the appellees, William C. McChesney and Joyce C. McChesney, husband and wife, a Right of First Refusal on a parcel of improved farmland. The agreement provided:

> (a) During the lifetime of said Steuarts, should said Steuarts obtain a Bona Fide Purchaser for Value, the said McChesneys may exercise their right to purchase said premises at a value equivalent to the market value of the premises according to the assessment rolls as maintained by the County of Warren and Commonwealth of Pennsylvania for the levying and assessing of real estate taxes; provided, however, that the date of valuation shall be that upon which the said Steuarts notify said McChesneys, in writing, of the existence of a Bona Fide Purchaser.

On July 6, 1977, the property in question was appraised by a real estate broker at a market value of $50,000. Subsequently, on October 10, 1977 and October 13, 1977 respectively, Steuart received bona fide offers of $35,000 and $30,000 for the land. Upon receiving notice of these offers, the McChesneys sought to exercise their right to purchase the property by tendering $7,820. This amount was exactly twice

---

[6] [4] Thus, by way of illustration, the second possible construction referred to in the text is demonstrated merely by reversing the order of the two key clauses in the second sentence of paragraph (2), viz., "In the event that the case is settled prior to the institution of a suit within thirty (30) days of this date, the client agrees to pay the attorneys $10,000."

[7] [5] We are mindful that the first sentence of paragraph (3) of the agreement provides that the defendants are entitled to a contingent fee if there is "any recovery by way of settlement or trial favorable to the Client. . . ." Neither party argues — and rightly so — that this clause, in the context of the remaining provisions, makes any sense at all.

the assessed value of the property as listed on the tax rolls maintained in Warren County.

Steuart refused to accept the tender, claiming that the exercise price for the Right of First Refusal must be that of the third party offer or fair market value. [In determining the intention of the parties, the court first examined the plain meaning rule:]

> It is well established that the intent of the parties to a written contract is to be regarded as being embodied in the writing itself, and when the words are clear and unambiguous the intent is to be discovered only from the express language of the agreement.

. . . Application of the plain meaning rule of interpretation has, however, been subjected to criticism as being unsound in theory. "The fallacy consists in assuming that there is or ever can be some one real or absolute meaning." 9 WIGMORE, EVIDENCE § 2462 (Chadbourn rev. 1981). "[S]ome of the surrounding circumstances always must be known before the meaning of the words can be plain and clear; and proof of the circumstances may make a meaning plain and clear when in the absence of such proof some other meaning may also have seemed plain and clear." 3 CORBIN, CONTRACTS § 542 (1960). "It is indeed desirable that it be made as difficult as is reasonably feasible for an unscrupulous person to establish a meaning that was foreign to what was in fact understood by the parties to the contract. However, this result can be achieved without the aid of an inflexible rule." MURRAY, CONTRACTS, § 110 (1974). . . .

[The Court cautioned that there are "dangers" posed by the plain meaning rule:]

> We are not unmindful of the dangers of focusing only upon the words of the writing in interpreting an agreement. A court must be careful not to "retire into that lawyer's Paradise where all words have a fixed, precisely ascertained meaning; where men may express their purposes, not only with accuracy, but with fullness; and where, if the writer has been careful, a lawyer, having a document referred to him, may sit in his chair, inspect the text, and answer all questions without raising his eyes." . . . Indeed, whether the language of an agreement is clear and unambiguous may not be apparent without cognizance of the context in which the agreement arose:
>
> > The flexibility of or multiplicity in the meaning of words is the principal source of difficulty in the interpretation of language. Words are the conduits by which thoughts are communicated, yet scarcely any of them have such a fixed and single meaning that they are incapable of denoting more than one thought. In addition to the multiplicity in meaning of words set forth in the dictionaries there are the meanings imparted to them by trade customs, local uses, dialects, telegraphic codes, etc. One meaning crowds a word full of significance, while another almost empties the utterance of any import.

Hurst v. Lake & Co., Inc., 141 Or. 306, 310, 16 P.2d 627, 629 (1932), quoted in 4 WILLISTON, CONTRACTS § 609 (3d. ed. 1961). . . . [Recognizing, however, that] 'It is not the province of the court to alter a contract by construction or to make a new contract for the parties; its duty is confined to the interpretation of the one which they have made for themselves, without regard to its wisdom or folly,' [the court found the language of the Right of First Refusal is] express and clear [and is not] reasonably or fairly susceptible to being understood in more than one sense so as to be regarded as ambiguous. [Consequently, there was no need for] extrinsic clarification.

NOTES & QUESTIONS

1. In examining the rationale behind the plain meaning rule, the court in *Steuart* stressed its role in ensuring the predictable enforcement of contractual obligations:

> The plain meaning approach enhances the extent to which contracts may be relied upon by contributing to the security of belief that the final expression of consensus ad idem will not later be construed to import a meaning other than that clearly expressed. Likewise, resort to the plain meaning of language hinders parties dissatisfied with their agreement from creating a myth as to the true meaning of the agreement through subsequently exposed extrinsic evidence. Absent the plain meaning rule, nary an agreement could be conceived, which, in the event of a party's later disappointment with his stated bargain, would not be at risk to having its true meaning obfuscated under the guise of examining extrinsic evidence of intent. Even if the dissatisfied party in good faith believed that the agreement, as manifest, did not express the consensus ad idem, his post hoc judgment would be inclined to be colored by belief as to what should have been, rather than what strictly was, intended. Hence, the plain meaning approach to interpretation rests upon policies soundly based, and the judiciousness of that approach warrants reaffirmation.

444 A.2d at _.

2. Although parties often attempt to construe a written agreement to "make a better bargain" than the one evidenced by the written document(s), courts rely on the parol evidence rule and the plain meaning rule to reject such reformation attempts. As the court recognized in *Steuart:*

> The court may not rewrite the contract for the of accomplishing that which, in its opinion, may appear proper, or, on general principles of abstract justice . . . make for [the parties] a better contract than they chose, or saw fit, to make for themselves, or remake a contract, under the guise of construction, because it later appears that a different agreement should have been consummated in the first instance. . . .

Id. at _.

3. In determining whether a document is clear on its face, courts often consider whether the written agreement has a patent or latent ambiguity. A patent ambiguity is one which appears on the face of the instrument, and arises from the defective, obscure, or insensible language used. BLACK'S LAW DICTIONARY 105 (rev. 4th ed. 1968). A latent ambiguity "arises from extraneous or collateral facts which make the meaning of a written agreement uncertain even though on its face the language appears clear and unambiguous." *Id.* Latent ambiguities often occur when a writing refers to a particular person or thing and is, consequently, apparently clear on its face, but upon examination of extrinsic evidence, the language could apply to one or more objects or persons. Thus, for example, although an agreement to ship cotton "ex rel Peerless" on its face appears unambiguous, external evidence

shows there are two ships named "Peerless," thereby creating a latent ambiguity. *See Raffles v. Wichelhaus,* discussed in Chapter 5.

4. In holding that an ambiguity is present in an agreement, a court cannot rely upon a strained reading to establish one. Consequently, the meaning of language "cannot be distorted to establish the ambiguity." *Anstead v. Cook,* 291 Pa. 335, 337, 140 A.139, 140 (1927). Nevertheless, as the case below demonstrates, one person's ambiguity is another person's clarity.

ETHYL CORPORATION v. FORCUM-LANNOM ASSOCIATES, INC.
433 N.E.2d 1214 (Ind. App. 1982)

MILLER, Judge:

In the fall of 1977 appellant owner desired to build an addition to his Capitol Products plant in Kentland, Indiana, and to that end contacted appellee builder. On December 22, 1977 the parties executed a written contract whereby the builder would "design and construct" an approximately 45,000 square foot addition to the plant for a sum in excess of $667,700. The contract called for the removal of the west wall of the existing building, resulting in a single, undivided building whose approximate size was in excess of 100,000 square feet. The transaction proceeded without incident until February 17, 1978 when the Indiana State Fire Marshal wrote to the builder and informed him that the builder's plans and specifications for the project did not comply with all required rules and regulations, specifically, that the building "shall have smoke and heat vents . . . in accordance with Sec. 3205, U.B.C. 1973," and "an annunciator panel in accordance with Sec. 3113-E, [Uniform Building Code] 1973." The contract was silent with respect to the vents and annunciator, but the "Scope of the Work" section did specifically obligate the builder to "install an ordinary hazard wet sprinkler fire protection system" in the addition. However, the agreement also provided the "CONTRACTOR. . . shall be responsible for all work which is implicit or accessory to this Scope of Work whether or not such work is expressly called for. . . [a]ll work. . . shall be in conformance with all current and applicable codes, rules, regulations, and standards."

The critical question in this case is whether or not the builder was bound under the contract to pay for the smoke and heat vents and annunciator panel required by the State Fire Marshal. . . .

"In deciding cases involving disputes over the meaning of written contracts, courts resort to the application of rules of construction and the receipt of extrinsic evidence only after their careful study of the entire contract itself has failed to make clear its meaning." *Evansville-Vanderburgh School Corp. v. Moll,* (1976) 264 Ind. 356, 362, 344 N.E.2d 831, 837. In the absence of ambiguity it is not within the function of the judiciary to look outside the instrument to arrive at the parties' intent. In other words Indiana applies the so-called "four corners" rule in the construction of written instruments. This rule provides that in construing written instruments, the express language found within the four corners of the instrument, if unambiguous, determines the intent of the parties such that parol or extrinsic evidence is inadmissible to expand, vary or explain the instrument unless there has been a showing of fraud, mistake, ambiguity, illegality, duress or undue influence (defect in the formation of the contract). While an ambiguous adhesion contract is construed in the non-drafting party's favor, an unambiguous contract must be enforced according to its terms. A contract is ambiguous only where reasonable people could find its terms susceptible to more than one interpretation. *Marksill Specialties, Inc. v. Barger*, (1981) Ind. App., 428 N.E.2d 65. Further, ambiguity is not established by the mere fact the parties assert different interpretations of the contract. Finally, whether an ambiguity exists must be determined by the application of the following principles:

1) Words used in a contract must be given their common meaning unless, from the entire contract and its subject-matter, it is clear that some other meaning was intended, and

2) Words, phrases, sentences and paragraphs of a contract are not to be read alone; the intention of the parties must be gathered from the entire contract.

We find the contract in the present case is not ambiguous as the builder contends because the express language of the instrument taken as a whole shows the parties contemplated the cost of compliance with state administrative regulations and assigned this responsibility to the builder.

The instant agreement stated the "CONTRACTOR [builder] shall provide all required engineering, labor, supervision, materials, construction equipment, tools, facilities and supplies to: design and construct a building addition, equipment foundations and utility services" at the owner's plant in Kentland, Indiana. We noted earlier other significant language in the agreement. It provided, generally, the builder "shall be responsible for all work which is implicit or accessory to this Scope of Work whether or not such work is expressly called for," and "[a]ll work shall be done in a good and workmanlike manner, to the satisfaction of OWNER, and shall be in conformance with all current and applicable codes, rules, regulations, and standards." Moreover, the "General Conditions" section of the contract expressly declared:

PERMITS, REGULATIONS AND RECORDINGS

a. The Contractor (builder) shall give all notices, comply with all laws, ordinances, rules and regulations bearing on the Work. The Contractor agrees to indemnify and hold Owner harmless from any loss, liability or penalty which might be imposed by reason of asserted or established failure of the Contractor or its employees or agents and/or its subcontractors and or their employees or agents to comply with any applicable laws, ordinances, rules or regulations.

Clearly the plain meaning of the contract called for the builder to "design and construct" the addition "in conformance with all current and applicable codes, rules, regulations and standards," and it placed responsibility on the builder for all work "implicit or accessory" to the project. We conclude, therefore, the contract is unambiguous on this issue and thus it would be erroneous to apply rules of construction or to consider extrinsic evidence as there were no allegations or evidence of a defect in the formation of the contract.

NOTES & QUESTIONS

1. Would you reach a different result if the extrinsic evidence included a letter from the contractor dated before the written agreement, clarifying that he would not be responsible for installing additional air vents to conform with any applicable

building codes or regulations?

2. Would you reach a different result if extrinsic evidence demonstrated that the custom in the construction industry was to put the burden on the hiring party to pay for any additions required to meet fire code requirements?

3. The "plain meaning rule," is one principle courts use to determine the meaning of written contracts. Other principles that courts consider include the following:

> 1. *Noscitur a suciis* — the meaning of a word in a series is affected by others in the same series.

> 2. An interpretation that makes the contract valid is preferred to one that makes it invalid.

> 3. The contract should be construed against the draftsman in selecting between potentially conflicting meanings.

> 4. Each term should be interpreted as part of the whole contract, and not in isolation.

> 5. Handwritten provisions generally control over printed ones.

> 6. Specific exceptions are construed to qualify more general provisions.

> 7. Technical terms and words of art are given their technical meaning when used in a transaction within their technical field.

> 8. Express terms are given greater weight than course of performance; specific terms are given greater weight than general language.

> 9. Separately negotiated terms are given greater weight than standardized terms.

> 10. Meanings that serve the public interest are preferred in agreements which affect a public interest.

See generally RESTATEMENT (SECOND) OF CONTRACTS §§ 202-208. *See also* Edwin Patterson, *The Interpretation and Construction of Contracts,* 64 COLUM. L. REV. 833 (1964). Applying these principles to *Ethyl Corp.* would you have reached the same result?

4. When should the failure to include a provision be considered evidence that the subject was not intended to be covered by the written agreement?

5. *Practice Points:* One method for avoiding ambiguity is by looking forward into the future to anticipate possible problems that might arise if performance does not meet the parties' expectations. In using your "crystal ball" to anticipate problems, make a list of unspoken assumptions which the parties are relying on. Be certain your agreement anticipates the failure of those assumptions. For example, in the joint venture agreement which you considered at the beginning of this subsection concerning commercialization of the rapid growth formula, what assumptions did both parties make regarding the ultimate goal of their agreement? What provisions should have been included to resolve problems arising from the disappointment of these expectations? Perhaps the unspoken assumptions should be written down and embodied in the contract, such as in a preamble or "whereas" section introducing the agreement.

PROBLEMS

1. Company B is in the business of constructing low-income housing. It has just been awarded a city contract to construct low-income housing on an unreconstructed lot owned by the city on the outside of town. Company B hires Removal, Inc. to prepare the lot for construction, including "laying all foundations required in accordance with plans filed with the city authorities, which plans are incorporated herein in full by reference." The agreement contains a merger and entirety clause. Removal, Inc. fails to prepare the foundations in accordance with the specified plans. Is the contract ambiguous? What if Removal, Inc. claims that it did not build the foundations because two inconsistent plans were filed with City Hall and the Land Planning Commission. Is the contract ambiguous then?

2. Removal, Inc. has constructed the foundations in accordance with the specifications filed at the Land Planning Commission. Company B claims that the plans referred to in the written document were those filed with City Hall and wants to present evidence regarding prior negotiations, course of dealing, and industry meaning to support its claims. Can it do so?

3. Paul agrees to hire Terry as a tutor in the art school which he owns and operates. According to the written agreement, Terry will be paid "on an hourly basis for her work as an individual tutor for students enrolled in the Art School at a rate of $25/hour." The agreement further provides that Terry "will be reimbursed for the cost of all materials used in connection with her tutoring activities." While employed by the Art School, Terry tutored Ruth and Bob in joint tutoring sessions. Paul has refused to pay Terry $25/hour for each student. He has also refused to reimburse her for the art supplies she bought. He claims the school has a policy against reimbursing supplies that are available from the school store. Terry has sued Paul for breach of contract and is seeking both the extra $25/hour for tutoring and the cost of her supplies. What result?

D. THE PAROL EVIDENCE RULE AND RELIANCE ON THE WRITTEN WORD

Despite early common law declarations of the parol evidence rule that excluded consideration of extrinsic evidence where a written instrument contained no ambiguity on its face and was intended as a complete expression of the parties' agreement, as you have seen from previous cases, the application of the rule has proven problematic. The parol evidence rule remains a major source of conflict in contract law. So many potential exceptions exist to this rule that some courts have questioned whether it qualifies as a "rule" at all. *See Zell v. American Seating Co.,* 138 F.2d 641, 643–44 (2d Cir. 1943). The parol evidence rule itself has been phrased in a variety of ways. Among those versions of the rule that are most often relied upon in interpreting contracts are the following:

(A) Common law formulation:

When parties have deliberately put their engagements in writing, and such writing is complete on its face, and is certain and definite as to the objects of their engagement, . . . [the written contract] cannot be contradicted, altered, added to, or varied by parol or extrinsic evidence.

Busnell v. Elkins, 34 Wyo. 495, 502, 245 P. 304, 306 (1926).

(B) RESTATEMENT (FIRST) OF CONTRACTS formulation:

[T]he integration of an agreement makes inoperative to add to or to vary the agreement all contemporaneous oral agreements relating to the same subject-matter; and also, unless the integration is void, or voidable and avoided, all prior oral or written agreements relating thereto.

RESTATEMENT (FIRST) OF CONTRACTS § 237 (1932).

(C) Williston's formulation:

Briefly stated, this rule requires, in the absence of fraud, duress, mutual mistake, or something of the kind, the exclusion of extrinsic evidence, oral or written, where the parties have reduced their agreement to an integrated writing.

4 WILLISTON ON CONTRACTS § 631 (1961).

(D) RESTATEMENT (SECOND) OF CONTRACTS formulation:

The interpretation of an integrated agreement is directed to the meaning of the terms of the writing or writings in the light of the circumstances. . . .

RESTATEMENT (SECOND) OF CONTRACTS § 212(2).

(E) Corbin's formulation:

When two parties have made a contract and have expressed it in a writing to which they have both assented as the complete and accurate integration of that contract, evidence, whether parol or otherwise, of antecedent understandings and negotiations will not be admitted for the purpose of varying or contradicting the writing.

3A CORBIN ON CONTRACTS § 573 (rev. ed. 1960).

(F) Uniform Commercial Code formulation:

Final Written Expression: Parol or Extrinsic Evidence.-Terms with respect to which the confirmatory memoranda of the parties agree or which are otherwise set forth in a writing intended by the parties as a final expression of their agreement with respect to such terms as are included therein may not be contradicted by evidence of any prior agreement or of a contemporaneous oral agreement but may be explained or supplemented

(a) by course of dealing or usage of trade . . . or by course of performance. . . and

(b) by evidence of consistent additional terms unless the court finds the writing to have been intended also as a complete and exclusive statement of the terms of the agreement.

U.C.C. § 2-202.

While these formulations share significant similarities, they also have marked differences that underscore the major problems with the so-called *parol evidence rule*. Among the major differences in various courts' reliance upon extrinsic evidence in determining the parties' intent are: (1) the emphasis placed upon the need for a patent ambiguity before extrinsic evidence may be considered; (2) the lack of suspicion with which extrinsic evidence is viewed in determining latent ambiguities; (3) the role of industry meaning, trade usage and custom in interpreting potentially unambiguous terms; (4) the balance struck between the need for predictability and fairness when the written document appears one-sided; and (5) the presence of fraud or mutual mistake.

ESKIMO PIE CORPORATION v. WHITELAWN DAIRIES, INC.
284 F. Supp. 987 (S.D.N.Y. 1968)

Mansfield, District Judge:

The actions arise out of written contracts between Eskimo Pie Corporation ("Eskimo" herein), Whitelawn Dairies, Inc. ("Whitelawn" herein) and Supermarket Advisory Sales, Inc. ('SAS' herein) (Whitelawn and SAS are collectively referred to herein as "Whitelawn-SAS") entered into on or about December 30, 1960, and modified in various respects in 1961 and 1962. These contracts are referred to by the parties as the "Package Deal." All parties agree that the Package Deal is an integrated agreement setting forth in several writings all of the essential terms agreed upon by Eskimo and Whitelawn-SAS. Under the terms of the Package Deal Eskimo granted to Whitelawn, an ice cream manufacturer, the right to manufacture certain ice cream products bearing "Eskimo" wrappers and labels and to SAS the right to purchase such Eskimo-branded products from Eskimo or an Eskimo-authorized manufacturer for sale in the New York City Metropolitan Area as follows:

> During the term of this Agreement [SAS] shall have the non-exclusive right to purchase the Eskimo stock and stickless products listed in Exhibit A hereto, which may be amended from time to time by addition or deletion, from Eskimo or from a manufacturer authorized by Eskimo to manufacture such products within the New York City metropolitan area. . . .

The present lawsuits were instituted after Eskimo, beginning sometime in 1962 and 1963, sold its Eskimo-branded products to others in the New York City Metropolitan Area, and entered into agreements with M. H. Renken Dairy Co. ("Renken" herein) to manufacture, and with Food Enterprises, Inc. ("Food Enterprises" herein) to sell, such products, and assisted Harry L. Darnstaedt and Imperial Ice Cream Novelties, Inc. ("Imperial" herein) in selling such products in the New York City Metropolitan Area. This led to a deterioration in the relationship between the parties to the Package Deal; a purported termination by Whitelawn and SAS of purchases and sales thereunder; and mutual claims of breach of contract, since Whitelawn and SAS appear to have refused to accept and pay for certain products. . . .

A threshold question, which appears to be central to the entire dispute between the parties, arises out of the meaning of the word "non-exclusive" as used in the above quotation from the Package Deal, and the proposal of Whitelawn-SAS to offer parol evidence with respect to its meaning. Whitelawn and SAS contend that the word "non-exclusive" as used in the Package Deal meant that Eskimo would have the right to continue existing licenses granted by it to others in the New York City Metropolitan Area and to grant new licenses to national companies (such as the Borden Company, National Dairy Products Corporation), but not to grant licenses to so called "independent" companies unless required to do so by order of a court or governmental agency, and that Eskimo itself was not to compete with Whitelawn and SAS in the sale of Eskimo-branded ice cream products. Eskimo denies such contentions as to the meaning of the word "non-exclusive" and asserts that it plainly meant that Eslumo was granting a bare non-exclusive right to Whitelawn and SAS to manufacture and sell Eskimo products, while retaining the unfettered right to license others as it saw fit to manufacture and sell Eskimo-branded ice cream products.

Whitelawn-SAS proposes . . . to introduce not only the written agreements constituting the Package Deal, but also parol and extrinsic evidence as to what the parties understood and intended the term "non-exclusive" to mean, including earlier drafts of the Package Deal, correspondence and conversations between the parties leading up to its execution, and subsequent conduct of the parties, including a letter written by Darnstaedt on February 12, 1963 stating that the parties "had a gentlemen's agreement that Eskimo would not solicit any stick franchises in New York City except any of the national companies that Eskimo is serving around the country." More specifically, Whitelawn-SAS would offer testimony of its lawyers and others who negotiated the Package Deal on its behalf to the effect that earlier drafts, including one submitted by an Eskimo official named Gunn (now deceased) contained a clause which would have obligated Eskimo not to license or franchise the Eskimo mark, or sell Eskimo-branded ice cream products, to anyone in the New York City Metropolitan Area other than existing licensees or national dairy organizations, unless Eskimo should be required to do so by court or governmental order; that thereafter Eskimo refused to sign an agreement containing the express clause because of a fear expressed by Eskimo's counsel that the proposed clause might violate the federal antitrust laws; and that accordingly, after a series of conferences, the proposed clause was deleted on the understanding that its meaning would be deemed incorporated into the word "non-exclusive" used in the above quoted license to Whitelawn-SAS. . . .

Whitelawn-SAS argues that parol evidence should be admitted on the ground that the term "non-exclusive" is ambiguous, and that even if it in fact lacks ambiguity such evidence may be received to show that the parties gave the term special or particular meaning not to be gathered from the language by a reasonably intelligent person having knowledge of the custom, usage and surrounding circumstances. In support of their position, Whitelawn-SAS relies principally on § 2-202 of the Uniform Commercial Code ("U.C.C." herein). . . .

Section 2-202 of New York's U.C.C. provides:

> Terms with respect to which the confirmatory memoranda of the parties agree or which are otherwise set forth in a writing intended by the parties as a final expression of their agreement with respect to such terms as are included therein may not be contradicted by evidence of any prior agreement or of a contemporaneous oral agreement but may be explained or supplemented
>
> (a) by course of dealing or usage of trade (§ 1-205) or by course of performance (§ 2-208). . . .

Since the Package Deal predated the effective date of the U.C.C., and since the U.C.C. was not intended to have retroactive effect, § 2-202 does not apply and the Court must look to prior law.

. . . The courts of New York have never subscribed to the view that, in the absence of ambiguity, evidence as to the subjective intent of the parties may be substituted for the plain meaning that would otherwise be ascribed to the language of a written agreement by a reasonably intelligent person having knowledge of the surrounding circumstances, customs and usages. On the contrary, prior New York law adhered to time-honored objective standards to determine the meaning of language found in writings which represent as did the Package Deal here the final and complete integrated agreement reached by the parties. *Mitchell v. Lath*, 247 N.Y. 377, 160 N.E. 646, 648 (1928). The cardinal principles forming the cornerstone of those standards are (1) that the meaning to be attributed to the language of such an instrument is that which a reasonably intelligent person acquainted with general usage, custom and the surrounding circumstances would attribute to it; and (2) that in the absence of ambiguity parol evidence will not be admitted to determine the meaning that is to be attributed to such language. . . .

[P]lain meanings may not be changed by parol, and the courts will not make a new contract for the parties under the guise of interpreting the writing. . . .

The first question to be determined in the present case, therefore, is whether the term "non-exclusive" as used in the Package Deal is ambiguous, which must be decided by the Court. An "ambiguous" word or phrase is one capable of more than one meaning when viewed objectively by a reasonably intelligent person who has examined the context of the entire integrated agreement and who is cognizant of the customs, practices, usages and terminology as generally understood in the particular trade or business. In the absence of proof that the term "non-exclusive" could possibly have the meaning, among others, attributed to it by Whitelawn-SAS, parol evidence must be excluded.

Applying the foregoing principles, the word "non-exclusive" when used — as was the case here — in an integrated license agreement drafted by legal counsel, has an established legal meaning that is usually accepted in the absence of a qualifying context, custom, usage or similar surrounding circumstance. The term has repeatedly been defined as meaning that the licensee is granted a bare right to use the trademark or patent being licensed without any right to exclude others, including other licensees taking from the grantor, from utilizing the mark or invention involved. . . .

Despite the meaning thus usually ascribed by the law to the term "non-exclusive" Whitelawn-SAS urge that here the legal draftsmen intended it to have a contrary meaning. . . . In a business world not noted for its economy of language (the Package Deal covers 70 typewritten pages, including amendments) no business reason, custom or usage is advanced for attaching such an elaborate and paradoxical meaning to the term "non-exclusive," when legal counsel negotiating for both sides could easily have spelled out such specifics in comprehensible terms. Whitelawn-SAS's assertion that the term was used to conceal a detailed secret "gentlemen's agreement" that was feared by Eskimo to violate the antitrust laws hardlycomports with the word's having a secondary meaning as a matter of generalized trade usage or custom. On the contrary, such evidence would indicate that the term, despite the definite and plain meaning usually attributed to it, was being used to express a particular, subjective meaning initially conceived by the parties solely for the purpose at hand, and not because the term would be recognized by others as having such a special meaning. Unless the language is meaningless on its face (e.g. "abracadabra") or ambiguous, however, the test for admission of parol evidence is not a secret code meaning given to it by the parties but whether it might objectively be recognized by a reasonably intelligent person acquainted with applicable customs, usages and the surrounding circumstances as having such a special meaning. . . . If the law were otherwise, not only the term "non-exclusive" but every apparently clear term in a written agreement, such as a specific purchase price (e.g., "$10,000") could be changed by secret oral agreement to mean something different (e.g., "$25,000").

Nevertheless, although the term "non-exclusive" as used in the Package Deal does not on its face appear to be ambiguous, Whitelawn-SAS will be afforded the opportunity to offer proof showing that the term is ambiguous, and Eskimo the opportunity to rebut such proof. In accordance with the principles hereinabove outlined, proof on the issue of ambiguity may encompass the terms of the Package Deal itself, the surrounding circumstances, common usage and custom as to the meaning attributed to it, and subsequent conduct of the parties under the Package Deal, but evidence of the subjective understanding of the parties as to the meaning attributed by them to the term "non-exclusive" will not be received. . . .

So ordered.

NOTES & QUESTIONS

1. The court in *Eskimo Pie* did not apply the U.C.C. to the package deal because it predated the adoption of the U.C.C. Assuming the U.C.C. applied, could the court consider the extra-contractual evidence? If it did so, what result would it have reached?

2. Although the court in *Eskimo Pie* rejected any party's efforts to alter the clear and unambiguous meaning of a contract's terms by "secret agreement," it still agreed to consider extrinsic evidence. If the evidence shows that a "secret agreement" existed regarding the meaning of "non-exclusive," should the plaintiff's claim succeed?

3. Some of the extrinsic evidence which the plaintiff tried to rely on in *Eskimo Pie* post-dated the execution of the written agreement. In its purest form, the parol evidence rule only applies to prior and contemporaneous agreements. It does not, theoretically, bar the introduction of post-execution evidence of intent. Nor does it bar evidence of subsequent modification of a contract.

4. Contrast *Eskimo Pie* with *Hurst v. W.J. Luke & Co., Inc.*, 16 P.2d 627 (Ore. 1932). On March 20, 1930, the plaintiff and the defendant entered into a written agreement for the purchase of "horsemeat scraps . . . Minimum 50% protein, ground and sacked in 100 lb. net each." In a separate contemporaneous letter, Hurst stated:

> Dear Sir: In case any of the Horse Meat Scraps, covered by our purchase order No. 1352 analyzes less than 50% of protein, it is understood that W. J. Lake & Company, Inc., the buyers, are to receive a discount of $5.00 per ton.

Pursuant to the contract, the plaintiff delivered to the defendant 349.25 tons of horse meat scraps which contained the following percentages of protein, and for which the defendant paid the following sums of money:

180 tons contained an excess of 50 per cent. protein, and the defendant paid for it $50 per ton; 29.25 tons contained 48.66 per cent. protein, and the defendant paid therefor $45 per ton; 140 tons contained protein varying from 49.53 per cent. to 49.96 per cent., for which the defendant paid $45 per ton.

Extrinsic evidence proved that both parties had long been engaged in the buying and selling of horse meat scraps and that at the time the agreement was entered into there was a "custom and usage of trade that . . . the terms 'minimum 50% protein' and 'less than 50% protein' when used in a contract for the sale of horse meat scraps meant that a protein content of not less than 49.5% was equal to and the same as a content of 50% protein."

The court rejected the defendant's contention that the absence of ambiguity on the face of the contract precluded consideration of trade usage in defining the terms used in the written agreement. Recognizing that a rule which rejects evidence of custom "has the advantage of simplicity," the court nevertheless found that "in the absence of evidence to the contrary . . . when tradesmen employ trade terms, they attach to them their trade significance." The court stated:

> The flexibility of or multiplicity in the meaning of words is the principal source of difficulty in the interpretation of language. Words are the conduits by which thoughts are communicated, yet scarcely any of them have such a fixed and single meaning that they are incapable of denoting more than one thought. In addition to the multiplicity in meaning of words set forth in the dictionaries, there are the meanings imparted to them by trade customs, local uses, dialects, telegraphic codes, etc. One meaning crowds a word full of significance, while another almost empties the utterance of any import. Various groups . . . are constantly amplifying our language; in fact, they are developing what may be called languages of their own. Thus one is justified in saying that the language of the dictionaries is not the only language spoken in America. For instance, the word "thousand" as commonly used has a very specific meaning; it denotes ten hundreds or fifty scores, but the language of the various trades and localities has assigned to it meanings quite different from that just mentioned. Thus in the bricklaying trade a contract which fixes the bricklayer's compensation at "$5.25 a thousand" does not contemplate that he need lay actually 1,000 bricks in order to earn $5.25, but that he should build a wall of a certain size. . . . Thus it must be evident that one cannot understand accurately the language of such sciences and trades without knowing the peculiar meaning attached to the words which they use. It is said that a court in construing the language of the parties must put itself into the shoes of the parties. That alone would not suffice; it must also adopt their vernacular.

> Where tradesmen use trade terms and "mean to strip the terms of their special significance and demote them to their common import, it would seem reasonable to believe that they would so state in their agreement. Otherwise they would refrain from using the trade term and express themselves in other language. . . . So (with Prof. Williston) we think that any one contracting with knowledge of a usage will naturally say nothing about the matter unless desirous of excluding its operation; if he does wish to exclude, he will say so in express terms."

5. *Practice Points:* If there is a special meaning that the parties attach to a particular word or phrase, that meaning should be specified in the written contract to avoid subsequent disputes. Indeed, you should consider whether to include a "definitions" section in a contract, where you would gather all words and phrases that need to be defined or explained.

6. *Practice Points:* In order to determine if there are special meanings, all important terms of an agreement should be clarified during negotiations so that the contract can reflect the actual intention of the parties. Such clarification will reduce subsequent disputes. Be sure to retain all drafts of a contract in the file until the contract has expired and the period of limitations for possible legal actions has run.

COLUMBIA NITROGEN CORPORATION v. ROYSTER COMPANY
451 F.2d 3 (4th Cir. 1971)

BUTZNER, Circuit Judge:

Columbia Nitrogen Corp. appeals a judgment in the amount of $750,000 in favor of F. S. Royster Guano Co. for breach of a contract for the sale of phosphate to Columbia by Royster. Columbia defended on the grounds that the contract, construed in light of the usage of the trade and course of dealing, imposed no duty to accept at the quoted prices the minimum quantities stated in the contract. . . . The jury found for Royster on . . . the contract claim. . . .

Royster manufactures and markets mixed fertilizers, the principal components of which are nitrogen, phosphate and potash. Columbia is primarily a producer of nitrogen, although it manufactures some mixed fertilizer. For several years Royster had been a major purchaser of Columbia's products, but Columbia had never been a significant customer of Royster. In the fall of 1966, Royster constructed a facility which enabled it to produce more phosphate than it needed in its own operations. After extensive negotiations, the companies executed a contract for Royster's sale of a minimum of 31,000 tons of phosphate each year for three years to Columbia, with an option to extend the term. The contract stated the price per ton, subject to an escalation clause dependent on production costs.[8]

---

[8] [2] In pertinent part, the contract provides:

"Contract made as of this 8th day of May between COLUMBIA NITROGEN CORPO-RATION, a Delaware corporation, (hereinafter called the Buyer) hereby agrees to purchase and accept from F. S. ROYSTER GUANO COMPANY, a Virginia corporation, (hereinafter called the Seller) agrees to furnish quantities of Diammonium Phosphate 18-46-0, Granular Triple Superphosphate 0-46-0, and Run-of-Pile Triple Superphosphate 0-46-0 on the following terms and conditions.

"Period Covered by Contract-This contract to begin July 1, 1967, and continue through June 30, 1970, with renewal privileges for an additional three year period based upon notification by Buyer and acceptance by Seller on or before June 30, 1969. Failure of notification by either party on or before June 30, 1969, constitutes an automatic renewal for an additional one-year period beyond June 30, 1970, and on a year-to-year basis thereafter unless notification of cancellation is given by either party 90 days prior to June 30 of each year.

"Products Supplied Under Contract

Minimum Tonnage Per Year

Diammonium Phosphate 18-46-0 15,000

Granular Triple Superphosphate 0-46-0 15,000

Run-of-Pile Triple Superphosphate 0-46-0 1,000

"Seller agrees to provide additional quantities beyond the minimum specified tonnage for

Phosphate prices soon plunged precipitously. Unable to resell the phosphate at a competitive price, Columbia ordered only part of the scheduled tonnage. At Columbia's request, Royster lowered its price for diammonium phosphate on shipments for three months in 1967, but specified that subsequent shipments would be at the original contract price. Even with this concession, Royster's price was still substantially above the market. As a result, Columbia ordered less than a tenth of the phosphate Royster was to ship in the first contract year. When pressed by Royster, Columbia offered to take the phosphate at the current market price and resell it without brokerage fee. Royster, however, insisted on the contract price. When Columbia refused delivery, Royster sold the unaccepted phosphate for Columbia's account at a price substantially below the contract price.

Columbia . . . offered the testimony of witnesses with long experience in the trade that because of uncertain crop and weather conditions, farming practices, and government agricultural programs, express price and quantity terms in contracts for materials in the mixed fertilizer industry are mere projections to be adjusted according to market forces.

Columbia also offered proof of its business dealings with Royster over the six-year period preceding the phosphate contract. Since Columbia had not been a significant purchaser of Royster's products, these dealings were almost exclusively nitrogen sales to Royster or exchanges of stock carried in inventory. The pattern which emerges, Columbia claimed, is one of repeated and substantial deviation from the stated amount or price, including four instances where Royster took none of the goods for which it had contracted. Columbia offered proof that the total variance amounted to more than $500,000 in reduced sales. This experience, a Columbia officer offered to testify, formed the basis of an understanding on which he depended in conducting negotiations with Royster.

---

products listed above provided Seller has the capacity and ability to provide such additional quantities.

* * *

"Price-In Bulk F.O.B. Cars, Royster, Florida.

Diammonium Phosphate 18-46-0

Granular Triple Superphosphate 0-46-0 $40.90 Per Ton

Run-of-Pile Triple Superphosphate 0-46-0 $0.86 Per Unit

"Default — If Buyer fails to pay for any delivery under this contract within 30 days after Seller's invoice to Buyer and then if such invoice is not paid within an additional 30 days after the Seller notifies the Buyer of such default, then after that time the Seller may at his option defer further deliveries hereunder or take such action as in their judgment they may decide including cancellation of this contract.

Any balances carried beyond 30 days will carry a service fee of ¾ of 1% per month.

* * *

"Escalation — The escalation factor up or down shall be based upon the effects of changing raw material cost of sulphur, rock phosphate, and labor as follows.

These escalations up or down to become effective against shipments of products covered by this contract 30 days after notification by Seller to Buyer.

* * *

"No verbal understanding will be recognized by either party hereto; this contract expresses all the terms and conditions of the agreement, shall be signed in duplicate and shall not become operative until approved in writing by the Seller."

The district court held that the evidence should be excluded. It ruled that "custom and usage or course of dealing are not admissible to contradict the express, plain, unambiguous language of a valid written contract, which by virtue of its detail negates the proposition that the contract is open to variances in its terms. . . ."

A number of Virginia cases have held that extrinsic evidence may not be received to explain or supplement a written contract unless the court finds the writing is ambiguous. This rule, however, has been changed by the Uniform Commercial Code which Virginia has adopted. The Code expressly states that it "shall be liberally construed and applied to promote its underlying purposes and policies," which include "the continued expansion of commercial practices through custom, usage and agreement of the parties. . ." Va. Code Ann. § 8.1-102 (1965).

The importance of usage of trade and course of dealing between the parties is shown by § 8.2-202, which authorizes their use to explain or supplement a contract. The official comment states this section rejects the old rule that evidence of course of dealing or usage of trade can be introduced only when the contract is ambiguous. . . . We hold, therefore, that a finding of ambiguity is not necessary for the admission of extrinsic evidence about the usage of the trade and the parties' course of dealing.

We turn next to Royster's claim that Columbia's evidence was properly excluded because it was inconsistent with the express terms of their agreement. There can be no doubt that the Uniform Commercial Code restates the well established rule that evidence of usage of trade and course of dealing should be excluded whenever it cannot be reasonably construed as consistent with the terms of the contract. Royster argues that the evidence should be excluded as inconsistent because the contract contains detailed provisions regarding the base price, escalation, minimum tonnage, and delivery schedules. The argument is based on the premise that because a contract appears on its face to be complete, evidence of course of dealing and usage of trade should be excluded. We believe, however, that neither the language nor the policy of the Code supports such a broad exclusionary rule. § 8.2-202 expressly allows evidence of course of dealing or usage of trade to explain or supplement terms intended by the parties as a final expression of their agreement. When this section is read in light of Va. Code. Ann. § 8.1-205(4),[9] it is clear that the test of admissibility is not whether the contract appears on its face to be complete in every detail, but whether the proffered evidence of course of dealing and trade usage reasonably can be construed as consistent with the express terms of the agreement.

The proffered testimony sought to establish that because of changing weather conditions, farming practices, and government agricultural programs, dealers adjusted prices, quantities, and delivery schedules to reflect declining market conditions. For the following reasons it is reasonable to construe this evidence as consistent with the express terms of the contract:

> The contract does not expressly state that course of dealing and usage of trade cannot be used to explain or supplement the written contract.

---

[9] [7] Va. Code Ann. § 8.1-205(4) states: "The express terms of an agreement and an applicable course of dealing or usage of trade shall be construed wherever reasonable as consistent with each other; but when such construction is unreasonable express terms control both course of dealing and usage of trade and course of dealing controls usage of trade."

The contract is silent about adjusting prices and quantities to reflect a declining market. It neither permits nor prohibits adjustment, and this neutrality provides a fitting occasion for recourse to usage of trade and prior dealing to supplement the contract and explain its terms.

Minimum tonnages and additional quantities are expressed in terms of "Products Supplied Under Contract." Significantly, they are not expressed as just "Products" or as "Products Purchased Under Contract." The description used by the parties is consistent with the proffered testimony.

Finally, the default clause of the contract refers only to the failure of the buyer to pay for delivered phosphate. During the contract negotiations, Columbia rejected a Royster proposal for liquidated damages of $10 for each ton Columbia declined to accept. On the other hand, Royster rejected a Columbia proposal for a clause that tied the price to the market by obligating Royster to conform its price to offers Columbia received from other phosphate producers. The parties, having rejected both proposals, failed to state any consequences of Columbia's refusal to take delivery — the kind of default Royster alleges in this case. Royster insists that we span this hiatus by applying the general law of contracts permitting recovery of damages upon the buyer's refusal to take delivery according to the written provisions of the contract. This solution is not what the Uniform Commercial Code prescribes. Before allowing damages, a court must first determine whether the buyer has in fact defaulted. It must do this by supplementing and explaining the agreement with evidence of trade usage and course of dealing that is consistent with the contract's express terms. VA. CODE ANN. §§ 8.1-205(4), 8.2-202. Faithful adherence to this mandate reflects the reality of the market-place and avoids the overly legalistic interpretations which the Code seeks to abolish.

Nor can we accept Royster's contention that the testimony should be excluded under the contract clause:

> No verbal understanding will be recognized by either party hereto; this contract expresses all the terms and conditions of the agreement, shall be signed in duplicate, and shall not become operative until approved in writing by the Seller.

Course of dealing and trade usage are not synonymous with verbal understandings, terms and conditions. § 8.2-202 draws a distinction between supplementing a written contract by consistent additional terms and supplementing it by course of dealing or usage of trade. Evidence of additional terms must be excluded when "the court finds the writing to have been intended also as a complete and exclusive statement of the terms of the agreement." Significantly, no similar limitation is placed on the introduction of evidence of course of dealing or usage of trade. Indeed the official comment notes that course of dealing and usage of trade, unless carefully negated, are admissible to supplement the terms of any writing, and that contracts are to be read on the assumption that these elements were taken for granted when the document was phrased.[10] Since the Code assigns course of dealing and trade

---

[10] [10] Va. Code Ann. § 8.2-202, Comment 2 states:

> Paragraph (a) [of § 8.2-202] makes admissible evidence of course of dealing, usage of trade and course of performance to explain or supplement the terms of any writing stating the

usage unique and important roles, they should not be conclusively rejected by reading them into stereotyped language that makes no specific reference to them. Indeed, the Code's official commentators urge that overly simplistic and overly legalistic interpretation of a contract should be shunned.[11]

We conclude, therefore, that Columbia's evidence about course of dealing and usage of trade should have been admitted. Its exclusion requires that the judgment against Columbia must be set aside and the case retried.

NOTES & QUESTIONS

1. If ambiguity on the face of the written document were required, would the evidence of course of dealing have been admitted in *Columbia Nitrogen?* Does the course of performance or course of dealing between two parties as to one type of contract become the trade usage between those parties as to all types of contract between them?

2. Assume that the U.C.C. has not been adopted. Would the RESTATEMENT (SECOND) OF CONTRACTS have allowed admission of evidence of course of dealing?

3. Would it matter if one of the parties was not aware of industry custom?

4. What evidence is required to establish a trade usage or custom sufficient to be read into a contact as part of the intention of the parties? Scholars have criticized *Columbia Nitrogen* for allowing the introduction of evidence of a usage that was not sufficiently well-established and that was not clearly applicable to the particular facts of so detailed a contract. *See* Roger Kirst, *Usage of Trade and Course of Dealing: Subversion of the U.C.C. Theory,* 1977 LAW FORM 811; Note, *Commercial Law Course of Dealing and Usage of Trade Affect Express Terms,* 1973 WIS. L. REV. 934.

5. *Practice Points:* Notice the importance in the previous case of the contents of previous drafts of a contract. Although we made this point before, it is so important as to be worth repeating.

NANAKULI PAVING AND ROCK COMPANY v. SHELL OIL COMPANY, INC.
664 F.2d 772 (9th Cir. 1981)

HOFFMAN, District Judge:

---

agreement of the parties in order that the true understanding of the parties as to the agreement may be reached. Such writings are to be read on the assumption that the course of prior dealings between the parties and the usages of trade were taken for granted when the document was phrased. Unless carefully negated they have become an element of the meaning of the words used. Similarly, the course of actual performance by the parties is considered the best indication of what they intended the writing to mean.

See also Levie, *Trade Usage and Custom under the Common Law and the Uniform Commercial Code,* 40 N.Y.U. L. REV. 1101, 1111 (1965).

[11] [11] Referring to the general provisions about course of dealing and trade usage, Va. Code Ann. § 8.1-205, Comment 1 states: "This Act rejects both the 'lay dictionary' and the 'conveyancer's' reading of a commercial agreement. Instead the meaning of the agreement of the parties is to be determined by the language used by them and by their actions, read and interpreted in the light of commercial practices and other surrounding circumstances. The measure and background for interpretation are set by the commercial context, which may explain and supplement even the language of a formal or final writing."

Appellant Nanakuli Paving and Rock Company (Nanakuli) initially filed this breach of contract action against appellee Shell Oil Company (Shell) in Hawaiian State Court in February, 1976. Nanakuli, the second largest asphaltic paving contractor in Hawaii, had bought all its asphalt requirements from 1963 to 1974 from Shell under two long-term supply contracts; its suit charged Shell with breach of the later 1969 contract.[12] The jury returned a verdict of $220,800 for Nanakuli on its first claim, which is that Shell breached the 1969 contract in January, 1974, by failing to price protect Nanakuli on 7200 tons of asphalt at the time Shell raised the price for asphalt from $44 to $76. Nanakuli's theory is that price-protection, as a usage of the asphaltic paving trade in Hawaii, was incorporated into the 1969 agreement between the parties, as demonstrated by the routine use of price protection by suppliers to that trade, and reinforced by the way in which Shell actually performed the 1969 contract up until 1974. Price protection, appellant claims, required that Shell hold the price on the tonnage Nanakuli had already committed because Nanakuli had incorporated that price into bids put out to or contracts awarded by general contractors and government agencies. . . .

Nanakuli . . . argues [that] all material suppliers to the asphaltic paving trade in Hawaii followed the trade usage of price protection and thus it should be assumed, under the U.C.C., that the parties intended to incorporate price protection into their 1969 agreement. This is so, Nanakuli continues, even though the written contract provided for price to be "Shell's Posted Price at time of delivery," F.O.B. Honolulu. Its proof of a usage that was incorporated into the contract is reinforced by evidence of the commercial context, which under the U.C.C. should form the background for viewing a particular contract. The full agreement must be examined in light of the close, almost symbiotic relations between Shell and Nanakuli on the island of Oahu, whereby the expansion of Shell on the island was intimately connected to the business growth of Nanakuli. The U.C.C. looks to the actual performance of a contract as the best indication of what the parties intended those terms to mean. Nanakuli points out that Shell had price protected it on the two occasions of price increases under the 1969 contract other than the 1974 increase. In 1970 and 1971 Shell extended the old price for four and three months, respectively, after an announced increase. This was done, in the words of Shell's agent in Hawaii, in order to permit Nanakuli to "chew up" tonnage already committed at Shell's old price.[13]

Shell presents three arguments for upholding the judgment n.o.v. or, on cross appeal, urging that the District Judge erred in admitting certain evidence. First, it says, the District Court should not have denied Shell's motion in limine to define trade, for purposes of trade usage evidence, as the sale and purchase of asphalt in Hawaii, rather than expanding the definition of trade to include other suppliers of materials to the asphaltic paving trade. Asphalt, its argument runs, was the subject matter of the disputed contract and the only product Shell supplied to the asphaltic

---

[12] [2] The parties agree this act is governed by the Uniform Commercial Code, as enacted in HAWAII REV. STAT. § 490:1-101 *et seq.*

[13] [4] Price protection was practiced in the asphaltic paving trade by either extending the old price for a period of time after a new one went into effect or charging the old price for a specified tonnage, which represented work committed at the old price, In addition, several months' advance notice was given of price increases.

paving trade.[14] Shell protests that the judge, by expanding the definition of trade to include the other major suppliers to the asphaltic paving trade, allowed the admission of highly prejudicial evidence of routine price protection by all suppliers of aggregate. Asphaltic concrete paving is formed by mixing paving asphalt with crushed rock, or aggregate, in a "hot-mix" plant and then pouring the mixture onto the surface to be paved. Shell's second complaint is that the two prior occasions on which it price protected Nanakuli, although representing the only other instances of price increases under the 1969 contract, constituted mere waivers of the contract's price term, not a course of performance of the contract. A course of performance of the contract, in contrast to a waiver, demonstrates how the parties understand the terms of their agreement. Shell cites two U.C.C. Comments in support of that argument: (1) that, when the meaning of acts is ambiguous, the preference is for the waiver interpretation, and (2) that one act alone does not constitute a relevant course of performance. Shell's final argument is that, even assuming its prior price protection constituted a course of performance and that the broad trade definition was correct and evidence of trade usages by aggregate suppliers was admissible, price protection could not be construed as reasonably consistent with the express price term in the contract, in which case the Code provides that the express term controls.

We hold that the judge did not abuse his discretion in defining the applicable trade, for purposes of trade usages, as the asphaltic paving trade in Hawaii, rather than the purchase and sale of asphalt alone, given the unusual, not to say unique, circumstances: the smallness of the marketplace on Oahu; the existence of only two suppliers on the island; the long and intimate connection between the two companies on Oahu, including the background of how the development of Shell's asphalt sales on Oahu was inextricably linked to Nanakuli's own expansion on the island; the knowledge of the aggregate business on the part of Shell's Hawaiian representative, Bohner; his awareness of the economics of Nanakuli's bid estimates, which included only two major materials, asphalt and aggregate; his familiarity with realities of the Hawaiian market-place in which all government agencies refused to include escalation clauses in contract awards and thus pavers would face tremendous losses on price increases if all their material suppliers did not routinely offer them price protection; and Shell's determination to build Nanakuli up to compete for those lucrative government contracts with the largest paver on the island, Hawaiian Bitumuls (H.B.), which was supplied by the only other asphalt company on the islands, Chevron, and which was routinely price protected on materials. We base our holding on the reading of the Code Comments as defining trade more broadly than the transaction and as binding parties not only to usages of their particular trade but also to usages of trade in general in a given locality. This latter seems an equitable application of usage evidence where the usage is almost universally practiced in a small market such as was Oahu in the 1960's before Shell signed its 1969 contract with Nanakuli. Additionally, we hold

---

[14] [5] Shell's argument would, in effect, eliminate all trade usage evidence. First, it argues that its own acts were irrelevant as mere waivers, not acts in the course of the performance of the contract. Second, it contends that all acts of price protection by the only other asphalt supplier in Hawaii, Chevron, the marketing division of Standard Oil Company, were irrelevant to prove trade usage because Chevron at one time owned all or part of the paving company it supplied and routinely price protected Hawaiian Bitumuls (H.B.). The court correctly refused to bar that evidence since the one-time relationship between the two went to the weight, not the admissibility, of the evidence. Nanakuli was given permission to offer evidence in rebuttal that Chevron price protected other customers in California with whom it had no such relationship in the event Shell tried to impeach that evidence.

that, under the facts of this case, a jury could reasonably have found that Shell's acts on two occasions to price protect Nanakuli were not ambiguous and therefore indicated Shell's understanding of the terms of the agreement with Nanakuli rather than being a waiver by Shell of those terms.

Lastly we hold that, although the express price terms of Shell's posted price of delivery may seem, at first glance, inconsistent with a trade usage of price protection at time of increases in price, a closer reading shows that the jury could have reasonably construed price protection as consistent with the express term. We reach this holding for several reasons. First, we are persuaded by a careful reading of the U.C.C., one of whose underlying purposes is to promote flexibility in the expansion of commercial practices and which rather drastically overhauls this particular area of the law. The Code would have us look beyond the printed pages of the contract to usages and the entire commercial context of the agreement in order to reach the "true understanding" of the parties. . . . [Second,] the delineation by thoughtful commentators of the degree of consistency demanded between express terms and usage is that a usage should be allowed to modify the apparent agreement, as seen in the written terms, as long as it does not totally negate it. We believe the usage here falls within the limits set forth by commentators and generally followed in the better reasoned decisions. The manner in which price protection was actually practiced in Hawaii was that it only came into play at times of price increases and only for work committed prior to those increases on non-escalating contracts. Thus, it formed an exception to, rather than a total negation of, the express price term of "Shell's Posted Price at time of delivery." Our decision is reinforced by the overwhelming nature of the evidence that price protection was routinely practiced by all suppliers in the small Oahu market of the asphaltic paving trade and therefore was known to Shell; that it was a realistic necessity to operate in that market and thus vital to Nanakuli's ability to get large government contracts and to Shell's continued business growth on Oahu; and that it therefore constituted an intended part of the agreement, as that term is broadly defined by the Code, between Shell and Nanakuli. . . .

A party is always held to conduct generally observed by members of his chosen trade because the other party is justified in so assuming unless he indicates otherwise. He is held to more general business practices to the extent of his actual knowledge of those practices or to the degree his ignorance of those practices is not excusable: they were so generally practiced he should have been aware of them. . . .

Perhaps one of the most fundamental departures of the Code from prior contract law is found in the parol evidence rule and the definition of an agreement between two parties. Under the U.C.C., an agreement goes beyond the written words on a piece of paper. " 'Agreement' means the bargain of the parties in fact as found in their language or by implication from other circumstances including course of dealing or usage of trade or course of performance as provided in this chapter." *Id.* § 490:1-201(3). Express terms, then, do not constitute the entire agreement, which must be sought also in evidence of usages, dealings, and performance of the contract itself.

. . . A commercial agreement, [therefore], is broader than the written paper and its meaning is to be determined not just by the language used by them in the written contract but "by their action, read and interpreted in the light of commercial practices and other surrounding circumstances. The measure and background for interpretation are set by the commercial context, which may explain and supplement even the language of a formal or final writing." *Id.*, Comment 1. Performance, usages, and prior dealings are important enough to be admitted always, even for a final and complete agreement; only if they cannot be reasonably reconciled with the express terms of the contract are they not binding on the parties.

. . . Some guidelines can be offered as to how usage evidence can be allowed to modify a contract. First, the court must allow a check on usage evidence by demanding that it be sufficiently definite and widespread to prevent unilateral post-hoc revision of contract terms by one party. . . .

Evidence of a trade usage does not need to be protected against perjury because, as one commentator has written, "an outside standard does exist to help judge the truth of the assertion that the parties intended the usage to control the particular dispute: the existence and scope of the usage can be determined from other members of the trade."

. . .

Here the evidence was overwhelming that all suppliers to the asphaltic paving trade price protected customers under the same types of circumstances. . . . [T]he express price term was "Shell's Posted Price at time of delivery." A total negation of that term would be that the buyer was to set the price. It is a less than complete negation of the term that an unstated exception exists at times of price increases, at which times the old price is to be charged, for a certain period or for a specified tonnage, on work already committed at the lower price on nonescalating contracts. Such a usage forms a broad and important exception to the express term, but does not swallow it entirely. Therefore, we hold that, under these particular facts, a reasonable jury could have found that price protection was incorporated into the 1969 agreement between Nanakuli and Shell and that price protection was reasonably consistent with the express term of seller's posted price at delivery.

Because the jury could have found for Nanakuli on its price protection claim . . . we reverse the judgment of the District Court and reinstate the jury verdict for Nanakuli in the amount of $220,800, plus interest according to law.

NOTES & QUESTIONS

1. The agreement with Nanakuli also contained a merger clause that stated that no oral agreements existed. The court held that this language did not preclude consideration of trade usage and custom. Finding that the U.C.C. "assigns dealing and usage evidence 'unique and important roles,'" the court found reliance on such evidence "reflects the reality of the marketplace and avoids overly legalistic interpretations which the Code seeks to abolish." Cf. *KFC v. Darsam Corp.*, 543 F. Supp. 222 (W.D. Ky. 1982).

2. In *Nanakuli* and *Columbia Nitrogen*, the court emphasized that trade usage and custom could be considered, in part, because such custom did not wholly negate the provisions at issue. In *Michael Schiavone & Sons, Inc. v. Securalloy Co.*, 312 F. Supp. 801, 804 (D. Conn. 1970), the court ruled that defendant-seller could attempt to prove that the quantity term specifying delivery of 500 tons of stainless steel solids was modified by an oral understanding, in line with a trade usage, that the seller would only supply as many tons as he could, with 500 tons the

upper limit. The court reasoned that an additional term with a lesser effect than total contradiction or negation of a contract term can be a consistent term and "[e]vidence that the quantity to be supplied by defendant was orally understood to be up to 500 tons cannot be said to be inconsistent with the terms of the written contract which specified the quantity as '500 Gross Ton'." Some scholars have suggested that usage and dealing evidence may be used *not only* to supplement or qualify express terms but "in appropriate circumstances, may even override express terms." *See* J. White & R. Summers, UNIFORM COMMERCIAL CODE § 3-3 (3d ed. 1988). Others have suggested that consideration of usage and trade does not depend on whether the usage is contrary to the express term. Instead, they suggest consideration of the commercial setting is always required to determine whether, in fact, an inconsistency exists.

3. *Practice Points:* Standard form agreements are often used in commercial transactions. Over time, members of the trade may consistently ignore obsolete clauses at variance with these practices and yet still continue to use the form. Virtually all trade customs or usages can be stated fairly readily in written provisions. Standard form documents should never be used without a careful review of its provisions. You should also inquire into special customs and practices, and draft documents that do not need supplementation.

4. In *Southern Concrete Services, Inc. v. Mableton Contractors, Inc.*, 407 F. Supp. 581 (N.D. Ga. 1975), in the absence of prior dealings by parties to a contract for the sale of approximately 70,000 cubic feet of concrete the court refused to consider custom and trade usage evidence that the buyer would only be liable for concrete actually delivered. The court stated:

> [T]he contract sets out fairly specific quantity, price, and time specifications. To allow such specific contracts to be challenged by extrinsic evidence might jeopardize the certainty of the contractual duties which parties have a right to rely on. Certainly customs of the trade should be relevant to the interpretation of certain terms of a contract and should be considered in determining what variation in specifications is considered acceptable, but this court does not believe that section 2-202 was meant to invite a frontal assault on the essential terms of a clear and explicit contract.

Id. at _.

Can this case be reconciled with *Nanukuli?* Which do you believe presents the better rule?

TRIDENT CENTER v. CONNECTICUT GENERAL LIFE INSURANCE COMPANY
847 F.2d 564 (9th Cir. 1988)

KOZINSKI, Circuit Judge:

The parties to this transaction are, by any standard, highly sophisticated business people: Plaintiff is a partnership consisting of an insurance company and two of Los Angeles' largest and most prestigious law firms; defendant is another insurance company. Dealing at arm's length and from positions of roughly equal bargaining strength, they negotiated a commercial loan amounting to more than $56 million. The contract documents are lengthy and detailed; they squarely address the precise issue that is the subject of this dispute; to all who read English, they appear to resolve the issue fully and conclusively.

Plaintiff nevertheless argues here, as it did below, that it is entitled to introduce extrinsic evidence that the contract means something other than what it says. This case therefore presents the question whether parties in California can ever draft a contract that is parol evidence proof. Somewhat surprisingly, the answer is no. . . .

The facts are rather simple. Sometime in 1983 Security First Life Insurance Company and the law firms of Mitchell, Silberberg & Knupp and Manatt, Phelps, Rothenberg & Tunney formed a limited partnership for the purpose of constructing an office building complex on Olympic Boulevard in West Los Angeles. The partnership, Trident Center, the plaintiff herein, sought and obtained financing for the project from defendant, Connecticut General Life Insurance Company. The loan documents provide for a loan of $56,500,000 at 12 ¼ percent interest for a term of 15 years, secured by a deed of trust on the project. The promissory note provides that "[m]aker shall not have the right to prepay the principal amount hereof in whole or in part" for the first 12 years. . . . In years 13–15, the loan may be prepaid, subject to a sliding prepayment fee. The note also provides that in case of a default during years 1-12, Connecticut General has the option of accelerating the note and adding a 10 percent prepayment fee.

Everything was copacetic for a few years until interest rates began to drop. The 12 ¼ percent rate that had seemed reasonable in 1983 compared unfavorably with 1987 market rates and Trident started looking for ways of refinancing the loan to take advantage of the lower rates. Connecticut General was unwilling to oblige, insisting that the loan could not be prepaid for the first 12 years of its life, that is, until January 1996.

Trident then brought suit in state court seeking a declaration that it was entitled to prepay the loan now, subject only to a 10 percent prepayment fee. Connecticut General promptly removed to federal court and brought a motion to dismiss, claiming that the loan documents clearly and unambiguously precluded prepayment during the first 12 years. The district court agreed and dismissed Trident's complaint. The court also "sua sponte, sanction[ed] the plaintiff for the filing of a frivolous lawsuit." . . . Trident appeals both aspects of the district court's ruling.

Trident makes two arguments as to why the district court's ruling is wrong. First, it contends that the language of the contract is ambiguous and proffers a construction that it believes supports its position. Second, Trident argues that, under California law, even seemingly unambiguous contracts are subject to modification by parol or extrinsic evidence. Trident faults the district court for denying it the opportunity to present evidence that the contract language did not accurately reflect the parties' intentions.

[T]he promissory note provides that Trident "shall not have the right to prepay the principal amount hereof in whole or in part before January 1996." It is difficult to imagine language that more clearly or unambiguously expresses the idea that Trident may not unilaterally prepay the loan during its first 12 years. Trident, however, argues that there is an ambiguity because another clause of the note provides that "[i]n the event of a prepayment resulting from a default hereunder or the Deed of Trust prior to January 10, 1996 the prepayment fee will be ten percent

(10%).". . . Trident interprets this clause as giving it the option of prepaying the loan if only it is willing to incur the prepayment fee.

We reject Trident's argument out of hand. In the first place, its proffered interpretation would result in a contradiction between two clauses of the contract; the default clause would swallow up the clause prohibiting Trident from prepaying during the first 12 years of the contract. The normal rule of construction, of course, is that courts must interpret contracts, if possible, so as to avoid internal conflict.

In any event, the clause on which Trident relies is not on its face reasonably susceptible to Trident's proffered interpretation. Whether to accelerate repayment of the loan in the event of default is entirely Connecticut General's decision. The contract makes this clear at several points. See Note at 4 ("in each such event [of default], the entire principal indebtedness, or so much thereof as may remain unpaid at the time, shall, at the option of Holder, become due and payable immediately"); *id.* at 7 ("[i]n the event Holder exercises its option to accelerate the maturity hereof. . ."); Deed of Trust ¶ 2.01, at 25 ("in each such event [of default], Beneficiary may declare all sums secured hereby immediately due and payable . . ."). Even if Connecticut General decides to declare a default and accelerate, it "may rescind any notice of breach or default." *Id.* ¶ 2.02, at 26. Finally, Connecticut General has the option of doing nothing at all: "Beneficiary reserves the right at its sole option to waive noncompliance by Trustor with any of the conditions or covenants to be performed by Trustor hereunder." . . .

Once again, it is difficult to imagine language that could more clearly assign to Connecticut General the exclusive right to decide whether to declare a default, whether and when to accelerate, and whether, having chosen to take advantage of any of its remedies, to rescind the process before its completion. Trident nevertheless argues that it is entitled to precipitate a default and insist on acceleration by tendering the balance due on the note plus the 10 percent prepayment fee. The contract language, cited above, leaves no room for this construction. It is true, of course, that Trident is free to stop making payments, which may then cause Connecticut General to declare a default and accelerate. But that is not to say that Connecticut General would be required to so respond. The contract quite clearly gives Connecticut General other options: It may choose to waive the default, or to take advantage of some other remedy such as the right to collect "all the income, rents, royalties, revenue, issues, profits, and proceeds of the Property." Deed of Trust ¶ 1.18, at 22. By interpreting the contract as Trident suggests, we would ignore those provisions giving Connecticut General, not Trident, the exclusive right to decide how, when and whether the contract will be terminated upon default during the first 12 years.

Trident argues in the alternative that, even if the language of the contract appears to be unambiguous, the deal the parties actually struck is in fact quite different. It wishes to offer extrinsic evidence that the parties had agreed Trident could prepay at any time within the first 12 years by tendering the full amount plus a 10 percent prepayment fee. As discussed above, this is an interpretation to which the contract, as written, is not reasonably susceptible. Under traditional contract principles, extrinsic evidence is inadmissible to interpret, vary or add to the terms of an unambiguous integrated written instrument.

Trident points out, however, that California does not follow the traditional rule. Two decades ago the California Supreme Court in *Pacific Gas & Electric Co. v.*

G.W. Thomas Drayage & Rigging Co., 69 Cal. 2d 33, 69 Cal. Rptr. 561, 442 P.2d 641 (1968), turned its back on the notion that a contract can ever have a plain meaning discernible by a court without resort to extrinsic evidence.

. . . Under *Pacific Gas*, it matters not how clearly a contract is written, nor how completely it is integrated, nor how carefully it is negotiated, nor how squarely it addresses the issue before the court: the contract cannot be rendered impervious to attack by parol evidence. If one side is willing to claim that the parties intended one thing but the agreement provides for another, the court must consider extrinsic evidence of possible ambiguity. If that evidence raises the specter of ambiguity where there was none before, the contract language is displaced and the intention of the parties must be divined from self-serving testimony offered by partisan witnesses whose recollection is hazy from passage of time and colored by their conflicting interests. We question whether this approach is more likely to divulge the original intention of the parties than reliance on the seemingly clear words they agreed upon at the time.

Pacific Gas casts a long shadow of uncertainty over all transactions negotiated and executed under the law of California. As this case illustrates, even when the transaction is very sizeable, even if it involves only sophisticated parties, even if it was negotiated with the aid of counsel, even if it results in contract language that is devoid of ambiguity, costly and protracted litigation cannot be avoided if one party has a strong enough motive for challenging the contract. While this rule creates much business for lawyers and an occasional windfall to some clients, it leads only to frustration and delay for most litigants and clogs already overburdened courts.

It also chips away at the foundation of our legal system. By giving credence to the idea that words are inadequate to express concepts, *Pacific Gas* undermines the basic principle that language provides a meaningful constraint on public and private conduct. If we are unwilling to say that parties, dealing face to face, can come up with language that binds them, how can we send anyone to jail for violating statutes consisting of mere words lacking "absolute and constant referents"? How can courts ever enforce decrees, not written in language understandable to all, but encoded in a dialect reflecting only the "linguistic background of the judge"? Can lower courts ever be faulted for failing to carry out the mandate of higher courts when "perfect verbal expression" is impossible? Are all attempts to develop the law in a reasoned and principled fashion doomed to failure as "remnant[s] of a primitive faith in the inherent potency and inherent meaning of words"? Be that as it may. While we have our doubts about the wisdom of *Pacific Gas*, we have no difficulty understanding its meaning, even without extrinsic evidence to guide us. As we read the rule in California, we must reverse and remand to the district court in order to give plaintiff an opportunity to present extrinsic evidence as to the intention of the parties in drafting the contract. It may not be a wise rule w e are applying, but it is a rule that binds us. *Erie R.R. Co. v. Tompkins*, 304 U.S. 64, 78 (1938).

NOTES & QUESTIONS

1. In *Pacific Gas & Electric Co. v. G.W. Thomas Drayage & Rigging Co., Inc.*, 69 Cal. 2d 33, 69 Cal. Rptr. 561, 442 P.2d 641 (1968) criticized by the court in *Trident*, the court permitted consideration of extrinsic (extra-contractual) evidence

to demonstrate that an indemnity clause, apparently clear on its face, was limited to injury to the property of third parties only. The court defended its action on the basis of the impossibility of determining the meaning the parties gave to their words from the written document alone. The court stated:

> If words had absolute and constant referents, it might be possible to discover contractual intention in the words themselves and in the manner in which they were arranged. Words, however, do not have absolute and constant referents. "A word is a symbol of thought but has no arbitrary and fixed meaning like a symbol of algebra or chemistry. . . ." (*Pearson v. State Social Welfare Board* (1960) 54 Cal. 2d 184, 195, 5 Cal. Rptr. 553, 559, 353 P.2d 33, 39.) The meaning of particular words or groups of words varies with the . . . "verbal context and surrounding circumstances and purposes in view of the linguistic education and experience of their users and their hearers or readers (not excluding judges). . . . A word has no meaning apart from these factors; much less does it have an objective meaning, one true meaning." (Corbin, *The Interpretation of Words and the Parol Evidence Rule* (1965) 50 Cornell L.Q. 161, 187.) Accordingly, the meaning of a writing . . . "can only be found by interpretation in the light of all the circumstances that reveal the sense in which the writer used the words. The exclusion of parol evidence regarding such circumstances merely because the words do not appear ambiguous to the reader can easily lead to the attribution to a written instrument of a meaning that was never intended."

Id.

2. As the questions of whether a contract is clear and whether it is complete are questions of law for the judge to decide, some courts follow the provisional admission approach in making those determinations. That is, outside the presence of the jury, the judge will provisionally allow parol evidence on one or both of the above questions. If the judge thereafter concludes the contract is ambiguous or unclear, the judge will allow the jury to hear the parol evidence in order to decide the factual question of the meaning of the contract.

3. Do you agree with the court's criticism of *Pacific Gas*? What standard would you apply for determining whether extrinsic evidence should be considered?

4. *Drafting Exercise:* Draft a contract for the sale of an iceberg for $10,000. Make it clear in the contract that no outside custom or trade practices may be considered to alter the expressed terms of the contract. Can you be certain this exclusion will be followed by the court in a breach of contract suit?

DELLCAR & CO. v. HICKS
685 F. Supp. 679 (N.D. Ill. 1988)

Zagel, United States District Judge:

In 1986, Treesdale, Inc. ("Treesdale") owned Continental Bearings Corp. ("Continental"). Charles Carson ("Carson") owned Treesdale; he was also Dellcar's general partner. Treesdale, as Continental's parent corporation, funded Continental's payroll and operating bank accounts. Due to its own financial problems, however, Treesdale was unable to fund these accounts adequately; and, as a result, by September 1986, Continental owed one of its suppliers, Import

Sales, Inc. ("Import"), more than $200,000.

Hicks, Continental's then-president and CEO, appealed to Carson for money to cover the debt. Carson replied that neither Treesdale nor Continental had the necessary funds. But Dellcar did. Accordingly, Carson sent a check for $20,000 payable to Hicks from Dellcar, and a promissory note, for the same amount, in Dellcar's favor for Hicks's signature. Hicks contacted Carson and asked him why the check and note were made out to him personally. (Hicks had expected a Continental or Treesdale check payable to Import.) Carson answered that only by structuring the transaction in this manner could he obtain the money to pay Import. Carson then told Hicks to endorse the check and to sign the promissory note and return it to him. Most important, however, Carson assured Hicks that Dellcar would never look to him for payment of the note. Relying on this assurance, Hicks endorsed the check, signed the note, and mailed it back to Carson.

Approximately one month later, Hicks received two more Dellcar checks from Carson (totaling $30,000) and another promissory note. Once again Hicks questioned Carson about the form of the papers; and once more Carson assured Hicks that he would not be held liable. Accordingly, Hicks endorsed the checks, and signed and returned the note. In May of 1987, Dellcar made written demand on Hicks for payment. Hicks refused, and this suit followed. . . .

Dellcar's argument in support of its motion is clear enough: Hicks signed the notes and he is bound by his agreement. Hicks, however, contends that he was fraudulently induced into signing the notes, and therefore that he cannot not be held liable on them. Dellcar responds that Hicks is barred from presenting evidence of fraudulent inducement by the parol evidence rule. . . .

In our view, under Illinois law, the parol evidence rule does not preclude a party from presenting evidence that he was fraudulently induced into executing an agreement, even though the false promise involved is flatly inconsistent with the express terms of the writing. Corbin agrees. *See* A. Corbin, *The Parol Evidence Rule*, 53 YALE L.J. 603, 626 (1944) ("[I]t is in no case denied that oral testimony is admissible to prove fraud . . . even though the testimony contradicts the terms of a complete integration in writing . . ."); *see also* J. Sweet, *Promissory Fraud and the Parol Evidence Rule*, 49 CALIF. L. REV. 877, 896–97 (1961) (arguing that the parol evidence rule should not bar evidence of antecedent promissory fraud, even where it is inconsistent with the terms of the subsequently executed writing). Accordingly, we believe that Hicks is entitled to present evidence that Carson fraudulently induced him into signing the promissory notes as part of a scheme to defraud him out of $50,000.

BENYON BUILDING CORPORATION v. NATIONAL GUARDIAN LIFE INSURANCE CO.
455 N.E.2d 246 (Ill. App. 1983)

Unverzagt, Justice:

The plaintiff, Benyon Building Corporation, appeals a judgment denying its complaint for a release from a mortgage held consecutively by the defendants, Rockford Mortgage Co. (hereafter, "Rockford") and National Guardian Life Insurance Co. (hereafter, "National"), and reforming the mortgage and note secured by the mortgage. Although Rockford was named as a defendant, it was no longer in business and did not participate in the lawsuit. The following issues are presented for review: . . .

(4) Whether National met its burden of proving that a mistake was in fact made on the mortgage and note.

On October 23, 1964, the plaintiff executed a mortgage and note with Rockford.

The mortgage document provided that the plaintiff would pay:

> the principal sum of Eighty-Five Thousand and no/100 Dollars ($85,000.00) as evidenced by a principal promissory note of even date herewith, payable in 180 equal monthly installments of Six Hundred Forty-Nine and 60/100 Dollars ($649.60) beginning December 15, 1964 and with a final payment November 15, 1979.

The installment note provided that the plaintiff would pay Rockford $85,000 as follows:

> Six Hundred Forty-Nine and 60/100 Dollars on the Fifteenth day of December A.D. 1964; Six Hundred Forty-nine and 60/100 Dollars on the Fifteenth day of each and every month beginning on the Fifteenth day of January A.D. 1965 for 178 months succeeding, and a final payment of Six Hundred Forty-nine and 60/100 Dollars on the Fifteenth day of November A.D., 1979, with interest at the rate of 5½ per cent. per annum, payable Monthly. . . .

Rockford assigned the mortgage and note to National by a document also dated October 23, 1964.

The plaintiff made 178 monthly payments of $649.60. In September 1979, the plaintiff sent National a check for $1,299.20, with an accompanying letter explaining that it was to cover the final two payments and requesting a release of the mortgage. National refused to accept the check as the final payment and sent a reply letter explaining that an error had been made in drafting the original promissory note in that the correct monthly payments should have been $694.60 rather than $649.60.

When further attempts to obtain a release from the mortgage based on the 180th payment failed, the plaintiff filed a complaint for release from the mortgage on January 9, 1980. National filed an answer denying that the payments tendered by the plaintiff were in full payment of the mortgage. National also asserted as an affirmative defense that there was an inadvertent mistake in the amount of monthly payments shown on the note, that the mistake was discovered and in 1965 a new amortization schedule was sent to the plaintiff showing that amortization would take 200 rather than 180 months, and that the plaintiff's former president acknowledged the longer loan term in a letter written to National in 1973. The loan amortization schedule was dated November 18, 1965, and showed that payments of $649.60 at 5½% interest would take 200 months, with the final payment due on August 15, 1981. The letter written by the plaintiff's former president in 1973 was a request for additional financing from National and stated, "The present mortgage balance is $51,695.06 and calls for payments of $649.60 through August of 1981 at 5½% interest."

A hearing was held before the court. The general counsel for National testified that, according to an amortization booklet, the monthly payments necessary to amortize an $85,000 loan at 5½% interest over 15 years (or 180 months) was $694.60. He concluded that a mistake had been made in the monthly payment figures but stated that National's records did not indicate that the discrepancy was discovered until 1979 when the "final payment" was tendered. No one from Rockford who was involved in the loan transaction was available to testify. . . .

It is undisputed that, given an $85,000 loan to be paid in 180 monthly payments, a 5½% interest rate and $649.60 payments do not compute. It is also clear that the interest rate was specified only in the note, as 5½%, and that the mortgage did not specify an interest rate. The other three terms — $85,000 for 180 months at $649.60 per month — were listed on both documents. . . .

A mutual mistake exists when the contract has been written in terms that violate the understanding of both parties. It is well settled that the parol evidence rule is no bar to the admission of evidence on the question of mutual mistake, and this is so even when the instrument to be reformed is clear and unambiguous on its face. Thus parol evidence may be used to show the real agreement between the parties when a mistake has been made and the evidence is for the purpose of making the contract conform to the original intent of the parties. Since National alleged that a mutual mistake was made on the mortgage document as to the correct amount of the monthly payments, the note was admissible as extrinsic evidence to establish the real intention of the parties. . . .

A written agreement is presumed to express the intention of the parties and will not be reformed unless the evidence of mutual mistake or other ground for reformation is strong, clear, and convincing. The mistake must be one of fact rather than law, the proof clear and convincing that a mistake was made, and the mistake mutual and common to both parties to the instrument.

In the present case, there is no question that the terms on the written documents were inconsistent. Moreover, there is sufficient evidence to justify a conclusion that at some point the monthly payment figure was transposed to read $649.60 when it should have been $694.60, since the $694.60 figure was exactly consistent with the other terms. The suggestion that the interest rate was the mistaken term is less convincing since amortizing $85,000 over 15 years at $649.60 produces an interest rate of approximately 4½%.

The remaining question is whether the mistake was mutual. There is no testimony that the plaintiff was aware of the $694.60 figure and agreed to it before the mistake in drafting the documents was made. However, the 5½% interest rate was clear on the face of the note, was never challenged by the plaintiff during the 15 years it made payments, and was affirmed in the 1973 letter. There was thus sufficient evidence for the trial court to conclude that the true intent of the parties was to secure an $85,000 loan at 5½% interest for 15 years, justifying reformation of the instruments to reflect the correct monthly payment as $694.60.

The judgment of the circuit court of Winnebago County is affirmed.

BAKER v. BAILEY
782 P.2d 1286 (Mont. 1989)

McDONOUGH, Justice:

In June of 1976, Arthur and Elma Bailey moved a mobile home onto property owned by their daughter and son-in-law. With their permission, the Baileys hooked onto the water line which serviced their daughter's home and installed a pipeline which would provide water for their trailer.

Approximately six years later, in the spring of 1982, the Bailey's daughter and son-in-law made the decision to sell their residence and the surrounding property. Because they were concerned about taking care of their parents, however, they transferred one acre of the property to the Baileys. This one acre surrounded the mobile home. The remaining property, consisting of forty-five acres, was sold to the Bakers.

In order to insure that the Bailey's continued to have access to water, a Water Well Use Agreement was prepared. Mrs. Baker was concerned about future ownership of the one-acre plot. In particular, she was worried that "a bunch of hippies" would move in next to her and consequently she wanted some control over the type of person who may, in the future, buy the Bailey's land. In order to address this concern, the well agreement specifically provided that the right to use water would only extend to the Baileys. In the event the Baileys conveyed the property, the Bakers were under no obligation to provide the new owners with water.

Despite the plain language used in the agreement, the Baileys believed that although not specifically set forth, the Bakers would transfer the right to use the water well to a subsequent "reasonable purchaser" of the Bailey property. The language of the agreement, according to testimony of both the Baileys and the Bakers, was included for the purpose of addressing Mrs. Baker's concern over potentially undesirable neighbors. This purpose was not, however, articulated within the contract.

In addition to the water well use agreement, the Bakers, at the time of purchase, asked for and received a right of first refusal in the event the Baileys received an offer to purchase their property. If an offer was received, the Baileys were to notify the Bakers of the offer in writing. The Bakers would then have the opportunity to exercise their "right of first refusal" within fifteen days of the offer.

Following sale of the land, the Bakers and Baileys lived next to one another and in fact became friends. The Baileys, however, decided to move to Butte, Montana, in the spring of 1984. On June 30, 1984, they executed a standard form listing contract with a local realty company. Under the terms of the listing, the Baileys represented that the property would be sold with "shared well water." Based upon the realtor's valuation of the property with water, it was listed for $47,500.00.

Shortly after the decision was made to sell the property, the water system developed several problems. As a result of these problems pressure in the line was reduced and the Baileys were unable to obtain sufficient water to meet their needs. As a result, they found it necessary to bring water to their residence in plastic jugs.

The Bakers were not as significantly affected by the problems. The Bakers always had sufficient water. In fact, during the entire period the Baileys were deprived of water, the Bakers had enough water to irrigate their lawn. Despite the fact this use adversely affected the Baileys' water supply, the Bakers refused to reduce their consumption. This problem persisted until August when the water system was finally repaired.

After the problems with the water well surfaced, the Bakers informed the Baileys that they would not share the water supply with any new purchaser.

Consequently, the property would have to be sold without access to water from the well. The Baileys searched for alternative sources of water, but unfortunately none was available. They approached the Bakers and offered to purchase joint use of the well. This offer was refused.

Recognizing that they would not be able to provide water for the property, the Baileys realized that the property was virtually without value. They, therefore, agreed to sell it for $8,000.00, which was the fair market value of the trailer and other improvements on the land.

After the Baileys made the decision to accept the $8,000.00 offer, they gave the Bakers notice of its terms in compliance with the right of first refusal provisions in the contract. On August 20, 1984, the Bakers exercised their option and purchased the property for $8,000.00. The transaction was closed on September 10, 1984. At that time, the Bakers acquired the Baileys' one-acre parcel which, if supplied with water, allegedly could be marketed for $40,000.00 — $47,500.00. . . .

The facts of this case present a classic parol evidence problem. The parol evidence rule, briefly stated, requires that in the absence of fraud, duress, or mutual mistake, all extrinsic evidence must be excluded if the parties have reduced their agreement to an integrated writing. Under this rule, all prior and contemporaneous negotiations or understandings of the contract are merged, once that contract is reduced to writing. WILLISTON ON CONTRACTS, Third Edition § 631.

As this case illustrates, application of the rule can work to create harsh results. However, the policies behind the rule compel its consistent, uniform application. Commercial stability requires that parties to a contract may rely upon its express terms without worrying that the law will allow the other party to change the terms of the agreement at a later date.

The Baileys maintain that all of the parties to the Water Well Use Agreement, shared a common understanding that the Bakers would continue to share the well water with subsequent purchasers provided that the purchasers were acceptable to the Bakers. This contention may be true; however it is not found within the terms of the contract.

The Water Well Use Agreement is very explicit concerning the rights and obligations of the parties. Its terms provide: "it being specifically understood that this Agreement is solely for the benefit of [the Baileys] and shall terminate in the event [the Baileys] no longer occupy [the land]." It further provides that "it is the intent of the parties to fully set forth their understanding concerning the utilization of the domestic water supplies for the respective tracts. . . ." There are no terms within the contract which state that the Bakers will provide water to subsequent "reasonable" purchasers.

Therefore, the fact there may have been further oral understandings between the parties is not admissible. The language of the Water Well Use Agreement is clear. Where the language of a written contract is clear and unambiguous, there is nothing for the court to construe. Rather, the duty of the court is simply to apply the language as written to the facts of the case and decide the case accordingly. The lower court's reliance upon evidence of the parties' oral negotiations was therefore in error, and there was no breach of contract.

In order to prove that a party acted unreasonably in violation of the implied covenant of good faith and fair dealing, one must show as an element there was a breach of the express terms of the contract. We have concluded that the Bakers did not breach the terms of the Water Well Use Agreement and accordingly, there was no violation of the covenant of good faith and fair dealing even if all other elements of the violation were met.

NOTES & QUESTIONS

1. Is it sufficient simply to allege that fraud occurred in order to permit parol evidence to be admitted, or must a party demonstrate some likelihood that fraud occurred? Taken to the extreme, would the court's willingness to introduce parol evidence in instances of alleged fraud have the potential to eliminate the parol evidence rule? What limitations, if any, would you impose on a party's ability to use extrinsic evidence to demonstrate fraud in the inducement?

2. In *Hield v. Thyberg*, 347 N.W.2d 503 (Minn. 1984), on June 10, 1977, plaintiff-respondent Willard R. Hield sold his half-interest in a corporation, Beauticians Supply, Inc., to defendant-appellant Edwin R. Thyberg, owner of the other half-interest. The sale was accomplished by a written document titled "Assignment," signed by Hield, which provided in part:

> For and in consideration of Fifteen Thousand Dollars ($15,000.00), Willard R. Hield, of Minneapolis, Minnesota, does hereby assign, order and transfer to Edwin R. Thyberg, of Sioux Falls, South Dakota, all of my right, title and interest in Beauticians Supply, Inc., a corporation, including but not limited to any and all advances made by me to the said corporation and all of my common shares of capital stock. . . .

> The undersigned assignor hereby acknowledges that the assignee assumes no other personal liability toward assignor. . . .

The $15,000 was paid at the time the assignment was signed by Hield. Sometime thereafter, Hield transferred his stock certificates to Thyberg. In January 1979, plaintiff Hield sued defendant Thyberg, alleging in his complaint that he had sold his corporate shares "for a total consideration of $50,000, $15,000 cash at closing and $35,000 in a promissory note." Plaintiff further alleged that Thyberg, by agreeing to pay $50,000 and then refusing to perform, had committed fraud.

The court held that "where the parties have entered into a written contract, complete and unambiguous on the consideration to be paid, but it is claimed that the consideration was not as stated so that the contract might be used to mislead or deceive a third party, parol evidence is usable; but the party seeking to vary the terms of the written contract in this situation has the burden of establishing his claim by clear and convincing evidence." *Id.* Would the court have reached the same conclusion if there had been no allegation of fraud?

3. What policy is the court upholding in the *Baker* decision? Should predictability ever be given precedence over fairness? Would the court in *Pacific Gas* have reached the same decision? Would you?

John D. Calamari & Joseph M. Perillo,
The Parol Evidence Rule, Is It Necessary?
44 N.Y.U.L. Rev. 972 (1969)

The difficulty in applying the parol evidence rule springs from the fact that the rule is not self-executing. Taken alone, the rule merely states that where parties have reduced their final agreement to writing, the writing cannot be varied or contradicted. But the rule gives no indication of how courts are to determine whether the writing before them is "final" or "integrated," or how courts should decide whether to give the terms of the writing their normal meaning as opposed to one suggested by one of the parties. As a result, courts have had to develop various tests for applying the rule. The standards have ranged from the rigid "four corners" test — holding that the court will look only within the four corners of the document to determine whether it constitutes a complete expression of the parties' agreement — to tests almost as ambiguous as the parol evidence rule itself, such as those requiring the court to determine whether an alleged collateral agreement might "naturally and normally" have been made as a separate agreement.

Consistent application of the parol evidence rule has been further hindered by the maze of exceptions that have developed around it. Further, since parol evidence questions depend heavily upon the facts of the particular case, the value of one case as precedent for a future decision is limited. The opinions usually indicate only the test utilized by the court and the court's conclusion that the proffered evidence passed or failed it. The cases thus indicate the type of evidence which has been included or excluded under varying formulations of the parol evidence rule but provide little guidance for an analytical approach to future cases. Consequently, reliable counseling or prediction of litigation on parol evidence questions is virtually impossible.

A more important criticism of the parol evidence rule has been that even where consistently applied, it results in injustice. In the name of protecting the parties' "agreement," the rule excludes evidence of the parties' true intentions. Under the stricter formulations of the rule, a party may be prevented from taking his case to the trier of fact whenever the written document "appears" to be complete or "appears" to be free of ambiguity. Unfairness seems inevitable where subjective questions of the parties' intentions are decided by reference to rigid objective standards. Since parties do make oral agreements outside their written contract and do use words in other than the usual sense, the exclusion of this evidence by the parol evidence rule may force upon the parties a contract that they never intended to make. Thus, because the parol evidence rule may exclude as much truthful testimony as it does perjurious testimony, the rule constitutes a major source of injustice in contract law.

PROBLEMS

1. The Bollingers entered into a written agreement allowing the defendant to deposit construction waste on the Bollingers' property. The Bollingers did not read the contract before signing it and did not realize that it did not contain a provision requiring the defendants to remove the topsoil from the Bollingers property, pile in the waste material and then restore the topsoil so it would cover the deposited waste. The Bollingers want to introduce evidence regarding the parties' oral agreement regarding the replacement of topsoil. Can they do so? On what

grounds? *See Bollinger v. Central Quarry Stripping and Construction*, 229 A.2d 1967 (Pa. 1967).

2. The parties enter into a written agreement to ship 125 bales of cotton "ex rel Peerless from Bombay." There are two ships named "Peerless," that sail from Bombay, one in October, one in December. Can the plaintiff offer evidence to demonstrate that they both intended the December Peerless? *See Raffles v. Wichelhaus*, 2 H. & C. 906 (Ex. 1864).

3. Plaintiffs have entered into a written sales contract to sell defendant-Buyer their customized yacht. The written agreement describes the yacht to be purchased as "Seller's customized yacht, including all furnishings." On delivery of the yacht, the Buyer claims that "furnishings" includes all deck equipment. The Seller claims that they had orally agreed that the Seller could keep the deck equipment. Can any of this extra-contractual evidence be admitted? Who would ultimately win on the claim for breach of contract?

E. PROVING THE MEANING OF PARTICULAR TERMS

As earlier cases have demonstrated, determining the intent of the parties to a written contract requires interpreting the meaning of the terms used. Such interpretation may depend on the ability of the court to consider extrinsic evidence regarding trade usage or custom, the apparent ambiguity of a particular phrase (for example, when does "non-exclusive" actually mean "exclusive"?) and the right of the courts to look beyond the four corners of the document to determine if a "clear term" is actually an ambiguous one — based on custom, trade usage, or the circumstances surrounding the agreement. The following cases examine particular instances where extra-contractual evidence is considered to define the meaning of such terms as "chicken," "best efforts" and "aesthetic effect."

FRIGALIMENT IMPORTING CO., LTD. v. B.N.S. INTERNATIONAL SALES CORP.
190 F. Supp. 116 (S.D.N.Y. 1960)

FRIENDLY, District Judge:

The issue is, what is chicken? Plaintiff says "chicken" means a young chicken, suitable for broiling and frying. Defendant says "chicken" means any bird of that genus that meets contract specifications on weight and quality, including what it calls "stewing chicken" and plaintiff pejoratively terms "fowl." Dictionaries give both meanings, as well as some others not relevant here. To support its claim, plaintiff sends a number of volleys over the net; defendant essays to return them and adds a few serves of its own. Assuming that both parties were acting in good faith, the case nicely illustrates Holmes' remark "that the making of a contract depends not on the agreement of two minds in one intention, but on the agreement of two sets of external signs — not on the parties" having meant the same thing but on their having said the same thing." The Path of the Law, in Collected Legal Papers, p. 178. I have concluded that plaintiff has not sustained its burden of persuasion that the contract used "chicken" in the narrower sense.

. . . Two contracts are in suit. In the first, dated May 2, 1957, defendant, a New York sales corporation, confirmed the sale to plaintiff, a Swiss corporation, of

US Fresh Frozen Chicken, Grade A, Government Inspected, Eviscerated 2½-3 lbs. and 1½-2 lbs. each all chicken individually wrapped in cryovac, packed in secured fiber cartons or wooden boxes, suitable for export

75,000 lbs. 2½-3 lbs. . . . . @$33.00

25,000 lbs. 1½-2 lbs. . . . . @$36.50

per 100 lbs. FAS New York

scheduled May 10, 1957 pursuant to instructions from Penson & Co., New York.

The second contract, also dated May 2, 1957, was identical save that only 50,000 lbs. of the heavier "chicken" were called for, the price of the smaller birds was $37 per 100 lbs., and shipment was scheduled for May 30. The initial shipment under the first contract was short but the balance was shipped on May 17. When the initial shipment arrived in Switzerland, plaintiff found, on May 28, that the 2½-3 lbs. birds were not young chicken suitable for broiling and frying but stewing chicken or "fowl"; indeed, many of the cartons and bags plainly so indicated. Protests ensued. Nevertheless, shipment under the second contract was made on May 29, the 2½-3 lbs. birds again being stewing chicken. Defendant stopped the transportation of these at Rotterdam.

This action followed. . . .

Since the word "chicken" standing alone is ambiguous, I turn first to see whether the contract itself offers any aid to its interpretation. Plaintiff says the 1½-2 lbs. birds necessarily had to be young chicken since the older birds do not come in that size, hence the 2½-3 lbs. birds must likewise be young. This is unpersuasive — a contract for "apples" of two different sizes could be filled with different kinds of apples even though only one species came in both sizes. Defendant notes that the contract called not simply for chicken but for "US Fresh Frozen Chicken, Grade A, Government Inspected." It says the contract thereby incorporated by reference the Department of Agriculture's regulations, which favor its interpretation; . . .

Plaintiff's . . . contention is that there was a definite trade usage that "chicken" meant "young chicken." Defendant showed that it was only beginning in the poultry trade in 1957, thereby bringing itself within the principle that 'when one of the parties is not a member of the trade or other circle, his acceptance of the standard must be made to appear' by proving either that he had actual knowledge of the usage or that the usage is "so generally known in the community that his actual individual knowledge of it may be inferred." Here there was no proof of actual knowledge of the alleged usage; indeed, it is quite plain that defendant's belief was to the contrary. In order to meet the alternative requirement, the law of New York demands a showing that "the usage is of so long continuance, so well established, so notorious, so universal and so reasonable in itself, as that the presumption is inviolate that the parties contracted with reference to it, and made it a part of their agreement."

Plaintiff endeavored to establish such a usage by the testimony of three witnesses and certain other evidence. Strasser, resident buyer in New York for a large chain of Swiss cooperatives, testified that "on chicken I would definitely understand a broiler." However, the force of this testimony was considerably weakened by the fact that in his own transactions the witness, a careful business-man, protected himself by using "broiler" when that was what he wanted and "fowl" when he wished older birds. . . . Niesielowski, an officer of one of the companies that had furnished the stewing chicken to defendant, testified that "chicken" meant "the male species of the poultry industry. That could be a broiler, a fryer or a roaster," but not a stewing chicken; however, he also testified that upon receiving defendant's inquiry for "chickens," he asked whether the desire was for "fowl or frying chickens" and, in fact, supplied fowl, although taking the precaution of asking defendant, a day or two after plaintiff's acceptance of the contracts in suit, to change its confirmation of its order from "chickens," as defendant had originally prepared it, to "stewing chickens," Dates, an employee of Urner-Barry Company, which publishes a daily market report on the poultry trade, gave it as his view that the trade meaning of "chicken" was "broilers and fryers." In addition to this opinion testimony, plaintiff relied on the fact that the Urner-Barry service, the Journal of Commerce, and Weinberg Bros. & Co. of Chicago, a large supplier of poultry, published quotations in a manner which, in one way or another, distinguish between "chicken," comprising broilers, fryers and certain other categories, and "fowl," which, Bauer acknowledged, included stewing chickens. This material would be impressive if there were nothing to the contrary. However, there was, as will now be seen.

Defendant's witness Weininger, who operates a chicken eviscerating plant in New Jersey, testified "Chicken is everything except a goose, a duck, and a turkey. Everything is a chicken, but then you have to say, you have to specify which category you want or that you are talking about," Its witness Fox said that in the trade "chicken" would encompass all the various classifications, Sadina, who conducts a food inspection service, testified that he would consider any bird coming within the classes of "chicken" in the Department of Agriculture's regulations to be a chicken. The specifications approved by the General Services Administration include fowl as well as broilers and fryers under the classification "chickens." Statistics of the Institute of American Poultry Industries use the phrases "Young chickens" and "Mature chickens," under the general heading "Total chickens." and the Department of Agriculture's daily and weekly price reports avoid use of the word 'chicken' without specification. . . .

Defendant makes a further argument based on the impossibility of its obtaining broilers and fryers at the 33 cents price offered by plaintiff for the 2½-3 lbs. birds. There is no substantial dispute that, in late April, 1957, the price for 2½-3 lbs. Broilers was between 35 and 37 cents per pound, and that when defendant entered into the contracts, it was well aware of this and intended to fill them by supplying fowl in these weights. It claims that plaintiff must likewise have known the market since plaintiff had reserved shipping space on April 23, three days before plaintiff's cable to Stovicek, or, at least, that Stovicek was chargeable with such knowl-edge. . . .

When all the evidence is reviewed, it is clear that defendant believed it could comply with the contracts by delivering stewing chicken in the 2½-3 lbs. size. Defendant's subjective intent would not be significant if this did not coincide with an objective meaning of "chicken." Here it did coincide with one of the dictionary meanings, with the definition in the Department of Agriculture Regulations to which the contract made at least oblique reference, with at least some usage in the trade, with the realities of the market, and with what plaintiff's spokesman had said.

Plaintiff asserts it to be equally plain that plaintiff's own subjective intent was to obtain broilers and fryers; the only evidence against this is the material as to market prices and this may not have been sufficiently brought home. In any event it is unnecessary to determine that issue. For plaintiff has the burden of showing that "chicken" was used in the narrower rather than in the broader sense, and this it has not sustained.

MORIN BUILDING PRODUCTS COMPANY, INC.
v. BAYSTONE CONSTRUCTION, INC.
717 F.2d 413 (7th Cir. 1983)

Posner, Circuit Judge:

This appeal from a judgment for the plaintiff in a diversity suit requires us to interpret Indiana's common law of contracts. General Motors, which is not a party to this case, hired Baystone Construction, Inc., the defendant, to build an addition to a Chevrolet plant in Muncie, Indiana. Baystone hired Morin Building Products Company, the plaintiff, to supply and erect the aluminum walls for the addition. The contract required that the exterior siding of the walls be of "aluminum type 3003, not less than 18 B & S gauge, with a mill finish and stucco embossed surface texture to match finish and texture of existing metal siding." The contract also provided "that all work shall be done subject to the final approval of the Architect or Owner's [General Motors'] authorized agent, and his decision in matters relating to artistic effect shall be final, if within the terms of the Contract Documents"; and that "should any dispute arise as to the quality or fitness of materials or workmanship, the decision as to acceptability shall rest strictly with the Owner, based on the requirement that all work done or materials furnished shall be first class in every respect. What is usual or customary in erecting other buildings shall in no wise enter into any consideration or decision."

Morin put up the walls. But viewed in bright sunlight from an acute angle the exterior siding did not give the impression of having a uniform finish, and General Motors' representative rejected it. Baystone removed Morin's siding and hired another subcontractor to replace it. General Motors approved the replacement siding. Baystone refused to pay Morin the balance of the contract price ($23,000) and Morin brought this suit for the balance, and won. . . .

Some cases hold that if the contract provides that the seller's performance must be to the buyer's satisfaction, his rejection — however unreasonable — of the seller's performance is not a breach of the contract unless the rejection is in bad faith. But most cases conform to the position stated in section 228 of the RESTATEMENT (SECOND) OF CONTRACTS (1979): if "it is practicable to determine whether a reasonable person in the position of the obligor would be satisfied, an interpretation is preferred under which the condition [that the obligor be satisfied with the obligee's performance] occurs if such a reasonable person in the position of the obligor would be satisfied."

We do not understand the majority position to be paternalistic; and paternalism would be out of place in a case such as this, where the subcontractor is a substantial multistate enterprise. The requirement of reasonableness is read into a contract not to protect the weaker party but to approximate what the parties would have expressly provided with respect to a contingency that they did not foresee, if they had foreseen it. Therefore the requirement is not read into every contract, because it is not always a reliable guide to the parties' intentions. In particular, the presumption that the performing party would not have wanted to put himself at the mercy of the paying party's whim is overcome when the nature of the performance contracted for is such that there are no objective standards to guide the court. It cannot be assumed in such a case that the parties would have wanted a court to second-guess the buyer's rejection. So "the reasonable person standard is employed when the contract involves commercial quality, operative fitness, or mechanical utility which other knowledgeable persons can judge. . . . The standard of good faith is employed when the contract involves personal aesthetics or fancy."

We have to decide which category the contract between Baystone and Morin belongs in. The particular in which Morin's aluminum siding was found wanting was its appearance, which may seem quintessentially a matter of "personal aesthetics," or as the contract put it, "artistic effect." But it is easy to imagine situations where this would not be so. Suppose the manager of a steel plant rejected a shipment of pig iron because he did not think the pigs had a pretty shape. The reasonable-man standard would be applied even if the contract had an "acceptability shall rest strictly with the Owner" clause, for it would be fantastic to think that the iron supplier would have subjected his contract rights to the whimsy of the buyer's agent. At the other extreme would be a contract to paint a portrait, the buyer having reserved the right to reject the portrait if it did not satisfy him. Such a buyer wants a portrait that will please him rather than a jury, even a jury of connoisseurs, so the only question would be his good faith in rejecting the portrait.

This case is closer to the first example than to the second. The building for which the aluminum siding was intended was a factory — not usually intended to be a thing of beauty. That aesthetic considerations were decidedly secondary to considerations of function and cost is suggested by the fact that the contract specified mill-finish aluminum, which is unpainted. There is much debate in the record over whether it is even possible to ensure a uniform finish within and among sheets, but it is at least clear that mill finish usually is not uniform. If General Motors and Baystone had wanted a uniform finish they would in all likelihood have ordered a painted siding. Whether Morin's siding achieved a reasonable uniformity amounting to satisfactory commercial quality was susceptible of objective judgment; in the language of the RESTATEMENT, a reasonableness standard was "practicable."

But this means only that a requirement of reasonableness would be read into this contract if it contained a standard owner's satisfaction clause, which it did not; and since the ultimate touchstone of decision must be the intent of the parties to the contract we must consider the actual language they used. The contract refers explicitly to "artistic effect," a choice of words that may seem deliberately designed to put the contract in the "personal aesthetics" category whatever an outside observer might think. But the reference appears as number 17 in a list of conditions in a general purpose form contract. And the words "artistic effect" are immediately followed by the qualifying phrase, "if within the terms of the Contract Documents," which suggests that the "artistic effect" clause is limited to contracts in which artistic effect is one of the things the buyer is aiming for; it is not clear that he was here. The other clause on which Baystone relies, relating to the quality or fitness of workmanship and materials, may seem all-encompassing, but it is qualified by the phrase, "based on the requirement that all work done or materials furnished shall be first class in every respect" — and it is not clear that Morin's were not. This clause also was not drafted for this contract; it was incorporated by reference to another form contract (the Chevrolet Division's "Contract General Conditions"), of which it is paragraph 35. We do not disparage form contracts, without which the commercial life of the nation would grind to a halt. But we are left with more than a suspicion that the artistic-effect and quality-fitness clauses in the form contract used here were not intended to cover the aesthetics of a mill-finish aluminum factory wall. . . .

[I]f it appeared from the language or circumstances of the contract that the parties really intended General Motors to have the right to reject Morin's work for failure to satisfy the private aesthetic taste of General Motors' representative, the rejection would have been proper even if unreasonable. But the contract is ambiguous because of the qualifications with which the terms "artistic effect" and "decision as to acceptability" are hedged about, and the circumstances suggest that the parties probably did not intend to subject Morin's rights to aesthetic whim.

JOYCE BEVERAGES OF NEW YORK, INC. v. ROYAL CROWN COLA CO.
555 F. Supp. 271 (S.D.N.Y. 1983)

POLLACK, District Judge:

Defendant Royal Crown Cola Co. (Royal Crown) is principally engaged in the licensing of its trademarks and the sale of secret soft drink concentrates to its independent bottlers. Under license from Royal Crown, the bottler uses the secret concentrates to produce finished soft drink products, which the bottler then promotes and distributes. Royal Crown products include ROYAL CROWN COLA, DIET-RITE COLA, RC-100, and DECAFFEINATED RC.

In the calendar year ending December 31, 1981, combined sales of the Royal Crown cola brands accounted for approximately 5 per cent of United States cola sales. Plaintiff, Joyce Beverages of New York, Inc. (Joyce), manufactures and sells soft drinks under license from several trademark licensors, including Royal Crown. In addition to the Royal Crown cola products, Joyce distributes 7-UP lemon-lime soft drinks, DIET 7-UP, A&W root beer, SUGAR-FREE A&W, PERRIER carbonated water, NESTEA iced tea, HAWAIIAN PUNCH and Royal Crown's NEHI fruit flavored soft drinks.

Since its origin in the last century, the United States soft drink industry has utilized the franchise system of distribution. Trademark licensors supply certain secret ingredients under license to local-independent bottlers, who produce, promote and distribute the finished soft drink products in designated territories. The market is highly competitive. The local bottlers engage in intense price and nonprice competition with one another.

Under its license and franchise agreements with Royal Crown, Joyce received long-term (and in some cases potentially perpetual) exclusive rights to manufacture and sell the Royal Crown cola products within defined territories in the States of New York, New Jersey and Connecticut.

. . . The bottler's agreements for DECAFFEINATED RC and RC-100 . . . contain "exclusive efforts" clauses which expressly preclude the bottler from distributing any "substantially or reasonably similar" soft drinks and which provide that "any cola shall be deemed substantially or reasonably similar to any . . . cola [and] any diet cola to any . . . diet cola. . . ." The "best efforts" clause in these agreements provides that Joyce "shall devote its best efforts to the sale and promotion of sales of the beverages within and only within the territory . . . so as to achieve maximum distribution and sale for the beverages within the territory."

Joyce is planning to commence the distribution of a decaffeinated cola product named LIKE, manufactured by the Seven-Up Company, which will be distributed for the first time in this area beginning not later than February 7, 1983. . . .

A best efforts clause is not per se breached by a mere undertaking of a competitive product line. It depends on the circumstances. However, the circumstances demonstrated by the record of the hearing establish beyond peradventure of doubt that Joyce's proposed effort to sell the new line of product to the established customers of the old product and the plan to use advertising and distribution methods developed in the promotion of the first for the promotion of the second product breaches the best efforts clause both factually and legally. The evidence establishes that the activity of Joyce would be so manifestly harmful to Royal Crown that it justifies the Court in finding that the new obligations to which Joyce has committed itself and its intended conduct breach its covenant to promote the product of Royal Crown. Joyce will control pricing, placement of local advertisements, special promotions, feature advertising and special displays of the two competitive products. It is important to emphasize that as a LIKE bottler, Joyce has already begun to convince retailers to purchase and display that product in their stores, and in connection therewith plans to offer them a massive give-away, without charge, of LIKE to induce promotion thereof by the retailers and to gain good will therefor. Retailers have been and will be asked to devote a portion of their limited cola budgets and to edge into their shelf space a cola product competitive to Royal Crown. In addition, Joyce will begin seeking and seizing promotional and merchandising opportunities on behalf of LIKE cola. These activities will necessarily dilute Joyce's efforts on behalf of the Royal Crown colas. Joyce has thus impaired and disabled itself from devoting its "best efforts" to Royal Crown and from promoting the Royal Crown sales in a "manner. . . satisfactory" to Royal Crown. The described conduct and promotional plans of Joyce are a breach of the best efforts clauses contained in the Royal Crown contracts.

Plaintiff argues that the contract clause providing for best efforts should not be interpreted to require exclusive efforts. This Court does not hold that the clause is violated merely as another cola has been signed. Instead, it is violated under the facts and circumstances disclosed in the evidence overall. . . . The entire pattern of industry practice since the beginning of the soft drink industry has been for distributors to distribute only one cola. This best efforts clause is properly read in terms of the trade practice and usage. In addition, credible evidence demonstrates that the adoption of a new contract form by Royal Crown in which an exclusive dealing clause was expressed alongside of the best efforts clause was meant only to reflect and solidify what already was the understanding of the parties and the industry regarding the best efforts clause. The obligations of Joyce were the same for all the colas it was handling for Royal Crown — no new ones in the regard here discussed were added for the new drinks. Joyce gave no testimony that it had been asked to add a further restriction in this regard when it was presented with the new form.

In sum, the actions of Joyce are and constitute a material breach of its obligations to Royal Crown under their agreements. Under all the facts and circumstances presented here, cancellation of the Royal Crown franchises and licenses to Joyce would not be a breach on the part of Royal Crown.

NOTES & QUESTIONS

1. An auto parts distributor agrees to use its "best efforts" to distribute plaintiff's new gaskets. The distributor advertises the new product in exactly the same method and manner as the products by other manufacturers which he sells. Has the distributor breached the agreement by not using additional efforts to market plaintiff's gaskets? What evidence would you consider in deciding the meaning of "best efforts"? What steps could you take in drafting the contract to avoid future arguments over this issue?

2. *Drafting Exercise:* Your client wants to enter into an agreement with a publishing company to publish her new novel. The contract provides that the publisher "shall have the sole discretion to determine whether the submitted manuscript is of publishable quality." Is the clause enforceable? Can the publisher refuse to publish the submitted manuscript because the subject matter is no longer popular? Because he hates the author's style? Because the story offends the publisher's personal tastes? Draft a clause that will best protect your client's interests.

PROBLEM

Cohen is the owner of the copyright in a musical composition. He grants the defendant a license to use the composition in a film and to exhibit the film "in theatres and on television." The defendant wants to put the film on videocassette. Can it do so under the written agreement? *Compare Cohen v. Paramount Pictures Corp.,* 845 F.2d 851 (9th Cir. 1988) *with Bartsch v. Metro-Goldwyn-Mayer Inc.,* 391 F.2d 150 (2d Cir. 1967).

F.   FILLING IN THE GAPS

Potential agreements may fail because they lack sufficient specificity to demonstrate that the parties have manifested a reasonable expectation to be bound. *See* Chapter 5. Even where there is sufficient specificity to demonstrate that the parties intended to enter into an enforceable contract, the written or oral manifestation of that agreement may be missing terms (such as price, delivery dates and the like) which need to be "interpreted" in order to ascertain completely the obligations of the contracting parties. "Filling the gaps" posed by these missing terms requires the court to consider such diverse factors as the nature of the transaction, course of dealing and the circumstances surrounding the execution and performance of the contract at issue.

HAINES v. CITY OF NEW YORK
364 N.E.2d 820 (N.Y. 1977)

GABRIELLI, Judge:

In the early 1920's, respondent City of New York and intervenors Town of Hunter and Village of Tannersville embarked upon negotiations for the construction of a sewage system to serve the village and a portion of the town. These negotiations were prompted by the city's need and desire to prevent the discharge of untreated sewage by residents of the area into Gooseberry Creek, a stream which fed a reservoir of the city's water supply system in the Schoharie watershed.

In 1923, the Legislature enacted enabling legislation authorizing the city to enter into contracts with municipalities in the watershed area "for the purpose of providing, maintaining (and) operating systems and plants for the collection and disposal of sewage" (L.1923, ch. 630, § 1). The statute further provided that any such contracts would be subject to the approval of the New York City Board of Estimate and Apportionment.

The negotiations culminated in an agreement in 1924 between the city and intervenors. By this agreement, the city assumed the obligation of constructing a sewage system consisting of a sewage disposal plant and sewer mains and laterals, and agreed that "all costs of construction and subsequent operation, maintenance and repair of said sewerage system with the house connections thereof and said disposal works shall be at the expense" of the city. The agreement also required the city to extend the sewer lines when "necessitated by future growth and building constructions of the respective communities". The village and town were obligated to and did obtain the necessary easements for the construction of the system and sewage lines. . . .

Presently, the average flow of the plant has increased from an initial figure of 118,000 gallons per day to over 600,000 gallons daily and the trial court found that the plant "was operating substantially in excess of design capacity". The city asserts, and it is not disputed by any of the parties in this action, that the system cannot bear any significant additional "loadings" because this would result in inadequate treatment of all the sewage and consequently harm the city's water supply. The instant controversy arose when plaintiff, who is the owner of a tract of unimproved land which he seeks to develop into 50 residential lots, applied to the city for permission to connect houses, which he intends to construct on the lots, to existing sewer lines. The city refused permission on the ground that it had no obligation to further expand the plant, which is presently operating at full capacity, to accommodate this new construction. . . .

We conclude that the city is presently obligated to maintain the existing plant but is not required to expand that plant or construct any new facilities to accommodate plaintiff's substantial, or any other, increased demands on the sewage system. The initial problem encountered in ascertaining the nature and extent of the city's obligation pursuant to the 1924 agreement, is its duration. We reject, as did the courts below, the plaintiff's contention that the city is perpetually bound under the agreement. The contract did not expressly provide for perpetual performance and both the trial court and the Appellate Division found that the parties did not so intend. Under these circumstances, the law will not imply that a contract calling for continuing performance is perpetual in duration.

On the other hand, the city's contention that the contract is terminable at will because it provides for no express duration should also be rejected. In the absence of an express term fixing the duration of a contract, the courts may inquire into the intent of the parties and supply the missing term if a duration may be fairly and reasonably fixed by the surrounding circumstances and the parties' intent. It is generally agreed that where a duration may be fairly and reasonably supplied by implication, a contract is not terminable at will.

While we have not previously had occasion to apply it, the weight of authority supports the related rule that where the parties have not clearly expressed the duration of a contract, the courts will imply that they intended performance to continue for a reasonable time. For compelling policy reasons, this rule has not been, and should not be, applied to contracts of employment or exclusive agency, distributorship, or requirements contracts which have been analogized to employment contracts. The considerations relevant to such contracts do not obtain here. Thus, we hold that it is reasonable to infer from the circumstances of the 1924 agreement that the parties intended the city to maintain the sewage disposal facility until such time as the city no longer needed or desired the water, the purity of which the plant was designed to insure. The city argues that it is no longer obligated to maintain the plant because State law now prohibits persons from discharging raw sewage into streams such as Gooseberry Creek. However, the parties did not contemplate the passage of environmental control laws which would prohibit individuals or municipalities from discharging raw, untreated sewage into certain streams. Thus, the city agreed to assume the obligation of assuring that its water supply remained unpolluted and it may not now avoid that obligation for reasons not contemplated by the parties when the agreement was executed, and not within the purview of their intent, expressed or implied. . . .

NOTES & QUESTIONS

1. So, how long is the term of the duration of the contract in *Haines*? Who decides?

2. The U.C.C. recognizes that missing terms may be supplied by a determination of reasonableness (§ 2-305 for open price terms; § 2-309 for delivery times), and by an implied best efforts requirement for exclusive dealing agreements (§ 2-306). Indeed, there is a whole series of gap-filling U.C.C. provisions (*see* §§ 2-309–2-315).

3. Gaps may also be filled by implied conditions. *See* Chapter 13.

G. THE ROLE OF GOOD FAITH

Parties do not have to agree that each shall act in good faith in performing their agreed-upon obligations. Instead courts will impose such a duty as a matter of public policy. As the cases below demonstrate, the presence of this implied obligation of good faith and fair dealing may, in certain instances, have a direct impact on the interpretation of the parties' responsibilities under the agreement at issue.

WOOD v. LUCY, LADY DUFF-GORDON
222 N.Y. 88, 118 N.E. 214 (N.Y. 1917)

CARDOZO, Judge:

The defendant styles herself "a creator of fashions." Her favor helps a sale. Manufacturers of dresses, millinery, and like articles are glad to pay for a certificate of her approval. The things which she designs, fabrics, parasols, and what not, have a new value in the public mind when issued in her name. She employed the plaintiff to help her to turn this vogue into money. He was to have the exclusive right, subject always to her approval, to place her indorsements on the designs of others. He was also to have the exclusive right to place her own designs on sale, or to license others to market them. In return she was to have one-half of "all profits and revenues" derived from any contracts he might make. The exclusive right was to last at least one year from April 1, 1915, and thereafter from year to year unless terminated by notice of 90 days. The plaintiff says that he kept the contract on his part, and that the defendant broke it. She placed her indorsement on fabrics, dresses, and millinery without his knowledge, and withheld the profits. He sues her for the damages, and the case comes here on demurrer.

The agreement of employment is signed by both parties. It has a wealth of recitals. The defendant insists, however, that it lacks the elements of a contract. She says that the plaintiff does not bind himself to anything. It is true that he does not promise in so many words that he will use reasonable efforts to place the defendant's indorsements and market her designs. We think, however, that such a promise is fairly to be implied. The law has outgrown its primitive stage of formalism when the precise word was the sovereign talisman, and every slip was fatal. It takes a broader view today. A promise may be lacking, and yet the whole writing may be "instinct with an obligation," imperfectly expressed. If that is so, there is a contract.

The implication of a promise here finds support in many circumstances. The defendant gave an exclusive privilege. She was to have no right for at least a year to place her own indorsements or market her own designs except through the agency of the plaintiff. The acceptance of the exclusive agency was an assumption of its duties. We are not to suppose that one party was to be placed at the mercy of the other. Many other terms of the agreement point the same way. We are told at the outset by way of recital that:

> The said Otis F. Wood possesses a business organization adapted to the placing of such indorsements as the said Lucy, Lady Duff-Gordon, has approved.

The implication is that the plaintiff's business organization will be used for the purpose for which it is adapted. But the terms of the defendant's compensation are even more significant. Her sole compensation for the grant of an exclusive agency is to be one-half of all the profits resulting from the plaintiff's efforts. Unless he gave his efforts, she could never get anything. Without an implied promise, the transaction cannot have such business "efficacy, as both parties must have intended that at all events it should have." Bowen, L. J., in *The Moorcock*, 14 P.D. 64, 68. But the contract does not stop there. The plaintiff goes on to promise that he will account monthly for all moneys received by him, and that he will take out all such patents and copyrights and trade-marks as may in his judgment be necessary to protect the rights and articles affected by the agreement. It is true, of course, as the

Appellate Division has said, that if he was under no duty to try to market designs or to place certificates of indorsement, his promise to account for profits or take out copyrights would be valueless. But in determining the intention of the parties the promise has a value. It helps to enforce the conclusion that the plaintiff had some duties. His promise to pay the defendant one-half of the profits and revenues resulting from the exclusive agency and to render accounts monthly was a promise to use reasonable efforts to bring profits and revenues into existence. For this conclusion the authorities are ample.

FORTUNE v. NATIONAL CASH REGISTER COMPANY
364 N.E.2d 1251 (Mass. 1977)

ABRAMS, Judge:

Orville E. Fortune (Fortune), a former salesman of The National Cash Register Company (NCR), brought a suit to recover certain commissions allegedly due as a result of a sale of cash registers to First National Stores Inc. (First National) in 1968. Counts 1 and 2 of Fortune's amended declaration claimed bonus payments under the parties' written contract of employment. [The jury awarded the plaintiff $45,649.62.].

Fortune was employed by NCR under a written "salesman's contract" which was terminable at will, without cause, by either party on written notice. The contract provided that Fortune would receive a weekly salary in a fixed amount plus a bonus for sales made within the "territory" (i.e., customer accounts or stores) assigned to him for "coverage or supervision," whether the sale was made by him or someone else. The amount of the bonus was determined on the basis of "bonus credits," which were computed as a percentage of the price of products sold. Fortune would be paid a percentage of the applicable bonus credit as follows: (1) 75% if the territory was assigned to him at the date of the order, (2) 25% if the territory was assigned to him at the date of delivery and installation, or (3) 100% if the territory was assigned to him at both times.

The contract further provided that the "bonus interest" would terminate if shipment of the order was not made within eighteen months from the date of the order unless (1) the territory was assigned to him for coverage at the date of delivery and installation, or (2) special engineering was required to fulfil the contract. In addition, NCR reserved the right to sell products in the salesman's territory without paying a bonus. However, this right could be exercised only on written notice.

In 1968, Fortune's territory included First National. This account had been part of his territory for the preceding six years; he had been successful in obtaining several orders from First National, including a million dollar order in 1963. Sometime in late 1967, or early 1968, NCR introduced a new model cash register, Class 5. Fortune corresponded with First National in an effort to sell the machine. He also helped to arrange for a demonstration of the Class 5 to executives of First National on October 4, 1968. NCR had a team of men also working on this sale. . . .

On November 29, 1968, First National signed an order for 2,008 Class 5 machines to be delivered over a four-year period at a purchase price of approximately $5,000,000. Although Fortune did not participate in the negotiation of the terms of the order, his name appeared on the order form in the space entitled "salesman credited." The amount of the bonus credit as shown on the order was \$92,079.99.

On January 6, 1969, the first working day of the new year, Fortune found an envelope on his desk at work. It contained a termination notice addressed to his home dated December 2, 1968. Shortly after receiving the notice, Fortune spoke to the Boston branch manager with whom he was friendly. The manager told him, "You are through," but, after considering some of the details necessary for the smooth operation of the First National order, told him to "stay on," and to "[k]eep on doing what you are doing right now." Fortune remained with the company in a position entitled "sales support." In this capacity, he coordinated and expedited delivery of the machines to First National under the November 29 order as well as servicing other accounts.

Commencing in May or June, Fortune began to receive some bonus commissions on the First National order. Having received only 75% of the applicable bonus due on the machines which had been delivered and installed, Fortune spoke with his manager about receiving the full amount of the commission. Fortune was told "to forget about it." Sixty-one years old at that time, and with a son in college, Fortune concluded that it "was a good idea to forget it for the time being."

NCR did pay a systems and installations person the remaining 25% of the bonus commissions due from the First National order although contrary to its usual policy of paying only salesmen a bonus. NCR, by its letter of November 27, 1968, had promised the services of a systems and installations person; the letter had claimed that the services of this person, Bernie Martin (Martin), would have a forecasted cost to NCR of over \$45,000. As promised, NCR did transfer Martin to the First National account shortly after the order was placed. Approximately eighteen months after receiving the termination notice, Fortune, who had worked for NCR for almost twenty-five years, was asked to retire. When he refused, he was fired in June of 1970. Fortune did not receive any bonus payments on machines which were delivered to First National after this date. . . .

The central issue on appeal is whether this "bad faith" termination constituted a breach of the employment at will contract. Traditionally, an employment contract which is "at will" may be terminated by either side without reason. Although the employment at will rule has been almost uniformly criticised, it has been widely followed.

The contract at issue is a classic terminable at will employment contract. It is clear that the contract itself reserved to the parties an explicit power to terminate the contract without cause on written notice. It is also clear that under the express terms of the contract Fortune has received all the bonus commissions to which he is entitled. Thus, NCR claims that it did not breach the contract, and that it has no further liability to Fortune. According to a literal reading of the contract, NCR is correct.

However, Fortune argues that, in spite of the literal wording of the contract, he is entitled to a jury determination on NCR's motives in terminating his services under the contract and in finally discharging him. We agree. We hold that NCR's written contract contains an implied covenant of good faith and fair dealing, and a termination not made in good faith constitutes a breach of the contract. . . .

Recent decisions in other jurisdictions lend support to the proposition that good faith is implied in contracts terminable at will. In a recent employment at will case, *Monge v. Beebe Rubber Co.*, 114 N.H. 130, 133, 316 A.2d 549, 552 (1974), the plaintiff alleged that her oral contract of employment had been terminated because she refused to date her foreman. The New Hampshire Supreme Court held that "(i)n all employment contracts, whether at will or for a definite term, the employer's interest in running his business as he sees fit must be balanced against the interest of the employee in maintaining his employment, and the public's interest in maintaining a proper balance between the two. . . . We hold that a termination by the employer of a contract of employment at will which is motivated by bad faith or malice . . . constitutes a breach of the employment contract. . . . Such a rule affords the employee a certain stability of employment and does not interfere with the employer's normal exercise of his right to discharge, which is necessary to permit him to operate his business efficiently and profitably."

We believe that the holding in the *Monge* case merely extends to employment contracts the rule that "in every contract there is an implied covenant that neither party shall do anything which will have the effect of destroying or injuring the right of the other party to receive the fruits of the contract, which means that in every contract there exists an implied covenant of good faith and fair dealing."

. . . Where the principal seeks to deprive the agent of all compensation by terminating the contractual relationship when the agent is on the brink of successfully completing the sale, the principal has acted in bad faith and the ensuing transaction between the principal and the buyer is to be regarded as having been accomplished by the agent. RESTATEMENT (SECOND) OF AGENCY § 454, and Comment a (1958). The same result obtains where the principal attempts to deprive the agent of any portion of a commission due the agent. . . .

NCR argues that there was no evidence of bad faith in this case; therefore, the trial judge was required to direct a verdict in any event. We think that the evidence and the reasonable inferences to be drawn there from support a jury verdict that the termination of Fortune's twenty-five years of employment as a salesman with NCR the next business day after NCR obtained a $5,000,000 order from First National was motivated by a desire to pay Fortune as little of the bonus credit as it could. The fact that Fortune was willing to work under these circumstances does not constitute a waiver or estoppel; it only shows that NCR had him "at their mercy." . . .

We think that NCR's conduct in June, 1970 permitted the jury to find bad faith.

NOTES & QUESTIONS

1. Does the imposition of the obligation of good faith alter the meaning of the term "at will"? Can an employee be terminated only "for cause"?

2. Can parties agree to expressly exclude a good faith duty? Should they be able to do so as a matter of policy?

THOMPSON v. ST. REGIS PAPER COMPANY
685 P.2d 1081 (Wash. 1984)

BRACHTENBACH, Justice:

Does a terminable at will employee have a cause of action for wrongful discharge when his employer summarily discharges him and gives no reason for so doing? . . .

The appellant, Kenneth L. Thompson, began working for St. Regis Paper Company (hereinafter St. Regis) in 1963. There is no written agreement concerning his employment. In 1973 he was promoted into a management position, reaching the rank of divisional controller for the Distribution Yards and Industrial Supply Division of St. Regis in Tacoma, Washington. From 1973 through 1979 he received regular bonuses under the Management Incentive Compensation Plan. Throughout this period the appellant received no complaints or criticism from his superiors concerning his work. In December 1979, he received a merit pay raise.

Despite this apparent satisfactory service, on January 17, 1980, after 17 years of service, he was asked to resign for the benefit of himself and the company. The only reason given was that he "stepped on somebody's toes." Ironically, the next day he was awarded a $10,000 bonus for his last year's performance. St. Regis has refused to give any other reason for the discharge. Appellant's personnel records classify his termination as an involuntary separation and state that it was a "mutual separation for the best interest of employee and Company." His severance benefits were awarded under the St. Regis Policy and Procedural Guide section applicable to employees terminated for no cause.

. . . The language . . . in the [St. Regis] Policy and Procedural Guide states that terminations "will be processed in a manner which will at all times be fair, reasonable and just"; . . . [Appellant] also quotes an internal memoranda stating termination of controllers will be discussed before the fact between the corporate controller and divisional operations managers.

Appellant's principal argument was that the fact he was doing a good job, coupled with the quoted corporate policies, created an implied contract he would be fired only for cause.

The St. Regis Policy and Procedural Guide states that terminations will be handled in a fair, just and equitable manner and, thus, merely implements a company policy to treat employees in a fair and consistent manner. Our examination of the Policy and Procedural Guide and the entire record shows no evidence of an implied contract that appellant was to be discharged only for cause. The appellant only had a subjective understanding that he would be discharged only for cause which is insufficient to establish an implied contract to that effect. . . .

An employer's interest in running his business as he sees fit must be balanced against the interest of the employee in maintaining his employment and this exception does not strike the proper balance. We believe that:

> . . . to imply into each employment contract a duty to terminate in good faith would . . . subject each discharge to judicial incursions into the amorphous concept of bad faith.

Parnar v. Americana Hotels, Inc., 65 Hawaii 370, 377, 652 P.2d 625, 629 (1982). Moreover, while an employer may agree to restrict or limit his right to discharge an employee, to imply such a restriction on that right from the existence of a contractual right, which, by its terms has no restrictions, is internally inconsistent. Such an intrusion into the employment relationship is merely a judicial substitute for collective bargaining which is more appropriately left to the legislative process. . . .

NOTES & QUESTIONS

1. Compare *Fortune* with *Thompson*. Which court do you think gave the proper weight to the duty of good faith?

2. What advice would you give to an employer that wants to fire an at-will employee, but has no good cause to do so?

3. *Drafting Exercise:* Draft an employment agreement for the plaintiff in *Fortune* that permits the employer to fire an employee without good cause.

4. *Practice Points:* The treatment of employee manuals as forming enforceable promises depends upon the claims made in the manual, statements made by the employer regarding the manual, and references in any employment contracts. When creating employment contracts, policy manuals should be closely examined to be certain the employer has not undertaken additional obligations.

PATTERSON v. MEYERHOFER
97 N.E. 472 (N.Y. 1912)

Willard Bartlett, Judge:

The parties to this action entered into a written contract whereby the plaintiff agreed to sell, and the defendant agreed to buy, four parcels of land with the houses thereon for the sum of $23,000, to be partly in cash and partly by taking title subject to certain mortgages upon the property. When she executed this contract, the defendant knew that the plaintiff was not then the owner of the premises which he agreed to sell to her, but that he expected and intended to acquire title thereto by purchasing the same at a foreclosure sale. Before this foreclosure sale took place, the defendant stated to the plaintiff that she would not perform the contract on her part, but intended to buy the premises for her own account without in any way recognizing the said contract as binding upon her, and this she did, buying the four parcels for *$5,595* each. The plaintiff attended the foreclosure sale, able, ready, and willing to purchase the premises, and he bid for the same, but in every instance of a bid made by him the defendant bid a higher sum. The result was that she acquired each lot for $155 less than she had obligated herself to pay the plaintiff therefor under the contract or $620 less in all. . . .

In the case of every contract there is an implied undertaking on the part of each party that he will not intentionally and purposely do anything to prevent the other party from carrying out the agreement on his part.

This proposition necessarily follows from the general rule that a party who causes or sanctions the breach of an agreement is thereby precluded from recovering damages for its nonperformance or from interposing it as a defense to an action upon the contract.

"Where a party stipulates that another shall do a certain thing, he thereby impliedly promises that he will himself do nothing which may hinder or obstruct that other in doing that thing." *Gay v. Blanchard*, 32 La. Ann. 497.

By entering into the contract to purchase from the plaintiff property which she knew he would have to buy at the foreclosure sale in order to convey it to her, the defendant impliedly agreed that she would do nothing to prevent him from acquiring the property at such sale. The defendant violated the agreement thus implied on her part by bidding for and buying the premises herself. Although the plaintiff bid therefor, she uniformly outbid him. Presumably, if she had not interfered, he could have bought the property for the same price which she paid for it. He would then have been able to sell it to her for the price specified in the contract (assuming that she fulfilled the contract), which was $620 more. This sum, therefore, represents the loss which he has suffered. It is the measure of the plaintiff's damages for the defendant's breach of contract.

I see no escape from this conclusion. It is true that the contract Contemplated that the four houses should go to the defendant and they have gone to her; but that is not all. The contract contemplated that they should go to the plaintiff first. In that event the plaintiff would have received $620 which he has not got. This would have had to be paid by the defendant if she had fulfilled her contract; and she should be required to pay it now unless she can present some better defense than is presented in this record. This will place both parties in the position contemplated by the contract. The defendant will have paid no more than the contract obligated her to pay. The plaintiff will have received all to which the contract entitled him.

NOTES & QUESTIONS

1. In *Market Street Associates v. Frey*, 941 F.2d 588 (7th Cir. 1991), the court used the implied obligation of good faith to find that the plaintiff had a duty to advise the other party to a sale and leaseback arrangement that if that party did not negotiate with regard to additional funding, the plaintiff would be entitled to repurchase the property. The Court acknowledged that "[t]he duty of honesty, of good faith even expansively conceived, is not a duty of candor." Nevertheless, "[i]t is another thing to say that you can take deliberate advantage of an oversight by your contract partner concerning his rights under the contract. Such taking advantage is not the exploitation of superior knowledge or the avoidance of unbargained-for expense; it is sharp dealing." How do you decide whether a party is merely taking advantage of a business opportunity or is engaging in "sharp dealing"?

2. In *Centronics Corp. v. Genicom Corp.*, 562 A.2d 187, 190 (N.H. 1989), the court recognized three categories of contract cases where the implied duty of good faith attaches: "Those dealing with standards of conduct in contract formation, with termination of at-will employment contracts, and with limits on discretion in contractual performance." Which of these categories, if any, applies to *Patterson*?

3. The scope of the obligation of good faith has been hotly debated. Some courts treat the obligation of good faith as "excluding behavior inconsistent with common standards of decency, fairness and reasonableness, and with the parties' agreed-upon common purposes and justified expectation." *See Centronics Corp. v. Genicom Corp.*, 562 A.2d 187 (N.H. 1989). Others treat the obligation as permitting the recapture of foregone opportunities. *See Fortune, supra.* Which definition do you believe makes more sense?

4. The U.C.C. defines good faith as "honesty in fact," and, in transactions between merchants, as "the observance of reasonable commercial standards of fair

dealing in the trade." U.C.C. §§ 1-201(19) and 2-103(1)(b), respectively.

5. Failure to meet the implied duty of good faith may also lead to recovery under tort law in certain instances. Such recovery for breach of an implied covenant of good faith and fair dealing is often limited to situations where there is a "special relationship" between the parties, such as a confidential or fiduciary relationship. *See, e.g., Commonwealth Department of Transportation v. E-Z Paks, Inc.*, 620 A.2d 712 (Pa. 1993); *Wilder v. Cody County Chamber of Commerce*, 868 P.2d 211 (Wyo. 1994). In the employment field, the tort of retaliatory discharge has been recognized.

PROBLEM

A distributor of automotive gas caps enters into an exclusive distribution agreement with New Company. The agreement requires the distributor to use its best efforts in distributing New Company's products. Two weeks after entering into the New Company deal, the distributor enters into an exclusive distribution agreement with New Company's largest competitor. Because it earns a larger profit on the competitor's products, the distributor ceases distributing New Company's products. Has it breached the contract with New Company?

CHAPTER 13

CONDITIONAL CONTRACTS

In this chapter we will study conditions. RESTATEMENT (SECOND) OF CONTRACTS § 224 defines a condition as "an event, not certain to occur, which must occur, unless its non-occurrence is excused, before performance under a contract becomes due." This definition will be used as a basis for understanding each of the sections that follow in this chapter, which primarily addresses conditions precedent.[1] Generally, the operative effect of including a condition in an agreement is to safeguard a party's duty of performance. For example, if A's duty is conditional upon the happening of an event in the control of B, then A's duty of performance does not arise until the happening of the event by B. Moreover, if the event that constitutes the condition never arises, then A's duty is discharged. This practical result or strategic aspect of conditional agreements has been described as "risk allocation":

> In general, the function of a contractual condition is to place the risk of the non-occurrence of the critical event on one party rather than the other. One speaks of "risk" in this connection because the failure of a condition would often entail a loss, or at least a disadvantage, to one of the parties, with some sort of corresponding advantage or immunity to the other. If the parties bargained for that outcome — if the risk of nonoccurrence was consciously assumed and priced into the deal — then, obviously, the law ought not to intervene and the disadvantaged party must simply take her lumps. Inevitably, however, there are instances in which the intention of the parties is less than clear. Where there is doubt about the meaning of the contract and the promisee has relied substantially on the expectation of the agreed exchange, the courts . . . usually seek an interpretation that avoids or minimizes the promisee's reliance loss. Supporting this effort, RESTATEMENT § 227 states that in case of uncertainty with respect to the intended effect of a condition, the "preferred" interpretation is one that will reduce the risk of "forfeiture." M. Chirelstein, CONCEPTS AND CASE ANALYSIS IN THE LAW OF CONTRACTS (1990).

Whether a court will find that a transaction is premised upon a condition depends upon the court's interpretation of the words of the contract, the intent of the parties, the surrounding circumstances and the interests of justice. The cases that follow demonstrate that conditions can be categorized generally as either express or constructive.

---

[1] The RESTATEMENT (SECOND) OF CONTRACTS does not follow the language "condition subsequent" or "condition precedent." Rather, what has traditionally been called a condition precedent is referred to as a "condition" under the RESTATEMENT (SECOND) OF CONTRACTS, and which has been termed a "condition subsequent" is dealt with in RESTATEMENT (SECOND) OF CONTRACTS § 230 under the rules on discharge rather than the rules on condition.

A. EXPRESS CONDITIONS

Because an express condition is an expression of the parties' intention, it is included in a contract by the parties at the time of its making. Generally, a court interprets an agreement to include an express condition based upon the language of the contract, e.g., provisional language such as "provided that," "on condition that," "if," "when," "while," "after," "so that," etc. However, express conditions include not only those conditions that arise from the intentions of the parties as expressed in the language of the agreement, but also include those conditions that arise from the intentions of the parties as revealed in the words and conduct of the parties. The latter type of express condition is referred to as "implied in fact," which is consistent with an express condition in theory because it reflects the intentions of the parties. As you review the following cases, ask yourself whether the issue involves a condition or a promise. If it involves a condition, how can it be satisfied? On what basis did the court reach its conclusion regarding the existence of a condition? As demonstrated in the following excerpt from Corbin, whether an agreement regarding future performance is a promise or a condition has a direct impact on the obligations arising under it.

1. Promise vs. Condition

. . . One who makes a promise thereby expresses an intention that some future performance will be rendered and gives assurance of its rendition to the promisee. Whether the promise is express or implied, there must be either words or conduct by the promisor by the interpretation of which the court can discover promissory intention; a condition is a fact or an event and is not an expression of intention or an assurance. A promise in a contract creates a legal duty in the promisor and a right in the promisee; the fact or event constituting a condition creates no right or duty and is merely a limiting or modifying factor. . . .

A promise is always made by the act or acts of one of the parties, such acts being words or other conduct expressing intention; a fact can be made to operate as a condition only by the agreement of both parties or by the construction of the law. The purpose of a promise is the creation of a duty in the promisor; the purpose of constituting some facts as a condition is always the postponement or discharge of an instant duty (or other specified legal relation). The non-fulfillment of a promise is called a breach of contact, and creates in the other party a secondary right to damages; it is the failure to perform that which was required by a legal duty. The non-occurrence of a condition will prevent the existence of a duty in the other party; but it may not create any remedial rights and duties at all, and it will not unless someone has promised that it shall occur. . . .

The first step, therefore, in interpreting an expression in a contract, with respect to condition as opposed to promise, is to ask oneself the question: Was this expression intended to be an assurance by one party to the other that some performance by the first would be rendered in the future and that the other could rely upon it? If the answer is yes, we have found the expression to be a promise that the specified performance will take place. The alternative question to be asked is: Was this expression intended to make a duty of one party conditional and dependent upon some performance by the other (or on some other fact or event)? If the answer to this question is yes, we have found that the specified performance is a condition of duty, but we have not found that anyone has promised that the performance will take place. It is not difficult to draw the logical distinction between a promise that a specified performance will be rendered, and a provision that makes a specified performance a condition of the legal duty of a party who promises to render another performance. The first creates a legal duty in the promisor; the second limits and postpones a promisor's duty.

CORBIN ON CONTRACTS § 633.

JONES ASSOCIATES, INC. v. EASTSIDE PROPERTIES, INC.
41 Wash. App. 462, 704 P.2d 681 (1985)

SWANSON, Judge:

Jones Associates, Inc. (Jones Associates) appeals the superior court judgment (1) dismissing its action against Eastside Properties, Inc., et al., (Eastside) for money due under a professional services contract of $15,030 plus interest. . . . We reverse and remand for trial.

In early 1977 Jones Associates, an engineering, consulting, and surveying firm, and Eastside Properties, a real estate development corporation, entered into a professional services agreement. The contract signed by the parties was a preprinted form commonly used by Jones Associates which was modified by an Eastside representative.

Under the contract for a $17,480 fixed fee, including short plat application fees, Jones Associates was to provide a feasibility study, master plan, nine record surveys, and nine short plats for Eastside's 180-acre land parcel. In May, 1978 Jones Associates submitted Eastside's short plat application to the King County Building and Land Development Division, which in July, 1978, gave its preliminary approval with numerous conditions attached. Eastside unsuccessfully appealed the conditions imposed.

To enable Eastside to comply with the imposed conditions, the parties entered into a June 19, 1979 amendment to the original contract, which amendment expressly incorporated all of the original contract's terms. For a $12,550 fixed fee, under the change order Jones Associates was to provide an updated feasibility study, a roadway plan and profile, a design for a water system if not provided by the water district, storm drainage plans submitted for approval, and revised short plats filed for recordation.

Jones Associates claims that it performed all required services under the original contract and the change order. According to Eastside Properties, however, the following two conditions precedent to payment were not met: the original and the updated feasibility studies were not proven to be satisfactory to Eastside, and King County final plat approval was not obtained.

Eastside paid $15,000 to Jones Associates in April, 1980. In March, 1981 Jones Associates brought a money due action against Eastside. At the time of trial Eastside's short plat application still had not been approved, and the extension period to obtain final county approval had expired.

At the end of the plaintiff's evidence the trial court granted Eastside's motion to dismiss the complaint. . . . The court's oral decision stated that the dismissal was based upon its interpretation of the unambiguous contract language that obtaining county approval was a condition precedent to contractual payment, which condition had not been met. Jones Associates' reconsideration' motion was denied, and this appeal followed.

The issue is whether the trial court erred in dismissing Jones Associates' action against Eastside Properties. Eastside Properties claims that the following contract provision creates a condition precedent to payment: "Engineer shall be responsible for obtaining King County approval for all platting as set forth above." Jones Associates, however, contends that the provision is not a condition precedent but rather merely states that it was to perform all necessary engineering, consulting, and surveying services related to Eastside's short plat application. We conclude that the provision is a promise rather than a condition precedent; thus dismissing the action was error.

Here upon the defendant's motion at the close of the plaintiff's case, the trial court dismissed the action as a matter of law and thus entered no findings of fact or conclusions of law. . . . In such a case the appellate court, like the trial court, looks upon the plaintiff's evidence in its most favorable light and determines whether the trial court correctly applied the law in dismissing the action. . . . Absent disputed facts, the construction of a contract is a matter of law, and the appellate court is in as good a position as the trial court to interpret a contract's meaning. . . .

A condition precedent is an event occurring after the making of a valid contract which must occur before a right to immediate performance arises. . . . In contrast to the breach of a promise, which subjects the promisor to liability for damages but does not necessarily discharge the other party's duty of performance, the nonoccurrence of a condition prevents the promisee from acquiring a right or deprives him of one but subjects him to no liability. *Ross v. Harding*, 64 Wash. 2d 231, 236, 391 P.2d 526 (1964); 5 S. WILLISTON, CONTRACTS § 665, at 132 (3d ed. 1961).

Whether a provision in a contract is a condition, the nonfulfillment of which excuses performance, depends upon the intent of the parties, to be ascertained from a fair and reasonable construction of the language used in the light of all the surrounding circumstances. 5 WILLISTON, CONTRACTS (3d ed.) § 663, p. 127.

. . .

Where it is doubtful whether words create a promise or an express condition, they are interpreted as creating a promise. Ross, *supra*.

An intent to create a condition is often revealed by such phrases and words as "provided that," "on condition," "when," "so that," "while," "as soon as," and "after." . . .

Here no such words were used, and it is unclear whether the parties intended obtaining King County approval to be a condition precedent to payment under the contract.

Where the parties' contractual language is ambiguous, the principal goal of construction is to search out the parties' intent. . . .

Determination of the intent of the contracting parties is to be accomplished by viewing the contract as a whole, the subject matter and objective of the contract, all the circumstances surrounding the making of the contract, the subsequent acts and conduct of the parties to the contract, and the reasonableness of respective interpretations advocated by the parties.

Stender v. Twin City Foods, Inc., 82 Wash. 2d 250, 254, 510 P.2d 221 (1973), quoted in *Leija v. Materne Bros., Inc.*, 34 Wash. App. 825, 829, 664 P.2d 527 (1983). Here an examination of the entire contract, circumstances surrounding the contract's formation, the parties' subsequent conduct, and the reasonableness of the parties' respective interpretations indicates that the parties intended Jones Associates' assumption of responsibility for obtaining King County approval to be a duty under the contract but not a condition precedent to payment.

First, the relevant provision's language in the second typewritten paragraph under "Scope of Services" does not expressly indicate that if King County approval was not obtained, Eastside would not be responsible for any costs whatsoever, as does the preceding typewritten paragraph[2] containing an express condition precedent regarding a satisfactory economic feasibility study. Since the two typewritten paragraphs were inserted into the contract by Eastside, the first typewritten paragraph provides evidence of Eastside's ability clearly and unambiguously to express a condition precedent to payment. Moreover, ambiguous contract language is strictly construed against the drafter. . . .

Further, other portions of the original contract support Jones Associates' contention that it contemplated its contractual duty to be to perform necessary services related to the short plat application rather than that obtaining King County final plat approval was to be a condition precedent to payment. The "Description of Final Product" lists, besides a development feasibility report and master plan, nine record surveys and nine short plats "in King County format," not "approved by King County." Similarly, the contract states under "Completion of Assignment" that the short plats were to be ready for submission by a certain date, not that they were to have King County approval by a certain date. In addition, while the change order is in accord with Jones Associates' assuming responsibility for obtaining King County final plat approval, the language implies a duty rather than an express condition precedent: One of Jones Associates' services to be performed under the change order was to revise and "file for recordation," not obtain county approval of, the short plats.

Moreover, the respondent's conduct subsequent to the making of the contract supports the interpretation that the parties did not intend the relevant provision to be a condition precedent. First, rather than refusing to pay the fixed fee because of the nonoccurrence of a condition precedent, Eastside did tender in April, 1980, $15,000 of the $30,030 that was due under the original contract and its amendment. In addition, Eastside did, though not without argument, enter into a contractual amendment for $12,550 for Jones Associates to perform additional services so that it could comply with King County's imposed conditions rather than insisting that the condition precedent of obtaining King County approval contemplated that the

---

[2] [4] The first typewritten paragraph states: "Engineer shall promptly complete feasibility study and if said study establishes to Client's satisfaction that the development project is economic, the Engineer shall be required to fulfill the entire scope of services as set forth in this agreement.

In the event said feasibility study is not satisfactory to Client, this entire agreement shall be considered terminated and Client shall not be responsible for any costs or charges whatsoever."

original contract encompassed any necessary additional services to secure such approval.

Further, it is well-established that forfeitures are not favored in law and are never enforced in equity unless the right thereto is so clear as to permit of no denial.

Kaufman Bros. Constr. v. Olney, 29 Wash. App. 296, 300, 628 P.2d 838 (1981) (quoting *Dill v. Zielke*, 26 Wash. 2d 246, 252, 173 P.2d 977 (1946)).[3] The RESTATEMENT (SECOND) OF CONTRACTS § 227(1) (1981) states:

> In resolving doubts as to whether an event is made a condition of an obligor's duty, . . . an interpretation is preferred that will reduce the obligee's risk of forfeiture, unless the event is within the obligee's control or the circumstances indicate that he has assumed the risks.

The RESTATEMENT § 227 comment b continues:

> If the event is within [the obligee's] control, he will often assume this risk [of forfeiture]. If it is not within his control, it is sufficiently unusual for him to assume the risk that, in case of doubt, an interpretation is preferred under which the event is not a condition.

Here since obtaining King County final plat approval was not within Jones Associates' control, it was sufficiently unusual for it to assume the risk of forfeiture so that where doubt exists, as in this case, the preferred interpretation is that the event was not a condition. No circumstances have been shown to indicate that it assumed the risk of forfeiture; rather, Harry P. Jones, Jones Associates' president, testified to the contrary. Moreover, conditions precedent are not favored by the courts. . . . An examination of the entire contract, the circumstances of its formation, the parties' conduct and the reasonableness of their interpretations supports the conclusion that obtaining King County final plat approval was intended to be Jones Associates' duty under the contract but not a condition precedent to payment. . . .

The judgment is reversed and the cause is remanded for trial. . . .

NOTES & QUESTIONS

1. What guidelines did the *Jones* court set forth as helpful in determining whether a contract duty is premised upon an express condition? How did the language of the entire agreement affect the court's decision?

2. Corbin has described conditional as opposed to unconditional rights and duties as follows:

> The group of operative facts that cause us to say that A has a right against B do not occur at one moment of time. When we say that a right is "conditional," we mean that some of these operative facts exist, but that one or more other facts necessary to perfect the legal relation that we have in mind do not yet exist. Any one of these other necessary facts is a

---

[3] [5] The RESTATEMENT (SECOND) OF CONTRACTS § 227 comment b (1981) defines "forfeiture" as the resulting denial of compensation where the nonoccurrence of a condition of an obligor's duty causes the obligee to lose his right to the agreed exchange after he has relied substantially on the expectation of that exchange, as by preparation or performance.

"condition" of the existence of the contemplated legal relation. This indicates the difference between a conditional right and an unconditional one. If it is unconditional, all of the necessary creative facts exist; if it is conditional, at least one of these facts has still to occur.

CORBIN ON CONTRACTS § 626 (1952). Using Corbin's comments as instructive, do you agree with the court in *Jones* that "obtaining King County approval" was a duty assumed by Jones under the agreement?

3. If the court in *Jones* had decided that the contract was premised upon an express condition, what result? Would such a decision be consistent with RESTATE-MENT (SECOND) OF CONTRACTS § 227, which provides that in deciding whether an event is to be a condition of the obligor's duty, "an interpretation is preferred that will reduce the obligee's risk of forfeiture, unless the event is within the obligee's control . . ."?

4. *Drafting Exercise:* How would you rewrite the provision in the contract between Jones and Eastside, so that a court would interpret it as an express condition?

5. *Express conditions and literal performance.* Express conditions must be strictly complied with or courts will find that the promisor's duty of performance is extinguished under the contract or correspondingly, that the promisee's rights thereunder have been forfeited. To avoid the harsh consequences of the failure of a condition, courts often prefer to interpret contract language as that of promise as opposed to condition. However, when it is clear from the agreement that the parties' rights and duties are subject to an express condition, a court will enforce the harsh consequences of such a transaction. For example: Borrower and Lender enter a standard mortgage commitment providing for monthly repayment. Additionally, the contract contained an acceleration clause which became active in the event that a covenant to pay was breached. The acceleration clause provided: "prior to acceleration, [Lender] shall mail notice to Borrower . . . specifying: (1) the breach; (2) the action required to cure such breach; (3) a date . . . by which such breach must be cured; and (4) failure to cure such breach . . . may result in acceleration of the sums secured by this mortgage and foreclosure or sale of the property." By letter Lender notified Borrower that he was in default of the mortgage commit-ment, and demanded payment in full within 30 days. Borrower failed to pay in full. Lender commenced a foreclosure action. Borrower defended by stating that Lender's notice was insufficient to satisfy the express condition precedent to acceleration. What result? *See Wilshire Credit Corporation v. Sound Beach Associates,* 1996 LEXIS 3380 (Conn. Super. 1996).

CHIRICHELLA v. ERWIN
270 Md. 178, 310 A.2d 555 (1973)

LEVINE, Judge:

This appeal is from a decree for specific performance of a contract for the sale of real estate. Appellants (the Chirichellas) had contracted in June 1971 to sell their home in Silver Spring to appellees (the Erwins) for the sum of $39,200. Due to the refusal of the Chirichellas to settle, the Erwins finally sued them on August 31, 1972 for specific performance. At the conclusion of the trial, the Circuit Court for Montgomery County (Miller, J.) entered the decree from which this appeal is taken.

The contract entered into by the parties was the "standard" form used by the Montgomery County Board of Realtors. Paragraph Six of the form contract, entitled "Settlement," reads as follows:

> Within _ days from date of acceptance hereof by the Seller, or as soon there-after as a report of the title can be secured if promptly ordered, and/or survey, if required, and/or Government-insured loan, if used, can be processed, if promptly applied for, the Seller and Purchaser are required and agree to make full settlement in accordance with the terms hereof. . . .

Apparently when the real estate salesman initially submitted the contract to the Chirichellas, the words, "by Oct. 1, 1971 or sooner," had been inserted in the blank space. By mutual agreement, this language was amended to read, 'Coincide with settlement of New Home in Kettering Approx. Oct. "71." No other reference to the "New Home in Kettering" appears in the contract.

The Chirichellas had contracted to purchase the "New Home" in April 1971. Their agreement provided that they were to settle "within fifteen (15) days from the date of completion." Although construction of the new house had not yet commenced when the Erwin contract was executed in April, the Chirichellas were confident that it would be completed by October unless unforeseen developments intervened. Their confidence proved to be unwarranted as the first settlement of the "New Home" was scheduled for June 15, 1972. The record does not indicate when construction actually commenced.

The June settlement on the "New Home" never materialized because the Chirichellas claimed it was not completed "in a workmanlike manner." In July, their attorney wrote to the realtor handling that transaction and itemized 84 alleged defects in the house. The testimony at trial reflects a clear-cut difference of opinion in that regard between the Chirichellas and a representative of the builder. The latter maintained that the house had been satisfactorily completed and implied that the Chirichellas were being unreasonable. In any event, settlement was rescheduled for two separate dates in August, but the Chirichellas persisted in their claim that the house was not yet ready for occupancy. Settlement has never occurred on the "New Home" and it appears that it has been resold to another purchaser.

The first settlement of the contract on the house sold by the Chirichellas to the Erwins was also scheduled for June 15, 1972. Sometime prior to that date, but after October 1971, Mr. Erwin asked Mr. Chirichella to settle, but the latter refused because the "New Home" was not ready. The Chirichellas did not appear at the June 15 settlement, and it was rescheduled for August 9. When that proved to be futile, the Erwins filed their suit on August 31, 1972.

Although he was of the view that the Chirichellas' complaints concerning the "New Home" were justified, the chancellor concluded that the provision for settlement inserted in the Erwin contract was not a condition precedent to performance, but merely a requirement that settlement take place during the month of October 1971, or within a reasonable time thereafter. And, since more than a reasonable time had elapsed, the Erwins were entitled to a decree for specific performance. We agree, and therefore affirm.

Before this Court, the Chirichellas attack the chancellor's ruling on the same grounds raised below: That the contested provision was a condition precedent to performance on their part, and since that condition failed, the contract failed with it. They rely almost entirely on *Griffith v. Scheungrab*, 219 Md. 27, 146 A.2d 864 (1958) for this contention. This reliance is completely misplaced, as there we merely held that:

> . . . Where a contractual duty is subject to a condition precedent, . . . there is no duty of performance and . . . 'a decree for specific performance will not be granted unless conditions precedent, express, implied, or constructive, have all occurred or been performed.' (citations omitted)." 219 Md. at 34–35, 146 A.2d at 868.

This argument begs the question. The issue is not whether there was a failure of a condition precedent, but whether the disputed clause indeed constitutes a condition precedent. We have already indicated our agreement with the chancellor that it does not.

A condition precedent has been defined as "a fact, other than mere lapse of time, which, unless excused, must exist or occur before a duty of immediate performance of a promise arises," 17 AM. JUR. 2D, *Contracts*, § 320. . . . The question whether a stipulation in a contract constitutes a condition precedent is one of construction dependent on the intent of the parties to be gathered from the words they have employed and, in case of ambiguity, after resort to the other permissible aids to interpretation. . . . Although no particular form of words is necessary in order to create an express condition, such words and phrases as "if" and "provided that," are commonly used to indicate that performance has expressly been made conditional, . . . as have the words "when," "after," "as soon as," or "subject to,". . . .

We turn then to the question of whether the language in controversy here meets the definition of a condition precedent, i.e., whether it may be read to mean that settlement on the 'New Home in Kettering' must have occurred before the Chirichellas' duty to settle with the Erwins arose. We think the provision in issue no more accomplishes that purpose than the words which it replaced. As we read the clause, "Coincide with settlement of New Home in Kettering Approx. Oct. '71," it merely fixes a convenient and appropriate time for settlement.

Although the amendment attempted to link one settlement with the other, its only effect was to insure that the October 1971 time designation not be regarded as of the essence. Cf. *String v. Steven Development Corporation*, 269 Md. 569, 307 A.2d 713, 718 (1973) where, given a form contract identical to that used here with '130' inserted in the blank space of the 'settlement clause,' we held that time was not made of the essence; and that 'the parties were required to settle within a reasonable period' after the expiration of the time specified. . . .

Here, whatever might have been the consequence had the phrase, "Approx. Oct. '71," not been added to the insertion, its inclusion effectively defeats the Chirichellas' argument. The result, as the chancellor ruled, was not to allow them to "avoid the contract," but to "delay settlement for a reasonable period of time while the (new) house was completed."

In sum, the Chirichellas' duty to perform by settling under their contract with the Erwins was not subject to the condition precedent that they first settle on the new house. Hence, they were required to do so within a reasonable time after October 1971. As suggested by the chancellor, that time had long since expired by January 29,1973, the day of trial.

Decree affirmed; appellants to pay costs.

PEACOCK CONSTRUCTION CO., INC. v. MODERN AIR CONDITIONING, INC.
353 So. 2d 840 (Fla. 1977)

Boyd, Acting Chief Justice:

We issued an order allowing certiorari in these two causes because the decisions in them of the District Court of Appeal, Second District, conflict with the decision in *Edward J. Gerrits, Inc. v. Astor Electric Service, Inc.*, 328 So. 2d 522 (Fla. 3d DCA 1976). The two causes have been consolidated for all appellate purposes in this Court because they involve the same issue. That issue is whether the plaintiffs, Modern Air Conditioning and Overly Manufacturing, were entitled to summary judgments against Peacock Construction Company in actions for breaches of identical contractual provisions.

Peacock Construction was the builder of a condominium project. Modern Air Conditioning subcontracted with Peacock to do the heating and air conditioning work and Overly Manufacturing subcontracted with Peacock to do the "rooftop swimming pool" work. Both written subcontracts provided that Peacock would make final payment to the subcontractors,

> within 30 days after the completion of the work included in this sub-contract, written acceptance by the Architect and full payment therefor by the Owner.

. . .

Modern Air Conditioning and Overly Manufacturing completed the work specified in their contracts and requested final payment. When Peacock refused to make the final payments the two subcontractors separately brought actions in the Lee County Circuit Court for breach of contract. In both actions it was established that no deficiencies had been found in the completed work. But Peacock established that it had not received from the owner full payment for the subcontractors' work. And it defended on the basis that such payment was a condition which, by express term of the final payment provision, had to be fulfilled before it was obligated to perform under the contract.

On motions by the plaintiffs, the trial judges granted summary judgments in their favor. The orders of judgment implicitly interpreted the contract not to require payment by the owner as a condition precedent to Peacock's duty to perform.

The Second District Court of Appeal affirmed the lower court's judgment in the appeal brought by Modern Air Conditioning[4] In so doing it adopted the view of the majority of jurisdictions in this country that provisions of the kind disputed here do not set conditions precedent but rather constitute absolute promises to pay, fixing payment by the owner as a reasonable time for when payment to the subcontractor is to be made. When the judgment in the Overly Manufacturing case reached the Second District Court, Modern Air Conditioning had been decided and the

---

[4] [5] Peacock Construction Co. Inc. v. Modern Air Conditioning, 339 So. 2d 294 (Fla. 2d DCA 1976).

judgment, therefore, was affirmed on the authority of the latter decision.[5] These two decisions plainly conflict with *Gerrits, supra.*

In *Gerrits,* the Court had summarily ordered judgment for the plaintiff/ contractor against the defendant/general contractor on a contractual provision for payment to the subcontractor which read,

> "The money to be paid in current funds and at such times as the General Contractor receives it from the Owner." *Id.* at 523.

In its review of the judgment, the Third District Court of Appeal referred to the fundamental rule of interpretation of contracts that it be done in accordance with the intention of the parties. Since the defendant had introduced below the issue of intention, a material issue, and since the issue was one that could be resolved through a factual determination by the jury, the Third District reversed the summary judgment and remanded for trial.

Peacock urges us to adopt *Gerrits* as the controlling law in this State. It concedes that the Second District's decisions are backed by the weight of authority. But it argues that they are incorrect because the issue of intention is a factual one which should be resolved after the parties have had an opportunity to present evidence on it. Peacock urges, therefore, that the causes be remanded for trial. If there is produced no evidence that the parties intended there be condition precedents, only then, says Peacock, should the judge, by way of a directed verdict for the subcontractors, be allowed to take the issue of intention from the jury.

The contractual provisions in dispute here are susceptible to two interpretations. They may be interpreted as setting a condition precedent or as fixing a reasonable time for payment. The provision disputed in Gerrits is susceptible to the same two interpretations. The questions presented by the conflict between these decisions, then, are whether ambiguous contractual [provisions may be] interpreted as a matter of law by the court, and if so what provisions of the kind disputed here may be interpreted only by the factfinder, usually the jury, or if they should be interpreted as a matter of law by the Court, and if so what interpretation they should be given.

Although it must be admitted that the meaning of language is a factual question, the general rule is that interpretation of a document is a question of law rather than of fact. . . . If an issue of contract interpretation concerns the intention of parties, that intention may be determined from the written contract, as a matter of law, when the nature of the transaction lends itself to judicial interpretation. A number of courts, with whom we agree, have recognized that contracts between small subcontractors and general contractors on large construction projects are such transactions. . . . The reason is that the relationship between the parties is a common one and usually their intent will not differ from transaction to transaction, although it may be differently expressed.

That intent in most cases is that payment by the owner to the general contractor is not a condition precedent to the general contractor's duty to pay the subcontractors. This is because small subcontractors, who must have payment for their work in order to remain in business, will not ordinarily assume the risk of the owner's

---

[5] [6] Peacock Construction Co. v. Overly Mfg. Co., 343 So. 2d 850 (Ha. 1976).

failure to pay the general contractor. And this is the reason for the majority view in this country, which we now join.

Our decision to require judicial interpretation of ambiguous provisions for final payment in subcontracts in favor of subcontractors should not be regarded as anti-general contractor. It is simply a recognition that this is the fairest way to deal with the problem. There is nothing in this opinion, however, to prevent parties to these contracts from shifting the risk of payment failure by the owner to the subcontractor. But in order to make such a shift the contract must unambiguously express that intention. And the burden of clear expression is on the general contractor.

The decisions of the Second District Court of Appeal to affirm the summary judgments were correct. We adopt, therefore, these two decisions as the controlling law in Florida and we overrule Gerrits, to the extent it is inconsistent with this opinion.

The orders allowing certiorari in these two causes are discharged. It is so ordered.

MASCIONI v. I.B. MILLER, INC.
261 N.Y. 1, 184 N.E. 473 (1933)

LEHMAN, Judge:

The plaintiffs and the defendant entered into a written contract whereby the plaintiffs, described in the contract as the "Sub-Contractor," agreed to provide all the materials and all the work for the erection of concrete walls, and the defendant, described in the contract as the "Contractor," agreed to pay therefor the sum of 55 cents per cubic foot. The concrete walls were to be erected as "specified in a certain contract between the Contractor and Village Apartments, Inc., described therein as Owner," and the defendant's promise to pay contained the proviso, "Payments to be made as received from the Owner." In spite of the fact that the owner has made no payments to the defendant for the work and materials, or any part thereof, performed and furnished by the plaintiffs, the plaintiffs have recovered a judgment against the defendant for the agreed price.

The problem presented on this appeal is whether the defendant assumed an absolute obligation to pay, though for convenience payment might be postponed till moneys were received from the owner, or whether the defendant's obligation to pay arose only if and when the owner made payment to the defendant. At the trial, the plaintiffs, claiming that the contract was ambiguous, were permitted to introduce testimony to show that, before the written contract was signed, much of the work had been performed under an oral contract by which the defendant assumed an absolute obligation to pay; and the defendant, though claiming that the written contract, in unambiguous terms, annexed a contingency to the defendant's obligation to pay, produced parol testimony to show that the plaintiffs expressly assumed the risk that they might never be paid. A judgment in favor of the defendant was reversed by the Appellate Division on the ground that the contract is unambiguous and that the provision with respect to payment "merely fixed the time of payment and did not create a condition precedent."

A provision for the payment of an obligation upon the happening of an event does not become absolute until the happening of the event. Whether the defendant's express promise to pay is construed as a promise to pay "if" payment is made by the owner or "when" such payment is made, "the result must be the same; since, if the event does not befall, or a time coincident with the happening of the event does not arrive, in neither case may performance be exacted.". . .

True, a debt with consequent obligation to pay may exist aside from any express promise to pay. Then a condition annexed to an express promise to pay the debt may render the promise to pay conditional without making the debt subject to the same condition. "It must be admitted, however, that a condition annexed to a promise to pay a debt will commonly, upon the true construction of the instrument in which it is contained, extend to the debt itself. There is a difference also between a promise to pay a debt on a certain condition, and a proviso that the debt shall be payable only upon a certain condition; for the latter necessarily renders the debt itself conditional." . . . In this case, if there were no express promise to pay a stipulated price for stipulated work, such a promise would be implied. There is, however, an express promise to pay moneys "as received from the Owner," and the event upon which that promise would ripen into an absolute, immediate obligation has not occurred. From the express promise to pay upon the happening of an event, an inference may be drawn that the parties did not intend or impliedly agree that payment should be made even if the event does not occur.

In many cases, nevertheless, an inference that an express promise to pay a debt on a certain condition excludes an implication that the debt shall be paid, even though performance of the condition is impossible, would defeat the intention of the parties. The tests approved by the Law Institute in its RESTATEMENT OF THE LAW OF CONTRACTS, § 295, are whether "(a) a debt for performance rendered has already arisen and the condition relates only to the time when the debt is to be discharged, or (b) existence of the condition is no material part of the exchange for the promiser's performance, and the discharge of the promiser will operate as a forfeiture." In either case "impossibility that would discharge the duty to perform a promise excuses the performance of a condition."

Here on its face the contract provides for a promise to perform in exchange for a promise to pay as payments are "received from the Owner." Performance by the plaintiff would inure directly to the benefit of the owner and indirectly to the benefit of the defendant, because the defendant had a contract with the owner to perform the work for a stipulated price. The defendant would not profit by the plaintiffs' performance unless the owner paid the stipulated price. That was the defendant's risk, but the defendant's promise to pay the plaintiffs for stipulated work on condition that payment was received by the defendant shifted that risk to the plaintiffs, if the condition was a material part of the exchange of plaintiffs' promise to perform for defendant's promise to pay.

In many cases similar conditions in contracts for compensation of brokers have been enforced in accordance with the letter of the promise to pay. In principle, brokerage contracts cannot be distinguished from other contracts to pay compensation for services rendered or materials furnished. "In each case, the intention of the parties to make the debt contingent or otherwise, must be gathered from the language used, the situation of the parties, and the subject matter of the contract, as presented by the evidence.". . .

Here we are not called upon to decide whether the language of the contract, read in the light of the situation of the parties and the subject-matter of the contract, shows clearly and unambiguously that the condition attached to the debt or obligation to pay, and did not merely fix the time of payment. Certainly on its face it is open to the construction that the plaintiffs accepted the condition as a material part of the exchange for their own promise or performance. The trial judge, after receiving parol evidence of the actual intention of the parties, gave it this construction, and that construction was not erroneous as matter of law.

The judgment of the Appellate Division should be reversed, and that of the Special Term affirmed, with costs in this court and in the Appellate Division.

Judgment accordingly.

NOTES & QUESTIONS

1. Are the decisions in *Chirichella* and *Peacock* consistent with the preference of courts to find, in cases of ambiguity, a promise over a condition? How? Can you reconcile *Mascioni* with *Peacock* and *Chirichella?*

Generally, the "mere passage of time" is not interpreted as a condition. (RESTATEMENT (SECOND) OF CONTRACTS § 224, comment b.) Why do you think this is so? Does the RESTATEMENT (SECOND) OF CONTRACTS make this clear? *Compare* RESTATEMENT OF CONTRACTS § 250 (1932) *with* RESTATEMENT (SECOND) OF CONTRACTS § 224 (1981).

2. *Implied in fact conditions.* Generally, courts will find the existence of an express condition by construing the language of the contract with specific attention to such triggering language as "if, whether, provided" and other similar terms. Clearly, however, the rules of interpretation allow courts to determine whether certain language is sufficiently clear to constitute a condition. Additionally, courts may also find a condition to exist by its interpretation of the conduct of the parties and the facts of the case. Such conditions are called " 'implied in fact' conditions," which have been described as follows:

> . . . A condition implied in fact is an express (true) condition. It is not spelled out in so many words but rather is gathered from the terms of the contract as a matter of interpretation.
>
> In a given agreement it may be difficult to determine whether a condition has been expressed in so many words or whether it is implied in fact by virtue of the words and conduct of the parties. It is not important that this determination be made since the same general rule applies to both, that is, a true condition must be literally complied with. Since there is no difference in consequences, implied in fact conditions and conditions set forth in so many words are both denominated as express (true) conditions.

John D. Calamari & Joseph M. Perillo, CONTRACTS HORNBOOK SERIES § 11-8 (3d ed. 1987). Bearing in mind that courts are reluctant to find the existence of an express condition, and prefer to find a promise over a condition, do you think that implied in fact conditions are seen very often?

The case of the engagement ring. Plaintiff asked defendant to marry him and upon defendant's acceptance of plaintiff's marriage proposal, plaintiff gave defendant a valuable diamond engagement ring. After receiving the ring, defendant refused to marry the plaintiff. Plaintiff brought suit demanding the return of the diamond ring on the grounds that the ring was given to the defendant upon the condition that she marry the plaintiff. What do you think the court held with regard to plaintiff's implied in fact theory? *See Beck v. Cohen*, 262 N.Y.S. 716 (1933).

The case of two loans. Suppose Lender issued a loan commitment to Borrower which provided for one loan to go to Borrower for the purchase of an airplane and a second loan to go to Borrower for the purchase of an engine for that plane. Borrower failed to make timely payment on the first loan and Lender repossessed the airplane. When Lender then refused to disburse the second loan, Borrower brought suit for breach of contract. Should possession of the airplane be an implied in fact condition precedent to receiving the second loan? *See CIT Group/Equipment Financing, Inc. v. Integrated Financial Services, Inc.*, 910 S.W. 2d 722 (Mo. 1995).

3. *Condition precedent to formation of a contract.* With regard to conditions precedent, courts distinguish between conditions precedent to performance under a contract, and conditions precedent to the formation of a contract. For the applicability of the parol evidence rule to conditions precedent to formation, consider the following. Owner of Company A executed a written agreement with owner of Company B under which they agreed to merge their corporate interests into a single company. The document recited that A and B would subscribe for a specified number of shares in the new company and that the subscriptions were to take place within five days after the date of the agreement. As consideration for the subscriptions in the new company the parties agreed to transfer stock they each owned to the new company. A failed to transfer his stock to the new company and thus did not receive joint stock in the new company. A sued for breach. B defended by asserting that the parties orally agreed that the "deal" would not become effective until they procured the necessary expansion funds. Will the parol evidence rule prevent B from proving the existence of the condition precedent? *See Hicks v. Bush*, 10 N.Y.2d 488, 225 N.Y.S.2d 34, 180 N.E.2d 425 (1962).

INTERNATIO-ROTTERDAM, INC. v. RIVER BRAND RICE MILLS, INC.
259 F.2d 137 (2d Cir. 1958)

HINCKS, Circuit Judge:

Appeal from the United States District Court, Southern District of New York, Walsh, Judge, upon the dismissal of the complaint after plaintiff's case was in.

The defendant-appellee, a processor of rice, in July 1952 entered into an agreement with the plaintiff-appellant, an exporter, for the sale of 95,600 pockets of rice. The terms of the agreement, evidenced by a purchase memorandum, indicated that the price per pocket was to be "$8.25 F.A.S. Lake Charles and/or Houston, Texas"; that shipment was to be "December, 1952, with two weeks call from buyer"; and that payment was to be by "irrevocable letter of credit to be opened immediately payable against' dock receipts and other specified documents. In the fall, the appellant, which had already committed itself to supplying this rice to a Japanese buyer, was unexpectedly confronted with United States export restrictions upon its December shipments and was attempting to get an export license from the government. December is a peak month in the rice and cotton seasons in Louisiana and Texas, and the appellee became concerned about shipping instructions under the contract, since congested conditions prevailed at both the mills and the docks. The appellee seasonally elected to deliver 50,000 pockets at

Lake Charles and on December 10 it received from the appellant instructions for the Lake Charles shipments. Thereupon it promptly began shipments to Lake Charles which continued until December 23, the last car at Lake Charles being unloaded on December 31. December 17 was the last date in December which would allow appellee the two week period provided in the contract for delivery of the rice to the ports and ships designated. Prior thereto, the appellant had been having difficulty obtaining either a ship or a dock in this busy season in Houston. On December 17, the appellee had still received no shipping instructions for the 45,600 pockets destined for Houston. On the morning of the 18th, the appellee rescinded the contract for the Houston shipments, although continuing to make the Lake Charles deliveries. It is clear that one of the reasons for the prompt cancellation of the contract was the rise in market price of rice from $8.25 per pocket, the contract price, to $9.75. The appellant brought this suit for refusal to deliver the Houston quota.

The area of contest is also considerably reduced by the appellant's candid concession that the appellee's duty to ship, by virtue of the two-week notice provision, did not arise until two weeks after complete shipping instructions had been given by the appellant. Thus on brief the appellant says: "we concede (as we have done from the beginning) that on a fair interpretation of the contract appellant had a duty to instruct appellee by December 17, 1952 as to the place to which it desired appellee to ship — at both ports, and that, being late with its instructions in this respect, appellant could not have demanded delivery (at either port) until sometime after December 31, 1952." This position was taken, of course, with a view to the contract provision for shipment "December, 1952": a two-week period ending December 31 would begin to run on December 17. But although appellant concedes that the two weeks' notice to which appellee was entitled could not be shortened by the failure to give shipping instructions on or before December 17, it stoutly insists that upon receipt of shipping instructions subsequent to December 17 the appellee thereupon became obligated to deliver within two weeks thereafter. We do not agree.

It is plain that a giving of the notice by the appellant was a condition precedent to the appellee's duty to ship. . . . Obviously, the appellee could not deliver free alongside ship, as the contract required, until the appellant identified its ship and its location. . . . Thus the giving of shipping instructions was what Professor Corbin would classify as a "promissory condition": the appellant promised to give the notice and the appellee's duty to ship was conditioned on the receipt of the notice. . . . The crucial question is whether that condition was performed. And that depends on whether the appellee's duty of shipment was conditioned on notice on or before December 17, so that the appellee would have two weeks wholly within December within which to perform, or whether, as we understand the appellant to contend, the appellant could perform the condition by giving the notice later in December, in which case the appellee would be under a duty to ship within two weeks thereafter. The answer depends upon the proper interpretation of the contract: if the contract properly interpreted made shipment in December of the essence then the failure to give the notice on or before December 17 was nonperformance by the appellant of a condition upon which the appellee's duty to ship in December depended.

In the setting of this case, we hold that the provision for December delivery went to the essence of the contract. In support of the plainly stated provision of the contract there was evidence that the appellee's mills and the facilities appurtenant thereto were working at full capacity in December when the rice market was at peak activity and that appellee had numerous other contracts in January as well as in December to fill. It is reasonable to infer that in July, when the contract was made, each party wanted the protection of the specified delivery period; the appellee so that it could schedule its production without undue congestion of its storage facilities and the appellant so that it could surely meet commitments which it in turn should make to its customers. There was also evidence that prices on the rice market were fluctuating. In view of this factor it is not reasonable to infer that when the contract was made in July for December delivery, the parties intended that the appellant should have an option exercisable subsequent to December 17 to postpone delivery until January. . . . That in effect would have given the appellant an option to postpone its breach of the contract, if one should then be in prospect, to a time when, so far as could have been foreseen when the contract was made, the price of rice might be falling. A postponement in such circumstances would inure to the disadvantage of the appellee who was given no reciprocal option. Further indication that December delivery was of the essence is found in the letter of credit which was provided for in the contract and established by the appellant. Under this letter, the bank was authorized to pay appellee only for deliveries "during December, 1952." It thus appears that the appellant's interpretation of the contract, under which the appellee would be obligated, upon receipt of shipping instructions subsequent to December 17, to deliver in January, would deprive the appellee of the security for payment of the purchase price for which it had contracted.

Since, as we hold, December delivery was of the essence, notice of shipping instructions on or before December 17 was not merely a "duty' of the appellant — as it concedes: it was a condition precedent to the performance which might be required of the appellee. The nonoccurrence of that condition entitled the appellee to rescind or to treat its contractual obligations as discharged. . . . On December 18th the appellant unequivocally exercised its right to rescind. Having done so, its obligations as to the Houston deliveries under the contract were at an end. And of course its obligations would not revive thereafter when the appellant finally succeeded in obtaining an export permit, a ship and a dock and then gave shipping instructions; when it expressed willingness to accept deliveries in January; or when it accomplished a "liberalization' of the outstanding letter of credit whereby payments might be made against simple forwarder's receipts instead of dock receipts. . . .

Affirmed.

NOTES & QUESTIONS

1. In *Internatio-Rotterdam* the agreement did not expressly provide that "time was of the essence," yet the court seemed to conclude that it was. How is this consistent with *Chirichella* above? With RESTATEMENT (SECOND) OF CONTRACTS § 226 (a)?

2. In RESTATEMENT (SECOND) OF CONTRACTS § 227 comment (b), the word *forfeiture* is defined as the "denial of compensation." Would forfeiture result under the decision in *Internatio-Rotterdam?* What risk did the plaintiff in that case assume? What point in time is relevant to the court in assessing risk allocation —

the time the contract is made or the time of performance?

3. *Practice Point*: If time is of the essence, the contract should state that fact in clear and unequivocal terms.

PROBLEMS

1. A painting subcontractor contracted with the general contractor to paint the interior of a public housing construction project. The contract provided that the subcontractor would be paid when the general contractor received payment from the housing authority. The contract provided in pertinent part: "Partial payments subject to all applicable provisions of the Contract shall be made when and as payments are received by the Contractor. The Subcontractor may be required as a condition precedent to any payment to furnish evidence satisfactory to the Contractor that all payrolls, material bills, and other indebtedness applicable to the work have been paid." The subcontractor completed all required work but did not receive payment for services rendered. The subcontractor brought a breach of contract action against the general contractor. The general contractor defended by asserting that the "pay when paid" clause was a condition precedent. What result? Why? *See Koch v. Construction Technology, Inc.*, 924 S.W.2d 68 (Tenn. 1996).

2. Purchasers contracted to buy a home owned by sellers for $85,000. Purchasers made an $8500 deposit to sellers. The contract was "subject to and conditional upon the purchasers first obtaining mortgage financing from a lending institution in the amount of $45,000 for a term of not less than 20 years at an interest rate which does not exceed 8% per annum." The parties further agreed that if purchasers could not obtain financing as provided in the contract, and notified the seller of such, all deposits made would be refunded and the contract would terminate without further obligation. Purchasers were only able to obtain financing at 8%. Since this failed to meet the contract requirements, timely notice was given to the sellers and purchasers demanded a return of their deposit. Sellers agreed to make up the difference between the interest rate obtained by the purchasers and the 8% rate which the contract provided by reducing the sale price. Purchasers refused, and when sellers refused to refund purchasers' deposit, purchasers brought suit for the return of their deposit on the grounds that the condition precedent to performance under the contract was not met. Do you think literal compliance was necessary here? What role does good faith play on the part of the purchasers? What result? *See Luttinger v. Rosen*, 164 Conn. 45, 316 A.2d 757 (1972).

3. A purchaser and builder entered into a contract for the construction and purchase of a new home. The contract provided, in pertinent part, "all disputes shall be settled by arbitration in accordance with the Construction Industry Arbitration Rules of the American Arbitration Association and any award rendered may be enforced in any court having jurisdiction. The parties shall first mediate these disputes in accordance with Construction Industry Mediation Rules of the American Arbitration Association." The purchaser was dissatisfied with the construction of the home and brought suit against the builder. The builder moved to stay the proceedings in the trial court and compel arbitration on the basis that arbitration was the proper initial means to settle the dispute as provided in the contract. What result? *See Weekley Homes, Inc. v. Jennings*, 936 S.W.2d 16, 18 (Tex. App. San Antonio 1996).

As you read the following cases, ask yourself: have the conditions imposed by the parties been met? Do the courts' decisions enforce the expectations of the parties or are other policies at work?

2.   Conditions of Satisfaction

The satisfaction cases are discussed here because for the most part they relate to the excuse of an express condition. To some extent they also relate to excuse of conditions because of forfeiture. . . . One of the key issues in most cases is whether the provision in the contract calls for personal (actual) satisfaction or reasonable satisfaction. The discussion is divided into two parts — the satisfaction of a party to a contract and the satisfaction of a third party. . . .

There is no question that in the case of the satisfaction of a party most of the courts tend to group the cases into two categories. (1) Those which involve taste, fancy or personal judgment, the classical example being a commission to paid a portrait. In such cases the promisor is the sole judge of the quality of the work, and his right to reject, if in good faith, is absolute and may not be reviewed by a court or jury. (2) Those which involve utility, fitness or value, which can be measured against a more or less objective standard. In these cases, although there is some conflict, we think the better view is that performance need only be reasonably satisfactory, and if the promisor refuses the proffered performance, the correctness of his decision and the adequacy of his grounds are subject to review. . . .

In the construction industry it is quite common to have a provision in the contract expressly conditioning the owner's promise to make progress payments, or at least the final payment, upon the personal satisfaction or approval of a named architect or engineer, evidenced by his certificate. Although the third person whose personal approval is made a condition precedent is usually retained by the party for whom the structure is to be built, the parties have agreed to rely on his professional integrity. Generally, courts have applied the same standard to this type of express condition precedent that has been applied to other express conditions: Strict compliance with the condition is the rule. The court will not substitute the approval or satisfaction of judge or jury for that of the chosen expert. Nevertheless, if it can be established that the expert acted dishonestly or in bad faith the condition that he expressed his approval in a certificate or otherwise will be excused. Under the modern view this is also true of gross mistake unless this risk has been assumed. The expert's misconduct is a question of fact and the burden of proof is on the party who alleges it. . . .

John D. Calamari & Joseph M. Perillo, CONTRACTS HORNBOOK SERIES § 11-37 (3d ed. 1987).

GIBSON v. CRANAGE
39 Mich. 49 (1878)

MARTSON, Judge:

Plaintiff in error brought assumpsit to recover the contract price for the making and execution of a portrait of the deceased daughter of the defendant. It appeared from the testimony of the plaintiff that he at a certain time called upon the defendant and solicited the privilege of making an enlarged picture of his deceased daughter. He says "I was to make an enlarged picture that he would like, a large one from a small one, and one that he would like and recognize as a good picture of his little girl, and he was to pay me."

The defendant testified that the plaintiff was to take the small photograph and send it away to be finished, "and when returned if it was not perfectly satisfactory to me in every particular, I need not take it or pay for it. I still objected and he urged me to do so. There was no risk about it. If it was not perfectly satisfactory to me I need not take it or pay for it."

There was little if any dispute as to what the agreement was. After the picture was finished it was shown to defendant who was dissatisfied with it and refused to accept it. Plaintiff endeavored to ascertain what the objections were, but says he was unable to ascertain clearly, and he then sent the picture away to the artist to have it changed.

On the next day he received a letter from defendant reciting the original agreement, stating that the picture shown him the previous day was not satisfactory and that he declined to take it or any other similar picture, and countermanded the order. A farther correspondence was had, but it was not very material and did not change the aspect of the case. When the picture was afterwards received by the plaintiff from the artist, he went to see defendant and to have him examine it. This defendant declined to do or to look at it, and did not until during the trial, when he examined and found the same objections still existing.

We do not consider it necessary to examine the charge in detail, as we are satisfied it was as favorable to plaintiff as the agreement would warrant.

The contract (if it can be considered such) was an express one. The plaintiff agreed that the picture when finished should be satisfactory to the defendant, and his own evidence showed that the contract in this important particular had not been performed. It may be that the picture was an excellent one and that the defendant ought to have been satisfied with it and accepted it. But under the agreement the defendant was the only person who had the right to decide this question. Where parties thus deliberately entered into an agreement which violates no rule of public policy and which is free from all taint of fraud or mistake, there is no hardship whatsoever in holding them bound by it.

Artists or third parties might consider a portrait an excellent one, and yet it prove very unsatisfactory to the person who had ordered it and who might be unable to point out with clearness or certainty the defects or objections. And if the person giving the order stipulates that the portrait when finished must be satisfactory to him or else he will not accept or pay for it, and this is agreed to, he may insist upon his right as given him by the contract. . . .

The judgment must be affirmed with costs.

DEVOINE CO. v. INTERNATIONAL CO.
136 A. 37 (Md. 1927)

BOND, Chief Judge:

In this case a buyer of goods appeals from a judgment against it, in favor of the seller, for damages from an alleged breach of the contract by the buyer's refusal to receive further deliveries after delivery of part.

On February 8, 1924, the appellee sold to the appellant, a manufacturer of candies, under a written contract for the sale, 400 barrels, of 50 gallons each, of cherries and syrup, "quality satisfactory" at specified prices, and, on November 26, 1924, after 97 of the 400 barrels had been delivered the appellant refused to receive any more and declared that the quantity of goods was not satisfactory. The appellee, the seller, in the regular course of its business, purchased green cherries in Italy, where they were grown, in amounts calculated to meet the demands for its product, and imported the cherries preserved in brine and sulfur. At its factory or place of business in Baltimore city, the cherries were put through a process which removed the brine or sulfur, and after that through further processes of boiling, coloring, and flavoring, and then were sorted and put in syrup. Thereafter they were shipped out to customers as the customers called for them. The Devoine Company, one of the customers, put such cherries up in candies, in its factory in Baltimore. At the trial of the suit below, the seller produced evidence to prove that the buyer's repudiation of the contract for further deliveries was not due to a conclusion on the buyer's part that the cherries were unsatisfactory in quality or condition, but to its preference of a plan by which it would get its supply at a lower cost. Declarations to that effect by the president of the Devoine Company were testified to, and evidence of high quality was offered by the seller and received in evidence. The buyer, on the other hand, produced evidence to substantiate its declaration that the quality of the cherries was unsatisfactory.

The exceptions bring up [two] principal questions for review. The first is that of the construction of the contract clause, "quality satisfactory." The buyer contends that this referred all question of continued acceptance of the cherries to its unrestrained choice, and that there could not properly be any inquiry into the reasons or motives for its decision, such as the trial court permitted. The seller, on the other hand, contends that the decision of the buyer had no effect on the contract, if it was not rendered as a bona fide decision as to its satisfaction with the goods delivered. And the trial court adopted the latter view, and admitted evidence and instructed the jury accordingly. A second principal question is one of the legal sufficiency of the evidence to prove any such lack of good faith in the refusal of goods. . . .

Taking up the first question, that of the construction and effect of the provision, "quality satisfactory," we assume there can be no doubt that this means of a quality satisfactory to the buyer. The arguments preceded upon that assumption. Contracts referring questions of quality or measure to the decision of a party or his agent have been construed by this court in several cases in the past, and it seems to us that, as a result of the discussions and decisions in those cases, we have a definite, clear principle of construction, and one that is in harmony with the best of later authority elsewhere. *Lynn v. B. & O. R.R. Co.*, 60 Md. 404, . . . *B. & O. R.R. Co. v. Brydon*, 65 Md. 198, 611.

When the parties to a valid contract refer any question of performance to the decision of the other party, or of a third person, the decision contracted for is final. "To substitute for it the opinions and judgments of other persons, whether judge, jury or witnesses," said Judge Miller, in *Lynn v. B. & O. R.R. Co.*, *supra*, "would be to annul the contract, and would make another in its place." And Williston (1 WILLISTON, SALES, § 191) says it would be "an arbitrary refusal by the court to enforce the contract that the parties have made, and seems unwarranted." But it is only the decision contracted for that is final. If the question referred does not arise, as if a title to be accepted as satisfactory should turn out to be clearly free from question, then a decision which pretends to be upon that question might have no effect. . . . And in those cases in which there may be a question open to decision, if the person to whom it is referred decides, not on the question submitted, but on some question of interest or advantage not made the basis of rights or obligations by the contract, the decision is outside of the contract and is given no effect by it. Apart from any possible difficulty in proof, and assuming it to be clear in any case, as, for instance, by a clear admission to that effect, that the tendered performance did meet the test stipulated for, that it was satisfactory or sufficient, as the case might be, a rejection on the ground of dissatisfaction or insufficiency would be beyond the right of the party who is to approve, in bad faith, and ineffectual. The appellant urges suggestions made in the separate concurring opinion in *B. & O. R.R. Co. v. Brydon*, *supra*, page 226, . . . that when a party to the contract is himself to be satisfied, there can be no inquiry to the reason or motives for his rejection, but that when a third person, even the party's agent is to be satisfied, his rejection is valid only if made in good faith. That view of the law was not adopted by the court in the Brydon Case, and although urged in later cases has not been adopted in any one of them. And is not accepted generally in other courts. . . . It may be added that if the suggested distinction had been adopted, it is not clear that it would ever have given any greater freedom to a corporation buyer which must always act by agents.

It is furthermore settled by our decisions that, on the issue of good faith in rejection of performance, the evidence may take a wide range, and facts such as the appellant sough to elicit in this case against objections of the appellee should be admitted. In *B. & O. R.R. Co. v. Brydon*, *supra*, coal bought by the company was required to be of a quality satisfactory to its master of transportation and master of machinery, and, after part had been delivered, acceptance of any further deliveries was refused because these agents had condemned the coal delivered as unsatisfactory, and in that case the seller, suing for a breach of the contract, offered evidence to prove expressions of satisfaction by the agents, and deliveries of coal of the proper grade, and that the rejection was due to some objection made to the coal by steamers, and to a reversal of the company's choice between this grade of coal and another. The court, page 220, of 65 Md. . . . said:

> Certainly they were not obliged to accept the coal, if they thought it was not fit for the uses contemplated by the contract; neither on the other hand would they be justified in rejecting it for the reason that it did not possess qualities, which at the time of the contract it was known by the parties that it did not possess. By the terms of the contract the whole decision was committed to them; if they made their decision against the coal in good faith, the defendant would not be obliged to accept it, but if they fraudulently rejected it, their judgment would be without effect in law, and the defendant would not be excused by it. . . . On the question of fraud, it

was proper that the evidence should take a wide range. . . . It was proper also to show whether the coal fulfilled these expectations, and whether the officers who were to decide on its rejection knew, or had the means of knowing, its quality; and whether there were any circumstances which might induce them to make an unjust decision in the interest of the defendant. It was proper also to prove acts, declarations or statements of these officers which would show what opinion they really had of the merits of this coal.

In the case at bar, the question referred to the buyer by the clause, "quality satisfactory," concerned a supply of foodstuff, to be put up for an exacting trade, and seems clearly enough one on which there would be room for judgment and choice. And an honest decision by the buyer of that question of satisfactory quality must, according to the principles stated, be accepted, however mistaken or unreasonable a judge or jury might consider it. On the other hand, as only the decision of that question must be accepted as final, the seller was at liberty to prove, if he could, that his goods were rejected not because the quality was unsatisfactory, but because the buyer had found a cheaper source of supply, and having proved rejection for that reason, the seller was not bound to accept it, but could take it as a breach of contract, as he has taken it, and recover his damages. He was at liberty to introduce evidence of a wide range tending to prove such a reason outside of the contract, and incidentally to prove a high quality in his goods.

He accordingly introduced testimony that of the 97 barrels of cherries delivered on the contract before refusal of further deliveries, none were rejected, and there was no complaint. Testimony was given of careful selection and putting up of the cherries in the seller's factory, and of a quality up to the highest grade known to the trade. A letter written by the buyer during the progress of deliveries, and expressing satisfaction, was read in evidence. It had been used by the seller as an advertisement. Further testimony was given to the effect that calls from this buyer for deliveries slackened to such an extent as to cause the seller some inconvenience, and the when the president of the seller company called on the buyer, the president of the latter explained, first, that his own sales had slackened, and, later, that he had an arrangement for putting up his own supply of cherries and therefore could not use the undelivered portion of the International Company's cherries, but would try to dispose of them to other consumers. Two letters followed from the International Company to the Devoine Company on a suggestion for deliveries in small installments, and these were answered by the final letter from the Devoine Company, stating that, as the International Company's president had previously been informed, the Devoine company found the cherries unsatisfactory and would take no more. This evidence was met by contradictory testimony on behalf of the Devoine Company, but no exception brings that up for review. Our conclusion is that the evidence of the International Company just outlined was relevant to prove a rejection for reasons other than dissatisfaction with the cherries . . . and that it was sufficient, no matter how strong the evidence of the Devoine Company may have been to the contrary, to require submission to the jury of the question of good faith in making the rejection. . . .

Judgment affirmed with costs to the appellee.

NOTES & QUESTIONS

1. *Personal aesthetics or fancy?* In both *Gibson* and *DeVoine*, the duty of the obligor was conditional on the obligor's personal satisfaction. How did the court determine whether that event, i.e., satisfaction, occurred? What guidelines were used to ensure that the obligor was not capricious? Could the obligor be unreasonable? How does good faith apply here? How is it proven? *See* RESTATEMENT (SECOND) OF CONTRACTS §§ 228, 205.

MORIN BUILDING PRODUCTS COMPANY, INC. v. BAYSTONE CONSTRUCTION, INC.
717 F.2d 413 (7th Cir. 1983)

POSNER, Circuit Judge:

This appeal from a judgment for the plaintiff in a diversity suit requires us to interpret Indiana's common law of contracts. General Motors, which is not a party to this case, hired Baystone Construction, Inc., the defendant, to build an addition to a Chevrolet plant in Muncie, Indiana. Baystone hired Morin Building Products Company, the plaintiff, to supply and erect the aluminum walls for the addition. The contract required that the exterior siding of the walls be of "aluminum type 3003, not less than 18 B & S gauge, with a mill finish and stucco embossed surface texture to match finish and texture of existing metal siding." The contract also provided "that all work shall be done subject to the final approval of the Architect or Owner's [General Motors'] authorized agent, and his decision in matters relating to artistic effect shall be final, if within the terms of the Contract Documents"; and that "should any dispute arise as to the quality or fitness of materials or workmanship, the decision as to acceptability shall rest strictly with the Owner, based on the requirement that all work done or materials furnished shall be first class in every respect. What is usual or customary in erecting other buildings shall in no wise enter into any consideration or decision."

Morin put up the walls. But viewed in bright sunlight from an acute angle the exterior siding did not give the impression of having a uniform finish, and General Motors' representative rejected it. Baystone removed Morin's siding and hired another subcontractor to replace it. General Motors approved the replacement siding. Baystone refused to pay Morin the balance of the contract price ($23,000) and Morin brought this suit for the balance, and won.

The only issue on appeal is the correctness of a jury instruction which, after quoting the contractual provisions requiring that the owner (General Motors) be satisfied with the contractor's (Morin's) work, states: "Notwithstanding the apparent finality of the foregoing language, however, the general rule applying to satisfaction in the case of contracts for the construction of commercial buildings is that the satisfaction clause must be determined by objective criteria. Under this standard, the question is not whether the owner was satisfied in fact, but whether the owner, as a reasonable person, should have been satisfied with the materials and workmanship in question." There was much evidence that General Motors' rejection of Morin's exterior siding had been totally unreasonable. Not only was the lack of absolute uniformity in the finish of the walls a seemingly trivial defect given the strictly utilitarian purpose of the building that they enclosed, but it may have been inevitable; "mill finish sheet" is defined in the trade as "sheet having a nonuniform finish which may vary from sheet to sheet and within a sheet, and may not be entirely free from stains or oil." If the instruction was correct, so was the judgment. But if the instruction was incorrect — if the proper standard is not whether a reasonable man would have been satisfied with Morin's exterior siding but whether General Motors' authorized representative in fact was — then there must be a new trial to determine whether he really was dissatisfied, or whether he was not and the rejection therefore was in bad faith.

Some cases hold that if the contract provides that the seller's performance must be to the buyer's satisfaction, his rejection — however unreasonable — of the seller's performance is not a breach of the contract unless the rejection is in bad faith. . . . But most cases conform to the position stated in § 228 of the RESTATEMENT (SECOND) OF CONTRACTS (1979): if "it is practicable to determine whether a reasonable person in the position of the obligor would be satisfied, an interpretation is preferred under which the condition [that the obligor be satisfied with the obligee's performance] occurs if such a reasonable person in the position of the obligor would be satisfied." . . .

We do not understand the majority position to be paternalistic; and paternalism would be out of place in a case such as this, where the subcontractor is a substantial multistate enterprise. The requirement of reasonableness is read into a contract not to protect the weaker party but to approximate what the parties would have expressly provided with respect to a contingency that they did not foresee, if they had foreseen it. Therefore the requirement is not read into every contract, because it is not always a reliable guide to the parties' intentions. In particular, the presumption that the performing party would not have wanted to put himself at the mercy of the paying party's whim is overcome when the nature of the performance contracted for is such that there are no objective standards to guide the court. It cannot be assumed in such a case that the parties would have wanted a court to second-guess the buyer's rejection. So "the reasonable person standard is employed when the contract involves commercial quality, operative fitness, or mechanical utility which other knowledgeable persons can judge. . . . The standard of good faith is employed when the contract involves personal aesthetics or fancy." . . .

We have to decide which category the contract between Baystone and Morin belongs in. The particular in which Morin's aluminum siding was found wanting was its appearance, which may seem quintessentially a matter of "personal aesthetics," or as the contract put it, "artistic effect." But it is easy to imagine situations where this would not be so. Suppose the manager of a steel plant rejected a shipment of pig iron because he did not think the pigs had a pretty shape. The reasonable-man standard would be applied even if the contract had an "acceptability shall rest strictly with the Owner" clause, for it would be fantastic to think that the iron supplier would have subjected his contract rights to the whimsy of the buyer's agent. At the other extreme would be a contract to paint a portrait, the buyer having reserved the right to reject the portrait if it did not satisfy him. Such a buyer wants a portrait that will please him rather than a jury, even a jury of connoisseurs, so the only question would be his good faith in rejecting the portrait. . . .

This case is closer to the first example than to the second. The building for which the aluminum siding was intended was a factory — not usually intended to be a thing of beauty. That aesthetic considerations were decidedly secondary to considerations of function and cost is suggested by the fact that the contract specified mill-finish aluminum, which is unpainted. There is much debate in the record over whether it is even possible to ensure a uniform finish within and among sheets, but it is at least clear that mill finish usually is not uniform. If General Motors and Baystone had wanted a uniform finish they would in all likelihood have ordered a painted siding. Whether Morin's siding achieved a reasonable uniformity amounting to satisfactory commercial quality was susceptible of objective judgment; in the language of the RESTATEMENT, a reasonableness standard was "practicable."

But this means only that a requirement of reasonableness would be read into this contract if it contained a standard owner's satisfaction clause, which it did not; and since the ultimate touchstone of decision must be the intent of the parties to the contract we must consider the actual language they used. The contract refers explicitly to "artistic effect," a choice of words that may seem deliberately designed to put the contract in the "personal aesthetics" category whatever an outside observer might think. But the reference appears as number 17 in a list of conditions in a general purpose form contract. And the words "artistic effect" are immediately followed by the qualifying phrase, "if within the terms of the Contract Documents," which suggests that the "artistic effect" clause is limited to contracts in which artistic effect is one of the things the buyer is aiming for; it is not clear that he was here. The other clause on which Baystone relies, relating to the quality or fitness of workmanship and materials, may seem allencompassing, but it is qualified by the phrase, "based on the requirement that all work done or materials furnished shall be first class in every respect" — and it is not clear that Morin's were not. This clause also was not drafted for this contract; it was incorporated by reference to another form contract (the Chevrolet Division's "Contract General Conditions"), of which it is paragraph 35. We do not disparage form contracts, without which the commercial life of the nation would grind to a halt. But we are left with more than a suspicion that the artistic-effect and quality-fitness clauses in the form contract used here were not intended to cover the aesthetics of a mill-finish aluminum factory wall.

If we are right, Morin might prevail even under the minority position, which makes good faith the only standard but presupposes that the contract conditioned acceptance of performance on the buyer's satisfaction in the particular respect in which he was dissatisfied. Maybe this contract was not intended to allow General Motors to reject the aluminum siding on the basis of artistic effect. It would not follow that the contract put Morin under no obligations whatsoever with regard to uniformity of finish. The contract expressly required it to use aluminum having "a mill finish . . . to match finish . . . of existing metal siding." The jury was asked to decide whether a reasonable man would have found that Morin had used aluminum sufficiently uniform to satisfy the matching requirement. This was the right standard if, as we believe, the parties would have adopted it had they foreseen this dispute. It is unlikely that Morin intended to bind itself to a higher and perhaps unattainable standard of achieving whatever perfection of matching that General Motors' agent insisted on, or that General Motors would have required Baystone to submit to such a standard. Because it is difficult — maybe impossible — to achieve a uniform finish with mill-finish aluminum, Morin would have been running a considerable risk of rejection if it had agreed to such a condition, and it therefore could have been expected to demand a compensating increase in the contract price. This would have required General Motors to pay a premium to obtain a freedom of action that it could not have thought terribly important, since its objective was not aesthetic. If a uniform finish was important to it, it could have gotten such a finish by specifying painted siding.

All this is conjecture; we do not know how important the aesthetics were to General Motors when the contract was signed or how difficult it really would have been to obtain the uniformity of finish it desired. The fact that General Motors accepted the replacement siding proves little, for there is evidence that the replacement siding produced the same striped effect, when viewed from an acute angle in bright sunlight, that Morin's had. When in doubt on a difficult issue of state law it is only prudent to defer to the view of the district judge, *Murphy v. White Hen Pantry Co.*, 691 E2d 350, 354 (7th Cir. 1982), here an experienced Indiana lawyer who thought this the type of contract where the buyer cannot unreasonably withhold approval of the seller's performance.

Lest this conclusion be thought to strike at the foundations of freedom of contract, we repeat that if it appeared from the language or circumstances of the contract that the parties really intended General Motors to have the right to reject Morin's work for failure to satisfy the private aesthetic taste of General Motors' representative, the rejection would have been proper even if unreasonable. But the contract is ambiguous because of the qualifications with which the terms "artistic effect" and "decision as to acceptability" are hedged about, and the circumstances suggest that the parties probably did not intend to subject Morin's rights to aesthetic whim.

AFFIRMED.

NOTES & QUESTIONS

1. The court in *Morin* notes that "[I]n the language of the RESTATEMENT, a reasonableness standard was "practicable'." What is meant by practicable? How is a standard of reasonableness different from a good faith requirement under RESTATEMENT (SECOND) OF CONTRACTS § 228?

2. Partnership Unlimited was comprised of four limited partners and a general partner. Pursuant to the partnership agreement, the limited partners removed the general partner and elected a new one. The clause of the agreement that the limited partners relied upon provides that "if the limited partners determine that the general partner has failed to perform satisfactorily, the limited partners are at liberty to remove the general partner and elect a new one." What standard applies here in determining satisfaction? *See Wilmington Leasing Inc. v. Parrish Leasing Company*, 1996 Del. Ch. LEXIS 155.

ANDERSON-ROSS FLOORS, INC. v. SCHERRER CONSTRUCTION CO., INC.
62 Ill. App. 3d 713, 19 Ill. Dec. 914, 379 N.E.2d 786 (1978)

SEIDENFELD, Presiding Justice:

Anderson-Ross, Inc., as a subcontractor filed suit against the general contractor, Scherrer Construction Co., Inc., the architectural firm of Orput-Orput, Inc., and the construction manager for the architect Marshall S. Stevens, to recover payment for the installation of a gymnasium floor in a grade school. Following a bench trial judgment was entered in favor of plaintiff and against the general contractor for $5180 and costs and Scherrer appeals. No judgment was entered against the other defendants. In issue is whether the plaintiff performed in accordance with his agreement "to the satisfaction of the architect" and whether recovery may be had when no architect's certificate has been issued and the school board owner has refused to accept the work.

The record of the trial is before us on a stipulated report of proceedings, no actual transcript having been prepared. Robert E. Ross, the president of the plaintiff company, testified that Stevens was present as the representative of the architect during the installation of the flooring, had an opportunity to observe the work but made no adverse comment. He said that his corporation had been installing floors for fifteen years during which time between three hundred and four hundred of such floors had been laid.

He explained the "Robbins lock-type floor system" which was the method he used. In February or March of 1971 he had the following conversation with Marshall Stevens:

> Q (by ROSS): What's the matter, MARSHALL?
>
> A (by MARSHALL STEVENS): There are complaints of spaces between the boards.
>
> Q (by ROSS): Sure there are a few but, you are bound to get them.
>
> A (by MARSHALL STEVENS): Yes, BOB, it looks all right to me.

On cross-examination the witness testified that he did not return to the site after March of 1971 although the Scherrer Construction Company requested meetings.

Marshall Stevens testified as an adverse witness to his employment as a construction manager and to the fact that he was not a registered architect. He said he had a conversation with Ross at the site in the early part of 1971 but he could not remember whether he had told Ross that in his opinion the floor was typical and adequate and he would recommend payment. He identified a letter which he wrote to the general contractor on March 19, 1971, which states in part:

> We have reviewed your gym floor installation thoroughly and cannot recommend that the Owner accept and make payment until the current deficiencies are corrected. The floor throughout must have tight end joints and side horizontal joints no matter what humidity may exist in the areas. You are directed to remove all portions of floor and replace in manner to meet these requirements and all of normal requirements.

(Plaintiff's Exhibit 3)

Stevens also identified a letter which he wrote to the school board on January 25, 1971, which included the following statement:

> Several specific locations were noted with cracks of 1/8 in width between boards. It was felt that normal expansion of boards in unheated months would help to close these gaps. The Architect, Marshall S. Stevens, agreed to release of payment to Scherrer Construction Company as requested in their Periodic Estimate 12 which is 90% of wood floors retaining 10% or $1,590.00. This action automatically releases "hold action' of Orput-Orput letter to Scherrer Construction Company of January 8, 1971. This decision was based upon fact that General Contractor guarantees this floor for one

(1) year and flooring contractor guarantees for five (5) years during which time it was felt that any minor problems would be corrected.

(Defendant's Exhibit 1)

Stevens also testified that it was possible to have tight joints at all times. He further testified that he had observed the spaces open and close over a period of time and also that the last time he visited the gymnasium it was being put to its intended use. He said that he had advised the school board that the spaces would not adversely affect its use and that he knew of no repairs having been made to the floor.

Professor Henry L. Mikolajczyk, testified on behalf of the plaintiff, that he had been teaching for thirty-one years, and that for the past twelve years he was a professor at the University of Illinois in the matter of the technical nature of materials; that he was a registered architect in engineering in charge of design of all Chicago facilities for the University of Illinois; that he did research in the area of materials and building construction materials and was a consultant architect, a member of the Illinois Society of Architects.

Professor Mikolajczyk testified that he had examined the second grade maple used in the floor construction and its moisture content. The stipulated substance of his testimony included the following:

> He further stated that there was a relationship between the air and the wood, and that wood absorbs moisture and gives off moisture, depending upon the relative humidity in the heated building; that if no humidification equipment in the building is present, then humidity is twenty (20%) percent or less; he examined the Antioch Upper Grade School's specifications and found no humidification equipment; that to have an eight (8%) percent moisture content you need forty-five (45%) percent relative humidity and that in heated buildings that twenty (20%) percent relative humidity the moisture content of the wood would be about four (4%) percent; that if the floor was laid with an eight (8%) percent moisture content there would be a forty (40%) percent loss in the moisture content and in twelve (12) inches of second grade maple board that shrink moisture loss would be approximately three sixteenths (3/16) of an inch or less or to relate the matter to width of coins, it would allow 2-five cent pieces to be put together between the cracks in the boards with space left over.

> The witness further testified that he visited the Antioch Grade School on June 23, 1976, at the end of the heating season and close to its dryest maximum shrinking potential. He spent one and one-half (1½%) hours inspecting the floors. The witness further identified Plaintiff's Exhibit No. (13), being a picture of the floors representing the spaces between the floors allowing coins to be inserted therein. The witness further testified that generally maple floors will expand when the humidity increases and shrink when the humidity decreases; that there is no uniformity but would depend on what part of the log the wood was cut from. The witnesses (sic) asked if it were possible to have tight ends regardless of the humidity and the witness answered, "No". The witness further testified that there was no humidification equipment present at the time he made the examination. . . .

The subcontract was also placed in evidence (Plaintiff's Exhibit 1) showing a contract price of $10,500. As pertinent the subcontract included the following:

(a). To furnish all materials and perform all labor for Antioch Upper Grade School Antioch, Illinois in accordance with the drawings, plans, and specifications prepared by Orput & Orput Rockford, Illinois, hereinafter called the architect, the receipt of a true and complete copy of said drawings, plans and specifications being acknowledged by the Sub-contractor and being incorporated herein as though fully set forth at length, as the same pertains to the Sub-Contractor as follows, to-wit: Division 9-E Gym Floor furnished and installed per plans and specifications. Also includes fir flooring on stage #C105, sanded and finished. . . .

(c). Payments to be made on or about the 10th day of each month at the rate of 90% of the value of the work erected in place during the preceding month, as determined by the Contractor or the architect and the remaining 10% within fifteen days after the completion and acceptance of this work.

Neither the contract between Scherrer and the School Board nor the plans and specifications have been made part of the record.

Essentially Scherrer argues that plaintiff's action must fail because performance under the agreement was to be to the satisfaction of the architect and he was not satisfied; and further that the acceptance by the school board was required but not obtained with the result that the contractor has not been paid for the disputed portion of the contract. Scherrer further argues that plaintiff is not entitled to recover on the basis of substantial performance arguing that the record shows gross defects. Plaintiff in turn argues that the floor was installed to the satisfaction of the architect but that he wrongfully withdrew his approval presumably because the school board rejected the work after the architect's representative had agreed to release payment. Plaintiff further argues that it is not barred from recovery since the architect acted unreasonably and without exercising his independent judgment when he refused to issue a certificate of approval. It also argues that the installation is in accordance with the requirements of the contract and that there is no support in the record for the claim that the school board must approve the work as a condition of recovery by the subcontractor.

The meaning of the phrase in a construction contract that a claimant must fulfill his contract "to the satisfaction of" another has been construed to require a judgment reasonably, and not merely arbitrarily, exercised. . . . An architect who inspects the work and accepts it as being in compliance with the contract but refuses without good reason to deliver his certificate is guilty of bad faith which will excuse the certificate. . . . If a certificate is withheld because the owner has directed the superintendent of construction not to issue it where it otherwise would be properly issued the failure to comply with that exact term is waived. . . . It has been held that "it is the architect's judgment, not his arbitrary will, that the contract makes conclusive on the questions submitted to his decision." . . .

These long established rules in the Illinois cases are consistent with the RESTATEMENT OF CONTRACTS in which the meaning of the term "to the satisfaction of the architect" is specifically addressed:

Where a certificate of an architect, surveyor or engineer is a condition precedent to a duty of immediate payment for work, the condition is excused if the architect, surveyor or engineer

(a) dies or becomes incapacitated, or

(b) refuses to give a certificate because of collusion with the promisor, or

(c) refuses to give a certificate after making examination of the work and finding it adequate, or

(d) fails to make proper examination of the work, or

(e) fails to exercise an honest judgment, or

(f) makes a gross mistake with reference to facts on which a refusal to give a certificate is based.

(RESTATEMENT OF CONTRACTS, § 303 (1932)). *See also* CORBIN ON CONTRACTS, § 650 at 618 (1952).

It is first noted that the record does not include the drawings, plans and specifications against which we might measure the evidence of plaintiff's performance. In a sense this may be viewed as irrelevant since defendant does not claim a failure to comply with these items nor did the architect so testify. Defendant alleges instead a failure to comply with the provision that the architect must be satisfied. While the defendant argues that the plaintiff was required to install a floor with "tight joints" this phrase is not a part of the record as an element of the contract but rather is the judgment of the architect. It appears, however, from the testimony of Professor Mikolajczyk, which the trier of facts could find more credible than that of Stevens to the contrary, that tight joints were not possible during all seasons without humidification equipment. He testified that absent humidification equipment there would be a space of approximately 3/16ths of an inch in each twelve inch section of the maple flooring. He also testified that it would be impossible to have tight ends as specified in Stevens' letter regardless of humidity. The trial court could conclude from the evidence that Stevens made a gross factual error with respect to the humidity and that his requirement that the floor have "tight end joints" was impossible.

The trial court could also conclude from the record that the certificate of the architect was excused because Stevens, after examining the work and finding it adequate, subsequently refused to issue a certificate. There is testimony in the record from Ross that there was a discussion between Stevens and Ross relative to the School Board's complaints in early 1971. Ross testified that Stevens stated at that time "It looks all right to me." While Stevens could not remember the conversation the trial court could consider this as an implied admission by him that he found the work adequate. . . . It also appears that Stevens was satisfied with the floor installation on January 25, 1971, except as to what he characterized as "minor problems," when he stated in a letter that he "agreed to release payment" for the wood flooring. Under these circumstances the trial court could conclude that Stevens initially found the work to be adequate and subsequently refused to issue the certificate. . . .

Defendant has argued that there is testimony that two nickels could be inserted in some of the cracks in the floor and that the floor is patently unsuitable for use by school children. However, defendants' own witness Stevens testified that he advised the school board that the use of the floor would not be adversely affected by the cracks. He further testified that he observed the floor being put to its intended use.

And the record shows that the floor has been in use.

We are not persuaded by defendant's contention that the contract required acceptance by the school board. Defendant relies on § 2(c) of the Contract which in substance provides that the payments will be made each month at the rate of 90% of the value of the work in place during the preceding months as determined by the contractor or architect; with the provision that the remaining 10% is due fifteen days after the completion and "acceptance of this work." It is apparent that the phrase "acceptance of the work" applies to acceptance by the architect and not to the acceptance by the owner. Nor are we persuaded by the defendant's additional argument that since the subcontract is controlled by the general contract, the school board's refusal to pay the general contractor indicates that the general contractor should not be required to pay the subcontractor. As previously noted the general contract is not before us and, in any event, there is nothing in the record to indicate that plaintiff's work was conditioned on acceptance of the work by the owner in addition to approval of the architect.

The judgment of the trial court is affirmed.

NOTES & QUESTIONS

1. What standard did the court in *Anderson-Ross* use to determine whether the condition of satisfaction, i.e., the architect's certificate, occurred? Would it have made a difference in this case if the architect had never come out to the school to inspect the job, but still failed to issue a certificate? What if the general contractor had never requested the certificate? What result if there was collusion between the school board owner and the architect in a fraudulent effort to prevent issuance of the certificate? *See* RESTATEMENT (SECOND) OF CONTRACTS §§ 84, 227, 235 & 245.

2. With regard to a condition of satisfaction by a third party, Corbin has stated:

> In the absence of fraud or mistake, courts generally deny that they can or will ever set aside an express condition, even though it is the personal state of mind of an interested party. But they often can and do produce the same result by indulging in a process of pseudo-interpretation, finding that the language used means the "satisfaction of a reasonable man." When this is in fact what is done, it is a substitution by the court of a reasonable condition precedent in place of what seems to the court an unreasonable condition precedent.

CORBIN ON CONTRACTS § 648. Do you agree with Corbin? How do these comments impact upon the requirement of courts to interpret express conditions literally? Would parties ever agree to a condition based on the personal whim of a particular individual? Should such an agreement be enforced as a matter of public policy?

3.   Policy Considerations and Underlying Principles

a.   Waiver, Estoppel, and Election

Waiver is intentional, voluntary action of the promisor which excuses the non-occurrence of a condition. Therefore, where the promisor is under a conditional duty to perform under a contract, the promisor may agree to perform, notwithstanding the nonoccurrence of the condition.

The doctrine of estoppel involves the consequences of waiver upon the promisor. Generally, once a promisor has waived a condition, and the promisee has relied upon the waiver, the promisor is said to be estopped from re-asserting the requirement of the condition.

Finally, election is a binding choice of the promisor after the failure of a condition. For example, upon the failure of a condition to occur, the promisor may choose between disregarding the non-occurrence of the condition and treating the duty as unconditional or regarding the duty as discharged. *See* RESTATEMENT (SECOND) OF CONTRACTS § 84.

As you read the following cases, ask yourself whether the parties' intentions were carried out by the courts. What types of actions will lead courts to impose a waiver of agreed-upon conditions? What policies do the court's decision uphold?

WHALEN v. K-MART CORPORATION
166 Ill. App. 3d 339, 116 Ill. Dec. 776, 519 N.E.2d 991 (1988)

Justice BILANDIC delivered the opinion of the court:

The plaintiff, Holly Whalen, brought an action under the Structural Work Act against the general contractor, Schostak Brothers, Inc., K-Mart and the landowners. (Ill. Rev. Stat. 1985, ch. 48, par. 60 *et seq.*) The general contractor and the landowners, as third-party plaintiffs (hereinafter collectively referred to a Schostak), filed a third-party complaint against A.W. Christianson & Sons, Inc., the painting subcontractor, for contribution and indemnity based on Christianson's agreement to procure insurance naming third-party plaintiffs as an insured. They also filed a counterclaim against Martin Cement Company, the cement subcontractor, for contribution and indemnity based on Martin's agreement to procure insurance naming the general contractor and landowners as an insured. The subcontractors moved to dismiss the third-party complaint and counterclaim pursuant to section 2-619 of the Code of Civil Procedure alleging that the general contractor and landowners waived the contractual insurance requirement. . . . The trial court sustained the motion and dismissed the third-party complaint and counterclaim with prejudice. This timely appeal followed.

The subcontracts with Christianson and Martin were drafted by Schostak, the general contractor. The "Supplemental Subcontract Conditions," involved in this appeal, are identical. They state:

> "SECTION 10. The Subcontractor shall not commence work under this Subcontract until he has obtained all insurances required by the General Conditions and as hereinafter set forth and certificates of insurance delivered to the Contractor. All policies or certifications of insurance to be furnished by Subcontractor shall provide that the insurance cannot be cancelled or modified until the expiration of twenty (20) days after receipt of written notice thereof by the Contractor."

> "SECTION 12. The subcontractor agrees to indemnify, save harmless and defend the contractor and owner from any liability for damages to any person or property upon, or at, or about the development that may arise as a result of or in connection with the work hereunder and the Subcontractor agrees to procure at his own expense, before the commencement of the work comprehensive general liability including Contractors protective

liability insurance, completed operations and contractual liability insurance and automobile liability insurance including the ownership, maintenance and operation of any automotive equipment owned, hired and non-owned for the benefit of the contractor and owner, in the sum of Two Hundred Fifty Thousand ($250,000) Dollars for damages resulting to one person and Five Hundred Thousand ($500,000) Dollars for damage to persons resulting from one occurrence and One Hundred Thousand ($100,000) Dollars for damages to property arising out of each occurrence, and to keep such insurance in force until the construction of development is fully completed, and to immediately and before commencing work deliver such policy or policies or certificates of insurance to the Contractor."

"SECTION 15. The Subcontractor agrees to indemnify and hold the Contractor harmless from all claims, losses, expenses or liability from the payment of:

. . . all the insurance required to be furnished by Subcontractor under this agreement shall be in a company or companies which are satisfactory to the Contractor and/or Owner. Subcontractor agrees to obtain and maintain the above-described insurance during the entire period of this agreement. Evidence of all insurance indicated within this Paragraph 12 shall be furnished to Contractor and/or Owner in writing and shall indicate that Contractor and/or Owner are additional or co-insured parties. No payments will be made until necessary proof of insurance has been made."

In substance, the affidavits in support of Martin's and Christianson's section 2-619 motions to dismiss state that the general contractor did not insist upon the respective subcontractor's compliance with the contractual insurance requirements of their respective subcontracts. Both subcontractors performed under their contracts and were paid i n full after the date of plaintiff's accident. Schostak and the landowners did not submit any counteraffidavits.

The trial court dismissed the general contractor's and landowners' third-party complaint and counterclaim with prejudice on the grounds that they waived their rights to enforce the insurance provisions of their subcontracts with Martin and Christianson. The orders were made final and appealable pursuant to Illinois Supreme Court Rule 304. . . .

I.

The first issue on appeal is whether the trial court properly found that Schostak waived any breach of contract claims against the subcontractors.

The express language of the contracts show that the subcontractors agreed to obtain insurance before commencement of any work. Proof of insurance was to be submitted to Schostak for approval prior to any performance and prior to any payment.

A condition precedent is a condition that must be performed before the contract becomes effective or which is to be performed by one party to the existing contract before the other party is obligated to perform. . . . In the case at bar, the subcontract plainly and unambiguously states that "[t]he Subcontractor shall not commence work under this subcontract until he has obtained all insurance required. . ." and "[n]o payments will be made until necessary proof of insurance has been made." Thus, obtaining the required insurance was a condition precedent to commencement of work and a condition precedent to receiving payment.

Parties to a contract have the power to waive provisions placed in the contract for their benefit and such a waiver may be established by conduct indicating that strict compliance with the contractual provisions will not be required. . . . An implied waiver of a legal right may arise when conduct of the person against whom waiver is asserted is inconsistent with any other intention than to waive it. . . .

Waiver is either an express or implied voluntary and intentional relinquishment of a known and existing right. . . . The determination as to what facts are sufficient to constitute waiver is a question of law. . . . An analysis of whether there was in fact a waiver of contractual provisions focuses on the intent of the non-breaching party. If he has intentionally relinquished a known right, either expressly or by conduct inconsistent with an intent to enforce that right, he has waived it and may not thereafter seek judicial enforcement. . . ,

A party to a contract may not lull another into a false assurance that strict compliance with a contractual duty will not be required and then sue for noncompliance. . . . While nonaction by both parties constitutes a waiver and mutual negation of that particular provision, the rest of the contract remains in force where the parties, by their acts and statements, show that they consider the agreement to retain its vitality. . . .

In the case sub judice, it is undisputed that Schostak drafted the contracts. The requirement that proof of insurance be submitted before the subcontractors could commence work and be paid was clearly for Schostak's benefit. Schostak's argument that they didn't know Martin and Christianson failed to obtain insurance until Schostak asked Martin and Christianson to defend this lawsuit is not persuasive. Schostak is presumed to know those things which reasonable diligence on their part would bring to their attention, namely, the absence of proof of insurance. . . . The record shows that Schostak never demanded any proof of insurance; both Martin and Christianson completed their performance under the contract; and, both were paid in full for their services.

We, therefore, conclude that the trial court did not err when it determined that Schostak waived its claim for breach of contract against the subcontractors.

II.

Next, Schostak contends that the trial court erred in granting the subcontractors' section 2-619 motions to dismiss because a disputed question of fact existed regarding the waiver. Schostak argues that its failure to insist on compliance by the subcontractors can be interpreted as ignorance of the noncompliance. Schostak concludes that without proof of its knowledge that the subcontractors did not comply with the insurance requirement, there could be no waiver. We disagree. A motion brought under section 2-619 provides for involuntary dismissal of a cause of action based on certain defects or defenses. The section provides:

> That the claim asserted against defendant is barred by other affirmative matter avoiding the legal effect of or defeating the claim.

(Ill. Rev. Stat. 1985, ch. 110, par. 2-619(a)(9).) Additionally:

If, upon the hearing of the motion, the opposite party presents affidavits or other proof denying the facts alleged or establishing facts obviating the grounds of defect, the court may hear and determine the same and may grant or deny the motion. If a material and genuine disputed question of fact is raised the court may decide the motion upon the affidavits and evidence offered by the parties. . . .

(Ill. Rev. Stat. 1985, ch. 110, par. 2-619(c).) Where the pleadings before a court fail to raise an issue of material fact, or where material fact issues are refuted by affirmative matter, the motion is properly granted. . . . The court may, in its discretion, decide questions of fact upon hearing the motion. . . .

Martin and Christianson raised the affirmative defense that Schostak waived any breach of their failure to obtain insurance because Schostak allowed them to commence work and made full payment to both subcontractors upon completion of their duties. Both Martin and Christianson submitted affidavits to that effect with their motions. Schostak did not submit any counter-affidavits to rebut the affiants' statements. There is no factual support for Schostak's argument that it did not have knowledge of the subcontractors' failure to comply with the insurance requirement. Their failure to challenge Martin's and Christianson's affidavits constitutes an admission of the facts set forth therein. . . . Thus, Schostak failed to raise a disputed question of fact.

Schostak would have us create the disputed question of fact by reading into the contract the fact that Schostak's failure to insist on compliance was caused by its lack of knowledge of the noncompliance. Under the facts of this case, we will not raise by implication or interpretation facts which should have been affirmatively stated in a counter-affidavit. Schostak drafted the contract. The provisions at issue are in the contract for the benefit of Schostak. They are presumed to know those things which reasonable diligence on their part would bring to their attention, namely, the absence of proof of insurance. . . .

We, therefore, conclude that a disputed issue of fact did not exist.

For the forgoing reasons the judgment of the circuit court of Cook County is affirmed.

ROSS v. HARDING
64 Wash. 2d 231, 391 P.2d 526 (1964)

JAMES, Judge:

The appellant and the respondents undertook the accomplishment of what must have seemed to them an uncomplicated business transaction. Involved was the sale of an almost extinct species of American free enterprise — a Mom and Pop grocery store. Unhappily, they now find that their efforts have brought them into court in a difficult and complex field of law. Their "legal rights" must be determined by a consideration of the law of contracts and specifically by the application of "interpretive rules which are extremely subtle and artificial." 12 AM. JUR. § 295, p. 848.

On October 21, 1958, appellant, Charlotte M. Harding, and her then living husband, entered into a conditional sale contract for the purchase of the grocery store from plaintiffs, Thomas B. Ross and Mildred H. Ross, his wife. Appellant and her husband gave plaintiffs a real estate mortgage to secure performance of the conditional sale contract. On the same day, appellant and her husband signed, as lessees, an instrument signed, as lessor, by one Henry A. Keil, as administrator of the estate of Anna E. Pentland, deceased, covering "That certain store building and living quarters situate at No. 4221 East 11th Street, Tacoma, Washington." These were the premises in which the grocery store was established. The term provided in the instrument was 5 years with an option to lessees for an additional 5-year period. These premises, which were more fully described in the "lease" by metes and bounds, were also identified by the same street address in the conditional sale contract and were referred to therein as "Toddhaven Grocery."

Appellant's husband died in August of 1959.

The transaction between appellant (individually and as administratrix of her deceased husband's estate) and respondents is encompassed in three instruments:

(1) Earnest Money Agreement and Sale of Personal Property, dated October 6, 1959. This document contains the following language of significance here:

"It is specifically understood and agreed that this offer is made subject to the written consent of the lessor of the said building to the assignment and/or renewal of the existing lease."

(2) Assignment of Conditional Sales Contract, dated October 9, 1959. This document contains the following language of significance here:

"Also all interest in a certain lease dated October 21, 1958 made by Henry A. Keil as Administrator."

(3) A paper which, in its entirety, is as follows:

"Tacoma, Washington
October 10, 1959

"I, Henry A. Keil, executor for the business known as Toddhaven Grocery, located at 4221 East 11th Street, Tacoma, Washington, give consent to Mrs. Mercedes Harding to underlet these premises to Mr. and Mrs. Max Lieb under the same conditions as in her present lease.

"Henry A. Keil
4114 Marine View Dr."

Pursuant to instrument No. 1, the respondents paid appellant $1,500 in cash. By the terms of the agreement, respondents assumed an unpaid balance on the conditional sale contract of $7,044.37 payable in monthly installments of $100, which included interest on deferred balances at 6 per cent per annum.

Respondents went into possession as directed by appellant's attorney, made monthly payments on the conditional sale contract to a bank for plaintiffs' account and monthly rental payments of $100 to Henry A. Keil. After April of 1960, respondents ceased making payments on either the contract or for rent, and, in May, abandoned the premises. The fixtures were left on the premises and the stock, which had been inventoried at less than $40 at the time of the sale to respondents, was entirely depleted.

Plaintiffs commenced this action for specific performance and joined both appellant and respondents as defendants. Plaintiffs sought judgment against both for the unpaid balance on the conditional sale contract and a decree of foreclosure of the real estate mortgage executed by appellant and her husband. In appellant's answer and cross-complaint her alternative prayer was for dismissal of the action against her or for judgment over against respondents in the event of judgment against her.

The trial court entered judgment for the plaintiffs against the appellant for the balance due on the conditional sale contract and decreed a foreclosure of the real-estate mortgage. Both the plaintiffs' complaint and appellant's cross-complaint against respondents were dismissed.

Appellant's assignments of error all relate to the trial court's conclusion that the respondents never became legally bound to perform because of the failure of appellant to fulfill a "condition precedent" which was a material part of the contract of sale.

The trial court's finding of fact No. 5 is as follows:

Said "Earnest Money Agreement and Sale of Personal Property" provides as follows:

It is specifically understood and agreed that this offer is made subject to the written consent of the lessor of the said building to the assignment and/or renewal of the existing lease.

The building referred to was the building in which the business of the Todd Haven Store was conducted. The "existing lease" referred to is in evidence herein. It was executed by Henry A. Keil "as Administrator of the Estate of Anna E. Pentland, Deceased," on October 21st, 1958. Said Henry A. Keil was discharged as Administrator of said Estate on July 29, 1957. Title to said building was at all times pertinent to this action vested in Esther A. Marbut, Myrtle A. Keil and Evelyn E. Stein, as their separate property in equal undivided shares. Said purported lease was for a term of five years from November 1, 1958, renewable at Lessees' option for an additional term of five years, and was not assignable, nor was underletting or occupancy by any person permitted, without the written consent of lessor. No consent of any person was ever obtained to the assignment and/or renewal of said lease or any lease of said property to Defendants Lieb or either of them. That Henry A. Keil did execute a written consent to subletting by Mercedes Harding to Mr. and Mrs. Max Lieb. That except as to the above lease there was no evidence of fraud or misrepresentation by anyone. HBS.

The trial court entered the following conclusions of law:

No. 7:

"The purported lease of the Todd Haven Store premises was made without authority, and was null and void from its inception. Defendant Harding by implication represented to Defendant Max E. Lieb that it was a valid lease and expressly represented that it was an 'existing lease.' Said representation was a material, substantive term and condition of the 'Earnest Money Agreement and Sale of Personal Property.' The leasehold, if valid, would have constituted a valuable estate."

No. 8:

"The language concerning the lease which is quoted in Finding of Fact V embodies a material condition precedent which had not been complied with."

There is no evidence to controvert the trial court's finding of fact No. 5. Neither is there any explanation whatever for the puzzling performance of Mr. Keil. Neither he nor any one of the owners of the real property which he purported to lease was called as a witness. Nor was any explanation tendered concerning their nonappearance.

Appellant's argument, when considered in its entirety, poses three questions, all referable to the provision in the sale agreement calling for a written consent to assignment or renewal of the "existing lease."

The first question to be determined is whether or not the provision in question constitutes a "promise' or a "condition precedent."

A "condition" whether it be "precedent" or "subsequent" may be either express, implied in fact, or constructive. 5 WILLISTON, CONTRACTS (3d ed.) § 668, p. 152; 3A CORBIN, CONTRACTS, §§ 631, 632, pp. 21, 22.

"Conditions precedent" are those facts and events, occurring subsequently to the making of a valid contract, that must exist or occur before there is a right to immediate performance, before there is a breach of contract duty, before the usual judicial remedies are available. 3A CORBIN, CONTRACTS, § 628, p. 16; *Partlow v. Mathews*, 43 Wash. 2d 398, 261 P.2d 394. A breach of a "promise' subjects the promissor to liability in damages, but does not necessarily excuse performance on the other side. Nonperformance or nonoccurrence of a "condition' prevents the promissee from acquiring a right, or deprives him of one, but subjects him to no liability. 5 WILLISTON, CONTRACTS (3d ed.) § 665, p. 132. Where it is doubtful whether words create a "promise' or an "express condition," they are interpreted as creating a "promise." RESTATEMENT, CONTRACTS § 261, p. 375; 5 WILLISTON, CONTRACTS (3d ed.) § 665, p. 133.

Whether a provision in a contract is a condition, the nonfulfillment of which excuses performance, depends upon the intent of the parties, to be ascertained from a fair and reasonable construction of the language used in the light of all the surrounding circumstances. 5 WILLISTON, CONTRACTS (3d ed.) § 663, p. 127.

Any words which express, when properly interpreted, the idea that the performance of a promise is dependent on some other event will create a condition. Phrases and words such as "on condition," "provided that," "so that," "when," "while," "after," or "as soon as' are often used. 12 AM. JUR. § 295, p. 849; 5 WILLISTON, CONTRACTS (3d ed.) § 671, p. 161.

It would be difficult to choose words to more precisely express an intention to create a condition precedent than those used in the contract here to be construed.

"It is specifically understood and agreed that this offer is made *subject to the written consent. . . .*" (Italics ours.)

This language leaves no room for interpretation. As stated in *Schwieger v. Harry W. Robbins & Co.*, 48 Wash. 2d 22, 24, 290 P.2d 984, 986:

"The release is in plain and unambiguous language. We often have said that the courts will not interpret the meaning of unambiguous contracts.

Silen v. Silen, 1954, 44 Wash. 2d 884, 271 P.2d 674. . . ."

The sale of a grocery business was also involved in the case of *Brier v. Orenberg*, 90 A.2d 832 (D.C. Mun. App. 1952). The contract there provided that it was "contingent in its entirety" upon the procuring of a valid assignment of the lease on the premises from the landlord. The court there held:

> ". . . This, quite clearly, made the securing of the lease assignment a condition precedent: a fact which must exist or occur before a duty of immediate performance of a promise could arise, *Creighton v. Brown*, D.C. Mun. App., 77 A.2d 559; RESTATEMENT, CONTRACTS, § 250 (1932)."

We hold that the procuring of the written consent of the lessor to the assignment or renewal of a valid lease of the premises occupied by the grocery store was a condition precedent to the appellant's right to specific performance against the respondents.

The second question then is: Was the condition precedent fulfilled by the written consent to underlet procured from Henry A. Keil? In asserting that the answer to this question should be in the affirmative, appellant seems to argue that the true owners of the real estate involved are in some way estopped from repudiating the purported lease and the purported consent to assignment thereof by Keil. In her brief, appellant stated:

> ". . . The three sisters, true owners of the property, saw him clothed with apparent authority to make the lease, sat by for over a year and a half, were charged with knowledge that the property was rented, and presumably received the benefits of the agreement which their agent had made under a continuation of his former agency as executor."

This astonishing assertion is unsupported by even a scintilla of evidence. The numerous cases cited by appellant applying the principles of estoppel to factual situations involving landlord and tenant, probate and agency are not apposite to the facts (or rather the absence of facts) in this case.

Equitable estoppel or estoppel in pais in its simplest terms means estoppel by conduct. Here the only evidence of conduct concerns that of the alleged agent. As to the principals, the true owners, the record is silent.

> . . . Equitable estoppel or estoppel in pais is the principal by which a party who knows or should know the truth is absolutely precluded, both at law and in equity, from denying or asserting the contrary of, any material fact which, by his words or conduct, affirmative or negative, intentionally or through culpable negligence, he has induced another, who was excusably ignorant of the true facts and who had a right to rely upon such words or conduct, to believe and act upon them thereby, as a consequence reasonably to be anticipated, changing his position in such a way that he would suffer injury if such denial or contrary assertion were allowed.

19 AM. JUR. § 34, p. 634; *Carruthers v. Whitney*, 56 Wash. 327, 105 P. 831.

This leaves the third question: Did respondents waive their right to require performance of the condition precedent or are they estopped from denying the validity of the lease because of the part performance on their part? Appellant argues in her brief as follows:

Did the furnishing of a lease, the greatest objection to which is that it was at most voidable, constitute such a partial failure of consideration that went to the root of the contract? The respondents got all they contracted for the store, the equipment, the stock, and peaceful possession of the property as long as they wanted possession, without any indication that their tenancy would be terminated. The relations between Keil and respondent Lieb, as testified to by him, certainly justify the inference that, had Lieb at any time objected to the voidability of the lease, a lease signed by the three sisters could be obtained.

*   *   *

"Appellant had a valid lease covering the store building. Respondent set up an affirmative defense alleging the lease was void. He did nothing to prove this defense against appellant's establishment of the lease, except to show that legal title to the property was not then in the executor. He had the burden of proof, and failed to establish that the lease was unauthorized. And having stepped into appellant's shoes as lessee, he is estopped to deny the validity of the lease.

This argument proceeds from a false major premise. Here there was no lease at all. Title to the property was not in the estate of Anna E. Pentland, deceased. The true owners of the property neither signed the purported lease nor authorized Henry A. Keil to execute the lease in their behalf.

The contract was prepared by appellant's counsel. The language used in the critical provision calling for the lessor's "written consent' to the assignment of "the existing lease' is plain and unambiguous. It can mean nothing other than that there is an existing valid lease.

The trial court expressly found that "except as to the above lease there was no evidence of fraud or misrepresentation by anyone." This does not amount to a finding that there were fraudulent misrepresentations concerning the existence of a lease. But, absent fraud, the undenied misrepresentation would at least necessarily have to be characterized as a mutual mistake of fact. Where there is a clear bona fide mutual mistake regarding material facts, equity will grant a rescission. *Stahl v. Schwartz*, 67 Wash. 25, 120 P. 856; *Lindeberg v. Murray*, 117 Wash. 483, 201 P. 759; *Sutton v. Peterson*, 193 Wash. 175, 74 P.2d 884.

That such an equitable principal has long been a part of the common law is demonstrated by the opinion in *Alien v. Hammond*, 11 Pet. 63, 36 U.S. 63, 71, 9 L. Ed. 633 (1837), in language appropriate to the facts of this case:

In 1 Fonbl Eq. 114, it is laid down, that where there is an error in the thing for which an individual bargains, by the general rules of contracting, the contract is null, as in such a case, the parties are supposed not to give their assent. And the same doctrine is laid down in Puffendorff's *Law of Nature and Nations*, b.1, c.3, § 12. The law on this subject is clearly stated, in the case of *Hitchcock v. Giddings*, Daniel's Exch. 1 (s.c. 4 Price 135); where it is said, that a vendor is bound to know that he actually has that which he professes to sell. . . .

The mistake of fact must, however, be as to a fact which is material. 12 AM. JUR. § 126, p. 618. It has been said that the true test as to materiality is whether the contract would have been entered into had there been no mistake. *Lindeberg v.*

Murray, supra. As was said in Lindeberg, we are clear that there was such a mistake here. That a valid lease with approximately 3 years to run plus a 5-year renewal option is a material and substantial part of the consideration for the agreement to purchase the grocery business is self evident.

The term "waiver" when used in connection with the required performance of a condition is usually defined as "the voluntary and intentional relinquishment of a known right." 5 WILLISTON, CONTRACTS § 678, p. 239. There is no evidence whatever that respondents had any knowledge that there was, in fact, no valid lease, until after this action was begun and respondents, for the first time, had legal counsel.

Appellant argues that respondents had the burden of establishing that the lease was void. The rule of law is to the contrary. Proof of performance of an express condition precedent is a burden which must be met by the party who seeks enforcement of the contract.

> . . . A plaintiff, in order to maintain an action on the contract, must have complied with the conditions precedent contained therein. That is to say, a breach by a plaintiff of a material condition precedent relieves a defendant of liability under a contract. 2 RESTATEMENT, CONTRACTS, 746, § 395; 3 WILLISTON, CONTRACTS, 1936, § 674; 6 CORBIN, CONTRACTS, 2, § 1252." *Atkinson v. Thrift Super Markets, Inc.*, 56 Wash. 2d 593, 594, 354 P.2d 709, 710.

In the case at bar, the appellant, if she was to prevail, had the burden of proof that she had met the express conditions precedent — the written consent to an assignment of a valid lease. She did not sustain her burden. The trial court correctly dismissed her cross-complaint against respondents.

The judgment is affirmed.

NOTES & QUESTIONS

1. Carla Consumer bought a Porsche from dealer contracting to make 48 monthly payments due on the 1st of every month. For thirteen months, Carla sent her payment out on the 11th of every month. Before the fourteenth payment was due, dealer repossessed consumer's Porsche. Immediately after repossession, Carla brought her account up to date, and sued for conversion. Did dealer waive its right to timely payments? *See Mercedes-Benz Credit Corp. v. Morgan, 850* S.W.2d 297 (Ark. 1993).

2. *Retraction.* Landlord and Tenant entered into a written lease agreement which provided that rental payments would be due no later than the 1st of every month. Tenant consistently mailed the rental payments in after the 1st of every month and Landlord regularly accepted the late payments. After several months of these late payments, Landlord brought an action to eject Tenant from the premises for breach of contract. Tenant defended by stating that Landlord waived his right to timely payments. In response, Landlord points to this clause in the lease agreement:

> If tenant shall be in default in the payment of rent more than ten (10) days, Landlord, at his option, shall have the right, notwithstanding any former waiver, to demand Tenant vacate the premises.

Who is correct, Tenant or Landlord? *See S.H.V.C. Inc. v. Roy,* 188 Conn. 503, 450 A.2d 351 (1982).

b.   Avoidance of Forfeiture

We have already seen that the preference with regard to conditions is for the court to interpret an agreement so as to reduce the promisee's risk of forfeiture. RESTATEMENT (SECOND) OF CONTRACTS § 227. However, where the language of the agreement is clear, the underlying policy favoring freedom of contract may result in a forfeiture; unless in appropriate circumstances the condition may be excused. *See* RESTATEMENT (SECOND) OF CONTRACTS § 229.

MILES v. CEC HOMES, INC.
753 P.2d 1021 (Wyo. 1988)

CARDINE, Justice:

In this contract action, appellants Maurice Miles and Meadowbrook Development, Inc. appeal from judgments entered against them in favor of appellees CEC Homes, Inc. and Inberg Surveying, Inc. Appellants present the following issues on appeal: . . . Whether Meadowbrook Development, Inc. should have been excused from its duty to pay CEC Homes, Inc. because of the failure of a condition precedent. . . .

We affirm in part, reverse in part, and modify.

Appellant Meadowbrook Development, Inc. (Meadowbrook) and appellee CEC Homes, Inc. (CEC) are Wyoming corporations which were engaged in the development of residential homes in Fremont County, Wyoming in the early 1980's. The two corporations owned subdivisions located on opposite sides of 18th Street in Riverton, Wyoming, and on December 3, 1980, they entered into an agreement to share the costs of developing the street. The common improvements contemplated by the agreement were the domestic water line, storm sewers, street construction and paving, and curb, gutter and sidewalk construction. The contract provided that there was "no priority as to which of the parties shall develop which common improvement" and that either party could proceed with development of the common improvements "as may be necessary for the development of the party's subdivision."

Early in 1981, Stanley Smalley, acting for CEC, and appellant Maurice Miles, president and majority shareholder of Meadowbrook, held discussions concerning the start of construction on the common improvements. CEC began developing the improvements in May 1981 and completed them in October or November of that year. On July 19, 1984, CEC billed Meadowbrook for its share of the costs, which amounted to $25,587.90. Meadowbrook failed to pay the bill.

Appellee Inberg Surveying, Inc. (Inberg) provided engineering services for both the Meadowbrook and CEC projects. The initial engineering and plat work for the Meadowbrook subdivision was completed by Inberg in 1981. Meadowbrook paid Inberg for those services in October 1981. In March 1983, market forces prompted a decision to replat the Meadowbrook land. The cost of Inberg's services for the replatting was $8,203.11. Meadowbrook never paid for those services.

On February 15, 1985, appellees CEC and Inberg filed an action to recover payment on CEC's contract with Meadowbrook and payment on the Inberg account. Both Meadowbrook and Maurice Miles were named as defendants. Appellees' claim against Miles was predicated on a theory of piercing the corporate veil.

After a bench trial, the court entered judgment against Meadowbrook and Miles. CEC was awarded $25,587.90, which represented the amount due under the cost-sharing contract, and $6,201.12 for attorney fees. Inberg was awarded $8,203.11 for services and $5,364.23 in interest on its account with Meadowbrook. . . .

The cost-sharing contract between Meadowbrook and CEC contained the following provision:

> 4. DEVELOPMENT: The parties agree that there is no priority as to which of the parties shall develop which common improvement. It is agreed, however, that the party taking on the activity of contracting for supplies, labor, and equipment for installation of any common improvement shall, prior to entering into any binding contract, inform the other party of the specifications of such proposed contract. The non-active party shall withhold its permission to proceed with the proposed contract only if such fails to present a reasonable cost and quality of supplies, labor, and equipment or a reasonable delivery and completion day.

Meadowbrook contended that this provision created a condition precedent to its obligation of payment, that the condition did not occur, and therefore it could not be liable on the contract.

A condition precedent is "an act or event, other than a lapse of time, which must exist or occur before a duty of immediate performance of a promise arises." *Robert W. Anderson Housewrecking and Excavating, Inc. v. Board of Trustees, School District No. 25, Fremont County, Wyoming*, Wyo. 681 P.2d 1326, 1331 (1984) (quoting Calamari and Perillo, *Law of Contracts* § 11-3 (1977)). The distinction between conditions and promises, and the significance of this distinction, is succinctly discussed by Corbin as follows:

> "A promise is always made by the act or acts of one of the parties, such acts being words or other conduct expressing intention; a fact can be made to operate as a condition only by the agreement of both parties or by the construction of the law. The purpose of a promise is the creation of a duty in the promisor; the purpose of constituting some fact as a condition is always the postponement or discharge of an instant duty (or other specified legal relation). The non-fulfillment of a promise is called a breach of contract, and creates in the other party a secondary right to damages; it is the failure to perform that which was required by a legal duty. The non-occurrence of a condition will prevent the existence of a duty in the other party; but it may not create any remedial rights and duties at all, and it will not unless someone has promised that it shall occur.

3A CORBIN ON CONTRACTS § 633, p. 26 (1960).

It is possible that a single contractual provision may operate as both a condition and a promise:

> Of course a contract can be so made as to create a duty that the fact operative as a condition shall come into existence. . . . The non-performance would then have double operation, on the one hand preventing any instant duty in the [promisee] . . . and on the other creating a secondary duty in the [promisor] to pay damages. Such a condition might be described as a promissory condition.

Id. at 27–28.

In the present case, paragraph four of the cost-sharing contract clearly contains an exchange of promises. CEC, the party initiating construction, promised that it "shall" inform Meadowbrook of the specifications of any contract prior to entering such a contract. These "specifications" are identified as the "cost and quality of supplies, labor, and equipment" and a "delivery and completion day." In exchange, Meadowbrook promised that it "shall" withhold its permission to proceed with the proposed contract only if those specifications were unreasonable.

Appellants contend that these words of promise also created an implied condition precedent. They apparently feel that because the contract gave Meadowbrook the right to review specifications and withhold its permission to proceed if those specifications were unreasonable, it necessarily followed that Meadowbrook's duty to pay its share of the proposed contracts did not arise unless and until CEC informed Meadowbrook of the specifications. While we question this premise, CEC never seriously challenged Meadowbrook's interpretation of paragraph four. Instead, it attempted to show that it had performed its duty of informing Meadowbrook of the contract specifications. The parties have treated the obligation of CEC as a condition precedent to Meadowbrook's duty to pay; we will do the same for purposes of this appeal.

The traditional rule is that conditions precedent are to be strictly complied with. *Frank v. Stratford-Handcock*, 13 Wyo. 37, 77 P. 134 (1904). More recently we have held that substantial performance in good faith is sufficient in most cases to meet the harsh rule of complete and exact performance of a condition precedent. *Leitner v. Lonabaugh*, Wyo. 402 P.2d 713 (1965). Even applying the substantial performance standard, it is clear from the record that CEC did not comply with paragraph four. Smalley testified that he informed Miles of the cost of the excavating contractor. Meadowbrook was never informed of the cost and quality of supplies, labor and equipment, or a specific delivery day and completion day for any other contract.

As previously stated, the general rule is that a non-occurrence of a condition precedent excuses a party's duty of performance. This general rule is not without exceptions. One exception is stated in § 229 of the RESTATEMENT (SECOND) OF CONTRACTS:

> To the extent that the non-occurrence of a condition would cause disproportionate forfeiture, a court may excuse the non-occurrence of that condition *unless its occurrence was a material part* of the agreed exchange. (Emphasis added.)

Section 241 of the RESTATEMENT, *supra*, describes circumstances to be considered in determining whether a failure to render performance is material:

> (a) the extent to which the injured party will be deprived of the benefit which he reasonably expected;

> (b) the extent to which the injured party can be adequately compensated for the part of that benefit of which he will be deprived;

> (c) the extent to which the party failing to perform or to offer to perform will suffer forfeiture;

(d) the likelihood that the party failing to perform or to offer to perform will cure his failure, taking account of all the circumstances including any reasonable assurances;

(e) the extent to which the behavior of the party failing to perform or to offer to perform comports with standards of good faith and fair dealing.

Applying these considerations to the present case, we conclude that occurrence of the condition must be excused. It appears that appellants were deprived of a benefit which they reasonably expected — they were not given an opportunity to review contract specifications before construction began. But if any of the contract specifications were unreasonable, and appellants suffered any harm in this respect, they could be adequately compensated in damages for breach of contract. Appellants have made no such claim. In fact, throughout the course of this litigation, appellants have never contended that the quality and cost of labor and materials or the start up and completion dates were unreasonable. Yet appellants seek to totally avoid their obligation to pay their share of the cost of the improvements. This would amount to a total forfeiture of CEC's rights under the contract.

Appellants should not escape liability under the contract because of the failure of a non-material condition. We affirm the trial court's finding of liability. . . .

Affirmed in part, reversed in part, and modified as to interest.

NOTES & QUESTIONS

1. A corporation entered into a contract with an armored car carrier in which the armored car carrier agreed to provide armored car services for the corporation and further agreed to provide for timely reimbursements of any service-related losses. The contract specifically provided that the armored car carrier's responsibility to provide timely reimbursements for service related losses "shall begin when . . . bags or packages have been accepted and receipted for. . . ." by the armored car carrier or one of its employees. The armored car carrier was robbed after accepting possession of one of the corporation's cashbags but before it provided a receipt for the cashbag. The corporation requested timely reimbursement of the money which was lost in the robbery. The armored car carrier refused to reimburse, claiming that since it never provided a receipt for the cashbag, it never became liable under the contract. The corporation filed suit. According to § 229 of the RESTATEMENT (SECOND) OF CONTRACTS, what result? *See Acme Markets, Inc. v. Federal Armored Express, Inc.*, 648 A.2d 1218 (Pa. 1994).

c. Prevention

The RESTATEMENT (SECOND) OF CONTRACTS provides that the parties to a contract have an implicit duty of good faith and fair dealing in performing and enforcing that contract. RESTATEMENT (SECOND) OF CONTRACTS § 205 (1981). In the context of a conditional contract, the duty of good faith and fair dealing has been interpreted to mean that a party to a contract cannot benefit from the nonoccurrence of a condition if that party has in some way caused the non-occurrence. Therefore, if "X" has prevented the occurrence of a condition to "X's" duty of performance, "X" cannot rely on that non-occurrence to excuse "X's" duty. This has come to be known as the prevention doctrine, which is discussed in the following case.

KEYSTONE BUS LINES, INC. v. ARA SERVICES, INC.
214 Neb. 813, 336 N.W.2d 555 (1983)

SHANAHAN, Justice:

Plaintiff, Keystone Bus Lines, Inc. (Keystone), appeals dismissal of its action against defendant, ARA Services, Inc. (ARA), to enforce a provision contained in a contract for purchase of certain assets of Keystone. The provision required ARA to pay Keystone $100,000 if ARA obtained specified revenues from busing operations. Keystone alleged that ARA intentionally prevented occurrence of a condition precedent, i.e., attainment of the prescribed revenues, so the court should disregard the condition and order ARA to pay $100,000 The trial court directed a verdict for ARA, finding no evidence that ARA intentionally prevented revenues from reaching the specified levels of sales. Keystone assigns as error the directed verdict and dismissal of Keystone's petition. We affirm.

In March 1976 the Omaha Public Schools (OPS) awarded a busing contract to ARA. This contract, a result of court-ordered busing and integration, involved OPS' busing second, third, and ninth graders. After obtaining the OPS contract, ARA began searching for bus facilities and in the spring discussed with Keystone possible purchase of its Omaha bus facilities. On July 30, 1976, Keystone signed a contract to sell certain assets to ARA, including its buses and busing contracts. The contract stated that, in addition to the $555,000 purchase price, ARA would pay $50,000 if sales for 1976-77 reached $1 million, and $50,000 if sales for 1977-78 reached $1.2 million. Sales, as defined in the agreement, was gross income from bus service conducted by ARA in Omaha, including charter service for school districts other than OPS and "parent-pay" routes where parents paid for busing their children to school. Specifically excluded from sales was revenue derived from bus service for OPS.

After signing its contract with Keystone, ARA sought drivers for the routes previously served by Keystone and utilized television, newspaper ads, flyers, and the Nebraska Job Service in the search. Outside factors thwarted the recruiting efforts by ARA. Women, fearing violence in the integrated school system, were reluctant to apply as drivers, and many of the drivers recruited by ARA failed the Department of Motor Vehicles' licensing test. Also, ARA faced the problem that recruiting too early could result in losing the drivers before the school year started.

When school began in 1976, ARA was responsible for transportation of OPS pupils and Keystone's obligations, including a Millard school contract and parent-pay routes. ARA did not have enough drivers for all bus routes and made a business decision to allocate its drivers to the OPS and Millard routes. There was some decline in the parent-pay routes, because busing necessitated in the integrated school system supplied free transportation for pupils. Due to the driver shortage ARA was not able to provide full service for the parent-pay routes until the end of October.

For the year 1976-77, revenues from the operations acquired by ARA from Keystone were $760,902, and in the year 1977-78 the revenues were $373,310. According to the levels of revenue specified in the agreement, sales did not obligate ARA to pay an additional $50,000 in either of those years. Keystone contends that ARA demonstrated bad faith by initially neglecting the parent-pay routes, which resulted in a permanent loss of revenue and prevented ARA's attaining the specified levels of revenue.

Robert Wakin, president of Keystone who had negotiated the sales contract, testified that sales in 1975-76, i.e., the year before the sale to ARA, exceeded $1 million and that he had conservatively projected that sales in 1976-77 would be in excess of $1.1 million. Wakin stated that ARA should have recruited drivers earlier than August and that the initial absence of service on parent-pay routes caused parents to stop using services of ARA. Wakin also testified that beginning in August 1976, ARA made a good faith effort to acquire drivers. On account of ARA's initial erratic service, both Ralston High School and Marian High School transferred transportation to another bus company.

ARA presented evidence that it made efforts to acquire sufficient drivers for the parent-pay routes before school began in 1976.

In considering a directed verdict the Supreme Court must assume the truth of the material and relevant evidence Keystone presents, find every controverted fact in its favor, and give it the benefit of every reasonable inference deducible from the evidence.

If the promisor prevents or hinders the occurrence of a condition precedent and if the condition would have occurred except for such prevention or hindrance, the condition is excused. . . . This rule is based on the maxim one cannot profit from or escape liability for his own wrongdoing, but application of such maxim requires demonstration that the promisor took deliberate steps to impede occurrence of the condition precedent.

In viewing the evidence in the light most favorable to Keystone, we find no evidence that ARA in bad faith caused the revenues to fall below the specified levels. Even if ARA's initial, erratic service regarding the parent-pay routes did cause a decline in revenues, Keystone failed to show that ARA deliberately discouraged or impeded use of the parent-pay routes, To the contrary, the undisputed evidence shows that ARA made good faith efforts to obtain sufficient drivers to staff the parent-pay routes before school commenced in 1976. When to recruit drivers and where to allocate drivers were business decisions left to the discretion and judgment of ARA. In selling the bus business to ARA, Keystone relinquished control over such business decisions and accepted the risk that good faith decisions and business judgments by ARA could cause revenues to fall below the specified levels which obligated ARA to pay the additional amounts to Keystone. Good faith governed the business decisions which ARA made after the parties entered into their agreement.

AFFIRMED.

NOTES & QUESTIONS

1. Contractor was the lowest bidder on a heating and ventilating project for a Manhattan public school. Contractor was awarded the contract which contained a clause providing that the agreement would become binding only when the city comptroller indorsed on it his certification that there were sufficient funds in the city's school renovation budget to pay for the work. The city later embarked upon an austerity program in an attempt to save New York from default and bankruptcy. As a result, the comptroller refused to certify the contract and the city

sought to rescind it even though it was undisputed that there were sufficient funds to complete the work. Contractor sued for breach. What result? *See Kooleraire Service & Installations Corp. v. Board of Education of City of New York*, 320 N.Y.S.2d 46, 286 N.E.2d 782 (1971).

2. *Practice Point*: In determining waiver, estoppel or completion, courts often consider the course of conduct between the parties. Where avoidance based on waiver or estoppel is sought, the facts surrounding this avoidance should be carefully documented.

B. CONSTRUCTIVE CONDITIONS

> A fact or event may be a condition of a contractual right or duty, even though the parties had no intention that it should so operate, said nothing about it in words, and did nothing from which an inference of intention can be drawn. When such is the case, the condition is one that can be described as neither an express condition nor an implied [in fact] condition. Such a fact or event will be called herein a constructive condition. It is operative as a condition for the reason that courts have held or will hold it so on grounds of justice that are independent of expressed intention. Frequently, however, the holding of the court will be so stated as to make it appear that it is based upon a "presumed" intention or even upon actual intention that is discovered by some mysterious kind of interpretation or inference. In many cases, indeed, it may be difficult to determine whether the parties intended such a condition or not; and this need not be determined at all if the court is willing to hold that justice requires the condition whether the parties intended it or not.

CORBIN ON CONTRACTS § 632.

In this section, we will explore the second category of conditions: those that arise in the interests of justice or "constructive conditions of exchange." As the above quote from Corbin indicates, these are not true conditions, in the sense that they are not a reflection of the parties' intent, but are construed into the contract by the court in an effort to achieve justice. The inquiry by the court begins with an agreement that is bilateral, i.e., where there has been an exchange of promises by the parties. However, the court is faced with the dilemma as to the time when each performance is due. If the promises are said to be independent of one another, then each is due irrespective of the happening of the other and a failure of either performance gives rise to breach. However, where the promises are dependent, then the issue arises as to which performance is due first or whether they are due at the same time. If this is the case, then a court will find that the promises are conditional, and the court will as a matter of law so hold. Such court-created conditions are termed "constructive conditions of exchange" or "implied in law" conditions.

NICHOLS v. RAYNBRED
Hobart, 88 (K.B. 1615)

Nichols brought an assumpsit against Raynbred, declaring that in consideration that Nichols promised to deliver the defendant to his own use a cow, the defendant promised to deliver him 50 shillings: adjudged for the plaintiff in both courts, that the plaintiff need not aver the delivery of the cow, because it is promise for promise. Note here the promises must be at one instant, for else they will be *nuda pacta*.

KINGSTON v. PRESTON
2 Doug. 689, 99 Eng. Rep. 437 (K.B. 1773)

[This] was an action of debt, for non-performance of covenants contained in certain articles of agreement between the plaintiff and the defendant. The declaration stated: That, by articles made the 24th of March, 1770, the plaintiff, for the considerations thereinafter mentioned, covenanted with the defendant to serve him for one year and a quarter next ensuing, as a covenant-servant, in his trade of a silkmercer, at £200 a year, and in consideration of the premises, the defendant covenanted that at the end of the year and a quarter, he would give up his business of a mercer to the plaintiff, and a nephew of the defendant, or some other person to be nominated by the defendant, and give up to them his stock in trade at a fair valuation; and that, between the young traders, deeds of partnership should be executed for fourteen years, and from and immediately after the execution of the said deeds the defendant would permit the said young traders to carry on the said business in the defendant's house. Then the declaration stated a covenant by the plaintiff, that he would accept the business and stock in trade, at a fair valuation, with the defendant's nephew, or such other person, &c., and execute such deeds of partnership, and, further, that the plaintiff should and would, at and before, the sealing and delivery of the deeds, cause and procure good and sufficient security to be given to the defendant to be approved of by the defendant for the payment of £250 monthly to the defendant in lieu of a moiety of the monthly produce of the stock in trade, until the value of the stock should be reduced to £4000. Then the plaintiff averred that he had performed and been ready to perform his covenants, and assigned for breach on the part of the defendant, that he had refused to surrender and give up his business at the end of the said year and a quarter. The defendant pleaded: 1. That the plaintiff did not offer sufficient security; and 2. That he did not give sufficient security for the payment of the £250, &c. And the plaintiff demurred generally to both pleas. On the part of the plaintiff, the case was argued by Mr. Buller, who contended that the covenants were mutual and independent, and therefore a plea of the breach of one of the covenants to be performed by the plaintiff was no bar to an action for a breach by the defendant of one of which he had bound himself to perform, but that the defendant might have his remedy for the breach by the plaintiff in a separate action. On the other side, Mr. Grose insisted, that the covenants were dependent in their nature, and therefore performance must be alleged. The security to be givenfor the money, was manifestly the chief object of the transaction, and it would be highly unreasonable to construe the agreement so as to oblige the defendant to give up a beneficial business, and valuable stock-in-trade, and trust to the plaintiff's personal security, (who might, and, indeed, was admitted to be worth nothing), for the performance of his part.

In delivering the judgment of the Court, Lord Mansfield expressed himself to the following effect: There are three kinds of covenants: 1. Such as are called mutual and independent, where either party may recover damages from the other for the injury he may have received by a breach of the covenants in his favour, and where it is no excuse for the defendant to allege a breach of the covenants on the part of the plaintiff. 2. There are covenants which are conditions and dependent, in which the performance of one depends on the prior performance of another, and therefore, till this prior condition is performed, the other party is not liable to an action on his covenant. 3. There is also a third sort of covenants, which are mutual conditions to be performed at the same time; and in these, if one party was ready, and offered to perform his part, and the other neglected or refused to perform his, he who was ready and offered has fulfilled his engagement, and may maintain an action for the default of the other; though it is not certain that either is obliged to do the first act. His Lordship then proceeded to say, that the dependence, or independence, of covenants, was to be collected from the evident sense and meaning of the parties, and that, however transposed, they might be in the deed, their precedency must depend on the order of time in which the intent of the transaction requires their performance. That, in the case before the Court, it would be the greatest injustice if the plaintiff should prevail. The essence of the agreement was, that the defendant should not trust to the personal security of the plaintiff, but, before he delivered up his stock and business, should have good security for the payment of the money. The giving such security, therefore, must necessarily be a condition precedent. Judgment was accordingly given for the defendant, because the part to be performed by the plaintiff was clearly a condition precedent.

NOTES & QUESTIONS

1. Is *Nichols* consistent with RESTATEMENT (SECOND) OF CONTRACTS § 234? What are the advantages of this rule?

2. RESTATEMENT (SECOND) OF CONTRACTS § 234 Comment b states:

> Cases in which simultaneous performance is possible under the terms of the contract can be grouped into five categories: (1) where the same time is fixed for the performance of each party; (2) where a time is fixed for the performance of one of the parties and no time is fixed for the other; (3) where no time is fixed for the performance of either party; (4) where the same period is fixed within which each party is to perform; (5) where different periods are fixed within which each party is to perform. The requirement of simultaneous performance applies to the first four categories. . . .

3. Under what category in the above comment does *Nichols* belong? *Kingston?*

SPIRTOS v. MORENO
154 B.R. 550 (B.A.P. 9th Cir. 1993)

PERRIS, Bankruptcy Judge:

Under a marital settlement agreement, the debtor, Thelma Spirtos, assumed one-half of a judgment debt owed by her ex-husband, Dr. Basil Spirtos ("Dr. Spirtos") to the appellee, Irene Moreno. The debtor objected to Moreno's proof of claim, contending that Moreno's claim against her should be precluded or reduced by the damages she suffered because of Dr. Spirtos' breach of the settlement agreement. The debtor appeals from the bankruptcy court's order allowing Moreno's claim for one-half of the amount of the judgment. We AFFIRM the bankruptcy court's decision.

FACTS

On April 18, 1983, Moreno, as the guardian ad litem for Raymond Guerna, obtained a state court medical malpractice judgment against Dr. Spirtos in the approximate amount of $826,000. The debtor was not a party to the malpractice action and was not named in the judgment. In 1985, Moreno's judgment against Dr. Spirtos was affirmed on appeal.

The debtor and Dr. Spirtos were married through April of 1983. In 1982, however, the debtor filed a petition in state court to dissolve their marriage. On July 1, 1983, the debtor and Dr. Spirtos entered into a Marriage Settlement Agreement ("MSA"), which divided their substantial liabilities and community property assets. Under the MSA, the debtor agreed, inter alia, to assume, pay, indemnify, and hold Dr. Spirtos harmless from several debts, including the following:

> An undetermined amount not to exceed one-half of the Civil Judgment in the case of *Moreno v. Spirtos*, Case No. C242972. Husband and wife acknowledge that the community estate is liable for the payment of the judgment . . . and that each party takes the property hereunder subject to said judgment, both individually and jointly.

In addition, the agreement contemplated the sale of several community assets in order to pay certain community debts and imposed upon Dr. Spirtos several continuing obligations, including the obligation to pay spousal and child support and to pay monthly mortgage payments, taxes and insurance on properties awarded to the debtor pending the sale of certain other community assets. The MSA also provided that in the event the parties obtained an interlocutory judgment in the dissolution proceeding, the MSA would be submitted to the court for its approval and all executory provisions of the MSA would be incorporated in and become part of the judgment.

On December 23, 1983, the state court entered an interlocutory judgment in the dissolution proceeding ("the interlocutory judgment"). The interlocutory judgment incorporated all pertinent provisions of the MSA.[6] Pursuant to the interlocutory judgment, the debtor was awarded substantial community property. On March 2, 1984, the state court entered the final judgment of the dissolution of the marriage of Dr. Spirtos and the debtor. The debtor was represented by counsel at all phases of the dissolution proceeding, including the negotiation of the MSA.

The debtor contends that Dr. Spirtos failed to perform his obligations under the MSA in several substantial respects. The debtor contends that Dr. Spirtos' breach of the MSA caused the foreclosure or forced sale of several properties, damaged the debtor in excess of $3,000,000 and precipitated the filing of her Chapter 11 petition.

The debtor filed her voluntary Chapter 11 petition on June 28, 1984. Moreno filed a proof of claim against the debtor's estate in the amount of $828,576.78 plus interest and post-judgment costs. The debtor objected. The bankruptcy court initially determined that Moreno did not have a judgment lien against the debtor's property and that the debtor's property was not liable for the Moreno judgment by virtue of the fact that it was formerly community property. After trial, the

---

[6] [1] All further references to the MSA refer to the agreement as incorporated into the dissolution judgment, unless the context indicates otherwise.

bankruptcy court further determined that one-half of the Moreno judgment was assigned for payment by and unconditionally assumed by the debtor under the MSA. According to the court, this created a direct debtor/creditor relationship between the debtor and Moreno, and the debtor, therefore, was not allowed to offset against the amounts due Moreno any damages arising from any breach of the MSA by Dr. Spirtos. The debtor filed this timely appeal from the bankruptcy court's order allowing Moreno an unsecured claim for one-half of her judgment plus interest.

ISSUE

Whether the bankruptcy court erred in determining that Moreno's enforcement against the debtor of that portion of the judgment debt assumed by the debtor under the MSA was not precluded or affected by any breach by Dr. Spirtos of his obligations under the MSA.

STANDARD OF REVIEW

This appeal turns upon questions of law concerning the interpretation and effect of the MSA under applicable law. We review such questions of law de novo.

DISCUSSION

The debtor contends that Dr. Spirtos' breach of the MSA prevents or impairs Moreno's enforcement of the assumption provision of the MSA, which is the sole source of her liability to Moreno, for the following reasons: (1) the debtor's agreement to assume part of the Moreno judgment was conditioned upon Dr. Spirtos' performance under the MSA; and (2) the defenses or offsets that the debtor could assert against Dr. Spirtos because of his breach may be asserted against Moreno as a third party beneficiary of the MSA. Moreno contends that the debtor is not entitled to rely upon any breach of the MSA by Dr. Spirtos nor offset any damages arising from such breach against sums owed Moreno because the debtor unconditionally assumed liability for one-half of the Moreno judgment, thereby creating a direct debtor/creditor relationship with Moreno.[7]

Our resolution of this appeal turns upon the parties' rights and obligations under the MSA and Cal. Civ. Code § 5120.160 (West Supp. 1993) and whether the debtor's assumption of the obligation was unconditional.

A. § 5120.160(a).

California Civ. Code § 5120.160(a) provides that property received by a person in the division of community property is liable for a debt incurred by the person's

---

[7] [6] Moreno also contends that the merger of the MSA into the interlocutory judgment extinguished any executory conditional provisions of the agreement, thereby replacing the future performance obligations under the MSA with the obligations imposed by the judgment and effectively eliminated any conditions or contract defenses as a barrier to the enforcement of the interlocutory judgment. Because we determine that Moreno has a statutory rather than a contractual right to enforce her claim against the debtor and that the debtor unconditionally assumed one half of the Moreno judgment, we need not address the effect of such a merger on the obligations under the MSA, on Moreno's rights as a third party beneficiary or on the availability of contract defenses arising from any breach by Dr. Spirtos.

spouse during the marriage, and the person is personally liable for the debt, if the debt was assigned for payment by the person in the division of property. The parties do not dispute the bankruptcy court's determination that § 5120.160(a) applies to this attempt to enforce the debt after the effective date of the section. . . .

The plain language of § 5120.160(a) imposes personal liability on a nondebtor spouse if payment of the debt is assigned to the nondebtor spouse in the division of community property. Although there is a paucity of cases construing this section, if the section is to have any meaning at all, it must necessarily confer upon creditors the right to enforce the personal liability of a nondebtor spouse to the extent the debt is assigned to that spouse for payment.

The debtor's reliance upon the limitations of contract principles attempts to read into this section limitations which are not there. If the debt is assigned to a person for payment, the rights to enforce the personal liability of the assignee are created by § 5120.160(a)(3) and do not depend upon principles of contract law. The assignment or assumption of a debt pursuant to a division of property and § 5120.160(a)(3) create a direct debtor/creditor relationship without regard to the rights of a creditor as a third party beneficiary of a marital settlement agreement. The determinative question, therefore, is whether the debtor unconditionally assumed part of the Moreno judgment or whether the assignment of the judgment to the debtor was contingent upon some unperformed condition.

B. Was the assumption conditional?

The MSA provides that one-half of the Moreno judgment is assumed by and assigned to the debtor for payment. We reject the debtor's contention that her assumption was conditioned upon Dr. Spirtos' performance under the MSA and since Dr. Spirtos breached the MSA, the assumption is not enforceable.

A condition is a fact, the happening or nonhappening of which creates or extinguishes a duty of performance on the part of the promisor. . . . A condition is distinguished from a covenant or promise to perform, the breach of which will give rise to a right of action for damages, but will not necessarily extinguish the obligation of performance.

There are essentially three types of conditions: (1) express conditions — those that are determined by the intention of the parties as disclosed in the agreement; (2) conditions implied in fact by the interpretation of the agreement and surrounding circumstances; and (3) constructive conditions, or conditions implied by law, irrespective of the parties' intent, to avoid injustice. Conditions are not favored and an intent to create a condition must appear expressly or by clear implication in the agreement.

There are two bases upon which courts find constructive conditions. The first is in bilateral contracts where the duties are to be performed at the same time and place, the law will ordinarily imply concurrent constructive conditions making each party's obligation dependent upon the performance by the other. This test looks to whether the covenants at issue are dependent or independent, which turns upon the intention of the parties as reflected in the agreement.[8] Under another theory, in

---

[8] [9] Because this type of constructive condition turns upon the intent of the parties as reflected in the

bilateral contracts for an agreed exchange, when one party has materially failed to perform his promise and the failure is excusable and therefore not a breach which would justify an action for damages, the other party's duty to perform is discharged. *See* WITKIN, CONTRACTS, § 757. Thus, failure of consideration operates as a constructive condition on the theory that it is unjust to compel one party to perform when he does not receive the other's performance and cannot recover damages on account of the other's failure to perform. . . .

The debtor's promise to pay part of the Moreno judgment is not conditional under any of these tests. The intent to condition the debtor's obligation to Moreno upon Dr. Spirtos' performance does not appear expressly in the agreement nor is there any sort of implication arising from the language or surrounding circumstances that such is the parties' intent. Although the debtor's promise to pay part of the Moreno judgment is part of the agreed exchange of property rights and obligations between the parties, there is no indication this particular promise is dependent upon the promises to pay support and make mortgage, property tax and insurance payments that Dr. Spirtos is alleged to have breached. The MSA does not require these promises to be performed at the same time or place. Given the principle that courts favor a construction of promises as independent, a constructive condition does not exist on the basis that these promises are dependant. Neither does a constructive condition exist on the basis that a failure of consideration makes it unjust to compel one party to perform when he does not receive the other's performance. While this theory may apply in an action between the debtor and Dr. Spirtos, it should not apply as between the debtor and Moreno. The debtor received substantial community property pursuant to the MSA which, at the time of the dissolution proceeding, was subject to Moreno's judgment, as the MSA acknowledged. Even though the debtor has not received all of the agreed performance from Dr. Spirtos, the debtor retains her rights to pursue Dr. Spirtos for any damages suffered by virtue of his failure to perform. Given these circumstances, there is nothing unjust about applying a portion of the community property received by the debtor to satisfy one-half of Moreno's judgment. This is especially true given that fact that nothing in the MSA made the debtor's obligation to Moreno contingent or conditional upon performance by Dr. Spirtos. Any subsequent breach by Dr. Spirtos should not be used to imply a condition.

Because the debtor unconditionally assumed and agreed to pay one-half of the Moreno judgment, she became personally liable on the judgment pursuant to § 5120.160(a)(3). This section created a direct debtor/creditor relationship between the debtor and Moreno. Moreno's rights under this section supports the allowance of her claim against the estate.

CONCLUSION

For the reasons set forth above, we AFFIRM the bankruptcy court's order allowing Moreno's claim for one-half of the amount of the judgment.

---

agreement and surrounding circumstances, it is more properly characterized as an implied in fact condition rather than an implied in law or constructive condition.

NOTES & QUESTIONS

1. Do you agree with the court in *Spirtos* with regard to its holding that the debtor's duty was neither expressly nor constructively conditional upon the conduct of Dr. Spirtos?

2. *Drafting Exercise:* How would you rewrite the Marital Settlement Agreement so that the court would have found the debtor's duty expressly conditional upon Dr. Spirtos' performance under the MSA? How would you, as attorney for the debtor, draft a complaint alleging that Dr. Spirtos' performance under the MSA was a constructive condition of the debtor's duty of performance to Moreno? If constructive conditions were imposed in the *Spirtos* case, what justice would you be seeking to achieve?

3. Once a court determines that the exchange of promises under an agreement is dependent, the court must decide the order of performances and then determine whether the degree to which one party has performed is sufficient to give rise to a duty on the other party. This inquiry is based upon the premise that while express conditions require strict or literal compliance, constructive conditions require only substantial compliance. Constructive conditions of exchange can hardly be introduced without setting forth the doctrine of Substantial Performance, the doctrine under which they arise. Under this doctrine, in an effort to effectuate agreements and reduce the risk of forfeiture, courts have allowed a party to be compensated notwithstanding the fact that the party has not performed fully, so long as the party has performed substantially.

In the next chapter, we will discuss the issues that arise in the context of performance and breach, including *inter alia,* substantial performance. These concepts of conditional exchange, performance, and breach are separated only for pedagogical, as opposed to theoretical reasons. The following quote from *MXL Industries, Inc. v. Mulder,* 623 N.E.2d 369 (Ill. 1993), is a good segue to Chapter 14.

Illinois courts define a condition precedent as one which must be performed either before a contract becomes effective or which is to be performed by one party to an existing contract before the other party is obligated to perform. . . . The satisfaction of a condition is generally subject to the rule of strict compliance. . . . Professor Williston explains, "[s]ince an express condition . . . depends for its validity on the manifested intention of the parties, it has the same sanctity as the promise itself. Though the court may regret the harshness of such a condition, as it may regret the harshness of a promise, it must, nevertheless, generally enforce the will of the parties. . . ." (E. Farnsworth, FARNSWORTH ON CONTRACTS§ 8.3, at 353 (1990), quoting 5 S. Williston, CONTRACTS § 669 (3d ed. 1961).) A party seeking the benefit of a condition precedent, however, may waive strict compliance by conduct indicating that strict compliance with the provision will not be required.

Distinctly different, although analogous to the concept of a condition, are constructive conditions of exchange. The concept of constructive conditions of exchange was developed by the courts in order to allow the court to supply terms under which a party's duties to perform are conditioned on the performance to be given in return. . . . The purpose of constructive conditions of exchange is to play an integral role in assuring the parties to a bilateral contract that they will actually receive the performance that they have been promised. . . . A common application of the concept occurs when one party seeks to justify its own refusal to perform on the ground that the other party has committed a breach of the contract. In sum, the doctrine serves the salutary purpose of assuring each party to a bilateral contract that it will receive the promised return performance, and it expresses a judicial preference for dependent promises. . . .

Because constructive conditions of exchange invoked the concept that one party's duty to perform was conditioned on the other party's performance, the need arose to ameliorate the rule of strict compliance ordinarily applied to express conditions. As explained by Professor Farnsworth, "[t]he doctrine evolved that if one party's performance is a constructive condition of the other party's duty, only "substantial performance is required of the first party before that party can recover under the contract." " (E. Farnsworth, FARNSWORTH ON CONTRACTS § 8.12, at 415 (1990).) Farnsworth further notes, however, that "[t]his flexible requirement of substantial performance stands in sharp contrast to the requirement of strict compliance that protects a party that has taken the precaution of making its duty expressly conditional." (E. Farnsworth, FARNSWORTH ON CONTRACTS § 8.12, at 415 (1990).) Stated differently, the doctrine does not address substantial performance of a condition; rather, it focuses on substantial performance by one party of its obligations arising out of an agreed exchange of performances. Accordingly, an express condition precedent, unless otherwise excused, operates by agreement of the parties to define the satisfaction of a necessary antecedent to a party's performance under the contract and is subject to the rule of strict compliance, unless such compliance is waived. In contrast, constructive or implied conditions of exchange operate to regulate the parties' course of performance and are subject to the rule of substantial performance.

Practice Point: If a condition is clearly intended, the contract should clearly state both the condition and the order of performance. Similarly, where complete performance is required of the condition, words such as "only if" should be used to make it clear that substantial performance will *not* be sufficient. Even if no condition is intended, the parties' actions may well alter the intended risk set forth in the contract. To limit the effect of any apparent "waiver," the terms of that waiver should be clearly set forth in unity.

PERFORMANCE AND BREACH OF CONTRACT

To this point, we have concentrated largely on issues that concern the *formation* of a contract. This section and succeeding sections, however, assume the existence of a binding agreement, and explore issues that arise concerning *performance, breach* and *remedies* in contract cases. The topics that will be addressed in this section include material breach, substantial performance, divisibility, and anticipatory repudiation, and some of the defenses available to parties accused of breaching their contracts.

CHAPTER 14

REPUDIATION, DEFAULT AND BREACH

A. MATERIAL BREACH

If a contract promisor, without lawful cause, totally repudiates or fails to perform on the contract at all, the promisor is said to be in complete or total breach. If that promisor has performed in part, but performance is less than substantially complete so that non-performance breaches the essence of the promisor's contract obligation, the promisor's breach is a *material breach*. Rights and remedies can differ, based on whether a contract breach is a material breach or is an immaterial breach.

With regard to whether a breach is material, Section 241 of the RESTATEMENT (SECOND) OF CONTRACTS provides:

> § 241. Circumstances Significant In Determining Whether a Failure Is Material
>
> In determining whether a failure to render or to offer performance is material, the following circumstances are significant:
>
> (a) the extent to which the injured party will be deprived of the benefit which he reasonably expected;
>
> (b) the extent to which the injured party can be adequately compensated for the part of that benefit of which he will be deprived;
>
> (c) the extent to which the party failing to perform or to offer to perform will suffer forfeiture;
>
> (d) the likelihood that the party failing to perform or to offer to perform will cure his failure, taking account of all the circumstances including any reasonable assurances;
>
> (e) the extent to which the behavior of the party failing to perform or to offer to perform comports with standards of good faith and fair dealing.

WALKER & CO. v. HARRISON
347 Mich. 630, 81 N.W.2d 352 (1957)

SMITH, Justice: This is a suit on a written contract. The defendants are in the dry-cleaning business. Walker & Company, plaintiff sells, rents, and services advertising signs and billboards. These parties entered into an agreement pertaining to a sign. The agreement is in writing and is termed a "rental agreement." It specifies, in part, that:

> The lessor agrees to construct and install, at its own cost, one 18 feet 9 inch high × 8 feet 8 inch wide pylon type d.f. neon sign with electric clock

and flashing lamps. . . . The lessor agrees to and does hereby lease or rent unto the said lessee the said sign for the term, use and rental and under the conditions, hereinafter set out, and the lessee agrees to pay said rental. . . .

"(a) The term of this lease shall be 36 months. . . .

"(b) The rental to be paid by lessee shall be $148.50 per month for each and every calendar month during the term of this lease; . . .

"(d) Maintenance. Lessor at its expense agrees to maintain and service the sign together with such equipment as supplied and installed by the lessor to operate in conjunction with said sign under the terms of this lease; this service is to include cleaning and repainting of sign in original color scheme as often as deemed necessary by lessor to keep sign in first-class advertising condition and make all necessary repairs to sign and equipment installed by lessor. . . .

At the "expiration of this agreement," it was also provided, "title to this sign reverts to lessee." This clause is in addition to the printed form of agreement and was apparently added as a result of defendants' concern over title, they having expressed a desire "to buy for cash" and the salesman, at one time, having "quoted a cash price."

The sign was completed and installed in the latter part of July, 1953. The first billing of the monthly payment of $148.50 was made August 1, 1953, with payment thereof by defendants on September 3, 1953. This first payment was also the last. Shortly after the sign was installed, someone hit it with a tomato. Rust, also, was visible on the chrome, complained defendants, and in its corners were "little spider cobwebs." In addition, there were "some children's sayings written down in here." Defendant Herbert Harrison called Walker for the maintenance he believed himself entitled to under subparagraph (d) above. It was not forthcoming. He called again and again. "I was getting, you might say, sorer and sorer. . . . Occasionally, when I started calling up, I would walk around where the tomato was and get mad again. Then I would call up on the phone again." Finally, on October 8, 1953, plaintiff not having responded to his repeated calls, he telegraphed Walker that:

> YOU HAVE CONTINUALLY VOIDED OUR RENTAL CONTRACT BY NOT MAINTAINING SIGNS AS AGREED AS WE NO LONGER HAVE A CONTRACT WITH YOU DO NOT EXPECT ANY FURTHER REMUNERATION.

Walker's reply was in the form of a letter. After first pointing out that "your telegram does not make any specific allegations as to what the failure of maintenance comprises," and stating that "We certainly would appreciate your furnishing us with such information," the letter makes reference to a prior collateral controversy between the parties, "wondering if this refusal on our part prompted your attempt to void our rental contract," and concludes as follows:

> We would like to call your attention to paragraph G in our rental contract, which covers procedures in the event of a breach of agreement. In the event that you carry out your threat to make no future monthly payments in accordance with the agreement, it is our intention to enforce

the conditions outlined under paragraph G¹ through the proper legal channels. We call to your attention that your monthly rental payments are due in advance at our office not later than the 10th day of each current month. You are now approximately 30 days in arrears on your September payment. Unless we receive both the September and October payments by October 25th, this entire matter will be placed in the hands of our attorney for collection in accordance with paragraph G which stipulates that the entire amount is forthwith due and payable.

No additional payments were made and Walker sued in assumpsit for the entire balance due under the contract, $5,197.50, invoking paragraph (g) of the agreement. Defendants filed answer and claim of recoupment, asserting that plaintiff's failure to perform certain maintenance services constituted a prior material breach of the agreement, thus justifying their repudiation of the contract and grounding their claim for damages. The case was tried to the court without a jury and resulted in a judgment for the plaintiff. The case is before us on a general appeal.

Defendants urge upon us again and again, in various forms, the proposition that Walker's failure to service the sign, in response to repeated requests, constituted a material breach of the contract and justified repudiation by them. Their legal proposition is undoubtedly correct. Repudiation is one of the weapons available to an injured party in event the other contractor has committed a material breach. But the injured party's determination that there has been a material breach, justifying his own repudiation, is fraught with peril, for should such determination, as viewed by a later court in the clam of its contemplation, be unwarranted, the repudiator himself will have been guilty of material breach and himself have become the aggressor, not an innocent victim.

What is our criterion for determining whether or not a breach of contract is so fatal to the undertaking of the parties that it is to be classed as "material"? There is no single touchstone. Many factors are involved. They are well stated in section 275 of RESTATEMENT OF THE LAW OF CONTRACTS, in the following terms:

---

¹ [*] (g) Breach of agreement. Lessee shall be deemed to have breached this agreement by default in payment of any installment of the rental herein provided for; abandonment of the sign or vacating premises where the sign is located; termination or transfer of lessee's interest in the premises by insolvency, appointment of a receiver for lessee's business; filing of a voluntary or involuntary petition in bankruptcy with respect to lessee or the violation of any of the other terms or conditions hereof. In the event of such default, the lessor may, upon notice to the lessee, which notice shall conclusively be deemed sufficient if mailed or delivered to the premises where the sign was or is located, take possession of the sign and declare the balance of the rental herein provided for to be forthwith due and payable, and lessee hereby agrees to pay such balance upon any such contingencies. Lessor may terminate this lease and without notice, remove and repossess said sign and recover from the lessee such amounts as may be unpaid for the remaining unexpired term of this agreement. Time is of the essence of this lease with respect to the payment of rentals herein provided for. Should lessee after lessor has declared the balance of rentals due and payable, pay the full amount of rental herein provided, he shall then be entitled to the use of the sign, under all the terms and provisions hereof, for the balance of the term of this lease. No waiver by either party hereto of the nonperformance of any term, condition or obligation hereof shall be a waiver of any subsequent breach of, or failure to perform the same, or any other term, condition or obligation hereof. It is understood and agreed that the sign is especially constructed for the lessee and for use at the premises now occupied by the lessee for the term herein provided; that it is of no value unless so used and that it is a material consideration to the lessor in entering into this agreement that the lessee shall continue to use the sign for the period of time provided herein and for the payment of the full rental for such term.

In determining the materiality of a failure fully to perform a promise the following circumstance are influential:

"(a) The extent to which the injured party will obtain the substantial benefit which he could have reasonably anticipated;

"(b) The extent to which the injured party may be adequately compensated in damages for lack of complete performance;

"(c) The extent to which the party failing to perform has already partly performed or made preparations for performance;

"(d) The greater or less hardship on the party failing to perform in terminating the contract;

"(e) The willful, negligent or innocent behavior of the party failing to perform;

"(f) The greater or less uncertainty that the party failing to perform will perform the remainder of the contract."

We will not set forth in detail the testimony offered concerning the need for servicing. Granting that Walker's delay (about a week after defendant Herbert Harrison sent his telegram of repudiation Walker sent out a crew and took care of things) in rendering the service requested was irritating, we are constrained to agree with the trial court that it was not of such materiality as to justify repudiation of the contract, and we are particularly mindful of the lack of preponderant evidence contrary to his determination. . . . The trial court, on this phase of the case, held as follows:

Now Mr. Harrison phoned in, so he testified, a number of times. He isn't sure of the dates but he set the first call at about the 7th of August and he complained then of the tomato and of some rust and some cobwebs. The tomato, according to the testimony, was up on the clock; that would be outside of his reach, without a stepladder or something. The cobwebs are within easy reach of Mr. Harrison and so would the rust be. I think that Mr. Bueche's argument that these were not materially a breach would clearly be true as to the cobwebs and I really can't believe in the face of all the testimony that there was a great deal of rust 7 days after the installation of this sign. And that really brings it down to the tomato. And, of course, when a tomato has been splashed all over your clock, you don't like it. But he says he kept calling their attention to it, although the rain probably washed some of the tomato off. But the stain remained, and they didn't come. I really can't find that that was such a material breach of the contract as to justify rescission. I really don't think so.

Nor, we conclude, do we. There was no valid ground for defendants' repudiation and their failure thereafter to comply with the terms of the contract was itself a material breach, entitling Walker, upon this record, to judgment. . . .

Affirmed. Costs to appellee.

NOTES & QUESTIONS

1. *Can failure to obtain consent be material?* Landlord and tenant entered into a commercial lease wherein the tenant agreed that it would not assign its interest in the leases without prior consent of the landlord. Tenant notified landlord that it planned on merging into its wholly owned subsidiary on the following day, so the name of the tenant would change. Landlord did not provide written consent, but the tenant went through with the merger anyway. The landlord notified the "new" tenant that the merger was an assignment of interest without prior consent and a violation of the no-assignment provision of the contract. Was the tenant's failure to obtain the prior written consent of the landlord a material breach of the commercial lease? See *Pacific First Bank v. New Morgan Park Corporation*, 122 Or. App. 401, 857 P.2d 895 (1993), reversing the trial court holding that tenant had not breached; and the Oregon Supreme Court's opinion affirming the appellate court. Note also dissenting opinions in both the appellate and supreme courts.

2. *Employment Contract.* In *Gibson v. City of Cranston*, 37 F.3d 731 (1st Cir. 1994), plaintiff, a superintendent of schools in Cranston, Rhode Island, brought suit against the city for breach of her city employment contract. Plaintiff claimed that defendant had failed to provide her with a performance evaluation and further failed to provide her with a statement of goals, and as a result of these alleged breaches plaintiff resigned her position. In holding that the conduct of the defendant did not constitute a material breach, the court stated (at 737-738):

> While a material breach of an employment contract need not completely frustrate the entire purpose of the contract, it must be so important that it makes continued performance by the plaintiff virtually pointless, . . . Thus, if Cranston refused to pay appellant, or, conversely, if appellant completely withheld her services for no valid reason, the ensuing breach would reach the essence of the Contract.

> But that is not what transpired here. We think it is readily apparent that, under the stringent standard that obtains, the Committee's alleged breaches of the Contract are, as a matter of law, not material. The superintendent's job encompasses a complex and varied set of responsibilities. Under a provision of the Rhode Island General Laws, which is incorporated into the Contract by explicit reference, the post includes a vast array of administrative, supervisory, managerial, and policymaking functions. . . . This elaborate compendium of responsibilities, complemented by the multifarious provisions of the Contract itself, put appellant's grievances into proper perspective. And so viewed, we are unable to see how a reasonable jury could find that the Committee's conduct involved matters of sufficient significance to constitute a material breach.

> Appellant's flagship claim pirouettes around the Committee's failure to provide her with a unified evaluation. Given the admitted feedback that appellant received from a majority of the individual Committee members, we cannot discern how the failure to reduce the feedback to a unified evaluation or the other shortcomings in the evaluation process could be deemed a material breach. Without the evaluation, appellant was still able to carry out virtually all of her responsibilities. She still received the overwhelming majority of the benefits to which the Contract entitled her. Her mere testimony that without the evaluation provision she would not

have signed the employment agreement cannot make this otherwise unremarkable provision into one that "goes to the essence of the contract." . . . The determination of materiality, like other aspects of contract interpretation, must be based largely on a standard of objective reasonableness rather than purely subjective belief. . . . In other words, a party cannot transmogrify a provision that, from an objective standpoint, has only marginal significance into one of central salience by the simple expedient of saying in retrospect that she believed it to be very important.

Here, notwithstanding plaintiff's *post hoc* rationalization, the Committee's failure to provide a unified evaluation seems much more a matter of form than of substance. It did not in any way shrink plaintiff's major duties or deprive her of the principal benefits of her contractual bargain. Nothing about the failure betokens bad faith or an unfair course of conduct. And the sockdolager is that, at the time Dr. Gibson resigned, there was a high likelihood that the Committee would soon cure its breach by providing an evaluation; a special meeting for this purpose was scheduled to occur less than one week after she precipitously resigned.

Appellant's fallback position is that the Committee never furnished her with a written statement of goals. But appellant had ample contact with the Committee and its members to get a sense of the school system's objectives. Thus, as with the first alleged breach, this failure did not interfere significantly with either her duties or her benefits under the Contract. Consequently, it could not be deemed a material breach.

3. *Employer reduction of compensation.* By written contract, employees agree to work for employer for a specified amount of compensation and further agree not to compete directly against employer for two years after termination of employment. If employer unilaterally reduces the specified amount of employees' compensation and employees quit, must employees still conform to the covenant not to compete on the grounds that the reduction in compensation was not a material breach of the contract? *See Matheny v. McClain*, 248 Miss. 842, 161 So. 2d 516 (1964), where the court ruled that "Payment in the manner agreed upon is a vital part of the contract, and a failure to perform this essential is such a breach as to discharge appellees from performing their part of their separate contracts. The appellees were therefore released from performing their agreement in the contract unless it can be said that they waived the breach of the contract previously made by appellants."

4. *Employee's willful refusal to obey employer's instructions.* VP of defendant company had an employment contract with the defendant company, which provided that the VP would perform such duties as reasonably directed and would report directly to the CEO. During a dispute at defendant company, VP informed the CEO that he would be taking a vacation. The CEO advised VP that he was not authorized to take the vacation and instructed him not to do so. VP ignored the instructions and took the vacation. The CEO sent VP a letter stating that his conduct was a material breach of the employment agreement and gave him one day to return to work. If VP does not return to work by the close of business the following day, can CEO terminate VP's employment on the ground that VP's disobedience of CEO's direction was a material breach of the employment contract? See *Reilly v. Polychrome Corp.*, 872 F. Supp. 1265 (S.D.N.Y. 1995), applying New York law and holding that:

The primary issue in this case is whether plaintiff's refusal to obey his superior's instruction to report to work constitutes a "material breach" of his employment agreement. Because plaintiff's refusal in this case does constitute a "material breach," defendant was justified as a matter of law in dismissing plaintiff . . ." and ". . . an employee materially breaches his contract when he disobeys the employer's instruction to report to work. In the absence of serious injury or emergency, an employee who disobeys such an instruction is "guilty of insubordination" and has violated the contract as a matter of law. . . .

SAHADI v. CONTINENTAL ILL. NAT. BANK AND TRUST CO. OF CHICAGO
706 F.2d 193 (7th Cir. 1983)

HARLINGTON WOOD, JR., Circuit Judge:

This is an appeal from the district court's order granting partial summary judgment in favor of the defendant-appellee Continental Illinois Bank (the Bank) in an action alleging that the Bank breached its agreement with the plaintiff-appellant's business, Great Lakes and European Lines, Inc. (GLE), by calling a $7 million loan when GLE tendered interest payments less than one day after they were due. On appeal, the plaintiffs argue that the district court erred in granting summary judgment because there existed an array of genuine and material disputed factual issues concerning . . . whether GLE's day-late tender of payment was a "material" breach of the underlying agreement warranting the Bank's calling of the loan, whether the Bank's conduct in accepting late interest payments under the predecessor loan agreement with GLE resulted in a waiver of its right to call the loan for the delayed tender without notice, and whether the Bank's calling of the loan without notice violated its duty of "good faith" under the Uniform Commercial Code and the common law. Because there existed a genuine factual dispute at least as to the question of whether there was a "material" breach of the agreement, we find that the district court's award of summary judgment to defendant on the question of breach was inappropriate, and we remand for a trial.

I.

Viewing the facts in the light most favorable to the plaintiffs, as we must, there emerges a story of financial brinkmanship and opaque dealing in which neither side emerges wholly blameless. GLE, an international shipping line, began its relationship with the Bank in 1976 with a $3 million loan, personally guaranteed by the Sahadis. The Bank increased its loan commitment to $11 million in 1977, a commitment upon which GLE relied in expanding its business, but which was repudiated by the Bank, to the detriment of GLE, when personal and institutional friction developed between the parties. The parties quickly reached a stalemate, with GLE threatening to sue the Bank for breach of its loan commitment and the Bank threatening to call the loans already extended. Meanwhile, GLE successfully interested another lender which conditioned its backing on GLE's settlement of it differences with the Bank.

Negotiations ensued in which, the evidence indicated, the Bank primarily sought to obtain release from the Sahadis and GLE of their claims stemming from the Bank's purported breach of its loan commitment, and to obtain further collateral from the Sahadis to secure their guarantee of the outstanding loan. The Bank also sought to have GLE's outstanding interest payments, which had been withheld during the several months of the dispute, brought up to date.

The negotiations resulted in two agreements executed on October 25, 1977. One agreement ran between the Sahadis and the Bank, completely releasing the Bank from any claims stemming from its failure to fulfill the loan commitment; it also extensively collateralized the Sahadis' guarantee of the Bank's outstanding loan to GLE. The other agreement, cross-referenced to the first and running between GLE and the Bank, provided in turn for the payment of interest and for the Bank's forbearance from demanding payment of the entire outstanding loan and accrued interest:

> 1. [The Bank] hereby agrees to forbear from demanding payment of the Liabilities during the period ending December 31, 1977, except for payment of current interest thereon as more fully set forth in clause (i) of paragraph 3 below.

The agreement went on to state:

> 3. Notwithstanding the foregoing, [the Bank] may demand payment in full of the Liabilities prior to December 31, 1977 if . . . (i) [GLE] shall fail to make payment of interest accrued on the Liabilities through September 30, 1977 on or before November 15, 1977.

This latter paragraph, as initially drafted, provided for October 7, 1977 as the deadline for the payment of accrued interest. This date was changed to November 15, 1977 at Sahadi's request with no objection by the Bank; moreover, there was no evidence that the precise date on which accrued interest was to be paid was ever a point of contention in the negotiations.

Despite the seeming air of reconciliation surrounding these agreements and despite the fact that the Bank had routinely accepted late interest payments from GLE under the underlying loan which the agreement modified, plaintiff's evidence established that after October 25, the Bank furtively prepared to take advantage of GLE's propensity for late payment to call the loan under the technical letter of the new agreement. Although the Bank sent a billing to GLE headquarters on November 9, 1977 reminding GLE of the interest due on November 15 and referring to the October 25, 1977 agreement, the letter made no mention of the Bank's intent to call the loan if payment did not arrive on the precise contractually specified date. In speaking with top GLE representatives on November 14 and 15, the Bank made no mention of its intent to call the loan.

Sahadi was reminded by a subordinate on November 14 of the November 15 interest payment date, but Sahadi responded that the payment should be delayed so that GLE monies in Chicago would be available to satisfy other immediate liabilities. As Sahadi noted in his affidavit, "There was no great significance attached to the payment of interest in this covenant; it did not occur to us that the bank would treat the interest payment date any differently than it had treated previous payment dates." On the morning of November 16, a GLE representative was queried by the Bank as to whether the interest payments had been made; when the GLE representative responded negatively but indicated that the payment would be made by the end of the week, the Bank representative responded that the matter could be discussed later that day. At that later meeting, the Bank presented the surprised GLE representative with notification that the loan was called. The GLE representative immediately offered to tender payment for the due interest from the company's account with the Bank, but the Bank refused. The calling of the loan destroyed GLE and subjected the Sahadis to liability on the personal guarantee.

The Sahadis, indirectly as assignees of GLE, thereafter filed this action against the Bank, seeking release from their personal guarantee agreement and damages for the destruction of GLE. Chiefly, they contended that GLE's brief delay in tender of the November 15 interest payment did not amount to a "material" breach of the October 25 agreements justifying the Bank's cessation of forbearance, . . .

In granting partial summary judgment to the Bank, the district court . . . did not directly address their "material" breach . . . contentions, . . . the Sahadis argued, required a trial to assess the conflicting evidence. Instead, the district court chose the alternative analytical framework of "ambiguity" and held that, since the November 15 date was not "ambiguous," there was no room for factual difference as to whether a brief delay in payment was permitted. After the district court denied the Sahadis' motion for reconsideration, this appeal followed.

II.

The limitations upon the use of summary judgment are stringent, and we may not affirm the district court's order unless the record reveals the absence of any genuine issue of material fact. . . . We cannot agree with the district court that under Illinois law, expressly made applicable in the agreements here, this record presents no issues of material fact requiring a full trial. . . .

It is black letter law in Illinois and elsewhere that only a "material" breach of a contract provision by one party will justify non-performance by the other party. . . . Moreover, the determination of "materiality" is a complicated question of fact, involving an inquiry into such matters as whether the breach worked to defeat the bargained-for objective of the parties or caused disproportionate prejudice to the nonbreaching party, whether custom and usage considers such a breach to be material, and whether the allowance of reciprocal non-performance by the non-breaching party will result in his accrual of an unreasonable or unfair advantage. . . . All of these issues must be resolved with reference to the intent of the parties as evidenced in large part by the full circumstances of the transaction, thus making these issues especially unsuited to resolution by summary judgment. . . .

The need for a complete factual inquiry into the underlying circumstances and commercial custom is especially acute where, as here, the purportedly breaching party claims that time was not of the essence of the contract. Even where the contract contains a provision, not present here, explicitly stipulating that "time is of the essence," the Illinois courts will inquire into the situation of the parties and the underlying equities to determine whether a delay in performance resulted in a "material" breach. . . . The record in the case at bar discloses evidence that would permit a trier of fact to find that payment of the interest due precisely on November 15 was not "of the essence" of the agreement from the Bank's point of view. For example, Sahadi himself was allowed unilaterally to choose the payment date, and there was no contention in negotiations over the fixing of that date; the prejudice to the Bank's rights stemming from a payment delay of several hours was de minimis in view of the Bank's retention of the enhanced collateralization, its retention of the complete release of legal claims stemming from the reneged-upon loan commitment, and the Bank's clear knowledge that GLE had on hand in the Bank, and tendered, funds sufficient to satisfy the interest requirement; the Bank had previously accepted late payments in its course of dealings with GLE; and there was evidence that calling a loan for such a brief delay was without precedent in the banking community. Significantly, even the Bank conceded at oral argument on appeal, "The important thing . . . is not the date of the fifteenth in that sense; it's the fact of the promise." Whether or not these facts would be sufficient to prove non-materiality in light of all the other evidence adduced at trial, they at least raise a genuine issue as to whether the "promise" was in any important way defeated by the hours of delay in tender of payment. Indeed, it would be difficult to posit a set of alleged facts making summary resolution of the issue of "materiality" in favor of the defendant less appropriate.

The Bank launches three lines of attack against such a conclusion. First, it argues, the contract before us presents a uniquely attractive case for the rigid and summary application of time requirements because it contains a specific provision allowing the cessation of the Bank's forbearance if interest was not paid on or before November 15, 1977. However, this argument merely assumes what it seeks to prove: that the payment of interest on precisely the named date was an essential part of that specific provision, and that whether the precise day of payment was essential can be determined without the benefit of a full inquiry at trial.

The Illinois courts have rightly spurned such conclusory logic. In *Janssen Bros. v. Northbrook Trust & Savings Bank*, 12 Ill. App. 3d 840, 299 N.E.2d 431 (2d Dist. 1973), for example, a real estate contract specifically provided that time was of the essence and that if certain payments were not made by the named date, certain deeds would be automatically recorded and the purchase price refunded. . . . Notwithstanding this explicit recitation of the consequences of late payment, the court refused to undertake a wooden reading of the provision, let alone to do so through a summary procedure. Noting that even where the parties clearly intended to regard a specific payment date as crucial, "equity will refuse to enforce such a provision when to do so would be unconscionable or would give one party an unfair advantage over the other," *id.* at 434, the court also underscored that "summary procedure is not . . . suited to situations in which substantial questions are present relating to the formation and terms of a settlement agreement or its construction, and evidence or testimony is required to satisfactorily resolve the issue," *id.* at 433. . . . Significantly, none of the Illinois cases cited by the Bank to illustrate the strict and summary application of explicit consequential provisions involve the enforceability of time requirements; rather, the provisions and defaults in those cases concern far more substantive matters, such as absolute failure to properly maintain and improve municipally granted property or the failure of a real estate purchaser to obtain required mortgage financing.[2] By contrast, the Illinois case

---

[2] [2] In addition, of the three Illinois cases cited by the Bank, we note that two — City of Belleville v. Citizens' Horse Railway, 152 Ill. 171, 38 N.E. 584 (1894) and People v. Central Union Telephone Co., 232 Ill. 260, 83 N.E. 829 (1900) — were decided in the salad days of American legal formalism which were marked by an unprecedented adherence to the letter of contractual texts — a jurisprudential posture that has since been eclipsed by the kind of common sense equity approach embodied in *Janssen Bros.*, *supra. See, e.g.*, Horwitz, *The Transformation of American Law, 1780-1860* 160-210, 253-69 (1977) (legal formalism in contract law described as attempt to displace customary fairness considerations from common law adjudication in favor of "objective" standards favoring economic rationalization); Gilmore, *The Death of Contract* 87-103 (1974) (describing attachment of contractual formalism's fate to the brief triumph and subsequent decline of laissez-faire economic doctrines). In the third Illinois case cited by the

most directly on point, *Janssen Bros., supra*, well expresses the special equitable principles extended to the enforcement of time requirements even when attached to explicit termination provisions, in view of the fact that performance dates are by their nature accessory rather than central aspects of most contracts. . . .

The Bank contends alternatively that no room for a "materiality" analysis and its concomitant factual inquiry exists here because the payment of the interest on or before November 15 was an "express condition" of the Bank's forbearance, and thus its terms were required to be exactly fulfilled. This second argument, like the Bank's first, suffers from its conclusory assumption of what it seeks to prove — that the payment of the interest on the precise named date rather than payment of the interest in a reasonably prompt manner was of threshold importance to the completion of the contract. In short, asking whether a provision is a "condition" is similar to stating the "materiality" question: both seek to determine whether its performance was a *sine qua non* of the contract's fulfillment. And that determination may not be made through a mechanical process.

In general, contractual terms are presumed to represent independent promises rather than conditions. . . . Determining whether this presumption may be upset entails a full inquiry into the "intention of the parties and the good sense of the case" including such factors as whether the protected party can achieve its principal goal without literal performance of the contractual provision. . . . So reluctant are courts to elevate a term to the status of a condition that the factual and equitable inquiry will often be undertaken in spite of the existence of explicit language, not present here, creating liability only "on condition" of the occurrence of a required, prior act. . . . The Bank points to a confirmatory telex message from Sahadi stating that the Bank's forbearance was to be "on condition" that interest was paid by the named date, but such evidence is but one tile in the evidentiary mosaic; the law requires that the Sahadis be given the opportunity to present evidence that the parties only considered the payment of the interest, not its payment by an exact hour, to be the relevant "condition," if, indeed, that term as used in the telex is to be given its formal legal meaning. The Sahadis have been denied this opportunity by the district court's summary disposition.

Moreover, even if the payment of interest by the named date could be summarily construed as a necessary "condition," the district court would still be required to conduct a full-ranging factual inquiry into whether that condition had been "materially" breached or whether the technical breach was without "pecuniary

---

Bank, *Dodson v. Nink*, 72 Ill. App. 3d 59, 28 Ill. Dec. 379, 390 N.E.2d 546 (2d Dist. 1979), the court considered the question of whether a variation in performance amounted to a cognizable breach of a termination clause "under the circumstances," emphasizing that the variation had placed a new substantive duty on the other party. 390 N.E.2d at 547, 550. Such a fact-sensitive, contextual review is markedly different from the summary procedure the Bank would have us sustain here.

The non-Illinois cases cited by the Bank fail to persuade us for similar reasons. In Ritter v. Perma-Stone Co., 325 P.2d 442 (Okla. 1958), there was no question of whether a brief delay of payment worked a "material" breach of a termination provision; the defaulting party had simply failed to tender at any time payment required under that provision. And in King v. Stevenson, 445 F.2d 565 (7th Cir. 1971), the reviewing court merely noted the hypothetical dictum of the trial court that the existence of a time contingency provision might have been conclusive; moreover, the time provision in that case concerned the performance of a condition, i.e., the obtaining of an appraisal of the value of stock to be sold, whose occurrence was, unlike here, a logical precondition to the consummation of the entire transaction. 445 F.2d at 569, 570. In any event, to the extent that these decisions may be read to permit summary disposition of the issue of the materiality of time in this termination clause, they must yield to the law of Illinois as clearly stated in *Janssen Bros., supra*.

importance.". . . RESTATEMENT (SECOND) OF CONTRACTS § 229 (1979) ("To the extent that the non-occurrence of a condition would cause disproportionate forfeiture, a court may excuse the non-occurrence of that condition unless its occurrence was a material part of the agreed exchange."); *see also* RESTATEMENT (SECOND) OF CONTRACTS § 229, Illustrations 3 and 4 (demonstrating that day-late payments are not "material" breaches).[3] At either level of the "promise/condition" analysis, then, summary judgment would not be appropriate in this case.

The Bank finally contends that the factual elements and general equitable principles of the "materiality" requirement are inapplicable to the kind of loan-calling provisions present here because, it argues, contracts involving commercial paper are more strictly and literally construed than are other contracts. The Illinois cases cited by the Bank, however, do not support this premise, for they state no more than that loan acceleration clauses are not inequitable per se; they do not consider whether such clauses may be enforced where there is a breach of an arguably incidental element of the clause such as exact time of payment. . . . Moreover, we would decline to speculate that the strong equitable principles embodied in later Illinois cases like *Janssen Bros., supra*, involving an arm's length corporate real estate transaction, would be held inapplicable by the Illinois courts to loan contracts like those present here.

CONCLUSION

. . . [W]e hold that . . . [summary judgment] was an inappropriate short-cut in resolving the necessarily fact-bound, complex question of "material" breach. The "materiality" issue cannot be avoided. The holding that the deadline date for interest payments in the contract was "unambiguous" does not resolve the matter. The plaintiffs concede the existence of an unambiguous, contractually specified date, but this is merely the beginning, not the end, of the required factfinding analysis.

Reversed and Remanded.

---

[3] [3] Contrary to the Bank's assertion, the "forfeiture" required to trigger the equitable analysis of RESTATEMENT § 229 describes without strain the effect of a technical reading of the contract here. Comment (b) of that section defines a "forfeiture" as a denial of compensation that results when the obligee loses his right to the agreed exchange after he has relied substantially, as by preparation or performance on the expectation of that exchange." Construing, as we must under Illinois law, both the Sahadi/Bank agreement and the simultaneous GLE/Bank agreement together as part of the same transaction, [citations], it is apparent that the Sahadis surrendered their legal claims against the Bank for its breach of the $11 million loan commitment and posted substantial additional collateral as a result of reliance upon the Bank's forbearance which is now sought to be negated through a technical interpretation. At the very least, this is the kind of circumstance which demands careful weighing of "the extent of the forfeiture by the obligee against the importance to the obligor of the risk from which he sought to be protected and the degree to which that protection will be lost if the non-occurrence of the condition is excused to the extent required to prevent forfeiture." RESTATEMENT (SECOND) OF CONTRACTS § 229, comment b (1979). Moreover, we note that, the RESTATEMENT standard aside, under Illinois law, this equitable inquiry may be undertaken even when the breach of a condition does not result in a "forfeiture." *See Janssen Bros.*, 299 N.E.2d at 434.

K & G CONSTR. CO. v. HARRIS
223 Md. 305, 164 A.2d 451 (1960)

PRESCOTT, Judge: Feeling aggrieved by the action of the trial judge of the Circuit Court for Prince George's County, sitting without a jury, in finding a judgment against it in favor of a subcontractor, the appellant, the general contractor on a construction project, appealed.

The principal question presented is: Does a contractor, damaged by a subcontractor's failure to perform a portion of his work in a workmanlike manner, have a right, under the circumstances of this case, to withhold, in partial satisfaction of said damages, an installment payment, which, under the terms of the contract, was due the subcontractor, unless the negligent performance of his work excused its payment?

The appeal is presented on a case stated in accordance with Maryland Rule 826 g. The statement, in relevant part, is as follows:

> . . . K & G Construction Company, Inc. (hereinafter called Contractor), plaintiff and counter-defendant in the Circuit Court and appellant herein, was owner and general contractor of a housing subdivision project being constructed (herein called Project). Harris and Brooks (hereinafter called Subcontractor), defendants and counter-plaintiffs in the Circuit Court and appellees herein, entered into a contract with Contractor to do excavating and earth-moving work on the Project. Pertinent parts of the contract are set forth below:

> "Section 3. The Subcontractor agrees to complete the several portions and the whole of the work herein sublet by the time or times following:

> (a) Without delay, as called for by the Contractor.

> (b) It is expressly agreed that time is of the essence of this contract, and that the Contractor will have the right to terminate this contract and employ a substitute to perform the work in the event of delay on the part of Subcontractor, and Subcontractor agrees to indemnify the Contractor for any loss sustained thereby, provided, however, that nothing in this paragraph shall be construed to deprive Contractor of any rights or remedies it would otherwise have as to damage for delay.

> "Section 4. . . .

> (b) Progress payments will be made each month during the performance of the work. Subcontractor will submit to Contractor, by the 25th of each month, a requisition for work performed during the preceding month. Contractor will pay these requisitions, less a retainer equal to ten per cent (10%), by the 10th of the months in which such requisitions are received.[4]

> (c) No payments will be made under this contract until the insurance requirements of Sec. 9 hereof have been complied with.

> "Section 5. The Contractor agrees —

---

[4] [2] This section is not a model for clarity.

(1) That no claim for services rendered or materials furnished by the Contractor to the Subcontractor shall be valid unless written notice thereof is given by the Contractor to the Subcontractor during the first ten days of the calendar month following that in which the claim originated.

*   *   *

"Section 8. * * * All work shall be performed in a workmanlike manner, and in accordance with the best practices.

"Section 9. Subcontractor agrees to carry, during the progress of the work, * * * liability insurance against * * * property damage, in such amounts and with such companies as may be satisfactory to Contractor and shall provide Contractor with certificates showing the same to be in force."

While in the course of his employment by the Subcontractor on the Project, a bulldozer operator drove his machine too close to Contractor's house while grading the yard, causing the immediate collapse of a wall and other damage to the house. The resulting damage to contractor's house was $3,400.00. Subcontractor had complied with the insurance provision (Sec. 9) of the aforesaid contract. Subcontractor reported said damages to their liability insurance carrier. The Subcontractor and its insurance carrier refused to repair damage or compensate Contractor for damage to the house, claiming that there was no liability on the part of the Subcontractor.

"Contractor gave no written notice to Subcontractor for any services rendered or materials furnished by the Contractor to the Subcontractor.

*   *   *

"Contractor was generally satisfied with Subcontractor's work and progress as required under Sections 3 and 8 of the contract until September 12, 1958, with the exception of the bulldozer accident of August 9, 1958.

"Subcontractor performed work under the contract during July, 1958, for which it submitted a requisition by the 25th of July, as required by the contract, for work done prior to the 25th of July, payable under the terms of the contract by Contractor on or before August 10, 1958. Contractor was current as to payments due under all preceding monthly requisitions from Subcontractor. The aforesaid bulldozer accident damaging Contractor's house occurred on August 9, 1958. Contractor refused to pay Subcontractor's requisition due on August 10, 1958, because the bulldozer damage to Contractor's house had not been repaired or paid for. Subcontractor continued to work on the project until the 12th of September, 1958, at which time they discontinued working on the project because of Contractor's refusal to pay the said work requisition and notified Contractor by registered letters of their position and willingness to return to the job, but only upon payment. At that time, September 12, 1958, the value of the work completed by Subcontractor on the project for which they had not been paid was $1,484.50.

"Contractor later requested Subcontractor to return and complete work on the Project which Subcontractor refused to do because of nonpayment of work requisitions of July 25 and thereafter. Contractor's house was not repaired by Subcontractor nor compensation paid for the damage.

"It was stipulated that Subcontractor had completed work on the Project under the contract for which they had not been paid in the amount of $1,484.50 and that if they had completed the remaining work to be done under the contract, they would have made a profit of $1,340.00 on the remaining uncompleted portion of the contract. It was further stipulated that it cost the Contractor $450.00 above the contract price to have another excavating contractor complete the remaining work required under the contract. It was the opinion of the Court that if judgment were in favor of the Subcontractor, it should be for the total amount of $2,824.50.

". . . Contractor filed suit against the Subcontractor in two counts: (1), for the aforesaid bulldozer damage to Contractor's house, alleging negligence of the Subcontractor's bulldozer operator, and (2) for the $450.00 costs above the contract price in having another excavating subcontractor complete the uncompleted work in the contract. Subcontractor filed a counterclaim for recovery of work of the value of $1,484.50 for which they had not received payment and for loss of anticipated profits on uncompleted portion of work in the amount of $1,340.00. By agreement of the parties, the first count of Contractor's claim, i.e., for aforesaid bulldozer damage to Contractor's house, was submitted to jury who found in favor of Contractor in the amount of $3,400.00. Following the finding by the jury, the second count of the Contractor's claim and the counterclaims of the Subcontractor, by agreement of the parties, were submitted to the Court for determination, without jury. All of the facts recited herein above were stipulated to by the parties to the Court. Circuit Court Judge Fletcher found for counter-plaintiff Subcontractor in the amount of $2,824.50 from which Contractor has entered this appeal.

The $3,400 judgment has been paid.

It is immediately apparent that our decision turns upon the respective rights and liabilities of the parties under that portion of their contract whereby the subcontractor agreed to do the excavating and earth-moving work in "a workmanlike manner, and in accordance with the best practices," with time being of the essence of the contract, and the contractor agreed to make progress payments therefor on the 10th day of the months following the performance of the work by the subcontractor. The subcontractor contends, of course, that when the contractor failed to make the payment due on August 10, 1958, he breached his contract and thereby released him (the subcontractor) from any further obligation to perform. The contractor, on the other hand, argues that the failure of the subcontractor to perform his work in a workmanlike manner constituted a material breach of the contract, which justified his refusal to make the August 10 payment; and, as there was no breach on his part, the subcontractor had no right to cease performance on September 12, and his refusal to continue work on the project constituted another breach, which rendered him liable to the contractor for damages. The vital question, more tersely stated, remains: Did the contractor have a right, under the circumstances, to refuse to make the progress payment due on August 10, 1958?

The answer involves interesting and important principles of contract law. Promises and counter-promises made by the respective parties to a contract have certain relations to one another, which determine many of the rights and liabilities of the parties. Broadly speaking, they are (1) independent of each other, or (2) mutually dependent, one upon the other. They are independent of each other if the parties intend that performance by each of them is in no way conditioned upon performance by the other. . . . In other words, the parties exchange promises for promises, not the performance of promises for the performance of promises. . . . A failure to perform an independent promise does not excuse non-performance on the part of the adversary party, but each is required to perform his promise, and, if one does not perform, he is liable to the adversary party for such non-performance. (Of course, if litigation ensues questions of setoff or recoupment frequently arise.) Promises are mutually dependent if the parties intend performance by one to be conditioned upon performance by the other, and, if they be mutually dependent, they may be (a) precedent, i.e., a promise that is to be performed before a corresponding promise on the part of the adversary party is to be performed, (b) subsequent, i.e., a corresponding promise that is not to be performed until the other party to the contract has performed a precedent covenant, or (c) concurrent, i.e., promises that are to be performed at the same time by each of the parties, who are respectively bound to perform each. . . .

Professor Page, op. cit., para. 2971, says there are three classes of independent promises left: (1) those in which the acts to be performed by the respective parties are, by the terms of the contract, to be performed at fixed times or on the happening of certain events which do not bear any relation to one another; (2) those in which the covenant in question is independent because it does not form the entire consideration for the covenants on the part of the adversary party, and ordinarily forms but a minor part of such consideration; and (3) those in which the contract shows that the parties intended performance of their respective promises without regard to performance on the part of the adversary, thus relying upon the promises and not the performances. . . .

In the early days, it was settled law that covenants and mutual promises in a contract were *prima facie* independent, and that they were to be so construed in the absence of language in the contract clearly showing that they were intended to be dependent. . . . In the case of *Kingston v. Preston*, 2 Doug. 689, decided in 1774, Lord Mansfield, contrary to three centuries of opposing precedents, changed the rule, and decided that performance of one covenant might be dependent on prior performance of another, although the contract contained no express condition to that effect. . . . The modern rule, which seems to be of almost universal application, is that there is a presumption that mutual promises in a contract are dependent and are to be so regarded, whenever possible. . . .

While the courts assume, in deciding the relation of one or more promises in a contract to one or more counter-promises, that the promises are dependent rather than independent, the intention of the parties, as shown by the entire contract as construed in the light of the circumstances of the case, the nature of the contract, the relation of the parties thereto, and the other evidence which is admissible to assist the court in determining the intention of the parties, is the controlling factor in deciding whether the promises and counter-promises are dependent or independent. . . .

Considering the presumption that promises and counter-promises are dependent and the statement of the case, we have no hesitation in holding that the promise and counter-promise under consideration here were mutually dependent, that is to say, the parties intended performance by one to be conditioned on performance by the other; and the subcontractor's promise was, by the explicit wording of the contract, precedent to the promise of payment, monthly, by the contractor. . . . [I]t is the general rule that where a total price for work is fixed by a contract, the work is not rendered divisible by progress payments. It would, indeed, present an unusual situation if we were to hold that a building contractor, who has obtained someone to do work for him and has agreed to pay each month for the work performed in the previous month, has to continue the monthly payments, irrespective of the degree of skill and care displayed in the performance of work, and his only recourse is by way of suit for ill-performance. If this were the law, it is conceivable, in fact, probable, that many contractors would become insolvent before they were able to complete their contracts. . . .

We hold that when the subcontractor's employee negligently damaged the contractor's wall, this constituted a breach of the subcontractor's promise to perform his work in a "workmanlike manner, and in accordance with the best practices.". . . And there can be little doubt that the breach was material: the damage to the wall amounted to more than double the payment due on August 10. . . . 3 A Corbin, Contracts, para. 708, says: "The failure of a contractor's [in our case, the subcontractor's] performance to constitute 'substantial' performance may justify the owner [in our case, the contractor] in refusing to make a progress payment. . . . If the refusal to pay an installment is justified on the owner's [contractor's] part, the contractor [subcontractor] is not justified in abandoning work by reason of that refusal. His abandonment of the work will itself be a wrongful repudiation that goes to the essence, even if the defects in performance did not." *See also* RESTATEMENT, CONTRACTS, para. 274. . . . Professor Corbin, in para. 954, states further: "The unexcused failure of a contractor to render a promised performance when it is due is always a breach of contract. . . . Such failure may be of such great importance as to constitute what has been called herein a 'total' breach. . . . For a failure of performance constituting such a 'total' breach, an action for remedies that are appropriate thereto is at once maintainable. Yet the injured party is not required to bring such an action. He has the option of treating the non-performance as a 'partial' breach only. . . ." In permitting the subcontractor to proceed with work on the project after August 9, the contractor, obviously, treated the breach by the subcontractor as a partial one. As the promises were mutually dependent and the subcontractor had made a material breach in his performance, this justified the contractor in refusing to make the August 10 payment; hence, as the contractor was not in default, the subcontractor again breached the contract when he, on September 12, discontinued work on the project, which rendered him liable (by the express terms of the contract) to the contractor for his increased cost in having the excavating done — a stipulated amount of $450. . . .

Judgment against the appellant reversed; and judgment entered in favor of the appellant against the appellees for $450, the appellees to pay the costs.

NOTES & QUESTIONS

Time of payments/materiality. When parties to a contract agree that payment for services shall be made on a certain date, does the payer's failure to submit payment on that date amount to a material breach thereby excusing further performance by the payee? Suppose a contract required a construction company to haul fill, perform grading work to level a large yard area, grade layers of bank run gravel and crushed run gravel over the entire yard, apply coats of oil topped by peastone, and then roll the surface, in exchange for $33,000.00 payable in five monthly installments due on the 15th of each month. If the preliminary work up to applying and grading the crushed run gravel is completed in two months, but the construction company only receives one month of payment, can the construction company consider the failure to make timely payments a material breach and stop further work? *See Aiello Construction Inc. v. Nationwide Tractor Trailer Training and Placement Corp.*, 122 R.I. 861, 413 A.2d 85 (1980). What if, instead of monthly payments, a purchaser who had contracted to buy a business (a) was to pay seller the agreed purchase price at scheduled closing, (b) failed to pay and refused to proceed and left the closing, angry that seller would receive certain bonuses that did not violate the contract and of which he was aware weeks before the closing, and (c) thereafter submitted a new contract proposal to seller containing some substantially different terms that seller rejected? Can the buyer consider seller's conduct in now failing to close the deal and in subsequently selling the business to another purchaser a material breach of the initial contract? *See Baysden v. W.P. Hitchcock*, 553 N.W.2d 901 (Iowa 1996).

CARTER v. KRUEGER
916 S.W.2d 932 (Tenn. Ct. App. 1995)

McMurray, Judge: This is an action arising from a suit to enforce a materialman's and laborer's lien against a building belonging to the appellant. The appellant insists that the appellee breached his contract with her and that he, therefore, is not entitled to enforce a lien. Additionally, appellant filed a counter-complaint seeking damages for breach of contract. The trial court, after a bench trial, entered judgment in favor of the appellee. This appeal resulted.

The defendant-appellant, Sylvia L. Krueger, M.D., is a medical doctor practicing her profession in Cleveland. Her professional practice offices are located in a building owned by her. The plaintiff-appellee is a building contractor also practicing his profession in the Cleveland area. The parties apparently have been acquaintances for some time. The appellee had previously constructed an addition to the appellant's professional office building.

In the case at hand, the parties entered into an oral agreement whereby the appellee was to construct a new addition to the appellant's building of some 3400 to 3500 additional square feet. The appellant presented to the appellee a simple sketch of the floor plan of the addition. The appellant hired an engineer to redraw the plan in such a fashion that it could be used to obtain a building permit. Other than the sketch of the floor plan there was no other written documentation relating to the addition. There were no specifications agreed upon.

By subsequent agreement the parties increased the finished area of the building to 6700 square feet by finishing the attic space and basement. Appellee asserts that he was to be paid fifty dollars ($50.00) per square foot for the construction based upon finished area. There appears to be no real dispute that $50.00 was the agreed upon price. The appellant, although verbose in her explanation of the costs for the project, does admit that the agreed upon price was $50.00 per square foot. In her testimony, the appellant was asked the following questions and gave the following answers:

> Q. . . . . You entered into a contract and agreement with Mr. Carter to construct this addition to your building; is that correct?

> A. That's correct.

Q. And the price was agreed to at $50.00 per square foot of finished space; is that correct?

A. That was the price we agreed to later on, not originally, no.

* * *

Q. You stated in your deposition that the price was $50.00 per square foot.

A. That's what Richard [the appellee] told me, but it was really on this one meeting that day, as I remember, that he gave me the total figure because originally as we said, the floor plan was for 3500 square feet.

The appellant moved into the new addition before a certificate of occupancy had been issued by the City of Cleveland. After his inspection the city building inspector presented the appellee with a punch list of items to be completed before a certificate would be issued. In due course, the items were corrected and a certificate of occupancy was issued.

The appellee, Mr. Carter, acknowledged that there was some $2,000.00 of work that had not been completed and that some of the work that had been done was improperly done. He complains primarily that he was not allowed to correct the problems or deficiencies; that the appellant removed him from the job and that she [the appellant] began paying the appellee's subcontractors directly; that she hired an architect and professional engineer to inspect the new premises and report any problems they found to her; and subsequently, she hired another contractor, ISI General Contractor, to make the repairs deemed necessary by the architect and engineer to complete the project. She claims to have expended $41,790.58 in payment to the appellee's subcontractors and $127,420.00 in repair costs to the substitute contractor. (Payments to the architect and engineer resulted in a total cost of $134,217.78).

The trial court entered a judgment against the appellant in the amount of $70,000.00. He ordered "that plaintiff, James R. Carter, shall have a valid and enforceable lien and a judgment against the defendant, Sylvia L. Krueger, M.D., after giving defendant all credits and offsets for her counter-complaint. . . ."

From this judgment the appellant appeals to this court and asks us to review the following issue:

The trial judge erred in failing to award judgment to the appellant for $77,508.00 on her counter-claim and erred in awarding judgment against appellant in favor of appellee for $70,000.00 when the appellee breached his contract with appellant.

Firstly, we note that the appellant's issue is argumentative in that it asserts as a fact that the appellee breached his contract with the appellant. This is a matter of fact which is properly addressed to the trier of fact. We, therefore, will consider the issue as a challenge to the preponderance of the evidence.

The appellee also asserts two issues for our consideration. The first is basically a restatement of the issue raised by the appellant. The second issue raised by the appellee is whether it was error for the trial court to allow a $52,000.00 credit to the appellant in computation of the amount of the judgment. Again, we observe that these issues are nothing more than a challenge to the preponderance of the evidence. . . .

BREACH OF CONTRACT

In this case, the material facts leading up to the cessation of work by the appellee are basically undisputed. It is clear from the record that the appellant failed to give notice to the appellee of the deficiencies in the structure and offer him an opportunity to correct any substantial and material defects falling below the standard of workmanship prevailing in the area. We are of the opinion that, in the absence of express plans and specifications, the standard of workmanship prevailing in the area coupled with conformity to the applicable codes adopted by the City of Cleveland is the standard by which the appellee's performance is to be tested. The findings of the architect, engineer and new contractor are immaterial unless it is shown that the conditions found to be defective by them fell below the applicable standard.

The appellee relies heavily upon the case of *McClain v. Kimbrough Construction Co.*, 806 S.W.2d 194 (Tenn. App. 1990). In *McClain*, the court held that Kimbrough [the contractor] was under a duty to give McClain [subcontractor] notice and a reasonable opportunity to correct its defective work before terminating the contract. The appellant argues that *McClain* has no application to this case because *McClain* was a case involving a contractor and a subcontractor. We do not perceive this to be a material distinction. In *McClain* it is said:

> Requiring notice is a sound rule designed to allow the defaulting party to repair the defective work, to reduce the damages, to avoid additional defective performance, and to promote the informal settlement of disputes. . . . Thus, even when the parties have not included a "take over" clause in their contract, courts have imposed upon contractors the duty to give subcontractors notice and an opportunity to cure before terminating the contract for faulty performance. . . .

In *McClain*, it is also said that "contracting parties should endeavor to define their respective rights and obligations precisely." Citing *V.L. Nicholson Co. v. Transcon Inv., Fin. Ltd.*, 595 S.W.2d 474, 482 (Tenn. 1980). . . . We can conceive of no case or circumstance where the advice imparted by *McClain* would have been more apropos.

We concur with the chancellor's conclusion that the appellant was in material breach of the contract by failure to give notice of the claimed defects and afford the appellee a reasonable opportunity to cure the defects. . . .

DAMAGES

. . . "There can be no recovery for damages on the theory of breach of contract by the party who himself breached the contract." . . .

A party who has materially breached a contract is not entitled to damages stemming from the other party's later material breach of the same contract. . . . Thus, in cases where both parties have not fully performed, it is necessary for the courts to determine which party is chargeable with the first *uncured material breach*. See RESTATEMENT (SECOND) OF CONTRACTS § 237 comment b (1979). (Emphasis added [by the court]). Without question, the first breach was attributable to the appellee in that he failed to construct the addition to the appellant's building in accordance with the standards imposed upon him. We cannot say, however, that his breach was an "uncured material breach" because he was never given proper notice of the claimed defects or an opportunity to "cure" the breach. In the construction context, we have imposed upon contractors the obligation to give their subcontractors a reasonable opportunity to perform. . . .

We are unable to calculate "lost net profits" from the record as it now stands. We, therefore, vacate the damage award and remand the case to the trial court for a recalculation of damages, if any, in a manner consistent with this opinion.

In our discretion, we tax the costs of this appeal equally between the parties.

NOTE

With regard to the concept of cure in the context of material breach, see RESTATEMENT (SECOND) OF CONTRACTS § 242, Comment a.

B. SUBSTANTIAL PERFORMANCE

Substantial performance is performance that is less than what the contract requires, yet sufficient enough to entitle the non-complying party to recovery under the contract. As a doctrine of contract law, it arises in the context of constructive conditions, and operates to avoid the harsh consequences which might result if courts were to require perfect or literal performance in all situations. This doctrine, therefore, allows the performing party, who is technically in breach, to collect part of the benefit to which he is entitled pursuant to the contract. Most often you will see the issue of substantial performance arise in the context of construction contracts.

This section should prompt the following questions: (1) What factors do courts look at to determine if performance is substantial? (2) How do courts calculate damages where performance, although not perfect, is substantial? (3) What is the policy behind this doctrine? The cases that follow help to answer these questions.

JACOB & YOUNGS, INC. v. KENT
230 N.Y. 239, 129 N.E. 889 (N.Y. 1921)

CARDOZO, Judge:
The plaintiff built a country residence for the defendant at a cost of upwards of $77,000, and now sues to recover a balance of $3,483.46, remaining unpaid. The work of construction ceased in June, 1914, and the defendant then began to occupy the dwelling. There was no complaint of defective performance until March, 1915. One of the specifications for the plumbing work provides that —

> [A]ll wrought iron pipe must be well galvanized, lap welded pipe of the grade known as "standard pipe" of Reading manufacture.

The defendant learned in March, 1915, that some of the pipe, instead of being made in Reading, was the product of other factories. The plaintiff was accordingly directed by the architect to do the work anew. The plumbing was then encased within the walls except in a few places where it had to be exposed. Obedience to the order meant more than the substitution of other pipe. It meant the demolition at great expense of substantial parts of the completed structure. The plaintiff left the work untouched, and asked for a certificate that the final payment was due. Refusal of the certificate was followed by this suit.

The evidence sustains a finding that the omission of the prescribed brand of pipe was neither fraudulent nor willful. It was the result of the oversight and inattention of the plaintiff's subcontractor. Reading pipe is distinguished from Cohoes pipe and other brands only by the name of the manufacturer stamped upon it at intervals of between six and seven feet. Even the defendant's architect, though he inspected the pipe upon arrival, failed to notice the discrepancy. The plaintiff tried to show that the brands installed, though made by other manufacturers, were the same in quality, in appearance, in market value and in cost as the brand stated in the contract — that they were, indeed, the same thing, though manufactured in another place. The evidence was excluded, and a verdict directed for the defendant. The Appellate Division reversed, and granted a new trial.

We think the evidence, if admitted, would have supplied some basis for the inference that the defect was insignificant in its relation to the project. The courts never say that one who makes a contract fills the measure of his duty by less than full performance. They do say, however, that an omission, both trivial and innocent, will sometimes be atoned for by allowance of the resulting damage, and will not always be the breach of a condition to be followed by a forfeiture. . . . The distinction is akin to that between dependent and independent promises, or between promises and conditions. . . . Some promises are so plainly independent that they can never by fair construction be conditions of one another. . . . Others are so plainly dependent that they must always be conditions. Others, though dependent and thus conditions when there is departure in point of substance, will be viewed as independent and collateral when the departure is insignificant. . . . Considerations partly of justice and partly of presumable intention are to tell us whether this or that promise shall be placed in one class or in another. The simple and the uniform will call for different remedies from the multifarious and the intricate. The margin of departure within the range of normal expectation upon a sale of common chattels will vary from the margin to be expected upon a contract for the construction of a mansion or a "skyscraper." There will be harshness sometimes and oppression in the implication of a condition when the thing upon which labor has been expended is incapable of surrender because united to the land, and equity and reason in the implication of a like condition when the subject-matter, if defective, is in shape to be returned. From the conclusion that promises may not be treated as dependent to the extent of their uttermost minutiae without a sacrifice of justice, the progress is a short one to the conclusion that they may not be so treated without a perversion of intention. Intention not otherwise revealed may be presumed to hold in contemplation the reasonable and probable. If something else is in view, it must not be left to implication. There will be no assumption of a purpose to visit venial faults with oppressive retribution.

Those who think more of symmetry and logic in the development of legal rules than of practical adaptation to the attainment of a just result will be troubled by a classification where the lines of division are so wavering and blurred. Something, doubtless, may be said on the score of consistency and certainty in favor of a stricter standard. The courts have balanced such considerations against those of equity and fairness, and found the latter to be the weightier. The decisions in this state commit us to the liberal view, which is making its way, nowadays, in jurisdictions slow to welcome it. . . . Where the line is to be drawn between the important and the trivial cannot be settled by a formula. "In the nature of the case precise boundaries are impossible" (2 WILLISTON ON CONTRACTS, § 841). The same omission may take on one aspect or another according to its setting. Substitution of equivalents may not have the same significance in fields of art on the one side and in those of mere utility on the other. Nowhere will change be tolerated, however, if it is so dominant or pervasive as in any real or substantial measure to frustrate the purpose of the contract. . . . There is no general license to install whatever, in the builder's judgment, may be regarded as "just as good". . . . The question is one of degree, to be answered, if there is doubt, by the triers of the facts . . . and, if the inferences are certain, by the judges of the law. . . . We must weigh the purpose to be served, the desire to be gratified, the excuse for deviation from the letter, the cruelty of enforced adherence. Then only can we tell whether literal fulfilment is to be implied by law as a condition. This is not to say that the parties are not free by apt and certain words to effectuate a purpose that performance of every term shall be a condition of recovery. That question is not here. This is merely to say that the law will be slow to impute the purpose, in the silence of the parties, where the significance of the default is grievously out of proportion to the oppression of the forfeiture. The willful transgressor must accept the penalty of his transgression. . . . For him there is no occasion to mitigate the rigor of implied conditions. The transgressor whose default is unintentional and trivial may hope for mercy if he will offer atonement for his wrong. . . .

In the circumstances of this case, we think the measure of the allowance is not the cost of replacement, which would be great, but the difference in value, which would be either nominal or nothing. Some of the exposed sections might perhaps have been replaced at moderate expense. The defendant did not limit his demand to them, but treated the plumbing as a unit to be corrected from cellar to roof. In point of fact, the plaintiff never reached the stage at which evidence of the extent of the allowance became necessary. The trial court had excluded evidence that the defect was unsubstantial, and in view of that ruling there was no occasion for the plaintiff to go farther with an offer of proof. We think, however, that the offer, if it had been made, would not of necessity have been defective because directed to difference in value. It is true that in most cases the cost of replacement is the measure. . . . The owner is entitled to the money which will permit him to complete, unless the cost of completion is grossly and unfairly out of proportion to the good to be attained. When that is true, the measure is the difference in value. Specifications call, let us say, for a foundation built of granite quarried in Vermont. On the completion of the building, the owner learns that through the blunder of a subcontractor part of the foundation has been built of granite of the same quality quarried in New Hampshire. The measure of allowance is not the cost of reconstruction. "There may be omissions of that which could not afterwards be supplied exactly as called for by the contract without taking down the building to its foundations, and at the same time the omission may not affect the value of the building for use or otherwise, except so slightly as to be hardly appreciable" *Handy v. Bliss*, 204 Mass. 513, 519, 90 N.E. 864. . . . The rule that gives a remedy in cases of substantial performance with compensation for defects of trivial or inappreciable importance, has been developed by the courts as an instrument of justice. The measure of the allowance must be shaped to the same end.

The order should be affirmed, and judgment absolute directed in favor of the plaintiff upon the stipulation, with costs in all courts.

McLaughlin, J. I dissent. The plaintiff did not perform its contract. Its failure to do so was either intentional or due to gross neglect which, under the uncontradicted facts, amounted to the same thing, nor did it make any proof of the cost of compliance, where compliance was possible.

Under its contract it obligated itself to use in the plumbing only pipe (between 2,000 and 2,500 feet) made by the Reading Manufacturing Company. The first pipe delivered was about 1,000 feet and the plaintiff's superintendent then called the attention of the foreman of the subcontractor, who was doing the plumbing, to the fact that the specifications annexed to the contract required all pipe used in the plumbing to be of the Reading Manufacturing Company. They then examined it for the purpose of ascertaining whether this delivery was of that manufacture and found it was. Thereafter, as pipe was required in the progress of the work, the foreman of the subcontractor would leave word at its shop that he wanted a specified number of feet of pipe, without in any way indicating of what manufacture. Pipe would thereafter be delivered and installed in the building, without any examination whatever. Indeed, no examination, so far as appears, was made by the plaintiff, the subcontractor, defendant's architect, or any one else, of any of the pipe except the first delivery, until after the building had been completed. Plaintiff's architect then refused to give the certificate of completion, upon which the final payment depended, because all of the pipe used in the plumbing was not of the kind called for by the contract. After such refusal, the subcontractor removed the covering or insulation from about 900 feet of pipe which was exposed in the basement, cellar and attic, and all but 70 feet was found to have been manufactured, not by the Reading Company, but by other manufacturers, some by the Cohoes Rolling Mill Company, some by the National Steel Works, some by the South Chester Tubing Company, and some which bore no manufacturer's mark at all. The balance of the pipe had been so installed in the building that an inspection of it could not be had without demolishing, in part at least, the building itself.

I am of the opinion the trial court was right in directing a verdict for the defendant. The plaintiff agreed that all the pipe used should be of the Reading Manufacturing Company. Only about two-fifths of it, so far as appears, was of that kind. If more were used, then the burden of proving that fact was upon the plaintiff, which it could easily have done, since it knew where the pipe was obtained. The question of substantial performance of a contract of the character of the one under consideration depends in no small degree upon the good faith of the contractor. If the plaintiff had intended to, and had complied with the terms of the contract except as to minor omissions, due to inadvertence, then he might be allowed to recover the contract price, less the amount necessary to fully compensate the defendant for damages caused by such omissions. . . . But that is not this case. It installed between 2,000 and 2,500 feet of pipe, of which only 1,000 feet at most complied with the contract. No explanation was given why pipe called for by the contract was not used, nor was any effort made to show what it would cost to remove the pipe of other manufacturers and install that of the Reading Manufacturing Company. The defendant had a right to contract for what he wanted. He had a right before making payment to get what the contract called for. It is no answer to this suggestion to say that the pipe put in was just as good as that made by the Reading Manufacturing Company, or that the difference in value between such pipe and the pipe made by the Reading Manufacturing Company would be either "nominal or nothing." Defendant contracted for pipe made by the Reading Manufacturing Company. What his reason was for requiring this kind of pipe is of no importance. He wanted that and was entitled to it. It may have been a mere whim on his part, but even so, he had a right to this kind of pipe, regardless of whether some other kind, according to the opinion of the contractor or experts, would have been "just as good, better, or done just as well." He agreed to pay only upon condition that the pipe installed were made by that company and he ought not to be compelled to pay unless that condition be performed. . . . *Smith v. Brady*, 17 N.Y. 173. . . .

What was said by this court in *Smith v. Brady (supra)* is quite applicable here:

> I suppose it will be conceded that everyone has a right to build his house, his cottage or his store after such a model and in such style as shall best accord with his notions of utility or be most agreeable to his fancy. The specifications of the contract become the law between the parties until voluntarily changed. If the owner prefers a plain and simple Doric column, and has so provided in the agreement, the contractor has no right to put in its place the more costly and elegant Corinthian. If the owner, having regard to strength and durability, has contracted for walls of specified materials to be laid in a particular manner, or for a given number of joists and beams, the builder has no right to substitute his own judgment or that of others. Having departed from the agreement, if performance has not been waived by the other party, the law will not allow him to allege that he has made as good a building as the one he engaged to erect. He can demand payment only upon and according to the terms of his contract, and if the conditions on which payment is due have not been performed, then the right to demand it does not exist. To hold a different doctrine would be simply to make another contract, and would be giving to parties an encouragement to violate their engagements, which the just policy of the law does not permit." (17 N.Y. 186, 72 Am. Dec. 422).

I am of the opinion the trial court did not err in ruling on the admission of evidence or in directing a verdict for the defendant.

For the foregoing reasons I think the judgment of the Appellate Division should be reversed and the judgment of the Trial Term affirmed.

NOTES & QUESTIONS

1. The Court in *Jacob* found that the brand of pipe used was of the same quality, appearance, market value, and cost as the pipe required by the contract, so the doctrine of substantial performance enabled the court to direct a judgment in favor of the plaintiff. What do you think the result would have been if the appearance of the substituted pipe was different? What if there was a difference in market value or cost instead? Do you think it made any difference that the defendant's architect failed to notice the discrepancy upon inspection?

2. Although the doctrine of substantial performance is used most commonly in the context of construction contracts, it is applicable in other areas of contract law. For example, do you think the doctrine of substantial performance can be applied to personal service contracts?

3. Suppose Client contracts with Attorney to pursue a personal injury action against Insurance Company, where the claim arises out of an automobile collision. Client enters into a contingency fee contract with Attorney which provides in pertinent part, "Clients will make final determination in accepting any monies . . .

however, no settlement will be made in such a way as to exclude the Attorney from contingency fee and repayment of costs advanced." Attorney negotiates a $225,000 settlement offer from the insurance company on the eve of the trial. Client rejects this offer and soon thereafter fires the attorney. Client then contacts Insurance Company directly and negotiates a $272,000 settlement offer which Client accepts. Attorney then files an attorney lien for $75,000, which represents the amount of his contingency fee based upon the $225,000 settlement offer Attorney had procured. Can the attorney recover under a theory of substantial performance? In *Taylor v. Shigaki*, 930 P.2d 340 (Wash. 1997), the Washington Supreme Court said yes:

> Here, the evidence supports the trial court's finding that the $225,000 settlement offer was obtained through [attorney's] efforts. [The client's] attorneys were responsible for completing discovery, obtaining favorable medical examinations, establishing liability, negotiating with [the insurance company], and pressuring the insurer to pay the liability policy limits. A discharged attorney has substantially performed his or her duties when the attorney's efforts make a settlement 'practically certain,' even if the settlement occurs after the client fires the attorney.

3. Do you think the doctrine of substantial performance should be applicable to the sale of goods? Section 2-601 of the U.C.C. provides that ". . . if the goods or the tender of delivery fail in any respect to conform to the contract, the buyer may (a) reject the whole. . . ." *But see* U.C.C. §§ 2-504, 2-508, 2-608 and 2-612.

VANCE v. MY APARTMENT STEAK HOUSE OF SAN ANTONIO, INC.
677 S.W.2d 480, 27 Tex. Sup. J. 388 (Tex. 1984)

BARROW, Justice:

This is an appeal by John H. Vance, d/b/a Vance Construction Company (Vance) from a take-nothing judgment rendered in his suit against My Apartment Steak House of San Antonio, Inc. (Steak House) to recover on a construction contract. The court of appeals affirmed. We reverse the judgments of the lower courts and remand the cause to the trial court.

In March of 1978, Vance entered into a construction contract with Steak House whereby Vance agreed to construct a restaurant to be completed by August 10, 1978 in return for payment of $116,000. Various delays occurred for which each party blames the other. Finally, on September 25, 1978, Steak House notified Vance the contract was terminated and thereafter denied him access to the property for further work. It is undisputed that the contract was not fully performed although the restaurant had been substantially completed. The sum of $20,000 was withheld by Steak House from the contract price.

One subcontractor, Consolidated Interior Systems, Inc., was not paid, and it brought this suit against both Vance and Steak House seeking to recover the sum of $2,484. Vance answered and filed a cross-action against Steak House seeking to recover the sum of $8,298 remaining due and owing under the original contract. In his petition, Vance conceded that the contract had not been fully performed, but urged that he was prevented by Steak House from completing the contract. Steak House then filed a cross-claim against Vance seeking the sum of $43,488.75 for defective construction and failure to complete the contract. It was stipulated by all parties that Consolidated Interiors was entitled to recover on its claim, and it is not a party to this appeal.

At the conclusion of all evidence, the trial court granted motions for instructed verdict against both Vance and Steak House on the cross-actions filed by each. Only Vance perfected an appeal. The court of appeals affirmed after concluding that Vance had failed to prove the cost of remedying the defects or omissions necessary to make the building conform to the contract.

At the outset, we shall restate the well-established Texas rules concerning the measure of damages in a building contract dispute such as this. We first note that both Vance and Steak House are alleged to have breached their contract. They both have filed affirmative claims for relief via their cross-actions. Moreover, the evidence indicates that Vance did substantially perform the contract and that all of the building defects were remediable.

When a contractor has substantially performed a building contract, he is entitled to recover the full contract price less the cost of remedying those defects that are remediable. *Atkinson v. Jackson Bros.*, 270 S.W. 848, 850 (Tex. Comm'n App. 1925, holding approved) [additional citations].

Steak House also has a claim for damages under Texas law. The measure of damages for an owner when the contractor is alleged to be in breach of a construction contract is the cost of completing the job or of remedying those defects that are remediable. If only part of the contract price has been paid to the contractor, then the amount of the owner's damages is credited against the balance of his payments still unpaid. [Citations.]

The formulae of recovery we have just set forth comprise the damage elements of the contractor's and the owner's causes of action. It is a well accepted postulate of the common law that a civil litigant who asserts an affirmative claim for relief has the burden to persuade the finder of fact of the existence of each element of his cause of action. [Citations.] Therefore, when Vance alleged facts entitling him to recover for his performance and his allegations were denied by Steak House, Vance was placed in the position of having to prove every fact essential to his case. [Citation.]

The primary contention raised by Vance is that this Court should re-examine the holding in *Atkinson v. Jackson Bros.*, 270 S.W. 848, and shift the burden of proof on the cost of remedying building defects to the owner in all instances, even when the contractor is asserting a claim for relief. After consideration of the arguments for and against this change, we decline to overrule *Atkinson*.

The *Atkinson* court correctly stated that the doctrine of substantial performance is merely an equitable doctrine that was adopted to allow a contractor who has substantially completed a construction contract to sue on the contract rather than being relegated to his cause of action for quantum meruit. The doctrine does not, however, permit the contractor to recover the full consideration provided for in the contract. By definition, this doctrine recognizes that the contractor has not totally fulfilled his bargain under the contract — he is in breach. Nonetheless, he is allowed to sue on the contract, but his recovery is decreased by the cost of remedying those defects for which he is responsible. "To allow full recovery without deductions for defects is to award compensation for something [the contractor has] not done." *Id.* at 851.

The court in *Atkinson* announced the following rule "for measuring compensation or damages . . . to both the contractor and the owner:"

> In cases of substantial performance, the amount recoverable by the contractor is the contract price, less the reasonable cost of remedying the defects or omissions in such a way as to make the building conform to the contract. This deduction measures the damages allowed the owner for failure on the part of the contractor to fully comply with the specifications.

The court concluded that when a contractor seeks recovery on a substantial performance theory he has the burden to prove the reasonable cost of remedying the defects. Because the cross-plaintiff contractor failed to present any evidence on the damage element of its cause of action, the Commission held that it was not entitled to recover.

We recognize that some courts and commentators argue in favor of placing the burden of proving the cost of defects on the owner in all instances; however, we have concluded that the rationale underlying such a change in our law does not justify the proposal. One reason suggested for placing the burden of proof upon the owner is that the owner is in a better position to know of the existence and extent of defects and the cost of remedying such defects. While this may be true in some instances, the Texas Rules of Civil Procedure contain various tools by which a contractor may require the owner to define and enumerate the alleged defects in a building. [Citation.] Further, the contractor may obtain the right to enter the owner's premises for the purpose of inspecting and observing what defects are present. [Citation.] Therefore, we refuse to conclude that a lack of access or control justifies changing the *Atkinson* rule.

On a related point, it has been urged that the owner may establish a defense to the contractor's cause of action simply by raising a fact issue concerning a defect not addressed by the contractor. Again, our rules of discovery permit a party to limit his opponent to certain facts and defenses. [Citation.] Under these rules, a contractor would be allowed to require the owner to set forth his list of alleged defects. Thereafter, the contractor may forego any discussion of undisputed defects at trial simply by proffering the interrogatories or other discovery into evidence. This will effectively preclude the owner from raising an issue on a defect not previously disclosed to the contractor.

We today reaffirm the holding in *Atkinson*. Therefore, when a breaching contractor brings suit to recover for his substantial performance and the owner alleges remediable defects in the construction, the contractor is required to prove that he did substantially perform, the consideration due him under the contract, and the cost of remedying the defects due to his errors or omissions.

We must now decide whether the court of appeals was correct in affirming the trial court's action in directing a verdict in favor of Steak House against Vance. A defendant is entitled to a directed verdict only when reasonable minds could reach but one conclusion under the available evidence. That is, there must be no evidence to raise a fact issue regarding the cost of remedying the defects in Steak House's building. In our review, we must consider all of the evidence in the light most favorable to Vance, disregarding all contrary evidence and inferences. [Citation.]

The record of this case is replete with testimony and other evidence concerning the cost of repairing the defects alleged to have been left by Vance. To begin with,

Robert Bare, who was a part-owner and manager of Steak House, testified that he retained $20,000 of the contract price of $116,000. Of that amount, Bare estimated that he had paid $14,000 to $15,000 to subcontractors for work done or for repairs on the building. Bare later stated that the total amount paid to suppliers and subcontractors was $13,549.41; in addition, Bare spent around $2,000 for maintenance and repair work.

The lien filed by Vance was for $8,298. Vance testified that he derived this figure by deducting the amount of bills that he was aware of Bare having paid — $11,702 — from the $20,000 withheld from Vance by Bare. The $8,298 claimed by Vance included the $2,484 bill owed to and sued upon by Consolidated. Thus, Vance's net claim was for $5,814. A third witness on cost of repairs was an expert called by Steak House, Bernie Fuller. He testified that he estimated the cost of repairing the defects in the building at $12,684. Fuller was not, however, able to itemize the specific matters that gave rise to this total.

Bare's testimony concerning the amounts paid by him to workmen and suppliers was competent evidence of the cost of repairs. Likewise, the estimate related to the jury by Bernie Fuller constituted some evidence as to the cost of repairing the defects in the structure. Finally, the testimony of Vance was sufficient to enable the jury to confront and resolve the issue concerning the cost of remedying the defects in the building.

There was a substantial conflict in the evidence with regard to the exact cost of repairs. Moreover, Vance's and Bare's testimony was in conflict on what items were "extras" and what items were called for by the contract. These inconsistencies and conflicts do not, however, negate the existence of a fact question. If an injured party has produced the best evidence available, and if it is sufficient to afford a reasonable basis for determining his loss, he is not to be denied a recovery because the exact amount of the damage is incapable of ascertainment. [Citations.]

We hold that the evidence in this record is sufficient to raise a question of fact as to the cost of remedying the defects in Steak House's building. The jury should have been permitted to determine what repairs, if any, were necessitated by the substandard building practices of Vance. The court of appeals erred in affirming the trial court's directed verdict in this cause.

The judgments of the lower courts' are reversed and the cause is remanded for a trial on the merits.

ROBERTSON, Justice:

I concur in the result of the majority. The facts and procedural history of the case at bar and *Atkinson v. Jackson Bros.*, 270 S.W. 848 (Tex. Comm'n App. 1925, holding approved) are similar. In *Atkinson*, suit was brought by a lumber company against the builder, Jackson Bros. and the owner, Atkinson, for the balance due on lumber and materials furnished for the construction of the Atkinson residence. Jackson Bros. filed a cross-action against Atkinson for the balance due on the construction contract. In response, Atkinson sought damages for various defects in the workmanship and material used in the construction of the building. The jury found that Jackson Bros. had substantially complied with the contract and had built the house in accordance with the plans and specifications agreed upon. The trial court awarded Jackson Bros. recovery for the full amount owed on the contract.

On appeal, Atkinson complained that the trial court erred in awarding Jackson Bros. the full contract price because the jury, although it found Jackson Bros. had substantially complied with the contract, also found several defects in the construction. 259 S.W. 280 (Tex. Civ. App.— Austin 1924), *rev'd and remanded in part*, 270 S.W. 848 (Tex. Comm'n App. 1925, holding approved). The court of civil appeals held that since Jackson Bros. had substantially complied with the contract, their performance is deemed equivalent to full performance for purposes of suit on the contract. The court reasoned that since Jackson Bros. had fully performed for purposes of suit on the contract, it was entitled to recover the contract price in the absence of *pleading* and *proof* of facts *by the Atkinsons* showing what amount would reasonably cover the cost of remedying any defects so as to fulfill the terms of the contract. 259 S.W. at 285.

The commission of appeals reversed the holding of the court of civil appeals and held:

> It being made to appear from the pleadings and the proof that there was not a full compliance with the plans and specifications, Jackson Bros. could not recover at all without invoking the equitable doctrine of substantial performance. We therefore think the burden was on them to furnish the evidence to properly measure the deductions allowable necessary to remedy the defects and omissions. 270 S.W. at 851.

This court approved the holding of the commission of appeals. 270 S.W. at 852.

As stated by the majority, the major issue before this court is whether Texas should continue to follow the *Atkinson* rule of placing the burden of proof of the measure of a defendant's damages on the party bringing suit on a substantially complete construction contract. In nonsubstantial performance cases, the general rule in Texas is that the party asserting a claim has the burden of proving, by a preponderance of the evidence, every element necessary to sustain his claim. [Citations.] The *Atkinson* court, however, departed from the traditional burden of proof by effectively requiring the contractor to establish the damages element of the owner's cause of action. This departure was founded on the belief that at common law the contractor could not recover under the contract in the absence of the doctrine of substantial performance. "No such rule has ever been a part of the common law, much less a rule of equity." A.L. Corbin, 3A Corbin on Contracts § 709 (1960). Furthermore, this reasoning ignores that, in cases such as *Atkinson* and the present dispute, *both* parties have breached the contract and *both* parties are seeking damages for the breach of the other.

In both *Atkinson* and this case, the owner sued for damages based upon the contractor's failure to render complete performance, and the contractor sued for damages based upon the owner's failure to pay. In both cases, each contracting party alleged an independent breach of contract. In such a case, assuming the owner proves the contractor has not completely performed, but the contractor proves he has substantially performed, the owner is entitled to recover damages resulting from the contractor's less-than-complete performance. Likewise, the contractor is entitled to recover his damages that result from the owner's failure to pay. Of course, as a practical matter, the damage claims will be offset against each other and only the party proving the larger amount of damages will actually recover against the other party. Placing the burden of proof on each party to prove his own damages in such a case allows each party to recover exactly that to which he is entitled under the contract.

In an independent action against a contractor for breach of a construction contract, the burden of proof is on the owner to establish the contract's existence, [citation], the alleged breach [citation], and any damages sustained. [Citation.] [S]ee *Franks v. Associated Air Center, Inc.*, 663 F.2d 583, 590 (5th Cir. 1981) ("Under Texas law, the reasonable cost of repairs is an essential element in plaintiff's proof of damages.") In a suit by an owner against a contractor for failure to complete the contract on time, the owner must meet the burden of proof as to the measure of damages. [Citations.] Similarly, in a suit by an owner for a contractor's failure to complete construction, the owner must satisfy the burden of proof as to the measure of damages to complete the structure. [Citations.]

However, under Texas law following *Atkinson*, when a contractor brings a cause of action for the owner's failure to pay, after substantially performing on the contract, and the owner counterclaims for defective workmanship, the contractor effectively has the burden of proof of the damage element of the owner's cause of action by furnishing evidence on "deductions allowable necessary to remedy the defects and omissions." *Matador Drilling Co., Inc. v. Post*, 662 F.2d 1190, 1195 (5th Cir. 1981). In addition to proving his own damages, a contractor must prove the owner's damages, to his own disadvantage, or risk forfeiture of his right to enforce the contract. *BPR Construction & Engineering, Inc. v. Rivers*, 608 S.W.2d 248, 249-50 (Tex. Civ. App. — Dallas 1980, writ ref'd n.r.e.). It is anomalous that the contractor, in suing on the contract, must prove breach on his own part and the value of that breach. *Todd Shipyards Corp. v. Jasper Electric Service Co.*, 414 F.2d 8, 15 (5th Cir. 1969) (placing of the burden on the owner is a "better view"). In the absence of such proof the contractor can recover nothing in his suit and the owner receives what may be, depending upon how much has already been paid under the contract, a substantial windfall. *See generally Ryan v. Thurmond*, 481 S.W.2d 199 (Tex. Civ. App. — Corpus Christi 1972, writ ref'd n.r.e.). Additionally, the contractor is faced with the risk of proving the owner's damages so convincingly that the finder of fact determines he, the contractor, *did not* substantially perform. If the contractor attempts to meet the burden imposed by the rule of *Atkinson* and the fact finder thereafter finds he did not substantially perform, he cannot receive a judgment on the contract and is left with only a quantum meruit claim. *Atkinson v. Jackson Bros.*, 270 S.W. at 851. In this way, the rule of *Atkinson* may require the contractor to defeat his own suit. The contractor's alternative to this delicate balancing act is to forego suit on the contract altogether and sue only for the value of his services. From the contractor's perspective, neither alternative is desirable. From the juristic perspective, neither alternative is fair.

An additional compelling reason for placing the burden of proof on the owner is found in the general rule long recognized by this state that the party having peculiar knowledge of the facts to be proved has the burden of proof of such facts. [Citation.] In a substantial performance case the same measure of damages applies to both the contractor and the owner. *Atkinson v. Jackson Bros.*, 270 S.W. at 850. Those damages are expressed as the contract price less the reasonable cost of repair of the defect or omission. The alleged defect is exclusively within the control and access of the owner. In both the case at bar and *Atkinson*, the owner either made or had the repairs made. The contractor did not know and should not have been expected to know without investigation the measure of damages. "Ultimately, it is the dissatisfied party who knows best what particular phase of the construction is unsatisfactory to it." *Hopkins Construction Co. v. Reliance Ins. Co.*, 475 P.2d 223, 226 (Alaska 1970). The owner, having responsibility for and usually supervising any repair work, is in the better position to establish the measure of damages.

By placing on the contractor the burden of proving the cost to remedy defects, the *Atkinson* court created a good defense to any suit on the contract by the contractor. As observed by a concurring opinion in *BPR Construction & Engineering, Inc. v. Rivers*, 608 S.W.2d at 250:

> According to the logic of *Atkinson*, if [the contractor] proves the cost of remedying one or more defects asserted by the owner, the dilemma still exists because *the court or jury* [emphasis added (by the court)] may find another defect raised by the evidence, but concerning which the amount of the owner's damage has not been shown. All an owner needs to do in order to establish a defense to the contractor's entire claim, while retaining the benefit of the contractor's work, is to raise a fact issue concerning any defect, no matter how slight in relation to the total of the work performed.

The possibility of the owner's unjustifiably alleging a series of defects presents the contractor with a most onerous burden. The contractor must present evidence regarding the cost to remedy every defect, and in the absence of such proof forfeits his contract rights. The smaller his breach, the greater the forfeiture. A.L. Corbin, 3A CORBIN ON CONTRACTS § 710 (1960).

The majority urges the fact an owner has peculiar knowledge of the damages to be proved and the onerous burden placed upon the contractor of presenting evidence of every defect alleged by an owner may be avoided by use of Texas' broad discovery rules. Although these problems may be lessened by our discovery rules, the prodigiously unfair and awkward position of a contractor attempting to show compliance with a construction contract while simultaneously being required to establish damages from his alleged breach of that same contract is indefensible. Therefore, I would overrule our previous decision in *Atkinson v. Jackson Bros.* and adopt the rule that in an action by a party for collection of the contract price of a substantially completed construction contract the defendant, in order to avail himself of a set-off for damages sustained from incomplete or defective work, has the burden of proof as to the measure of such damages. [Citations.] A.L. Corbin, 3A CORBIN ON CONTRACTS § 710 (2d ed. 1960 and 1962 supplement) (stating the rule requiring the placing of the burden on the owner is "sensible and self-evident"); S. Williston, 6 WILLISTON ON CONTRACTS § 842 (3d ed. 1962) ("The burden of establishing the amount of the allowance for defective work falls upon the owner").

WALLACE and KILGARLIN, J.J., join in this concurring opinion.

NOTES

1. When a contractor files suit seeking recovery based on the substantial performance doctrine, that contractor has the burden, of course, of proving substantial performance. If proved, the doctrine allows recovery of the contract price less the cost to the other party of obtaining completion of the contractor's remaining contract obligations.

2. When the contractor has substantially performed, some relevant further questions are: (a) the costs to remedy the contractor's deficiencies or defects in

performance, and (b) which party must bear the burden of proof as to those costs. On this latter question there are two views. A number of jurisdictions place the burden of proof of the amount required to correct the contractor's deficiencies on the *owner* or other contracting party, claiming that the contractor's performance was incomplete. On the other hand, Texas and New York, and probably Maine, place the burden on the *contractor* to prove the extent of the other party's damages due to the contractor's incomplete performance.

3. The concurring opinion in the *Vance* case above refers to opinions from the following jurisdictions in support of the position that Texas should rescind from its *Atkinson* case rule and should place the burden of proving costs to complete the work on the contractor's opponent: U.S. Courts of Appeals for the Second, Eighth and Tenth Circuits, and state courts in Alaska, Louisiana, Michigan, Nebraska, New Jersey, Ohio, Pennsylvania, Vermont and Washington, to support his position that Texas should change its law. Connecticut, Minnesota, Maryland, Iowa, New Hampshire and Wisconsin also place the burden of proof of costs to complete the work on the defendant or owner when contractor has established substantial, albeit not complete, performance.

4. New York's burden of proof rule as to costs to remedy the contractor's insubstantial deficiencies, equivalent to Texas' *Atkinson* rule, was first set forth in *Spence v. Ham*, 163 N.Y. 220, 57 N.E.412 (1900). Holding, as does Texas, that the burden is on the contractor to prove the extent of those costs, the *Spence* case states that:

> When the plaintiff shows that he performed his contract he is entitled to judgment for the contract price, but when he shows that he performed his contract except that through inadvertence he omitted to do some unsubstantial things, he is not entitled to recover anything until he shows that the things omitted, if worthy of any attention whatever, can be supplied for a comparatively small sum, in which event he can recover the contract price after deducting that sum. This rule is liberal to the contractor, for it allows him to recover when he has not fully performed, and it cannot be extended without danger to the integrity of the contract. As he does not show full performance, it is not requiring too much of him to show what it will cost to remedy the defects in order to permit him to recover the contract price less the sum allowed for defective performance. It is for him to show this, for otherwise the owner could say "am I to pay according to my promise when the contractor does not perform according to his?" The one who fails in fully performing and who invokes the doctrine of substantial performance must furnish the evidence to measure the compensation for the defects, as that is the substitute for his failure to do as he agreed.

5. Maine is another state that is said to espouse the so-called minority view. In *Northeast Drilling, Inc. v. Inner Space Servs.*, 2000 U.S. Dist. Lexis 20254 (D. Me. 2000), *aff'd*, 243 F.3d 25 (1st Cir. 2001), the U.S. District Court for Maine noted that: "*Skowhegan Water Co. v. Skowhegan Village Corp.*, 102 Me. 323, 66 A. 714 (Me. 1906), seems to say that the burden of proving damages lies with the contractor even in a substantial performance case and that he cannot simply seek the contract price, expecting the defendant to prove any reduction."

VINCENZI v. CERRO
186 Conn. 612, 442 A.2d 1352 (1982)

SHEA, Justice:

In this suit on a building contract the trial court found that a balance of $20,015.40 plus interest was owed by the defendant owners for their home which the plaintiffs had constructed. From the judgment rendered the defendants have appealed claiming error in the conclusion of the trial court that the plaintiffs were entitled to recover on the basis of the contract price by virtue of their substantial performance of the work; in allowing the plaintiffs to be compensated for certain extra work not included in the original contract; in disallowing wholly or partially the setoffs claimed by the defendants for delay, correction of defective work, and finishing some items of the contract which the plaintiffs failed to complete; and in awarding the amount of interest included in the judgment. The plaintiffs have cross appealed claiming only that the calculation of interest was erroneous and prejudicial to them. . . .

In a memorandum of decision the trial court set forth the facts in commendable detail. On October 5, 1976, the parties signed a written contract for the plaintiffs to construct a three-family house on land owned by the defendants in Bridgeport. The contract price was $91,000, to be paid in five installments as various stages of the work were finished. The house was to be completed within 150 days from the date of the execution of the contract, which would make the projected completion date March 4, 1977. Except for $2000 withheld for incomplete items, the first four scheduled payments were made. The payments made totaled $67,100, leaving a balance of $23,900 on the contract price. In August, 1977, the plaintiffs demanded this balance, but the defendants refused on the ground that the house was not complete and that some work was defective. The court found that the work was not finished at that time because the heating system was not approved until October, 1977, and a certificate of occupancy was not issued until November 9, 1977. This date, when the certificate of occupancy was obtained, was deemed by the trial court to be the date when the contract had been substantially performed by the plaintiffs.

The judgment awarded the plaintiffs the balance of the contract price, $23,900, plus certain extras totaling $1118.30, but deducted therefrom $5002.90 for defective or incomplete work and for the loss of rent suffered by the defendants for the period of unjustifiable delay.

The principal claim of the defendants is that the doctrine of substantial performance was inapplicable in this case because the plaintiffs were guilty of a willful or intentional breach of contract by failing to complete all of the work required. "There is no reason why one who has substantially performed such a contract, but unintentionally failed of strict performance in the matter of minor details, should have imposed upon him as a condition of recovery for that of which the other party has received the benefit, the burden of showing by direct evidence its reasonable value, or why he should be deprived of all benefit of the contract which he has substantially performed." *Daly & Sons v. New Haven Hotel Co.*, 91 Conn. 280, 287-88, 99 A. 853 (1917). The defendants rely on this articulation of the doctrine of substantial performance, which is also quoted in the memorandum of decision, as indicating that a builder who has failed to complete his contract fully may not invoke its benefit unless he was prevented from doing so by some circumstance beyond his control, such as interference by the owner. We have in several cases approved the common statement that a contractor who is guilty of a "willful" breach cannot maintain an action upon the contract. See 3A Corbin, CONTRACTS § 707. The contemporary view, however, is that even a conscious and intentional departure from the contract specifications will not necessarily defeat recovery, but may be considered as one of the several factors involved in deciding whether there has been full performance. The pertinent inquiry is not simply whether the breach was "willful" but whether the behavior of the party in default "comports with standards of good faith and fair dealing." 2 RESTATEMENT (SECOND) OF CONTRACTS§ 241 (e), *and see* comment f. Even an adverse conclusion on this point is not decisive but is to be weighed with other factors, such as the extent to which the owner will be deprived of a reasonably expected benefit and the extent to which the builder may suffer forfeiture, in deciding whether there has been substantial performance. . . .

The reference in the memorandum of decision to the "willful default" qualification of the doctrine of substantial performance indicates the court considered this factor as well as others in concluding that the plaintiffs were entitled to recover on the contract. The court allowed the defendants $2060.40 on their claim for defective or incomplete items, $1527 for repairing stress cracks in the foundation walls and $533.40 for five minor items. Upon a contract price of $91,000 the proportion of unperformed work, therefore, was so minimal as to warrant the conclusion of substantial performance drawn by the court. The reliance upon the certificate of occupancy as indicating substantial performance was entirely appropriate, despite the fact that two minor items were still to be performed, installing two electric plates and building a railing for the front steps.

The remaining claims, which relate to the amounts allowed to the plaintiffs for extras and to the defendants for defective work and for delay, raise only the question of whether the discretion of the trier was abused in the light of the evidence presented. We cannot retry the case. . . . We have reviewed the evidence relating to the various items involved and conclude that the decision of the trial court with respect to each of them was not "clearly erroneous.". . .

There is error in the amount of the judgment only with respect to those items in which error has been confessed by the parties as set forth in this opinion. The judgment is set aside and the case is remanded to the trial court with direction to correct the amount of damages awarded accordingly.

In this opinion the other judges concurred.

NOTES & QUESTIONS

1. *Compare* RESTATEMENT (FIRST) OF CONTRACTS (1932) § 275, to RESTATEMENT (SECOND) OF CONTRACTS § 241 (1981). Note the omission of the words "wilful, negligent or innocent behavior of the party failing to perform" in the RESTATEMENT (SECOND) OF CONTRACTS section. Do you think a willful breach should preclude the application of the doctrine of substantial performance? If not, under what circumstances would willfulness be significant to the courts? *See* RESTATEMENT (SECOND) OF CONTRACTS § 241, Comment f:

> f. *Absence of good faith or fair dealing.* A party's adherence to standards
> of good faith and fair dealing (§ 205) will not prevent his failure to perform

a duty from amounting to a breach (§ 236(2)). Nor will his adherence to such standards necessarily prevent his failure from having the effect of the non-occurrence of a condition (§ 237; cf. § 238). The extent to which the behavior of the party failing to perform or to offer to perform comports with standards of good faith and fair dealing is, however, a significant circumstance in determining whether the failure is material (Subsection (e)). In giving weight to this factor courts have often used such less precise terms as "wilful." Adherence to the standards stated in Subsection (e) is not conclusive, since other circumstances may cause a failure to be material in spite of such adherence. Nor is non-adherence conclusive, and other circumstances may cause a failure not to be material in spite of such non-adherence.

2. Buyer and seller entered into a purchase agreement wherein buyer purchased all assets and rights to manufacture improved patient care equipment in exchange for 5% royalties payable to the seller over 10 years. Seller assured buyer that the patient care equipment was patent pending. However, seller did not file the patent application until after the contract was executed, and due to the late filing, the patent was denied. As a result, buyer did not have the exclusive right to manufacture and market the patient care equipment. Buyer thereafter refused to pay seller any royalties. Can seller assert a claim for substantial performance and collect royalties pursuant to the contract or is seller's conduct the type of conduct which precludes the application of the doctrine of substantial performance as explained in Comment f of § 241 of the RESTATEMENT (SECOND) OF CONTRACTS?

> The contract reveals that the very essence of the transaction was to enable Dutton-Lainson to manufacture, market, and distribute the improvements which were the subject of the patent application. While Dutton-Lainson took the risk that, for reasons beyond the control of the parties, a patent might not issue, Dutton-Lainson did not bargain for the certainty that a patent would not issue because, contrary to the representation made to it, no application had been filed.

> Thus, VRT's failure to deliver and assign a filed application was not a relatively minor and unimportant deviation from VRT's obligation. As a consequence, VRT's misrepresentation with regard to the application means there was no honest endeavor in good faith on its part to perform its part of the contract. It therefore necessarily follows that there was no substantial performance on its part and that it is precluded from maintaining this action against Dutton-Lainson.

VRT, Inc. v. Dutton-Lainson Co., 247 Neb. 845, 530 N.W.2d 619 (1995).

PLANTE v. JACOBS
10 Wis. 2d 567, 103 N.W.2d 296 (1960).

HALLOWS, Justice:

The defendants argue that the plaintiff cannot recover any amount because he has failed to substantially perform the contract. The plaintiff conceded he failed to furnish the kitchen cabinets, gutters and downspouts, sidewalk, closet clothes poles, and entrance seat amounting to $1,601.95. This amount was allowed to the defendants. The defendants claim some 20 other items of incomplete or faulty performance by the plaintiff and no substantial performance because the cost of completing the house in strict compliance with the plans and specifications would amount to 25 or 30 per cent of the contract price. The defendants especially stress the misplacing of the wall between the living room and the kitchen, which narrowed the living room in excess of one foot. The cost of tearing down this wall and rebuilding it would be approximately $4,000. The record is not clear why and when this wall was misplaced, but the wall is completely built and the house decorated and the defendants are living therein. Real-estate experts testified that the smaller width of the living room would not affect the market price of the house.

The defendants rely on *Manitowoc Steam Boiler Works v. Manitowoc Glue Co.*, (1903) 120 Wis. 1, 97 N.W. 515, for the proposition that there can be no recovery on the contract as distinguished from quantum meruit unless there is substantial performance. This is undoubtedly the correct rule at common law. . . . The question here is whether there has been substantial performance. The test of what amounts to substantial performance seems to be whether the performance meets the essential purpose of the contract. In the Manitowoc case the contract called for a boiler having a capacity of 150 per cent of the existing boiler. The court held there was no substantial performance because the boiler furnished had a capacity of only 82 per cent of the old boiler and only approximately one half of the boiler capacity contemplated by the contract. In *Houlahan v. Clark*, (1901), 110 Wis. 43, 85 N.W. 676, the contract provided that the plaintiff was to drive pilings in the lake and place a boathouse thereon parallel and in line with a neighbor's dock. This was not done and the contractor so positioned the boathouse that it was practically useless to the owner. *Manthey v. Stock*, (1907), 133 Wis. 107, 113 N.W. 443, involved a contract to paint a house and to do a good job, including the removal of the old paint where necessary. The plaintiff did not remove the old paint, and blistering and roughness of the new paint resulted. The court held that the plaintiff failed to show substantial performance. The defendants also cite *Manning v. School Dist.* (1905), 124 Wis. 84, 102 N.W. 356. However, this case involved a contract to install a heating and ventilating plant in the school building which would meet certain tests which the heating apparatus failed to do. The heating plant was practically a total failure to accomplish the purposes of the contract. . . .

Substantial performance as applied to construction of a house does not mean that every detail must be in strict compliance with the specifications and the plans. Something less than perfection is the test of specific performance unless all details are made the essence of the contract. This was not done here. There may be situations in which features or details of construction of special or of great personal importance, if not performed, would prevent a finding of substantial performance of the contract. In this case the plan was a stock floor plan. No detailed construction of the house was shown on the plan. There were no blueprints. The specifications were standard printed forms with some modifications and additions written in by the parties. Many of the problems that arose during the construction had to be solved on the basis of practical experience. No mathematical rule relating to the percentage of the price, of cost of completion, or of completeness can be laid down to determine substantial performance of a building contract. Although the defendants received a house with which they are dissatisfied in many respects, the trial court was not in error in finding the contract was substantially performed.

The next question is, what is the amount of recovery when the plaintiff has substantially, but incompletely, performed? For substantial performance, the plaintiff should recover the contract price less the damages caused the defendant by the incomplete performance. Both parties agree *Venzke v. Magdanz* (1943), 243 Wis. 155, 9 N.W. (2d) 604, states the correct rule for damages due to faulty construction amounting to such incomplete performance, which is the difference between the value of the house as it stands with faulty and incomplete construction and the value of the house if it had been constructed in strict accordance with the plans and specifications. This is the diminished-value rule. The cost of replacement or repair is not the measure of such damage, but is an element to take into consideration in arriving at value under some circumstances. The cost of replacement or the cost to make whole the omissions may equal or be less than the difference in value in some cases and, likewise, the cost to rectify a defect may greatly exceed the added value to the structure as corrected. The defendants argue that under the Venzke rule their damages are $10,000. The plaintiff on review argues that the defendants' damages are only $650. Both parties agree the trial court applied the wrong rule to the facts.

The trial court applied the cost-of-repair or replacement rule as to several items, relying on *Stern v. Schlafer*, 1943, 244 Wis. 183, 11 N.W.2d 640, 12 N.W.2d 678, wherein it was stated that when there are a number of small items of defect or omission which can be remedied without the reconstruction of a substantial part of the building or a great sacrifice of work or material already wrought in the building, the reasonable cost of correcting the defect should be allowed. However, in *Mohs v. Quarton*, 1950, 257 Wis. 544, 44 N.W.2d 580, the court held when the separation of defects would lead to confusion, the rule of diminished value could apply to all defects.

In this case no such confusion arises in separating the defects. The trial court disallowed certain claimed defects because they were not proven. This finding was not against the great weight and clear preponderance of the evidence and will not be disturbed on appeal. Of the remaining defects claimed by the defendants, the court allowed the cost of replacement or repair except as to the misplacement of the living-room wall. Whether a defect should fall under the cost-of-replacement rule or be considered under the diminished-value rule depends upon the nature and magnitude of the defect. This court has not allowed items of such magnitude under the cost-of-repair rule as the trial court did. Viewing the construction of the house as a whole and its cost we cannot say, however, that the trial court was in error in allowing the cost of repairing the plaster cracks in the ceilings, the cost of mud jacking, and repairing the patio floor, and the cost of reconstructing the nonweight-bearing and nonstructural patio wall. Such reconstruction did not involve an unreasonable economic waste.

The item of misplacing the living-room wall under the facts of this case was clearly under the diminished-value rule. There is no evidence that defendants requested or demanded the replacement of the wall in the place called for by the specifications during the course of construction. To tear down the wall now and rebuild it in its proper place would involve a substantial destruction of the work, if not all of it, which was put into the wall and would cause additional damage to other parts of the house and require replastering and redecorating the walls and ceilings of at least two rooms. Such economic waste is unreasonable and unjustified. The rule of diminished value contemplates the wall is not going to be moved. Expert witnesses for both parties, testifying as to the value of the house, agreed that the misplacement of the wall had no effect on the market price. The trial court properly found that the defendants suffered no legal damage, although the defendants' particular desire for specified room size was not satisfied. . . .

On review, the plaintiff raises two questions: Whether he should have been allowed compensation for the disallowed extras, and whether the cost of reconstructing the patio wall was proper. The trial court was not in error in disallowing the claimed extras. None of them was agreed to in writing as provided by the contract, and the evidence is conflicting whether some were in fact extras or that the defendants waived the applicable requirements of the contract. The plaintiff had the burden of proof on these items. The second question raised by the plaintiff has already been disposed of in considering the cost-of-replacement rule.

It would unduly prolong this opinion to detail and discuss all the disputed items of defects of workmanship or omissions. We have reviewed the entire record and considered the points of law raised and believe the findings are supported by the great weight and clear preponderance of the evidence and the law properly applied to the facts.

Judgment affirmed.

NOTES & QUESTIONS

1. *Drafting exercise.* Review the facts of *Plante* and note the measure of damages that the court found to be applicable. Draft an appropriate instruction to the jury on how to measure damages in that case.

2. *Restitution as a remedy for less than substantial performance.* A plumbing contractor was to install the sewer system for a new subdivision. Time was of the essence. Work commenced in May and the completion date was specified as November 1. After numerous delays and three months of work the contractor was commanded to stop working by the county inspector as much of the work performed to date did not conform to county specifications. The original contract price was $150,265.38, of which the contractor had only received $3,172.66 at the time the work was stopped. The contractor sued to recover additional compensation for the labor and material conferred by the performance. Even though the court found that performance was less than substantial, recovery was still allowed. What do you think the limits of this basis of recovery should be? *See* RESTATEMENT (SECOND) OF CONTRACTS § 374.

3. The facts in note 2 above are from the case of *Murray v. Marbro Builders Inc.*, 53 Ohio App. 2d 1, 3, 371 N.E.2d 218, 220 (1977), where the court stated that it "is inclined to follow the more modern and, we believe, more equitable rule," and quoted with approval from an earlier Ohio appellate opinion (*Kirkland v. Archbold*, 113 N.E.2d 496, 499-500, 68 Ohio Law Abs 481, 485). One quoted sentence reads: "The drastic rule of forfeiture against a defaulting contractor who has by his labor and materials materially enriched the estate of the other party, should, in natural justice, be afforded relief to the reasonable value of the work done, less whatever damage the other party has suffered."

4. As previously noted, the doctrine of substantial performance does not specifically apply to the sale of goods according to the U.C.C. Is restitution an available remedy under the Code when performance is less than substantial? *See* U.C.C. § 2-718(2)(b).

C. DIVISIBLE CONTRACTS

You have already seen that where a party fails to render full performance under a contract, that party may still recover on the contract under the doctrine of substantial performance. Furthermore, you have seen that even when performance is less than substantial, courts may still allow recovery to a limited degree under the equity-related doctrine of restitution. In addition to substantial performance or restitution as a means of recovery for less than full performance, courts allow recovery for a partial, but less than substantial performance, under the theory of divisibility (also known as severability), depending upon whether the contract in question is entire or divisible. Section 240 of the RESTATEMENT (SECOND) OF CONTRACTS provides:

> If the performances to be exchanged under an exchange of promises can be apportioned into corresponding pairs of part performances so that the parts of each pair are properly regarded as agreed equivalents, a party's performance of his part of such a pair has the same effect on the other's duties to render performance of the agreed equivalent as it would have if only that pair of performances had been promised.

GILL v. JOHNSTOWN LUMBER CO.
151 Pa. 534, 25 Atl. 120 (1892)

HEYDRICK, Justice:

The single question in this cause is whether the contract upon which the plaintiff sued is entire or severable. If it is entire it is conceded that the learned court below properly directed a verdict for the defendant; if severable, it is not denied that the cause ought to have been submitted to the jury. The criterion by which it is to be determined to which class any particular contract shall be assigned is thus stated in 1 PARSONS ON CONTRACTS, 29-31:

> If the part to be performed by one party consists of several and distinct items, and the price to be paid by the other is apportioned to each item to be performed, or is left to be implied by law, such a contract will generally be held to be severable. . . . But if the consideration to be paid is single and entire the contract must be held to be entire, although the subject of the contract may consist of several distinct and wholly independent items. . . .

[This rule] was also applied in *Ritchie v. Atkinson*, 110 East, 295, a case not unlike the present. There the master and freighter of a vessel of four hundred tons mutually agreed that the ship should proceed to St. Petersburg, and there load from the freighter's factors a complete cargo of hemp and iron and deliver the same to the freighter at London on being paid freight for hemp £5 per ton, for iron 5s. per ton, and certain other charges, one half to be paid on delivery and the other at three months. The vessel proceeded to St. Petersburg, and when about half loaded was compelled by the imminence of a Russian embargo upon British vessels to leave, and returning to London delivered to the freighter so much of the stipulated cargo as had been taken on board. The freighter, conceiving that the contract was entire and the delivery of a complete cargo a condition precedent to a recovery of any compensation, refused to pay at the stipulated rate for so much as was delivered. Lord Ellenborough said: "The delivery of the cargo is, in its nature, divisible, and therefore I think it is not a condition precedent; but the plaintiff is entitled to recover freight in proportion to the extent of such delivery; leaving the defendant to his remedy in damages for the short delivery."

Applying the test of an apportionable or apportioned consideration to the contract in question, it will be seen at once that it is severable. The work undertaken to be done by the plaintiff consisted of several items, viz., driving logs, first, of oak, and second of various other kinds of timber, from points upon Stony creek and its tributaries above Johnstown to the defendant's boom at Johnstown, and also driving cross-ties from some undesignated point or points, presumably understood by the parties, to Bethel in Somerset county, and to some other point or points below Bethel. For this work the consideration to be paid was not an entire sum, but was apportioned among the several items at the rate of one dollar per thousand feet for the oak logs; seventy-five cents per thousand feet for all other logs; three cents each for cross-ties driven to Bethel, and five cents each for cross-ties driven to points below Bethel. But while the contract is severable, and the plaintiff entitled to compensation at the stipulated rate for all logs and ties delivered at the specified points, there is neither reason nor authority for the claim for compensation in respect to logs that were swept by the flood to and through the defendant's boom, whether they had been driven part of the way by the plaintiff or remained untouched by him at the coming of the flood. In respect to each particular log the contract in this case is like a contract of common carriage, which is dependent upon the delivery of the goods at the designated place, and if by casus the delivery is prevented the carrier cannot recover pro tanto for freight for part of the route over which the goods were taken: Whart. Cont. § 714. Indeed this is but an application of the rule already stated. The consideration to be paid for driving each log is an entire sum per thousand feet for the whole distance and is not apportioned or apportionable to parts of the drive.

The judgment is reversed and a venire facias de novo is awarded.

NOTES & QUESTIONS

1. As a historical note, the flood mentioned in the *Gill* case is the infamous Johnstown Flood of May 31, 1889, that killed 2,209 people from the Pennsylvania towns of South Fork, Mineral Point, Woodvale, East Conemaugh and Johnstown. The flood was caused by the failure of the earthen South Fork Dam upstream of these communities.

2. Vendor and prospective purchaser entered into a contract for the sale of property. The contract contained a financing contingency, which made the contract contingent upon the purchaser obtaining financing by May 22, and further provided that the contract would be null and void and all earnest money would be returned if such financing was not obtained. The contract also contained a clause which provided, "[I]n the event of any litigation between the parties the prevailing party, in addition to and cumulative with any other right or remedy, shall be entitled to recover its costs incurred in such litigation, including a reasonable attorney's fee." The contingency date was extended twice at the prospective purchaser's request. Upon a third request for extension, vendor replied that it would only extend the date if purchaser agreed to deposit additional earnest money and pay an increased price for the property. Prospective purchaser refused and sued for specific performance of the contract. Vendor answered by claiming that the contract was null and void and counterclaimed for attorney's fees incurred as a result of the litigation as provided for in the contract. Can vendor collect

attorney's fees pursuant to the provision in the contract even if the remainder of the sales contract is declared void? In *Grease Monkey International, Inc. v. Godat*, 916 S.W.2d 257 (Mo. 1996), the court applied the divisibility doctrine and held "yes":

> . . . [A]ppellant argues the trial court erred in finding the contract null and void yet premising the attorney's fee award on a provision of that same contract. We find the contract was divisible and, therefore, the trial court did not error. Severable or divisible contracts are, in legal effect, independent agreements about different subjects though made at the same time. *Sanfillippo v. Oehler*, 869 S.W.2d 159, 161 (Mo. App. E.D. 1994). The question of divisibility is primarily a question of the intent of the parties determined by the language used and the subject matter of the agreements. *Id.* A contract is entire if the performance of one party is dependent upon the performance of the other but is divisible if the contract embraces separate distinct promises that admit to separate execution. *Id.* The contract at issue in this case contained an agreement for the sale of real estate contingent upon financing availability and approval by the seller. Failure of the contingency voided the contract. An additional term provided for litigation costs, including attorney's fees, to the prevailing party in the event of any litigation. Clearly, these two promises were not dependent upon one another. The agreement as to litigation reimbursement only arose if and when a suit was brought by one of the parties to the contract. The sales agreement in no way depended upon the litigation clause. The words used by the parties also indicate they intended two distinct promises. The litigation clause stated the prevailing party would be reimbursed in the event of "any litigation" between the parties. This contract provision does not condition effect of this clause upon the court's legal conclusions. We find the language expresses a clear intent the cost reimbursement would apply to all litigation, just as it says. Because the contract meets the tests for divisibility, we find it encompassed two independent agreements and, therefore, the trial court did not err in giving effect to the fee agreement while holding the sales agreement void.

HOGAN v. COYNE INTERNATIONAL ENTERPRISES CORP.
996 S.W.2d 195 (Tenn. App. 1999)

CANTRELL, Judge:

This action is based on a series of contracts executed in the sale of an industrial dust control and laundry business. The Chancery Court of Davidson County dismissed the claims of the sellers, held that one of the sellers had breached one of the agreements but that the buyer had failed to prove its damages, and awarded the buyer attorneys' fees. We reverse the dismissal of the sellers' action and modify the award of attorneys' fees.

I.

Roger P. Hogan owned seventy-five percent of Music City Dust-Tex Service, Inc. (Dust-Tex), a Nashville industrial laundry business; Fred Dance, a Nashville attorney, owned the other twenty-five percent. Hogan owned the building that housed the operation. Dust-Tex rented to its customers dust control products such as mats, dust mops, wet mops, aprons, bar towels, table linens, and napkins. In addition, Dust-Tex cleaned some of the goods that actually belonged to its customers. . . .

In the fall of 1993, Mr. Hogan and Mr. Dance met with the president and vice-president of Coyne International Enterprises Corporation, a national industrial laundry business, to discuss the terms of a sale of Dust-Tex to Coyne. The negotiations led to a series of agreements on December 28, 1993 in which Coyne agreed to purchase the assets of Dust-Tex, including the trade name, the goodwill, and the customer contracts. In separate agreements, Coyne hired Hogan as the general manager of the Nashville operation, and leased the building from him. Hogan and Dance executed a negative covenant agreement in which they agreed to refrain from competing with Coyne in the industrial laundry business, or from assisting any others in such competition. Hogan signed a similar negative covenant agreement on behalf of Dust-Tex.

Coyne agreed to pay the sellers $552,500. Although the sellers quoted a lump sum price based on $85 per dollar of weekly rental business, Coyne got the sellers to agree at the closing to allocate the sales price in the following manner.

		Payable to	Date Due
Laundry Equipment, Office: Furniture, etc.	$32,500	corp.	July 1, 1994
Merchandise Inventory: Supplies, etc.	$100,000	corp.	Dec. 31, 1993
Building Rent: $2,000 per month × 60 months	$120,000	Roger Hogan	monthly starting Jan. 1, 1994
Sales Commission:	$175,000	Roger Hogan	$17,500 Apr. 1 and Oct. 1, 10 payments starting Apr. 1, 1994
Consulting & Neg. Covenant:	$125,000	jointly Roger Hogan & Fred Dance	$12,500 Apr. 1 and Oct. 1, 10 payments starting Apr. 1, 1994
Total	$552,500		

Within four months of the purchase, Coyne moved the cleaning and processing operation to London, Kentucky. Hogan had to terminate his sales people and pick up the duties of a salesman and route person. He viewed this change as a demotion from the position of general manager, and he experienced a drop in efficiency because of the problem of getting the goods back from Kentucky. . . . and he filed suit against Coyne for a breach of the employment agreement in September of 1995.

Coyne paid the $100,000 down payment, the $32,500 on July 1, 1994, and the installment payments through April of 1995. Coyne also tendered the October 1995 payments but stopped payment on the checks when Hogan sued Coyne over his employment agreement. When Coyne refused to make the payments called for in the purchase agreement, Hogan, Dance, and Dust-Tex sued to collect the remaining payments. Coyne counterclaimed for damages, alleging that the plaintiffs breached the agreement and that they were guilty of fraudulent misrepresentations. Coyne continued to make the lease payments through August of 1996, when they moved out, alleging the building was unsafe and had not been repaired by Hogan.

II. The Sales Agreement

The contract of sale includes several parts. The principal part is a letter from Coyne dated December 28, 1993 in which Coyne confirms an agreement to purchase the assets, inventory, goodwill, customer contracts, and the Dust-Tex trade name. Hogan and Dance warranted that the Dust-Tex rental volume amounted to $6,336 per week and the N.O.G. volume amounted to $465 per week. The two figures were to be verified in a four week test period in January of 1994, and if the volume fell below the warranted figures, the purchase price would be reduced by $85 for every one dollar of rental volume below $6,336 per week and $30 for every N.O.G. dollar below $465 per week.

Coyne signed two purchase orders. One covered the inventory and supplies ($100,000) and the other the laundry equipment and office furniture ($32,500). Another sheet attached to the letter agreement called for payments to Hogan for "sales commissions" of $175,000 in ten installments of $17,500 each due on April 1 and October 1 beginning in 1994. The final attachment called for payments to Hogan and Dance jointly for "Consulting and Agreement Not to Compete" of $125,000, payable in ten installments on the same schedule as the installment payments to Hogan. Coyne also bargained for the right to designate $120,000 of the purchase price as "building rent," consisting of $2,000 per month for sixty months. (The building was actually owned by Hogan, and was leased by Coyne in a separate lease.)

When Coyne stopped payment on the checks issued to Hogan and Dance for the October 1, 1995 installment, Hogan and Dance filed an action for breach of contract. Coyne did not plead an affirmative defense to the contract action; instead Coyne filed a counter-claim based on (1) a breach of the restrictive covenant in Hogan's employment agreement, (2) Hogan's failure to perform his duties under the employment agreement, (3) fraudulent misrepresentations concerning the volume of Dust-Tex's business, and (4) a violation of the negative covenants signed by Hogan and Dance. Coyne asked for rescission and restitution, damages, and a declaration that it had no further obligations under the agreement to purchase Dust-Tex or under the lease agreement with Hogan. In an amendment to its counterclaim, Coyne alleged that the plaintiffs had induced a breach of Coyne's contract with its customers.

The chancellor dismissed the fraud claims, citing a lack of proof of any misrepresentations by Hogan or Dance. (The proof shows that the figures warranted in the contract checked out in the 1994 test period — although Coyne alleged that the test period billings were inflated.) On the negative covenants, the chancellor found that Dance had not breached the agreement but that Hogan had committed a breach by being involved in a company known as Dust-Tex Mat and Mop. As to any damages suffered by Coyne, the court found that Coyne's losses were attributable to its own "poor service to its customers, including rudeness, forgery and shortages."

The chancellor refused to rescind the agreement because the parties could not be placed in status quo. The court dismissed Coyne's damage claims, but held that Coyne had no further obligation to make the installment payments on the purchase price.

Hogan and Dance allege that the chancellor erred in holding that Coyne had no further obligation on the asset purchase agreement. We agree. Although we agree with the chancellor's findings of fact, the findings do not support a cancellation of the balance of the contract.

A contract may have several parts. A breach of one part will excuse all of the promised performance by the other party where the contract is to be performed only as a whole. . . . In such a case, we call the contract "entire," and "the complete fulfillment of the contract by either side is required as a condition precedent to the fulfillment of any part of the contract by the other." . . .

If, however, "several things are to be done under a contract, and the money consideration to be paid is apportioned to each of the items, the contract is ordinarily regarded as severable." . . . In that case, "neither party can claim more than an equivalent for the actual consideration on his part." *Bradford and Carson v. Montgomery Furniture Co.*, 115 Tenn. 610, 92 S.W. 1104 at 1109 (Tenn. 1906).

In this case, Coyne specifically assigned a money value to the separate parts of the agreement. We think it is clear that the contract was severable, and a breach of one part would not excuse the promised performance for the other parts. It should be obvious therefore that Mr. Hogan's breach of the negative covenant or his breach of his separate employment agreement would not defeat Dance's right to recover what was promised to him. Coyne received full performance from Dance and should deliver what was promised in return.

What about Hogan? There is another level of severability that has been applied by our courts. That is severability within a specific part of a contract. The point is best illustrated by *Bradford and Carson v. Montgomery, supra,* where the sellers sold their furniture business and entered into a covenant not to engage in the furniture business for a period of three years. The parties valued the goodwill of the business and the covenant not to compete at $3,000 and the purchaser gave the sellers a note for that amount, due in one year. The sellers breached the covenant not to compete within a year, but the Supreme Court held that the sellers could collect the note. The court recognized that the buyers did have a claim for the amount they had been damaged by the sellers' breach, but the buyers had the burden of proving the amount of their damages. The Court reasoned that the note covered two different things and that the buyers "have received by far the larger part of the consideration of their note, the good will of the firm of Bradford and Carson, and the performance of their contract to close business for nearly one-third of the time agreed upon.". . . The performance of the contract not to re-enter the furniture business was therefore not a condition precedent to collecting the note.

This court reached a similar result in *Young v. Jones*, 36 Tenn. App. 333, 255 S.W.2d 703 (Tenn. App. 1952), where the plaintiff sold his veterinary business for $10,000 and agreed not to practice veterinary medicine "for as long as the contract was not breached" (by the buyer, we assume). The purchase price was to be paid in monthly installments of $166.67. When the seller resumed a veterinary practice, the buyer asked for a cancellation of the unpaid purchase price. Relying on *Bradford and Carson v. Montgomery*, this court held that the contract was severable and that performance by either party was not subject to performance by the other as a condition precedent. To demonstrate the independence of the covenant and the promise to pay the purchase price the court said:

> The only difference in those facts and the instant case is the covenant not to compete was to run for the rest of Jones' life and the price was to be paid in installments over approximately a five-year period. It is obvious that, if

Jones lived longer than five years, the price would have been applied before he could fully perform, and if Jones had died, say the first year, the purchaser was not bound to perform fully for five years in paying the note; immediate performance by neither was expected, nor was performance of one dependent upon performance by the other of these parts of the contract.

255 S.W.2d at 706.

The order of time in which promises are to be performed may control whether they are independent of dependent. "Where the acts to be done are to be done at different times the stipulations are to be construed as independent of each other.". . . In this case Coyne was obligated to pay the balance of the purchase price over five years. The negative covenants signed by Hogan and Dance included a five year provision (not to engage in or assist another in engaging in the industrial laundry business) and a ten year provision (not to solicit Coyne's customers or any Dust-Tex employees hired by Coyne). Although the chancellor held that the ten year provision was unreasonable (and therefore unenforceable beyond five years) the contract demonstrates that payment was not conditioned on performance by the sellers. Coyne could set off against the purchase price any damages it suffered from the sellers' breach, but Coyne had the burden of proof. The chancellor found that Coyne had failed to carry that burden and Coyne has not taken issue with that determination on appeal. We have examined the record and we are satisfied that there is no proof on which to base a judgment for damages for a breach of the negative covenant. Coyne, therefore, remains obligated to pay the balance of the purchase price, except for the balance due on the lease payments. We will deal with that part of the case in Part IV of this opinion.

One other thing remains to be said about this part of the controversy. The breakdown of the contract into its several parts was Coyne's own invention — for tax purposes, apparently. The reference to "commissions" in Hogan's payments and "consulting" in the payments to Hogan and Dance were merely Coyne's labels, and not an indication of specific services that were actually due from Hogan and Dance. Hogan was not due any commissions under the sales agreement. He had a separate employment agreement under which he could earn a bonus if the company achieved a certain sales level, but there is no proof in the record of how he was to earn the $175,000 Coyne was to pay him over five years. The same is true of the "consulting" services for Dance. There is no proof of any duties he had in that regard. We therefore conclude that the separate categories were just for Coyne's convenience in accounting for the purchase price.

The sellers should be allowed to recover the balance of the $175,000 due to Hogan and the $125,000 due to Hogan and Dance jointly.

III. Hogan's Employment Agreement

Hogan sued Coyne for a breach of his separate employment agreement. . . . Since we concur in the chancellor's findings and conclusions regarding the alleged breach by Coyne, we also agree with her conclusion that Hogan voluntarily abandoned his employment contract.

IV. The Lease

When Coyne acquired Dust-Tex in December of 1993, it also entered into a five year lease of the space owned by Hogan, that formerly served as the base of Dust-Tex's operations. The lease stipulated that the premises were received in good order and condition. It also included a provision that Coyne would maintain the premises in good order and make all necessary repairs except for pre-existing and structural conditions.

The proof showed that in 1996 the roof leaked to such an extent that Coyne employed a roofing expert to assess the problem. The expert concluded that the leaks made the building unsafe and that the deficiencies in that respect existed prior to December of 1993. Coyne called on Hogan to make the necessary repairs, but Hogan refused to do so. On July 23, 1996 Coyne vacated the building.

The chancellor found that "the premises were not in good order and condition upon receipt by Coyne and that the problems which required Coyne to vacate the premises were pre-existing."

Hogan maintains that the proof showing the defective roof was a pre-existing condition violated the parol evidence rule; it contradicted the lease provision that the premises were received in good order and condition. It should be noted, however, that the two lease provisions should be read together. The provision imposing on the tenant a duty to make repairs "except for pre-existing conditions, and structural repairs" indicates that the parties knew such things might exist. Therefore, parol evidence that the roof was defective on the date of the lease would not vary or contradict the contract.

We think the chancellor's findings are supported by the proof. Therefore, the building condition amounted to a constructive eviction.

With respect to the lease payments of $2,000 per month mentioned in the sales agreement, Hogan argues that the true rent was $4,500 per month and that the $2,000 payment was actually part of the purchase price. In effect, Hogan argues that the reference to rent in the sales agreement was just another of Coyne's slick accounting practices.

We note, however, that the lease actually recites that $6,500 per month will be paid for forty-eight months and that $2,000 per month will be paid for an additional twelve months. If Mr. Hogan is correct it means that in the fifth year Coyne would be occupying the building rent-free. The issue is not free from doubt, so we will accept Coyne's argument that the $2,000 monthly payments in the sales agreement actually represented rent. Therefore, the chancellor's finding that Hogan breached the lease is a defense to any further claim for the $2,000 lease payments.

V. The Negative Covenants

Hogan asserts that the restrictive covenant in his employment agreement and the negative covenant he and Dance signed are void because they are used to restrain ordinary competition. . . .

Our Supreme Court has said that such covenants are enforceable "if they are reasonable under the particular circumstances.". . . "Reasonableness" includes a time and geographical component. . . . But it also includes a requirement that the restraint imposed must not exceed what is needed to protect the employer's legitimate interests. . . . The employer's legitimate interests do not include a restraint on "ordinary" competition. . . . But it is reasonable for an employer to restrict a former employee's contact with the employer's customers where customers tend to associate the employer's business with the employee. . . . Outside the employer/employee relationship, covenants restricting competition have generally been upheld when they are incidental to the sale of a business. . . .

We think Coyne had a legitimate business interest to protect by putting Hogan under a non-compete agreement. Hogan was the business in this area, and he agreed to the restrictions in connection with the sale. He posed more than an ordinary threat of competition to Coyne. On appeal, Hogan argues at length that the proof shows he did not personally cause any of Coyne's customers to take their business elsewhere. Therefore, he argues, he was not closely associated with the business in the customer's minds. The reasonableness of the restriction, however, must be measured as of the time of the agreement. . . .

As to the time restrictions, Hogan does not argue on appeal that the agreements were per se invalid. While a ten year restriction might be unreasonable, the court has the option to refuse to enforce a restriction beyond a reasonable time or outside a reasonable area. . . . Since the chancellor held that the negative covenants would not be enforced beyond a three year period, the problem with the length of the restriction has now become moot.

VI. Attorneys' Fees

The chancellor awarded Coyne $65,000 in attorneys' fees against Hogan. On appeal Hogan argues that the fees were not justified by the negative covenant agreement nor by the proof in this case.

The American Rule prohibits an award of attorney's fees as a part of the costs of litigation except where the award is provided by statute or contract. . . . In this case the Negative Covenant agreement signed by Hogan provided:

> In the event of a breach of this Agreement, the party enforcing the Agreement shall be entitled to reasonable attorneys' fees and reasonable costs and expenses associated with the enforcement thereof.

The trial court held a hearing on the attorneys' fees issue. The only proof on the amount was contained in the records kept by Coyne's lawyers, one firm in Nashville and another in New York. The records detailed the time and expenses spent on the series of cases consolidated for trial, but the records do not break down the costs incurred in defending or enforcing the negative covenant. The total fees and expenses for the two firms came to $129,388.52. There is no dispute over the reasonableness of the hourly rates charged or the total hours spent in the litigation.

The sole question here, then, is how much of the overall fee should be apportioned to the controversy over Hogan's breach of the Negative Covenant. There were actually three actions consolidated for trial. The first was an action by Hogan alleging a breach of his employment agreement. Coyne filed a counterclaim against Hogan, Dance and Dust-Tex, alleging a violation of the negative covenant by Hogan and Dance, a breach of the employment contract, and fraud on the part of all of the counter-defendants. The second action was filed by Hogan, Dance, and Dust-Tex for a breach of the asset purchase agreement. Coyne filed a counterclaim, essentially raising the same issues that were raised in the prior action. In addition,

Coyne alleged in the counterclaim that it was no longer obligated on the lease. . . . The third action was an appeal of a General Sessions action in which Hogan and Dance sought to repossess the equipment transferred to Coyne in the sale.

As we have indicated, the only provision for the recovery of attorneys' fees is in the Negative Covenant. A major part of the whole controversy involved other matters — the fraud claims, the allegation that Dance violated the Negative Covenant, the lease, and Hogan's employment agreement. While we acknowledge that Hogan's Negative Covenant played a part in all of the claims, we are satisfied that allocating almost one-half of the total fees and expenses to that item alone results in an unreasonable fee for its enforcement or defense. We are handicapped, as the trial court was, by the refusal of Coyne's attorneys to make any allocation on their own. In fact, the summaries in the record delete all references to the specific activities for which the charges were made. If the specifics are to be kept secret, some other method could have been employed to give a better approximation of the time devoted to the Negative Covenant.

Based on our review of the record, we think one-fourth of the expense should be allocated to the enforcement of the Negative Covenant. We, therefore, modify the judgment against Hogan for attorneys' fees to $32,347.13.

The judgment of the court below is reversed in part, and modified in part, as indicated herein. In all other respects it is affirmed. The cause is remanded to the Chancery Court of Davidson County for the entry of a judgment in accordance with this opinion. Pre-judgment interest on the award to Hogan and Dance for the breach of the asset purchase agreement in the amount of 10% per annum shall run from the dates the installment payments came due. Post-judgment interest on Coyne's $32,347.13 judgment against Hogan shall run from November 17, 1997, the date of the final judgment below. Tax the costs on appeal equally to Hogan and Coyne.

NOTES & QUESTIONS

1. Is a contract for lifetime membership at a private club, where dues are paid monthly, divisible or severable? What effect does finding a contract divisible have on the Statute of Limitations? *See Greene v. THGC, Inc.*, 915 S.W.2d 809 (Tenn. 1995).

2. In *Nayles v. Best Manufacturing & Supply, Inc.*, 1996 WL 27832, 1996 Ohio LEXIS 186 (Ohio App. 2 Dist. 1996), where business partners decided to go their separate ways, one partner bought out the other partner using a complex payment scheme to spread out the costs for the buyer and spread the seller's income over a 20-year period. The pertinent portion of the buy and sell agreement stated:

> The seller agrees to sell all the shares of stock that he owns in Best Mfg. And Supply, Inc., including any interest he has in Buildings, Land, Equipment, Inventory, Bank Accounts, Assets, or Liabilities of all kinds, as of the day of the signing of this agreement. Seller agrees to sell all the above, *and buyer agrees to buy and pay all of the following contracts and Promissory Notes.* (Emphasis added [by the court]).

The agreement established three different payment streams that totaled $4,500,000 over 20 years. Litigation ensued when buyer failed to perform, and the appeals court stated:

In her conclusions of law, the referee concluded that the two notes for two million dollars each were for past consideration and were unenforceable for want of consideration. The referee also concluded that the contract was divisible and recommended that plaintiff be granted judgment on only the note in the amount of $500,000. . . .

The seminal Ohio case on divisible or separable contracts is *Huntington & Fink Co. v. Lake Erie Lumber & Supply Co.* (1924) 109 Ohio St. 488. The first paragraph of the syllabus in this case provides:

"Whether a contract of sale is entire or divisible depends generally upon the intention of the parties, and this must be ascertained by the ordinary rules of construction, considering not only the language of the contract, but also, in cases of uncertainty, the subject-matter, the situation of the parties, and circumstances surrounding the transaction, and the construction placed upon the contract by the parties themselves. If the part to be performed by one party consists of several distinct and separate items, and the price is apportioned to each item, payable at the time of delivery, the contract will generally be held severable."

. . . The primary criteria in determining whether a contract is entire or divisible "is the intention of the parties as determined by a fair consideration of the terms and provision of the contract itself, by the subject matter to which it has reference, and by the circumstances of the particular transaction giving rise to the question." "A factor in determining whether a contract is entire or severable is whether the parties reached an agreement regarding the various items as a whole or whether the agreement was reached by regarding each item as a unit." 17A AM. JUR. 2d § 415.

We think that it is reasonably clear that when Kenneth Nayles and Lawrence Parr negotiated their buy and sell agreement both parties intended that Nayles would sell all of his interest in the defendant company for four and one half million dollars in installments as set forth in the three notes.

In our view the July 31, 1991 contract was entire and not divisible as a matter of law.

D. BREACH BY ANTICIPATORY REPUDIATION

The doctrine of anticipatory breach or — more accurately — breach by anticipatory repudiation, addresses the situation where a party has declared unwillingness to perform prior to the time performance is due under the contract. The issues that arise in this context are: (1) when does the aggrieved party bring suit — at the time of the anticipatory repudiation or at the time performance is due? (2) what constitutes a repudiation? (3) when is retraction of a repudiation permissible? and (4) what effect does the aggrieved party's urging performance have in such a situation?

An historic case on anticipatory breach is *Hochster v. De La Tour*, 2 EL. & BL. 678 (1853), where the court framed the issue as whether it was possible to breach a contract prior to the time of performance. There, the plaintiff entered into an employment contract with the defendant to work as a courier and travel with the defendant in Europe, commencing June 1, 1852. On May 11, 1852, the defendant wrote to the plaintiff, declined plaintiff's services, but refused to compensate the plaintiff in any way. The plaintiff brought suit on May 22. The court found for the plaintiff and stated as follows:

> If the plaintiff has no remedy for breach of the contract unless he treats the contract as in force, and acts upon it down to the 1st of June 1852, it follows that, till then he must enter into no employment which will interfere with his promise "to start with the defendant on such travels on the day and year" and that he must then be properly equipped in all respects as a courier for a three months' tour on the continent of Europe. But it is surely much more rational, and more for the benefit of both parties, that, after the renunciation of the agreement by the defendant, the plaintiff should be at liberty to consider himself absolved from any future performance of it, retaining his right to sue for any damages he has suffered from the breach of it. Thus, instead of remaining idle and laying out money on preparations which must be useless, he is at liberty to seek service under another employer, which would go in mitigation of damages to which he would otherwise be entitled for a breach of contract. It seems strange that the defendant, after renouncing the contract, and absolutely declaring that he will never act under it, should be permitted to object that faith is given to his assertion, and that an opportunity is not left to him of changing his mind. If the plaintiff is barred of any remedy by entering into an engagement inconsistent with starting as a courier with the defendant on the 1st of June, he is prejudiced by putting faith in the defendant's assertion: and it would be more consonant with the principle, if the defendant were precluded from saying that he had not broken the contract when he declared that he entirely renounced it.

A statement or an act can be a repudiation. The RESTATEMENT (SECOND) OF CONTRACTS § 250 provides that:

> A repudiation is:
>
> (a) a statement by the obligor to the obligee indicating that the obligor will commit a breach that would of itself give the obligee a claim for damages for total breach under § 243, or
>
> (b) a voluntary affirmative act which renders the obligor unable or apparently unable to perform without such a breach.

CITY OF FAIRFAX v. WASHINGTON METROPOLITAN AREA TRANSIT AUTHORITY
582 F.2d 1321 (4th Cir. 1978).

RUSSELL, Circuit Judge:

This is an action on contract. The contract arose in connection with the construction of a Metrorail system to serve the Washington (D.C.) area. To effectuate this end, the Washington Metropolitan Area Transit Authority (hereinafter referred to as the Authority) had been created as a body politic by an Interstate Compact between Maryland, Virginia and the District of Columbia, for the purpose of constructing a rapid rail transit system in the Washington Transit Zone. Such Zone covered the political entities of Prince George's County (Maryland) Montgomery County (Maryland), Fairfax County (Virginia), Arlington County (Virginia), the Cities of Alexandria, Fairfax and Falls Church (Virginia) and the District of Columbia. The terms of the Compact contemplated that the Authority should develop, subject to the approval of the several political entities to be served, a mass transit plan in line with the Compact's purposes, along with a proposed method of financing construction of such transit system to be approved and participated in by the several political entities involved, as well as the Federal Government.

In 1969, the Authority adopted, with the approval of the eight local jurisdictions within the Transit Zone, a mass transit plan, described by the parties to this appeal as ARS-68 (Revised). Such plan provided for a 100-mile Metrorail system, consisting of a number of routes designated on the plan by letters of the alphabet. The one with which this appeal is particularly concerned was designated as Route K, beginning at Rosslyn, Virginia, and terminating at Nutley Road near Vienna, approximately three-quarters of a mile from the boundaries of the City of Fairfax. This particular Route was designed primarily to serve the residents in the area of the City of Fairfax. The entire plan was premised upon an estimated construction cost for the system as a whole of $2.5 billion, to be financed from three sources: 1. Contributions, representing two-thirds of the estimated costs, from the Federal Government; 2. Contributions from the eight local political entities within the Zone; and 3. The proceeds of revenue bonds to be issued by the Authority. This method of financing was adopted because the Authority had no independent taxing authority, and, except for the proceeds of revenue bonds and grants from the Federal Government, was dependent upon contributions committed to it by the eight local political entities.

In January, 1970, the several local political units, including the plaintiff City of Fairfax, entered into a Capital Contributions Agreement, under the terms of which each of the units promised to contribute a certain sum, calculated under a formula set forth in the Agreement, toward the fulfillment of the planned development. It was recognized in the Agreement, however, that the costs of construction could exceed this initial estimate and the local entities promised their "faithful cooperation and best efforts" to raise any additional local share required. The Agreement, in turn, obligated the Authority to use the funds contributed by the local units and funds realized from the other two sources of financing to construct the planned system "with all practical dispatch" substantially in accordance with ARS-68 (Revised) "as the same may hereafter from time to time be altered, revised or amended in accordance with the Compact," subject to this provision set forth as paragraph 2.1 of the Agreement:

> No such revision, alteration or amendment which would reduce the facilities to be constructed in accordance with the Adopted Regional System 1968 (Revised) within any Political Subdivision (or in the case of the City of Fairfax and the City of Falls Church, reduce the facilities serving such Political Subdivision) shall be adopted without the consent of such Political Subdivision.

Since it was "understood and agreed that definitive net project costs for the Transit System will not be determined until . . . completed," the Agreement, also, required the Authority, as the construction proceeded to make a recomputation of the contributions required of each local entity under the established formula on the basis of any increase in the estimated costs of completing the project beyond those originally contemplated. If, as a result of such increase in costs, an additional contribution were required, the local jurisdiction would be requested to contribute to such increased cost in accordance with the established formula. All the jurisdictions also agreed to use their "best efforts" to make such additional contributions as were requested of them because of such additional costs. The first date fixed for such recomputation was "a date five years after the start of construction of the Transit System, or July 1, 1974, whichever is the later date." Other recomputations were to be made "at least every two years" thereafter. This Agreement further incorporated a design and construction schedule in order to assure a sequence of construction of the System, "in which the construction activity would be carried out to achieve essentially equitable treatment of each of the jurisdictions as monies became available and work was accomplished."

As the project proceeded costs did escalate beyond the initial estimate. At the time of the trial, the completion of the system was estimated to cost in excess of five billion dollars. However, by 1975, the funds raised by the political subdivisions under the first financing plan were practically exhausted. Moreover, the Congressional appropriation for the project was likewise near exhaustion. The Authority was accordingly confronted with the problem of devising a new or revised financing plan in order to keep the project going and to avoid costly delays in the orderly prosecution of the project. The most important problem in connection with such financing plan was the federal support for the project, which had been increased from two-thirds to four-fifths of the cost of the program. Any additional federal funds could only be secured promptly from the Highway Trust Fund under the Federal-Aid Highway Act of 1973. The Administrator of the Urban Mass Transportation Administration, in order to make these increased Highway Trust funds available for the construction of certain parts of the proposed system, demanded that some parts of the system be deferred until an alternatives analysis study was completed for the purpose of determining whether another mode of transportation would be more cost effective for the corridors to be served by certain parts of the routes which included Route K from Glebe Road to Nutley Road Station. Until this alternatives study was completed, final completion of Route K was to be deferred. Moreover, any construction of Route K beyond Glebe Road was impossible because of the unavailability of a right-of-way in the median of proposed Interstate 66 along which the rail line was to run from Glebe Road to Nutley Road Station. Until Interstate 66 was free of litigation, it was uncertain whether that highway would be constructed and whether there would be a median in such highway along which the Metro system could run.

Confronted with these difficulties, the Authority sought to reach an agreement with the local jurisdictions which would permit the continued construction of that part of the entire project for which there was federal financing then available and the construction of which was not impeded by pending litigation or delayed pending an alternatives study. To this end, the local jurisdictions (other than the City of Fairfax) entered into an Interim Capital Contributions Agreement whereby the local political units would contribute sufficient local funds, which supplemented by federal highway transfer funds, would permit the construction of those parts of the project then approved for the use of federal funds. This Interim Plan, as originally drafted in October of 1976, included this provision pertinent to the controversy between the parties:

> No signatory of this Agreement shall be obligated to fund construction not included in this Agreement or to pay in excess of the amounts specified above, except for interest penalties in accordance with Paragraph 1 above. Funding of additional construction beyond that covered in this Agreement shall be dependent upon the adoption of a financial plan and a new or revised Capital Contributions Agreement.

However, at least two of the political units which were to execute the Interim Capital Contributions Agreement expressed dissatisfaction with the inclusion in the Plan of the quoted provision. Thus Prince George's County at the meeting of its Council on December 21, 1976, conditioned its agreement to the Plan on the understanding "that this Agreement in no way abridges the rights and responsibilities of the various parties to the January 9, 1970, WMATA Capital Contributions Agreement to complete the Metrorail system" and "that the Office of Law is authorized to change the language of Paragraph 3 (the quoted provision) to further carry out the concept that there be no such abridgment." After some discussion among the parties to the Plan, it was agreed to "delete Paragraph 3 (the quoted provision) in its entirety" from the Plan and to provide that "(n)o language will be included in the revised Interim Agreement, in other words, which might be read to compromise or modify the 1970 Agreement." Confirmatory of this change, the Montgomery County Council formally approved on January 11, 1977, the deletion of "Paragraph 3" from the Interim Capital Contributions Agreement and added "that the Montgomery County Council understands that the amended Interim Capital Contributions Agreement is not intended to alter the obligations of the respective signatories to the original Capital Contributions Agreement as set forth in that Agreement."

In the meantime, the plaintiff City of Fairfax filed this action on December 13, 1976, against the Authority and the local jurisdictions which were signatories to the Interim Plan. The basic claim made by the plaintiff was that the Interim Capital Contributions Agreement of 1976 "constitute(d) a repudiation and breach of the Capital Contributions Agreement (of 1970) and represent(ed) a refusal to perform thereon on the parts" of the other signatories to the Agreement of 1970. It accordingly sought both injunctive relief and damages against the Authority and the other local political entities which were signatories of that Agreement. After a trial, the District Court found that the defendants had breached the 1970 Capital Contributions Agreement, but denied any injunctive relief, holding that plaintiff's remedy was for damages, which it proceeded to assess as the amount of the plaintiff's contribution to the project. From this judgment entered on these findings, the defendants have appealed. We reverse.

Plaintiff premised its right of recovery on the doctrine of anticipatory breach or, as it is sometimes described, a "breach by anticipatory repudiation." Under this doctrine, if one party to a contract declares in advance that he will not perform at the time set for his performance, the other party may bring an immediate action for total breach of the contract. That doctrine, though sometimes criticized as a harsh remedy, has been generally accepted both in federal and state decisions, including those of Virginia and Maryland. It is included in the RESTATEMENT OF CONTRACTS as well as in the Uniform Commercial Code. But "(t)o constitute an 'anticipatory breach,' (within this rule) it must appear that the party bound under a contract has unequivocally refused to perform," or, as the Supreme Court put it in *Dingley v. Oler, supra*, at 502 of 117 U.S., at 854 of 6 S. Ct., there must be "a positive, unconditional, and unequivocal declaration of fixed purpose not to perform the contract in any event or at any time."

The strictness of this requirement of an absolute and unequivocal refusal to perform is illustrated by a number of cases in this and other circuits as well as in the Supreme Court itself. In *Frank F. Pels Co. v. Saxony Spinning Co.* (4th Cir. 1923) 287 F. 282, 288, there had been much controversy over the contract, which was the subject of the litigation, and the defendant, which had had considerable difficulty in securing performance by the plaintiff, refused to proceed unless the plaintiff made "satisfactory arrangements with (it)" for the latter's performance under the contract. This conditional refusal was found not to satisfy the test of "an absolute, positive, and unequivocal refusal to comply" required under the doctrine of anticipatory breach.

Similarly, in *Suburban Improvement Co. v. Scott Lumber, supra*, at 337 of 67 F.2d, the defendant had denied it was bound under the contract, contending that the agreement was a mere option. This was held not "equivalent to refusing to take the lots which it was obligated to take" under the contract and insufficient to support a claim of anticipatory breach.

Nor are these decisions of our Circuit out of line with the rule as it has been applied either by other Circuits or by the Supreme Court itself. Thus, in *Dingley v. Oler, supra*, the defendant, while declining to deliver ice in the 1880 season as agreed, did suggest that if the price increased, they might deliver. In finding error in the trial court for holding on those facts an anticipatory breach, the Supreme Court said:

> Although in this extract they decline to ship the ice that season, it is accompanied with the expression of an alternative intention, and that is, to ship it, as must be understood, during that season, if and when the market price should reach the point which, in their opinion, the plaintiffs ought to be willing to accept as its fair price between them. It was not intended, we think, as a final and absolute declaration that the contract must be regarded as altogether off, so far as their performance was concerned, and it was not so treated by the plaintiffs. . . .

> This, we think, is very far from being a positive, unconditional, and unequivocal declaration of fixed purpose not to perform the contract in any event or at any time. 117 U.S. at 501–502, 6 S. Ct. at 853–54.

In *McCloskey & Co. v. Minweld Steel Co.* (3d Cir. 1955) 220 F.2d 101, 104, the defendant, a subcontractor, had agreed to supply the steel required in the construction of a major hospital. There was delay in performance by the defendant and the plaintiff, the primary contractor, sought from the defendant assurance of the latter's ability to perform under its contract. The defendant replied that it was unable to secure the steel needed for performance, that it had been turned down by all the steel suppliers and it requested the assistance of the plaintiff itself in securing the steel. The plaintiff charged that such a reply represented a plain manifestation of an inability to perform. The Court held, however, that there had been no anticipatory breach because the defendant had not declared that it "had definitely abandoned all hope of otherwise receiving the steel and so finishing its undertaking."

McCloskey emphasized what is another essential element in the anticipatory breach doctrine, i.e., that it must be a repudiation of the very essence of the contract. It cannot consist of a mere partial breach; nor can it be based on mere delay unless the contract makes time of the very essence. The rule is that, in order to give rise to an anticipatory breach which will support an action for breach of the contract, the breach must be "so material and substantial in nature that it affects the very essence of the contract and serves to defeat the object of the parties;" it must be a "refusal to perform . . . of the whole contract or of a covenant going to the whole consideration;" and it must be "of such substantial character as to defeat the object of the parties in making the contract." As Corbin summarizes it, the non-performance or breach of a part of the contract "not going to the essence" of the contract will not support an action "for a total non-performance of the contract, unless he awaits the occurrence of an additional breach by the other party that is so material in character that, when added to the partial breach, the two taken together go to the essence and make the breaches so substantial as to be total." 4 CORBIN ON CONTRACTS, § 972, p. 901.

Of course, the repudiation, though it must be unconditional and total, need not be express or dependent on "spoken words" alone; it may rest on a defendant's conduct evidencing a clear intention "to refuse performance in the future," such as placing himself "in a position in which performance . . . would be impossible . . . ."

In the application of these principles to the facts of a particular case, the initial inquiry to be addressed centers on the determination of the basic object sought to be secured by the plaintiff from the agreement and the consideration for which the plaintiff bargained in entering into such contract. This is so because, as we have noted, an anticipatory breach which will support an action for breach of the contract must go "to the whole consideration" of the contract and must relate to "the essence of the contract," so far as the complaining party is concerned. To repeat, it cannot rest on a "partial breach" or on a breach of a provision in the contract or agreement which is not "so substantial as to defeat the object of the parties in making the contract."

Considered in the light of these criteria, the record makes it crystal clear that the plaintiff's real object in executing the 1970 Agreement was to secure the construction of Route K of the Metrorail for the benefit of its citizens. That manifestly was the consideration it bargained for in return for its agreement to contribute to the costs of the project. That for the plaintiff was the "essence" of the agreement. The language of the 1970 Agreement itself makes this plain. The relief demanded by the plaintiff in its complaint also attests to this fact: The plaintiff asked the Court in the alternative either to issue a mandatory injunction which would require the completion of Route K or for damages in the amount of its contributions, either in dollars or credit, to the overall project. In addition, the plaintiff's city manager, in his testimony, declared unequivocally that this was the object of the plaintiff in executing the 1970 Agreement. In answer to the question, "Assuming that Nutley Road station (now referred to as the Vienna Station) could be built by, say, between 1982 and 1984, would Metro have complied with its obligations under the Capital Contributions Agreement of 1970?", he candidly conceded, "In my opinion, yes." The repudiation in this case thus must consist of an absolute, positive and unequivocal refusal to construct Route K on the part of the defendants, or some act on the part of the defendants which made it impossible for Route K to be completed. If the record will not support such a finding, there is no anticipatory breach and there can be no recovery by the plaintiff in the present action for breach of the 1970 Agreement.

The record is wholly insufficient to support a finding of an unequivocal repudiation or abandonment by the defendants of the plan to construct the full length of Route K as provided in the 1970 Agreement. The only basis on which the plaintiff asserted there was such an express repudiation or abandonment was the execution by the defendants of the Interim Capital Contributions Agreement in 1977. When the Authority considered the initial draft of this Interim Capital Contributions Agreement, however, it firmly disclaimed any purpose of effecting thereby "an abrogation of the existing Agreement (i.e., the 1970 Agreement)" and it restated at the time it approved such draft for submission to the local jurisdictions "the intention of the Authority that the entire 100-mile system (would) be built." When this initial draft was submitted to the local jurisdictions for their approval and execution, those defendants, as we have said, expressed concern whether the proposed Plan was sufficiently clear on their common resolve to complete the project as planned under the 1970 Agreement, particularly in the light of Paragraph 3 of such draft. The general counsel of the Authority sought to allay their concern by assuring the local jurisdictions, including the plaintiff, that in his opinion all the terms of the 1970 Agreement "will remain viable after execution of the Interim Agreement." Despite this assurance of the Authority's general counsel who was presumably responsible for the initial draft of the Plan, some of the local jurisdictions still found Paragraph 3 of the initial draft of the Interim Plan objectionable because of what they considered its possible ambiguity on the continued resolve of the parties to construct as planned the entire Metrorail system, including Route K. Typical was the action of the County Council of Prince George's County. That Council, in a formal resolution, conditioned its execution of the Interim Plan upon the following specific understandings:

> First, that it is understood by Prince George's County that this Agreement in no way abridges the rights and responsibilities of the various parties to the January 9, 1970, WMATA Capital Contributions Agreement to complete the Metrorail system; second, that the Office of Law is authorized to change the language of Paragraph No. 3 to further carry out the concept that there be no such abridgement; and, third, that the Agreement itself not be executed until after a satisfactory Memorandum of Understanding with Montgomery County has been signed by that County and concurred in by the Department of Transportation, State of Maryland.

The initial Interim Plan, as originally approved for submission to the local jurisdictions for approval, was accordingly changed and, in its final, executed form, Paragraph 3, which the plaintiff as well as other local jurisdictions had found inappropriate, was deleted and the clear intention of all the parties not to abandon or repudiate their obligations under the 1970 Agreement to complete the system in accordance with ARS-68 (Revised), including Route K, was reaffirmed.

It is accordingly manifest that whether Paragraph 3 of the initial draft of the Interim Capital Contributions Agreement could be read as suggesting that the parties to that Plan had repudiated their 1970 Agreement to complete the project as outlined in ARS-68 (Revised) is irrelevant. This is so because, as we have already pointed out, that Paragraph was deleted from the final draft of the Interim Plan, which the defendants executed and to which they agreed. And it was deleted because the defendants did not want to leave any doubt about their intention and resolve to complete the full project as planned. Yet, despite all this, the plaintiff has persisted in arguing that the initial draft of the Interim Plan, adopted by the Authority on December 2, 1976, and thereafter submitted to the local jurisdictions for their approval with the challenged Paragraph 3 included, represented the agreement of the parties. And the District Court appears to have accepted this argument and to have rested its conclusion largely on a finding to this effect. Thus, it found:

> The breach in this case occurred when WMATA approved the interim capital contributions agreement on December 2, 1976. That amendment terminated the K Route at Glebe Road in Arlington a substantial reduction in facilities serving the City of Fairfax.

What both the plaintiff and the District Court would disregard is that the Authority had no authority to bind any of the local jurisdictions to any obligation or, for that matter, to absolve them from any obligation which they had previously assumed. The Authority was merely the agent to carry out the agreements made by the local jurisdictions and to perform such functions as were delegated to it by those jurisdictions. This was the reason the Authority submitted the initial draft of the Interim Plan to the local jurisdictions for approval and it was the reason that the Interim Plan was not treated as operative and effective until it had been duly executed by the local jurisdictions. At best the Interim Plan as considered by the Authority on December 2, 1976 was no more than a proposal and, until it had been approved and executed by the local jurisdictions which were to be bound by it, it remained a mere proposal, an incomplete agreement without binding effect on the parties named. It only gained the stature of an agreed contract when all the parties thereto had joined in its execution. Indeed, it is difficult to understand how the plaintiff could assume that a proposed contract, which the necessary parties never actually signed or even approved could be a valid and binding contract until all those parties to be bound had actually approved and executed such contract. The reliance of the plaintiff, as well as the District Court, upon the initial draft of the Interim Plan and its Paragraph 3, which was deleted from the Final executed Plan, is thus misplaced. The omission of Paragraph 3 from the final, approved Interim Plan the only Plan actually approved and signed by all the parties was not a modification or retraction of any previously existing, binding, effective Interim Plan; it was, and is the only Interim Plan actually approved and executed by the parties.

Even if the defendants did not expressly repudiate their obligations under the 1970 Agreement to construct Route K as a whole, the plaintiff seems to suggest that, in effect, the defendants, by their voluntary execution and implementation of the final Interim Plan, as approved and executed by the parties, made it impossible for them to perform their obligation to complete Route K as contemplated by the 1970 Agreement. This contention is predicated upon an assumption that the parties will never enter into another Plan to finance the construction of that part of Route K which was deferred in the Interim Plan, that they have indicated as much, and that the Interim Plan represents the final agreement of the parties to contribute to the construction of a Metrorail system for the Washington area. The flaw in this argument is that it does not square with the facts and the District Court recognized that this was the case. Thus, the Court conceded that "it is not conclusive that the interim capital contributions agreement is the final round of financing for the

Metrorail construction." Indeed, the record, and especially action officially taken after the hearings in the District Court were concluded, demonstrate that the parties are not only intending but are actually engaged in preparing plans for the further financing required for the completion of Route K, as well as certain other segments of the projected system which were deferred by the Interim Plan. Nor is there anything in the Interim Plan of 1977 as finally executed, which suggests even obliquely that the parties did not intend further financing in order to complete the system. Paragraph 3 of the proposed draft of the Interim Plan was disapproved simply because it was feared that such paragraph might be construed to have this effect. And it was to make perfectly clear and positive that the parties intended no abandonment of the plan to construct the full system, as outlined in ARS-68 (Revised), and no repudiation, in any particular, of the obligations assumed by them in the 1970 Agreement, that the parties excised from the final executed Interim Plan paragraph 3 of the earlier draft.

Moreover, it must be emphasized that the District Court never found that Route K would not be completed as contemplated under the 1970 Agreement. And the plaintiff emphasizes this in its brief in this appeal; in fact, it seems to take the position that such a finding was unnecessary in order to support an action to recover damages for an anticipatory breach of the Agreement. Yet the very essence of the plaintiff's right of action is that either the defendants have unequivocally repudiated any intention "at any time" to construct such a system with Route K included or have so completely disqualified themselves voluntarily that they cannot construct such a system. Absent such a finding, the plaintiff's action for a total breach of the 1970 Agreement is premature.

As a matter of fact, the plaintiff seems during trial to have departed from the theory that the defendants had repudiated or abandoned any intention "at any time" of completing Route K and to have adopted the view that the defendants' failure to conform to two subsidiary provisions of the 1970 Agreement were sufficient to give the plaintiff a right of action for damages for total breach of that Agreement in advance of the time fixed in the Agreement for performance of the object which was the consideration bargained for by the plaintiff (i.e., the construction of Route K).

This is no more than an argument that, if one party to a contract violates any provision of a contract, whatever its materiality, such violation will represent an anticipatory breach, giving the other party the right to recover damages for the breach of the entire contract. But this, as we have seen, is just what the doctrine of anticipatory breach does not authorize. The Courts and text writers have repeatedly declared that an anticipatory breach cannot be predicated on a partial breach of the contract or on a breach which is not "of such substantial character as to defeat the object of the parties in making the contract." Neither of the breaches relied on by the plaintiff and identified by the District Court as a basis for its findings will meet this test.

The failure to make the computations called for under Section 3.3(b) of the 1970 Agreement, which was the first of the omissions relied on by the plaintiff, was immaterial, so far as the accomplishment of the objective of that Agreement itself was concerned. The plaintiff argues, and the District Court seems to accept this argument, however, that, if the computations had been made beginning in 1974, followed by calls for contributions upon the local jurisdictions, there would have been no reason to defer the construction of Route K in 1976 and the Authority would have had adequate funds at that time for the completion of the project as planned under ARS-68 (Revised) when the Interim Plan was executed. The argument disregards the clearly established facts. The deferment of Route K was not caused by any delay on the part of the local jurisdictions in making their contributions to its costs. In fact, there was no basis on which such computation could have been intelligently made in 1974 or 1975. The amount and timing of such contributions depended on the availability of the federal share of the construction costs. The federal government's share of the costs for completing the project, it is true, had been increased, during the progress of the project, from two-thirds to four-fifths but the federal appropriation for the project was, as a practical matter, exhausted. Any additional federal funds required for the federal share of the construction costs, could only be secured by transfers from the highway trust fund. Such transfers required the authorization of the Secretary of Transportation. The Secretary of Transportation, however, was unwilling to authorize such transfers until an alternatives study had been prepared and submitted in connection with the completion of Route K beyond Glebe Road and of four other routes. It would accordingly have been an entirely futile exercise to compute and demand contributions from local jurisdictions until the Authority knew the federal contribution was available. Moreover, any computation prior to this knowledge would have been useless, since between its preparation and the time when the federal contribution might be assured, construction costs, interest charges, and demographic changes in the various parts of the zone to be served would have changed, invalidating completely any earlier computation of costs and anticipated revenue.

The second departure from the strict language of the 1970 Agreement, on which the plaintiff relies, is the provision which states that there shall be no revision, alteration or amendment altering the facilities to be constructed under ARS-68 (Revised) without the consent of the local jurisdiction to be served by the facility. The plaintiff contends the deferment in the construction of Route K beyond Glebe Road was not consented to by it and was therefore a violation of the above provision. Without tarrying to consider whether such deferment was a revision within the terms of the 1970 Agreement, the fact is the Authority had no choice but to defer at that time further construction beyond Glebe Road. In the first place, it could not have proceeded with construction beyond Glebe Road as contemplated under the express language of ARS-68 (Revised), whether it wished to or not. ARS-68 (Revised) provided specifically that from Glebe Road to Nutley Station the system should run along the median of Interstate 66. But concededly, when the Interim Plan was formulated, the construction of Interstate 66 was enjoined under pending litigation. Certainly, under those circumstances, the Authority could not be expected to stop all construction simply because, in the absence of the necessary right-of-way, it could not at the moment proceed with construction of Route K beyond Glebe Road. The Interim Plan was no more than a reasonable solution for what the parties assumed and hoped was merely a temporary problem, which in time would be solved. Subsequent events have shown that this assumption was sound, since construction of Interstate 66 appears now to have surmounted all legal challenges. In addition, the federal government refused at the time the Interim Plan was agreed upon to advance any funds for construction of Route K beyond Glebe Road until after an alternatives study had been concluded. Again, it would have been unreasonable to expect all construction on other parts of the system, for which adequate financing was available, to be deferred until the alternatives study had been concluded and considered by the Secretary. But the important fact is that, despite these tentative roadblocks, the defendants have aggressively pressed on with plans for the construction of the system along Route K beyond Glebe Road. They have completed the alternatives study and have reaffirmed their commitment to the completion of Route K. They are even now engaged in the preparation of a contribution and construction schedule for the project. The defendants are confident that within the time provided for the completion of the system Route K beyond Glebe Road will be constructed. The District Courtrecognized this. Under such circumstances, it cannot be said the defendants have repudiated the real objective of the 1970 Agreement or abandoned the firm intention to complete the construction of a 100-mile Metro system for the Washington area. There has thus been no anticipatory breach of that Agreement by the defendants, authorizing a suit to recover damages for such "total breach." The findings of the District Court to the contrary were clearly erroneous.

The judgment of the District Court is accordingly vacated, with directions to dismiss the action of the plaintiff as premature, without prejudice to plaintiff's right, if it develops that the defendants have unequivocally abandoned hope of constructing Route K beyond Glebe Road, as provided in the 1970 Agreement, or if Route K is not completed within the time fixed for the completion of the system in the 1970 Agreement, to file such other actions as may then be appropriate.

REVERSED.

NOTES & QUESTIONS

1. *Unilateral Contracts*. Can a party to a unilateral contract treat the other party's repudiation as an absolute breach and sue under the contract at the time that the party repudiates or must he wait until the other party's performance is due? Suppose season ticket holders for college football games were given an option to purchase Rose Bowl tickets if the football game were to be played at their stadium. If their stadium was selected but the ticket seller refused to comply with the option offer, could the season ticket holders sue for breach of contract before the Rose Bowl game was played on the grounds of anticipatory repudiation? *See Diamond v. University of Southern California*, 11 Cal. App. 3d 49, 89 Cal. Rptr. 302 (1970); see also *Rosenfeld v. City Paper Co.*, 527, 527 So. 2d 704 (Ala. 1988).

2. *What constitutes repudiation*? Horse owner contracts with the horse breeder to perform breeding services upon two mares in 1966 for the fee of $3500.00. In April 1966, the horse owner tried to reserve a breeding time for her two mares, but was advised by the horse breeder that the stud's schedule was full. This continued through the mares' heat periods until June 1966 when the horse owner finally had her two mares bred by another stud and sued the horse breeder for breach of contract. What result? Did the breeder's conduct constitute anticipatory repudiation? *See H.B. Taylor v. Johnson*, 15 Cal. 3d 130, 5309 P.2d 425, 123 Cal. Rptr. 641 (1975).

3. Suppose that a contractor and subcontractor enter into a written contract for the erection of structural steel, which was required for two new buildings. Due to a shortage of steel, the subcontractor writes the contractor a letter stating that it was unable to acquire the requisite steel and needed the contractor's help. Can the contractor treat the subcontractor's apparent inability to procure the steel as an anticipatory repudiation of the contract and hire a new subcontractor? Would it make any difference if, with the contractor's help, the required steel could be

obtained by the subcontractor? *See McCloskey & Co. v. Minweld Steel Co.*, 220 F.2d 101 (3d Cir. 1955).

TRUMAN L. FLATT & SONS CO., INC. v. SCHUPF
271 Ill. App. 3d 983, 649 N.E.2d 990 (Ill. App. 4th Dist. 1995).

KNECHT, Justice:

Plaintiff Truman L. Flatt & Sons Co., Inc., filed a complaint seeking specific performance of a real estate contract made with defendants Sara Lee Schupf, Ray H. Neiswander, Jr., and American National Bank and Trust Company of Chicago (American), as trustee under trust No. 23257. Defendants filed a motion for summary judgment, which the trial court granted. Plaintiff now appeals from the trial court's grant of the motion for summary judgment. We reverse and remand.

In March 1993, plaintiff and defendants entered a contract in which defendants agreed to sell plaintiff a parcel of land located in Springfield, Illinois. The contract stated the purchase price was to be $160,000. The contract also contained the following provisions:

> 1. This transaction shall be closed on or before June 30, 1993, or upon approval of the relief requested from the Zoning Code of the City of Springfield, Illinois, whichever first occurs ("Closing Date"). The closing is subject to contingency set forth in paragraph 14.

> * * *

> 14. This Contract to Purchase Real Estate is contingent upon the Buyer obtaining, within one hundred twenty (120) days after the date hereof, amendment of, or other sufficient relief of, the Zoning Code of the City of Springfield to permit the construction and operation of an asphalt plant. In the event the City Council of the City of Springfield denies the request for such use of the property, then this contract shall be voidable at Buyer's option and if Buyer elects to void this contract Buyer shall receive a refund of the earnest money paid.

On May 21, plaintiff's attorney sent a letter to defendants' attorney informing him of substantial public opposition plaintiff encountered at a public meeting concerning its request for rezoning. The letter concluded:

> The day after the meeting all of the same representatives of the buyer assembled and discussed our chances for successfully pursuing the rezoning request. Everyone who was there was in agreement that our chances were zero to none for success. As a result, we decided to withdraw the request for rezoning, rather than face almost certain defeat.

> The bottom line is that we are still interested in the property, but the property is not worth as much to us a 35-acre parcel zoned I-1, as it would be if it were zoned I-2. At this juncture, I think it is virtually impossible for anyone to get that property re-zoned I-2, especially to accommodate the operation of an asphalt plant. In an effort to keep this thing moving, my clients have authorized me to offer your clients the sum of $142,500.00 for the property, which they believe fairly represents its value with its present zoning classification. Please check with your clients and advise whether or not that revision in the contract is acceptable. If it is, I believe we can

accelerate the closing and bring this matter to a speedy conclusion. Your prompt attention will be appreciated. Thanks.

Defendants' attorney responded in a letter dated June 9, the body of which stated, in its entirety:

> In reply to your May 21 letter, be advised that the owners of the property in question are not interested in selling the property for $142,500 and, accordingly, the offer is not accepted.
>
> I regret that the zoning reclassification was not approved.

Plaintiff's attorney replied back in a letter dated June 14, the body of which stated, in its entirety:

> My clients received your letter of June 9, 1993[,] with some regret, however upon some consideration they have elected to proceed with the purchase of the property as provided in the contract. At your convenience please give me a call so that we can set up a closing date.

After this correspondence, plaintiff's attorney sent two more brief letters to defendants' attorney, dated June 23 and July 6, each requesting information concerning the status of defendants' preparation for fulfillment of the contract. Defendants' attorney replied in a letter dated July 8. The letter declared it was the defendants' position plaintiff's failure to waive the rezoning requirement and elect to proceed under the contract at the time the rezoning was denied, coupled with the new offer to buy the property at less than the contract price, effectively voided the contract. Plaintiff apparently sent one more letter in an attempt to convince defendants to honor the contract, but defendants declined. Defendants then arranged to have plaintiff's earnest money returned.

Plaintiff filed a complaint for specific performance and other relief against defendants and American, asking the court to direct defendants to comply with the terms of the contract. Defendants responded by filing a "motion to strike, motion to dismiss or, in the alternative, motion for summary judgment." The motion for summary judgment sought summary judgment on the basis plaintiff repudiated the contract.

Prior to the hearing on the motions, plaintiff filed interrogatories requesting, among other things, information concerning the current status of the property. Defendants' answers to the interrogatories stated defendants had no knowledge of any third party's involvement in a potential sale of the property, defendants had not made any offer to sell the property to anyone, no one had made an offer to purchase the property or discussed the possibility of purchasing the property, and defendants had not sold the property to, received any offer from, or discussed a sale of the property with, any other trust member.

After a hearing on the motions, the trial court granted the defendants' motion for summary judgment without explaining the basis for its ruling. Plaintiff filed a post-trial motion to vacate the judgment. The trial court denied the post-trial motion, declaring defendants' motion for summary judgment was granted because plaintiff had repudiated the contract. Plaintiff now appeals the trial court's grant of summary judgment, arguing the trial court erred because (1) it did not repudiate the contract, and (2) even if it did repudiate the contract, it timely retracted that repudiation.

Plaintiff contends the trial court erred in granting summary judgment. Summary judgment is proper when the resolution of a case hinges on a question of law and the moving party's right to judgment is clear and free from doubt. In considering a motion for summary judgment, the court must consider the affidavits, depositions, admissions, exhibits, and pleadings on file and has a duty to construe the evidence strictly against the movant and liberally in favor of the nonmoving party. The motion will be granted if the court finds there is no genuine issue as to any material fact and the moving party is entitled to judgment as a matter of law. . . . A triable issue of fact exists where there is a dispute as to material facts or where the material facts are undisputed but reasonable persons might draw different inferences from those facts. In a case involving summary judgment, a reviewing court reviews the evidence in the record de novo. . . Here, there are no facts in dispute. Thus, the question is whether the trial court erred in declaring defendant was entitled to judgment as a matter of law based on those facts.

Plaintiff first argues summary judgment was improper because the trial court erred in finding plaintiff had repudiated the contract. "The doctrine of anticipatory repudiation requires a clear manifestation of an intent not to perform the contract on the date of performance. . . . That intention must be a definite and unequivocal manifestation that he will not render the promised performance when the time fixed for it in the contract arrives. [Citation.] Doubtful and indefinite statements that performance may or may not take place are not enough to constitute anticipatory repudiation." . . .

These requirements exist because "anticipatory breach is not a remedy to be taken lightly." The RESTATEMENT (SECOND) OF CONTRACTS adopts the view of the Uniform Commercial Code (U.C.C.) and states "language that under a fair reading 'amounts to a statement of intention not to perform except on conditions which go beyond the contract' constitutes a repudiation. Comment 2 to Uniform Commercial Code § 2-610." (RESTATEMENT (SECOND) OF CONTRACTS § 250 Comment, b, at 273 (1981).) Whether an anticipatory repudiation occurred is a question of fact and the judgment of the trial court thereon will not be disturbed unless it is against the manifest weight of evidence. . . .

As can be seen, whether a repudiation occurred is determined on a case-by-case basis, depending on the particular language used. Both plaintiff and defendants, although they cite Illinois cases discussing repudiation, admit the cited Illinois cases are all factually distinguishable from the case at hand because none of those cases involved a request to change a term in the contract. According to the commentators, a suggestion for modification of the contract does not amount to a repudiation. . . . Plaintiff also cites cases in other jurisdictions holding a request for a change in the price term of a contract does not constitute a repudiation. . . . Defendants attempt to distinguish these cases by arguing here, under the totality of the language in the letter and the circumstances surrounding the letter, the request by plaintiff for a decrease in price clearly implied a threat of nonperformance if the price term was not modified. We disagree.

The language in the May 21 letter did not constitute a clearly implied threat of nonperformance. First, although the language in the May 21 letter perhaps could be read as implying plaintiff would refuse to perform under the contract unless the price was modified, given the totality of the language in the letter, such an inference is weak. More important, even if such an inference were possible, Illinois law requires a repudiation be manifested clearly and unequivocally. Plaintiff's May 21 letter at most created an ambiguous implication whether performance would occur. Indeed, during oral argument defense counsel conceded the May 21 letter was "ambiguous" on whether a repudiation had occurred. This is insufficient to constitute a repudiation under well-settled Illinois law. Therefore, the trial court erred in declaring the May 21 letter anticipatorily repudiated the real estate contract as a matter of law.

Moreover, even if plaintiff had repudiated the contract, the trial court erred in granting summary judgment on this basis because plaintiff timely retracted its repudiation. Only one published decision has discussed and applied Illinois law regarding retraction of an anticipatory repudiation, *Refrigeradora Del Noroeste, S.A. v. Appelbaum* (1956), 138 F. Supp. 354 (holding the repudiating party has the power of retraction unless the injured party has brought suit or otherwise materially changed position), aff'd in part & rev'd in part on other grounds (1957), 248 F.2d 858. The RESTATEMENT (SECOND) OF CONTRACTS states:

> The effect of a statement as constituting a repudiation under § 250 or the basis for a repudiation under § 251 is nullified by a retraction of the statement if notification of the retraction comes to the attention of the injured party before he materially changes his position in reliance on the repudiation or *indicates* to the other party that he considers the repudiation to be final. (Emphasis added [by the court].) (RESTATEMENT (SECOND) OF CONTRACTS § 256(1), at 293 (1981).)

The U.C.C. adopts the same position:

> Retraction of Anticipatory Repudiation. (1) Until the repudiating party's next performance is due he can retract his repudiation unless the aggrieved party has since the repudiation cancelled or materially changed his position or otherwise *indicated* that he considers the repudiation final. (Emphasis added [by the court].) (810 ILCS 5/2-611(1) (West 1992).)

Professors Calamari and Perillo declare section 2-611 of the U.C.C.:

> . . . is in general accord with the common law rule that an anticipatory repudiation may be retracted until the other party has commenced an action thereon or has otherwise changed his position. The Code is explicit that no other act of reliance is necessary where the aggrieved party *indicates* 'that he considers the repudiation final.' " (Emphasis added [by the court]) (Calamari § 12.7, at 528.)

"The majority of the common law cases appear to be in accord with this position." (Calamari § 12.7, at 528 n.93.) Other commentators are universally in accord. Professor Farnsworth states: "The repudiating party can prevent the injured party from treating the contract as terminated by retracting before the injured party has acted in response to it." (2 E. Farnsworth, CONTRACTS § 8.22, at 482 (1990).) Professor Corbin declares one who has anticipatorily repudiated his contract has the power of retraction until the aggrieved party has materially changed his position in reliance on the repudiation. (4 A. Corbin, CORBIN ON CONTRACTS § 980, at 930-31 (1951) (hereinafter Corbin).) Corbin goes on to say the assent of the aggrieved party is necessary for retraction only when the repudiation is no longer merely anticipatory, but has become an actual breach at the time performance is due. (4 Corbin § 980, at 935.) Williston states an anticipatory repudiation can be retracted by the repudiating party "unless the other party has, before the withdrawal, *manifested* an election to rescind the contract, or changed his position in reliance on the repudiation." (Emphasis added [by the court]) 11 W. Jaeger, WILLISTON ON CONTRACTS § 1335, at 180 (3d ed. 1968) (hereinafter WILLISTON).

Defendants completely avoid discussion of the common-law right to retract a repudiation other than to say Illinois is silent on the issue. Defendants then cite *Stonecipher v. Pillatsch* (1975), 30 Ill. App. 3d 140, 332 N.E.2d 151, *Builder's Concrete Co. v. Fred Faubel & Sons, Inc.* (1978), 58 Ill. App. 3d 100, 15 Ill. Dec. 517, 373 N.E.2d 863, and *Leazzo v. Dunham* (1981), 95 Ill. App. 3d 847, 51 Ill. Dec. 437, 420 N.E.2d 851, as well as Williston § 1337, at 185-86. These authorities stand for the proposition that after an anticipatory repudiation, the aggrieved party is entitled to choose to treat the contract as rescinded or terminated, to treat the anticipatory repudiation as a breach by bringing suit or otherwise changing its position, or to await the time for performance. The U.C.C. adopts substantially the same position. . . . Defendants here assert they chose to treat the contract as rescinded, as they had a right to do under well-settled principles of law.

Plaintiff admits the law stated by defendants is well settled, and admits if the May 21 letter was an anticipatory breach, then defendants had the right to treat the contract as being terminated or rescinded. However, plaintiff points out defendants' assertions ignore the great weight of authority, discussed earlier, which provides a right of the repudiating party to retract the repudiation before the aggrieved party has chosen one of its options allowed under the common law and listed in Stonecipher, Builder's Concrete, and Leazzo. Plaintiff argues defendants' letter of June 9 failed to treat the contract as rescinded, and absent notice or other manifestation defendants were pursuing one of their options, plaintiff was free to retract its repudiation. Plaintiff is correct.

Defendants' precise theory that plaintiff should not be allowed to retract any repudiation in this instance is ambiguous and may be given two interpretations. The first is Illinois should not follow the common-law rule allowing retraction of an anticipatory repudiation before the aggrieved party elects a response to the repudiation. This theory warrants little discussion, because the rule is well settled. Further, defendants have offered no public policy reason to disallow retraction of repudiation other than the public interest in upholding the "sanctity of the contract."

The second possible interpretation of Defendants' precise theory is an aggrieved party may treat the contract as terminated or rescinded without notice or other indication being given to the repudiating party, and once such a decision is made by the aggrieved party, the repudiating party no longer has the right of retraction. It is true no notice is required to be given to the repudiating party if the aggrieved party materially changes its position as a result of the repudiation. . . . Here, however, the defendants admitted in their answers to plaintiff's interrogatories they had not entered another agreement to sell the property, nor even discussed or considered the matter with another party. Defendants had not changed their position at all, nor do defendants make any attempt to so argue. As can be seen from the language of the RESTATEMENT, the U.C.C., and the commentators, shown earlier, they are in accord that where the aggrieved party has not otherwise undergone a material change in position, the aggrieved party must indicate to the other party it is electing to treat the contract as rescinded. This can be accomplished either by bringing suit, by notifying the repudiating party, or by in some other way manifesting an election to treat the contract as rescinded. Prior to such indication, the repudiating party is free to retract its repudiation. The RESTATEMENT (SECOND) OF CONTRACTS provides the following illustrations:

> 2. On February 1, A contracts to supply B with natural gas for one year beginning on May 1, payment to be made each month. On March 1, A repudiates. On April 1, before B has taken any action in response to the repudiation, A notifies B that he retracts his repudiation. B's duties under the contract are not discharged, and B has no claim against A.

*　*　*

> 4. The facts being otherwise as stated in Illustration 2, on March 15, B *notifies* A that he cancels the contract. B's duties under the contract are discharged and B has a claim against A for damages for total breach . . . ." (Emphasis added [by the court].) RESTATEMENT (SECOND) OF CONTRACTS § 256, Comments a, c (1981).

This rule makes sense as well. If an aggrieved party could treat the contract as rescinded or terminated without notice or other indication to the repudiating party, the rule allowing retraction of an anticipatory repudiation would be eviscerated. No repudiating party ever would be able to retract a repudiation, because after receiving a retraction, the aggrieved party could, if it wished, simply declare it had already decided to treat the repudiation as a rescission or termination of the contract. Defendants' theory would effectively rewrite the common-law rule regarding retraction of anticipatory repudiation so that the repudiating party may retract an anticipatory repudiation only upon assent from the aggrieved party. This is not the common-law rule, and we decline to adopt Defendants' proposed revision of it.

Applying the actual common-law rule to the facts here, plaintiff sent defendants a letter dated June 14, which clearly and unambiguously indicated plaintiff intended to perform under the contract. However, defendants did not notify plaintiff, either expressly or impliedly, of an intent to treat the contract as rescinded until July 8. Nor is there anything in the record demonstrating any indication to plaintiff, prior to July 8, of an intent by defendants to treat the contract as rescinded or terminated. Thus, assuming plaintiff's May 21 request for a lower purchase price constituted an anticipatory repudiation of the contract, plaintiff successfully retracted that repudiation in the letter dated June 14 because defendants had not yet materially changed their position or indicated to plaintiff an intent to treat the contract as rescinded. Therefore, because plaintiff had timely retracted any alleged repudiation of the contract, the trial court erred in granting summary judgment for defendants on the basis plaintiff repudiated the contract. Defendants were not entitled to judgment as a matter of law.

The trial court's grant of summary judgment for defendants is reversed, and the cause is remanded. Reversed and remanded.

NOTES & QUESTIONS

1. *Reliance on repudiation.* Doctor entered into a two-year employment contract to teach medicine at a university which commenced on July 1, 1976. In January of the following year the chairman of the Department of Medicine informed Doctor that his training was limited and that he should plan to relocate by July 1, 1977. The chairman further advised Doctor that if he planned to stay,

there was no guarantee that his salary or his office and laboratory space would be available. During a subsequent phone conversation, chairman requested Doctor's resignation. Doctor refused and immediately hired an attorney to pursue a breach of employment contract claim against the university. Doctor then began a job search in the area. Finding nothing in the immediate area available, Doctor decided he would go into private practice in the next state when he left the university in July. In March, the university got notice of the Doctor's suit and contacted Doctor's attorney to advise him that the university intended to honor the two-year contract. Doctor continued to work until July and then left to establish his private practice. Did the university effectively retract its repudiation or did Doctor materially change his position in reliance on the repudiation prior to the university's retraction? *See Lowe v. Beatty*, 145 Vt. 215, 485 A.2d 1255 (1984).

2. *Conduct or Contract?* The government entered into a contract with a contractor for the supply of gas. The contractor repudiated the contract by letter. The government gave the contractor notice that if it did not retract its repudiation within three days, the government was going to start taking new bids. When the government did not hear from the contractor within three days, it began bidding. The government accepted the lowest bid even though it was higher than the cost of performance under the original contract. Prior to the signing of the contract between the new contractor and the government, the contractor tried to retract its repudiation. The government sued contractor for damages in the amount of the difference between the old contract and the new one. The contractor defended by stating that it retracted its repudiation before the government entered into a new contract. What result? *See United States v. Seacoast Gas Co.*, 204 F.2d 709 (5th Cir. 1953).

3. For a discussion of the RESTATEMENT's view of retraction, see § 256 of the RESTATEMENT (SECOND) OF CONTRACTS:

§ 256 Nullification of Repudiation or Basis for Repudiation

(1) The effect of a statement as constituting a repudiation under § 250 or the basis for a repudiation under § 251 is nullified by a retraction of the statement if notification of the retraction comes to the attention of the injured party before he materially changes his position in reliance on the repudiation or indicates to the other party that he considers the repudiation to be final.

(2) The effect of events other than a statement as constituting a repudiation under § 250 or the basis for a repudiation under § 251 is nullified if, to the knowledge of the injured party, those events have ceased to exist before he materially changes his position in reliance on the repudiation or indicates to the other party that he considers the repudiation to be final.

UNITED CORPORATION v. REED, WIBLE
AND BROWN, INC.
626 F. Supp. 1255 (D. V.I. 1986).

PER CURIAM. The issue presented in this appeal from the Territorial Court is whether the failure of a contracting party to comply with a condition precedent prevents application of the doctrine of anticipatory breach. We affirm the trial court's decision and hold that performance of a condition is excused where the breaching party induced the non-compliance.

I. FACTS

This appeal involves the second lawsuit arising out of the parties' contract for the sale and lease back of construction equipment. Executed in February, 1980, the agreement was to last through the completion of two building projects specified by the seller, United Corporation ("United"). It contained the following provision:

> BUYER shall maintain, operate and deliver to SELLER within SEVENTY-TWO (72) HOURS from the time of request, the following listed equipment for the hourly rental rates as stated below, said accrued rental sums to be deducted from the total purchase price as above stated.

The buyer, Reed, Wible & Brown, Inc. ("RWB"), was unhappy with the deal from the onset due to repeated breakdowns in the machinery and, therefore, ignored United's rental requests. United, in turn, rented equipment from other sources and brought its first action against RWB for the difference in the rental rates. The Territorial Court, rejecting RWB's counterclaim which alleged that the sale of defective equipment breached the contract, found RWB in partial breach and awarded damages to United.

With its contract still in force, United made several requests to rent equipment. When these went unanswered, it again turned to other suppliers but never abandoned the contract. The record shows that 14 requests were made overall and RWB failed to deliver equipment — or even respond — on all but one occasion and on that day heavy rains made work impossible. On another occasion, a face-to-face demand yielded only smiles from RWB personnel. Finally, United turned exclusively to its other sources, renting equipment on 46 occasions. United again sued RWB and judgment of $33,822.97 was entered in its favor.

RWB now appeals the amount of this second award, arguing that it was excused from performance on each of the 32 occasions where United failed to request equipment. United maintains in justification of the trial court's judgment that RWB repudiated the contract.

II. DISCUSSION

Repudiation occurs when a party to a contract makes clear his intent to breach the agreement before the time to perform has arrived. . . . The remedy for anticipatory breach, as repudiation is also known, is the right of the non-breaching party to immediately seek damages for a total breach of the contract. . . .

Two elements must exist in order to support a finding of repudiation. First, the obligation repudiated must be so essential to the purpose of the contract that non-performance makes the agreement worthless. . . . Otherwise, only a partial breach may be found. Secondly, there must be an "absolute and unequivocal refusal to perform.". . . Thus, courts have refused to find repudiation where a party has merely threatened non-performance or has offered to rescind the contract. . . .

It is not required that the breaching party make a point blank declaration, because an act may also constitute repudiation. . . . It must, however, be "a voluntary affirmative act which renders the obligor unable or apparently unable to perform without such a breach.". . . Nonfeasance, such as United was faced with, cannot support a finding of repudiation under the RESTATEMENT's definition. Instead, where suspicion regarding future performance exists, a party may demand assurances of the other's intent and ability to perform and the contract is repudiated if none are provided. . . . This right is drawn from § 2-609 of the Uniform Commercial Code and recognizes that a sense of security is an implicit feature of every contract. . . .

United's right to demand assurances arose when RWB failed to respond to the rental requests made in the wake of the decision of the first lawsuit. From United's point of view, these requests tested RWB's intent to honor the contract. Not only did RWB fail to perform but its employees all but laughed at United's in-person demand for assurances. Moreover, each written rental request also included a demand,[5] all of which were, of course, ignored. It is clear, then, that this continued abstinence constituted repudiation under section 251 of the RESTATEMENT.

RWB contends, however, that its duty to rent out equipment was conditioned upon United's giving notice of its needs. It concedes on appeal that a partial breach resulted from its failure to perform when notice was given but argues that it was discharged from performing in United's other 32 rentals. Thus, RWB concludes, the trial court erred in awarding damages for a total breach of the contract.

A condition precedent is an event which must occur before there is a right to performance and a resulting breach of duty. . . .

Although the trial judge did not specifically rule on whether the notice provision was a condition, this issue is not essential to affirming the judgment. If notice was intended as a mere time frame for performance, then RWB's repeated failure to provide the assurances demanded by United supports a finding of repudiation. And even if performance was conditioned on notice, United was excused from this prerequisite because conditions are excused where a party's conduct has caused the non-occurrence. . . .

The same conduct that gave rise to United's right to demand assurances, namely RWB's failure to respond to the rental requests as well as to the demands themselves, supports a finding that notice, if it were a condition, was excused. After repeated attempts to secure performance, particularly in light of the earlier judgment, United was justified in concluding that further efforts would be futile and then seeking the equipment it needed elsewhere.

Accordingly, the damages awarded by the trial judge properly encompassed all of the additional rental costs incurred over the contract's term.

III. CONCLUSION

The record clearly supports the trial court's finding that RWB breached the rental contract. Therefore, we affirm the award of cover damages. . . .

---

[5] [1] Each rental request issued after the first trial bore the following warning:

If you do not confirm the availability to us of the above mentioned equipments, we have no choice but to rent from the open rental market and bill you for same.

NOTES

1. *Demand for adequate assurance of due performance.* Under U.C.C. § 2-609, where a party to a contract manifests prospective inability or unwillingness to perform, the other party is entitled to demand adequate assurance of due performance. RESTATEMENT (SECOND) OF CONTRACTS § 251 parallels the U.C.C. § 2-609 provision and provides that:

§ 251 When a Failure to Give Assurance May Be Treated as a Repudiation

(1) Where reasonable grounds arise to believe that the obligor will commit a breach by non-performance that would of itself give the obligee a claim for damages for total breach under § 243, the obligee may demand adequate assurance of due performance and may, if reasonable, suspend any performance for which he has not already received the agreed exchange until he receives such assurance.

(2) The obligee may treat as a repudiation the obligor's failure to provide within a reasonable time such assurance of due performance as is adequate in the circumstances of the particular case.

2. *See also Cohen v. Kranz,* 12 N.Y.2d 242, 238 N.Y.S.2d 928, 189 N.E.2d 473 (1963). In this case, Cohen agreed to purchase a home from Kranz. At the signing of the contract, Cohen paid a deposit of $4000 to Kranz with the rest of the payment due upon delivery of the deed. Due to problems with the title, Cohen sent a letter to Kranz rejecting the title and demanding the return of the $4000. However, in the letter, Cohen failed to advise Kranz of the defects in the title so that Kranz could remedy them before transfer of the deed. The court found that Cohen's objections to the title could have been cured by Kranz if Cohen would have given proper and timely notice. Further, the court concluded that if Cohen was insecure about Kranz performing his end of the contract, Cohen should have demanded good title from Kranz and given Kranz a reasonable time to cure the defects of the title. Cohen's conduct therefore amounted to an anticipatory repudiation and Cohen was not entitled to return of deposit. *Cohen* is a fact pattern exemplifying grounds for insecurity as set forth in RESTATEMENT (SECOND) OF CONTRACTS § 280. Demand for adequate assurance is a concept that generally arises under the topic of inability or unwillingness to perform. *See* RESTATEMENT (SECOND) OF CONTRACTS § 280. On the other hand, for effects on the non-repudiating party, see RESTATEMENT (SECOND) OF CONTRACTS § 257.

CHAPTER 15

DEFENSES TO ALLEGED BREACH

The absence of any element required to form an enforceable contractual obligation can be raised in defense of an alleged breach of contract. Thus, lack of an offer, an invalid acceptance, or the absence of binding consideration can be used to defend against a purported breach. Similarly, issues of interpretation, fraud, mistake, duress or minority status can be used to challenge the enforceability of the purported obligation. This chapter will examine those defenses that can be raised when the contractual obligation is not only enforceable, but plainly has not been performed. Under certain circumstances, an apparently clear breach will be excused because of supervening events which make the party's performance impossible, impracticable or otherwise excusable under law. This chapter examines the available defenses to otherwise valid, enforceable contracts which have not been performed.

In determining the success of these defenses, courts often purport to base their decisions on the unexpressed intentions of the parties. Thus, for example, a court may excuse a breach when performance becomes physically impossible, such as, for example, when a contracted-for concert hall burns down, on the basis that the parties intended that the concert hall exist or performance would be discharged. A breach may also be excused by the non-breaching party's waiver of their contractual benefit. A court may excuse a party's repeated failure to make timely deliveries if the non-breaching party has not insisted on timeliness. The court may treat the party's earlier failure as evidence of an intention to waive future timely performance. In each instance the court interprets an unexpected situation and imposes a judicial construction of intent the parties probably never considered at the time the contract was entered into.

As you consider the defenses examined in this chapter, ask yourself what factors the court should consider in deciding when an agreed-upon performance should be excused? As you explore the answers to these questions, consider what effect these judicially imposed excuses have upon the predictability of contract enforcement.

A. IMPOSSIBILITY AND IMPRACTICABILITY

One of the primary principles of U.S. contract law is the right of parties to make an economically based decision to breach otherwise enforceable contracts. So long as the non-breaching party is "made whole," the other party is free to walk away from a less than desirable deal. Thus, for example, if Farmer A agrees to sell his oranges to Buyer B for 10¢ apiece and Buyer C offers to pay Farmer A 20¢ apiece for the same oranges Farmer A may decide to sell the oranges to Buyer C. So long as Farmer A reimburses Buyer B for the harm caused by Farmer A's breach (through payment of compensatory damages designed to put Farmer B in as good a position as if the contract had been fully performed) *and* Farmer A is paid enough to make it profitable for him to sell the oranges to Buyer C, Farmer A may elect to breach the contract.

Situations may arise where a contracting party must breach contractual obligations because of events that are beyond his control. Thus, for example, although Farmer A may have a binding obligation to sell oranges to Buyer B, he may be unable to do so because all of his oranges have been destroyed in a freak frost. Similarly, due to an unforeseen raise in the cost of fertilizer, Farmer A may discover that he needs to sell his oranges for 20¢ apiece in order to cover these unexpected costs and remain solvent. In each of these cases, Farmer A has allegedly breached his contractual obligations to Buyer B. So long as the original contract between Farmer A and Buyer B is enforceable, Farmer A's sole defense must be based on the supervening "impossibility" or "impracticability" of performance.

Early common law cases allowed no defense to breach of contract based on supervening impossibility. Unless the parties expressly agreed that Farmer A would be excused from performance in the event of a frost, courts would hold Farmer A "strictly liable" for his breach. Modern courts have moderated this principle and, in certain situations where performance is physically impossible, or where it is commercially or financially impracticable, will excuse the alleged breach and will hold that the breaching party's performance as discharged.

In deciding whether physical impossibility of performance or financial or commercial impracticability "excuse" an alleged breach, courts have considered a variety of factors, including the foreseeability of the "impossibility" of performance, the parties' express intention regarding the effects of "force majeure" clauses and the intended allocation of risk of loss between the parties. Ultimately, these defenses serve to shift the risk of loss for breach from the breaching party to the non-breaching party. For example, if Farmer A is held contractually liable for his failure to deliver the oranges, Farmer A will bear the risk of loss caused by the frost. By contrast, if Farmer A is excused from performing, Buyer B will bear the risk of loss.

As you read the cases below, ask yourself whether the court's decision reflects the true intention of the parties. Would the parties have reached the same decision if they had considered the matter? And, if not, what impact, if any, should the parties' failure to address the issue have on the court's decision?

PARADINE v. JANE
Hil. 22 Car. Rot. 1178 & 1179 (1670)

In debt the plaintiff declares upon a lease for years rendering rent at the four usual feasts; and for rent behind for three years, ending at the Feast of the Annunciation, 21 Car. brings this action; the defendant pleads, that a certain German prince, by name Prince Rupert, an alien born, enemy to the King and kingdom had invaded the realm with an hostile army of men; and with the same force did enter upon the defendant's possession, and him expelled, and held out of possession from the 19 of July 18 Car. til the Feast of the Annunciation, 21 Car. whereby he could not take the profits.

. . . It was resolved, that the matter of the plea was insufficient; for though the whole army had been alien enemies, yet he ought to pay his rent. And this difference was taken, that where the law creates a duty or charge, and the party is disabled to perform it without any default in him, and hath no remedy over, there the law will excuse him. As in the case of waste, if a house be destroyed by tempest, or by enemies, the lessee is excused. . . . [B]ut when the party by his own contract creates a duty or charge upon himself, he is bound to make it good, if he may, notwithstanding any accident by inevitable necessity, because he might have provided against it by his contract. And therefore if the lessee covenant to repair a house, though it be burnt by lightning, or thrown down by enemies, yet he ought to repair it. Now the rent is a duty created by the parties upon the reservation, and had there been a covenant to pay it, there had been no question but the lessee must have made it good, notwithstanding the interruption by enemies, for the law would not protect him beyond his own agreement, no more than in the case of reparations; this reservation then being a covenant in law, and whereupon an action of covenant hath been maintained it is all one as if there had been an actual covenant. Another reason was added, that as the lessee is to have the advantage of casual profits, so he must run the hazard of casual losses, and not lay the whole burthen of them upon his lessor; that though the land be surrounded, or gained by the sea, or made barren by wildfire, yet the lessor shall have his whole rent: and judgment was given for the plaintiff.

TAYLOR v. CALDWELL
3 B. & S. 826, 122 Eng. Rep. 309 (K.B. 1863)

BLACKBURN J.:

In this case the plaintiffs and defendants had, on the 27th May, 1861, entered into a contract by which the defendants agreed to let the plaintiffs have the use of The Surrey Gardens and Music Hall on four days then to come, viz., the 17th June, 15th July, 5th August and 19th August, for the purpose of giving a series of four grand concerts, and day and night fetes at the Gardens and Hall on those days respectively; and the plaintiffs agreed to take the Gardens and Hall on those days, and pay 100£ for each day.

After the making of the agreement, and before the first day on which a concert was to be given, the Hall was destroyed by fire. This destruction, we must take it on the evidence, was without the fault of either party, and was so complete that in consequence the concerts could not be given as intended. And the question we have to decide is whether, under these circumstances, the loss which the plaintiffs have sustained is to fall upon the defendants. The parties when framing their agreement evidently had not present to their minds the possibility of such a disaster, and have made no express stipulation with reference to it, so that the answer to the question must depend upon the general rules of law applicable to such a contract.

There seems no doubt that where there is a positive contract to do a thing, not in itself unlawful, the contractor must perform it or pay damages for not doing it, although in consequence of unforeseen accidents, the performance of his contract has become unexpectedly burthensome or even impossible. . . . But this rule is only applicable when the contract is positive and absolute, and not subject to any condition either express or implied: and there are authorities which, as we think, establish the principle that where, from the nature of the contract, it appears that the parties must from the beginning have known that it could not be fulfilled unless when the time for the fulfillment of the contract arrived some particular specified thing continued to exist, so that, when entering into the contract, they must have contemplated such continuing existence as the foundation of what was to be done; there, in the absence of any express or implied warranty that the thing shall exist, the contract is not to be construed as a positive contract, but as subject to an implied condition that the parties shall be excused in case, before breach, performance becomes impossible from the perishing of the thing without default of the contractor.

There seems little doubt that this implication lends to further the great object of making the legal construction such as to fulfil the intention of those who entered into the contract. For in the course of affairs men in making such contracts in general would, if it were brought to their minds, say that there should be such a condition.

Accordingly, in the Civil law, such an exception is implied in every obligation of the class which they call obligatio de certo corpore. . . .

There is a class of contracts in which a person binds himself to do something which requires to be performed by him in person; and such promises, e.g. promises to marry, or promises to serve for a certain time, are never in practice qualified by an express exception of the death of the party; and therefore in such cases the contract is in terms broken if the promisor dies before fulfillment. Yet it was very early determined that, if the performance is personal, the executors are not liable. . . .

It seems that in those cases the only ground on which the parties or their executors, can be excused from the consequences of the breach of the contract is, that from the nature of the contract there is an implied condition of the continued existence of the life of the contractor, and, perhaps in the case of the painter of his eyesight.

. . . These are instances where the implied condition is of the life of a human being, but there are others in which the same implication is made as to the continued existence of a thing. For example, where a contract of sale is made amounting to a bargain and sale, transferring presently the property in specific chattels, which are to be delivered by the vendor at a future day; there, if the chattels, without the fault of the vendor, perish in the interval, the purchaser must pay the price and the vendor is excused from performing his contract to deliver, which has thus become impossible.

. . . In the present case, looking at the whole contract, we find that the parties contracted on the basis of the continued existence of the Music Hall at the time when the concerts were to be given; that being essential to their performance.

We think, therefore, that the Music Hall having ceased to exist, without fault of either party, both parties are excused, the plaintiffs from taking the gardens and paying the money, the defendants from performing their promise to give the use of the Hall and Gardens and other things. Consequently the rule must be absolute to enter the verdict for the defendants.

NOTES & QUESTIONS

1. Compare *Paradine v. Jane* with *Taylor v. Caldwell*. Which decision do you think most accurately reflects the intention of the parties at the time they entered into the contracts in question? What were the influencing factors the court considered in deciding who should bear the economic risk?

2. What if the concert hall in *Taylor v. Caldwell* had been burnt down as a result of arson? Should that change the court's decision? What if the arsonist had been hired by the owner of the concert hall? Would you reach a different result? Why?

3. What if the parties in *Taylor v. Caldwell* had discussed the possibility of the concert hall being unavailable due to flood or some other natural disaster and had decided that this event would not excuse performance under the contract? Would this change the court's decision? Should it?

4. *Practice Points*: Parties often draft clauses, referred to as "force majeure" clauses, that provide that performance will be excused in the event of certain natural disasters ("Acts of God"), strikes, war or other foreseeable "unforeseen" occurrences. Such clauses usually exempt performance for as long as the "unforeseen" event delays performance. You should consider the need for such clauses whenever your client is agreeing to complete a performance that might be adversely affected by events beyond his or her control.

5. *Drafting Exercise.* Draft a contract clause that will excuse the orange farmer's performance in the case of a catastrophic frost, but that will not excuse performance because of fluctuation of either the market price or supply prices of fertilizer.

PROBLEMS

1. A well-known actor has signed a contract to perform the leading role in a local theatre production for a six-month run. Two days before the play is scheduled to begin performances, the actor catches pneumonia and is unable to perform for the run of the play. Is the actor's performance excused? *See Wasserman Theatrical Enterprises v. Harris*, 137 Conn. 371, 77 A.2d 329 (1950). *See also* Restatement (Second) of Contracts § 262.

2. Ben Builder enters into a written contract to construct two log houses "made 100% out of cedar construction." Before Builder begins to construct the two houses, the City Council passes a local ordinance prohibiting the future construction of any wooden structures. Assuming the ordinance is a valid and enforceable exercise of authority, and that Builder's construction of the contracted-for houses will violate the ordinance, is Builder's performance excused? *See L.N. Jackson & Co. v. Royal Norwegian Government*, 177 F.2d 694 (2d Cir. 1949), *cert. denied*, 339 U.S. 914 (1950). *See also* Restatement (Second) of Contracts § 263.

In the following cases, pay attention to what factors the court addresses in determining if performance may be excused.

TRANSATLANTIC FINANCING CORPORATION
v. UNITED STATES
363 F.2d 312 (D.C. Cir. 1966)

J. Skelly Wright, Circuit Judge:

This appeal involves a voyage charter between Transatlantic Financing Corporation, operator of the *SS CHRISTOS*, and the United States covering carriage of a full cargo of wheat from a United States Gulf port to a safe port in Iran. . . .

On July 26, 1956, the Government of Egypt nationalized the Suez Canal Company and took over operation of the Canal. On October 2, 1956, during the international crisis which resulted from the seizure, the voyage charter in suit was executed between representatives of Transatlantic and the United States. The charter indicated the termini of the voyage but not the route. On October 27, 1956, the SS CHRISTOS sailed from Galveston for Bandar Shapur, Iran, on a course which would have taken her through Gibraltar and the Suez Canal. On October 29, 1956, Israel invaded Egypt. On October 31, 1956, Great Britain and France invaded the Suez Canal Zone. On November 2, 1956, the Egyptian Government obstructed the Suez Canal with sunken vessels and closed it to traffic.

On or about November 7, 1956, Beckmann, representing Transatlantic, contacted Potosky, an employee of the United States Department of Agriculture, who appellant concedes was unauthorized to bind the Government, requesting instructions concerning disposition of the cargo and seeking an agreement for payment of additional compensation for a voyage around the Cape of Good Hope. Potosky advised Beckmann that Transatlantic was expected to perform the charter according to its terms, that he did not believe Transatlantic was entitled to additional compensation for a voyage around the Cape, but that Transatlantic was free to file such a claim. Following this discussion, the CHRISTOS changed course for the Cape of Good Hope and eventually arrived in Bandar Shapur on December 30, 1956.

Transatlantic's claim is based on the following train of argument. The charter was a contract for a voyage from a Gulf port to Iran. Admiralty principles and practices, especially stemming from the doctrine of deviation, require us to imply into the contract the term that the voyage was to be performed by the "usual and customary" route. The usual and customary route from Texas to Iran was, at the time of contract, via Suez, so the contract was for a voyage from Texas to Iran via Suez. When Suez was closed this contract became impossible to perform. Consequently, appellant's argument continues, when Transatlantic delivered the cargo by going around the Cape of Good Hope, in compliance with the Government's demand under claim of right, it conferred a benefit upon the United States for which it should be paid in quantum meruit.

The doctrine of impossibility of performance has gradually been freed from the earlier fictional and unrealistic strictures of such tests as the "implied term" and the parties' "contemplation." It is now recognized that "A thing is impossible in legal contemplation when it is not practicable; and a thing is impracticable when it can only be done at an excessive and unreasonable cost." *Mineral Park Land Co. v. Howard*, 172 Cal. 289, 293, 156 P. 458, 460 (1916). The doctrine ultimately represents the ever-shifting line, drawn by courts hopefully responsive to commercial practices and mores, at which the community's interest in having contracts enforced according to their terms is outweighed by the commercial senselessness of requiring performance. When the issue is raised, the court is asked to construct a condition of performance based on the changed circumstances, a process which involves at least three reasonably definable steps. First, a contingency — something unexpected — must have occurred. Second, the risk of the unexpected occurrence must not have been allocated either by agreement or by custom. Finally, occurrence of the contingency must have rendered performance commercially impracticable. Unless the court finds these three requirements satisfied, the plea of impossibility must fail.

The first requirement was met here. It seems reasonable, where no route is mentioned in a contract, to assume the parties expected performance by the usual and customary route at the time of contract. Since the usual and customary route from Texas to Iran at the time of contract was through Suez, closure of the Canal made impossible the expected method of performance. But this unexpected development raises rather than resolves the impossibility issue, which turns additionally on whether the risk of the contingency's occurrence had been allocated and, if not, whether performance by alternative routes was rendered impracticable.

Proof that the risk of a contingency's occurrence has been allocated may be expressed in or implied from the agreement. Such proof may also be found in the surrounding circumstances, including custom and usages of the trade. The contract in this case does not expressly condition performance upon availability of the Suez route. Nor does it specify "via Suez" or, on the other hand, "via Suez or Cape of Good Hope." Nor are there provisions in the contract from which we may properly imply that the continued availability of Suez was a condition of performance. Nor is there anything in custom or trade usage, or in the surrounding circumstances generally, which would support our constructing a condition of performance. The numerous cases requiring performance around the Cape when Suez was closed indicate that the Cape route is generally regarded as an alternative means of performance. So the implied expectation that the route would be via Suez is hardly adequate proof of an allocation to the promisee of the risk of closure. In some cases, even an express expectation may not amount to a condition of performance. The doctrine of deviation supports our assumption that parties normally expect performance by the usual and customary route, but it adds nothing beyond this that is probative of an allocation of the risk.

If anything, the circumstances surrounding this contract indicate that the risk of the Canal's closure may be deemed to have been allocated to Transatlantic. We know or may safely assume that the parties were aware, as were most commercial men with interests affected by the Suez situation, that the Canal might become a dangerous area. No doubt the tension affected freight rates, and it is arguable that the risk of closure became part of the dickered terms. We do not deem the risk of closure so allocated, however. Foreseeability or even recognition of a risk does not necessarily prove its allocation. Compare UNIFORM COMMERCIAL CODE § 2-615, Comment 1; RESTATEMENT, CONTRACTS § 457 (1932). Parties to a contract are not always able to provide for all the possibilities of which they are aware, sometimes because they cannot agree, often simply because they are too busy. Moreover, that some abnormal risk was contemplated is probative but does not necessarily establish an allocation of the risk of the contingency which actually occurs. In this case, for example, nationalization by Egypt of the Canal Corporation and formation of the Suez Users Group did not necessarily indicate that the Canal would be blocked even if a confrontation resulted. The surrounding circumstances do indicate, however, a willingness by Transatlantic to assume abnormal risks, and this fact should legitimately cause us to judge the impracticability of performance by an alternative route in stricter terms than we would were the contingency unforeseen.

We turn then to the question whether occurrence of the contingency rendered performance commercially impracticable under the circumstances of this case. The goods shipped were not subject to harm from the longer, less temperate Southern route. The vessel and crew were fit to proceed around the Cape. Transatlantic was no less able than the United States to purchase insurance to cover the contingency's occurrence. If anything, it is more reasonable to expect owner-operators of vessels to insure against the hazards of war. They are in the best position to calculate the cost of performance by alternative routes (and therefore to estimate the amount of insurance required), and are undoubtedly sensitive to international troubles which uniquely affect the demand for and cost of their services. The only factor operating here in appellant's favor is the added expense, allegedly $43,972.00 above and beyond the contract price of $305,842.92, of extending a 10,000 mile voyage by approximately 3,000 miles. While it may be an overstatement to say that increased cost and difficulty of performance never constitute impracticability, to justify relief there must be more of a variation between expected cost and the cost of performing by an available alternative than is present in this case, where the promisor can legitimately be presumed to have accepted some degree of abnormal risk, and where impracticability is urged on the basis of added expense alone.

. . . If the performance rendered has value, recovery in quantum meruit for the entire performance is proper. But here Transatlantic has collected its contract price, and now seeks quantum meruit relief for the additional expense of the trip around the Cape. If the contract is a nullity, Transatlantic's theory of relief should have been quantum meruit for the entire trip, rather than only for the extra expense. Transatlantic attempts to take its profit on the contract, and then force the Government to absorb the cost of the additional voyage. When impracticability without fault occurs, the law seeks an equitable solution, and quantum meruit is one of its potent devices to achieve this end. There is no interest in casting the entire burden of commercial disaster on one party in order to preserve the other's profit. Apparently the contract price in this case was advantageous enough to deter appellant from taking a stance on damages consistent with its theory of liability. In any event, there is no basis for relief.

NOTES & QUESTIONS

1. In *Taylor v. Caldwell*, the concert could not be performed because the building was destroyed. Performance was *physically* impossible at the contracted-for site. Is performance physically impossible in the *Transatlantic Financing* case? Is there any valid reason to extend the impossibility doctrine of *Taylor v. Caldwell* to instances of non-physical impossibility? What should the limits of the doctrine be?

2. While early common law cases discussed the availability of discharge based on the "impossibility" of performance, modern law acknowledges that performance may be discharged even if performance is not physically "impossible," but simply "impracticable."

Section 261 of the RESTATEMENT (SECOND) OF CONTRACTS provides that a person's duty may be discharged "[w]here, after a contract is made, a party's performance is made impracticable without his fault by the occurrence of an event the non-occurrence of which was a basic assumption on which the contract was made . . . unless the language or the circumstances indicate the contrary."

Similarly, § 2-615(a) of the U.C.C. provides:

> Except so far as a seller may have assumed a greater obligation . . .
> [d]elay in delivery or non-delivery in whole or in part . . . is not a breach
> of his duty under a contract of sale if performance as agreed has been made
> impracticable by the occurrence of a contingency the nonoccurrence of
> which was a basic assumption on which the contract was made. . . .

3. What four requirements must be met to establish impracticability under the
RESTATEMENT (SECOND) OF CONTRACTS and the U.C.C.? Are they identical?

4. To what extent, if any, should considerations of altered market conditions or
financial adversity play a role in deciding whether performance has become
"impracticable"?

5. What is the basic assumption on which both parties made the contract in
Transatlantic Financing? Was it the use of the Suez Canal as a trade route? Or the
use of any commercially reasonable route? How did the Court decide on the
assumption of a reasonable route as opposed to the assumption that the route was
to be the Suez Canal? Does the court's assumption matter in this case?

6. How did the *Transatlantic* Court decide who should bear the risk of the canal
closure?

7. Which party should bear the risk of loss if performance becomes impracticable? The carrier or the shipping party? On which party did the court place the
risk in *Transatlantic Financing*?

8. Would you reach a different decision if the parties had signed the shipping
contract after the outbreak of hostilities but before the actual closure of the Suez
Canal?

OPERA COMPANY OF BOSTON, INC. v. WOLF TRAP
FOUNDATION FOR THE PERFORMING ARTS
817 F.2d 1094 (4th Cir. 1987)

DONALD RUSSELL, Circuit Judge:

This is a breach of contract suit by the plaintiff to recover the agreed payment
from the defendant for four operatic performances at the Filene Center in The
Wolf Trap Park. The plaintiff asserts it was prepared, able and willing to perform
as agreed but that it was prevented from giving one of the performances because
of cancellation by the defendant of the performance on the ground it considered
the performance impossible as a result of an electrical storm which terminated
power to the pavilion during the time this performance was to be given. The court
found against defendant's claim of cancellation of the performance because of an
unexpected occurrence and granted judgment in favor of plaintiff. Defendant has
appealed.

The parties in this suit are The Opera Company of Boston, Inc., an operatic
organization recognized both nationally and internationally. The defendant The
Wolf Trap Foundation for the Performing Arts is an organization for the
advancement of the performing arts headquartered at Vienna, Virginia, and as
such sponsors at the Filene Center in the Wolf Trap Park operatic performances
and similar artistic programs. The Filene Center is located in the Wolf Trap
National Park and is a part of the various facilities maintained and controlled by
the National Park Service. It consists of a main stage tower, an auditorium and an

open lawn. The main stage tower contains the stage, dressing rooms and space for the scenery and electrical effects. In front of the tower is a covered auditorium seating approximately 3,500 people. Beyond this is the uncovered lawn providing seating for an additional 3,000 people. The Park provides parking space. This parking area is separated from the Center itself. A number of pathways leading from the parking area to the Filene Center are available. The distance of the parking area from the Center varies from approximately 300 to 700 yards. Ordinarily, when there are any night performances at the Center, the roads in the park, the parking area and the pathways to the Center are lighted for the guidance of patrons at performances at the Center.

This suit between the parties arises under a contract between the plaintiff The Opera Company of Boston, Inc. (Opera Company) and the defendant The Wolf Trap Foundation for the Performing Arts (Wolf Trap) by which the Opera Company for its part agreed to give four "fully staged orchestrally accompanied [operatic] performances to the normally recognized standards" of the Opera Company on the nights of June 12, 13, 14 and 15, 1980 at the Filene Center. For this the Opera Company was to be paid by Wolf Trap $272,000 payable under a schedule providing for payment of $20,000 at the signing of the contract and a further $40,000 on April 1, 1980, with the balance payable in four equal installments before the rise of the curtain on each performance. Wolf Trap, in turn, for its part under the contract was obliged to make the above payments and also to furnish the place of performance including an undertaking "to provide lighting equipment as shall be specified by the Opera Company of Boston's lighting designer." Both parties to the contract performed apparently all their obligations under the contract through the operatic performance on June 14. These performances had been fully sold as well as had the remaining performance on June 15. During this final day, the weather was described as hot and humid, with rain throughout the day. Sometime between 6:00 and 6:30 p.m. a severe thunderstorm arose causing an electrical power outage. As a result all electrical service in the Park, in its roadways, parking area, pathways and auditorium were out. Conferences were had among representatives of the Park Service and that of Wolf Trap. The public utility advised that it would be at least after eleven o'clock before any service by it could be resumed in the Park and that it was likely power might not be available before morning. Various alternatives for supplying power were considered but none was regarded as relieving the situation. Already some 3,000 people were in the Park for the performance; 3,500 more were expected before 8:00 p.m. when the performance was to begin. The Park Service recommended the immediate cancellation of the performance and advised Wolf Trap if the performance were not cancelled, it disclaimed any responsibility for the safety of the people who were to attend as well as those who were to perform. It was the Park Service's view that a prompt cancellation was necessary to enable the parties to leave the park safely and to prevent others from coming. Wolf Trap agreed and the performance was cancelled. While some of these discussions were being carried on a representative of the Opera Company was present but she took no part in the decision to cancel, though she voiced no objection. Since the performancewas cancelled, Wolf Trap failed to make the final payment under the contract to the Opera Company. Five years after the cancellation, the Opera Company filed this suit to recover the balance due under the contract. Wolf Trap defended on the ground that performance by it of its obligation under the contract was excused under the doctrine of impossibility of performance. The basis for this defense was that the final performance by the Opera Company for which payment was claimed had been cancelled because a performance was impracticable as a result of the power outage.

The single question on appeal is whether th[e] dismissal of Wolf Trap's defense of impossibility of performance was proper. The resolution of this issue requires a review of the doctrine of impossibility. We proceed first to that review.

The doctrine of impossibility of performance as an excuse or defense for a breach of contract was for long smothered under a declared commitment to the principle of sanctity of contracts. This rationale for constrained application of the doctrine was expressed by the United States Supreme Court in *Dermott v. Jones* (2 Wall.), 69 U.S. 1, 8, 17 L. Ed. 762 (1864):

> The principle which controlled the decision of the cases referred to rests upon a solid foundation of reason and justice. It regards the sanctity of contracts. It requires parties to do what they have agreed to do. If unexpected impediments lie in the way, and a loss must ensue, it leaves the loss where the contract places it. If the parties have made no provision for a dispensation, the rule of law gives none. It does not allow a contract fairly made to be annulled, and it does not permit to be interpolated what the parties themselves have not stipulated.

The growth of commercial activity in the nineteenth century, however, made this rigidity of the doctrine of impossibility both "economically and socially unworkable," *see Cook v. Deltona Corp.*, 753 F.2d 1552, 1558 (11th Cir. 1985), and in *Taylor v. Caldwell*, 3 B.&S. 826, 122 Eng. Rep. 309, 324, 6 R.C. 603 (1863), the English courts recognized these changed conditions and, relying largely on civil law precedents, relaxed the constraints on the doctrine by the principle of sanctity of contracts as followed by the English courts since *Paradine v. Jayne*, Alleyn, 27, 23d Charles II (1670). It based such relaxation on the theory of an implied condition arising without express condition in the contract itself. In stating this new rule on impossibility of performance as a defense to a breach of contract suit, the court said:

> The principle seems to us to be that in contracts in which the performance depends on the continued existence of a given person or thing, a condition is implied that the impossibility arising from the perishing of the person or thing shall excuse the performance. In none of the cases is the promise in words other than positive, nor is there any express stipulation that the destruction of the person or thing shall excuse the performance, but that excuse is by law implied, because from the nature of the contract it is apparent that the parties contracted on the basis of the continued existence of the particular person or chattel.

Though the United States Supreme Court had not taken note of *Taylor v. Caldwell* in its decision in *Dermott v. Jones*, rendered the year after *Taylor v. Caldwell*, it, two decades later, adopted the reasoning and the restatement of the doctrine of impossibility as enunciated in *Taylor v. Caldwell* in its decision in *The Tornado*, 108 U.S. 342, 351, 2 S. Ct. 746, 752, 27 L. Ed. 747 (1883). In that case the Court said:

> In *Taylor v. Caldwell*, 3 Best & Smith, 826, it is laid down as a rule, that, "in contracts in which the performance depends on the continued existence of a given person or thing, a condition is implied, that the impossibility of

performance arising from the perishing of the person or thing shall excuse the performance." The reason given for the rule is, that without "any express stipulation that the destruction of the person or thing shall excuse the performance," "that excuse is by law implied, because, from the nature of the contract, it is apparent that the parties contracted on the basis of the continued existence of the particular person or chattel."

. . . *Taylor v. Caldwell*, the United States Supreme Court cases and the Virginia cases all relied in their statement of the doctrine on an implied, though unstated, condition in the contract. Increasingly, though, commentators and text writers were uncomfortable with the implied condition rationale for the new doctrine of impossibility of performance. In 6 CORBIN ON CONTRACTS, § 1331, p. 360 (1962 ed.), the author puts his objection to the implied condition theory strongly and rephrased the rationale for the doctrine thus:

> Though it has been constantly said by high authority, including Lord Sumner, that the explanation of the rule is to be found in the theory that it depends on an implied condition of the contract, that is really no explanation. It only pushes back the problem a single stage. It leaves the question what is the reason for implying a term. Nor can I reconcile that theory with the view that the result does not depend on what the parties might, or would as hard bargainers, have agreed. The doctrine is invented by the court in order to supplement the defects of the actual contract. The parties did not anticipate fully and completely, if at all, or provide for what actually happened.[1]

18 WILLISTON ON CONTRACTS, § 1937, p. 33 (3d. ed. Jaeger 1978) is equally forceful in its rejection of the implied condition theory:

> Any qualification of the promise is based on the unfairness or unreasonableness of giving it the absolute force which its words clearly state. In other words, because the court thinks it fair to qualify the promise, it does so and quite rightly; but clearness of thought would be increased if it were plainly recognized that the qualification of the promise or the defense to it is not based on any expression of intention by the parties.

Moreover, in line with the "tendency of the law . . . towards an enlargement," modern authorities also abandoned any absolute definition of impossibility and, following the example of the Uniform Commercial Code,[2] have adopted impracticability or commercial impracticability as synonymous with impossibility in the application of the doctrine of impossibility of performance as an excuse for breach of contract.[3]

---

[1] [5] The RESTATEMENT (SECOND) OF CONTRACTS accepts this statement of the doctrine in its Introductory Note to Chapter 11 ("Impracticability of Performance and Frustration of Purpose") at pp. 310-11.

[2] [7] *See* U.C.C. § 2-615(a) (1978).

[3] [8] Impossibility or impracticability may not be "subjective" but must be "objective," and the difference between the two concepts has been summarized in the phrases "the thing cannot be done" (this being objective impossibility or impracticability) and "I cannot do it" (classified as subjective impossibility or impracticability). B's Company, Inc. v. Barber & Associates, Inc., 391 F.2d 130, 137 (4th Cir. 1968); Ballou v. Basic Construction Co., 407 F.2d 1137, 1140-41 (4th Cir. 1969). It is often necessary in this connection to consider when the performance, as stipulated, is objectively impossible, whether there is an alternative form of performance and, if there is, if it is not "so excessive [in cost of performance] as to make performance extremely impracticable," there is no objective impracticability so

Under these revisions the doctrine of impossibility of performance is basically according to Corbin one "invented by the court in order to supplement the defects of the actual contract" in the interest of reason, justice and fairness. 6 CORBIN ON CONTRACTS § 1331, p. 360. Williston is equally specific in recognizing that the revision in the doctrine as envisioned by both it and Corbin had made the doctrine "essentially an equitable defense, [which could] . . . be asserted in an action at law." 18 WILLISTON ON CONTRACTS, § 1931, p. 6. . . .

The modern doctrine of impossibility or impracticability, deduced from these authorities, has been formulated in § 265 of the RESTATEMENT (SECOND) OF CONTRACTS in these words:

> Where, after a contract is made, a party's principal purpose is substantially frustrated without his fault by the occurrence of an event the non-occurrence of which was a basic assumption on which the contract was made, his remaining duties to render performance are discharged, unless the language or the circumstances indicate the contrary.

Supplementing this statement of the doctrine, the RESTATEMENT in § 263 defines the event the "non-occurrence of which [may be] a basic assumption on which the contract was made":

> If, . . . the existence of a specific thing is necessary for the performance of a duty . . . its failure to come into existence or its destruction or deterioration makes performance impracticable, [is an event] . . . "the non-occurrence of which was a basic assumption on which the contract was made."

This statement of the revised doctrine is restated in 2-615(a) of the Uniform Commercial Code which excuses non-delivery under a contract "if performance as agreed has been made impracticable by the occurrence of a contingency the non-occurrence of which was a basic assumption on which the contract was made. . . ."

In *Eastern Air Lines, Inc. v. McDonnell Douglas Corp.*, 532 F.2d 957, 991 (5th Cir. 1976), the court, adopting the modern statement of the doctrine, said impossibility- impracticability arises as a defense to breach of contract when "the circumstances causing the breach has made performance so vitally different from what was anticipated that the contract cannot reasonably be thought to govern."

. . . Probably, though, the fullest statement of the modern doctrine of impossibility or impracticability is that of Judge Wright, speaking for the Court, in *Transatlantic Financing Corporation v. United States*, 363 F.2d 312, 315 (D.C. Cir. 1966):

> The doctrine of impossibility of performance has gradually been freed from the earlier fictional and unrealistic strictures of such tests as the "implied term" and the parties' "contemplation." Page, *The Development of the Doctrine of Impossibility of Performance*, 18 MICH. L. REV. 589, 596 (1920). *See generally* 6 CORBIN, CONTRACTS §§ 1320-1372 (rev. ed. 1962); 6 WILLISTON, CONTRACTS §§ 1931-1979 (rev. ed. 1938). It is now recognized that "A thing is impossible in legal contemplation when it is not practicable; and

---

far as the obligor is concerned. *See* Waegemann v. Montgomery Ward & Co., Inc., 713 F.2d 452, 454 (9th Cir. 1983).

a thing is impracticable when it can only be done at an excessive and unreasonable cost." (citing authorities) The doctrine ultimately represents the ever-shifting line, drawn by courts hopefully responsive to commercial practices and mores, at which the community's interest in having contracts enforced according to their terms is outweighed by the commercial senselessness of requiring performance. When the issue is raised, the court is asked to construct a condition of performance based on the changed circumstances, a process which involves at least three reasonably definable steps.

In line with these cases, we accept as the correct statement of the modern and prevailing doctrine of impossibility of performance as a defense to a breach of contract to be essentially as equitable in character "based [to quote WILLISTON] on the unfairness or unreasonableness of giving [the contract] the absolute force which its words clearly state" and to be applied under the circumstances so well stated in Transatlantic.

Applying the law as above stated to the facts of this case, we conclude, as did the district judge, that the existence of electric power was necessary for the satisfactory performance by the Opera Company on the night of June 15. While he seems to conclude that public safety was the main consideration on which the cancellation was based, he found that the power outage was the reason assigned for cancellation, and in that connection he found it to be questionable that "a generator could [have been] set up to provide additional light for the theater itself (when power from the utility company became unavailable) and still provide adequate light for the people who had to move backstage." Such findings meet the requirement of the RESTATE-MENT (SECOND) OF CONTRACTS § 263 for an event, the "non-occurrence of which was a basic assumption on which the contract was made" and accordingly satisfies the definition of an impracticability which will relieve the obligor of his duty to perform as declared in section 265 of such RESTATEMENT (which we have accepted as the proper present statement of the doctrine of impossibility of performance as a defense to a breach of contract suit). Moreover, the facts as found make out impracticability of performance. . . . The district judge, however, refused to sustain the defense because he held that if the contingency that occurred was one that could have been foreseen reliance on the doctrine of impossibility as a defense to a breach of contract suit is absolutely barred. As we have said, this is not the modern rule and he found that the power outage was foreseeable. In this the district judge erred. Foreseeability, as we have said, is at best but one fact to be considered in resolving first how likely the occurrence of the event in question was and, second whether its occurrence, based on past experience, was of such reasonable likelihood that the obligor should not merely foresee the risk but, because of the degree of its likelihood, the obligor should have guarded against it or provided for non-liability against the risk. This is a question to be resolved by the trial judge after a careful scrutiny of all the facts in the case. The trial judge in this case made no such findings. The cause must be remanded for such findings. In connection with that remand, the parties may be permitted to offer additional evidence on the matters in issue.

McMILLAN, District Judge, dissenting in part and concurring in part:

The majority opinion does an admirable job of analyzing and declaring the state of the court decisions on the doctrine of impossibility of performance.

However, I believe that the District Court takes that law into account and that although he did not fully articulate a classic statement of the law, he reached the right result for the right reasons and ought to be affirmed.

Evening opera on an indoor stage obviously requires power and lights. Supplying power and lights was a necessary part of Wolf Trap's undertaking, a cost figured into their charges for the facility.

The financing and the preparation for the delivery of the essential power required nothing esoteric, inspirational, unforeseeable or expensive.

Mr. Craig Hankenson, a representative of Wolf Trap who apparently negotiated the contract, made a detailed statement about the situation immediately after the cancellation of the concert. On pertinent matters, his statement included the following:

> From my experience in theatres with which I have been affiliated prior to Wolf Trap, I know it is possible to install at the main service panel for the theatre a switchover system so that within 10 minutes an external portable generator or an emergency stage lighting generator can provide emergency service for minimal theatrical lighting and sound. This is not a major investment. . . .

> It is my feeling that a theater without this capacity is incomplete. I attach a memo to Claire which I wrote last summer voicing this opinion along with her response.

> My memo addressed two equally critical issues: public safety and the ability to continue the performance. Her reply seems to be based solely on public safety and a very "let's wait to see it if it ever happens and then maybe we'll do something" attitude.

> The facts are that we have experienced power outages on several occasions. It is perhaps a matter of opinion as to how many occurrences can be called frequent. There have been many other occasions of power outage at Wolf Trap has been very lucky they did not occur during the evening when the performance would have been affected. It can perhaps be said that tonight, too we were lucky. What if the failure had occurred after 9:30 in the middle of the performance in darkness?

> I recommend that this situation be addressed immediately. The cost to the Foundation, the Park Service and the Opera Company of Boston for the evening's cancellation would go along way if not all the way toward providing emergency backup equipment to prevent such a recurrence.

From this evidence, the trial court could rationally have concluded, and did obviously conclude, that performance of this contract was not "impossible"; that power failures were not only foreseeable in an abstract sense, but were, in fact, inevitable; that a theater without emergency capacity to carry on in case of a power outage is "incomplete"; that Hankenson had advised "Claire," chairman of the theater board, of this opinion during the previous summer; that power outages had occurred on several previous occasions; that "Wolf Trap has been very lucky they did not occur during the evening when the performance would have been affected"; and that the "cost to the Foundation, the Park Service and the Opera Company of Boston for the evening's cancellation would go along [sic] way if not all the way toward providing emergency backup equipment to prevent such a recurrence."

It would have taken only a few seconds to write into the contract a sentence which said, in effect, "If the electric power fails, Wolf Trap will not be responsible for any losses caused by the power failure."

If the parties had agreed to such a provision I would not raise my voice.

They did not so agree.

I do not think we should write for the defendant a defense it did not write for itself.

I would affirm the decision of the trial court.

NOTES & QUESTIONS

1. Which decision do you believe more accurately reflects the contracting parties' intentions — the majority or the dissent?

2. Would your conclusion regarding the impracticability of performance be changed if the following information were in evidence:

> a. Severe storms have required the cancellation of performances two times in the past year? Twenty times?

> b. Theaters of comparable size have bought the required generator?

> c. Every other open-air theater in the country has bought the required generator?

3. Which of the parties is in the best position to ensure against the risk posed by the lack of electricity? The Opera Company or Wolf Trap? What impact, if any, should this have on the court's decision?

4. On the one hand, the impracticability defense is an outgrowth of the courts' recognition that events occur for which parties could not have planned and, as a result of which, the non-performing party should be excused (or discharged) from performing. On the other hand, the defense can be seen as merely another instance of the court re-writing the contract to include never-anticipated provisions. In *Opera Company*, should the court in effect step in to write a contract provision that excuses Wolf Trap from performing when the parties could have included such a provision if they had wanted to do so?

5. *Practice Points*: Whenever drafting an agreement, you should consider all the potential problems that might arise in the performance of the contract and include express provisions that address the effect of such problems on each party's responsibilities. For example, in the contract between Wolf Trap and the Opera Company, what happens if a performance is cancelled due to inclement weather? If the lead singers are unable to perform due to illness? If the stage hands go on strike? Who should bear the risk of loss in each situation? Draft a contract clause(s) that cover these and any other contingencies you can imagine arising.

MARCOVICH LAND CORPORATION v. J.J. NEWBERRY COMPANY

413 N.E.2d 935 (Ind. Ct. App. 1980)

MILLER, Judge:

. . . Newberry, former tenant in a building owned by Marcovich located in East Chicago, Indiana, was awarded lost business profits for a period of three years because Marcovich refused to rebuild the structure occupied by Newberry after it was destroyed by fire. The parties had a written lease which the trial court determined was enforceable and required such reconstruction by Marcovich. . . .

Because of its significance to the instant appeal, the so-called "fire clause" relied upon by both parties is quoted herein at the outset. That language in the lease provides as follows:

> In the event the demised premises are damaged or destroyed by fire or other casualty, or damaged by the demolition of any portion of the building necessitated by the enforcement of any law or Ordinance, or declared unsafe by any public authority, the Landlord shall, at own cost (sic) and expense, immediately repair, reconstruct and replace the demised premises, including improvements, extensions, alterations and additions to building made by Landlord or Tenant, all such work to be done in compliance with State Laws and City Ordinances. If the extent or character of such damage, destruction or unsafe condition renders the demised premises unfit for the proper conduct of the business of the Tenant, all rent shall cease and abate during the cessation of business of the Tenant and until the complete restoration of the demised premises ready for occupancy. If, however, the Tenant is able to and does continue its business in said premises pending the restoration or reconstruction of the demised premises, then a fair and just proportion of the rent shall abate until the demised premises are restored and ready for occupancy. Any rent paid in advance beyond the happening of any of the contingencies above mentioned shall be returned by the Landlord to the Tenant.

Before applying such provision in its judgment and conclusions of law, the trial court, which decided this case without intervention of a jury, arrived at the following findings of fact significant to the rights of Newberry and the successors to Marcovich's interest:

> 6. That at the time the lease of September 30, 1953 was negotiated between the parties, the defendants, Paul March and Michael March, deceased, principals of the defendant, Marcovich Land Corporation, were experienced and competent real estate brokers and landlords.

> *   *   *

> 9. That at all times during the negotiation of the lease agreement of September 30, 1953, both the plaintiff and the defendants had equal bargaining power for the purposes of negotiating said lease.

> 10. That from September 30, 1953 until the time of the fire (December 30, 1971) both parties to the lease had completely performed pursuant to the terms of the lease and that neither of the parties to the lease had in any way breached the lease or its terms and conditions.

11. That on December 30, 1971, the building which was the subject-matter of the lease of September 30, 1953, was complete (sic) destroyed by fire. The building was a total loss and nothing was saved.

13. That on December 31, 1971 the defendants were advised by J.J. Newberry Company that the plaintiff wanted the building rebuilt pursuant to the lease agreement.

16. That there is no express covenant or provision in the lease of September 30, 1953 requiring the plaintiff to extend the term of years on the original lease agreement should the fire clause be invoked; or requiring the plaintiff to supply architectural plans and specifications for the purposes of rebuilding the demised premises should the fire clause be invoked.

*   *   *

18. If the defendants had complied with the fire clause in the lease agreement of September 30, 1953, one (1) year would have provided them with a reasonable time within which to build such a structure.

19. That as of December 30, 1971, the lease of September 30, 1953, had a period of six (6) years nine (9) months and one (1) day to run and that said lease would expire on September 30, 1978.

. . . The Marches . . . contend . . . that under the circumstances of this particular case, the fire clause would achieve an "unconscionable" result, and that in fact performance by rebuilding was impossible — a defense which the Marches regard as being synonymous with "impractical," or with performance which "can be done only at excessive and unreasonable cost." . . .

Significantly . . . it does not appear the Marches argue it was absolutely impossible to rebuild the structure rented by Newberry at the time of the fire, since they suggest in their brief "[p]erformance is possible, but the value (benefit) (investment) has been destroyed by an unforeseen event, a totally and completely destroyed building. . . ." Indeed, the only evidence presented at trial which was arguably intended to show such absolute impossibility of performance concerned the purported inability of the Marcovich representatives to obtain financing for a new building under the existing lease terms with Newberry. In this regard, however, we must note not only that there was no showing such financing was essential to permit rebuilding, but also that the depositions of defendant-appellant Paul March and Michael March, deceased (for whom defendant-appellant Walter March acts as executor), suggest the family in fact never tried to obtain financing based on the remaining lease term. . . .

The Marches maintain, however, that apart from any issue of "absolute" impossibility, the essential question raised by this appeal is whether in Indiana impossibility of performance should include the defense that performance is "impractical" where it involves "excessive and unreasonable cost." They concede such issue is unanswered in any Indiana precedent, but contend their position should be adopted in light of the practice in other jurisdictions, citing *Transatlantic Financing Corp. v. United States, supra,* a case in which Judge Wright acknowledged such a defense but concluded it was not "commercially impractical" under a contract to require a ship carrying wheat to travel 3,000 additional miles on an original 10,000-mile trip, at an alleged cost of almost $44,000, because of the closing of the Suez Canal.

In response to such argument, we conclude, even assuming arguendo the affirmative defense in Indiana extends beyond "absolute" impossibility to encompass the doctrine urged by the Marches, that the trial court could properly have determined there was no evidence before it of the kind of commercially senseless expense contended by the Marches, but rather that the parties had anticipated and allocated between them the unextraordinary risk which in fact occurred. . . .

Turning to the evidence relied on by the Marches in support of their theory we note the uncontroverted (though challenged by objection) testimony of the Marches' expert, Richard J. Kestle, that it would cost at least $452,000 in 1972 to construct a building on the site in accordance with certain rough plans prepared by Newberry. Additionally, the Marches presented evidence they received only $200,000 in insurance proceeds, such lesser figure presumably being attributable to the fact the Marches chose not to insure the structure for its replacement cost.[4] The Marches also presented evidence in this regard, however, in the form of testimony from a real estate appraiser using the $452,000 reconstruction figure and a six-year lease, that rebuilding would not be economically or commercially "feasible," a conclusion which he explained in an offer to prove took into account what return a prudent investor would want for his money invested in a new building in 1972, assuming such an investor "would want at least 8% on his money and we said that the recapture or depreciation rate would be 2½% or a total capitalization rate of 10½%." The same expert observed the property in question was in an "urban renewal" area in 1974 or 1975 (though not in 1972), and concluded, "I would advise my client that this is a very poor deal to get into."

In viewing such evidence we are cognizant that even under the standard advocated by the Marches, the test is not simply whether a particular performance would be a bad business risk or even a "very poor deal" for a prudent investor, but rather whether there was "extreme . . . difficulty, expense, injury, or loss" which goes well beyond the normal range of what might have been expected, and whether the parties failed to allocate such risk. We believe the trial court could properly have concluded the evidence in the instant case, involving regrettable but unextraordinary rebuilding considerations, did not rise to such a level, but that the risk was anticipated by the parties, and thus not expected, and that such risk was, moreover, intended to be allocated between them by the "fire clause" itself. As was observed in *Transatlantic Financing Corp. v. United States, supra* at 319:

> While it may be an overstatement to say that increased cost and difficulty of performance never constitute impracticability, to justify relief there must be more of a variation between expected cost and the cost of performing . . . than is present in this case, where the promisee can legitimately be presumed to have accepted some degree of abnormal risk. . . .

. . . [W]e believe the trial court did not err in its ultimate determination, in light of the fact "it is only where the evidence is without conflict and leads to only one

---

[4] [8] We are cognizant the trial court implicitly found the building had been insured for its "reasonable insurable value" when it concluded neither party had breached the lease, but we do not find such determination to be inconsistent with the Marches' right, if they chose, to protect themselves against their ultimate liability for rebuilding by insuring for the replacement cost.

conclusion, and the trial court has reached a contrary conclusion, that such judgment will be disturbed as contrary to law." Indeed, we find that in light of the nature of the evidence which was presented, the trial court was not required (as the Marches contend) to enter specific factual findings on the defense of impossibility of performance, since the record does not show there was probative testimony of impossibility upon which such findings could be founded. . . .

NOTES & QUESTIONS

1. Would labor disputes be considered extraordinary in the course of modern commerce? Under what circumstances would you consider a labor dispute to be extraordinary? What role, if any, would the following factors have on your decision: the historic frequency of labor disputes for the party? In the industry in general? The length of the dispute? The reasonableness of the party's refusal to settle the strike or make alternate arrangements? (*See Mishara Construction Co., Inc. v. Transit-Mixed Concrete Corp.*, 310 N.E.2d 363 (Mass. 1974), for the proposition that labor disputes may not be "extraordinary in the course of modern commerce" such as to excuse performance.

2. Do you consider the following events as extraordinary or not: terrorist acts in countries undergoing political turmoil? Floods along the Nile River? Hurricanes in the Gulf Coast? If they are not "extraordinary," how would you protect a client doing business under these conditions?

KARL WENDT FARM EQUIPMENT CO., INC.
v. INTERNATIONAL HARVESTER CO.
931 F.2d 1112 (6th Cir. 1991)

NATHANIEL R. JONES, Circuit Judge:

. . . This diversity action arises out of IH's decision to go out of the farm equipment business after a dramatic downturn in the market for farm equipment. In the fall of 1974, Wendt and IH entered into a "Dealer Sales and Service Agreement" ("agreement") which established Wendt as a dealer of IH goods in the area of Marlette, Michigan. The agreement set forth the required method of sale, provisions for the purchase and servicing of goods, as well as certain dealer operating requirements. The agreement also provided specific provisions for the termination of the contract upon the occurrence of certain specified conditions.

In light of a dramatic recession in the farm equipment market, and substantial losses on the part of IH, IH negotiated an agreement with J.I. Case Co. and Tenneco Inc. ("Case/Tenneco") to sell its farm equipment division to Case/Tenneco. The sale took the form of a sale of assets. The base purchase price was $246,700,000.00 in cash and $161,300,000.00 to be paid in participating preferred stock in Tenneco. While IH asserts that it lost $479,000,000.00 on the deal, it also noted that this was a "paper loss" which will result in a tax credit offsetting the loss. J. App. at 405.

In its purchase of IH's farm equipment division, Casemenneco did not acquire IH's existing franchise network. Rather, it received "access" to IH dealers, many of whom eventually received a Case franchise. However, there were some 400 "conflicted areas" in which both a Case and an IH dealership were located. In these areas Case offered only one franchise contract. In nearly two-thirds of the conflicted areas, the IH dealer received the franchise. However, Marlette, Michigan was such a "conflicted area" and Wendt was not offered a Case franchise.

Wendt filed this action alleging breach of IH's Dealer Agreement and several other causes of action, but all Wendt's allegations save the breach of contract action were disposed of before trial. IH filed a counter-claim against Wendt for debts arising out of farm equipment and parts advanced to Wendt on credit.

At trial, the court allowed IH's defense of impracticability of performance to go to the jury on the contract action. The jury returned a verdict of no cause of action on the contract and the district court denied Wendt's motion for J.N.O.V./new trial, which was based on the invalidity of the impracticability defense. These actions by the court form a substantial basis of Wendt's appeal. . . .

Generally, under Michigan law, "[e]conomic unprofitableness [sic] is not the equivalent to impossibility of performance. Subsequent events which in the nature of things do not render performance impossible, but only render it more difficult, burdensome, or expensive, will not operate to relieve [a party of its contractual obligations]."

In *Bissell*, the Michigan Court of Appeals, relying on the RESTATEMENT OF CONTRACTS § 457, concluded that the doctrine of impossibility is a valid defense not only when performance is impossible, but also when supervening circumstances make performance impracticable. § 457 of the RESTATEMENT OF CONTRACTS, now § 261 of the RESTATEMENT (SECOND) OF CONTRACTS (1981) provides:

Discharge by Supervening Impracticability

> Where, after a contract is made, a party's performance is made impracticable without his fault by the occurrence of an event the non-occurrence of which was a basic assumption on which the contract was made, his duty to render that performance is discharged, unless the language or the circumstances indicate the contrary. . . .

. . . The commentary to § 261 of the RESTATEMENT (SECOND) provides extensive guidance for determining when economic circumstances are sufficient to render performance impracticable. Comment d to § 261 makes clear that mere lack of profit under the contract is insufficient: " '[I]mpracticability' means more than 'impracticality.' A mere change in the degree of difficulty or expense due to such causes as increased wages, prices of raw materials or costs of construction, unless well beyond the normal range, does not amount to impracticability since it is this sort of risk that a fixed price contract is intended to cover." Comment d also provides:

> A severe shortage of raw materials or of supplies due to war, embargo, local crop failure, unforeseen shutdown of major sources of supply, or the like, which either causes a marked increase in cost or prevents performance altogether may bring the case within the rule stated in this Section.

More guidance is provided in Comment b to section 261. Comment b states: "In order for a supervening event to discharge a duty under this Section, the non-occurrence of that event must have been a 'basic assumption' on which both parties made the contract." Comment b goes on to provide that the application of the "basic assumption" criteria:

is also simple enough in the cases of market shifts or the financial inability of one of the parties. The continuation of existing market conditions and of the financial situation of one of the parties are ordinarily not such assumptions, so that mere market shifts or financial inability do not usually effect discharge under the rule stated in this Section.

Comment b also provides two helpful examples. In Illustration 3 of comment b, A contracts to employ B for two years at a set salary. After one year a government regulation makes A's business unprofitable and he fires B. A's duty to employ B is not discharged due to impracticability and A is liable for breach. In Illustration 4, A contracts to sell B a machine to be delivered by a certain date. Due to a suit by a creditor, all of A's assets are placed in receivership. A is not excused for non-performance under the doctrine of impracticability.

In our view, section 261 requires a finding that impracticability is an inappropriate defense in this case. The fact that IH experienced a dramatic downturn in the farm equipment market and decided to go out of the business does not excuse its unilateral termination of its dealership agreements due to impracticability. IH argues that while mere unprofitability should not excuse performance, the substantial losses and dramatic market shift in the farm equipment market between 1980 and 1985 warrant the special application of the defense in this case. IH cites losses of over $2,000,000.00 per day and a drop in the company's standing on the Fortune 500 list from 27 to 104. IH Brief at 7 (citing trial record). IH also put on evidence that if it had not sold its farm equipment division, it might have had to declare bankruptcy. While the facts suggest that IH suffered severely from the downturn in the farm equipment market, neither market shifts nor the financial inability of one of the parties changes the basic assumptions of the contract such that it may be excused under the doctrine of impracticability. RESTATEMENT (SECOND) OF CONTRACTS, section 261, comment b. To hold otherwise would not fulfill the likely understanding of the parties as to the apportionment of risk under the contract. The agreement provides in some detail the procedure and conditions for termination. IH may not have been entirely responsible for the economic downturn in the company, but it was responsible for its chosen remedy: to sell its farm equipment assets. An alternative would have been to terminate its Dealer Agreements by mutual assent under the termination provisions of the contract and share the proceeds of the sale of assets to Case/Tenneco with its dealers. Thus, we find that IH had alternatives which could have precluded unilateral termination of the contract. Further, application of the impracticability defense in this case would allow IH to avoid its liability under franchise agreements, allow Case/Tenneco to pick up only those dealerships its sees fit and leave the remaining dealers bankrupt. In such circumstance, application of the doctrine of impracticability would not only be a misapplication of law, but a windfall for IH at the expense of the dealers.

. . . The fact that IH's losses in this case involved millions of dollars does not change the scope of the doctrine. . . .

In the end, IH simply asserts that it would have been unprofitable to terminate its agreements with its dealers by invoking the six-month notice and other termination procedures embodied in the Dealer Agreement, or by sharing the proceeds of its sale of its farm equipment assets with dealers. This assertion does not excuse IH's performance under the agreement.

RYAN, Circuit Judge (dissenting):

The court has held that the district court erred in submitting the defendants' defense of impracticability of performance to the jury. I disagree. . . .

It appears that the majority opinion rejects the impracticability defense "in the circumstances of this case" because, in the court's view, the economic reverses confronted by International Harvester were not so "extreme and unreasonable," severe, or catastrophic as to excuse performance of the franchise agreement with the plaintiffs. Although claiming to recognize that whether impracticability of performance has been proved is a question of fact for the jury, the court appears to disagree with the jury that International Harvester was confronted with economic circumstances sufficiently disastrous to justify discharge for impracticability. There were "alternatives," the court says, "which might have precluded unilateral termination of the contract." One such alternative open to International Harvester, the court suggests, might have been "to terminate [the] Dealer Agreements by mutual assent under the termination provisions of the contract and share the proceeds of the sale of assets to Case/Tenneco with its dealers."

Whether the "alternative" the court suggests ever occurred to International Harvester's management, or, if considered, was a feasible business solution, is entirely irrelevant on this appeal because it is the jury, not this court, that is empowered to determine whether International Harvester proved impracticability of performance as that defense was defined by the trial court. . . .

The "event" International Harvester relies upon is a sudden, massive, near total collapse of the farm equipment industry that was nationwide, drove two major suppliers into bankruptcy, and resulted in losses to International Harvester of over $2 billion in four years. . . .

When all facts and reasonable inferences therefrom are taken in a light most favorable to International Harvester, they reveal a sudden, unforeseen, nationwide collapse of the farm implement industry so severe and so widespread that International Harvester, after losing over $2 billion in four years, was faced, in its business judgment, with no alternative but bankruptcy or selling off its farm implement division. Those are the facts as we must view them for purposes of this appeal. The question for us, then, is whether "reasonable people could differ" that those facts amounted to "an event, the non-occurrence of which was a basic assumption on which the contract was made." RESTATEMENT (SECOND) OF CONTRACTS, *supra*. Manifestly, they could. The majority opinion is an indication of that.

Since there is nothing in the jurisprudence of the impracticability defense to suggest that a market collapse of the kind shown by International Harvester is not, as a matter of law, within the doctrine, we are not free to disturb the jury's verdict.

NOTES & QUESTIONS

1. Which decision in *Karl Wendt* do you agree with — the majority's or the dissent's? Why?

2. Which case presents a stronger case for impossibility (impracticability): *Karl Wendt* or *Marcovich Land Corporation v. J.J. Newberry Company*? Why?

3. Courts are generally reluctant to find impracticability on the basis of mere financial difficulty. Such impracticability is generally considered to be a form of "subjective" impracticability — not that the performance cannot be done

(objective) but I cannot do what I promised (subjective). Is the plaintiff seeking relief on the basis of objective or subjective impracticability in *Karl Wendt*? In *Marcovich Land Corporation v. J.J. Newberry Company*? The RESTATEMENT (SECOND) OF CONTRACTS does not use the term "objective" or "subjective." Comment e to Section 261 states, in pertinent part:

> This Section recognizes that if the performance remains practicable and it is merely beyond the party's capacity to render it, he is ordinarily not discharged, but it does not use the terms "objective" and "subjective" to express this. Instead, the rationale is that a party generally assumes the risk of his own inability to perform his duty. . . .

4. Is there a point where financial difficulty becomes an objective bar to performance? Is something less than bankruptcy required to establish objective financial impracticability? What should the test be? *See* U.C.C. § 2-615, comment 4 ("Increased cost alone does not excuse performance unless the rise in cost is due to some unforeseen contingency which alters the essential nature of the performance. Neither is a rise or collapse in the market in itself a justification, for that is exactly the type of business risk which business contracts made at fixed prices are intended to cover.").

5. There is often a close doctrinal relationship between impracticability and mutual mistake. Both doctrines concern the "excuse" of performances when an underlying assumption of the contract has not been met. For a review of the doctrine of mutual mistake, see Chapter 8. Where the impracticability existed *before* the contract arose, the defense will generally be raised in terms of mistake. *See* RESTATEMENT (SECOND) OF CONTRACTS § 266. Where the impracticability arose *after* the contract, the defense is usually raised in terms of impossibility or impracticability. *See* RESTATEMENT (SECOND) OF CONTRACTS § 262. For an early case demonstrating the role of mistake and impracticability, *see Mineral Park Land Co. v. Howard*, 172 Cal. 289, 156 P. 458 (1916).

6. *Practice Points*: The transaction underlying the *Karl Wendt* case was an asset purchase agreement. Under this agreement, the buyer buys the assets of a company — its inventory, name, going business value and, often, its existing contracts. In this case the buyer elected *not* to assume the existing contract with Wendt. Once the underlying business was sold, International Harvester had no control over whether Wendt would be given a franchise agreement. Consequently, it would have been advisable for IH to set aside some of the monies from the sale to either buy out Wendt's contract or to have available to pay anticipated damages for its probable breach.

FREIDCO OF WILMINGTON, DELAWARE, LTD. v. FARMERS BANK OF THE STATE OF DELAWARE
529 F. Supp. 822 (D. Del. 1981)

STAPLETON, District Judge:

. . . Freidco of Wilmington, Ltd. ("FW") a limited partnership, was created for the purpose of developing land in downtown Wilmington as a site for a new headquarters office building for the Farmers Bank of Delaware ("Farmers"). . . .

Farmers and FW's predecessor in interest signed the lease on May 14, 1965. Under its terms, Farmers rents approximately 79,800 square feet of space on the basement through the sixth floor of the Farmers Bank Building ("FBB"). Farmers' space comprises roughly 40% of the leasable area of the building. It pays a rental of $4.31 per square foot. Farmers also pays its proportionate share of property tax increases, and the "actual costs charged to FW for water, electricity and heating and air conditioning furnished or used on the premises, provided, however, that the annual cost to Tenant therefore shall not exceed $1.10 per square foot of occupied space." In 1979, the last year for which we have facts of record, Farmers paid $344,121 in rent; $27,150 in property taxes; and $90,489 for its pro rata share of utility costs.

In this litigation, FW's Trustee in Bankruptcy asks that the $1.10 limitation, or "cap," on Farmers' obligation to reimburse FW for utility service be set aside as commercially impracticable in view of the dramatic increase in the cost of that service. Farmers insists that the utility provision is not impracticable and has counterclaimed for alleged overpayments to FW for utilities between 1967 and 1974. This Opinion comprises the Court's Findings of Fact and Conclusions of Law.

In recent years, courts have abandoned the restrictive doctrine of "impossibility of performance" for the more flexible "impracticability" standard. . . .

Discharge by reason of impracticability requires proof of three elements. First, the party claiming discharge must establish the occurrence of an event the non-occurrence of which was a basic assumption of the contract. The event need not be unexpected, unforeseeable, or even unforeseen. RESTATEMENT (SECOND) § 261, Comment c; § 265, Comment a. *Transatlantic Financing Corp. v. United States*, 363 F.2d 312, 318 (D.C. Cir. 1966). The non-occurrence of that event, however, must have been a fundamental assumption on which both parties made the contract. "The continuation of existing market conditions and the financial situation of the parties are ordinarily not such assumptions, so that mere market shifts or financial inability do not usually effect discharge under the rule stated in [Section 261]." RESTATEMENT (SECOND) § 261, Comment b.

Second, it must be shown that continued performance is not commercially practicable. Although the standard of impracticability is not impossibility, neither is it mere impracticality. RESTATEMENT (SECOND) § 261, Comment d. "A mere change in the degree of difficulty or expense due to such causes as increased wages, prices of raw materials or costs of construction, unless well beyond the normal range, does not amount to impracticability since this is the sort of risk that a fixed price contract is intended to cover." *Id.* As the Third Circuit Court of Appeals recently explained in *Gulf Oil Co. v. FPC*:

> The crucial question in applying [the doctrine of commercial impracticability] to any given situation is whether the cost of performance has in fact become so excessive and unreasonable that failure to excuse performance would result in grave injustice. . . .

> The party seeking to excuse [its] performance must not only show that [it] can perform only at a loss but also that the loss will be especially severe and unreasonable.

563 F.2d 588 at 599-600.

Finally, the party claiming discharge must show that it did not expressly or impliedly agree to perform in spite of impracticability that would otherwise justify his nonperformance. Both the U.C.C. and the RESTATEMENT provide that contracting parties may override or control the application of the "discharge by supervening impracticability" rule if they agree to do so. Thus, a court in a case of alleged commercial impracticability must examine the agreement of the parties and the circumstances surrounding their negotiations in order to determine if they contemplated that the commercial risk involved would be borne by the party claiming discharge, despite the impracticability of performance. If so, he is not excused and may be held liable for damages.

. . . I turn . . . to the third element of the commercial impracticability claim in this case because it poses a substantial issue which, if resolved in Farmers' favor, would be dispositive.

The parties to the 1965 lease did not ignore the possibility of changing utility costs. The price which Farmers was to pay for the utility service supplied by FW was to vary with changes in the rate paid by FW for that utility service until that rate reached the $1.10/sq. ft. cap. The lease thus assigned the burden of any increase in utility rates below that cap to Farmers. Further, the cap itself was an assignment of a potential burden from increased utility costs; it allocated the risk of increases above the $1.10/sq. ft. to FW.

The risk allocation inherent in the utility cap does not require, however, that FW be left with the burden of all increased costs above $1.10. The doctrine of commercial impracticability assumes contractual allocation of a burden to the party claiming discharge and operates to relieve a party who has assumed a duty without expressly qualifying that undertaking to exclude the changed circumstances. RESTATEMENT (SECOND) § 261, Comment a. Accordingly, the focus cannot be on the unqualified nature of the language of the contract. Rather, the inquiry is whether the parties, by virtue of their implicit assumptions, have contracted in a universe more limited than the literal undertaking, or whether they intended to allocate a duty without regard to the possibility of change, foreseeable or otherwise.

A fixed price contract for the manufacture and delivery of goods, in effect, assigns the risk of increased costs to the seller. Courts enforce that assignment in the context of increased costs within the normal range. The existence of such a risk assignment does not preclude a discharge by supervening impracticability, however, where a disaster results in an abrupt tenfold increase in cost to the seller. In such a circumstance, the seller may be relieved of his duty because the contract, having been made on a different "basic assumption," is regarded as not covering the extreme case that has arisen. As the RESTATEMENT puts it, it "is an omitted case, falling within a 'gap' in the contract."

In a case in which the parties have allocated the risks associated with increasing costs at a variety of levels, it is, of course, less likely than in the fixed price case, that the risk at a particular level was beyond the universe in which the parties contracted. Nevertheless, contracting parties may allocate the risks at levels which they recognize as being realistic possibilities during the term of the contract without assigning risks that are wholly unforeseeable at the time of their negotiations or which are so remote at that time as to be deemed unworthy of express treatment. Or, stated in the context of this case where the estimated utility cost during negotiations was $.52/sq. ft., the fact that the parties allocated the burden associated with a 111% increase does not mean, for example, that they allocated the burden of a tenfold increase. If the latter burden was a wholly unforeseeable one at the inception of the term or was so remote as to be of minimal importance, this would suggest that non-occurrence of such a burden was a "basic assumption" within the meaning of the RESTATEMENT.

This is not a case in which a party has expressly undertaken to assume all risks, known or unknown, associated with a particular kind of change of circumstance. It is thus unlike the Gulf case where the court found that Gulf, by "warranting, rather than merely promising, the availability of sufficient quantities of gas [to meet the purchaser's needs] . . . , assumed for itself the entire risk that future conditions would . . ." require it to transport the gas over a long distance at substantial additional expense. 563 F.2d at 599.[5]

Having concluded that the utility cap itself does not preclude relief, I turn to an analysis of the other two elements.

As the comments to the RESTATEMENT and the U.C.C. point out, the parties to any contract to be performed over a term normally assume that the cost of performance may fluctuate during the term, and, as a result, courts ordinarily do not conclude that an increase in the cost of performance is an event the non-occurrence of which was a basic assumption of the contract. In addition, in this case we know from the terms of the contract itself that the parties in fact assumed that the cost of FW's performance of the utility provisions might vary over a range the high end of which would be greater than $1.10. . . .

[T]he evidence relating to the inclusion of the utility cap also suggests that the parties expected, at most, a gradual rise in utility rates over the term of the lease. While the record does not disclose how the concept of a utility cap originated, it does reflect that this provision was not regarded as a matter of major importance in the negotiating process.

Regardless, however, of what the parties and others thought would be the most likely course of events with respect to utility rates, FW and Farmers recognized the possibility of utility costs in excess of $1.10/sq. ft. during the term of the lease and expressly assigned the burden of costs above that level to FW. During 1979, the last year for which figures are in the record, the cost to FW for the utility service supplied to Farmers was $1.43/sq. ft. Accordingly, the relevant issue, I believe, is whether it can be said that the non-existence of a situation producing utility costs of $1.43 is a basic assumption of a lease which assigns such costs above $1.10 to the landlord. To state the question is to answer it. While there is undoubtedly a level of utility cost beyond the universe in which these parties contracted, one would have to ignore the utility cap provision itself to conclude that that level had been reached. . . .

[T]he record reveals that the utility cap provision has resulted in FW's paying $23,544 in utility expenses for Farmers' space in 1979 which was not reimbursed by Farmers. This represents 5.14% of the total consideration received from Farmers under the lease in that year. It is not altogether clear from the record whether or not this 5% reduction in revenue resulted in a negative cash flow in 1979. The

---

[5] [3] Nor is this case like Aluminum Co. of America ("ALCOA") v. Essex Group, Inc., 499 F. Supp. 53 (W.D. Pa. 1980). The parties there had agreed upon a formula which provided a sliding scale for the price of the goods to be sold over a potentially infinite range of cost increases. It is far easier to argue in that context that the parties have expressly allocated the burden associated with all theoretically conceivable price changes, even those not reasonably foreseeable at the inception of the bargain. Even in that situation, however, the court concluded that an unforeseeable rise in the seller's non-labor production costs imposed a burden outside the scope of the contract.

Trustee asserts that it did; Farmers argues to the contrary. Even if the record as a whole suggested that FW performed its lease obligations at a loss in 1979, however, I would remain unpersuaded that the loss has been, in the words of the Gulf opinion, "so excessive and unreasonable that the failure to excuse performance would result in grave injustice." 563 F.2d at 588.

The Trustee's commercial impracticability claim will be denied.

NOTES & QUESTIONS

Practice Points: As *Freidco* amply demonstrates, every provision in a contract has more than one role to play. In *Freidco* although the utility cap was used for one reason (to establish a type of fixed costs under the agreement), the court used the cap to reflect the parties' intent with regard to risk allocation for purposes of determining impracticability. Whenever drafting an agreement, consider the adverse consequences of every provision. Don't include a provision without a strong, readily articulated reason for doing so.

PROBLEMS

1. Defendants contracted to purchase a house for $135,000. The principal asset the defendants owned at the time of the contract was stock with a market value of $150,000. By the time of closing, the stock fell in value to $50,000. The defendants were relying on the sale of the stock to help finance their acquisition and refused to close. Was their duty to buy the house discharged? *See Rothman Realty Co. v. Bereck*, 140 N.J. Super. 72, 355 A.2d 201 (1976).

2. Mark owns a factory in a small nation overseas. The factory manufactures truck tires. Mark contracts with Perry to sell Perry the output of his factory for the next two years. A civil war breaks out and the government orders Mark to sell the output of his factory to it. Mark complies with the government's orders. Is his performance under the contract with Perry excused?

3. Fred Farmer owns a lemon grove. He contracts with Laura Lemonuser to sell her "all the lemons from my grove" for a "fixed price of $2.00 per bushel." An unseasonable frost destroys Fred's crops. His neighbor's crops are unaffected because they had the standard heaters to keep the crops sufficiently warm to avoid frost damage. Fred's heaters had broken down a month before and he had forgotten to repair them. Is his performance under the contract excused?

B.   COMMERCIAL FRUSTRATION

Closely related to the doctrines of impossibility and impracticability, the doctrine of commercial frustration excuses a party's performance when an unforeseen event substantially frustrates the principal purpose of the contract. Thus, for example, suppose that you had a ticket to attend the concert that was the subject of *Taylor v. Caldwell* and you had hired a limousine specifically to take you to the concert. Once the concert is canceled, should you be excused from paying for the limousine rental? Performance is *not* impracticable, but the value of the performance to one of the parties has been substantially reduced, if not wholly eliminated. As you read the following cases, consider what limits should be used in deciding when one party's "frustration" excuses performance.

KRELL v. HENRY
2 K.B. 740 (C.A. 1903)

The plaintiff, Paul Krell, sued the defendant, C.S. Henry, for 50£., being the balance of a sum of 75£., for which the defendant had agreed to hire a flat at 56A, Pall Mall on the days of June 26 and 27, for the purpose of viewing the processions to be held in connection with the coronation of His Majesty. The defendant denied his liability, and counterclaimed for the return of the sum of 25£., which had been paid as a deposit, on the ground that, the processions not having taken place owing to the serious illness of the King, there had been a total failure of consideration for the contract entered into by him.

VAUGHAN WILLIAMS L.J. read the following written judgment: The real question in this case is the extent of the application in English law of the principle of the Roman law which has been adopted and acted on in many English decisions, and notably in the case of *Taylor v. Caldwell*. That case at least makes it clear that "where from the nature of the contract, it appears that the parties must from the beginning have known that it could not be fulfilled unless, when the time for the fulfillment of the contract arrived, some particular specified thing continued to exist, so that when entering into the contract they must have contemplated such continued existence as the foundation of what was to be done; there, in the absence of any express or implied warranty that the thing shall exist, the contract is not to be considered a positive contract, but as subject to an implied condition that the parties shall be excused in case, before breach, performance becomes impossible from the perishing of the thing without default of the contractor."

I do not think that the principle of the civil law as introduced into the English law is limited to cases in which the event causing the impossibility of performance is the destruction or non-existence of some thing which is the subject-matter of the contract or of some condition or state of things expressly specified as a condition of it. I think that you first have to ascertain, not necessarily from the terms of the contract, but, if required, from necessary inferences, drawn from surrounding circumstances recognized by both contracting parties, what is the substance of the contract, and then to ask the question whether that substantial contract needs for its foundation the assumption of the existence of a particular state of things. If it does, this will limit the operation of the general words, and in such case, if the contract becomes impossible of performance by reason of the non-existence of the state of things assumed by both contracting parties as the foundation of the contract, there will be no breach of the contract thus limited. . . . In my judgment the use of the rooms was let and taken for the purpose of seeing the Royal procession. It was not a demise of the rooms, or even an agreement to let and take the rooms. It is a license to use rooms for a particular purpose and none other. And in my judgment the taking place of those processions on the days proclaimed along the proclaimed route, which passed 56A, Pall Mall, was regarded by both contracting parties as the foundation of the contract; and I think that it cannot reasonably be supposed to have been in the contemplation of the contracting parties, when the contract was made, that the coronation would not be held on the proclaimed days, or the processions not take place on those days along the proclaimed route; and I think that the words imposing on the defendant the obligation to accept and pay for the use of the rooms for the named days, although general and unconditional, were not used with reference to the possibility of the particular contingency which afterwards occurred. It was suggested in the course of the argument that if the occurrence, on the proclaimed days, of the coronation and the procession in this case were the foundation of the contract, and if the general words are thereby limited or qualified, so that in the event of the non-occurrence of the coronation and procession along the proclaimed route they would discharge both parties from further performance of the contract, it would follow that if a cabman was engaged to take some one to Epsom on Derby Day at a suitable enhanced price for such a journey, say 10£, both parties to the contract would be discharged in the contingency of the race at Epsom for some reason becoming impossible; but I do notthink this follows, for I do not think that in the cab case the happening of the race would be the foundation of the contract. No doubt the purpose of the engager would be to go to see the Derby, and the price would be proportionately high; but the cab had no special qualifications for the purpose which led to the selection of the cab for this particular occasion. Any other cab would have done as well. Moreover, I think that, under the cab contract, the hirer, even if the race went off, could have said, "Drive me to Epsom; I will pay you the agreed sum; you have nothing to do with the purpose for which I hired the cab," and that if the cabman refused he would have been guilty of a breach of contract, there being nothing to qualify his promise to drive the hirer to Epsom on a particular day. Whereas in the case of the coronation, there is not merely the purpose of the hirer to see the coronation procession, but it is the coronation procession and the relative position of the rooms which is the basis of the contract as much for the lessor as the hirer; and I think that if the King, before the coronation day and after the contract, had died, the hirer could not have insisted on having the rooms on the days named. It could not in the cab case be reasonably said that seeing the Derby race was the foundation of the contract, as it was of the license in this case. Whereas in the present case, where the rooms were offered and taken, by reason of their peculiar suitability from the position of the rooms for a view of the coronation procession, surely the view of the coronation procession was the foundation of the contract, which is a very different thing from the purpose of the man who engaged the cab — namely, to see the race — being held to be the foundation of the contract. Each case must be judged by its own circumstances. In each case one must ask oneself, first, what, having regard to all the circumstances, was the foundation of the contract? Secondly, was the performance of the contract prevented? Thirdly, was the event which prevented the performance of the contract of such a character that it cannot reasonably be said to have been in the contemplation of the parties at the date of the contract? If all these questions are answered in the affirmative (as I think they should be in this case), I think both parties are discharged from further performance of the contract.

NOTES & QUESTIONS

1. Was performance under the *Krell* contract "impracticable"? Could Henry have still let his rooms even if the coronation had not occurred? Could Krell have rented the rooms?

2. What was the primary purpose of the contract? To let rooms? Or to let rooms for the coronation?

3. *Practice Points:* What evidence would you put on at a trial to demonstrate the primary purpose of the contract?

4. *Drafting Exercise.* Draft a contract for *Krell v. Henry* that expresses the parties' intent to rent the rooms for the coronation and that adequately protects both parties in the event the concert is canceled.

CHASE PRECAST CORPORATION v. JOHN J. PAONESSA COMPANY, INC.
566 N.E.2d 603 (Mass. 1991)

LYNCH, Justice:

This appeal raises the question whether the doctrine of frustration of purpose may be a defense in a breach of contract action in Massachusetts, and, if so, whether it excuses the defendant John J. Paonessa Company, Inc. (Paonessa), from performance.

The claim of the plaintiff, Chase Precast Corporation (Chase), arises from the cancellation of its contracts with Paonessa to supply median barriers in a highway reconstruction project of the Commonwealth. Chase brought an action to recover its anticipated profit on the amount of median barriers called for by its supply contracts with Paonessa but not produced. Paonessa brought a cross action against the Commonwealth for indemnification in the event it should be held liable to Chase. After a jury-waived trial, a Superior Court judge ruled for Paonessa on the basis of impossibility of performance. Chase and Paonessa cross appealed. The Appeals Court affirmed, noting that the doctrine of frustration of purpose more accurately described the basis of the trial judge's decision than the doctrine of impossibility. We agree. We allowed Chase's application for further appellate review, and we now affirm.

The pertinent facts are as follows. In 1982, the Commonwealth, through the Department of Public Works (department), entered into two contracts with Paonessa for resurfacing and improvements to two stretches of Route 128. Part of each contract called for replacing a grass median strip between the north and southbound lanes with concrete surfacing and precast concrete median barriers. Paonessa entered into two contracts with Chase under which Chase was to supply, in the aggregate, 25,800 linear feet of concrete median barriers according to the specifications of the department for highway construction. The quantity and type of barriers to be supplied were specified in two purchase orders prepared by Chase.

The highway reconstruction began in the spring of 1983. By late May, the department was receiving protests from angry residents who objected to use of the concrete median barriers and removal of the grass median strip. Paonessa and Chase became aware of the protest around June 1. On June 6, a group of about 100 citizens filed an action in the Superior Court to stop installation of the concrete median barriers and other aspects of the work. On June 7, anticipating modification by the department, Paonessa notified Chase by letter to stop producing concrete barriers for the projects. Chase did so upon receipt of the letter the following day. On June 17, the department and the citizens' group entered into a settlement which provided, in part, that no additional concrete median barriers would be installed. On June 23, the department deleted the permanent concrete median barriers item from its contracts with Paonessa.

Before stopping production on June 8, Chase had produced approximately one-half of the concrete median barriers called for by its contracts with Paonessa, and had delivered most of them to the construction sites. Paonessa paid Chase for all that it had produced, at the contract price. Chase suffered no out-of-pocket expense as a result of cancellation of the remaining portion of barriers.

This court has long recognized and applied the doctrine of impossibility as a defense to an action for breach of contract. Under that doctrine, "where from the nature of the contract it appears that the parties must from the beginning have contemplated the continued existence of some particular specified thing as the foundation of what was to be done, then, in the absence of any warranty that the thing shall exist . . . the parties shall be excused . . . [when] performance becomes impossible from the accidental perishing of the thing without the fault of either party."

On the other hand, although we have referred to the doctrine of frustration of purpose in a few decisions, we have never clearly defined it. Other jurisdictions have explained the doctrine as follows: when an event neither anticipated nor caused by either party, the risk of which was not allocated by the contract, destroys the object or purpose of the contract, thus destroying the value of performance, the parties are excused from further performance.

In *Mishara Constr. Co.*, 310 N.E.2d 363, we called frustration of purpose a "companion rule" to the doctrine of impossibility. Both doctrines concern the effect of supervening circumstances upon the rights and duties of the parties. The difference lies in the effect of the supervening event. Under frustration, "[p]erformance remains possible but the expected value of performance to the party seeking to be excused has been destroyed by [the] fortuitous event. . . ." The principal question in both kinds of cases remains "whether an unanticipated circumstance, the risk of which should not fairly be thrown on the promisor, has made performance vitally different from what was reasonably to be expected."

Since the two doctrines differ only in the effect of the fortuitous supervening event, it is appropriate to look to our cases dealing with impossibility for guidance in treating the issues that are the same in a frustration of purpose case. The trial judge's findings with regard to those issues are no less pertinent to application of the frustration defense because they were considered relevant to the defense of impossibility.

Another definition of frustration of purpose is found in the RESTATEMENT (SECOND) OF CONTRACTS § 265 (1981):

> Where, after a contract is made, a party's principal purpose is substantially frustrated without his fault by the occurrence of an event the non-occurrence of which was a basic assumption on which the contract was made, his remaining duties to render performance are discharged, unless the language or the circumstances indicate the contrary.

This definition is nearly identical to the defense of "commercial impracticability," found in the Uniform Commercial Code, § 2-615. . . . It follows, therefore, that the RESTATEMENT's formulation of the doctrine is consistent with this court's previous treatment of impossibility of performance and frustration of purpose.

Paonessa bore no responsibility for the department's elimination of the median barriers from the projects. Therefore, whether it can rely on the defense of frustration turns on whether elimination of the barriers was a risk allocated by the contracts to Paonessa. *Mishara Constr. Co.*, 310 N.E.2d 363, articulates the relevant test:

> The question is, given the commercial circumstances in which the parties dealt: Was the contingency which developed one which the parties could reasonably be thought to have foreseen as a real possibility which could affect performance? Was it one of that variety of risks which the parties were tacitly assigning to the promisor by their failure to provide for it explicitly? If it was, performance will be required. If it could not be so considered, performance is excused.

This is a question for the trier of fact.

Paonessa's contracts with the department contained a standard provision allowing the department to eliminate items or portions of work found unnecessary. The purchase order agreements between Chase and Paonessa do not contain a similar provision. This difference in the contracts does not mandate the conclusion that Paonessa assumed the risk of reduction in the quantity of the barriers. It is implicit in the judge's findings that Chase knew the barriers were for department projects. The record supports the conclusion that Chase was aware of the department's power to decrease quantities of contract items. The judge found that Chase had been a supplier of median barriers to the department in the past. The provision giving the department the power to eliminate items or portions thereof was standard in its contracts. The judge found that Chase had furnished materials under and was familiar with the so-called "Unit Price Philosophy" in the construction industry, whereby contract items are paid for at the contract unit price for the quantity of work actually accepted. Finally, the judge's finding that "[a]ll parties were well aware that lost profits were not an element of damage in either of the public works projects in issue" further supports the conclusion that Chase was aware of the department's power to decrease quantities, since the term prohibiting claims for anticipated profit is part of the same sentence in the standard provision as that allowing the engineer to eliminate items or portions of work.

In *Mishara Constr. Co.*, 310 N.E.2d 363, we held that, although labor disputes in general cannot be considered extraordinary, whether the parties in a particular case intended performance to be carried out, even in the face of a labor difficulty, depends on the facts known to the parties at the time of contracting with respect to the history of and prospects for labor difficulties. In this case, even if the parties were aware generally of the department's power to eliminate contract items, the judge could reasonably have concluded that they did not contemplate the cancellation for a major portion of the project of such a widely used item as concrete median barriers, and did not allocate the risk of such cancellation.

NOTES & QUESTIONS

1. Section 265 of the RESTATEMENT (SECOND) OF CONTRACTS recognizes that a supervening frustration may discharge a party's performance. It provides:

> Where, after a contract is made, a party's principal purpose is substantially frustrated without his fault by the occurrence of an event the non-occurrence of which was a basic assumption in which the contract was made, his remaining duties to render performance are discharged, unless the language or the circumstances indicate the contrary.

Compare this provision to Section 262, which concerns discharge by virtue of impracticability. What are the differences and similarities between the two?

2. Does a supervening frustration always result in impracticability?

Never? Sometimes?

3. The U.C.C. does not contain an express provision recognizing frustration as an excuse. Section 1-103, which provides, "Unless displaced by the particular provision of this Act, the principles of law and equity . . . shall supplement its provisions," has been used to incorporate the defense of frustration.

PROBLEM

Hannah owns a hotel; Clem owns a country club. They enter into a written contract under which Hannah will pay Clem $1,000 a month and Clem will make the club's membership privileges available to the hotel's guests free of charge. Without her fault, Hannah's hotel burns to the ground. Hannah refuses to make further monthly payments under the contract. Has her duty been discharged? Why or why not? *See Smith v. Roberts*, 54 Ill. App. 3d 910, 370 N.E.2d 271 (1971); *407 East 61st Garage v. Savoy Fifth Ave. Corp.*, 23 N.Y.2d 275, 296 N.Y.S.2d 338, 244 N.E.2d 37 (1968).

DOWNING v. STILES
635 P.2d 808 (Wyo. 1981)

Rooney, Justice:

Appellants-plaintiffs carried on a retail liquor business (hereinafter referred to as Rustler Bar) in a building owned by them in Basin, Wyoming. They were also partners with appellee-defendant Stiles (hereinafter referred to as Stiles) in a restaurant business styled Maverick Recreation Center (hereinafter referred to as Maverick), which was carried on in the basement of the same building. Much of Maverick's business resulted from patronage by Rustler Bar's customers.

Appellants sold Rustler Bar and the building to Dennis D. Morris, the person who had been managing Rustler Bar for appellants. Subsequently, on June 12, 1976, appellants sold their half interest in Maverick to Stiles. The terms of this sale were set forth in a purchase agreement. The purchase price was $25,000.00 to be paid in semi-annual installments. . . . Stiles also gave appellants a promissory note dated June 12, 1976 for $25,000.00 payable in semi-annual installments and with interest at 10% per annum. With appellants' help, Stiles obtained a five-year lease from Rustler Bar for the basement of the building.

Thereafter, the business of Rustler Bar decreased, and the bar finally ceased doing business in June 1978. On January 21, 1979, a fire destroyed the building and its contents. Stiles stopped making payments on the note on December 12, 1978. . . .

FRUSTRATION

With reference to "frustration," the trial court made the following two findings upon which Stiles was "relieved of any further obligation under the purchase agreement . . . and the note. . . .":

5. That the evidence shows that the Maverick Recreation Center, owned by the Defendant, Stiles, was dependent on the business with the Rustler Bar, and that without it, the center was not a viable operation. That the value of performance was destroyed by the frustrating event, which was the failure of the Rustler Bar.

6. That under the doctrine of commercial frustration, the Defendant, Stiles, should be relieved from any further payments under and by virtue of her Contract with the Plaintiffs.

The doctrine of "commercial frustration" or "frustration of the venture" or "discharge of commercial contract by supervening frustration" in the law of contracts "has been said to be a relatively modern one." It grew out of the so-called coronation cases initiated in *Krell v. Henry*, 2 K.B. 740 (1903) wherein a defendant was excused from payment for use of an apartment from which to view the coronation proceedings of King Edward VII because the proceedings were cancelled when the king became ill. It is akin to the doctrine of impossibility of performance of a contract, and the two doctrines are often treated under the same heading in encyclopedias and textbooks. However, the generally recognized distinction between the two doctrines lies in the inability to literally perform (impossibility) and the impracticability to perform (commercial frustration).

> . . . The doctrine of commercial frustration is close to but distinct from the doctrine of impossibility of performance. Both concern the effect of supervening circumstances upon the rights and duties of the parties but in cases of commercial frustration "[p]erformance remains possible but the expected value of performance to the party seeking to be excused has been destroyed by a fortuitous event, which supervenes to cause an actual but not literal failure of consideration."

More than one rationale has been advanced for the doctrine of commercial frustration:

> In construing contracts, the doctrine reads into them, in the absence of repellent circumstances, an implied condition that the promisor shall be absolved from performance if, through a supervening circumstance for which neither party is responsible, a thing, event, or condition which was essential so that performance would yield to the promisor the result which the parties intended him to receive, fails. The general principle underlying the doctrine of commercial frustration is that where the purpose of a contract is completely frustrated and rendered impossible of performance by a supervening event or circumstance, the contract will be discharged. The doctrine is predicated on the premise of giving relief in a situation where the parties could not provide themselves, by the terms of the contract, against the happening of subsequent events, so, if the intervening or supervening event was reasonably foreseeable, or was controllable by the parties, they may not invoke the principles of the doctrine as a defense to escape their obligations. It applies to executory contracts alone.

. . . Contract liability stems from consent. If an event occurs which is totally outside the contemplation of the parties and which drastically shifts the nature of the risks ostensibly consented to, is consent real?

Second, the doctrines of impossibility and frustration are closely allied to the doctrine of mutual mistake. The distinction is that mutual mistake as a doctrine is applicable only if the parties are mistaken as to a vital existing fact, while frustration and impossibility relate to future events. . . . [I]deas of unjust enrichment are heavily involved. Before applying the doctrine one must search the facts for unexpected, unbargained for gain on the one hand and unexpected, unbargained for loss on the other.

Third, notions of conscionability and fairness tend to support the doctrines. The law deems it to be unconscionably sharp practice to take advantage of the mistake of another. It may equally be deemed unconscionable to take advantage of a mistake as to the course of future events.

From the point of view of legal analysis, the doctrines of impossibility and frustration have been explained by two different conceptual models: (1) the existence of an implied term; and (2) the imposition by law of a constructive condition. The former is rooted in the idea that one can infer from the facts that the parties did not intend that performance would have to be rendered if an unexpected obstacle would create a radical change in the nature of the performance. This is the prevailing approach in England. In the United States, despite some discrepancy in the cases, it is generally believed that the excuse for non-performance created by the doctrines discussed here are more realistically understood as stemming from rules of law rather than from inferences drawn from the parties' agreement.

The question of foreseeability of the unexpected occurrence is frequently discussed in cases where impossibility or frustration are raised. First, it must be pointed out that the parties are free to allocate the risks of even unforeseen occurrences. Where they have neither foreseen the subsequent event nor allocated the risks of the unforeseen, various more or less standardized rules have been formulated to allocate some of the risks of this kind. All of these rules involve consideration of whom would the community normally expect to assume the risk of the unexpected occurrence. If the occurrence is reasonably foreseeable, courts often take the position that the promisor has assumed the risk of impossibility or frustration. . . .

The importance of foreseeability ought not to be exaggerated, however. As recently pointed out by the Supreme Court of California, "the question whether a risk is foreseeable is quite distinct from the question whether it was contemplated by the parties." The relevance of foreseeability is that a party's consent to the contract can generally be extended to foreseeable risks. The proper inquiry ought to be whether the risk was assumed; and the basic test is not foreseeability but whether the parties took the risk into account or whether the contract failed to provide for the situation.

Calamari & Perillo, CONTRACTS 2d ed. § 13-13, pp. 498-501.

* * *

Section 285, RESTATEMENT CONTRACTS (SECOND), sets forth the rule for Discharge By Supervening Frustration:

Where, after a contract is made, a party's principal purpose is substantially frustrated without his fault by the occurrence of an event the non-occurrence of which was a basic assumption on which the contract was made, his remaining duties to render performance are discharged, unless the language or the circumstances indicate the contrary.

Comment a thereto states in part:

> . . . First, the purpose that is frustrated must have been a principal purpose of that party in making the contract. It is not enough that he had in mind*some specific object without which he would not have made the contract. The object must be so completely the basis of the contract that, as both parties understand, without it the transaction would make little sense. Second, the frustration must be substantial. It is not enough that the transaction has become less profitable for the affected party or even that he will sustain a loss. The frustration must be so severe that it is not fairly to be regarded as within the risks that he assumed under the contract. Third, the non-occurrence of the frustrating event must have been a basic assumption on which the contract was made. . . .

(1) In consideration of the foregoing, we conclude that the court should apply the doctrine of commercial frustration to relieve a party to a contract from further performance thereunder only if:

1. The contract is at least partially executory.
2. A supervening event occurred after the contract was made.
3. The non-occurrence of such event was a basic assumption on which the contract was made.
4. Such occurrence frustrated the party's principal purpose for the contract.
5. The frustration was substantial, and
6. The party has not agreed, expressly or impliedly, to perform in spite of the occurrence of the event.

(2) In this case, Stiles did not contend that the supervening event was the fire. The discontinuance of the Rustler Bar business was the event designated as supervening. The contract was partly executory, the event occurred subsequent to the making of the contract, and appellants had not agreed, expressly or impliedly, to perform in spite of the occurrence of the event. Although subject to considerable dispute, it may even be said that the non-occurrence of the event was a basic assumption on which the contract was made. But the evidence does not establish the continuation of Rustler Bar's business as the principal purpose for which the contract was made, and, therefore, that the frustration was substantial. Certainly, the frustration was not "total or nearly total."

The principal purpose of the purchase was to carry on a restaurant business. The fact is that such restaurant business was continued to be carried on for six or seven months after the Rustler Bar ceased doing business. It was not until just prior to the fire that Stiles refused to make payment under the contract. This fact reflects the recognition that one of the risks assumed by Stiles under the contract was the decrease and discontinuance of Rustler Bar's business. Because of the lease, Stiles could not be evicted.

But Stiles had not sought any provision in the agreement whereby Rustler Bar was bound to use Stiles for its food service. If such were the principal purpose of the purchase agreement between Stiles and appellants, assurance of such should have been secured along with the lease. And such assurance should designate the extent of such service. For otherwise, where is the line drawn? Can Stiles be discharged from performance of her contract with appellants when service to Rustler Bar's customers falls off 10%? or 25%? or 90%? In the language of Comment a to § 285, RESTATEMENT, CONTRACTS 2D, *supra*: ". . . It is not enough that the transaction has become less profitable for the affected party or even that he will sustain a loss. The frustration must be so severe that it is not fairly to be regarded as within the risks that he assumed under the contract.

Accordingly, it was error to apply the doctrine of commercial frustration to the circumstances of this case.

NOTES & QUESTIONS

1. Consider the problem after *Chase Precast* in light of the *Downing* decision. Would you reach a different result?

2. *Drafting Exercise*: Draft an agreement for the problem after *Chase* Precast which would clearly release Hannah from an obligation to pay in the event Clem's fee becomes financially impracticable. How would you define such an occurrence?

LLOYD v. MURPHY
153 P.2d 47 (Cal. 1944)

TRAYNOR, Justice:

. . . The question in cases involving frustration is whether the equities of the case, considered in the light of sound public policy, require placing the risk of a disruption or complete destruction of the contract equilibrium on defendant or plaintiff under the circumstances of a given case, and the answer depends on whether an unanticipated circumstance, the risk of which should not be fairly thrown on the promisor, has made performance vitally different from what was reasonably to be expected. The purpose of a contract is to place the risks of performance upon the promisor, and the relation of the parties, terms of the contract, and circumstances surrounding its formation must be examined to determine whether it can be fairly inferred that the risk of the event that has supervened to cause the alleged frustration was not reasonably foreseeable. If it was foreseeable there should have been provision for it in the contract, and the absence of such a provision gives rise to the inference that the risk was assumed. . . .

PROBLEM

Ed has been hired to excavate Paul's land in order to install an Olympic-sized swimming pool for a fixed price of $1,000. Halfway through the project, Ed hits granite. He had run the standard tests but had not discovered the granite before signing the contract. Ed has the necessary equipment to remove the granite but it will cost him more than $5,000 to do so. Is his performance "excused"?

Richard A. Posner & Andrew M. Rosenfeld
Impossibility and Related Doctrines in Contract Law: An Economic Analysis
6 J. LEGAL STUD. 83 (1977)

1. *Of contract law in general.* The process by which goods and services are shifted into their most valuable uses is one of voluntary exchange. The distinctive problems of contract law arise when the agreed-upon exchange does not take place instantaneously (for example, A agrees to build a house for B and construction will take several months). The fact that performance is to extend into the future introduces uncertainty, which in turn creates risks. A fundamental purpose of contracts is to allocate these risks between the parties to the exchange.

One purpose of contract law, but not a particularly interesting one here, is to assure compliance with the allocation of risks that the parties have agreed upon (that is, to prevent bad faith). A second purpose, central to our subject, is to reduce the costs of contract negotiation by supplying contract terms that the parties would probably have adopted explicitly had they negotiated over them.

If the purpose of the law of contracts is to effectuate the desires of the contracting parties, then the proper criterion for evaluating the rules of contract law is surely that of economic efficiency. Since the object of most voluntary exchanges is to increase value or efficiency, contracting parties may be assumed to desire a set of contract terms that will maximize the value of the exchange. It is true that each party is interested only in the value of the contract to it. However, the more efficiently the exchange is structured, the larger is the potential profit of the contract for the parties to divide between them.

The use of economic efficiency as a criterion for legal decision-making is of course controversial. In the area of contract, however, the criterion is well-nigh inevitable once it is conceded that the parties to a contract have the right to vary the terms at will. If the rules of contract law are inefficient, the parties will (save as transaction costs may sometimes outweigh the gains from a more efficient rule) contract around them. A law of contract not based on efficiency considerations will therefore be largely futile. This is a powerful reason for expecting that the law of contract has, in fact, been informed by efficiency considerations, even if judges and lawyers may have found it difficult to articulate the underlying economic premises of the law.

2. *The economics of impossibility.* The typical case in which impossibility or some related doctrine is invoked is one where, by reason of an unforeseen or at least unprovided-for event, performance by one of the parties of his obligations under the contract has become so much more costly than he foresaw at the time the contract was made as to be uneconomical (that is, the costs of performance would be greater than the benefits). The performance promised may have been delivery of a particular cargo by a specified delivery date — but the ship is trapped in the Suez Canal because of a war between Israel and Egypt. Or it may have been a piano recital by Gina Bachauer — and she dies between the signing of the contract and the date of the recital. The law could in each case treat the failure to perform as a breach of contract, thereby in effect assigning to the promisor the risk that war, or death, would prevent performance (or render it uneconomical). Alternatively, invoking impossibility or some related notion, the law could treat the

failure to perform as excusable and discharge the contract, thereby in effect assigning the risk to the promisee.

From the standpoint of economics — and disregarding, but only momentarily, administrative costs — discharge should be allowed where the promisee is the superior risk bearer; if the promisor is the superior risk bearer, nonperformance should be treated as a breach of contract. "Superior risk bearer" is to be understood here as the party that is the more efficient bearer of the particular risk in question, in the particular circumstances of the transaction. Of course, if the parties have expressly assigned the risk to one of them, there is no occasion to inquire which is the superior risk bearer. The inquiry is merely an aid to interpretation.

A party can be a superior risk bearer for one of two reasons. First, he may be in a better position to prevent the risk from materializing. This resembles the economic criterion for assigning liability in tort cases. It is an important criterion in many contract settings, too, but not in this one. Discharge would be inefficient in any case where the promisor could prevent the risk from materializing at a lower cost than the expected cost of the risky event. In such a case efficiency would require that the promisor bear the loss resulting from the occurrence of the event, and hence that occurrence should be treated as precipitating a breach of contract.

But the converse is not necessarily true. It does not necessarily follow from the fact that the promisor could not at any reasonable cost have prevented the risk from materializing that he should be discharged from his contractual obligations. Prevention is only one way of dealing with risk; the other is insurance. The promisor may be the superior insurer. If so, his inability to prevent the risk from materializing should not operate to discharge him from the contract, any more than an insurance company's inability to prevent a fire on the premises of the insured should excuse it from its liability to make good the damage caused by the fire.

The fact that people are willing to pay to avoid risk shows that risk is a cost. Accordingly, insurance is a method (alternative to prevention) of reducing the costs associated with the risk that performance of a contract may be more costly than anticipated. It is a particularly important method of cost avoidance in the impossibility context because the risks with which that doctrine is concerned are generally not preventable by the party charged with nonperformance.

The factors relevant to determining which party to the contract is the cheaper insurer are (1) risk-appraisal costs and (2) transaction costs. The former comprise the costs of determining (a) the probability that the risk will materialize and (b) the magnitude of the loss if it does materialize. The amount of risk is the product of probability of loss and of the magnitude of the loss if it occurs. Both elements — probability and magnitude — must be known in order for the insurer to know how much to ask from the other party to the contract as compensation for bearing the risk in question.

The relevant transaction costs are the costs involved in eliminating or minimizing the risk through pooling it with other uncertain events, that is, diversifying away the risk. This can be done either through self-insurance or through the purchase of an insurance policy (market insurance). . . .

An easy case for discharge would be one where (1) the promisor asking to be discharged could not reasonably have prevented the event rendering his performance uneconomical, and (2) the promisee could have insured against the occurrence of the event at lower cost than the promisor because the promisee (a) was in a better position to estimate both (i) the probability of the event's occurrence and (ii) the magnitude of the loss if it did occur, and (b) could have self-insured, whereas the promisor would have had to buy more costly market insurance. . . .

The discharge question arises only in those cases where the contract does not assign the risk in question and the event giving rise to the discharge claim was not avoidable by any cost-justified precautions. When these threshold conditions have been satisfied, economic analysis suggests that the loss should be placed on the party who is the superior (that is, lower cost) risk bearer. To determine which party is the superior risk bearer three factors are relevant — knowledge of the magnitude of the loss, knowledge of the probability that it will occur, and (other) costs of self- or market-insurance.

NOTES & QUESTIONS

1. Consider the cases you have read regarding impossibility, impracticability and commercial frustration. Does the economic analysis contained in this article explain the courts' decisions in these cases? What role should the economic analysis in this article play in interpreting a party's intent?

2. How is a party's risk-bearing capability relevant to interpreting contractual obligations?

3. What role, if any, is risk-bearing capacity given in the RESTATEMENT (SECOND) OF CONTRACTS in determining liability for breach? In the U.C.C.? What role should it be given?

C. WAIVER AND EXCUSE

An alleged breach may be "excused" by the non-breaching party's conduct. Thus, for example, if a builder's obligation to construct an office building is conditioned upon the owner's making timely progress payments, the builder may forfeit his right to timely payments through words or actions that demonstrate a waiver of his rights under the contract. A waiver has often been defined as "the intentional relinquishment of a known right." This definition, however, is not precisely accurate. As you will see from the following cases, parties can waive performance without actually intending to do so. Furthermore, waiver may occur either prior to, or after, the time for performance is required. Waivers may be retracted, but only if such retraction does not work an injustice upon the other party.

As you read the following cases, ask yourself whether the party in question actually intended to waive strict compliance with the contract terms. Are there other policy issues that are being enforced?

MERCEDES-BENZ CREDIT CORPORATION v. MORGAN
312 Ark. 225, 850 S.W.2d 297 (1993)

GLAZE, Justice:

This tort of conversion case was commenced by Dr. Jerry Morgan after his 1984 Porsche had been repossessed by Mercedes-Benz Credit Corporation (MBCC). Morgan purchased the Porsche from Riverside Motors and afterwards, Riverside assigned the purchase installment contract to MBCC. Under the contract, Morgan was to make a payment of $253.37 on the first day of each month for forty-eight months commencing March 1, 1990. Morgan was indisputably late in his payments, and on March 22, 1991, MBCC decided to exercise its right under statutory law and the parties' contract to self-help repossession. MBCC peacefully and without incident gained possession of the Porsche on April 8, 1991. Following repossession, Dr. Morgan brought his account current. MBCC then offered to return the Porsche to Morgan, but he refused, choosing instead to file this conversion action against MBCC.

Prior to trial, MBCC moved for summary judgment which the trial court denied. The parties tried the case to a jury which returned a verdict for Dr. Morgan in the sum of $11,900.00. MBCC filed motions for directed verdict and for judgment notwithstanding the verdict, all of which were denied. The trial court also awarded attorney's fees to Morgan. MBCC brings this appeal arguing the trial court erred in denying its motions for directed verdict and judgment notwithstanding the verdict and in awarding Morgan attorney's fees.

Morgan proceeded below on two theories, namely (1) he was not in default when MBCC decided to repossess Morgan's car, and alternatively (2) if Morgan was in default, MBCC had established a course of dealing by accepting late payments, so MBCC was required to put Morgan on notice that it would no longer allow late payments and would require strict compliance with the parties' contract. Both of these theories were presented to the jury, and if Morgan is correct on either argument, we must affirm.

As to Morgan's first point, our review of the record shows he was clearly in default at the time MBCC repossessed Morgan's car. Morgan makes much of the argument that MBCC had miscalculated the receipt of his late February 1 and March 1, 1991 payments. He showed MBCC had misapplied his February 1 payment to the wrong account and mistakenly delayed in crediting this payment to Morgan's correct account until April 15, 1991. Morgan argued MBCC had actually accepted his late February 1 payment well in advance of its declaring Morgan in default. Morgan also claimed that MBCC had accepted his late March 1 payment on April 1, 1991. In both cases, Morgan asserts his account was current prior to MBCC's repossession of Morgan's car on April 8, 1991.

Although the record appears to support Morgan's argument as to his February and March payments, the evidence also reflects he still was late on his payment due on April 1, 1991, which was not received by MBCC until on or about April 11, 1991 — several days after MBCC repossessed Morgan's car. In sum, we conclude MBCC is correct in its argument that Morgan was, indeed, in default when it regained possession of Morgan's car. That being so, MBCC argues it was not liable for conversion. . . .

In pre-code cases, this court adhered to the principle that acceptance of late payments waives strict compliance with contract terms specifying time of payments. . . .

See Ford Motor Credit Co. v. Waters, 273 So. 2d 96 (Fla. Dist. Ct. App. 1973), (where seller of automobile had consistently accepted late payments from the buyer, who had made more than half of the thirty-six monthly payments when the vehicle was repossessed at time buyer was two months behind, the court held the seller's conduct led buyer to believe late payments would be accepted and therefore buyer had a right to be notified, prior to repossession, of any modification of such conduct, and in absence of such notice, buyer was entitled to recover for wrongful repossession.) . . .

In the present case, Dr. Morgan made only one timely payment of the fourteen monthly payments required prior to MBCC having repossessed Morgan's automobile. The thirteen late payments ranged from a few days to more than thirty days delinquent from the due date required under the parties' agreement. MBCC's personnel had contacted Morgan concerning his delinquent payments, but no one at MBCC ever informed Morgan that MBCC intended to commence strict enforcement of its rights under their contract. The record shows that shortly before it repossessed Morgan's Porsche on April 8, 1991, MBCC had again accepted another late payment (March) on April 1, 1991, and it also accepted Morgan's delinquent April payment on April 11, 1991. In fact, MBCC even tendered the car's return to Morgan when Morgan became current on his account. Clearly, a jury, under the above authority, could have found that (1) MBCC, by its course of dealing, had waived its right to repossession based on its having repeatedly accepted late payments, and (2) in order to reinstate its right under the parties' contract, MBCC was required to give Morgan notice that MBCC expected strict compliance in future dealings. If MBCC failed to give such notice in these circumstances, it would then not have the right to declare a default and repossess its collateral. . . .

Because substantial evidence was presented that Morgan never received notice from MBCC that it would henceforth require prompt payments under the parties' contract, the jury could have readily determined MBCC wrongfully repossessed Morgan's vehicle when it did. This is especially true since MBCC continued its pattern of accepting late payments from Morgan by accepting his late April 1 payment on April 11, 1991, and offering to return Morgan his car. We note further that it was MBCC's burden to demonstrate error and having failed to do so, we must affirm.

STINEMEYER v. WESCO FARMS, INC.
260 Or. 109, 487 P.2d 65 (1971)

MCALLISTER, Justice:

This is a suit for the strict foreclosure of a land sale contract. The basic question is whether the acceptance by the vendor of late payments precludes him from declaring the entire balance due and filing suit for strict foreclosure without first giving purchasers a reasonable time to cure any defaults. . . .

There is little dispute about the facts. On May 14, 1969, F.H. and Betty Haugland, as vendors, contracted to sell the Starfish Cove Motel in Lincoln County to defendant *Wesco Arms, Inc.* The selling price was $97,500 of which $10,000 was paid in cash, $5,000 in property, and $26,567.96 by the assumption of a mortgage on the motel held by Hollis and Isabel Evans.

The balance of the purchase price bore interest at seven per cent from July 15, 1969, and Wesco was required for the first year to pay only this interest in monthly installments commencing August 15, 1969. Time was made of the essence of the contract. We are concerned here only with delay in the monthly interest payments of $326.26 each and are not concerned with the large monthly payments required commencing August 15, 1970.

On July 15, 1969, Wesco contracted to sell the motel and a major portion of the real property which it was buying from the Hauglands to the defendant Ocean Eleven, Inc.

On November 20, 1969, the Hauglands assigned all their interest in the May 14, 1969, contract to the plaintiff Frank G. Stinemeyer, to whom we will refer herein as if he were the sole plaintiff.

On March 18, 1970, Stinemeyer, by letter to Wesco, declared the entire balance of the purchase price due and payable and also instructed National Security Bank of Newport, as the escrow agent of the parties, not to accept any further payment less than the entire balance of the contract. . . .

As to the monthly installments of interest, the evidence shows the following payment record:

Date due	Date paid
August 15, 1969	August 20, 1969
September 15, 1969	
October 15, 1969	November 21, 1969
November 15, 1969	
December 15, 1969	Paid late
January 15, 1970	Paid late
February 15, 1970	Still unpaid on
March 15, 1970	March 18, 1970

It will be noted that on November 20, 1969, the date of the assignment to plaintiff, Wesco was in default in three payments. After the assignment those three payments were made in a lump sum, and the next two monthly payments were made late and accepted by plaintiff. On March 18, 1970, when plaintiff declared the full balance due and payable, the February installment of $326.26 was slightly more than one month overdue and the March installment was three days delinquent.

Wesco argues that by accepting late payments over a period of time, plaintiff had waived the contract provision making time of the essence, and that Wesco was therefore entitled to notice of plaintiff's intention to require strict performance as well as an opportunity to make up the delinquent payments before plaintiff could accelerate the debt and bring this suit.

. . . Although there are cases to the contrary, a number of courts have held that a creditor who has, by his past actions, led his debtor to believe that the terms of their agreement requiring prompt payment will not be strictly enforced must, before taking advantage of an acceleration option, give the debtor a reasonable opportunity to make up his delinquent payments. . . .

We hold that this general rule, which we have applied in cases involving attempted forfeitures, is applicable as well when the vendor is seeking to foreclose a land sale contract.

. . . The evidence clearly shows that plaintiff's behavior gave Wesco the right to expect that late payments would be accepted. Plaintiff wrote Wesco a letter on March 3, 1970, reading as follows:

> I am concerned with the repeated delay in payments to the undersigned under the captioned escrowed contract.

> I have been advised by the Hauglands that the remittance has not been made to them, and that they have on several occasions given explicit instructions that the payments, in accordance with the terms of Assignments executed by each of you, were to be made to the undersigned at the above address.

> I am hopeful that the past due February payment and future monthly payments will be made without the delays I have thus far experienced. I feel that it is reasonable that additional interest should be assessed on all past due payments. It appears to me that the scheduled deferment to the 15th of each month should be more than sufficient time past the beginning of the month to afford the obligors an opportunity to deposit the payments with the escrowee.

> I will expect additional interest to be paid on all payments not made by the end of the month in which payments accrue (on the 15th thereof).

> I trust that it will not be necessary that I take further action to enforce payment.

> Very truly yours,

> /s/ FRANK G. STINEMEYER

The above letter is, effect, a declaration by plaintiff that he will accept monthly payments without penalty if paid before the end of the month in which they fall due and will accept payments after the month in which they fall due if they include "additional interest."

By his inaction in the face of prior late payments, and by the position he took in the letter of March 3, plaintiff indicated that he would not insist upon timely payments of the installments due under the contract. It would be inequitable to permit the acceleration of the entire contract balance and a foreclosure based on that acceleration without first requiring that Wesco be given an opportunity to bring its payments up to date.

Wesco, by its tender into court, cured all existing delinquencies, and plaintiff was entitled to no more. The trial court properly dismissed the suit.

The decree of the trial court is affirmed.

NOTES & QUESTIONS

1. Waivers are closely related to the doctrine of modification of an executory contract. For example, in *Stinemeyer*, assume that the parties had met and discussed the problem of the late payments. In consideration of resolving their current dispute, the parties agree that late payments will be acceptable so long as such payments are no more than 30 days overdue. Does this agreement have a different legal impact on the ultimate outcome of a dispute between the parties than the waiver argument posited by the defendant if he is late with a payment?

2. Waiver generally permits greater flexibility in dealing with a party's conduct. In order to establish a modification, there must be assent *and* consideration. By contrast, a waiver arises *without* mutual assent or consideration.

3. Section 84(2) of the RESTATEMENT (SECOND) OF CONTRACTS provides that a previously waived conditional duty can be reinstated "before the time for the occurrence of the condition has expired" if "the condition is within the control of the promisee or a beneficiary" so long as the promisor notifies the promisee of his intention to reinstate the promise. The notification must be "received while there is still a reasonable time to cause the condition to occur under the antecedent terms or an extension given by the promisor, *and* reinstatement of the requirement of the condition is not unjust because of a material change of position by the promisee or beneficiary." *See also* U.C.C. § 2-209(5) ("A party who has made a waiver affecting an executory portion of the contract may retract the waiver by reasonable notification received by the other party that strict performance will be required of any term waived, unless the retraction would be unjust in view of a material change of position in reliance on the waiver."

4. Under Section 84 of the RESTATEMENT (SECOND) OF CONTRACTS, "a promise to perform all or part of a conditional duty under an antecedent contract in spite of the non-occurrence of the condition is binding whether the promise is made before or after the time for condition to occur. . . ." In *Mercedes-Benz* and *Stinemeyer* when were the promises to perform made? Which presents a stronger case for the application of the waiver, a pre-performance promise or a post-performance promise? Why?

5. In *Mercedes-Benz*, the purchaser had failed to make a single timely payment. What if the buyer had made two late payments? Does Mercedes-Benz have to give him notice before reasserting its right to timely payments? If yes, what kind of notice is required? How far in advance of the next payment date must such notice be given?

6. What steps could the parties in *Mercedes-Benz* and *Stinemeyer* have taken to make it clear that they were not waiving their right to future timely payments?

SECTION H

REMEDIES FOR BREACH

Introduction to Remedies

The law provides remedies in contract cases when there has been a breach, and sometimes when there is a threatened breach, of contract duties. Usually, of course, the party in breach is the one against whom a remedy is assessed. However, in some situations the party from whom a remedy may be available is not always the so-called breaching party, and the party to whom a remedy is available is not always the so-called innocent party. In addition, there are cases in which both parties may have defaulted; and cases in which a party entitled to a remedy is the one who initially failed to perform, or to perform in full.

There are three general categories of remedies available to an aggrieved party under contract law. Which one, or more, of the various types of remedies will be available in a particular contract case depends upon a number of factors. The first category of remedy we will study is the remedy known as *money damages*. The second is *restitutionary relief*, which ordinarily involves the payment of money but is different in nature and purpose from the money damage remedy. The third is *equitable relief*, which generally involves court orders directing parties to perform or refrain from performing particular acts.

CHAPTER 16

MONEY DAMAGES

Introduction to Damages

Money damages is the remedy most often sought and most often discussed in contract cases. It is one of the so-called common-law remedies, and is often referred to as "the remedy at law." Its primary purpose in contract cases is to provide compensation for an aggrieved party to, or intended beneficiary of, the contract when a breach of that contract by another party to the contract has caused or will cause loss (i.e., injury or damage).

Judges and scholars have developed and discussed various principles for determining the sum that properly compensates a plaintiff for losses proximately caused by a defendant's breach of contract. One formulation defines the aggrieved party's interests to be served by money damages into the *expectation* interest, the *reliance* interest, and the *restitution* interest, and divides the remedy into *expectation* damages, *reliance* damages, and *restitution* damages. Expectation damages provide compensation for the loss of value of the benefits originally expected to be received under the contract that has been breached. Thus, *expectation* damages are often also referred to as *benefit of the bargain damages*. *Reliance* damages provide compensation for losses sustained by reason of actions taken or withheld by the innocent party, including the expending or withholding of funds, in reasonable reliance that the contract will be performed. *Restitution* damages are generally viewed as compensation for benefits (e.g., money, property or services) already received by the breaching party from the innocent party pursuant to the contract. Another formulation suggests the applicability of *economic* theory in assessing the existence of loss and the quantum of money to compensate for that loss.

When there is a breach of contract that results in damage to the innocent party, courts are often required to draw the line between losses for which the breaching party should pay and losses that are too remote to be properly chargeable to the breaching party. Here, too, they utilize various concepts and formulations. One such formula defines and divides losses for which money damages are available from losses for which damages are withheld, by establishing a distinction between *general* damages and *special* damages. Under this formulation: *general* damages compensate for losses normally expected to arise by reason of this kind of breach of this kind of contract; and *special* damages, to cover further losses, are awarded only if, when the contract was made, the party at fault was aware of special circumstances and thus contemplated that such further losses could occur in the event of that contract breach. Another formulation distinguishes between *loss of value of the contract* damages, *incidental* damages, and *consequential* damages.

In the United States, rules governing the award of money damages in contract cases are generally based upon common law principles described in reported judicial decisions. The RESTATEMENT (SECOND) OF CONTRACTS (American Law Institute, 1979), which does not itself have the force of law, sets forth in RESTATEMENT chapter 16 (Remedies) many of the common law rules and principles about which the drafters have concluded there is general agreement under state law.

State and federal statutes and regulations, and international treaties, also establish rules and formulae by which to measure money damages in certain types of contract cases. Some examples: The Uniform Commercial Code (the U.C.C.), which has been enacted into law in almost all states of the United States, contains in Article 2 (Sales) a number of sections that provide rules by which to measure recoverable damages for breach of contracts that involve the sale and purchase of goods. *See* U.C.C., Art. 2, Part 7, §§ 2-701 to 2-725. The Convention on Contracts for the International Sale of Goods (CISG), approved at a United Nations Diplomatic Conference in 1980 and ratified by a number of countries including with certain allowable reservations the United States in 1986, contains in Chapter V, Sections II and III (Damages, Interest) articles that deal with the money damage remedy. Statutes and regulations that concern government procurement contracts and contracts financially supported with government funds, often define the circumstances in which money damages and liquidated damages are required.

In the international sphere, rules have been proposed for determining when and to what extent the money damages remedy applies in the full range of international commercial contract disputes. The UNIDROIT Principles of International Commercial Contracts, completed in 1994 as a project of the International Institute for the Unification of Private Law to serve as a model for agreements, for legislation, and to assist in dispute resolution, contains in Section 4 (Damages) a number of articles dealing with money damages.

Although many of the same general remedies rules are utilized in the wide variety of contract cases, a more complete understanding of how the rules actually operate can be gained by examining their application in different types of cases. Note both the similarities and the differences in the cases presented below.

A. EXPECTANCY (BENEFIT OF THE BARGAIN) DAMAGES

1. General Expectancy Damages Rules

HADLEY v. BAXENDALE
Court of Exchequer, 1854
9 Ex. 341, 156 Eng. Rep. 145

At the trial before Crompton, J., at the last Gloucester Assizes, it appeared that the plaintiffs carried on an extensive business as millers at Gloucester; and that, on the 11th of May, their mill was stopped by a breakage of the crank shaft by which the mill was worked. The steam-engine was manufactured by Messrs. Joyce & Co., the engineers, at Greenwich, and it became necessary to send the shaft as a pattern for a new one to Greenwich. The fracture was discovered on the 12th, and on the 13th, the plaintiffs sent one of their servants to the office of the defendants, who are the well known carriers trading under the name of Pickford & Co., for the purpose of having the shaft carried to Greenwich. The plaintiffs' servant told the clerk that the mill was stopped, and that the shaft must be sent immediately; and in answer to the inquiry when the shaft would be taken, the answer was, that if it was sent up by twelve o'clock any day, it would be delivered at Greenwich on the following day. On the following day the shaft was taken by the defendants, before noon, for the purpose of being conveyed to Greenwich, and the sum of 2£. 4s. was paid for its carriage for the whole distance; at the same time the defendants' clerk was told that a special entry, if required, should be made to hasten its delivery. The delivery of the shaft at Greenwich was delayed by some neglect; and the consequence was, that the plaintiffs did not receive the new shaft for several days after they would otherwise have done, and the working of their mill was thereby delayed and they thereby lost the profits they would otherwise have received.

On the part of the defendants, it was objected that these damages were too remote, and that the defendants were not liable with respect to them. The learned Judge left the case generally to the jury, who found a verdict with 25£, damages beyond the amount paid into Court.

Whateley, in last Michaelmas Term, obtained a rule nisi for a new trial, on the ground of misdirection.

Keating and Dowdeswell (Feb. 1) showed cause. The plaintiffs are entitled to the amount awarded by the jury as damages. These damages are not too remote, for they are not only the natural and necessary consequence of the defendants' default, but they are the only loss which the plaintiffs have actually sustained. The principle upon which damages are assessed is founded upon that of rendering compensation to the injured party. This important subject is ably treated in Sedgwick on the Measure of Damages. And this particular branch of it is discussed in the third chapter. . . . In. speaking of the rule respecting the breach of a contract to transport goods to a particular place, and in actions brought on agreements for the sale and delivery of chattels, the learned author lays it down, that, "In the former case, the difference in value between the price at the point where the goods are and the place where they were to be delivered, is taken as the measure of damages, which, in fact, amounts to an allowance of profits; and in the latter case, a similar result is had by the application of the rule, which gives the vendee the benefit of the rise of the market price." The several cases, English as well as American, are there collected and reviewed.

PARKE, B.
The sensible rule appears to be that which has been laid down in France, and which is declared in their code — Code Civil, liv. iii, tit, iii, sections 1149, 1150, 1151 — and which is thus translated in Sedgwick: "The damages due to the creditor consist in general of the loss that he has sustained, and the profit which he has been prevented from acquiring, subject to the modifications hereinafter contained. The debtor is only liable for the damages foreseen, or which might have been foreseen, at the time of the execution of the contract, when it is not owing to his fraud that the agreement has been violated. Even in the case of non-performance of the contract, resulting from the fraud of the debtor, the damages only comprise so much of the loss sustained by the creditor, and so much of the profit which he has been prevented from acquiring, as directly and immediately results from the nonperformance of the contract."

Keating and Dowdeswell. If that rule is to be adopted, there was ample evidence in the present case of the defendants' knowledge of such a state of things as would necessarily result in the damage the plaintiffs suffered through the defendants' default. . . .

ALDERSON, B. We think that there ought to be a new trial in this case; but, in so doing, we deem it to be expedient and necessary to state explicitly the rule which the Judge, at the next trial, ought, in our opinion, to direct the jury to be governed by when they estimate the damages.

It is, indeed, of the last importance that we should do this; for if the jury are left without any definite rule to guide them, it will, in such cases as these, manifestly lead to the greatest injustice. The Courts have done this on several occasions; and, in *Blake v. Midland Railway Company*, 21 L.J., Q.B. 237, the Court granted a new trial on this very ground, that the rule has not been definitely laid down to the jury by the learned judge at Nisi Prius.

"There are certain established rules," this Court says, in *Alder v. Keighley*, 15 M&W. 117, "according to which the jury ought to find." And the court, in that case, adds: "and here there is a clear rule, that the amount which would have been received if the contract had been kept, is the measure of damages if the contract is broken."

Now we think the proper rule in such a case as the present is this: Where two parties have made a contract which one of them has broken, the damages which the other party ought to receive in respect of such breach of contract should be such as may fairly and reasonably be considered either arising naturally, i.e., according to the usual course of things, from such breach of contract itself, or such as may reasonably be supposed to have been in the contemplation of both parties, at the time they made the contract, as the probable result of the breach of it. Now, if the special circumstances under which the contract was actually made were communicated by the plaintiffs to the defendants, and thus known to both parties, the damages resulting from the breach of such a contract, which they would reasonably contemplate, would be the amount of injury which would ordinarily follow from a breach of contract under these special circumstances so known and communicated. But, on the other hand, if these special circumstances were wholly unknown to the party breaking the contract, he, at the most, could only be supposed to have had in his contemplation the amount of injury which would arise generally, and in the great multitude of cases not affected by any special circumstances, from such a breach of contract. For, had the special circumstances been known, the parties might have specially provided for the breach of contract by special terms as to the damages in that case; and of this advantage it would be very unjust to deprive them. Now the above principles are those by which we think the jury ought to be guided in estimating the damages arising out of any breach of contract. It is said, that other cases such as breaches of contract in the nonpayment of money, or in the not making a good title to land, are to be treated as exceptions from this, and as governed by a conventional rule. But as, in such cases, both parties must be supposed to be cognizant of that well-known rule, these cases may, we think be more properly classed under the rule above enunciated as to cases under known special circumstances, because there both parties may reasonably be presumed to contemplate the estimation of the amount of damages according to the conventional rule. Now, in the present case, if we are to apply the principles above laid down, we find that the only circumstances here communicated by the plaintiffs to the defendants at the time the contract was made, were, that the article to be carried was the broken shaft of a mill, and that the plaintiffs were the millers of that mill. But how do these circumstances show reasonably that the profits of the mill must be stopped by an unreasonable delay in the delivery of the broken shaft by the carrier to the third person? Suppose the plaintiffs had another shaft in their possession put up or putting up at the time, and that they only wished to send back the broken shaft to the engineer who made it; it is clear that this would be quite consistent with the above circumstances, and yet the unreasonable delay in the delivery would have no effect upon the intermediate profits of the mill. Or, again, suppose, that, at the time of the delivery to the carrier, the machinery of the mill had been in other respects defective, then, also, the same results would follow. Here it is true that the shaft was actually sent back to serve as a model for a new one, and that the want of a new one was the only cause of the stoppage of the mill, and that the loss of profits really arose from not sending down the new shaft in proper time, and that this arose from the delay in delivering the broken one to serve as a model. But it is obvious that, in the great multitude of cases of millers sending off broken shafts to third persons by a carrier under ordinary circumstances, such consequences would not, in all probability, have occurred; and these special circumstances were here never communicated by the plaintiffs to the defendants.

It follows, therefore, that the loss of profits here cannot reasonably be considered such a consequence of the breach of contract as could have been fairly and reasonably contemplated by both the parties when they made this contract. For such loss would neither have flowed naturally from the breach of this contract in the great multitude of such cases occurring under ordinary circumstances, nor were the special circumstances, which, perhaps, would have made it a reasonable and natural consequence of such breach of contract, communicated to or known by the defendants. The Judge ought, therefore, to have told the jury that, upon the facts then before them, they ought not to take the loss of profits into consideration at all in estimating the damages. There must therefore be a new trial in this case.

Rule absolute.

NOTES

1. The rules in *Hadley v. Baxendale* have been widely accepted by courts and writers as a basis for distinguishing between losses due to contract breach that are recoverable and those that are not recoverable. They have been applied to many different kinds of contracts and to many different kinds of contract breaches.

2. A 2003 opinion from the U.S. Court of Appeals for the Fifth Circuit restates the distinction between general damages and special damages in words that remind of us those in the 1854 *Hadley* case. Dealing, as did *Hadley*, with damage issues in a carrier of goods case, the Fifth Circuit held: "That [plaintiff] actually incurred the disputed expenses is uncontroverted; the only issue is whether it is entitled to recover them as consequential, or 'special,' damages, which are those unusual or indirect costs that, although caused by the defendant's conduct in a literal sense, are beyond what one would reasonably expect to be the ordinary consequences of a breach. As a general rule, special damages are not recoverable in an action for breach of contract. Instead, to recover special damages, a plaintiff must establish that the defendant 'had notice of the special circumstances from which such damages would flow.' Accordingly, a carrier is liable for special damages caused by an unreasonable and unnecessary delay in the transportation of goods only if it has notice of the special circumstances leading to those

damages." *Tex. A&M Research Foundation v. Magna Transp., Inc.*, 338 F.3d 394, 404 (5th Cir. 2003). [footnotes omitted]

3. *See* WILLISTON ON CONTRACTS, § 64:12. Distinction between general and special damages. "[D]amages resulting from a breach of contract may be divided into those which flow naturally and usually from the breach itself, or general damages, and those which do not naturally and usually flow from such a breach, but did in this case, or special or consequential damages. As to the former, the parties need not actually have considered the possibility of their occurrence, as long as they may fairly be supposed to have considered them, while, as to the latter, to be recoverable, they must meet the requirements of causation, certainty, and foreseeability, that is, be such as may reasonably be supposed to have been in the contemplation of both parties at the time they made the contract. Stated another way, when a defendant has reason to know, before entering into the contract in question, of facts indicating that particular, though unusual, damages will follow or may follow the defendant's failure to perform its agreement, the defendant is liable for such damages."

4. *Practice Point*: In the United States today, statutes and administrative rules regulate the operations and responsibilities of most common carriers and contract carriers. The extent of liability of carriers for breach of contracts of carriage is often set forth in tariffs that carriers file pursuant to statute with state or federal agencies, and tariff terms that define and limit carrier liability may be incorporated by law into the contract of carriage. In all cases, but especially in cases involving regulated industries (such as the transportation industry), lawyers should not rely only on common-law cases as authority, but must also review provisions of applicable federal and state statutes and regulations, and even relevant international treaties and conventions. Some such provisions follow. (*Also see* Order of Civil Aeronautics Board, below, in the section on Limitation of Liability Laws.)

5. *Carriage by air*: So long as an airline ticket or airway bill received by a passenger or shipper contains a notice that states "The contract of carriage may incorporate terms and conditions by reference" and customer "may inspect the full text of each applicable incorporated term" at any of the carrier's airport locations or ticket sales offices, including the text of contract terms in published tariffs, federal regulation (14 C.F.R. § 221.107) does not require airline companies to expressly notify customers (except for foreign air travel) of contractual "Limits on the carrier's liability for personal injury or death of passengers . . . , and for loss, damage, or delay of goods and baggage, including fragile or perishable goods."

6. *Carriage by motor vehicle. Carriage generally*: Federal statute (49 U.S.C.A. § 14706) imposes liability on carriers that provide transportation or service subject to federal jurisdiction "for the actual loss or injury to the property" caused by the receiving carrier, delivering carrier, or other carrier over whose line the property is transported. *Carriers of passengers and baggage by motor vehicle:* Motor common carriers subject to federal law are allowed under 49 C.F.R. § 374.401 to publish tariff provisions limiting their liability for loss or damage to checked baggage when the limitation is $250 or greater per adult fare, and when the passenger for additional charge may declare and recover (up to actual loss) a value exceeding the limited amount in the event of loss or damage. *Carriage of household goods by motor vehicle:* Federal law (49 C.F.R. § 375.203) allows motor common carriers that transport household goods in interstate or foreign commerce to limit

their liability for loss or damage to $100 per pound, per article, for specific articles that exceed that value. If the shipper specifically notifies the carrier in writing that an identified article with a value greater than $100 per pound will be included in the shipment, the shipper will be entitled to full recovery up to the declared value of the article or articles, not to exceed the declared value of the entire shipment.

7. *Carriage by railroad*: Federal law (49 C.F.R. Pt. 1035, App. B) provides that "where a lower value than actual value has been represented in writing by the shipper or has been agreed upon in writing as the released value of the property as determined by the classification or tariffs upon which the rate is based, such lower value plus freight charges if paid shall be the maximum amount to be recovered, whether or not such loss or damage occurs from negligence."

HANDICAPPED CHILDREN'S EDUC. BD. v. LUKASZEWSKI
112 Wis. 2d 197, 332 N.W.2d 774 (1983)

CALLOW, Justice:

This review arises out of an unpublished decision of the court of appeals which affirmed in part and reversed in part a judgment of the Ozaukee county circuit court, Judge Warren A. Grady.

In January of 1978 the Handicapped Children's Education Board (the Board) hired Elaine Lukaszewski to serve as a speech and language therapist for the spring term. Lukaszewski was assigned to the Lightfoot School in Sheboygan Falls which was approximately 45 miles from her home in Mequon. Rather than move, she commuted to work each day. During the 1978 spring term, the Board offered Lukaszewski a contract to continue in her present position at Lightfoot School for the 1978-79 school year. The contract called for an annual salary of $10,760. Lukaszewski accepted.

In August of 1978, prior to the beginning of the school year, Lukaszewski was offered a position by the Wee Care Day Care Center which was located not far from her home in Mequon. The job paid an annual salary of $13,000. After deciding to accept this offer, Lukaszewski notified Thomas Morrelle, the Board's director of special education, that she intended to resign from her position at the Lightfoot School. Morrelle told her to submit a letter of resignation for consideration by the Board. She did so, and the matter was discussed at a meeting of the Board on August 21, 1978. The Board refused to release Lukaszewski from her contract. On August 24, 1978, the Board's attorney sent a letter to Lukaszewski directing her to return to work. The attorney sent a second letter to the Wee Care Day Care Center stating that the Board would take legal action if the Center interfered with Lukaszewski's performance of her contractual obligations at the Lightfoot School. A copy of this letter was sent to the Department of Public Instruction.

Lukaszewski left the Wee Care Day Care Center and returned to Lightfoot School for the 1978 fall term. She resented the actions of the Board, however, and retained misgivings about her job. On September 8, 1978, she discussed her feelings with Morrelle. After this meeting Lukaszewski felt quite upset about the situation. She called her doctor to make an appointment for that afternoon and subsequently left the school.

Dr. Ashok Chatterjee examined Lukaszewski and found her blood pressure to be high. Lukaszewski asked Dr. Chatterjee to write a letter explaining his medical findings and the advice he had given her. In a letter dated September 11, 1978, Dr. Chatterjee indicated that Lukaszewski had a hypertension problem dating back to 1976. He reported that on the day he examined Lukaszewski she appeared agitated, nervous, and had blood pressure readings up to 180/100. It was his opinion that, although she took hypotensive drugs, her medical condition would not improve unless the situation which caused the problem was removed. He further opined that it would be dangerous for her to drive long distances in her agitated state.

Lukaszewski did not return to work after leaving on September 8, 1978. She submitted a letter of resignation dated September 13, 1978, in which she wrote: "I enclose a copy of the doctor's statement concerning my health. On the basis of it, I must resign. I am unwilling to jeopardize my health and I am also unwilling to become involved in an accident. For these reasons, I tender my resignation." A short time later Lukaszewski reapplied for and obtained employment at the Wee Care Day Care Center.

After Lukaszewski left, the Board immediately began looking for a replacement. Only one qualified person applied for the position. Although this applicant had less of an educational background than Lukaszewski, she had more teaching experience. Under the salary schedule agreed upon by the Board and the teachers' union, this applicant would have to be paid $1,026.64 more per year than Lukaszewski. Having no alternative, the Board hired the applicant at the higher salary.

In December of 1978 the Board initiated an action against Lukaszewski for breach of contract. The Board alleged that, as a result of the breach, it suffered damage in the amount of the additional compensation it was required to pay Lukaszewski's replacement for the 1978-79 school year ($1,026.64). A trial was held before the court. The trial court ruled that Lukaszewski had breached her contract and awarded the Board $1,249.14 in damages ($1,026.64 for breach of contract and $222.50 for costs).

Lukaszewski appealed. The court of appeals affirmed the circuit court's determination that Lukaszewski breached her contract. However, the appellate court reversed the circuit court's damage award, reasoning that, although the Board had to pay more for Lukaszewski's replacement, by its own standards it obtained a proportionately more valuable teacher. Therefore, the court of appeals held that the Board suffered no damage from the breach. We granted the Board's petition for review.

There are two issues presented on this review: (1) whether Lukaszewski breached her employment contract with the Board; and (2) if she did breach her contract, whether the Board suffered recoverable damages therefrom. . . .

II.

This court has long held that an employer may recover damages from an employee who has failed to perform an employment contract. *Walsh v. Fisher*, 102 Wis. 172, 179, 78 N.W. 437 (1899). Damages in breach of contract cases are ordinarily measured by the expectations of the parties. The nonbreaching party is entitled to full compensation for the loss of his or her bargain — that is, losses necessarily flowing from the breach which are proven to a reasonable certainty and were within contemplation of the parties when the contract was made. *Lommen v. Danaher*, 165 Wis. 15, 19, 161 N.W. 14 (1917); *Pleasure Time, Inc. v. Kuss*, 78 Wis. 2d 373, 385, 254 N.W.2d 463 (1977). Thus damages for breach of an employment contract include the cost of obtaining other services equivalent to that promised but not performed, plus any foreseeable consequential damages. *Roth v. Speck*, 126 A.2d 153, 155 (D.C. 1956); Annot., 61 A.L.R.2d 1008 (1958).

In the instant case it is undisputed that, as a result of the breach, the Board hired a replacement at a salary exceeding what it had agreed to pay Lukaszewski. There is no question that this additional cost ($1,026.64) necessarily flowed from the breach and was within the contemplation of the parties when the contract was made. Lukaszewski argues and the court of appeals held, however, that the Board was not damaged by this expense. The amount a teacher is paid is determined by a salary schedule agreed upon by the teachers' union and the Board. The more education and experience a teacher has the greater her salary will be. Presumably, then, the amount of compensation a teacher receives reflects her value to the Board. Lukaszewski argues that the Board suffered no net loss because, while it had to pay more for the replacement, it received the services of a proportionately more valuable teacher. Accordingly, she maintains that the Board is not entitled to damages because an award would place it in a better position than if the contract had been performed.[1]

We disagree. Lukaszewski and the court of appeals improperly focus on the objective value of the services the Board received rather than that for which it had bargained. Damages for breach of contract are measured by the expectations of the parties. The Board expected to receive the services of a speech therapist with Lukaszewski's education and experience at the salary agreed upon. It neither expected nor wanted a more experienced therapist who had to be paid an additional $1,026.64 per year. Lukaszewski's breach forced the Board to hire the replacement and, in turn, to pay a higher salary. Therefore, the Board lost the benefit of its bargain. Any additional value the Board may have received from the replacement's greater experience was imposed upon it and thus cannot be characterized as a benefit. We conclude that the Board suffered damages for the loss of its bargain in the amount of additional compensation it was required to pay Lukaszewski's replacement.

This is not to say that an employer who is injured by an employee's breach of contract is free to hire the most qualified and expensive replacement and then recover the difference between the salary paid and the contract salary. An injured party must take all reasonable steps to mitigate damages. *Kuhlman, Inc. v. G. Heileman Brewing Co.*, 83 Wis. 2d 749, 752, 266 N.W.2d 382 (1978). Therefore, the employer must attempt to obtain equivalent services at the lowest possible cost. In the instant case the Board acted reasonably in hiring Lukaszewski's replacement even though she commanded a higher salary. Upon Lukaszewski's breach, the Board immediately took steps to locate a replacement. Only one qualified person applied for the position. Having no alternative, the Board hired this applicant. Thus the Board properly mitigated its damages by hiring the least expensive, qualified replacement available.

---

[1] [2] We have held that an injured party is not entitled to be placed in a better position because of a breach of contract. Dehnart v. Waukesha Brewing Co., 21 Wis. 2d 583, 595-96, 124 N.W.2d 664 (1963); Pleasure Time, Inc. v. Kuss, 78 Wis. 2d 373, 385, 254 N.W.2d 463 (1977). However, because we find that the Board was damaged by Lukaszewski's breach, this problem does not arise.

We hold that the Board is entitled to have the benefit of its bargain restored. Therefore, we reverse that portion of the court of appeals' decision which reversed the trial court's damage award.

The decision of the court of appeals is affirmed in part and reversed in part.

DAY, JUSTICE (dissenting).

I dissent. The majority opinion correctly states, "The only question is whether her resignation is somehow justified." I would hold that it was. . . .

I would reverse the court of appeals decision that held she breached her contract.

Because I would hold that on this record there was no breach, I would not reach the damage question.

NOTE

Assume that the school board in the *Handicapped Children's Educ. Bd.* case had lost $1,000 in state funding of its special education program for the period that the program ceased to function while the school searched for a replacement special education teacher. Consider and discuss whether the school board would have the right to recover that $1,000 amount as part of its claim for damages. How might the court rule if the *Hadley* distinction between *general* damages and *special* damages is included in arguments on that question?

SPANG INDUS., INC., FT. PITT BRIDGE DIV. v. AETNA CASUALTY & SURETY CO.
512 F.2d 365 (2d Cir. 1975)

MULLIGAN, Circuit Judge: Torrington Construction Co., Inc. (Torrington), a Connecticut corporation, was the successful bidder with the New York State Department of Transportation for a highway reconstruction contract . . . . Before submitting its bid, Torrington received an oral quotation from Spang Industries, Inc., Fort Pitt Bridge Division (Fort Pitt), a Pennsylvania corporation, for the fabrication, furnishing and erection of some 240 tons of structural steel at a unit price of 27.5 cents per pound; . . . to be utilized to construct a 270 foot long, double span bridge over the Battenkill River as part of the highway reconstruction. The quotation was confirmed in a letter from Fort Pitt to Torrington dated September 5, 1969, which stated in part: "Delivery to be mutually agreed upon." On November 3, 1969, Torrington, in response to a request from Fort Pitt, advised that its requirements for delivery and erection of the steel would be late June, 1970. On November 12, 1969, Fort Pitt notified Torrington that it was tentatively scheduling delivery in accordance with these requirements. On January 7, 1970, Fort Pitt wrote to Torrington asking if the June, 1970 erection date was still valid; Torrington responded affirmatively on January 13, 1970. However, on January 29, 1970, Fort Pitt advised that it was engaged in an extensive expansion program and that "[d]ue to unforeseen delays caused by weather, deliveries from suppliers, etc., it is our opinion that the June date cannot be met." On February 2, 1970, Torrington sent a letter requesting that Fort Pitt give a delivery date and, receiving no response, wrote again on May 12, 1970 requesting a written confirmation of the date of delivery and threatening to cancel out if the date was not reasonably close to the originally scheduled date. On May 20, 1970, Fort Pitt responded and promised that the structural steel would be shipped early in August, 1970.

Although some 25 tons of small steel parts were shipped on August 21, 1970, the first girders and other heavy structural steel were not shipped until August 24, 26, 27, 31 and September 2 and 4, 1970. Fort Pitt had subcontracted the unloading and erection of the steel to Syracuse Rigging Co. but neglected to advise it of the August 21st shipment. The steel began to arrive at the railhead in Shushan, New York about September 1st and the railroad demanded immediate unloading. Torrington was therefore compelled to do the unloading itself until Syracuse Rigging arrived on September 8, 1970. Not until September 16 was there enough steel delivered to the job site to permit Syracuse to commence erection. The work was completed on October 8, 1970 and the bridge was ready to receive its concrete deck on October 28, 1970. Because of contract specifications set by the State requiring that concrete be poured at temperatures of 40° Fahrenheit and above, Torrington had to get special permission from the State's supervising engineer to pour the concrete on October 28, 1970, when the temperature was at 32°.

Since the job site was in northern New York near the Vermont border and the danger of freezing temperatures was imminent, the pouring of the concrete was performed on a crash basis in one day, until 1 a.m. the following morning, which entailed extra costs for Torrington in the form of overtime pay, extra equipment and the protection of the concrete during the pouring process.

[Subcontractor Fort Pitt filed suit for the unpaid balance of the price to be paid under the subcontract. Thereafter general contractor Torrington sued Fort Pitt, seeking damages of $23,290.81 caused by Fort Pitt's delay in furnishing the steel. The U.S. District Court for the Northern District of N.Y., in which the cases were ultimately consolidated and tried, entered findings of fact and conclusions of law holding that Fort Pitt had breached its contract by its delayed delivery, for which Torrington was entitled to damages in the amount of $7,653.57; and that Fort Pitt was entitled to recover from Torrington the sum of $23,290.12, which was the balance due on its contract price plus interest, less the $7,653.57 damages sustained by Torrington. Judgment was entered for Fort Pitt against Torrington and Aetna Casualty and Surety Co. (the latter having posted a general contractor's labor and material bond) on their joint and several liability for $15,636.55 with interest from November 12, 1970.]

Fort Pitt on this appeal does not take issue with any of the findings of fact of the court below but contends that the recovery by Torrington of its increased expenses constitutes special damages which were not reasonably within the contemplation of the parties when they entered into the contract.

I.

While the damages awarded Torrington are relatively modest ($7,653.57) in comparison with the subcontract price ($132,274.37), Fort Pitt urges that an affirmance of the award will do violence to the rule of *Hadley v. Baxendale*, 156 Eng. Rep. 145 (Ex. 1854), and create a precedent which will have a severe impact on the business of all subcontractors and suppliers.

While it is evident that the function of the award of damages for a breach of contract is to put the plaintiff in the same position he would have been in had there been no breach, *Hadley v. Baxendale* limits the recovery to those injuries which the parties could reasonably have anticipated at the time the contract was entered into. If the damages suffered do not usually flow from the breach, then it must be established that the special circumstances giving rise to them should reasonably have been anticipated at the time the contract was made.[2]

There can be no question but that *Hadley v. Baxendale* represents the law in New York and in the United States generally. . . . There is no dispute between the parties on this appeal as to the continuing viability of Hadley v. Baxendale and its formulation of the rule respecting special damages, and this court has no intention of challenging or questioning its principles, which Chief Judge Cardozo characterized to be, at least in some application, "tantamount to a rule of property," *Kerr S.S. Co. v. Radio Corporation of America*, 245 N.Y. 284, 291, 157 N.E. 140, 142 (1927).

The gist of Fort Pitt's argument is that, when it entered into the subcontract to fabricate, furnish and erect the steel in September, 1969, it had received a copy of the specifications which indicated that the total work was to be completed by December 15, 1971. It could not reasonably have anticipated that Torrington would so expedite the work (which was accepted by the State on January 21, 1971) that steel delivery would be called for in 1970 rather than 1971. Whatever knowledge Fort Pitt received after the contract was entered into, it argues, cannot expand its liability, since it is essential under Hadley v. Baxendale and its Yankee progeny that the notice of the facts which would give rise to special damages in case of breach be given at or before the time the contract was made. The principle urged cannot be disputed. . . . We do not, however, agree that any violence to the doctrine was done here.

Fort Pitt also knew from the same specifications that Torrington was to commence the work on October 1, 1969. The Fort Pitt letter of September 5, 1969, which constitutes the agreement between the parties, specifically provides: "Delivery to be mutually agreed upon." On November 3, 1969, Torrington, responding to Fort Pitt's inquiry, gave "late June 1970" as its required delivery date and, on November 12, 1969, Fort Pitt stated that it was tentatively scheduling delivery for that time. Thus, at the time when the parties, pursuant to their initial agreement, fixed the date for performance which is crucial here, Fort Pitt knew

---

[2] [2] The rule of *Hadley v. Baxendale* was stated by Alderson, B., as follows:

> Where two parties have made a contract which one of them has broken, the damages which the other party ought to receive in respect of such breach of contract should be such as may fairly and reasonably be considered either arising naturally, i.e., according to the usual course of things, from such breach of contract itself, or such as may reasonably be supposed to have been in the contemplation of both parties, at the time they made the contract, as the probable result of the breach of it. Now, if the special circumstances under which the contract was actually made were communicated by the plaintiffs to the defendants, and thus known to both parties, the damages resulting from the breach of such a contract, which they would reasonably contemplate, would be the amount of injury which would ordinarily follow from a breach of contract under these special circumstances so known and communicated. But, on the other hand, if these special circumstances were wholly unknown to the party breaking the contract, he, at the most, could only be supposed to have had in his contemplation the amount of injury which would arise generally, and in the great multitude of cases not affected by any special circumstances, from such a breach of contract.

156 Eng. Rep. at 151.

that a June, 1970 delivery was required. It would be a strained and unpalatable interpretation of *Hadley v. Baxendale* to now hold that, although the parties left to further agreement the time for delivery, the supplier could reasonably rely upon a 1971 delivery date rather than one the parties later fixed. The behavior of Fort Pitt was totally inconsistent with the posture it now assumes. In November, 1969, it did not quarrel with the date set or seek to avoid the contract. It was not until late January, 1970 that Fort Pitt advised Torrington that, due to unforeseen delays and its expansion program, it could not meet the June date. None of its reasons for late delivery was deemed excusable according to the findings below, and this conclusion is not challenged here. It was not until five months later, on May 20, 1970, after Torrington had threatened to cancel, that Fort Pitt set another date for delivery (early August, 1970) which it again failed to meet, as was found below and not disputed on this appeal.

We conclude that, when the parties entered into a contract which, by its terms, provides that the time of performance is to be fixed at a later date, the knowledge of the consequences of a failure to perform is to be imputed to the defaulting party as of the time the parties agreed upon the date of performance. This comports, in our view, with both the logic and the spirit of Hadley v. Baxendale. Whether the agreement was initially valid despite its indefiniteness or only became valid when a material term was agreed upon is not relevant. At the time Fort Pitt did become committed to a delivery date, it was aware that a June, 1970 performance was required by virtue of its own acceptance. There was no unilateral distortion of the agreement rendering Fort Pitt liable to an extent not theretofore contemplated.

Having proceeded thus far, we do not think it follows automatically that Torrington is entitled to recover the damages it seeks here; further consideration of the facts before us is warranted. Fort Pitt maintains that, under the *Hadley v. Baxendale* rubric, the damages flowing from its conceded breach are "special" or "consequential" and were not reasonably to be contemplated by the parties. Since Torrington has not proved any "general" or "direct" damages, Fort Pitt urges that the contractor is entitled to nothing. We cannot agree. It is commonplace that parties to a contract normally address themselves to its performance and not to its breach or the consequences that will ensue if there is a default. . . . As the New York Court of Appeals long ago stated: "[A] more precise statement of this rule is, that a party is liable for all the direct damages which both parties to the contract would have contemplated as flowing from its breach, if at the time they entered into it they had bestowed proper attention upon the subject, and had been fully informed of the facts. [This] may properly be called the fiction of law. . . ." *Leonard v. New York, Albany & Buffalo Electro-Magnetic Telegraph Co.*, 41 N.Y. 544, 567 (1870).[3]

It is also pertinent to note that the rule does not require that the direct damages must necessarily follow, but only that they are likely to follow; as Lord Justice Asquith commented in *Victoria Laundry, Ltd. v. Newman Industries, Ltd.*, (1949) 2 K.B. 528, 540, are they "on the cards"? We believe there that the damages sought to be recovered were also "in the cards."

---

[3] [3] A second fiction, added as an embellishment to *Hadley v. Baxendale* by Mr. Justice Holmes as federal common law in *Globe Ref.. Co. v. Landa Cotton Oil Co.*, 190 U.S. 540, 23 S. Ct. 754, 47 L. Ed. 1171 (1903), would require not only knowledge of the special circumstances but a tacit agreement on the part of the party sought to be charged to accept the liability imposed by the notice. This second test has generally been rejected by the courts and commentators.

It must be taken as a reasonable assumption that, when the delivery date of June, 1970 was set, Torrington planned the bridge erection within a reasonable time thereafter. It is normal construction procedure that the erection of the steel girders would be followed by the installation of a poured concrete platform and whatever railings or super-structure the platform would require. Fort Pitt was an experienced bridge fabricator supplying contractors and the sequence of the work is hardly arcane. Moreover, any delay beyond June or August would assuredly have jeopardized the pouring of the concrete and have forced the postponement of the work until the spring. The work here, as was well known to Fort Pitt, was to be performed in northern New York near the Vermont border. The court below found that continuing freezing weather would have forced the pouring to be delayed until June, 1971.[4] Had Torrington refused delivery or had it been compelled to delay the completion of the work until the spring of 1971, the potential damage claim would have been substantial. Instead, in a good faith effort to mitigate damages, Torrington embarked upon the crash program we have described. It appears to us that this eventuality should have reasonably been anticipated by Fort Pitt as it was experienced in the trade and was supplying bridge steel in northern climes on a project requiring a concrete roadway.

Torrington's recovery under the circumstances is not substantial or cataclysmic from Fort Pitt's point of view. It represents the expenses of unloading steel from the gondola due to Fort Pitt's admitted failure to notify its erection subcontractor, Syracuse Rigging, that the steel had been shipped, plus the costs of premium time, extra equipment and the cost of protecting the work, all occasioned by the realities Torrington faced in the wake of Fort Pitt's breach. In fact, Torrington's original claim of $23,290.81 was whittled down by the court below because of Torrington's failure to establish that its supervisory costs, overhead and certain equipment costs were directly attributable to the delay in delivery of the steel.

Professor Williston has commented: The true reason why notice to the defendant of the plaintiff's special circumstances is important is because, just as a court of equity under circumstances of hardship arising after the formation of a contract may deny specific performance, so a court of law may deny damages for unusual consequences where the defendant was not aware when he entered into the contract *how serious an injury would result from its breach.* . . . (emphasis added [by the court]).

In this case, serious or catastrophic injury was avoided by prompt, effective and reasonable mitigation at modest cost.[5] Had Torrington not acted, had it been forced to wait until the following spring to complete the entire job and then sued to recover the profits it would have made had there been performance by Fort Pitt according to the terms of its agreement, then we might well have an approximate setting for a classical Hadley v. Baxendale controversy. As this case comes to us, it hardly presents that situation. We therefore affirm the judgment below permitting Torrington to offset its damages against the contract price.

---

[4] [6] The contract specifications required that concrete be poured only when the temperature was at 40° Fahrenheit and above. The president of Fort Pitt testified at trial that, before his company quotes a price for steel to a general contractor, it obtains the state's specifications on the job in question, and that that was done in this case.

[5] [7] It is well understood that expenses incurred in a reasonable effort, whether successful or not, to avoid harm that the defendant had reason to foresee as a probable result of the breach when the contract was made may be recovered as an item of damage flowing from the breach.

II.

The only other question raised on this appeal involves the computation of interest. The total contract price due to Fort Pitt was $132,274.73, payable 30 days from the date of invoice. The invoices rendered here required payment by Torrington on October 8, November 12 and December 30, 1970. Torrington made a partial payment of $60,000 on December 11, 1970 but refused to pay the balance. After Fort Pitt commenced suit against Aetna for the balance due plus interest, Torrington paid $20,000 on February 4, 1972 and $28,983.92 on September 7, 1972. There is no question but that under the law of New York Fort Pitt is entitled to interest for the sums due under the subcontract. N.Y.C.P.L.R. § 5001(a); *United States v. Walsh*, 240 F. Supp. 1019 (N.D.N.Y. 1965). The court below, by order dated December 12, 1973, denied Fort Pitt's motion to amend the judgment to reflect its entitlement to interest on late payments made in February and September, 1972, on the theory that this interest had not been demanded and that acceptance of partial payments without protest barred the interest award. Since interest was recoverable as a matter of law and since Fort Pitt had demanded interest in its counterclaim to Torrington's complaint, the right to interest cannot be considered to have been waived. *Crane v. Craig*, 230 N.Y. 452, 130 N.E. 609 (1921), relied upon below, held that, where interest is not payable by the terms of the contract but is allowable as a mere incident to it, receipt of the principal bars a subsequent claim for interest since the debt is extinguished by the payment of the principal. But here the payment was partial and did not extinguish the debt. The proper rule, set forth by this court in *Ohio Savings Bank & Trust Co. v. Willys Corp.*, 8 F.2d 463, 466-67 (1925) (relying upon, inter alia, New York cases), is that when partial payments have been made, the payment must be applied first to the interest then due, with the surplus discharging the principal pro tanto.

It seems to be conceded that the court below was in error in calculating the rate of interest at 7½% from November 12, 1970. By amendment of N.Y.C.P.L.R. § 5004 effective September 1, 1972, the rate was changed to 6%. Thus, the interest should be computed at these rates for the relevant periods.

We therefore remand this case to the district court to compute the interest in accordance with this opinion and further to enter amended and separate judgments against Torrington and Aetna.

Affirmed in part, reversed in part and remanded. No costs.

NOTES

1. States vary in their rules on the availability of prejudgment interest in actions at law. Two examples: In *Spang Industries* the Second Circuit Court of Appeals held that New York law (CPLR § 5001(a)) entitled Fort Pitt to prejudgment interest on the unpaid portion of sums due it under its subcontract. And in 2006 the Illinois Supreme Court, in *Tri-G, Inc. v. Burke, Bosselman & Weaver*, 222 Ill. 2d 218, 856 N.E.2d 389, a legal professional negligence action, held that in actions entirely at law, Illinois allows prejudgment interest only where authorized by agreement of the parties or by statute and that no such agreement or statute applied in that case; and further cited with approval a ruling that "Illinois courts decline to apply the rule governing equitable awards of prejudgment interest to cases at law."

2. *Practice Point*: In the principal case some payments pursuant to the contract were received by Fort Pitt, apparently without the recipient or counsel stating that the amounts were received without waiver of or prejudice to remaining claims, including claims for the balance due and for prejudgment interest. Because of the possibility that such sums may in certain circumstances be deemed to preclude further or other recovery by the recipient, an attorney will seriously consider the value of providing written receipts that identify the nature and allocation of sums so received and that deny any intent or effect to waive, prejudice, or preclude claims that remain.

NATIVE ALASKAN RECLAMATION AND PEST CONTROL, INC. v. UNITED BANK ALASKA
685 P.2d 1211 (1984)

[This was a suit against the UBA bank for breach of a loan agreement to provide funds to finance plaintiff's plan to purchase surplus military aircraft and convert them for fire fighting purposes. The trial court held that the bank was in breach, allowed plaintiff NAR-PC mitigation damages ($86,705.97), but refused to allow either expectation damages ($2,385,605) or reliance damages ($97,344.22). Its refusal to allow those damages was on the ground that the bank did not have reason to foresee such consequences as a probable result of its future refusal to perform, since the bank when issuing its letter of commitment believed that plaintiff could obtain replacement loans if plaintiff sought them in the event of the bank's nonperformance. Remanding for reconsideration of plaintiff's expectation damages, the Alaska Supreme Court approved trial court findings that the bank had breached the agreement by refusing to disburse funds under a letter of credit, that plaintiff could have successfully completed the project and paid off the loan had the bank not breached, that plaintiff acted reasonably in its failed efforts to mitigate, and that plaintiff presented sufficiently certain evidence of market value of the aircraft to be delivered. The Court's discussion is particularly instructive concerning the recoverability of reliance or expectation damages if at the time of contracting plaintiff's inability to obtain replacement financing and the resultant loss of the project were foreseeable as a probable result of the bank's failure to perform.]

BURKE, Chief Justice: . . . We must first ascertain the appropriate standard of review. NAR-PC argues that since the underlying facts are not in dispute, the trial court's ruling on foreseeability is a question of law, not fact. However, 5 A. Corbin, CORBIN ON CONTRACTS § 1012, at 89 (1964) provides: The question whether or not the defendant did in fact foresee, or had reason to foresee, the injury that the plaintiff has suffered is a question of fact for the jury. . . . *E.g., Continental Plants Corp. v. Measured Marketing Service, Inc.*, 274 Or. 621, 547 P.2d 1368, 1372 (1976). We will therefore apply the "clearly erroneous" standard of review.

Alaska's law on foreseeability of damages is somewhat confused. In *Skagway City School Board v. Davis*, 543 P.2d 218 (Alaska 1975), the court quoted the *Hadley v. Baxendale* test. It then noted that the test had undergone "some refinement at the hand of Mr. Justice Holmes" in *Globe Refining Co. v. Landa Cotton Oil Co.*, 190 U.S. 540, 23 S. Ct. 754, 47 L. Ed. 1171 (1903). In *Globe*, Justice Holmes, speaking for the court, stated:

> It is true that, as people when contracting contemplate performance, not breach, they commonly say little or nothing as to what shall happen in the

latter event, and the common rules have been worked out by common sense, which has established what the parties probably would have said if they had spoken about the matter. But a man never can be absolutely certain of performing any contract when the time of performance arrives, and, in many cases, he obviously is taking the risk of an event which is wholly, or to an appreciable extent, beyond his control. The extent of liability in such cases is likely to be within his contemplation, and, whether it is or not, should be worked out on terms which it fairly may be presumed he would have assented to if they had been presented to his mind . . . We have to consider, therefore, what the plaintiff would have been entitled to recover . . . and that depends on what liability the defendant fairly may be supposed to have assumed consciously, or to have warranted the plaintiff reasonably to suppose that it assumed, when the contract was made.

Globe, 190 U.S. at 543-44, 23 S. Ct. at 755-56, 47 L. Ed. at 1173. This language is commonly referred to as the "tacit or presumed agreement" test of foreseeability of damages.

In a later case, *Arctic Contractors, Inc. v. State*, 564 P.2d 30, 44-45 (Alaska 1977), this court, *in dicta*, recommended the *Hadley* rule, but mentioned Justice Holmes' "tacit agreement" test in a footnote. In *City of Whittier v. Whittier Fuel & Marine Corp.*, 577 P.2d 216, 220 (Alaska 1978), after stating that the *Hadley v. Baxendale* rule is "the applicable rule in Alaska," we used language more closely aligned with Justice Holmes' "tacit agreement" test.

The "tacit agreement" test has come under attack in modern times. RESTATEMENT (SECOND) OF CONTRACTS section 351 comment a, at 135-36 (1981) states: "Furthermore, the party in breach need not have made a 'tacit agreement' to be liable for the loss. Nor must he have had the loss in mind when making the contract, for the test is an objective one based on what he had reason to foresee." Moreover, 5 A. Corbin, CORBIN ON CONTRACTS § 1009, at 77 (1964) provides: "The existing rule requires only reason to foresee, not actual foresight. It does not require that the defendant should have had the resulting injury actually in contemplation *or should have promised either impliedly or expressly to pay therefor in case of breach*." (Emphasis [by the court]). To the extent that prior Alaska case law suggests adoption of the "tacit agreement" test, it is expressly disapproved. We find the RESTATEMENT test to be the clearest expression of Alaska's test of foreseeability of damages.

RESTATEMENT (SECOND) OF CONTRACTS section 351, at 135 (1981) provides:

(1) Damages are not recoverable for loss that the party in breach did not have reason to foresee as a probable result of the breach when the contract was made.

(2) Loss may be foreseeable as a probable result of a breach because it follows from the breach (a) in the ordinary course of events, or (b) as a result of special circumstances, beyond the ordinary course of events, that the party in breach had reason to know.[6]

---

[6] [5] This rule is applicable to breach of a contract to lend money. Comment e to § 351 states: "Because credit is so widely available, a lender often has no reason to foresee at the time the contract is made that the borrower will be unable to make substitute arrangements in the event of breach. . . . In most cases, then, the lender's liability will be limited to the relatively small additional amount that it would ordinarily cost to get a similar loan from another lender. However, in the less common situation

The trial court found that damages which would have flowed from UBA's repudiation of the loan "in the ordinary course of events" were limited to mitigation damages, i.e., the expenses of (1) obtaining a replacement loan, (2) higher interest charges on the replacement loan, (3) demobilizing the project and preserving the aircraft while seeking the replacement loan, and (4) remobilizing the project after the replacement loans were obtained. The court found that NAR-PC reasonably incurred expenses of this type worth $86,705.97. . . .

It is a close question whether or not the trial court clearly erred in concluding that it was not foreseeable that NAR-PC would be unable to obtain replacement financing. . . .

We find the trial court's ruling on the foreseeability issue clearly erroneous. . . . The actions and testimony of UBA's own officers amply demonstrate that it was foreseeable that a reasonable lender would not have issued a replacement loan in reliance upon the planes as collateral and Risley's [NAR-PC's executive officer and principal shareholder] personal statement of self-worth.

On remand, the trial court should reconsider its award of damages in light of RESTATEMENT (SECOND) OF CONTRACTS section 351(3) at 135 (1981).[7]

E. CERTAINTY OF DAMAGES

The trial court found that NAR-PC's expectation damages consisted of the net value of the eleven S-2's, minus the total of the interest payments that would have been incurred as a result of the UBA S-2 loan and the alternative long term financing. The court found this figure to be $2,385,605.[8] UBA attacks this finding on several grounds.

UBA first argues that the evidence regarding the plane's fair market value was insufficient, unreliable and speculative. . . . UBA's argument as to the lower court's finding on fair market value is without merit. The record clearly supports the trial court's finding as to market value.

UBA next asserts that the lower court's finding of a cost of $139,149.54 for purchase, conversion and delivery of each plane was speculative and, therefore, clearly erroneous. . . .

---

in which the lender has reason to foresee that the borrower will be unable to borrow elsewhere or will be delayed in borrowing elsewhere, the lender may be liable for much heavier damages based on the borrower's inability to take advantage of a specific opportunity . . . , his having to postpone or abandon a profitable project . . . , or his forfeiture of security for failure to make prompt payment. . . ." *See also* 5 A. Corbin, CORBIN ON CONTRACTS § 1078, at 447 (1964).

[7] [6] RESTATEMENT (SECOND) OF CONTRACTS section 351(3) at 135 (1981) provides: "A court may limit damages for foreseeable loss by excluding recovery for loss of profits, by allowing recovery only for loss incurred in reliance, or otherwise if it concludes that in the circumstances justice so requires in order to avoid disproportionate compensation." We note, however, that the mere fact that UBA only stood to gain interest payments on its loan under the contract, i.e. that it would not receive any profits of the S-2 purchase venture, is not sufficient reason to warrant a limitation on NAR-PC's damages recovery. We leave for the trial court's determination whether any other factors may warrant application of a disproportionality theory. *See* RESTATEMENT (SECOND) OF CONTRACTS § 351(3) comment f (1981).

[8] [7] The trial court found that "the fair market value of the S-2's, after being converted, rendered airworthy and delivered to the United States, would have been $404,750.00 each." Cost of purchase, conversion, and delivery of each plane was found to be $139,149.54, leaving a net value of $265,600.46 per plane. Total loss of value to NAR-PC on all eleven S-2's was found to be $2,921,605.

RESTATEMENT (SECOND) OF CONTRACTS section 352, at 144 (1981) provides:

> Damages are not recoverable for loss beyond an amount that the evidence permits to be established with reasonable certainty.

Comment (a) to the above cited section states:

> Doubts are generally resolved against the party in breach. A party who has, by his breach, forced the injured party to seek compensation in damages should not be allowed to profit from his breach where it is established that a significant loss has occurred. A court may take into account all the circumstances of the breach, including willfulness, in deciding whether to require a lesser degree of certainty, giving greater discretion to the trier of the facts. Damages need not be calculable with mathematical accuracy and are often at best approximate.

Given the willfulness of UBA's breach in this case and the fact that UBA did not directly attack the accuracy of any of the figures contained in Exhibit 96, which contained a detailed and specific breakdown of the costs, we find UBA's allegation of error concerning the S-2's purchase, conversion and delivery cost per plane to be without merit.

The trial court's findings on the amount of expectation damages are affirmed.

F. INTEREST DEDUCTION

The trial court found that if its foreseeability ruling were later held to be incorrect, NAR-PC would only be entitled to recover the net value of the eleven S-2's ($2,921,605) "minus the total of the interest payments on the UBA loan and the long term financing ($536,000)." NAR-PC asserts that this interest deduction was erroneous as it resulted in NAR-PC being under compensated, especially since NAR-PC was denied lost profits based on certainty of proof grounds.

This argument is without merit. RESTATEMENT (SECOND) OF CONTRACTS § 347, at 112 (1981) provides: Subject to the limitations stated in §§ 350-53, the injured party has a right to damages based on his expectation interest as measured by (a) the loss in the value to him of the other party's performance caused by its failure or deficiency, plus (b) any other loss, including incidental or consequential loss, caused by the breach, less (c) *any cost or other loss that he has avoided by not having to perform.* (Emphasis [by the court]). See also 5 A. Corbin, CORBIN ON CONTRACTS § 1038, at 236 (1964).

Clearly, NAR-PC would have had to pay interest on the money loaned to finance the S-2 project. Because of UBA's breach, NAR-PC avoided having to pay the interest cost. The interest cost was therefore properly deducted from the value of the S-2's. . . .

Affirmed in part, Reversed and Remanded in part.

PIPKIN v. THOMAS & HILL, INC.
298 N.C. 278, 258 S.E.2d 778 (1979)

Plaintiffs, as individuals and general partners doing business under the name of P.W.D.&W., brought this action for damages against defendant, a West Virginia corporation engaged in the mortgage banking business, to recover damages for its breach of an alleged contract to make plaintiffs a long-term loan to repay a construction loan from Central Carolina Bank (CCB). . . .

. . . We allowed defendant's petition for discretionary review for the sole purpose of considering what damages plaintiffs are entitled to recover for defendant's breach of contract.

SHARP, Chief Justice:

. . . Initially, the primary relief which plaintiffs sought in this action was a decree ordering defendant to specifically perform its commitment to provide long-term or "permanent" financing to enable plaintiffs to take up CCB's interim construction loan on their motel-restaurant project. Historically, courts of equity refused to decree specific performance of a contract to lend money on the ground that the disappointed borrower could be fully compensated by damages because, presumably, money could always be found elsewhere. . . . More recently, however, courts have employed the equitable remedy of specific performance when the circumstances of the particular case demonstrate the inadequacy of money damages to afford appropriate relief. . . . In this case the parties' stipulation that defendant is financially unable to comply with its contract rendered the availability of the remedy of specific performance immaterial. Plaintiffs, therefore, are relegated to such damages as they are legally entitled to recover, and are able to collect, from defendant.

A borrower's claim for damages resulting from a lender's breach of a contract to lend money is primarily circumscribed by the rule of *Hadley v. Baxendale*, 156 Eng. Rep. 145, 151 (Ex. 1854). This rule limits generally the recovery of damages in actions for breach of contract. To recover, a disappointed borrower must not only prove his damages with reasonable certainty, he must also show that they resulted naturally according to the usual course of things from the breach or that, at the time the contract was made, such damages were in the contemplation of the parties as a probable result of the breach. Additionally, the borrower must demonstrate that, upon the lender's breach, he minimized his damages by securing the money elsewhere if available. When alternative funds are unavailable, however, the borrower may recover the damages actually incurred because of the breach, subject to the general rules of foreseeability and certainty of proof. . . .

The rule governing damages for breach of a contract to lend money is nowhere stated more succinctly than in RESTATEMENT OF CONTRACTS section 343 (1932):

> Damages for breach of a contract to lend money are measured by the cost of obtaining the use of money during the agreed period of credit, less interest at the rate provided in the contract, plus compensation for other unavoidable harm that the defendant had reason to foresee when the contract was made.

> Comment:

> a. This Section is an application of the general rules of damages to a special class of contracts. The damages awarded are affected by the fact that money is nearly always obtainable in the market. If the loan was to be repayable on demand, or if the contract rate of interest is as much as the current market rate and the money is available to the borrower in the market, his recoverable damages are nominal only. He is expected to avoid other harm by borrowing elsewhere if he can, the reasonable expenses

being chargeable to the defendant. Sometimes inability to borrow elsewhere or the delay caused by the lender's action results in loss of a specific
advantageous bargain, an unfinished building, or an equity of redemption in
mortgaged land; damages are recoverable for losses if the lender had
reason to foresee them.

Clearly, the plaintiffs in this case have been injured by defendant's breach of
contract. Without defendant's commitment to provide long-term financing they
would not have begun construction of the motel project. When it was completed and
the construction loan from CCB became due they were unable to obtain alternative
long-term financing because none was available at any rate of interest. Plaintiffs
were able to forestall foreclosure only by refinancing the construction loan with a
demand note at a fluctuating rate of interest which varied from 2 to 3% *above* CCB's
prime rate and was always in excess of the contract rate. . . .

Specifically, the question for our determination is the following:

What is the measure of damages for breach of a contract to make a loan of
$1,162,500 at 9½% *interest per annum*, the loan to be amortized over 300 monthly
installments and to be used to take out a short-term construction loan, when a
substitute loan was unobtainable upon any terms at the time of the breach and, in
order to forestall foreclosure, the borrowers had to refinance the construction loan
by a demand note at a fluctuating rate of interest for a period of 18 months?

At trial plaintiffs sought to recover and the judge purported to assess their past,
present and prospective damages. The case was tried upon the fiction that at the
time of trial plaintiffs had obtained a permanent loan at 10½% Interest, which the
court found was the lowest prevailing rate of interest for a comparable long-term
commercial loan as of 1 October 1974, the date of the breach. In attempting to
fashion a rule which would appropriately measure plaintiffs' damages the trial
judge analogized this case to those in which the borrower actually obtained another
loan. On this theory, the trial court awarded plaintiffs general damages in the
amount of $120,000, this amount being the difference between the interest on a
25-year loan of $1,162,500 at 10½% *per annum* and a similar loan at 9½%, reduced
to present value *and* "discounted for the likelihood of early payment." As special
damage, Judge McKinnon awarded plaintiffs $5,888.12, the total of amounts which
plaintiffs reasonably expended in refinancing their construction loan with CCB to
prevent foreclosure, and in their unsuccessful attempts over 18 months to secure a
replacement long-term loan. The judge, however, refused to allow any recovery of
the $184,619.49 in interest which plaintiffs paid CCB on the demand note during
that 18-month interim.

The Court of Appeals affirmed the trial judge's award of $5,888.12 in special
damages. This ruling was clearly correct, and we affirm it. As the Court of Appeals
pointed out, additional title insurance and brokerage, accounting and appraisal fees
"were foreseeable expenses which, but for the breach, plaintiffs would not have
incurred." . . .

In our view, plaintiffs have reasonably demonstrated that as a consequence of
defendant's breach of its loan commitment they will suffer prospective losses; and
we agree with the Court of Appeals that the trial court's use of the lowest prevailing
rate for comparable long-term loans as a figure to be compared with the contract
interest rate represents effort to provide relief from these prospective damages. We
also agree that the trial judge erred in reducing the present worth of plaintiff's

prospective damages ($143,282.03) to the amount of $120,000 "for the likelihood of early payment."

. . . [T]here was no evidence that plaintiffs contemplated early payment of the loan. The Court of Appeals, therefore, properly ordered this reduction stricken, and we affirm.

Finally, the Court of Appeals concluded that the trial judge erred in refusing to allow plaintiffs to recover the $184,618.49 in interest which they paid CCB on the demand notes during the 18 months elapsing between the date of defendant's breach of its contract and the date of the trial. This interest, that court said, was recoverable as special damages which defendant should have foreseen as the probable consequence of its failure to provide plaintiffs the promised long-term financing. Thus, the question remaining is whether, in order to avoid foreclosure, a disappointed borrower to whom a defaulting lender had committed long-term financing to pay off a temporary construction loan, is entitled to obtain temporary refinancing at a higher rate of interest and to recover the cost of this refinancing as special damages.

On the ground that such refinancing was an unforeseeable consequence of the breach defendant argues that the trial court properly denied plaintiffs any recovery of the interest they paid on the demand note which refinanced the temporary construction loan. In our view, this contention by a defaulting lender, fully aware of the purpose for which plaintiffs had secured its commitment, is entirely unrealistic. In 11 Williston on Contracts section 1411 (3d Ed. Jaeger 1968), it is stated:

> It will frequently happen that the borrower is unable to get money elsewhere, and, if the defendant had notice of the purpose for which the money was desired, he will be liable for damages caused by the plaintiff's inability to carry out his purpose, if the performance of the promise would have enabled him to do so.

The case of *St. Paul at Chase Corp. v. Manufacturers Life Ins. Co.*, 262 Md. 192, 278 A.2d 12, *cert. denied*, 404 U.S. 857, 92 S. Ct. 104, 30 L. Ed. 2d 98 (1971), grew out of the defendant's breach of a commitment to provide the plaintiff with permanent financing "to take out" a construction loan on a high rise apartment building. When the defendant canceled its commitment and the plaintiff was unable to obtain a substitute loan, the bank carrying the construction loan foreclosed the property and obtained a deficiency judgment against the plaintiff, which then sued the defendant for damages. In affirming the trial court's award of compensatory damages which would enable the plaintiff to pay the deficiency judgment and other "consequential damages," the Court of Appeals of Maryland also adopted both the judge's rationale and his succinct statement of it. After noting that in loan transactions such as the one in suit "the parties, of course, anticipate that everything will proceed according to Hoyle that there will be no breach by either party," Judge Proctor added:

> On the other hand, the would be permanent mortgage lender must contemplate that if, at the last minute, it cancels its commitment such action would be disastrous to the borrower; that in such event obtaining a new permanent mortgage loan would be well-nigh impossible, for the reason that whatever brought about the cancellation would in all likelihood prevent another lender from entering the fray; that one doesn't find someone willing and able to lend $4,800,000 at a moment's notice; that,

under such circumstances, foreclosure under the construction mortgage would not only be a probability, it would be almost inevitable. (Emphasis added [by the court].) 262 Md. at 243, 278 A.2d at 36.

Whether the loan commitment be for $4,800,000 or $1,162,500, we harbor no doubt that a committed permanent lender on a substantial building project certainly must foresee that a breach of his commitment a relatively short time before the date he has contracted to provide the money to pay off the interim construction loan will result in substantial harm to the borrower.

. . . In a reasonable effort to minimize their losses, while they continued their search for another permanent loan plaintiffs refinanced the construction loan to prevent foreclosure of property in which they had acquired equity of approximately $627,500. That their search during the subsequent 18 months proved futile is no reason to deny them compensation for the resulting damages they sustained during that period.

However, our conclusion that plaintiffs should recover as foreseeable damages their losses arising from the interest payments on the demand notes does not necessarily entail an award for the full amount of interest actually paid to CCB. On the contrary, we hold that the Court of Appeals erred insofar as it awarded plaintiffs both the full amount of interest actually paid CCB from the date of the breach until the date of trial *and* the present value of the difference between the interest on $1,162,500 amortized over 25 years from the date of the trial at the hypothetical rate of 10½% *per* year and the contract rate of 9½%. . . .

We are of the opinion that the Wisconsin Court in Bridgkort Racquet Club [*Bridgkort Racquet Club v. University Bank*, 85 Wis. 2d 706, 271 N.W.2d 165 (1978)], was correct in determining the plaintiffs' damages to be the differential between the cost of obtaining new financing and the interest payments specified in the contract. Based on this principle, plaintiffs' recovery of interest payments made to CCB during this 18-month period must be reduced by the amount of interest which would have been payable to defendant at the contract rate of 9½%.

Having concluded that plaintiffs are entitled to compensatory damages for the cost of refinancing during the 18-month period between the date of defendant's breach and trial, and a general damages award resulting from defendant's breach, we believe the most equitable remedy will be achieved by compensating plaintiffs for the amount of their actual losses up until the date of trial and using the difference between the hypothetical interest rate of 10½% *and* the contract rate as the basis for determining the damages sustained after the trial. The record shows that for each of the 300 months of the loan plaintiffs contracted for, the amount of interest which plaintiffs would have been obligated to pay defendant can be determined with exactitude. Therefore the amount of plaintiffs' actual damages prior to trial can be computed by subtracting from the $184,619.49 actually paid CCB by March 31, 1976, the amount of interest plaintiffs would have paid to defendant under the contract by that date. As to plaintiffs' prospective losses from the contractual breach, they can be calculated by using the differential between the 10½% *per annum* rate which the trial court hypothesized to be the lowest prevailing rate of interest on 1 October 1974 for a long-term commercial loan on a project such as plaintiffs' and the contract rate of 9½%. Plaintiffs are therefore entitled to the present value of the difference in interest payments owed under the contract from 1 April 1976, the date of the trial, until 1 October 1999 and the interest which would have been paid during the same period for a loan bearing interest at 10½% Per annum.

This cause is returned to the Court of Appeals for remand to the Superior Court of Wake County with instructions that, after hearing such additional evidence as may be necessary to make the calculations required to determine the amounts defined in subsections (b) and (c) below, that court shall enter judgment that plaintiff recover of defendant as damages the sum of the amounts specified in subsections (a), (b), and (c) as follows:

(a) $5,888.12 expended for additional title insurance, brokerage, accounting, and appraisal fees necessitated by defendant's breach;

(b) $184,619.49, less the amount of interest plaintiffs contracted to pay defendant from 1 October 1974 until 31 March 1976;

(c) the present value of the amount determined by subtracting the interest payments which were to have been made by plaintiffs pursuant to the contract from 1 April 1976 until 1 October 1999, from the interest payable during the same period on a loan of $1,162,500, amortized over 300 months from 1 October 1974 bearing an interest rate of 10½% Per annum.

The judgment entered shall also provide that the damages therein awarded plaintiff shall bear interest at the legal rate of six percent from 28 May 1976, the date of the judgment from which the parties appealed. . . .

For the reasons stated and specified above, the decision of the Court of Appeals is Affirmed in part, and Reversed in part.

Central Coordinates, Inc. v. Morgan Guar. Trust Co., 129 Misc. 2d 804, 494 N.Y.S.2d 602 (N.Y. Supp. 1985). This was an action against a bank on theories of negligence, breach of contract, and strict products liability, to recover damages resulting from the bank's delay in arranging a wire transfer of funds. The defendant bank moved for partial summary judgment dismissing plaintiff's claims to the extent they sought consequential damages, and plaintiff moved for summary judgment for its alleged loss of profits of $458,500. The court granted the bank's motion, stating that under common law principles plaintiff could not receive consequential damages whether its claim is characterized as one in contract, tort or strict liability. On the contract remedy issue the court referred to the rule of *Hadley v. Baxendale* as limiting liability "to those damages within the contemplation of the parties at the time the contract was made"; pointed out that plaintiff did not allege that when defendant entered into the agreement defendant was informed of plaintiff's purpose in sending the wire "or of the possibility that damages in an amount five times the wired amount would result if the transmittal was not completed before the close of business on July 14, 1983"; noted that defendant was told only of the source and destination of the amount to be transferred; and held that the mere fact that the funds were being transferred by wire did not place defendant on notice "that time was of the essence or that extraordinary consequences could occur if the transfer went awry."

NOTE

Assume that an automobile dealer breached its contract to record a bank's first lien on the application for title to a car purchased by a borrower. The lien was to secure the borrower's debt to the bank of $4,525.92. Assume further that after making several loan payments the borrower defaulted and left the state with the car, leaving a $3,771.98 balance due the bank. If the dealer had fulfilled its contractual obligation the bank would have been protected by a first lien on the title certificate issued in the name of the borrower covering the amount of his indebtedness to the bank. On behalf of the bank in an action against the dealer, set forth your position as to the types and amounts of damages that would have been in the contemplation of the parties at the time the contract was made. *See United Virginia Bank of Fairfax v. Dick Herriman Ford, Inc.*, 215 Va. 373, 210 S.E.2d 158 (1974).

2.   Special Expectancy Damages Situations

a.   Lost profits

FERA v. VILLAGE PLAZA, INC.
396 Mich. 639, 242 N.W.2d 372 (1976)

T.G. KAVANAGH, Chief Justice:

Plaintiffs received a jury award of $200,000 for loss of anticipated profits in their proposed new business as a result of defendants' breach of a lease. The Court of Appeals reversed. 52 Mich. App. 532, 218 N.W.2d 155 (1974). We reverse and reinstate the jury's award.

FACTS

On August 20, 1965 plaintiffs and agents of Fairborn-Village Plaza executed a ten-year lease for a "book and bottle" shop in defendants' proposed shopping center. This lease provided for occupancy of a specific location at a rental of $1,000 minimum monthly rent plus 5% Of annual receipts in excess of $240,000. A $1,000 deposit was paid by plaintiffs.

After this lease was executed, plaintiffs gave up approximately 600 square feet of their leased space so that it could be leased to another tenant. In exchange, it was agreed that liquor sales would be excluded from the percentage rent override provision of the lease.

Complications arose, including numerous work stoppages. Bank of the Commonwealth received a deed in lieu of foreclosure after default by Fairborn and Village Plaza. Schostak Brothers managed the property for the bank.

When the space was finally ready for occupancy, plaintiffs were refused the space for which they had contracted because the lease had been misplaced, and the space rented to other tenants. Alternative space was offered but refused by plaintiffs as unsuitable for their planned business venture.

Plaintiffs initiated suit in Wayne Circuit Court, alleging Inter alia a claim for anticipated lost profits. The jury returned a verdict for plaintiffs against all defendants for $200,000.

The Court of Appeals reversed and remanded for new trial on the issue of damages only, holding that the trial court "erroneously permitted lost profits as the measure of damages for breach of the lease." 52 Mich. App. 532, 542, 218 N.W.2d 155, 160.

In *Jarrait v. Peters*, 145 Mich. 29, 31-32, 108 N.W. 432 (1906), plaintiff was prevented from taking possession of the leased premises. The jury gave plaintiff a judgment which included damages for lost profits. This Court reversed:

> It is well settled upon authority that the measure of damages when a lessor fails to give possession of the leased premises is the difference between the actual rental value and the rent reserved. 1 Sedgwick on Damages (8th Ed.) ¶ 185. Mr. Sedgwick says: "If the business were a new one, since there could be no basis on which to estimate profits, the plaintiff must be content to recover according to the general rule." The rule is different where the business of the lessee has been interrupted. . . .

> The evidence admitted tending to show the prospective profits plaintiff might have made for the ensuing two years should therefore have been excluded under the objections made by defendant, and the jury should have been instructed that the plaintiff's damages, if any, would be the difference between the actual rental value of the premises and the rent reserved in the lease.

Six years later, in *Isbell v. Anderson Carriage Co.*, 170 Mich. 304, 318, 136 N.W. 457, 462 (1912), the Court wrote:

> It has sometimes been stated as a rule of law that prospective profits are so speculative and uncertain that they cannot be recognized in the measure of damages. This is not because they are profits, but because they are so often not susceptible of proof to a reasonable degree of certainty. Where the proof is available, prospective profits may be recovered, when proven, as other damages. But the jury cannot be asked to guess. They are to try the case upon evidence, not upon conjecture.

These cases and others since should not be read as stating a rule of law which prevents every new business from recovering anticipated lost profits for breach of contract. The rule is merely an application of the doctrine that "(i)n order to be entitled to a verdict, or a judgment, for damages for breach of contract, the plaintiff must lay a basis for a reasonable estimate of the extent of his harm, measured in money." 5 CORBIN ON CONTRACTS, § 1020, p. 124. The issue becomes one of sufficiency of proof. "The jury should not (be) allowed to speculate or guess upon this question of the amount of loss of profits." *Kezeli v. River Rouge Lodge IOOF*, 195 Mich. 181, 188, 161 N.W. 838, 840 (1917).

> "Assuming, therefore, that profits prevented may be considered in measuring the damages, are profits to be divided into classes and kinds? Does the term "speculative profits" express one of these classes, differing in nature from nonspeculative profits? Do "uncertain" profits differ in kind from "certain" profits? The answer is assuredly, No. There is little that can be regarded as "certain," especially with respect to what would have happened if the march of events had been other than it in fact has been. Neither court nor jury is required to attain "certainty" in awarding

damages; and this is just as true with respect to "value' as with respect to "profits." Therefore, the term "speculative and uncertain profits" is not really a classification of profits, but is instead a characterization of the evidence that is introduced to prove that they would have been made if the defendant had not committed a breach of contract. The law requires that this evidence shall not be so meager or uncertain as to afford no reasonable basis for inference, leaving the damages to be determined by sympathy and feelings alone. The amount of evidence required and the degree of its strength as a basis of inference varies with circumstances.

5 Corbin on Contracts, § 1022, pp. 139–140.

The rule was succinctly stated in *Shropshire v. Adams*, 40 Tex. Civ. App. 339, 344, 89 S.W. 448, 450 (1905):

> Future profits as an element of damage are in no case excluded merely because they are profits but because they are uncertain. In any case when by reason of the nature of the situation they may be established with reasonable certainty they are allowed.

It is from these principles that the "new business"/"interrupted business" distinction has arisen. "If a business is one that has already been established a reasonable prediction can often be made as to its future on the basis of its past history. . . . If the business . . . has not had such a history as to make it possible to prove with reasonable accuracy what its profits have been in fact, the profits prevented are often but not necessarily too uncertain for recovery." 5 Corbin on Contracts, § 1023, pp. 147, 150–151. Cf. *Jarrait v. Peters, supra.*

The Court of Appeals based its opinion reversing the jury's award on two grounds: First, that a new business cannot recover damages for lost profits for breach of a lease. We have expressed our disapproval of that rule. Secondly, the Court of Appeals held plaintiffs barred from recovery because the proof of lost profits was entirely speculative. We disagree.

The trial judge in a thorough opinion made the following observations upon completion of the trial.

> On the issue of lost profits, there were days and days of testimony. The defendants called experts from the Michigan Liquor Control Commission and from Cunningham Drug Stores, who have a store in the area, and a man who ran many other stores. The plaintiffs called experts and they, themselves, had experience in the liquor sales business, in the book sales business and had been representatives of liquor distribution firms in the area.

> The issue of the speculative, conjectural nature of future profits was probably the most completely tried issue in the whole case. Both sides covered this point for days on direct and cross-examination. The proofs ranged from no lost profits to two hundred and seventy thousand dollars over a ten-year period as the highest in the testimony. A witness for the defendants, an expert from Cunningham Drug Company, testified the plaintiffs probably would lose money. Mr. Fera, an expert in his own right, testified the profits would probably be two hundred and seventy thousand dollars. The jury found two hundred thousand dollars. This is well within

the limits of the high and the low testimony presented by both sides, and a judgment was granted by the jury.

The Court cannot invade the finding of fact by the jury, unless there is no testimony to support the jury's finding. There is testimony to support the jury's finding. We must realize that witness Stein is an interested party in this case, personally. He is an officer or owner in Schostak Brothers. He may personally lose money as a result of this case. The jury had to weigh this in determining his credibility. How much credibility they gave his testimony was up to them. How much weight they gave to counter-evidence was up to them. . . .

The Court must decide whether or not the jury had enough testimony to take this fact from the speculative-conjecture category and find enough facts to be able to make a legal finding of fact. This issue (damages for lost profits) was the most completely tried issue in the whole case. Both sides put in testimony that took up days and encompassed experts on both sides. This fact was adequately taken from the category of speculation and conjecture by the testimony and placed in the position of those cases that hold that even though loss of profits is hard to prove, if proven they should be awarded by the jury. In this case, the jury had ample testimony to make this decision from both sides.

The jury award was approximately seventy thousand dollars less than the plaintiffs asked and their proofs showed they were entitled to. The award of the jury was well within the range of the proofs and the Court cannot legally alter it, as determination of damages is a jury function and their finding is justified by the law in light of the evidence in this case.

The loss of profits are often speculative and conjectural on the part of witnesses. When this is true, the Court should deny loss of profits because of the speculative nature of the testimony and the proofs. However, the law is also clear that where lost profits are shown, and there is ample proof on this point, they should not be denied merely because they are hard to prove. In this case, both parties presented testimony on this issue for days. This testimony took the lost profits issue out of the category of speculation and conjecture. The jury was given an instruction on loss of profits and what the proofs must show, and the nature of the proofs, and if they found them to be speculative they could not award damages therefor. The jury, having found damages to exist, and awarded the same in this case in accord with the proper instructions, the Court cannot, now, overrule the jury's finding.

As Judge Wickens observed, the jury was instructed on the law concerning speculative damages. The case was thoroughly tried by all the parties. Apparently, the jury believed the plaintiffs. That is its prerogative. . . .

While we might have found plaintiffs' proofs lacking had we been members of the jury, that is not the standard of review we employ. "As a reviewing court we will not invade the fact finding of the jury or remand for entry of judgment unless the factual record is so clear that reasonable minds may not disagree." *Hall v. Detroit*, 383 Mich. 571, 574, 177 N.W.2d 161, 163 (1970). This is not the situation here.

The Court of Appeals is reversed and the trial court's judgment on the verdict is reinstated. Costs to plaintiffs.

COLEMAN, JUSTICE (concurring in part, dissenting in part).

Although anticipated profits from a new business may be determined with a reasonable degree of certainty such was not the situation regarding loss of profits from liquor sales as proposed by plaintiffs.

First, plaintiffs had no license and a Liquor Control Commission regional supervisor and a former commissioner testified that the described book and bottle store could not obtain a license. Further, the proofs of possible profits from possible liquor sales — if a license could have been obtained — were too speculative. The speculation of possible licensing plus the speculation of profits in this case combine to cause my opinion that profits from liquor sales should not have been submitted to the jury.

I agree with Judge O'Hara in his Court of Appeals dissent and would have allowed proof of loss from the bookstore operation to go to the jury, but not proof of loss from liquor sales. His remedy is also approved. I would affirm the trial court judgment conditioned upon plaintiffs' consenting within 30 days following the release of this opinion, to "remitting that portion of the judgment in excess of $60,000. Otherwise, the judgment should be reversed and a new trial had." Plaintiffs are also entitled to the $1,000 deposit.

NOTES

1. *See Kenford Co., Inc. v. Erie County*, 108 App. Div. 2d 132, 489 N.Y.S.2d 939 (1985) below, in the section on "E. Defenses to Damage Claims" "1. Insufficient Proof," for additional discussion on when lost profits are recoverable for breach of contract.

2. In *Lewis Jorge Const. Management, Inc. v. Pomona Unified School Dist.*, 34 Cal. 4th 960, 22 Cal. Rptr. 3d 340, 102 P.3d 257 (2004), the court discussed lost profits and their availability under the *Hadley v. Baxendale* set of principles. Holding in that case that lost profits plaintiff contractor may have earned on future projects were not recoverable either as general damages or as special damages, the court also noted that "Contract damages, unlike damages in tort . . . , do not permit recovery for unanticipated injury." (34 Cal. 4th at 969, 102 P.3d at 262, 22 Cal. Rptr. 3d at 345.)

b.   Cost to repair vs. diminution in value

KANGAS v. TRUST
110 Ill. App. 3d 876, 441 N.E.2d 1271 (1982)

SEIDENFELD, Justice:

Antti Kangas, d/b/a Kangas Construction Company, appeals from a judgment denying recovery under his suit for a mechanic's lien, and awarding the homeowners, Anthony Trust and Madeline Trust, his wife, $25,155.21 on their counterclaim. On appeal Kangas does not challenge the dismissal of his lien claim but contends that several items were improperly included in the damages awarded.

On November 7, 1977, the Trusts contracted with Kangas for construction of a duplex house on property owned by the Trusts. Mrs. Trust testified that it was intended as a home that they planned to live in as a retirement home with an apartment for her parents. The original contract price was $132,496 payable in two installments, the first due when the house was under roof and the balance when the house was completed to the Trusts' satisfaction; with extras, the price by later agreement was $144,482.60. The house was to be completed within 120 days from the ground breaking.

The house was under roof in January 1978 when problems developed. The asphalt roof shingles would not flatten out because workmen placed the shingles over accumulated ice and snow; and the roof sagged because the rafters were set at different levels. According to Mrs. Trust, Kangas told her that the shingles would flatten out in the summer heat, but they never did.

At trial, workmen who inspected and did repairs testified to other construction problems which indicated that work done by Kangas was not good and workmanlike. The entire house was "out of plumb." The exterior walls leaned out 1½ inches; the floor tilted down 2½ inches; the house sagged because the center beam in the basement was not level; the heating and air conditioning ducts were crooked and the standard fittings were nonexistent. The floor joist was single rather than double as called for in the contract, and the upstairs and downstairs floor joists had been reversed; as a result the joists ran in opposite directions and there was no bearing wall to support the second floor, which sagged.

A particular item challenged on appeal is the basement floor, which was poured at least four inches higher than called for in the contract. Ken Olson, the architectural designer who had drawn up the plans, testified that the basement walls were poured 4½ inches too short and the only way to conform to the contract would have been to dig out the foundation and excavate further. He admitted that he was on the site when the floor was poured but denied the Trusts had authorized the basement floor at the level of seven foot six inches rather than seven foot 10 inches specified in the contract. The actual height variance from the plans was never definitely established. According to Kangas, from footing to the top of the foundation the height was seven foot six inches with a two-by-six plate on top of the concrete adding 1½ inches. According to Olson, the variance was originally 6½ inches, but ended up 4½ inches after the concrete on the footing was depressed two inches. In his reply to the Trusts' counterclaim, Kangas admitted that the basement height was four inches shorter than specified in the plan.

The Trusts terminated the contract with Kangas in October 1978, and contracted with Olson to correct and complete construction. Olson said that his repairs, including installation of a new cedar roof, were done in the least expensive way and cost $45,000. The Trusts sold the house and lot together for $155,000.

In its judgment order the trial judge computed damages:

> [The parties] have made the following expenditures, had the following losses or would have had to expend the following sums to build, finish or correct the building. . . :

Kangas	$63,000.00
Olson (Construction)	45,000.00
Olson (Inspection)	1,162.50
Items admitted by Kangas	1,710.00
Glue	66.00
Air Comfort	5,510.00

Blacktop	1,600.00
Rough Grading	1,126.42
Painting	2,150.00
Value of Lot	35,000.00
Carpet Allowance	2,976.00
Fence Replacement	267.09
Wallpaper	477.20
Brick above window	2,860.00
Lowering of basement floor	20,000.00
	$182,905.21

That there should be deducted from the above the sum of $2,750.00 being one-half of the cost of finishing part of the basement and $155,000.00 being the price for which Defendants sold the premises in question.

The judge expressed additional findings that time was intended to be of the essence of the contract; that Kangas substantially breached the contract by not completing it within time; that there was bad workmanship, and that in various instances there was a "total failure to look at the plans and specifications." He also found that the roof was done in an unworkmanlike manner with no effort to cure the defective construction; that the basement height provided in the contract "was important to the Trusts"; that Kangas "didn't pay any attention to the plans and specifications" as to the basement height, and that by Kangas' own testimony he "built it the way he usually builds a house."

1. The Roof

Both parties agree that as to the roof the cost or remedying the defect is the proper rule of damages. (*See Park v. Sohn* (1982), 89 Ill. 2d 453, 464.) A witness for Kangas testified that new shingles could have been nailed over the rippled shingles for $4,000 but did not estimate the cost of correcting the uneven rafters underlying the shingles. Olson, testifying for the Trusts, said that the repairmen "would have had to have taken the roof apart in certain areas, rebuilt it, eliminated all the shingles that were on the roof at the time, and reshingled it." In Olson's opinion, the cedar shakes roof was less expensive than insisting on full performance requiring the roof to be rebuilt. In oral argument Kangas has conceded that the cedar roof was the less expensive method of remedying the roof defects, but he further contends, citing *St. Joseph Hospital v. Corbetta Construction Co.* (1974), 21 Ill. App. 3d 925, that the Trusts were unjustly enriched by installation of a higher grade roof over the defective shingles. On this question of fact the judge chose to believe Olson; and his award of the installation cost of the cedar shakes as a remedy for the defect is not against the manifest weight of the evidence.

St. Joseph Hospital v. Corbetta Construction Co. (1974), 21 Ill. App. 3d 925, is distinguishable. The court held that the hospital (owner) was not entitled to indemnity from the contractor for the extra cost of installing a more expensive fire retardant paneling, which the local building code required, where the hospital's architect (an "exclusive agent") failed to specify the more expensive paneling, approved initial installation of the less retardant paneling, and performance by the general contractor was good and workmanlike. By contrast, the trial court here found that Kangas had breached the contract by failing to construct the roof in a good, workmanlike manner, and the owners stand blameless.

The Trusts received a better roof than they contracted for only because Kangas made the cheaper roof more costly to rebuild.

The trial court did not err in refusing to grant a setoff to Kangas of $22,384 which represented the increased costs of installing the cedar shake shingles over reshingling the defective roof.

2. The Basement

The plans called for the height of the basement to be seven feet 10 inches. Prior to entering into the contract Mrs. Trust had pointed out to Kangas the basement in her previous house which had this admittedly high basement. There was evidence that the basement walls had been poured short before either the Trusts or Olson had seen the construction. When Olson first noticed the variance from the plans he said he told Kangas that the basement walls were poured too short but Kangas merely said it was his standard height. Olson suggested that they could "buy" two inches of ceiling height by lowering the floor, laying two inches of concrete and gravel base over the footing instead of the four inches called for by the plans. He said the only alternative at that time would have been to excavate, destroy one foundation wall, remove the footing and lower the floor the necessary amount. He said at that time this would have cost between $18,000 and $20,000.

a. Equitable Estoppel

Under these facts we are not persuaded by Kangas' argument that the Trusts were equitably estopped by the agreement of Olson, found to be their agent, to go ahead with the pouring of the basement floor. At that time the basement walls were already 4½ inches too short and the ceiling would have been 6½ inches shorter than the contract called for except for Olson's agreement to lower the floor by diminishing the base material, ending up with a seven foot six inch ceiling height instead of the seven foot 10 inches called for in the contract. The cost to repair at that time could not have been changed by Olson's assent to the partial cure. True, there was testimony that the cost of repair would have been $26,800 when Kangas left the job, but the court did not award damages on this basis.

For a voluntary acceptance of defective performance to work a complete discharge, the acceptance must be absolute and unconditional (*Broncata v. Timbercrest Estates, Inc.* (1968), 100 Ill. App. 2d 49, 54), based on facts and circumstances indicating that the owner intentionally relinquished a known right (*Lempera v. Karner* (1979), 79 Ill. App. 3d 221, 223). The acts relied on by the party in breach must be inconsistent with an intention by the injured party to insist on rights to performance under the contract. (*John Kubinski & Sons, Inc. v. Dockside Development Corp.* (1975), 33 Ill. App. 3d 1015, 1020.) The mere receipt of defective performance does not discharge a claim for damages for the breach. (CORBIN, CONTRACTS § 1245, at 1000 (1952).) There must also be an expression of assent to accept defective performance in satisfaction and as a complete discharge. (RESTATEMENT OF CONTRACTS § 411 (1932); RESTATEMENT (SECOND) OF CONTRACTS § 277(2) (1981).) Assent is required because defective performance alone cannot discharge the duty to perform; the discharge is effected solely by the expression of assent to discharge. (CORBIN, CONTRACTS § 1245, at 1000 (1981).) The burden of proving acceptance is on the party pleading it. (*Intaglio Service Corp. v. J. L. Williams & Co.* (1981), 95 Ill. App. 3d 708, 714.) We conclude that the Trusts did not accept the defective performance.

b. Measure of Damages

There are various formulas which may be applied in fixing damages in building construction cases, as the trial court properly noted, but the circumstances dictate the method to be used. Kangas argues that the proper formula here is to determine the amount the fair market value of the house was diminished by the failure to follow the plans and that since the Trusts presented no evidence to show any diminution in value when they sold the house without changing the basement they were not entitled to be credited with the $20,000 awarded.

Kangas relies principally on language in *Brewer v. Custom Builders Corp.* (1976), 42 Ill. App. 3d 668, to support his position. In *Brewer*, the trial court awarded $7,500 in damages for defects in the work based on diminution in the value of the house.

The appellate court noted that although the contractor's performance of his agreement was less than substantial the builder's omissions of performance, a number of unspecified interior defects, "would involve a substantial tearing down and rebuilding of the structure" and "to avoid economic waste the measure of damages is not the cost of repair, but rather is the difference in value. . . ." 42 Ill. App. 3d 668, 679; *see also Mayfield v. Swafford* (1982), 106 Ill. App. 3d 610, 614.

We do not believe that the circumstances of this case appropriately call for application of the diminution in value rule. Granted, the cost of remedying the defect is substantial, but it is evident that the damage arose from a wilful violation of the building contract. The trial court found as a fact that failure to conform was because Kangas "didn't pay any attention to the plans and specifications," and "built it the way he usually builds a house." Mrs. Trust wanted a seven foot 10 inch ceiling in the basement of the duplex that she then intended to live in as a retirement home, which would contain an apartment for her parents; she showed Kangas a basement with that height in her previous house; she particularly expressed her desire that the height be the same in her new home and pointed out the 12-inch I beams; and she specified it in the plans. On the record we cannot say the four to 4½ inch variance was trivial, but conclude that the basement height was of "special value" to Mrs. Trust. *Cf.* RESTATEMENT (SECOND) OF CONTRACTS § 348, illust. 4 (1981).

The cases in Illinois which have been cited and which we have seen do not involve a wilful violation of the contract by a builder.

Cases in other jurisdictions, however, have directly confronted this issue and appear to have qualified the diminution of value rule by holding that it applies only if the breach is not wilful. (*See Shell v. Schmidt* (1958), 164 Cal. App. 2d 350, 359, 363, 330 P.2d 817, 823, 825-26, *cert. denied* (1959), 359 U.S. 959, 79 S. Ct. 799, 3 L. Ed. 2d 766; *Hourihan v. Grossman Holdings Ltd.* (Fla. App. 1981), 396 So. 2d 753, 755; *American Standard, Inc. v. Schectman* (1981), 80 A.D.2d 318, 322-23, 439 N.Y.S.2d 529, 532-33. *See generally* Annot., 76 A.L.R.2d 805, 825-26 (1961).) It has also been recognized that awarding damages equal to the amount required to reconstruct the dwelling so as to make it conform to the specifications is proper when the contract is one to construct a dwelling for the owner who plans to live in it as distinguished from a commercial structure "where the aesthetic taste of the owner is not so deeply involved." *Fox v. Webb* (1958), 268 Ala. 111, 119, 105 So. 2d 75, 82-83; *Carter v. Quick* (1978), 263 Ark. 202, 209, 563 S.W.2d 461, 465.

We, however, do not conclude that every wilful breach requires that the cost of repair be automatically used as the measure of damages. Obviously, every variation from specifications does not mandate this result. If the builder does not perform in the manner called for in the contract, but in good faith, although intentionally, does something equally as good he should not be required to pay for substantial repairs. (*See* 3A CORBIN, CONTRACTS § 707, at 330 (1960).) Otherwise, the penalty and forfeiture, with no real damage to the owner, may be grossly disproportionate to the nature of the breach. (5 CORBIN, CONTRACTS § 707, at 331 (1960).) But we agree with Corbin that where the variance from the contract does not result in a lesser market value than would result from exact performance, it may still be less than substantial performance; and that under that circumstance the wilful violation of the contract by the builder is a factor which may be considered by the trier of fact in determining whether the breach requires application of cost of repair or diminution in value as the measure of damages. (5 CORBIN, CONTRACTS § 1089, at 491 (1964).) We also conclude that in addition to the determination of wilfulness, the owner's purpose in constructing a dwelling for his own use and therefore to his own tastes is also a factor to be considered. *Fox v. Webb* (1958), 268 Ala. 111, 119, 105 So. 2d 75, 82-83; *Carter v. Quick* (1978), 263 Ark. 202, 209, 563 S.W.2d 461, 465.

We hold that the trial court's resolution of the measure of damages and the amount was proper on this record.

3. Value of the Vacant Lot

Kangas finally argues that the trial court improperly included the value of the lot, $35,000, in computing damages. We do not agree. The trial judge included the lot as an item in adding up the Trusts' costs before subtracting from this sum ($182,905.21) the sales proceeds of the house and lot together ($155,000). This sales price was unallocated between the house and lot. The court properly included the lot since the lot had been included in the sale. Kangas was not prejudiced thereby in computing damages since the same result is reached if the lot is excluded both from the cost of completion ($147,905.21) and the sales proceeds of the house alone ($120,000). The value of the lot on either side of the equation cancelled each other out.

The judgment of the circuit court of Lake County is therefore affirmed.

NOTE

The Florida District Court of Appeals' decision in the *Hourihan* case (cited in the *Kangas* case above at b. Measure of Damages, paragraph 6) that plaintiff purchasers were entitled to damages measured by the cost to reconstruct the house that defendant contractor had built as a "mirror image" of the house provided for in their contract, was rejected by the Florida Supreme Court a year later. The Supreme Court's opinion holds that the "unreasonable economic waste doctrine" is applicable to both residential and non-residential construction, and that the contractor's willfulness did not render the economic waste doctrine inapplicable. The opinion further states that "Punitive damages are not recoverable for breach of contract, but where the acts constituting the breach also amount to a cause of action in tort, punitive damages may be recovered. . . . The Hourihans, however, presented only the breach of contract issue to the district court. The amount of compensatory damages flowing from a breach of contract is not affected by the manner of the breach." *Grossman Holdings, Ltd. v. Hourihan*, 414 So. 2d 1037 (1982).

c.   Lost volume sellers

WIRED MUSIC, INC. v. CLARK
26 Ill. App. 2d 413, 168 N.E.2d 736 (1960)

SPIVEY, Justice:

The County Court of Winnebago County, in a nonjury case, entered judgment in favor of the plaintiff for $302.95 for defendant's breach of a written contract. The action was brought to the County Court on an appeal from a Justice of Peace Court judgment in favor of the plaintiff. There are no pleadings in the cause.

On appeal, defendant contends that the plaintiff failed to prove any damages and further, that by reason of the plaintiff's obligation to mitigate damages, no damages could be shown.

There was no dispute in the evidence, and we have presented to us solely a question of the legal obligations of the parties. Plaintiff distributes recorded music to various locations in Rockford, by means of direct wires supplied by the local telephone company. The music is supplied from a tape and is transmitted to each customer over the telephone company wires to individual equipment in the various customers' locations. For defendant's particular installation, plaintiff charged $24.30 for the service monthly. This charge represents a line charge of $8.75 and profit of $15.55 to the plaintiff. In addition, there was a connection charge of $7.50.

Defendant executed a contract with the plaintiff requiring plaintiff to furnish and defendant to pay for three years service. The contract provided that there could be no assignment without the written consent of the plaintiff. There was also a provision that defendant was not to be relieved of the obligation to make monthly payments if he discontinued service, but obviously, no contention is made that the damages awarded were pursuant to this clause, since the damages are less than the remaining contract installments.

After using the music and paying promptly for seventeen months of the three year contract, defendant moved his business and discontinued the service. However, the tenant who rented the space formerly occupied by the defendant requested and was refused the right to take an assignment of defendant's contract, and so, entered into another contract for the service at the same location. In this regard, it should be noted that this latter contract was for one year only and called for a five per cent increase in cost because it was for only a one year term, rather than a three year term. For this reason, defendant contends that the plaintiff fails to show damages for the breach of contract since plaintiff will realize more revenue from defendant's former location than plaintiff would have received if defendant were still the tenant.

There is no dispute between the parties that the defendant breached his contract. The only question is the measure of damages. We said, in *Meyer v.*

Buckman, 7 Ill. App. 2d 385, 129 N.E.2d 603, 613, "The measure of damages where one engaged in the performance of a contract of this type is wrongfully prevented by the other party from completing it is the difference shown by the evidence between the contract price and what it would have cost the plaintiff to have done and completed the work according to the terms of the contract: *Hayes v. Wagner*, 1906, 220 Ill. 256, 77 N.E. 211; *Ryan v. Miller*, 1893, 52 Ill. App. 191; Id., 153 Ill. 138, 38 N.E. 642; *Kingman & Co. v. Hanna Wagon Co.*, 1898, 176 Ill. 545, 52 N.E. 328."

Plaintiff's testimony that his profit on this contract was $15.55 per month is not disputed in any way. This figure for nineteen months plus the disconnection charge of $7.50 was the judgment of the court, and according to our understanding of the law and uncontradicted evidence, was exactly right. The court reduced the total contract price by the expenses of $8.75 per month for line rental.

> Our courts have held that the measure of damages plaintiff can recover under such circumstances is the total benefit of the contract, less expenses; and without evidence to the contrary, the amount which would have been made as profit if the contract had been kept. *Nestler v. Pure Silk Hosiery Mills*, 242 Ill. App. 151; *Anderson v. Pan American Motors Corp.*, 232 Ill. App. 37; *Barnett v. Caldwell Furniture Co.*, 277 Ill. 286, 115 N.E. 389.

Capitol Paper Box, Inc. v. Belding Hosiery Mills, 350 Ill. App. 68, 111 N.E.2d 858, 860.

> The burden of proving that the damages were not correct or unfair was on the defendant that breached the contract.

Behn v. Southern Pac. Co., 2 Ill. App. 2d 62, 118 N.E.2d 625, 627.

Finally, defendant contends that plaintiff is under a duty to mitigate damages and since he did supply music to defendant's location and received greater revenue than defendant's contract called for, plaintiff has not been damaged. In this contention, the defendant is in error. "It is inaccurate to say that plaintiff has a 'duty' for if he breaches the 'duty' by failing to mitigate damages, he incurs no legal liability. The law does not assess damages against him, it just fails to compensate him for any injury he reasonably could have avoided." RESTATEMENT OF CONTRACTS, 3336 [*sic* 336], Comment d.

Again, the evidence is uncontradicted that plaintiff could supply any number of additional customers without incurring further expenses except for wire rental. If defendant's contention were adopted by this court, it would have the effect of denying to the plaintiff the benefit of his bargain. This case is not at all like the situation where a plaintiff has one house to rent or one car to sell or a fixed quantity of personal property or real estate. Here, plaintiff has so far as the evidence shows, an unlimited supply of music, limited in its distributions only by the number of contracts which plaintiff can secure. One who has a parcel of real estate cannot multiply it. If he retakes possession he has regained usually the full consideration for which he parted with it. But one who manufactures an article capable of infinite production destroys new outlets with full profits when he reclaims and resells his products. *Electrical Products Corporation v. Mosko*, 88 Colo. 447, 297 P. 991, 993.

The so-called rule of "avoidable damages" if applied in this case would serve to deprive the plaintiff of the true measure of damages. "The rule, however, has never been carried to the extent of requiring the injured party to surrender important and valuable rights." *Pittsburgh, Ft. W. & C. R.R. Co. v. Reno et al.*, 22 Ill. App. 470.

The guiding rule and the basic principle is that compensation is the general purpose of the law in fixing the measure of damages. Williston and Thompson, WILLISTON ON CONTRACTS, Revised Edition, ¶ 1338. But much careless language has pervaded judicial opinions dealing with the element of damages. Trouble is created when this careless language, used for instance in a case involving the sale of a single unique parcel of land, is again used to define the rights and duties existing by virtue of a contract to sell limitless quantities of taped music.

It is true that after a breach of contract, damages may be reduced by another sale of the article which was the subject of the breach. But this rule should be limited in its application to those situations where the innocent party will not lose any valuable rights under the contract. We are unable to say that the music sold in the location that defendant abandoned could not have been sold but for the breach of the defendant. And so we distinguish for the purposes of fixing damages, between the types of sales involved. We cannot remake the contract from one of a term of three years to that of a contract from month to month. Here, the evidence shows that the plaintiff received five per cent per month less on a three year contract than he is receiving on the one year contract with the customer who rented the premises abandoned by the defendant. In effect, plaintiff has purchased, by this discount given, the right to call for the money equivalent to performance for a three year term. He acquired his right to call upon the defendant to perform for three years and not just the right to supply music to a particular location for three years. Obviously, plaintiff's stimulus is the expectation of a profit rather than a maudlin gratification from having supplied music in a particular place. We have mentioned "profits" several times as being the desire of the plaintiff, and profits may be recovered in a proper case.

> It (profit) can well be a just measure of damages where the product involved is in itself for sale on the market and, as a matter of fact, there is little difference between that and the general rule that the measure of damages is the difference in value between what is tendered and what was agreed to be delivered. There is also an area within which courts have at times as a matter of justice resorted to loss of profit as a measure of damages when there is no other measure or other damages are difficult to prove. Whatever may be the inducement, the purpose of the court is always to find a measure of damages which will be fairly compensatory to the vendee, and not unjust to the vendor. *Flug v. Craft Mfg. Co.*, 3 Ill. App. 2d 56, 120 N.E.2d 666, 671.

Here, the proof of the loss was precise and whether we call damages profit or the difference between the contract price and the cost of performance, in this case, they are the same.

The judgment of the County Court of Winnebago County is affirmed.

NOTES

1. One of the rulings in *Wired Music* was that the *avoidable damage* doctrine was inapplicable as a basis to reduce damages otherwise due to this plaintiff in its capacity as a *volume seller*. It appears, thus, that the *lost volume seller* concept is applicable to sellers of services as well as to sellers of tangible goods.

2. Some more recent decisions holding that providers other than traditional sellers of tangible goods are entitled to the benefit of the *lost volume seller* principle: *Collins Entertainment Corp. v. Coats and Coats Rental Amusement*, 368 S.C. 410, 629 S.E.2d 635 (2006) (video poker machine lessor, noting that lost volume sellers may recover lost profits despite resales of the products or services, and that such resales do not mitigate (reduce) lost profits damages); *Gianetti v. Norwalk Hospital*, 266 Conn. 544, 844 A.2d 891 (2003) (holding that although "the Appellate Court properly determined, as a matter of law, that the lost volume seller theory applies to personal services contracts," whether plaintiff-surgeon in that case was a lost volume seller must be determined at trial); *Jetz Service Co., Inc. v. Salina Properties*, 19 Kan. App. 2d 144, 865 P.2d 1051 (1993) (lessor of coin-operated laundry equipment); *Lone Star Ford, Inc. v. McCormick*, 838 S.W.2d 734 (Tex. App. 1992) (advertising spokesman for automobile dealership was lost volume seller of his personal services); *David Sloane, Inc. v. Stanley G. House & Associates Inc.*, 311 Md. 36, 532 A.2d 694 (1987) (advertising agency contract to supply services).

R.E. DAVIS CHEMICAL CORP. v. DIASONICS, INC.
826 F.2d 678 (7th Cir. 1987)

Cudahy, Circuit Judge:

Diasonics, Inc. appeals from the orders of the district court denying its motion for summary judgment and granting R.E. Davis Chemical Corp.'s summary judgment motion. Diasonics also appeals from the order dismissing its third-party complaint against Dr. Glen D. Dobbin and Dr. Galdino Valvassori. We affirm the dismissal of the third-party complaint, reverse the grant of summary judgment in favor of Davis and remand for further proceedings.

I.

Diasonics is a California corporation engaged in the business of manufacturing and selling medical diagnostic equipment. Davis is an Illinois corporation that contracted to purchase a piece of medical diagnostic equipment from Diasonics. On or about February 23, 1984, Davis and Diasonics entered into a written contract under which Davis agreed to purchase the equipment. Pursuant to this agreement, Davis paid Diasonics a $300,000 deposit on February 29, 1984. Prior to entering into its agreement with Diasonics, Davis had contracted with Dobbin and Valvassori to establish a medical facility where the equipment was to be used. Dobbin and Valvassori subsequently breached their contract with Davis. Davis then breached its contract with Diasonics; it refused to take delivery of the equipment or to pay the balance due under the agreement. Diasonics later resold the equipment to a third party for the same price at which it was to be sold to Davis.

Davis sued Diasonics, asking for restitution of its $300,000 down payment under section 2-718(2) of the Uniform Commercial Code (the "U.C.C." or the "Code"). Ill. Rev. Stat. ch. 26, para. 2-718(2) (1985).[9] Diasonics counterclaimed. Diasonics did

---

[9] [1] The pertinent portion of section 2-718 provides:

§ 2-718. Liquidation or Limitation of Damages; Deposits . . . . (2) Where the seller justifiably withholds delivery of goods because of the buyer's breach, the buyer is entitled to

not deny that Davis was entitled to recover its $300,000 deposit less $500 as provided in section 2-718(2)(b). However, Diasonics claimed that it was entitled to an offset under section 2-718(3). Diasonics alleged that it was a "lost volume seller," and, as such, it lost the profit from one sale when Davis breached its contract. Diasonics' position was that, in order to be put in as good a position as it would have been in had Davis performed, it was entitled to recover its lost profit on its contract with Davis under section 2-708(2) of the U.C.C. Ill. Rev. Stat. ch. 26, para. 2-708(2) (1985). Section 2-708 provides:

§ 2-708. Seller's Damages for Non-acceptance or Repudiation

(1) Subject to subsection (2) and to the provisions of this Article with respect to proof of market price (Section 2-723), the measure of damages for non-acceptance or repudiation by the buyer is the difference between the market price at the time and place for tender and the unpaid contract price together with any incidental damages provided in this Article (Section 2-710), but less expenses saved in consequence of the buyer's breach. (2) If the measure of damages provided in subsection (1) is inadequate to put the seller in as good a position as performance would have done then the measure of damages is the profit (including reasonable overhead) which the seller would have made from full performance by the buyer, together with any incidental damages provided in this Article (Section 2-710), due allowance for costs reasonably incurred and due credit for payments or proceeds of resale.

Diasonics subsequently filed a third-party complaint against Dobbin and Valvassori, alleging that they tortiously interfered with its contract with Davis. Diasonics claimed that the doctors knew of the contract between Davis and Diasonics and also knew that, if they breached their contract with Davis, Davis would have no use for the equipment it had agreed to buy from Diasonics.

The district court dismissed Diasonics' third-party complaint for failure to state a claim upon which relief could be granted, finding that the complaint did not allege that the doctors intended to induce Davis to breach its contract with Diasonics. The court also entered summary judgment for Davis. The court held that lost volume sellers were not entitled to recover damages under 2-708(2) but rather were limited to recovering the difference between the resale price and the contract price along with incidental damages under section 2-706(1). Ill. Rev. Stat. ch. 26, ¶ 2-706(1) (1985). Section 2-706(1) provides:

§ 2-706. Seller's Resale Including Contract for Resale

(1) Under the conditions stated in Section 2-703 on seller's remedies, the seller may resell the goods concerned or the undelivered balance thereof.

---

restitution of any amount by which the sum of his payments exceeds (a) the amount to which the seller is entitled by virtue of terms liquidating the seller's damages in accordance with subsection (1), or (b) in the absence of such terms, 20% of the value of the total performance for which the buyer is obligated under the contract or $500, whichever is smaller. (3) The buyer's right to restitution under subsection (2) is subject to offset to the extent that the seller establishes (a) a right to recover damages under the provisions of this Article other than subsection (1), and (b) the amount or value of any benefits received by the buyer directly or indirectly by reason of the contract.
Ill. Rev. Stat. ch. 26, ¶ 2-718(2)&(3) (1985).

Where the resale is made in good faith and in a commercially reasonable manner the seller may recover the difference between the resale price and the contract price together with any incidental damages allowed under the provisions of this Article (Section 2-710), but less expenses saved in consequence of the buyer's breach.

Davis was awarded $322,656, which represented Davis' down payment plus prejudgment interest less Diasonics' incidental damages. Diasonics appeals the district court's decision respecting its measure of damages as well as the dismissal of its third-party complaint.

II.

We consider first Diasonics' claim that the district court erred in holding that Diasonics was limited to the measure of damages provided in 2-706 and could not recover lost profits as a lost volume seller under 2-708(2). Surprisingly, given its importance, this issue has never been addressed by an Illinois court, nor, apparently, by any other court construing Illinois law. Thus, we must attempt to predict how the Illinois Supreme Court would resolve this issue if it were presented to it. Courts applying the laws of other states have unanimously adopted the position that a lost volume seller can recover its lost profits under 2-708(2). . . . Contrary to the result reached by the district court, we conclude that the Illinois Supreme Court would follow these other cases and would allow a lost volume seller to recover its lost profit under 2-708(2).

We begin our analysis with 2-718(2) and (3). Under 2-718(2)(b), Davis is entitled to the return of its down payment less $500. Davis' right to restitution, however, is qualified under 2-718(3)(a) to the extent that Diasonics can establish a right to recover damages under any other provision of Article 2 of the U.C.C. Article 2 contains four provisions that concern the recovery of a seller's general damages (as opposed to its incidental or consequential damages): 2-706 (contract price less resale price); 2-708(1) (contract price less market price); 2-708(2) (profit); and 2-709 (price). The problem we face here is determining whether Diasonics' damages should be measured under 2-706 or 2-708(2).[10] To answer this question, we need to engage in a detailed look at the language and structure of these various damage provisions.

The Code does not provide a great deal of guidance as to when a particular damage remedy is appropriate. The damage remedies provided under the Code are catalogued in section 2-703, but this section does not indicate that there is any hierarchy among the remedies.[11] One method of approaching the damage sections

---

[10] [4] An action for the price, provided for under 2-709, is not an option in this case because Diasonics resold the equipment that it had intended to sell to Davis.

[11] [5] Section 2-703 provides:

§ 2-703. Seller's Remedies in General.

Where the buyer wrongfully rejects or revokes acceptance of goods or fails to make a payment due on or before delivery or repudiates with respect to a part or the whole, then with respect to any goods directly affected and, if the breach is of the whole contract (Section 2-612), then also with respect to the whole undelivered balance, the aggrieved seller may (a) withhold delivery of such goods; (b) stop delivery by any bailee as hereafter provided (Section 2-705); (c) proceed under the next section respecting goods still unidentified to the contract; (d) resell and recover damages as hereafter provided (Section 2-706); (e) recover damages for non-acceptance (Section 2-708) or in a proper case the price (Section 2-709); (f) cancel.

is to conclude that 2-708 is relegated to a role inferior to that of 2-706 and 2-709 and that one can turn to 2-708 only after one has concluded that neither 2-706 nor 2-709 is applicable.[12] Under this interpretation of the relationship between 2-706 and 2-708, if the goods have been resold, the seller can sue to recover damages measured by the difference between the contract price and the resale price under 2-706. The seller can turn to 2-708 only if it resells in a commercially unreasonable manner or if it cannot resell but an action for the price is inappropriate under 2-709. The district court adopted this reading of the Code's damage remedies and, accordingly, limited Diasonics to the measure of damages provided in 2-706 because it resold the equipment in a commercially reasonable manner.

The district court's interpretation of 2-706 and 2-708, however, creates its own problems of statutory construction. There is some suggestion in the Code that the "fact that plaintiff resold the goods [in a commercially reasonable manner] does not compel him to use the resale remedy of § 2-706 rather than the damage remedy of § 2-708." Harris, *A Radical Restatement of the Law of Seller's Damages: Sales Act and Commercial Code Results Compared*, 18 Stan. L. Rev. 66, 101 n.174 (1965) (emphasis in original). Official comment 1 to 2-703, which catalogues the remedies available to a seller, states that these "remedies are essentially cumulative in nature" and that "[w]hether the pursuit of one remedy bars another depends entirely on the facts of the individual case." *See also* State of New York, Report of the Law Revision Comm'n for 1956, 396-97 (1956).[13]

Ill. Rev. Stat. ch. 26, ¶ 2-703 (1985).

[12] [6] Evidence to support this approach can be found in the language of the various damage sections and of the official comments to the U.C.C. See § 2-709(3) ("a seller who is held not entitled to the price under this Section shall nevertheless be awarded damages for non-acceptance under the preceding section [§ 2-708]"); U.C.C. comment 7 to § 2-709 ("[i]f the action for the price fails, the seller may nonetheless have proved a case entitling him to damages for non-acceptance [under § 2-708]"); U.C.C. comment 2 to § 2-706 ("[f]ailure to act properly under this section deprives the seller of the measure of damages here provided and relegates him to that provided in Section 2-708"); U.C.C. comment 1 to § 2-704 (describes § 2-706 as the "primary remedy" available to a seller upon breach by the buyer); *see also* Commonwealth Edison Co. v. Decker Coal Co., 653 F. Supp. 841, 844 (N.D. Ill. 1987) (statutory language and case law suggest that "§ 2-708 remedies are available only to a seller who is not entitled to the contract price" under § 2-709); Childress & Burgess, Seller's Remedies: The Primacy of U.C.C. 2-708(2), 48 N.Y.U.L. Rev. 833, 863-64 (1973). As one commentator has noted, 2-706 is the Code section drafted specifically to define the damage rights of aggrieved reselling sellers, and there is no suggestion within it that the profit formula of section 2-708(2) is in any way intended to qualify or be superior to it. Shanker, *The Case for a Literal Reading of U.C.C. Section 2-708(2) (One Profit for the Reseller)*, 24 Case W. Res. 697, 699 (1973).

[13] [7] U.C.C. comment 2 to 2-708(2) also suggests that 2-708 has broader applicability than suggested by the district court. U.C.C. comment 2 provides: "This section permits the recovery of lost profits in all appropriate cases, which would include all standard priced goods. The normal measure there would be list price less cost to the dealer or list price less manufacturing cost to the manufacturer." The district court's restrictive interpretation of 2-708(2) was based in part on U.C.C. comment 1 to 2-704 which describes 2-706 as the aggrieved seller's primary remedy. The district court concluded that, if a lost volume seller could recover its lost profit under 2-708(2), every seller would attempt to recover damages under 2-708(2) and 2-706 would become the aggrieved seller's residuary remedy. This argument ignores the fact that to recover under 2-708(2), a seller must first establish its status as a lost volume seller. . . . The district court also concluded that a lost volume seller cannot recover its lost profit under 2-708(2) because such a result would negate a seller's duty to mitigate damages. This position fails to recognize the fact that, by definition, a lost volume seller cannot mitigate damages through resale. Resale does not reduce a lost volume seller's damages because the breach has still resulted in its losing one sale and a corresponding profit. *See Autonumerics*, 144 Ariz. at 192, 696 P.2d at 1341.

Those courts that found that a lost volume seller can recover its lost profits under 2-708(2) implicitly rejected the position adopted by the district court; those courts started with the assumption that 2-708 applied to a lost volume seller without considering whether the seller was limited to the remedy provided under 2-706. None of those courts even suggested that a seller who resold goods in a commercially reasonable manner was limited to the damage formula provided under 2-706. We conclude that the Illinois Supreme Court, if presented with this question, would adopt the position of these other jurisdictions and would conclude that a reselling seller, such as Diasonics, is free to reject the damage formula prescribed in 2-706 and choose to proceed under 2-708.

Concluding that Diasonics is entitled to seek damages under 2-708, however, does not automatically result in Diasonics being awarded its lost profit. Two different measures of damages are provided in 2-708. Subsection 2-708(1) provides for a measure of damages calculated by subtracting the market price at the time and place for tender from the contract price.[14] The profit measure of damages, for which Diasonics is asking, is contained in 2-708(2). However, one applies 2-708(2) only if "the measure of damages provided in subsection (1) is inadequate to put the seller in as good a position as performance would have done. . . ." Ill. Rev. Stat. ch. 26, ¶ 2-708(2) (1985). Diasonics claims that 2-708(1) does not provide an adequate measure of damages when the seller is a lost volume seller.[15] To understand Diasonics' argument, we need to define the concept of the lost volume seller. Those cases that have addressed this issue have defined a lost volume seller as one that has a predictable and finite number of customers and that has the capacity either to sell to all new buyers or to make the one additional sale represented by the resale after the breach. According to a number of courts and commentators, if the seller would have made the sale represented by the resale whether or not the breach occurred, damages measured by the difference between the contract price and market price cannot put the lost volume seller in as good a position as it would have been in had the buyer performed.[16] The breach effectively cost the seller a "profit," and the seller can only be made whole by awarding it damages in the amount of its "lost profit" under 2-708(2).

We agree with Diasonics' position that, under some circumstances, the measure of damages provided under 2-708(1) will not put a reselling seller in as good a position as it would have been in had the buyer performed because the breach resulted in the seller losing sales volume. However, we disagree with the definition of "lost volume seller" adopted by other courts. Courts awarding lost profits to a lost volume seller have focused on whether the seller had the capacity to supply the

---

[14] [9] There is some debate in the commentaries about whether a seller who has resold the goods may ignore the measure of damages provided in 2-706 and elect to proceed under 2-708(1). Under some circumstances the contract-market price differential will result in overcompensating such a seller. *See* J. White & R. Summers, *Handbook of the Law under the Uniform Commercial Code* § 7-7, at 271-73 (2d ed. 1980); Sebert, *Remedies under Article Two of the Uniform Commercial Code: An Agenda for Review*, 130 U. PA. L. REV. 360, 380-83 (1981). We need not struggle with this question here because Diasonics has not sought to recover damages under 2-708(1).

[15] [10] This is also the position adopted by those courts that have held that a lost volume seller can recover its lost profits under 2-708(2). *See, e.g., Snyder*, 38 Md. App. at 153-54, 380 A.2d at 624-25.

[16] [11] According to one commentator, Resale results in loss of volume only if three conditions are met: "(1) the person who bought the resold entity would have been solicited by plaintiff had there been no breach and resale; (2) the solicitation would have been successful; and (3) the plaintiff could have performed that additional contract." *Harris, supra* p. 682, at 82 (footnotes omitted).

breached units in addition to what it actually sold. In reality, however, the relevant questions include, not only whether the seller could have produced the breached units in addition to its actual volume, but also whether it would have been profitable for the seller to produce both units. Goetz & Scott, *Measuring Sellers' Damages: The Lost-Profits Puzzle*, 31 STAN. L. REV. 323, 332-33, 346-47 (1979). As one commentator has noted, "under the economic law of diminishing returns or increasing marginal costs[,] . . . as a seller's volume increases, then a point will inevitably be reached where the cost of selling each additional item diminishes the incremental return to the seller and eventually makes it entirely unprofitable to conclude the next sale." *Shanker, supra* p. 7 n. 6, at 705. Thus, under some conditions, awarding a lost volume seller its presumed lost profit will result in overcompensating the seller, and 2-708(2) would not take effect because the damage formula provided in 2-708(1) does place the seller in as good a position as if the buyer had performed. Therefore, on remand, Diasonics must establish, not only that it had the capacity to produce the breached unit in addition to the unit resold, but also that it would have been profitable for it to have produced and sold both. Diasonics carries the burden of establishing these facts because the burden of proof is generally on the party claiming injury to establish the amount of its damages; especially in a case such as this, the plaintiff has easiest access to the relevant data. *Finance America Commercial Corp. v. Econo Coach, Inc.*, 118 Ill. App. 3d 385, 390, 73 Ill. Dec. 878, 882, 454 N.E.2d 1127, 1131 (2d Dist. 1983) ("A party seeking to recover has the burden not only to establish that he sustained damages but also to establish a reasonable basis for computation of those damages.") (citation omitted); *see also Snyder*, 38 Md. App. at 158-59 & n. 7, 380 A.2d at 627 & n. 7.[17]

One final problem with awarding a lost volume seller its lost profits was raised by the district court. This problem stems from the formulation of the measure of damages provided under 2-708(2) which is "the profit (including reasonable overhead) which the seller would have made from full performance by the buyer, together with any incidental damages provided in this Article (Section 2-710), due allowance for costs reasonably incurred and *due credit for* payments or *proceeds of resale.*" Ill. Rev. Stat. ch. 26, ¶ 2-708(2) (1985) (emphasis added). The literal language of 2-708(2) requires that the proceeds from resale be credited against the amount of damages awarded which, in most cases, would result in the seller recovering nominal damages. In those cases in which the lost volume seller was awarded its lost profit as damages, the courts have circumvented this problem by concluding that this language only applies to proceeds realized from the resale of uncompleted goods for scrap. *See, e.g., Neri*, 30 N.Y.2d at 399 & n.2, 334 N.Y.S.2d at 169 & n.2, 285 N.E.2d at 314 & n.2; *see also* J. White & R. Summers, HANDBOOK OF THE LAW UNDER THE UNIFORM COMMERCIAL CODE § 7-13, at 285 ("courts should simply ignore the 'due credit' language in lost volume cases") (footnote omitted). Although neither the text of 2-708(2) nor the official comments limit its application to resale of goods for scrap, there is evidence that the drafters of 2-708 seemed to have had this more limited application in mind when they proposed amending 2-708 to include the phrase "due credit for payments or proceeds of resale."[18] We

---

[17] [14] As some commentators have pointed out, the cost of calculating a loss of profit may be very high. *Goetz & Scott, supra*, at 353 ("the complexity of the lost-volume problem suggests that the information costs of exposing an overcompensatory rule are relatively high").

[18] [15] In explaining its recommendation that 2-708 be amended to include the requirement that due credit be given for resale, the Enlarged Editorial Board stated that its purpose was "to clarify the privilege of the seller to realize junk value when it is manifestly useless to complete the operation of

conclude that the Illinois Supreme Court would adopt this more restrictive interpretation of this phrase rendering it inapplicable to this case.

We therefore reverse the grant of summary judgment in favor of Davis and remand with instructions that the district court calculate Diasonics' damages under 2-708(2) if Diasonics can establish, not only that it had the capacity to make the sale to Davis as well as the sale to the resale buyer, but also that it would have been profitable for it to make both sales. Of course, Diasonics, in addition, must show that it probably would have made the second sale absent the breach. . . .

Affirmed in part, reversed in part and remanded.

NOTE

After remand there was a second appeal in the *Diasonics* case, concerning the District Court's calculation of Diasonics' lost profits damages under U.C.C. § 2-708(2) and its $153,050 judgment for Diasonics ($453,050 lost profit less a $300,000 deposit which Diasonics retained). On this appeal the Seventh Circuit held, *inter alia*, that lost volume seller Diasonics was not foreclosed from recovering lost profits even though it was unable to specify which particular MRI unit the defaulting buyer had contracted for or to trace an exact resale buyer for that unit. *R.E. Davis Chemical Corp. v. Diasonics, Inc.*, 924 F.2d 709 (7th Cir. 1991).

B. RELIANCE DAMAGES

WARTZMAN v. HIGHTOWER PRODUCTIONS, LTD.
53 Md. App. 656, 456 A.2d 82 (1983)

James S. Getty, Judge (Specially Assigned): Woody Hightower did not succeed in breaking the Guiness World Record for flagpole sitting; his failure to accomplish this seemingly nebulous feat, however, did generate protracted litigation. We are concerned here with whether Judge Robert L. Karwacki, presiding in the Superior Court of Baltimore City, correctly permitted a jury to consider the issue of "reliance damages" sustained by the appellees. Additionally, we are requested by the appellees, as cross-appellants, to determine if the trial court's refusal to permit the jury to consider prejudgment interest is error.

Hightower Productions Ltd. (appellees and cross-appellants) came into being in 1974 as a promotional venture conceived by Ira Adler, Frank Billitz and J. Daniel Quinn. The principals intended to employ a singer-entertainer who would live in a specially constructed mobile flagpole perch from April 1, 1975, until New Years Eve at which time he would descend in Times Square in New York before a nationwide television audience having established a new world record for flagpole sitting.

The young man selected to perform this feat was to be known as "Woody Hightower." The venture was to be publicized by radio and television exposure, by adopting a theme song and by having the uncrowned champion make appearances from his perch throughout the country at concerts, state fairs and shopping centers.

manufacture." Supplement No. 1 to the 1952 Official Draft (1955), quoted in *Harris, supra* p. 682, at 98.

In November, 1974, the three principals approached Michael Kaminkow of the law firm of Wartzman, Rombro, Rudd and Omansky, P.A., for the specific purpose of incorporating their venture. Mr. Kaminkow, a trial attorney, referred them to his partner, Paul Wartzman.

The three principals met with Mr. Wartzman at his home and reviewed the promotional scheme with him. They indicated that they needed to sell stock to the public in order to raise the $250,000 necessary to finance the project. Shortly thereafter, the law firm prepared and filed the articles of incorporation and Hightower Productions Ltd. came into existence on November 6, 1974. The Articles of Incorporation authorized the issuance of one million shares of stock of the par value of 10 cents per share, or a total of $100,000.00.

Following incorporation, the three principals began developing the project. With an initial investment of $20,000, they opened a corporate account at Maryland National Bank and an office in the Pikesville Plaza Building. Then began the search for "Woody Hightower." After numerous interviews, twenty-three year old John Jordan emerged as "Woody Hightower."

After selecting the flagpole tenant, the corporation then sought and obtained a company to construct the premises to house him. This consisted of a seven foot wide perch that was to include a bed, toilet, water, refrigerator and heat. The accommodations were atop an hydraulic lift system mounted upon a flat bed tractor trailer.

Hightower employed two public relations specialists to coordinate press and public relations efforts and to obtain major corporate backers. "Woody" received a proclamation from the Mayor and City Council of Baltimore and after a press breakfast at the Hilton Hotel on "All Fools Day" ascended his home in the sky.

Within ten days, Hightower obtained a live appearance for "Woody" on the Mike Douglas Show, and a commitment for an appearance on the Wonderama television program. The principals anticipated a "snow-balling" effect from commercial enterprises as the project progressed with no substantial monetary commitments for approximately six months.

Hightower raised $43,000.00 by selling stock in the corporation. Within two weeks of "Woody's" ascension, another stockholders' meeting was scheduled, because the corporation was low on funds. At that time, Mr. Wartzman informed the principals that no further stock could be sold, because the corporation was "structured wrong," and it would be necessary to obtain the services of a securities attorney to correct the problem. Mr. Wartzman had acquired this information in a casual conversation with a friend who recommended that the corporation should consult with a securities specialist.

The problem was that the law firm had failed to prepare an offering memorandum and failed to assure that the corporation had made the required disclosures to prospective investors in accordance with the provisions of the Maryland Securities Act Article 32A. (The Act was repealed and re-enacted in 1975 as C A Sec. 11-101 to 11-805). Mr. Wartzman advised Hightower that the cost of the specialist would be between $10,000.00 and $15,000.00. Hightower asked the firm to pay for the required services and the request was rejected.

Hightower then employed substitute counsel and scheduled a shareholders' meeting on April 28, 1975. At that meeting, the stockholders were advised that

Hightower was not in compliance with the securities laws; that $43,000.00, the amount investors had paid for issued stock, had to be covered by the promoters and placed in escrow; that the fee of a securities specialist would be $10,000.00 to $15,000.00 and that the additional work would require between six and eight weeks. In the interim, additional stock could not be sold, nor could "Woody" be exhibited across state lines. Faced with these problems, the shareholders decided to discontinue the entire project.

On October 8, 1975, Hightower filed suit alleging breach of contract and negligence for the law firm's failure to have created a corporation authorized to raise the capital necessary to fund the venture. At the trial, Hightower introduced into evidence its obligations and expenditures incurred in reliance on the defendant law firm's creation of a corporation authorized to raise the $250,000.00, necessary to fund the project. The development costs incurred included corporate obligations amounting to $155,339 including: initial investments by Adler and Billitz, $20,000; shareholders, excluding the three promoters, $43,010; outstanding liabilities exclusive of salaries, $58,929; liability to talent consultants, $25,000; and accrued salaries to employees, $8,400.

Individual liabilities to the three promoters, Adler, Billitz and Quinn, totaled $88,608, including loans to the corporation $44,692; repayment of corporate debt to Maryland National Bank, $8,016; and loss of salaries $36,000. The trial court disposed of the individual suit filed by the promoters, Adler, Billitz and Quinn and the cross complaint filed by the appellants. The only claim submitted for the jury's consideration was the claim of the corporation, Hightower, against the defendant law firm.

The jury returned a verdict in favor of Hightower in the amount of $170,508.43. Wartzman, Rombro, Rudd and Omansky, P.A., appealed to this Court. Hightower filed a cross appeal alleging that the jury should have been permitted to consider prejudgment interest.

The appellants raise four issues for our consideration:

1. The trial court erred in permitting Hightower to recover "reliance damages" or "development costs."
2. If "reliance damages" were recoverable, the trial court failed to properly instruct the jury on the law concerning their recovery.
3. The trial court erred in refusing to instruct the jury on the duty to mitigate damages.
4. The trial court erroneously permitted a member of the plaintiff's law firm to testify as a witness in the case.

Reliance Damages

The appellants first contend that the jury verdict included all of Hightower's expenditures and obligations incurred during its existence resulting in the law firm being absolute surety for all costs incurred in a highly speculative venture. While they do not suggest the analogy, the appellants would no doubt equate the verdict as tantamount to holding the blacksmith liable for the value of the kingdom where the smith left out a nail in shoeing the king's horse, because of which the shoe was lost, the horse was lost, the king was lost and the kingdom was lost. Appellants contend that there is a lack of nexus or causation between the alleged failure of Mr. Wartzman to discharge his duties as an attorney and the loss claimed by Hightower.

Stated differently, an unjust result will obtain where a person performing a collateral service for a new venture will, upon failure to fully perform the service, be liable as full guarantor for all costs incurred by the enterprise.

Ordinarily, profits lost due to a breach of contract are recoverable. Where anticipated profits are too speculative to be determined, monies spent in part performance, in preparation for or in reliance on the contract are recoverable. 5 CORBIN, CONTRACTS, § 1031, RESTATEMENT OF CONTRACTS, § 333, cited with approval in *Dialist Co. v. Pulford*, 42 Md. App. 173, 399 A.2d 1374 (1979).

In *Dialist, supra*, a distributor, Pulford, brought suit for breach of an exclusive contract that he had with Dialist. Pulford paid $2500.00 for the distributorship, terminated his employment with another company and expended funds in order to begin developing the area where the product was to be sold. When Pulford learned that another distributor was also given part of his territory he terminated his services.

This Court upheld the award of development costs to Pulford which included out of pocket expenses, telephone installation, office furniture, two months of forfeited salary and the value of medical insurance lost. The Court determined that the expenditures were not in preparation for or part performance of a contract, but in reliance upon it. "Such expenditures are not brought about by reason of the breach. They are induced by reliance on the contract itself and rendered worthless by its breach." *Id.* at 181, 399 A.2d 1374.

Recovery based upon reliance interest is not without limitation. If it can be shown that full performance would have resulted in a net loss, the plaintiff cannot escape the consequences of a bad bargain by falling back on his reliance interest. Where the breach has prevented an anticipated gain and made proof of loss difficult to ascertain, the injured party has a right to damages based upon his reliance interest, including expenditures made in preparation for performance, or in performance, less any loss that the party in breach can prove with reasonable certainty the injured party would have suffered had the contract been performed. RESTATEMENT (SECOND) OF CONTRACTS, § 349, *Holt v. United Security Life Ins. & Trust Co.*, 76 N.J. 585, 72 A. 301 (1909); *In Re Yeager Company*, 227 Fed. Supp. 92 (N.D. Ohio, E.D. 1963).

The appellants' contention that permitting the jury to consider reliance damages in this case rendered the appellants insurers of the venture is without merit. Section 349 of the RESTATEMENT, cited above, expressly authorizes the breaching party to prove any loss that the injured party would have suffered had the contract been performed. Such proof would avoid making the breaching party a guarantor of the success of the venture.

As Judge Learned Hand stated in *Albert & Son v. Armstrong Rubber Company*, 178 F.2d 182 (2d Cir. 1949), "It is often very hard to learn what the value of the performance would have been; and it is a common expedient, and a just one, in such situations to put the peril of the answer upon that party who by his wrong has made the issue relevant to the rights of the other. On principle therefore the proper solution would seem to be that the promisee may recover his outlay in preparation for the performance, subject to the privilege of the promisor to reduce it by as much as he can show that the promisee would have lost if the contract had been performed."

In the present case the appellants knew, or should have known, that the success of the venture rested upon the ability of Hightower to sell stock and secure advertising as public interest in the adventure accelerated. Appellants' contention that their failure to properly incorporate Hightower was collateral and lacked the necessary nexus to permit consideration of reliance damages is not persuasive. The very life blood of the project depended on the corporation's ability to sell stock to fund the promotion. This is the reason for the employment of the appellants. In reliance thereon, Hightower sold stock and incurred substantial obligations. When it could no longer sell its stock, the entire project failed. No greater nexus need be established. Aside from questioning the expertise of the promoters based upon their previous employment, the appellants were unable to establish that the stunt was doomed to fail. The inability to establish that financial chaos was inevitable does not make the appellants insurers and does not preclude Hightower from recovering reliance damages. The issue was properly submitted to the jury.

Appellants contend that the appellees should be limited to the recovery of damages under traditional contract and negligence concepts, citing *Meyerberg, Sawyer and Rue v. Agee*, 51 Md. App. 711, 446 A.2d 69 (1982).

Meyerberg, supra, involved a breach of contract action for certification of a title that was not marketable. The trial judge permitted the jury, in assessing damages, to consider: 1. Economic loss occasioned by increased costs of construction and financing. 2. Attorneys' fees expended to establish access to the property. 3. Capital gains taxes paid for failure to purchase another property within the time limitations prescribed by law. 4. The amount of earned hazard insurance premium the appellees were required to purchase.

In affirming the decision of the trial court, this Court acknowledged that a contracting party is expected to take account of only those risks that are foreseeable at the time he makes the contract and is not liable in the event of breach for loss that he did not at the time of contracting have reason to foresee as a probable result of such a breach. This limitation is set forth in RESTATEMENT (SECOND) OF CONTRACTS, section 351.

In *Meyerberg*, we noted that exceptional perception is not relevant to the test of foreseeability when applied to an attorney who is relied upon by a layman to protect his investment from pitfalls which are not readily apparent to those in foreign fields of endeavor.

Relying on *Cochrane v. Little*, 71 Md. 323, 18 A. 698 (1889), we further stated: "A client who has employed an attorney has a right to his diligence, his knowledge and his skill; and whether he had not so much of these qualities as he was bound to have, or having them, neglected to employ them, the law properly makes him liable for the loss that has accrued to his employer." We find little solace for the appellants' cause in the cases cited above.

The appellants are aggrieved by the amount of the verdict which they consider to be excessive. According to the docket entries, the appellants did not seek any modification of the verdict. It is difficult and arduous for this court to determine precisely the various costs that were presented for the jury's consideration. Jury arguments were not transcribed and the court apparently gave limiting instructions and permitted counsel to argue specific development cost items. After reviewing nine hundred and seventy-five pages of testimony and a maze of exhibits, we note that in answer to interrogatories filed in October, 1981, corporate damages were stated to be $155,339.00. This figure included shareholders investments and accrued salaries amounting to $51,410. The court's instructions precluded inclusion of these items as recoverable damages. It would appear, therefore, that the verdict may well have exceeded the guidelines set forth by the trial court. That issue is not before us, however, except that the appellants contend generally that reliance damages are improper in this case.

Instructions on Reliance Damages

Appellant's primary exception to the court's damage instruction relates to the failure to include suggested instruction 23b which states:

> You are instructed that you may not award any damages for unpaid expense of Hightower unless you find that these expenses were incurred by Hightower in justifiable reliance on the defendant's causing Hightower to comply with the securities laws. If you find that the expenses were not incurred in reliance on the defendant's performance, or if such reliance was not justified, then you may not award unpaid expenses as damages.

The Court instructed the jury that in order to find liability that the plaintiff must prove three things:

> First, the employment of the defendants in behalf of the Plaintiff and the extent of the duties for which the Defendants were employed; secondly, that the Defendants neglected the duties undertaken in the employment; and, thirdly, that such negligence resulted in and was the proximate cause of loss by the Plaintiff, that is that the Plaintiff was deprived of any right or parted with anything of value in reliance upon the negligence of the Defendants.

The instruction given fairly apprised the jury of the Plaintiffs' burden and adequately covered the reliance damage concept. Additionally, the court instructed the jury that they could not consider unpaid salaries due its officers or employees or amounts invested by stockholders as recoverable damages.

Appellants further object to the court's refusal to grant its suggested instructions 23C and D designed to forbid recovery if the jury found that Hightower would not have been able to secure funds to remain in business regardless of the defendants' breach. The instruction was properly refused. The very nature of reliance damages is that future gain cannot be measured with any reasonable degree of reliability. Had Hightower been able to show lost profits the theory of their right to recover may not have been development costs in reliance on the contract but loss based upon expectation interest instead. Appellants had the opportunity to minimize the recovery by showing that the venture could not succeed. This was difficult, but their failure to do so does not entitle them to an instruction that requires the jury to speculate on the ultimate success of the venture. We find no error in the instructions given by Judge Karwacki.

Duty to Mitigate Damages

Appellants further except to the trial court's refusal to grant any instruction on the issue of Hightower's obligation to mitigate its damages. The instruction offered by appellants is a correct statement of the law. Correctness alone, however, is insufficient to require the court to grant the prayer; there must be evidence to support the proposition to which it relates. *Dorough v. Lockman*, 224 Md. 168, 167 A.2d 129 (1961).

The evidence in this case establishes that Hightower did not have the $43,000.00 to place in escrow covering stock sold, did not have the $10,000.00 or $15,000.00 to employ a securities specialist and could not continue stock sales or exhibitions to obtain the necessary funds. Mr. Wartzman's offer to set up an appointment for Hightower with an expert in security transactions at Hightower's expense can hardly be construed as a mitigating device that Hightower was obligated to accept. The party who is in default may not mitigate his damages by showing that the other party could have reduced those damages by expending large amounts of money or incurring substantial obligations. Myerberg, *supra*. Since such risks arose because of the breach, they are to be borne by the defaulting party. 22 AM. JUR. 2d, DAMAGES, § 37, *Griffin v. Bredouw (Okla.)*, 420 P.2d 546 (1966).

The doctrine of avoidable consequences, moreover, does not apply where both parties have an equal opportunity to mitigate damages. Appellants had the same opportunity to employ and pay a securities specialist as they contend Hightower should have done. They refused. Having rejected Hightower's request to assume the costs of an additional attorney, they are estopped from asserting a failure by Hightower to reduce its loss. *See* D. Dobbs, Remedies, § 37 (1973), 11 WILLISTON, CONTRACTS § 1353 (1979).

There is no evidence in this case that the additional funds necessary to continue the operation pending a restructuring of the corporation were within the financial capabilities of Hightower. The Court properly declined to instruct the jury on the issue of mitigation.

Disqualification of Counsel . . .

Prejudgment Interest

Hightower, in its cross-appeal, alleges that the issue of pre-judgment interest should have been presented to the jury for its consideration. Applicable Maryland law provides that where a claim is for unliquidated damages, interest may run from the date of the judgment, but not before. *Affiliated Distillers*, 213 Md. 509, 132 A.2d 582, (1957), *Taylor v. Wahby*, 271 Md. 101, 314 A.2d 100, (1974).

The reliance damages sought in this case are not subject to pre-judgment valuation. "Reasonable and justified" damages incurred by reason of Mr. Wartzman's representation of Hightower were not reasonably ascertainable until the jury rendered its verdict. Refusal to permit the jury to consider prejudgment interest, therefore, was not an abuse of discretion.

In conclusion, the final comment of Judge Lowe in Myerberg, *supra*, is equally apposite here. "The unfortunate oversight on which this case was based was a costly one, but it was made by one who was hired precisely for the purpose of averting the consequent losses. It is he, and his firm, who must bear them."

Judgment Affirmed. Costs Assessed to Appellants.

NOTES

1. The text of RESTATEMENT (SECOND) OF CONTRACTS § 349 (1981) refers to *reliance* damages as follows:

§ 349. DAMAGES BASED ON RELIANCE INTEREST

As an alternative to the measure of damages stated in § 347, the injured party has a right to damages based on his reliance interest, including expenditures made in preparation for performance or in performance, less any loss that the party in breach can prove with reasonable certainty the injured party would have suffered had the contract been performed.

Section 347 ("Measure of damages in general") identifies *expectation* damages as the generally applicable measure.

2. As noted in *Wartzman*, in breach of contract cases, damages based on the injured party's reliance interest are often allowed when damages based on lost expectations are uncertain or cannot be measured. For another example, see *Brennan v. Carvel Corp.*, 929 F.2d 801 (1st Cir. 1991) where after their business failed franchisees successfully sued and recovered damages from their franchisor although the trial court noted that plaintiffs "have not proffered evidence of loss of actual profits expected in the enterprise and hence, this court cannot grant expectation damages." The court agreed with the district court that in cases where damages are suffered by a business, lost profits are often too uncertain to measure, and held that the district court did not err in granting the plaintiff's reliance damages because damages based on lost profits were too uncertain to measure.

3. *Practice Point*: In *Wartzman* the Maryland Special Appeals Court held that defendant attorneys could have defended against plaintiff's reliance damages claim by presenting evidence showing that plaintiff's venture could not have succeeded. Defendants apparently did not present any such evidence, or sufficient evidence (in the courts' view) to warrant submitting the question to the jury. "Appellants had the opportunity to minimize the recovery by showing that the venture could not succeed. This was difficult, but their failure to do so does not entitle them to an instruction that requires the jury to speculate on the ultimate success of the venture." Financial and business experts, as well as experts in other fields, are available to testify and state their opinions on matters relevant to values and probable success of various ventures. Consider, then, the possibility that counsel for the *Wartzman* defendants might have presented sufficient evidence on that reliance damages defense to make it a jury question, had they found and introduced supporting expert testimony.

4. *See Sullivan v. O'Connor*, 363 Mass. 579, 296 N.E.2d 183 (1973), *supra*, for a discussion of reliance damages. There a professional entertainer sued a plastic surgeon seeking damages for breach of contract and professional negligence in performing plastic surgery on plaintiff's nose. On the contract count she claimed that the surgeon promised a positive outcome, which would enhance her beauty and improve her appearance. The surgery failed to achieve the promised result, caused her physical and emotional pain, and subjected her to other damages and expense. The Massachusetts Supreme Court held that on the contract claim plaintiff could recover under a reliance theory of damages, observing that:

Suffering or distress resulting from the breach going beyond that which was envisaged by the treatment as agreed, should be compensable on the same ground as the worsening of the patient's condition because of the breach. Indeed it can be argued that the very suffering or distress "contracted for" — that which would have been incurred if the treatment [had] achieved the promised result — should also be compensable on the theory underlying the New York cases. For that suffering is "wasted" if the treatment fails. Otherwise stated, compensation for this waste is arguably required in order to complete the restoration of the status quo ante.

C. RESTITUTION DAMAGES

OSTEEN v. JOHNSON
473 P.2d 184 (Colo. App. 1970)

DUFFORD, Judge: . . . This was an action for breach of an oral contract. Trial was to the court, which found that the plaintiffs had paid the sum of $2,500. In exchange, the defendant had agreed to "promote" the plaintiffs' daughter, Linda Osteen, as a singer and composer of country-western music. More specifically, it was found that the defendant had agreed to advertise Linda through various mailings for a period of one year; to arrange and furnish the facilities necessary for Linda to record several songs; to prepare two records from the songs recorded; to press and mail copies of one of the records to disc jockeys throughout the country; and, if the first record met with any success, to press and mail out copies of the second record.

The trial court further found that the defendant did arrange for several recording sessions, at which Linda recorded four songs. A record was prepared of two of the songs, and 1,000 copies of the record were then pressed. Of the pressed records, 340 copies were mailed to disc jockeys, 200 were sent to the plaintiffs, and the remainder were retained by the defendant. Various mailings were made to advertise Linda; flyers were sent to disc jockeys throughout the country; and Linda's professional name was advertised in trade magazines. The record sent out received a favorable review and a high rating in a trade magazine.

Upon such findings the trial court concluded that the defendant had substantially performed the agreement. However, a judgment was entered in favor of the plaintiffs in the sum of $1.00 and costs on the basis that the defendant had wrongfully caused the name of another party to appear on the label of the record as co-author of a song which had been written solely by Linda. The trial court also ordered the defendant to deliver to the plaintiffs certain master tapes and records in the defendant's possession.

1. Right Of Restitution

Although plaintiffs' reasons are not clearly defined, they argue here that the award of damages is inadequate, and that the trial court erred in concluding that the defendant had substantially performed the agreement. However, no evidence was presented during the trial of the matter upon which an award of other than nominal damages could be based. In our opinion, the remedy which plaintiffs proved and upon which they can rely is that of restitution. *See* 5 A. CORBIN,

CONTRACTS § 996. This remedy is available where there has been a contract breach of vital importance, variously defined as a substantial breach or a breach which goes to the essence of the contract. See 5 A. Corbin, CONTRACTS section 1104, where the author writes:

> In the case of a breach by non-performance, . . . the injured party's alternative remedy by way of restitution depends upon the extent of the non-performance by the defendant. The defendant's breach may be nothing but a failure to perform some minor part of his contractual duty. Such a minor non-performance is a breach of contract and an action for damages can be maintained. The injured party, however, can not maintain an action for restitution of what he has given the defendant unless the defendant's non-performance is so material that it is held to go to the "essence"; it must be such a breach as would discharge the injured party from any further contractual duty on his own part. Such a vital breach by the defendant operates, with respect to the right of restitution, in the same way that a repudiation of the contractual obligation would operate. A minor breach by one party does not discharge the contractual duty of the other party; and the latter being still bound to perform as agreed can not be entitled to the restitution of payments already made by him or to the value of other part performances rendered.

This rule is modified somewhat where the damages which might have been awarded would be difficult or impossible to determine or inadequate. *See* 17 AM. JUR. 2d *Contracts* § 504; and *Briggs v. Robinson*, 82 Colo. 1, 256 P. 639.

2. Breach Of Contract

The essential question here then becomes whether any breach on the part of the defendant is substantial enough to justify the remedy of restitution. Plaintiffs argue that the defendant breached the contract in the following ways: First, the defendant did not promote Linda for a period of one year as agreed; secondly, the defendant wrongfully caused the name of another party to appear on the label as co-author of the song which had been composed solely by Linda; and thirdly, the defendant failed to press and mail out copies of the second record as agreed.

The first argument is not supported by the record. Plaintiffs brought the action within the one-year period for which the contract was to run. There was no evidence that during this period the defendant had not continued to promote Linda through the use of mailings and advertisements. Quite obviously the mere fact that the one-year period had not ended prior to the commencement of the action does not justify the conclusion that the defendant had breached the agreement. Plaintiffs' second argument overlooks the testimony offered on behalf of the defendant that listing the other party as co-author of the song would make it more likely that the record would be played by disc jockeys.

The plaintiffs' third argument does, however, have merit. It is clear from the record and the findings of the trial court that the first record had met with some success. It is also clear that copies of the second record were neither pressed nor mailed out. In our opinion the failure of the defendant to press and mail out copies of the second record after the first had achieved some success constituted a substantial breach of the contract and, therefore, justifies the remedy of restitution. . . . Both parties agree that the essence of their contract was to publicize

Linda as a singer of western songs and to make her name and talent known to the public. Defendant admitted and asserted that the primary method of achieving this end was to have records pressed and mailed to disc jockeys.

We find no merit in the defendant's argument that the sole issue raised by the pleadings was whether the defendant had *totally* failed to perform the agreement. . . .

3. Determining Damages

It is clear that the defendant did partially perform the contract and, under applicable law, should be allowed compensation for the reasonable value of his services. *See* 5 A. Corbin, CONTRACTS section 1114, where the author writes:

> [A]ll courts are in agreement that restitution by the defendant will not be enforced unless the plaintiff returns in some way what he has received as a part performance by the defendant.

It shall, therefore, be the ultimate order of this court that prior to restoring to the plaintiffs the $2,500 paid by them to the defendant further proceedings be held during which the trial court shall determine the reasonable value of the services which the defendant rendered on plaintiffs' behalf.

The judgment is reversed, and this case is remanded with directions that a new trial be held to determine the one issue of the amount to which the plaintiffs are entitled by way of restitution. Such amount shall be the $2,500 paid by plaintiffs to defendant less the reasonable value of the services which the defendant performed on behalf of plaintiffs.

NOTES

1. Damages by way of *restitution* of money or value of other benefits conferred may be an available alternative when a contract has been breached. A section of the RESTATEMENT (SECOND) OF CONTRACTS (1981) that deals with this damages remedy in the context of contract breach reads:

§ 373. Restitution When Other Party Is In Breach

> (1) Subject to the rule stated in Subsection (2), on a breach by non-performance that gives rise to a claim for damages for total breach or on a repudiation, the injured party is entitled to restitution for any benefit that he has conferred on the other party by way of part performance or reliance.

> (2) The injured party has no right to restitution if he has performed all of his duties under the contract and no performance by the other party remains due other than payment of a definite sum of money for that performance.

2. *Practice Point*: Restitution of fees paid to an attorney is an available remedy in situations where the attorney is found to have failed to perform. Example: In *Singleton v. Stegall*, 580 So. 2d 1242 (Miss. 1991) an inmate sued his attorney seeking compensatory and punitive damages for alleged breaches of trust and contract. The inmate, who had paid the attorney $5,000 to pursue post-conviction

proceedings, claimed that the attorney substantially failed to perform. Reversing a trial court dismissal and remanding for trial, the court held that by establishing an attorney-client relationship the attorney owed the inmate a number of contractual duties, the nonperformance of which might entitle the inmate to restitution.

3. In *Kim v. Conway & Forty, Inc.*, 772 S.W.2d 723 (Mo. App. 1989), plaintiff home buyers were held entitled to elect restitution as their remedy in a breach of contract action filed against the sellers after sellers refused to transfer title, although buyers attended the closing and tendered a check for the contract balance due. The damages claimed and awarded included return of the earnest money deposit and sums for flooring and lighting improvements.

4. Because *restitution* is generally treated as an alternative method of measurement of damages for breach of contract, the non-breaching party is not entitled to recover *restitution* as well as lost profits (*expectancy* damages). *See Morris v. Homco Intern., Inc.*, 853 F.2d 337 (5th Cir. 1988) where buyer of a business sued seller for breach of seller's noncompetition obligation under the contract, seeking damages to compensate for lost profits and seeking to avoid contract payments due to seller pursuant to the breached noncompetition agreement.

5. *Restitution* of any benefit conferred by the innocent party is an appropriate measure of damages if there is breach by nonperformance going to the essence of the contract. In *Ed Hackstaff Concrete v. Powder Ridge Condo.*, 679 P.2d 1112 (Colo. App. 1984), where a contractor sued to foreclose a mechanic's lien against a condominium owners' association for which he had contracted to repair a carport deck, and the association filed a counterclaim asserting defective workmanship, it was held that a finding that the contractor's repair work was valueless entitled the association to restitution of the total amount it had paid under the contract. *See also Harris v. Metropolitan Mall*, 112 Wis. 2d 487, 334 N.W.2d 519 (1983), an action by a real estate investor seeking restitution of his investment in a shopping mall being developed by defendants under a sale and leaseback arrangement, where defendants breached the lease and plaintiff stopped making his financing payments. There the court held that plaintiff had met the requirements for restitution because there had been a total breach of the lease agreement, the plaintiff still owed duties under the lease, and the plaintiff had conferred a benefit on the defendants with the purchase of the mall.

D. DAMAGE RULES AND THE UNIFORM COMMERCIAL CODE

The first principal case and the summary case noted below preceded the Uniform Commercial Code (U.C.C.).

MISSOURI FURNACE CO. v. COCHRAN
8 Fed. 463 (W.D. Pa 1881)

ACHESON, D.J.:

This suit, brought February 26, 1880, was to recover damages for the breach by John M. Cochran of a contract for the sale and delivery by him to the plaintiff of 36,621 tons of standard Connellsville coke, at the price of $1.20 per ton, (subject to an advance in case of a rise in wages,) deliverable on cars at his works, at the rate of nine cars of 13 tons each per day on each working day during the year 1880.

After 3,765 tons were delivered, Cochran, on February 13, 1880, notified the plaintiff that he had rescinded the contract, and thereafter delivered no coke. After Cochran's refusal further to deliver coke, the plaintiff made a substantially similar contract with one Hutchinson for the delivery during the balance of the year of 29,587 tons of Connellsville coke at four dollars per ton, which was the market rate for such a forward contract, and rather below the market price for present deliveries on February 27, 1880, the date of the Hutchinson contract. The plaintiff claimed to recover the difference between the price stipulated in the contract sued on, and the price which the plaintiff agreed to pay Hutchinson under the contract of February 27, 1880. But the court refused to adopt this standard of damages, and instructed the jury that the plaintiff was "entitled to recover, upon the coke which John M. Cochran contracted to deliver and refused to deliver to the plaintiff, the sum of the difference between the contract price — that is, the price Cochran was to receive — and the market price of standard Connellsville coke, at the place of delivery, at the several dates when the several deliveries should have been made under the contract." Under this instruction there was a verdict for the plaintiff for $22,171.49. As the plaintiff had in its hands $1,521.10 coming to the defendant for coke delivered, the damages as found by the jury amounted to the sum of $23,692.50.

The plaintiff moved the court for a new trial; and, in support of the motion, an earnest and certainly very able argument has been made by plaintiff's counsel. But we are not convinced that the instruction complained of was erroneous.

Undoubtedly it is well settled, as a general rule, that when contracts for the sale of chattels are broken by the vendor failing to deliver, the measure of damages is the difference between the contract price and the market value of the article at the time it should be delivered. SEDGWICK ON THE MEASURE OF DAMAGES, (7th Ed.) 552. In *Shepherd v. Hampton*, 3 Wheat. 200, this rule was distinctly sanctioned. Chief Justice Marshall there says: "The unanimous opinion of the court is that the price of the article at the time it was to be delivered is the measure of damages." *Id.* 204. Nor does the case of *Hopkins v. Lee*, 6 Wheat. 118, promulgate a different doctrine; for, clearly, "the time of the breach" there spoken of is the time when delivery should have been made under the contract.

It is said in SEDGWICK ON MEASURE OF DAMAGES, (7th Ed.) 558, note b: "Where delivery is required to be made by installments, the measure of damages will be estimated by the value at the time each delivery should have been made." In accordance with this principle the damages were assessed in *Brown v. Muller*, Law Rep. 7 Ex. 319, and *Roper v. Johnson*, Law Rep. 8 C.P. 167, which were suits by vendee against vendor for damages for failure to deliver iron, in the one case, and coal, in the other, deliverable in monthly installments. In one of these cases suit was brought after the contract period had expired; in the other case before its expiration; but in both cases the vendor had given notice to the plaintiff that he did not intend to fulfill his contract. To the argument, there urged on behalf of the vendor, that upon receiving such notice it is the duty of the vendee to go into the market and provide himself with a new forward contract, Kelly, C.B., in *Brown v. Muller*, said:

> He is not bound to enter into such a contract, which might be to his advantage or detriment, according as the market might fall or rise. If it fell, the defendant might fairly say that the plaintiff had no right to enter into a speculative contract, and insist that he was not called upon to pay a

greater difference than would have existed had the plaintiff held his hand.

Where the breach is on the part of the vendee, it seems to be settled law that he cannot have the damages assessed as of the date of his notice that he will not accept the goods. SEDGWICK ON MEASURE OF DAMAGES, 601. The date at which the contract is considered to have been broken by the buyer is that at which the goods were to have been delivered, not that at which he may give notice that he intends to break the contract. BENJAMIN ON SALES, § 759. And, indeed, it is a most rational doctrine that a party, whether vendor or vendee, may stand upon his contract and disregard a notice from the other party of any intended repudiation of it. If this were not so, the party desiring to be off from a contract might choose his own time to discharge himself from further liability.

The law as to the effect of such notice is clearly and most satisfactorily stated by Cockburn, C.J., in *Frost v. Knight*, Law Rep. 7 Ex. 112:

> The promisee, if he pleases, may treat the notice of intention as inoperative, and wait the time when the contract is to be executed, and then hold the other party responsible for all the consequences of non-performance; but in that case he keeps the contract alive for the benefit of the other party as well as his own; he remains subject to all his own obligations and liabilities under it, and enables the other party not only to complete the contract, if so advised, notwithstanding his previous repudiation of it, but also to take advantage of any supervening circumstances which would justify him to decline to complete it. On the other hand, the promisee may, if he thinks proper, treat the repudiation of the other party as a wrongful putting an end to the contract, and may at once bring his action as on a breach of it; and in such action he will be entitled to such damages as would have arisen from the non-performance of the contract at the appointed time, subject, however, to abatement in respect of any circumstances which may have afforded him the means of mitigating his loss. . . .

I see nothing in the present case to distinguish it from the ordinary case of a breach by the vendor of a forward contract to supply a manufacturer with an article necessary to his business. For such breach what is the true measure of damages? Says Kelly, C.B., in *Brown v. Muller*: "The proper measure of damages is that sum which the purchaser requires to put himself in the same condition as if the contract had been performed." That result — which is compensation — is secured, it seems to me, by the rule given to the jury here, unless the case is exceptional. The vendee's real loss, whether delivery is to be made at one time or in installments, ordinarily is the difference between the contract price and the market value at the times the goods should be delivered. If, however, the article is of limited production, and cannot, for that or other reason, be obtained in the market, and the vendee suffers damage beyond that difference, the measure of damages may be the actual loss he sustains. *McHose v. Fulmer*, 73 Pa. St. 367; *Richardson v. Chynoweth*, 26 Wis. 656; SEDGWICK, DAMAGES 554. With this qualification to meet exceptional cases, the rule that the damages are to be assessed with reference to the times the contract should be performed, furnishes, I think, a safe and just standard from which it would be hazardous to depart.

In this case I fail to perceive anything to call for a departure from that standard. There was no evidence of any special damage to the plaintiff by the stoppage of its furnaces or otherwise. Furthermore, the contract with Hudson, February 27, 1880, was made at a time when the coke market was excited and in an extraordinary condition. Unexpectedly and suddenly coke had risen to the unprecedented price of four dollars per ton; but this rate was of brief duration. The market declined about May 1, 1880, and by the middle of that month the price had fallen to one dollar and thirty cents per ton. The good faith of the plaintiff in entering into the new contract cannot be questioned, but it proved a most unfortunate venture. By the last of May the plaintiff had in its hands more coke than was required in its business, and it procured — at what precise loss does not clearly appear — the cancellation of contracts with Hutchinson to the extent of 20,000 tons. As the plaintiff was not bound to enter into the new forward contract, it seems to me it did so at its own risk, and cannot fairly claim that the damages chargeable against the defendant shall be assessed on the basis of that contract.

The motion for a new trial is denied.

Illinois Cent. R. Co. v. Crail, 281 U.S. 57, 50 S. Ct. 180 (1930). Crail, a Minneapolis coal dealer who purchased while in transit a carload of coal that when shipped weighed 88,700 pounds, sued the carrier when, upon delivery at plaintiff's industrial siding, the shipment was short by 5,500 pounds. The dealer had not resold any of the coal, the shipment was intended to be and was added to his stock of coal for resale, he lost no sales by reason of the shortage, and he purchased no coal to replace the shortage except via his usual practice of purchasing in carload lots of 60,000 pounds or more. Before and after the subject shipment, Crail purchased coal of like quality in carload loads delivered to his siding at $5.50 per ton plus freight. In Minneapolis the *retail* market price for like coal in less than carload lots was $13 per ton including a $3.30 freight charge. The question was whether Crail's damages should be measured by the *wholesale* or by the *retail* value of the coal. By statute (the Cummins Amendment of March 4, 1915, 49 U.S.C. § 20(11)) "the holder of a bill of lading issued for an interstate rail shipment is entitled to recover for failure to make delivery of any part of the shipment without legal excuse, 'the full actual loss, damage, or injury to such property' at point of destination." Craig contended that the Court of Appeals had correctly ruled that the measure of damage for nondelivery of a shipment of merchandise is the sum required to replace the exact amount of the shortage at the stipulated time and place of delivery "which, in this case, would be its retail value, and that convenience and the necessity for a uniform rule require its application here." The Supreme Court held, however, that this contention ignored the basic principle underlying common law remedies "that they shall afford only compensation for the injury suffered, . . . and leaves out of account the language of the amendment, which likewise gives only a right of recovery for 'actual loss.' " The Court rejected Crail's contention, noting that in the actual circumstances the cost of replacing the shortage at retail price was not the measure of Crail's loss, "since it was capable of replacement, and was, in fact, replaced in the course of [Crail's] business from purchases made in carload lots at wholesale market price without added expense." Absent special circumstances, the Court continued, "the damage for shortage in delivery by the seller of fungible goods sold by quantity is measured by the bulk price rather thanthe price for smaller quantities, both at common law . . . and under section 44 of the Uniform Sales Act. Likewise, we think that the wholesale market price is to be preferred as a test over the retail when, in circumstances like the present, it is clearly the more accurate measure."

NOTES

1. The Uniform Sales Act, referred to by the Court in the *Crail* case, preceded and has been replaced by Article 2 ("Sales") of the Uniform Commercial Code.

2. Under the U.C.C. concept of "cover," the replacement cost of goods actually purchased by a buyer in substitution for goods not delivered is a factor in the calculation of damages. U.C.C. § 2-712.

OLOFFSON v. COOMER
11 Ill. App. 3d 918, 296 N.E.2d 871 (1973)

ALLOY, Presiding Justice: Richard Oloffson, d/b/a Rich's Ag Service appeals from a judgment of the circuit court of Bureau County in favor of appellant against Clarence Coomer in the amount of $1,500 plus costs. The case was tried by the court without a jury.

Oloffson was a grain dealer. Coomer was a farmer. Oloffson was in the business of merchandising grain. Consequently, he was a "merchant" within the meaning of section 2–104 of the Uniform Commercial Code. (Ill. Rev. Stat. 1969, ch. 26 § 2–104). Coomer, however, was simply in the business of growing rather than merchandising grain. He, therefore, was not a "merchant" with respect to the merchandising of grain.

On April 16, 1970, Coomer agreed to sell to Oloffson, for delivery in October and December of 1970, 40,000 bushels of corn. Oloffson testified at the trial that the entire agreement was embodied in two separate contracts, each covering 20,000 bushels and that the first 20,000 bushels were to be delivered on or before October 30 at a price of $1.12¾ per bushel and the second 20,000 bushels were to be delivered on or before December 15, at a price of $1.12¼ per bushel. Coomer, in his testimony, agreed that the 40,000 bushels were to be delivered but stated that he was to deliver all he could by October 30 and the balance by December 15.

On June 3, 1970, Coomer informed Oloffson that he was not going to plant corn because the season had been too wet. He told Oloffson to arrange elsewhere to obtain the corn if Oloffson had obligated himself to deliver to any third party. The price for a bushel of corn on June 3, 1970, for future delivery, was $1.16. In September of 1970, Oloffson asked Coomer about delivery of the corn and Coomer repeated that he would not be able to deliver. Oloffson, however, persisted. He mailed Coomer confirmations of the April 16 agreement. Coomer ignored these. Oloffson's attorney then requested that Coomer perform. Coomer ignored this request likewise. The scheduled delivery dates referred to passed with no corn delivered. Oloffson then covered his obligation to his own vendee by purchasing 20,000 bushels at $1.35 per bushel and 20,000 bushels at $1.49 per bushel. The judgment from which Oloffson appeals awarded Oloffson as damages, the difference between the contract and the market prices on June 3, 1970, the day upon which Coomer first advised Oloffson he would not deliver.

Oloffson argues on this appeal that the proper measure of his damages was the difference between the contract price and the market price on the dates the corn should have been delivered in accordance with the April 16 agreement. Plaintiff does not seek any other damages. The trial court prior to entry of judgment, in an opinion finding the facts and reviewing the law, found that plaintiff was entitled to recover judgment only for the sum of $1,500 plus costs as we have indicated which is equal to the amount of the difference between the minimum contract price and the price on June 3, 1970, of $1.16 per bushel (taking the greatest differential from $1.12¼ per bushel multiplied by 40,000 bushels). We believe the findings and the judgment of the trial court were proper and should be affirmed.

It is clear that on June 3, 1970, Coomer repudiated the contract "with respect to performance not yet due." Under the terms of the Uniform Commercial Code the loss would impair the value of the contract to the remaining party in the amount as indicated. (Ill. Rev. Stat. 1969, ch. 26, § 2–610.) As a consequence, on June 3, 1970, Oloffson, as the "aggrieved party," could then: "(a) for a commercially reasonable time await performance by the repudiating party; or (b) resort to any remedy for breach (Section 2–703 or Section 2–711), even though he has notified the repudiating party that he would await the latter's performance and has urged retraction; . . ."

If Oloffson chose to proceed under subparagraph (a) referred to, he could have awaited Coomer's performance for a "commercially reasonable time." As we indicate in the course of this opinion, that "commercially reasonable time" expired on June 3, 1970. The Uniform Commercial Code made a change in existing Illinois law in this respect, in that, prior to the adoption of the Code, a buyer in a position as Oloffson was privileged to await a seller's performance until the date that, according to the agreement, such performance was scheduled. To the extent that a "commercially reasonable time" is less than such date of performance, the Code now conditions the buyer's right to await performance. (See Ill. Rev. Stat. Ann. 1969, ch. 26, § 2–610, Illinois Code Comment, Paragraph (a)).

If, alternatively, Oloffson had proceeded under subparagraph (b) by treating the repudiation as a breach, the remedies to which he would have been entitled were set forth in section 2–711 (Ill. Rev. Stat. 1969, ch. 26, § 2–711), which is the only applicable section to which section 2–610(b) refers, according to the relevant portion of 2–711:

> (1) Where the seller fails to make delivery or repudiates or the buyer rightfully rejects or justifiably revokes acceptance then with respect to any goods involved, and with respect to the whole if the breach goes to the whole contract (Section 2–612), the buyer may cancel and whether or not he has done so may in addition to recovering so much of the price as has been paid

> (a) "cover" and have damages under the next section as to all the goods affected whether or not they have been identified to the contract; or

> (b) recover damages for non-delivery as provided in this Article (Section 2–713). . . .

Plaintiff, therefore, was privileged under Section 2–610 of the Uniform Commercial Code to proceed either under subparagraph (a) or under subparagraph (b). At the expiration of the "commercially reasonable time" specified in subparagraph (a), he in effect would have a duty to proceed under subparagraph (b) since subparagraph (b) directs reference to remedies generally available to a buyer upon a seller's breach.

Oloffson's right to await Coomer's performance under section 2–610(a) was conditioned upon his:

(i) waiting no longer than a "commercially reasonable time"; and

(ii) dealing with Coomer in good faith.

Since Coomer's statement to Oloffson on June 3, 1970, was unequivocal and since "cover" easily and immediately was available to Oloffson in the well-organized and easily accessible market for purchases of grain to be delivered in the future, it would be unreasonable for Oloffson on June 3, 1970, to have awaited Coomer's performance rather than to have proceeded under Section 2–610(b) and, thereunder, to elect then to treat the repudiation as a breach. Therefore, if Oloffson were relying on his right to effect cover under section 2–711(1)(a), June 3, 1970, might for the foregoing reason alone have been the day on which he acquired cover.

Additionally, however, the record and the finding of the trial court indicates that Oloffson adhered to a usage of trade that permitted his customers to cancel the contract for a future delivery of grain by making known to him a desire to cancel and paying to him the difference between the contract and market price on the day of cancellation. There is no indication whatever that Coomer was aware of this usage of trade. The trial court specifically found, as a fact, that, in the context in which Oloffson's failure to disclose this information occurred, Oloffson failed to act in good faith. According to Oloffson, he didn't ask for this information:

> I'm no information sender. If he had asked I would have told him exactly what to do. . . . I didn't feel my responsibility. I thought it his to ask, in which case I would tell him exactly what to do.

We feel that the words "for a commercially reasonable time" as set forth in Section 2–610(a) must be read relatively to the obligation of good faith that is defined in Section 2–103(1)(b) and imposed expressly in Section 1–203. (Ill. Rev. Stat. 1969, ch. 26, § 2–103(1)(b) and § 1–03.)

The Uniform Commercial Code imposes upon the parties the obligation to deal with each other in good faith regardless of whether they are merchants. The Sales Article of the Code specifically defines good faith, "in the case of a merchant . . . [as] honesty in fact and the observance of reasonable commercial standards of fair dealing in the trade." For the foregoing reasons and likewise because Oloffson's failure to disclose in good faith might itself have been responsible for Coomer's failure to comply with the usage of trade which we must assume was known only to Oloffson, we conclude that a commercially reasonable time under the facts before us expired on June 3, 1970.

Imputing to Oloffson the consequences of Coomer's having acted upon the information that Oloffson in good faith should have transmitted to him, Oloffson knew or should have known on June 3, 1970, the limit of damages he probably could recover. If he were obligated to deliver grain to a third party, he knew or should have known that unless he covered on June 3, 1970, his own capital would be at risk with respect to his obligation to his own vendee. Therefore, on June 3, 1970, Oloffson, in effect, had a duty to proceed under subparagraph (b) of Section 2–610 and under subparagraphs (a) and (b) of subparagraph 1 of Section 2–711. If Oloffson had so proceeded under subparagraph (a) of Section 2–711, he should have effected cover and would have been entitled to recover damages all as provided in section 2–712, which requires that he would have had to cover in good faith without unreasonable delay. Since he would have had to effect cover on June 3, 1970, according to section 2–712(2), he would have been entitled to exactly the damages which the trial court awarded him in this cause.

Assuming that Oloffson had proceeded under subparagraph (b) of Section 2–711, he would have been entitled to recover from Coomer under Section 2–713 and Section 2–723 of the Commercial Code, the difference between the contract price and the market price on June 3, 1970, which is the date upon which he learned of the breach. This would produce precisely the same amount of damages which the trial court awarded him. (*See*: Ill. Rev. Stat. 1969, ch. 26 § 2–723(1)).

Since the trial court properly awarded the damages to which plaintiff was entitled in this cause, the judgment of the circuit court of Bureau County is, therefore, affirmed.

Affirmed.

TONGISH v. THOMAS
251 Kan. 728, 840 P.2d 471 (1992)

McFarland, Justice:

This case presents the narrow issue of whether damages arising from the nondelivery of contracted-for sunflower seeds should be computed on the basis of K.S.A. 84-1-106 or K.S.A. 84-2-713. That is, whether the buyer is entitled to its actual loss of profit or the difference between the market price and the contract price. The trial court awarded damages on the basis of the buyer's actual loss of profit. The Court of Appeals reversed the judgment, holding that the difference between the market price and the contract price was the proper measure of damages (*Tongish v. Thomas*, 16 Kan. App. 2d 809, 829 P.2d 916 [1992]). The matter is before us on petition for review.

The pertinent facts are as follows. Denis Tongish entered into a contract on April 28, 1988, with the Decatur Coop Association (Coop) where Tongish agreed to grow 160 acres of sunflower seeds, said crop to be purchased by Coop at $13 per hundredweight for large seeds and $8 per hundredweight for small seeds. By agreement, the acreage was subsequently reduced to 116.8 acres. The crop was to be delivered in increments of one-third by December 31, 1988, March 31, 1989, and May 31, 1989.

Coop had a contract to deliver the seeds purchased to Bambino Bean & Seed, Inc. Coop was to be paid the same price it paid the farmers less a 55 cent per hundredweight handling fee. Coop's only anticipated profit was the handling fee.

In October and November 1988, Tongish delivered sunflower seeds to Coop. In January, a dispute arose over the amount of dockage charged against Tongish's seeds. Tongish's seeds were of higher quality than those of many other farmers selling to Coop, and Coop's practice of commingling seeds prior to sampling was disadvantageous to Tongish. This was resolved by Coop issuing an additional check to Tongish reflecting a lower dockage charge.

Due to a short crop, bad weather, and other factors, the market price of sunflower seeds in January 1989 was double that set forth in the Tongish/Coop contract. On January 13, Tongish notified Coop he would not deliver any more sunflower seeds.

In May 1989, Tongish sold and delivered 82,820 pounds of sunflower seeds to Danny Thomas for approximately $20 per hundredweight. Tongish was to receive

$14,714.89, which was $5,153.13 more than the Coop contract price. Thomas paid for approximately one-half of the seeds. Tongish brought this action to collect the balance due. Thomas paid the balance of $7,359.61 into court and was ultimately dismissed from the action.

Meanwhile, Coop intervened in the action, seeking damages for Tongish's breach of their contract. Following a bench trial, the district court held that Tongish had breached the contract with no basis therefor. Damages were allowed in the amount of $455.51, which was the computed loss of handling charges. Coop appealed from said damage award. The Court of Appeals reversed the district court and remanded the case to the district court to determine and award damages pursuant to K.S.A. 84-2-713 (the difference between the market price and the contract price).

The analyses and rationale of the Court of Appeals utilized in resolving the issue are sound and we adopt the following portion thereof:

"The trial court decided the damages to Coop should be the loss of expected profits. Coop argues that K.S.A. 84-2-713 entitles it to collect as damages the difference between the market price and the contract price. Tongish argues that the trial court was correct and cites K.S.A. 84-1-106 as support for the contention that a party should be placed in as good a position as it would be in had the other party performed. Therefore, the only disagreement is how the damages should be calculated.

"The measure of damages in this action involves two sections of the Uniform Commercial Code: K.S.A. 84-1-106 and K.S.A. 84-2-713. The issue to be determined is which statute governs the measure of damages. Stated in another way, if the statutes are in conflict, which statute should prevail? The answer involves an ongoing academic discussion of two contending positions. The issues in this case disclose the problem.

"If Tongish had not breached the contract, he may have received under the contract terms with Coop about $5,153.13 less than he received from Danny Thomas. Coop in turn had an oral contract with Bambino to sell whatever seeds it received from Tongish to Bambino for the same price Coop paid for them. Therefore, if the contract had been performed, Coop would not have actually received the extra $5,153.13.

"We first turn our attention to the conflicting statutes and the applicable rules of statutory construction. K.S.A. 84-1-106(1) states:

'The remedies provided by this act shall be liberally administered to the end that the aggrieved party may be put in as good a position as if the other party had fully performed but neither consequential or special nor penal damages may be had except as specifically provided in this act or by other rule of law.'

"If a seller breaches a contract and the buyer does not 'cover,' the buyer is free to pursue other available remedies. K.S.A. 84-2-711 and 84-2-712. One remedy, which is a complete alternative to 'cover' (K.S.A. 84-2-713, Official comment), is K.S.A. 84-2-713(1), which provides:

'Subject to the provisions of this article with respect to proof of market price (section 84-2-723), the measure of damages for nondelivery or repudiation by the seller is the difference between the market price at the time when the buyer learned of the breach and the contract price together with any incidental and consequential damages provided in this article (section 84-2-715), but less expenses saved in consequence of the seller's breach.'

"Neither party argues that the Uniform Commercial Code is inapplicable. Both agree that the issue to be determined is which provision of the U.C.C. should be applied. As stated by the appellee: 'This is really the essence of this appeal, i.e., whether this general rule of damages [K.S.A. 84-1-106] controls the measure of damages set forth in K.S.A. 84-2-713.' However, Tongish then offers no support that K.S.A. 84-1-106 controls over K.S.A. 84-2-713. The authority he does cite (*M&W Development, Inc. v. El Paso Water Co.*, 6 Kan. App. 2d 735, 634 P.2d 166 [1981]) is not a U.C.C. case and K.S.A. 84-2-713 was not applicable.

"The statutes do contain conflicting provisions. On the one hand, K.S.A. 84-1-106 offers a general guide of how remedies of the U.C.C. should be applied, whereas K.S.A. 84-2-713 specifically describes a damage remedy that gives the buyer certain damages when the seller breaches a contract for the sale of goods.

"The cardinal rule of statutory construction, to which all others are subordinate, is that the purpose and intent of the legislature govern. *State ex rel. Stephan v. Kansas Racing Comm'n*, 246 Kan. 708, 719, 792 P.2d 971 (1990); *Cedar Creek Properties, Inc. v. Board of Johnson County Comm'rs*, 246 Kan. 412, 417, 789 P.2d 1170 (1990); and *Stauffer Communications, Inc. v. Mitchell*, 246 Kan. 492, Syl. P. 1, 789 P.2d 1153 (1990). When there is a conflict between a statute dealing generally with a subject and another statute dealing specifically with a certain phase of it, the specific statute controls unless it appears that the legislature intended to make the general act controlling. *State v. Wilcox*, 245 Kan. 76, Syl. P. 1, 775 P.2d 177 (1989). The Kansas Supreme Court stated in *Kansas Racing Management, Inc. v. Kansas Racing Comm'n*, 244 Kan. 343, 353, 770 P.2d 423 (1989): 'General and special statutes should be read together and harmonized whenever possible, but to the extent a conflict between them exists, the special statute will prevail unless it appears the legislature intended to make the general statute controlling.'

"K.S.A. 84-2-713 allows the buyer to collect the difference in market price and contract price for damages in a breached contract. For that reason, it seems impossible to reconcile the decision of the district court that limits damages to lost profits with this statute.

"Therefore, because it appears impractical to make K.S.A. 84-1-106 and K.S.A. 84-2-713 harmonize in this factual situation, K.S.A. 84-2-713 should prevail as the more specific statute according to statutory rules of construction.

"As stated, however, Coop protected itself against market price fluctuations through its contract with Bambino. Other than the minimal handling charge, Coop suffered no lost profits from the breach. Should the protection require an exception to the general rule under K.S.A. 84-2-713? . . . .

"There is authority for appellee's position that K.S.A. 84-2-713 should not be applied in certain circumstances. In *Allied Canners & Packers, Inc. v. Victor Packing Co.*, 162 Cal. App. 3d 905, 209 Cal. Rptr. 60 (1984), Allied contracted to purchase 375,000 pounds of raisins from Victor for 29.75 cents per pound with a 4% discount. Allied then contracted to sell the raisins for 29.75 cents per pound expecting a profit of $4,462.50 from the 4% discount it received from Victor. 162 Cal. App. 3d at 907-08 [209 Cal. Rptr. 60].

"Heavy rains damaged the raisin crop and Victor breached its contract, being unable to fulfill the requirement. The market price of raisins had risen to about 80 cents per pound. Allied's buyers agreed to rescind their contracts so Allied was not bound to supply them with raisins at a severe loss. Therefore, the actual loss to Allied was the $4,462.50 profit it expected, while the difference between the market price and the contract price was about $150,000. 162 Cal. App. 3d at 908-09 [209 Cal. Rptr. 60].

"The California appellate court, in writing an exception, stated: 'It has been recognized that the use of the market-price contract-price formula under section 2-713 does not, absent pure accident, result in a damage award reflecting the buyer's actual loss. [Citations omitted.]' 162 Cal. App. 3d at 912 [209 Cal. Rptr. 60]. The court indicated that section 2-713 may be more of a statutory liquidated damages clause and, therefore, conflicts with the goal of section 1-106. The court discussed that in situations where the buyer has made a resale contract for the goods, which the seller knows about, it may be appropriate to limit 2-713 damages to actual loss. However, the court cited a concern that a seller not be rewarded for a bad faith breach of contract. 162 Cal. App. 3d at 912-14 [209 Cal. Rptr. 60].

"In Allied, the court determined that if the seller knew the buyer had a resale contract for the goods, and the seller did not breach the contract in bad faith, the buyer was limited to actual loss of damages under section 1-106. 162 Cal. App. 3d at 915 [209 Cal. Rptr. 60].

"The similarities between the present case and Allied are that the buyer made a resale contract which the seller knew about. (Tongish knew the seeds eventually went to Bambino, although he may not have known the details of the deal.) However, in examining the breach itself, Victor could not deliver the raisins because its crop had been destroyed. Tongish testified that he breached the contract because he was dissatisfied with dockage tests of Coop and/or Bambino. Victor had no raisins to sell to any buyer, while Tongish took advantage of the doubling price of sunflower seeds and sold to Danny Thomas. Although the trial court had no need to find whether Tongish breached the contract in bad faith, it did find there was no valid reason for the breach. Therefore, the nature of Tongish's breach was much different than Victor's in Allied.

"Section 2-713 and the theories behind it have a lengthy and somewhat controversial history. In 1963, it was suggested that 2-713 was a statutory liquidated damages clause and not really an effort to try and accurately predict what actual damages would be. Peters, *Remedies for Breach of Contracts Relating to the Sale of Goods Under the Uniform Commercial Code: A Roadmap for Article Two*, 73 YALE L.J. 199, 259 (1963).

"In 1978, Robert Childres called for the repeal of section 2-713. Childres, *Buyer's Remedies: The Danger of Section 2-713*, 72 Nw. U. L. REV. 837 (1978). Childres reflected that because the market price/contract price remedy 'has been the cornerstone of Anglo-American damages' that it has been so hard to see that this remedy 'makes no sense whatever when applied to real life situations.' 72 Nw. U. L. REV. at 841-42.

"In 1979, David Simon and Gerald A. Novack wrote a fairly objective analysis of the two arguments about section 2-713 and stated:

'For over sixty years our courts have divided on the question of which measure of damages is appropriate for the supplier's breach of his delivery obligations. The majority view, reinforced by applicable codes, would award market damages even though in excess of plaintiff's loss. A persistent minority would reduce market damages to the plaintiff's loss, without regard to whether this creates a windfall for the defendant. Strangely enough, each view has generally tended to disregard the arguments, and even the existence, of the opposing view.' Simon and Novack, *Limiting the Buyer's Market Damages to Lost Profits: A Challenge to the Enforceability of Market Contracts*, 92 HARV. L. REV. 1395, 1397 (1979).

"Although the article discussed both sides of the issue, the authors came down on the side of market price/contract price as the preferred damages theory. The authors admit that market damages fly in the face 'of the familiar maxim that the purpose of contract damages is to make the injured party whole, not penalize the breaching party.' 92 HARV. L. REV. at 1437. However, they argue that the market damages rule discourages the breach of contracts and encourages a more efficient market. 92 HARV. L. REV. at 1437.

"The Allied decision in 1984, which relied on the articles cited above for its analysis to reject market price/contract price damages, has been sharply criticized. In Schneider, *U.C.C. Section 2-713: A Defense of Buyers' Expectancy Damages*, 22 CAL. W. L. REV. 233, 266 (1986), the author stated that Allied 'adopted the most restrictive [position] on buyer's damages. This Article is intended to reverse that trend.' Schneider argued that by following section 1-106, 'the court ignored the clear language of section 2-713's compensation scheme to award expectation damages in accordance with the parties' allocation of risk as measured by the difference between contract price and market price on the date set for performance.' 22 CAL. W. L. REV. at 264.

"Recently in Scott, *The Case for Market Damages: Revisiting the Lost Profits Puzzle*, 57 U. CHI. L. REV. 1155, 1200 (1990), the Allied result was called 'unfortunate.' Scott argues that section 1-106 is 'entirely consistent' with the market damages remedy of 2-713. 57 U. CHI. L. REV. at 1201. According to Scott, it is possible to harmonize sections 1-106 and 2-713. Scott states, 'Market damages measure the expectancy ex ante, and thus reflect the value of the option; lost profits, on the other hand, measure losses ex post, and thus only reflect the value of the completed exchange.' 57 U. CHI. L. REV. at 1174. The author argues that if the nonbreaching party has laid off part of the market risk (like Coop did) the lost profits rule creates instability because the other party is now encouraged to breach the contract if the market fluctuates to its advantage. 57 U. CHI. L. REV. at 1178.

"We are not persuaded that the lost profits view under Allied should be embraced. It is a minority rule that has received only nominal support. We believe the majority rule or the market damages remedy as contained in K.S.A. 84-2-713 is more reasoned and should be followed as the preferred measure of damages. While application of the rule may not reflect the actual loss to a buyer, it encourages a more efficient market and discourages the breach of contracts." *Tongish v. Thomas*, 16 Kan. App. 2d at 811-17 [829 P.2d 916].

At first blush, the result reached herein appears unfair. However, closer scrutiny dissipates this impression. By the terms of the contract Coop was obligated to buy Tongish's large sunflower seeds at $13 per hundredweight whether or not it had a market for them. Had the price of sunflower seeds plummeted by delivery time, Coop's obligation to purchase at the agreed price was fixed. If loss of actual profit pursuant to K.S.A. 84-1-106(1) would be the measure of damages to be applied herein, it would enable Tongish to consider the Coop contract price of $13 per hundred weight plus 55 cents per hundredweight handling fee as the "floor" price for his seeds, take advantage of rapidly escalating prices, ignore his contractual obligation, and profitably sell to the highest bidder. Damages computed under K.S.A. 84-2-713 encourage the honoring of contracts and market stability.

As an additional argument, Tongish contends that the application of K.S.A. 84-2-713 would result in the unjust enrichment of Coop. This argument was not presented to the trial court.

Even if properly before us, the argument lacks merit. We discussed the doctrine of unjust enrichment in *J.W. Thompson Co. v. Welles Products Corp.*, 243 Kan. 503, 758 P.2d 738 (1988), stating: "The basic elements on a claim based on a theory of unjust enrichment are threefold: (1) a benefit conferred upon the defendant by the plaintiff; (2) an appreciation or knowledge of the benefit by the defendant; and (3) the acceptance or retention by the defendant of the benefit under such circumstances as to make it inequitable for the defendant to retain the benefit without payment of its value." 243 Kan. at 512, 758 P.2d 738.

Before us is which statutory measure of damages applies. This is not a matter of one party conferring a benefit upon another.

The judgment of the Court of Appeals reversing the district court and remanding the case for the determination and award of damages pursuant to the provisions of K.S.A. 84-2-713 is affirmed. The judgment of the district court is reversed.

NOTES

1. Section 2-713 of the U.C.C. (identical to K.S.A. 84-2-713 referred to in the *Tongish* case) substantially codifies for sales-of-goods cases one of the general common law rules for measuring damages in contract breach situations. This common law rule states that, where appropriate, damages may be measured by the difference between the contract price of the subject item and its market value/price at the time and place of the contract breach.

2. Question: U.C.C. § 2-713 ("Buyer's damages for non-delivery or repudiation") provides that buyer's damages in cases to which the section applies are measured by "the difference between the market price at the time when the buyer learned of the breach and the contract price together with incidental and consequential damages provided in [Article 2], but less expenses saved in consequence of the seller's breach." In a rising market (one in which prices are moving up), to what extent, if any, does the U.C.C. rule result in a different measure of damages than the similar common law rule? What about in a declining market?

KOENEN v. ROYAL BUICK CO.
162 Ariz. 376, 783 P.2d 822 (1989)

ROLL, Judge:

Defendant Royal Buick Company (Royal Buick) appeals from a judgment entered in favor of Thomas Koenen in connection with an alleged breach of contract involving a limited edition automobile. Because sufficient evidence was presented that Koenen entered into a contract with Royal Buick and that Royal Buick breached that contract, we affirm.

FACTS

In September 1986, Thomas Koenen learned from automobile literature that General Motors planned to manufacture 500 special editions of the Buick Regal Grand National automobile. The vehicle, dubbed the Grand National Experimental (GNX) was the quickest limited production car in the United States at that time. The GNX, like the Grand National, was available only in black and had a 3.8 turbo-charged fuel-injected hand-built motor. The GNX, however, had additional features including an intercooled turbo-charged V-6 engine with special body, special tires and suspension, and special wheels. The GNX was featured on the cover of Autoweek and Popular Mechanics. . . .

Several months before Royal Buick, a Tucson-based automobile dealership, received official notification that it would receive one of the 500 GNX autos, Koenen contacted salesperson William Yalen at Royal Buick. Koenen, along with his father and brother, collected cars under the name of Koenen Classic Cars. Their collection was stored in an air-conditioned California warehouse. Koenen had previously conducted transactions with Royal Buick and Yalen. In March 1986, Koenen purchased a 1986 Grand National from Royal Buick for cash. Yalen was the salesperson. In August 1986, Koenen purchased a 1987 Grand National through Yalen from Royal Buick for cash.

In November 1986, Koenen went to Yalen and told him that he wished to buy a GNX. Koenen showed Yalen current literature regarding Buick's plan to offer a limited number of this special edition. During discussions with Yalen and new car sales manager Robert Sagar, Koenen agreed to pay the window sticker price for the vehicle, that is, the price placed on the car at the factory.

In December 1986, Royal Buick General Manager Tom Bird orally agreed to sell the GNX to Gary Gerovac. No purchase order was completed, however. On January 5, 1987, Jeff Buchner signed a purchase order agreement to purchase a GNX from Royal Buick. Although Buchner offered to give Royal Buick a $1000 deposit in connection with the purchase order, he was told that a $100 deposit was satisfactory. At that time, sales manager Sagar assured Buchner that he was "first in line."

On February 16, 1987, a purchase order form was signed by Koenen, Yalen, and Sagar regarding the GNX. The document contained the notation: Order is not binding on Seller until accepted in writing by officer, or Sales-manager of Seller, and until Purchaser's credit has been approved. The purchase order also contained the notation "Price and Availability To Be Determined?" Koenen was listed on the form as the purchaser. Koenen told Sagar and Yalen that he was willing to pay up to $30,000 if that was the sticker price. Sagar and Yalen told Koenen that no one else had made a deposit and that Koenen was number one to receive a GNX. Koenen gave Yalen a check for $500 as a deposit for the GNX but asked that the check not be cashed. On February 17, 1987, Royal Buick filled out a purchase order form for David Woon and accepted a $500 deposit from him for purchase of the

GNX. On February 20, 1987, Koenen replaced the February 16, 1987 check with a $500 check from his father.

In a letter dated April 21, 1987, General Motors notified Royal Buick that it would receive one GNX. The window sticker price for the vehicle was $29,290. Royal Buick General Manager Tom Bird placed a market value of $44,900 on the vehicle. Yalen contacted Koenen to see if Koenen wanted to bid on the vehicle.

On May 8, 1987, Royal Buick returned the deposits to Koenen, Buchner, and Woon. When Buchner received the letter, he contacted Sagar to protest. Sagar asked Buchner if he would be interested in bidding on the vehicle. Royal Buick received the GNX in September 1987. Royal Buick placed a price of $44,900 on the vehicle. Bird testified as to the process by which he arrived at the $44,900 figure:

> Q: Who came up with the price?
>
> A: I did.
>
> Q: And how did you come up with that price?
>
> A: In doing a little search as to what the cars were bringing around the country, that that [sic] seemed to be somewhat of a mean figure.
>
> Q: About $45,000?
>
> A: Right. We wanted to be a little cheaper than anybody else, so we cut it down a hundred dollars.
>
> Q: Four hundred?
>
> A: Forty-four nine.
>
> Q: Forty-four nine?
>
> A: I was being facetious in that last comment, but it was forty-four nine.

In April 1988, Royal Buick sold the vehicle for $39,750 to an Oklahoma physician.

PROCEDURAL HISTORY

Koenen received Royal Buick's May 8, 1987 letter informing him that he would not be able to purchase the GNX. The letter included a check in the amount of Koenen's $500 deposit, but Koenen declined to cash the check. Koenen proceeded to file a civil complaint alleging breach of contract on the part of Royal Buick. As part of the complaint, Koenen sought a temporary restraining order preventing Royal Buick from selling the GNX. By stipulation of the parties, Royal Buick agreed not to sell the vehicle. On November 30, 1987, a preliminary injunction was denied and Royal Buick was permitted to sell the GNX.

Koenen's complaint against Royal Buick was joined with a complaint filed by Buchner, who also sought damages based upon Royal Buick's refusal to sell the GNX to him. [Koenen's complaint was amended adding allegations of fraud and negligence.]

The matter was tried to the court without a jury. The trial court awarded Koenen and Buchner $15,610 each, representing the difference between the manufacturer's suggested retail price ($29,290) and the fair market value of the automobile ($44,900). [Buchner and Royal Buick later stipulated to dismissal of Royal Buick's appeal as to the judgment in favor of Buchner.]

ISSUES ON APPEAL

On appeal, Royal Buick argues that (1) no enforceable contract was entered between Royal Buick and Koenen, (2) the purchase order did not satisfy the statute of frauds, (3) parol evidence was improperly admitted to explain the terms of the purchase order, (4) the contract was illegal and void, and (5) Koenen failed to prove the damages awarded by the court.

Standards of Review

This court must view the evidence and reasonable inferences therefrom in the light most favorable to the prevailing party. If there is any evidence to support the judgment, we are required to affirm. *Paul Schoonover, Inc. v. Ram Construction, Inc.*, 129 Ariz. 204, 205, 630 P.2d 27, 28 (1981). Questions of law are reviewed de novo. *Tovrea Land & Cattle Co. v. Linsenmeyer*, 100 Ariz. 107, 114, 412 P.2d 47, 52 (1966).

Proof of Damages

Finally, Royal Buick argues that the trial court should have computed damages as the difference between the cost to cover the loss and the contract price, and that Koenen failed to prove the cost of cover.

The U.C.C. permits a buyer to elect the remedy when damaged by the actions of the seller. A.R.S. § 47-2711. Here, Koenen elected the difference between the fair market value and the contract price. A.R.S. § 47-2713.

Koenen's father purchased a GNX for the family collection from another source. No evidence was introduced as to the purchase price of that particular vehicle. Royal Buick argues that because Koenen's father succeeded in obtaining a GNX from a different source, Koenen suffered no damages or, alternatively, that Koenen was required to introduce evidence as to the purchase price for the other GNX so that the court would be able to determine the fair market value of the GNX which Koenen was unable to purchase from Royal Buick.

We disagree. First, the fact that Koenen's father purchased a substitute vehicle is not dispositive. If the father's purchase was proven to be a reasonable substitute for the contracted car then the measure of damages would be the difference between the cost of cover and the contract price. No evidence shows that the vehicle was purchased specifically to substitute for the lost bargain under the Royal Buick contract. The car was purchased in April or May 1988, some 11 or 12 months after Royal Buick repudiated the contract. Also, Koenen testified that even after acquiring the GNX, he was still possibly in the market for another one.

"The burden of proof as to mitigation of damages is on the party asserting the requirement." *Harper & Associates v. Printers, Inc.*, 46 Wash. App. 417, 424, 730 P.2d 733, 736-37 (1986). Royal Buick failed to introduce any evidence that the father's purchase substituted for the Royal Buick contract or that the purchase of that car in any way mitigated the damages under the contract. Therefore, Royal Buick cannot claim that the buyer elected the remedy of cover. *Jamestown Farmers Elevator, Inc. v. General Mills, Inc.*, 552 F.2d 1285, 1293 (8th Cir. 1977).

Royal Buick also argues that Koenen was required to introduce evidence as to the purchase price for the other GNX so the court could determine the fair market value of the contracted GNX. We disagree. A.R.S. Section 47-2713 requires that market price be determined at the time the buyer learned of the breach. Royal Buick breached its contract with Koenen on May 8, 1987. Evidence of the purchase price of a GNX one year later is not dispositive of the fair market value of the vehicle in 1987. Significantly, when the Royal Buick general manager testified regarding the fair market value of the GNX which Royal Buick was selling, he testified that he surveyed Buick dealerships and determined that $45,000 was a fair market value for the GNX. This concession by Royal Buick could certainly be considered by the trial court.

The trial court correctly computed damages as the difference between the fair market value and the contract price. Sufficient evidence was presented to support the trial court's conclusion that $44,900 was the market value of the vehicle.

We affirm.

Attorneys' Fees

A.R.S. § 12-341.01 authorizes an award to the successful party in any contested action arising out of contract. Section 12-341.01 applies to appeals as well as trials. *Wenk v. Horizon Moving & Storage Co.*, 131 Ariz. 131, 133, 639 P.2d 321, 323 (1982). Appellee Koenen is awarded attorneys' fees incurred in the defense of this appeal.

NOTES

1. *Question:* The court in *Koenen* stated, among other things, that "The U.C.C. permits a buyer to elect the remedy when damaged by the actions of the seller. A.R.S. § 47-2711. Here, Koenen elected the difference between the fair market value and the contract price. A.R.S. § 47-2713." The alternate remedy available to an innocent buyer under the U.C.C. is the difference between cover price and contract price (§ 2–712). If the GNX automobile purchased by Koenen's father a year after the dealer's breach *had* been a cover purchase, and if the cover price were less than market price, would Koenen really have been allowed to elect the 2–713 remedy? What are the arguments in favor of and what are those against allowing that election under those circumstances?

2. Under the mitigation of damages principle referred to by the court in *Koenen*, the non-breaching party is refused recovery for increased damages accruing by reason of unreasonable action or inaction by the non-breaching party taken or omitted after learning of the breach. The principle does not impose a *duty* on the non-breaching party to mitigate; it simply denies recovery for that portion of the party's damages that accrue by reason of his failure to mitigate.

3. The RESTATEMENT (SECOND) OF CONTRACTS (1981) refers to the concept as one of *avoidability*. The text of § 350 of the RESTATEMENT reads:

§ 350. AVOIDABILITY AS A LIMITATION ON DAMAGES

(1) Except as stated in Subsection (2), damages are not recoverable for loss that the injured party could have avoided without undue risk, burden or humiliation.

(2) The injured party is not precluded from recovery by the rule stated in Subsection (1) to the extent that he has made reasonable but unsuccessful efforts to avoid loss.

4. *Problem*: Assume the same facts as in the *Koenen* case, except that shortly after its breach Royal Buick offered to sell the vehicle to Koenen for $39,900 ($5,000 less than its then-fair market value), stating that "We wish to mitigate the situation and renew your confidence in our firm. For this reason we are providing you the opportunity to purchase the car anew for $39,900." In response Koenen, after speaking with his counsel, advised: "I do want the car, and I am willing to mitigate at a cover price of $39,900. However, I am reserving and am not waiving all rights to which I have become entitled." What do the parties mean by their respective statements, and what are the legal implications of the situation now?

LAREDO HIDES CO. V. H&H MEAT PRODUCTS CO.
513 S.W.2d 210 (Tex. Civ. App. 1974)

BISSETT, Justice:

This is a breach of contract case. Laredo Hides Company, Inc., the buyer, sued H&H Meat Products Company, Inc., the seller, to recover damages for breach of a written contract for the sale of cattle hides. Trial was to the court without a jury. A take nothing judgment in favor of defendant was rendered. Plaintiff has appealed.

[Laredo Hides corporation, located in Laredo, Texas, purchases cattle hides from various meat packers and ships them to tanneries in Mexico. Laredo had a contract to purchase all of H&H's byproduct hides for a fixed period of time, with payment in cash at pickup. When Laredo sent a truck to pick up a load of hides on March 18, 1972, they forgot to send a check along. When Laredo called H&H to see how to handle the situation, the owner of H&H told him to just mail the check, which Laredo did later that day. Three days later the check had not reached H&H and the owner called and asked where the check was? He was assured during two different phone calls that it had been mailed. Then, during the second phone call, the owner of H&H told Laredo Hides that if H&H did not receive the check by 4:30 that afternoon H&H would never "sell [Laredo] another hide." Laredo arranged for a bank transfer of the required funds directly into H&H's bank account, but it was not credited to H&H's account until the fourth day after the original pickup date of the hides. H&H "treated the failure to make payment before 4:30 p.m. on March 21, 1972, as a breach of the agreement which gave H&H a right to cancel the contract." and the owner of H&H advised Laredo that he had "made up his mind to terminate the contract."]

Laredo Hides, on March 3, 1972, had contracted with a Mexican tannery for the sale of all the hides which it expected to purchase from H&H under the February 29, 1972, contract. Following the cancellation by H&H of the contract, Laredo Hides, in order to meet the requirements of its contract with the tannery, was forced to purchase hides on the open market in substitution for the hides which were to have been delivered to it under the contract with H&H.

[Laredo purchased 17,218 hides at the total replacement cost of about $142,254.48 over what it would have paid H&H, and suffered additional handling costs of $3,448.95 to satisfy their obligations under its sales contract with the tannery. During the course of the contract period the market price of hides tripled in price.]

The trial court filed findings of fact and conclusions of law. The findings are, in substance, as follows: 1) time was of the essence of the written contract; 2) on March 18, 1972, plaintiff breached the contract by failure to make payment upon delivery of the hides; 3) defendant (after March 18, 1972) orally agreed with plaintiff to accept payment if the money was in defendant's possession by 4:30 p.m. on March 21, 1972, but if plaintiff did not make such payment within the time limited therefor, that no further hides would be sold to plaintiff under the contract; and, 4) payment was not received until the inter-bank transfer deposit on March 23, 1972. Based on these findings, the court concluded: ". . . that the cancellation by defendant of its contract with plaintiff, upon plaintiff's original breach of such contract and subsequent failure to make such payment to defendant within the time as extended, was legally justified, and that plaintiff is not entitled to recover of defendant its money damages thereafter allegedly accruing.". . .

The record before us will neither allow time to be made the essence of the contract by implication, nor permit an oral extrinsic showing that such was the intention of the parties to the written contract, the terms of which are expressed in clear, explicit and unequivocal language. Time of payment was not of the essence under the contract sued on by Laredo Hides.

There are two reasons why the finding that Laredo Hides breached the contract on March 18, 1972, when it failed to make payment upon delivery of the hides cannot be sustained. First, payment was made on March 18, 1972, when the check was mailed to H&H pursuant to instructions by Hinojosa. Second, the actual payment of cash upon delivery of the hides was waived.

Since this case must be reversed, we now confront the issue of damages. The guidelines for determining a buyer's remedies in a case where there is a breach of a contract for the sale of goods by a seller are found in Chapter 2 of the Texas Business and Commerce Code. Among other remedies afforded by the Code, when there is a repudiation of the contract by the seller or a failure to make delivery of the goods under contract, the buyer may cover under section 2.711. He may have damages under section 2.712 "by making in good faith and without unreasonable delay any reasonable purchase of or contract to purchase goods in substitution for those due from the seller," and "may recover from the seller as damages the difference between the cost of cover and the contract price together with any incidental or consequential damages" provided by the chapter; or, he may, under section 2.713, have damages measured by "the difference between the market price at the time when the buyer learned of the breach and the contract price together with any incidental and consequential damages" provided by the chapter. . . .

Laredo Hides offered uncontroverted evidence of the hide production of H&H from April to December, 1972. It also established the price for the same number of hides which it was forced to buy elsewhere. There was testimony that purchases had to be made periodically throughout 1972 since Laredo Hides had no storage facilities, and the hides would decompose if allowed to age. Furthermore, White, a C.P.A., testified as to statistical summaries which he made showing the cost of buying substitute hides. These summaries were made from invoices which are also in evidence. All of this evidence was admitted without objection. Clearly, Laredo Hides elected to pursue the remedy provided by section 2.712 of the Code, and by its pleadings and evidence brought itself within the purview of the "cover" provisions contained therein.

It is not necessary under section 2.712 that the buyer establish market price. . . . Where the buyer complies with the requirements of section 2.712, his purchase is presumed proper and the burden of proof is on the seller to show that 'cover' was not properly obtained. . . . There was no evidence offered by H&H to negate this presumption or to "establish expenses saved in consequence of the seller's breach," as permitted by § 2.712.

The difference between the cover price and the contract price is shown to be $134,252.82 for steer hides and $8,001.66 for bull hides, or a total of $142,254.48. In addition, Laredo Hides offered evidence of increased transportation costs of $1,435.77, and increased handling charges of $2,013.18. These are clearly recoverable as incidental damages where the buyer elects to "cover." §§ 2.715(a); 2.712(b). . . .

The rule in Texas is that prejudgment interest will be allowed as damages when the principal damages are determinable and established at a definite time, either by rules of evidence or known standards of value. When such is the case, interest is recoverable from the date of the injury. . . . Such interest (as damages) may only be recovered where there is either a specific claim for the interest, or a prayer for general relief and a claim for damages in such a sum as to include interest as well as specific damages. . . .

In the absence of a special exception, the general rule allows a recovery of interest as damages under a prayer for general relief without the necessity of a specific prayer therefor, provided that the amount claimed in the pleadings is sufficient to cover the loss at the time of accrual of the cause of action and interest thereon from that date to time of trial. . . .

There is no evidence that Laredo Hides, in any manner, endeavored to increase its damages sustained when H&H refused to deliver any more hides to it. Laredo Hides, in purchasing the hides in substitution of the hides which should have been delivered under the contract, acted promptly and in a reasonable manner. The facts of this case regarding the issue of liability of H&H and the issues pertaining to damages suffered by Laredo Hides, have been fully and completely developed in the court below. The facts upon which judgment should have been rendered for Laredo Hides by the trial court are conclusively established. It, therefore, becomes the duty of this Court to render judgment which the trial court should have rendered. . . .

Applying the rules announced by the above cited cases and authorities to the instant case, we hold that the record does not support the findings of fact made by the trial judge and there is no legal justification for the conclusion of law reached by the court. Accordingly, the judgment of the trial court is reversed, and judgment is here rendered for Laredo Hides in the amount of $152,960.04, together with interest thereon at the rate of 6% Per annum from August 6, 1973, the date judgment was rendered by the trial court, until paid.

Reversed and rendered.

NYE, Chief Justice (dissenting):

I concur in and with that part of the opinion that calls for a reversal of the trial court's judgment. Since all of the essential facts upon which judgment can be rendered were not conclusively established, nor were they a part of the trial court's finding of fact, the judgment should not be rendered. I would remand the case for a new trial.

TRANS WORLD METALS, INC. v. SOUTHWIRE CO.
769 F.2d 902 (2d Cir. 1985)

[Trans World Metals brought suit against Southwire for breach of a long-term commodity supply contract in which Southwire had agreed to purchase 12,000 tons of aluminum from Trans World. The jury determined that Southwire was the breaching party and awarded Trans World $7,122,141.84 in damages "consisting of $6,702,529.00 for repudiation of the remaining purchase obligations of the contract and $419,232.84 for shipments accepted without payment by Southwire in February." The District Court applied the New York prejudgment interest rate and awarded Trans World $1,304,804.88 in prejudgment interest, for a total of $8,426,946.72. Its motions for judgment notwithstanding the verdict and for a new trial having been denied, Southwire filed an appeal. On appeal, the Second Circuit rejected Southwire's contention that Trans World was the breaching party. Even though Trans World had not shipped the complete first month's allotment of aluminum in January 1982, it was held that this did not constitute a breach, and the jury having found that the "time is of essence" and "termination" clauses of Southwire's "purchase contract confirmation" were not a part of the contract, Southwire did not have the right to repudiate.]

Jon O. Newman, Circuit Judge: . . . .

Southwire complains that the damage award, calculated by the difference between contract and market prices, gave Trans World an unwarranted windfall. Southwire favors an alternative measure of damages based on the rate of profit earned by Trans World on the first month's completed shipments projected over the twelve-month life of the contract. Such a measure, Southwire argues, would better estimate the amount Trans World would have made had the contract been completed. We reject this alternative as contrary to the Uniform Commercial Code.

Seller's damages for repudiation are governed by section 2-708 of the Uniform Commercial Code. Subsection 1 of this section sets forth the general rule that damages are to be calculated by the difference between the contract and market prices:

> (1) Subject to subsection (2) and to the provisions of this Article with respect to proof of market price (Section 2-723), the measure of damages for non-acceptance or repudiation by the buyer is the difference between the market price at the time and place for tender and the unpaid contract price together with any incidental damages provided in this Article (Section 2-710), but less expenses saved in consequence of the buyer's breach." N.Y.U.C.C. Law § 2-708(1).

The drafters of the Uniform Commercial Code recognized that this measure would not adequately compensate certain types of sellers, generally referred to as "lost volume sellers." *See* J. White & R. Summers, Uniform Commercial Code § 7-9, at 274-76 (2d ed. 1980) ("White & Summers"). Therefore, an alternative measure of damages was provided for those sellers who would be inadequately compensated by the standard contract/market price differential:

> (2) If the measure of damages provided in subsection (1) is inadequate to put the seller in as good a position as performance would have done then the measure of damages is the profit (including reasonable overhead) which the seller would have made from full performance by the buyer, together with any incidental damages provided in this Article (Section 2-710), due allowance for costs reasonably incurred and due credit for payments or proceeds of resale." N.Y.U.C.C. Law § 2-708(2).

This measure of damages is often preferred by sellers who have not acquired the goods to be sold prior to the buyer's repudiation because such sellers often would be undercompensated by the contract/market price measure of damages.[19]

Southwire argues that the "lost profits" measure should also apply when the seller would be overcompensated by section 2-708(1). We disagree. We do not doubt that the contract/market price differential "will seldom be the same as the seller's actual economic loss from breach." White & Summers § 7-7, at 269; *see* Peters, *Remedies for Breach of Contracts Relating to the Sale of Goods Under the Uniform Commercial Code: A Roadmap for Article Two*, 73 YALE L.J. 199, 259 (1963). However, nothing in the language or history of section 2-708(2) suggests that it was intended to apply to cases in which section 2-708(1) might overcompensate the seller. *See* White & Summers § 7-12, at 283. Nor has Southwire cited any New York case that interprets section 2-708(2) as Southwire urges us to interpret it. As a federal court sitting in diversity, we will not extend the application of this state law.

Nor are we convinced that Trans World has been overcompensated. No measure other than the contract/market price differential will award Trans World the "benefit of its bargain," that is, the "amount necessary to put [it] in as good a position as [it] would have been if the defendant had abided by the contract." *Western Geophysical Co. of America, Inc. v. Bolt Associates, Inc.*, 584 F.2d 1164, 1172 (2d Cir. 1978) (quoting *Perma Research & Development Co. v. Singer Co.*, 402 F. Supp. 881, 898 (S.D.N.Y.1975), *aff'd*, 542 F.2d 111 (2d Cir.), *cert. denied*, 429 U.S. 987, 97 S. Ct. 507, 50 L. Ed. 2d 598 (1976)). The contract at issue in this case is an aluminum supply contract entered into eight months prior to the initial deliveries called for by its terms. The last of the anticipated deliveries of aluminum would not have been completed until a full twenty months after the negotiations took place. It simply could not have escaped these parties that they were betting on which way aluminum prices would move. Trans World took the risk that the price would rise; Southwire took the risk that the price would fall. Under these circumstances, Trans World should not be denied the benefit of its bargain, as reflected by the

---

[19] [3] Professors White and Summers refer to such sellers as "jobbers." "By 'jobber' we refer to a seller who satisfies two conditions. First, he is a seller who never acquires the contract goods. Second, his decision not to acquire those goods after learning of the breach is commercially reasonable under 2-704. . . . Since he has no goods on hand to resell, he cannot even resell on the market at the time of tender and so recoup the amount necessary to make him whole by adding such proceeds to his 2-708(1) recovery. Thus the only recovery which grossly approximates the "jobber's" economic loss is a recovery based on lost profits." White & Summers § 7-10, at 278. In a case involving a commodity like aluminum that fluctuates rapidly in price — as compared to standard-priced goods like cars, see 67 AM. JUR. 2D *Sales* § 1129 — the lost profits of a selling jobber may well be adequately reflected by the contract/market price differential.

contract/market price differential.[20] Cf. *Apex Oil Co. v. Vanguard Oil & Service Co.*, 760 F.2d 417 (2d Cir. 1985) (defaulting seller obliged to pay damages based on contract/market price differential).

The decision primarily relied upon by Southwire is distinguishable from this case. *Nobs Chemical, U.S.A., Inc. v. Koppers Co., Inc.*, 616 F.2d 212 (5th Cir. 1980), involved a seller acting as a middleman. The seller in Nobs had entered into a second fixed-price contract with its own supplier for purchase of the goods to be sold under the contract sued upon; its "market price" thus had been fixed in advance by contract. Because the seller had contractually protected itself against market price fluctuation, the Fifth Circuit concluded that it would have been unfair to permit the seller to reap a riskless benefit. As that Court noted, "the difference between the fallen market price and the contract price is [not] necessary to compensate the plaintiffs for the breach. Had the transaction been completed, their 'benefit of the bargain' would not have been affected by the fall in the market price. . . ." *Id.* at 215. Whether or not we would have reached the same result in Nobs, here the benefit of the bargain under a completed contract would have been affected by the fall in aluminum prices.[21] Because Trans World accepted the risk that prices would rise, it is entitled to benefit from their fall.

Southwire raises a number of further points on appeal. The first involves the proper determination of the market price for purposes of calculating the contract/market price differential. The jury relied upon Trans World's damage calculations, which were based on the market price as reflected by bids received on April 26 (and projections discussed below). Southwire argues that because the contract was repudiated on March 4, the market price figure used to calculate damages should be the March 4 price. We do not agree. The measure of damages set forth in section 2-708(1) is "the difference between the market price at the time and place for tender and the unpaid contract price." N.Y.U.C.C. Law § 2-708(1) (emphasis added [by the court]); cf. *id.* § 2-713(1) (buyer's damages for repudiation by seller measured by contract/market price differential "at the time when the buyer learned of the breach"). Thus, the pertinent market price date is not the date of repudiation but the date for tender.

We would accept Southwire's argument that the date Trans World learned of the repudiation would be the correct date on which to calculate the market price had this action been tried before the time for full performance under the contract. *See* N.Y.U.C.C. § 2-723(1) (market price at time aggrieved party learned of repudiation used to calculate damages in action for anticipatory repudiation that "comes to trial before time for performance with respect to some or all of the goods"). However, where damages are awarded after the time for full performance, as in this case, the calculation of damages under section 2-708(1) should reflect the actual market price at each successive date when tender was to have been made under the repudiated

---

[20] [4] Southwire presented no evidence and made no claim concerning any expenses saved by Trans World as a result of Southwire's breach. Such expenses, if established, would have reduced the recoverable damages. N.Y.U.C.C. Law § 2-708(1); *see* Katz Communications, Inc. v. The Evening News Association, 705 F.2d 20, 26-27 (2d Cir. 1983).

[21] [5] Although Trans World had available to it about 78,000 tons of aluminum at the time of the breach, Trans World had corresponding obligations to deliver about 76,000 tons of aluminum to buyers other than Southwire. Absent any indication that Trans World had "identified" any of this metal to the Southwire contract, *see* N.Y.U.C.C. Law § 2-501(b), we cannot say, as could the court in Nobs, that a change in the market price would not affect the seller's "benefit of the bargain."

installment contract. This was the rule prior to enactment of the Uniform Commercial Code. *United States v. Burton Coal Co.*, 273 U.S. 337, 340, 47 S. Ct. 351, 352, 71 L. Ed. 670 (1927) (following repudiation of supply contract, "seller may recover the difference between the contract price and the market value at the times when and the places where deliveries should have been made"); *L.W. Foster Sportswear Co. v. Goldblatt Brothers*, Inc., 356 F.2d 906, 910 & n.6 (7th Cir. 1966) (recognizing same standard under pre-U.C.C. law and U.C.C. § 2-708); *see* 67A AM. JUR. 2D *Sales* § 1115, at 505 n.19 (2d ed. 1985); *id.* § 1118, at 510 n. 50. New York did not intend to deviate from this measure of damages upon adoption of the Uniform Commercial Code. The Official Comment to section 2-708 indicates that the "prior uniform statutory provision is followed generally in setting the current market price at the time and place for tender as the standard by which damages for non-acceptance are to be determined." N.Y.U.C.C. Law § 2-708 Official Comment 1. The "prior uniform statutory provision" indicated that where " 'there is an available market for the goods . . . [damages should be measured by] the difference between the contract price and the market or current price . . . when the goods ought to have been accepted, or, if no time was fixed for acceptance, then at the time of the refusal to accept.' " *Id.* § 2-708 Practice Commentary (*quoting* Sales Act § 64 (McKinney's Personal Property Law § 145)).

We therefore conclude that when calculating damages for a buyer's repudiation of an installment contract by the contract/market price differential, "time . . . for tender" under section 2-708(1) is the date for each successive tender of an installment, as specified in the contract. *See* 67A AM. JUR. 2D *Sales* § 1118, at 510 ("[W]here the breach is of an installment contract, damages should be measured by the market price at the time of each delivery." (footnote omitted)). In this case the successive dates for tender were the last day of each month in 1982, at which time Trans World was authorized to invoice that month's shipments even if such shipments had not been "released" by Southwire's delivery instructions. A contract/market price differential should have been calculated for each month during 1982.

We recognize that the jury relied upon a damage calculation prepared for Trans World that did not use actual market prices for each month of scheduled tenders. Instead, Trans World's expert took the actual price for April 1982 and projected forward from that date "anticipated" increases of $15 per metric ton for each month thereafter. Though the use of such an estimate was inappropriate because the actual market price for each successive month was known by the date of the trial, Southwire has no basis for complaint. Trans World's projected monthly market prices were closer to the contract price than were the actual market prices. Trans World therefore received less in damages using its expert's projection than it would have received using the correct measure. Furthermore, Southwire did not preserve at trial the factual issue as to the correct market price on each successive date of tender. Southwire did not object to Trans World's use or the accuracy of projected prices nor otherwise raise the issue with the jury, relying instead on its unsuccessful effort to convince the jurors that the contract/market price differential was not an appropriate method for calculating damages. Having failed to preserve the point for appeal, Southwire may not now raise the issue for the first time. *See, e.g., Schmidt v. Polish People's Republic*, 742 F.2d 67, 70 (2d Cir. 1984).

Southwire contends that it was improper for the District Court to award prejudgment interest because Georgia law governs this case and Georgia does not permit prejudgment interest except on liquidated damages. *See United States ex rel. Georgia Electric Supply Co., Inc. v. United States Fidelity and Guaranty Co.,* 656 F.2d 993, 997 (5th Cir. 1981). Southwire argues that Georgia law applies to this case both because of the inclusion of a choice-of-law provision on the back of the purchase contract confirmation and because under New York choice-of-law rules Georgia is the place of "most significant contacts." *See, e.g., Transatlantic Cement, Inc. v. Lambert Freres et Cie,* 462 F. Supp. 363, 364-65 (S.D.N.Y. 1978). In ruling on this issue the District Court stated that "[i]n view of the numerous contacts with the State of New York, we believe that New York law is applicable, that plaintiffs are entitled to [prejudgment] interest and the appropriate rate is nine percent per annum." Because the District Court would not have undertaken this conflict-of-laws analysis had it determined that the choice-of-law provision in the purchase contract confirmation was part of the contract between the parties, we take the District Court's statement as an implicit ruling that, like the delivery time and termination clauses of the purchase contract confirmation, the choice-of-law provision was not part of the contract. This implicit finding is not clearly erroneous. Nor can we say that the choice-of-law ruling was in error. Though both Georgia and New York had contacts with this transaction, it would be anomalous to reject the holding that New York was the state with the most significant contacts when there was serious doubt that Trans World had sufficient contacts in Georgia even to subject it to personal jurisdiction there. . . .

We have considered Southwire's remaining claims and find them to lack merit. The judgment of the District Court is affirmed.

NOTES

1. *Prejudgment interest,* discussed by the court at the end of its *Trans World* opinion, can accrue as either: (a) interest calculated from the date of breach to the date of judgment, or (b) interest calculated from the date the suit was filed to the date of judgment. In jurisdictions that allow prejudgment interest as defined by "(a)," prejudgment interest traditionally was limited to claims that by their nature or by agreement were liquidated (meaning certain) in amount, or as to which the damage amount could be set by fixed standards of valuation. Some jurisdictions, as in New York, make the *prejudgment interest* remedy available in other selected situations, too. *See* examples below: *New York* (statutory), *Florida* (statutory), *Maine* (statutory), *New Jersey* (case law).

2. The New York *prejudgment interest* rule is statutory (CPLR § 5001). The statute reads in part:

§ 5001. Interest to verdict, report or decision

(a) Actions in which recoverable. Interest shall be recovered upon a sum awarded because of a breach of performance of a contract, or because of an act or omission depriving or otherwise interfering with title to, or possession or enjoyment of, property, except that in an action of an equitable nature, interest and the rate and date from which it shall be computed shall be in the court's discretion.

(b) Date from which computed. Interest shall be computed from the earliest ascertainable date the cause of action existed, except that interest upon damages incurred thereafter shall be computed from the date incurred. Where such damages were incurred at various times, interest shall be computed upon each item from the date it was incurred or upon all of the damages from a single reasonable intermediate date.

3. *Practice Point*: When state law mandates prejudgment interest only for actions *at law*, and allows it in the court's discretion for actions *in equity*, questions can arise as to whether a quantum meruit (or similar) claim is legal or equitable. A 2005 commentary concerning New York's CPLR § 5001 states that "Reviewing the contents of a quantum meruit claim substantively, the Third Department in *Precision Foundations v. Ives*, 4 A.D.3d 589, 772 N.Y.S.2d 116 (3d Dep't 2004), holds implicitly that it is a claim in equity. Whether to award interest on it is therefore subject to the court's discretion, says *Precision*, and, on an exercise of discretion on the facts, the court denies the interest."

4. The Maine *prejudgment interest* statute (14 M.R.S.A. § 1602(1)), reads in part as follows:

§ 1602-B. Interest before judgment (eff. July 1, 2003)

1. In small claims. In small claims actions, prejudgment interest is not recoverable unless the rate of interest is based on a contract or note.

2. On contracts and notes. In all civil and small claims actions involving a contract or note that contains a provision relating to interest, prejudgment interest is allowed at the rate set forth in the contract or note.

3. Other civil actions; rate. In civil actions other than those set forth in subsections 1 and 2, prejudgment interest is allowed at the one-year United States Treasury bill rate plus 3%. . . .

5. Accrual; suspension; waiver. Prejudgment interest accrues from the time of notice of claim setting forth under oath the cause of action, served personally or by registered or certified mail upon the defendant until the date on which an order of judgment is entered. . . . If the prevailing party at any time requests and obtains a continuance for a period in excess of 30 days, interest is suspended for the duration of the continuance. On petition of the nonprevailing party and on a showing of good cause, the trial court may order that interest awarded by this section be fully or partially waived.

5. A Florida statute that includes a *prejudgment interest* provision (F.S. 57.105(1)) provides: "57.105. Attorney's fee; sanctions for raising unsupported claims or defenses. . . . If the court awards attorney's fees to a claimant pursuant to this subsection, the court shall also award prejudgment interest. . . ." In *RDR Computer Consulting Corp. v. Eurodirect, Inc.*, 884 So. 2d 1053 (Fla. App. 2 Dist. 2004), the Florida appeals court held that counterclaimant RDR was entitled to prejudgment interest on its award against plaintiff customer for breach of contract, and held that the damages were liquidated by the jury's verdict and the judgment as of and from the date certain when the contract terminated and damages first became due.

6. New Jersey cases defining that state's pre-1993 prejudgment interest rule are summarized in *Performance Leasing Corp. v. Irwin Lincoln-Mercury*, 262 N.J. Super. 23, 619 A.2d 1024 (N.J. Super. A.D., 1993), which notes (a) that the rule limiting prejudgment interest awards to cases where damages were liquidated or clearly ascertainable in advance has been significantly eroded, and (b) that it can now be awarded whether either liquidated or unliquidated damages are recovered

and the equities are in the injured party's favor. *See also, e.g.*, N.J.S.A. 59:13-8. Interest on judgments (eff. 2001): "No interest shall accrue prior to the entry of judgment in a court of competent jurisdiction, except that the court, in its discretion, may award prejudgment interest on the whole or part of a judgment arising out of or relating to claims for the construction or installation of improvements to real property in accordance with principles of equity."; N.J. R. Law Div. Civ. Pt. R. 6:6-3. Judgment by Default: "(a) Entry by the Clerk; Judgment for Money. . . . If prejudgment interest is demanded in the complaint the clerk shall add that interest to the amount due provided the affidavit of proof states the date of defendant's breach and the amount of such interest. If the judgment is based on a document of obligation that provides a rate of interest, prejudgment interest shall be calculated in accordance therewith; . . ."

7. The U.S. Supreme Court, in its 2004 opinion awarding damages to Kansas against Colorado for unlawful water depletion contrary to the Arkansas River Compact, held that prejudgment interest accruing as of the time the original suit was filed (1985), would be based on damages incurred only from that time until the date of judgment, rather than from the time when Colorado knew or should have known it was in violation. The Court ruled that the goal of the prejudgment interest award in the special context of the case was to balance the equities and to apply the Court's own "considerations of fairness," rather than to provide compensation for all of Kansas' lost investment opportunities. *State of Kansas v. State of Colorado*, 543 U.S. 86, 125 S. Ct. 526, 160 L. Ed. 2d 418 (Dec. 7, 2004).

E.   DEFENSES TO DAMAGE CLAIMS

1.   Insufficient Proof

FREUND v. WASHINGTON SQUARE PRESS, INC.
34 N.Y.2d 379, 357 N.Y.S.2d 857, 314 N.E.2d 419 (1974)

[Freund, an author, sued publisher Washington Square Press, for breach of contract for failing to publish his book as promised. The contract provided that unless the contract were terminated defendant agreed to publish the work in hardbound edition within 18 months and afterwards in paperbound edition. In addition to a $2,000 advance which was paid to the author, the contract provided that he was to receive, not the books themselves, but a percentage of receipts on sales of books published and sold. The publisher had a 60-day right to terminate which it did not exercise, but refused to publish the manuscript. After trial, finding that the loss of hardcover publication was the natural and probable consequence of the breach and based upon expert testimony, the trial court awarded plaintiff $10,000 to cover the cost of publication. The Appellate Division by split decision (3-2) affirmed the conclusion that cost of publication was the proper measure of damages, drawing an analogy to construction contract cases in which the cost of completion could be the proper measure for a builder's failure to complete a house or for use of wrong materials. The dissent, however, with which the Court of Appeals agreed in this opinion, would have allowed plaintiff only nominal damages.]

SAMUEL RABIN, Judge:

. . . It is axiomatic that, except where punitive damages are allowable, the law awards damages for breach of contract to compensate for injury caused by the breach — injury which was foreseeable, *i.e.*, reasonably within the contemplation of the parties, at the time the contract was entered into. (*Swain v. Schieffelin*, 134 N.Y. 471, 473, 31 N.E. 1025, 1026.) Money damages are substitutional relief designed in theory "to put the injured party in as good a position as he would have been put by full performance of the contract, at the least cost to the defendant and without charging him with harms that he had no sufficient reason to foresee when he made the contract." (5 CORBIN, CONTRACTS, § 1002, pp. 31-32; 11 WILLISTON, CONTRACTS (3d ed.), § 1338, p. 198.) In other words, so far as possible, the law attempts to secure to the injured party the benefit of his bargain, subject to the limitations that the injury — whether it be losses suffered or gains prevented — was foreseeable, and that the amount of damages claimed be measurable with a reasonable degree of certainty and, of course, adequately proven. (*See generally* Dobbs, LAW OF REMEDIES, p. 148; *see also* Farnsworth, *Legal Remedies for Breach of Contract*, 70 COL. L. REV. 1145, 1159.) But it is equally fundamental that the injured party should not recover more from the breach than he would have gained had the contract been fully performed. (*Baker v. Drake*, 53 N.Y. 211, 217; *see generally* Dobbs, LAW OF REMEDIES, p. 810.)

Measurement of damages in this case according to the cost of publication to the plaintiff would confer greater advantage than performance of the contract would have entailed to plaintiff and would place him in a far better position than he would have occupied had the defendant fully performed. Such measurement bears no relation to compensation for plaintiff's actual loss or anticipated profit. Far beyond compensating plaintiff for the interests he had in the defendant's performance of the contract — whether restitution, reliance or expectation (*see* Fuller & Perdue, *Reliance Interest in Contract Damages*, 46 YALE L.J. 52, 53-56) an award of the cost of publication would enrich plaintiff at defendant's expense.

Pursuant to the contract, plaintiff delivered his manuscript to the defendant. In doing so, he conferred a value on the defendant which, upon defendant's breach, was required to be restored to him. Special Term, in addition to ordering a trial on the issue of damages, ordered defendant to return the manuscript to plaintiff and plaintiff's restitution interest in the contract was thereby protected. (Cf. 5 CORBIN, CONTRACTS, § 996, p. 15.)

At the trial on the issue of damages, plaintiff alleged no reliance losses suffered in performing the contract or in making necessary preparations to perform. Had such losses, if foreseeable and ascertainable, been incurred, plaintiff would have been entitled to compensation for them. (Cf. *Bernstein v. Meech*, 130 N.Y. 354, 359, 29 N.E. 255, 257.)

As for plaintiff's expectation interest in the contract, it was basically two-fold — the "advance" and the royalties. (To be sure, plaintiff may have expected to enjoy whatever notoriety, prestige or other benefits that might have attended publication, but even if these expectations were compensable, plaintiff did not attempt at trial to place a monetary value on them.) There is no dispute that plaintiff's expectancy in the "advance" was fulfilled — he has received his $2,000. His expectancy interest in the royalties — the profit he stood to gain from sale of the published book — while theoretically compensable, was speculative. Although this work is not plaintiff's first, at trial he provided no stable foundation for a reasonable estimate of royalties he would have earned had defendant not breached its promise to publish. In these circumstances, his claim for royalties falls for uncertainty. (Cf. *Broadway Photoplay Co. v. World Film Corp.*, 225 N.Y. 104, 121 N.E. 756; *Hewlett v. Caplin*, 275 App. Div. 797, 88 N.Y.S.2d 428.)

Since the damages which would have compensated plaintiff for anticipated royalties were not proved with the required certainty, we agree with the dissent in the Appellate Division that nominal damages alone are recoverable. (Cf. *Manhattan Sav. Inst. v. Gottfried Baking Co.*, 286 N.Y. 398, 36 N.E.2d 637.) Though these are damages in name only and not at all compensatory, they are nevertheless awarded as a formal vindication of plaintiff's legal right to compensation which has not been given a sufficiently certain monetary valuation. (Cf. *Baker v. Hart*, 123 N.Y. 470, 474, 25 N.E. 948, 949; *see, generally,* Dobbs, LAW OF REMEDIES, p. 191; 11 WILLISTON, CONTRACTS (3d ed.), § 1339A, pp. 206-208.)

In our view, the analogy by the majority in the Appellate Division to the construction contract situation was inapposite. In the typical construction contract, the owner agrees to pay money or other consideration to a builder and expects, under the contract, to receive a completed building in return. The value of the promised performance to the owner is the properly constructed building. In this case, unlike the typical construction contract, the value to plaintiff of the promised performance — publication — was a percentage of sales of the books published and not the books themselves. Had the plaintiff contracted for the printing, binding and delivery of a number of hardbound copies of his manuscript, to be sold or disposed of as he wished, then perhaps the construction analogy, and measurement of damages by the cost of replacement or completion, would have some application.

Here, however, the specific value to plaintiff of the promised publication was the royalties he stood to receive from defendant's sales of the published book. Essentially, publication represented what it would have cost the defendant to confer that value upon the plaintiff, and, by its breach, defendant saved that cost. The error by the courts below was in measuring damages not by the value to plaintiff of the promised performance but by the cost of that performance to defendant. Damages are not measured, however, by what the defaulting party saved by the breach, but by the natural and probable consequences of the breach *to the plaintiff*. In this case, the consequence to plaintiff of defendant's failure to publish is that he is prevented from realizing the gains promised by the contract — the royalties. But, as we have stated, the amount of royalties plaintiff would have realized was not ascertained with adequate certainty and, as a consequence, plaintiff may recover nominal damages only.

Accordingly, the order of the Appellate Division should be modified to the extent of reducing the damage award of $10,000 for the cost of publication to six cents, but with costs and disbursements to the plaintiff. . . .

ESTATE OF HENDERSON v. HENDERSON
804 So. 2d 191 (Ala. 2001)

[June M. Henderson sued the estate of Hiliary H. Henderson, Jr. ("the Estate"), and her three stepsons in their capacities as coexecutors of the Estate, alleging a breach of a prenuptial contract. At trial, "the jury returned a verdict in favor of Ms. Henderson, awarding her damages of $250,000 on the breach-of-contract claim against the Estate . . . ." The Estate appealed arguing "that the damages awarded for breach of contract were not supported by the evidence."]

We affirm conditionally.

Facts

On January 28, 1975, Dr. Hiliary H. Henderson, Jr., and June Massey Wood (now known as June M. Henderson) entered into a prenuptial agreement, which stated, in pertinent part:

> In the event Mrs. Wood [June M. Henderson] survives Dr. Henderson, Dr. Henderson will cause to be paid to her for and during her lifetime, or until her remarriage, the income from his security account, which he presently estimates to be a sum of approximately $250,000. Upon the death or remarriage of Mrs. Wood, these securities shall be transferred to Dr. Henderson's three sons or their surviving issue. Nothing herein contained shall prohibit Dr. Henderson from changing investments in his security account or from selling securities and investing in other assets at any time after this marriage." Ms. Henderson agreed that accepting the provisions of the prenuptial agreement precluded her from taking any future interest in Dr. Henderson's estate. . . .

The Hendersons were married on February 9, 1975. In 1976, Dr. Henderson executed a will naming his three sons from a prior marriage as coexecutors. The will incorporated the prenuptial agreement. Before his death in January 1996, Dr. Henderson asked his sons to help him arrange his estate. The sons hired an attorney to review Dr. Henderson's estate plan. The attorney drafted a trust agreement and a new will for Dr. Henderson, but the attorney never had any direct contact with him. The new will and the trust agreement were executed in July 1995. At the time of Dr. Henderson's death, his security account contained eight stocks.

Ms. Henderson claimed that the trust agreement conflicted with the Hendersons' prenuptial agreement — which guaranteed her the income from all of the stocks in the security account — in that it provided Ms. Henderson the income from only two of the eight stocks held in Dr. Henderson's security account at the time of his death. The remaining six stocks were bequeathed in the new will to the coexecutors as part of the residuary estate. The coexecutors sold these six stocks after Dr. Henderson's death and invested the proceeds in certificates of deposit. Ms. Henderson testified that she was not aware the new will and the trust agreement had been prepared until after Dr. Henderson's death.

Ms. Henderson sued the Estate, alleging breach of the prenuptial agreement and seeking relief in the nature of specific performance and seeking damages. She argued that the breach occurred when Dr. Henderson signed the trust agreement and the new will, dividing his security account and thus depriving her of the dividends agreed upon in the prenuptial agreement. The jury returned a verdict in favor of Ms. Henderson. The trial court entered a judgment on the jury's verdict, ordering that the damages award against the Estate be paid from the certificates of deposit that had been purchased from the proceeds of the sale of the six stocks, and that the remainder of those certificates of deposit be delivered to the corpus of the trust benefiting Ms. Henderson, in order to effectuate the terms of the prenuptial agreement.[22]

---

[22] [1] The trial court's order stated:

II. Excessiveness of the Damages Award for Breach of Contract

The Estate does not challenge the trial court's finding that at the time of Dr. Henderson's death his security account included all eight of the stocks. Nor does it challenge the court's final order instructing the Estate in what manner to satisfy the judgment and implement the provisions of the prenuptial agreement. The Estate does, however, contest the damages award of $250,000 for breach of contract because, it claims, the award was not supported by the evidence.

The Estate argues that the only evidence Ms. Henderson offered to support her claim for damages for breach of contract was introduced in the form of a chart detailing the amount of dividend income the six stocks would have earned during the four years following the death of Dr. Henderson had those stocks remained in the trust and not been invested in certificates of deposit. The dividend income indicated by that chart totaled $64,343. 29. The Estate also argues that the only other evidence offered that supported Ms. Henderson's claim for damages was offered by the Estate itself. Brooks Henderson testified that the certificates of deposit purchased from the proceeds of the sale of six stocks yielded the Estate approximately $25,000 per year in income, totaling $100,000 over the four years following Dr. Henderson's death.

Ms. Henderson argues that without knowing what elements the jury considered in making its decision to award her $250,000 in damages for breach of contract, this Court "is not in the position to take exception with [the jury's] findings."

The trial court instructed the jury that the measure of the damages recoverable for a breach of contract was "what amount would be sufficient to place [Ms. Henderson] in the same shoes she would have been in had the contract not been breached." While the prenuptial agreement may be susceptible to an interpretation that Ms. Henderson was due the principal amount of $250,000 at Dr. Henderson's death, the first appeal held that Ms. Henderson was due only the income from all the securities held in Dr. Henderson's security account, which was valued at $250,000 at the time of the agreement.

Ms. Henderson cites *Donavan v. Fandrich*, 265 Ala. 439, 92 So. 2d 1 (1957), for the proposition that if the jury verdict is supported by any reasonable hypothesis presented by the evidence, it should not be set aside. She argues that there was substantial evidence presented to the jury from which it could have arrived at the verdict, and she suggests several hypotheses as to how the jury reached that verdict. In Donavan, the plaintiff sued to recover $2,185 that he claimed the defendant owed him for seed. The jury, however, returned a verdict in favor of the plaintiff in the amount of $1,427.68. In reversing the judgment based on that verdict, this Court stated:

> We have searched the record with considerable care and we are unable to find any evidence which tends to justify a finding of the amount fixed by the jury and for which judgment was rendered. Where, as here, the jury

---

(1) The Two Hundred Fifty Thousand Dollar ($250,000.00) judgment against the estate in this case is to be paid from the CD's or time deposits and the interest earned thereon held by the estate and which were purchased from the proceeds of sale of the six securities.

(2) The remainder of said CD's or time deposits with an accounting thereof shall be delivered to the trustee of the Henderson Security Account Trust Agreement dated July 14, 1995 as additional corpus of said trust and in full satisfaction of the duty of the estate to effectuate the terms of the antenuptial agreement.

verdict cannot be justified upon any reasonable hypothesis presented by the evidence, it ought to be set aside upon proper proceedings as being the result of compromise or mistake, for neither the court nor [the] jury have the right to arbitrate or compromise differences between the parties. It is no adequate answer to say that a judgment for a larger amount might have been justified as a legal possibility. In this state of the case appellant's motion for a new trial should have been granted. *Donavan*, 265 Ala. at 440-41, 92 So. 2d at 2; . . .

Similarly, the only evidence suggesting the proper amount of damages that could be awarded on Ms. Henderson's breach-of-contract claim was the chart, which represented the dividend income from the six stocks as totaling $64,343.29, and the testimony of Brooks Henderson indicating that the certificates of deposit yielded $100,000 in interest income over the four years following Dr. Henderson's death. Ms. Henderson's closing argument to the jury acknowledged that the damages award could be, at most, $100,000, and her attempt to justify a larger sum is a grasp at straws. In stating the "reasonable hypotheses" she suggests in her brief, Ms. Henderson overlooks the undisputed evidence, distorts the reasonable import of the testimony, and disregards the law of the case established in the earlier appeal.

After carefully considering the record, we find no evidence to support the jury's $250,000 damages award for breach of contract. The greatest amount of compensatory damages a jury could have awarded based on the evidence would have been $100,000. The trial court erred in denying the Estate's postjudgment motion for a new trial or, in the alternative, a remittitur of the damages. Therefore, we order a remittitur of the damages award to $100,000. If Ms. Henderson chooses not to accept this remittitur, the judgment will be reversed and the cause remanded for a new trial.

III. Motion to Dismiss Appeal

Ms. Henderson also asks that this appeal be dismissed, based on the acceptance-of-benefits doctrine. She claims that the Estate used the judgment against it in order to obtain a tax benefit and that it should now be precluded from appealing that judgment.

Following the jury's verdict, the Estate amended its 1996 income-tax return, on which it had claimed approximately $21,000 in income from the stocks it had retained. The Estate delivered the amended tax return to Ms. Henderson. The document reflected that the dividend income was properly payable to Ms. Henderson for the year 1996. Ms. Henderson amended her 1996 income-tax return; the amendment caused her to have to pay additional taxes and interest for that year. When questioned by Ms. Henderson as to why it filed the amended return, the Estate responded in a letter:

> All of the income which had been received from the six stocks or the funds invested as the result of their sale had been reported as income to the Estate. As I understand the jury's verdict, [it] found that Mrs. Henderson, not the Estate, is entitled to that income. Therefore, the 1996 return was amended, which according to the accountants[,] had to be done by April 15, 2000. It is my clients' intention to go ahead and pay Mrs. Henderson the amount of income received during this period, since our only issue on appeal is the amount the jury awarded.

Ms. Henderson claims that because the Estate is now entitled to a refund of the tax that it had previously paid on the $21,000 in income, it has waived its right to proceed with this appeal.

Generally, where an appellant is shown to have accepted the benefits of the judgment, the appeal will be dismissed. *Barnett v. Wooldridge*, 494 So. 2d 459, (Ala. Civ. App. 1986). This notion is based on the principle of quasi-estoppel by election, which precludes a party from asserting, to the disadvantage of an adverse party, a right that is inconsistent with a position previously taken by him. *Barnett*, 494 So. 2d at 460. Here, however, the Estate does not take an inconsistent position to the disadvantage of Ms. Henderson. The Estate, in amending its 1996 tax return, was simply acknowledging its liability to Ms. Henderson for the dividend income. The letter to Ms. Henderson clearly reserved the issue of alleged excessiveness of the damages award. Therefore, Ms. Henderson's motion to dismiss the appeal is denied.

IV. Conclusion

The judgment is affirmed on the condition that Ms. Henderson file with this Court within 21 days a remittitur of damages on her contract claim to the sum of $100,000; otherwise, the judgment will be reversed and the cause remanded for a new trial.

Motion To Dismiss Denied; Affirmed Conditionally.

KENFORD CO., INC. v. ERIE COUNTY
108 App. Div. 2d 132, 489 N.Y.S.2d 939 (1985)

DOERR, Justice: This appeal presents for our review the extent to which plaintiffs may recover damages following defendant's breach of contract.

In the late 1960s the County of Erie obtained enabling legislation permitting it to finance and construct a sports stadium. Edward Cottrell, a local businessman, put together an assemblage of properties in the Town of Lancaster. Cottrell eventually obtained options to purchase in excess of 700 acres of land, some of which he tried to interest the County in purchasing for the purpose of building a domed stadium facility. Cottrell, who formed plaintiff Kenford Co., Inc. in 1968 [hereinafter Kenford] planned to develop the land surrounding the stadium and he also hoped to acquire a major league baseball franchise to play in the stadium. When Cottrell's efforts to interest the County in buying his land were unsuccessful, he consulted Judge Roy Hofheinz, who had developed the Houston Astrodome. Hofheinz suggested donating the Lancaster property to the County in exchange for the County permitting Hofheinz and Cottrell to lease or manage the stadium, which was to be built by the County. In May of 1969 Cottrell and Hofheinz formed plaintiff Dome Stadium, Inc. [DSI], which was owned two-thirds by Hofheinz and one-third by Cottrell. The two also agreed to share the peripheral land development scheme.

In June 1969 the Erie County Legislature passed a resolution authorizing the plan suggested by Hofheinz. Cottrell, as agent for Kenford, thereafter exercised his options on the Lancaster property, paying some $2.6 million for the total assemblage. On August 8, 1969 the County, Kenford, and DSI signed a contract by which Kenford agreed to convey 178 acres of land in exchange for the County's promise to construct a domed stadium facility. The contract further provided that the County would either lease the stadium to DSI for 40 years, or permit DSI to manage the stadium for 20 years in accordance with an attached management agreement, if no acceptable lease could be arranged within three months. Title to the property was duly conveyed, but the parties thereafter failed to agree to lease terms, and the management contract came into being automatically.

The County sought bids on the stadium, but they were $20 million over budget. On August 8, 1970 the County Legislature voted to abandon the project. Cottrell unsuccessfully sought to obtain substitute funding. Plaintiffs commenced the instant action alleging breach of contract and seeking specific performance or, alternatively, $90 million in damages. Plaintiffs were granted summary judgment on the issue of liability (*Kenford Co. v. County of Erie*, 88 A.D.2d 758, 451 N.Y.S.2d 1021) and a trial was ordered on the issue of damages.[23]

The damage trial lasted nine months, consuming over 25,000 pages of transcript. Plaintiffs attempted to prove that the breach caused them to suffer $495 million in damages, including lost profits on a baseball franchise, a theme park, three hotels, an office park, a golf course, and a specialty retail center. Plaintiffs also sought to recover lost profit on the management contract, loss of appreciation in the value of the land surrounding the stadium site, and out-of-pocket expenses incurred in reliance on the contract. The trial court dismissed Kenford's claims of lost profits on the peripheral land development and the baseball franchise as being too speculative, but the court submitted the other items of damage to the jury, which awarded DSI lost profits of $25.6 million on the management contract. The jury also awarded Kenford $18 million for its lost appreciation in land value and it granted Kenford over $6 million in out-of-pocket expenses. On appeal, the recoverability of all elements is challenged.

I. Lost Profits on the Peripheral Development

In a breach of contract case, the goal of a damage award is to place plaintiff in the position he would have been in absent the breach, no worse but no better. . . . Only such damages as are the natural and probable result of the breach may be recovered. Ordinarily, plaintiff may not recover for a collateral enterprise upon which he might have embarked, had defendant not breached the contract. . . . This rule is derived from the doctrine enunciated in *Hadley v. Baxendale* (156 Eng. Rep. 145, 151). Under this rule, recovery is limited to such damages as may fairly and reasonably have been in the contemplation of the parties when the contract was made (*Kerr S.S. Co. v. Radio Corp. of Am.*, 245 N.Y. 284, 157 N.E. 140). Thus, damages may not be recovered where the consequences of the breach are remote and indirect. "No one is answerable in law for all the remote consequences of his own acts" (36 N.Y. JUR. 2d, DAMAGES, § 13, citing *Hoffman v. King*, 160 N.Y. 618, 55 N.E. 401; *Coppola v. Kraushaar*, 102 App. Div. 306, 92 N.Y.S. 436).

In addition to the foreseeability requirement, to be recoverable "damages must be not merely speculative, possible and imaginary, but they must be reasonably certain. . . . They may be so uncertain, contingent and imaginary as to be incapable of adequate proof, and then they cannot be recovered because they

---

[23] [1] Thereafter, plaintiffs were granted permission to increase their ad damnum clause to $495 million (Kenford Co. v. County of Erie, 93 A.D.2d 998, 461 N.Y.S.2d 628), but a motion to change venue was denied (Kenford Co. v. County of Erie, 97 A.D.2d 982, 468 N.Y.S.2d 1019).

cannot be proved" (*Najjar Inds. v. City of New York*, 87 A.D.2d 329, 334, 451 N.Y.S.2d 410, quoting *Wakeman v. Wheeler & Wilson Mfg. Co.*, 101 N.Y. 205, 209, 4 N.E. 264). Damages may not be awarded on the basis of conjecture and guesswork. . . . Damages that are uncertain contingent, or speculative may not be recovered. . . . It is for the court to determine, in the first instance, whether as a matter of law the damages claimed are too remote to permit recovery. . . .

Application of these rules to the instant case leads to the inescapable conclusion that the trial court properly refused to submit to the jury Kenford's claims pertaining to the peripheral land development and the baseball franchise. Although it was known that Kenford would try to buy a baseball franchise and would try to develop the land surrounding the stadium, it was by no means certain that Kenford would have been successful in doing so or that these enterprises would have thrived. Not all business ventures prove to be profitmaking. . . . The office buildings, golf course, and theme park for which plaintiff now seeks lost profits were nothing more than visions at the time the parties entered into the contract. No specific plans had been drawn for any of these ventures. The proposed baseball franchise was equally speculative. It was by no means certain that Cottrell would have been able to purchase a baseball franchise since such a purchase would have required approval of a percentage of league owners. Moreover, it is completely speculative to say that the franchise would have been a profitable one.

II. Loss of Appreciation in Peripheral Land Values

There is no dispute that Kenford suffered a monetary loss in land appreciation as a result of defendant's breach of contract. Defendant's own expert admitted that construction of the Dome would have caused the peripheral land to appreciate in value fourfold. Nor can it be doubted that both parties contemplated this appreciation, since the contract itself states that the County expected to receive increased property taxes from the peripheral lands purchased by Cottrell and/or Kenford.[24] Unlike Kenford's specific development plans, which were remote and uncertain at the time of contracting, the purchase of the land was a completed fact of which the County had full notice. Also, while it was uncertain whether any particular development scheme would prove profitable, there was no possibility of the land depreciating in value. Thus damage was certain. It is well settled in New York that in a breach of contract case a plaintiff may recover not only losses sustained, but also gains prevented . . . , and where damage is certain, recovery will not be denied because the amount is uncertain; the breaching party bears the risk of the uncertainty created by his breach. . . . In our view, Kenford's loss was both foreseeable and certain, and plaintiff is entitled to recover for its loss.

Nevertheless, we conclude that the award of damages on this issue must be reversed because it was based on improper appraisal evidence. Plaintiff's appraiser valued the land as of projected completion dates ranging from 1973 to 1979 and based his estimates on the assumption that the property was improved with the specific items that we now find speculative as a matter of law, i.e., theme park, office buildings, and golf course. Plaintiff should have produced appraisal

---

[24] [4] The contract obligated the parties to attempt to negotiate a lease calling for $63.75 million in revenues over 40 years, the revenues to be derived from, inter alia, "increased real property taxes . . . generated by the peripheral lands and development thereof (peripheral lands shall mean those lands presently owned, contracted for or hereafter acquired by Edward H. Cottrell or Kenford."

testimony indicating what the land would have been worth as raw acreage immediately following construction of the stadium. Any further appreciation to the land resulting from theme parks and the like makes the evidence of value too speculative to permit recovery. . . .

Upon retrial, the proper measure of damages will be the value of the land as raw acreage following construction of the Dome less the value of the land when purchased. The sales price of the subject property may be the best evidence of value (*W.T. Grant Co. v. Srogi*, 52 N.Y.2d 496, 511, 438 N.Y.S.2d 761, 420 N.E.2d 953), particularly the early sales before it was widely known that Cottrell was acquiring an assemblage. A post-construction estimate of value may similarly be derived by using the market data approach. The experts may rely on the appreciation experienced by lands surrounding other major developments in Western New York as well as in other similar metropolitan areas. . . .

III. Lost Profits on the Management Contract

The issue of DSI's lost profits on the management contract involves two questions: whether an unestablished business may recover lost profits in New York and, if so, whether plaintiff's proof was adequate.

a. Per Se Rule v. Rule of Evidence

We begin our analysis by noting that we found no case from a New York State court permitting a recovery of lost profits to a new business. The seminal case on the subject is *Cramer v. Grand Rapids Show Case Co.*, 223 N.Y. 63, 119 N.E. 227. The defendant in Cramer breached its contract to deliver furniture to plaintiffs thereby preventing the latter from opening their ladies clothing store in a timely fashion. In reversing an award of lost profits, the court noted that evidence of plaintiffs' subsequent profit, earned after they were able to open their store, was insufficient proof of what their lost profits would have been had defendant not breached the contract. The court did not establish a per se rule of nonrecovery of lost profits; the court merely stated that, as an evidentiary matter, a new business would almost never be able to establish sufficient proof to recover lost profits. New York has thus been characterized as having a per se rule of nonrecoverability of lost profits to a new business. . . .

In juxtaposition to the New York State cases, there are several Federal cases in New York permitting new businesses to recover lost profits. The key case was *Perma Research & Devel. Co. v. Singer Co.*, 402 F. Supp. 881, *aff'd*, 542 F.2d 111, *cert. den.* 429 U.S. 987, 97 S. Ct. 507, 50 L. Ed. 2d 598. In *Perma Research*, the court cited *Cramer v. Grand Rapids Show Case Co.* (*supra*) for the proposition that lost profits in a new venture are not ordinarily recoverable, but then went on to hold that lost profits may be awarded if plaintiff establishes three elements: that the lost profits are the direct and proximate result of the breach; that profits were contemplated by the parties; and that there is a rational basis on which to calculate the lost profits (*Perma Research & Devel. Co. v. Singer Co.*, *supra*, p. 898). . . .

Although the issue was not directly raised, we gave tacit approval to the rule as enunciated by the Federal courts in our recent decision in *Whitmier & Ferris Co. v. Buffalo Structural Steel Corp.*, 104 A.D.2d 277, 482 N.Y.S.2d 927. The plaintiff in Whitmier was not a new business, but a tenant not yet in possession. Nevertheless, the rationale for precluding recovery to tenants not in possession was the same justification for denying recovery to new businesses — lack of any certain basis for measuring lost profits (*see Whitmier & Ferris Co. v. Buffalo Structural Steel Corp., supra*, p. 284, 482 N.Y.S.2d 927 [Moule, J., dissenting]). The majority agreed with the view expressed in the dissent that a per se rule of nonrecoverability should give way to a rule of evidence permitting recovery of lost profits if there is some rational basis on which to calculate such an award. In accordance with our view expressed in *Whitmier & Ferris Co.*, we now hold that there is no per se rule precluding a new business from recovering lost profits and we adopt the test employed by the Second Circuit Court of Appeals in *Perma Research & Devel. Co. v. Singer Co. (supra)*.

The first two Perma Research criteria are clearly met. The County's failure to build the stadium was clearly the proximate cause of any loss of profits stemming from the management contract and it is unquestionable that profits by DSI from the management contract were contemplated by the parties. We conclude, however, that plaintiff has failed to establish a rational basis upon which lost profits may be calculated.

Profit, of course, involves two variables — income less expenses. The management contract provided that DSI would receive 11% of gross revenues from major events (i.e., professional baseball and football) and 89% of gross revenues on "open time" events. The contract further provided that DSI would do the negotiating for all contracts, but that major event contracts would be between the performer and the County while open time events would be between the performer and DSI. To establish its lost profits, plaintiff called an expert who prepared a series of projections based on the experience of other domed facilities as well as an analysis of the market in the Buffalo area. The expert opined that the facility would hold 10 professional football games a year, as well as 42 open time events including three consumer shows, six high school football games, five circuses and seven musical or entertainment events. The expert then developed an average ticket price per event, which was multiplied by his estimate of anticipated attendance. The expert also developed an approximation of what each person would spend on parking and concessions. These figures were then computed to arrive at an anticipated revenue stream. The expert also gave his opinion of what the expenses of running the operation would be. He used a flat figure for salaries and then estimated that other expenses, such as advertising and legal fees, would be a percentage of gross revenue. His projected expenses were then subtracted from his projected revenue to arrive at a before-tax net income figure. One sheet summarizing the foregoing information was prepared for each of the 20 years of the management contract. The expert's opinion of net profit for each year ranged from just under $1 million for the first year to over $4 million in the twentieth year. Based upon these projections of net income, the jury found lost profits totalling over $28 million, which the court reduced to $25.6 million after applying a formula to arrive at present value. The issue is whether the figures supplied by the expert are sufficient, as a matter of law, upon which to base an award of lost profits. Once again, we find a decided split between the New York State cases and the Federal cases. Several Federal cases have permitted statistical analyses to support an award of lost profits to a new business. Significantly, however, all of those cases involved only a royalty payment or the sale of a single product. The common thread running through those cases is that only one variable was involved, i.e., how many of the product would have been sold. Thus it was certain that plaintiff would have made money and theonly uncertainty was the amount. The instant case, by contrast, is filled with conjecture. The expert had to estimate, first, how many, if any, events would be held at the stadium; how many people would attend each event; and how much each person would spend on parking and concessions. Additionally, and even more compelling, the expert also had to estimate all expense items. Highly significant in our view is that the expert assumed that various expenses would be a percentage of gross revenue, such as advertising. In short, the expert was assuming the fact to be proved, to wit, that revenues would exceed expenses. It is not inconceivable that DSI could have ended up spending more promoting events than it took in as receipts . . . .

The cases from New York State courts are even more restrictive than the Federal cases, since they have precluded projections even in the context of a royalty case. . . . Moreover, not only have the New York State cases excluded evidence of projections to justify lost profits, but New York cases have even excluded proof of plaintiff's own subsequent profits. . . . [T]he projections used in the instant case simply involve too many variables to permit them to support an award of lost profits. Although a breaching party bears the risk of any uncertainty as to the amount of damage, . . . plaintiff must first establish that he has, in fact, suffered lost profits. . . . We find plaintiff's projections insufficient as a matter of law to support an award of lost profits.

IV. Out-of-Pocket Expenses

Lastly, defendant seeks reversal of the $6 million awarded Kenford as reliance and mitigation damages. It is well settled, of course, that a party may not recover both the expense of performing his side of the contract and the profit to be received under it, since "an award of lost profits . . . will make plaintiff whole" (*R&I Electronics v. Neuman*, 66 A.D.2d 836, 837, 411 N.Y.S.2d 401; . . .). By contrast, a party may recover mitigation expenses in addition to lost profit, because mitigation expenses would not have been incurred had defendant not breached the contract, and hence there is no double recovery. We view all damages awarded after the date of breach (August 8, 1970) as mitigation damages properly submitted to the jury, and accordingly we affirm the jury's finding of mitigation damages of $6,160,030.46. The jury's finding of expenses prior to that date ($6,218.17 and $636,502.34), however, is reversed and the matter remitted for a new trial. Upon retrial, plaintiff's proof should not include any sums expended for land acquisition expenses (i.e., brokerage commissions, recording fees, etc.) or for interest paid on the mortgages, since these sums would have been paid even without the breach and since plaintiff will be compensated for these sums by being awarded loss of appreciation of land value. Only expenses incurred as preparatory to the aborted management agreement, for which no lost profits are recoverable, may be awarded.[25]

Accordingly, the judgment should be modified and the matter remitted for further proceedings in accordance with this opinion.

---

[25] [12] We feel compelled to note that the Court is unanimous in its determination of all major issues raised on this appeal, save one — loss of appreciation of peripheral land values — the dissenters differing views on this single issue being expressed at pages 956-957 of the dissenting opinion.

Judgment modified, on the law, and as modified, affirmed, without costs, and matter remitted to Supreme Court, Erie County, for a new trial, in accordance with this opinion.

HANCOCK, JUSTICE PRESIDING, with whom BOOMER, J., concurs (dissenting in part).

NOTES

1. Ruling only on the "prospective profits" question in the *Kenford Company* case, the N.Y. Court of Appeals in May 1986 affirmed the Appellate Division and agreed that the plaintiff in this breach of contract action may not recover loss of prospective profits for its expected 20-year operation of the domed stadium that was to be constructed by the county. Although plaintiffs presented a "massive" quantity of proof on the "most advanced and sophisticated method for predicting the probable results of contemplated projects," those proofs were found insufficient under the requirements (a) that damages may not be merely speculative, possible or imaginary, but must be reasonably certain and directly traceable to the breach, (b) that the particular damages be fairly within the contemplation of the parties when the contract was made, and (c) that when a new business seeks to recover for loss of future profits, a stricter standard of proof is imposed because there is no reasonable basis of experience upon which to estimate lost profits with the requisite degree of reasonable certainty. 67 N.Y.S.2d 257, 493 N.E.2d 234, 502 N.Y.S.2d 131.

2. In March 1988 the Appellate Division, affirming a new trial court judgment that awarded the *Kenford Company* plaintiffs-promoters $6.5 million for loss of appreciation of peripheral land, held that plaintiffs had presented sufficient proof of both preconstruction and postconstruction values of land surrounding the site of the proposed domed stadium. 138 App. Div. 946, 526 N.Y.S.2d 282. However, in an opinion that appears to have ended the litigation, the Court of Appeals ruled in February 1989 that, there being no evidence that when the contract was made the parties contemplated that upon breach the county would be liable for loss of anticipated appreciation in the value of such land, plaintiffs were not entitled to those damages. 73 N.Y.2d 312, 540 N.Y.S.2d 1, 537 N.E.2d 176.

3. RESTATEMENT (SECOND) OF CONTRACTS § 352, Uncertainty as a Limitation on Damages, sets out the generally applicable standard for evidence required to establish the amount of damages for a contract breach: "Damages are not recoverable for loss beyond an amount that the evidence permits to be established with reasonable certainty." Comment *a* on the requirement for certainty notes:

> *a. Requirement of certainty.* A party cannot recover damages for breach of a contract for loss beyond the amount that the evidence permits to be established with reasonable certainty. . . . Courts have traditionally required greater certainty in the proof of damages for breach of a contract than in the proof of damages for a tort. The requirement does not mean, however, that the injured party is barred from recovery unless he establishes the total amount of his loss. It merely excludes those elements of loss that cannot be proved with reasonable certainty. The main impact of the requirement of certainty comes in connection with recovery for lost profits. Although the requirement of certainty is distinct from that of foreseeability (§ 351), its impact is similar in this respect. Although the requirement applies to damages based on the reliance as well as the

expectation interest, there is usually little difficulty in proving the amount that the injured party has actually spent in reliance on the contract, even if it is impossible to prove the amount of profit that he would have made. In such a case, he can recover his loss based on his reliance interest instead of on his expectation interest. . . .

Doubts are generally resolved against the party in breach. A party who has, by his breach, forced the injured party to seek compensation in damages should not be allowed to profit from his breach where it is established that a significant loss has occurred. A court may take into account all the circumstances of the breach, including willfulness, in deciding whether to require a lesser degree of certainty, giving greater discretion to the trier of the facts. Damages need not be calculable with mathematical accuracy and are often at best approximate. . . . This is especially true for items such as loss of good will as to which great precision cannot be expected. . . . Furthermore, increasing receptiveness on the part of courts to proof by sophisticated economic and financial data and by expert opinion has made it easier to meet the requirement of certainty.

2. Avoidability and Mitigation

ROCKINGHAM COUNTY v. LUTEN BRIDGE CO.
35 F.2d 301 (4th Cir. 1929)

[Plaintiff bridge contractor filed this action in the District Court to recover an amount alleged due from Rockingham County, North Carolina, under a contract to construct a bridge. The County Board of Commissioners had awarded the contract on January 7, 1924; but by resolution of February 21, 1924, a new majority declared that the contract was not legal and valid. The board also directed the clerk of the board to notify plaintiff that the board refused to recognize the award as a valid contract, and that plaintiff should proceed no further under it. That notice was given to the bridge company before erection of the bridge was commenced, and defendant contends that it is liable only for the damages, some $1,900, which the company would have sustained had it abandoned construction at that time. In its complaint filed November 24, 1924, plaintiff sought to recover for work done up until November 3, 1924, claiming the sum of $18,301.07. The judge below directed a verdict for plaintiff for the full amount of its claim. From judgment on this verdict the county appealed.]

PARKER, Circuit Judge:

. . . As the county now admits the execution and validity of the contract, and the breach on its part, the ultimate question in the case is one as to the measure of plaintiff's recovery, . . . [w]hether plaintiff, if the notices are to be deemed action by the county, can recover under the contract for work done after they were received, or is limited to the recovery of damages for breach of contract as of that date. . . .

Coming, then, to the third question — i.e., as to the measure of plaintiff's recovery — we do not think that, after the county had given notice, while the contract was still executory, that it did not desire the bridge built and would not pay for it, plaintiff could proceed to build it and recover the contract price. It is true that the county had no right to rescind the contract, and the notice given plaintiff amounted to a breach on its part; but, after plaintiff had received notice of the breach, it was its duty to do nothing to increase the damages flowing therefrom. If A enters into a binding contract to build a house for B, B, of course, has no right to rescind the contract without A's consent. But if, before the house is built, he decides that he does not want it, and notifies A to that effect, A has no right to proceed with the building and thus pile up damages. His remedy is to treat the contract as broken when he receives the notice, and sue for the recovery of such damages, as he may have sustained from the breach, including any profit which he would have realized upon performance, as well as any other losses which may have resulted to him. In the case at bar, the county decided not to build the road of which the bridge was to be a part, and did not build it. The bridge, built in the midst of the forest, is of no value to the county because of this change of circumstances. When, therefore, the county gave notice to the plaintiff that it would not proceed with the project, plaintiff should have desisted from further work. It had no right thus to pile up damages by proceeding with the erection of a useless bridge.

The contrary view was expressed by Lord Cockburn in *Frost v. Knight*, L.R. 7 Ex. 111, but, as pointed out by Prof. Williston (WILLISTON ON CONTRACTS, vol. 3, p. 2347), it is not in harmony with the decisions in this country. The American rule and the reasons supporting it are well stated by Prof. Williston as follows:

> There is a line of cases running back to 1845 which holds that, after an absolute repudiation or refusal to perform by one party to a contract, the other party cannot continue to perform and recover damages based on full performance. This rule is only a particular application of the general rule of damages that a plaintiff cannot hold a defendant liable for damages which need not have been incurred; or, as it is often stated, the plaintiff must, so far as he can without loss to himself, mitigate the damages caused by the defendant's wrongful act. The application of this rule to the matter in question is obvious. If a man engages to have work done, and afterwards repudiates his contract before the work has been begun or when it has been only partially done, it is inflicting damage on the defendant without benefit to the plaintiff to allow the latter to insist on proceeding with the contract. The work may be useless to the defendant, and yet he would be forced to pay the full contract price. On the other hand, the plaintiff is interested only in the profit he will make out of the contract. If he receives this it is equally advantageous for him to use his time otherwise.

The leading case on the subject in this country is the New York case of *Clark v. Marsalis*, 1 Denis (N.Y.) 317, 43 Am. Dec. 670. In that case defendant had employed plaintiff to paint certain pictures for him, but countermanded the order before the work was finished. Plaintiff, however, went on and completed the work and sued for the contract price. In reversing a judgment for plaintiff, the court said:

> The plaintiff was allowed to recover as though there had been no countermand of the order; and in this the court erred. The defendant, by requiring the plaintiff to stop work upon the paintings, violated his contract, and thereby incurred a liability to pay such damages as the plaintiff should sustain. Such damages would include a recompense for the labor done and materials used, and such further sum in damages as might, upon legal principles, be assessed for the breach of the contract; but the plaintiff had no right, by obstinately persisting in the work, to make the

penalty upon the defendant greater than it would otherwise have been."

. . .

. . . The judgment below will accordingly be reversed, and the case remanded for a new trial.

SOMMER v. KRIDEL
RIVERVIEW REALTY CO. v. PEROSIO
74 N.J. 446, 378 A.2d 767 (1977)

PASHMAN, Justice:

We granted certification in these cases to consider whether a landlord seeking damages from a defaulting tenant is under a duty to mitigate damages by making reasonable efforts to re-let an apartment wrongfully vacated by the tenant. Separate parts of the Appellate Division held that, in accordance with their respective leases, the landlords in both cases could recover rents due under the leases regardless of whether they had attempted to re-let the vacated apartments. Although they were of different minds as to the fairness of this result, both parts agreed that it was dictated by *Joyce v. Bauman*, 113 N.J.L. 438, 174 A. 693 (E. & A. 1934), a decision by the former Court of Errors and Appeals. We now reverse and hold that a landlord does have an obligation to make a reasonable effort to mitigate damages in such a situation. We therefore overrule *Joyce v. Bauman* to the extent that it is inconsistent with our decision today.

I.

A. Sommer v. Kridel

This case was tried on stipulated facts. On March 10, 1972 the defendant, James Kridel, entered into a lease with the plaintiff, Abraham Sommer, owner of the "Pierre Apartments" in Hackensack, to rent apartment 6-L in that building.[26] The term of the lease was from May 1, 1972 until April 30, 1974, with a rent concession for the first six weeks, so that the first month's rent was not due until June 15, 1972.

One week after signing the agreement, Kridel paid Sommer $690. Half of that sum was used to satisfy the first month's rent. The remainder was paid under the lease provision requiring a security deposit of $345. Although defendant had expected to begin occupancy around May 1, his plans were changed. He wrote to Sommer on May 19, 1972, explaining:

> I was to be married on June 3, 1972. Unhappily the engagement was broken and the wedding plans cancelled. Both parents were to assume responsibility for the rent after our marriage. I was discharged from the U.S. Army in October 1971 and am now a student. I have no funds of my own, and am supported by my stepfather. In view of the above, I cannot take possession of the apartment and am surrendering all rights to it. Never having received a key, I cannot return same to you. I beg your understanding and compassion in releasing me from the lease, and will of

---

[26] [1] Among other provisions, the lease prohibited the tenant from assigning or transferring the lease without the consent of the landlord. If the tenant defaulted, the lease gave the landlord the option of re-entering or re-letting, but stipulated that failure to re-let or to recover the full rental would not discharge the tenant's liability for rent.

course, in consideration thereof, forfeit the 2 month's rent already paid. Please notify me at your earliest convenience.

Plaintiff did not answer the letter.

Subsequently, a third party went to the apartment house and inquired about renting apartment 6-L. Although the parties agreed that she was ready, willing and able to rent the apartment, the person in charge told her that the apartment was not being shown since it was already rented to Kridel. In fact, the landlord did not re-enter the apartment or exhibit it to anyone until August 1, 1973. At that time it was rented to a new tenant for a term beginning on September 1, 1973. The new rental was for $345 per month with a six week concession similar to that granted Kridel.

Prior to re-letting the new premises, plaintiff sued Kridel in August 1972, demanding $7,590, the total amount due for the full two-year term of the lease. Following a mistrial, plaintiff filed an amended complaint asking for $5,865, the amount due between May 1, 1972 and September 1, 1973. The amended complaint included no reduction in the claim to reflect the six week concession provided for in the lease or the $690 payment made to plaintiff after signing the agreement. Defendant filed an amended answer to the complaint, alleging that plaintiff breached the contract, failed to mitigate damages and accepted defendant's surrender of the premises. He also counterclaimed to demand repayment of the $345 paid as a security deposit.

The trial judge ruled in favor of defendant. Despite his conclusion that the lease had been drawn to reflect "the 'settled law' of this state," he found that "justice and fair dealing" imposed upon the landlord the duty to attempt to re-let the premises and thereby mitigate damages. He also held that plaintiff's failure to make any response to defendant's unequivocal offer of surrender was tantamount to an acceptance, thereby terminating the tenancy and any obligation to pay rent. As a result, he dismissed both the complaint and the counterclaim. The Appellate Division reversed in a *per curiam* opinion, 153 N.J. Super. 1 (1976), and we granted certification. 69 N.J. 395, 354 A.2d 323 (1976).

B. Riverview Realty Co. v. Perosio

This controversy arose in a similar manner. On December 27, 1972, Carlos Perosio entered into a written lease with plaintiff Riverview Realty Co. The agreement covered the rental of apartment 5-G in a building owned by the realty company at 2175 Hudson Terrace in Fort Lee. As in the companion case, the lease prohibited the tenant from subletting or assigning the apartment without the consent of the landlord. It was to run for a two-year term, from February 1, 1973 until January 31, 1975, and provided for a monthly rental of $450. The defendant took possession of the apartment and occupied it until February 1974. At that time he vacated the premises, after having paid the rent through January 31, 1974.

The landlord filed a complaint on October 31, 1974, demanding $4,500 in payment for the monthly rental from February 1, 1974 through October 31, 1974. Defendant answered the complaint by alleging that there had been a valid surrender of the premises and that plaintiff failed to mitigate damages. The trial court granted the landlord's motion for summary judgment against the defendant, fixing the damages at $4,050 plus $182.25 interest.[27]

The Appellate Division affirmed the trial court, holding that it was bound by prior precedents, including *Joyce v. Bauman, supra.*, 138 N.J. Super. 270, 350 A.2d 517 (App. Div. 1976). Nevertheless, it freely criticized the rule which it found itself obliged to follow:

> There appears to be no reason in equity or justice to perpetuate such an unrealistic and uneconomic rule of law which encourages an owner to let valuable rented space lie fallow because he is assured of full recovery from a defaulting tenant. Since courts in New Jersey and elsewhere have abandoned ancient real property concepts and applied ordinary contract principles in other conflicts between landlord and tenant there is no sound reason for a continuation of a special real property rule to the issue of mitigation.. . .

(138 N.J. Super. at 273-74, 350 A.2d at 519; citations omitted). We granted certification. 70 N.J. 145, 358 A.2d 191 (1976).

II.

As the lower courts in both appeals found, the weight of authority in this State supports the rule that a landlord is under no duty to mitigate damages caused by a defaulting tenant. . . . This rule has been followed in a majority of states, Annot. 21 A.L.R.3d 534, § 2(a) at 541 (1968), and has been tentatively adopted in the American Law Institute's RESTATEMENT OF PROPERTY. RESTATEMENT (SECOND) OF PROPERTY, § 11.1(3) (Tent. Draft No. 3, 1975).

Nevertheless, while there is still a split of authority over this question, the trend among recent cases appears to be in favor of a mitigation requirement. Compare *Dushoff v. Phoenix Co.*, 23 Ariz. App. 238, 532 P.2d 180 (App. 1975); Hirsch v. Merchants National Bank & Trust Co., 336 N.E.2d 833 (Ind. App. 1975); *Wilson v. Ruhl*, 277 Md. 607, 356 A.2d 544 (1976) (by statute); *Bernstein v. Seglin*, 184 Neb. 673, 171 N.W.2d 247 (1969); *Lefrak v. Lambert*, 89 Misc. 2d 197, 390 N.Y.S.2d 959 (N.Y. Cty. Ct. 1976); *Howard Stores Corp. v. Rayon Co., Inc.*, 36 A.D.2d 911, 320 N.Y.S.2d 861 (App. Div. 1971); *Ross v. Smigelski*, 42 Wis. 2d 185, 166 N.W.2d 243 (1969); with *Chandler Leas. Div. v. Florida-Vanderbilt Dev. Corp.*, 464 F.2d 267 (5 Cir. 1972) *cert. den.* 409 U.S. 1041, 93 S. Ct. 527, 34 L. Ed. 2d 491 (1972) (applying Florida law to the rental of a yacht); *Winshall v. Ampco Auto Parks, Inc.*, 417 F. Supp. 334 (E.D. Mich. 1976) (finding that under Michigan law a landlord has a duty to mitigate damages where he is suing for a breach of contract, but not where it is solely a suit to recover rent); *Ryals v. Laney*, 338 So. 2d 413 (Ala. Civ. App. 1976); *B.K.K. Co. v. Schultz*, 7 Cal. App. 3d 786, 86 Cal. Rptr. 760 (App. 1970) *(dictum)*; *Carpenter v. Riddle*, 527 P.2d 592 (Okl. Sup. Ct. 1974); *Hurwitz v. Kohm*, 516 S.W.2d 33 (Mo. App. 1974).

The majority rule is based on principles of property law which equate a lease with a transfer of a property interest in the owner's estate. Under this rationale the lease conveys to a tenant an interest in the property which forecloses any control by

---

27 [2] The trial court noted that damages had been erroneously calculated in the complaint to reflect ten months rent. As to the interest awarded to plaintiff, the parties have not raised this issue before this Court. Since we hold that the landlord had a duty to attempt to mitigate damages, we need not reach this question.

the landlord; thus, it would be anomalous to require the landlord to concern himself with the tenant's abandonment of his own property. *Wright v. Baumann*, 239 Or. 410, 398 P.2d 119, 120-21, 21 A.L.R.3d 527 (1965).

For instance, in *Muller v. Beck, supra* [94 N.J.L. 311, 110 A. 831 (Sup. Ct. 1920)], where essentially the same issue was posed, the court clearly treated the lease as governed by property, as opposed to contract, precepts.[28] The court there observed that the "tenant had an estate for years, but it was an estate qualified by this right of the landlord to prevent its transfer," 94 N.J.L. at 313, 110 A. at 832, and that "the tenant has an estate with which the landlord may not interfere." *Id.* at 314, 110 A. at 832. . . .

Yet the distinction between a lease for ordinary residential purposes and an ordinary contract can no longer be considered viable. As Professor Powell observed, evolving "social factors have exerted increasing influence on the law of estates for years." 2 POWELL ON REAL PROPERTY (1977 ed.), § 221(1) at 180-81. The result has been that (t)he complexities of city life, and the proliferated problems of modern society in general, have created new problems for lessors and lessees and these have been commonly handled by specific clauses in leases. This growth in the number and detail of specific lease covenants has reintroduced into the law of estates for years a predominantly contractual ingredient. (*Id.* at 181) Thus in 6 WILLISTON ON CONTRACTS (3 ed. 1962), § 890A at 592, it is stated: "There is a clearly discernible tendency on the part of courts to cast aside technicalities in the interpretation of leases and to concentrate their attention, as in the case of other contracts, on the intention of the parties, . . ."

This Court has taken the lead in requiring that landlords provide housing services to tenants in accordance with implied duties which are hardly consistent with the property notions expressed in *Muller v. Beck, supra*, and *Heckel v. Griese, supra* [12 N.J. Misc. 211, 171 A. 148 (Sup. Ct. 1934)]. *See Braitman v. Overlook Terrace Corp.*, 68 N.J. 368, 346 A.2d 76 (1975) (liability for failure to repair defective apartment door lock); *Berzito v. Gambino*, 63 N.J. 460, 308 A.2d 17 (1973) (construing implied warranty of habitability and covenant to pay rent as mutually dependent); *Marini v. Ireland*, 56 N.J. 130, 265 A.2d 526 (1970) (implied covenant to repair); *Reste Realty Corp. v. Cooper*, 53 N.J. 444, 251 A.2d 268 (1969) (implied warranty of fitness of premises for leased purpose). In fact, in *Reste Realty Corp. v. Cooper, supra*, we specifically noted that the rule which we announced there did not comport with the historical notion of a lease as an estate for years. 53 N.J. at 451-52, 251 A.2d 268. And in *Marini v. Ireland, supra*, we found that the "guidelines employed to construe contracts have been modernly applied to the construction of leases." 56 N.J. at 141, 265 A.2d at 532.

Application of the contract rule requiring mitigation of damages to a residential lease may be justified as a matter of basic fairness.[29] Professor McCormick first

---

[28] [3] It is well settled that a party claiming damages for a breach of contract has a duty to mitigate his loss. *See* Frank Stamato & Co. v. Borough of Lodi, 4 N.J. 14, 71 A.2d 336 (1950); Sandler v. Lawn-A-Mat Chem. & Equip. Corp., 141 N.J. Super. 437, 455, 358 A.2d 805 (App. Div. 1976); Wolf v. Marlton Corp., 57 N.J. Super. 278, 154 A.2d 625 (App. Div. 1956); 5 CORBIN ON CONTRACTS (1964 ed.), § 1039 at 241 *et seq.*; McCormick, Damages, § 33 at 127 (1935). *See also* N.J.S.A. 12A:2-708.

[29] [4] We see no distinction between the leases involved in the instant appeals and those which might arise in other types of residential housing. However, we reserve for another day the question of whether a landlord must mitigate damages in a commercial setting. Cf. Kruvant v. Sunrise Market, Inc., 58 N.J. 452, 456, 279 A.2d 104 (1971), modified on other grounds, 59 N.J. 330, 282 A.2d 746 (1971).

commented upon the inequity under the majority rule when he predicted in 1925 that eventually

> the logic, inescapable according to the standards of a "jurisprudence of conceptions" which permits the landlord to stand idly by the vacant, abandoned premises and treat them as the property of the tenant and recover full rent, while yield to the more realistic notions of social advantage which in other fields of the law have forbidden a recovery for damages which the plaintiff by reasonable efforts could have avoided. (McCormick, *The Rights of the Landlord Upon Abandonment of the Premises by the Tenant* 23 MICH. L. REV. 211, 221-22 (1925))

Various courts have adopted this position. *See* Annot., *supra*, § 7(a) at 565, and *ante* at 770-771.

The pre-existing rule cannot be predicated upon the possibility that a landlord may lose the opportunity to rent another empty apartment because he must first rent the apartment vacated by the defaulting tenant. Even where the breach occurs in a multi-dwelling building, each apartment may have unique qualities which make it attractive to certain individuals. Significantly, in *Sommer v. Kridel*, there was a specific request to rent the apartment vacated by the defendant; there is no reason to believe that absent this vacancy the landlord could have succeeded in renting a different apartment to this individual.

We therefore hold that antiquated real property concepts which served as the basis for the pre-existing rule, shall no longer be controlling where there is a claim for damages under a residential lease. Such claims must be governed by more modern notions of fairness and equity. A landlord has a duty to mitigate damages where he seeks to recover rents due from a defaulting tenant.

If the landlord has other vacant apartments besides the one which the tenant has abandoned, the landlord's duty to mitigate consists of making reasonable efforts to re-let the apartment. In such cases he must treat the apartment in question as if it was one of his vacant stock.

As part of his cause of action, the landlord shall be required to carry the burden of proving that he used reasonable diligence in attempting to re-let the premises. We note that there has been a divergence of opinion concerning the allocation of the burden of proof on this issue. *See* Annot., *supra*, § 12 at 577. While generally in contract actions the breaching party has the burden of proving that damages are capable of mitigation, *see Sandler v. Lawn-A-Mat Chem. & Equip. Corp.*, 141 N.J. Super. 437, 455, 358 A.2d 805 (App. Div. 1976); McCormick, DAMAGES, § 33 at 130 (1935), here the landlord will be in a better position to demonstrate whether he exercised reasonable diligence in attempting to re-let the premises. Cf. *Kulm v. Coast to Coast Stores Central Org.*, 248 Or. 436, 432 P.2d 1006 (1967) (burden on lessor in contract to renew a lease).

III.

The *Sommer v. Kridel* case presents a classic example of the unfairness which occurs when a landlord has no responsibility to minimize damages. Sommer waited 15 months and allowed $4658.50 in damages to accrue before attempting to re-let the apartment. Despite the availability of a tenant who was ready, willing and able to rent the apartment, the landlord needlessly increased the damages by turning her away. While a tenant will not necessarily be excused from his obligations under a lease simply by finding another person who is willing to rent the vacated premises, *see, e.g., Reget v. Dempsey-Tegler & Co.*, 70 Ill. App. 2d 32, 216 N.E.2d 500 (Ill. App. 1966) (new tenant insisted on leasing the premises under different terms); *Edmands v. Rust & Richardson Drug Co.*, 191 Mass. 123, 77 N.E. 713 (1906) (landlord need not accept insolvent tenant), here there has been no showing that the new tenant would not have been suitable. We therefore find that plaintiff could have avoided the damages which eventually accrued, and that the defendant was relieved of his duty to continue paying rent. Ordinarily we would require the tenant to bear the cost of any reasonable expenses incurred by a landlord in attempting to re-let the premises, *see Ross v. Smigelski, supra*, 166 N.W.2d at 248-49; 22 Am. Jur. 2d *Damages*, § 169 at 238, but no such expenses were incurred in this case.[30]

In *Riverview Realty Co. v. Perosio*, no factual determination was made regarding the landlord's efforts to mitigate damages, and defendant contends that plaintiff never answered his interrogatories. Consequently, the judgment is reversed and the case remanded for a new trial. Upon remand and after discovery has been completed, R. 4:17 *et seq.*, the trial court shall determine whether plaintiff attempted to mitigate damages with reasonable diligence, *see Wilson v. Ruhl, supra*, 356 A.2d at 546, and if so, the extent of damages remaining and assessable to the tenant. As we have held above, the burden of proving that reasonable diligence was used to re-let the premises shall be upon the plaintiff. *See* Annot., *supra*, § 11 at 575.

In assessing whether the landlord has satisfactorily carried his burden, the trial court shall consider, among other factors, whether the landlord, either personally or through an agency, offered or showed the apartment to any prospective tenants, or advertised it in local newspapers. Additionally, the tenant may attempt to rebut such evidence by showing that he proffered suitable tenants who were rejected. However, there is no standard formula for measuring whether the landlord has utilized satisfactory efforts in attempting to mitigate damages, and each case must be judged upon its own facts. Compare *Hershorin v. La Vista, Inc.*, 110 Ga. App. 435, 138 S.E.2d 703 (App. 1964) ("reasonable effort" of landlord by showing the apartment to all prospective tenants); *Carpenter v. Wisniewski*, 139 Ind. App. 325, 215 N.E.2d 882 (App. 1966) (duty satisfied where landlord advertised the premises through a newspaper, placed a sign in the window, and employed a realtor); *Re Garment Center Capitol, Inc.*, 93 F.2d 667, 115 A.L.R. 202 (2 Cir. 1938) (landlord's duty not breached where higher rental was asked since it was known that this was merely a basis for negotiations); *Foggier v. Dix*, 265 Or. 315, 509 P.2d 412, 414 (1973) (in mitigating damages, landlord need not accept less than fair market value or "substantially alter his obligations as established in the pre-existing lease"); with *Anderson v. Andy Darling Pontiac, Inc.*, 257 Wis. 371, 43 N.W.2d 362 (1950) (reasonable diligence not established where newspaper advertisement placed in one issue of local paper by a broker); *Scheinfeld v. Muntz T.V., Inc.*, 67 Ill. App. 2d 8, 214 N.E.2d 506 (Ill. App. 1966) (duty breached where landlord refused to accept suitable subtenant); *Consolidated Sun Ray, Inc. v. Oppenstein*, 335 F.2d 801, 811 (8

---

[30] [5] As to defendant's counterclaim for $345, representing the amount deposited with the landlord as a security deposit, we note that this issue has not been briefed or argued before this Court, and apparently has been abandoned. Because we hold that plaintiff breached his duty to attempt to mitigate damages, we do not address defendant's argument that the landlord accepted a surrender of the premises.

Cir. 1964) (dictum) (demand for rent which is "far greater than the provisions of the lease called for" negates landlord's assertion that he acted in good faith in seeking a new tenant).

IV.

The judgment in *Sommer v. Kridel* is reversed. In *Riverview Realty Co. v. Perosio*, the judgment is reversed and the case is remanded to the trial court for proceedings in accordance with this opinion.

For reversal in *Sommer* and reversal and remandment in *Riverview Realty Co.*: CHIEF JUSTICE HUGHES, JUSTICES MOUNTAIN, PASHMAN, CLIFFORD and SCHREIBER and JUDGE CONFORD.

For affirmance: None.

NOTES

1. The rule precluding or reducing recovery from a defaulting lessee by a lessor who has not attempted reasonably to relet the property (as in *Sommer v. Kridel*) has been held not to apply where the lessee has failed to pay rent but has not abandoned the property. *See Consolidated AG of Curry, Inc. v. Rangen, Inc.*, 128 Idaho 228, 912 P.2d 115 (1996) (commercial lease situation).

2. In the commercial lease context, at least one court has held that a commercial lessor did not conclusively fail to mitigate damages arising by reason of the lessee's default simply by requesting, when attempting to relet the premises, a higher rent than that paid by lessee. Whether the lessor had taken reasonable steps to mitigate remained for the trial court to determine in light of all the evidence. *Bavosi v. Harrington*, 1995 Mass. App. Div. 57, 58 (1995).

PARKER v. TWENTIETH CENTURY-FOX FILM CORP.
3 Cal. 3d 176, 89 Cal. Rptr. 737, 474 P.2d 689 (1970)

BURKE, Justice:

Defendant Twentieth Century-Fox Film Corporation appeals from a summary judgment granting to plaintiff the recovery of agreed compensation under a written contract for her services as an actress in a motion picture. As will appear, we have concluded that the trial court correctly ruled in plaintiff's favor and that the judgment should be affirmed.

Plaintiff is well known as an actress, and in the contract between plaintiff and defendant is sometimes referred to as the "Artist." Under the contract, dated August 6, 1965, plaintiff was to play the female lead in defendant's contemplated production of a motion picture entitled "Bloomer Girl." The contract provided that defendant would pay plaintiff a minimum "guaranteed compensation" of $53,571.42 per week for 14 weeks commencing May 23, 1966, for a total of $750,000. Prior to May 1966 defendant decided not to produce the picture and by a letter dated April 4, 1966, it notified plaintiff of that decision and that it would not "comply with our obligations to you under" the written contract.

By the same letter and with the professed purpose "to avoid any damage to you," defendant instead offered to employ plaintiff as the leading actress in another film tentatively entitled "Big Country, Big Man" (hereinafter, "Big Country"). The compensation offered was identical, as were 31 of the 34 numbered provisions or articles of the original contract.[31] Unlike "Bloomer Girl," however, which was to have been a musical production, "Big Country" was a dramatic "western type" movie. "Bloomer Girl" was to have been filmed in California; "Big Country" was to be produced in Australia. Also, certain terms in the proffered contract varied from those of the original.[32] Plaintiff was given one week within which to accept; she did not and the offer lapsed. Plaintiff then commenced this action seeking recovery of the agreed guaranteed compensation.

The complaint sets forth two causes of action. The first is for money due under the contract; the second, based upon the same allegations as the first, is for damages resulting from defendant's breach of contract. Defendant in its answer admits the existence and validity of the contract, that plaintiff complied with all the conditions, covenants and promises and stood ready to complete the performance, and that defendant breached and "anticipatorily repudiated" the contract. It denies, however, that any money is due to plaintiff either under the contract or as a result of its breach, and pleads as an affirmative defense to both causes of action plaintiff's allegedly deliberate failure to mitigate damages, asserting that she unreasonably refused to accept its offer of the leading role in "Big Country."

Plaintiff moved for summary judgment under Code of Civil Procedure section 437c, the motion was granted, and summary judgment for $750,000 plus interest was entered in plaintiff's favor. This appeal by defendant followed. . . .

As stated, defendant's sole defense to this action which resulted from its deliberate breach of contract is that in rejecting defendant's substitute offer of employment plaintiff unreasonably refused to mitigate damages.

---

[31] [1] Among the identical provisions was the following found in the last paragraph of Article 2 of the original contract: "We (defendant) shall not be obligated to utilize your (plaintiff's) services in or in connection with the Photoplay hereunder, our sole obligation, subject to the terms and conditions of this Agreement, being to pay you the guaranteed compensation herein provided for."

[32] [2] Article 29 of the original contract specified that plaintiff approved the director already chosen for "Bloomer Girl" and that in case he failed to act as director plaintiff was to have approval rights of any substitute director. Article 31 provided that plaintiff was to have the right of approval of the "Bloomer Girl" dance director, and Article 32 gave her the right of approval of the screenplay. Defendant's letter of April 4 to plaintiff, which contained both defendant's notice of breach of the "Bloomer Girl" contract and offer of the lead in "Big Country," eliminated or impaired each of those rights. It read in part as follows:

The terms and conditions of our offer of employment are identical to those set forth in the 'BLOOMER GIRL' Agreement, Articles 1 through 34 and Exhibit A to the Agreement, except as follows:

1. Article 31 of said Agreement will not be included in any contract of employment regarding "BIG COUNTRY, BIG MAN" as it is not a musical and it thus will not need a dance director.

2. In the "BLOOMER GIRL" agreement, in Articles 29 and 32, you were given certain director and screenplay approvals and you had preapproved certain matters. Since there simply is insufficient time to negotiate with you regarding your choice of director and regarding the screenplay and since you already expressed an interest in performing the role in "BIG COUNTRY, BIG MAN," we must exclude from our offer of employment in "BIG COUNTRY, BIG MAN" any approval rights as are contained in said Articles 29 and 32; however, we shall consult with you respecting the director to be selected to direct the photoplay and will further consult with you with respect to the screenplay and any revisions or changes therein, provided, however, that if we fail to agree . . . the decision of . . . (defendant) with respect to the selection of a director and to revisions and changes in the said screenplay shall be binding upon the parties to said agreement.

The general rule is that the measure of recovery by a wrongfully discharged employee is the amount of salary agreed upon for the period of service, less the amount which the employer affirmatively proves the employee has earned or with reasonable effort might have earned from other employment. . . .[33] However, before projected earnings from other employment opportunities not sought or accepted by the discharged employee can be applied in mitigation, the employer must show that the other employment was comparable, or substantially similar, to that of which the employee has been deprived; the employee's rejection of or failure to seek other available employment of a different or inferior kind may not be resorted to in order to mitigate damages. . . .

In the present case defendant has raised no issue of *reasonableness of efforts* by plaintiff to obtain other employment; the sole issue is whether plaintiff's refusal of defendant's substitute offer of "Big Country" may be used in mitigation. Nor, if the "Big Country" offer was of employment different or inferior when compared with the original "Bloomer Girl" employment, is there an issue as to whether or not plaintiff acted reasonably in refusing the substitute offer. Despite defendant's arguments to the contrary, no case cited or which our research has discovered holds or suggests that reasonableness is an element of a wrongfully discharged employee's option to reject, or fail to seek, different or inferior employment lest the possible earnings therefrom be charged against him in mitigation of damages.[34]

---

[33] [4] Although it would appear that plaintiff was not *discharged* by defendant in the customary sense of the term, as she was not permitted by defendant to enter upon performance of the "Bloomer Girl" contract, nevertheless the motion for summary judgment was submitted for decision upon a stipulation by the parties that "plaintiff Parker was discharged."

[34] [5] Instead, in each case the reasonableness referred to was that of the *efforts* of the employee to obtain other employment that was not different or inferior; his right to reject the latter was declared as an unqualified rule of law. Thus, Gonzales v. Internat. Assn. of Machinists, *supra*, 213 Cal. App. 2d 817, 823-824, 29 Cal. Rptr. 190, 194, holds that the trial court correctly instructed the jury that plaintiff union member, a machinist, was required to make "such *efforts* as the average (member of his union) desiring employment would make at that particular time and place" (italics added); but, further, that the court *properly* rejected defendant's *offer of proof* of the *availability of other kinds of employment* at the same or higher pay than plaintiff usually received and all outside the jurisdiction of his union, as plaintiff could not be required to accept different employment or a nonunion job.

In Harris v. Nat. Union, etc., Cooks and Stewards, *supra*, 116 Cal. App. 2d 759, 761, 254 P.2d 673, 676, the issues were stated to be, *inter alia*, whether comparable employment was open to each plaintiff employee, and if so whether each plaintiff made a *reasonable effort* to secure such employment. It was held that the trial court *properly sustained an objection to an offer to prove a custom of accepting a job in a lower rank* when work in the higher rank was not available, as "The duty of mitigation of damages . . . does not require the plaintiff 'to seek or to accept other employment of a different or inferior kind.'" (p. 764(5), 254 P.2d 676.) *See also*: Lewis v. Protective Security Life Ins. Co. (1962) 208 Cal. App. 2d 582, 583, 584, 25 Cal. Rptr. 213, 214: "*honest effort* to find similar employment. . . ." (Italics added.) De La Falaise v. Gaumont-British P. Corp., *supra*, 39 Cal. App. 2d 461, 469, 103 P.2d 447: "reasonable effort." Erler v. Five Points Motors, Inc. (1967) 249 Cal. App. 2d 560, 562, 57 Cal. Rptr. 516, 518. Damages may be mitigated "by a showing that the employee, by the exercise of *reasonable diligence and effort*, could have procured comparable employment. . . ." (Italics added.) Savitz v. Gallaccio (Pa. 1955) 179 Pa.Super. 589, 118 A.2d 282, 286; Atholwood Development Co. v. Houston (1941) 179 Md. 441, 19 A.2d 706, 708; Harcourt & Co. v. Heller (1933) 250 Ky. 321, 62 S.W.2d 1056; Alaska Airlines v. Stephenson (9th Cir. 1954) 217 F.2d 295, 299, 15 Alaska 272; United Protective Workers of America, Local No. 2 v. Ford Motor Co. (7th Cir. 1955) 223 F.2d 49, 52; Chisholm v. Preferred Bankers' Life Assur. Co. (1897) 112 Mich. 50, 70 N.W. 415; each of which held that the *reasonableness of the employee's efforts*, or his excuses for failure, to find other similar employment was properly submitted to the jury as a question of fact. NB: Chisholm additionally *approved a jury Instruction that a substitute offer* of the employer to work for a lesser compensation was *not* to be considered in mitigation, as the employee was not required to accept

Applying the foregoing rules to the record in the present case, with all intendments in favor of the party opposing the summary judgment motion — here, defendant — it is clear that the trial court correctly ruled that plaintiff's failure to accept defendant's tendered substitute employment could not be applied in mitigation of damages because the offer of the "Big Country" lead was of employment both different and inferior, and that no factual dispute was presented on that issue. The mere circumstance that "Bloomer Girl" was to be a musical review calling upon plaintiff's talents as a dancer as well as an actress, and was to be produced in the City of Los Angeles, whereas "Big Country" was a straight dramatic role in a "Western Type" story taking place in an opal mine in Australia, demonstrates the difference in kind between the two employments; the female lead as a dramatic actress in a western style motion picture can by no stretch of imagination be considered the equivalent of or substantially similar to the lead in a song-and-dance production.

Additionally, the substitute "Big Country" offer proposed to eliminate or impair the director and screenplay approvals accorded to plaintiff under the original "Bloomer Girl" contract (*see* fn.2, *ante*), and thus constituted an offer of inferior employment. No expertise or judicial notice is required in order to hold that the deprivation or infringement of an employee's rights held under an original employment contract converts the available "other employment" relied upon by the employer to mitigate damages, into inferior employment which the employee need not seek or accept. (*See Gonzales v. Internat. Assn. of Machinists, supra*, 213 Cal. App. 2d 817, 823-824, 29 Cal. Rptr. 190; and fn.[4], *ante*.)

Statements found in affidavits submitted by defendant in opposition to plaintiff's summary judgment motion, to the effect that the "Big Country" offer was not of employment different from or inferior to that under the "Bloomer Girl" contract, merely repeat the allegations of defendant's answer to the complaint in this action, constitute only conclusionary assertions with respect to undisputed facts, and do not give rise to a triable factual issue so as to defeat the motion for summary judgment. . . .

In view of the determination that defendant failed to present any facts showing the existence of a factual issue with respect to its sole defense — plaintiff's rejection of its substitute employment offer in mitigation of damages — we need not consider plaintiff's further contention that for various reasons, including the provisions of the original contract set forth in footnote 1, *ante*, plaintiff was excused from attempting to mitigate damages.

The judgment is affirmed.

MCCOMB, PETERS, and TOBRINER, JJ., and KAUS, J. PRO TEM., and ROTH, J. PRO TEM., concur.

SULLIVAN, Acting Chief Justice (dissenting):

The basic question in this case is whether or not plaintiff acted reasonably in rejecting defendant's offer of alternate employment. The answer depends upon whether that offer (starring in "Big Country, Big Man") was an offer of work that was substantially similar to her former employment (starring in "Bloomer Girl") or

---

it. Williams v. National Organization, Masters, etc. (1956) 384 Pa. 413, 120 A.2d 896, 901(13): "Even assuming that plaintiff . . . could have obtained employment in ports other than . . . where he resided, *legally* he was not compelled to do so in order to mitigate his damages." (Italics added.)

of work that was of a different or inferior kind. To my mind this is a factual issue which the trial court should not have determined on a motion for summary judgment. The majority have not only repeated this error but have compounded it by applying the rules governing mitigation of damages in the employer-employee context in a misleading fashion. Accordingly, I respectfully dissent.

The familiar rule requiring a plaintiff in a tort or contract action to mitigate damages embodies notions of fairness and socially responsible behavior which are fundamental to our jurisprudence. Most broadly stated, it precludes the recovery of damages which, through the exercise of due diligence, could have been avoided. Thus, in essence, it is a rule requiring reasonable conduct in commercial affairs. This general principle governs the obligations of an employee after his employer has wrongfully repudiated or terminated the employment contract. Rather than permitting the employee simply to remain idle during the balance of the contract period, the law requires him to make a reasonable effort to secure other employment.[35] He is not obliged, however, to seek or accept any and all types of work which may be available. Only work which is in the same field and which is of the same quality need be accepted.[36]

Over the years the courts have employed various phrases to define the type of employment which the employee, upon his wrongful discharge, is under an obligation to accept. Thus in California alone it has been held that he must accept employment which is "substantially similar" (*Lewis v. Protective Security Life Ins. Co.* (1962) 208 Cal. App. 2d 582, 584, 25 Cal. Rptr. 213; *De La Falaise v. Gaumont-British P. Corp.* (1940) 39 Cal. App. 2d 461, 469, 103 P.2d 447); "comparable employment" (*Erler v. Five Points Motors, Inc.* (1967) 249 Cal. App. 2d 560, 562, 57 Cal. Rptr. 516; *Harris v. Nat. Union, etc., Cooks and Stewards* (1953) 116 Cal. App. 2d 759, 761, 254 P.2d 673); employment "in the same general line of the first employment" (*Rotter v. Stationers Corporation* (1960) 186 Cal. App. 2d 170, 172, 8 Cal. Rptr. 690, 691); "equivalent to his prior position" (*De Angeles v. Roos Bros., Inc.* (1966) 244 Cal. App. 2d 434, 443, 52 Cal. Rptr. 783); "employment in a similar capacity" (*Silva v. McCoy* (1968) 259 Cal. App. 2d 256, 260, 66 Cal. Rptr. 364); employment which is "not . . . of a different or inferior kind. . . ." (*Gonzales v. Internat. Assn. of Machinists* (1963) 213 Cal. App. 2d 817, 822, 29 Cal. Rptr. 190, 193.)

For reasons which are unexplained, the majority cite several of these cases yet select from among the various judicial formulations which contain one particular phrase, "Not of a different or inferior kind," with which to analyze this case. I have discovered no historical or theoretical reason to adopt this phrase, which is simply

---

[35] [1] The issue is generally discussed in terms of a duty on the part of the employee to minimize loss. The practice is long-established and there is little reason to change despite Judge Cardozo's observation of its subtle inaccuracy. "The servant is free to accept employment or reject it according to his uncensored pleasure. What is meant by the supposed duty is merely this: That if he unreasonably reject, he will not be heard to say that the loss of wages from then on shall be deemed the jural consequence of the earlier discharge. He has broken the chain of causation, and loss resulting to him thereafter is suffered through his own act." (McClelland v. Climax Hosiery Mills (1930) 252 N.Y. 347, 359, 169 N.E. 605, 609, concurring opinion.)

[36] [2] This qualification of the rule seems to reflect the simple and humane attitude that it is too severe to demand of a person that he attempt to find and perform work for which he has no training or experience. Many of the older cases hold that one need not accept work in an inferior rank or position nor work which is more menial or arduous. This suggests that the rule may have had its origin in the bourgeois fear of resubmergence in lower economic classes.

a negative restatement of the affirmative standards set out in the above cases, as the exclusive standard. Indeed, its emergence is an example of the dubious phenomenon of the law responding not to rational judicial choice or changing social conditions, but to unrecognized changes in the language of opinions or legal treatises. [Footnote citing early California and annotation authorities.] However, the phrase is a serviceable one and my concern is not with its use as the standard but rather with what I consider its distortion.

The relevant language excuses acceptance only of employment which is of a *different kind. . . .* It has never been the law that the mere existence of *differences between two jobs in the same field* is sufficient, as a matter of law, to excuse an employee wrongfully discharged from one from accepting the other in order to mitigate damages. Such an approach would effectively eliminate any obligation of an employee to attempt to minimize damage arising from a wrongful discharge. The only alternative job offer an employee would be required to accept would be an offer of his former job by his former employer.

Although the majority appear to hold that there was a difference "in kind" between the employment offered plaintiff in "Bloomer Girl" and that offered in "Big Country" . . . , an examination of the opinion makes crystal clear that the majority merely point out differences between the two *films* (an obvious circumstance) and then apodically assert that these constitute a difference in the *kind of employment.* The entire rationale of the majority boils down to this: that the *"mere circumstances"* that "Bloomer Girl" was to be a musical review while "Big Country" was a straight drama "demonstrates the difference in kind" since a female lead in a western is not "the equivalent of or substantially similar to" a lead in a musical. This is merely attempting to prove the proposition by repeating it. It shows that the vehicles for the display of the star's talents are different but it does not prove that her employment as a star in such vehicles is of necessity different *in kind* and either inferior or superior.

I believe that the approach taken by the majority (a superficial listing of differences with no attempt to assess their significance) may subvert a valuable legal doctrine.[37] The inquiry in cases such as this should not be whether differences between the two jobs exist (there will always be differences) but whether the differences which are present are substantial enough to constitute differences in the Kind of employment or, alternatively, whether they render the substitute work employment of an *inferior kind.*

It seems to me that *this inquiry involves, in the instant case at least, factual determinations* which are improper on a motion for summary judgment. Resolving whether or not one job is substantially similar to another or whether, on the other hand, it is of a different or inferior kind, will often (as here) require a critical appraisal of the similarities and differences between them in light of the importance of these differences to the employee. This necessitates a weighing of the evidence, and it is precisely this undertaking which is forbidden on summary judgment. (*Garlock v. Cole* (1962) 199 Cal. App. 2d 11, 14, 18 Cal. Rptr. 393.)

---

[37] [5] The values of the doctrine of mitigation of damages in this context are that it minimizes the unnecessary personal and social (e.g., nonproductive use of labor, litigation) costs of contractual failure. If a wrongfully discharged employee can, through his own action and without suffering financial or psychological loss in the process, reduce the damages accruing from the breach of contract, the most sensible policy is to require him to do so. I fear the majority opinion will encourage precisely opposite conduct.

This is not to say that summary judgment would never be available in an action by an employee in which the employer raises the defense of failure to mitigate damages. . . . [T]here may well be cases in which the substitute employment is so manifestly of a dissimilar or inferior sort, the declarations of the plaintiff so complete and those of the defendant so conclusionary and inadequate that no factual issues exist for which a trial is required. This, however, is not such a case.

It is not intuitively obvious, to me at least, that the leading female role in a dramatic motion picture is a radically different endeavor from the leading female role in a musical comedy film. Nor is it plain to me that the rather qualified rights of director and screenplay approval contained in the first contract are highly significant matters either in the entertainment industry in general or to this plaintiff in particular. Certainly, none of the declarations introduced by plaintiff in support of her motion shed any light on these issues. . . .

Nor do they attempt to explain why she declined the offer of starring in "Big Country, Big Man." Nevertheless, the trial court granted the motion, declaring that these approval rights were "critical" and that their elimination altered "the essential nature of the employment." . . .

I cannot accept the proposition that an offer which eliminates *any* contract right, regardless of its significance, is, as a matter of law, an offer of employment of an inferior kind. Such an absolute rule seems no more sensible than the majority's earlier suggestion that the mere existence of differences between two jobs is sufficient to render them employment of different kinds. Application of such per se rules will severely undermine the principle of mitigation of damages in the employer-employee context.

I remain convinced that the relevant question in such cases is whether or not a particular contract provision is so significant that its omission creates employment of an inferior kind. This question is, of course, intimately bound up in what I consider the ultimate issue: whether or not the employee acted reasonably. This will generally involve a factual inquiry to ascertain the importance of the particular contract term and a process of weighing the absence of that term against the countervailing advantages of the alternate employment. In the typical case, this will mean that summary judgment must be withheld.

In the instant case, there was nothing properly before the trial court by which the importance of the approval rights could be ascertained, much less evaluated. Thus, in order to grant the motion for summary judgment, the trial court misused judicial notice. In upholding the summary judgment, the majority here rely upon per se rules which distort the process of determining whether or not an employee is obliged to accept particular employment in mitigation of damages.

I believe that the judgment should be reversed so that the issue of whether or not the offer of the lead role in "Big Country, Big Man" was of employment comparable to that of the lead role in "Bloomer Girl" may be determined at trial.

Soules v. Independent School Dist. No. 518, 258 N.W.2d 103 (Minn. 1977). Soules, wrongfully terminated as a part-time teacher, charged breach of contract and sought reinstatement as an elementary school teacher. After reinstatement pursuant to order of the court, trial was conducted on the issue of damages. *Held,* the trial court was correct when it reduced the damages award after finding that the plaintiff teacher had failed to mitigate her loss; the evidence sustained the finding that the teacher failed to exert reasonable efforts to pursue or accept other suitable employment in the same locality under the rule of "avoidable consequences"; and the most that the trial court may properly deduct because of the part-time teacher's failure to accept a full-time teaching position at a private school was one-half the full-time teaching salary. The following rules and decisions are set forth in the syllabus by the court:

1. The measure of damages for wrongful discharge of an employee under contract with an employer is the amount of compensation specified by the contract.

2. Under the rule of avoidable consequences, the amount of a wrongfully discharged employee's damages may be reduced if it is established that he made no reasonable effort to pursue or unreasonably declined to accept other similar employment in the same locality.

3. The burden of proof is on the employer to establish that a wrongfully discharged employee failed to exert reasonable effort to pursue or unreasonably declined to accept other employment, and the amount that such employee, compatible with the working hours required by his prior employment, could have earned in avoiding the consequences of wrongful discharge.

4. Where plaintiff's continuing elementary teacher's contract for half-time employment was wrongfully terminated by defendant school district, Minn. St. 125.12, subd. 4, the court properly reduced the damages awarded upon findings that plaintiff failed to exert reasonable efforts to pursue and unreasonably declined to accept similar employment in the same locality, but improperly applied the rule of avoidable consequences by ordering a reduction of what plaintiff would have earned for full-time teaching to offset damages awarded for half-time teaching.

Indiana State Symphony Soc., Inc. v. Ziedonis, 171 Ind. App. 292, 359 N.E.2d 253 (1976). After plaintiff Ziedonis, a member of the Symphony's violin section, was terminated for alleged unexcused absences, he sued for breach of his written employment contract which also incorporated the terms of the Symphony's Master Agreement. On appeal, it was held unanimously (3-0) that although the evidence sustained the jury's finding that the discharge violated the contract, the verdict for plaintiff in the amount of $6,335 must be reversed on the issue of damages and a remittitur of $3,430 or a new trial on that issue held in the court below. The appellate panel disagreed, however, on the extent of the respective burdens borne by plaintiff and defendant in the case. The plaintiff's own evidence showing that he had earnings of $3,430 from other employment after the discharge, the majority of the court concluded (2-1) that the burden then shifted to the musician to show the amount of expense he incurred because of the discharge in order to avoid a reduction of his damages by the full amount of those earnings. The majority in its opinion noted that Indiana law requires that "one wrongfully discharged must attempt to seek alternate employment in order to mitigate damages"; that "in no event could he recover more than what his actual loss might have been had he made such reasonable effort to obtain employment"; that "the burden [is] on the Defendant Symphony of showing that other employment was available to plaintiff or that the plaintiff did not use diligence in seeking other employment"; that the Symphony is not required "to show that this employment was profitable to Ziedonis, i.e., because Ziedonis had certain expenses of a unspecified amount during the time he earned the $3,430, the Symphony has failed to show that such employment was profitable"; that "defendant is in no position to know plaintiff's

expenses and should not reasonably be saddled with the burden of proving them";
and that "If [Ziedonis] had expenses which reduced his income, he should have
proved them."

NOTES

1. Failure to mitigate does not always result in a zero recovery for a lessor; it
may result in recovery of a reduced amount. For example, in a case involving
termination of a farm lease, it was held that if lessor had properly mitigated its
damages, it would have saved lessee the sum of $23,000 in farming expenses.
Therefore, lessee was not required to pay lessor that sum. *Fox Grain and Cattle
Co. v. Maxwell*, 267 Mont. 528, 885 P.2d 432 (1994).

2. Mitigation by a lessor does not operate to release the lessee from the
obligation to pay lessor the damage balance due lessor over and above damages
recouped or prevented by the mitigation principle. *See Southwest Securities v.
AMFAC, Inc.*, 110 Nev. 1036, 879 P.2d 755 (1994) ("Nevada law does not espouse
the theory that a landlord's procurement of a mitigation-tenant automatically
works a discharge or release of the former occupant, the defaulting lessee, or of
any guarantor from liability from past defaults and damages accruing therefrom.");
Holly Farm Foods, Inc. v. Kuykendall, 114 N.C. App. 412, 442 S.E.2d 94 (1994)
("the measure of damages is the amount of rent the lessor would have received in
rent for the remainder of the term, less the amount received from the new
tenant.").

3. A lessor's damages may also include amounts expended by the lessor in
reasonable efforts to mitigate, often called *mitigation damages*. See *Properties
Inv. Group of Mid-America v. JBA, Inc.*, 242 Neb. 439, 495 N.W.2d 624 (1993),
where the lessor's damages were held to include attorney fees expended in
attempting to mitigate its damages from the lessee's breach of the lease.

F.   MENTAL DISTRESS DAMAGE CLAIMS

B & M HOMES, INC. v. HOGAN
376 So. 2d 667, 7 A.L.R. 4th 1162 (Ala. 1979)

Embry, Justice:

. . . [J]udgment in favor of appellees/plaintiffs Thomas J. Hogan and Carol Ann
Hogan. The judgment was entered on a jury verdict for $75,000 reduced by
remittitur to $50,000. Although the Hogans accepted the remittitur, B&M and
Morrow appeal and the Hogans urge reinstatement of the original verdict. . . .

We affirm but reinstate the verdict in the full amount of $75,000.

The Hogans' action was submitted to the jury on two theories: (1) breach of a
covenant, implied within their written purchase contract, to build their home in a
workmanlike manner using first class materials; and (2) breach of an express
warranty to build their home in substantial conformity to plans and specifications
approved by the FHA (Federal Housing Administration) or the VA (Veterans
Administration).

The issues are: (1) whether damages for mental anguish may be recovered in an action for breach of contract or breach of warranty to construct a house; (2) whether the trial court committed reversible error by admitting in evidence, over objection, certain hearsay testimony; (3) whether the trial court committed reversible error by failing to grant a directed verdict in favor of appellants on grounds of variance between appellees' pleadings and proof; (4) whether the trial court erred by admitting parol evidence as to B&M Homes' liability on the purchase contract; (5) whether the trial court committed reversible error by admitting evidence regarding appellees' VA financing; (6) whether the trial court erred by not entering summary judgment in behalf of, or directing a verdict for, appellant Morrow; and (7) whether the original jury verdict should be reinstated.

This is the second appeal to this court of this case. *See B&M Homes, Inc. v. Hogan*, 347 So.2d 1331 (Ala. 1977). On the first appeal we reversed on the sole basis that a remittitur was ordered without affording the Hogans an opportunity to choose it or a new trial.

On remand a corrected order of remittitur was entered and the remitted judgment was accepted by the Hogans. Nonetheless, B&M Homes and Morrow each perfected their appeal.

The Hogans entered into a written agreement to buy both a lot and a house to be constructed on that lot. . . .

During the construction of the house, Mrs. Hogan discovered a hairline crack in the concrete slab that extended from the front porch through the den and informed Morrow of this. He informed her that such cracks were common and told her not to worry about it. B&M Homes completed construction of the house and the Hogans received a warranty of completion of construction signed by Morrow on behalf of B&M Homes. The Hogans then moved into the house. After they moved in they reported several defects in the house to Morrow and repairmen were sent to fix those defects. After a couple of months the crack in the slab widened and extended through the house causing severe damage.

Again, Morrow was notified. He sent a man to repair some of the damage caused by the crack in the slab; however, nothing was done to repair the slab itself. There is expert testimony to the effect the slab probably could not be permanently repaired. There is also testimony the defective slab seriously decreased the value of the house; the Hogans' expert witness testified the defective slab made the house worthless. Evidence of what caused the crack in the slab is in conflict.

I.

Appellants contend the trial court erred by failing to grant their motion to strike mental anguish as an element of damages from the Hogans' complaint. We find mental anguish a proper element of damages in this case.

As noted at the outset, the Hogans' case was submitted to the jury on two theories stated in separate counts: one for breach of an implied covenant, to their written purchase contract, to build their home in a workmanlike manner using first class materials; and one for breach of express warranty. In both counts, appellees alleged damages for mental anguish as follows: ". . . the plaintiffs have suffered mental anguish and are still suffering mental anguish with regard to the condition of such home in that they fear for their safety in the house not being structurally sound; . . . ." At the close of the trial, B&M Homes filed a motion to strike the above allegation from both causes of action. The motion was denied. It can be assumed the jury awarded damages for mental anguish since the verdict was for $75,000 and the highest appraisal of the value of the house had it been built without defects was $42,500.

Evidence was introduced, over appellants' objection, that the Hogans were worried and concerned for their safety due to these facts: (1) the house was structurally defective and they believed its defective condition might cause the gas and water lines to burst; and (2) they were forced to live in the defective house because they could not afford to move.

In Alabama the general rule is that mental anguish is not a recoverable element of damages arising from breach of contract. *Sanford v. Western Life Insurance Co.*, 368 So. 2d 260 (Ala. 1979); *Stead v. Blue Cross-Blue Shield of Alabama*, 346 So. 2d 1140 (Ala. 1977). This court, however, has traditionally recognized exceptions to this rule in certain cases. [Citations] The exceptions are stated in the following excerpt from *F. Becker Asphaltum Roofing Co. v. Murphy* [224 Ala. 655, 141 So. 630 (1932)], which was quoted in *Stead v. Blue Cross-Blue Shield of Alabama, supra*:

> The general rule is that damages cannot be recovered for mental anguish in an action of assumpsit. *Birmingham Water Works Co. v. Vinter*, 164 Ala. 490, 51 So. 356. The ground on which the right to recover such damages is denied, is that they are too remote, were not within the contemplation of the parties, and that the breach of the contract is not such as will naturally cause mental anguish. *Westesen v. Olathe State Bank*, 78 Colo. 217, 240 P. 689, 44 A.L.R. 1484. "Yet where the contractual duty or obligation is so coupled with matters of mental concern or solicitude, or with the feelings of the party to whom the duty is owed, that a breach of that duty will necessarily or reasonably result in mental anguish or suffering, it is just that damages therefor be taken into consideration and awarded." 8 R.C.L. p. 529, § 83; . . .

> Another exception is where the breach of the contract is tortious, or attended with personal injury, damages for mental anguish may be awarded. *Vinson v. Southern Bell Tel. & Tel. Co.*, 188 Ala. 292, 66 So. 100, L.R.A. 1915C, 450.

> The facts of this case, if the plaintiff's evidence was believed, brings the case within these two exceptions.

> The contract related to placing a roof on the plaintiff's residence, her 'castle,' the habitation which she had provided to protect her against the elements, and to shelter her belongings that she thought essential to her comfort and well-being, the very things against which she made the contract to protect herself and her property, and as a result of the breach of the obligation which defendants assumed, the roof leaked to such extent that she was disturbed in her comfort, her household belongings were soaked with water, her house was made damp, she was made sick, as the jury were authorized to find. And the defendants, though repeatedly notified, took no steps to meet their obligation, were not only guilty of a breach of the contract, but were negligent in respect to the performance of

the duty which it imposed on them. Charge 12 was therefore refused without error.

> She was also entitled to recover for inconvenience and annoyance, resulting proximately from such breach. *Alabama Water Co. v. Knowles*, 220 Ala. 61, 124 So. 96 [224 Ala. 655 at 657, 141 So. 630 at 631, *quoted in* 346 So. 2d 1140 at 1143].

This case clearly falls within the first exception delineated in *F. Becker Asphaltum*. It was reasonably foreseeable by appellants that faulty construction of appellees' house would cause them severe mental anguish. The largest single investment the average American family will make is the purchase of a home. The purchase of a home by an individual or family places the purchaser in debt for a period ranging from twenty (20) to thirty (30) years. While one might expect to take the risk of acquiring a defective home if that person bought an older home, he or she certainly would not expect severe defects to exist in a home they contracted to have newly built. Consequently, any reasonable builder could easily foresee that an individual would undergo extreme mental anguish if their newly constructed house contained defects as severe as those shown to exist in this case. In any event, this court long ago set down the principle that the person who contracts to do work concerning a person's residence subjects himself to possible liability for mental anguish if that work is improperly performed and causes severe defects in that residence or home. The court clearly indicated this when it referred to the plaintiff's residence in *F. Becker Asphaltum* as "her 'castle,' the habitation which she had provided to protect her against the elements . . . ." 224 Ala. at 657, 141 So. at 631. While such language might be dramatic, it is a clear indication that contracts dealing with residences are in a special category and are exceptions to the general damages rule applied in contract cases which prohibits recovery for mental anguish.

In the recent case of *Hill v. Sereneck*, 355 So. 2d 1129 (Ala. Civ. App. 1978), the Court of Civil Appeals dealt with the issue of damages for mental anguish where a builder had breached an agreement to build a residence in a workmanlike manner. The major defects in the house in *Hill* were almost exactly the same as the major defects in the house in this case. The appellate court in *Hill* found that cases of this type fall within the first exception set out in *F. Becker Asphaltum* and that evidence of mental anguish caused by such defects was relevant and admissible. The *Hill* court stated:

> . . . Such evidence was relevant to the first exception to the general proposition that damages cannot be recovered for mental anguish in a civil action for breach of contract. In instances where it is demonstrated that the breach of the contractual duty actually caused the complaining party mental anguish or suffering and that the breach was such that it would necessarily result in emotional or mental detriment to the plaintiff, damages for annoyance and inconvenience may be awarded.
> 355 So. 2d at 1132.

We concur with the Court of Civil Appeals in the accuracy of the above statement. Appellants contend, that before recovery for mental anguish or suffering can be allowed, the mental anguish has to be corroborated by physical symptoms, i.e., becoming physically sick or ill. We reject this contention. The cases have not required mental anguish to be corroborated by the presence of physical symptoms. This is demonstrated by the fact that the cases have allowed recovery for annoyance and inconvenience. *See Alabama Water Service Co. v. Wakefield, supra; F. Becker*

Asphaltum Roofing Co. v. Murphy, supra; and *Birmingham Water Works Co. v. Ferguson, supra.* Appellees were only required to present evidence of their mental anguish, which they did; the question of damages for mental anguish then became a question of fact for the jury to decide. . . .

V.

B&M Homes asserts the trial court committed reversible error by admitting evidence which disclosed that appellees had financed their house with VA financing and they would not be able to obtain future VA financing for the purchase of another home. B&M Homes objected to such evidence as being immaterial and irrelevant. We cannot agree with this contention. Damages for breach of contract or warranty should restore the injured party to the condition he or she would have occupied if the contract had not been breached, or had been fully performed. *Geohagan v. General Motors Corp.*, 291 Ala. 167, 279 So. 2d 436 (1973). VA financing is a pecuniary benefit to those eligible to receive it because of the low interest rate applicable to the loan. Consequently, evidence as to the Hogans' inability to obtain additional VA financing was relevant because other evidence disclosed the house could not be repaired; thus, the probability the Hogans would be compelled to purchase another.

We also reject the argument by B&M Homes that appellees did not prove their damages. There is ample evidence in the record to authorize the jury to arrive at the amount of damages reflected by its verdict. . . .

VII.

The final question we address is whether the original jury verdict of $75,000 should be reinstated. We consider that it should. Only when it is shown that a verdict is based on bias, passion, prejudice, corruption or other improper motive does a court have authority to order a remittitur. The verdict may not be set aside because the trial court is of the opinion the jury awarded too much. *Central of Georgia Railway Co. v. Steed*, 287 Ala. 64, 248 So. 2d 110 (1971). The trial judge may not substitute his personal preference for the judgment of the jury. *Holcombe v. Whitaker*, 294 Ala. 430, 318 So. 2d 289 (1975). We find the jury award of $75,000 neither excessive nor based upon improper motive, prejudice, bias, passion or corruption. We, therefore, reinstate the original jury award of $75,000 and direct that the judgment be modified accordingly.

For the reasons assigned the jury award of $75,000 is due to be, and is hereby, reinstated and the judgment below is hereby directed to be modified to that extent and is hereby affirmed as modified.

Modified and Affirmed.

On Rehearing

EMBRY, Justice: The original opinion is hereby modified by striking the concluding paragraph and substituting therefor the following: For the reasons assigned, the original verdict and judgment of $75,000 are hereby reinstated by the judgment of this court. The trial court in all other respects is hereby affirmed.

Application for Rehearing Overruled.

DEITSCH v. MUSIC CO.

6 Ohio Misc. 2d 6, 453 N.E.2d 1302 (1983)

PAINTER, Judge:

This is an action for breach of contract. Plaintiffs and defendant entered into a contract on March 27, 1980, whereby defendant was to provide a four-piece band at plaintiffs' wedding reception on November 8, 1980. The reception was to be from 8:00 p.m. to midnight. The contract stated "wage agreed upon — $295.00," with a deposit of $65, which plaintiffs paid upon the signing of the contract.

Plaintiffs proceeded with their wedding, and arrived at the reception hall on the night of November 8, 1980, having employed a caterer, a photographer and a soloist to sing with the band. However, the four-piece band failed to arrive at the wedding reception. Plaintiffs made several attempts to contact defendant but were not successful. After much wailing and gnashing of teeth, plaintiffs were able to send a friend to obtain some stereo equipment to provide music, which equipment was set up at about 9:00 p.m.

This matter came on to be tried on September 28, 1982. Testimony at trial indicated there were several contacts between the parties from time to time between March and November 1980. The testimony of plaintiff Carla Deitsch indicated that she had taken music to the defendant several weeks prior to the reception and had received a telephone call from defendant on the night before the wedding confirming the engagement. Defendant's president testified that he believed the contract had been cancelled, since the word "cancelled" was written on his copy of the contract. There was no testimony as to when that might have been done, and no one from defendant-company was able to explain the error. There was also testimony that defendant's president apologized profusely to the mother of one of the plaintiffs, stating that his "marital problems" were having an effect on his business, and it was all a grievous error.

The court finds that defendant did in fact breach the contract and therefore that plaintiffs are entitled to damages. The difficult issue in this case is determining the correct measure and amount of damages.

Counsel for both parties have submitted memoranda on the issue of damages. However, no cases on point are cited. Plaintiffs contend that the entire cost of the reception, in the amount of $2,643.59, is the correct measure of damages. This would require a factual finding that the reception was a total loss, and conferred no benefit at all on the plaintiffs. Defendant, on the other hand, contends that the only measure of damages which is proper is the amount which plaintiffs actually lost, that is, the $65 deposit. It is the court's opinion that neither measure of damages is proper; awarding to plaintiffs the entire sum of the reception would grossly overcompensate them for their actual loss, while the simple return of the deposit would not adequately compensate plaintiffs for defendant's breach of contract.

Therefore, we have to look to other situations to determine whether there is a middle ground, or another measure of damages which would allow the court to award more than the deposit, but certainly less than the total cost of the reception.

It is hornbook law that in any contract action, the damages awarded must be the natural and probable consequence of the breach of contract or those damages which were within the contemplation of the parties at the time of making the contract. *Hadley v. Baxendale* (1854), 9 Exch. 341, 156 Eng. Rep. 145.

Certainly, it must be in the contemplation of the parties that the damages caused by a breach by defendant would be greater than the return of the deposit — that would be no damages at all.

The case that we believe is on point is *Pullman Company v. Willett* (Richland App. 1905), 7 Ohio C.C. (N.S.) 173, affirmed (1905), 72 Ohio St. 690, 76 N.E. 1131. In that case, a husband and wife contracted with the Pullman Company for sleeping accommodations on the train. When they arrived, fresh from their wedding, there were no accommodations, as a result of which they were compelled to sit up most of the night and change cars several times. The court held that since the general measure of damages is the loss sustained, damages for the deprivation of the comforts, conveniences, and privacy for which one contracts in reserving a sleeping car space are not to be measured by the amount paid therefor. The court allowed compensatory damages for the physical inconvenience, discomfort and mental anguish resulting from the breach of contract, and upheld a jury award of $125. The court went on to state as follows:

> It is further contended that the damages awarded were excessive. We think not. The peculiar circumstances of this case were properly [a] matter for the consideration of the jury. The damages for deprivation of the comforts, conveniences and privacy for which he had contracted and agreed to pay *are not to be measured by the amount to be paid therefor.* He could have had cheaper accommodations had he so desired, but that he wanted these accommodations under the circumstances of this case was but natural and commendable, and we do not think that the record fails to show any damages, but, on the contrary it fully sustains the verdict and would, in our opinion, sustain even a larger verdict had the jury thought proper to fix a larger amount. (Emphasis added.)

Pullman Company v. Willett, supra, at 177-78; *see also* 49 Ohio Jurisprudence 2d 191, *Sleeping Car Companies,* Section 6.

Another similar situation would be the reservation of a room in a hotel or motel. Surely, the damages for the breach of that contract could exceed the mere value of the room. In such a case, the Hawaii Supreme Court has held the plaintiff was "not limited to the narrow traditional contractual remedy of out-of-pocket losses alone." *Dold v. Outrigger Hotel* (1972), 54 Haw. 18, 22, 501 P.2d 368, at 371-372.

The court holds that in a case of this type, the out-of-pocket loss, which would be the security deposit, or even perhaps the value of the band's services, where another band could not readily be obtained at the last minute, would not be sufficient to compensate plaintiffs. Plaintiffs are entitled to compensation for their distress, inconvenience, and the diminution in value of their reception. For said damages, the court finds that the compensation should be $750. Since plaintiffs are clearly entitled to the refund of their security deposit, judgment will be rendered for plaintiffs in the amount of $815 and the costs of this action.

Judgment accordingly.

Lamm v. Shingleton, 231 N.C. 10, 55 S.E.2d 810 (N.C. 1949). A claim was brought for the failure of a funerary establishment to properly inter the remains of the plaintiff's husband. Within a few weeks of the burial, and after a period of heavy rain, the vault containing the casket had risen out of the ground, and flooded the casket. The North Carolina Supreme Court held that there is a developing trend that allows an exception to the rule that mental anguish may not be considered as an element of damages for contract claims.

The court noted that "[s]ome courts qualify the rule by holding that such damages are recoverable when the breach amounts in substance to a willful or independent tort or is accompanied by physical injury. 15 A.J. 599, 603; *Hall v. Jackson*, 24 Colo. App. 225, 134 P. 151. Still others treat the breach as an act of negligence and decide the question as though the action were cast in tort, and thus confuse the issue. Thus, to some extent the courts have modified the common law rule."

The Court did not want to recognize either of those doctrines in this case, but they noted a generally accepted exception to the rule against emotional damages for contract claims, saying that "[w]here the contract is personal in nature and the contractual duty or obligation is so coupled with matters of mental concern or solicitude, or with the sensibilities of the party to whom the duty is owed, that a breach of that duty will necessarily or reasonably result in mental anguish or suffering, and it should be known to the parties from the nature of the contract that such suffering will result from its breach, compensatory damages therefor may be recovered." It went on to say that, "[i]n such case the party sought to be charged is presumed to have contracted with reference to the payment of damages of that character in the event such damages should accrue on account of his breach of the contract."

The Court noted that, "[t]he tenderest feelings of the human heart center around the remains of the dead. When the defendants contracted with plaintiff to inter the body of her deceased husband in a workmanlike manner they did so with the knowledge that she was the widow and would naturally and probably suffer mental anguish if they failed to fulfill their contractual obligation in the manner here charged. The contract was predominantly personal in nature and no substantial pecuniary loss would follow its breach. Her mental concern, her sensibilities, and her solicitude were the prime considerations for the contract, and the contract itself was such as to put the defendants on notice that a failure on their part to inter the body properly would probably produce mental suffering on her part. It cannot be said, therefore, that such damages were not within the contemplation of the parties at the time the contract was made."

NOTES

1. Some recent cases in accord with the view that damages for mental anguish, anxiety or distress caused by breach of a funeral contract are recoverable and within the contemplation of the parties: *Flores v. Baca*, 117 N.M. 306, 871 P.2d 962 (1994); *Holland v. Edgerton*, 85 N.C. App. 567, 355 S.E.2d 514 (1987); *McDaniel v. Bass-Smith Funeral Home, Inc.*, 80 N.C. App. 629, 343 S.E.2d 228, 54 A.L.R. 4th 891 (1986).

2. There are, however, jurisdictions that refuse to allow, or have limitations upon, recovery of contract damages for mental anguish, anxiety or distress, even when the contract is of the manifestly personal character as that in *Lamm*. The following are examples.

3. *Contreraz v. Michelotti-Sawyers*, 271 Mont. 300, 896 P.2d 1118 (1995), denied mental distress damages for breach of a funeral contract on the authority of a state

statute (MCA Section 27-1-310) that provides:

> Damages for emotional or mental distress prohibited in contract actions
> — exception. In an action for breach of an obligation or duty arising from
> contract, recovery is prohibited for emotional or mental distress, except in
> those actions involving actual physical injury to the plaintiff. Emotional or
> mental distress, as used in this section, includes mental anguish or
> suffering, sorrow, grief, fright, shame, embarrassment, humiliation, anger,
> chagrin, disappointment, or worry.

4. *Sackett v. St. Mary's Church Soc.*, 18 Mass. App. Ct. 186, 464 N.E.2d 956
(1984), held that the special nature of a funeral contract would not entitle the
decedent's children to recover damages for mental distress on a contract theory
which would go beyond what they might have recovered in tort. "While the duty of
the defendants may have its origin in contract, the damages for mental distress
recoverable in contract would probably be governed by the principles of tort and
would not exceed those recoverable under the rules applicable to negligence
actions."

5. Claims for damages for mental anguish have been made where employers have
breached employment contracts by discharging employees, and claims for such
damages are typically denied. In *Valentine v. General American Credit, Inc.*, 420
Mich. 256, 362 N.W.2d 628 (1984), the court refused to allow the plaintiff mental
distress damages for her employer's breach of the employment contract. *Valentine*
had relied on the rule of *Hadley v. Baxendale*, "which provides that damages
recoverable for a breach of contract are those that 'may fairly and reasonably be
considered either arising naturally, i.e., according to the usual course of things,
from such breach of contract itself, or such as may reasonably be supposed to have
been in the contemplation of both parties at the time they made the contract, as the
probable result of the breach of it.'"

6. The *Valentine* opinion also notes that "Although courts frequently begin
analysis with a reference to the rule stated in *Hadley v. Baxendale*, that rule has
not been applied scrupulously. As stated by Professor Dobbs in his treatise on
remedies, a "difficulty in the *Hadley* type case is that the test of foreseeability [i.e.,
whether damages 'arise naturally'] has little or no meaning. The idea is so readily
subject to expansion or contraction that it becomes in fact merely a technical way
in which the judges can state their conclusion.'" Quoting from Dobbs, REMEDIES,
§ 12.3, p. 14 and 804; and also suggesting examination of 5 CORBIN ON CONTRACTS,
§ 1007, pp. 70-71. After citing Dobbs and Corbin, and in support of its decision
denying Valentine mental distress damages, the Michigan court continued:

> Yet the general rule, with few exceptions, is to "uniformly den[y]"
> recovery for mental distress damages although they are "foreseeable
> within the rule of *Hadley v. Baxendale*." [quoting GRISMORE, CONTRACTS
> (rev. ed.), § 203, p. 320.] The rule barring recovery of mental distress
> damages — a gloss on the generality of the rule stated in *Hadley v.
> Baxendale* — is fully applicable to an action for breach of an employment
> contract. [citing McCormick, DAMAGES, § 163, p. 637-638.]

7. The Hawaii Supreme Court, in *Francis v. Lee Enterprises, Inc.*, 89 Hawaii 234,
971 P.2d 707 (1999), referred with approval to Michigan's 1984 *Valentine* decision,
noted important distinctions between theories of contract and of tort, and held that
"damages for emotional distress will rarely, if ever, be recoverable for breaches of

an employment contract, where the parties did not bargain for such damages or where the nature of the contract does not clearly indicate that such damages were within the contemplation or expectation of the parties."

8. *Question*: Can you suggest the kinds of employment, or employment contract provisions, that would support awards of mental distress damages to discharged employees in actions predicated only on claims for breach of contract? For this exercise do not include claims based on or relating to tort theories, such as fraud, fraudulent inducement, intentional or negligent misrepresentation or deceit, or intentional or negligent infliction of mental or emotional distress.

9. *Consider*: In *Birmingham-Jefferson County Transit Authority v. Arvan*, 669 So. 2d 825 (Ala. 1995), a jury award and judgment of $685,000 for plaintiff discharged employee — some portion of which may have included damages for mental anguish — was affirmed on appeal. In its opinion the state supreme court noted that "the evidence indicated . . . he had suffered mental anguish as a result of his discharge," and the court then stated, in parentheses, that: "(The jury was instructed, without objection, that it could award damages for mental anguish if it found for [plaintiff] on his contract claim.)."

G.   ATTORNEY FEES DAMAGE CLAIMS

BUNNETT v. SMALLWOOD
793 P.2d 157 (Colo. 1990)

Justice Mullarkey delivered the Opinion of the Court:
We granted certiorari in this case in order to decide if attorney fees could be awarded as damages in a case where the lawsuit was barred because of an agreement not to sue. The court of appeals held in *Bunnett v. Smallwood*, 768 P.2d 736 (Colo. Ct. App. 1988), that the defendant was entitled to recover his attorney fees and costs where the legal proceedings were instituted in violation of an agreement not to sue. We reverse the court of appeals and hold that, absent a contractual agreement or statutory or rule authority, the non-breaching party to a release is not entitled to attorney fees and costs.

I.

This case involves two consolidated appeals arising from a series of business transactions between the parties. We summarize only the facts which are relevant to the issue before us.

In 1974, William E. Bunnett and Donald E. Smallwood formed Bunnett/Smallwood & Co., Inc., a company engaged in the business of buying and selling fertilizer, feed supplements, and hay. Bunnett/Smallwood was incorporated in Texas and had its principal place of business in Colorado. Both Bunnett and Smallwood were fifty percent shareholders in the corporation.

Several points of contention arose between the two parties. In February 1984, Smallwood resigned his office at Bunnett/Smallwood and started another company in competition with Bunnett/Smallwood. Bunnett filed a claim against Smallwood in August 1984 charging that Smallwood had obtained certain raw materials by misrepresentation that he was still a Bunnett/Smallwood officer. For his part, Smallwood was concerned about his potential liability to a Texas bank for a separate personal guaranty that he had signed as a Bunnett/Smallwood officer in return for the bank extending an open line of credit to the company. Smallwood wanted to avoid liability for both the claims filed against him by Bunnett and the personal guaranty. After previous unsuccessful negotiations, Smallwood and Bunnett met at a Denver-area restaurant on October 3, 1984 in order to discuss the Bunnett/Smallwood Company stock still owned by Smallwood. Smallwood told Bunnett that he wanted to end all of the "hassle" in exchange for giving his stock to Bunnett.[38]

The effect of the parties' informal, oral agreement was raised in the two lawsuits which were consolidated in this appeal. Smallwood contended that he received a release from liability for "any and all claims of any kind or nature which Bunnett or Bunnett/Smallwood had against Smallwood." Bunnett, on the other hand, claimed that Smallwood received a release from liability for the August 1984 claim, but not for any other claims. It is undisputed that after Bunnett received the stock, he dropped the August 1984 suit against Smallwood and notified the Texas bank that Smallwood was no longer personally liable for Bunnett/Smallwood debts.

Bunnett, however, instituted two other lawsuits against Smallwood after the meeting of October 3, 1984. In the first case, *Bunnett v. Smallwood*, No. 86CA1302 (Bunnett case), Bunnett claimed that Smallwood converted partnership property and Smallwood counterclaimed for breach of the October 1984 agreement. In the second case, *Bunnett/Smallwood & Co. v. Smallwood*, No. 87CA0469 (Bunnett/Smallwood case), Bunnett claimed that Smallwood had breached his fiduciary duty to Bunnett/Smallwood prior to February 1984, usurped a corporate opportunity, and tortiously interfered with a Bunnett/Smallwood contract. Smallwood moved for summary judgment and dismissal on the ground that Bunnett was collaterally estopped from contesting the exclusivity of the October 1984 release.

The jury in the Bunnett case held against Bunnett on June 20, 1986, finding that Bunnett had breached a contract which released Smallwood of all future claims, and granted damages to Smallwood of $30,000, equal to his attorney fees and costs for defending both the Bunnett case and Bunnett/Smallwood case. The trial court in the Bunnett/Smallwood case granted Smallwood's motions concluding that because of the judgment in the Bunnett case, the doctrine of collateral estoppel barred relitigation of a vital issue involved in the Bunnett/Smallwood case. Both cases were appealed. The court of appeals consolidated the appeals and affirmed the trial court judgments. The validity of the settlement agreement or Bunnett's breach are not before us. Rather, we granted certiorari in order to address the following question: whether the prevailing party in a lawsuit can recover attorney fees and costs for breach of an agreement not to sue.

---

[38] [1] The parties testified to slightly different versions of Smallwood's "hassle" comment which both parties agreed was made after some initial small talk. According to Bunnett, Smallwood pulled his Bunnett/Smallwood stock certificates from his pocket and said "I've got enough money. This company has served a useful purpose for me, and I'm tired of hassling on the deal, and I'm just giving you the stock." When Bunnett questioned why Smallwood wanted to give him the stock, Smallwood said, "Well, I'm just tired of this deal, and I have got my own company going, and there is no use hassling anymore." Smallwood testified that when Bunnett raised the subject of the stock, Smallwood said, "Bill, the hassling we have been doing is getting us nowhere. I would like for you to accept this stock and just end all of the hassle, all of it."

II.

The jury found that the agreement between Bunnett and Smallwood constituted a release of all claims and controversies.[39] A release is the relinquishment of a vested right or claim to the person against whom the claim is enforceable. *Neves v. Potter*, 769 P.2d 1047 (Colo. 1989); *see also* RESTATEMENT (SECOND) OF CONTRACTS, § 284 (1981). Furthermore, a release is an agreement to which general contractual rules of interpretation and construction apply. *Rocky Mountain Ass'n of Credit Mgmt. v. Hessler Mfg. Co.*, 37 Colo. App. 551, 553 P.2d 840 (1976).

Smallwood's claim for attorney fees and costs after his successful defense must be analyzed against the background of the caselaw, statutes, and court rules regarding the award of attorney fees and costs. In the absence of a statute or private contract to the contrary, attorney fees and costs generally are not recoverable by the prevailing party in a breach of contract case. *Alyeska Pipeline Serv. Co. v. Wilderness Soc'y*, 421 U.S. 240, 247, 95 S. Ct. 1612, 1616-17, 44 L. Ed. 2d 141 (1975); *Cement Asbestos Prods. Co. v. Hartford Accident & Indem. Co.*, 592 F.2d 1144, 1148 (10th Cir. 1979); *Buder v. Sartore*, 774 P.2d 1383, 1390 (Colo. 1989); *Beebe v. Pierce*, 185 Colo. 34, 38, 521 P.2d 1263, 1265 (1974). Requiring each party in such cases to pay its own legal expenses is based on the well-established American rule. *See generally* 1 M. Derfner & A. Wolfe, COURT AWARDED ATTORNEY FEES ¶ 1.01 (1990). Numerous rationales are advanced in support of the American rule. For example, attorney fees and costs are not considered actual damages "because they are not the legitimate consequences of the tort or breach of contract sued upon." Taxpayers for the *Animas-LaPlata Referendum v. Animas-LaPlata Water Conservancy Dist.*, 739 F.2d 1472, 1480 (10th Cir. 1984) (construing Colorado law). Additional rationales include that the rule promotes equality among litigants, does not penalize parties for merely asserting their legal positions, and does not substantially burden judicial administration. M. Derfner & A. Wolfe, at ¶ 1.03.

In affirming the trial court judgments, the court of appeals reasoned that, if a party must defend a suit despite a release, then the attorney fees and costs which the party incurs are the measure of actual damages because they represent the direct consequences of the breach. *Bunnett*, 768 P.2d at 739 (citing *Anchor Motor Freight, Inc. v. International Bhd. of Teamsters*, 700 F.2d 1067 (6th Cir.), *cert. denied* 464 U.S. 819, 104 S. Ct. 81, 78 L. Ed. 2d 92 (1983)). As such, the court of appeals concluded that Smallwood was entitled to compensatory damages sufficient to place him in the position in which he would have been if the breach had not occurred. *Id.*; *see also General Ins. Co. v. City of Colorado Springs*, 638 P.2d 752, 759 (Colo. 1981); *Combined Communications Corp. v. Bedford Motors, Inc.*, 702 P.2d 281, 282 (Colo. Ct. App. 1985); *Kniffin v. Colorado W. Dev. Co.*, 622 P.2d 586 (Colo. Ct. App. 1980) (damages awarded in contract dispute to make the nonbreaching party whole).

The court of appeals followed a line of cases which has held that attorney fees are recoverable as damages for breach of a release. *See Anchor Motor Freight, Inc.*, 700 F.2d 1067; *Widener v. Arco Oil and Gas Co.*, 717 F. Supp. 1211 (N.D. Tex. 1989); *Borbely v. Nationwide Mut. Ins. Co.*, 547 F. Supp. 959 (D.N.J. 1981); *Desroches v. Ryder Truck Rental, Inc.*, 429 So. 2d 1010 (Ala. 1983); *Colton v. New*

---

[39] [2] The parties have used the terms "release," "covenant not to sue" and "settlement agreement" interchangeably. For purposes of this opinion, we will use the term "release."

York Hospital, 53 A.D.2d 588, 385 N.Y.S.2d 65 (1976); *Scott v. Reedy*, 5 Ohio Dec. Reprint 388 (Ohio 1876). These cases provide little explanation for their holdings, and several of the cases merely state that a party breaching a release "may be compelled to respond in damages." *Colton*, 53 A.D.2d at 589, 385 N.Y.S.2d at 66. *See also Borbely*, 547 F. Supp. at 977. We find two general theories underlying the award of attorney fees in the jurisdictions which have followed this practice. First, several cases maintain that the traditional American rule, providing that each party to a lawsuit pays its own attorney fees and costs, is not applicable in this situation because the attorney fees are the subject of the lawsuit itself rather than an award to the successful litigant. *Anchor Motor Freight, Inc.*, 700 F.2d at 1072 (citing *Scott v. Local Union 377*, 548 F.2d 1244, 1266 (6th Cir.), *cert. denied*, 431 U.S. 968, 97 S. Ct. 2927, 53 L. Ed. 2d 1064 (1977)).

Secondly, it is argued that attorney fees should be awarded for breach of a release based on equitable principles. For example, the court in Widener stated, "[b]ecause the purpose of entering into a release is to avoid litigation, the damages a releasor suffers when the release is breached are its costs and attorneys' fees incurred in defending against the wrongfully brought action." 717 F. Supp. at 1217. Moreover, in urging us to affirm the court of appeals, Smallwood argues that to hold otherwise would create unfair results, would enable some defendants to evade damages despite wrongdoing, and would preclude damaged parties from receiving redress or being made whole for their losses. We reject the theories underlying the cases followed by the court of appeals.

As to the first theory, we agree that there is an exception to the American rule when the attorney fees are the subject of the lawsuit. Properly construed, however, this exception applies to cases such as suits brought by attorneys to enforce their fee agreements. The exception should not be construed to extend to an action which is defended on the grounds that the action is barred by a release. The subject of the action in such a case is the claim or claims pled by the plaintiff. Attorney fees and costs necessarily are incurred as part of the defense based on breach of a release but they are not the subject of the suit. Smallwood's position in this respect is no different from that of any other defendant who prevails in a lawsuit and does not have a successful counterclaim for damages. Unless we are prepared to abandon the American rule and award attorney fees and costs to the prevailing party, it is difficult to construct any principled way to contain the "exception" to the American rule which would be created by characterizing attorney fees as the subject of the lawsuit because a release is raised as a defense.

We also reject the equitable argument for awarding attorney fees. Although Smallwood argues that he has been damaged by Bunnett's unlawful breach of the release and that failure to award attorney fees would mean that he has received nothing in exchange for the agreement, we disagree. Smallwood has obtained a valid release which he has employed as a successful defense in the Bunnett and Bunnett/Smallwood cases. The intent of the release having now been adjudicated, the release may be used as an effective defense to possible future litigation. *See Isaacs v. Caterpillar, Inc.*, 702 F. Supp. 711 (C.D. Ill. 1988). Furthermore, parties who enter into a release are aware of the potential legal costs if the agreement is breached. It is not unfair to require each party to pay its own legal costs if the parties did not find it necessary to include a fee shifting provision when they entered into the agreement.

III.

Contrary to the line of cases upon which the court of appeals relied, most jurisdictions have applied the American rule barring the award of attorney fees and costs to cases involving a breach of a release. Such jurisdictions award attorney fees for breach of release only if an agreement or statute specifically authorizes such fees. *See Isaacs v. Caterpillar, Inc.*, 702 F. Supp. 711; *Dodge v. United Services Auto Ass'n*, 417 A.2d 969 (Me. 1980); *Child v. Lincoln Enter., Inc.*, 51 Ill. App. 2d 76, 200 N.E.2d 751 (1964). Alternatively, the courts which adhere to the American rule will award attorney fees only if the suit is brought in obvious breach of a release or is brought in bad faith which is one of the established exceptions to the American rule. *See Artvale, Inc. v. Rugby Fabrics Corp.*, 363 F.2d 1002 (2d Cir. 1966); *Bellefonte Re Ins. Co. v. Argonaut Ins. Co.*, 757 F.2d 523 (2d Cir. 1985); *Quill Co., Inc. v. A.T. Cross Co.*, 477 A.2d 939 (R.I. 1984). Discussion of the leading cases explains the analyses developed by these jurisdictions.

In *Dodge v. United Services Auto Ass'n*, 417 A.2d 969, 975, the Maine Supreme Court discussed the policy reasons against awarding attorney fees for breach of a release: Lawyers settle cases against the background of the American rule that firmly and with only very limited exceptions denies attorney's fees as an element of costs or damages. . . . Because of the pervasiveness and vigor of the American rule making each party bear his own attorney's fees, parties to a settlement agreement — in absence of an express contractual provision to the contrary — must be taken to intend to exclude attorney's fees from the damages that otherwise would be recoverable as a foreseeable and probable consequence of a breach of the agreement. The court reasoned that there were strong public policy reasons for denying normal contract damages for breach of settlement agreements. For example if such contract damages were allowed, a lawyer conceivably would be more "wary of informal settlement discussions for fear of subjecting his client to the added expense of the opposing party's attorney's fees if it were later determined that those discussions had in fact reached the point of a binding bilateral agreement." *Id.* at 976. Hence, the court found it preferable to encourage free settlement negotiations without the risk of heavy damages which could result in the relatively rare case where one party failed to perform his agreement. *Id.* Finally, the court stated that "lawyers who wish to swim against the tide of the American rule are perfectly capable of including an express undertaking that the damages resulting from any breach of the settlement agreement shall include attorney's fees." *Id.*

Artvale, Inc. v. Rugby Fabrics Corp., 363 F.2d 1002, and its progeny follow a slightly different test for awarding attorney fees for breach of a release. In Artvale, the Second Circuit Court of Appeals held that the question of whether a party who has breached a release is liable for litigation expenses is to be solved by seeking to determine what the parties intended by their contract. However, in the absence of contrary evidence, liability for attorney fees and costs would be imposed only for suits brought in obvious breach of the release or otherwise brought in bad faith. Also, in *Winchester Drive-In Theater, Inc. v. Warner Bros. Pictures Distrib. Corp.*, 358 F.2d 432 (9th Cir. 1966), the court did not support an absolute bar on the recovery of attorney fees, but rather held that when the very existence of a release is disputed in good faith, attorney fees and costs may not be recovered.

In our view, attorney fees and costs should not be awarded for breach of a release unless (1) the agreement expressly provides that remedy, or (2) such an award is permitted by statute or court rule. The first alternative is consistent with normal rules of contract interpretation and the second alternative, given Colorado's extensive and detailed provisions for awarding attorney fees, should serve to adequately protect the non-breaching party. Our state has various statutory and rule exceptions to the American rule regarding attorney fees which allow attorney fees to be imposed for suits brought in bad faith. In general, section 13-17-101, 6A C.R.S. (1987), provides that attorney fees may be recovered at the discretion of the trial court if it is determined that the bringing or defense of an action has been "substantially frivolous, substantially groundless, or substantially vexatious." Furthermore, section 13-17-101 instructs the courts to construe the provisions of the article regarding attorney fees liberally. *See Western United Realty, Inc. v. Isaacs*, 679 P.2d 1063 (Colo. 1984) (attorney fees awarded for bad faith which includes conduct which is arbitrary, vexatious, abusive, or stubbornly litigious, and conduct aimed at unwarranted delay or disrespectful of truth and accuracy). Also, our rules of civil procedure explicitly authorize the award of attorney fees in certain circumstances. *See, e.g.*, C.R.C.P. 3(a) (civil action vexatiously commenced); C.R.C.P. 11 (willful violation of rule regarding the signing of pleadings); C.R.C.P. 30(g) (failure to attend deposition or failure to serve a subpoena for attendance to deposition); C.R.C.P. 37(a)(3) (failure to respond to discovery requests); C.R.C.P. 37(c) (failure to admit the genuineness of any documents or the truth of requests for admission); C.R.C.P. 56(g) (affidavits made in bad faith); C.R.C.P. 107(d) (sanction for civil contempt). Consequently, the trial courts have ample authority to award attorney fees in appropriate cases.

In adopting a test for determining when attorney fees and costs are properly awarded in this context, we reject the rule of Artvale allowing such award in the case of a clear breach of a release. We do so because that standard seems to invite litigation over whether a breach was "clear." Furthermore, our existing statutes and rules are adequate to protect the interests of the non-breaching party by, for example, allowing the award of attorney fees if the suit is "substantially frivolous" or "substantially groundless." We also decline to follow the language of Winchester which awarded attorney fees unless the very existence of the release was disputed in good faith. Again, this standard invites unnecessary litigation and is covered in part by our statutes and rules imposing attorney fees for suits brought in bad faith.

The facts in the instant case illustrate why attorney fees should not be recoverable absent express contractual, statutory or rule liability. The oral agreement here was imprecise at best. What each party understood by the term "hassle" was not spelled out. Only two disputed matters actually were discussed by the parties and Bunnett disposed of both matters as requested by Smallwood. There was no description of any other claims which Bunnett was to surrender and the parties did not specifically discuss or agree that liability or consequences would result from a breach of the agreement. Bunnett and Smallwood were experienced businessmen who presumably knew the importance of formalizing an agreement if they meant it to be binding. In the absence of a plain, unambiguous agreement for the award of attorney fees and costs, we will not create such a remedy for the parties. The existing law providing for the award of attorney fees and costs upon a finding that the litigation is frivolous or groundless is adequate to protect the prevailing party's interest in the truly unmeritorious case. But where, as here, the nature and scope of the agreement itself is ambiguous, award of attorney fees and costs in the absence of an express contractual provision would be unfair. A party should not be penalized because its judgment about the scope of agreement simply proves to be wrong. Here, there was no finding that Bunnett acted in bad faith or that attorney fees and costs were justified under the relevant statutes or rules. Hence, the award was erroneous.

We think that the general rule which allows attorney fees and costs only where there is contractual agreement or the award is authorized by statute or rule promotes settlement negotiations and greater contractual autonomy among parties and their attorneys. If parties and lawyers wish to abandon the general rule and provide for the award of attorney fees for a breach of an agreement not to sue, they can do so expressly within the agreement.

In conclusion, we hold that the non-breaching party to a release who successfully defends a lawsuit brought in violation of the agreement is not entitled to the award of attorney fees and costs absent contractual, statutory or rule authorization for such award. The judgment of the court of appeals is reversed on this issue, with directions to remand to the trial court for dismissal of the counterclaim in accord with this opinion.

NOTES

1. To the same effect is *Raymond v. Feldmann*, 124 Or. App. 543, 863 P.2d 1269 (1993), where the court, refusing to allow a personal injury defendant to recover from the plaintiff the attorney's fees defendant incurred in defending an action brought after plaintiff had settled with and released defendant's insurer, noted: (a) that the general rule is that attorney fees are not recoverable in contract actions, and held (b) that since this action did not involve a claim for damages arising from a separate litigation with a third party, that exception to the general rule could not apply.

2. The American rule that attorney fees are not recoverable absent a contract provision or statute authority therefor is generally applied whether attorney fees are claimed as "damages" or as "costs." Quoting from previous cases, the Alabama Supreme Court in *Tolar Construction, LLC v. Keane Electric Co., Inc.*, 944 So. 2d 138, 2006 Ala. LEXIS 109 (Ala. 2006), has held that "In Alabama and most other jurisdictions, the general rule is that attorney's fees and expenses of litigation are not recoverable as damages, in [the] absence of a contractual or statutory duty, other than [by] a few recognized . . . equity principles."

3. *See Danzl v. Heidinger*, 677 N.W.2d 924 (N.D. 2004), where the court noted that "attorney fees and expenses may be recovered if they constitute damages from the breach of a contract, but not if they are incurred in proving the breach"; and *Ferrell v. Glenwood Brokers, Ltd.*, 848 P.2d 936 (Colo. 1993), where the court distinguished between attorney fees as *damages* and as *costs*, stating that "If attorney fees are part of the substance of a lawsuit, that is, if the fees being sought are 'the legitimate consequences of the tort or breach of contract sued upon,' . . . such as in an insurance bad faith case, then such fees are clearly damages."

4. *Practice Point*: There are situations in which the question whether a request or an award for attorney fees is one for *damages* or for *costs* may be important. For example, in the *Ferrell* case (see paragraph above) the court noted that in a case where the only remaining item to be decided is a request for attorney fees, the time to file an appeal can expire earlier in one instance (*costs*) than in the other (*damages*).

H. STIPULATED CONTRACT DAMAGES

1. Liquidated Damage Agreements

TRUCK RENT-A-CENTER, INC. v. PURITAN FARMS 2nd, INC.
41 N.Y.2d 420, 393 N.Y.S.2d 365, 361 N.E.2d 1015 (1977)

JASEN, Judge:

The principal issue on this appeal is whether a provision in a truck lease agreement which requires the payment of a specified amount of money to the lessor in the event of the lessee's breach is an enforceable liquidated damages clause, or, instead, provides for an unenforceable penalty.

Defendant Puritan Farms 2nd, Inc. (Puritan), was in the business of furnishing milk and milk products to customers through home delivery. In January, 1969, Puritan leased a fleet of 25 new milk delivery trucks from plaintiff Truck Rent-A-Center for a term of seven years commencing January 15, 1970. Under the provisions of a truck lease and service agreement entered into by the parties, the plaintiff was to supply the trucks and make all necessary repairs. Puritan was to pay an agreed upon weekly rental fee. It was understood that the lessor would finance the purchase of the trucks through a bank, paying the prime rate of interest on the date of the loan plus 2%. The rental charges on the trucks were to be adjusted in the event of a fluctuation in the interest rate above or below specified levels. The lessee was granted the right to purchase the trucks, at any time after 12 months following commencement of the lease, by paying to the lessor the amount then due and owing on the bank loan, plus an additional $100 per truck purchased.

Article 16 of the lease agreement provided that if the agreement should terminate prior to expiration of the term of the lease as a result of the lessee's breach, the lessor would be entitled to damages, "liquidated for all purposes," in the amount of all rentals that would have come due from the date of termination to the date of normal expiration of the term less the "re-rental value" of the vehicles, which was set at 50% of the rentals that would have become due. In effect, the lessee would be obligated to pay the lessor, as a consequence of breach, one half of all rentals that would have become due had the agreement run its full course. The agreement recited that, in arriving at the settled amount of damage, "the parties hereto have considered, among other factors, Lessor's substantial initial investment in purchasing or reconditioning for Lessee's service the demised motor vehicles, the uncertainty of Lessor's ability to re-enter the said vehicles, the costs to Lessor during any period the vehicles may remain idle until re-rented, or if sold, the uncertainty of the sales price and its possible attendant loss. The parties have also considered, among other factors, in so liquidating the said damages, Lessor's saving in expenditures for gasoline, oil and other service items."

The bulk of the written agreement was derived from a printed form lease which the parties modified by both filling in blank spaces and typing in alterations. The agreement also contained several typewritten indorsements which also made changes in the provisions of the printed lease. The provision for lessee's purchase of the vehicles for the bank loan balance and $100 per vehicle was contained in one such indorsement. The liquidated damages clause was contained in the body of the printed form.

Puritan tendered plaintiff a security deposit, consisting of four weeks' rent and the lease went into effect. After nearly three years, the lessee sought to terminate the lease agreement. On December 7, 1973, Puritan wrote to the lessor complaining that the lessor had not repaired and maintained the trucks as provided in the lease agreement. Puritan stated that it had "repeatedly notified" plaintiff of these defaults, but plaintiff had not cured them. Puritan, therefore, exercised its right to terminate the agreement "without any penalty and *without purchasing the trucks*." (Emphasis added [by the court].) On the date set for termination, December 14, 1973, plaintiff's attorneys replied to Puritan by letter to advise it that plaintiff believed it had fully performed its obligations under the lease and, in the event Puritan adhered to the announced breach, would commence proceedings to obtain the liquidated damages provided for in article 16 of the agreement. Nevertheless, Puritan had its drivers return the trucks to plaintiff's premises, where the bulk of them have remained ever since. At the time of termination, plaintiff owed $45,134.17 on the outstanding bank loan.

Plaintiff followed through on its promise to commence an action for the payment of the liquidated damages. Defendant counterclaimed for the return of its security deposit. At the nonjury trial, plaintiff contended that it had fully performed its obligations to maintain and repair the trucks. Moreover, it was submitted, Puritan sought to cancel the lease because corporations allied with Puritan had acquired the assets, including delivery trucks, of other dairies and Puritan believed it cheaper to utilize this "shadow fleet." The home milk delivery business was on the decline and plaintiff's president testified that efforts to either re-rent or sell the truck fleet to other dairies had not been successful. Even with modifications in the trucks, such as the removal of the milk racks and a change in the floor of the trucks, it was not possible to lease the trucks to other industries, although a few trucks were subsequently sold. The proceeds of the sales were applied to the reduction of the bank balance. The other trucks remained at plaintiff's premises, partially protected by a fence plaintiff erected to discourage vandals. The defendant countered with proof that plaintiff had not repaired the trucks promptly and satisfactorily.

At the close of the trial, the court found, based on the evidence it found to be credible, that plaintiff had substantially performed its obligations under the lease and that defendant was not justified in terminating the agreement. Further, the court held that the provision for liquidated damages was reasonable and represented a fair estimate of actual damages which would be difficult to ascertain precisely. "The parties, at the time the agreement was entered into, considered many factors affecting damages, namely: the uncertainty of the plaintiff's ability to re-rent the said vehicles; the plaintiff's investment in purchasing and reconditioning the vehicles to suit the defendant's particular purpose; the number of man hours not utilized in the non-service of the vehicles in the event of a breach; the uncertainty of reselling the vehicles in question; the uncertainty of the plaintiff's savings or expenditures for gasoline, oil or other service items, and the amount of fluctuating interest on the bank loan." The court calculated that plaintiff would have been entitled to $177,355.20 in rent for the period remaining in the lease and, in accordance with the liquidated damages provision, awarded plaintiff half that amount, $88,677.60. The resulting judgment was affirmed by the Appellate Division, with two Justices dissenting. (51 A.D.2d 786, 380 N.Y.S.2d 37.)

The primary issue before us is whether the "liquidated damages" provision is enforceable. Liquidated damages constitute the compensation which, the parties have agreed, should be paid in order to satisfy any loss or injury flowing from a breach of their contract. . . . In effect, a liquidated damage provision is an estimate, made by the parties at the time they enter into their agreement, of the extent of the injury that would be sustained as a result of breach of the agreement. (5 WILLISTON, CONTRACTS (3d ed.), § 776, p. 668.) Parties to a contract have the right to agree to such clauses, provided that the clause is neither unconscionable nor contrary to public policy. . . . Provisions for liquidated damage have value in those situations where it would be difficult, if not actually impossible, to calculate the amount of actual damage. In such cases, the contracting parties may agree between themselves as to the amount of damages to be paid upon breach rather than leaving that amount to the calculation of a court or jury. (14 N.Y. JUR., *Damages*, § 155, pp. 4-5.)

On the other hand, liquidated damage provisions will not be enforced if it is against public policy to do so and public policy is firmly set against the imposition of penalties or forfeitures for which there is no statutory authority. . . . It is plain that a provision which requires, in the event of contractual breach, the payment of a sum of money grossly disproportionate to the amount of actual damages provides for penalty and is unenforceable. . . . A liquidated damage provision has its basis in the principle of just compensation for loss. (Cf. RESTATEMENT, CONTRACTS, § 339, and Comment thereon.) A clause which provides for an amount plainly disproportionate to real damage is not intended to provide fair compensation but to secure performance by the compulsion of the very disproportion. A promisor would be compelled, out of fear of economic devastation, to continue performance and his promisee, in the event of default, would reap a windfall well above actual harm sustained. . . . As was stated eloquently long ago, to permit parties, in their unbridled discretion, to utilize penalties as damages, "would lead to the most terrible oppression in pecuniary dealings." (*Hoag v. McGinnis*, 22 Wend. 163, 166; . . .)

The rule is now well established. A contractual provision fixing damages in the event of breach will be sustained if the amount liquidated bears a reasonable proportion to the probable loss and the amount of actual loss is incapable or difficult of precise estimation. (. . . RESTATEMENT, CONTRACTS, § 339.) If, however, the amount fixed is plainly or grossly disproportionate to the probable loss, the provision calls for a penalty and will not be enforced. (. . . 14 N.Y. JUR., *Damages* § 155.) In interpreting a provision fixing damages, it is not material whether the parties themselves have chosen to call the provision one for "liquidated damages," as in this case, or have styled it as a penalty. . . . Such an approach would put too much faith in form and too little in substance. Similarly, the agreement should be interpreted as of the date of its making and not as of the date of its breach. . . .

In applying these principles to the case before us, we conclude that the amount stipulated by the parties as damages bears a reasonable relation to the amount of probable actual harm and is not a penalty. Hence, the provision is enforceable and the order of the Appellate Division should be affirmed.

Looking forward from the date of the lease, the parties could reasonably conclude, as they did, that there might not be an actual market for the sale or re-rental of these specialized vehicles in the event of the lessee's breach. To be sure, plaintiff's lost profit could readily be measured by the amount of the weekly rental fee. However, it was permissible for the parties, in advance, to agree that the re-rental or sale value of the vehicles would be 50% of the weekly rental. Since there was uncertainty as to whether the trucks could be re-rented or sold, the parties could reasonably set, as they did, the value of such mitigation at 50% of the amount the lessee was obligated to pay for rental of the trucks. This would take into consideration the fact that, after being used by the lessee, the vehicles would no longer be "shiny, new trucks," but would be used, possibly battered, trucks, whose value would have declined appreciably. The parties also considered the fact that, although plaintiff, in the event of Puritan's breach, might be spared repair and maintenance costs necessitated by Puritan's use of the trucks, plaintiff would have to assume the cost of storing and maintaining trucks idled by Puritan's refusal to use them. Further, it was by no means certain, at the time of the contract, that lessee would peacefully return the trucks to the lessor after lessee had breached the contract.

With particular reference to the dissent at the Appellate Division, it is true that the lessee might have exercised an option to purchase the trucks. However, lessee would not be purchasing 25 "shiny, new trucks" for a mere $2,500. Rather, lessee, after the passage of one year from the commencement of the term, could have purchased trucks that had been used for at least one year for the amount outstanding on the bank loan, in addition to the $2,500. Of course, the purchase price would be greater if the option were exercised early in the term rather than towards the end of the term since plaintiff would be making payments to the bank all the while. More fundamental, the existence of the option clause has absolutely no bearing on the validity of the discrete, liquidated damages provision. The lessee could have elected to purchase the trucks but elected not to do so. In fact, the lessee's letter of termination made a point of the fact that the lessee did not want to purchase the trucks. The reality is that the lessee sought, by its wrongful termination of the lease, to evade all obligations to the plaintiff, whether for rent or for the agreed upon purchase price. Its effort to do so failed. That lessee could have made a better bargain for itself by purchasing the trucks for $48,134.17[40] pursuant to the option, instead of paying $92,341.79 in damages for wrongful breach of the lease is not availing to it now. Although the lessee might now wish, with the benefit of hindsight, that it had purchased the trucks rather than default on its lease obligations, the simple fact is that it did not do so.

We attach no significance to the fact that the liquidated damages clause appears on the preprinted form portion of the agreement. The agreement was fully negotiated and the provisions of the form, in many other respects, were amended. There is no indication of any disparity of bargaining power or of unconscionability. The provision for liquidated damages related reasonably to potential harm that was difficult to estimate and did not constitute a disguised penalty. We also find no merit in the claim of trial error advanced by Puritan.

Accordingly, the order of the Appellate Division should be affirmed, with costs.

John T. Brady & Co. v. Form-Eze Systems, Inc., 623 F.2d 261 (2d Cir. 1980), affirmed a trial court order that had confirmed and refused to vacate under the Federal Arbitration Act an arbitrator's award allowing damages to a manufacturer-lessor of concrete forming equipment against the lessee. The award

---

[40] [3] This sum represents the $45,634.17 still owed by plaintiff on the bank loan, plus $2,500 ($100 for each of the 25 trucks).

allowed both $45,590 for the value of unreturned and damaged equipment, and $90,000 representing six months of rent at $15,000 per month. The $90,000 portion of the award was made pursuant to a contract provision stating that if any equipment was lost or damaged the lessee would be responsible not only for its value but also for monthly rental of all equipment until the amount due for the unreturned and damaged equipment was paid. Rejecting the lessee's contention that the clause permitting recovery of the monthly rental amounts constituted a penalty clause and not merely a liquidated damages provision, the court of appeals ruled that: (a) the clause was not one providing for payment of a fixed amount upon breach of any provision in the contract, no matter how trivial the breach, and was not contrary to N.Y. public policy; (b) the arbitrator did not label the $90,000 award as punitive, there was nothing to indicate a genuine intention that the award be punitive, and the failure of the arbitrator's opinion to discuss the public policy argument was not fatal to confirmation; (c) because lessee-appellant did not include a transcript of the arbitration proceeding as part of the record, the court had no basis to infer that the amount assessed for withholding payment for the damaged or lost equipment bore no relationship *to* the actual damage suffered by the lessor-appellee and was therefore punitive in nature; and (d) arbitrators are not required to disclose the basis upon which their awards are made, the court is bound even by a "barely colorable" interpretation given to the instrument by the arbitrator, and the court generally refuses to second-guess an arbitrator's resolution of a contract dispute.

Layton Mfg. Co. v. Dulien Steel, Inc., 277 Or. 343, 560 P.2d 1058 (1977). Action was brought to recover damages for breach of a lease agreement under which lessee agreed to pay $100 for the leasehold, promised to remove debris by a certain date, and was to pay an additional $30 per day for each day after the designated date until completion of the work. Reversing and remanding the case on plaintiff's appeal from rulings that the clause was a penalty provision and that plaintiff could not file an amended complaint, the Oregon Supreme Court held that the evidence presented below was inconclusive on the issue of whether $30 per day was a reasonable forecast for loss of use of the land, and that the defendant having assumed the burden of proof on the issue of whether the provision was for a penalty rather than liquidated damages, the trial court erred in placing the burden of proof on the plaintiff. The Court also noted that: (a) agreed damage provisions are unenforceable where designed only to secure performance of a contract rather than to pre-estimate the anticipated damages; (b) whether a contract damage provision is essentially designed to operate as a penalty is a question of law for the court; (c) a contract provision that states the amount to be paid to a damaged party will not be construed as an enforceable liquidated damages provision unless actual damages resulting from a breach are difficult or impossible to ascertain and unless the agreed damages have a reasonable relationship to probable losses; (d) generally the denomination given by the parties to an agreed damages clause — here termed a "penalty" — is not conclusive; and (e) ordinarily the burden is on a defendant to prove matter in avoidance, special, or affirmative defenses, and other new matter urged as ground for denying plaintiff relief, but he does not, by specially pleading matter which he could prove under a denial of the plaintiff's allegations, assume the burden of proof on such matters.

NOTES

1. Under statutes establishing rules for court proceedings to confirm or to vacate arbitration awards, courts may not have the right to consider the validity or enforceability of a liquidated damages clause considered by the arbitrator in entering the award. In *City of Lenexa v. C.L. Fairley Const. Co., Inc.*, 15 Kan. App. 2d 207, 805 P.2d 507 (1991), it was held that the trial court exceeded its authority by considering whether a construction contractor's claims for liquidated damages, back charges, and increased overhead were procedurally correct under the arbitration provision of the construction contract.

2. The Convention on the Recognition and Enforcement of Foreign Arbitral Awards provides procedures applicable to court proceedings involving such awards. *See National Oil Corp. v. Libyan Sun Oil Co.*, 733 F. Supp. 800 (D. Del. 1990), where an oil company owned by the Libyan government sued to enforce a foreign arbitral award against a U.S. oil company, arising from the domestic company's failure to perform under an exploration and production sharing agreement. The court held that the award of $20 million under the liquidated damages clause of the agreement was not completely irrational or in excess of the power of the arbitration tribunal, but that a reduction of the amount of liquidated damages to be recovered was warranted in light of the good faith of the domestic company in incorrectly claiming the *force majeure* defense, the Libyan company's failure to mitigate, and a drop in oil prices.

LAKE RIVER CORP. v. CARBORUNDUM CO.
769 F.2d 1284 (7th Cir. 1985)

Posner, Circuit Judge:

This diversity suit between Lake River Corporation and Carborundum Company requires us to consider questions of Illinois commercial law, and in particular to explore the fuzzy line between penalty clauses and liquidated-damages clauses.

Carborundum manufactures "Ferro Carbo," an abrasive powder used in making steel. To serve its midwestern customers better, Carborundum made a contract with Lake River by which the latter agreed to provide distribution services in its warehouse in Illinois. Lake River would receive Ferro Carbo in bulk from Carborundum, "bag" it, and ship the bagged product to Carborundum's customers. The Ferro Carbo would remain Carborundum's property until delivered to the customers.

Carborundum insisted that Lake River install a new bagging system to handle the contract. In order to be sure of being able to recover the cost of the new system ($89,000) and make a profit of 20 percent of the contract price, Lake River insisted on the following minimum-quantity guarantee: In consideration of the special equipment [i.e., the new bagging system] to be acquired and furnished by LAKE-RIVER for handling the product, CARBORUNDUM shall, during the initial three-year term of this Agreement, ship to LAKE-RIVER for bagging a minimum quantity of [22,500 tons]. If, at the end of the three-year term, this minimum quantity shall not have been shipped, LAKE-RIVER shall invoice CARBORUNDUM at the then prevailing rates for the difference between the quantity bagged and the minimum guaranteed. If Carborundum had shipped the full minimum quantity that it guaranteed, it would have owed Lake River roughly $533,000 under the contract.

After the contract was signed in 1979, the demand for domestic steel, and with it the demand for Ferro Carbo, plummeted, and Carborundum failed to ship the guaranteed amount. When the contract expired late in 1982, Carborundum had shipped only 12,000 of the 22,500 tons it had guaranteed. Lake River had bagged the 12,000 tons and had billed Carborundum for this bagging, and Carborundum had paid, but by virtue of the formula in the minimum — guarantee clause Carborundum still owed Lake River $241,000 — the contract price of $533,000 if the full amount of Ferro Carbo had been shipped, minus what Carborundum had paid for the bagging of the quantity it had shipped.

When Lake River demanded payment of this amount, Carborundum refused, on the ground that the formula imposed a penalty. At the time, Lake River had in its warehouse 500 tons of bagged Ferro Carbo, having a market value of $269,000, which it refused to release unless Carborundum paid the $241,000 due under the formula. Lake River did offer to sell the bagged product and place the proceeds in escrow until its dispute with Carborundum over the enforceability of the formula was resolved, but Carborundum rejected the offer and trucked in bagged Ferro Carbo from the East to serve its customers in Illinois, at an additional cost of $31,000.

Lake River brought this suit for $241,000, which it claims as liquidated damages. Carborundum counterclaimed for the value of the bagged Ferro Carbo when Lake River impounded it and the additional cost of serving the customers affected by the impounding. The theory of the counterclaim is that the impounding was a conversion, and not as Lake River contends the assertion of a lien. The district judge, after a bench trial, gave judgment for both parties. Carborundum ended up roughly $42,000 to the good: $269,000 + $31,000 − $241,000 − $17,000, the last figure representing prejudgment interest on Lake River's damages. (We have rounded off all dollar figures to the nearest thousand.) Both parties have appealed. . . .

The hardest issue in the case is whether the formula in the minimum-guarantee clause imposes a penalty for breach of contract or is merely an effort to liquidate damages. Deep as the hostility to penalty clauses runs in the common law, *see* Loyd, *Penalties and Forfeitures*, 29 HARV. L. REV. 117 (1915), we still might be inclined to question, if we thought ourselves free to do so, whether a modern court should refuse to enforce a penalty clause where the signator is a substantial corporation, well able to avoid improvident commitments. Penalty clauses provide an earnest of performance. The clause here enhanced Carborundum's credibility in promising to ship the minimum amount guaranteed by showing that it was willing to pay the full contract price even if it failed to ship anything. On the other side it can be pointed out that by raising the cost of a breach of contract to the contract breaker, a penalty clause increases the risk to his other creditors; increases (what is the same thing and more, because bankruptcy imposes "deadweight" social costs) the risk of bankruptcy; and could amplify the business cycle by increasing the number of bankruptcies in bad times, which is when contracts are most likely to be broken. But since little effort is made to prevent businessmen from assuming risks, these reasons are no better than makeweights.

A better argument is that a penalty clause may discourage efficient as well as inefficient breaches of contract. Suppose a breach would cost the promisee $12,000 in actual damages but would yield the promisor $20,000 in additional profits. Then there would be a net social gain from breach. After being fully compensated for his loss the promisee would be no worse off than if the contract had been performed, while the promisor would be better off by $8,000. But now suppose the contract contains a penalty clause under which the promisor if he breaks his promise must pay the promisee $25,000. The promisor will be discouraged from breaking the contract, since $25,000, the penalty, is greater than $20,000, the profits of the breach; and a transaction that would have increased value will be forgone.

On this view, since compensatory damages should be sufficient to deter inefficient breaches (that is, breaches that cost the victim more than the gain to the contract breaker), penal damages could have no effect other than to deter some efficient breaches. But this overlooks the earlier point that the willingness to agree to a penalty clause is a way of making the promisor and his promise credible and may therefore be essential to inducing some value-maximizing contracts to be made. It also overlooks the more important point that the parties (always assuming they are fully competent) will, in deciding whether to include a penalty clause in their contract, weigh the gains against the costs — costs that include the possibility of discouraging an efficient breach somewhere down the road — and will include the clause only if the benefits exceed those costs as well as all other costs.

On this view the refusal to enforce penalty clauses is (at best) paternalistic — and it seems odd that courts should display parental solicitude for large corporations. But however this may be, we must be on guard to avoid importing our own ideas of sound public policy into an area where our proper judicial role is more than usually deferential. The responsibility for making innovations in the common law of Illinois rests with the courts of Illinois, and not with the federal courts in Illinois. And like every other state, Illinois, untroubled by academic skepticism of the wisdom of refusing to enforce penalty clauses against sophisticated promisors, *see, e.g.,* Goetz & Scott, *Liquidated Damages, Penalties and the Just Compensation Principle,* 77 COLUM. L. REV. 554 (1977), continues steadfastly to insist on the distinction between penalties and liquidated damages. . . . To be valid under Illinois law a liquidation of damages must be a reasonable estimate at the time of contracting of the likely damages from breach, and the need for estimation at that time must be shown by reference to the likely difficulty of measuring the actual damages from a breach of contract after the breach occurs. If damages would be easy to determine then, or if the estimate greatly exceeds a reasonable upper estimate of what the damages are likely to be, it is a penalty. . . .

The distinction between a penalty and liquidated damages is not an easy one to draw in practice but we are required to draw it and can give only limited weight to the district court's determination. Whether a provision for damages is a penalty clause or a liquidated-damages clause is a question of law rather than fact, . . . and unlike some courts of appeals we do not treat a determination by a federal district judge of an issue of state law as if it were a finding of fact, and reverse only if persuaded that clear error has occurred, though we give his determination respectful consideration. . . .

Mindful that Illinois courts resolve doubtful cases in favor of classification as a penalty, . . . we conclude that the damage formula in this case is a penalty and not a liquidation of damages, because it is designed always to assure Lake River more than its actual damages. The formula — full contract price minus the amount already invoiced to Carborundum — is invariant to the gravity of the breach. When a contract specifies a single sum in damages for any and all breaches even though it is apparent that all are not of the same gravity, the specification is not a reasonable effort to estimate damages; and when in addition the fixed sum greatly exceeds the actual damages likely to be inflicted by a minor breach, its character as a penalty becomes unmistakable. . . . This case is within the gravitational field of these principles even though the minimum-guarantee clause does not fix a single sum as damages.

Suppose to begin with that the breach occurs the day after Lake River buys its new bagging system for $89,000 and before Carborundum ships any Ferro Carbo. Carborundum would owe Lake River $533,000. Since Lake River would have incurred at that point a total cost of only $89,000, its net gain from the breach would be $444,000. This is more than four times the profit of $107,000 (20 percent of the contract price of $533,000) that Lake River expected to make from the contract if it had been performed: a huge windfall.

Next suppose (as actually happened here) that breach occurs when 55 percent of the Ferro Carbo has been shipped. Lake River would already have received $293,000 from Carborundum. To see what its costs then would have been (as estimated at the time of contracting), first subtract Lake River's anticipated profit on the contract of $107,000 from the total contract price of $533,000. The difference — Lake River's total cost of performance — is $426,000. Of this, $89,000 is the cost of the new bagging system, a fixed cost. The rest ($426,000 − $89,000 = $337,000) presumably consists of variable costs that are roughly proportional to the amount of Ferro Carbo bagged; there is no indication of any other fixed costs. Assume, therefore, that if Lake River bagged 55 percent of the contractually agreed quantity, it incurred in doing so 55 percent of its variable costs, or $185,000. When this is added to the cost of the new bagging system, assumed for the moment to be worthless except in connection with the contract, the total cost of performance to Lake River is $274,000. Hence a breach that occurred after 55 percent of contractual performance was complete would be expected to yield Lake River a modest profit of $19,000 ($293,000 − $274,000). But now add the "liquidated damages" of $241,000 that Lake River claims, and the result is a total gain from the breach of $260,000, which is almost two and a half times the profit that Lake River expected to gain if there was no breach. And this ignores any use value or salvage value of the new bagging system, which is the property of Lake River — though admittedly it also ignores the time value of money; Lake River paid $89,000 for that system before receiving any revenue from the contract.

To complete the picture, assume that the breach had not occurred till performance was 90 percent complete. Then the "liquidated damages" clause would not be so one-sided, but it would be one-sided. Carborundum would have paid $480,000 for bagging. Against this, Lake River would have incurred its fixed cost of $89,000 plus 90 percent of its variable costs of $337,000, or $303,000. Its total costs would thus be $392,000, and its net profit $88,000. But on top of this it would be entitled to "liquidated damages" of $53,000, for a total profit of $141,000 — more than 30 percent more than its expected profit of $107,000 if there was no breach.

The reason for these results is that most of the costs to Lake River of performing the contract are saved if the contract is broken, and this saving is not reflected in the damage formula. As a result, at whatever point in the life of the contract a breach occurs, the damage formula gives Lake River more than its lost profits from the breach — dramatically more if the breach occurs at the beginning of the contract; tapering off at the end, it is true. Still, over the interval between the beginning of Lake River's performance and nearly the end, the clause could be expected to generate profits ranging from 400 percent of the expected contract profits to 130 percent of those profits. And this is on the assumption that the bagging system has no value apart from the contract. If it were worth only $20,000 to Lake River, the range would be 434 percent to 150 percent.

Lake River argues that it would never get as much as the formula suggests, because it would be required to mitigate its damages. This is a dubious argument on several grounds. First, mitigation of damages is a doctrine of the law of court-assessed damages, while the point of a liquidated-damages clause is to substitute party assessment; and that point is blunted, and the certainty that liquidated-damages clauses are designed to give the process of assessing damages impaired, if a defendant can force the plaintiff to take less than the damages specified in the clause, on the ground that the plaintiff could have avoided some of them. It would seem therefore that the clause in this case should be read to eliminate any duty of mitigation, that what Lake River is doing is attempting to rewrite the clause to make it more reasonable, and that since actually the clause is designed to give Lake River the full damages it would incur from breach (and more) even if it made no effort to find a substitute use for the equipment that it bought to perform the contract, this is just one more piece of evidence that it is a penalty clause rather than a liquidated-damages clause. . . .

But in any event mitigation would not mitigate the penal character of this clause. If Carborundum did not ship the guaranteed minimum quantity, the reason was likely to be — the reason was — that the steel industry had fallen on hard times and the demand for Ferro Carbo was therefore down. In these circumstances Lake River would have little prospect of finding a substitute contract that would yield it significant profits to set off against the full contract price, which is the method by which it proposes to take account of mitigation. At argument Lake River suggested that it might at least have been able to sell the new bagging equipment to someone for something, and the figure $40,000 was proposed. If the breach occurred on the first day when performance under the contract was due and Lake River promptly sold the bagging equipment for $40,000, its liquidated damages would fall to $493,000. But by the same token its costs would fall to $49,000. Its profit would still be $444,000, which as we said was more than 400 percent of its expected profit on the contract. The penal component would be unaffected.

. . . Here, . . . it is apparent from the face of the contract that the damages provided for by the "liquidated damages" clause are grossly disproportionate to any probable loss and penalize some breaches much more heavily than others regardless of relative cost.

We do not mean by this discussion to cast a cloud of doubt over the "take or pay" clauses that are a common feature of contracts between natural gas pipeline companies and their customers. Such clauses require the customer, in consideration of the pipeline's extending its line to his premises, to take a certain amount of gas at a specified price — and if he fails to take it to pay the full price anyway. The resemblance to the minimum-guarantee clause in the present case is obvious, but perhaps quite superficial. Neither party has mentioned take-or-pay clauses, and we can find no case where such a clause was even challenged as a penalty clause — though in one case it was argued that such a clause made the damages unreasonably low. *See National Fuel Gas Distribution Corp. v.*

Pennsylvania Public Utility Comm'n, 76 Pa. Commw. 102, 126-27 n.8, 464 A.2d 546, 558 n.8 (1983). If, as appears not to be the case here but would often be the case in supplying natural gas, a supplier's fixed costs were a very large fraction of his total costs, a take-or-pay clause might well be a reasonable liquidation of damages. In the limit, if all the supplier's costs were incurred before he began supplying the customer, the contract revenues would be an excellent measure of the damages from breach. But in this case, the supplier (Lake River, viewed as a supplier of bagging services to Carborundum) incurred only a fraction of its costs before performance began, and the interruption of performance generated a considerable cost saving that is not reflected in the damage formula.

The fact that the damage formula is invalid does not deprive Lake River of a remedy. The parties did not contract explicitly with reference to the measure of damages if the agreed-on damage formula was invalidated, but all this means is that the victim of the breach is entitled to his common law damages. *See, e.g.*, RESTATEMENT (SECOND) OF CONTRACTS § 356, comment a (1981). In this case that would be the unpaid contract price of $241,000 minus the costs that Lake River saved by not having to complete the contract (the variable costs on the other 45 percent of the Ferro Carbo that it never had to bag). The case must be remanded to the district judge to fix these damages. . . .

The judgment of the district court is affirmed in part and reversed in part, and the case is returned to that court to redetermine both parties' damages in accordance with the principles in this opinion. The parties may present additional evidence on remand, and shall bear their own costs in this court. . . .

Affirmed in Part, Reversed in Part, and Remanded.

NOTES

1. In *Lake River* the court held that the minimum guaranty formula provision in the contract would be considered to constitute a liquidated damages clause. Because the clause failed to satisfy applicable Illinois state rules for establishing that such a clause is valid, the court then concluded that the clause was invalid and unenforceable.

2. Acceleration clauses in leases, providing that upon lessee's breach prior to the end of the lease term, the amount of rent to the end of the lease term would become immediately due and payable, have been construed to be liquidated damage clauses. *See Aurora Business Park Associates, L.P. v. Michael Albert, Inc.*, 548 N.W.2d 153 (Iowa 1996), a commercial lease case, where the court concluded that the clause was valid and enforceable and did not provide for a penalty.

3. Contract provisions in promissory notes requiring prepayment premiums in the event of default have also been viewed as purported liquidated damages clauses. In *TMG Life Ins. Co. v. Ashner*, 21 Kan. App. 2d 234, 898 P.2d 1145 (1995), the court held that the prepayment premium provision there was to be evaluated pursuant to Kansas law rules applicable to other liquidated damages clauses. *Compare C.C. Port, Ltd. v. Davis-Penn Mortg. Co.*, 891 F. Supp. 371 (S.D. Tex. 1994), where the court held that a prepayment premium clause in a note would not form the basis for a usury claim under Texas law, since Texas views prepayment premiums as charges made for borrowers to exercise the option to pay off loans

early and not as "interest" within the meaning of usury statutes; *West Raleigh Group v. Massachusetts Mut. Life Ins. Co.*, 809 F. Supp. 384 (E.D.N.C. 1992), where a prepayment provision in a promissory note was held to be an enforceable contract term, not an illegal penalty under North Carolina law, even though the note called the prepayment premium a "penalty," because the prepayment "penalty" or premium was bargained-for consideration for the option to prepay.

4. A contract term providing for specific performance upon breach is not a liquidated damages clause. It has been said that such a clause is different in kind from a liquidated damages clause, and enforcement of the contract obligation freely agreed to by the defendant could not be considered unreasonable or a penalty. *Martin v. Sheffer*, 102 N.C. App. 802, 403 S.E.2d 555 (1991).

5. As an alternative to invalidating in its entirety a liquidated damages clause that amounts to a penalty, some courts have the power to reduce liquidated damages to a reasonable sum, thus validating the clause to that extent. *See Philippi v. Viguerie*, 606 So. 2d 577 (La. App. 1992), where by statute the court had "power to modify stipulated damages if those damages are so manifestly unreasonable as to be contrary to public policy," and where the stipulated amount of $1,000 due for each violation of a noncompetition agreement was reduced by the court to $200 per violation.

6. *Practice Points*: Unenforceability of a contract provision based on the theory that the provision amounts to a penalty is generally considered to be an affirmative defense that must be specially pleaded. Example: *D&D Leasing Co. of South Carolina, Inc. v. David Lipson, Ph.D., P.A.*, 305 S.C. 540, 409 S.E.2d 794 (S.C. App. 1991), where it was held, pursuant to that state's civil procedure rules, that because defendant did not plead unenforceability based on the alleged penalty nature of the contract termination provision, he waived that defense.

7. In *Wilt v. Waterfield*, 273 S.W.2d 290 (Mo. 1954), the Missouri Supreme Court held that the $1,900 liquidated damages provision was invalid as an impermissible penalty, in part because the provision was disproportionately *below* the actual loss plaintiff sustained. Contract provisions that limit the amount recoverable by a party ("limitation of liability" clauses) are ordinarily upheld. Might the *Wilt* court have decided differently had the provision been identified in the contract — or in argument — as a limitation of liability clause, rather than as a liquidated damages clause? See limitation of liability clauses below, in section 2.

8. In *Wilt* the parties used a standardized sales form which included a printed liquidated damages clause. In determining intent in liquidated damage cases, should it matter whether the provision is a standard-form term?

Southwest Engineering v. United States, 341 F.2d 998 (8th Cir. 1965). In this case contractor Southwest Engineering appealed from a trial court summary judgment that upheld the government's decision to withhold partial payment of the contract price as liquidated damages. A liquidated damages clause had been included in the contract and the contractor had been tardy in completing performance. One of the contractor's two arguments on appeal was that "the Government, in order to enforce a contract provision for liquidated damages for delay, must not cause or contribute to such delay, and if the Government does cause or contribute to such delay, it cannot assess liquidated damages." The court, rejecting this argument, further quoted from several Supreme Court opinions dealing with the law applicable to federal contracts: "'Federal law controls in the construction and determination of rights under federal contracts.' *Priebe & Sons, Inc. v. United States*, 332 U.S. 407, 411, 68 S. Ct. 123, 92 L. Ed. 32 . . . [and] " 'It is customary, where Congress has not adopted a different standard, to apply to the construction of government contracts the principles of general contract law. *United States v. Standard Rice Co.*, 323 U.S. 106, 111, (65 S. Ct. 145, 147, 89 L. Ed. 104) . . .' " The court then held that "[t]he fact that the government's action caused some of the delay presents no legal ground for denying it compensation for loss suffered wholly through the fault of the contractor. Since the contractor agreed to pay at a specified rate for each day's delay not caused by the government, it was clearly the intention that it should pay for some days' delay at that rate, even if it were relieved from paying for other days, because of the government's action. . . ."

As to the contractor's alternative argument, the court said "Southwest's second point in substance is that the parties' stipulation that the Government suffered no actual damage bars any recovery of liquidated damages." While the parties had stipulated that the government had not suffered any damages when the work was completed, the court held that the stipulation "does not go to the extent of agreeing that the parties at the time of contracting did not reasonably contemplate that damages would flow from a delay in performance. . . . There is no showing that the liquidated damages for delay provided for are beyond damages reasonably contemplated by the parties at the time of the contract." The Eighth Circuit then restated the generally applicable rules as to when a liquidated damages clause will be considered valid, binding and enforceable: "Two requirements must be considered to determine whether the provision included in the contract fixing the amount of damages payable on breach will be interpreted as an enforceable liquidated damage clause rather than an unforceable penalty clause: First, the amount so fixed must be a reasonable forecast of just compensation for the harm that is caused by the breach, and second, the harm that is caused by the breach must be one that is incapable or very difficult of accurate estimation. . . ." RESTATEMENT, CONTRACTS § 339. Whether these requirements have been complied with must be viewed as of the time the contract was executed rather than when the contract was breached or at some other subsequent time." The Supreme Court's *Bethlehem Steel* case, 205 U.S. 105, 119, 27 S. Ct. 450, 455, 51 L. Ed. 731, the court said, establishes "the standard to be applied for determining whether a liquidated damage provision can be upheld as follows: 'The question always is, What did the parties intend by the language used? When such intention is ascertained it is ordinarily the duty of the court to carry it out.'. . . Here Southwest has failed to establish that the intention of the parties was to do anything other than execute a valid liquidated damage provision."

The court also quotes the Supreme Court's view in *Priebe & Sons v. United States*, 332 U.S. 407, 411-412, 68 S. Ct. 123, 126, on a current trend to allow the use of liquidated damages clauses: "Today the law does not look with disfavor upon 'liquidated damages' provisions in contracts. When they are fair and reasonable attempts to fix just compensation for anticipated loss caused by breach of contract, they are enforced. . . . They serve a particularly useful function when damages are uncertain in nature or amount or are unmeasurable, as is the case in many government contracts. . . . And the fact that the damages suffered are shown to be less than the damages contracted for is not fatal. These provisions are to be judged as of the time of making the contract." The Court concluded by saying, "We believe that the cases holding that the situation existing at the time of the contract is controlling in determining the reasonableness of liquidated damages are based upon sound reasoning and represent the weight of authority. Where parties have by their contract agreed upon a liquidated damage provision as a reasonable forecast of just compensation for breach of contract and damages are difficult to estimate accurately, such provision should be enforced. If in the course of subsequent developments, damages prove to be greater than those stipulated, the party entitled to damages is bound by the liquidated damage agreement. It is not unfair to hold the contractor performing the work to such agreement if by reason of later developments damages prove to be less or nonexistent. Each party by entering into such contractual provision took a calculated risk and is bound by reasonable contractual provisions pertaining to liquidated damages."

NOTES

1. The court in *Southwest Engineering* upheld the validity and application for that case of the liquidated damage provision in the subject U.S. government contract. Courts have not held that all damage clauses in contracts with governments or government agencies are valid and enforceable. *Telenois, Inc. v. Village of Schaumburg*, 256 Ill. App. 3d 897, 628 N.E.2d 581 (1993), involved a dispute between a village and its cable television franchisee, and a clause in their contract which provided that the village would collect on a $100,000 letter of credit if the franchisee failed to complete performance by a specified date. The village manager and its cable consultant testified that the clause was intended to ensure performance by the franchisee and serve as a penalty in case of breach. The court agreed with the trial judge that this clause constituted an impermissible penalty and was unenforceable as against public policy.

2. Non-breaching parties may waive rights under liquidated damages provisions, waiver being defined as the voluntary relinquishment of a known right. In *Village of Fox Lake v. Aetna Cas. & Sur. Co.*, 178 Ill. App. 3d 887, 534 N.E.2d 133 (1989), it was held that waiver by plaintiff of its right to liquidated damages against the defendant contractor and its surety in connection with a sewer and water system installation was valid, notwithstanding the village's contention that the waiver did not constitute modification of the contract because it was not supported by consideration.

3. The U.S. Court of Appeals for the Federal Circuit has noted that some state courts are hostile to liquidated damages clauses in contracts, but that federal law does not look with disfavor upon them. *DJ Mfg. Corp. v. United States*, 86 F.3d 1130 (Fed. Cir. 1996), where the court also noted that: (a) it is rare for a federal court to refuse to enforce the parties' bargain on this issue, and that (b) generally, when the amount of prospective damages is difficult to determine at the outset and the parties agree upon a fixed amount or rate to pay in the event of a breach, thereby bypassing the trouble and expense of litigating the damages issue, federal courts have regularly upheld liquidated damages clauses.

4. Although the amount set forth in a bail bond is not usually thought of as liquidated damages, at least one federal judge has viewed it as such. In *United States v. Gonzalez*, 912 F. Supp. 242 (S.D. Tex. 1995), the court declared that bail bonds are in effect contracts between the government and defendants pursuant to which defendants are released from confinement upon their promise to appear when required, and when they breach that promise they and their bond sureties

essentially become liable to the government for liquidated damages.

2.   Limitation of Liability Agreements

WEDNER v. FIDELITY SEC. SYSTEMS, INC.
228 Pa. Super. 67, 307 A.2d 429 (1973)

PER CURIAM. The six Judges who heard this appeal being equally divided, the judgment is affirmed.

WATKINS, J., files an opinion in support of affirmance in which JACOBS and SPAULDING, J.J., join. CERCONE, J., files an opinion in support of reversal in which WRIGHT, PRESIDENT JUDGE and HOFFMAN, J., join.

WATKINS, Judge, in support of affirmance:

This is an appeal from the judgment of the Court of Common Pleas of Allegheny County entered after a non-jury trial on a burglar alarm system contract, in the amount of $312.00 in favor of Charles Wedner, doing business as Wedner Furs, the appellant, and against Fidelity Security Systems, Inc., the appellee.

This action involved a contract for a burglar alarm system. There was a burglary involving the loss of $46,180.00 in furs. It was first tried by Judge Silvestri without a jury and a nonsuit resulted. The nonsuit was removed and a new trial granted. It was then tried by Judge McLean without a jury and although he found the contract had been negligently breach, the appellant was only entitled to liquidated damages in the amount of $312.00 by the terms of the contract. Exceptions were filed and the Court En Banc by a majority vote dismissed the exceptions. This appeal followed.

The appellant suffered a loss of $46,180.00 due to the appellee's wrongful failure to perform under a burglary protection service contract, but because of a contract provision he was allowed recovery of only $312.00. The contract provided that the appellee, FEPS, was not to be liable for any loss or damages to the goods of the appellant and then continued: "If there shall, notwithstanding the above provisions, at any time arise any liability on the part of FEPS by virtue of this agreement, whether due to the negligence of FEPS or otherwise, such liability is and shall be limited to a sum equal in amount to the yearly service charge hereunder, which sum shall be paid and received by the Subscriber as liquidated damages." The appellant contends that this is an unreasonable forecast of the probable damages resulting from a breach of the contract.

The court below treated the matter as one of liquidated damages and said: "In his decision the trial judge pointed out, and the parties agree, that there is a well settled general principle that courts will not give effect to a provision in a contract which is a penalty, but will give effect to a provision in a contract which is deemed a liquidated damages provision. The trial judge further noted that deciding which is which can be difficult. In the absence of any Pennsylvania cases making the determination in the context of a contract for burglary alarm protection, the trial judge determined that the instant provision was one for liquidated damages, rather than a penalty, on the reasoning and analysis of *A.G. Schepps v. American District Telegraph Company of Texas*, 286 S.W.2d 684 (Texas Court of Appeals) (1956); *Better Food Markets v. American Dist. Tel. Co.*, 40 Cal. 2d 179, (253) 353 P.2d 10

(1953); *Atkinson v. Pacific Fire Extinguisher Company*, 40 Cal. 2d 192, 253 P.2d 18 (1953)."

However, although he ably supported his judgment on the theory of liquidated damages, he did not have to decide the matter on the premise alone.

Much reliance is placed upon the RESTATEMENT OF CONTRACTS § 339, but the appellant disregards Comment, which provides: "An agreement limiting the amount of damages recoverable for breach is not an agreement to pay either liquidated damages or a penalty. Except in the case of certain public service contracts, the contracting parties can by agreement limit their liability in damages to a specified amount, either at the time of making their principal contract, or subsequently thereto. Such a contract, or subsequent thereto, does not purport to make an estimate of the harm caused by a breach; nor is its purpose to operate in terrorem to induce performance." It can hardly be contended that the words "liability is and shall be limited" to the yearly service charge of $312 are anything but a limitation of liability and not really a liquidated damage clause. Surely, if the loss to the customer was $150, the expressed mutual assent was that recovery should be $150 and not $312.

The fact that the words "liquidated damages" were used in the contract has little bearing on the nature of the provision. It is well settled that in determining whether a particular clause calls for liquidated damages or for a penalty, the name given to the clause by the parties "is but of slight weight, and the controlling elements are the intention of the parties and the special circumstances of the case." *Laughlin v. Baltalden, Inc.*, 191 Pa. Super. 611, 617, 159 A.2d 26, 29 (1960). The same principle applies here. Nor can it be argued that the use of these words automatically creates an ambiguity to be resolved against the appellee as the drafter of the instrument. The meaning of the words is clear — the fixed limit of liability was $312. We are, therefore, not dealing with a liquidated damage problem.

The real question is whether any reason exists why the limitation on liability should not be given effect. There is no doubt as to its legality as between ordinary business men. "The Validity of a contractual provision which exculpates a person from liability for his own acts of negligence is well settled if the contract is between persons relating entirely to their own private affairs." *Dilks v. Flohr Chevrolet*, 411 Pa. 425, 433, 192 A.2d 682, 687 (1963). That was the common law rule and is illustrated by *Bechtold v. Murray Ohio Mfg. Co.*, 321 Pa. 423, 428–429, 184 A. 49, 51 (1936), where the court stated:

> It is not suggested that the transaction is affected by fraud or mistake. The parties agree that they said what they meant. Both parties and their counsel participated in stating the terms of the contract. The seller says that it was performed, but, if it has not done so in the respect complained of, the buyer has agreed that he shall have no right to recover damages.

In accord is the RESTATEMENT OF CONTRACTS, §§ 574, 575.

It is also the rule with respect to the sale of goods under the Uniform Commercial Code, 12A P.S. § 2–719(3), which provides:

> Consequential damages may be limited or excluded unless the limitation or exclusion is unconscionable. Limitation of consequential damages for injury to the person in the case of consumer goods is prima facie

unconscionable but limitation of damages where the loss is commercial is not.

The common law exception as to public utilities, *Turek v. Pennsylvania R.R. Co.*, 361 Pa. 512, 64 A.2d 779 (1949), has been expanded to some extent by *Thomas v. First Nat. Bank of Scranton*, 376 Pa. 181, 185-186, 101 A.2d 910, 912 (1954), where the court concluded:

> Banks, like common carriers, utility companies, etc., perform an important public service. The United States Government and the Commonwealth respectively stipulate how banks under their respective jurisdictions shall be incorporated and organized. All banks are examined and supervised by government or state officers with extreme particularity. The United States insures deposits in banks up to a stipulated amount. If a person desires to deposit money in a bank, necessarily, he is relegated to a governmental or state regulated banking institution. The situation of a depositor is quite analogous to that of a passenger on a public carrier who is required to accept such means of transportation and to purchase a ticket in the nature of a contract. This Court has consistently decided that it is against public policy to permit a common carrier to limit its liability for its own negligence: . . .

In this case, however, we have a private arrangement between two firms without the attendant state regulation that exists with banks and public utilities. The appellant had a choice as to how to protect his property, and whether or not he should obtain insurance. Although protection against burglary is becoming increasingly important, we believe that it has not yet reached the level of necessity comparable to that of banking and other public services.

Nor do we consider this a case of an unconscionable provision, assuming that unconscionability is applicable by adoption of the prevailing rule with respect to the sale of goods. Even under the foregoing reference to the Uniform Commercial Code the limitation of liability under the facts of the case is prima facie conscionable. Furthermore, there is this significant fact pointed out in the opinion of the trial judge:

> In our case both plaintiff and defendant are experienced, established business persons. Additionally, plaintiff had for some 20 years prior to the instant contract had a similar type protection service with similar type clause, with a competitor of defendant.

Thus in this respect the case is comparable to *K&C, Inc. v. Westinghouse Elec. Corp.*, 437 Pa. 303, 308, 263 A.2d 390, 393 (1970), where the court concluded that "it is clear that the exclusion was not unconscionable here, where the buyer was hardly the sheep keeping company with wolves that it would have us believe."

I would affirm the judgment of the court below. JACOBS and SPAULDING, JJ., join in this opinion.

CERCONE, judge, in support of reversal:

The facts in this case as found by the trial judge who sat as the fact-finder are as follows:

Plaintiff, who was in the retail fur business, entered into a contract with defendant Security Systems whereby defendant was to provide plaintiff's store with electronic burglar alarm protection. While this contract was in full force and effect, and had been for several years, a burglary occurred, setting off devices at defendant's headquarters. Plaintiff brought suit in trespass against defendant for losses ensuing from the said burglary, plaintiff alleging negligence, willfulness, and wantonness of the defendant in failing to carry out its duties towards plaintiff's establishment. After trial, the trial judge found, as stated in his opinion, "defendant negligently failed to carry out those duties and render those services which its contract required of it upon the receipt of such alarm, with the result that the burglars were able to get away with merchandise of the value of $38,862.00. The loss of merchandise put plaintiff out of business until he could replenish his stock of goods, to the further loss of $7,318." The trial judge entered an award for the plaintiff, but limited that award to the amount of $312 (plus interest from the date of loss). This award was based on the trial judge's conclusion that this was the sum of the "liquidated damages" provided for in the contract. The provision so relied upon by the trial judge reads as follows:

> If there shall, notwithstanding the above provisions, at any time arise any liability on the part of FEPS by virtue of this agreement, whether due to the negligence of FEPS or otherwise, such liability is and shall be limited to a sum equal in amount to the yearly service charge hereunder, which sum shall be paid and received by the Subscriber as liquidated damages.

The plaintiff took exceptions to the findings and conclusions of the trial judge, which exceptions were dismissed by the court en banc with one judge dissenting. This appeal by plaintiff followed.

Neither the court below nor any of the parties to this action at any time prior to oral argument before this court regarded the provision in question as other than what the parties expressed it to be, to-wit: a "liquidated damages" clause. The affirming opinion, however, views the language differently than did the lower court and the parties and refers to it as a "limitation of liability" clause. It apparently views a "limitation of liability" clause as more binding than a "liquidated damages" clause under the circumstances. I cannot agree. If the parties can escape their contractual provisions for liquidated damages because the amount stated is unreasonably disproportionate (either higher or lower) to the actual damages involved, there is no logical reason why the same test of reasonableness should not apply to a contractual limitation of liability. I would hold therefore, that a contractual Limitation, as well as a contractual Liquidation of damages, is not binding where unreasonable and bearing no relation to the loss that would result from defendant's failure to fulfill the terms of its contract. The limitation in this case "to a sum equal in amount to the yearly service charge hereunder" was clearly unreasonable and arbitrary, bearing no relationship whatever to the damages flowing from defendant's breach. In my opinion this provision, whether viewed as one of liquidated damages or as a limitation of damages, should not be enforced.

Section 2–718 of the Uniform Commercial Code of Sales, which by its expressed title "Liquidation *or Limitation of Damages*" necessarily refers to limitation as well as liquidation of damages, provides:

> (1) Damages for breach by either party may be liquidated in the agreement but only at an amount which is reasonable in the light of the anticipated or actual harm caused by the breach, the difficulties of proof of loss, and the inconvenience or nonfeasibility of otherwise obtaining an

adequate remedy. A term fixing unreasonably large liquidated damages is void as a penalty.

The Uniform Commercial Code comment to that subsection 1 is:

> A term fixing unreasonably large liquidated damages is expressly made void as a penalty. *An unreasonably small amount would be subject to similar criticism and might be stricken under the section on unconscionable contracts or clauses.*

(emphasis added [by the court])

Section 2–719 of the Code is entitled "Contractual Modification or *Limitation of Remedy*" and subsection 1 of that section states that "subject to the provisions . . . of the preceding section on liquidation *and limitation of damages,* (a) the agreement . . . may limit or alter the measure of damages recoverable under this Article . . . ." The official comment to that section is:

> 1. Under this section parties are left free to shape their remedies to their particular requirements and *reasonable* agreements *limiting* or modifying remedies are to be given effect.
>
> However, it is of the very essence of a sales contract that at least minimum adequate remedies be available. If the parties intend to conclude a contract for sale within this Article they must accept the legal consequence that there be at least a fair quantum of remedy for breach of the obligations or duties outlined in the contract. *Thus any clause purporting to modify or limit the remedial provisions of this Article in an unconscionable manner is subject to deletion* and in that event the remedies made available by this Article are applicable as if the stricken clause had never existed. Similarly, under subsection (2), where an apparently fair and reasonable clause because of circumstances fails in its purpose or operates to deprive either party of the substantial value of the bargain, it must give way to the general remedy provisions of this Article. (Emphasis added [by the court].)

The clause here in question (whether viewed as a liquidated damages clause or a limitation of damages clause) unreasonably limits plaintiff's recovery to a return of the service charge and deprives plaintiff of the bargain of his contract. As construed in the affirming opinion, the clause in effect works a rescission of the contract, completely freeing defendant from proper performance of its terms and requiring only a return of the service charge when defendant has failed to properly perform thereunder. The contract thus becomes, in effect, an illusory one with defendant not being bound to perform and plaintiff not being entitled to performance by defendant. By limiting plaintiff's remedy upon defendant's breach to a return of the service charge, the defendant is permitted to effectuate a cancellation of its duties to perform under the contract, leaving plaintiff without the bargained-for performance and without any reasonable compensation for defendant's failure to perform as contracted.

It is my opinion, therefore, that the clause in question is unreasonable and unconscionable and should not be enforced.

I therefore respectfully, but vigorously, dissent from the affirming opinion in this case. WRIGHT, PRESIDING JUDGE, and HOFFMAN, J., join.

Better Food Markets v. American Dist. Telegraph Co., 40 Cal. 2d 179, 253 P.2d 10 (1953). In this action plaintiff sought damages resulting from delay by defendants in transmitting burglar alarm signals to their own guards and to the municipal police department, allegedly allowing the burglar to escape with $35,930 from plaintiff's food market. The California Supreme Court ruled that the trial court should not have allowed defendant's motion for directed verdict, but granted only qualified reversal of the judgment since it also held (one justice dissenting) that plaintiff's recovery if he were to prevail on a retrial was limited to $50. The basis for that damage limitation was a contract provision and facts in the case which the Court concluded were sufficient to limit plaintiff's recoverable damages to the smaller amount, notwithstanding plaintiff's claim that the amount of money stolen should be the measure of damage allowed. The contract provision read:

> It is agreed by and between the parties that the Contractor is not an insurer, that the payments hereinbefore named are based solely on the value of the service in the maintenance of the system described, that it is impracticable and extremely difficult to fix the actual damages, if any, which may proximately result from a failure to perform such services and in case of failure to perform such services and a resulting loss its liability hereunder shall be limited to and fixed at the sum of fifty dollars as liquidated damages, and not as a penalty, and this liability shall be exclusive.

The court further held that since there was no reasonable basis when contracting upon which to predict the nature and extent of any loss, nor the portion of any such loss the defendant's failure of performance might account for, the statutory prerequisite for finding a contract damage provision valid — that it be "impracticable or extremely difficult to fix the actual damage" (Cal. Civ. Code, §§ 1670, 1671) — was satisfied. The dissent argued, among other things, that a provision disproportionately lower than the actual loss is as much a penalty provision as one that is disproportionately higher, and that the $50 provision here bore no reasonable relation to the losses contemplated by the parties when they entered into the contract.

Johnson v. Mobil Oil Corp., 415 F. Supp. 264, 20 U.C.C. Rep. Serv. 637 (E.D. Mich. 1976). Plaintiff service station operator sought to recover losses suffered when the service station, operated under defendant's retail dealer contract, was destroyed by fire allegedly caused by events which followed defendant's delivery of gasoline containing water. Defendant's motion for partial summary judgment, seeking dismissal of plaintiff's claim for consequential damages based on a contract provision that "In no event shall Seller be liable for prospective profits or special, indirect or consequential damages," was denied. Applying Michigan's enactment of U.C.C. § 2-719(3) (M.C.L.A. § 440.2719(3)), "Consequential damages may be limited or excluded unless the limitation or exclusion is unconscionable," the court: (a) noted that even commercial contracts may be found to be unconscionable under certain circumstances, (b) quoted from an Indiana Supreme Court case (*Weaver v. American Oil Co.*, 1971, 276 N.E.2d 144) holding unconscionable clauses in a service station lease that exculpated the oil company lessor from any liability for its negligence and obliged lessee to indemnify the oil company for any loss, (c) noted that other courts had found elements of unconscionability in transactions between oil companies and their retail dealers, as well as in a variety of other commercial settings, (d) cited a Michigan Court of Appeals case (*Allen v. Michigan Bell*

Telephone Co., 1969, 18 Mich. App. 632, 171 N.W.2d 687) holding unconscionable a clause exculpating Bell from any liability to yellow page advertisers for failure to include advertising, and (e) delineated various procedural as well as substantive categories of factors considered by the courts in deciding questions of unconscionability. The court concluded that in this case the contract provision excluding defendant's liability for consequential damages was unenforceable since Michigan law does not permit such a clause to be enforced when plaintiff, who could not read except perhaps certain newspaper sports section items, was not made aware that the contract contained such a clause. This conclusion was not affected, the court said, by the failure of plaintiff to indicate to defendant's representative his inability to read or to ask that the contract be explained to him, nor by the fact that the representative was not guilty of unfair or oppressive conduct.

I. STATUTORY MANDATES AND LIMITS FOR CONTRACT DAMAGES

1. Contract Damage Statutory Mandates

N. Y. STATE TEAMSTERS CONF. PENSION AND RETIREMENT FUND v. FRATTO CURBING CO., INC.
875 F. Supp. 129 (N.D.N.Y. 1995)

Memorandum Decision and Order

POOLER, District Judge:

Introduction and Background

Plaintiff New York State Teamsters Conference Pension and Retirement Fund, et al. ("Teamsters") moves for a default judgment against defendant Fratto Curbing Co., Inc. ("Fratto") in this action under the Employee Retirement Income Security Act ("ERISA") to collect $6,030.48 plus post-judgment interest for delinquent pension fund contributions, interest, penalties and costs and attorney's fees.

Fratto was party to a collective bargaining agreement with Teamsters Local No. 398 (the "union") and a fund participation agreement with Teamsters. Pursuant to these contracts, Fratto was obligated to make fringe benefit contributions on behalf of union workers to the pension plan administered by Teamsters. Teamsters conducted an audit on January 4, 1994, showing that Fratto had failed to make $3,432.45 in required payments. Teamsters commenced this action on July 25, 1994, to collect the delinquent contributions. Service on Fratto was effected on August 31, 1994. Fratto never filed an answer to plaintiffs' complaint. An entry of default was made by the Clerk of the Court on September 23, 1994, and Teamsters now moves for default judgment. Oral argument took place on January 23, 1995, at which Fratto failed to enter an appearance.

Discussion

I. Entry of Default Judgment

Pursuant to Rule 55(b) of the Federal Rules of Civil Procedure and Local Rule 55.1(b), entry by the court of a default judgment is permitted where a party has failed to make any response to a plaintiff's complaint. . . . Because plaintiff has fulfilled the requirements for a default judgment, its motion is granted.

II. Judgment Amount

ERISA is designed to ensure that pension funds not only are reimbursed for delinquent contributions but also that they will receive "significant extra funding at the delinquent employer's expense." *Parise v. Riccelli Haulers, Inc.*, 672 F. Supp. 72, 74 (N.D.N.Y.1987). ERISA accordingly permits the recovery of delinquent contributions, interest, liquidated damages, costs and attorney's fees. 29 U.S.C. §§ 1132(g)(2), 1145. The relevant contracts between Fratto and Teamsters also authorize such recovery.

As detailed in the supporting affidavits of Teamsters, defendant Fratto owed the fund $3,432.45 in benefit contributions due as of January 4, 1994. In its default judgment request, Fratto has requested this amount as well as prejudgment interest pursuant to 29 U.S.C. 1132(g)(2)(A) & (B). In addition, Teamsters has requested costs and attorney's fees pursuant to 29 U.S.C. § 1132(g)(2)(D). Teamsters requests fees totalling $1,143, and the rates upon which the fees are calculated — $125 to $150 per hour for attorneys — are reasonable. *See Onondaga County Laborers' Health, Welfare, Pension, Annuity and Training Funds v. Sal Masonry Contractors, Inc.*, 1992 U.S. Dist. LEXIS 4715, (N.D.N.Y. 1992) (awarding fees based on rates of $126 to $137 per hour for attorneys); *see also Cefali v. Buffalo Brass Co.*, 748 F. Supp. 1011, 1020 (W.D.N.Y. 1990) (awarding attorney's fee based on rate of $150 per hour in ERISA action).

One portion of the award requested by Teamsters must be reduced because it is not in accordance with ERISA. Teamsters requests liquidated damages of 10 percent of the unpaid contribution amount, or $343.25, as provided in its contract with Fratto. However, Teamsters also requests statutory liquidated damages of double interest in the amount of $359.47, relying on 29 U.S.C. § 1132(g)(2)(C). According to this provision of ERISA, the fund is entitled to the greater of interest or liquidated damages as provided for under the plan, but not both amounts. Specifically, statute provides for the award of "an amount equal to the greater of — (i) interest on the unpaid contributions, or (ii) liquidated damages provided for under the plan in an amount not in excess of 20 percent [of the unpaid contribution amount]." 29 U.S.C. § 1132(g)(2)(C) . . . .

By the plain language of the statute, Teamsters is entitled to the greater of double interest, which is $359.47, or liquidated damages, which is $343.25, but not both. At oral argument, counsel for Teamsters stated that "contractual liquidated damages" is distinct from the statutory liquidated damages in Section 1132(g)(2)(C). We disagree. The term "liquidated damages" in Section 1132(g)(2)(C) necessarily refers to the liquidated damages amount negotiated by the parties in their contract. This interpretation has been expressed by the Second Circuit, which explained that "an award under this section encompasses, in addition to interest on the unpaid contributions, an amount equal to the greater of such interest (hence, 'double interest') or the liquidated damages provided under the parties' agreement up to 20 percent of the amount of delinquent contributions." *Diduck v. Kaszycki & Sons Contractors, Inc.*, 974 F.2d 270, 285 (2d Cir. 1992) . . . . The Second Circuit further explained that "double interest (as a form of liquidated damages) is a statutorily-created remedy designed to compensate the plan for the loss occasioned or costs incurred as a result of an employer's failure to make required contributions." *Id.* Thus, the fund is fully compensated by the liquidated damages provided by Section 1132(g)(2)(C) and is not entitled to a double recovery. . . . Consequently, Teamsters is entitled only to $359.47 in liquidated damages.

Conclusion

A default judgment is entered against Fratto in favor of Teamsters in the amount of $5,687.23, which represents $3,432.45 in delinquent contributions, audit fees of $247.84, interest of $359.47, double interest liquidated damages of $359.47, and attorney's fees and costs of $1,288. Teamsters also is awarded post-judgment interest pursuant to 28 U.S.C. § 1961(a).

So Ordered.

NEWTON v. GULF OIL CORPORATION
180 F.2d 491 (3d Cir. 1950)

GOODRICH, Circuit Judge: This case presents the question whether the libelants may recover damages from libelee for a "discharge" under the terms of the federal statute, 46 U.S.C.A. § 594, which deals with "Right to wages in case of improper discharge."

The facts are simple and undisputed. These libelants and others signed shipping articles between May 1 and May 4, 1948, for a voyage on the S.S. Gulfmoon from New York to "one or more ports in Venezuela . . . for a term of time not exceeding three calendar months." The ship did not go to Venezuela, but went, instead, from New York to Harbor Island, Texas, and returned to Philadelphia. The date of return was on or about May 15, 1948. On May 15 articles were terminated and the seamen were signed off. Each man received his earned wages for the voyage. They protested and demanded the statutory one month's pay to which they claimed to be entitled. Upon this being refused, suit was brought to recover and the seamen won in the District Court. D.C.E.D. Pa. 1949, 87 F. Supp. 210. It appears that at the time the men were signed off, in the presence of a United States Shipping Commissioner, they could have signed on again for another voyage on the same ship. This proposed voyage was for coastwise points. It also appears that the time consumed in the trip to Texas was within a day of the time in which a trip to Venezuela and back could be made.

The statute under which the claim is made reads as follows:

§ 594. Right to wages in case of improper discharge

Any seaman who has signed an agreement and is afterward discharged before the commencement of the voyage or before one month's wages are earned, without fault on his part justifying such discharge, and without his consent, shall be entitled to receive from the master or owner, in addition to any wages he may have earned, a sum equal in amount to one month's wages as compensation, and may, on adducing evidence satisfactory to the court hearing the case, of having been improperly discharged, recover such compensation as if it were wages duly earned. R.S. § 4527.

For these men to recover the one month's pay they claim they must have been (1) discharged (2) before the commencement of the voyage or the earning of one month's wages (3) without fault and (4) without consent. There is no doubt that the men were signed off before one month's wages were earned. There is no suggestion that there was any fault justifying discharge on the part of the libelants. The libelee makes some argument about the necessity of showing lack of consent. We think that is answered by the protest made by the men at the time they were signed off.

The case turns, then, on the meaning of the term "discharged" as used in the statute. . . .

We think that the established custom in shipping to sign men on for a voyage and release them at the end contemplates "discharge" and "rehiring." The word "discharge" in that connection does not mean, as it tends in common parlance to mean, termination of a man's employment because he has not done well. The statute itself conditions the seaman's right upon the lack of "fault on his part justifying such discharge." We think the word in this connection is as impersonal as its usage in the process of discharging freight or passengers.

Furthermore, we think that this interpretation fits into legislation for the protection of seamen.[41] Whether under modern conditions all these provisions should stand is a legislative and not a judicial question. It is easy to find archaic provisions in the shipping articles as, for instance, when one inspects the scale of provisions required to be served the crew. Nevertheless, the protection of the seaman as a ward of the admiralty is by no means an obsolete concept in the law. Courts not only repeat the statement, but apply it constantly. We have no doubt that the libelants in this case come within the terms of the statute. The voyage was changed and they were discharged before earning a month's wages. That they probably could not show, in an ordinary action of contract, damages which amounted to as much as a month's pay is not the question. They are suing for damages which have been liquidated by legislative enactment.

The libelee predicts that if the decree in this case is sustained, a ship owner will not be able to sign on men for a foreign voyage for less than a month in duration

---

[41] [2] The scope of the protection given to seamen by statutes derived from the Act of 1872 is wide indeed. The statutes require the master or owner to execute a written agreement with every seaman carried to sea. The agreement, known as "articles," must inform the seaman of the duration of the voyage and the port of its termination, his duties and wages and the scale of provisions which are to be furnished. 46 U.S.C.A. § 564. Articles which are so vague that they are not informative are void. . . . The articles must be signed by the seaman in the presence of a United States shipping commissioner, who must certify that its terms were understood. 46 U.S.C.A. § 577. If the vessel is lost during the voyage, seamen are entitled to transportation to the port of shipment. 46 U.S.C.A. §§ 593, 678, 679, 681. Wages must be paid within two days after the termination of the voyage; failure to do so subjects the owner to double liability. 46 U.S.C.A. § 596. Payment of wages in advance is forbidden. 46 U.S.C.A. § 599. Crew quarters are to be inspected by the Bureau of Marine Inspection and Navigation at least once each month. 46 U.S.C.A. § 660. Broad though these protective statutes are, they do not supplant or limit the ancient right of seamen to maintenance and cure. . . . Moreover, the remedies of seamen for negligent injury are expanded by the Jones Act, 48 U.S.C.A. § 688.

without becoming liable under the statute. The libelants reply that this case presents no such problem and has in it no such implications because this ship owner did not take the voyage which the articles called for. In other words, there was a technical breach of contract. If this is not a sufficient answer to the libelee's fears we shall make the answer if and when the problem is presented for decision.

The decree will be affirmed.

DEPT. OF PUBLIC HEALTH v. WILEY
218 Ill. 2d 207, 843 N.E.2d 259 (2006)

McMorrow, Justice:

The Illinois Department of Public Health (Department) filed suit in the circuit court of Cook County against Thelma E. Wiley, M.D., alleging that Wiley violated scholarship contracts she entered into with the Department pursuant to the Family Practice Residency Act (110 ILCS 935/1 *et seq.*), and that the Department was entitled to treble damages under section 10 of the same statute (110 ILCS 935/10). The circuit court granted summary judgment in favor of the Department. The appellate court affirmed. 348 Ill. App. 3d 809, 284 Ill. Dec. 824, 810 N.E.2d 614. For the reasons that follow, we affirm the judgment of the appellate court.

BACKGROUND

Enacted in 1977, the Family Practice Residency Act (Act) (110 ILCS 935/1 *et seq.*) states that its purpose is to "establish a program in the Illinois Department of Public Health to upgrade primary health care services for all citizens of the State, by providing grants to family practice and preventive medicine residency programs, scholarships to medical students and a loan repayment program for physicians who will agree to practice in areas of the State demonstrating the greatest need for more professional medical care. The program shall encourage family practice physicians to locate in areas where health manpower shortages exist and to increase the total number of family practice physicians in the State." 110 ILCS 935/2.

To further this purpose, section 4.03 of the Act (110 ILCS 935/4.03) authorizes the Department to "establish a program of medical student scholarships and to award scholarships to eligible medical students." An "[e]ligible medical student" is defined, in part, as a person who "agrees to practice full-time in a Designated Shortage Area as a primary care physician one year for each year he or she is a scholarship recipient." 110 ILCS 935/3.07(d). Thus, rather than awarding conventional scholarships, which do not have to be repaid, the Department awards "scholarship contracts," whereby students agree to a service commitment in exchange for receiving funds for medical schooling.

In addition to authorizing the creation of scholarship contracts, the Act also includes a penalty provision for scholarship recipients who fail to fulfill their statutory service obligation. Section 10 of the Act states that if a scholarship recipient fails to fulfill the obligation of serving as a full-time primary care physician in a designated shortage area, then the recipient "shall pay to the Department a sum equal to 3 times the amount of the annual scholarship grant for each year the recipient fails to fulfill such obligation." 110 ILCS 935/10.

In the case at bar, Wiley attended medical school from 1985 through 1989. During each of her four years of school, Wiley entered into a scholarship contract with the Department as authorized by the Act. The combined amount of the scholarships awarded to Wiley during the four years totaled $52,465.

Although the language in portions of the four contracts varies somewhat, the central obligation under the agreements is the same. Each contract states that, in exchange for receiving scholarship funds, Wiley agrees "to serve as a full-time primary care physician in direct patient care in only the designated shortage areas in Illinois approved as a practice site(s)."

Each of the four contracts also contains the following provision regarding the starting date of Wiley's term of service:

> Student's service term shall begin within thirty (30) days of Student's licensure to practice medicine, except that service may be deferred until completion of an approved residency program in primary care. In all cases where service is deferred, service shall begin within thirty (30) days after Student leaves residency program.

In addition, each of the contracts states that the Act is fully incorporated into the terms of the agreements and that, if the student fails to fulfill the terms of the contract, the Department is entitled to three times the amount of the scholarship awarded. Finally, each contract states that, if the student is required to reimburse the Department monetarily, then "[p]ayments shall begin within 30 days" from the date when the failure to perform occurs.

Wiley graduated from medical school in June of 1989. A month after her graduation, she began a three-year residency in internal medicine at the University of Illinois Medical Center at Chicago. . . .

[Her residency was approved and her service obligation was deferred until 30 days after she completed the residency. The Department communicated with her during the period of her residency concerning selecting a position in designated shortage areas, and she also talked by phone with the Department concerning the possibility of deferring her service while she completed a post residency in gastroenterology. She was told this is not an approved program, but was told that "something might be worked out as far as repaying the service." She then applied and obtained the post residency fellowship in gastroenterology at the University of Illinois Chicago. She did not select or begin working as a primary care physician in a designated shortage area at the end of her residency deferment. The Department repeatedly attempted to communicate with her by mail and certified mail concerning the requirements of her scholarship obligations. Finally the Department informed her that she had not fulfilled her service requirement to pay her grant contracts back, and therefore the Department assumed that she "had 'elected to monetarily repay [her] scholarship obligation.' The Department noted that she was required to pay three times the amount of the scholarships, or $157,395" and that payments were to begin immediately.]

In December 1992, the Department sent Wiley a repayment contract stating that Wiley had "elected to repay required funds in lieu of completing practice commitment," that the total amount owed, $157,395, would be paid off in 36 installments, and that the first payment was due January 1, 1993. In a cover letter, the Department asked Wiley to sign the contract and return it as soon as possible. Wiley did not return the contract or respond to the letter. . . .

[There were further attempts by the Department and its collection agency to obtain payment; the Illinois Comptroller's office withheld certain sums from her paycheck for work at the University of Illinois Medical Center at Chicago; there were communications with the state Attorney General's office and a follow-up $100 per month "Installment Agreement" subsequently terminated by the Attorney General's office for arrearages and at the Department's request; and the Department elected to continue with salary offsets of $500 a month.]

On August 17, 1995, the Department filed a two-count verified complaint against Wiley in the circuit court of Cook County. Count I alleged that Wiley breached the four scholarship contracts by, *inter alia*, failing to serve, within 30 days after her residency, as a full-time primary care physician in a designated shortage area approved by the Department. Count I further alleged that, pursuant to the Act, the Department was entitled to treble damages of $157,395. . . . [Count II, asserting breach of contract of the "Installment Agreement" that was abandoned when the Department asked the Attorney General to terminate it, was dismissed on defendant's motion.]

Wiley and the Department filed cross-motions for summary judgment with respect to count I. The circuit court determined that there was no question of material fact that Wiley failed to fulfill her service obligation because neither the type of medicine she practiced nor the locations where she practiced satisfied the terms of the scholarship contracts and the Act. The circuit court therefore entered judgment in favor of the Department on count I in the amount of $157,395.

On appeal, Wiley argued that the installment agreement was a settlement agreement that merged all claims based on the scholarship contracts and, therefore, the Department was precluded from proceeding under count I. The appellate court rejected this argument, concluding that the installment agreement was a payment plan, rather than a settlement. 348 Ill. App. 3d at 818-19, 284 Ill. Dec. 824, 810 N.E.2d 614. In addition, the appellate court held that there was no question of material fact that Wiley breached the four scholarship contracts. . . . The appellate court additionally held that, pursuant to the scholarship contracts and the Act, Wiley was required to reimburse the Department three times the amount of the scholarships awarded. In so holding, the appellate court noted that the treble damages provision in the contracts arose from a statutory directive, rather than through negotiations of the parties. Thus, the appellate court determined that common law contract defenses, such as the doctrine of substantial performance, could not be raised in an attempt to avoid the treble damages requirement. In reaching this conclusion, the appellate court rejected the reasoning of *Department of Public Health v. Jackson*, 321 Ill. App. 3d 228, 237, 254 Ill. Dec. 434, 747 N.E.2d 474 (2001), wherein the court held that treble damages are appropriate only in cases "where there has been a substantial failure to perform."

ANALYSIS

[The Supreme Court stated that the case arose from a grant of summary judgment and that the standard of review is *de novo*. The Court also rejected Wiley's argument that the installment payment was a settlement agreement which would have precluded the Department's first claim.]

Breach of the Scholarship Contracts

Wiley also argues that the circuit court erred in granting the Department summary judgment on count I because there are material questions of fact as to whether she breached any of the scholarship contracts. As noted, the appellate court rejected this argument, holding that, among other things, Wiley breached the scholarship contracts by failing to work in a location approved by the Department and by failing to begin her service commitment within 30 days of the completion of her residency. 348 Ill. App. 3d at 820, 284 Ill. Dec. 824, 810 N.E.2d 614.

Each of Wiley's scholarship contracts required her to work as a full-time primary care physician in a designated shortage area "approved as a practice site(s) by the Department. Each contract also required Wiley to begin fulfilling her service obligation within 30 days of the completion of her residency. Wiley did not fulfill either of these requirements. . . . [The Court noted that none of her subsequent actions satisfied her obligations and that the Department had notified her that her fellowship in gastroenterology also was not approved to satisfy her service obligation.]

[The Court also rejected Wiley's argument] that obtaining approval from the Department for a practice site and beginning her service obligation within the 30 day period are merely "administrative requirements" and that the failure to fulfill those requirements resulted in no harm to the Department. Wiley then points to the common law doctrine of *de minimis non curat lex,* [meaning "the law does not concern itself with trifles."] . . . . Relying on this doctrine, Wiley contends that she did not breach the scholarship contracts.

The Department, in response, contends that the defense of *de minimis non curat lex* is not available in this case because common law contract defenses may not be applied to contracts whose terms are established by the Act, rather than through negotiations conducted by the parties. . . . [The Court analyzed the statutory text and concluded:] [b]ecause these requirements have not been imposed by the General Assembly, we conclude that ordinary contract principles apply to them and that Wiley may raise the doctrine of *de minimis non curat lex.*

However, while Wiley may invoke this defense, it is not successful here. The requirements that the Department approve the scholarship recipients' practice locations and that the service commitments begin in a timely fashion are critical to the efficacy of the scholarship program. Departmental approval of a practice site is needed to ensure that medical services are being distributed throughout the state and being provided to those who are most in need. The Department must be able to retain control over where and when the scholarship recipients serve or the program will be ineffective and the purpose of the Act frustrated. . . . Wiley's failure to obtain approval of her practice location and begin working within 30 days were not "slight" or "technical" matters. Rather, these were material breaches of core obligations contained in the scholarship contracts. Accordingly, we decline to find that the doctrine of *de minimis non curat lex* is applicable in this case. We therefore affirm the judgment of the appellate court that Wiley breached the scholarship contracts.

Treble Damages

Wiley also contends that the circuit court erred in awarding the Department treble damages. Wiley notes that, under Illinois law, damages may not be recovered in an action for breach of contract if the purpose of those damages is merely to secure a party's performance of the agreement. . . . Such damages are considered "an unenforceable penalty unless: (1) the amount so fixed is a reasonable forecast of just compensation of the harm that is caused by the breach; and (2) the harm caused is difficult or impossible to estimate." . . . Wiley argues that the treble damages at issue here are an improper penalty and may not be imposed.

Wiley also relies on *Department of Public Health v. Jackson*, 321 Ill. App. 3d 228, 254 Ill. Dec. 434, 747 N.E.2d 474 (2001). In that case, the appellate court concluded that treble damages under the Act should be imposed in those instances "where there has been a substantial failure to perform" on the part of the scholarship recipient. . . . Wiley maintains that she substantially performed under the scholarship contracts and, therefore, that treble damages are inappropriate.

Wiley may be correct that, at common law, the treble damages provision in her scholarship contracts would be unenforceable. However, we need not consider that issue here because the imposition of treble damages in this case is not governed by common law. Rather, the treble damages are required by statute.

Each of Wiley's scholarship contracts incorporates the Act into the terms of the agreements. In addition, three of the four contracts specifically state that the treble damages requirement is imposed "in accordance with the Family Practice Residency Act." . . . Wiley does not argue that the legislature may not, as a general matter, modify the common law on the issue of damages for breaches of scholarship contracts, nor does she contend that section 10 of the Act is unconstitutional. We are not free to ignore the requirements set forth by the General Assembly in constitutionally valid legislation. Accordingly, we conclude that, so long as the statutory requirements of section 10 of the Act are met, treble damages may be imposed in this case.

Further, we decline to apply the position advanced in *Jackson* that, in determining whether treble damages may be imposed, the relevant inquiry is whether the scholarship recipient failed to substantially perform the scholarship contract. The question in this case is not whether Wiley did, or did not, substantially perform the terms and conditions of her scholarship contracts. Instead, in accordance with sections 10 and 3.07(d) of the Act, the question is whether Wiley (1) practiced full time (2) as a primary care physician (3) in a designated shortage area. *See* 110 ILCS 935/10, 3.07(d).

The Department contends that there is no question of material fact that Wiley failed to fulfill each of the foregoing requirements. According to the Department, Wiley did not work as a primary care physician because her practice was in gastroenterology, a subspecialty of internal medicine, and hepatology, a sub-subspecialty of internal medicine. The Department also maintains that, even if portions of her practice were in primary care, she was not working as a primary care physician full time. Finally, the Department contends that Wiley was not working in a designated shortage area because her practice locations were not listed in any of the directories of designated shortage areas prepared by the Department.

Wiley, in response, maintains that testimony from expert witnesses obtained during discovery raises questions of material fact as to whether she was practicing full time as a primary care physician. Moreover, Wiley argues that, under the definition of designated shortage area contained in section 3.04 of the Act, she satisfied the requirement that she practice in a designated shortage area as well. We address this latter contention first. The Act defines a designated shortage area as:

> an area designated by the Director as a physician shortage area, a medically underserved area, or a critical health manpower shortage area as defined by the United States Department of Health, Education and Welfare, or as further defined by the Department to enable it to effectively fulfill the purpose stated in Section 2 of this Act. Such areas may include the following:
>
> (a) an urban or rural area which is a rational area for the delivery of health services;
>
> (b) a population group; or
>
> (c) a public or nonprofit private medical facility. 110 ILCS 935/3.04.

Wiley argues that the requirement of designation by the Director of the Department applies only to the first clause in section 3.04, *i.e.,* "physician shortage area," and not to any of the successive clauses. Thus, according to Wiley, the phrase "medically underserved area" is defined independently of any designation by the Director. Wiley then points to Census Bureau statistics, undisputed by the Department, which show that the median family income in the neighborhood where the University of Illinois at Chicago and Veteran's Administration medical centers are located is approximately one-third of the median citywide family income and that 55% of the population in the neighborhood live below the poverty line. Wiley further notes that a large percentage of the patients she treated received public assistance and had no other form of insurance. Wiley argues that it is precisely this type of low-income population that experiences difficulty receiving medical care because of its lack of resources. Thus, according to Wiley, her practice location was in a "medically underserved area" and treble damages are unwarranted. We disagree.

In light of the purpose of the Act, Wiley's reading of section 3.04 is not a reasonable one. Consider, for example, that a large and highly respected research hospital, though located in an impoverished neighborhood, may have no difficulty filling available medical positions because of the salary and career opportunities that those positions provide. A community clinic located in the same neighborhood, however, cannot offer the salaries and career options that the hospital can, and may struggle to hire physicians. The purpose of the Act is to improve primary health-care services in those areas "where health manpower shortages exist." 110 ILCS 935/2. Although both the large hospital and the community clinic may be located in the same neighborhood, they may face very different levels of "manpower shortages." For this reason, it cannot be left up to the scholarship recipient to determine, on her own, that her statutory service obligation has been met because the neighborhood in which she works is an impoverished one. The purpose of the Act cannot be effectuated unless the Director can designate those places where health services are actually needed. Consequently, we reject Wiley's interpretation of section 3.04. We conclude that a "designated shortage area" means just that —

an area designated by the Director of the Department as suffering from a shortage of professional medical care.

In this case, it is undisputed that Wiley's practice locations in gastroenterology and hepatology at the University of Illinois at Chicago and the Veteran's Administration medical centers were not in the directory of designated shortage areas prepared by the Department. Accordingly, Wiley violated section 10 of the Act and the Department is entitled to treble damages. Because we have determined that Wiley was not working in a designated shortage area, we need not consider whether she was working full time as a primary care physician.

CONCLUSION

For the foregoing reasons, the judgment of the appellate court is affirmed. *Affirmed.*

Chief Justice THOMAS and Justices FREEMAN, FITZGERALD, KILBRIDE, GARMAN, and KARMEIER concurred in the judgment and opinion.

NOTES

1. There are other state statutes that establish specific measures of damages for certain contract breaches. Some allow the court to exercise judicial discretion in imposing the statutory measure of damages, while others require that the statutory measure of damages be imposed. Usually the statutory measure doubles or triples the damage award, and may also require reasonable attorney's fees. A few examples:

California Civil Code § 1812.62 allows a judge the discretion to award treble damages and lawyer's fees to parties injured by a violation of Civil Code, Division 3, Part 4 (Obligations Arising from Particular Transactions), Title 2.4 (Contracts for Dance Studio Lessons and Other Services).

California Civil Code § 1812.123 allows a judge the discretion to award treble damages and lawyer's fees to parties injured by a violation of Civil Code, Division 3, Part 4 (Obligations Arising from Particular Transactions), Title 2.6 (Contracts for Discount Buying Services). If the court finds that there was a violation of § 1812.120 of the same Title 2.6, relating to untrue or misleading statements, judgment is to be for one thousand dollars plus reasonable attorney's fees or three times the amount of actual damages plus attorney's fees, whichever is greater.

2. Some states have statutes protecting commissioned salespersons working under a commission contract. The statutes may provide for treble damages plus reasonable attorney fees when a company breaches its commission sales contract and fails to pay commissions due on sales made by the salesman. For example, Code of Alabama, Title 8 — Commercial Law and Consumer Protection, Chapter 24 — Sales Representative's Commission Contracts, provides for treble damages and attorney's fees.

3. *See Duck Head Apparel Company, Inc. v. Ken Hoots, et. al.*, 659 So. 2d 897 (Ala. 1995), where the Alabama Supreme Court affirmed trial court jury instructions allowing treble damages and attorney fees authorized by the Alabama Sales Representative's Commission Contract statute. The Court also approved the trial

court decision to require plaintiffs to choose between treble damages for breach of contract, and straight contract damages plus tort punitive damages on fraud claims. The jury had assessed contract damages at $852,000, trebled to $2,556,353.60; and tort damages at $7,000,000 for mental anguish, plus $19,500,000 in punitive damages. After a hearing on the matter of the jury's punitive damages award, the trial judge entered an order for remittitur of the punitive damages to $15,000,000. Further, because the trial judge viewed the treble damages and the punitives as "double recovery or double punishment," and after the court required plaintiffs to choose between them, plaintiffs chose to remit the treble damages award down to straight contract damages. Final judgment was thus for the straight contract damage amount plus the compensatory and punitive tort damages. Based on its evaluation of the evidence offered at trial, the Alabama Supreme Court affirmed that judgment, except that it required a remittitur of the compensatory damages award for mental anguish from $7,000,000 to $4,000,000. Note that the punitive damages allowed in this case were not for the breach of contract, but for the additional tort claims brought by the plaintiffs.

4. Maryland has a similar statute that requires an employer to pay final wages of a terminated employee within two weeks, unless there is a bona fide dispute as to what is owed. Failure of the employer to pay entitles the employee to sue and request treble the unpaid wages plus reasonable attorney's fees. Maryland Wage Payment and Collection Law, LE §§ 3-501 to 3-509. In *Admiral Mortgage, Inc. v. Cooper*, 745 A.2d 1026 (Md. 2000), *Cooper* recovered treble damages plus legal fees for the employer's failure to pay outstanding commissions when the employer terminated the employee.

2.   Limitation of Liability Laws

SIEGEL v. WESTERN UNION TELEGRAPH CO.
312 Ill. App. 86, 37 N.E.2d 868 (1941)

FRIEND, Justice:

Plaintiff brought suit against the Western Union Telegraph Company for damages resulting from its failure to transmit promptly a telegraphic money order. The court limited his damages to the charge made for transmitting the money order and entered judgment accordingly for $1.92. Upon the theory that he had established damages in excess of $500, the maximum sum provided in the tariff regulation then on file with the Federal Communications Commission, plaintiff seeks reversal of the judgment and the entry of judgment here in the sum of $500 and costs.

The cause was submitted and tried by the court upon stipulated facts. It appears that on November 23, 1938, plaintiff delivered to the Western Union Telegraph Company $200 with instructions to transmit this sum to P. W. Gunkel, a friend of plaintiff residing at Rogers Smith Hotel in Washington, D.C. The money was to be wagered on a horse named Mintson, to win, at the pari mutuel machines at Bowie Race Track in Maryland, where pari mutuel wagering is legalized under the laws of that state. The money order was negligently misdirected to New York City and was ultimately delivered to Gunkel several hours after the race had been run November 24, 1938. Mintson won and the pari mutuel machines paid $18.50 for each $2 wagered. Had plaintiff's $200 been placed the odds would have been reduced to $16.50. Deducting the principal of the money order which was returned to plaintiff he claims to have sustained damages to the extent of $1,450 through defendant's negligence.

The suit is predicated on a tariff regulation then in effect and on file with the Federal Communications Commission, which also appears as one of the conditions set forth on the back of the money order application, providing:

> In any event, the Company shall not be liable for damages for delay, nonpayment or underpayment of this money order, whether by reason of negligence on the part of its agents or servants or otherwise, beyond the sum of $500, at which amount the right to have this money order promptly and correctly transmitted and promptly and fully paid is hereby valued, unless a greater value is stated in writing on the face of this application and an additional sum paid or agreed to be paid based on such value equal to one-tenth of one per cent thereof.

Prior to 1910 telegraph companies had a common law liability from which they might or might not extricate themselves according to views of policy prevailing in the several states. . . . In June of that year congress broadened the scope of the Act to Regulate Commerce so as to include telegraph, telephone and cable companies engaged in sending messages interstate and to any foreign country. c. 309, § 7, 36 Stat. 539, 49 U.S.C.A. § 1(1-9). This act "introduced a new principle into the legal relations of the telegraph companies with their patrons which dominated and modified the principles previously governing them. . . . Thereafter, for all messages sent in interstate or foreign commerce, the outstanding consideration became that of uniformity and equality of rates. Uniformity demanded that the rate represent the whole duty and the whole liability of the company. It could not be varied by agreement; still less could it be varied by lack of agreement. The rate became, not as before a matter of contract by which a legal liability could be modified, but a matter of law by which a uniform liability was imposed." *Western Union Telegraph Co. v. Esteve Bros. & Co.*, 256 U.S. 566, 41 S. Ct. 584, 65 L. Ed. 1094.

Pursuant to this enactment the Interstate Commerce Commission decided upon investigation that the existing rules and rates of the telegraph companies limiting their liability for negligence were unreasonable and prescribed rules and rates therefor which fixed the maximum liability in case of unrepeated messages at not less than $500. *Cultra v. Western Union Telegraph Co.*, 1921, 61 I.C.C. 541. In accordance with the order entered in the Cultra case the Western Union Telegraph Company prepared its new rules and tariffs relating to messages and subsequently extended them to money orders by including the provision in question.

Wernick v. Western Union Telegraph Company, 1937, 290 Ill. App. 569, 9 N.E.2d 72, was one of the earliest cases requiring the construction of the tariff regulation in question. We were there called upon to decide whether the amount of $500 as stipulated therein constituted liquidated damages for nonpayment or underpayment of a money order transmitted through the Western Union Telegraph Company or whether it was merely a limitation on the liability of the company to the extent of actual damages sustained. We construed the regulation as a limitation upon the liability of the company for rate-making purposes and held that plaintiff could recover for actual damages shown, but not to exceed the sum of $500. This conclusion was predicated upon the historical origin and effect given to similar tariff regulations governing public carriers in *Western Union Telegraph Co. v. Esteve Bros. & Co.*, 256 U.S. 566, 41 S. Ct. 584, 65 L. Ed. 1094, and *Western Union Telegraph Co. v. Priester*, 276 U.S. 252, 48 S. Ct. 234, 72 L. Ed. 555.

Plaintiff relies on *Western Union Telegraph Co. v. Nester*, 1939, 106 F.2d 587, wherein the circuit court of appeals (ninth district), with one of the justices dissenting, construed this precise regulation as an agreement for liquidated damages, despite the sender's failure to prove actual damages. The Supreme Court of the United States granted *certiorari*, 309 U.S. 643, 60 S. Ct. 468, 84 L. Ed. 997, and, since briefs were filed in this cause, has reversed the decision of the circuit court of appeals, quoting with approval the construction we placed upon the tariff regulation in the Wernick case. 309 U.S. 582, 60 S. Ct. 769, 84 L. Ed. 960, 128 A.L.R. 628. The precise question was also considered in *Miazza v. Western Union Telegraph Co.*, 1935, 50 Ga. App. 521, 178 S.E. 764, with the same result. All these decisions discuss the origin and effect of the stipulated value of the regulation and leave no doubt that the amount of $500 stated in the contract is for the purpose of limiting, but not of fixing, the damages. Under these decisions plaintiff is required to prove actual damages and recovery is limited in any event to the stipulated amount of $500. The cogent reasons for this limitation are twofold: telegraph rates imposed by the federal government are framed on the basis of determining the cost of rendering the service of rapid transmission to the public at reasonable rates and with a fair margin of profit to the carrier, and if liability were to be unlimited, the company's ability to continue business might be seriously endangered; certainly it could not continue in business operating under the present rate structure. On the other hand, if the rates should be increased sufficiently to offset the higher expense resulting from unlimited liability, the carrier's volume of business would materially decrease and its services would not be available at prices within reach of the general public. *Cultra v. Western Union Telegraph Co.*, 61 I.C.C. 541.

The case at bar involved an interstate transaction. Under the stipulated facts plaintiff was deprived of winning $1,450 on Mintson through misdirection of the money order. The company's negligence is conceded. The question therefore presented is whether plaintiff should have been awarded as special damages the maximum amount of $500 stipulated in the contract.

Under the rule generally applied to the nonpayment or underpayment of money orders transmitted through telegraph companies, the measure of damages is the interest on the money from the time it should have been delivered to the time it was actually delivered, together with the cost of the message. This rule was followed in *Lust v. Western Union Telegraph Co.*, 1926, 243 Ill. App. 624, not reported general number 31035, wherein the court held that any other loss would be too remote and said that "ordinarily, the measure of damages for the nonpayment of money when due is interest from the time of the default to the time the money is paid; and this rule applies to the failure on the part of a telegraph company to perform its agreement to transmit money to a person at a distant point." [*Citing* Jones on Telegraph & Telephone Companies, § 567; 37 Cyc. 1775; and *Smith v. Western Union Telegraph Co.*, 150 Pa. 561, 24 A. 1049.] In an earlier case, *Churches v. Western Union Telegraph Co.*, 1921, 108 Kan. 431, 195 P. 610, a farmer purchased two teams of horses at Kansas City, Missouri, and telegraphed his bank at Lawrence, Nebraska, to forward him $600 to pay for them. Defendant failed to transmit the money and plaintiff sued the telegraph company for board for himself and his teams and other damages, including his traveling expenses and the cost of the message. The court stated the rule as follows:

> The defendant contends that the measure of damages is the cost of transmitting the telegram and interest on the $600 for the time it was held by the telegraph company, about 10 days. The authorities support this contention.

The same rule was applied under similar circumstances in *Robinson v. Western Union Telegraph Co.*, 68 S.W. 656, 24 Ky. Law Rep. 452, 57 L.R.A. 611; *Loudon v. Taxing District*, 1881, 104 U.S. 771, 26 L. Ed. 923; and *Green Briar Drainage Dist. v. Clark*, 7th Cir., 292 F. 828.

However, the authorities recognize an exception to this rule in cases where the telegraph company has notice, at the time of making the contract, of such special facts or circumstances as to justify the conclusion that special or unusual damages are within the contemplation of the parties. *Lust v. Western Union Telegraph Co.*, 243 Ill. App. 624; 37 Cyc. 1775. The exception dates back to the early case of *Hadley v. Baxendale*, 9 Exchequer 341 (1854), and it has since been generally held that whether or not a telegraph company incurs any special liability, for its default in transmitting money, depends on whether it has been put on notice of circumstances such as would reasonably have led an ordinarily prudent person to anticipate consequential losses or injuries from a failure to deliver the message. . . . It was stipulated in the case at bar that defendant had no notice or knowledge of the purpose for which the money was being transmitted.

. . . Neither of these cases supports the contention that the common law rule for ascertaining damages has been superseded by the tariff regulations. Under the established rule for construing the regulation in question, the extent of the common law liability of telegraph companies for negligence has been limited by their tariff provisions, unless the sender places a greater value than $500 on his money order and pays or agrees to pay therefor. Plaintiff must in each instance prove actual damages and the company is liable under the common law, to the extent for which it is liable under its tariff. We conceive no reason for holding that the control of interstate business of telegraph companies by the federal government, through published rules, regulations and tariffs, was intended to change or affect the long established rule that recovery for special damages can only be had in cases where the special damage was within the contemplation of the parties, and we find no authority so holding.

Judgment of the Municipal court is affirmed.

ORDER OF CIVIL AERONAUTICS BOARD APPROVING INCREASES IN LIABILITY LIMITATIONS OF WARSAW CONVENTION AND HAGUE PROTOCOL

Adopted by the Civil Aeronautics Board, Washington, D.C., on the 13th day of May 1966.

The Convention for the Unification of Certain Rules Relating to International Transportation by Air, generally known as the Warsaw Convention, creates a uniform body of law with respect to the rights and responsibilities of passengers, shippers, and air carriers in international air transportation. The United States became a party to the Convention in 1934, and eventually over 90 countries likewise became parties to the Convention. [The Convention was amended by the Protocol signed at Hague in 1955 which has never been ratified by the United States. The

Convention (subject to certain provisions) limits carriers' liability for death or injury to passengers in international transportation to 125,000 gold francs, or approximately $8,300. The Protocol, subject to certain provisions, provides for liability limitations of approximately $16,600.] On November 15, 1965, the U.S. Government gave notice of denunciation of the Convention, emphasizing that such action was solely because of the Convention's low limits of liability for personal injury or death to passengers. Pursuant to Article 39 of the Convention this notice would become effective upon 6 months' notice, in this case, May 15, 1966. Subsequently, the International Air Transport Association (IATA) made efforts to effect an arrangement among air carriers, foreign air carriers, and other carriers (including carriers not members of IATA) providing the major portions of international air carriage to and from the United States to increase the limitations of liability now applicable to claims for personal injury and death under the Convention and the Protocol. The purpose of such action is to provide a basis upon which the United States could withdraw its notice of denunciation.

The arrangement proposed has been embodied in an agreement (Agreement CAB 18900) between various air carriers, foreign air carriers, and other carriers which has been filed with the Board pursuant to section 412(a) of the Federal Aviation Act of 1958 and Part 261 of the Board's economic regulations and assigned the above designated CAB number.

By this agreement, the parties thereto bind themselves to include in their tariffs, effective May 16, 1966, a special contract in accordance with Article 22(1) of the Convention or the Protocol providing for a limit of liability for each passenger for death, wounding, or other bodily injury of $75,000 inclusive of legal fees, and, in case of a claim brought in a State where provision is made for separate award of legal fees and costs, a limit of $58,000 exclusive of legal fees and costs. These limitations shall be applicable to international transportation by the carrier as defined in the Convention or Protocol which includes a point in the United States as a point of origin, point of destination, or agreed stopping place. . . .

Steps have been taken by the signing carriers to have tariffs become effective May 16, 1966, upon approval of this agreement, which will increase by special contract their liability for personal injury or death as described herein. The signatory carriers provide by far the greater portion of international transportation to, from, and within the United States. The agreement will result in a salutary increase in the protection given to passengers from the increased liability amounts and the waiver of defenses under Article 20(1) of the Convention or Protocol. The U.S. Government has concluded that such arrangements warrant withdrawal of the Notice of Denunciation of the Warsaw Convention. Implementation of the agreement will permit continued adherence to the Convention with the benefits to be derived therefrom, but without the imposition of the low liability limits therein contained upon most international travel involving travel to or from the United States. The stipulation that no tariff provision shall be deemed to affect the rights and liabilities of the carrier with regard to any claim brought by, on behalf of, or in respect of any person who has willfully caused damage which results in death, wounding or other bodily injury of a passenger operates to diminish any incentive for sabotage.

Upon consideration of the agreement, and of matters relating thereto of which the Board takes notice, the Board does not find that the agreement is adverse to the public interest or in violation of the Act and it will be approved.

Accordingly, pursuant to the provisions of the Federal Aviation Act of 1958, and particularly sections l02,204(a), and 412 thereof:

It is ordered, That: 1. Agreement CAB 18900 is approved.

J. PUNITIVE (EXEMPLARY) DAMAGES

WHITE v. BENKOWSKI
37 Wis. 2d 285, 155 N.W.2d 74 (1967)

[In November 1962 the Whites and the Benkowskis, owners of neighboring homes, entered into a written agreement by which the Benkowskis promised to supply water from their well to the White home for 10 years or until an earlier date when either water would be supplied by the municipality, the well would become inadequate, or the Whites drilled their own well. The Whites were to pay $3 a month for the water and one-half the cost of any future repairs or maintenance that the Benkowski well might require. Not included in the written agreement, but as part of the transaction, the Whites gave the Benkowskis $400 which was used to purchase and install a new pump and an additional tank to increase the well's capacity. After a time the relationship between the neighbors deteriorated. In 1964 the water supply controlled by the Benkowskis was shut off on a number of occasions concerning which Mrs. White kept records. Mr. Benkowski claimed that the water was shut off either to allow sand in the pipes to settle or to remind the Whites that they were using excessive water.]

WILKIE, Justice:

Two issues are raised on this appeal. 1. Was the trial court correct in reducing the award of compensatory damages from $10 to $1? 2. Are punitive damages available in actions for breach of contract? . . .

Punitive Damages.

"If a man shall steal an ox, or a sheep, and kill it, or sell it; he shall restore five oxen for an ox, and four sheep for a sheep." [Exodus 22:1]

Over one hundred years ago this court held that, under proper circumstances, a plaintiff was entitled to recover exemplary or punitive damages. [*McWilliams v. Bragg*, 3 Wis. 377 (1854)]

Kink v. Combs [28 Wis. 2d 65, 135 N.W.2d 789 (1965)] is the most recent case in this state which deals with the practice of permitting punitive damages. In *Kink* the court relied on *Fuchs v. Kupper* [22 Wis. 2d 107, 125 N.W.2d 360 (1963)] and reaffirmed its adherence to the rule of punitive damages.

In Wisconsin compensatory damages are given to make whole the damage or injury suffered by the injured party. [*Malco, Inc. v. Midwest Aluminum Sales*, 14 Wis. 2d 57, 66, 109 N.W.2d 516, 521 (1961).] On the other hand, punitive damages are given

> . . . on the basis of punishment to the injured party not because he has been injured, which injury has been compensated with compensatory damages, but to punish the wrongdoer for his malice and to deter others from like conduct. [*Id.*]

Thus we reach the question of whether the plaintiffs are entitled to punitive damages for a breach of the water agreement.

The overwhelming weight of authority supports the proposition that punitive damages are not recoverable in actions for breach of contract. [Annot. (1933), 84 A.L.R. 1345, 1346.] In CHITTY ON CONTRACTS, the author states that the right to receive punitive damages for breach of contract is now confined to the single case of damages for breach of a promise to marry. [1 CHITTY, CONTRACTS, (22d ed. 1961), p. 1339.]

Simpson states: "Although damages in excess of compensation for loss are in some instances permitted in tort actions by way of punishment . . . in contract actions the damages recoverable are limited to compensation for pecuniary loss sustained by the breach." [SIMPSON, CONTRACTS, (2d ed. hornbook series), p. 394, § 195.]

Corbin states that as a general rule punitive damages are not recoverable for breach of contract. [5 CORBIN, CONTRACTS, p. 438, § 1077.]

In Wisconsin, the early case of *Gordon v. Brewster* [7 Wis. 309 (1858)] involved the breach of an employment contract. The trial court instructed the jury that if the nonperformance of the contract was attributable to the defendant's wrongful act of discharging the plaintiff, then that would go to increase the damages sustained. On appeal, this court said that the instruction was unfortunate and might have led the jurors to suppose that they could give something more than actual compensation in a breach of contract case. We find no Wisconsin case in which breach of contract (other than breach of promise to marry) [*Simpson v. Black*, 27 Wis. 206 (1870)] has led to the award of punitive damages.

Persuasive authority from other jurisdictions supports the proposition (without exception) that punitive damages are not available in breach of contract actions. . . . This is true even if the breach, as in the instant case, is willful. . . .

Although it is well recognized that breach of a contractual duty may be a tort . . . , in such situations the contract creates the relation out of which grows the duty to use care in the performance of a responsibility prescribed by the contract. [38 AM. JUR., *Negligence*, p. 661, § 20]. Not so here. No tort was pleaded or proved.

Reversed in part by reinstating the jury verdict relating to compensatory damages and otherwise affirmed. Costs to appellant.

U.S. Naval Institute v. Charter Communications, Inc., and Berkley Publishing Group, 936 F.2d 692 (2d Cir. 1991). In 1984, Naval Institute (Naval), assignee of the author's copyright for the book *Red October*, entered into a licensing agreement with Charter and Berkley (Berkley), granting Berkley the exclusive right to publish a paperback edition of the book "not sooner than October 1985." Berkley, however, printed and shipped a paperback edition to retailers early, allowing retail sales to begin September 15, 1985, and these early sales were so substantial that the book was near the top of paperback bestseller lists before the end of September. On this appeal the Court of Appeals concluded that Naval was not entitled to recover for copyright infringement or lost profits due to such alleged infringement or attorney fees, but was entitled to recover actual damages and prejudgment interest. In addition, it held that the district court did not err in finding that Naval suffered $35,380 in actual damages, or in finding that Berkley's alleged $724,300 profits did not define Naval's loss because many who bought the paperback in September 1985 would not have bought the hardcover book but would merely have waited until the paperback edition became available. "While on occasion the defendant's profits are used as the measure of damages, . . . this generally occurs when those profits tend to define the plaintiff's loss, for an award of the defendant's profits where they greatly exceed the plaintiff's loss and there has been no tortious conduct on the part of the defendant would tend to be punitive, and punitive awards are not part of the law of contract damages."

NOTES

1. Punitive damages are generally not awarded in contract cases unless the breach of the contract "is also an independent tort for which punitive damages are recoverable and proper allegations of malice, wantonness, or oppression are made." *Morrow v. L.A. Goldschmidt Assoc., Inc.*, 112 Ill. 2d 87 (1986). However, different states apply this rule with varied rigor. In *Mulder v. Donaldson, Lufkin & Jenrette*, 161 Misc. 2d 698, 611 N.Y.S.2d 1019 (Supp. 1994), affirmed 208 A.D.2d 301, 623 N.Y.S.2d 560 (N.Y.A.D. 1995), the court said, "[p]unitive damages can be awarded for the breach of contract where there is a bad faith or dishonest failure to carry out contract or where defendant conduct is deemed to be truly egregious." And "[p]unitive damages will not generally be available in contract actions, but the rule is not without exceptions." *Kocse v. Liberty Mut. Ins. Co.*, 152 N.J. Super. 371, 377 A.2d 1234 (Law Div. 1977).

2. There appears to be one common exception to the rule against the award of punitive damages for a breach of contract, and that is a breach of contract to marry. See, *Stanback v. Stanback*, 297 N.C. 181, 254 S.E.2d 611 (1979), and 84 A.L.R. 1345 (Punitive or exemplary damages for breach of contract, other than contracts to marry and actions on statutory bonds).

3. The previous edition of this text included two cases in which punitive damages were allowed for contract complaints. They were *Nicholson v. United Pacific Ins. Co.*, 219 Mont. 32, 710 P.2d 1342 (1985), and *Seaman's Direct Buying Service, Inc. v. Standard Oil Co. of California*, 36 Cal. 3d 752, 206 Cal. Rptr. 354, 686 P.2d 1158 (1984). The respective state supreme courts have essentially receded from or overruled both cases, reasserting the rule that punitive damages are unavailable for breach of contract claims, unless the breach also constitutes an independent tort.

CHAPTER 17

RESTITUTIONARY RELIEF
AND EQUITABLE REMEDIES

A. RESTITUTIONARY RELIEF

Remedies sought when claims are based on *implied contract* (and related theories such as *promissory estoppel, quasi-contract, unjust enrichment,* and *quantum meruit*) are referred to generally as *restitutionary* remedies.

Restitution in Money. If the relief sought in an implied contract case is the return of a specific amount of money deposited with or improperly obtained by the defendant, that sum is the measure of restitution allowed. Except when the return of such a specific sum of money is involved, restitution by way of monetary relief in implied contract cases is measured by reasonable *value* — ordinarily the value of the benefit conferred upon or retained by the defendant, but occasionally the value of the detriment sustained by the plaintiff.

Restitution in Kind. When restitution is sought of property interests withheld or improperly obtained (rather than the value of the property) relief is generally in the form of a remedy available through the exercise by the court of its equitable powers. The nature of the case determines the type of equitable remedy allowed. Some examples are: an order directing the conveyance or delivery of property; an order establishing a *constructive trust* over the property and declaring defendant to be the constructive trustee; and an order impressing an *equitable lien* on the property. Equitable remedies are more fully explored in part B of this chapter.

1. Availability of Restitution — Value Provided

UNITED STATES ex rel. COASTAL STEEL ERECTORS, INC.
v. ALGERNON BLAIR, INC.
479 F.2d 638 (4th Cir. 1973)

CRAVEN, Circuit Judge:

May a subcontractor, who justifiably ceases work under a contract because of the prime contractor's breach, recover in quantum meruit the value of labor and equipment already furnished pursuant to the contract irrespective of whether he would have been entitled to recover in a suit on the contract? We think so, and, for reasons to be stated, the decision of the district court will be reversed.

The subcontractor, Coastal Steel Erectors, Inc., brought this action under the provisions of the Miller Act, 40 U.S.C.A. § 270a *et seq.*, in the name of the United States against Algernon Blair, Inc., and its surety, United States Fidelity and Guaranty Company. Blair had entered a contract with the United States for the construction of a naval hospital in Charleston County, South Carolina. Blair had then contracted with Coastal to perform certain steel erection and supply certain equipment in conjunction with Blair's contract with the United States. Coastal commenced performance of its obligations, supplying its own cranes for handling and placing steel. Blair refused to pay for crane rental, maintaining that it was not obligated to do so under the subcontract. Because of Blair's failure to make payments for crane rental, and after completion of approximately 28 percent of the subcontract, Coastal terminated its performance. Blair then proceeded to complete the job with a new subcontractor. Coastal brought this action to recover for labor and equipment furnished.

The district court found that the subcontract required Blair to pay for crane use and that Blair's refusal to do so was such a material breach as to justify Coastal's terminating performance. This finding is not questioned on appeal. The court then found that under the contract the amount due Coastal, less what had already been paid, totaled approximately $37,000. Additionally, the court found Coastal would have lost more than $37,000 if it had completed performance. Holding that any amount due Coastal must be reduced by any loss it would have incurred by complete performance of the contract, the court denied recovery to Coastal. While the district court correctly stated the " 'normal' rule of contract damages," we think Coastal is entitled to recover in quantum meruit.

In *United States for Use of Susi Contracting Co. v. Zara Contracting Co.*, 146 F.2d 606 (2d Cir. 1944), a Miller Act action, the court was faced with a situation similar to that involved here — the prime contractor had unjustifiably breached a subcontract after partial performance by the subcontractor. The court stated:

> For it is an accepted principle of contract law, often applied in the case of construction contracts, that the promisee upon breach has the option to forego any suit on the contract and claim only the reasonable value of his performance. 146 F.2d at 610.

The Tenth Circuit has also stated that the right to seek recovery under quantum meruit in a Miller Act case is clear. Quantum meruit recovery is not limited to an action against the prime contractor but may also be brought against the Miller Act surety, as in this case. Further, that the complaint is not clear in regard to the theory of a plaintiff's recovery does not preclude recovery under quantum meruit. *Narragansett Improvement Co. v. United States*, 290 F.2d 577 (1st Cir. 1961). A plaintiff may join a claim for quantum meruit with a claim for damages from breach of contract.

In the present case, Coastal has, at its own expense, provided Blair with labor and the use of equipment. Blair, who breached the subcontract, has retained these benefits without having fully paid for them. On these facts, Coastal is entitled to restitution in quantum meruit. The "restitution interest," involving a combination of unjust impoverishment with unjust gain, presents the strongest case for relief. If, following Aristotle, we regard the purpose of justice as the maintenance of an equilibrium of goods among members of society, the restitution interest presents twice as strong a claim to judicial intervention as the reliance interest, since if A not only causes B to lose one unit but appropriates that unit to himself, the resulting discrepancy between A and B is not one unit but two. Fuller & Perdue, *The Reliance Interest in Contract Damages*, 46 YALE L.J. 52, 56 (1936).

The impact of quantum meruit is to allow a promisee to recover the value of services he gave to the defendant irrespective of whether he would have lost money on the contract and been unable to recover in a suit on the contract. *Scaduto v.*

Orlando, 381 F.2d 587, 595 (2d Cir. 1967). The measure of recovery for quantum meruit is the reasonable value of the performance, RESTATEMENT OF CONTRACTS § 347 (1932); and recovery is undiminished by any loss which would have been incurred by complete performance. 12 WILLISTON ON CONTRACTS § 1485, at 312 (3d ed. 1970). While the contract price may be evidence of reasonable value of the services, it does not measure the value of the performance or limit recovery.[1] Rather, the standard for measuring the reasonable value of the services rendered is the amount for which such services could have been purchased from one in the plaintiff's position at the time and place the services were rendered.

Since the district court has not yet accurately determined the reasonable value of the labor and equipment use furnished by Coastal to Blair, the case must be remanded for those findings. When the amount has been determined, judgment will be entered in favor of Coastal, less payments already made under the contract. Accordingly, for the reasons stated above, the decision of the district court is

Reversed and remanded with instructions.

NOTES & QUESTIONS

1. The restitution remedy, which seeks to restore a party to his or her original position as it was prior to loss or injury, is also applied in various cases to place a party in the position in which he or she would have been, had a breach or a supervening impediment to contract performance, not occurred. It often has the object of preventing unjust enrichment and unjust detriment. Restitution can be sought in situations other than those involving promises, and is treated generally in the RESTATEMENT OF RESTITUTION (American Law Institute, 1937).

2. The RESTATEMENT (SECOND) OF CONTRACTS deals with the remedy of restitution in some seven areas that involve or are otherwise closely related to contracts.

> The first is that in which the other party is in breach and the party seeking restitution has chosen it as an alternative to the enforcement of the contract between them (§ 373). In the second the party seeking restitution claims the benefit that he has conferred under the contract because he is precluded by his own breach from enforcing the contract (§ 374). In the third situation the party seeking restitution claims the benefit that he has conferred under the contract because he is precluded from enforcing it against the other party because of the Statute of Frauds (§ 375). The fourth situation is that in which a party claims restitution upon avoidance of a contract on the ground, for example, of mistake, misrepresentation or duress (§ 376). The fifth is that in which he claims restitution on the ground that his duty of performance did not arise or was discharged as a result of impracticability of performance, frustration of purpose, non-occurrence of a condition or disclaimer by a beneficiary (§ 377).

Introduction to RESTATEMENT (SECOND), CONTRACTS. The sixth area involves a party's right to restitution under a contract unenforceable because of public policy (*see*

---

[1] [7]. . .It should be noted, however, that in suits for restitution there are many cases permitting the plaintiff to recover the value of benefits conferred on the defendant, even though this value exceeds that of the return performance promised by the defendant. In these cases it is no doubt felt that the defendant's breach should work a forfeiture of his right to retain the benefits of an advantageous bargain. Fuller & Perdue, *supra* at 77.

REST. (SECOND), CONTRACTS, Chapter 8, Topic 5); and the seventh area deals with the right to restitution consequent upon an agreement of rescission (*see* REST. (SECOND), CONTRACTS, § 283, comment c).

3. In *Algernon-Blair* the court held that the non-breaching subcontractor could sue the breaching contractor in quantum meruit (i.e., an action founded on an implied promise, in which recovery is based on the reasonable value of services rendered), and is not limited to suit on the express contract that had been terminated by the contractor's breach. The court also held that such implied contract recovery is available even if the plaintiff would not have been entitled to recover in the breach of contract suit.

4. *Problem (a).* Assume that the subject subcontract contains the following clause: "In the event of any suit by either party against the other arising out of this contract or relating to duties undertaken or performed pursuant to this contract, recovery is hereby agreed to be limited to $50.00." What effect, if any, do you expect that clause would have on the quantum meruit claim filed by the subcontractor against the contractor?

5. *Problem (b).* Assume that the subcontract contains the following provision: "In the event of breach by the contractor, the parties agree that recovery by the subcontractor shall not exceed the actual net profit to be earned by the subcontractor under this contract." What effect would this clause have on the quantum meruit claim?

American Trading & Production Corp. v. Shell Intern. Marine Ltd., 453 F.2d 939 (2d Cir. 1972). In this suit a ship owner sued the charterer, seeking additional shipping charges for delivering a cargo of oil from Texas to India via a route around the Cape of Good Hope, rather than via the shorter Suez Canal route rendered unavailable when the Suez Canal was closed to shipping. The additional expense involved in using the longer route was $131,978.44, an increase of somewhat less than one-third over the agreed-upon rate of $417,327.36. On appeal, the trial court's dismissal of the claim was affirmed. In its opinion the appeals court held that (a) the closing of the Suez Canal route did not under the doctrine reflected in RESTATEMENT OF CONTRACTS § 460 (1932) render the contract legally impossible to perform, discharge unperformed contract obligations, and render the charterer liable in quantum meruit for the benefit conferred by delivery via the Cape of Good Hope route; and (b) there existed no commercial impracticability within the principle referred to in RESTATEMENT OF CONTRACTS § 454 (1932) sufficient to excuse performance of the charter even though additional expense of about one-third was involved. The court also noted that (a) the charter party did not refer to a fixed route, (b) the agreement merely contemplated that passage via the Suez Canal would be the probable route, (c) it was understood in the shipping industry that the Cape route was an acceptable alternative in voyages of this nature, and (d) the ability to use the Suez Canal route was not made a condition to performance even though the agreed rate was in accordance with a rate schedule based on passage via the Suez Canal.

ALBRE MARBLE & TILE CO. v. JOHN BOWEN CO.
338 Mass. 394, 155 N.E.2d 437 (1959)

SPALDING, Justice:

The declaration in this action of contract contains four counts. The plaintiff in counts 1 and 2 seeks damages for the defendant's alleged breach of two subcontracts under which the plaintiff agreed to supply labor and materials to the defendant as general contractor of the Chronic Disease Hospital and Nurses' Home in Boston. In counts 3 and 4 the plaintiff seeks to recover the value of work and labor furnished by it to the defendant at the defendant's request. The defendant's substitute answer in defence to the first two counts states that the performance of the subcontracts became impossible when the defendant's general contract with the Commonwealth was declared invalid by this court in *Gifford v. Commissioner of Public Health*, 328 Mass. 608, 105 N.E.2d 476. The defendant's answer to counts 3 and 4 (based on quantum meruit) states that no payment could be demanded because the plaintiff did not possess an architect's certificate for the work done; and that in no event could the defendant be required to pay the plaintiff until it was itself paid by the Commonwealth, and it had received no such payments except those which had been made before the *Gifford* decision. . . .

The first question is whether the pleadings and affidavits show that a genuine issue of fact exists as to counts 1 and 2, alleging breach of contract.

. . . The plaintiff . . . attempted to avoid the defence of impossibility by asserting that the invalidity of the general contract was caused by the wrongful acts of the defendant.

. . . We are of opinion . . . that the granting of the defendant's motion for judgment on counts 1 and 2 was right.

We turn now to counts 3 and 4 by which the plaintiff seeks a recovery for the fair value of work and labor furnished to the defendant prior to the termination of the general contract. The plaintiff seeks recovery in count 3 for "preparation of samples, shop drawings, tests and affidavits" in connection with the tile work; in count 4 recovery for similar work in connection with the marble contract is sought.

The defendant in its affidavit maintains that the tile and marble work to be furnished by the plaintiff could not have been done until late in the construction process; that no tile or marble was actually installed in the building; and that the expenses incurred by the plaintiff prior to the time the general contract was declared invalid consisted solely of expenditures in preparation for performance. Relying on the decision in *Young v. Chicopee*, 186 Mass. 518, 72 N.E. 63, the defendant maintains that where a building contract has been rendered impossible of performance a plaintiff may not recover for expenses incurred in preparation for performance, but may recover only for the labor and materials "wrought into" the structure. Therefore, the defendant says, the plaintiff should take nothing here.

The plaintiff places its reliance upon a clause appearing in both contracts which provides in part: "It is agreed you [the plaintiff] will furnish and submit all necessary or required samples, shop drawings, tests, affidavits, etc., for approval, all as ordered or specified. . . ." The plaintiff in effect concedes that no labor or materials were actually wrought into the structure, but argues that the contract provision quoted above placed its preparatory efforts under the supervision of the defendant, and that this circumstance removes this case from the ambit of those decisions which apply the "wrought-in" principle.

In *Boston Plate & Window Glass Co. v. John Bowen Co., Inc.*, 335 Mass. 697, 141 N.E.2d 715, a case involving the same general factual situation as is presented here, it was pointed out that the declaration did not contain a count based on quantum meruit, and for that reason it was unnecessary to decide whether "recovery may be had for payments made or obligations reasonably incurred in preparation for performance of a contract after it has been executed and delivered and is reasonably understood to be in effect." 335 Mass. 697, at page 702, 141 N.E.2d 715, 718. That question is now before us.

The problem of allocating losses where a building contract has been rendered impossible of performance by a supervening act not chargeable to either party is a vexed one. In situations where the part performance of one party measurably exceeds that of the other the tendency has been to allow recovery for the fair value of work done in the actual performance of the contract and to deny recovery for expenditures made in reliance upon the contract or in preparing to perform. This principle has sometimes been expressed in terms of "benefit" or "lack of benefit." In other words, recovery may be had only for those expenditures which, but for the supervening act, would have enured to the benefit of the defendant as contemplated by the contract. [Citation] The "wrought-in" principle applied in building contract cases is merely a variant of this principle. It has long been recognized that this theory is unworkable if the concept of benefit is applied literally. In *M. Ahern Co. v. John Bowen Co. Inc.*, 334 Mass. 36, 41, 133 N.E.2d 484, 487, we quoted with approval the statement of Professor Williston that "It is enough that the defendant has actually received in part performance of the contract something for which when completed he had agreed to pay a price." WILLISTON ON CONTRACTS (Rev. ed.) § 1976.

Although the matter of denial of reliance expenditures in impossibility situations seems to have been discussed but little in judicial opinions, it has, however, been the subject of critical comment by scholars. *See* Fuller and Perdue, *The Reliance Interest in Contract Damages*, 46 YALE L.J. 52, 373, 379–383. *Note* 46 MICH. L. REV. 401. In England the recent frustrated contracts legislation provides that the court may grant recovery for expenditures in reliance on the contract or in preparation to perform it where it appears "*just to do so having regard to all the circumstances of the case*" (emphasis supplied [by the court]). 6 & 7 George VI, c. 40.

We are of opinion that the plaintiff here may recover for those expenditures made pursuant to the specific request of the defendant as set forth in the contract clause quoted above. A combination of factors peculiar to this case justifies such a holding without laying down the broader principle that in every case recovery may be had for payments made or obligations reasonably incurred in preparation for performance of a contract where further performance is rendered impossible without fault by either party. . . .

The factors which determine the holding here are these: First, this is not a case of mere impossibility by reason of a supervening act. The opinion of this court in *M. Ahern Co. v. John Bowen Co. Inc.*, 334 Mass. 36, 133 N.E.2d 484, points out that the defendant's involvement in creating the impossibility was greater than that of its subcontractors. . . . Although the defendant's conduct was not so culpable as to render it liable for breach of contract [citation], nevertheless, it was a contributing factor to a loss sustained by the plaintiff which as between the plaintiff and the defendant the latter ought to bear to the extent herein permitted.

We attach significance to the clause in the contract, which was prepared by the defendant, specifically requesting the plaintiff to submit samples, shop drawings, tests, affidavits, etc., to the defendant. This is not a case in which all efforts in preparation for performance were solely within the discretion and control of the subcontractor. We are mindful that in *Young v. Chicopee*, 186 Mass. 518, 72 N.E. 63, recovery of the value of materials brought to the construction site at the specific request of the defendant therein was denied. But in that case the supervening act rendering further performance impossible was a fire not shown to have been caused by the fault of either party. We are not disposed to extend that holding to a situation in which the defendant's fault is greater than the plaintiff's.

Moreover, the acts requested here by their very nature could not be "wrought into" the structure. In *Angus v. Scully*, 176 Mass. 357, 57 N.E. 674, 49 A.L.R. 562, recovery for the value of services rendered by house movers was allowed although the house was destroyed midway in the moving. The present case comes nearer to the rationale of the *Angus* case than to that of the *Young* case.

The defense that the defendant was not required to pay until it had been paid by the Commonwealth under the general contract was declared to be without merit in *M. Ahern Co. v. John Bowen Co. Inc.*, 334 Mass. 36, 133 N.E.2d 484, and need not be dealt with here.

We hold that the damages to be assessed are limited solely to the fair value of those acts done in conformity with the specific request of the defendant as contained in the contract. Expenses incurred prior to the execution of the contract, such as those arising out of preparing the plaintiff's bid, are not to be considered.

The plaintiff's exceptions as to counts 1 and 2 are overruled and are sustained as to counts 3 and 4; as to those counts the case is remanded to the Superior Court for further proceedings in conformity with this opinion. The appeal is dismissed.

So ordered.

2.   Restitution and Promissory Estoppel

WHEELER v. WHITE
398 S.W.2d 93 (Tex. 1965)

SMITH, Justice: This is a suit for damages brought by petitioner, Ellis D. Wheeler, against respondent, S. E. White. Wheeler alleged that White had breached a contract to secure a loan or furnish the money to finance the construction of improvements upon land owned by Wheeler. Wheeler further pleaded, in the alternative, that if the contract itself was not sufficiently definite, then nevertheless White was estopped from asserting such insufficiency. White filed special exceptions to all of Wheeler's Third Amended Original Petition. The special exceptions asserted that the pleaded contract did not contain essential elements to its enforceability in that it failed to provide the amount of monthly installments, the amount of interest due upon the obligation, how such interest would be computed, when such interest would be paid, and that the alternative plea of estoppel was, as a matter of law, insufficient to establish any ground of recovery. All special exceptions were sustained, and upon Wheeler's declination to amend his pleadings, the trial court entered its judgment dismissing the case and ordered that Wheeler take nothing from White by reason of his suit. The Court of Civil Appeals has affirmed the judgment of the trial court. 385 S.W.2d 619. We have concluded that the trial court did not err in sustaining the special exceptions directed at the sufficiency of the contract itself, but that Wheeler's pleadings on the theory of estoppel state a cause of action. Accordingly, we reverse the judgments of the trial court and the Court of Civil Appeals and remand the cause for trial.

Since the trial court sustained White's special exceptions to wheeler's petition, we necessarily must assume that all the alleged material facts are true. Wheeler alleged that as the owner of a three-lot tract of land in Port Arthur, Texas, he desired to construct a commercial building or shopping center thereon. He and White entered into an agreement, embodied in the written contract involved here, whereby White was to obtain the necessary loan for Wheeler from a third party or provide it himself on or before six months from the date of the contract. The loan as described in the contract, was to be ". . . in the sum of SEVENTY THOUSAND AND 00/100 ($70,000.00) DOLLARS and to be payable in monthly installments over a term of fifteen (15) years and bear interest at a rate of not more than six (6%) per cent per annum." Additionally, under the contract White was to be paid $5,000.00 for obtaining the loan and a five per cent commission on all rentals received from any tenants procured by White for the building. Wheeler alleged that he has been ready and willing to comply with his part of the agreement at all times since the contract was made.

After the contract had been signed by both parties, White assured Wheeler that the money would be available and urged him to proceed with the necessary task of demolishing the buildings presently on the site so as to make way for construction of the new building. The buildings on the site had a reasonable value of $58,500.00 and a rental value of $400.00 per month. By way of reassurance, White stressed the fact that in the event the money was unobtainable elsewhere, he would make the loan himself. Pursuant to such promises Wheeler proceeded to raze the old building and otherwise prepare the land for the new structure; thereafter, he was told by White that there would be no loan. After White's refusal to perform, Wheeler made reasonable efforts to obtain the loan himself but was unsuccessful. In the pleadings Wheeler pleaded the necessary elements of inducement and reliance which entitle him to recover if he can prove the facts alleged.

Where a promisee acts to his detriment in reasonable reliance upon an otherwise unenforceable promise, courts in other jurisdictions have recognized that the disappointed party may have a substantial and compelling claim for relief. The RESTATEMENT, CONTRACTS, section 90, says: "A promise which the promisor should reasonably expect to induce action or forbearance of a definite and substantial character on the part of the promisee and which does induce such action or forbearance is binding if injustice can be avoided only by enforcement of the promise." According to Dean Hildebrand's Texas Annotation to the Restatement, Texas follows Section 90, *supra*. *See Ferguson v. Getzendaner*, 83 S.W. 374, 98 Tex. 310 (1904); *Morris v. Gaines*, 17 S.W. 538, 82 Tex. 255 (1891); and others. These early cases do not speak of the doctrine of promissory estoppel in specific terms since those cases were written before the compilation of the RESTATEMENT, but, while many of them dealt with subscription transactions or transactions within the statute of frauds, it is readily apparent that the equities involved in those cases are applicable to the instant case. . . .

The binding thread which runs through the cases applying promissory estoppel is the existence of promises designedly made to influence the conduct of the promisee, tacitly encouraging the conduct, which conduct, although not necessarily constituting any actual performance of the contract itself, is something that must be done by the promisee before he could begin to perform, and was a fact known to the promisor. As to the argument that no new cause of action may be created by such a promise regardless of its established applicability as a defense, it has been answered that where one party has by his words or conduct made to the other a promise or assurance which was intended to affect the legal relations between them and to be acted on accordingly, then, once the other party has taken him at his word and acted on it, the party who gave the promise cannot afterward be allowed to revert to the previous relationship as if no such promise had been made. This does not create a contract where none existed before, but only prevents a party from insisting upon his strict legal rights when it would be unjust to allow him to enforce them. *See* 1 Williston, CONTRACTS, §§ 139-40 (Rev. ed. 1936); and 48 A.L.R.2d 1069 (1956).

The function of the doctrine of promissory estoppel is, under our view, defensive in that it estops a promisor from denying the enforceability of the promise. It was said in the case of *Dickerson v. Colgrove*, 100 U.S. 578, 580, 25 L. Ed. 618, that:

> The vital principle is that he who by his language or conduct leads another to do what he would not otherwise have done, shall not subject such person to loss or injury by disappointing the expectations upon which he acted. Such a change of position is sternly forbidden . . . . This remedy is always so applied as to promote the ends of justice.

In the case of *Goodman v. Dicker*, 169 F.2d 684, 83 U.S. App. D.C. 353 (1948), the trial court held that a contract had not been proven but that ". . . appellants were estopped from denying the same by reason of their statements and conduct upon which appellees relied to their detriment." In that case, Dicker relied upon a promise by Goodman that a franchise to sell radios would be granted and radios would be supplied. In reliance upon the promise, Dicker incurred expenses in making preparations to engage in the business of selling radios. The franchise was not granted and Goodman failed to deliver the radios. The appellate court in holding that Dicker was entitled to damages for moneys expended in preparing to do business, said:

> We are dealing with a promise by appellants that a franchise would be granted and radios supplied, on the faith of which appellees with the knowledge and encouragement of appellants incurred expenses in making preparations to do business. Under these circumstances we think that appellants cannot now advance any defense inconsistent with their assurance that the franchise would be granted. Justice and fair dealing require that one who acts to his detriment on the faith of conduct of the kind revealed here should be protected by estopping the party who has brought about the situation from alleging anything in opposition to the natural consequences of his own course of conduct. . . .

The Court, having so held, rendered its judgment that Goodman was liable for moneys expended in preparing to do business under the promised dealer franchise, but was not liable for loss of profits on the radios which were never delivered.

The Court in the *Goodman* case, in refusing to allow damages based on a loss of anticipated profits, apparently acted in harmony with the theory that promissory estoppel acts defensively so as to prevent an attack upon the enforceability of a contract. Under this theory, losses of expected profits will not be allowed even if expected profits are provable with certainty. The rule thus announced should be followed in the present case. We agree with the reasoning announced in those jurisdictions that, in cases such as we have before us, where there is actually no contract the promissory estoppel theory may be invoked, thereby supplying a remedy which will enable the injured party to be compensated for his foreseeable, definite and substantial reliance. Where the promisee has failed to bind the promisor to a legally sufficient contract, but where the promisee has acted in reliance upon a promise to his detriment, the promisee is to be allowed to recover no more than reliance damages measured by the detriment sustained. Since the promisee in such cases is partially responsible for his failure to bind the promisor to a legally sufficient contract, it is reasonable to conclude that all that is required to achieve justice is to put the promisee in the position he would have been in had he not acted in reliance upon the promise. . . .

The judgments of the trial court and the Court of Civil Appeals are both reversed and judgment is here entered remanding the cause to the trial court for trial on its merits in accordance with this opinion.

GREENHILL, Justice (concurring):

The Court of Civil Appeals denied a recovery of damages here because the contract, it felt, was too indefinite in its provisions under *Bryant v. Clark*, 358 S.W.2d 614, 163 Tex. 596 (1962). The holding in *Bryant v. Clark* was that the contract was not sufficiently definite to be specifically enforceable. The contract here in question, viewed in context, is different in some respects from that in the *Bryant* case; and I would not extend *Bryant v. Clark*. See the criticism of that case in FA CORBIN, CONTRACTS 283 (1964).

But assuming that the contract here, under *Bryant v. Clark*, is not definite enough to be specifically enforced, it is sufficiently definite to support an action for damages. RESTATEMENT, CONTRACTS § 370, comment b.

There are Texas cases in which damages have been denied after a holding that the contract was not specifically enforceable. . . . In each of these cases, however, the contracts were held to be within the Statute of Frauds and not enforceable for that reason in a suit for damages. 1 WILLISTON, CONTRACTS § 16 (Rev. ed. 1936). The contract here in question is not within the Statute of Frauds and will support an action for damages.

While I agree with the judgment entered by the Court, it seems to me that the above is a sounder ground upon which to rest our decision.

NOTES & QUESTIONS

1. The majority opinion in *Wheeler* includes rulings to the effect that: (a) the promissory estoppel principle operates defensively; (b) when it applies the injured party may recover for losses due to his foreseeable, definite and substantial reliance; and (c) losses of expected profits will not be allowed even if expected profits are provable with certainty.

2. *Questions*: If the promissory estoppel principle operates (defensively) to prevent the promisor from attacking the enforceability of his promise, why should the promise not be treated as any other enforceable contractual promise? Is it not true that recovery for breach of enforceable contractual promises includes compensation for loss of the benefit of the bargain? If the theory of the concurring

opinion in *Wheeler* were adopted by the majority, would expectancy damages as well as reliance losses be recoverable?

3. When setting forth their respective theories, both the majority and the concurring opinions in *Wheeler* made mention of the statute of frauds. In *Whiteco Industries, Inc. v. Kopani*, 514 N.E.2d 840 (Ind. App. 1987), the court rejected a contention by plaintiff employees that the statute of frauds defense raised by defendant employer should be inapplicable because of promissory estoppel or constructive fraud, and held that an estoppel that will remove a case from the operation of the statute of frauds requires a showing that the other party's refusal to carry out the terms of the agreement has resulted:

> not merely in a denial of the rights which the agreement was intended to confer, but the infliction of an unjust and unconscionable injury and loss . . . In other words, neither the benefit of the bargain itself, nor mere inconvenience, incidental expenses, etc. short of a reliance injury so substantial and independent as to constitute an unjust and unconscionable injury and loss are sufficient to remove the claim from the operation of the Statute of Frauds.

Whiteco Industries further concludes that the law of Indiana defines avoidance of "injustice" more narrowly than is proposed in RESTATEMENT (SECOND) OF CONTRACTS § 139 ("Enforcement by virtue of action in reliance"), and notes that the drafters of that restatement section envisioned defining the term by use of a more "flexible principle" than do the courts of Indiana.

4. Consider what remedies may be appropriate for a promissory estoppel case in light of RESTATEMENT (SECOND) OF CONTRACTS § 139. The *Whiteco Industries* court quotes that RESTATEMENT section in full:

> (1) A promise which the promisor should reasonably expect to induce action or forbearance on the part of the promisee or a third person and which does induce the action or forbearance is enforceable notwithstanding the Statute of Frauds if injustice can be avoided only by enforcement of the promise. The remedy granted for breach is to be limited as justice requires.

> (2) In determining whether injustice can be avoided only by enforcement of the promise, the following circumstances are significant:

> (a) the availability and adequacy of other remedies, particularly cancellation and restitution;

> (b) the definite and substantial character of the action or forbearance in relation to the remedy sought;

> (c) the extent to which the action or forbearance corroborates evidence of the making and terms of the promise, or the making and terms are otherwise established by clear and convincing evidence;

> (d) the reasonableness of the action or forbearance;

> (e) the extent to which the action or forbearance was foreseeable by the promisor.

3.   Restitution and Rescinded or Discharged Contracts

CBS, INC. v. MERRICK
716 F.2d 1292 (9th Cir. 1983)

SOLOMON, Senior District Judge:

CBS, Inc., appellee, filed an action against David Merrick in the Los Angeles County Superior Court for rescission seeking restitution and consequential damages. Merrick removed the action on the grounds of diversity of citizenship to the federal court where he filed an answer and also a counterclaim for damages for breach of contract. Thereafter, CBS filed an amended complaint containing a separate cause of action for damages for breach of contract. After a court trial, the district court found that Merrick had breached his contract with CBS and awarded CBS the amount it had paid Merrick and his agent but denied CBS recovery for the amount paid out to Friedkin, the director, and Green, the screenwriter, after execution of and in reliance on the contract. The court denied Merrick any relief. Both parties appeal.

CBS contends that the district court erred in refusing to award reliance damages in addition to the award for restitution.

Facts

David Merrick is a well known producer of entertainment programs for stage and screen. CBS is a major television network.

In early 1977, Merrick acquired the motion picture and television rights to the novel Blood and Money. CBS negotiated with Merrick for the right to do a mini-series based on that novel, and on August 1, 1977, the parties signed two documents — a Rights Agreement and a Production Agreement.

In the Rights Agreement, CBS agreed to pay Merrick $1,250,000 for the right to do a television series based on Blood and Money. CBS paid Merrick $833,333.34 when the agreement was executed and agreed to pay Merrick the balance in installments when various stages of production were completed. It was agreed that if photography did not commence within two years, that is, by August 1, 1979, the agreement would terminate and CBS would pay Merrick the balance owed on the contract. In addition, the rights to Blood and Money would revert to Merrick. The agreement required all modifications to be in writing.

In the Production Agreement, CBS agreed to pay Merrick an additional $250,000 to produce the show. The parties agreed to consult on the selection of the writer, director and principal actors. Merrick would then negotiate the terms and conditions of their employment, and CBS would then enter into contracts with these persons containing the terms negotiated by Merrick.

. . . CBS had ninety days from the delivery of the final screenplay to notify Merrick whether it would proceed with the project. If CBS elected not to proceed and if Merrick had not breached the contract and was ready, willing and able to perform his duties as producer, CBS was obligated to pay Merrick the entire $250,000 and all rights to the story Blood and Money would revert to him.

Merrick promptly selected a director and screenwriter. The fee for the director was $500,000 regardless of whether the show was produced. The fee for the screenwriter was $250,000. When Merrick hired them, he knew that they were working on another project and that they could not immediately start to work on Blood and Money. Merrick failed to tell them about the deadline, and he ignored suggestions that he hire a second writer.

The first segment of the screenplay was not delivered until September, 1978, and the screenplay was not completed until June, 1979. However, by April, 1979, it was apparent that the August 1, 1979 deadline could not be met because at that time the screenplay had not been completed and at least six months' pre-production work was required before photography could start.

On April 9, 1979, Merrick met with CBS executives, and he orally agreed to extend the deadline. CBS sent Merrick proposed drafts of a written amendment. Although Merrick did not object to the basic terms, he objected to their form and complexity. CBS delivered a simplified draft to Merrick, but he never signed it.

On May 17, 1979, Merrick's attorney sent a telex to CBS stating that Merrick would not agree to any changes in the original agreements. Nevertheless, Merrick continued to act as though the deadline had been extended, and later he described the telex as "lawyer stuff." Five days before the August 1 deadline, CBS told Merrick of its decision to proceed with the production of the show. Merrick expressed enthusiasm for the project. Twelve days after the deadline, CBS and Merrick met to plan the project.

On August 24, 1979, CBS met with Merrick's agents to discuss a budget and a tentative production schedule, but in the following month Merrick notified CBS that all rights to the story had reverted to him because CBS had not met the August 1 deadline. No further work was ever done on the project.

The district court found in favor of CBS and against Merrick on six separate grounds: (1) Merrick waived his right to enforce the deadline; (2) Merrick was estopped from asserting the deadline; (3) CBS's failure to meet the deadline was excused because Merrick contributed to the failure; (4) Merrick breached his oral agreement to extend the deadline; (5) Merrick failed to meet an express condition precedent of the contract in that he was not ready, willing and able to perform; and (6) Merrick breached the agreement before the deadline.

The court awarded CBS the $833,333.34 it had paid Merrick and also $83,333.33, the amount that CBS had paid William Morris Agency, Merrick's agents. The court denied CBS the $750,000 which CBS was contractually liable to pay the director and screenwriter for their services. The court also denied Merrick any recovery on his counterclaim.

I. Merrick's Appeal

Merrick, in this appeal, asserts that under New York law, which the contract provides and the parties agree shall govern their controversy, the district court erred in awarding CBS rescission and restitution and any damages, and in refusing to award Merrick any relief. Specifically, Merrick asserts that the district court was clearly in error when it found in favor of CBS on the six separate grounds, including findings that Merrick had no excuse for his refusal to perform his contract with CBS and that he waived his right to have the photography commence before August 1, 1979.

Waiver is the intentional relinquishment of a known right with knowledge of its existence and the intent to relinquish it. . . . A contractual deadline may be waived by acts, words or conduct inconsistent with the deadline. . . .

The existence of a waiver is usually a fact question; therefore, the trial court's finding should be upheld unless it is clearly erroneous. Fed. R. Civ. P. 52(a). The district court found Merrick's conduct and words inconsistent with the August 1, 1979 deadline. . . . He orally agreed to waive the deadline, and he met with CBS and encouraged the development of the project both before and after the deadline had passed. These discussions amply support the district court's finding that Merrick waived his right to enforce the deadline and that CBS relied on that waiver to its detriment.

There is no merit in Merrick's contention that any amendment to the agreements must be in writing. The contract so provides, but a clause in a contract that requires amendments to be in writing may itself be waived. [Citation] By his words and conduct, Merrick waived the provision. CBS's detrimental reliance on the oral modification also prevents Merrick from invoking the clause to prevent proof of the modification. . . .

There was ample evidence to support the court's other findings that Merrick refused to perform and had breached his contract with CBS.

II. CBS's Cross-Appeal

The district court found that CBS's complaint sought rescission and restitution and in a separate cause of action sought damages for breach of contract. A party injured by a breach of a contract may recover both restitution and reliance damages. . . . A party may rescind a contract if there was fraud in the inception or if there was a substantial breach. . . . The district court listed many reasons why Merrick's refusal to perform was unjustified and held that "Merrick materially breached the Rights Agreement and the Production Agreement by repudiating them without justification."

In its findings on damages, the district held that "Merrick must return to CBS the amounts which it paid him under the contract." The court also found that CBS is entitled to rescission "both because Merrick expressly repudiated the modified contract and because he breached the original contract," and it therefore awarded CBS $916,666.67, the amount it paid both to Merrick and his agent, the William Morris Agency.

This award of restitution damages is proper under either rescission or breach of contract. When a breach occurs after the execution of the contract, the injured party in a contract action is entitled to both restitution and reliance damages.

Here, the district court found substantial breaches of contract. Nevertheless, the court limited recovery to restitution, the only recovery available when the contract is illegal or void from its inception. The court refused to allow reliance damages even though it found breaches of the contract.

This was error. This action must therefore be remanded to the district court to determine what part, if any, of the $750,000 paid to the director and screenwriter are legitimate reliance damages. In connection with this determination, the court should consider questions like reasonable reliance on the agreement, attempts to mitigate damages, the value of the screenplay delivered to CBS, and the foreseeability of the loss.

The district court's finding that Merrick is liable to CBS for breach of contract is Affirmed. The award to CBS of $916,666.67 it paid to Merrick and his agent is also Affirmed. The denial of amounts paid to Friedkin, the director, and Green, the screenwriter, by CBS in reliance on its contract with Merrick is Reversed and Remanded for proceedings consistent with this opinion.

NELSON, Circuit Judge, concurring: I concur in the majority opinion but believe that the applicable law in section II requires further clarification.

The proper measure of damages in this case depends on an interpretation of an unclear area of New York law. Although CBS denominated its complaint below as one for rescission, I believe CBS's lawsuit was effectively a breach of contract action. The complaint sought restitution instead of lost profits because of the speculative nature of the breached contract. The question presented to us, then, is whether an award of restitution when used as a substitute for speculative lost profits in a breach of contract action should preclude the recovery of additional measures of damages.

In seeking to answer this question of New York law, I have found neither a New York statute that is directly controlling nor a decision by the New York Court of Appeals that is directly on point. I would therefore have this court turn to other relevant sources of New York law and sit, in effect, as a New York state court. *Commissioner v. Estate of Bosch*, 387 U.S. 456, 465, 87 S. Ct. 1776, 1782, 18 L. Ed. 2d 886 (1967).

The phrase "rescission and restitution" has two meanings in New York. *Richard v. Credit Suisse*, 242 N.Y. 346, 152 N.E. 110, 111 (1926) (Cardozo, J.). When used in the context of a voidable or mutually rescinded contract, "rescission and restitution" means that a contract is treated as void *ab initio*. *Id.* On the other hand, a party seeking rescission and restitution in a breach of contract action does not seek to undo the contract from its beginning. *Id.; see generally* D. Dobbs, HANDBOOK ON THE LAW OF REMEDIES § 12.1, at 793 (1973); 5 A. Corbin, CORBIN ON CONTRACTS §§ 1104-1106 (1964). Instead, a plaintiff may request restitution in a breach of contract action as a substitute measure of lost profits where, as here, the true measure of lost profits would be purely speculative. *Nelson v. Hatch*, 70 A.D. 206, 75 N.Y.S. 389, 393 (1902), *aff'd* 174 N.Y. 596, 67 N.E. 1085 (1903) (law firm breached contract to prosecute lawsuit and was required to return pre-paid fee).

New York law is unclear on whether the two different meanings of the phrase "rescission and restitution" produce two different answers to the question whether a plaintiff can recover restitution plus additional damages. I conclude that they do. A plaintiff who elects to rescind his voidable contract cannot avoid the contract for purposes of restitution and invoke it for purposes of recovering special damages.[2] *See Sheridan Drive-In, Inc. v. New York*, 16 A.D.2d 400, 407, 228 N.Y.S.2d 576

---

[2] In 1941, New York created a narrow exception to its rule denying reliance and consequential damages when a voidable contract is rescinded. Such damages are recoverable in addition to restitution when the contract was induced by fraud or misrepresentation. N.Y. CIV. PRAC. LAW § 3002(e) (McKinney 1974). In arguing that this statute describes the only circumstance in which a plaintiff can recover both

(1962) (no consequential damages where contract rescinded because of mistake that either was mutual or resulted from innocent misrepresentation); *Rodriguez v. Northern Auto Auction, Inc.*, 35 Misc. 2d 395, 396, 225 N.Y.S.2d 107 (Sup. Ct. 1962) (no consequential damages where contract rescinded because of infancy), *Naimoli v. Massa*, 81 Misc. 2d 431, 366 N.Y.S.2d 573 (City Ct. 1975) (no reliance damages where contract mutually rescinded). In such cases, a plaintiff suing for rescission and restitution can recover only those benefits that he has conferred on the defendant. RESTATEMENT (SECOND) OF CONTRACTS § 370 (1981).

In contrast, because it does not actually "rescind" the breached contract, an award of restitution in a breach of contract action should not preclude the award of additional measures of damages. I have found only two cases that reach this conclusion under New York law. *See Nelson v. Hatch*, 75 N.Y.S. at 394 (where lost profits from contract were speculative, plaintiff properly "permitted to prove the moneys which he advanced, and the expenses which he incurred in connection with it") (dictum); *Sperry & Hutchinson Co. v. O'Neill-Adams Co.*, 185 F. 231, 239–40 (2d Cir. 1911) (where trading stamp suppliers' breach caused unknown loss of profits, New York law held to permit recovery of restitution of price paid for unused trading stamps plus consequential damages incurred in redeeming already distributed stamps). Neither case is binding on this court, and both predate *Richard v. Credit Suisse*, *supra*, the opinion that gives them their analytical underpinning. Still, the conclusion of each case, although not black letter law in New York, accords with a report by New York's Law Revision Commission[3] and with the position of most commentators.

I therefore concur with the majority's conclusion that a New York court would permit recovery of restitution plus additional measures of contract damages in this case. I also concur with the necessity of a remand. In rejecting CBS's claim for full contract damages and relying instead on a purely restitutionary measure, the district court failed to pass on several issues necessary to measure breach of contract damages. Both parties address these issues in their briefs on appeal, but these are topics best left to the trier of fact.

4.   Restitution for a party in breach

Vines v. Orchard Hills, Inc., 181 Conn. 501, 435 A.2d 1022 (1980). Purchasers of condominium real estate defaulted on their contract, their breach arising out of a transfer to a more distant place of employment. Thereafter they filed suit against the seller, seeking to recover the sum they had given the seller as a down payment upon the signing of the contract. The contract price was $78,800, and the 10% down payment was $7,880. Although the Supreme Court of Connecticut concluded that the evidence here was insufficient to sustain a judgment in favor of the purchasers and remanded for further proceedings, the Court held that the plaintiffs did,

---

restitution and reliance damages, Merrick ignores the second meaning of "rescission and restitution" under New York law.

[3] [3] "One party to a bilateral contract is entitled, upon the ground of repudiation or material breach by the other, to treat the contract as terminated and to maintain an action against the other for 'restitution', for the reasonable value of the injured party's part performance of the contract. . . . Certainly the measure of recovery is not limited to the benefits conferred on the defendant; the purpose of the action is to restore the *plaintiff* to the situation existing before the contract was made." Leg. Doc. No. 65(b), Report of Law Commission at 46–47 (1946) . . . (emphasis in original).

indeed, have a restitutionary claim to recover sums paid that unjustly enrich the seller. Although "it is the purchasers and not the seller whose breach precipitated the present cause of action," and although "[t]he right of a contracting party, despite his default, to seek restitution for benefits conferred and allegedly unjustly retained has been much disputed in the legal literature and in the case law," the Court approved the principle that restitution is allowed notwithstanding the plaintiffs' own breach in order to prevent unjust enrichment and to avoid forfeiture. The Court noted also: (a) that to recognize a claim in restitution is "consistent with the economic functions that the law of contracts is designed to serve"; (b) that a party injured by a contract breach "is entitled to retain nothing in excess of that sum which compensates him for the loss of his bargain"; (c) that a claim for restitution "although legal in form, is equitable in nature, and permits a trial court to balance the equities, to take into account a variety of competing principles to determine whether the defendant has been unjustly enriched"; (d) that this basis for recovery is available to purchasers whose breach, as appears from this record, is not willful; and (e) that this right of restitutionary recovery requires that the purchaser establish that the seller has been unjustly enriched.

LANCELLOTTI v. THOMAS
341 Pa. Super. 1, 491 A.2d 117 (1985)

[The buyer of a luncheonette business contracted to buy the business name, goodwill, and equipment in consideration of $25,000 payable on signing of the agreement, his promise that only he would be the owner and operator of the business, and his promise to complete by May 1, 1973, 75% of a 16' × 16' addition to the existing building, costing at least $15,000. Buyer also signed a lease, pursuant to which he was to rent from sellers for a 5-year term at $8,000 per year the premises on which the business was located. Buyer, having paid sellers the $25,000 as agreed, began operating the business. When problems developed concerning the building addition buyer refused to begin construction; and a year later buyer was no longer interested in operating the business. Sellers resumed possession of the business and found that some of their equipment was missing. Buyer sued for the return of the $25,000 plus interest. Sellers counterclaimed for damages.]

SPAETH, President Judge:

This appeal raises the question of whether a defaulting purchaser of a business who has also entered into a related lease for the property can recover any part of his payments made prior to default. The common law rule precluded a breaching buyer from recovering these payments. Today, we reject this rule, which created a forfeiture of the breaching buyer's payments and unjustly enriched the nonbreaching seller, and adopt section 374 of the RESTATEMENT (SECOND) CONTRACTS (1979), which permits limited restitution. This case is remanded for further proceedings so that the trial court may apply the RESTATEMENT rule. . . .

-2-

At one time the common law rule prohibiting a defaulting party on a contract from recovering was the majority rule. J. Calamari & J. Perillo, THE LAW OF CONTRACTS § 11-26, at 427 (2d ed. 1977). However, a line of cases, apparently beginning with *Britton v. Turner*, 6 N.H. 481 (1834), departed from the common law rule. The merit of the common law rule was its recognition that the party who breaches should not be allowed "to have advantage from his own wrong." Corbin, *The Right of a Defaulting Vendee to the Restitution of Installments Paid*, 40 YALE L.J. 1013, 1014 (1931). As Professor Perillo states, allowing recovery "invites contract-breaking and rewards morally unworthy conduct." *Restitution in the Second Restatement of Contracts*, 81 COLUM. L. REV. 37, 50 (1981). Its weakness, however, was its failure to recognize that the nonbreaching party should not obtain a windfall from the breach. The party who breaches after almost completely performing should not be more severely penalized than the party who breaches by not acting at all or after only beginning to act. Under the common law rule the injured party retains more benefit the more completely the breaching party has performed prior to the default. Thus it has been said that "to allow the injured party to retain the benefit of the part performance . . . , without making restitution of any part of such value, is the enforcement of a penalty or forfeiture against the contract-breaker." Corbin, *supra*, at 1013.

Critics of the common law rule have been arguing for its demise for over fifty years. *See* Corbin, *supra*. *See also* Calamari & Perillo, *supra*, at § 11-26; 5A CORBIN ON CONTRACTS §§ 1122-1135 (1964); 12 S. Williston, A TREATISE ON THE LAW OF CONTRACTS §§ 1473-78 (3d ed. 1970). In response to this criticism an alternative rule has been adopted in the RESTATEMENT OF CONTRACTS.

The first RESTATEMENT OF CONTRACTS (1932) adopted the following rule:

§ 357. Restitution in Favor of a Plaintiff Who Is Himself in Default.

(1) Where the defendant fails or refuses to perform his contract and is justified therein by the plaintiff's own breach of duty or non-performance of a condition, but the plaintiff has rendered a part performance under the contract that is a net benefit to the defendant, the plaintiff can get judgment, except as stated in Subsection (2), for the amount of such benefit in excess of the harm that he has caused to the defendant by his own breach, in no case exceeding a ratable proportion of the agreed compensation, if (a) the plaintiff's breach or non-performance is not wilful and deliberate; or (b) the defendant, with knowledge that the plaintiff's breach of duty or non- performance of condition has occurred or will thereafter occur, assents to the rendition of the part performance, or accepts the benefit of it, or retains property received although its return in specie is still not unreasonably difficult or injurious.

(2) The plaintiff has no right to compensation for his part performance if it is merely a payment of earnest money, or if the contract provides that it may be retained and it is not so greatly in excess of the defendant's harm that the provision is rejected as imposing a penalty.

(3) The measure of the defendant's benefit from the plaintiff's part performance is the amount by which he has been enriched as a result of such performance unless the facts are those stated in Subsection (1b), in which case it is the price fixed by the contract for such part performance, or, if no price is so fixed, a ratable proportion of the total contract price.

In 1979, this rule was liberalized. RESTATEMENT (SECOND) OF CONTRACTS § 374 (1979) provides:

§ 374. Restitution in Favor of Party in Breach

(1) Subject to the rule stated in Subsection (2), if a party justifiably refuses to perform on the ground that his remaining duties of performance have been discharged by the other party's breach, the party in breach is entitled to restitution for any benefit that he has conferred by way of part performance or reliance in excess of the loss that he has caused by his own breach.

(2) To the extent that, under the manifested assent of the parties, a party's performance is to be retained in the case of breach, that party is not entitled to restitution if the value of the performance as liquidated damages is reasonable in the light of the anticipated or actual loss caused by the breach and the difficulties of proof of loss.

Thus the first RESTATEMENT's exclusion of the willful defaulting purchaser from recovery was deleted, apparently in part due to the influence of the Uniform Commercial Code's permitting recovery by a buyer who willfully defaults. *Id.*, Reporter's Note at 218. Professor Perillo suggests that the injured party has adequate protection without the common law rule. Choosing "the just path," he therefore rejects the common law rule, explaining this choice by saying that times have changed. "What appears to be just to one generation may be viewed differently by another." Perillo, *supra*, at 50. *See also* 12 S. Williston, *supra*, § 1473, at 222 ("The mores of the time and place will often determine which policy will be followed.").

Many jurisdictions have rejected the common law rule and permit recovery by the defaulting party. . . .

This development has been called the modern trend. . . . Indeed, the common law rule is no longer intact even with respect to land sales contracts. . . .

In Pennsylvania, the common law rule has been applied to contracts for the sale of real property. . . . In such cases, however, the seller has several remedies against a breaching buyer, including, in appropriate cases, an action for specific performance or for the purchase price. *See Trachtenburg v. Sibarco Stations, Inc.*, 477 Pa. 517, 384 A.2d 1209 (1978). *See also* 5A CORBIN ON CONTRACTS, *supra*, § 1145. As long as the seller remains ready, able, and willing to perform a contract for the sale of real property, the breaching buyer has no right to restitution of payments made prior to default. *See* 5A CORBIN ON CONTRACTS, *supra*, at § 1130. . . .

The viability of the common law rule permitting forfeiture has also been undermined in other areas of Pennsylvania law. In *Estate of Cahen*, 483 Pa. 157, 168 n.10, 394 A.2d 958, 964 n.10 (1978), the Supreme Court held that assuming that a breaching fiduciary could recover in unjust enrichment, the basis would be RESTATEMENT OF CONTRACTS section 357 (1932), which allows recovery by a breaching party to the extent that the benefits exceed the losses sustained by the other party. . . .

-3-

In regard to the present case, section 374 of the RESTATEMENT (SECOND) OF CONTRACTS represents a more enlightened approach than the common law rule. "Rules of contract law are not rules of punishment; the contract breaker is not an outlaw." Perillo, *supra*, at 50. The party who committed a breach should be entitled to recover "any benefit . . . in excess of the loss that he has caused by his own breach." RESTATEMENT (SECOND) OF CONTRACTS § 374(1).

This conclusion leads to the further conclusion that we should remand this case to the trial court. The trial court rested its decision on the common law rule. . . . Thus it never considered whether appellant is entitled to restitution (RESTATEMENT (SECOND) OF CONTRACTS § 374(1)) nor, if appellant is not entitled to restitution, whether retention of the $25,000 was "reasonable in the light of the anticipated or actual loss caused by the breach and the difficulties of proof of loss," *id.*, § 374(2). . . .

Remanded for further proceedings consistent with this opinion. Jurisdiction relinquished.

TAMILIA, JUDGE, dissenting:

I strongly dissent. In the first instance, the majority does not and cannot cite any Pennsylvania authority adopting the rule cited in section 374 of the RESTATEMENT (SECOND) OF CONTRACTS. Although the ostensible basis for remand is the trial court's reliance on outmoded law, the majority relies on law so new as to be virtually unknown in this jurisdiction. The law in Pennsylvania has been and continues to be that where a binding contract exists, and there is no allegation that the contract itself is void or voidable, a breaching party is not entitled to recovery. . . . While our Supreme Court may yet abrogate the forfeiture principle in this Commonwealth, it has not yet seen fit to do so, and we may not usurp its prerogatives, particularly when the result would be unjust.

Secondly, the Uniform Commercial Code § 2718, cited by the majority in (partial) support, is applicable only to the sale of goods, and, while it and some of the equally inapplicable cases referred to by the majority may be part of a trend, the mainstream of contract law in Pennsylvania has not yet been diverted by it. Indeed the identification of the jurisdictions cited as the vanguard of change is for the most part questionable, as of those states relied upon to confer legitimacy on the majority's somewhat arbitrary conclusion, only one may be termed authoritative.

Lastly, and given the current state of the law, the most important determinant of the proper result in this case is the trial judge's assessment of the witness' credibility, here resolved in appellee's favor. The majority, far from according these findings their due, ignores them, contrary to law and our mandate. . . .

The trial court correctly points out that the understanding of the parties is clearly evidenced by the agreements they signed. In breaching those agreements, appellant has engaged in what might charitably be termed sharp practice. The facts reasonably support the inference that appellant learned the hoagie business, benefited from the acquired trade and good will at appellees' place of business, then conducted the hoagie business at its previously owned pizza shop in the following season. Restitution in this instance constitutes a wholly unmerited reward for bad faith. We do not feel that such a result is consistent with the intent of law or the expectations of equity.

QUESTION

The majority in the *Lancelotti* case reject the common law rule that denies restitution for benefits earlier conferred under a contract by the party who later breaches that contract. What is your view on whether the common law rule should be rejected? In the event that it is rejected, should it be rejected for all situations, or only for certain kinds of situations? If only for certain situations, identify the factors that you believe must exist in a case in order to allow restitution to the breaching party.

B.   EQUITABLE REMEDIES

Equitable remedies may be available as an alternative to, and sometimes along with, the common law remedy of money damages, when a party fails or refuses to perform the contract. When money damages would be inadequate and in other situations authorized under cases or statutes in particular jurisdictions, an equitable remedy may be sought.

The principal equitable remedy applicable in contract cases is the remedy of *specific performance.* There are others, however, such as court-ordered *rescissions, injunctions, foreclosures, constructive trusts, equitable liens,* and *receiverships.*

In addition to equitable remedies, the statutory or court-rule remedy of *declaratory judgments* (derived originally from the equitable remedy known as the *declaration of rights*) may be available in certain cases.

1.   Specific Performance of Contracts

a.   Inadequacy of remedies at law — irreparable harm

TAMARIND LITHOGRAPHY WORKSHOP, INC. v. SANDERS
143 Cal. App. 3d 571, 193 Cal. Rptr. 409 (1983)

Stephens, Associate Justice:

The essence of this appeal concerns the question of whether an award of damages is an adequate remedy at law in lieu of specific performance for the breach of an agreement to give screen credits. Our saga traces its origin to March of 1969, at which time appellant, and cross-complainant below, Terry Sanders (hereinafter "Sanders" or "appellant"), agreed in writing to write, direct and produce a motion picture on the subject of lithography for respondent, Tamarind Lithography Workshop, Inc. (hereinafter referred to as "Tamarind" or "respondent").

Pursuant to the terms of the agreement, the film was shot during the summer of 1969, wherein Sanders directed the film according to an outline/treatment of his authorship, and acted as production manager by personally hiring and supervising personnel comprising the film crew. Additionally, Sanders exercised both artistic control over the mixing of the sound track and overall editing of the picture.

After completion, the film, now titled the "Four Stones for Kanemitsu," was screened by Tamarind at its tenth anniversary celebration on April 28, 1970. Thereafter, a dispute arose between the parties concerning their respective rights and obligations under the original 1969 agreement. Litigation ensued and in January 1973 the matter went to trial. Prior to the entry of judgment, the parties entered into a written settlement agreement, which became the premise for the instant action. Specifically, this April 30, 1973, agreement provided that Sanders would be entitled to a screen credit entitled "A Film by Terry Sanders."

Tamarind did not comply with its expressed obligation pursuant to that agreement, in that it failed to include Sanders' screen credits in the prints it distributed. As a result a situation developed wherein Tamarind and co-defendant Wayne filed suit for declaratory relief, damages due to breach of contract, emotional distress, defamation and fraud.

Sanders cross-complained, seeking damages for Tamarind's breach of contract, declaratory relief, specific performance of the contract to give Sanders screen credits, and defamation. Both causes were consolidated and brought to trial on May 31, 1977. A jury was impaneled for purposes of determining damage issues and decided that Tamarind had breached the agreement and awarded Sanders $25,000 in damages.

The remaining claims for declaratory and injunctive relief were tried by the court. The court made findings that Tamarind had sole ownership rights in the film, that "both June Wayne and Terry Sanders were each creative producers of the film, that Sanders shall have the right to modify the prints in his personal possession to include his credits." All other prayers for relief were denied.

It is from the denial of appellant's request for specific performance upon which appellant predicates this appeal.

Since neither party is contesting the sufficiency of Sanders' $25,000 jury award for damages, the central issue thereupon becomes whether that award is necessarily preclusive of additional relief in the form of specific performance, i.e., that Sanders receive credit on all copies of the film. Alternately expressed, the issue is whether the jury's damage award adequately compensates Sanders, not only for injuries sustained as a result of the prior exhibitions of the film without Sanders' credits, but also for future injuries which may be incurred as a result of any future exhibitions of the film without his credit. Commensurate with our discussion below, we find that the damages awarded raise an issue that justifies a judgment for specific performance. Accordingly, we reverse the judgment of the lower court and direct it to award appellant the injunctive relief he now seeks.

Our first inquiry deals with the scope of the jury's $25,000 damage award. More specifically, we are concerned with whether or not this award compensates Sanders not only for past or preexisting injuries, but also for future injury (or injuries) as well.

Indeed, it is possible to categorize respondent's breach of promise to provide screen credits as a single failure to act from which all of Sanders' injuries were caused. However, it is also plausible that damages awarded Sanders were for harms already sustained at the date of trial, and did not contemplate injury as a result of future exhibitions of the film by respondent, without appropriate credit to Sanders.

Although this was a jury trial, there are findings of facts and conclusions of law necessitated by certain legal issues that were decided by the court. Finding of Fact No. 12 states:

"By its verdict the jury concluded that Terry Sanders and the Terry Sanders Company are entitled to the sum of $25,000.00 in damages for all damages suffered by them arising from Tamarind's breach of the April 30th agreement." The exact wording of this finding was also used in Conclusion of Law No. 1. Sanders argues that use of the word "suffered" in the past tense is positive evidence that the jury assessed damages only for breach of the contract up to time of trial and did not award possible future damages that might be suffered if the film was subsequently exhibited without the appropriate credit. Tamarind on the other hand, contends that the jury was instructed that if a breach occurred the award would be for all damages past and future arising from the breach. The jury was instructed: "For the breach of a contract, the measure of damages is the amount which will compensate the party aggrieved, for the economic loss, directly and proximately caused by the breach, or which, in the ordinary course of things, would be likely to result therefrom" and ". . . economic benefits including enhancement of one's professional reputation resulting in increased earnings as a result of screen credit, if their loss is a direct and natural consequence of the breach, may be recovered for breach of an agreement that provides for screen credit. Economic benefits lost through breach of contract may be estimated, and where the plaintiff [Tamarind], by its breach of the contract, has given rise to the difficulty of proving the amount of loss of such economic benefit, it is proper to require of the defendant [Sanders] only that he show the amount of damages with reasonable certainty and to resolve uncertainty as to the amount of economic benefit against the plaintiff [Tamarind]."

The trial court agreed with Tamarind's position and refused to grant the injunction because it was satisfied that the jury had awarded Sanders all the damages he was entitled to including past and possible future damages. The record does not satisfactorily resolve the issue. However, this fact is not fatal to this appeal because, as we shall explain, specific performance as requested by Sanders will solve the problem.

The availability of the remedy of specific performance is premised upon well established requisites. These requisites include: A showing by plaintiff of (1) the inadequacy of his legal remedy; (2) an underlying contract that is both reasonable and supported by adequate consideration; (3) the existence of a mutuality of remedies; (4) contractual terms which are sufficiently definite to enable the court to know what it is to enforce; and (5) a substantial similarity of the requested performance to that promised in the contract. (*See Henderson v. Fisher* (1965) 236 Cal. App. 2d 468, 473, 46 Cal. Rptr. 173, and Civ. Code, §§ 3384, 3386, 3390, 3391.)

It is manifest that the legal remedies available to Sanders for harm resulting from the future exhibition of the film are inadequate as a matter of law. The primary reasons are twofold: (1) that an accurate assessment of damages would be far too difficult and require much speculation, and (2) that any future exhibitions might be deemed to be a continuous breach of contract and thereby create the danger of an untold number of lawsuits.

There is no doubt that the exhibition of a film, which is favorably received by its critics and the public at large, can result in valuable advertising or publicity for the artists responsible for that film's making. Likewise, it is unquestionable that the non-appearance of an artist's name or likeness in the form of screen credit on a successful film can result in a loss of that valuable publicity. However, whether that loss of publicity is measurable dollar wise is quite another matter.

By its very nature, public acclaim is unique and very difficult, if not sometimes impossible, to quantify in monetary terms. Indeed, courts confronted with the dilemma of estimating damages in this area have been less than uniform in their disposition of same. Nevertheless, it is clear that any award of damages for the loss of publicity is contingent upon those damages being reasonably certain, specific, and unspeculative.[4](*See Ericson v. Playgirl, Inc.* (1977) 73 Cal. App. 3d 850, 140 Cal. Rptr. 921.)

The varied disposition of claims for breach of promise to provide screen credits encompasses two schools of thought. On the one hand, there is the view that damages can be ascertained (to within a reasonable degree of certainty) if the trier of fact is given sufficient factual data. (*See Paramount Productions, Inc. v. Smith* (1937) 91 F.2d 863, *cert. den.* 302 U.S. 749, 58 S. Ct. 266, 82 L. Ed. 579.) On the other hand, there is the equally strong stance that although damages resulting from a loss of screen credits might be identifiable, they are far too imponderable and ethereal to define in terms of a monetary award. (*See Poe v. Michael Todd Co.* (S.D.N.Y. 1957) 151 F. Supp. 801.) If these two views can be reconciled, it would only be by an independent examination of each case on its particular set of facts.

In *Paramount Productions, Inc. v. Smith, supra,* 91 F.2d 863, 866–867, the court was provided with evidence from which the ". . . jury might easily compute the advertising value of the screen credit." (*Id.,* at p. 867.) The particular evidence presented included the earnings the plaintiff/writer received for his work on a previous film in which he did not contract for screen credits. This evidence was in turn easily compared with earnings that the writer had received for work in which screen credits were provided as contracted. Moreover, evidence of that artist's salary, prior to his receipt of credit for a play when compared with earnings received subsequent to his actually receiving credit, was ". . . if believed, likewise sufficient as a gauge for the measure of damages." (*Id.,* at p. 867.)

In another case dealing with a request for damages for failure to provide contracted for screen credits, the court in *Zorich v. Petroff* (1957) 152 Cal. App. 2d 806, 313 P.2d 118 demonstrated an equal awareness of the principle. The court emphasized ". . . that there was no evidence from which the [trial] court could have placed a value upon the screen credit to be given plaintiff as an associate producer. (Civ. Code, § 3301.)" (*Id.,* at p. 811, 313 P.2d 118.) Incident to this fact, the court went on to surmise that because the motion picture which was at the root of the litigation was an admitted financial failure, that screen credit, if given, ". . . could reasonably have been regarded as a detriment to him." (*Id.,* at p. 811, 313 P.2d 118.)

At the other extreme, it has been held that failure to give an artist screen credit would constitute irreparable injury. In *Poe v. Michael Todd Co., supra,* 151 F. Supp. 801, the New York District Court was similarly faced with an author's claim that his contractual right to screen credit was violated. The court held: "Not only would money damages be difficult to establish, but at best they would hardly compensate for the real injury done. A writer's reputation, which would be greatly enhanced by public credit for authorship of an outstanding picture, is his stock in trade; it is clear that irreparable injury would follow the failure to give screen

---

[4] [5] California codifies this doctrine in section 3301 of the Civil Code which provides in pertinent part: "No damages can be recovered for a breach of contract which are not clearly ascertainable in both their nature and origin."

credit if in fact he is entitled to it." (*Id.*, at p. 803.)

Notwithstanding the seemingly inflexible observation of that court as to the compensability of a breach of promise to provide screen credits, all three cases equally demonstrate that the awarding of damages must be premised upon calculations, inferences or observations that are logical. Just how logical or reasonable those inferences are regarded serves as the determining factor. Accordingly, where the jury in the matter sub judice was fully apprised of the favorable recognition Sanders' film received from the Academy of Motion Picture Arts and Sciences, the Los Angeles International Film Festival, and public television, and further, where they were made privy to an assessment of the value of said exposure by three experts, it was reasonable for the jury to award monetary damages for that ascertainable loss of publicity. However, pecuniary compensation for Sanders' future harm is not a fully adequate remedy. (*See* REST., CONTRACTS, § 361, p. 648)

We return to the remaining requisites for Sanders' entitlement to specific performance. The need for our finding the contract to be reasonable and supported by adequate consideration is obviated by the jury's determination of respondent's breach of that contract. The requisite of mutuality of remedy has been satisfied in that Sanders had fully performed his obligations pursuant to the agreement (i.e., release of all claims of copyright to the film and dismissal of his then pending action against respondents). (*See* Civ. Code, § 3386.) Similarly, we find the terms of the agreement sufficiently definite to permit enforcement of the respondent's performance as promised.

In the present case it should be obvious that specific performance through injunctive relief can remedy the dilemma posed by the somewhat ambiguous jury verdict. The injunction disposes of the problem of future damages, in that full compliance by Tamarind moots the issue. Of course, violation of the injunction by Tamarind would raise new problems, but the court has numerous options for dealing with the situation and should choose the one best suited to the particular violation.

In conclusion, the record shows that the appellant is entitled to relief consisting of the damages recovered, and an injunction against future injury.

Subsequent to the initial filing of this opinion, it was brought to this court's attention that Terry Sanders entered into a settlement agreement which it is alleged may have a mooting effect on the instant action.

. . . [R]espondents petitioned this court to dismiss the instant appeal or alternatively allow them to produce evidence in addition to their supporting declarations. . . .

Considering the extent of this controversy, in conjunction with our decision to reverse the judgment below, we think it in the best interests of all parties concerned for the trial court to determine what effect, if any, the agreement should have on the action. In effect, respondents' petition is tantamount to a motion to dismiss the entire action, as opposed to the mere dismissal of this appeal. It would appear that the trial court is the more appropriate forum to receive evidence and adjudicate the merits of this issue. If it were to reach a determination unfavorable to petitioners, it would be in position to grant the relief we have determined appellants are entitled to. On the other hand, a contrary determination by the trial court would still leave that court with the authority to take the action requested by petitioners.

The judgment denying appellants' prayer for injunctive relief is hereby reversed and the action, with the addition of this new issue, is remanded to the trial court to take appropriate action in conformity with the views expressed in this opinion, including the taking of additional evidence, oral or written, if deemed appropriate, on the motion to dismiss.

Rubinstein v. Rubinstein, 23 N.Y. 2d 293, 296 N.Y.S. 2d 354, 244 N.E.2d 49 (1968). After many years, two cousins, Henry and Leo, had a falling out and agreed to divide and sever their business relationship, which involved owning and operating a grocery store and a delicatessen at separate sites. The agreement provided for the division of business assets, one business for each of them and an escrow payment of $5,000 by each to be used to cover legal fees and contingencies. One clause of the agreement said, "[i]n the event that either of the parties hereto shall default or refuse to consummate the transaction, then the aforesaid $5,000.00 deposited by such defaulting party shall be forfeited as liquidated damages and such sum shall be paid by the escrowee thereof to the other party."

When they could not agree on who would get which business, Henry brought suit against Leo for defaulting on the contract. Henry asked for specific performance and Leo initially also counterclaimed for specific performance, but after a change of counsel claimed that Henry's recovery for the default was limited to $5,000 as the liquidated damages specified in the agreement. The trial court and the appellate court both held that Henry was entitled to summary judgment, but the liquidated damages clause limited Henry's remedy to the terms of the clause, and refused to grant specific performance.

Henry appealed to the New York Court of Appeals, which started its opinion by saying that liquidated damages provisions do not, standing alone, bar the remedy of specific performance — without some express statement in the contract to that effect. The Court said, "[n]othing in the language of the contract explicitly states that the liquidated damages provision was to be the plaintiff's sole and exclusive remedy, ..." The Court also said, "[a]bsent, therefore, an unambiguous provision, the majority below was in error in finding that the language precluded specific performance . . . [T]he law presumes that the primary purpose of a contract not expressly stated to be an option, is performance of the act promised and not nonperformance."

The Court also found that the agreement did not intend the escrow deposit to guarantee performance, but to be used in connection with the performance of the agreement itself. The Court held that since the original purpose of the agreement was to sever the business relationship between the parties, granting money damages would have the effect of perpetuating their interactions, and would be contrary to the intent of the parties. As Henry had no viable remedy at law, specific performance was the appropriate remedy.

Madariaga v. Morris, 639 S.W.2d 709 (Tex. App. 1982). This was an action arising from the sale of a hot sauce business where the plaintiff had entered into a lease contract with defendant containing an option to buy the manufacturing and retail business, the formula for the sauce, and its associated goodwill. The contract also included a royalty payment clause which required plaintiff to pay defendant a set fee for each case of hot sauce he sold. Plaintiff fully complied with the terms of the lease contract and chose to exercise the option to purchase the business. He requested the defendant to convey the business to him, but defendant refused unless the plaintiff would continue to pay the royalties in perpetuity. Plaintiff brought suit requesting specific performance, which the trial court granted, and defendant appealed.

On appeal, the court first found that by the terms of the contract, royalty payments were "in addition to the payment of said rental payments" and therefore tied to the rental payments, and as such, the obligation to pay royalties terminated at the end of the lease and the completion of the sale. Appellant raised several other issues, including: the construction of the contract; the trial court's refusal to consider the testimony of Mrs. Madariaga stating her intention that the royalty payments be perpetual in nature; and that the contract was not specific enough to grant specific performance. In dealing with the first issues the Court said, "if the terms of the agreement clearly invest it with a definite legal meaning, all necessity for inquiry as to the intent of the parties is at an end." The Court addressed the second issue by saying the contract was "clear and certain," and "there is no showing of fraud or mistake, the instrument alone will be deemed to express the intention of the parties and will be enforced as written, no matter what their actual intention may have been."

Appellant also contended on appeal that "specific performance is not ordinarily available when the complaining party can be fully compensated through the legal remedy of damages." However, the court said, "[e]quity will generally decree specific performance at the instance of the buyer of personal property, which property he needs and which is not obtainable elsewhere." The court went on to note that while a plaintiff has to show he does not have a remedy at law, it "is not necessary for him to allege in express terms" in his claim that he does not have a remedy at law, "if the facts brought out in the pleadings show such is the case." The Court went on to say, ". . . the plaintiff, by the facts brought in his pleadings and evidence show that he does not have an adequate remedy at law and cannot be adequately compensated in damages. The business, including the hot sauce formula and goodwill, has a special, peculiar, unique value or character; it consists of property which Morris needs and could not be obtained elsewhere." The Court affirmed the trial court judgment.

NOTES & QUESTIONS

1. The advertising and publicity benefits contracted for in *Tamarind Lithography* were to derive from exhibitions or screenings of the subject film. Should courts grant specific performance remedies when such benefits are intended to derive from exhibitions of other kinds? What about art exhibits and billboards?

2. In *Whiteway Neon-Ad. Inc. v. Maddox*, 211 Ga. 27, 83 S.E.2d 676 (1954), specific performance was approved where a corporate defendant and its transferee failed to comply with the undertaking under a lease agreement to erect and maintain an electrical advertising display sign fabricated to the plaintiff's special order at a monthly rental of $160. Plaintiff alleged, among other things, that the sign and its location on designated land controlled by defendants were unique and

of great value as an advertising medium, the difficulty involved in establishing with exactitude such value to plaintiff and plaintiff's business, that there was no other location where such sign could be seen by as many people who would be influenced to trade with him, that after the sign had been partially erected the defendants refused to comply with their contract and removed the sign, and that defendants had falsely asserted that their nonperformance was due to refusal of municipal authorities to grant the necessary permit. In rejecting a number of defendants' claims, the court also held that: (a) Since plaintiff accepted the sign that was fabricated, the remedy was not precluded by reason of any contract indefiniteness involving details as to construction of the sign; (b) Personal services to be performed by way of maintenance, if any, were minor in nature; (c) The fact that the corporate defendant was subsequently without assets, funds or employees, did not relieve defendant of its duty to comply with the main part of the contract by allowing plaintiff to place the sign upon defendant's realty; and (d) Plaintiff would be entitled to compensation for having to erect the sign.

3. In *Klein v. Pepsico, Inc.*, 845 F.2d 76 (4th Cir. 1988), the Fourth Circuit reviewed a trial court decision using a traditional "abuse of discretion" standard of review applicable to decisions that grant or refuse to grant equitable remedies. The trial court, holding that defendant failed to perform a contract for the sale of its corporate jet and that the contract for sale had been properly formed, then granted specific performance on the ground of uniqueness of the property involved in the sale. The Fourth Circuit reversed the grant of specific performance, also noting that under the U.C.C. "Virginia Code § 8.2-716 permits a jilted buyer of goods to seek specific performance of the contract if the goods sought are unique, or in other proper circumstances." During its analysis of the trial court's rationale for granting specific performance, the court pointed out that the trial judge "repeatedly stated [in his findings] that money damages would make [the plaintiff] whole," and the court held that "an increase in the cost of a replacement [aircraft] does not merit the remedy of specific performance." The court rejected the lower court's conclusion that the plane in question "was unique because only three comparable aircraft existed on the market." The plaintiff had made offers on two other similar aircraft since the defendant had failed to perform, but did not close on them "because prices had started to rise." Ruling that money damages were an adequate remedy and the aircraft "is not unique within the meaning of the Virginia Commercial Code," the court reversed the grant of specific performance and remanded "for a trial on damages."

4. In *London Bucket Co. v. Stewart*, 312 Ky. 832, 237 S.W.2d 509 (1951), the Kentucky Supreme Court also reversed a judgment granting specific performance against a defendant. There plaintiff had contracted with defendant for defendant to provide a heating system, and the system was never completed and did not perform as required. Plaintiff requested a judgment directing specific performance, also that performance be completed before the arrival of cold weather, and an additional $8250 in damages. The trial court considered the general rule that equitable remedies are unavailable unless damages would be an "inadequate and incomplete remedy" for the injury, but still ordered specific performance of the terms of defendant's contract with the plaintiff. On appeal the court said, "[i]n the present case the decree was in effect to direct a building contractor to go back, correct defective work and complete its job. It is the general rule that contracts for building construction will not be specifically enforced because ordinarily damages are an adequate remedy and, in part, because of the

incapacity of the court to superintend the performance. . . . That there may be difficulty in proving the damages as appellee suggests, is not enough to put the case within the exceptions."

5. In *Kohrs v. Barth*, 212 Ill. App. 3d 468, 570 N.E.2d 1273 (1991), the court affirmed a specific performance judgment awarded to the vendor in his suit against the real estate contract purchaser, holding that specific performance should be available as a matter of right where a contract for the sale of real estate has been entered into without misunderstanding on the part of the purchaser and without misrepresentation on the part of the vendor. The court also held that the fact that a contract provides for liquidated damages in case of failure to perform does not of itself prevent an award of specific performance.

6. *Practice Point*: As noted in the *Kohrs* case, a contract term providing for liquidated damages does not preclude a request for or the granting of the equitable specific performance remedy. The provision can, however, have that effect if it is: (1) a valid liquidated damages clause enforceable in the subject jurisdiction; (2) it is drafted to reflect the intention of the parties that the specified damages are to be the sole remedy for default to the exclusion of any specific performance remedy; and (3) if the law in that jurisdiction will give effect to that expression of intent.

7. In *Dixon v. City of Monticello*, 223 Ill. App. 3d 549, 585 N.E.2d 609 (1991), vendors were allowed specific performance of their contract to sell a single-family residence to a purchaser planning to place a restaurant parking lot on the property, after purchaser attempted to terminate the contract for its failure to obtain conclusive permission from the city to construct the parking facility. The court noted that under the contract purchaser had the duty to use reasonable efforts to secure such permission from the city, and purchaser failed to act in good faith to make reasonable efforts to effect a change in zoning or obtain a variance or conditional use permit. The court further held that the vendors also were entitled to recover from the purchaser interest expense damages incurred by them in connection with the purchase of a new residence, since specific performance alone would not have provided the vendor with complete relief.

b.   Discretion and specific performance

WALGREEN CO. v. SARA CREEK PROPERTY CO., B.V.
966 F.2d 273 (7th Cir. 1992).

[Plaintiff tenant, which operated a pharmacy business on premises in Southgate Mall in Milwaukee, Wisconsin, was informed by the landlord that the latter intended to replace a failing anchor tenant with a tenant whose business included the operation of a pharmacy. In its suit against the landlord and the proposed competitor Phar-Mor, plaintiff sought an injunction against the letting of premises to the competitor, claiming that such would constitute breach of contract and violate an exclusivity clause in the lease whereby the landlord had promised not to lease mall space to a competing pharmacy or to a store containing a pharmacy. The trial court granted, and the court of appeals approved, a permanent injunction enforcing the exclusivity clause.]

POSNER, Circuit Judge:

This appeal from the grant of a permanent injunction raises fundamental issues concerning the propriety of injunctive relief. . . .

. . . After an evidentiary hearing, the judge found a breach of Walgreen's lease and entered a permanent injunction against Sara Creek's letting the anchor tenant premises to Phar-Mor until the expiration of Walgreen's lease. He did this over the defendants' objection that Walgreen had failed to show that its remedy at law — damages — for the breach of the exclusivity clause was inadequate. Sara Creek had put on an expert witness who testified that Walgreen's damages could be readily estimated, and Walgreen had countered with evidence from its employees that its damages would be very difficult to compute, among other reasons because they included intangibles such as loss of goodwill.

Sara Creek reminds us that damages are the norm in breach of contract as in other cases. Many breaches, it points out, are "efficient" in the sense that they allow resources to be moved into a more valuable use. *Patton v. Mid-Continent Systems, Inc.*, 841 F.2d 742, 750–51 (7th Cir. 1988). Perhaps this is one — the value of Phar-Mor's occupancy of the anchor premises may exceed the cost to Walgreen of facing increased competition. If so, society will be better off if Walgreen is paid its damages, equal to that cost, and Phar-Mor is allowed to move in rather than being kept out by an injunction. That is why injunctions are not granted as a matter of course, but only when the plaintiff's damages remedy is inadequate. *Northern Indiana Public Service Co. v. Carbon County Coal Co.*, 799 F.2d 265, 279 (7th Cir. 1986). Walgreen's is not, Sara Creek argues; the projection of business losses due to increased competition is a routine exercise in calculation. Damages representing either the present value of lost future profits or (what should be the equivalent, *Carusos v. Briarcliff, Inc.*, 76 Ga. App. 346, 351–52, 45 S.E.2d 802, 806–07 (1947)) the diminution in the value of the leasehold have either been awarded or deemed the proper remedy in a number of reported cases for breach of an exclusivity clause in a shopping-center lease. . . . Why, Sara Creek asks, should they not be adequate here?

Sara Creek makes a beguiling argument that contains much truth, but we do not think it should carry the day. For if, as just noted, damages have been awarded in some cases of breach of an exclusivity clause in a shopping-center lease, injunctions have been issued in others. . . . The choice between remedies requires a balancing of the costs and benefits of the alternatives. *Hecht Co. v. Bowles*, 321 U.S. 321, 329, 64 S. Ct. 587, 591, 88 L. Ed. 754 (1944); *Yakus v. United States*, 321 U.S. 414, 440, 64 S. Ct. 660, 674, 88 L. Ed. 834 (1944). The task of striking the balance is for the trial judge, subject to deferential appellate review in recognition of its particularistic, judgmental, fact-bound character. . . . As we said in an appeal from a grant of a preliminary injunction — but the point is applicable to review of a permanent injunction as well — "The question for us [appellate judges] is whether the [district] judge exceeded the bounds of permissible choice in the circumstances, not what we would have done if we had been in his shoes." *Roland Machinery Co. v. Dresser Industries, Inc.*, 749 F.2d 380, 390 (7th Cir. 1984).

The plaintiff who seeks an injunction has the burden of persuasion — damages are the norm, so the plaintiff must show why his case is abnormal. But when, as in this case, the issue is whether to grant a permanent injunction, not whether to grant a temporary one, the burden is to show that damages are inadequate, not that the denial of the injunction will work irreparable harm. "Irreparable" in the injunction context means not rectifiable by the entry of a final judgment. . . . It has nothing to do with whether to grant a permanent injunction, which, in the usual case anyway, is the final judgment. The use of "irreparable harm" or "irreparable injury" as synonyms for inadequate remedy at law is a confusing usage. It should be avoided. . . .

The benefits of substituting an injunction for damages are twofold. First, it shifts the burden of determining the cost of the defendant's conduct from the court to the parties. If it is true that Walgreen's damages are smaller than the gain to Sara Creek from allowing a second pharmacy into the shopping mall, then there must be a price for dissolving the injunction that will make both parties better off. Thus, the effect of upholding the injunction would be to substitute for the costly processes of forensic fact determination the less costly processes of private negotiation. Second, a premise of our free-market system, and the lesson of experience here and abroad as well, is that prices and costs are more accurately determined by the market than by government. A battle of experts is a less reliable method of determining the actual cost to Walgreen of facing new competition than negotiations between Walgreen and Sara Creek over the price at which Walgreen would feel adequately compensated for having to face that competition.

That is the benefit side of injunctive relief but there is a cost side as well. Many injunctions require continuing supervision by the court, and that is costly. . . . A request for specific performance (a form of mandatory injunction) of a franchise agreement was refused on this ground in *North American Financial Group, Ltd. v. S.M.R. Enterprises, Inc.*, 583 F. Supp. 691, 699 (N.D. Ill. 1984); *see* Edward Yorio, CONTRACT ENFORCEMENT: SPECIFIC PERFORMANCE AND INJUNCTIONS § 3.3.2 (1989). This ground was also stressed in *Rental Development Corp. v. Lavery*, 304 F.2d 839, 841–42 (9th Cir. 1962), a case involving a lease. Some injunctions are problematic because they impose costs on third parties. . . . A more subtle cost of injunctive relief arises from the situation that economists call "bilateral monopoly," in which two parties can deal only with each other: the situation that an injunction creates. . . . The sole seller of widgets selling to the sole buyer of that product would be an example. But so will be the situation confronting Walgreen and Sara Creek if the injunction is upheld. Walgreen can "sell" its injunctive right only to Sara Creek, and Sara Creek can "buy" Walgreen's surrender of its right to enjoin the leasing of the anchor tenant's space to Phar-Mor only from Walgreen. The lack of alternatives in bilateral monopoly creates a bargaining range, and the costs of negotiating to a point within that range may be high. Suppose the cost to Walgreen of facing the competition of Phar-Mor at the Southgate Mall would be $1 million, and the benefit to Sara Creek of leasing to Phar-Mor would be $2 million. Then at any price between those figures for a waiver of Walgreen's injunctive right both parties would be better off, and we expect parties to bargain around a judicial assignment of legal rights if the assignment is inefficient. R.H. Coase, *The Problem of Social Cost*, 3 J. LAW & ECON. 1 (1960). But each of the parties would like to engross as much of the bargaining range as possible — Walgreen to press the price toward $2 million, Sara Creek to depress it toward $1 million. With so much at stake, both parties will have an incentive to devote substantial resources of time and money to the negotiation process. The process may even break down, if one or both parties want to create for future use a reputation as a hard bargainer; and if it does break down, the injunction will have brought about an inefficient result. All these are in one form or another costs of the injunctive process that can be avoided by substituting damages.

The costs and benefits of the damages remedy are the mirror of those of the injunctive remedy. The damages remedy avoids the cost of continuing supervision and third-party effects, and the cost of bilateral monopoly as well. It imposes costs of its own, however, in the form of diminished accuracy in the determination of value, on the one hand, and of the parties' expenditures on preparing and presenting evidence of damages, and the time of the court in evaluating the evidence, on the other.

The weighing up of all these costs and benefits is the analytical procedure that is or at least should be employed by a judge asked to enter a permanent injunction, with the understanding that if the balance is even the injunction should be withheld. The judge is not required to explicate every detail of the analysis and he did not do so here, but as long we are satisfied that his approach is broadly consistent with a proper analysis we shall affirm; and we are satisfied here. The determination of Walgreen's damages would have been costly in forensic resources and inescapably inaccurate. . . . The lease had ten years to run. So Walgreen would have had to project its sales revenues and costs over the next ten years, and then project the impact on those figures of Phar-Mor's competition, and then discount that impact to present value. All but the last step would have been fraught with uncertainty.

We may have given too little weight to such uncertainties in *American Dairy Queen Corp. v. Brown-Port Co.*, 621 F.2d 255, 257 n.2 (7th Cir. 1980), but in that case the district judge had found that the remedy at law was adequate in the circumstances and the movant had failed to make its best argument for inadequacy in the district court. *Id.* at 259. It is difficult to forecast the profitability of a retail store over a decade, let alone to assess the impact of a particular competitor on that profitability over that period. Of course one can hire an expert to make such predictions, Glen A. Stankee, *Econometric Forecasting of Lost Profits: Using High Technology to Compute Commercial Damages*, 61 FLA. B.J. 83 (1987), and if injunctive relief is infeasible the expert's testimony may provide a tolerable basis for an award of damages. . . . [I]n . . . cases in which damages have been awarded for the breach of an exclusivity clause in a shopping-center lease . . . they are awarded in such circumstances not because anyone thinks them a clairvoyant forecast but because it is better to give a wronged person a crude remedy than none at all. It is the same theory on which damages are awarded for a disfiguring injury. No one thinks such injuries readily monetizable, . . . but a crude estimate is better than letting the wrongdoer get off scot-free (which, not incidentally, would encourage more such injuries). . . . Sara Creek presented evidence of what happened (very little) to Walgreen when Phar-Mor moved into other shopping malls in which Walgreen has a pharmacy, and it was on the right track in putting in comparative evidence. But there was a serious question whether the other malls were actually comparable to the Southgate Mall, so we cannot conclude, in the face of the district judge's contrary conclusion, that the existence of comparative evidence dissolved the difficulties of computing damages in this case. Sara Creek complains that the judge refused to compel Walgreen to produce all the data that Sara Creek needed to demonstrate the feasibility of forecasting Walgreen's damages. Walgreen resisted, on grounds of the confidentiality of the data and the cost of producing the massive data that Sara Creek sought. Those are legitimate grounds; and the cost (broadly conceived) they expose of pretrial discovery, in turn presaging complexity at trial, is itself a cost of the damages remedy that injunctive relief saves.

Damages are not always costly to compute, or difficult to compute accurately. In the standard case of a seller's breach of a contract for the sale of goods where the buyer covers by purchasing the same product in the market, damages are readily calculable by subtracting the contract price from the market price and multiplying by the quantity specified in the contract. But this is not such a case and here damages would be a costly and inaccurate remedy; and on the other side of the balance some of the costs of an injunction are absent and the cost that is present seems low. The injunction here, like one enforcing a covenant not to compete (standardly enforced by injunction, . . . is a simple negative injunction — Sara Creek is not to lease space in the Southgate Mall to Phar-Mor during the term of Walgreen's lease — and the costs of judicial supervision and enforcement should be negligible. There is no contention that the injunction will harm an unrepresented third party. It may harm Phar-Mor but that harm will be reflected in Sara Creek's offer to Walgreen to dissolve the injunction. (Anyway Phar-Mor is a party.) The injunction may also, it is true, harm potential customers of Phar-Mor — people who would prefer to shop at a deep-discount store than an ordinary discount store — but their preferences, too, are registered indirectly. The more business Phar-Mor would have, the more rent it will be willing to pay Sara Creek, and therefore the more Sara Creek will be willing to pay Walgreen to dissolve the injunction.

The only substantial cost of the injunction in this case is that it may set off a round of negotiations between the parties. In some cases, illustrated by *Boomer v. Atlantic Cement Co.*, 26 N.Y.2d 219, 309 N.Y.S.2d 312, 257 N.E.2d 870 (1970), this consideration alone would be enough to warrant the denial of injunctive relief. . . . There is nothing so dramatic here. Sara Creek does not argue that it will have to close the mall if enjoined from leasing to Phar-Mor. Phar-Mor is not the only potential anchor tenant. *Liza Danielle, Inc. v. Jamko, Inc.*, 408 So. 2d 735, 740 (Fla. App. 1982), on which Sara Creek relies, presented the converse case where the grant of the injunction would have forced an existing tenant to close its store. The size of the bargaining range was also a factor in the denial of injunctive relief in *Gitlitz v. Plankinton Building Properties, Inc.*, 228 Wis. 334, 339-40, 280 N.W. 415, 418 (1938).

To summarize, the judge did not exceed the bounds of reasonable judgment in concluding that the costs (including forgone benefits) of the damages remedy would exceed the costs (including forgone benefits) of an injunction. We need not consider whether, as intimated by Walgreen, exclusivity clauses in shopping-center leases should be considered presumptively enforceable by injunctions. Although we have described the choice between legal and equitable remedies as one for case-by-case determination, the courts have sometimes picked out categories of case in which injunctive relief is made the norm. The best-known example is specific performance of contracts for the sale of real property. . . . The rule that specific performance will be ordered in such cases as a matter of course is a generalization of the considerations discussed above. Because of the absence of a fully liquid market in real property and the frequent presence of subjective values (many a homeowner, for example, would not sell his house for its market value), the calculation of damages is difficult; and since an order of specific performance to convey a piece of property does not create a continuing relation between the parties, the costs of supervision and enforcement if specific performance is ordered are slight. The exclusivity clause in Walgreen's lease relates to real estate, but we hesitate to suggest that every contract involving real estate should be enforceable as a matter of course by injunctions. Suppose Sara Creek had covenanted to keep the entrance to Walgreen's store free of ice and snow, and breached the covenant. An injunction would require continuing supervision, and it would be easy enough if the injunction were denied for Walgreen to hire its own ice and snow remover and charge the cost to Sara Creek. . . . On the other hand, injunctions to enforce exclusivity clauses are quite likely to be justifiable by just the considerations present here — damages are difficult to estimate with any accuracy and the injunction is a one-shot remedy requiring no continuing judicial involvement. So there is an argument for making injunctive relief presumptively appropriate in such cases, but we need not decide in this case how strong an argument.

Affirmed.

Van Wagner Advertising Corp. v. S&M Enterprises, 67 N.Y.2d 186, 492 N.E.2d 756 (1986). In lessee's suit filed when lessor breached a lease for advertising space on the exterior wall of a building, the trial court awarded damages to the time of trial but refused to order specific performance. On this appeal it was held that the denial of specific performance did not constitute an abuse of discretion, and that lessee should have been awarded damages for the entire period through the expiration of the lease. In so holding the court concluded that specific performance of a lease agreement for "unique" billboard space is properly denied when: (a) the damage remedy is adequate to provide compensation to the tenant, and (b) an equitable remedy would impose a "disproportionate burden on the defaulting landlord," and pointed out that although specific performance may be available in appropriate cases of breach of commercial or residential leases, in New York specific performance of real property leases is not awarded as a matter of course. Further, when discussing the concept of "uniqueness" as a basis for finding that money damages are so inadequate as to warrant the grant of an equitable remedy, the court declared that a "distinction must be drawn between physical difference and economic interchangeability," and that physical uniqueness alone (except for real property sale situations) does not establish the propriety of equitable relief. In considering whether or not to order specific performance, the focus is not on inherent physical uniqueness of the property but on "the uncertainty of valuing it," and upon whether the risk of undercompensating the injured tenant by refusing equitable relief and providing money damages instead is "unacceptably high." In addition, the court discussed the principle that mandates that an equitable remedy must not itself work an inequity and that performance required by a specific performance order should not constitute an undue hardship on the defendant.

c.   Damages in addition to specific performance

BILLY WILLIAMS BUILDERS & DEVELOPERS, INC.
v. HILLERICH
446 S.W.2d 280 (Ky. 1969)

EDWARD P. HILL, Judge:

Appellees (hereinafter Hillerich) sued appellant (hereinafter Williams) for specific performance of a contract to convey a house and a lot, for damages growing out of the defective construction of the house, and for damages due to delay in performance. Equity directed specific performance and transferred the case to the common law docket, where a jury later returned a verdict for appellees for $3318 in damages resulting from defective construction and for $910.38 in damages occasioned by delay in performance. Williams appeals.

Williams forcefully argues that: (1) Hillerich cannot have specific performance and damages; (2) Hillerich did not prove damages; (3) the verdict is excessive; (4) Hillerich judicially admitted a breach of contract, precluding recovery; (5) Hillerich first breached the contract by failure to make a down payment; and (6) the court erred in directing a verdict for Hillerich on Williams' counterclaim.

The main thrust of Williams' argument concerns the right of the buyer to have two remedies (1) specific performance of a contract to purchase real estate (a house and a lot) and (2) damages for defective construction and for delay in performance. Williams argues that by complying with the judgment for specific performance and by accepting the deed to the property, Hillerich elected to have one of two inconsistent remedies; and by so doing, he cannot back up to the "forks of the road" and take a road different from the one on which he "first embarked."

In a proper case there can be little doubt that one may be entitled to the specific performance of a contract to purchase real estate and damages for delay in performance. . . . But damages for deficiency of quantity or quality present a more complex question, on which there is some conflict among the authorities. We look to the writings of text writers and then to the recorded opinions here and elsewhere for guidance.

First we note comments by text writers.

In RESTATEMENT OF THE LAW, volume 2, Contracts, section 365, at page 659, it is said:

> Specific Enforcement in Part, With Compensation for the Remainder. "The fact that a part of the promised performance cannot be rendered, or is otherwise such that its specific enforcement would violate some of the rules stated in §§ 360–380, does not prevent the specific enforcement of the remainder, if in all other respects the requisites for specific enforcement of that remainder exist. Compensation for the partial breach that still remains may be awarded in the same proceeding, either as damages, restitution, or an abatement in price." "A contracts to transfer land to B and also to make certain repairs and to complete an unfinished building on the land. In case of repudiation by A, B may be given a decree for specific performance, with an abatement in the price or other compensation sufficient in amount to enable him to make the repairs and complete the building himself."

See also 81 C.J.S. *Specific Performance* § 21b(2), and 49 AM. JUR., *Specific Performance*, §§§ 105, page 123.

We find in THOMPSON ON REAL PROPERTY, volume 8A, chapter 57, section 4482, at page 487, the remedies available to both vendor and purchaser clearly defined in this fashion:

> Whether the vendor or purchaser is the plaintiff there are three alternatives presented when the vendor is able to give only a performance nonconforming in quantity, *quality* or value: (1) to refuse the remedy of specific performance; (2) to enforce the contract without any regard to the partial failure; (3) to decree a conveyance and allow the vendee an abatement from price equal to the value of the deficiency in the perfor-

mance. If the vendor cannot convey the agreed quantity of the estate the vendee may have specific performance with pro tanto abatement of purchase price.

See also 95 A.L.R. page 228, which cites cases from fifteen states and POMEROY'S EQUITY JURISPRUDENCE, volume 1, § 237b.

As will be seen from annotations in some of the authorities above cited, the state courts are not of one accord in following the rule announced above. They seldom are.

Up to now, it has been extremely difficult to determine the position of this court on the specific questions here discussed. . . .

In *Rocks v. Brosius*, 241 Md. 612, 217 A.2d 531 (1966), the Maryland court allowed damages growing out of the construction of a "temporary haul road because of improper performance of the work itself," along with specific performance. The court held that such damages were "similar" to damages resulting "from delay" in performance.

South Carolina is not in accord with the rule that general damages may be awarded incidental to specific performance. It was held in *Spencer v. National Union Bank of Rock Hill*, 189 S.C. 197, 200 S.E. 721, that "special" damages may, but "general" damages may not be awarded with specific performance.

It is recognized that specific performance is an equitable remedy devised to apply in cases where common law actions for damages were found inadequate to afford a full remedy. . . . The doctrine, first adopted in England, met with formidable opposition, but it has survived. In fact, its scope has been enlarged down through the years.

We need to keep in mind that in the contract in question vendor (appellant) agreed to sell lot 102 and to construct a house according to "submitted plans and specifications." Not only did appellant agree to convey the lot and residence to be built, but he undertook to build the house according to the "plans and specifications."

Appellees argue that their purpose in entering into the contract was to obtain this particular property in this particular neighborhood due to aged relatives nearby; that they are entitled to specific performance notwithstanding appellant's breach of the contract to construct the house according to plans and specifications.

In POMEROY'S SPECIFIC PERFORMANCE OF CONTRACTS, 3d ed., section 438, p. 903, it is said:

> The general doctrine is firmly settled, both in England and in this country, that a vendor whose estate is less than or different from that which he agreed to sell, or who cannot give the exact subject-matter embraced in his contract, will not be allowed to set up his inability as a defense against the demand of a purchaser who is willing to take what he can get with a compensation. The vendee may, if he so elect (sic), enforce a specific performance to the extent of the vendor's ability to comply with the terms of the agreement, and may compel a conveyance of the vendor's deficient estate, or defective title or partial subject-matter, and have compensation for the difference between the actual performance, and the

performance which would have been an exact fulfillment of the terms of their contract.

This court decided in *Preece v. Wolford*, 196 Ky. 710, 246 S.W. 27, 28, that vendee may have "specific performance as to such title as the vendor can furnish, and may also have a just abatement from the purchase money for the deficiency of title or quantity or *quality* of the estate." (Our emphasis.) We can see no reason for a distinction between a deficiency in quantity (short acreage or lack of title) and deficiency of quality (defective construction).

We conclude that appellees' remedies were not inconsistent so as to require an election of remedies and that the chancellor did not err in granting specific performance and directing that damages be ascertained by the common law division of the court.

Appellant's second and third points, that appellees did not prove damages and that the amount of the verdict is excessive, will be treated as one.

Appellant reminds us that appellees' own qualified witness testified the value of the property was slightly in excess of the contract price and that although appellee Joseph L. Hillerich testified the market value was $18,000, they (appellees) are bound by the testimony of their own witness, who, according to appellant was more qualified than Mr. Hillerich. With this argument we cannot agree. Appellee, an engineer, purchased, owned, and occupied a residence in the vicinity eighteen months prior to the date of the contract in question. He testified he was familiar with real estate in this "particular area;" that he had watched want ads of real estate and had "studied pamphlets" showing listings and prices "put out" by the real estate board. Taking his evidence, there was a difference between the contract price and the value of the property in its so-called defective condition of $3846. The jury awarded $3318. On this item we conclude the evidence supported the verdict and that the amount is not excessive. In addition appellees introduced evidence of two architects that it would cost $4200 to $6000 to remedy the claimed defects in construction.

Concerning damages occasioned from delay in performance, appellee Hillerich testified to itemized damages amounting to $2638.44. The jury found $910.38 for appellees on this item. We do not find this part of the verdict excessive. . . .

The trial court, both the equity and the common law divisions, we think, correctly determined the issues favorable to appellees. . . .

The judgment is affirmed.

d.   Specific performance — some special situations

i.   Requirements contracts — the public interest

TENNESSEE VALLEY AUTHORITY v. MASON COAL, INC.
384 F. Supp. 1107 (E.D. Tenn., 1974)
aff'd mem., 513 F.2d 632 (1975)

ROBERT L. TAYLOR, District Judge:

Plaintiff, the Tennessee Valley Authority, seeks a preliminary injunction restraining defendant, Mason Coal, Inc., (hereafter Mason) from selling, delivering, or otherwise disposing of any coal until defendant has first fulfilled its obligations under a supply contract formerly entered into between plaintiff and defendants. Evidence and oral argument were received in support of and in opposition . . . .

Plaintiff is a wholly-owned corporation of the United States. 16 U.S.C. § 831 *et seq.* The Tennessee Valley Authority (hereinafter T.V.A.) currently operates the nation's largest electric power generating system, which serves approximately 80,000 square miles in Tennessee, Kentucky, Mississippi, Alabama, Georgia, North Carolina, and Virginia. Approximately 80 per cent of T.V.A.'s electrical output is generated by coal-burning steam plants which consume more than 35 million tons of coal annually.

Mason is incorporated and principally located in Virginia and has authorized Coal Development Corporation, a Tennessee corporation, as its exclusive sales agent.

In seeking to maintain a constant and reliable coal supply, T.V.A. has entered into numerous long-term contracts with coal producers for the sale and purchase of coal for delivery to T.V.A.'s coalburning steam plants. The award of these supply contracts is based upon a competitive bid system, requiring the coal supplier to affirmatively represent in his bid that he has the necessary experience and qualifications to produce the requisite quantity and quality of coal. . . .

Defendant's bid for a 12-month period to sell to T.V.A. 1,500 tons of coal per week was submitted on August 20, 1973 for public opening on August 21, 1973. Defendant's bid noted the appropriate mode of acceptance . . . . Pursuant to this bid, T.V.A. telephoned acceptance of Mason's bid on October 10, 1973, and thereafter confirmed this oral acceptance in writing . . . .

The parties thereafter agreed to supplement No. 1 on October 26, 1973, which permitted shipments to begin on October 29, 1973. Under the contract's terms, T.V.A. forwarded to Mason a "filled out" contract for the latter's signature. Mason has refused to sign this contract. Defendants delivered more than 4,000 tons of coal but since November 30, 1973 refused to deliver any coal under the contract.

In support of plaintiff's motion for preliminary injunction, it has filed with the Court the affidavit of C. R. Wilkerson, Chief of the Fuels Procurement Branch, Division of Purchasing. Mr. Wilkerson's affidavit is instrumental in aiding the Court's development of a factual setting in which to couch any extraordinary remedy at this preliminary stage. Mr. Wilkerson asserts that a number of economic factors, both inside and outside the coal industry, have led to a sharp decline in coal supplies and a concomitant reduction in T.V.A.'s coal reserves.

> Due to the energy shortage and other factors, an acute shortage of coal supply has developed in those areas serving TVA, and the situation is rapidly becoming critical. Shortages of transportation equipment, mining equipment, explosives, fuels, and roof belts have interrupted deliveries under existing TVA contracts . . . As of July 1, 1973, the John Sevier Steam Plant, the plant to which Mason's coal was being shipped, had a 64-day supply of coal in its stockpile. That stockpile has since dwindled to a 22-day supply in spite of a sharp reduction in generation at this plant in recent months. Coal is urgently needed now for this plant.

Of similar significance in controlling a grant of extraordinary relief at this stage is the additional remark by Mr. Wilkerson that:

. . . TVA's efforts to purchase coal for the TVA power system, including the John Sevier plant, have had very little success. (To date, only one 500 tons per week proposal has been received by TVA).

In summary, TVA has not been able to obtain offers from other sources to offset delivery losses under the Mason Coal contract, much less meet burn requirements and maintain satisfactory stockpiles. . . .

Conclusions of Law

It is against this factual background that the Court concludes that plaintiff is entitled to extraordinary relief in the form of specific performance. Although the Court is not aided by specific case law in point, it is guided by traditional prerequisites that must be established before specific performance is compelled. Thus, it is generally understood that a federal court in exercising its inherent equity power must conclude prior to compelling performance under a contract that a valid contract exists between the parties, that the obligations under the contract are sufficiently clear, that the subject matter of the contract must be unique in character and, finally, plaintiff's remedies at law are inadequate. *See generally*, 71 Am. Jur. 13 *et seq.* . . .

In determining the unique character of this contract, the Court must look beyond the property of the subject matter itself to the surrounding circumstances at the present time. Accordingly, the scarcity of raw fuel materials can make an otherwise common product assume a unique character. . . .

The supply contract under examination here provides for extensive contractual remedies both in the form of standard default procedures and the price escalation clause. In the absence of an alternative source of supply for plaintiff, it would appear that any legal remedies are both impractical and inadequate from plaintiff's standpoint. *Texas Co. v. Central Fuel Oil Co.*, 194 F. 1 (8th Cir. 1912); *Southwest Pipe Line Co. v. Empire Natural Gas Co.*, 33 F.2d 248 (8th Cir. 1929).

The fixed price contract with escalation does not guarantee a profit to the contractor. However, an inadequate profit margin does not necessarily constitute an inequitable hardship on defendants as it appears that the price escalation clause adequately protects defendant's financial recovery of increased costs.

In a similar case brought by T.V.A. in the United States District Court for the Western District of Kentucky, Judge James F. Gordon ordered the coal supplier: ". . . To begin immediate deliveries of coal to T.V.A. in accordance with the contract provision . . . ." *Tennessee Valley Authority v. First Pa. Bank & Trust Co.*, *Civ. No. 2525* (W.D. Ky., November 16, 1950). . . .

Summary and Conclusion

In conclusion, the Court finds that the contract under preliminary examination is neither inequitable nor one that imposes undue hardships against either party; that plaintiff's legal remedies under the circumstances are inadequate in light of the increased demand in coal, and that the inherent equity power of the Court permits a decree of specific performance.

The Court is also mindful of the various factors that are to be weighed in considering a motion for preliminary injunction, in particular, (a) substantial question, (b) probability of success on the merits, (c) balancing of injuries to parties, (d) and the public interest, which, under the circumstances, is of paramount importance. A continued and reliable supply of coal for the production of electricity is of important concern both to the industrial and private sectors of the region.

Accordingly, the motion is granted, except plaintiff shall be required to make payment to defendants for any amounts presently owing for past delivery of coal under the contract.

A final hearing on the merits shall be appropriately scheduled. . . .

MOTION FOR PERMANENT INJUNCTION

[After final hearing the court entered an order granting a permanent injunction, and issued its further memorandum opinion]

This case is again before the Court on the motion of Tennessee Valley Authority (TVA) for a permanent injunction requiring Mason Coal, Inc. (Mason) to supply certain coal for a one-year period. . . .

The findings and conclusions made by the Court in its March 5, 1974 memorandum are incorporated by reference in this memorandum. . . .

By order of March 18, 1974, the Court ordered Mason Coal to begin immediate coal deliveries under the contract to TVA, and preliminarily enjoined defendants from selling their coal to others until they had made the required deliveries to TVA pending final disposition of the case.

. . . Defendants contend that this Court lacks jurisdiction over the portion of this action seeking equitable relief affecting real property located beyond the Court's jurisdiction. An action for specific performance is by nature a proceeding in personam. Once the court acquires jurisdiction over the person of the defendant, it may decree specific performance of a contract affecting an interest in land located in another state or even another country. 71 AM. JUR., 2d, *Specific Performance* § 185 (1973); *Johnson v. Kimbro*, 40 Tenn. 557, 3 Head 557 (1859).

NOTES & QUESTIONS

1. The supply contract in *Curtice Bros. Co. v. Catts*, 72 N.J. Eq. 831, 66 A. 935 (1907) (tomatoes to be supplied for canning during packing season) was an output contract; and that in the *T.V.A.* case above was for a certain quantity of coal deliverable over a one-year period. For a case involving a *requirements* contract, see *Laclede Gas Co. v. Amoco Oil Co.*, 522 F.2d 33 (8th Circuit 1975), where the court held that the specific performance remedy should be granted against a propane producer on its contract to supply a utility with the latter's requirements of propane needed to serve retail customers in certain residential developments.

2. Is a supply contract in the nature of an *output* or a *requirements* contract more likely to be specifically enforced than a certain quantity contract? List the factors you believe are important in determining whether a contract to supply a certain quantity of goods should be specifically enforced. Are there any factors that you believe may operate as a basis for denial of specific performance if the supply

contract is an output or a requirements contract?

ii.   Impossibility of performance

SKELLY OIL CO. v. ASHMORE
365 S.W.2d 582 (Mo. 1963)

[Skelly Oil, vendee, entered into a contract with Ashmore, vendor, for the purchase and sale of property and the building thereon. The contract for sale contained no provision as to the assumption of risk occasioned by the destruction of the building. Shortly before the closing, the building was destroyed by fire. At closing, vendee informed vendor that they intended to close on the contract, regardless of the fire damage, but that vendee was entitled to the insurance proceeds received by the vendor for the value of the destroyed building. The vendor refused to assign the insurance proceeds, and the buyer filed suit seeking specific performance of the contract and a reduction in purchase price by the sum of the insurance proceeds received by the seller. The trial court determined that there had been a valid contract and that vendee was entitled to specific performance of the contract at a price reduced by the insurance payout to the vendor. On appeal the court listed five different views (one going back to an 1801 English case) for allocating "the burden of fortuitous loss between vendor and purchaser of real estate."]

HYDE, Judge:

. . . [W]e do not agree with the rule that arbitrarily places the risk of loss on the vendee from the time the contract is made. Instead we believe the Massachusetts rule is the proper rule. It is thus stated in *Libman v. Levenson*, 236 Mass. 221, 128 N.E. 13, 22 A.L.R. 560:

> [When] the conveyance is to be made of the whole estate, including both land and buildings, for an entire price, and the value of the buildings constitutes a large part of the total value of the estate, and the terms of the agreement show that they constituted an important part of the subject matter of the contract. . . the contract is to be construed as subject to the implied condition that it no longer shall be binding if, before the time for the conveyance to be made, the buildings are destroyed by fire. The loss by the fire falls upon the vendor, the owner; and if he has not protected himself by insurance, he can have no reimbursement of this loss; but the contract is no longer binding upon either party. If the purchaser has advanced any part of the price, he can recover it back. *Thompson v. Gould*, [*supra*] 20 Pick. [37 Mass.] 134, 138. If the change in the value of the estate is not so great, or if it appears that the building did not constitute so material a part of the estate to be conveyed as to result in an annulling of the contract, specific performance may be decreed, *with compensation for any breach of agreement*, or relief may be given in damages. . . .

. . . The reason for the Massachusetts rule is that specific performance is based on what is equitable; and it is not equitable to make a vendee pay the vendor for something the vendor cannot give him.

However, the issue in this case is not whether the vendee can be compelled to take the property without the building but whether the vendee is entitled to enforce the contract of sale, with the insurance proceeds substituted for the destroyed building. We see no inequity to defendants in such enforcement since they will receive the full amount ($20,000.00) for which they contracted to sell the property. Their contract not only described the land but also specifically stated they sold it "together with the buildings, driveways and all construction thereon." While the words "Service Station Site" appeared in the caption of the option contract and that no doubt was the ultimate use plaintiff intended to make of the land, the final agreement made by the parties was that plaintiff would take it subject to a lease of the building which would have brought plaintiff about $6,150.00 in rent during the term of the lease. Moreover, defendants' own evidence showed the building was valued in the insurance adjustment at $16,716.00 from which $4,179.00 was deducted for depreciation, making the loss $12,537.00. Therefore, defendants are not in a very good position to say the building was of no value to plaintiff. Furthermore, plaintiff having contracted for the land with the building on it, the decision concerning use or removal of the building, or even for resale of the entire property, was for the plaintiff to make. . . . The short of the matter is that defendants will get all they bargained for; but without the building or its value plaintiff will not.

We therefore affirm the judgment and decree of the trial court.

Storckman, J., dissents in separate opinion filed. Westhues, C.J., and Dalton, J., dissent and concur in separate dissenting opinion of Storckman, J.

Storckman, Judge (dissenting): I agree that the parties on March 7, 1958, entered into a valid contract for the transfer of the real estate, but in the circumstances I cannot assent to the holding that the plaintiff is entitled to specific performance on any terms other than those of the purchase contract without reduction in the contract price. . . .

The evidence is convincing that Skelly Oil Company was buying the lot as a site for a service station and that in so using it they not only wanted the Jones's lease terminated but intended to tear down and remove the building in question. The contract documents support this conclusion. Both the option and the letter of acceptance refer to the property as a "service station site" and contain escape clauses permitting Skelly to avoid the purchase agreement if proper permits could not be obtained or if zoning laws prohibited such use. . . . [P]laintiff's present contention [is] that the building and its rental under the lease represented a substantial part of the consideration for the purchase of the real estate. . . .

In spite of the issue made by Count 2 as to effect of the destruction of the building upon the value of the real estate, the trial court refused to permit cross-examination of plaintiff's witness to establish that the purpose and intent of Skelly was to remove the building from the premises when the lease was terminated, and the court rejected defendants' offer of proof to the same effect. In this equity action the testimony should have been received. . . .

The claim of neither party is particularly compelling insofar as specific performance in this case is concerned. The destruction of the building by fire, its insurance, and the disposition of the insurance proceeds were matters not contemplated by the parties and not provided for in the purchase contract documents. . . . Skelly's present claims are an afterthought inconsistent with its conduct throughout the negotiations and prior to the closing date.

In short, as to both Skelly and the Ashmores, the destruction of the insured building was a fortuitous circumstance supplying the opportunity to rid the property of a vexatious lease, to dispose of the building, and at the same time resulting in a windfall of $10,000. And the problem, in fact the only seriously contested issue between the parties, is which of them is to have the advantage of this piece of good fortune. Skelly contracted to pay $20,000 for the property. If it is awarded the $10,000 windfall, it will receive a $20,000 lot for $10,000. If the Ashmores retain the $10,000, they will in fact have realized $30,000 for a piece of property they have agreed to sell for $20,000.

In claiming the proceeds of the Ashmores' fire insurance policy, Skelly did not contend that the value of the real estate as a service station site had decreased. . . .

A valid legal excuse is a sufficient reason for refusal of specific performance. 49 Am. Jur., *Specific Performance*, section 2, p. 7, states: "Neither party has any legal right to refuse to perform the obligations imposed, in the absence of a reservation of the right to terminate the contract upon some contingency, unless because of circumstances subsequently arising there exists some valid legal excuse for nonperformance." Destruction of a particular thing upon which the contract depends is generally regarded as a legal excuse for nonperformance . . .

> It long has been settled in the English courts and in those of this country, federal and state, that where parties entered into a contract on the assumption that some particular thing essential to its performance will continue to exist and be available for the purpose and neither agrees to be responsible for its continued existence and availability the contract must be regarded as subject to an implied condition that, if before the time for performance and without the default of either party the particular thing ceases to exist or be available for the purpose, the contract shall be dissolved and the parties excused from performing it. *Texas Co. v. Hogarth Shipping Corp.*, 256 U.S. 619, 41 S. Ct. 612, 614, 65 L. Ed. 1123. . . .

The plaintiff's petition alleges that the building destroyed by fire "was a valuable appurtenance on said real estate worth more than $10,000.00 and that its destruction reduced the value of said real estate more than the sum of $10,000.00." So far as Skelly's use of the property as a service station site is concerned, this allegation cannot be true if Skelly's intent was to tear down and remove the building. On the other hand, if the plaintiff retained the property or sold to an investor who proposed to rent the building for a store or a similar business purpose, then the loss would be substantial and the insurance proceeds would be necessary to restore a suitable building. The petition asserts that "as a matter of law" the defendant held "said $10,000.00 insurance proceeds in trust for the benefit of plaintiff as the vendee of the defendants." I know of no equitable or legal principle that justifies the award of the insurance proceeds automatically to the purchaser in the circumstances of this case.

I cannot see that this court is bound by any precedent that can only be changed by an act of the general assembly. Specific performance is an equitable remedy and a part of our common law. *Fidelity Loan Securities Co. v. Moore*, 280 Mo. 315, 217 S.W. 286, 289[9]. . . .

> As a general rule, the specific performance of a contract by a court of equity is not a matter of absolute right in the parties demanding it, but the grant of specific performance is a matter of grace, and applications for such

relief are addressed to the sound discretion of the court. 81 C.J.S. Specific Performance § 9, pp. 417–418. Numerous Missouri cases are cited in the footnotes in support of the above statement of law. I do not think that the evidence justifies the grant of the relief requested in Count 2 of plaintiff's petition. It is generally recognized that much less strength of proof is required to defeat specific performance than to enforce the remedy. *Eisenbeis v. Shillington*, 349 Mo. 108, 159 S.W.2d 641, 644.

. . . We would not be justified in making a new contract for the parties to cover the building insurance, and a court of equity will not decree specific performance of a contract that is incomplete, indefinite or uncertain. . . . Nor can the courts supply an important element that has been omitted from the contract. . . .

The precise problem presented by this appeal has not heretofore been considered by the supreme court. The facts of this case demonstrate the unsoundness of a rigid and exclusive adherence to the doctrine that equity regards that as done which ought to be done. I would apply general equitable principles and first determine whether Skelly has established by clear, cogent and convincing evidence that it is entitled to have a trust declared in the insurance proceeds in accordance with the allegations of Count 2 of its petition. It is not enough to say that the Ashmores have been unjustly enriched because giving the fund to Skelly would result in its being unjustly enriched. . . . This would result in Skelly acquiring for $10,000 a filling station site for which it solemnly agreed to pay $20,000. Swapping one inequity for another is no justification for disturbing the legal title. . . .

[T]he majority opinion, employs conflicting rules or theories. It purports to adopt one but applies another. It professes to repudiate the equitable conversion theory and to adopt unequivocally the Massachusetts rule . . . . This rule as shown by the opinion's quotation from *Libman v. Levenson*, 236 Mass. 221, 128 N.E. 13, 22 A.L.R. 560, is that the sales contract will no longer be binding if the buildings are destroyed by fire and "the value of the buildings constitutes a large part of the total value of the estate, and the terms of the agreement show that they constituted an important part of the subject matter of the contract." In the same quotation from the Libman case, the circumstances and terms under which specific performance is granted are stated as follows: "If the change in the value of the estate is not so great, or if it appears that the buildings did not constitute so material a part of the estate to be conveyed as to result in an annulling of the contract, specific performance may be decreed, *with compensation for any breach of agreement, or relief may be given in damages*." Emphasis added.

Obviously the majority opinion did not find that the value of the building constituted "a large part of the total value of the estate" or "an important part of the subject matter of the contract," else it would have declared the sales contract no longer binding under the Massachusetts rule. What it had to find was that the value of the building was not so great or such a material part of the estate to be conveyed as to interfere with the decree of specific performance.

But at this point the majority opinion abandons any pretense of following the Massachusetts rule and switches back to the equitable conversion theory and awards the insurance proceeds as such to the vendee without a determination of compensation for breach or relief to be given in damages. . . . Logically the majority opinion should have remanded the case for a determination of the amount of actual damages suffered by Skelly or the compensation to which it is entitled if it still wants specific performance. This is undoubtedly what the Massachusetts rule contemplates. I would find no fault with such a procedure. . . .

On the present record the plaintiff has failed to show a superior equity in the insurance proceeds under the Massachusetts rule or otherwise, and on well-established equitable principles I would leave the legal title to that fund where it is. I would find against the plaintiff on Count 2 of its petition, but award it specific performance under Count 1 on the condition that it pay to the defendants the agreed purchase price of $20,000 less the amount of compensation or damages, if any, that it could establish against the defendants (not the insurance funds) at a plenary hearing of that issue in the trial court.

Dixon v. Salvation Army, 142 Cal. App. 3d 463, 191 Cal. Rptr. 111 (1983). In a purchaser's suit filed against vendors seeking a declaration of rights after fire destroyed improvements on the subject property, the trial court entered an order authorizing purchaser to seek specific performance of the contract at an abated price. The appellate court disagreed, holding that "where a material part of the subject property is destroyed without the fault of either party and neither title nor possession has passed to the purchaser, the vendor's performance is excused and the purchaser is entitled to the return of any consideration paid." The court also noted its view that the more equitable approach and the approach most compatible with the Uniform Vendor and Purchaser Risk Act is to place the parties in their original position, free to make a new bargain.

> A rule that denies a vendor the ability to specifically enforce the sales agreement where the material part of the consideration is lost or destroyed calls out for the converse also to be applied. It would be grossly unfair to require either party to accept consideration less than the whole of what was bargained for under these circumstances. If it is unfair to force the purchaser to receive materially damaged property, it is equally unfair to compel the vendor to accept a price substantially below what he bargained for. . . . Specific performance with abatement of the purchase price is not an appropriate remedy for the purchaser.

NOTES

1. The Uniform Vendor and Purchaser Risk Act, approved by the National Conference of Commissioners on Uniform State Laws and by the American Bar Association in 1935, was drafted by Professor Samuel Williston. A prefatory note to the act advises that "The object of the act is to protect the purchaser of real estate where there is a binding contract of sale and the property is destroyed before the purchaser has gone into possession or has taken legal title, and to protect the vendor after transfer of possession."

2. Thirteen jurisdictions are noted as having adopted the Vendor and Purchaser Risk Act, some with modifications: California, Hawaii, Illinois, Michigan, Nevada, New Mexico, New York, North Carolina, Oklahoma, Oregon, South Dakota, Texas, and Wisconsin.

3. In *Schlosser v. Norwest Bank South Dakota, N.A.*, 506 N.W.2d 416 (S.D. 1993), buyers under a contract for deed sued the sellers seeking a reduction in amount due, equal to the value of a dwelling destroyed by fire in which sellers retained a joint life estate. Reversing the trial court's dismissal of the complaint

and remanding, the court held that buyers' complaint was sufficient with regard to issues of risk of loss, breach of contract, and the sellers' duty to repair. The court agreed with buyers' claim that risk of loss can be deemed allocated to a seller when under the contract seller has the obligation to purchase insurance on the subject dwelling, and when seller is in possession of the premises and has the contract duty to keep them in repair.

iii.   Specific performance in arbitration awards

Greyson-Robinson Stores, Inc. v. Iris Constr. Corp., 8 N.Y.2d 133, 168 N.E.2d 377 (1960). Defendant, the owner of vacant land, entered into a written agreement with plaintiff whereby defendant undertook to erect a building to be rented to plaintiff for use as a department store. The agreement called for arbitration of all disputes, and gave the arbitrator ability to award any equitable remedy, including specific performance. After the initial construction began, defendant notified plaintiff that, because of difficulties in obtaining financing, it could not go further unless plaintiff agreed to increase the agreed rent. Plaintiff declined, and proceeded with arbitration to enforce the contract. The arbitrator found that the agreement did not contain any language relieving defendant of its obligation in the event of its inability to secure financing. Based on this finding the arbitrator awarded the plaintiff specific performance. A trial court sustained the arbitrator's decision, and defendant appealed. The New York Court of Appeals affirmed the decision as within the discretion of the trial court. The Court stated, "[a]bitration is by consent and those who agree to arbitrate should be made to keep their solemn, written promises." The Court also said that if defendant failed to comply, plaintiff could use contempt of court proceedings to enforce the judgment. The dissent did not disagree with the principle that arbitration awards should be sustained by courts, but asserted that doing so blindly leads to impractical and illogical outcomes. Defendant was not able to obtain financing for the project in spite of applying at 27 different financial institutions, and the dissent pointed out that even were defendant held in contempt for not performing, it would still not be able to get the financing needed to perform. In addition, once the arbitrator had made his decision, he had washed his hands of the controversy, and it would be the court that would actually have to enforce the judgment and supervise the project, something courts generally try to avoid. The dissent would have remitted the matter to the arbitrator to determine whether specific performance was even possible and, if not possible, then have the arbitrator decide the question of damages.

e.   Specific performance — additional considerations

i.   Impracticability

MADISON PLAZA, INC. v. SHAPIRA CORP.
180 Ind. App. 141, 387 N.E.2d 483 (1979)

STATEMENT OF THE CASE

LOWDERMILK, Judge:

Plaintiff-appellant Madison Plaza, Inc. (Madison Plaza) brings this appeal after the Jefferson Circuit Court refused to issue an injunction requiring defendant-appellee Shapira Corporation (Shapira) to continue operating a retail store in Madison Plaza's shopping center pursuant to a lease executed by Madison Plaza and Shapira.

FACTS

Madison Plaza owns a shopping center in Jefferson County. Shapira executed a ten-year lease on April 19, 1974, and occupied approximately one fifth of the total space available at the shopping center.

Shapira's store in Jefferson County opened for business on October 21, 1974. Although Shapira made conscientious, persistent efforts to operate the store profitably, sales declined and losses mounted.

The trial court listed reasons for the financial problems suffered by Shapira in Jefferson County:

> A number of factors were responsible for the Madison store operating at a loss. The store sold medium-priced merchandise, nationally advertised branded merchandise, and was not discount oriented. The other stores in the center would not participate in any promotional activities such as rides, antique shows and the like, designed to attract customers to the center. This was another factor accounting for the loss operations of the Madison store. General economic conditions including layoffs and strikes resulted in higher unemployment in Madison. This contributed to the downfall of the Madison store.

On May 9, 1977, Shapira informed Madison Plaza that it intended to hold a final sale during May 1977 and then vacate the premises. Madison Plaza responded with a letter informing Shapira that Shapira would not be permitted to discontinue operation of its store in the shopping center.

Shapira did vacate the premises but has continued to pay its monthly rent, which amounts to $37,125 annually. The trial court listed the damages suffered by Madison Plaza as a result of Shapira's departure:

> A. One-fifth (1/5) of the center is vacant and is not contributing to the pulling power of the center;

> B. The vacancy projects an image of failure to the public;

> C. The closing has caused plaintiff's center to lose that group of customers shopping for clothing and shoes;

> D. Financing for future expansion will be more difficult to obtain because of the vacancy;

> E. Future expansion of the center will be more difficult because the vacancy projects an image of failure discouraging prospective tenants from locating in the center;

> F. Plaintiff is put in a difficult negotiating position with prospective tenants because of the vacancy;

G. The empty space is more difficult to lease when it is vacant than if Shapira Corporation were doing business;

H. The Shapira space will be difficult to lease to a new tenant because of its large size and because it was built specifically to Shapira Corporation specifications;

I. Plaintiff will not collect any additional percentage rent from defendant during the term of the lease if defendant is not doing business;

J. The loss of pulling power into the center by the Shapira vacancy will result in lower gross sales by the other tenants and will cause plaintiff to lose percentage rents from the other tenants in the center.

The trial court nevertheless refused to issue an injunction requiring Shapira to continue operating its store in Madison Plaza's shopping center. The trial court stated two reasons for its refusal, each of which is set forth hereinafter.

ISSUE

The issue presented by this appeal is not whether Shapira has breached its lease. The only issue is whether the trial court erred in refusing to grant an injunction requiring Shapira to continue operation of its store in Madison Plaza's shopping center.

DISCUSSION AND DECISION

We quote the first reason given by the trial court for denying Madison Plaza's request for an injunction:

> The provision in the lease entered into by the parties that the tenant shall keep the premises open and available for business "except when prevented by strikes, fire, casualty or other causes beyond the tenant's reasonable control" relieves the defendant from continuing to operate its store at Madison Plaza because all reasonable efforts were made by the defendant which were calculated to cause the store to operate profitably. Nevertheless, despite such efforts, the store lost very substantial sums of money in its operation and thus its successful, i.e. profitable, operation was beyond the reasonable control of the defendant. . . .

Madison Plaza contends that the inability of Shapira to operate its store profitably should not be deemed a cause beyond Shapira's control which would excuse Shapira from keeping the store open and available for business activity. We agree.

The general rule is that performance will not be excused simply because a contract causes hardship or proves to be unprofitable. . . . Justice Traynor explained in *Lloyd v. Murphy* (1944), 25 Cal. 2d 48, 153 P.2d 47, 50, that "(t)he purpose of a contract is to place the risks of performance upon the promisor. . . ."

Shapira executed a lease in which it promised that it would "during the entire term, continuously use the demised premises for the purpose stated in this lease, carrying on therein Tenant's business undertaking diligently, assiduously and energetically." Shapira further agreed that it would not vacate the premises without the consent of Madison Plaza.

When the trial court recognized unprofitability as an excuse releasing Shapira from its duty to operate its store on the leased premises, the trial court erroneously imposed upon Madison Plaza (the promisee) the risk of unprofitable performance by Shapira (the promisor). . . .

We hold that the trial court erred in concluding that Shapira's inability to earn a profit excused Shapira from its obligation to continue operation of its store on the leased premises.

We quote a portion of the second reason given by the trial court for denying Madison Plaza's request for an injunction:

A. The lease provides for the operation by the defendant of a junior department store on the leased premises for a period of ten years commencing October 21, 1974, and ending October 31, 1984. In order to operate a junior department store, the defendant must exercise special knowledge, taste, skill and judgment in selecting and investing in inventory, selecting and training and compensating adequate personnel needed to operate the store, and in making innumerable other day-to-day business decisions. A decree of specific performance would require the Court to maintain constant supervision over a long period of time of acts involving taste, skill, judgment and technical knowledge in order to enforce the decree.

* * *

F. Should the Court undertake specific performance of the lease, it would become involved in a long and complicated administration of the affairs of the defendant and such control over the affairs of the defendant is out of keeping with the character of the Court's primary function.

G. The enforcement of a decree of specific performance would unreasonably tax the time, attention and resources of the Court.

Madison Plaza contends that this conclusion of law is contrary to law and is not supported by sufficient evidence. More specifically, Madison Plaza insists that court supervision would not be required: The trial court would merely decree that Shapira must operate its store; Shapira, for its own benefit, would make efforts to operate its store profitably; if Shapira did not honor the injunction, Madison Plaza would file contempt proceedings.

Specific performance is an equitable remedy which is not available as a matter of right. It may be resisted on weaker grounds than are required for its maintenance. The granting of specific performance rests in the sound judicial discretion of the trial court. . . . A court may properly deny a request for specific performance if such a decree would require supervision by the court for a lengthy period of time. . . .

The findings of fact made by the trial court in the case at bar reveal the extensive and varied tasks and talents involved in operating Shapira's retail department store. . . . Although the entry of an order requiring Shapira to continue operation of its store would be a simple matter, such an order would be ill-advised if the trial court had insufficient ability to enforce its order. . . .

. . . In the case at bar we must search for an abuse of discretion in denying an injunction. An abuse of judicial discretion ". . . is an erroneous conclusion and judgment, one clearly against the logic and effect of the facts before the court or against the reasonable, probable and actual deductions to be drawn therefrom." *Guraly v. Tenta* (1956), 126 Ind. App. 527, 531, 132 N.E.2d 725, 727. Although Judge Sullivan made the following statement in *Henline, Inc. v. Martin* (1976), Ind. App., 348 N.E.2d 416, 420, in the context of reviewing a default judgment, the statement is appropriate also in the case at bar: ". . . the fact that another trial court might not have abused its discretion by granting . . . relief on these facts, does not necessarily mean that the court below abused its discretion by denying relief."

Due to the lengthy period of time involved, the nature and size of Shapira's business operation, and the detailed nature of the relief sought by Madison Plaza in its complaint, we cannot say that the Jefferson Circuit Court's judgment is clearly against the logic and effect of the facts before the court. We hold that the trial court did not abuse its discretion when it denied the equitable relief sought by Madison Plaza.

Judgment affirmed.

Jones v. Parker, 163 Mass. 564, 40 N.E. 1044 (1895). Plaintiff-lessee entered into a lease agreement with defendant-lessor in which lessor promised to deliver possession of a space in the basement of a building under construction and that the premises would be reasonably heated and lit. When the building was completed, defendant refused to install the heating and lighting apparatus and turn over possession to the plaintiff. The plaintiff brought this action requesting specific performance, claiming that possession of the building without heat and light was impracticable. The defendant demurred. The Court said no argument was necessary to show that the covenant was valid, and the only question was whether a remedy of specific performance was appropriate. Here, the agreement at hand made heating and lighting an integral and essential part of the lease, without which possession could not begin. The Court noted that enforcing a specific performance decree for construction would call on the court to do more than it had the habit of doing, but it was not beyond the capabilities and resources of the court in this case. "There is no universal rule that courts of equity never will enforce a contract which requires some building to be done . . . . Demurrer overruled."

Northern Delaware Indus. Development Corp. v. E.W. Bliss Co., 245 A.2d 431 (Del. Ch. 1968). Defendant agreed by written construction contract to furnish plaintiffs with all labor, services, materials and equipment necessary to expand and modernize plaintiffs' steel fabricating plant. This was a huge undertaking, involving an area of some 60 acres and a contract price of $27.5 million to be paid defendant. Defendant fell behind on the work completion schedules in the contract, and plaintiffs sued, seeking an order directing defendant to requisition 300 more workmen for a night shift. Plaintiffs alleged that under the contract defendant had promised to put on the job the number of men required to make up a full second shift at the plant site, and that at the time suit was filed defendant was operating only one shift. The court refused to enter that order, pointing out: (a) that a court of equity is not without "jurisdiction in a proper case to order the completion of an expressly designed and largely completed construction project, particularly where the undertaking to construct is tied in with a contract for the sale of land and the construction in question is largely finished"; (b) that the court should not "become committed to supervising the carrying out of a massive, complex, and unfinished construction contract, a result which would necessarily follow as a consequence of ordering defendant to requisition laborers as prayed for"; and (c) that unless there are special circumstances or the public interest is directly involved, a court of equity should not order specific performance of a building contract when it would be impractical to carry out such an order (citing the Massachusetts *Jones v. Parker* case as authority for this proposition). Finding also that the defendant had merely "contemplated" hiring a night shift, and that the building plan was not so "precisely definite as to make compliance therewith subject to effective judicial supervision," the court concluded that it "would not exercise jurisdiction over plaintiffs' application for an order for specific performance" since it would be "inappropriate in view of the imprecision of the contract provisions relied upon and the impracticability if not impossibility of effective enforcement by the Court of a mandatory order designed to keep a specific number of men on the job at the site of a steel mill which is undergoing extensive modernization and expansion."

NOTES & QUESTIONS

1. For a case in which a preliminary injunction was granted requiring an anchor tenant to continue to operate, at least through trial of the case, see *Massachusetts Mutual Life Insurance Co. v. Associated Dry Good Corp.*, 786 F. Supp. 1403 (N.D. Ind., 1992). There, after the tenant announced that it intended to close its store, the shopping mall owner sued, seeking temporary and permanent injunctive relief requiring the store to continue to operate for the 12 years remaining on its lease. The trial court order also required, as a precondition to the effectiveness of the injunction, that the owner post a $1 million bond against which the tenant could proceed to recover damages in the event of a subsequent finding that the injunction had been improvidently granted.

2. *Practice Point*: When seeking preliminary injunctive relief, counsel should not disregard the possibility that, if plaintiff is successful, the order will often also require plaintiff to post a surety bond. The injunction will be of no use to plaintiff if the bond is set so high that plaintiff is unable to obtain and post that bond. Thus, even when a court rules that preliminary injunctive relief is to issue, the defense may be able to establish the appropriateness of a bond amount that renders the injunction of no practical benefit to the plaintiff. Of course, applicable law may also authorize the court to waive bond, or allow individual bond not secured by property or surety, or reduce the bond amount from that otherwise required.

ii. Lack of specificity

AMMERMAN v. CITY STORES CO.
394 F.2d 950 (D.C. Cir. 1968)

PER CURIAM.

Appellants, builders and developers of Tyson's Corner Shopping Center in Fairfax County, Virginia, challenge the District Court's decision (1) that the builders had given City Stores Company, owners of Lansburgh's Department Store, a binding option to lease one of the major buildings to be constructed at the contemplated shopping center and (2) that the option-lease agreement is sufficiently definite and certain in terms of design, type of construction, and price to be specifically enforced.

The appellants in their statement of points have here contended that the District Court erred: in ordering specific performance in that the existence and terms of the contract had not been established by clear and convincing evidence; in granting equitable relief despite the appellants' claim that the appellee had been guilty of "laches and unclean hands"; and in ordering specific performance of the contract since some substantial details will require future negotiations and yet others are said to be unclear or can not be performed. . . .

At the core of the dispute is an undated letter (text, infra), from the appellants to one Jagels, then President of Lansburgh's, given at a time when the builders were attempting to obtain a ruling from the Fairfax Board of County Supervisors which would permit the rezoning of their tract of land for use as a shopping center. Prospects for a favorable outcome at a May 31, 1962, hearing, then yet in the future, were in doubt. . . .

Judge Gasch [in the trial court] agreed with the appellee that the Jagels letter was given in exchange for a promise that Lansburgh's be given an opportunity to become a major tenant at Tyson's Corner on terms equal to those given other major tenants. The trial judge further found that this promise had been memorialized in the following undated letter given to Mr. Jagels on or about May 29, 1962:

> Dear Mr. Jagels:
>
> We very much appreciate the efforts which you have expended in endeavoring to assist Mr. Gudelsky and me in our application for zoning at Tyson's Corner for a Regional Shopping Center.
>
> You have our assurance that in the event we are successful with our application, that we will give you the opportunity to become one of our contemplated center's major tenants with rental and terms at least equal to that of any other major department store in the center.
>
> Sincerely yours,
> (s) Isadore M. Gudelsky
> (s) Theodore N. Lerner

. . . At the time the contract was made, the builders themselves had no more than a "chance" or "opportunity" to succeed in their Tyson's Corner rezoning project. That it may thus have seemed futile to specify in detail the terms of the agreement, did not preclude a ruling that the Gudelsky-Lerner letter evidenced in Lansburgh's favor a legally binding option to take a lease at the shopping center. The District Judge, finding that an exercise of the option was conditioned upon the happening of certain events, concluded:

> The first condition precedent to the Lerner-Gudelsky obligation to Lansburgh's was the securing of necessary zoning for its Tyson's Corner tract. . . . The second . . . was its entering into leases with other major tenants for stores in the center, so the terms of those leases could provide the essential terms of a lease to be offered to (Lansburgh's). (Appellants) did secure the zoning, and they did, in the latter half of 1965, enter into leases with Woodward & Lothrop and Hecht department stores . . .(at which time appellants) were under an immediate contractual obligation to tender (Lansburgh's) a lease which in all its material terms would be at least as favorable . . . as the two other leases were to their respective

stores . . .. Both the Hecht and Woodward & Lothrop leases . . . contain clauses to the effect that their terms will be at least equal to those offered to other lessees in the center. Thus, even though none of the stores . . . will be identical in design, it is apparent . . . that complete equality of material terms governing occupancy, including amount of space and cost per square foot, and substantially equal terms on less material aspects of the lease, is within the customary contemplation of parties entering into shopping center agreements of the type at issue in this case.

. . . Judge Gasch found that Lansburgh's had exercised its option and was entitled to an order compelling the builders to grant it a lease equal in terms to that of the Hecht lease. The appellants argue that the option-lease agreement is too indefinite and uncertain to be specifically enforced because substantial terms have been left to future negotiation. We approve the trial judge's recognition as a rule of law that the mere fact that a contract, definite in material respects, contains some terms which are subject to further negotiation between plaintiff and defendant will not bar a decree for specific performance, if in the court's discretion specific performance should be granted. . . .

Treating the enforcement of construction contracts as a question novel to the District of Columbia, Judge Gasch emphasized that the essential basis for interposition by the court is the inadequacy or impracticability of the plaintiff's legal remedy rather than the generic subject matter of the contract.

Here it is apparent that Lansburgh's could have had no adequate remedy in damages for any attempt in that respect would have been impractical because of the impossibility of an appropriate measurement. Moreover, damages could hardly compensate for the loss of the sought for opportunity to raise Lansburgh's image and economic position in the Metropolitan Washington area by its anticipated expansion into the suburbs, and for that reason alone could have been deemed inadequate.

Thus, where the contractual obligation being enforced involves more than the mere construction of a building and the building is to be built on land controlled by its owner (making it impossible for the enforcing party to have the job done by another and charged to the defaulting owner), specific enforcement becomes entirely appropriate. Nor should relief be withheld merely because it would order construction unless the difficulties of supervision by the court outweigh the importance of enforcement to the plaintiff. In this case, as the District Judge found, the construction criteria set forth in the Hecht and Woodward & Lothrop leases are sufficiently detailed to allow the court, applying the standard of equality required by the option, to enforce the lease contract with little difficulty of supervision. The District Court here has retained jurisdiction and can appoint a special master to settle such details as the parties may not agree upon or which can not be resolved through arbitration.

Affirmed.

NOTES & QUESTIONS

1. A specific performance order is not the only equitable remedy available through which to seek enforcement of contract provisions. The injunction, another equitable remedy to which recourse may be had in an appropriate case, may

operate to require compliance with contracts and contract clauses.

2. If you were the trial judge in the *Walgreen v. Sara Creek Property Co.* case above, would you have preferred to provide a damage remedy, a specific performance remedy, or a remedy by way of injunction?

iii.   Personal services contracts

BLOCH v. HILLEL TORAH NORTH SUBURBAN DAY SCHOOL
100 Ill. App. 3d 204, 426 N.E.2d 976 (1981)

McNAMARA, Justice:

Plaintiffs appeal from an order of the trial court granting summary judgment in favor of defendant Hillel Torah North Suburban Day School. Helen Bloch is a grade school child who was expelled from defendant, a private Jewish school, at mid-year in 1980. Her parents brought this action seeking to enjoin expulsion and for specific performance of defendant's contract to educate Helen.

The complaint alleged that defendant arbitrarily and in bad faith breached its contract, and that Helen's expulsion was motivated by defendant's disapproval of plaintiffs' leadership role in combatting an epidemic of head lice at the school. The complaint also alleged that the school uniquely corresponded exactly to the religious commitments desired by plaintiffs. Defendant's answer stated that Helen was expelled, pursuant to school regulations, for excessive tardiness and absences. The parties also disputed the duration of the contractual obligation to educate. Defendant contended that the contract was to endure only for a school year since tuition for only that period of time was accepted by it. Plaintiffs maintained that the contract, as implied by custom and usage, was to endure for eight years, the first year's tuition creating irrevocable option contracts for the subsequent school years, provided that Helen conformed to defendant's rules.

After the trial court denied plaintiffs' request for a preliminary injunction, both sides moved for summary judgment. The trial court denied plaintiffs' motion and granted the motion of defendant. In the same order, the trial court gave plaintiffs leave to file an amended complaint for money damages.

Whether a court will exercise its jurisdiction to order specific performance of a valid contract is a matter within the sound discretion of the court and dependent upon the facts of each case. . . . Where the contract is one which establishes a personal relationship calling for the rendition of personal services, the proper remedy for a breach is generally not specific performance but rather an action for money damages. . . . The reasons for denying specific performance in such a case are as follows: the remedy at law is adequate; enforcement and supervision of the order of specific performance may be problematic and could result in protracted litigation; and the concept of compelling the continuance of a personal relationship to which one of the parties is resistant is repugnant as a form of involuntary servitude. . . .

Applying these principles to the present case, we believe that the trial court properly granted summary judgment in favor of defendant. It is beyond dispute that the relationship between a grade school and a student is one highly personal in nature. Similarly, it is apparent that performance of such a contract requires a rendition of a variety of personal services. Although we are cognizant of the difficulties in duplicating the personal services offered by one school, particularly one like defendant, we are even more aware of the difficulties pervasive in compelling the continuation of a relationship between a young child and a private school which openly resists that relationship. In such a case, we believe the trial court exercised sound judgment in ruling that plaintiffs are best left to their remedy for damages. . . . In *St. Joseph School v. Lamm* (1972), 288 Ala. 68, 257 So. 2d 318, the Supreme Court of Alabama held that specific performance was not available to compel a private grade school to educate a young child since such a contract calls for personal services. *See also Flint v. St. Augustus High School* (La. 1975), 323 So. 2d 229, 236; Cf. *Greene v. Howard Univ.* (D.D.C. 1967), 271 F. Supp. 609, *rev'd in part*, (1969), 412 F.2d 1128 (in action for private school's breach of contract to employ teacher, damages at law and not specific performance is the appropriate remedy.)

Plaintiffs' reliance on three Illinois cases is misplaced. In *DeMarco v. University of Health Services* (1976), 40 Ill. App. 3d 474, 352 N.E.2d 356, a mandatory injunction was issued compelling a school to confer a degree on plaintiff. The order did not compel the continuance of a personal relationship, but instead provided for the performance of a solitary ministerial act which recognized the termination of the parties' relationship. Similarly, in *Tanner v. Bd. of Trustees of Univ. of Illinois* (1977), 48 Ill. App. 3d 680, 6 Ill. Dec. 679, 363 N.E.2d 208, plaintiff sought to compel the issuance of a degree. In *Steinberg v. Chicago Medical School* (1977), 69 Ill. 2d 320, 13 Ill. Dec. 699, 371 N.E.2d 634, the court held that the plaintiff stated a valid class action for an injunction against a medical school's misrepresentation of admission standards in its brochure and for restitution of application fees. In so holding, the court noted that plaintiff did not seek to compel the school to admit him. There was no issue concerning the enforcement of a personal relationship between adverse parties.

Illinois law recognizes the availability of a remedy for monetary damages for a private school's wrongful expulsion of a student in violation of its contract. . . . And especially, where, as here, the issue involves a personal relationship between a grade school and a young child, we believe plaintiffs are best left to a remedy for damages for breach of contract.

For the reasons stated, the judgment of the circuit court of Cook County is affirmed, and the cause is remanded for further proceedings permitting plaintiffs to file an amended complaint for money damages.

NOTES & QUESTIONS

1. The rule that courts do not grant the specific performance remedy to require the performance of personal services contracts also finds support in provisions of the U.S. Constitution:

Amendment XIII. Slavery Abolished; Enforcement

> Section 1. Neither slavery nor involuntary servitude, except as a punishment for crime whereof the party shall have been duly convicted, shall exist within the United States, or any place subject to their jurisdiction.

Section 2. Congress shall have power to enforce this article by appropriate legislation.

2. The involuntary servitude principle is ordinarily utilized in cases that seek orders requiring contracting parties personally to perform services. For example, in *Beverly Glen Music, Inc. v. Warner Communications, Inc.*, 178 Cal. App. 3d 1142, 224 Cal. Rptr. 260 (1986), it was held that an unwilling employee cannot be compelled to continue to provide services to his employer, either by ordering specific performance of his contract or by injunction, and to do so runs afoul of the Thirteenth Amendment's prohibition against involuntary servitude.

3. Would it have been appropriate in the *Madison Plaza* scenario above (*Madison Plaza, Inc. v. Shapira Corp.*) to apply the "performance of personal services" or "involuntary servitude" principle as an additional ground upon which to deny the specific performance order sought by the plaintiff lessor? If you were counsel for the tenant how might you structure an argument based on the principle?

iv.   Mutuality of remedy

Bleecher v. Conte, 29 Cal. 3d 345, 698 P.2d 1154 (1981). Plaintiff-buyers entered into a negotiated agreement with defendant-seller for the purchase of land. The agreement contained a liquidated damages clause that limited seller's remedy to possession of any plans or reports prepared at the buyers' request and expense. After plaintiffs deposited earnest money into escrow, pursuant to the agreement, defendant refused to proceed with the sale unless plaintiffs paid the entire purchase price before the end of the calendar year. This was not part of the agreement, and plaintiffs brought suit for specific performance. At trial, defendant claimed that the presence of a clause where one party waived specific performance precluded such remedy for both parties. The court noted that although the traditional view had been that one party to a contract could not obtain specific performance if that remedy was not available to the other party, in 1969 the California legislature discarded the rigid requirement of mutuality of remedy. The court also referenced the RESTATEMENT OF CONTRACTS view that when specific performance of an agreed counter-performance would not be available, specific performance may be compelled if it would otherwise be an appropriate remedy. Thus, the court held that seller's waiver of her right to specific performance in the contract's liquidated damages clause did not prevent the buyers from seeking, or preclude the trial court from compelling, specific performance of this land sale agreement.

Converse v. Fong, 159 Cal. App. 3d 86, 205 Cal. Rptr. 242 (1984). Purchasers filed suit seeking specific performance of a contract entered into when seller, needing funds to pay state and local taxes and other debts, offered to sell her family home to plaintiffs, who owned property next door. Later a son of defendant came forward with a $20,000 loan to help his mother pay debts, and she then attempted to rescind the contract and returned plaintiffs' earnest money deposit. The trial court refused to grant specific performance, holding that in light of various provisions of the valid and enforceable contract there was no mutuality of remedy between the parties, and that defendant validly rescinded the contract prior to plaintiffs' performance. The appellate court reversed and remanded, holding that "Mutuality of remedy is not a prerequisite to granting specific performance if there is sufficient assurance of each party's performance of the agreed obligations," and directing the trial court to "determine if equitable considerations should otherwise justify specific performance." The court discussed the presumption that a breach of contract to sell real property cannot be adequately relieved by pecuniary compensation, and noted that the trial court may consider the equities in determining whether damages are indicated or whether it is appropriate to grant specific performance. In its opinion the court also held that the contract was binding and enforceable even though it obligated the parties to perform when specific contingencies were satisfied; buyers acted timely under a satisfaction clause conditioning the continued validity of the contract upon their approval of termite and roof inspection reports; and the change in seller's financial condition after signing the contract was not attributable to buyers and was not a lawful basis for rescission of the otherwise binding contract. Referring to *Bleecher v. Conte* and Civil Code § 3386 cited in *Bleecher*, the court also noted that mutuality of remedy is no longer strictly required under California law; that "If otherwise equitable, specific performance may be refused only if there is not sufficient assurance that the defendant will receive the performance promised to her"; and that California now follows a flexible mutuality rule that allows courts to adjust the equities and ensure fair treatment for both parties.

NOTE

Sellers of real estate, as well as buyers, may seek the remedy of specific performance. The fact that a seller entitled to specific performance seeks money (i.e., the purchase price) from the buyer is not ordinarily considered a basis to refuse the remedy. There is a substantive difference between a *specific performance* decree directing that money be paid by a defaulting buyer to the innocent seller, and a *damages* judgment for money against the breaching buyer in favor of the innocent seller. Specific performance has the effect of affirming the continued existence of the contract, requires performance of remaining contract duties by both buyer and seller, and directs payment of purchase price by buyer and conveyance of title by seller. The damages remedy, however, contemplates that contract obligations terminate by reason of buyer's breach, that seller will retain title to the property, and that buyer pay compensation for seller's loss caused by the breach.

v.   Laches

Patterson v. Amundson, 201 Or. App. 486, 119 P.3d 264, (Or. Ct. App. 2005). Laches is an equitable defense and is available against a claim for specific performance, but there are several elements required to establish it. This case involved an agreement for the sale and purchase of a house, with an $88,500 down payment toward a final purchase price of $275,000, based on two documents: a 1994 "Sale Agreement and Receipt for Earnest Money, and a 1995 "Lease With Purchase." On taking possession in May of 1995, the plaintiffs essentially assumed payment of the mortgage, taxes and insurance, along with routine maintenance, with closing to take place on or about December 31, 1995. A controversy developed over serious defects in the home and the purchasers/plaintiffs requested vendor/defendant to correct the defects before the closing. He did not, and the closing never occurred, though negotiations over the defects continued. Further complications arose in trying to close the transaction, including a rescission by the plaintiffs, a declaration of bankruptcy by the defendant rendering recovery of the down payment impossible and tax problems for the defendant resulting in an IRS lien on the house. Plaintiffs remained in possession of the house and continued to pay the mortgage, property taxes and insurance until June 2002 when they filed this action seeking to quiet title in their names. The trial court awarded the plaintiffs specific performance of the contract.

On appeal, defendant contended, among other theories, that plaintiffs were barred by laches from obtaining specific performance because plaintiffs had not complied with the contract's "time is of the essence" provision, and that they were not ready, willing and able to pay off the purchase price throughout the course of the dispute. The appellate court affirmed the lower court's rulings on specific performance, holding: "we do not think it equitable for defendant to receive plaintiffs' payment of $88,500, the benefit of [plaintiffs'] payments for principal, interest, taxes, and insurance on the property, the value of the repairs that plaintiffs made to the property, and the value of the appreciation of the property over what is now a ten-year period, all of which would occur if we denied specific performance of the contract." In addressing the "time is of the essence" issue, the court said, "if the vendor, for whose benefit the stipulation about time being of the essence of the contract is made, would insist upon it, he must act promptly upon that provision so that any indulgence upon his part will amount to a nullification of that feature of the covenant. Defendant's actions are inconsistent with an intent to enforce any time-of-the-essence provision."

The court then turned to defendant's assertion that the trial court erred in concluding that plaintiffs' action was not barred by laches, and restated rules from a 1986 opinion by Oregon's Supreme Court and a 1996 appellate court opinion:

> In order to prevail on [a] defense of laches, [a] defendant [generally] must. . . establish the following three elements: (1) [the] plaintiffs delayed asserting their claim for an unreasonable length of time, (2) with full knowledge of all relevant facts (and laches does not start to run until such knowledge is shown to exist), (3) resulting in such substantial prejudice to [the] defendant that it would be inequitable for the court to grant relief.
>
> If the action is commenced after the expiration of the analogous statute of limitations, the plaintiff must prove the absence of laches.

On these points defendant asserted that the period of the analogous limitation statute had expired and that plaintiffs failed to sustain their burden of proving the absence of laches. Plaintiffs in response claimed that the analogous statute had not expired and, even if it had, they met their burden on the laches issue by showing that defendant was not substantially prejudiced by delay in filing the action. The Court agreed with plaintiffs' second contention. "At trial, plaintiffs presented evidence that rebutted any presumption that defendant was substantially prejudiced by their failure to bring this action earlier. Plaintiffs demonstrated that defendant received all the equity that he had in the house in 1995. From then on, plaintiffs made monthly payments that covered the mortgage obligation, property taxes, and insurance. Thus, the mortgage was only nominally an obligation of defendant. The delay did not prejudice defendant, and plaintiffs' claim was not barred by laches." The trial court's judgment was affirmed.

NOTE

The equitable remedy of specific performance may be held time-barred when the equitable *laches* defense is raised, even though other breach of contract claims in that same case — claims seeking money damages — are not time-barred under applicable statutes of limitation. In *CertainTeed Corp. v. Celotex Corp. and Celotex Asbestos Settlement Trust*, No. 471, 2005 Del. Ch. LEXIS 11, (Del. Ch. 2005), involving claims of breach of a business asset agreement, certain of plaintiff's claims for money damages were held not time-barred because suit was filed within the period of the applicable statute of limitations. However, plaintiff's request for a specific performance remedy in that same suit was held time-barred, because "laches bars CertainTeed from seeking specific performance of these obligations after acting so slowly in bringing suit. A demand for specific performance is akin to a request for a mandatory injunction and it is not appropriate to measure promptness by analogy to a statute of limitations for a damages claim. CertainTeed's inexcusable torpidity in bringing suit prejudices Celotex." Also, "Once it had reason to suspect, despite the pre-Closing representations and historical environmental audits to be provided to it by Celotex, that some of the facilities did not comply with their warranted condition, [plaintiff] CertainTeed was not entitled to lean back in the recliner and not investigate whether, as to other of the facilities, similar breaches also existed."

vi.   Unclean hands and equitable estoppel

Ingram v. Kasey's Associates, 340 S.C. 98, 531 S.E.2d 287 (2000). Here, where the tenant of a restaurant sued the landlord and his subtenant operator of the restaurant for specific performance of an option to purchase the property, the trial court found for the defendants, the appellate court reversed for the plaintiff, and the South Carolina Supreme Court ruled that the trial court judgment had been correct. The four main reasons for the supreme court's ruling were: "(1) the Court of Appeals used no equity doctrines, even though Ingram sought an equitable remedy; (2) the Court of Appeals did not strictly construe the option contract in favor of the optionor and against the optionee; (3) the Court of Appeals disregarded specific findings of fact made by the trial judge that Ingram was unable to pay the purchase price within the lease period; and (4) the Court of Appeals recognized only the general rule of options, which does not apply to all option contracts in every context." On the issue of whether plaintiff had exercised the option, the supreme court noted that the option was included in a lease contract, by specific terms the lease contract called for payment before expiration of the lease, and the mere expression of intent to exercise the option without tendering payment was not adequate to exercise the option. The Court then addressed issues relating to the specific performance remedy, noting first that specific performance is a claim in equity, that the standard of review is *de novo*, and that an appellate court is not required to ignore the trial court's findings of fact, and continuing "In order to compel specific performance, a court of equity must find: (1) there is clear evidence of a valid agreement; (2) the agreement had been partly carried into execution on one side with the approbation of the other; and (3) the party who comes to compel performance has performed his or her part, or has been and remains able and willing to perform his or her part of the contract." In this case, however, plaintiff never demonstrated that he was ready and willing to perform his obligations under the options contract, and indeed the record below "indicates that [plaintiff] Ingram was not in a position to pay Kasey's the purchase price" on either the lease expiration date or the date plaintiff "brought the action for specific performance."

Holding that the equitable maxim "[h]e who seeks equity must do equity" is also applicable in this case, the supreme court noted that: (a) plaintiff had "misled the defendant by promising that he would not exercise his option" and defendant in reliance had negotiated a new agreement with the subtenant and was planning to purchase adjacent property for $135,000 based on the assurance; (b) plaintiff was also aware of the owner's need to continuously maintain operation of the restaurant or he would lose his grandfathered zoning rights; and (c) there was evidence that the plaintiff was using the option for the improper ulterior purpose of pressuring the subtenant in negotiations over the purchase of the restaurant business. Concluding that defendant must prevail in light of the record and the law, the Court ruled that "[t]he doctrines of unclean hands and equitable estoppel can be used to preclude Ingram from recovering in equity. Unclean hands precludes a plaintiff from recovering in equity if he acted unfairly in a matter that is the subject of the litigation to the prejudice of the defendant. Elements of equitable estoppel as to the party estopped are: (1) conduct by the party estopped which amounts to a false representation or concealment of material facts; (2) the intention that such conduct shall be acted upon by the other party; and (3) knowledge, actual or constructive, of the true facts. As to the party claiming the estoppel, the elements are: (1) lack of knowledge and of the means of knowledge of the truth as to the facts in question; and (2) reliance upon the conduct of the party estopped."

2. Rescission of Contracts

a. Rescission for mistake

SHERWOOD v. WALKER
66 Mich. 568, 33 N.W. 919, 11 Am. St. Rep. 531 (1887)

MORESE, Justice:

Replevin for a cow. Suit commenced in justice's court; judgment for plaintiff; appealed to circuit court of Wayne county, and verdict and judgment for plaintiff in that court. The defendants bring error, and set out 25 assignments of the same. . . .

It appears from the record that both parties supposed this cow was barren and would not breed, and she was sold by the pound for an insignificant sum as compared with her real value if a breeder. She was evidently sold and purchased on the relation of her value for beef, unless the plaintiff had learned of her true condition, and concealed such knowledge from the defendants. Before the plaintiff secured the possession of the animal, the defendants learned that she was with calf, and therefore of great value, and undertook to rescind the sale by refusing to deliver her. The question arises whether they had a right to do so. The circuit judge ruled that this fact did not avoid the sale and it made no difference whether she was barren or not. I am of the opinion that the court erred in this holding. I know that this is a close question, and the dividing line between the adjudicated cases is not easily discerned. But it must be considered as well settled that a party who has given an apparent consent to a contract of sale may refuse to execute it, or he may avoid it after it has been completed, if the assent was founded, or the contract made, upon the mistake of a material fact — such as the subject-matter of the sale, the price, or some collateral fact materially inducing the agreement; and this can be done when the mistake is mutual. . . .

If there is a difference or misapprehension as to the substance of the thing bargained for; if the thing actually delivered or received is different in substance from the thing bargained for, and intended to be sold, then there is no contract; but if it be only a difference in some quality or accident, even though the mistake may have been the actuating motive to the purchaser or seller, or both of them, yet the contract remains binding. "The difficulty in every case is to determine whether the mistake or misapprehension is as to the substance of the whole contract, going, as it were, to the root of the matter, or only to some point, even though a material point, an error as to which does not affect the substance of the whole consideration." *Kennedy v. Panama, etc., Mail Co.*, L.R. 2 Q.B. 580, 587. It has been held, in accordance with the principles above stated, that where a horse is bought under the belief that he is sound, and both vendor and vendee honestly believe him to be sound, the purchaser must stand by his bargain, and pay the full price, unless there was a warranty.

It seems to me, however, in the case made by this record, that the mistake or misapprehension of the parties went to the whole substance of the agreement. If the cow was a breeder, she was worth at least $750; if barren, she was worth not over $80. The parties would not have made the contract of sale except upon the understanding and belief that she was incapable of breeding, and of no use as a cow. It is true she is now the identical animal that they thought her to be when the contract was made; there is no mistake as to the identity of the creature. Yet the mistake was not of the mere quality of the animal, but went to the very nature of the thing. A barren cow is substantially a different creature than a breeding one. There is as much difference between them for all purposes of use as there is between an ox and a cow that is capable of breeding and giving milk. If the mutual mistake had simply related to the fact whether she was with calf or not for one season, then it might have been a good sale, but the mistake affected the character of the animal for all time, and for its present and ultimate use. She was not in fact the animal, or the kind of animal, the defendants intended to sell or the plaintiff to buy. She was not a barren cow, and, if this fact had been known, there would have been no contract. The mistake affected the substance of the whole consideration, and it must be considered that there was no contract to sell or sale of the cow as she actually was. The thing sold and bought had in fact no existence. She was sold as a beef creature would be sold; she is in fact a breeding cow, and a valuable one. The court should have instructed the jury that if they found that the cow was sold, or contracted to be sold, upon the understanding of both parties that she was barren, and useless for the purpose of breeding, and that in fact she was not barren, but capable of breeding, then the defendants had a right to rescind, and to refuse to deliver, and the verdict should be in their favor.

The judgment of the court below must be reversed, and a new trial granted, with costs of this court to defendants.

SHERWOOD, J., (dissenting.) I do not concur in the opinion given by my brethren in this case. I think the judgments before the justice and at the circuit were right. I agree with my Brother MORSE . . . that the plaintiff was entitled to a delivery of the property to him when the suit was brought, unless there was a mistake made which would invalidate the contract, and I can find no such mistake. There is no pretense there was any fraud or concealment in the case, and an intimation or insinuation that such a thing might have existed on the part of either of the parties would undoubtedly be a greater surprise to them than anything else that has occurred in their dealings or in the case. . . .

There is no question but that the defendants sold the cow representing her of the breed and quality they believed the cow to be, and that the purchaser so understood it. And the buyer purchased her believing her to be of the breed represented by the sellers, and possessing all the qualities stated, and even more. He believed she would breed. There is no pretense that the plaintiff bought the cow for beef, and there is nothing in the record indicating that he would have bought her at all only that he thought she might be made to breed. Under the foregoing facts — and these are all that are contained in the record material to the contract — it is held that because it turned out that the plaintiff was more correct in his judgment as to one quality of the cow than the defendants, and a quality, too, which could not by any possibility be positively known at the time by either party to exist, the contract may be annulled by the defendants at their pleasure. I know of no law, and have not been referred to any, which will justify any such holding, and I think the circuit judge was right in his construction of the contract between the parties. . . .

I entirely agree with my brethren that the right to rescind occurs whenever "the thing actually delivered or received is different in substance from the thing bargained for, and intended to be sold; but if it be only a difference in some quality or accident, even though the misapprehension may have been the actuating motive" of the parties in making the contract, yet it will remain binding. In this case the cow sold was the one delivered. What might or might not happen to her after the sale formed no element in the contract. . . .

According to this record, whatever the mistake was, if any, in this case, it was upon the part of the defendants, and while acting upon their own judgment. It is, however, elementary law, and very elementary, too, "that the mistaken party, without any common understanding with the other party in the premises as to the quality of an animal, is remediless if he is injured through his own mistake." Leake, Cont. 338; *Torrance v. Bolton*, L.R. 8 Ch. 118; *Smith v. Hughes*, L.R. 6 Q.B. 597. . . . The only pretense for avoiding this contract by the defendants is that they erred in judgment as to the qualities and value of the animal. . . . The judgment should be affirmed.

Elsinore Union Elementary School Dist. of Riverside County v. Kastorff, 54 Cal. 2d 380, 6 Cal. Rptr. 1, 353 P.2d 713 (1960). This was an action by a school district against a contractor and the surety on the latter's bid bond, to recover damages allegedly resulting from the contractor's refusal to sign a building contract pursuant to his previously submitted bid in the amount of $89,994. The contractor testified that to prepare his bid he used worksheets upon which he entered bids of various subcontractors for portions of the work, and that by mistake he had failed to include a sum for plumbing work, for which he would have included $9,500 more. Upon discovering his error the day after submitting his bid, the contractor immediately informed the school district and two days later wrote to the school board explaining his error and requesting permission to withdraw his bid. Permission was refused, this suit followed, and on appeal the trial court judgment for plaintiff school district was reversed when the California Supreme Court "concluded that because of an honest clerical error in the bid and defendant's subsequent prompt rescission he was not obliged to execute the contract." Quoting from its earlier *Kemper* case (*M.F. Kemper Const. Co. v. City of Los Angeles* (1951), 37 Cal. 2d 696, 235 P.2d 7) the court reaffirmed rulings that:

(1) Once opened and declared, the company's bid was in the nature of an irrevocable option, a contract right of which the city could not be deprived without its consent unless the requirements for rescission were satisfied. . . . (2) . . . the city had actual notice of the error in the estimates before it attempted to accept the bid, and knowledge by one party that the other is acting under mistake is treated as equivalent to mutual mistake for purposes of rescission. . . . (3) Relief from mistaken bids is consistently allowed where one party knows or has reason to know of the other's error and the requirements for rescission are fulfilled. . . . (4) Rescission may be had for mistake of fact if the mistake is material to the contract and was not the result of neglect of a legal duty, if enforcement of the contract as made would be unconscionable, and if the other party can be placed in status quo. . . . In addition, the party seeking relief must give prompt notice of his election to rescind and must restore or offer to restore to the other party everything of value which he has received under the contract. (5) Omission of the $301,769 item [in *Kemper*] from the company's bid was, of course, a material mistake. . . . [E]ven if we assume that the error was due to some carelessness, it does not follow that the company is without remedy. Civil Code section 1577, which defines mistake of facts for which relief may be allowed, describes it as one not caused by "the neglect of a legal duty" on the part of the person making the mistake. (6) It has been recognized numerous times that not all carelessness constitutes a "neglect of legal duty" within the meaning of the section. . . . On facts very similar to those in the present case, courts of other jurisdictions have stated that there was no culpable negligence and have granted relief from erroneous bids. . . . (7) The type of error here involved is one which will sometimes occur in the conduct of reasonable and cautious businessmen, and, under all the circumstances, we cannot say as a matter of law that it constituted a neglect of legal duty such as would bar the right to equitable relief. (8) The evidence clearly supports the conclusion that it would be unconscionable to hold the company to its bid at the mistaken figure. The city had knowledge before the bid was accepted that the company had made a clerical error which resulted in the omission of an item amounting to nearly one third of the amount intended to be bid, and, under all the circumstances, it appears that it would be unjust and unfair to permit the city to take advantage of the company's mistake. (9, 10) There is no reason for denying relief on the ground that the city cannot be restored to status quo. It had ample time in which to award the contract without readvertising, the contract was actually awarded to the next lowest bidder, and the city will not be heard to complain that it cannot be placed in status quo because it will not have the benefit of an inequitable bargain. . . . (11) Finally, the company gave notice promptly upon discovering the facts entitling it to rescind, and no offer of restoration was necessary because it had received nothing of value which it could restore. . . . We are satisfied that all the requirements for rescission have been met.

In so ruling the court also held that a finding below that the contractor had ample time and opportunity to complete and check his final bid did not warrant a conclusion of "neglect of legal duty" which would preclude relief from the inadvertent clerical error. Further, it concluded that he should not be denied relief "from an unfair, inequitable, and unintended bargain simply because, in response to inquiry from the board when his bid was discovered to be much the lowest submitted, he informed the board, after checking with his clerical assistant [at a time when he did not have access to his worksheets] that the bid was correct," since he did inspect the worksheets at the earliest practicable moment and then promptly notified the board and rescinded his bid. The court noted in addition that defendant's bid agreement was to execute the formal written contract only after receiving written notification that his bid had been accepted, and the notice was not given until two weeks following his rescission; that the "bargain" for which the board was contending appeared to be "too sharp for law and equity to sustain"; and that the omitted sum was "plainly material to the total."

b.   Rescission for breach of implied warranty

HINSON v. JEFFERSON
287 N.C. 422, 215 S.E.2d 102 (1975)

[Proceeding to review a N.C. Court of Appeals decision which had vacated and remanded the trial court judgment rendered on stipulations contained in a pretrial order. The action was filed by plaintiff to recover the $3,500 purchase price paid by plaintiff to defendants (husband and wife) for a parcel of land and for cancellation of the deed by which defendants had conveyed the lot to the plaintiff. Among the stipulated facts were the following:

(a) Included in the deed were restrictive covenants running with the land which required that the lot be used for residential purposes only, that no residence constructed thereon may cost less than $25,000 based on costs prevailing in October 1971, that the first residence on the lot could not be built without approval of the plans and specifications by defendants or their survivor, that no trailer, mobile home, basement, tent, shack, garage, barn or other outbuilding erected on the land may at any time be used as a temporary or permanent residence, that no building on the land may be built nearer than 50 feet to the front lot line or nearer than 20 feet from any side lot line, that no noxious or offensive trade may be carried on upon the land which may be or become an annoyance or nuisance, that no signs or billboards may be erected or maintained on the premises, that no trade materials or inventories or trucks or tractors may be stored on the land, that the lot must at all times be neat and clean in appearance, and that the lot may not be subdivided into smaller building lots;

(b) Defendants did approve certain plans submitted by plaintiff after defendants had purchased the lot; (c) A sewage disposal system for any residence constructed on the lot required the use of a septic tank or an on-site sewage disposal system; (d) Prior to commencement of construction, the Environmental Health Division of the county health department certified that the lot would not support such a tank or disposal system and determined that the lot is not suitable for residential building purposes and does not meet county health requirements, and the county Board of Health denied a permit to install either; (e) An evaluation of the lot by the U.S. Department of Agriculture, Soil Conservation Service, concluded that the subsurface condition could be corrected by extensive drainage procedures including channel improvements to Black Swamp and Little Contentnea Creek at a prospective cost of several hundred thousand dollars; (f) Plaintiff thereafter demanded that defendants refund the $3,500 purchase price, offering in exchange a reconveyance of the lot by plaintiff to defendants; (g) Defendants declined the plaintiff's offer and refused plaintiff's demand; (h) Prior to the conveyance of the lot to plaintiff, neither defendants nor plaintiff knew that the lot would not support a septic tank or on-site sewage disposal system; (i) There was no allegation in plaintiff's complaint of fraud or misrepresentation on the part of the defendants and the plaintiff does not contend that the defendants were guilty of any fraud or misrepresentation with respect to the condition of the lot prior to or at the time of the conveyance; (j) On the contrary the defendants in conveying the lot to plaintiff were totally unaware of any drainage or other soil condition respecting the lot which would or might prohibit the use of a septic tank or other on-site sewage system thereon; (k) The deed of conveyance contained no covenant of warranty that the lot conveyed was suitable for the on-site construction of a residence. . . .

In its judgment the District Court stated: "And based upon said stipulations entered into between the parties hereto, the Court is of the opinion and concludes as a matter of law that plaintiff is not entitled to the relief prayed for by her, or any part thereof;" and ordered "First: That this action be dismissed and plaintiff have and recover nothing of the defendants, either individually or jointly. Second: That the costs of this action be taxed against the plaintiff."]

COPELAND, Justice:

. . . Plaintiff states in her sole assignment of error that she relies on the following legal points in support of her exception to the judgment:

1. That the stipulated facts show that there was a mutual mistake of an existing material fact, common to both parties, and by reason thereof each has done what neither intended, coupled with a failure of consideration.

2. That in a conveyance of land by deed containing restrictions therein which restrict the use of the property for a certain purpose, the grantor thereby warrants that the property so conveyed and restricted can be used for the specific purpose to which its use is restricted by the deed of conveyance.

. . . Based on these uncontroverted facts, the Court of Appeals held that plaintiff was entitled to rescind the contract on the grounds of "mutual mistake of material fact" coupled with a "total failure of consideration." 24 N.C. App. at 238-39, 210 S.E.2d at 502-03. Assuming, *arguendo*, that the Court of Appeals was correct, and that this is a true mistake case, then it is one that must necessarily involve a mistaken *assumption* of the parties in the formation of the contract of purchase. In these mistaken assumption cases, unlike other kinds of mistake cases, the parties communicate their desires to each other perfectly; they intend to complete a sale, or a contract of sale, and their objective acts are in accord with their intent. Difficulties subsequently arise because at least one of the parties has, either consciously or unconsciously, mistaken beliefs concerning facts that make the sale appear more attractive to him than it actually is. . . .

In attempting to determine whether the aggrieved party is entitled to some kind of relief in these mistaken assumption cases, courts and commentators have suggested a number of factors as relevant. E.g., was the mistake bilateral or unilateral; was it palpable or impalpable; was one of the parties unjustly enriched; was the other party unjustly impoverished; was the risk assumed by one of the parties (*i.e.*, subjective ignorance); was the mistake fundamental or collateral; was the mistake related to present facts or to future expectations; etc. *See* Rabin, *A Proposed Black-Letter Rule Concerning Mistaken Assumptions in Bargain Transactions*, 45 TEX. L. REV. 1273 (1967) (hereinafter cited as Rabin). *See also* D. Dobbs, REMEDIES 716–84 (West 1973).

Our research has failed to disclose a prior North Carolina case applying the doctrine of mutual mistake pertaining to a physical condition of real property as a ground for rescission. . . However, we have found a few cases from other jurisdictions. . . .

The closest mistaken assumption case we have found to our fact situation is *A&M Land Development Co. v. Miller*, 354 Mich. 681, 94 N.W.2d 197 (1959). In that case, the court held that the trial judge was correct in refusing to rescind the sale of 42 building lots slated for subdivision and development, because of mutual mistake regarding the poor absorptive qualities of the soil that resulted in a tentative refusal of septic tank permits to the subdivider. The court concluded that assuming there was a mutual mistake, to grant rescission would be improper since the purchaser received the property for which he contracted, notwithstanding that it was less attractive and less valuable to him than he had anticipated.

There are, however, several important distinguishing factors between the Miller case and our case. First, the purchaser in Miller was a developer-speculator; in our case the purchaser is a consumer-widow. Second, the property in Miller was not rendered valueless for its intended use, but only rendered less valuable because it could not be developed as densely as originally anticipated; in our case the property was rendered totally valueless for the intended use. . . .

. . . At this moment, plaintiff has naked legal title to a tract of real estate whose use to her is limited by the restrictive covenants and by the facts as stipulated to what she calls "the dubious pleasure of viewing the same." On the other hand, defendants have $3,500 of plaintiff's money. There can be no question but that the parties to this transaction never contemplated this particular use of the subject property. In fact, the deed, by its very terms, makes it clear that the intended use was for the construction of a single-family residence, strictly limited as to costs and as to design. The stipulation further indicates that both prior to and at the time of the conveyance neither defendants nor plaintiff knew that the property would not support a septic tank or on-site sewage disposal system.

In the face of these uncontroverted facts, defendants rely upon the doctrine of *caveat emptor* as a legal defense to plaintiff's action for rescission.

The common law doctrine of caveat emptor historically applied to sales of both real and personal property. Its application to personal property sales, however, has been restricted by the Uniform Commercial Code. *See* G.S. § 25-2-314 *et seq.* Over the years, as to real property, the number of cases that strictly apply the rule of *caveat emptor* appears to be diminishing, while there is a distinct tendency to depart therefrom, either by way of interpretation, or exception, or by simply refusing to adhere to the rule where it would work injustice. . . .

In recent years the rule of *caveat emptor* has suffered severe inroads in sales of houses to be built or in the course of construction. . . . Today, it appears that a majority of the states imply some form of warranty in the purchase of a new home by a first purchaser from a builder-vendor. . . .

During the course of this litigation, and subsequent to the oral arguments of this case in the Court of Appeals, this Court decided the case of *Hartley v. Ballou*, 286 N.C. 51, 209 S.E.2d 776 (1974). In that case, this Court, in an opinion by Chief Justice Bobbitt, approved the "relaxation of the rule of caveat emptor" in respect of defects of which the purchaser of a recently completed or partially completed dwelling was unaware and could not discover by a reasonable inspection, and substituted therefore, for the first time in this State, an implied warranty defined as follows:

> (I)n every contract for the sale of a recently completed dwelling, and in every contract for the sale of a dwelling then under construction, the vendor, if he be in the business of building such dwellings, shall be held to impliedly warrant to the initial vendee that, at the time of the passing of the deed or the taking of possession by the initial vendee (whichever first occurs), the dwelling, together with all its fixtures, is sufficiently free from major structural defects, and is constructed in a workmanlike manner, so as to meet the standard of workmanlike quality then prevailing at the time and place of construction; and that this implied warranty in the contract of sale survives the passing of the deed or the taking of possession by the initial vendee.

Id. at 62, 209 S.E.2d at 783. At the same time, Hartley made it clear that such implied warranty falls short of "an absolute guarantee." "An implied warranty cannot be held to extend to defects which are visible or should be visible to a reasonable man . . . ." *Id.* at 61, 209 S.E.2d at 782. . . .

We believe that [a number] of the mutual mistake cases discussed *supra* [are] in fact embryo implied warranty cases. For example in *Davey v. Brownson* [3 Wash. App. 820, 478 P.2d 258 (1970), *cert. denied*, 78 Wash. 2d 997 (1971)], the purchaser obtained rescission because of termites on the ground of mutual mistake. Although the court denied its decision was based on implied warranty, it is difficult to understand the application of the mutual mistake doctrine. . . . In this context, Hartley could easily be classified as a mutual mistake case, i.e., both parties assumed that the basement wall was sufficiently free from structural defects so as to prevent any water leakage. But, in Hartley we recognized the implied warranty as a limited exception to the general rule of *caveat emptor*; if we had elected to totally abolish the doctrine, then perhaps application of the mutual mistake theory would have been appropriate. Hartley is not an abrogation of the doctrine of *caveat emptor*; on the contrary it is only a well-reasoned exception.

Concededly, this is not the Hartley fact situation. Hartley involved a builder-vendor of new homes and a consumer-vendee. Nonetheless, we believe that Hartley provides the legal precedent for deciding this case. The basic and underlying principle of Hartley is a recognition that in some situations the rigid common law maxim of *caveat emptor* is inequitable. We believe this is one of those situations. As a result, we hold that where a grantor conveys land subject to restrictive covenants that limit its use to the construction of a single-family dwelling, and, due to subsequent disclosures, both unknown to and not reasonably discoverable by the grantee before or at the time of conveyance, the property cannot be used by the grantee, or by any subsequent grantees through mesne conveyances, for the specific purpose to which its use is limited by the restrictive covenants, the grantor breaches an implied warranty arising out of said restrictive covenants.

Defendant contends that if plaintiff is permitted to rescind, then any contract or conveyance can be set aside under a set of circumstances rendering the land no longer attractive to a purchaser. If we applied the mutual mistake doctrine, then there might be some merit to this argument. But, under the rule we have announced, a purchaser is bound by patent defects or by facts a reasonable investigation would normally disclose. In the instant case, it is clear that a reasonable inspection by the grantee either before or at the time of conveyance would not have disclosed that the property could not support a septic tank or on-site sewage disposal system.

Therefore, under the facts of this case, we hold that defendant grantors have breached the implied warranty, as set out above, and that plaintiff, by timely notice of the defect, once it was discovered, is entitled to full restitution of the purchase price; provided that she execute and deliver a deed reconveying the subject lot to defendants. The judgment of the Court of Appeals, as modified herein, is thus affirmed.

Modified and affirmed.

NOTES & QUESTIONS

1. In *Hinson*, North Carolina's Supreme Court agreed with its intermediate appellate court that plaintiff's rescission of the contract was authorized under the law. However, it disapproved the legal theory pursuant to which the lower court had allowed plaintiff the benefit of that remedy. The intermediate appellate court had upheld rescission on the theory that there had been a "mutual mistake of an existing material fact" — the first theory offered by plaintiff to support her position. The supreme court, however, upheld rescission on the theory that the defendant grantors had breached an implied contract warranty "that the property can be used for the specific purpose to which its use is restricted by the deed of conveyance" — the second theory offered by plaintiff to support her position.

2. Why do you suppose that counsel for plaintiff asserted both theories — the "mutual mistake" theory and the "implied warranty" theory — to support plaintiff's claimed right to rescind the contract? Had you represented the plaintiff, would you have done the same? Why?

3. *Practice Points*: Courts of review have often said that they will affirm judgments, but will not reverse judgments, on theories not asserted in the courts below. *See, e.g., Consoer, Townsend and Associates v. Addis*, 37 Ill. App. 2d 105, 185 N.E.2d 97 (1962), where the reviewing court refused to consider two theories of defense where the defendants had not pleaded them in their answer and where no motion had been made to amend either before or after judgment; *Leone v. City of Chicago*, 156 Ill. 2d 33, 619 N.E.2d 119 (1993), where it was held that the city, having tried and lost the case on one theory, could not assail the circuit court's judgment on a wholly different basis on appeal. For a discussion of one of various exceptions to this rule, *see* 76 A.L.R. Fed. 522 (1986) ("When will federal court of

appeals review issue raised by party for first time on appeal where legal developments after trial affect issue").

4. In *C.B. & T. Co. v. Hefner*, 98 N.M. 594, 651 P.2d 1029 (App. 1982), it was held that the question whether the vendor was barred from obtaining rescission of its contract with purchasers because the vendor did not read the contract before signing, was not an issue on appeal since it had not been raised in the trial court. Also, in *Moschelle v. Hulse*, 190 Mont. 532, 622 P.2d 155 (1980), vendors in a contract of sale of a tavern were not allowed to argue laches for the first time on appeal with regard to purchasers' attempt to obtain rescission, where the vendors did not plead laches as an affirmative defense at trial as required by rule. *And see City of Chicago v. Supreme Sav. & Loan Ass'n*, 27 Ill. App. 3d 589, 327 N.E.2d 5 (1975), where purchasers who had lost in the trial court on their counter-complaints for rescission of real estate sale contract documents were not allowed to urge a theory on appeal (a) as to which they had not offered any evidence, and (b) upon which they had stated to the trial court that they did not rely.

3.   Injunctions in Contract Cases

STATE v. AVCO FINANCIAL SERVICE OF NEW YORK INC.
50 N.Y.2d 383, 429 N.Y.S.2d 181, 406 N.E.2d 1075 (1980)

FUCHSBERG, Judge:

The Attorney-General, acting on a consumer complaint, instituted this special proceeding under subdivision 12 of section 63 of the Executive Law to enjoin respondent Avco's use of a security clause in a loan agreement form. The petition alleged that the clause was illegal and void as against public policy on the theory that it constituted an impermissible waiver of the personal property exemption afforded a judgment debtor under CPLR 5205 (subd. (a)). Special Term summarily declared the clause invalid for this reason. Although the Appellate Division, over a single dissent, affirmed the order and judgment, it did so on the ground that the provision was unconscionable (70 A.D.2d 859, 418 N.Y.S.2d 52). We now reverse, holding that it is not illegal and that the determination of unconscionability was improperly made without any opportunity for an evidentiary presentation as to the commercial and bargaining context in which the clause appears.

The clause at issue is one regularly inserted by Avco, a finance company, in its loan agreements. Its terms unmistakably provide:

> This loan is secured by . . . all household goods, furniture, appliances, and consumer goods of every kind and description owned at the time of the loan secured hereby, or at the time of any refinance or renewal thereof, or cash advanced under the loan agreement secured hereby, and located about the premises at the Debtor's residence (unless otherwise stated) or at any other location to which the goods may be moved.

It is not denied that this language must be understood to create a security interest in items of personal property which include the ones made exempt from the reach of a judgment creditor by CPLR 5205 (subd. (a)).[5] From its inception, this

---

[5] [1] CPLR 5205 (subd. (a)) provides in pertinent part, as follows:

(a) Exemption for personal property. The following personal property when owned by any person is exempt from application to the satisfaction of a money judgment except where the judgment is for the purchase price of the exempt property or was recovered by a domestic,

statute along with its venerable antecedents has embodied the humanitarian policy that the law should not permit the enforcement of judgments to such a point that debtors and their families are left in a state of abject deprivation . . . .

It is well recognized, however, that simply because the law exempts such property from levy and sale upon execution by a judgment creditor does not mean that the exemption statute was intended to serve the far more paternalistic function of restricting the freedom of debtors to dispose of these possessions as they wish . . . . No statute precludes exempt property from being sold; nor is there any which expressly interdicts the less drastic step of encumbering such property. So, for example, while contractual waivers of a debtor's statutory exemptions are usually held to be void . . . , the law has not forbidden a debtor to execute a mortgage upon the property so protected and thus create a lien which may be foreclosed despite the property's exempt status . . . . The clause here permits no more and, hence, cannot be said to contravene the exemption statute.

The Attorney-General nevertheless argues that the clause should be invalidated under the doctrine of unconscionability. The contention, as accepted by the majority of the Appellate Division, is that "the inequality of bargaining position and the granting to the creditor of enforcement rights greater than those which the law confers upon a judgment creditor armed with execution, lead inevitably to the conclusion that the absence of choice on the part of the debtor left him with no recourse but to grant to his creditor rights which, in good conscience, the law should not enforce" (70 A.D.2d 859, 860, 418 N.Y.S.2d 52). The clause is also alleged to be unconscionable in that its broad terms create security interests even in items not sold or financed by Avco and function mainly as an in terrorem device to spur repayment.

In this connection, we note initially that the statute under which this proceeding was brought (EXECUTIVE LAW, § 63, subd. 12) lists "unconscionable contractual provisions" as a type of "fraudulent" conduct against which the Attorney-General is authorized to move. Furthermore, an application for injunctive or other relief under this provision is one which may properly look to the exercise of a sound judicial discretion . . . . But the petition here provided no opportunity for the operation of such discretion on the issue of unconscionability since it alleged only that the clause per se was "illegal" and "void as against public policy and contrary to law," theories which, as we have seen, are not consonant with established law. Indeed, the only ground presented to nisi prius was that the clause violated CPLR 5205 (subd. (a));

---

laboring person or mechanic for work performed by that person in such capacity:

1. all stoves kept for use in the judgment debtor's dwelling house and necessary fuel therefor for sixty days; one sewing machine with its appurtenances;

2. the family bible, family pictures, and school books used by the judgment debtor or in the family; and other books, not exceeding fifty dollars in value, kept and used as part of the family or judgment debtor's library;

5. all wearing apparel, household furniture, one mechanical, gas or electric refrigerator, one radio receiver, one television set, crockery, tableware and cooking utensils necessary for the judgment debtor and the family;

6. a wedding ring; a watch not exceeding thirty-five dollars in value; and

7. necessary working tools and implements, including those of a mechanic, farm machinery, team, professional instruments, furniture and library, not exceeding six hundred dollars in value, together with the necessary food for the team for sixty days, provided, however, that the articles specified in this paragraph are necessary to the carrying on of the judgment debtor's profession or calling.

the petitioner never raised an unconscionability argument until it arrived at the Appellate Division.

As a general proposition, unconscionability, a flexible doctrine with roots in equity . . . , requires some showing of "an absence of meaningful choice on the part of one of the parties together with contract terms which are unreasonably favorable to the other party". . . . The concept, at least as defined in the Uniform Commercial Code which both parties seem to agree governs the transactions at issue here is not aimed at "disturbance of allocation of risks because of superior bargaining power" but, instead, at "the prevention of oppression and unfair surprise" (MCKINNEY'S CONS. LAWS OF N.Y., Book 62 1/2, Uniform Commercial Code, § 2-302, Official Comment 1). To that extent at least it hailed a further retreat of caveat emptor.

By its nature, a test so broadly stated is not a simple one, nor can it be mechanically applied . . . . So, no doubt precisely because the legal concept of unconscionability is intended to be sensitive to the realities and nuances of the bargaining process, the Uniform Commercial Code goes on to provide: "When it is claimed or appears to the court that the contract or any clause thereof may be unconscionable the parties shall be afforded a reasonable opportunity to present evidence as to its commercial setting, purpose and effect to aid the court in making the determination" (Uniform Commercial Code, § 2-302, subd. 2). . . .

But as indicated, here a case on unconscionability was not presented to Special Term either in form or substance. Nor was that issue available when raised on appeal for the first time . . . . Specifically, at no point did the Attorney-General by affidavits from borrowers or otherwise make any factual showing as to such matters as, for instance, deception of borrowers as to the clause's content or existence . . . , or the presence of language difficulties or illiteracy affecting its execution, or any other reasons that would have made it unlikely that consent was freely and knowingly given . . . , all within the embrace of what is sometimes referred to as "procedural unconscionability" . . . . Nor, for that matter, in light of the limited scope of its petition, was there occasion to delve into, much less attempt to prove, the now belated assertion of so-called "substantive unconscionability" . . . .

Accordingly, the order of the Appellate Division should be reversed and the petition should be dismissed, without costs, with leave to the petitioner to commence a new proceeding, if it be so advised. . . .

Order reversed, etc.

NOTES & QUESTIONS

1. As we see from the *Avco Financial Service* case, there are situations in which the injunction remedy may be sought in an attempt to prevent enforcement of duties consensually undertaken by contract. Ordinarily, however, when injunctions are sought in contract cases, the purpose is to *require* performance of those duties. Section 357 of the RESTATEMENT (SECOND) OF CONTRACTS treats the injunction as a remedy that serves this latter purpose, and broadly defines situations in which specific performance orders and injunctions will be granted against contracting parties who have committed or threatened to commit breach of contract duties.

§ 357. AVAILABILITY OF SPECIFIC PERFORMANCE AND IN-JUNCTION

(1) Subject to the rules stated in §§ 359-69, specific performance of a contract duty will be granted in the discretion of the court against a party who has committed or is threatening to commit a breach of the duty.

(2) Subject to the rules stated in §§ 359-69, an injunction against breach of a contract duty will be granted in the discretion of the court against a party who has committed or is threatening to commit a breach of the duty if:

(a) the duty is one of forbearance, or

(b) the duty is one to act and specific performance would be denied only for reasons that are inapplicable to an injunction.

2. In *Avco Financial Service*, the decision of the New York Court of Appeals allowed the state's attorney general to commence a new proceeding, apparently to present in better form and with better proof the issue of *unconscionability*. The court also noted a possible distinction between "procedural unconscionability" and "substantive unconscionability." Compare the one with the other, and state what you propose would be a workable definition of each.

4.   Foreclosures in Contract Cases

SKENDZEL v. MARSHALL
261 Ind. 226, 301 N.E.2d 641 (1973)

Hunter, Justice:

Petitioners seek transfer to this Court as a result of an adverse ruling by the Court of Appeals. Plaintiff-respondents originally brought suit to obtain possession of certain real estate through the enforcement of a forfeiture clause in a land sale contract. Plaintiff-respondents suffered a negative judgment, from which they appealed. The Court of Appeals reversed, holding that the defendant-petitioners had breached the contract and that the plaintiff-respondents had not waived their right to enforce the forfeiture provisions of the contract.

In December of 1958, Mary Burkowski, as vendor, entered into a land sale contract with Charles P. Marshall and Agnes P. Marshall, as vendees. The contract provided for the sale of certain real estate for the sum of $36,000.00, payable [in installments]. The contract also contained a fairly standard section which provided for the treatment of prepayments — but which the Court of Appeals found to be of particular importance. It provided as follows:

> Should Vendees have made prepayments or paid in advance of the payments herein required, said prepayments, if any, shall at any time thereafter be applied in lieu of further principal payments required as herein stated, to the extent of such prepayments only. . . .

The following is the forfeiture/liquidated damages provision of the land sale contract:

> It is further agreed that if any default shall be made in the payment of said purchase price or any of the covenants and/or conditions herein

provided, and if any such default shall continue for 30 days, then, after the lapse of said 30 days' period, *all moneys and payments previously paid shall, at the option of the Vendor without notice or demand, be and become forfeited and be taken and retained by the Vendor as liquidated damages* and thereupon this contract shall terminate and be of no further force or effect; provided, however, that nothing herein contained shall be deemed or construed to prevent the Vendor from enforcing specific performance of this agreement in the event of any default on the part of the Vendees in complying, observing and performing any of the conditions, covenants and terms herein contained. . . (Emphasis added [by the court].)

The vendor, Mary Burkowski, died in 1963. The plaintiffs in this action are the assignees (under the vendor's will) of the decedent's interests in the contract. They received their assignment from the executrix of the estate of the vendor on June 27, 1968. One year after this assignment, several of the assignees filed their complaint in this action alleging that the defendants had defaulted through non-payment.

The schedule of payments made under this contract was shown by the evidence to be as follows:

Date	Amount Paid	Total of Paid Principal
12/1/1958	$ 500.00	$ 500.00
12/25/1958	500.00	1,000.00
3/26/1959	5,000.00	6,000.00
4/5/1960	2,500.00	8,500.00
5/23/1961	2,500.00	11,000.00
4/6/1962	2,500.00	13,500.00
1/15/1963	2,500.00	16,000.00
6/30/1964	2,500.00	18,500.00
2/15/1965	2,500.00	21,000.00

No payments have been made since the last one indicated above — $15,000.00 remains to be paid on the original contract price.

*   *   *

If forfeiture is enforced against the defendants, they will forfeit outright the sum of $21,000, or well over one-half the original contract price, as liquidated damages plus possession.

Forfeitures are generally disfavored by the law. . . . In fact, ". . . [e]quity abhors forfeitures and beyond any question has jurisdiction, which it will exercise in a proper case to grant relief against their enforcement." 30 C.J.S. *Equity* § 56 (1965) . . . .

Paragraph 17 of the contract, *supra*, provides that all prior payments "become forfeited and be taken and retained by the Vendor as liquidated damages." "Reasonable" liquidated damage provisions are permitted by the law. *See* 22 Am. Jur., 2d *Damages* § 212 (1965). However, the issue before this Court, is whether a $21,000 forfeiture is a "reasonable" measure of damages. If the damages are unreasonable, i.e., if they are disproportionate to the loss actually suffered, they must be characterized as penal rather then compensatory. . . . Under the facts of this case, a $21,000 forfeiture is clearly excessive.

The authors of AMERICAN LAW REPORTS have provided an excellent analysis of forfeiture provisions in land contracts:

> As is frequently remarked, there is no single rule for the determination of whether a contractual stipulation is one for liquidated damages or a penalty, each case depending largely upon its own facts and equities, and this apothegm is fully applicable to the decisions involving provisions in land contracts for the forfeiture of payments.
>
> There is a plethora of abstract tests and criteria for the determination of the nature of a contractual provision as one for a penalty or liquidated damages, and in most instances the courts struggle valiantly to make the result reached by them accord reasonably well with one or more of the more prominent of these abstract tests. But it must be observed that in the last analysis, these factors and criteria are so vague and indefinite that it is doubtful if they are of much aid in construing a specific contractual provision, even assuming that the court makes a conscious and conscientious effort to apply them. At any rate, a reading of the cases collected herein conveys the impression that the ultimate catalyst is the court's belief as to the equities of the case before it.
>
> Granting this, however, certain tendencies of decision are clearly discernible in the cases. If, for example, the contract involved calls for deferred payments of the purchase price which are relatively small in amount and extend over a number of years, and if it appears that at the time of the purchaser's breach and the consequent invocation of the forfeiture clause by the vendor a comparatively small proportion of the total price remains unpaid, the courts are prone to find that the forfeiture clause was one for a penalty, at least if, as is usually the case, such a holding will tend to give the purchaser another chance to complete the purchase.
>
> On the other hand, if the amount of the payments received by the vendor at the time the purchase was abandoned represents but a small percentage of the total purchase price, and if the purchaser's breach occurred soon after the execution of the agreement (and particularly if the circumstances indicate that the purchase was made for speculative purposes or that the breach represented an effort on the part of the purchaser to escape an unfortunate turn in the market), the courts tend to hold that the forfeiture clause was one for liquidated damages, which the result that the purchaser cannot recover back the payments made." 6 A.L.R.2d 1401 (1949).

If we apply the specific equitable principle announced above — namely, that the amount paid be considered in relation to the total contract price — we are compelled to conclude that the $21,000 forfeiture as liquidated damages is inconsistent with generally accepted principles of fairness and equity. The vendee has acquired a substantial interest in the property, which, if forfeited, would result in substantial injustice.

Under a typical conditional land contract, the vendor retains legal title until the total contract price is paid by the vendee. Payments are generally made in periodic installments. Legal title does not vest in the vendee until the contract terms are satisfied, but equitable title vests in the vendee at the time the contract is consummated. When the parties enter into the contract, all incidents of ownership accrue to the vendee. . . . The vendee assumes the risk of loss and is the recipient of all appreciation in value. . . . The vendee, as equitable owner, is responsible for taxes. . . . The vendee has a sufficient interest in land so that upon sale of that interest, he holds a vendor's lien. . . .

This Court has held, consistent with the above notions of equitable ownership, that a land contract, once consummated constitutes a present sale and purchase. The vendor "has, in effect, exchanged his property for the unconditional obligation of the vendee, the performance of which is secured by the retention of the legal title." . . . The Court, in effect, views a conditional land contract as a sale with a security interest in the form of legal title reserved by the vendor. Conceptually, therefore, the retention of the title by the vendor is the same as reserving a lien or mortgage. Realistically, vendor-vendee should be viewed as mortgagee-mortgagor. To conceive of the relationship in different terms is to pay homage to form over substance. . . .

The piercing of the transparent distinction between a land contract and a mortgage is not a phenomenon without precedent. . . .

It is also interesting to note that the drafters of the Uniform Commercial Code abandoned the distinction between a conditional sale and a security interest. Section 1-201 of the U.C.C. (IC 1971, 26-1-1-201 (IND. ANN. STAT. § 19-1-201 (1964 Repl.)) defines "security interest" as "an interest in personal property or fixtures which secures payment or performance of an obligation . . . retention or reservation of title by a seller of goods notwithstanding shipment or delivery to the buyer is limited in effect to a reservation of 'security interest.' " We can conceive of no rational reason why conditional sales of real estate should be treated any differently.

A conditional land contract in effect creates a vendor's lien in the property to secure the unpaid balance owed under the contract. This lien is closely analogous to a mortgage — in fact, the vendor is commonly referred to as an "equitable mortgagee." . . . In view of this characterization of the vendor as a lienholder, it is only logical that such a lien be enforced through foreclosure proceedings. Such a lien "[has] all the incidents of a mortgage" . . . one of which is the right to foreclose.

There is a multitude of cases upholding the vendor's right to foreclose. (*See* 77 A.L.R. 276, and the cases cited therein.) The remedy is most often referred to as a foreclosure of an executory contract. (A land contract is "executory" until legal title is actually transferred to the vendee.) . . .

. . . We believe there to be great wisdom in requiring judicial foreclosure of land contracts pursuant to the mortgage statute. Perhaps the most attractive aspect of judicial foreclosure is the period of redemption, during which time the vendee may redeem his interest, possibly through refinancing.

Forfeiture is closely akin to strict foreclosure — a remedy developed by the English courts which did not contemplate the equity of redemption. American jurisdictions, including Indiana, have, for the most part, rejected strict foreclosure in favor of foreclosure by judicial sale. . . . Guided by the above principles we are compelled to conclude that judicial foreclosure of a land sale contract is in consonance with the notions of equity developed in American jurisprudence. . . . This is not to suggest that a forfeiture is an inappropriate remedy for the breach of all land contracts. In the case of an abandoning, absconding vendee, forfeiture is a logical and equitable remedy. Forfeiture would also be appropriate where the vendee has paid a minimal amount on the contract at the time of default and seeks to retain possession while the vendor is paying taxes, insurance, and other upkeep in order to preserve the premises. Of course, in this latter situation, the vendee will have acquired very little, if any, equity in the property. However, a court of equity must always approach forfeitures with great caution, being forever aware of the possibility of inequitable dispossession of property and exorbitant monetary loss. We are persuaded that forfeiture may only be appropriate under circumstances in which it is found to be consonant with notions of fairness and justice under the law.

In other words, we are holding a conditional land sales contract to be in the nature of a secured transaction, the provisions of which are subject to all proper and just remedies at law and in equity.

. . . On the facts of this case, we are of the opinion that the trial court correctly refused the remedy sought by the vendor-assignees, but in so refusing it denied all remedial relief to the plaintiffs. . . . Where discretionary power is not exercised by a trial court, under the mistaken belief that it was without this power, a remand and direction by a court of review is necessary and proper. . . . This is not an unwarranted interference with the trial court's function. Upon appeal to this Court, we have the judicial duty to sua sponte direct the trial court to apply appropriate equitable principles in such a case. . . . Consistent with such above-stated rules, this Court has the undeniable authority to remand with guidelines which will give substantial relief to plaintiffs under their secured interests and will prevent the sacrifice of the vendees' equitable lien in the property.

For all of the foregoing reasons, transfer is granted and the cause is reversed and remanded with instructions to enter a judgment of foreclosure on the vendors' lien, pursuant to Trial Rule 69(C) and the mortgage foreclosure statute (IC 1971, 32-8-16-1 (IND. STAT. ANN., § 3-1801 (1968 Repl.))) as modified by Trial Rule 69(C). Said judgment shall include an order for the payment of the unpaid principal balance due on said contract, together with interest at 8% per annum from the date of judgment. The order may also embrace any and all other proper and equitable relief that the court deems to be just, including the discretion to issue a stay of the judicial sale of the property, all pursuant to the provisions of Trial Rule 69(C). Such order shall be consistent with the principles and holdings developed within this opinion.

Reversed and remanded with instructions.

PRENTICE, Justice (concurring): I have some concern that our opinion herein might be viewed by some as indicating an attitude of indifference towards the rights of contract vendors. Such a view would not be a true reflection.

Because the installment sales contract, with forfeiture provisions, is a widely employed and generally accepted method of commerce in real estate in this state, it is appropriate that a vendee seeking to avoid the forfeiture, to which he agreed, be required to make a clear showing of the inequity of enforcement. In any given transaction anything short of enforcing the forfeiture provision may be a denial of equity to the vendor. It has been set forth in the majority opinion that if the vendee has little or no real equity in the premises, the court should have no hesitancy in declaring a forfeiture. It follows that if the vendee has indicated his willingness to forego his equity, if any, whether by mere abandonment of the premises, by release or deed or by a failure to make a timely assertion of his claim, he should be barred from thereafter claiming an equity.

If the court finds that forfeiture, although provided for by the terms of the contract, would be unjust, it should nevertheless grant the vendor the maximum relief consistent with equity against a defaulting vendee. It so doing, it should consider that, had the parties known that the forfeiture provision would not be enforceable, other provisions for the protection of the vendor doubtlessly would have been incorporated into the agreement. Generally, this would require that the transaction be treated as a note and mortgage with such provisions as are generally included in such documents customarily employed in the community by prudent investors. Terms customarily included in such notes and mortgages but frequently omitted from contracts include provisions for increased interest during periods of default, provision for the acceleration of the due date of the entire unpaid principal and interest upon a default continuing beyond a reasonable grace period, provisions for attorneys' fees and other expenses incidental to foreclosure, for the waiver of relief from valuation and appraisement laws and for receivers.

NOTES & QUESTIONS

1. *Practice Points*: The sale of real estate pursuant to a "conditional land contract" or "installment land sale contract" or "land contract," or "articles of agreement for warranty deed," also known as a "sale of land on contract" or "sale on contract," is different from the usual arrangement for which lawyers attend a real estate closing. The ordinary real estate sale contract contemplates that the sale will be closed (i.e., buyer pays the purchase price and seller delivers a deed transferring title to the buyer) within a short time after the contract has been signed by both parties. In a sale on contract, seller retains title until buyer has made agreed periodic installment payments, generally covering a number of years.

2. *Lien enforcement procedures.* As noted in *Skendzel*, a court-administered foreclosure and judicial sale proceeding is the usual method used today to enforce a mortgage lien on *real estate*. With respect to *personal property*, however, a lien or security interest subject to the Uniform Commercial Code is ordinarily enforced by public or private sale that is not court-administered. *See, e.g.,* U.C.C. § 7-210 (Enforcement of warehouseman's lien), § 7-308 (Enforcement of carrier's lien), § 9-504 (Secured party's right to dispose of collateral after default — Effect of disposition).

3. The court in *Skendzel* uses the U.C.C.'s abandonment of the distinction between a conditional sale of goods and a security interest in goods, as one of the factors supporting its conclusion that a conditional sale of *real estate* may likewise be treated as creating a mortgage lien. The analogy does not, however, extend so far as to contemplate the same kind of enforcement mechanism. Thus, when as in *Skendzel* a land sale contract is construed as creating a mortgage lien, court-administered foreclosure and judicial sale is the remedy available to the contract seller for enforcement of that lien.

4. Statutes may also require that installment land sale contracts on which vendees have defaulted are enforceable by vendors by foreclosure rather than by forfeiture or other proceedings. For example, the *Forcible Entry and Detainer* article in the ILLINOIS CODE OF CIVIL PROCEDURE (735 ILCS 5/9-102(a)(5)) includes the following provision:

> (a) The person entitled to the possession of lands or tenements may be restored thereto under any of the following circumstances:

. . . (5) When a vendee having obtained possession under a written or verbal agreement to purchase lands or tenements, and having failed to comply with the agreement, withholds possession thereof, after demand in writing by the person entitled to such possession; provided, however, that any such agreement for residential real estate as defined in the Illinois Mortgage Foreclosure Law entered into on or after July 1, 1987 where the purchase price is to be paid in installments over a period in excess of 5 years and the amount unpaid under the terms of the contract at the time of the filing of a foreclosure complaint under Article XV, including principal and due and unpaid interest, is less than 80% of the original purchase price shall be foreclosed under the Illinois Mortgage Foreclosure Law.

See also In re Butler, 552 N.W.2d 226 (Minn. 1996), where the court, reviewing Minnesota law dealing with such contracts, noted:

Contracts for deed provide a useful alternative financing mechanism which promotes the availability of credit and the transferability of property, and the legislature has approved contracts for deed as being in Minnesota's best interest by enacting legislation which supports their continued use. . . . In Minnesota, one remedy available to a vendor upon the vendee's defaulting under the terms of the contract for deed is the vendor's ability to cancel the contract pursuant to Minnesota Statutes section 559.21. A statutory cancellation of a contract for deed results in the vendee's forfeiture of all payments made and restoration of full legal and equitable title in the property to the vendor. This result is different from that in a mortgage foreclosure sale, where the defaulting party may receive proceeds of a mortgage foreclosure sale above the amount owed on the property.

5.   Constructive Trusts in Contract Cases

SNEPP v. UNITED STATES
444 U.S. 507 (1980)

PER CURIAM. . . . Frank W. Snepp III seeks review of a judgment enforcing an agreement that he signed when he accepted employment with the Central Intelligence Agency (CIA). He also contends that punitive damages are an inappropriate remedy for the breach of his promise to submit all writings about the Agency for prepublication review. . . . [T]he United States conditionally cross petitions from a judgment refusing to find that profits attributable to Snepp's breach are impressed with a constructive trust. We grant the petitions for certiorari in order to correct the judgment from which both parties seek relief.

I.

Based on his experiences as a CIA agent, Snepp published a book about certain CIA activities in South Vietnam. Snepp published the account without submitting it to the Agency for prepublication review. As an express condition of his employment with the CIA in 1968, however, Snepp had executed an agreement promising that he would "not . . . publish . . . any information or material relating to the Agency, its activities or intelligence activities generally, either during or after the term of [his] employment . . . without specific prior approval by the

Agency." . . . The promise was an integral part of Snepp's concurrent undertaking "not to disclose any classified information relating to the Agency without proper authorization." . . .[6] Thus, Snepp had pledged not to divulge classified information and not to publish any information without prepublication clearance. The Government brought this suit to enforce Snepp's agreement. It sought a declaration that Snepp had breached the contract, an injunction requiring Snepp to submit future writings for prepublication review, and an order imposing a constructive trust for the Government's benefit on all profits that Snepp might earn from publishing the book in violation of his fiduciary obligations to the Agency.[7]

The District Court found that Snepp had "willfully, deliberately and surreptitiously breached his position of trust with the CIA and the [1968] secrecy agreement" by publishing his book without submitting it for prepublication review. 456 F. Supp. 176, 179 (E.D. Va. 1978). The court also found that Snepp deliberately misled CIA officials into believing that he would submit the book for prepublication clearance. Finally, the court determined as a fact that publication of the book had "caused the United States irreparable harm and loss." *id.*, at 180. The District Court therefore enjoined future breaches of Snepp's agreement and imposed a constructive trust on Snepp's profits.

The Court of Appeals accepted the findings of the District Court and agreed that Snepp had breached a valid contract.[8] It specifically affirmed the finding that Snepp's failure to submit his manuscript for prepublication review had inflicted "irreparable harm" on intelligence activities vital to our national security. . . . Thus, the court upheld the injunction against future violations of Snepp's prepublication obligation. The court, however, concluded that the record did not support imposition of a constructive trust. The conclusion rested on the court's perception that Snepp had a First Amendment right to publish unclassified information and the Government's concession — for the purposes of this litigation — that Snepp's book divulged no classified intelligence. . . . In other words, the court thought that Snepp's fiduciary obligation extended only to preserving the confidentiality of classified material. It therefore limited recovery to nominal

---

[6] [1] Upon the eve of his departure from the Agency in 1976, Snepp also executed a "termination secrecy agreement." That document reaffirmed his obligation "never" to reveal "any classified information, or any information concerning intelligence or CIA that has not been made public by CIA . . . without the express written consent of the Director of Central Intelligence or his representative."

[7] [2] At the time of suit, Snepp already had received about $60,000 in advance payments. His contract with his publisher provides for royalties and other potential profits. . . .

[8] [3] The Court of Appeals and the District Court rejected each of Snepp's defenses to the enforcement of his contract. 595 F.2d 926, 931–934 (CA4 1979); 456 F. Supp., at 180–181. In his petition for certiorari, Snepp relies primarily on the claim that his agreement is unenforceable as a prior restraint on protected speech. When Snepp accepted employment with the CIA, he voluntarily signed the agreement that expressly obligated him to submit any proposed publication for prior review. He does not claim that he executed this agreement under duress. Indeed, he voluntarily reaffirmed his obligation when he left the Agency. We agree with the Court of Appeals that Snepp's agreement is an "entirely appropriate" exercise of the CIA Director's statutory mandate to "protec[t] intelligence sources and methods from unauthorized disclosure," 50 U.S.C. § 403(d)(3). 595 F.2d, at 932. Moreover, this Court's cases make clear that — even in the absence of an express agreement — the CIA could have acted to protect substantial government interests by imposing reasonable restrictions on employee activities that in other contexts might be protected by the First Amendment. . . . The Government has a compelling interest in protecting both the secrecy of information important to our national security and the appearance of confidentiality so essential to the effective operation of our foreign intelligence service. . . . The agreement that Snepp signed is a reasonable means for protecting this vital interest.

damages and to the possibility of punitive damages if the Government — in a jury trial — could prove tortious conduct.

Judge Hoffman, sitting by designation, dissented from the refusal to find a constructive trust. The 1968 agreement, he wrote, "was no ordinary contract; it gave life to a fiduciary relationship and invested in Snepp the trust of the CIA." . . . Prepublication clearance was part of Snepp's undertaking to protect confidences associated with his trust. Punitive damages, Judge Hoffman argued, were both a speculative and inappropriate remedy for Snepp's breach. We agree with Judge Hoffman that Snepp breached a fiduciary obligation and that the proceeds of his breach are impressed with a constructive trust.

II.

Snepp's employment with the CIA involved an extremely high degree of trust. In the opening sentence of the agreement that he signed, Snepp explicitly recognized that he was entering a trust relationship. . . . The trust agreement specifically imposed the obligation not to publish any information relating to the Agency without submitting the information for clearance. Snepp stipulated at trial that — after undertaking this obligation — he had been "assigned to various positions of trust" and that he had been granted "frequent access to classified information, including information regarding intelligence sources and methods." . . .[9] Snepp published his book about CIA activities on the basis of this background and exposure. He deliberately and surreptitiously violated his obligation to submit all material for prepublication review. Thus, he exposed the classified information with which he had been entrusted to the risk of disclosure.

Whether Snepp violated his trust does not depend upon whether his book actually contained classified information. The Government does not deny — as a general principle — Snepp's right to publish unclassified information. Nor does it contend — at this stage of the litigation — that Snepp's book contains classified material. The Government simply claims that, in light of the special trust reposed in him and the agreement that he signed, Snepp should have given the CIA an opportunity to determine whether the material he proposed to publish would compromise classified information or sources. Neither of the Government's concessions undercuts its claim that Snepp's failure to submit to prepublication review was a breach of his trust.

Both the District Court and the Court of Appeals found that a former intelligence agent's publication of unreviewed material relating to intelligence activities can be detrimental to vital national interests even if the published information is unclassified. When a former agent relies on his own judgment about what information is detrimental, he may reveal information that the CIA — with its broader understanding of what may expose classified information and confidential sources — could have identified as harmful. In addition to receiving intelligence from domestically based or controlled sources, the CIA obtains

---

[9] [6] Quite apart from the plain language of the agreement, the nature of Snepp's duties and his conceded access to confidential sources and materials could establish a trust relationship. *See* 595 F.2d, at 939 (Hoffman, J., concurring in part and dissenting in part). Few types of governmental employment involve a higher degree of trust than that reposed in a CIA employee with Snepp's duties.

information from the intelligence services of friendly nations[10] and from agents operating in foreign countries. The continued availability of these foreign sources depends upon the CIA's ability to guarantee the security of information that might compromise them and even endanger the personal safety of foreign agents.

Undisputed evidence in this case shows that a CIA agent's violation of his obligation to submit writings about the Agency for prepublication review impairs the CIA's ability to perform its statutory duties. . . .[11]

In view of this and other evidence in the record, both the District Court and the Court of Appeals recognized that Snepp's breach of his explicit obligation to submit his material — classified or not — for prepublication clearance has irreparably harmed the United States Government. . . .[12]

III.

The decision of the Court of Appeals denies the Government the most appropriate remedy for Snepp's acknowledged wrong. Indeed, as a practical matter, the decision may well leave the Government with no reliable deterrent against similar breaches of security. No one disputes that the actual damages attributable to a publication such as Snepp's generally are unquantifiable. Nominal damages are a hollow alternative, certain to deter no one. The punitive damages recoverable after a jury trial are speculative and unusual. Even if recovered, they may bear no relation to either the Government's irreparable loss or Snepp's unjust gain. The Government could not pursue the only remedy that the Court of Appeals left it[13] without losing the benefit of the bargain it seeks to enforce. Proof of the

---

[10] [7] Every major nation in the world has an intelligence service. Whatever fairly may be said about some of its past activities, the CIA (or its predecessor the Office of Strategic Services) is an agency thought by every President since Franklin D. Roosevelt to be essential to the security of the United States and — in a sense — the free world. It is impossible for a government wisely to make critical decisions about foreign policy and national defense without the benefit of dependable foreign intelligence. . . .

[11] [8] . . . If in fact information is unclassified or in the public domain, neither the CIA nor foreign agencies would be concerned. The problem is to ensure in advance, and by proper procedures, that information detrimental to national interest is not published. Without a dependable prepublication review procedure, no intelligence agency or responsible Government official could be assured that an employee privy to sensitive information might not conclude on his own — innocently or otherwise — that it should be disclosed to the world. The dissent argues that the Court is allowing the CIA to "censor" its employees' publications. . . . Snepp's contract, however, requires no more than a clearance procedure subject to judicial review. If Snepp, in compliance with his contract, had submitted his manuscript for review and the Agency had found it to contain sensitive material, presumably — if one accepts Snepp's present assertion of good intentions — an effort would have been made to eliminate harmful disclosures. Absent agreement in this respect, the Agency would have borne the burden of seeking an injunction against publication. . . .

[12] [9] . . . [O]n the basis of a premise wholly at odds with the record, the dissent bifurcates Snepp's 1968 agreement and treats its interdependent provisions as if they imposed unrelated obligations. Mr. Justice STEVENS then analogizes Snepp's prepublication review agreement with the Government to a private employee's covenant not to compete with his employer. . . . A body of private law intended to preserve competition, however, simply has no bearing on a contract made by the Director of the CIA in conformity with his statutory obligation to "protec[t] intelligence sources and methods from unauthorized disclosure." 50 U.S.C. § 403(d)(3).

[13] [10] Judge Hoffman's dissent suggests that even this remedy may be unavailable if the Government must bring suit in a State that allows punitive damages only upon proof of compensatory damages. . . . The Court of Appeals majority, however, held as a matter of federal law that the nominal

tortious conduct necessary to sustain an award of punitive damages might force the Government to disclose some of the very confidences that Snepp promised to protect. The trial of such a suit, before a jury if the defendant so elects, would subject the CIA and its officials to probing discovery into the Agency's highly confidential affairs. Rarely would the Government run this risk. In a letter introduced at Snepp's trial, former CIA Director Colby noted the analogous problem in criminal cases. Existing law, he stated, "requires the revelation in open court of confirming or additional information of such a nature that the potential damage to the national security precludes prosecution." . . . When the Government cannot secure its remedy without unacceptable risks, it has no remedy at all.

A constructive trust, on the other hand, protects both the Government and the former agent from unwarranted risks. This remedy is the natural and customary consequence of a breach of trust.[14] It deals fairly with both parties by conforming relief to the dimensions of the wrong. If the agent secures prepublication clearance, he can publish with no fear of liability. If the agent publishes unreviewed material in violation of his fiduciary and contractual obligation, the trust remedy simply requires him to disgorge the benefits of his faithlessness. Since the remedy is swift and sure, it is tailored to deter those who would place sensitive information at risk. And since the remedy reaches only funds attributable to the breach, it cannot saddle the former agent with exemplary damages out of all proportion to his gain. The decision of the Court of Appeals would deprive the Government of this equitable and effective means of protecting intelligence that may contribute to national security. We therefore reverse the judgment of the Court of Appeals insofar as it refused to impose a constructive trust on Snepp's profits, and we remand the cases to the Court of Appeals for reinstatement of the full judgment of the District Court.

So ordered.

Mr. Justice Stevens, with whom Mr.. Justice Brennan and Mr. Justice Marshall join, dissenting:

. . . [T]he Court today grants the Government unprecedented and drastic relief in the form of a constructive trust over the profits derived by Snepp from the sale of the book. Because that remedy is not authorized by any applicable law and because it is most inappropriate for the Court to dispose of this novel issue summarily on the Government's conditional cross-petition for certiorari, I respectfully dissent.

---

damages recoverable for any breach of a trust agreement will support an exemplary award. . . .

[14] [11] . . . Mr. Justice Stevens concedes that, even in the absence of a written contract, an employee has a fiduciary obligation to protect confidential information obtained during the course of his employment. . . . He also concedes that all personal profits gained from the exploitation of such information are impressed with a constructive trust in favor of the employer. . . . In this case, he seems to think that the common law would not treat information as "confidential" unless it were "classified." . . . We have thought that the common-law obligation was considerably more expansive. . . . But since this case involves the breach of a trust agreement that specifically required the prepublication review of all information about the employer, we need not look to the common law to determine the scope of Snepp's fiduciary obligation.

I.

The rule of law the Court announces today is not supported by statute, by the contract, or by the common law. Although Congress has enacted a number of criminal statutes punishing the unauthorized dissemination of certain types of classified information, it has not seen fit to authorize the constructive trust remedy the Court creates today. Nor does either of the contracts Snepp signed with the Agency provide for any such remedy in the event of a breach. The Court's per curiam opinion seems to suggest that its result is supported by a blend of the law of trusts and the law of contracts. But neither of these branches of the common law supports the imposition of a constructive trust under the circumstances of this case.

Plainly this is not a typical trust situation in which a settlor has conveyed legal title to certain assets to a trustee for the use and benefit of designated beneficiaries. Rather, it is an employment relationship in which the employee possesses fiduciary obligations arising out of his duty of loyalty to his employer. One of those obligations, long recognized by the common law even in the absence of a written employment agreement, is the duty to protect confidential or "classified" information. If Snepp had breached that obligation, the common law would support the implication of a constructive trust upon the benefits derived from his misuse of confidential information.

But Snepp did not breach his duty to protect confidential information. Rather, he breached a contractual duty, imposed in aid of the basic duty to maintain confidentiality, to obtain prepublication clearance. In order to justify the imposition of a constructive trust, the majority attempts to equate this contractual duty with Snepp's duty not to disclose, labeling them both as "fiduciary." I find nothing in the common law to support such an approach.

. . . [E]ven assuming that Snepp's covenant to submit to prepublication review should be enforced, the constructive trust imposed by the Court is not an appropriate remedy. If an employee has used his employer's confidential information for his own personal profit, a constructive trust over those profits is obviously an appropriate remedy because the profits are the direct result of the breach. But Snepp admittedly did not use confidential information in his book; nor were the profits from his book in any sense a product of his failure to submit the book for prepublication review. . . .

Despite the fact that Snepp has not caused the Government the type of harm that would ordinarily be remedied by the imposition of a constructive trust, the Court attempts to justify a constructive trust remedy on the ground that the Government has suffered some harm. The Court states that publication of "unreviewed material" by a former CIA agent "can be detrimental to vital national interests even if the published information is unclassified." . . . It then seems to suggest that the injury in such cases stems from the Agency's inability to catch "harmful" but unclassified information before it is published. I do not believe, however, that the Agency has any authority to censor its employees' publication of unclassified information on the basis of its opinion that publication may be "detrimental to vital national interests" or otherwise "identified as harmful." . . . The CIA never attempted to assert such power over Snepp in either of the contracts he signed; rather, the Agency itself limited its censorship power to preventing the disclosure of "classified" information. Moreover, even if such a wide-ranging prior restraint would be good national security policy, I would have great difficulty reconciling it with the demands of the First Amendment. . . .

In any event, to the extent that the Government seeks to punish Snepp for the generalized harm he has caused by failing to submit to prepublication review and to deter others from following in his footsteps, punitive damages is, as the Court of Appeals held, clearly the preferable remedy "since a constructive trust depends on the concept of unjust enrichment rather than deterrence and punishment. *See* D. Dobbs, LAW OF REMEDIES § 3.9 at 205 and § 4.3 at 246 (1973)." 595 F.2d, at 937.

* * *

III.

The uninhibited character of today's exercise in lawmaking is highlighted by the Court's disregard of two venerable principles that favor a more conservative approach to this case.

First, for centuries the English-speaking judiciary refused to grant equitable relief unless the plaintiff could show that his remedy at law was inadequate. Without waiting for an opportunity to appraise the adequacy of the punitive damages remedy in this case, the Court has jumped to the conclusion that equitable relief is necessary.

Second, and of greater importance, the Court seems unaware of the fact that its drastic new remedy has been fashioned to enforce a species of prior restraint on a citizen's right to criticize his government. Inherent in this prior restraint is the risk that the reviewing agency will misuse its authority to delay the publication of a critical work or to persuade an author to modify the contents of his work beyond the demands of secrecy. The character of the covenant as a prior restraint on free speech surely imposes an especially heavy burden on the censor to justify the remedy it seeks. It would take more than the Court has written to persuade me that that burden has been met.

I respectfully dissent.

NOTES & QUESTIONS

1. The constructive trust remedy has been sought and has been allowed in many different contract situations. Breach of contract to make a will in return for services to the promisor is one of them. Some examples: In *Kelsey v. Pewthers*, 685 So. 2d 953 (Fla. App. 1996), an action by relatives (a nephew and his wife) against a widow for breach of contract to make a will leaving her assets to them, the court held that plaintiffs could not recover money damages representing the present value of the expected inheritance, but that plaintiffs could choose to seek: (a) damages in quantum meruit for the value of services that they had provided to defendant, or (b) imposition of a constructive trust on the widow's assets subject to her unrestricted, reasonable use of those assets during her lifetime. In *Estate of Brenzikofer*, 49 Cal. App. 4th 1461, 57 Cal. Rptr. 2d 401 (1996), where tenants sought specific performance of their deceased landlord's alleged oral agreement to convey to them the house they were renting from her, the case was remanded for trial, the court holding that when one devotes work, energy and effort for a promisor, and in reliance on a promise of being devised property forgoes

opportunities elsewhere, relief equivalent to specific performance may be allowed by impressing a constructive trust upon the property promised.

2. In *Estate of Jones by Blume v. Kvamme*, 449 N.W.2d 428 (Minn. 1989), the estate representative of a deceased seller of stock sued the buyer who had allegedly misrepresented that he was purchasing the stock on behalf of a corporation, while actually purchasing the stock for himself. The court held that the trial court properly awarded rescissionary damages and properly imposed a constructive trust in favor of the seller's estate on the proceeds of the stock, and ruled that where a defrauded transferor sues for rescission of the contract, the fraud-feasor holds the chattel in constructive trust for the transferor, and the constructive trust includes any proceeds of the chattel.

3. The "heir hunter" case: In *Wattles v. Plotts*, 120 N.J. 444, 577 A.2d 131 (1990), an heir hunter discovered out-of-state heirs of the last record owner of a 6.21 acre parcel of vacant land worth more than $162,000 concerning which suit was then pending to foreclose on a tax sale certificate purchased from the township by an adjacent landowner for $1,131. The contract between the heirs and the heir hunter gave heir hunter the right, if the heirs were successful in upsetting the tax foreclosure and in obtaining title to the property, to sell the property, reimburse itself for its expenses, and divide the net profits with the heirs. Although the court concluded that the heirs were entitled to redeem the property and thus prevent foreclosure of the tax sale certificate, the heir hunter did not fare as well. Based on precedent and statutes disapproving certain activities by heir hunters, the court further ruled that a constructive trust in favor of the tax sale certificate holder was to be imposed on the heir hunter's rights under its contract with the heirs, and the heir hunter would be entitled only to reimbursement for its reasonable expenses under the contract.

4. Constructive trust remedies have also been applied against third parties who hold property to which plaintiffs are entitled by contract. Some examples in a family law context are: *Flanigan v. Munson*, 175 N.J. 597, 818 A.2d 1275 (2003), an action brought by children's legal custodians, holding that the children had standing as third-party beneficiaries to enforce a provision in their deceased mother's divorce property settlement agreement requiring the children to be made beneficiaries of any life insurance policies, and that a constructive trust against their mother's widower from a second marriage who had obtained proceeds from the mother's insurance policies is the appropriate remedy. *Faulknier v. Shafer*, 264 Va. 210, 563 S.E.2d 755 (2002), holding that the deceased insured's former wife properly stated a cause of action against a life policy's named beneficiary for a constructive trust on the policy proceeds, and that when property is given or devised to a defendant in breach of a donor's or testator's contract with a plaintiff, equity will impose a constructive trust on that property held by the recipient even though (1) the transfer was not the result of breach of fiduciary duty or an actual or constructive fraud and (2) the donee or devisee had no knowledge of the wrongdoing or breach of contract. *Simonds v. Simonds*, 45 N.Y.2d 233, 380 N.E.2d 189 (1978), a suit by a former wife against her former husband's second wife claiming that the deceased former husband had breached a provision in a separation agreement requiring him to maintain certain life insurance policies in effect with his first wife as beneficiary, in which a constructive trust was imposed on proceeds of the former husband's life insurance policies. *Perry v. Perry*, 484 S.W.2d 257 (Mo. 1972), suit — on behalf of the deceased insured's minor children

against decedent's mother — in which a constructive trust was imposed on the proceeds of three life insurance policies where decedent had failed to comply with his contract, executed incident to a divorce, agreeing to change the beneficiary on his policies to make his children the beneficiaries. *Jones v. Harrison*, 250 Va. 64, 458 S.E.2d 766 (1995), where, based on decedent's breach of obligation under a divorce decree to maintain life insurance coverage for the benefit of decedent's children from his former marriage, the court: (a) upheld the request by those children for a constructive trust upon a portion of life insurance proceeds paid to decedent's second wife, and (b) declared that when property is given or devised in breach of a donor's or testator's contract, a constructivetrust will be imposed upon property in the hands of the recipient, even though the transfer was not the result of breach of fiduciary duty or an actual or constructive fraud practiced upon plaintiff, and even though the donee or devisee had no knowledge of wrongdoing or breach of contract. *Aetna Life Ins. Co. v. Hussey*, 63 Ohio St. 3d 640, 590 N.E.2d 724 (1992), an insurer's interpleader action in which it was determined that because a separation agreement required the husband to maintain a life insurance policy with his daughter as irrevocable beneficiary, decedent's attempt to change the beneficiary was unlawful, the daughter was entitled to a portion of the policy's proceeds for her education until age 22, and a constructive trust in her favor should be imposed upon those proceeds.

5. Mutual promises between spouses for the disposition of their property present another contract situation in which the constructive trust remedy is often invoked for and against persons other than the contracting parties. Some examples: *Garrett v. Read*, 278 Kan. 662, 102 P.3d 436 (2004), holding that the imposition of a constructive trust was appropriate when a testator who executed a contractual will pursuant to oral agreement with her spouse to leave a portion of estate assets to one another's children, had breached a duty imposed by the confidential relationship with her spouse by revoking her contractual will after her spouse's death and executing a subsequent will that disinherited her spouse's children. *Alvarez v. Coleman*, 642 So. 2d 361 (Miss. 1994), where the court held that a constructive trust arose by reason of the husband and wife's family trust agreement, that the deceased husband was bound by a contract contained in joint, mutual or reciprocal wills and the trust agreement with his previously deceased wife, and that the husband was estopped from revoking his will and could not dispose of the entire marital estate differently than originally agreed. In *Matter of Estate of Green*, 516 N.W.2d 326 (S.D. 1994), a suit by beneficiaries named in a joint will of the husband and wife alleging that the wife's subsequent will violated the contractual agreement in the joint will, the court approved entry of an order to distribute the wife's estate under a constructive trust imposed on the basis that the wife's subsequent will violated the contract contained in the prior joint will. *Robison v. Graham*, 799 P.2d 610 (Okla. 1990), where beneficiaries of a contractual will which decedent entered into with his first wife were granted a constructive trust on decedent's entire estate, it having been found that decedent's actions following his first wife's death were unconscionable and constituted a breach of their contractual will. Compare *Matter of Estate of Cohen*, 83 N.Y.2d 148, 629 N.E.2d 1356 (1994), where the court refused to allow recovery by legatees named in a will mutually executed by decedent and his surviving wife, the court holding that: (a) a finding that decedent had duly revoked the mutually executed will (due to loss of decedent's will and its presumed revocation) precluded enforcement of a contemporaneous agreement through the imposition of constructive trusts on all or

any portion of the decedent's estate, (b) a constructive trust could not be imposed upon the estate that the decedent's spouse took by intestacy, and (c) the wife who manifested her assent to revocation of decedent's will when she applied for letters of administration of his estate (rather than letters testamentary) thereby precluded third-party beneficiaries from asserting any vested rights under the agreement.

6.   Equitable Liens in Contract Cases

ROLFE v. VARLEY
860 P.2d 1152 (Wyo. 1993)

CARDINE, Justice: Harley and Pauline Rolfe, husband and wife, appeal from a judgment, awarding Jay Varley approximately $900,000.00, an equitable lien on all of the Rolfes' real estate holdings, and terminating the alleged partnership between the Rolfes and Varley. Underlying this controversy is a written document, signed by the parties, which was to formalize their agreement to develop a resort hotel facility in Jackson, Wyoming; but instead the agreement created a tangled web of rights and duties. After a four-day bench trial, the district court issued findings of fact and conclusions of law and a judgment in favor of Varley.

We affirm.

The Rolfes raise a number of issues: ISSUE I. The trial court erred in finding from the facts of record in the action below and concluding as a matter of law that Appellant Pauline Rolfe was jointly and severally liable for any judgment against or obligation of her husband, Appellant Harley Rolfe . . . ISSUE II. The court erred as a matter of law and of fact in awarding an equitable lien against the sole and separate property of Appellant Pauline Rolfe. ISSUE III. The court erred as a matter of law in awarding an equitable lien against the property of Appellant Harley Rolfe. ISSUE IV. The court erred as a matter of law in the manner in its construction and interpretation of the April 6, 1987 Agreement. . . .

I. FACTS

. . . Since purchasing the Western Motel, Harley had wanted to develop it into a resort complex.

. . . Varley first contacted Harley and Pauline in 1983 when he stayed at the Western Motel during a ski vacation in Jackson. . . . [M]eetings and contacts culminated in the drafting and signing of a document titled, Agreement, on April 6, 1987.

. . . The Agreement provided that the Rolfes and Varley would enter into another agreement forming a partnership within thirty days of the execution of the Agreement. The Agreement stated that the future partnership must include the following "rights and obligations of the parties": (1) Harley must contribute the Western Motel property to the partnership, and (2) Varley must "provide the means to satisfy all current and existing debts and obligations encumbering or relating to the [Western Motel] property." The Agreement also stated that Varley, "for the benefit of the partnership and proposed development, shall use his best effort to purchase six [6] lots" and that Varley will pay Harley and Pauline $10,000.00 for expenses already accrued. In addition, the Agreement described the possibility of a "wrap-mortgage" if Varley satisfied either part or all of the Western Motel debts; this section of the Agreement, however, was very ambiguous. The Rolfes and Varley never entered into the contemplated partnership agreement.

After the Agreement was signed, Harley and Varley vigorously pursued their dream of creating a resort complex on the Western Motel property. Using Varley's money, the parties hired a builder, an architect and several different consultants to assist in the development efforts. Originally, in 1987, the parties contemplated a $7,000,000.00 project; however, after several changes on advice from the consultants, the proposed cost of the project grew to an estimated cost of $30,000,000.00 in 1988. At this point, the project was in jeopardy, and the parties attempted to downsize the project to make it workable.

Over the two-year period, beginning in April of 1987 with the $10,000.00 described in the Agreement and ending in 1989 when the joint effort to develop collapsed, Varley advanced Harley and Pauline $397,316.45 for the payment of their debts on the Western Motel. During October 1989, after the $30,000,000.00 figure appeared and after attempts to downsize the project, Varley discontinued paying the Western Motel debts. Throughout this period of debt service by Varley, he made several demands from the Rolfes for a personal note and mortgage as security for the debt payments. The Rolfes, however, refused to execute a note and mortgage.

The debt, which the Rolfes had accrued on the Western Motel, was over $500,000.00. Several of these loans were secured, not only by the Western Motel property, but also by Pauline's property. When Varley signed the Agreement, it was his understanding that the payments he made for the Western Motel debt were to be secured by the same collateral as was securing the underlying debts.

In addition to the money Varley expended for servicing the Western Motel debt, he also spent $347,556.85 towards trying to develop the resort complex. These funds were payments made to the builder, the architect and the host of consultants the parties hired.

Finally, in September 1990, Varley filed this suit in district court. Following a four-day bench trial, the district court awarded judgment to Varley for his two years of Western Motel debt payment and for his expenditures in pursuit of the resort development. In addition, the district court granted Varley interest on those damages, an equitable lien on all of Harley's and Pauline's property, and terminated whatever formal relationship existed between the Rolfes and Varley. The Rolfes now appeal several aspects of the judgment and the district court's findings of fact and conclusions of law.

II. DISCUSSION

* * *

B. EQUITABLE LIEN

The first three arguments raised by the Rolfes involve the same issue, whether the court erred in granting Varley an equitable lien against the properties of Pauline and Harley. In making this argument, the Rolfes claim that the equitable lien placed on Pauline's and Harley's property was error because the equitable lien doctrine does not apply to these facts. Additionally, they argue that the equitable lien placed on Pauline's property is error because she was not jointly and severally liable under the Agreement.

The equitable lien has been described generally as a right, not recognized at law, which a court of equity recognizes and enforces as distinct from strictly legal rights, to have a fund or specific property, or the proceeds, applied in full or in part to the payment of a particular debt or demand. 53 C.J.S. *Liens* § 2 at 457 (1987). Equitable liens arise in two ways, either by a contract or by implication. Dan B. Dobbs, Law of Remedies § 4.3(3) at 401-02 (2nd ed. 1993); *see also* 53 C.J.S. *Liens* §§ 6 and 8 at 464, 467. An equitable lien created expressly by contract occurs where a contract states that certain property will act as security but for some reason or another it fails to create a lien enforceable at law and thus the court enforces it in equity. Dobbs, at 402; 53 C.J.S. *Liens* § 6 at 464. Where there is no contract, equitable liens are implied by courts to avoid unjust enrichment. Dobbs, at 402.

Equitable liens are related to several other equity concepts. They are imposed to prevent unjust enrichment where the unjust enrichment might result from the "receipt of particular property." *United States Through Farmers Home Admin. v. Redland*, 695 P.2d 1031, 1040 (Wyo. 1985). An equitable lien is said to be a "special, and limited, form of the constructive trust" and closely related to subrogation because each is a remedy used to prevent unjust enrichment or fraud, and to allow restitution. Dobbs, § 4.3(3) at 402, § 4.3(4) at 405; 53 C.J.S. *Liens* § 2(b) at 457, § 3(b) at 459.

The following four requirements must exist before an equitable lien can be imposed: (1) a duty or obligation from one person to another; (2) a res to which that obligation attaches; (3) which can be identified with reasonable certainty; and, (4) an intent that the property serve as security for that purpose. *Redland*, 695 P.2d at 1040.

The district court did not err in imposing an equitable lien on both Pauline's and Harley's properties. Both Pauline and Harley signed the Agreement and accepted Varley's payments, thus they are obligated to Varley for his payments towards the Western Motel debt. Varley's payments went toward debts for which both Pauline and Harley were personally liable and which were secured by the Western Motel property. In addition, at least one of the debts was secured by Pauline's four properties. Thus, their obligation to Varley attaches to a recognizable res. The record demonstrates that the parties intended Pauline's and Harley's property to serve as security because the Agreement described a "wrap-mortgage" and because Varley testified that he understood that he would get a wrap-mortgage. Therefore, applying the four element test for an equitable lien, the district court ruled in accordance with law when it imposed an equitable lien on Pauline's and Harley's property for the debt payments made by Varley.

There is further support for imposing an equitable lien. It is generally held that an equitable lien exists where one party has paid another party's liabilities or debts owed upon certain, identifiable property. The general rule is: Where debts or claims against property are paid in good faith by another on the express or implied request of the owner of the property, the one so paying is entitled to an equitable lien on the property for his reimbursement. However, a person is not entitled to such lien if he voluntarily pays the debts of another without such other's request . . . . 53 C.J.S. § 8(a) at 468; *see also Dobbs v. Bowling*, 339 So. 2d 985 (Miss. 1976) (equitable lien upheld because, where one party made another's mortgage payments, then the paying party is subrogated to the rights of the mortgagee). In addition, where money advances are made by one party to another "under an agreement or circumstances showing that it was the intention of the parties to pledge [certain] property as security for the advancements," equitable liens have been imposed. 53 C.J.S. § 8(c) at 469, *see also Beck v. Brooks*, 224 Kan. 300, 580 P.2d 882, 884–85 (1978) (equitable mortgage imposed where one party advanced another money upon the faith of an agreement of a mortgage security but mortgage never executed).

We agree that Pauline was properly found to be jointly and severally liable for the debt to Varley. Although the Rolfes testified to the contrary, it is clear from the Agreement and through the Rolfes' course of business, that Pauline was involved in the development process. . . ."

. . . The Agreement and the testimony of the parties clearly demonstrates that Harley and Pauline requested Varley to pay their Western Motel debts and that Varley did pay those debts for a period of two years. Both Pauline's and Harley's properties were pledged as security for the underlying debts, and they both were personally liable; hence, both of their properties benefitted from Varley's payments. The district court, therefore, did not err in imposing an equitable lien on the Rolfes' property.

C. THE "AGREEMENT"

. . . Both Harley and Varley testified that they believed that the above Agreement formed a partnership to develop the Western Motel property. . . . [A] partnership was formed because the parties intended to create one. Whether or not a partnership has been created is controlled by the parties' intent. . . . From both Varley's and Harley's testimony, it is apparent that they thought they had created a partnership and were acting as partners. . . .

We conclude, as did the district court, that the Agreement created a creditor/debtor relationship between the parties with respect to the payments of Rolfes' debts upon the Western Motel and a partnership or joint venture to develop the Western Motel into a resort hotel. We do so because: (1) the Agreement was drafted by Harley and Smith — the Kentucky attorney assisting the Rolfes, (2) the use of the term wrap-mortgage, and (3) because it is the most reasonable interpretation.

A wrap-mortgage or wraparound mortgage is a transaction which involves: "a second mortgage securing a promissory note, the face amount of which is the sum of the existing first mortgage liability plus the cash or equity advanced by the lender. The wrap-around borrower must make payments on the first mortgage debt to the wrap-around lender, who, as required by the wrap-around agreement, must in turn make payments on the first mortgage debt to the third party, the first mortgagee." Grant S. Nelson and Dale A. Whitman, REAL ESTATE FINANCE LAW § 5.16 at 297 (2d ed. 1985) (quoting Comment, *The Wrap-Around Mortgage: A Critical Inquiry*, 21 U.C.L.A. L. REV. 1529, 1529–30 (1974)). Clearly, the use of the term wrap-mortgage implies the creation of a creditor/debtor relationship. . . . The Agreement is clear in stating that Varley is to provide the means to satisfy all obligations on the Western motel property, all of which are personal obligations of the Rolfes. In addition, Varley testified that he believed, when the Agreement was signed, that the security for his debt service for the Rolfes would be the same as the underlying creditors he was paying off.

We think the only reasonable interpretation of this agreement is that it did create a creditor/debtor relationship between Varley and the Rolfes. Under the circumstances, common sense tells us that Varley wanted security, in the form of a wrap-around mortgage from the Rolfes, in return for taking on the motel obligations. Therefore, we affirm the district court's conclusion that the Agreement created a creditor/debtor relationship. . . .

III. CONCLUSION

We affirm the district court's judgment and findings of fact and conclusions of law. The district court properly invoked its equitable authority by imposing an equitable lien on the Rolfes' property. The written contract was ambiguous. The district court had no choice but to invoke equity in resolving the dispute between these parties.

Affirmed.

NOTES & QUESTIONS

1. *Vendor's equitable lien in land sale on contract.* Courts have held that the vendor in a contract for deed retains an implied equitable vendor's lien or security interest on the real property for the amount of the unpaid purchase price. *See In re Butler*, 552 N.W.2d 226 (Minn. 1996). The lien "provides the critical security to a seller that is essential for an installment land sale contract to be a commercially reasonable way of selling real estate." *Butler v. Wilkinson*, 740 P.2d 1244 (Utah 1987).

2. *Vendee's equitable lien in land sale on contract.* The vendee in an installment land contract sale also may be entitled to the benefits of an equitable lien. In *Sidney Federal Sav. & Loan Ass'n v. Jones*, 215 Neb. 225, 337 N.W.2d 779 (1983), the court held that the contract vendee's equitable lien, in the amount it had paid on the purchase price, is assertable against a subsequent creditor or purchaser from the vendor.

3. *Vendor or mortgagee equitable lien on insurance proceeds.* When a vendee or mortgagor have promised to insure property for the vendor's or mortgagee(s benefit, but the insurance policy procured fails to include a loss-payable clause naming vendor or mortgagee, the promisee has an equitable lien on the proceeds of that insurance. In *Rosario-Paolo, Inc. v. C&M Pizza Restaurant, Inc.*, 84 N.Y.2d 379, 643 N.E.2d 85 (1994), a restaurant vendor was allowed to enforce its equitable lien claim against the restaurant vendee and vendee's insurer to the extent of that lien — the unpaid portion remaining on the purchase price. Vendee had promised in its security agreement to insure the restaurant and name vendor as a loss-payee to the extent of vendor's interest, but had obtained insurance naming only itself as loss-payee. The insurer was held liable because it had improperly paid the insurance proceeds to the vendee after ignoring vendor's written notice and claim of interest, and had failed to preserve the proceeds for the rightful owner. In *Terra Western Corp. v. Berry and Co.*, 207 Neb. 28, 295 N.W.2d 693 (1980), it was similarly held that when a mortgagor contracts with a mortgagee to insure property for the latter's benefit but fails to have a loss payable clause covering mortgagee's interest included in the policy, the mortgagee has an equitable lien on the proceeds of the insurance policy. The insurer in this case was held not liable to

the mortgagee because it had paid the insurance proceeds to the mortgagor in good faith and without actual knowledge of the mortgagee's interest. The court also noted, however, that: (a) an insurer with actual notice of a mortgagee's lien and the mortgagor's promise to mortgagee before it pays the insured mortgagee, is liable to the mortgagee for its interest, and (b) even if the insurer has no notice of the promise, the mortgagee may, before the insurer has paid out the policy proceeds, bring a suit in equity to impress its equitable lien on those proceeds.

4. *Vendor or mortgagee equitable lien on condemnation proceeds.* In *Halfon v. Title Ins. and Trust Co.*, 97 Nev. 421, 634 P.2d 660 (1981), a suit by vendors of real property against the vendee seeking, among other things, recovery of a $52,000 condemnation award, vendors were held entitled to that portion of the award necessary to satisfy their equitable lien. As security the vendee had signed a deed of trust (in effect a mortgage, naming a trustee as mortgagee and designating as beneficiary the vendor or other party financing the purchase) naming vendors as beneficiary, which contained a provision purporting to assign to the beneficiary any condemnation award received concerning the secured property. The court held that even without a contractual provision for assignment to vendors of a condemnation award paid for the taking of secured property, when property subject to mortgage or deed of trust is taken by eminent domain proceedings, the award becomes a substitute for the property, the mortgagee or beneficiary has an equitable lien on the award, and the secured party is entitled only to that portion of the award necessary to satisfy the lien, even where the deed of trust specifically provides for assignment of the entire award to the secured party.

5. In *Embree Const. Group, Inc. v. Rafcor, Inc.*, 330 N.C. 487, 411 S.E.2d 916 (1992), a general contractor was held entitled to claim relief in the form of an equitable lien in order to reach the $70,000 balance of loan funds held by a construction lender bank, based upon the lender's unjust enrichment in acquiring the completed project as security for its loan without disbursing the balance of the agreed-upon construction loan funds. In its discussion of various theories pursuant to which attempts in other jurisdictions had been made to reach construction funds remaining with the lender, the court noted that: (a) equitable assignment, third-party beneficiary, and trust fund theories had been generally unsuccessful, and that (b) relief in the form of an equitable lien based on a theory of detrimental reliance or unjust enrichment had been more fruitful, notably in California and Florida, with some courts also considering completion of the plaintiff's work — or of the project itself — critical. The equitable lien remedy was deemed appropriate for this case, based also on plaintiff contractor's allegations that it had satisfactorily completed construction on the project prior to any default by the owner on its obligations to the bank, and in reliance upon contract terms that provided for the disbursements to be made.

6. In *Middlebrooks v. Lonas*, 246 Ga. 720, 272 S.E.2d 687 (1980), a complaint seeking equitable relief was deemed sufficient based on allegations that in reliance on defendants' promise to repay, plaintiff had loaned them $25,000 which they used to build a home on land which they owned; that defendants had mortgaged the home and lot; that defendants had refused to repay the loan; and that plaintiff's remedies at law were inadequate. Assuming that remedies at law are inadequate, the court said, if a plaintiff proves that a defendant promised to repay a loan and made that promise without a present intent to perform, plaintiff can enforce either a constructive trust or an equitable lien on the fund, and if plaintiff proves that

fraudulently procured funds were used by defendant to purchase other property, plaintiff can reach the other property by a proceeding in equity, and can enforce a constructive trust or an equitable lien.

7.   Receivers in Contract Cases

MADDEN v. ROSSETER
117 Misc. 244, 192 N.Y.S. 113 (N.Y. Sup. 1921)

Guy, Judge:

Motion by a receiver to fix the compensation due him; also his counsel's fees. The receiver was directed to and did take from the defendant in California and deliver to plaintiff in Kentucky a valuable stallion named Frair Rock. Plaintiff first owned the horse. In 1918 plaintiff sold defendant a half interest, and they became partners or joint adventurers in the horse, under a contract by which defendant was to keep the horse in California until the end of the season of 1920, and plaintiff was to keep him in Kentucky for the seasons of 1921 and 1922; thereafter new arrangements mutually satisfactory were to be made. The fees, wherever received, were to be divided equally. When the end of the season of 1920 came, defendant refused to deliver the horse to plaintiff. Plaintiff sued for a mandatory injunction for the delivery of the stallion to him, for a receivership to effect the delivery, and also for a dissolution of the joint adventure or partnership. In February, 1921, an order was made granting a mandatory injunction, directing the delivery of the horse to the plaintiff and appointing the receiver to carry out such delivery. The defendant appealed from the order, and, on appeal, the order was affirmed. Thereafter the receiver carried out the order with tact and diplomacy, avoiding any litigation or ancillary receivership in California. He delivered the horse to plaintiff on May 23, 1921, in good condition.

It is admitted that the receiver's services, if they can now be directed to be paid for prior to the dissolution of the partnership or joint adventure, were worth $5,000, and those of his counsel are proved to be worth $500. While the dissolution action does not appear to have been disposed of, as to the primary relief sought the plaintiff is the winner, and has prevailed by reason of the affirmance on appeal and execution of the mandatory injunction for the delivery of the horse to him under the contract, which entitles him to keep it during the 1921 and 1922 seasons. The receiver's commissions on the delivery of a valuable live animal are not limited or to be computed upon the cash collected by him; $5,000 upon a $200,000 or $250,000 live animal is just, proper, and reasonable. . . . How are such commissions to be paid or allowed? In several states the rule is that the costs of a receivership incurred by the assertion of a wrongful claim, which is determined or found to be wrongful, may be taxed against whichever party asserted such wrongful claim, instead of being taken from the receivership funds. . . .

By the affirmance of the mandatory injunction and its execution the plaintiff has been adjudged the winner and has prevailed, with the right to keep the horse during the seasons of 1921 and 1922. He is therefore entitled to be reimbursed for the taxable expenses caused by defendant's unwarranted acts. The cases holding that, where a receiver was illegally appointed and his appointment was vacated, the party procuring his appointment must pay him . . . have no application to the case at bar, where the appointment of receiver was the object of the action, and as such has been sustained on appeal. Receiver's fees fixed at $5,000; those of his counsel at $500 — to be paid by defendant.

Ordered accordingly.

NOTES & QUESTIONS

1. *Question*: The *Madden* case involves an unusual use of the receivership tool. Can you think of other situations in which appointment of a receiver might be used to enforce or otherwise effectuate court orders in contract cases?

2. In *First Interstate Bank of Lea County v. Heritage Square, Ltd.*, 113 N.M. 763, 833 P.2d 240 (1992) it was noted that a court's authority to appoint a receiver can be based upon a court's equity jurisdiction or statutory authority, that receivers may be provided for in a variety of contracts, and that receiverships are general or special depending on whether the receiver's duty is to administer all the assets of a person or corporation or to take control of a particular property such as that subject to a mortgage.

3. Appointment of a receiver will often operate to displace the existing management of property or a business, and is therefore a remedy that can have serious consequences. In *Panama Timber Co., Inc. v. Barsanti*, 619 P.2d 872 (1980), an action seeking rescission of a sales contract, foreclosure of a sales agreement, and appointment of a receiver, the court held that the trial court abused its discretion in appointing a receiver where plaintiff had failed to present any evidence in support of its assertion that the property which was the subject of the contract was in bad condition and stood a good chance of being lost.

4. Courts may, however, consider contract terms that acknowledge the right of one of the parties to the appointment of a receiver in the event of default by the other. The court in *Fleet Bank of Maine v. Zimelman*, 575 A.2d 731 (Me. 1990), held that in light of unambiguous language in a mortgage document the plaintiff mortgagee was entitled to appointment of a receiver to collect rental income from property involved in the subject foreclosure suit, regardless of the underlying cause of the mortgagor's default. The mortgagor had failed to make timely and sufficient payments required by the note and made no claim that the mortgage contract was anything other than a commercial loan agreement negotiated at arm's length between knowledgeable businesspersons.

5. In certain circumstances receivers may be authorized to "sequester" funds or other personal property belonging to defendants. *See, e.g., Daniello v. Daniello*, 30 Misc. 2d 855, 219 N.Y.S.2d 641 (N.Y. Sup. 1961), a sequestration proceeding in a matrimonial action in which the receiver's motion to require delivery of certain sums allegedly belonging to the defendant was refused. The court noted that in this case the right to sequester property was limited by the state's Civil Practice Act to property that belonged to the defendant without any reasonable question, and held that there was reasonable question as to whether a sum due the husband under an employment contract was to be deemed earnings subsequent to appointment of the receiver (not sequestrable) or part of the price paid for redemption of his stock (sequestrable).

8.   Declaratory Judgments in Contract Cases

TROSSMAN v. TROSSMAN
24 Ill. App. 2d 521, 165 N.E.2d 368 (Ill. App., 1st Dist, 1960)

McCormick, Justice:

[A husband and wife had entered an ante-nuptial agreement stating "the property rights of the parties to the contract should be and remain absolutely and forever separate and distinct as though marriage had not taken place, and that the contract should remain in full force and effect whether the marriage was terminated either by death or divorce." It also required that "at the request of the other party they would execute deeds necessary to convey the property of the other and extinguish any right of dower, curtesy, homestead, or inheritance in each others estate." The wife asserted that the agreement was invalid and she would "in the event of plaintiff's prior death, seek dower and an intestate share in the plaintiff's estate." The plaintiff asserted that the agreement was valid and binding. He filed for a declaratory judgment "declaring the rights and other legal relations of the parties with respect to the said antenuptial agreement and the positions of the respective parties thereto with respect to the same."] . . .

The defendant moved to strike and dismiss the plaintiff's complaint, and in the motion set up, among other things, that the complaint failed to state a cause of action; that the controversy therein set forth is not justiciable at the present time; and that the relief prayed for therein is prior to any actual injury to the plaintiff and is founded on speculation and conjecture. . . . The court dismissed the plaintiff's complaint and cause of action and ordered that the defendant go hence without day. From that judgment order this appeal is taken.

A declaratory judgment is a new concept in the law. . . .

The purpose of the Declaratory Judgment Act is well expressed in the Notes by Messrs. Jenner and Tone to section 57.1 of the Civil Practice Act found in the Annotated Statutes (Smith-Hurd, Ill. Ann. Stat. ch. 110, § 57.1):

> The remedy is not designed to supplant existing remedies, nor afford a new choice of tribunals. It supplies a new form of relief where needed. It is designed to afford security and relief against uncertainty with a view to avoiding litigation, rather than in aid of it, and to settle and fix rights before there has been an irrevocable change of position of the parties in disregard of their respective claims of right, and thus promote peace, quiet and justice, with the end always constantly in view that one of the chief purposes is to declare rights rather than to execute then. . . . As stated by the court in *Sheldon v. Powell*, 99 Fla. 782, 128 So. 258 (1930) the remedy is one to be employed in the interests of preventative justice and its scope should be kept wide and liberal, and not restricted by technicalities. . . .

The particular contention before us is a matter of first impression in this State. The trial court dismissed the complaint and based its conclusion on the ground that the complaint did not set up an actual and justiciable controversy as required under the Act.

It has been held that in order for the court to enter a declaratory judgment there must be an actual controversy. . . . It is also the law that since the declaratory judgment statute was not designed to supplant existing remedies declaratory relief as a general rule will not be granted for a cause of action which has already accrued which is justiciable in a well-recognized form of action. . . . It would seem to be clearly apparent that if an action for declaratory judgment could only lie when some other legal remedy was available the passage of the Act would have been idle. Between Scylla and Charybdis there is a narrow but plain channel. In *Exchange Nat. Bank of Chicago v. County of Cook, supra* [6 Ill. 2d 419, 129 N.E.2d 1 (1955)], the court says:

> The section of the Practice Act authorizing the use of declaratory judgment procedures provides, in part, as follows:
>
> "* * * the court may, in cases of actual controversy, make binding declarations of rights, having the force of final judgments, whether or not any consequential relief is or could be claimed, * * *." We have repeatedly held that such provision does not authorize the court to grant declarations of rights involving mere abstract propositions of law without regard to the interest of the parties, and that before a declaration of rights may be made there must be an actual controversy. . . . The controversy must be definite and concrete, touching the legal relations of parties having adverse legal interests. * * * It must be a real and substantial controversy admitting of specific relief through a decree of a conclusive character, as distinguished from an opinion advising what the law would be upon a hypothetical state of facts. * * * Where there is such a concrete case admitting of an immediate and definitive determination of the legal rights of the parties in an adversary proceeding upon the facts alleged, the judicial function may be appropriately exercised although the adjudication of the rights of the litigants may not require the award of process or the payment of damages."
>
> . . .

Again referring to the Historical Notes to Section 57.1 of the Practice Act in the Annotated Statutes, it is said:

> The remedy was by no means unusual or extraordinary or unheard of either in Illinois or in other jurisdictions at the time the Act was adopted. Proceedings in equity to construe trusts and wills, to instruct trustees, to quiet title, and (in interpleader suits brought by stakeholders) to settle conflicting claims to a fund are a few forms of declaratory remedy familiar to the bar which have been afforded by the courts with and without statutory sanction or authorization. * * *

In a case decided by the Supreme Court of Minnesota in 1910 without the benefit of a Declaratory Judgment Act, *Slingerland v. Slingerland*, 109 Minn. 407, 124 N.W. 19, 20, which was an action brought by a wife to cancel a purported antenuptial contract, the court held that such an action might be maintained by the wife during the life of the husband while the wife's rights in his property are still inchoate, and the court says: ". . . Her rights in defendant's property are, it is true, inchoate and susceptible of change; but she has a present right to have determined the validity of an instrument which she sufficiently alleges she was unduly influenced to execute. In addition it would seem that now, while the parties to the instrument are alive and capable of testifying fully to the facts, is the appropriate time for the adjustment of this controversy."

. . . In *Elward v. Peabody Coal Co.*, *supra*, [9 Ill. App. 2d 234, 132 N.E.2d 549] a declaratory judgment was sought to determine whether a stock option was invalid. At the time the action was brought no attempt had been made to exercise the option. The court held that a declaratory judgment was proper. The court in its opinion, after pointing out that the defendants contend that since no part of the option had as yet been exercised it is premature to entertain the action before the court, said:

> . . . We are of the opinion that plaintiff is entitled to a declaratory decree as to whether the stock option agreement is illegal. Section 57.1 of the Civil Practice Act (¶ 57.1, Ch. 110, ILL. REV. STAT. 1955) provides that no action or proceeding in any court of record shall be open to objection on the ground that a merely declaratory decree, judgment or order is sought thereby, and the court may, in cases of actual controversy, make binding declarations of rights having the force of final judgments, whether or not any consequential relief is or could be claimed, including the determination, at the instance of anyone interested in the controversy, of the construction of any deed, will, contract or other written instrument, and a declaration of the rights of the parties interested, but the foregoing enumeration shall not exclude other cases of actual controversy. As there is an actual controversy involving the construction and validity of the stock option agreement, the complaint is properly brought. . . .

In 26 C.J.S. *Declaratory Judgments* § 28, it is said:

> It is not essential to a proceeding for a declaratory judgment that there be a violation of a right, a breach of duty or a wrong committed by one party against the other. The mere existence of a cloud, the denial of a right, the assertion of an unfounded claim, the existence of conflicting claims, or the uncertainty or insecurity occasioned by new events may constitute the operative facts entitling a party to declaratory relief." . . .

In the case before us there was an actual controversy, definite and concrete. The parties had adverse legal interests. In actions for declaratory judgments, "just as in equitable actions to quiet title or *quia timet*, no wrong need be proved but merely the existence of a claim or record which disturbs the title, peace, or freedom of the plaintiff, so any claims, assertions, challenges, records, or adverse interests, which, by casting doubt, insecurity, and uncertainty upon the plaintiff's rights or status, damage his pecuniary or material interests, establish a condition of justiciability. * * * While actions for declaratory judgments may be brought either after wrong done or threatened, or prior thereto, the fact that the court must be convinced that its judgment will settle the controversy and quiet the disputed or endangered rights is an assurance against abuse of a remedy which has simplified the administration of justice and admirably served a considerable part of the civilized world." Borchard, DECLARATORY JUDGMENTS, 2nd ed., pp. 39, 40. Here the controversy was neither moot nor based on a hypothetical state of facts. The contention of the defendant that the antenuptial contract was invalid would prevent a comprehensive plan being made on the part of the plaintiff to dispose of his estate either by will or otherwise. Here are present the ripening seeds of litigation. Such a dispute under the declaratory judgment statute "may be tried at its inception before it has accumulated the asperity, distemper, animosity, passion, and violence of the full-blown battle which looms ahead. It describes a state of facts indicating 'imminent' and 'inevitable' litigation, provided the issue is not settled and stabilized by a tranquilizing declaration. The dispute may be determined before the *status quo* has been altered or disturbed by physical acts of either party." Borchard, DECLARATORY JUDGMENTS, 2nd Ed., p. 57.

The judgment of the Circuit Court of Cook County is reversed and the cause remanded for further proceedings consistent with this opinion. Reversed and remanded.

NOTES & QUESTIONS

1. Declaratory Judgment is a statutory or court rule construct that derives from the common law equitable remedy known as the Declaration of Rights. Declaratory judgments are an alternative form of procedure and are not actions at law or in equity per se, but may form the basis for subsequent proceedings that seek damages or equitable remedies. Declaratory judgment acts and rules provide a mechanism for a court with proper jurisdiction to make a binding declaration of a party's rights and duties having the force of a final judgment, possibly before actual harm is sustained. Plaintiff seeking a declaratory judgment must, however, have a cognizable interest in an actual controversy.

2. Examples of situations appropriate for declaratory judgments include: construing the meaning of a document or language of a deed, establishing marketability of title to real property, determining the validity of an antenuptial agreement, establishing obligations under an insurance policy, and determining the applicability, validity, or constitutionality of various laws, regulations, and ordinances.

3. The Illinois declaratory judgment statute, 735 ILCS 5/2-701, reads:

> § 2-701. **Declaratory judgments.** (a) No action or proceeding is open to objection on the ground that a merely declaratory judgment or order is sought thereby. The court may, in cases of actual controversy, make binding declarations of rights, having the force of final judgments, whether or not any consequential relief is or could be claimed, including the determination, at the instance of anyone interested in the controversy, of the construction of any statute, municipal ordinance, or other governmental regulation, or of any deed, will, contract or other written instrument, and a declaration of the rights of the parties interested. The foregoing enumeration does not exclude other cases of actual controversy. The court shall refuse to enter a declaratory judgment or order, if it appears that the judgment or order, would not terminate the controversy or some part thereof, giving rise to the proceeding. In no event shall the court entertain any action or proceeding for a declaratory judgment or order involving any political question where the defendant is a State officer whose election is provided for by the Constitution; however, nothing herein shall prevent the court from entertaining any such action or proceeding for a declaratory judgment or order if such question also involves a constitutional convention or the construction of a statute involving a constitutional convention.
>
> (b) Declarations of rights, as herein provided for, may be obtained by means of a pleading seeking that relief alone, or as incident to or part of a complaint, counterclaim or other pleading seeking other relief as well, and if a declaration of rights is the only relief asked, the case may be set for

early hearing as in the case of a motion.

(c) If further relief based upon a declaration of right becomes necessary or proper after the declaration has been made, application may be made by petition to any court having jurisdiction for an order directed to any party or parties whose rights have been determined by the declaration to show cause why the further relief should not be granted forthwith, upon reasonable notice prescribed by the court in its order.

(d) If a proceeding under this Section involves the determination of issues of fact triable by a jury, they shall be tried and determined in the same manner as issues of fact are tried and determined in other civil actions in the court in which the proceeding is pending.

(e) Unless the parties agree by stipulation as to the allowance thereof, costs in proceedings authorized by this Section shall be allowed in accordance with rules. In the absence of rules the practice in other civil actions shall be followed if applicable, and if not applicable, the costs may be taxed as to the court seems just.

SECTION I

THIRD PARTY INTERESTS

It has been thought, and very learned writers have said, that two parties can not by contract create rights in a third person; others, while recognizing the possibility that rights may be so created, doubted that it was sound legislative or juristic policy to give recognition to such rights. Fears were expressed that the enforcement of such rights might result in serious injustice to the contracting parties, and that in any case it would greatly complicate judicial procedure and lead to a flood of litigation.

4 CORBIN ON CONTRACTS § 772 at page 2.

Up to this point in your study of contract law, for the most part you have been concerned with the rights, powers and duties of two parties, e.g., the offeror and offeree, promisor and promisee, seller and buyer, employer and employee, etc. However, you have been astute enough, we are sure, to have recognized the fact that the performance of one's duty, or the breach of that duty, has occasionally had an effect, sometimes profound, sometimes less than profound, on persons who were not "privy" to the contract.

In chapters 18 and 19 we will attempt to determine if and when persons, including partnerships and corporations, who were not parties to the contract will be accorded rights under the contract, against whom those rights may be enforced, when those rights become indefeasibly vested, and whether those non-parties to the contract may also find themselves duty-bound to one of the original contracting parties. And who said that contract law was "ineffably dull"?

CHAPTER 18

THIRD PARTY BENEFICIARY CONTRACTS

A. PRIVITY vs. NON-PRIVITY

DUTTON v. POOL
B.R. Hill. 28 & 29 Car. 2, Rot. 1123

Assumpsit. 1 Danv. Ab. 64, p. 3. 1 Vent. 319, 332. 2 Lev. 210.2 Jones 102.3 Keb. 786, 814, 830, 836.

In trespass upon the case. The plaintiffs declare, that whereas Sir Edward Pool Knight, father of the said Grizil was possessed and lawfully interessed [sic] of and in certain timber-trees growing in a certain park called Oaksey-Park in Wiltshire, 1 May 26 Car. 2 intended to cut down and sell the same to raise portions for his children, of which said intention the said defendant having notice, he the said defendant then at Sherborn in the county of Gloucester, in consideration that the said Sir Edward at the defendant's special instance and request would forbear cutting the said trees, did promise the said Sir Edward, that he the said defendant would well and faithfully pay to the said Grizil 1000£. And the plaintiffs in fact say, that the said Sir Edward after the making the said promise did not cut any of the said trees, and yet the defendant did not pay the said Grizil whilst she was sole, nor the said Sir Ralph and Grizil, or either of them after their marriage, the said 1000£ though thereunto requested, *ad damnum* 1000£. Upon *non assumpsit* pleaded, and verdict for the plaintiff, and damages 1000£ and judgment, the defendant brings a writ of error, and assigns the general error.

Holt for the plaintiff in the writ of error. The promise is made to Sir Edward Pool, and the action is brought by Grizil and her husband, to whom the payment was agreed to be made, which ought not to be. 3 Cro. 369, Jordan, 619 and 652. *Levet versus Hawes*, 849 and 881. *Rippon versus Norton*, Roll. Abr. 1, 31, pl. 6 and 30, pl. 3, Archdale's case. A promise to pay money to the attorney of A, the action may be brought by A, or his attorney. Latch 206, Legat's case.

Pollexfen for the defendant in the writ of error. The action is maintainable by the party to whom the promise was made, or to the *cestuy que use*, the promise was indifferently, Roll. Abr. 1, 31 Z. pl. 8, Oldham versus Bateman, 269, Starkey versus Mills, and of this opinion were all the justices and Barons; and judgment was affirmed. 2 Co. 47 a. pl. 175, Sprat versus Agar, M. 1658, B.R.

DUTTON v. POOLE
83 Eng. Rep. 523 (K.B. 1677), *aff'd*, 83 Eng. Rep. 156 (Ex. Ch. 1679)

. . . *Assumpsit,* and declares, that the father of the plaintiff's wife being seised of a wood which he intended to sell to raise portions for younger children, the defendant being his heir, in consideration the father would forbear to sell it at his request, promised the father to pay his daughter, now the plaintiff's wife, 1000£ and avers, that the father at his request forbore, but the defendant had not paid the 1000£. After verdict for the plaintiff. . . it was moved in arrest of judgment, that the action ought not to be brought by the daughter, but by the father; . . . for the promise was made to the father, and the daughter is neither privy nor interested in the consideration, nothing being due to her: also the father, notwithstanding this agreement with the son, might have cut down the wood, and then there was no remedy for the son, nor could the daughter have released the promise, and therefore she cannot have an action against him for not performing the promise. . . .

On the other side it was said, if a man deliver goods or money to H to deliver or pay to B, B may have an action, because he is to have the benefit of the bailment; so here the daughter is to have the benefit of the promise: so if a man should say, Give me a horse, I will give your son 10£ the son may bring the action, because the gift was upon consideration of a profit to the son; and the father is obliged by natural affection to provide for his children; for which cause affection to children is sufficient to raise a use to them out of the father's estate; and therefore the daughter had an interest in the consideration, and in the promise; and the son had a benefit by this agreement, for by this means he hath the wood, and the daughter is without a portion, which otherwise in all probability the son would have been left to pay, if the wood had not been cut down, nor this agreement between him and his father. . . .

Upon the first argument Wylde and Jones, Justices, seemed to think, that the action ought to be brought by the father and his executors, though for the benefit of the daughter, and not by the daughter, being not privy to the promise, nor consideration. Twysden and Rainsford seemed *contra;* and afterwards two new Judges being made . . . the case was argued again upon the reasons aforesaid; and now Scroggs Ch. Just. said, that there was such apparent consideration of affection from the father to his children, for whom nature obliges him to provide, that the consideration and promise to the father may well extend to the children. . . . Dolben, Justice, concurred with him that the daughter might bring the action; Jones and Wylde *haesitabant.* But next day they also agreed to the opinion of the Chief Justice and Dolben; and so judgment was given for the plaintiff, for the son hath the benefit by having of the wood, and the daughter hath lost her portion by this means. And now Jones said, he must confess he was never well satisfied with the judgment in Norris & Pine's case; but being it was resolved, he was loth to give his opinion so suddenly against it. And *nota,* upon this judgment error was immediately brought; . . . and was affirmed in the Exchequer-Chamber.

NOTES & QUESTIONS

1. The graphics in *Dutton* would have looked something like this:

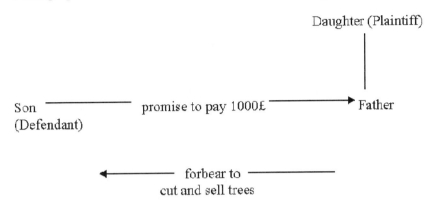

2. In *Tweddle v. Atkinson*, 121 Eng. Rep. 762 (Q.B. 1861), the court, speaking through Crompton J., rejected the rationale of *Dutton* and said:

> The modern cases have, in effect, overruled the old decisions; they shew that the consideration must move from the party entitled to sue upon the contract. It would be a monstrous proposition to say that a person was a party to the contract for the purpose of suing upon it for his own advantage, and not a party to it for the purpose of being sued. It is said that the father in the present case was agent for the son in making the contract, but that argument ought also to make the son liable upon it. I am prepared to overrule the old decisions, and to hold that, by reason of the principles which now govern the action of assumpsit, the present action is not maintainable.

3. Why did the English courts eventually hold that one not "in privity" with the defendant should be precluded from suing the defendant for his non-performance? In other words, why put a limitation on the type of plaintiff who is permitted to sue, if that plaintiff can show damage as a result of defendant's breach of his promised performance? Is such a limitation jurisprudentially sound?

4. Can you think of any modern scenarios where a third party not related to the major players prevailed against an alleged breacher? What about trusts? Life insurance policies?

B. TYPES OF PROPER PLAINTIFFS

LAWRENCE v. FOX
20 N.Y. 268 (1859)

. . . APPEAL from the Superior Court of the city of Buffalo. On the trial before Mr. Justice Masten, it appeared by the evidence of a bystander, that one Holly, in November, 1857, at the request of the defendant, loaned and advanced to him $300, stating at the time that he owed that sum to the plaintiff for money borrowed of him, and had agreed to pay it to him the then next day; that the defendant in consideration thereof, at the time of receiving the money, promised to pay it to the plaintiff the then next day. Upon this state of facts the defendant moved for a nonsuit, upon three several grounds, viz.: That there was no proof tending to show that Holly was indebted to the plaintiff; that the agreement by the defendant with Holly to pay the plaintiff was void for want of consideration, and that there was no privity between the plaintiff and defendant. The court overruled the motion, and the counsel for the defendant excepted. The cause was then submitted to the jury, and they found a verdict for the plaintiff for the amount of the loan and interest, $344.66, upon which judgment was entered; from which the defendant appealed to the Superior Court, at general term, where the judgment was affirmed, and the defendant appealed to this court. . . .

H. GRAY, Judge:

. . . It is claimed that notwithstanding this promise [of defendant Fox] was established by competent evidence, it was void for the want of consideration . . . In this case the promise was made to Holly and not expressly to the plaintiff; and this difference presents the question, raised by the defendant's objection, as to the want of privity between the plaintiff and defendant.

As early as 1806 it was announced by the Supreme Court of this State, upon what was then regarded as the settled law of England, "That where one person makes a promise to another for the benefit of a third person, that third person may maintain an action upon it." *Schermerhorn v. Vanderheyden* (1 John. R., 140) has often been reasserted by our courts and never departed from. . . . This question was subsequently, and in a case quite recent, again the subject of consideration by the Supreme Court, when it was held, that in declaring upon a promise, made to the debtor by a third party to pay the creditor of the debtor, founded upon a consideration advanced by the debtor, it was unnecessary to aver a promise to the creditor; for the reason that upon proof of a promise made to the debtor to pay the creditor, a promise to the creditor would be implied. And in support of this proposition, in no respect distinguishable, from the one now under consideration, the case of *Schermerhorn v. Vanderheyden*, with many intermediate cases in our courts, were cited, in which the doctrine of that case was not only approved but affirmed. The same principle is adjudged in several cases in Massachusetts. I will refer to but few of them. In *Hall v. Marston* the court say [sic]: "It seems to have been well settled that if A promises B for a valuable consideration to pay C, the latter may maintain assumpsit for the money;" and in *Brewer v. Dyer*, the recovery was upheld, as the court said, "upon the principle of law *long recognized and clearly established*, that when one person, for a valuable consideration, engages with another, by a simple contract, to do some act for the benefit of a third, the latter, who would enjoy the benefit of the act, may maintain an action for the breach of such engagement; that it does not rest upon the ground of any actual or supposed relationship between the parties as some of the earlier cases would seem to indicate, but upon the broader and more satisfactory basis, that the law operating on the act of the parties creates the duty, establishes a privity, and implies the promise and obligation on which the action is founded.". . . But it is urged that because the defendant was not in any sense a trustee of the property of Holly for the benefit of the plaintiff, the law will not imply a promise. I agree that many of the cases where a promise was implied were cases of trusts, created for the benefit of the promisor. The case of *Felton v. Dickinson* (10 Mass. 287), and others that might be cited, are of that class; but concede them all to have been cases of trusts, and it proves nothing against the application of the rule to this case. The duty of the trustee to pay the *cestuis que trust*, according to the terms of the trust, implies his promise to the latter to do so.

In this case the defendant, upon ample consideration received from Holly, promised Holly to pay his debt to the plaintiff; the consideratin received and the promise to Holly made it as plainly his duty to pay the plaintiff as if the money had been remitted to him for that purpose, and as well implied a promise to do so as if he had been made a trustee of property to be converted into cash with which to pay. The fact that a breach of the duty imposed in the one case may be visited, and justly, with more serious consequences than in the other, by no means disproves the payment to be a duty in both. The principle illustrated by the example so frequently quoted (which concisely states the case in hand) "that a promise made to one for the benefit of another, he for whose benefit it is made may bring an action for its breach," has been applied to trust cases, not because it was exclusively applicable to those cases, but because it was a principle of law, and as such applicable to those cases. It was also insisted that Holly could have discharged the defendant from his promise, though it was intended by both parties for the benefit of the plaintiff, and therefore the plaintiff was not entitled to maintain this suit for the recovery of a demand over which he had no control. It is enough that the plaintiff did not release the defendant from his promise, and whether he could or not is a question not now necessarily involved; but if it was, I think it would be found difficult to maintain the right of Holly to discharge a judgment recovered by the plaintiff upon confession or otherwise, for the breach of the defendant's promise; and if he could not, how could he discharge the suit before judgment, or the promise before suit, made as it was for the plaintiff's benefit and in accordance with legal presumption accepted by him, until his dissent was shown. The cases cited, and especially that of *Farley v. Cleaveland*, establish the validity of a parol promise; it stands then upon the footing of a written one. . . .

The judgment should be affirmed.

Johnson, Ch. J., Denio, Selden, Allen and Strong, Js., concurred.

Johnson, Ch. J., and Denio, J., were of opinion that the promise was to be regarded as made to the plaintiff through the medium of his agent, whose action he could ratify when it came to his knowledge, though taken without his being privy thereto.

Comstock, J. (Dissenting): The plaintiff had nothing to do with the promise on which he brought this action. It was not made to him, nor did the consideration proceed from him. If he can maintain the suit, it is because an anomaly has found its way into the law on this subject. In general, there must be privity of contract. The party who sues upon a promise must be the promisee, or he must have some legal interest in the undertaking. In this case, it is plain that Holly, who loaned the money to the defendant, and to whom the promise in question was made, could at any time have claimed that it should be performed to himself personally. He had lent the money to the defendant, and at the same time directed the latter to pay the sum to the plaintiff. This direction he could countermand, and if he had done so, manifestly the defendant's promise to pay according to the direction would have ceased to exist. The plaintiff would receive a benefit by a complete execution of the arrangement, but the arrangement itself was between other parties, and was under their exclusive control. . . .

The cases which have sometimes been supposed to have a bearing on this question, are quite numerous. In some of them, the dicta of judges, delivered upon very slight consideration, have been referred to as the decisions of the courts. Thus, *Schermerhorn v. Vanderheyden* (1 John., 140), the court is reported as saying, "We are of opinion, that where one person makes a promise to another, for the benefit of a third person, that third person may maintain an action on such promise." This remark was made on the authority of *Dalton* [sic] *v. Poole* (Vent., 318, 332), decided in England nearly two hundred years ago. It was, however, but a mere remark, as the case was determined against the plaintiff on another ground. Yet this decision has often been referred to as authority for similar observations in later cases. . . .

The cases in which some trust was involved are also frequently referred to as authority for the doctrine now in question, but they do not sustain it. If A delivers money or property to B, which the latter accepts upon a trust for the benefit of C, the latter can enforce the trust by an appropriate action for that purpose. . . . A fund received under such an agreement does not belong to the person who receives it. He must account for it specifically; and perhaps there is no gross violation of principle in permitting the equitable owner of it to sue upon an express promise to pay it over. Having a specific interest in the thing, the undertaking to account for it may be regarded as in some sense made with him through the author of the trust. But further than this we cannot go without violating plain rules of law. In the case before us there was nothing in the nature of a trust or agency. The defendant borrowed the money of Holly and received it as his own. The plaintiff had no right in the fund, legal or equitable. The promise to repay the money created an obligation in favor of the lender to whom it was made and not in favor of any one else.

I have referred to the dictum in *Schermerhorn v. Vanderheyden* (1 Johns., 140), as favoring the doctrine contended for. It was the earliest in this State, and was founded, as already observed, on the old English case of *Dutton v. Poole*, in Ventris. That case has always been referred to as the ultimate authority whenever the rule in question has been mentioned, and it deserves, therefore, some further notice. The father of the plaintiff's wife being seized of certain lands, which afterwards on his death descended to the defendant, and being about to cut £1,000 worth of timber to raise a portion for his daughter, the defendant promised the father, in consideration of his forbearing to cut the timber, that he would pay the said daughter the £1,000. After verdict for the plaintiff, upon the issue of non-assumpsit, it was urged in arrest of judgment, that the father ought to have brought the action, and not the husband and wife. It was held, after much discussion, that the action would lie. The court said, "It might be another case if the money had been to have been paid to a stranger; but there is such a manner of relation between the father and the child, and it is a kind of debt to the child to be provided for, that the plaintiff is plainly concerned." We need not criticise the reason given for this decision. It is enough for the present purpose, that the case is no authority for the general doctrine, to sustain which it has been so frequently cited. It belongs to a class of cases somewhat peculiar and anomalous, in which promises have been made to a parent or person standing in a near relationship to the person for whose benefit it was made, and in which, on account of that relationship, the beneficiary has been allowed to maintain the action. Regarded as standing on any other ground, they have long since ceased to be the law in England. . . .

The judgment of the court below should therefore be reversed, and a new trial granted.

Judgment affirmed.

NOTES & QUESTIONS

1. Graphically, the relationship would look something like this:

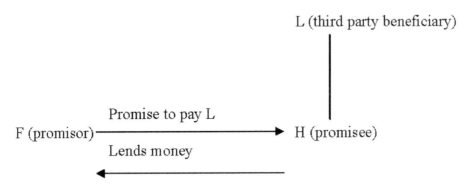

2. Once plaintiff has acquired a right against the defendant promisor, does the plaintiff thereby lose his right to collect the debt from his debtor, the promisee? *See* RESTATEMENT (SECOND) OF CONTRACTS § 310(1).

3. Once L, to enforce his right, begins to actually prosecute a cause of action against F for breach of his promise, does the plaintiff — L then lose his right against H his debtor, the promisee?

4. *Compare* RESTATEMENT OF CONTRACTS § 133 *with* RESTATEMENT (SECOND) OF CONTRACTS § 302.

§ 133. Definition of Donee Beneficiary, Creditor Beneficiary, Incidental Beneficiary.

(1) Where performance of a promise in a contract will benefit a person other than the promisee, that person is, except as stated in Subsection (3):

(a) a donee beneficiary if it appears from the terms of the promise in view of the accompanying circumstances that the purpose of the promisee in obtaining the promise of all or part of the performance thereof is to make a gift to the beneficiary or to confer upon him a right against the promisor to some performance neither due nor supposed or asserted to be due from the promisee to the beneficiary;

(b) a creditor beneficiary if no purpose to make a gift appears from the terms of the promise in view of the accompanying circumstances and performance of the promise will satisfy an actual or supposed or asserted duty of the promisee to the beneficiary, or a right of the beneficiary against the promisee which has been barred by the Statute of Limitations or by a discharge in bankruptcy, or which is unenforceable because of the Statute of Frauds;

(c) an incidental beneficiary if neither the facts stated in Clause (a) nor those stated in Clause (b) exist.

(2) Such a promise as is described in Subsection (1a) is a gift promise. Such a promise as is described in Subsection (1b) is a promise to discharge the promisee's duty.

(3) Where it appears from the terms of the promise in view of the accompanying circumstances that the purpose of the promisee is to benefit a beneficiary under a trust and the promise is to render performance to the trustee, the trustee, and not the beneficiary under the trust, is a beneficiary within the meaning of this Section.

§ 302. Intended and Incidental Beneficiaries

(1) Unless otherwise agreed between promisor and promisee, a beneficiary of a promise is an intended beneficiary if recognition of a right to performance in the beneficiary is appropriate to effectuate the intention of the parties and either:

(a) the performance of the promise will satisfy an obligation of the promisee to pay money to the beneficiary; or

(b) the circumstances indicate that the promisee intends to give the beneficiary the benefit of the promised performance.

(2) An incidental beneficiary is a beneficiary who is not an intended beneficiary.

5. Under the first RESTATEMENT OF CONTRACTS, there are two different kinds of protected third party beneficiaries: (a) a third party creditor beneficiary (cf. *Lawrence v. Fox*) and (b) a third party donee beneficiary (cf. next case).

Under the first RESTATEMENT OF CONTRACTS, the critical factor is to determine the purpose of the promisee — H — in extracting a promise from the promisor — F — that benefits L. If H wants F to perform his promise so that a debt of H to L will be discharged, then L is a third party "creditor" beneficiary.

If H simply wants L to receive a gratuitous right against F, then L becomes a third party "donee" beneficiary.

Query: Is F's intent equally, secondarily, or non-important?

The RESTATEMENT (SECOND) OF CONTRACTS combines both kinds of protected beneficiaries under one rubric, that of an "intended beneficiary." *See* RESTATEMENT (SECOND) OF CONTRACTS § 302, above.

The final kind of beneficiary is an "incidental beneficiary," that is, one who acquires no rights against the promisor F.

6. The argument has been made that there is no real need to accord L a right against F. Since L retains his right to collect from H, L need simply sue H, and H may thereafter join F as a third party defendant if H so wishes. In short, why is there a need to give L a new right against F, since F will eventually be ordered to abide by — or pay damages for the breach of — his promise? Persuasive?

7. Now that L has acquired a cause of action against F, does H retain a cause of action for F's breach? If so, then F is subject to two liabilities. Is this fundamentally

fair to F? *See* RESTATEMENT (SECOND) OF CONTRACTS § 305.

SEAVER v. RANSOM
224 N.Y. 233, 120 N.E. 639 (1918)

POUND, Judge:

Judge Beman and his wife were advanced in years. Mrs. Beman was about to die. She had a small estate, consisting of a house and lot in Malone and little else. Judge Beman drew his wife's will according to her instructions. . . .

Plaintiff was her niece, 34 years old, in ill health, sometimes a member of the Beman household. When the will was read to Mrs. Beman, she said that it was not as she wanted it. She wanted to leave the house to plaintiff. She had no other objection to the will, but her strength was waning, and, although the judge offered to write another will for her, she said she was afraid she would not hold out long enough to enable her to sign it. So the judge said, if she would sign the will, he would leave plaintiff enough in his will to make up the difference. He avouched the promise by his uplifted hand with all solemnity and his wife then executed the will. When he came to die, it was found that his will made no provision for the plaintiff.

This action was brought, and plaintiff recovered judgment in the trial court on the theory that Beman had obtained property from his wife and induced her to execute the will in the form prepared by him by his promise to give plaintiff $6,000, the value of the house, and that thereby equity impressed his property with a trust in favor of plaintiff. Where a legatee promises the testator that he will use property given him by the will for a particular purpose, a trust arises. Beman received nothing under his wife's will but the use of the house in Malone for life. Equity compels the application of property thus obtained to the purpose of the testator, but equity cannot so impress a trust, except on property obtained by the promise. Beman was bound by his promise, but no property was bound by it; no trust in plaintiff's favor can be spelled out.

An action on the contract for damages, or to make the executors trustees for performance, stands on different ground. The Appellate Division properly passed to the consideration of the question whether the judgment could stand upon the promise made to the wife, upon a valid consideration, for the sole benefit of plaintiff. The judgment of the trial court was affirmed by a return to the general doctrine laid down in the great case of *Lawrence v. Fox*, 20 N.Y. 268, which has since been limited as herein indicated.

Contracts for the benefit of third persons have been the prolific source of judicial and academic discussion. Williston, *Contracts for the Benefit of a Third Person*, 15 HARVARD LAW REVIEW, 767; Corbin, *Contracts for the Benefit of Third Persons*, 27 YALE LAW REVIEW, 1008. The general rule, both in law and equity, was that privity between a plaintiff and a defendant is necessary to the maintenance of an action on the contract. The consideration must be furnished by the party to whom the promise was made. The contract cannot be enforced against the third party, and therefore it cannot be enforced by him. On the other hand, the right of the beneficiary to sue on a contract made expressly for his benefit has been fully recognized in many American jurisdictions, either by judicial decision or by legislation, and is said to be "the prevailing rule in this country." It has been said that "the establishment of this doctrine has been gradual, and is a victory of practical utility over theory, of equity over technical subtlety." BRANTLY ON

CONTRACTS (2d Ed.) p. 253. The reasons for this view are that it is just and practical to permit the person for whose benefit the contract is made to enforce it against one whose duty it is to pay. Other jurisdictions still adhere to the present English rule (7 *Halsbury's Laws of England*, 342, 343; JENKS' DIGEST OF ENGLISH CIVIL LAW, § 229) that a contract cannot be enforced by or against a person who is not a party (*Exchange Bank v. Rice*, 107 Mass. 37, 9 Am. (Rep. 1). But *see also Forbes v. Thorpe*, 209 Mass. 570, 95 N.E. 955; *Gardner v. Denison*, 217 Mass. 492, 105 N.E. 359, 51 L.R.A. (N.S.) 1108.

In New York the right of the beneficiary to sue on contracts made for his benefit is . . . at present confined: First, to cases where there is a pecuniary obligation running from the promisee to the beneficiary, "a legal right founded upon some obligation of the promisee in the third party to adopt and claim the promise as made for his benefit." Secondly, to cases where the contract is made for the benefit of the wife, affianced wife (*De Cicco v. Schweizer*, 221 N.Y. 431, 117 N.E. 807, Ann. Cas. 1918C, 816), or child of a party to the contract. The close relationship cases go back to the early *King's Bench* case (1677), long since repudiated in England, of *Dutton v. Poole*, 2 Lev. 211 (s.c., 1 Ventris, 318, 332). *See Schermerhorn v. Vanderheyden*, 1 Johns. 139, 3 Am. Dec. 304. The natural and moral duty of the husband or parent to provide for the future of wife or child sustains the action on the contract made for their benefit. "This is the farthest the cases in this state have gone," says Cullen, J., in the marriage settlement case of *Borland v. Welch*, 162 N. Y. 104, 110, 56 N. E. 556.

[The court here discusses public contract cases where the third party beneficiary's right has been upheld and cases where the promise runs directly to the third party beneficiary.]

. . . It may be safely said that a general rule sustaining recovery at the suit of the third party would include but few classes of cases not included in these groups, either categorically or in principle.

The desire of the childless aunt to make provision for a beloved and favorite niece differs imperceptibly in law or in equity from the moral duty of the parent to make testamentary provision for a child. The contract was made for the plaintiff's benefit. She alone is substantially damaged by its breach. The representatives of the wife's estate have no interest in enforcing it specifically. . . . If plaintiff had been a child of Mrs. Beman, legal obligation would have required no testamentary provision for her, yet the child could have enforced a covenant in her favor identical with the covenant of Judge Beman in this case. *De Cicco v. Schweizer, supra.* The constraining power of conscience is not regulated by the degree of relationship alone. The dependent or faithful niece may have a stronger claim than the affluent or unworthy son. No sensible theory of moral obligation denies arbitrarily to the former what would be conceded to the latter. We might consistently either refuse or allow the claim of both, but I cannot reconcile a decision in favor of the wife in *Buchanan v. Tilden*, based on the moral obligations arising out of near relationship, with a decision against the niece here on the ground that the relationship is too remote for equity's ken. No controlling authority depends upon so absolute a rule. . . . KELLOG, P.J., writing for the court below well said:

The doctrine of *Lawrence v. Fox* is progressive, not retrograde. The course of the late decisions is to enlarge, not to limit, the effect of that case.

The court in that leading case attempted to adopt the general doctrine that any third person, for whose direct benefit a contract was intended, could sue on it . . . but *Vrooman v. Turner, supra,* confined its application to the facts on which it was decided. "In every case in which an action has been sustained," says Allen, J., "there has been a debt or duty owing by the promisee to the party claiming to sue upon the promise." 69 N.Y. 285, 25 Am. Rep. 195. As late as *Towsend v. Rackham,* 143 N.Y. 516, 523, 38 N. E. 731, 733, we find Peckham, J., saying that, "to maintain the action by the third person, there must be this liability to him on the part of the promisee." . . .

But, . . . [i]f Mrs. Beman had left her husband the house on condition that he pay the plaintiff $6,000, and he had accepted the devise, he would have become personally liable to pay the legacy, and plaintiff could have recovered in an action at law against him, whatever the value of the house. That would be because the testatrix had in substance bequeathed the promise to plaintiff, and not because close relationship or moral obligation sustained the contract. The distinction between an implied promise to a testator for the benefit of a third party to pay a legacy and an unqualified promise on a valuable consideration to make provision for the third party by will is discernible, but not obvious. The tendency of American authority is to sustain the gift in all such cases and to permit the donee beneficiary to recover on the contract. The equities are with the plaintiff, and they may be enforced in this action, whether it be regarded as an action for damages or an action for specific performance to convert the defendants into trustees for plaintiff's benefit under the agreement.

The judgment should be affirmed, with costs.

Judgment affirmed.

NOTES & QUESTIONS

1. Graphically, the relationship looks like this:

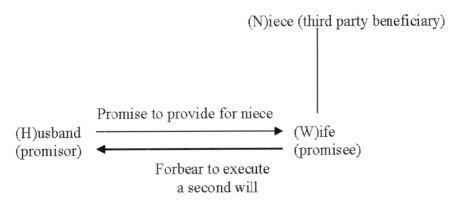

2. Whose intent should be controlling in determining whether a third party — here N — acquires a right to sue the promisor — here H? Should it be W's intent, H's intent, or equally W's and H's? *See* RESTATEMENT (SECOND) OF CONTRACTS § 302. Must the intent be expressed in the contract itself?

LUCAS v. HAMM
56 Cal. 2d 583, 364 P.2d 685 (1961)

GIBSON, Chief Justice:

Plaintiffs, who are some of the beneficiaries under the will of Eugene H. Emmick, deceased, brought this action for damages against defendant L.S. Hamm, an attorney at law who had been engaged by the testator to prepare the will. They have appealed from a judgment of dismissal entered after an order sustaining a general demurrer to the second amended complaint without leave to amend.

The allegations of the first and second causes of action are summarized as follows: Defendant agreed with the testator, for a consideration, to prepare a will and codicils thereto for him by which plaintiffs were to be designated as beneficiaries of a trust provided for by paragraph Eighth of the will and were to receive 15% of the residue as specified in that paragraph. Defendant, in violation of instructions and in breach of his contract, . . . prepared testamentary instruments containing phraseology that was invalid by virtue of [certain sections] of the Civil Code relating to restraints on alienation and the rule against perpetuities. . . .

After the death of the testator the instruments were admitted to probate. Subsequently defendant, as draftsman of the instruments and as counsel of record for the executors, advised plaintiffs in writing that the residual trust provision was invalid and that plaintiffs would be deprived of the entire amount to which they would have been entitled if the provision had been valid unless they made a settlement with the blood relatives of the testator under which plaintiffs would receive a lesser amount than that provided for them by the testator. As the direct and proximate result of . . . his breach of contract in preparing the testamentary instruments and the written advice referred to above, plaintiffs were compelled to enter into a settlement under which they received a share of the estate amounting to $75,000 less than the sum which they would have received pursuant to testamentary instruments drafted in accordance with the directions of the testator. . . .

It was held in *Buckley v. Gray*, 110 Cal. 339, 42 P. 900, 31 L.R.A. 862, that an attorney who made a mistake in drafting a will was not liable for negligence or breach of contract to a person named in the will who was deprived of benefits as a result of the error. The court stated that an attorney is liable to his client alone with respect to actions based on negligence in the conduct of his professional duties, and it was reasoned that there could be no recovery for mere negligence where there was no privity by contract or otherwise between the defendant and the person injured. The court further concluded that there could be no recovery on the theory of a contract for the benefit of a third person, because the contract with the attorney was not expressly for the plaintiff's benefit and the testatrix only remotely intended the plaintiff to be benefited as a result of the contract. For the reasons hereinafter stated the case is overruled.

The reasoning underlying the denial of tort liability in the *Buckley* case, *i.e.*, the stringent privity test, was rejected in *Biakanja v. Irving*, where we held that a notary public who, although not authorized to practice law, prepared a will but negligently failed to direct proper attestation was liable in tort to an intended beneficiary who was damaged because of the invalidity of the instrument. It was pointed out that since 1895, when *Buckley* was decided, the rule that in the absence of privity there was no liability for negligence committed in the performance of a contract had been greatly liberalized. In restating the rule it was said that the determination whether in a specific case the defendant will be held liable to a third person not in privity is a matter of policy and involves the balancing of various factors, among which are the extent to which the transaction was intended to affect the plaintiff, the foreseeability of harm to him, the degree of certainty that the plaintiff suffered injury, the closeness of the connection between the defendant's conduct and the injury, and the policy of preventing future harm. The same general principle must be applied in determining whether a beneficiary is entitled to bring an action for negligence in the drafting of a will when the instrument is drafted by an attorney rather than by a person not authorized to practice law.

Many of the factors which led to the conclusion that the notary public involved in *Biakanja* was liable are equally applicable here. As in *Biakanja*, one of the main purposes which the transaction between defendant and the testator intended to accomplish was to provide for the transfer of property to plaintiffs; the damage to plaintiffs in the event of invalidity of the bequest was clearly foreseeable; it became certain, upon the death of the testator without change of the will, that plaintiffs would have received the intended benefits but for the asserted negligence of defendant; and if persons such as plaintiffs are not permitted to recover for the loss resulting from negligence of the draftsman, no one would be able to do so, and the policy of preventing future harm would be impaired.

*   *   *

It follows that the lack of privity between plaintiffs and defendant does not preclude plaintiffs from maintaining an action in tort against defendant.

Neither do we agree with the holding in *Buckley* that beneficiaries damaged by an error in the drafting of a will cannot recover from the draftsman on the theory that they are third-party beneficiaries of the contract between him and the testator. It has been recognized in other jurisdictions that the client may recover in a contract action for failure of the attorney to carry out his agreement. (*See* 5 AM. JUR. 331; 49 A.L.R.2d 1216, 1219–1221; Prosser, SELECTED TOPICS ON THE LAW OF TORTS (1954) pp. 438, 422.) This is in accord with the general rule stated in *Comunale v. Traders & General Ins. Co.*, 50 Cal. 2d 654, 663, 328 P.2d 198, 68 A.L.R.2d 883, that where a case sounds in both tort and contract, the plaintiff will ordinarily have freedom of election between the two actions. Obviously the main purpose of a contract for the drafting of a will is to accomplish the future transfer of the estate of the testator to the beneficiaries named in the will, and therefore it seems improper to hold, as was done in *Buckley*, that the testator intended only "remotely" to benefit those persons. It is true that under a contract for the benefit of a third person performance is usually to be rendered directly to the beneficiary, but this is not necessarily the case. For example, where a life insurance policy lapsed because a bank failed to perform its agreement to pay the premiums out of the insured's bank account, it was held that after the insured's death the beneficiaries could recover against the bank as third-party beneficiaries. *Walker Bank & Trust Co. v. First Security Corp.*, 9 Utah 2d 215, 341 P.2d 944, 945 *et seq.* Persons who had agreed to procure liability insurance for the protection of the promisees but did not do so were also held liable to injured persons who would have been covered by the insurance, the courts stating that all persons who might be injured were third-party beneficiaries of the contracts to procure insurance. *Johnson v. Holmes Tuttle Lincoln-Merc., Inc.*, 160 Cal. App. 2d 290, 296 *et seq.*, 325 P.2d 193; *James Stewart & Co. v. Law*, 233 S.W.2d 558, 561-562, 149 Tex. 392, 22

A.L.R.2d 639. Since, in a situation like those presented here and in the *Buckley* case, the main purpose of the testator in making his agreement with the attorney is to benefit the persons named in his will and this intent can be effectuated, in the event of a breach by the attorney, only by giving the beneficiaries a right of action, we should recognize, as a matter of policy, that they are entitled to recover as third-party beneficiaries. *See* 2 WILLISTON ON CONTRACTS (3rd ed. 1959) pp. 843-844; 4 CORBIN ON CONTRACTS (1951) pp. 8, 20.

Section 1559 of the Civil Code, which provides for enforcement by a third person of a contract made "expressly" for his benefit, does not preclude this result. The effect of the section is to exclude enforcement by persons who are only incidentally or remotely benefited. As we have seen, a contract for the drafting of a will unmistakably shows the intent of the testator to benefit the persons to be named in the will, and the attorney must necessarily understand this.

Defendant relies on language in *Smith v. Anglo-California Trust Co.*, 205 Cal. 496, 502, 271 P. 898, and *Fruitvale Canning Co. v. Cotton*, 115 Cal. App. 2d 622, 625, 252 P.2d 953, that to permit a third person to bring an action on a contract there must be "an intent clearly manifested by the promisor" to secure some benefit to the third person. This language, which was not necessary to the decision in either of the cases, is unfortunate. Insofar as intent to benefit a third person is important in determining his right to bring an action under a contract, it is sufficient that the promisor must have understood that the promisee had such intent. (Cf. REST., CONTRACTS, § 133, subds. l(a) and l(b); 4 CORBIN ON CONTRACTS (1951) pp. 16–18; 2 WILLISTON ON CONTRACTS (3rd ed. 1959) pp. 836–839). No specific manifestation by the promisor of an intent to benefit the third person is required. . . .

We conclude that intended beneficiaries of a will who lose their testamentary rights because of failure of the attorney who drew the will to properly fulfill his obligations under his contract with the testator may recover as third-party beneficiaries.

However, an attorney is not liable either to his client or to a beneficiary under a will for errors of the kind alleged in the first [negligence] and second [breach of contract] causes of action.

[After finding that the Rule Against Perpetuities was a trap "for the unwary" the court said] . . . we have concluded that in any event an error of the type relied on by plaintiffs does not show negligence or breach of contract on the part of defendant. It is apparent that plaintiffs have not stated and cannot state causes of action with respect to the first two counts, and the trial court did not abuse its discretion in denying leave to amend as to these counts.

*   *   *

The judgment is affirmed.

NOTES & QUESTIONS

1. Regarding the field of negligence, more specifically legal malpractice, the rather clever holding in *Lucas* that no negligence cause of action could be maintained against the defendant-attorney Hamm because an attorney should not be expected to be able to fathom the intricacies of the "Rule Against Perpetuities" would not be followed today. The California Supreme Court deemed the Rule

Against Perpetuities to be a trap "for the unwary." Indeed, generations of law students have navigated its rocky shoals, and should be aware of the rule when drafting estate planning documents. "There is reason to doubt that the ultimate conclusion of *Lucas v. Hamm* is valid in today's state of the art. Draftsmanship to avoid the Rule Against Perpetuities seems no longer esoteric." (*See e.g., Cal. Will Drafting* (CONT. ED. BAR 1965) §§ 15.43-15.71; Bowman, *Ogden's Revised Cal. Real Property Law* (CONT. ED. BAR 1974) §§ 2.44-2.45.)

2. In *H.R. Moch Co. v. Renssalaer Water Co.*, 247 N.Y. 160, 159 N.E. 896 (1928), the plaintiff's building burned down. The New York Court of Appeals, speaking through Mr. Justice Cardozo, held that an individual citizen did not qualify as a protected third party beneficiary when the defendant water company breached its duty to the city to maintain adequate water pressure. The court held that the plaintiff was merely an incidental beneficiary. Can this holding be reconciled with *Lucas?*

Notwithstanding the overpowering presence and influence of Justice Cardozo in shaping the common law of contracts and torts in the early twentieth century, some states have refused to follow *H.R. Moch Co. v. Renssalaer Water Co.* "Plaintiffs have called to the court's attention the series of North Carolina cases upholding the rights of citizens to sue, sometimes as third party beneficiaries in contract and sometimes in tort, upon breach of a contract between a water company and a municipality to supply water to the latter." *E.g., Gorrell v. Greensboro Water Supply Co.*, 124 N.C. 328, 32 S.E. 720 (1899); *Jones v. Water Co.*, 135 N.C. 553 (1904); *Morton v. Washington Light and Water Co.*, 168 N.C. 582, 84 S.E. 1019 (1915); *Potter v. Carolina Water Co.*, 253 N.C. 112, 116 S.E.2d 374 (1960). North Carolina is in this regard one of only a handful of states which has rejected the reasoning of Justice Cardozo in the *Moch* case.

3. *See also LaMourea v. Rhude*, 209 Minn. 53, 295 N.W. 304 (1940). Defendant promised the city of Duluth that it would repair citizens' (like plaintiff's) property if defendant's explosives, used during the course of sewer construction, were to damage citizens' properties. The court found plaintiff to be a donee beneficiary. What policy reasons dictate that *Lucas* and *LaMourea* be considered protected beneficiaries, but that *Moch* be denied that status?

4. In a public contract case, if an individual citizen were to be given a right to sue a breaching contractor, the recovery would be given to the particular plaintiff. In a taxpayers' action, the damages would be deposited in the treasury for the benefit of the general public. Is this a factor that the courts should weigh when deciding whether or not to allow a cause of action to an individual citizen?

5. If the contract between the promisor and promisee requires that the promisor's promise be performed only after the promisee's death, must this contract then be in writing in order to comply with the Statute of Wills? *See* MURRAY ON CONTRACTS § 132 (3d ed.).

C.　CONSTRUCTION CASES

PORT CHESTER ELECTRICAL CONSTRUCTION CORP.
v. ATLAS
40 N.Y.2d 652, 357 N.E.2d 983 (1976)

Jasen, Judge:

Until his death in July, 1973, the late Sol G. Atlas was actively engaged in the acquisition and development of real property. Atlas organized his various ownership and construction ventures into a complex network of separate corporations in which he had both a controlling interest and an active leadership role. This case involves the efforts of an independent subcontractor on an Atlas project to collect a money judgment it obtained against an Atlas controlled general contractor. Since the general contractor was virtually judgment proof due to certain financial manipulations, the subcontractor endeavored to enforce its judgment against other corporations allied with Atlas in the venture, as well as against Atlas' estate. The trial court, by piercing the corporate veil of the various corporate defendants and holding that the subcontractor was a third-party beneficiary of contracts between these Atlas corporations, granted the relief sought. The Appellate Division affirmed, placing primary reliance upon the third-party beneficiary theory. While we disagree with the theories developed by the courts below, we are in accord with the result reached. In our view, the subcontractor was entitled to enforce its money judgment against the defendant corporations and the estate of Sol G. Atlas through a special proceeding authorized by CPLR article 52. Since all necessary parties are before the court, the court may convert the plenary action into a special proceeding and, on that basis, we would affirm the order of the Appellate Division.

. . . In 1957, the general contractor entered into a subcontract with plaintiff for performance of all electrical work on the project. The subcontract referred to certain provisions of the general contract that were to be incorporated therein. A clause provided for submission of controversies and claims to arbitration. Plaintiff completed its work in May, 1958, received a substantial amount on its contract and made a claim of $96,940 for extra work performed. The Contractor resisted the claim and counterclaimed for approximately $52,000 in offsets. When the parties were unable to reach an accommodation, plaintiff, in December, 1960, pursuant to the subcontract, demanded arbitration. The arbitration proceeding was unusually protracted. The plaintiff finally prevailed in June, 1966 and received an award of $73,000, plus interest. The award was confirmed by the Supreme Court and judgment was entered for $105,011 in favor of the plaintiff.

Plaintiff's efforts to collect its judgment against the Contractor were unsuccessful. As a result of certain financial manipulations directed by Atlas, the assets of the venture, the bulk of which had previously been lodged in the Owner, were transferred to Atlas and to his other allied corporations. Both the Owner and the general contractor were rendered virtually judgment proof. The plaintiff, to enforce its judgment, commenced this action against the defendant corporations which ended up with the assets, the estate of Atlas, and the Owner. In granting recovery to the plaintiff, Trial Term held that as a third-party beneficiary of the general contract, the plaintiff could enforce the Owner's obligation to pay the cost of the work performed under the electrical subcontract. The court also placed liability on the Owner by piercing its corporate veil. The Appellate Division affirmed, agreeing generally with the reasoning of Trial Term and noting particularly that plaintiff was a third-party creditor beneficiary . . .

We do not agree that the plaintiff is a third-party creditor beneficiary of the contract between the Owner, Essex Green, Inc., and the general contractor, Essex Construction. It is old law that a third party may sue as a beneficiary on a contract made for his benefit. (*Lawrence v. Fox*, 20 N.Y. 268; 17A C.J.S. *Contracts*, § 519(3); 10 N.Y. JUR., *Contracts*, § 237.) However, an intent to benefit the third party must be shown and, absent such intent, the third party is merely an incidental beneficiary with no right to enforce the particular contracts. Difficulty may be encountered, however, in applying the intent to benefit test in construction contracts because of the multiple contractual relationships involved and because performance ultimately, if indirectly, runs to each party of the several contracts. Hence, interpretational difficulties prevalent in third-party beneficiary contracts are compounded as a result of the peculiar problems presented by construction contracts.

Generally it has been held that the ordinary construction contract — i.e., one which does not expressly state that the intention of the contracting parties is to benefit a third party — does not give third parties who contract with the promisee the right to enforce the latter's contract with another. Such third parties are generally considered mere incidental beneficiaries. The text writers have uniformly designated these third parties only as incidental beneficiaries and not infrequently have posited the situation wherein the subcontractor sues the owner as an example of an action by an incidental beneficiary. (4 CORBIN, CONTRACTS, § 779D; RESTATEMENT, CONTRACTS, 2d, § 133, Illustration 18 (Tent. Draft No. 4, 1968); 2 WILLISTON, CONTRACTS (3d ed.), § 402. . . .

In this case, we cannot conclude from the record before us that the Contractor and the Owner intended that their contract run to the benefit of the subcontractor. Thus, it cannot be said that the subcontractor was a third-party beneficiary of that contract and the courts below erred in predicating liability on that theory.

Nor was it appropriate, in this case, to disregard the corporate forms and pierce the corporate veils. Corporations, of course, are legal entities distinct from their managers and shareholders and have an independent legal existence. Ordinarily, their separate personalities cannot be disregarded. . . .

. . . Since Atlas himself carefully respected the separate identities of the corporations, and each corporation was pursuing its separate corporate business, rather than the purely personal business of Atlas, we conclude that the corporate veils of the defendant corporations should not be "pierced."

* * *

[The subcontractor, however, was permitted to recover against the owner. Having already obtained a judgment against the general contractor, the subcontractor was allowed to collect the debt from the owner who in turn was indebted to the general contractor.]

We would, therefore, affirm the order of the Appellate Division. Order affirmed, with costs.

NOTE

Cf., *e.g.*, *Western Waterproofing Co. Inc. v. Springfield Housing Authority*, 669 F. Supp. 901 (C.D. Ill. 1987), in which the court held the subcontractors to be third party beneficiaries. The court distinguished between a contract made for the direct benefit of a third party, and one where the benefit to the third party was merely incidental. In this case, the benefit was direct, and therefore the subcontractor had the right to sue for breach of contract.

D. INSURANCE — UNBORN PLAINTIFFS

PETERSON v. NATIONWIDE MUTUAL INS. CO.
175 Ohio St. 551, 197 N.E.2d 194 (1964)

This cause originated in the Court of Common Pleas, of Columbiana County with Richard N. Peterson, administrator of the estate of Audrey F. Peterson, as plaintiff, and the Nationwide Mutual Insurance Company as defendant. Plaintiff seeks to recover the sum of $2,000 plus incidental expenses under an insurance policy or contract issued by defendant to Richard N. Peterson individually. There is but one matter for decision, and that embraces the meaning and scope of the undefined word, "person," as used in the "family compensation" clause of the insured's contract. In the instant case, the claimed "person" was a female infant delivered prematurely after a gestation period of about 24 weeks as a result of a miscarriage alleged to have been induced by physical injuries sustained by the infant and her mother.

In its pertinent parts, the clause referred to reads:

> To pay, in accordance with the schedule below . . . to or for the benefit of:

> "(1) any person who suffers bodily injury . . . or death by reason of any accident arising out of the . . . use of the described automobile.

> "(2) the policyholder, and while residents of the same household, his spouse, and the relatives of either who by accident suffer bodily injury . . . or death:

> "(a) by being struck by any other land motor vehicle. . . ."

The cause came on for hearing before the trial court, a jury having been waived, upon the petition, the answer in the form of a general denial, the evidence and certain exhibits. As shown by the judgment entry, the court found that plaintiff's decedent "was not a 'person' within the meaning of the policy contract and has no right of action on the policy contract — petition ordered dismissed at plaintiff's costs."

In its opinion in favor of defendant, the trial court said:

> The court feels that the common, usual, everyday meaning of "person" contemplates that the person must first be born — it starts with the birth of the individual and continues from there. . . .

> Therefore, under this contract, the court finds that it only covers injuries sustained after birth and not before. . . .

There was an appeal on questions of law to the Court of Appeals, where the judgment of the court below was reversed "and said cause is remanded to the Court of Common Pleas for a new trial with further proceedings according to law."

As shown by its opinion, the Court of Appeals took the position that, "so far as right of recovery in tort for injury resulting in death is concerned, the injuries to plaintiff's decedent who was subsequently born alive and lived 21 hours, were injuries done her in her person, within the doctrine of *Williams v. Marion Rapid Transit, supra* [152 Ohio St. 114, 87 N.E.2d 334, 10 A.L.R.2d 1051].

> It seems difficult to avoid the conclusion that a child who receives a certificate of live birth, who breathes, moves its limbs and cries, is a person within the concept of third party beneficiary contract, even more than in tort.

It is disclosed by the evidence that in the late afternoon of July 12, 1960, Patricia Peterson, wife of Richard N. Peterson, while operating the insured family automobile on a street of East Liverpool, Ohio, was run into from the rear by another motor vehicle, which resulted in claimed physical injuries — "whiplash of the neck and back injuries." Mrs. Peterson was then 21 to 22 weeks pregnant, and her physician testified, "The child was in normal condition for the period of pregnancy as far as I know."

Subsequently, Mrs. Peterson was hospitalized, and on July 31, 1960, she suffered a miscarriage and was delivered of a female infant. The infant was given the name of Audrey Fenton Peterson, and a certificate of live birth was issued. The infant lived about 21 hours, during which time she breathed, emitted vocal sounds and moved her limbs. An autopsy was performed by a physician, and the period of gestation was fixed at approximately 24 weeks or about five and one-half months. It is improbable that the infant could have survived and had [sic] a normal existence.

* * *

ZIMMERMAN, Judge:

An established principle of insurance law, recognized in many decisions of this court, is that an insurance contract, in case of doubt as to the meaning and intent thereof, is to be interpreted against the insurer, the one who drew it and who is responsible for the language employed, and in favor of the insured. In the clause of the insurance contract presently under examination, the term, "person," is not defined and should be given an interpretation as favorable as is reasonably possible for the insured.

This court held, as follows, in the second paragraph of the syllabus of the landmark case of *Williams, an Infant, v. Marion Rapid Transit, Inc., supra* (152 Ohio St. 114, 87 N.E.2d 334, 10 A.L.R.2d 1058):

> 2. Injuries wrongfully inflicted upon an unborn viable child capable of existing independently of the mother are injuries "done him in his . . . person" within the meaning of Section 16, Article I of the Constitution and, subsequent to his birth, he may maintain an action to recover damages for the injury so inflicted.

In the later case of *Jasinsky, Admr. v. Potts*, 153 Ohio St. 529, 92 N.E.2d 809, the syllabus reads:

Under the wrongful-death statute, Section 10509-166 *et seq.*, General Code, the administrator of the estate of a child who, while viable, suffered a prenatal injury through the alleged negligent act of another and who died approximately three months after its birth as a result of such injury has a cause of action against such other for damages for the benefit of the parents of such infant.

Thus, it is established in this state that an unborn viable child is a "person."

As used with reference to a foetus, the word, "viable," means that the foetus has reached such a state of development that it can live outside the uterus. *Bonbrest v. Kotz* (D.C.), 65 F. Supp. 138, 140.

In *Hall, Admr. v. Murphy*, 236 S.C. 257, 263, 113 S.E.2d 790, 793, the court remarked:

> We have no difficulty in concluding that a foetus having reached that period of prenatal maturity where it is capable of independent life apart from its mother is a person and, if such a child is injured, it may after birth maintain an action for such injuries. A few courts have gone further and held that such an action may be maintained even if the infant had not reached the state of a viable foetus at the time of the injury.

And in *Poliquin, Admx., v. MacDonald*, 101 N.H. 104, 107, 135 A.2d 249, 251, the court said:

> We are also of the opinion that a fetus having reached that period of prenatal maturity where it is capable of independent life apart from its mother is a person. . . .

* * *

Here, the infant showed definite physical signs of life upon delivery from her mother and had an independent existence for an appreciable length of time after separation from her mother, and a certificate of live birth was issued. Considering all these factors, we think the situation comes within the holding of the *Williams* case that liability exists for prenatal injuries suffered by a viable child delivered alive.

In other words, an unborn viable child capable of life outside its mother's womb is a person as that term is used in an insurance contract providing death benefits for persons killed as a result of a motor vehicle accident.

* * *

The judgment of the Court of Appeals is, therefore, affirmed.

Judgment affirmed.

NOTES & QUESTIONS

1. Consider the following scenario:

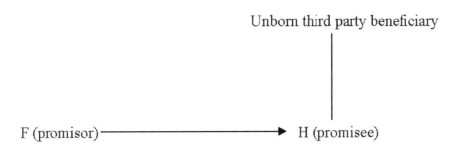

See RESTATEMENT (SECOND) OF CONTRACTS § 308, comment a. Does this comment place any limitations on unidentifiable parties being accorded a protected status as a third party intended beneficiary?

2. In *Sindell v. Abbott Labs*, 26 Cal. 3d 588, 607 P.2d 924 (1980), a negligence case, the court held that a plaintiff, who was in utero at the time her mother ingested DES, had a cause of action against multiple drug manufacturers. If negligence is difficult to prove (for example, the Illinois Supreme Court in *Smith v. Eli Lilly & Co.*, 137 Ill. 2d 222, 560 N.E.2d 324 (1990), rejected the "market share theory" adopted in *Sindell)*, would plaintiff have a better cause of action founded on a third party beneficiary theory?

3. But then see *Enright v. Eli Lilly & Co.*, 77 N.Y.2d 377, 570 N.E.2d 198 (1991), where the New York Court of Appeals refused to extend protection in a strict liability in tort case to the granddaughter of a woman who, during her pregnancy, ingested DES. Since "fault" need not be proved against the provider of the drug, but merely breach of an implied promise to furnish a safe and effective drug, would you suggest that the plaintiff bring a third party beneficiary contract theory instead of a tort case against the drug company? Why? Why not?

E.   REAL ESTATE AND BREAK IN ASSUMPTIONS

VROOMAN v. TURNER
69 N.Y. 280 (1877)

APPEAL from judgment of the General Term of the Supreme Court in the second judicial department, affirming a judgment in favor of plaintiff, entered upon the report of a referee.

This was an action to foreclose a mortgage.

The mortgage was executed in August, 1873, by defendant Evans, who then owned the mortgaged premises. He conveyed the same to one Mitchell, and through various mesne conveyances the title came to one Sanborn. In none of these conveyances did the grantee assume to pay the mortgage. Sanborn conveyed the same to defendant Harriet B. Turner, by deed which contained a clause stating that the conveyance was subject to the mortgage, "which mortgage the party hereto of the second part hereby covenants and agrees to pay off and discharge, the same forming part of the consideration thereof."

The referee found that said grantee, by so assuming payment of the mortgage, became personally liable therefore, and directed judgment against her for any deficiency. Judgment was entered accordingly.

* * *

ALLEN, J. The precise question presented by the appeal in this action has been twice before the courts of this State, and received the same solution in each. It first arose in *King v. Whitely*, 10 Paige, 465, decided in 1843. There the grantor of an equity of rede+mption in mortgaged premises, neither legally nor equitably interested in the payment of the bond and mortgage except so far as the same were a charge upon his interest in the lands, conveyed the lands subject to the mortgage, and the conveyance recited that the grantees therein assumed the mortgage, and were to pay off the same as a part of the consideration of such conveyance, and it was held that as the grantor in that conveyance was not personally liable to the holder of the mortgage to pay the same, the grantees were not liable to the holder of such mortgage for the deficiency upon a foreclosure and sale of the mortgaged premises. It was conceded by the chancellor that if the grantor had been personally liable to the holder of the mortgage for the payment of the mortgage debt, the holder of such mortgage would have been entitled in equity to the benefit of the agreement recited in such conveyance, to pay off the mortgage and to a decree over against the grantees for the deficiency. . . .

King v. Whitely was followed, and the same rule applied, by an undivided court in *Trotter v. Hughes*, 12 N.Y. 74. . . .

. . . Had the grantor in that case [*Trotter v. Hughes*, 12 N.Y. 74] been personally bound for the payment of the debt, I am of the opinion that an action would have been sustained against the grantee upon a promise implied from the terms of the grant accepted by him to pay it, and indemnify the grantor. It must have been so regarded by this court, otherwise no question would have been made upon it, and the court would not have so seriously and ably fortified and applied the doctrine of *King v. Whitely*, ... The rule which exempts the grantee of mortgaged premises subject to a mortgage, the payment of which is assumed in consideration of the conveyance as between him and his grantor, from liability to the holder of the mortgage when the grantee [sic] is not bound in law or equity for the payment of the mortgage, is founded in reason and principle, and is not inconsistent with that class of cases in which it has been held that a promise to one for the benefit of a third party may avail to give an action directly to the latter against the promissor, of which *Lawrence v. Fox* (20 N.Y. 268), is a prominent example. To give a third party who may derive a benefit from the performance of the promise an action, there must be, first, an intent by the promisee to secure some benefit to the third party, and second, some privity between the two, the promisee and the party to be benefited, and some obligation or duty owing from the former to the latter which would give him a legal or equitable claim to the benefit of the promise, or an equivalent from him personally.

It is true there need be no privity between the promissor and the party claiming the benefit of the undertaking, neither is it necessary that the latter should be privy to the consideration of the promise, but it does not follow that a mere volunteer can avail himself of it. . . . A mere stranger cannot intervene, and claim by action the benefit of a contract between other parties. There must be either a new consideration or some prior right to claim against one of the contracting parties, by which he has a legal interest in the performance of the agreement.

It is said in *Garnsey v. Rodgers* (47 N.Y. 233), that it is not every promise made by one person to another from the performance of which a third person would derive a benefit that gives a right of action to such third person, he being privy neither to the contract nor the consideration. In the language of Judge Rapallo, "to entitle him to an action, the contract must have been made for his benefit. He must be the party intended to be benefited." . . . The courts are not inclined to extend the doctrine of *Lawrence v. Fox* to cases not clearly within the principle of that decision. Judges have differed as to the principle upon which *Lawrence v. Fox* and kindred cases rest, but in every case in which an action has been sustained there has been a debt or duty owing by the promisee to the party claiming to sue upon the promise. Whether the decisions rest upon the doctrine of agency, the promisee being regarded as the agent for the third party, who, by bringing his action adopts his acts, or upon the doctrine of a trust, the promissor being regarded as having received money or other thing for the third party, is not material. In either case there must be a legal right, founded upon some obligation of the promisee, in the third party, to adopt and claim the promise as made for his benefit.

. . . It is claimed that *King v. Whitely* and the cases following it were overruled by *Lawrence v. Fox*. But it is very clear that it was not the intention to overrule them, and that the cases are not inconsistent. . . .

The court below erred in giving judgment against the appellant for the deficiency after the sale of the mortgaged premises, and so much of the judgment as directs her to pay the same must be reversed with costs.

All concur, except EARL, J., dissenting.

Judgment accordingly.

NOTES & QUESTIONS

1. Can the holdings in *Vrooman* and *Seaver* be reconciled? How?

2. The first RESTATEMENT OF CONTRACTS § 133(1)(b) disagrees with the holding in *Vrooman*.

The first RESTATEMENT says that the plaintiff in *Vrooman* should be considered a third party creditor beneficiary because the promisee thought that he might have an obligation to plaintiff. Promisee's motive was to preclude his own possible liability to the plaintiff.

RESTATEMENT (SECOND) OF CONTRACTS would call plaintiff an "intended" beneficiary under § 302(2)(b) since "the circumstances indicate that the promisee intends to give the beneficiary the benefit of the promised performance." See § 302 comment b. Under § 302(2)(a) where the performance of the promise satisfies "an obligation of the promisee to pay money to the beneficiary," there is a requirement that there be an actual obligation (not a supposed obligation) running from promisee to third party beneficiary.

Thus, where under the first RESTATEMENT a supposed obligation running from promisee to third party beneficiary would make third party beneficiary a "creditor beneficiary," under RESTATEMENT (SECOND) OF CONTRACTS, this plaintiff would turn into a "donee beneficiary," or perhaps even an "incidental beneficiary."

Is there any theoretical or practical difference to plaintiff in being characterized as a third party creditor beneficiary (under the first RESTATEMENT) or an intended beneficiary (under RESTATEMENT (SECOND) OF CONTRACTS)?

3. In a transfer of real estate whereby the grantee takes title to property that is already encumbered by a debt, there are fundamentally two kinds of assumptions:

(a) An assumption with release of the mortgagor (promisee). This, in effect, is a novation.

(b) An assumption without release of the mortgagor (promisee). The mortgagor remains liable to the mortgagee. However, once the grantee begins paying the mortgage indebtedness and the mortgagee knowingly accepts these payments, the relationship among mortgagee, mortgagor and grantee, *inter se*, changes. The grantee becomes primarily liable to the mortgagee, and the original mortgagor becomes merely a surety. *See* Nelson & Whitman, REAL ESTATE FINANCE LAW § 5.19 (3d ed. 1993).

4. The grantee may also take the property "subject to" the earlier mortgage, where the grantee does not agree to pay it. In this case, the mortgagee does not become an intended third party beneficiary. To "assume" a loan the courts usually require an unequivocal commitment by the grantee to pay the indebtedness. Cf. *Adams v. George*, 119 Idaho 973, 812 P.2d 280 (1991). But what if grantee starts paying the loan off to avoid foreclosure, and the mortgagee begins accepting payments. Does the mortgagee acquire third party beneficiary rights? *See Oswianza v. Wengler*, 358 Ill. 302 (1934).

5. In *Schneider v. Ferrigno*, 110 Conn. 86, 147 A. 303 (1929), the Connecticut Supreme Court held that even though there was a "break in assumptions," the last grantee who assumed the mortgage indebtedness could be held liable to the original mortgagee. This is the more modern rule. Cf. RESTATEMENT (SECOND) OF CONTRACTS § 312 Illustration 3.

F.   RESCISSION OF CONTRACT — "VESTING"

DETROIT BANK AND TRUST COMPANY v. CHICAGO FLAME HARDENING COMPANY, INC.
541 F. Supp. 1278 (N.D. Ind 1982)

LEE, District Judge:

This matter was tried before the Honorable Phil M. McNagny, Jr. without the intervention of a jury on December 22 and 23, 1980. . . . However, Judge McNagny became incapacitated before such [final] arguments could be held, and passed away without rendering a final decision in this instant case.

. . . This Court, having considered the entire record and being fully advised following said argument, hereby renders and enters the following Memorandum Opinion and Order pursuant to Rule 52(a), Federal Rules of Civil Procedure. The relevant facts as revealed by the record and adduced through the final argument are as follows.

* * *

On July 29, 1964, Marvin R. Scott, [President of Chicago Flame Hardening Co.,] Gainor D. Scott and John R. Keeler, the owners of the entire issue of Chicago Flame's capital stock, unanimously agreed by corporate resolution that upon the death of these specifically named shareholders (M. R. Scott, G. D. Scott and J. D. Keeler), the corporation would pay to his wife, if then living, commencing with the date of her husband's death, a graduated monthly stipend over a fifteen (15) year period totaling $150,300 to terminate in the event of her death if prior to the expiration of the payment period.[1]

The signatories to this 1964 resolution did not expressly reserve the right to alter and/or amend.

Despite the fact that the potential beneficiaries of this resolution lacked experience or independent expertise in the flame hardening industry, they were, as recipient widows under the terms of the resolution, to make themselves available for consulting work and to agree not to compete with Chicago Flame for the duration of their receipt of benefits as consideration for the same under this corporate agreement.

*　　*　　*

Within a reasonable time following the adoption of this resolution Marvin R. Scott's wife, Roxanne, became aware that this document's beneficial terms were potentially available to her in the future. She then "forgot the whole thing." . . .

The provisions of the 1964 widow's resolution were initially implemented on July 12, 1967 when Marjorie Scott Keeler signed the requisite statement agreeing to abide by the resolution's consideration requirements, following the July 8, 1967 death of her husband, John R. Keeler.

Marjorie Scott Keeler thereinafter continually received a monthly stipend pursuant to the express terms of this agreement, except for an eighteen (18) month period during 1971 and 1972 when she voluntarily consented to a postponement in recognition of Chicago Flame's deteriorating financial posture.

Marvin R. Scott's wife, Roxanne, was fully and continuously aware that Marjorie Scott Keeler (her sister-in-law) was receiving the benefits provided by the 1964 resolution for surviving spouses of the original signatories.

---

[1] [2] That resolution which specifically avoided naming the current wives of the signatories provides in pertinent part:

> That immediately following the death of each stockholder, his wife, if then living, will be asked to sign a statement agreeing to make herself available at all reasonable times to said corporation as a consultant for same and further agreeing to make available to said corporation any and all knowledge as to the business thereof as revealed to her by her husband during his lifetime including any and all technical know-how, and further agreeing that she will not for a 15 year period following the death of her husband compete with said corporation in any way, directly or indirectly, nor knowingly permit her husband's name, knowledge or reputation to be used in competition with the corporation during said period, in exchange for which undertakings, it is agreed that she shall, commencing with the date of her husband's death be paid a monthly salary by the corporation of $1,250 for the first five year period after her husband's death, a monthly salary of $835 for the second five year period following her husband's death, and a monthly salary of $420 for the third five year period following her husband's death, it being understood and agreed, however, that the aforesaid salary arrangement will take effect only in case said deceased stockholder is survived by his wife and that same will forthwith terminate in the event of her death at anytime prior to the expiration of the aforesaid 15 year period.

On February 15, 1971 Marvin R. Scott participated in and approved the adoption of a second corporate resolution along with the other owners of the entire issue of Chicago Flame's capital stock, Gainor D. Scott and Marjorie Scott Keeler. This subsequent agreement was executed to rescind the right of Marvin R. Scott's surviving spouse to receive graduated monthly payments as formerly provided in the 1964 resolution.

Marvin R. Scott's motivation for entering into this second resolution was to sustain the future financial integrity of Chicago Flame.

. . . Marvin R. Scott died on October 31, 1971 leaving plaintiff's current ward, Roxanne Scott, as his surviving spouse.

Although there remains conflicting testimony, it is the determination of the Court that, while Mrs. Roxanne Scott may not have actually seen the February 15, 1971 rescission document prior to the instigation of this suit, she became aware of her husband's relinquishment of the widow's benefits during the interim following his death and the filing of this suit.

Following the death of her husband, Roxanne Scott . . . was adjudicated incompetent by a Florida court and a guardianship was established in March of 1972 which was maintained for approximately two years.

Roxanne Scott returned to Michigan in 1975 where she suffered a recurrence of the same mental illness in August of 1975. She remained hospitalized in various facilities until her release in December of 1975. A guardianship was established solely over her estate in November, 1975. This same guardianship remains in force. Although mentally competent today, Mrs. Scott continues to be under a physician's care.

* * *

Mrs. Roxanne Scott made no expenditure, nor did she change position or perform any act in reliance on the 1964 widow's resolution prior to the commencement of this litigation.

Following the January, 1977 death of Gainor Scott, Chicago Flame executed the same "consideration" agreement with his widow, Cecelia Scott, as they had previously done with Marjorie Scott Keeler. Thereinafter, Chicago Flame continued to provide benefits to these two fully vested surviving spouses as mandated by the operative terms of the 1964 widow's resolution.

* * *

Plaintiff initiated this litigation on September 19, 1977 by way of a complaint which seeks to enforce the terms of the 1964 widow's resolution for the benefit of its ward, Mrs. Roxanne Scott. Plaintiff asserts its contentions on the basis of (1) the failure to expressly reserve the right to rescind, (2) a presumption of acceptance for a donee beneficiary, (3) Roxanne Scott's medical condition precluding the earlier assertion of her rights as a means of acceptance, and (4) that this agreement vested a right in its ward which could not be denied by the 1971 rescission. . . . Indiana law clearly controls and will dictate the determination of this matter. *Royal v. Kenny Co.*, 528 F.2d 184 (7th Cir. 1975).

The old RESTATEMENT rule provided that the promisor and promisee could make no change in the promise made to a donee beneficiary unless such a power is reserved.[2] RESTATEMENT OF CONTRACTS § 142 at 168 (1932). Nor could a change be made by the promisor and promisee in their promise to a creditor beneficiary if he has changed his position in reliance on that promise. *Id.*; *see* Page, *The Power of Contracting Parties to Alter a Contract for Rendering Performance to a Third Person*, 12 WIS. L. REV. 141, 149-50 (1937). Evolutionary changes in the law, however, have transformed the afore-mentioned position of the original RESTATE-MENT. The SECOND RESTATEMENT OF CONTRACTS, as adopted and promulgated, eliminates this distinction between a donee and creditor beneficiary and recognizes that modification on the part of the promisor and promisee is ineffective only if the agreement so provides, unless the third party beneficiary has changed his position in reliance on the promise or has accepted, adopted or acted upon it. RESTATEMENT (SECOND) OF CONTRACTS § 142 (1979).

Indiana specifically reaffirmed its adoption of this majority view as later expressed in the SECOND RESTATEMENT. In the case of *In re Estate of Fanning*, 263 Ind. 414, 333 N.E.2d 80 (1975), the Indiana Supreme Court examined the posture of a third party beneficiary and determined that the right to rescind or modify a third party beneficiary contract, without the assent of the beneficiary, ceases once the contract is accepted, adopted or acted upon by the third party.

The plaintiff, on behalf of its ward, asserts that the 1971 rescission was invalid for the parties failed to expressly reserve the right to rescind the 1964 widow's resolution. Indiana has long recognized that even a party without right may rescind a contract if the other party fails to object to it and permits the rescission to occur; such a rescission would be by mutual consent. In the case of contracts entered into for the benefit of a third party, Indiana follows the rule found in most jurisdictions. That is, the parties to a third party beneficiary contract may rescind, vary or abrogate the contract as they see fit, without the approval of the third party, at any time before the contract is accepted, adopted or acted upon by a third party beneficiary. *Fanning*, 333 N.E.2d at 84; accord *Jackman Cigar Co. v. Berger*, 114 Ind. App. 437, 52 N.E.2d 363 (1944). A rescission prior to the required change in position by a third party deprives that third party of any rights under or because of the contract. *See* 17 AM. JUR. 2D *Contracts* § 317 (1979).

In this case the 1964 agreement was adopted as a corporate resolution by Chicago Flame Hardening, Inc. All of the officers and shareholders of the corporation approved the initial agreement. On February 15, 1971 the officers and shareholders mutually agreed to rescind the July 29, 1964 resolution. Recognizing the majority view followed by Indiana, the rescission of the prior agreement is valid without a specific reservation of the power to rescind so long as the third-party beneficiary, Mrs. Roxanne Scott, had not accepted, adopted or acted upon the original widow's resolution. Therefore, an express reservation of the right to rescind is not required to abrogate the third party beneficiary agreement.

Plaintiff next contends that since Mrs. Roxanne Scott had knowledge of the original 1964 resolution, her acceptance of this beneficial agreement must be presumed. In support of this position plaintiff offers three vintage cases which recognize a presumption of acceptance.

---

[2] [9] This position promulgated by the initial RESTATEMENT was not followed by the vast majority of states even at the time of its adoption. The express reservation requirement was thereafter abandoned in tentative drafts and in the final adopted version of the RESTATEMENT (SECOND); *see* 2 WILLISTON, CONTRACTS §§ 396-97 (3d Ed. 1959).

These cases are clearly distinguishable from the present cause. The primary and controlling distinction is that while acceptance was presumed in cases cited by plaintiff, the intended beneficiaries were infants at the time of the transaction. A presumption is necessary in such instances to protect the interests of minor beneficiaries. Mrs. Scott, however, was an adult at the time of the 1964 widow's resolution, completely able to assert her own rights, and as such is not afforded the same protection. Moreover, the same authority submitted by plaintiff in support of a presumption of acceptance provides a fortiori a strong argument for the opposite proposition — a lack of such protection for a competent adult through negative implication.

Plaintiff's cases and contention here are effectively nothing more than a camouflaged application of gift theory which recognizes that once a gift is consummated, it remains irrevocable except by consent of the donee. Although the contract theory applicable to this cause has been extended in some instances as an equitable means of avoiding the delivery requirement necessitated by the gift theory, it would be an over-simplification to also attempt to inject into this same contract theory a substitute for acceptance. The determinative legal theory in this matter is therefore a stricter contract theory which does not provide the presumption of acceptance claimed by plaintiff for its beneficiary ward donee.

Plaintiff's next focus theorizes that "but for" Roxanne Scott's declining health, she would have instituted this litigation at an earlier date. Plaintiff attempts thereby to utilize its ward's acknowledged mental and physical difficulties as a vehicle to excuse not only the failure to sue before rescission, but also to demonstrate why prompt commencement of this action to preserve her benefits was prevented. The net effect of this proposition is to attempt to transform this 1977 litigation into a belated substitute for acceptance prior to rescission.

Although the Court recognizes that the filing of a suit by a third party beneficiary may be considered as acceptance by that individual, *Zimmerman v. Zehender*, 164 Ind. 466, 73 N.E. 920 (1905); *Blackard v. Monarch*, 131 Ind. App. 514, 169 N.E.2d 735 (1960), the Court may not consider Mrs. Scott's health as dispositive of the issue before it. Perhaps equity might demand some presumption of acceptance had Mrs. Scott been totally incapacitated prior to rescission; however, plaintiff's own evidence makes it clear that the February 15, 1971 rescission took place before Mrs. Scott's inhibiting physical and mental decline occurred and the appointment of guardians to represent her interests.

As early as 1903, the Indiana Supreme Court stated that "[A] contract for the benefit of a competent third person may become available to that person, provided that it is not rescinded by the parties thereto before such third person gives notice that he accepts it." *Johnson v. Central Co.*, 159 Ind. 605, 65 N.E. 1028 (1903). Therefore, this Court cannot accept plaintiff's novel preclusion argument. Mrs. Scott was a "competent" adult third party beneficiary at the time of this rescission. Consequently, this Court may not fictionalize the initiation of this suit as an act of acceptance prior to the 1971 rescission. *See Zimmerman, supra*, 73 N.E. at 922.

. . . Three cases which appear to be somewhat significant to this cause have emerged. . . . First, the case of *In re Estate of Fanning*, 263 Ind. 414, 333 N.E.2d 80 (1975) (previously cited), dealt with the ownership of certificates of deposit. Wildus Fanning purchased certificates of deposit which, upon their face, were payable to "Wildus Fanning or Marcella Seavey either of them with the right of survivorship and not as tenants in common." Since the certificates were discovered in Fanning's safety deposit box after her death and since no signature card or deposit agreement had been executed, her daughter (Seavey) could not claim the certificates under a gift theory as there was no actual or constructive delivery. The Indiana Supreme Court held that where a certificate of deposit creates a joint account with rights of survivorship in clear and unequivocal language, donative intent of the donor is presumptively established.

The thrust of the holding was that principles of contract law, rather than that of gifts, should be the governing substantive law due to the inherent contractual nature of certificates. The daughter who was unaware of the existence of the certificates until after the death of her mother, was found to be a third party beneficial owner. Therefore, the essence of *Fanning* is that as a third party contract, the donor could rescind during her lifetime. . . .

The Court's reading of *Fanning* does not support plaintiff's contention that knowledge on the part of the donee beneficiary constitutes acceptance. In fact, *Fanning* provides authority for this Court's position concerning rescission by citing with approval 17 Am. Jur. 2d *Contracts* § 314 (1964), which states in part, "[t]he parties to a contract entered into for the benefit of a third person may rescind, vary, or abrogate the contract as they see fit, without the assent of the third person, at any time before the contract is accepted, adopted, or acted upon by him. . . ."

[Next, the court discusses the case of *Matter of Estate of Bannon*, 358 N.E.2d 215 (1976).]

The Court's review of these cases fails to resolve the decisive question remaining before the Court. Neither plaintiff's assertions concerning acceptance, nor defendant's position on rescission are directly supported by the cases presented. The Court must therefore return to the issue of whether Roxanne Scott accepted, adopted or acted upon the 1964 resolution prior to the 1971 rescission.

The analysis above establishes that acceptance may not be presumed by this Court and that this contract for the benefit of a third party is enforceable only if the third party beneficiary has accepted, adopted or acted upon it prior to rescission. Because prior decisions fail to provide an adequate definition, the Court must examine the somewhat nebulous term "acceptance" in an effort to identify if some form of assent took place on the part of Mrs. Roxanne Scott if it is to conclude that the 1971 rescission was ineffective and that her derivative rights were preserved. *See e.g., United States v. Winnicki*, 151 F.2d 56, 57 (7th Cir. 1945) (words "receive" and "accept" are legal equivalents).

Acceptance may be an overt act, or the adoption of a benefit which is a question of intent and thereby also a factual determination. *See* Corbin, *supra*, §§ 782-793; Jones, *Legal Protection of Third Party Beneficiaries: On Opening Courthouse Doors*, 46 Cinn. L. Rev. 313 (1977). Nevertheless, even in instances such as this where plaintiff has provided no specific evidence of an overt act or of a change in position, it must still be remembered that "the power of promisor and promisee to vary the promisor's duty to an intended beneficiary is terminated when the beneficiary manifests assent to the promise in a manner invited by the promisor or promisee." Restatement (Second) Contracts, *supra*, § 311 at comment (h). This rule utilizes an analogy to the law of offer and acceptance by recognizing that a third party beneficiary may well rely in ways difficult or impossible to prove.

Fortunately for this Court, the narrow question currently before it does not present this circumstance characterized by an impossibility of proof. The converse is true as the Court's determination of the factual question regarding Roxanne Scott's intent to accept the benefits afforded by the 1964 resolution was answered in the negative by her own sworn testimony. While facing cross-examination, Mrs. Scott was specifically asked whether she made any long range plans or depended upon the 1964 widow's resolution.

Her answer was, "No, I forgot the whole thing." (Transcript of testimony, December 22, 1980, pp. 19–20). In addition to this testimonial controversion, the Court also failed to discern any other corroborative evidence which might sustain plaintiff's claim of acceptance or change in position in reliance on that resolution. . . . Furthermore, the Court's position regarding the failure to establish adoptive intent is not gleaned from this single negatory response, but is supported by a detailed review of the entire record. It is therefore the conclusion of the Court that Roxanne Scott failed to accept, adopt or act upon the 1964 resolution prior to the 1971 rescission. Consequently, the Court must hold that Mrs. Scott's failure to act or rely upon the original agreement extinguished any benefits which might have accrued to her from the 1964 agreement.

It is the final determination of the Court that Mrs. Roxanne Scott failed to accept, adopt or act upon the 1964 resolution prior to the contracting parties' valid rescission on February 15, 1971.

It is hereby ORDERED that Judgment be entered for the defendant, Chicago Flame Hardening Company, Inc., consistent with this Memorandum Decision and the findings and conclusions herein.

NOTES & QUESTIONS

1. In *Detroit Bank*, the court states that if the plaintiff had been an infant, his or her acceptance of the beneficial contract would be presumed. Why isn't this same presumption applicable to adults, especially when that beneficiary would have no correlative duties? The court goes on to say that those cases where there is found to be a presumption of acceptance for the benefit of infants "provides, a fortiori, a strong argument for the opposite proposition — a lack of such protection for a competent adult through negative implication." Persuasive?

2. Cf. *Hartman v. Pistorius*, 248 Ill. 568, 94 N.E. 131 (1911), where the court held that a purchaser "who assumes the mortgage indebtedness . . . becomes personally liable for such indebtedness and cannot defeat the mortgagee's right to hold him responsible by procuring a release from the mortgagor." However, because the contract in this case was only executory, the purchasers were not obligated to pay the mortgage debt.

3. In *Copeland v. Beard*, 217 Ala. 216, 115 So. 389 (1928), the court said:

> Coming then to the question of when the creditor's right of action against the promisor becomes fixed, we think it properly determinable on the basic law of contracts. So long as the contract to assume is between the debtor and his promisor only, the creditor is not a party thereto. He can become so only by his consent. At the same time, the contract, in the nature of it, is an open offer to the creditor. His assent while the offer is open is all that is required. When the minds of all parties consent to the same thing

at the same time, and such consent is communicated between them, the contract is complete.

Consent in such case may be proven in the same manner as in other contracts. The consideration for the promise passing between promisor and promisee is also consideration for the completed contract between all parties. The tripartite contract being consummated, it cannot be rescinded without the consent of all. It follows that the creditor's assent to the contract, made known to the promisor, who is expected to pay, is the only change of position required. But the assent must be to a promise in force at the time. The right of contract is the right to rescind or modify.

4. RESTATEMENT OF CONTRACTS states in § 142:

Variation of the Duty to a Donee Beneficiary by Agreement of Promisor and Promisee.

Unless the power to do so is reserved, the duty of the promisor to the donee beneficiary cannot be released by the promisee or affected by any agreement between the promisee and the promisor, but if the promisee receives consideration for an attempted release or discharge of the promisor's duty, the donee beneficiary can assert a right to the consideration so received, and on doing so loses his right against the promisor.

As to the vesting in a donee beneficiary situation involving a life insurance policy, what adverse effects would occur if the dictates of § 142 were followed to their logical conclusion? Should a gift, once given, be able to be withdrawn? Basic property law says no. Should contract law be different?

5. RESTATEMENT OF CONTRACTS § 143 states:

Variation of the Promisor's Duty to a Creditor Beneficiary by Agreement of Promisor and Promisee

A discharge of the promisor by the promisee in a contract or a variation thereof by them is effective against a creditor beneficiary if,

(a) the creditor beneficiary does not bring suit upon the promise or otherwise materially change his position in reliance thereon before he knows of the discharge or variation, and

(b) the promisee's action is not a fraud on creditors.

Here you can see that the third party's rights vest upon:

a) suit being brought by the third party, or

b) substantial reliance by the third party before modification or discharge.

Under the original RESTATEMENT, what kind of beneficiary, donee or creditor, has the more secure right? Does this make sense?

6. The position of RESTATEMENT (SECOND) OF CONTRACTS § 311 (1) per comments a and b, is that all intended beneficiaries' rights vest at the same time. Under § 311(1), rights vest when the plaintiff:

1) "materially changes his position in justifiable reliance on the promise, or"

2) "brings suit on it or"

3) "manifests assent to it at the request of the promisor or promisee."

G. DEFENSES TO THIRD PARTY BENEFICIARY'S CAUSE OF ACTION

ROUSE v. UNITED STATES
215 F.2d 872 (D.C. Cir. 1954)

EDGERTON, Circuit Judge:

Bessie Winston gave Associated Contractors, Inc., her promissory note for $1,008.37, payable in monthly installments of $28.01, for a heating plant in her house. The Federal Housing Administration guaranteed the note and the payee endorsed it for value to the lending bank, the Union Trust Company.

Winston sold the house to Rouse. In the contract of sale Rouse agreed to assume debts secured by deeds of trust and also "to assume payment of $850 for heating plant payable $28 per Mo." Nothing was said about the note.

Winston defaulted on her note. The United States paid the bank, took an assignment of the note, demanded payment from Rouse, and sued him for $850 and interest.

Rouse alleged as defenses: (1) that Winston fraudulently misrepresented the condition of the heating plant, and (2) that Associated Contractors did not install it satisfactorily. The District Court struck these defenses and granted summary judgment for the plaintiff. The defendant Rouse appeals.

Since Rouse did not sign the note he is not liable on it. . . . He is not liable to the United States at all unless his contract with Winston makes him so. The contract says the parties to it are not "bound by any terms, conditions, statements, warranties or representation, oral or written" not contained in it. But this means only that the written contract contains the entire agreement. It does not mean that fraud cannot be set up as a defense to a suit on the contract. [*Citing* 3 Williston, CONTRACTS § 811A (Rev. Ed. 1936).] Rouse's promise to "assume payment of $850 for heating plant" made him liable to Associated Contractors, Inc., only if and so far as it made him liable to Winston; one who promises to make a payment to the promisee's creditor can assert against the creditor any defense that the promisor could assert against the promisee. Accordingly Rouse, if he had been sued by the corporation, would have been entitled to show fraud on the part of Winston. He is equally entitled to do so in this suit by an assignee of the corporation's claim. It follows that the court erred in striking the first defense. . . .

We think the court was right in striking the second defense.

> If the promisor's agreement is to be interpreted as a promise to discharge whatever liability the promisee is under, the promisor must certainly be allowed to show that the promisee was under no enforceable liability. . . . On the other hand, if the promise means that the promisor agrees to pay a sum of money to A, to whom the promisee says he is indebted, it is immaterial whether the promisee is actually indebted to that amount or at all. . . . Where the promise is to pay a specific debt . . . this

interpretation will generally be the true one.

[*Citing* 2 WILLISTON, CONTRACTS § 399.]

The judgment is reversed and the cause remanded with instructions to reinstate the first defense.

Reversed and remanded.

NOTES & QUESTIONS

1. CORBIN ON CONTRACTS § 818 states:

> The claim of a beneficiary is dependent upon the validity of the contract that creates it. If that contract is void, voidable, or unenforceable, his claim is likewise affected. Thus an informal promise without consideration cannot be enforced by a beneficiary; nor can he enforce a promise void for illegality. If the promisor is lacking in legal capacity, or if the promise is void or voidable (as for fraud, mistake, infancy, insanity, or coverture) the claim of the beneficiary as well as that of the promisee is subject to the defect. If the promise as made is within the statute of frauds, the beneficiary cannot enforce it unless the provisions of the statute are complied with.
>
> Observe further that the promisee may have many good defenses in a suit brought against him by the third party that would not be operative in a suit against the promisor by the third party. The contract may have been made by the promisee for the purpose of settling some ill-founded claim of the third party. . . . The duty owed by the promisee to the third party may have become barred by statute of limitations or in bankruptcy; such a bar will not avail the promisor.

2. RESTATEMENT OF CONTRACTS § 309 states:

> § 309 Defenses Against the Beneficiary
>
> (1) A promise creates no duty to a beneficiary unless a contract is formed between the promisor and the promisee; and if a contract is voidable or unenforceable at the time of its formation the right of any beneficiary is subject to the infirmity.
>
> (2) If a contract ceases to be binding in whole or in part because of impracticability, public policy, non-occurrence of a condition, or present or prospective failure of performance, the right of any beneficiary is to that extent discharged or modified.
>
> (3) Except as stated in Subsections (1) and (2) and in § 311 or as provided by the contract, the right of any beneficiary against the promisor is not subject to the promisor's claims or defenses against the promisee or to the promisee's claims or defenses against the beneficiary.
>
> (4) A beneficiary's right against the promisor is subject to any claim or defense arising from his own conduct or agreement.

3. Even though the promisor may have a valid defense against the promisee that could, in theory, be raised against the third party beneficiary, there are occasions

where the third party beneficiary may insist that these defenses be deemed useless in any claim that the third party beneficiary may elect to bring. For example, casualty insurance policies for real estate frequently provide, where both owner and mortgagee are being provided insurance coverage, that any default by the owner-mortgagor, for example, due to non-payment of premium, fraud, misrepresentation, etc. by the mortgagor towards a casualty company will not operate to preclude coverage for the mortgagee if the property were to be destroyed by fire. Thus even though the owner-mortgagor neglected to pay the premium, the mortgagee would nevertheless be indemnified for a covered loss. 44 C.J.S. *Insurance* § 356(d). *See also General Credit Corp. v. Imperial Cas. and Indem. Co.,* 167 Neb. 833, 95 N.W.2d 145 (1959).

4. Should the promisor be able to counterclaim against the third party beneficiary for a loss caused the promisor by the promisee? *See* RESTATEMENT (SECOND) OF CONTRACTS § 309 comment c.

5. *Query:* If the third party beneficiary's rights have "vested," may the promisor nevertheless raise as a defense lack of consideration by the promisee? Is this logical?

CHAPTER 19

ASSIGNMENT AND DELEGATION

A. OVERVIEW

Assume an executory bilateral contract where S has contracted to sell his farm and B has agreed to purchase it for $100,000.

Their contractual relationship could be graphically depicted as follows:

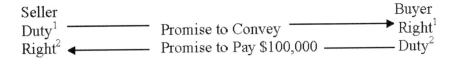

Thus, in a totally executory contract there are 2 duties: (1) the duty of seller to transfer title [Duty #1], out of which flows B's correlative right to the conveyance [Right #1]; and (2) the duty of buyer to pay $100,000 [Duty #2], out of which arises S's right to receive this payment [Right #2].

The threshold question that must be addressed is whether one party to a contract is legally able to transfer his contractual right to a third party. (Later we will address the question of whether he can delegate his duty to perform to another party).

In this scenario the graphic depiction would then look something like this:

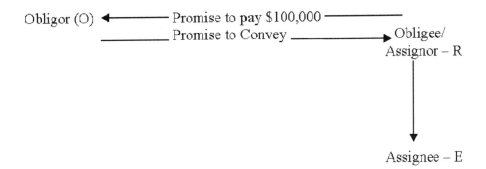

wherein R (the assignor) attempts to transfer his right to the land to E (the assignee) so that thereafter E may enforce the promise of O (the obligor of the promise to convey) against O.

At first glance the answer would seem to be obvious — one may give his right away, or sell it, to a third party. After all, it's a "credit" on the contractual ledger sheet, and who in the world could object when someone decides to divest himself of a right and transfer it to a third party?

It should be noted that "R" is also the obligor of a promise to pay $100,000; and O is the obligee of that promise. But at the moment, we are not concerning ourselves with whether O's right to receive payment is transferrable. We are simply attempting to determine if E (the putative assignee) may legally force O (the putative obligor of the promise to convey) to deed the farm to E rather than to R.

So once again, the question might be: what justification could O have in refusing to tender his performance to E rather than to R?

B.   ASSIGNMENT — ITS NATURE AND FUNCTION

ALLIANZ LIFE INSURANCE COMPANY OF NORTH AMERICA v. RIEDL
264 Ga. 395, 444 S.E.2d 736 (1994)

SEARS-COLLINS, Justice:

We granted certiorari in this case to consider whether an assignment of health care benefits under an insurance policy to a health care provider divests the assignor/insured of the right to bring an action against the insurer to collect benefits under the insurance policy. We find that it does and reverse the decision of the Court of Appeals. . . .

The appellee, Frank Riedl, was insured under a policy by the appellant, Allianz Life Insurance Company of North America (hereinafter "Allianz"). The policy also covered Riedl's wife and minor daughter, Jodie. In 1989, Jodie was treated at the Anneewakee Treatment Center in Douglasville, Georgia, incurring over $36,000 in charges. Upon Jodie's admission to Anneewakee, Ms. Riedl executed a document entitled, in relevant part, "ASSIGNMENT TO HOSPITAL/PHYSICIANS." The agreement provided that "in consideration for the services rendered by ANNEEWAKEE TREATMENT CENTER and/or ATTENDING PHYSICIANS . . . [Ms. Riedl] assign[ed] both BASIC and/or MAJOR MEDICAL to [Anneewakee] . . . under the [policy] with [Allianz] . . . insofar as they are necessary to cover both BASIC and/or MAJOR MEDICAL expenses."

Riedl filed this action against Allianz, claiming, among other things, that the charges at Anneewakee were compensable under the policy. Allianz moved to dismiss on the ground that Riedl was not the real party in interest, Allianz contended that Anneewakee was the real party in interest because the document executed by Ms. Riedl constituted an assignment to Anneewakee of the benefits under the policy. The trial court denied Allianz's motion, and the Court of Appeals granted Allianz's application for interlocutory appeal.

The Court of Appeals vacated the trial court's judgment, holding that the document executed by Ms. Riedl constituted an assignment of benefits due under the Allianz policy to Anneewakee, . . . but that both Riedl and Anneewakee, as assignor and assignee, were indispensable parties and, as such, both had to be joined in the action. . . . The court remanded with direction that "a reasonable opportunity be provided" the parties to comply with the opinion. We granted certiorari and now reverse.

The first issue for resolution is whether the document executed by Ms. Riedl is actually an assignment. We conclude that it is.

The document is entitled an "Assignment" and provides in the text that Ms. Riedl assigned "both BASIC and/or MAJOR MEDICAL" contractual benefits under the Allianz policy. Moreover, unlike other documents that some courts have held not to be an assignment, the document in this case does not merely direct or authorize the insurer to make direct payment to the health care provider. Such documents have been held to be a "mere power of attorney to the obligor. . . , empowering him to effectuate a transfer." *Piedmont, etc., Life Ins. Co. v. Gunter*, 108 Ga. App. 236, 240(2), 132 S.E.2d 527 (1963) (quoting 4 Corbin on Contracts 425, § 862). *Accord Jefferson Oncology v. Louisiana Health Services & Indem. Co.*, 545 So. 2d 1125 (La. Ct. App. 1989); *Kelly Health Care v. Prudential Ins. Co.*, 226 Va. 376, 309 S.E.2d 305 (1983). . . . In any event, because the provision in this case speaks in terms of assignments and not merely in terms of authorizing payments, we conclude that the provision did constitute an assignment of the contractual benefits under the Allianz policy. . . .

Having decided that Ms. Riedl did execute an assignment, we must next analyze whether the assignment of the right to benefits under the policy divested the Riedls of the right to bring an action against the insurer under the insurance policy. Although the Court of Appeals has issued several, sometimes conflicting, rulings on this issue, *see Riedl*, 209 Ga. App. 883, 434 S.E.2d 820; *Santiago v. Safeway Ins. Co.*, 196 Ga. App. 480(1), 396 S.E.2d 506 (1990); . . . for the reasons that follow, we hold that an assignment of benefits by an insured does divest the insured of the right to bring an action against the insurer.

An assignment is an "absolute, unconditional, and completed transfer of all right, title, and interest in the property that is the subject of the assignment. . . , with the concomitant total relinquishment of any control over the property." *Bank of Cave Spring v. Gold Kist, Inc.*, 173 Ga. App. 679, 680(1), 327 S.E.2d 800 (1985). Moreover, "[i]n the absence of a contrary intention, an assignment usually passes as incidents all ancillary remedies and rights of action which the assignor had or would have had for the enforcement of the right or chose assigned." 6A C.J.S. 721, Assignments, § 77 (1975). Further, other courts have concluded that an assignment of insurance benefits transfers the cause of action for the benefits to the health care provider. . . .

In this case, as there is no contrary intention appearing in the document executed by Ms. Riedl, we conclude that the assignment transferred to Anneewakee the right of action that the Riedls had to enforce their right to the benefits due under the policy for the expenses incurred at Anneewakee and thus divested Riedl of that right of action.

Because the assignment divested Riedl of and transferred to Anneewakee all right, title, and interest in the benefits due under the policy with Allianz, as well as the right of action necessary to enforce that right, we conclude that the Court of Appeals erred by concluding that both Anneewakee and Riedl were real parties in interest. The real party in interest is "the person, who, by the substantive governing law, has the right sought to be enforced." Wright, Miller & Kane, Federal Practice and Procedure: Civil 2d § 1543 (1990). Here, the substantive governing law is the law of assignment discussed above. *See* Wright, Miller & Kane, § 1545. Under the law of assignment, Anneewakee has the substantive right sought to be enforced; therefore, Anneewakee and not Riedl is the real party in interest for the claim seeking recovery of the expenses incurred at Anneewakee.

When an action is not being prosecuted by the real party in interest, a trial court should not dismiss the action "until a reasonable time has been allowed . . . for ratification of commencement of the action by . . . the real party in interest." OCGA § 9-11-17(a). Accordingly, on remand, the trial court should give Anneewakee a reasonable opportunity to ratify or join the action as to the claim for medical expenses incurred at Anneewakee or to be substituted for Riedl as to that claim.

For the foregoing reasons, we reverse the Court of Appeals' judgment in this case. Judgment reversed and case remanded.

NOTES & QUESTIONS

1. "An assignment operates to transfer some identifiable property right, interest or claim from the assignor to assignee." *In re Estate of Martinek*, 140 Ill. App. 3d 621, 628, 94 Ill. Dec. 939, 944, 488 N.E.2d 1332, 1337 (1986). "No particular words are necessary to demonstrate the existence of an assignment. . . . Rather, any document which sufficiently evidences the intent of the assignor to vest ownership of the subject matter of the assignment in the assignee is sufficient to effect an assignment."

Department of Transportation v. Heritage-Pullman Bank and Trust Co., 627 N.E.2d 191, 192 (Ill. App. 1993).

"To be enforceable against third parties under New York law, an assignment must be 'a complete transfer of the entire interest of the assignor in the particular subject of assignment, whereby the assignor is divested of all control over the things assigned.' 3 N.Y. Juris, *Assignments* § 28."

Continental Oil Co. v. United States, 326 F. Supp. 266, 269 (S.D.N.Y. 1971).

2. Note that although some courts and lawyers use the terms "assign the contract," a contracting party technically assigns rights and delegates duties. *See* Corbin, *Assignment of Contract Rights*, 74 U. Pa. L. Rev. 207 (1926). *See* Restatement (Second) of Contracts § 316, comment c. *See also* Restatement (Second) of Contracts § 328 comment a; Calamari & Perillo, The Law of Contracts § 18-1, at 722 (3d ed. 1987).

3. If R were to say that he promised to transfer his right to the land to E in two months, would this constitute an assignment? Why or why not?

> "A mere agreement to assign a debt or chose in action at some future time will not operate as an assignment thereof so as to vest any present interest in the assignee." *KC v. Milrey Development Co.*, 600 S.W.2d 660 (Mo. App. 1980).

4. Assume that S, a seller, makes B, a buyer, an offer to sell B a car for $10,000. May B assign his power of acceptance to C? Now assume that B pays $100 to S to secure an option to buy for 30 days. B now has the right to purchase the car, and the question is: is this right assignable to C? Bear in mind that the right would be

nugatory if B never accepts S's offer. *See* 1 CORBIN ON CONTRACTS § 57; *Cochran v. Taylor*, 273 N.Y. 172,7 N.E.2d 89 (1937).

5. In both a third party beneficiary scenario and an assignment scenario there are three "players." How do the two scenarios differ?

C. EFFECTIVE TRANSFERS

FARRELL v. PASSAIC WATER CO.
82 N.J. Eq. 97, 88 A. 627 (1913)

STEVENS, V.C., Judge:

This is a bill filed by the administratrix of Catherine Farrell against the Passaic Water Company and the executors of James Atkinson. It is alleged that Mr. Atkinson was engaged to be married to Mrs. Farrell, and that about the year 1895, and while so engaged, he handed her a coupon bond of the Passaic Water Company for $1,000, intending to make her a gift of it. The bond was, at the time of the alleged gift, and still is, registered, as to principal, in the name of Atkinson. . . . Mrs. Farrell drew the interest coupons during her life, and died in 1909. Atkinson died in 1902. Since the death of Mrs. Farrell, the bond has been in the possession of either her next of kin or her administratrix. On its face it provides that it is payable to the bearer or registered holder thereof, and that it 'may at any time be registered in the name of the owner on the books of the company,' . . . The bill prays that the bond may be declared to be a part of the estate of Catherine Farrell, and that the company may be decreed to register it in the name of her administratrix.

The defense is, first, that no gift is proven, and, second, that, if an intention to give has been shown, such gift was imperfect without registry, and a court of equity will not lend its aid to perfect it.

* * *

There is nothing in this case to indicate that Atkinson declared that he held the bond in controversy as trustee for Mrs. Farrell. What he did was, not to set it aside among his own papers, and to declare in any way that from that time forth he held it for her benefit, but to give her the possession of it, and, as far as appears, concern himself no further about it. . . . If, then, the complainant has a valid title, it must be because Atkinson completely divested himself of all title. . . .

By what formalities may title be vested in an assignee? At first it was held that an instrument under seal could only be assigned by an instrument of equal dignity. *Wood v. Partridge*, 11 Mass. 488; but this view has been abandoned, and it is now held that instruments such as bonds, mortgages, and policies of insurance may be assigned by writing without seal, or even by parol accompanied by delivery. . . . The effect of the assignment is precisely the same in any of these forms — it vests the legal title in the assignee. The proof of it may be more difficult in the case of an assignment by parol, but in any mode the debt theretofore owing to the obligee passes to the assignee; he is the creditor, and the only creditor.

These several modes of assignment are as applicable to the case of gifts as to those of transfers for value. The gift is just as completely vested by the one mode as by the other, and it is settled law that the fact that the bond is not payable to bearer or that the instrument is not negotiable does not prevent a valid gift of it by manual tradition without writing. . . . Proof of delivery, coupled with proof of intent to pass a present interest by way of gift, has precisely the same effect as a formal written transfer. A moment's consideration will show that this is necessarily so. The instrument given remains, in either case, unchanged. If payable by A. to B., it remains so payable on the face of it, whether transferred by writing or not; but by the effect of the transfer what theretofore was payable to B. has in law become payable to C., the transferee. In the case of *Green v. Tulane*, 52 N.J. Eq. 169, 28 A. 9, the question was not before the court. I do not think it can be fairly gathered from what Pitney, V.C., said that he thought that a writing was necessary; but, if he there so expressed himself, when the point came squarely before him, in the insurance case, he held otherwise. The question, then, is, Did Atkinson make a gift; that is, a perfect gift? Two objections are made: First, it is said that the proof fails to show delivery accompanied with a declaration of intent; and, secondly, that the instrument itself forbids the making of a gift in the manner in which it is alleged to have been made.

As to the first objection: The evidence is that Atkinson, a business man of mature years, possessed of considerable property, while engaged to be married to Mrs. Farrell, parted with the bond in question; how or when does not appear. Although he lived for six or seven years after it came into Mrs. Farrell's possession, he did not reclaim it; reclamation being all the more easy because of the fact that the bond stood registered in his name. He told a friend that he had made Mrs. Farrell a present of a bond of that description. She took the interest accruing upon it for 10 or 12 years before her death. It was natural that, situated as they were, he should have made a gift, and there is no evidence against it. Under these circumstances I think the inference that a gift was actually made is the only fair inference from the proofs. . . .

But it is said that the failure to direct the company to make a transfer on its books is evidence that Atkinson did not intend his gift to be irrevocable. If the facts justify the inference that he did so intend, proof that he failed to authorize the company by power of attorney to make a transfer is immaterial. He had, I have shown, the option of making the gift with or without writing. Such failure might indeed be a circumstance militating against the gift, if coupled with other circumstances throwing doubt upon it.

Standing by itself, it is without significance as long as it is the doctrine of this court that a valid gift may be made by parol. Proof of failure to make in one way is no proof of failure to make in another. . . .

[The court then ordered Passaic Water Co. to register the bond in the assignee's name.]

ADAMS v. MERCED STONE CO.
176 Cal. 415, 178 P. 498 (1917)

SHAW, Justice:

The plaintiff appeals from a Judgment in favor of the defendant, and from an order denying his motion for a new trial.

The complaint states a cause of action against the defendant, in favor of the decedent, Thomas Prather, upon an indebtedness alleged to be the sum of

$112,965.84. The defendant in its answer denied the existence of any indebtedness from it to said Thomas Prather at the time of his death, and on information and belief alleged that prior to his death said Thomas Prather made a gift of said indebtedness, due from the plaintiff [sic] to Thomas Prather, to one Samuel D. Prather, and that said Samuel then became and ever since has been the owner of said indebtedness.

The court found that during the last sickness of Thomas Prather, to wit, on April 17, 1913, said Thomas Prather made a gift to his brother Samuel D. Prather, of all of the indebtedness due from the defendant to said Thomas, being the indebtedness sued for by the plaintiff herein. That at that time Samuel was the president, the general manager, and a member of the board of directors of the defendant, said defendant being a corporation, and Thomas Prather knew that Samuel held said offices and by reason thereof had full and exclusive charge and control of defendant's books of account, including power to make or direct the making of entries and transfers in said books, and knew that by reason thereof Samuel D. Prather had the means of obtaining possession and control of the said indebtedness so given to him. The court further stated that by reason of the fact that Thomas Prather had this knowledge at the time he gave the indebtedness to Samuel, he therefore at that time gave to said Samuel the means of obtaining possession and control of the thing given, that is, of the said indebtedness. . . . The appellant contends that the transaction as stated in the findings did not constitute a valid gift of the indebtedness in question, and that the finding, so far as it states the ultimate fact of such gift, is contrary to the evidence.

It is conceded that at the time of the asserted gift Thomas Prather knew that Samuel D. Prather held the offices above mentioned, and that it was within his official power by reason thereof to make sufficient changes upon the books of account of the defendant to make them show that the said indebtedness had been transferred by Thomas Prather to Samuel D. Prather, and was owing by the defendant to Samuel D. Prather, instead of Thomas Prather. It is admitted that the asserted gift was made during the last sickness of Samuel (sic) Prather, two days before his death, which event occurred on April 19, 1913, and was therefore a gift in view of death. Civ. Code, § 1150. It is also admitted that no change was made upon the books of the defendant regarding said indebtedness, up to the time of the trial of this action, and that when the action was begun the account books of the defendant showed it to be indebted to the said Thomas Prather in the sum claimed in the complaint. The only evidence of the gift asserted in the answer is found in the testimony of Samuel D. Prather, and is as follows:

> In talking business matters my brother said to me, "Now, in reference to the account of Thomas Prather in the Merced Stone Company, I want to give you that account, all that is due me from that account. I don't know just how to do this, but I give it to you." . . . A little further in the conversation my brother said to me, "I give you the keys to my office, the combination of my safe and keys to my desk, and with these I give you all accounts, books, papers, letters, documents, furnishings, pictures, everything that belongs to me in that office. It is yours."

This he said occurred on April 17, 1913.

The case depends upon the meaning and effect of section 1147 of the Civil Code which reads as follows:

A verbal gift is not valid, unless the means of obtaining possession and control of the thing are given, nor, if it is capable of delivery, unless there is an actual or symbolical delivery of the thing to the donee.

The contention of the respondent is that this section is complied with in every case of gift of a chose in action where, at the time the donor makes such gift, he knows that the donee has it within his power to secure the possession and control of the thing given, and that in such a case no delivery or transmission from the donor to the donee of the means of obtaining possession and control of the subject of the gift is necessary. We do not think this is the correct construction of the section quoted. It contemplates that the donor shall do something at the time of making the gift which has the effect of placing in the hands of the donee the means of obtaining the control and possession of the thing given. That the fact that the thing was already in possession of the donee at the time of declaring the gift is not enough, is well settled by the authorities. . . .

In order to comply with the section the "means" must be "given." In the connection in which these words occur the effect is that such means must be given by the donor to the donee. This giving of the means is authorized, where the thing given is not capable of delivery, as a substitute for the actual or symbolical delivery of the thing by the donor to the donee required in cases where such thing is capable of delivery. No good reason can be given for supposing that a transmission or delivery by the donor to the donee of the means was not intended to be as essential in the case of intangible property, as the delivery, actual or symbolical, of the thing itself, where it is tangible.

In the case of a chose in action not evidenced by a written instrument, the only means of obtaining control that is recognized by the authorities is an assignment in writing, or some equivalent thereof.

"According to the weight of authority, in order to make a valid gift inter vivos of a chose in action not evidenced by a written instrument, there must be a written assignment, or some equivalent instrument." 20 Cyc. 1202.

"A written assignment of the demand by the donor to the donee is essential to complete the delivery in the case of gifts causa mortis." 20 Cyc. 1237; 14 Am. & Eng. Ency. of Law, 1022.

"If the thing be not capable of actual delivery, there must be some act equivalent to it. The donor must part not only with the possession, but with the dominion of the property. If the thing given be a chose in action, the law requires an assignment, or some equivalent instrument, and the transfer must be actually executed." 2 Kent Com. 439.

. . . In *Cook v. Lum*, 55 N.J. Law, 373, 26 A. 803, the court said that the test of an effectual gift was this:

That the transfer was such that, in conjunction with the donative intention, it completely stripped the donor of his dominion of the thing given, whether that thing was a tangible chattel or a chose in action.

In the present case it is true that Samuel D. Prather was possessed of the physical power and of the official authority, by reason of his relation to the defendant, to make the necessary changes on its books to show that the indebtedness was due to him and not to the decedent. But this power did not emanate from the decedent. Samuel possessed it before the asserted gift as well as after. The decedent did not even authorize him to make such changes, nor suggest that the gift might be effected in that way. It was not shown that such method was in the mind of the donor. . . . The law intends something more than a mere power to make physical entries in the books of the debtor in such a case. . . . If verbal gifts could be made in such loose manner as this it would open the door to innumerable frauds and perjuries. For this reason the authorities hold that something more than mere physical power is necessary; something more than the previous possession of the property or of the means of obtaining it; something emanating from the donor which operates to give to the donee the means of obtaining such possession and control.

The mere delivery of an order for the payment of a debt is therefore not sufficient to make a complete gift thereof. In the present case there was not even the delivery of an order, nor any suggestion thereof. All that was done was to declare the present intention to give the indebtedness to Samuel D. Prather. No means whatever were delivered by the donor to the donee by which the latter could obtain payment of the indebtedness. The fact that Samuel D. Prather was the managing officer of the defendant and had power to change its books did not make the gift effectual. The indebtedness was due from the defendant and not from Samuel D. Prather, and it was necessary that the defendant should have some authority from Thomas Prather before it could legally make a change upon the books of the company to show the change in the indebtedness. Thomas Prather gave no such authority to his brother or to any other person.

The conclusion of the court below upon the facts found was not in accordance with the law, and its finding of the ultimate fact that Thomas Prather transferred the debt to Samuel D. Prather by way of a verbal gift is not supported by the evidence. Consequently the judgment and order cannot be upheld.

The judgment and order are reversed and the cause is remanded, with directions to the court below to enter judgment upon the findings in favor of the plaintiff for the amount prayed for.

NOTES & QUESTIONS

1. Once an assignment has occurred, the right in R is extinguished and E alone possesses it. This is normally the case because on occasion the assignment might be able to be terminated, for example where the assignment from R to E was gratuitous and R thereafter dies before E exercises the right. *See* Restatement (Second) of Contracts § 332.

2. To whom must R manifest his intent that his right against O is assigned? If R tells O that O should thereafter pay to E whatever O owes R, does this constitute an effective assignment? Restatement (Second) of Contracts § 325, comment a. See also *Delbrueck & Co. v. Manufacturers Hanover Trust*, 609 F.2d 1047 (2d Cir. 1979), where the court held that a written credit slip received by the assignee made the transfer of funds to the assignee irrevocable.

3. Must the manifestation of an intent to assign be in writing? *See* Restatement (Second) of Contracts § 324.

See Anaconda v. Sharp, 136 So. 2d 585 (Miss. 1962) where the court stated:

The Chancellor held that these two conversations perfected the verbal assignment. It is the law in this state, and has been for many years, that an assignment of an account can be made verbally.

4. If O owed R $10,000, which debt arose out of a written contract, would R's delivery of that written contract to E be sufficient to create an assignment? What about a letter to E, signed by R, referring to his contract with O? A New York statute provides that "An assignment shall not be denied the effect of irrevocably transferring the assignor's rights because of the absence of consideration, if such assignment is in writing and signed by the assignor, or by his agent." N.Y. GEN. OBLIG. L. § 5-1107 (McKinney). In *Brooks v. Mitchell*, 161 A. 261 (Ct. of App. Md. 1932), the court held that delivery of a bank savings book created an assignment of a bank account from R to E.

5. Assume a lease, dated January 1, wherein the lessee O agrees to pay $1,000/month for one calendar year. O fails to make payments for January and February. On March 1 the lessor, for value, assigns his right to the entire year's rent to E. On March 5th the lessor dies. What rights to rentals does E possess? None? $2,000? $10,000? $12,000? What rights would E acquire if R assigned a lease that he intended to sign with X for the next year? See RESTATEMENT (SECOND) OF CONTRACTS § 321(2); *Speelman v. Pascal*, 10 N.Y.2d 313, 178 N.E.2d 723 (1961); FARNSWORTH ON CONTRACTS§ 11.5, at 770.

6. In the preceding hypothetical, if E were found to have no right to the rents that X would someday be obligated to pay, would E have any enforceable right at all? Against whom and on what theory? Would your answer depend on whether the purported assignment was for value or gratuitous? *See* Calamari & Perillo, THE LAW OF CONTRACTS § 18-9, at 733 (3d ed. 1987).

D. NON-ASSIGNABLE RIGHTS

CRANE ICE CREAM CO. v. TERMINAL FREEZING & HEATING CO.
128 A. 280 (Md. 1925)

PARKE, Judge:

The appellee (defendant) and one W.C. Frederick entered into a contract for the delivery of ice by the appellee to Frederick, and, before the expiration of the contract, Frederick executed an assignment of the contract to the appellant (plaintiff); and on the refusal of the appellee to deliver ice to the assignee it brought an action on the contract against the appellee to recover damages for the alleged breach. The common counts of the declaration were abandoned, leaving an amended special count on the contract and assignment to which a demurrer was filed and sustained. It is from the judgment against the appellant on this demurrer that the appeal was taken.

The demurrer admitted the following material allegations: At the execution of the contract the Terminal Freezing & Heating Company, appellee, was a corporation engaged in the manufacture and sale of ice at wholesale within the state of Maryland, and William C. Frederick made and sold ice cream in Baltimore, where his plant was located. The original contract between these two parties was made on April 2, 1917, and ran until April 2, 1920. The contract was modified on

June 3, 1918, by the increase of the original contract price of ice from $2.75 a ton to $3.25, and before its expiration the contract was renewed by the parties for another three years so that the contract was continued until April 2, 1923, without change, save as to the higher agreed cost of the ice delivered.

The contract imposed upon [Terminal] the liability to sell and deliver to Frederick such quantities of ice as he might use in his business as an ice cream manufacturer to the extent of 250 tons per week, at and for the price of $3.25 a ton of 2,000 pounds [sic] on the loading platform of Frederick. The contractual rights of [Terminal] were (a) to be paid on every Tuesday during the continuation of the contract, for all ice purchased by Frederick during the week ending at midnight upon the next preceding Saturday; (b) to require Frederick not to buy or accept any ice from any other source than [Terminal], except in excess of the weekly maximum of 250 tons; (c) to annul the contract upon any violation of the agreement by Frederick. . . .

There was a further provision that the contract in its entirety should continue in force from term to term, unless either party thereto gave to the other party at least 60 days' notice in writing before the expiration of the term of the intention to end the contract, The contract did not expressly permit or inhibit an assignment, but neither did it contain any word, such as assigns, to indicate that the parties contemplated an assignment by either.

Before the first year of the second term of the contract had expired, Frederick, without the consent or knowledge of [Terminal], executed and delivered to [Crane], for a valuable consideration, a written assignment dated February 15, 1921, of the modified agreement between him and [Terminal]. The attempted transfer of the contract was a part of the transaction between Frederick and [Crane] whereby [Crane] acquired by purchase the plant, equipment, rights, and credits, choses in action, "good will, trade, custom, patronage, rights, contracts," and other assets of Frederick's ice cream business, which had been established and conducted by him in Baltimore. The purchaser took full possession and continued the former business carried on by Frederick. . . .

As soon as [Terminal] learned of this purported assignment and the absorption of the business of Frederick by [Crane], it notified Frederick that the contract was at an end, and declined to deliver any ice to [Crane]. Until the day of the assignment the obligations of both original parties had been fully performed and discharged.

It may be stated as a general rule that a contract cannot be enforced by or against a person who is not a party to it, but there are circumstances under which either of the contracting parties may substitute another for himself in the rights and duties of the contract without obtaining the consent of the other party to the contract. The inquiry here is if the facts bring the case within the scope of the general rule, and the answer must be found from a consideration in detail of the relation of the parties concerned, the subject-matter of the contract, its terms, and the circumstances of its formation.

The basic facts upon which the question for solution depends must be sought in the effect of the attempted assignment of this executory bilateral contract on both the rights and liabilities of the contracting parties, as every bilateral contract includes both rights and duties on each side while both sides remain executory. 1 WILLISTON ON CONTRACTS, § 407. If the assignment of rights and the assignment of duties by Frederick are separated, they fall into these two divisions: (1) The rights of the assignor were (a) to take no ice, if the assignor used none in his business, but, if he did (b) to require [Terminal] to deliver, on the loading platform of the assignor, all the ice he might need in his business to the extent of 250 tons a week, and (c) to buy any ice he might need in excess of the weekly 250 tons from any other person; and (2) the liabilities of the assignor were (a) to pay to [Terminal] on every Tuesday during the continuance of the contact the stipulated price for all ice purchased . . . , and (b) not directly or indirectly, during the existence of this agreement, to buy or accept any ice from any other person, firm, or corporation than the said the Terminal Freezing & Heating Company, except such amounts as might be in excess of the weekly limit of 250 tons.

Whether the attempted assignment of these rights, or the attempted delegation of these duties must fail because the rights or duties are of too personal a character, is a question of construction to be resolved from the nature of the contact and the express or presumed intention of the parties. WILLISTON ON CONTRACTS, § 431.

The contract was made by a corporation with an individual, William C. Frederick, an ice cream manufacturer, with whom the corporation had dealt for 3 years, before it executed a renewal contract for a second like period. The character, credit, and resources of Frederick had been tried and tested by [Terminal] before it renewed the contract. Not only had his ability to pay as agreed been established, but his fidelity to his obligation not to buy or accept any ice from any other source up to 250 tons a week had been ascertained. In addition, [Terminal] had not asked in the beginning, nor on entering into the second period of the contract, for Frederick to undertake to buy a specific quantity of ice or even to take any. Frederick simply engaged himself during a definite term to accept and pay for such quantities of ice as he might use in his business to the extent of 250 tons a week. If he used no ice in his business, he was under no obligation to pay for a pound. . . .

When it is also considered that the ice was to be supplied and paid for, according to its weight on the loading platform of Frederick, at an unvarying price without any reference either to the quantity used, or to the fluctuations in the cost of production or to market changes in the selling price, throughout 3 years, the conclusion is inevitable that the inducement for [Terminal] to enter into the original contract and into the renewal lay outside the bare terms of the contract, but was implicit in them, and was [Terminal]'s reliance upon its knowledge of an average quantity of ice consumed, and probably to be needed, in the usual course of Frederick's business, at all times throughout the year, and its confidence in the stability of his enterprise, in his competency in commercial affairs, in his probity, personal judgment, and in his continuing financial responsibility. The contract itself emphasized the personal equation by specifying that the ice was to be bought for "use in his business as an ice cream manufacturer," and was to be paid for according to its weight "on the loading platform of the said W.C. Frederick."

When Frederick went out of business as an ice cream manufacturer, and turned over his plant and everything constituting his business to [Crane], it was no longer his business, or his loading platform, or subject to his care, control, or maintenance, but it was the business of a stranger, whose skill, competency, and requirement of ice were altogether different from those of Frederick. The assignor had his simple plant in Baltimore. The assignee, in its purchase, simply added another unit to its ice cream business which it had been, and is now, carrying on "upon a large and extensive scale in the city of Philadelphia and state of Pennsylvania, as well as in the city of Baltimore and state of Maryland." [Terminal] . . . was familiar with the quantities of ice he [Frederick] would require, from time to time, in his business at his plant in Baltimore, and it consequently could make its other commitments for ice with this knowledge as a basis.

[Crane], on the other hand, might wholly supply its increased trade acquired in the purchase of Frederick's business with its ice cream produced upon a large and extensive scale by its manufactory in Philadelphia, which would result in no ice being bought by the assignee of [Terminal], and so [Terminal] would be deprived of the benefit of its contract by the introduction of a different personal relation or element which was never contemplated by the original contracting parties. Again, should the price of ice be relatively high in Philadelphia in comparison with the stipulated price, the assignee could run its business in Baltimore and furnish its patrons, or a portion of them, in Philadelphia with this product from the weekly maximum consumption of 250 tons of ice throughout the year. There can be no denial that the uniform delivery of the maximum quantity of 250 tons a week would be a consequence not within the normal scope of the contract, and would impose a greater liability on [Terminal] than was anticipated. . . .

Moreover, the contract here to supply ice was undefined except as indicated from time to time by the personal requirements of Frederick in his specified business. The quantities of ice to be supplied to Frederick to answer his weekly requirements must be very different from, and would not be the measure of the quantities needed by his assignee, and manifestly, to impose on the seller the obligation to obey the demands of the substituted assignee is to set up a new measure of ice to be supplied and so a new term in the agreement that [Terminal] never bound itself to perform. Up to 250 tons of ice a week Frederick engaged not to buy or accept ice from any other party than [Terminal]. After Frederick had sold away his business, this covenant could not bind the assignee of his business, and, even if it continued to bind Frederick, his refraining from not buying ice elsewhere was not a contemplated consideration for selling ice to any one except Frederick himself. . . . It was argued that Frederick was entitled to the weekly maximum of 250 tons, and that he might have expanded his business so as to require this weekly limit of ice, and that therefore the burdens of the contract might have been as onerous to [Terminal], if Frederick had continued in business, as they could become under the purporting assignment by reason of the increased requirements of the larger business of the assignee. The unsoundness of this argument is that the law accords to every man freedom of choice in the party with whom he deals and the terms of his dealing. He cannot be forced to do a thing which he did not agree to do because it is like and no more burdensome than something which he did contract to do.

Under all the circumstances of the case, it is clear that the rights and duties of the contract under consideration were of so personal a character that the rights of Frederick cannot be assigned nor his duties be delegated without defeating the intention of the parties to the original contract. When Frederick went out of the business of making ice cream, he made it impossible for him to complete his performance of the contract, and his personal action and qualifications upon which [Terminal] relied were eliminated from a contract which presupposed their continuance. Frederick not only attempted an assignment, but his course is a repudiation of the obligations of the contract. . . .

While a party to a contract may as a general rule assign all his beneficial rights, except where a personal relation is involved, his liability under the contract is not assignable inter vivos, because any one who is bound to any performance whatever or who owes money cannot by any act of his own, or by any act in agreement with any other person than his creditor or the one to whom his performance is due, cast off his own liability and substitute another's liability. . . .

. . . [T]he analysis of the facts on this appeal leaves no room for doubt that the case at bar falls into the category of those assignments where an attempt is made both to transfer the rights and to delegate the duties of the assignor under an executory bilateral contract whose terms and circumstances make plain that the personal qualification and action of the assignor, with respect to both his benefits and burdens under the contract, were essential inducements in the formation of the contract, and further, that the assignment was a repudiation of any future liability of the assignor. The attempted assignment before us altered the conditions and obligations of the undertaking. [Terminal] would here be obliged not only to perform the subsequent stipulations of the contract for the benefit of a stranger and in conformity with his will, but also to accept the performance of the stranger in place of that of the assignor with whom it contracted, and upon whose personal integrity, capacity, and management in the course of a particular business he must be assumed to have relied by reason of the very nature of the provisions of the contract and of the circumstances of the contracting parties. . . .

The authorities cited on [plaintiff Crane's] brief have been examined, and they are not in conflict with the principals of law controlling this case, but rather serve to illustrate their application to other and different combinations of facts, which do not afford any ground for this court to change its conclusion on the nonassignable character of the burdens and benefits arising from the stipulations and the nature of the contract in this appeal. . . .

We take it to be sound doctrine that, where one contracting party repudiates his obligations, the other party has the right of declining to be bound to a stranger by its terms. *See* ANSON ON CONTRACTS (4th Am. Ed. by Corbin) note 2, pp. 378, 379; 1 WILLISTON ON CONTRACTS, § 420; *Hand v. Evans Marble Co.*, 88 Md. 226, 229, 230, 40 A. 899.

Judgment affirmed, with costs to [Terminal].

NOTES & QUESTIONS

1. If the requirements of E were less than those of R, would the assignment then be a valid one? *See* U.C.C. § 2-306, comment 4. The court also states that, by assigning his rights and delegating his duty to pay to Crane, Frederic repudiated his own duty towards Terminal. Does a repudiation necessarily follow from a delegation of duties?

2. RESTATEMENT (SECOND) OF CONTRACTS § 317(2)(a) provides:

> (2) A contractual right can be assigned unless
>
> (a) the substitution of a right of the assignee for the right of the assignor would materially change the duty of the obligor, or materially increase the burden or risk imposed on him by his contract, or materially impair his

chance of obtaining return performance, or materially reduce its value to him.

3. One reason R's right may not be assignable is because such assignment would materially impair O's chance of obtaining R's return performance. Of course any assignment by R would lessen R's incentive somewhat to perform his corresponding duty to O, since R no longer can anticipate the receipt of O's performance. However, if R doesn't perform he is subject to being sued by O and/or E. *See* 4 CORBIN ON CONTRACTS § 869.

4. A right to sue in federal court, where the basis of jurisdiction is diversity of citizenship, was held to be personal and not assignable to another where diversity would thereby be extinguished. *See RTC Commercial Loan Trust v. Winthrop Management,* 923 F. Supp. 83 (E.D. Va. 1996). Cf. RESTATEMENT (SECOND) OF CONTRACTS § 317(2)(b) regarding rights, the assignment of which are prohibited by statute and/or public policy. *See In re Persky,* 1998 U.S. Dist. LEXIS 15509 (E.D. Pa. 1998). Thrift Savings Plan accounts, pursuant to 5 U.S.C. § 8437(e)(2) "may not be assigned or alienated and are not subject to execution, levy, attachment, garnishment, or other legal process." Similarly, public policy prohibits the assignment of certain rights, e.g., claims against attorneys for legal malpractice. *Appletree v. O'Connor and Hannan,* 559 N.W.2d 711 (Minn. App. 1997) ("Such an assignment would convert these claims into commodities 'to be exploited and transferred to economic bidders who have never had a professional relationship with the attorney.' . . .") Reversed on other grounds 575 N.W.2d 102 (Minn. 1998).

HANIGAN v. WHEELER
19 Ariz. App. 49, 504 P.2d 972 (1972)

HOWARD, Judge:

[After motions to dismiss and for summary judgment were denied] a trial proceeded on the merits. A declaratory judgment was entered ruling in essence that the provisions in the Store Agreement disallowing assignment without the consent of the holder of the franchise was unenforceable as against public policy, amounting to an unreasonable restraint on the alienation of property; that defendant Hanigan acted unreasonably, arbitrarily and capriciously in withholding his approval of the sale; and that Hanigan had a duty to consent to the sale of the Dairy Queen franchise, the subject matter of the deposit receipt and agreement between plaintiffs Lemoine [sic] and Wheeler.

The facts leading to litigation are as follows. In August, 1962, George Hanigan entered into a "Dairy Queen Store Agreement" with appellee Eileen A. LeMoine. This bilateral contract provided for certain duties and services to be performed by each of the contracting parties. For purposes of this appeal, the only material provision of the contract stated:

> Second Party shall not assign or transfer this Agreement without the written approval of First Party.

On March 7, 1972, appellees LeMoine entered into a deposit and receipt agreement with appellees Wheeler for the sale of the Dairy Queen franchise in question, as well as the real property located and built specifically for that franchise.

The real estate agent, Robert A. Wackerly, who prepared the deposit and receipt agreement contacted Hanigan two days later concerning the sale and appears to have made subsequent attempts to gain Hanigan's approval of the sale and to arrange a meeting with the potential purchasers. Evidence consisting of two tape-recorded telephone conversations held on March 27th between Hanigan and Wackerly and between Hanigan and Mr. Moore, attorney for appellees, were admitted by the court. Among other reasons for refusing to approve the sale, Hanigan stated that the price of $90,000 was too high and that based on his experience an inflated sales price was detrimental to the Dairy Queen business.

Thereafter, litigation was commenced on March 31, 1972, and a meeting between Hanigan and the Wheelers took place on May 8th. After the meeting Hanigan advised appellees' counsel that he would not approve the sale for the reasons that the Wheelers were inexperienced in business matters and were too young to properly run a Dairy Queen franchise. Mr. Wheeler is a practicing dentist and Mrs. Wheeler is a housewife with no children. Their ages are 34 and 32 respectively.

The primary question dispositive of this appeal is whether the trial court erred in determining that the contract provision precluding the franchise transfer without the area franchise holder's approval is unenforceable as against public policy. A review of the record and the relevant law leads us to answer this question in the affirmative. Given the instant fact situation, the law in this area does not warrant the trial court's order requiring Hanigan to consent to the subject transaction:

> As a general rule, a contract is not assignable where the nature or terms of the contract make it nonassignable, (footnote omitted) unless such provision is waived. . . . The parties may in terms, by a provision in the contract, prohibit an assignment thereof. . . .

6 C.J.S. *Assignments* § 24.b (1937).

> Provisions in bilateral contracts which forbid or restrict assignment of the contract without the consent of the obligor have generally been upheld as valid and enforceable when called into question, (footnote omitted) although the meaning of such terms becomes a matter of interpretation. . . .

6 AM. JUR. 2D *Assignments* § 22 (1963).

These general statements are in accord with the RESTATEMENT OF THE LAW OF CONTRACTS § 151, which reads as follows:

> A right may be the subject of effective assignment unless, . . .

* * *

> (c) the assignment is prohibited by the contract creating the right.

The treatises on this subject are likewise in accord. *See* 3 S. Williston, A TREATISE ON THE LAW OF CONTRACTS § 422 (3d ed. 1960); J. Calamari & J. Perillo, THE LAW OF CONTRACTS § 267 (1970).

A leading case, *Allhusen v. Caristo Construction Corporation*, 303 N.Y. 446, 103 N.E.2d 891 (1952); 37 A.L.R.2d 1245 (1954), stated the law as follows:

> . . . we think it is reasonably clear that, while the courts have striven to uphold freedom of assignability, they have not failed to recognize the concept of freedom to contract. In large measure they agree that, where appropriate language is used, assignments of money due under contracts

may be prohibited. When "clear language" is used, and the "plainest words . . . have been chosen", parties may "limit the freedom of alienation of rights and prohibit the assignment." . . .

Such a holding is not violative of public policy. Professor Williston, in his treatise on Contracts, states (Vol. 2 § 422, p. 1214): "The question of the free alienation of property does not seem to be involved." 103 N.E.2d at 893.

In opposition to the above principles, appellees contend that more than a contract right is involved in the case at bench in that the subject clause restricting assignment without Hanigan's approval serves as an unreasonable and unlawful restraint on the right of alienation of property, since the Store Agreement provides no guidelines by which the area franchise holder is to base his approval or disapproval of potential buyers, and that hypothetically, through the whim or arbitrariness of the holder, the LeMoines could be prevented from ever selling their franchise and the property associated with the franchise.

We accept the fundamental principle that one of the primary incidents inherent in the ownership of property is the right of alienation or disposition. . . . However, this right is not limitless. The right to make an assignment of property can be defeated where there is a clear stipulation to that effect. The current state of the law in this area appears to be that a restraint on the alienation of property may be sustained when the restraint is reasonably designed to attain or encourage accepted social or economic ends. In *Gale v. York Center Community Cooperative, Inc.*, 21 Ill. 2d 86, 171 N.E.2d 30 (1960), the court upheld a partial restraint on the alienation of property interests of members of a co-operative housing association in order to assure the continued existence of the association. Likewise, in *Penthouse Properties, Inc. v. 1158 Fifth Avenue, Inc.*, 256 App. Div. 685, 11 N.Y.S.2d 417 (1939), the court upheld as valid contractual restrictions on the right to transfer stock and to assign a proprietary lease in a co-operative apartment house.

We also perceive that despite the restriction on assignment of the store agreement, the LeMoines are not entirely powerless. Where a contract contains a *promise* to refrain from assigning, an assignment which violates it would not be ineffective.[1] "The promise creates a *duty* in the promisor not to assign. It does not deprive the assignor of the *power* to assign and its breach, therefore, would simply subject the promisor to an action for damages while the assignment would be effective. . . ." . . .

In summary, we hold that the law as set forth above demonstrates that the contract limitation against assignment of the Store Agreement without the approval of the area franchise holder is proper and valid. The trial court erred in concluding that the provision limiting assignability was unenforceable as against public policy. The court also erred in ruling that defendants had a duty to consent to the franchise sale, for this is contrary to the manifested intention of the parties to the contract. The general proposition is that 'a covenantor is not to be held beyond his undertaking and he may make that as narrow as he likes.' 3 S. Williston, *supra*, § 422 at 128.

---

[1] This type of restriction is to be distinguished from a provision which renders the assignment void. Such a provision has been held to be valid and deprives the assignor of the *power* to assign. J. Calamari & J. Perillo, op. cit., p. 417.

The judgment below is reversed and the cause is remanded with directions to enter an appropriate declaratory judgment in accordance herewith.

NOTES & QUESTIONS

1. The general rule is stated in 4 CORBIN ON CONTRACTS § 873, at 491:

> We have substantial unanimity of authority to the effect that in contracts for the future conveyance of land or goods, the vendor can limit or forbid the purchaser's assignment of his right to transfer. The court may hesitate to interpret general words against assignment as being intended as such a prohibition; but such a prohibition, if made, is not invalid. Attention may again be called, however, to the difference between forbidding the assignment of a contract right to a future transfer, and forbidding a future conveyance of land or goods by the buyer after their transfer to him. The latter may be invalid for various reasons; it is the former that is now being considered.

2. If your client wishes a contract to be drafted in such a way that he/she will be dealing exclusively with the other contracting party, i.e., your client wants a contractual prohibition against assignment, what terminology would you suggest for inclusion in the contract? Based on *Hanigan*, is it enough to simply say: "This contract cannot be assigned"? What additional language would you recommend for inclusion in the contract?

3. The U.C.C. § 2-210(3) provides:

> (2) Unless the circumstances indicate the contrary a prohibition of assignment of "the contract" is to be construed as barring only the delegation to the assignee of the assignor's performance.

Similarly, the U.C.C. § 9-318(4) provides:

> (4) A term in any contract between an account debtor and an assignor is ineffective if it prohibits assignment of an account or prohibits creation of a security interest in a general intangible for money due or to become due or requires the account debtor's consent to such assignment or security interest.

See American Bank of Commerce v. City of McAlester, 555 P.2d 581 (Okla. 1976).

What is the reason for the Code's bias towards assignment? RESTATEMENT (SECOND) OF CONTRACTS § 322 is to the same effect.

4. If a contract right were not, per se, assignable but if the contract contained a provision — as many contracts do — that "this contract shall inure to the benefit of the heirs and assigns of the parties," does this make the otherwise non-assignable right assignable? *See Standard Chautauqua System v. Gift*, 120 Kan. 101, 242 P. 145 (1926). *See also* RESTATEMENT (SECOND) OF CONTRACTS § 323, comment b. Would your answer be any different if the attempted assignment ran counter to the public policy of the jurisdiction?

5. Assume that the prohibition against assignment is valid, but assume further that the obligee executes an assignment to assignee. Does the assignee have any rights? "The contractual prohibition of assignment of contract rights ordinarily serves to protect the obligor alone and does not affect the legal or equitable rights

of the assignor and assignee as between themselves." *Paul v. Chromalytics Corp.,* 343 A.2d 622, 625 (Del. 1975). RESTATEMENT (SECOND) OF CONTRACTS § 322(2)(c) is to the same effect.

6. In the next to last paragraph of the opinion, the court states:

> The promise creates a duty in the promisor not to assign. It does not deprive the assignor of the power to assign . . . .

Is this logical? If the assignor is duty-bound not to assign, then how can he have the "power" to assign?

E.   DEFENSES TO ASSIGNEE'S CAUSE OF ACTION

FIRST INVESTMENT COMPANY v. ANDERSEN
621 P.2d 683 (Utah 1980)

MAUGHAN, Justice:

Plaintiff, the transferee of the payee of two promissory notes, initiated this action to recover the unpaid balance from the makers, the defendants. The trial court found the notes were not negotiable instruments; plaintiff was not a holder in due course; and there was a failure of consideration on the part of the payee. Defendants were awarded a judgment of no cause of action. Plaintiff appeals therefrom. The judgment of the trial court is affirmed; costs are awarded to defendants.

On September 6, 1965, defendants entered into a franchise agreement with Great Lakes Nursery Corporation, hereinafter identified as the "Nursery," a Wisconsin corporation. Defendants, as the franchisees, were to grow and sell nursery stock and Christmas trees. The Nursery was to provide and to deliver 65,000 trees as planting stock for the purchase price of $9,500.00. The franchisor, the Nursery, under the agreement was to provide the number, size, and variety therein specified, as well as to furnish replanting stock, chemicals, fertilizers, and other articles to be used in the production and sale of the trees; to root prune the trees; to provide technical training and supervision necessary for the planting, sheering, pruning, marketing and sale and other technical information affecting the growth, production, harvest and sale of the trees.

Contemporaneously with the franchise agreement, the defendants, as makers, executed two promissory notes, with the Nursery as payee; each in the amount of $6,412.00. The notes recited:

> For value received, Robert Andersen of Nephi, Utah, promises to pay to Great Lakes Nursery Corp. at Waukesha, Wisconsin six thousand four hundred twelve dollars payable as follows: $100 per month beginning Oct. 1, 1965 for 24 months and then $111.30 per month for 36 months including interest computed at 7% per annum added to the principal amount of $4,750.00. . . .
>
> Robert Andersen. . .
>
> Donna Andersen

> This note is received in full payment for the trees described in Article III-A (Planting Stock) of the Santa's Forest Franchise Agreement. Great

Lakes Nursery Corporation. . . .

Prior to the delivery of any trees to defendants, the Nursery transferred the note to plaintiff on September 20, 1965. The following was written on the reverse side of the note:

> For value received, the undersigned does hereby endorse, sell, assign and transfer with full recourse the within note and mortgage to First Investment Company or order, and authorizes it to do every act and thing necessary to collect and discharge the same.
>
> September 20, 1965. . . .

Defendants were notified by plaintiff of the transfer of the note by a letter dated September 28, 1965. Defendants made payments of $1,350.00 on each of these notes between April 2, 1966, and January 7, 1967. In response to plaintiff's demand, the Nursery made payments on each note in the sum of $1,033.30 as of August, 1968. . .

During 1967, defendants made no further payments on their notes for the reason that the Nursery had failed to perform in accordance with the franchise agreement. In their answer, defendants pleaded a failure of consideration as an affirmative defense. The trial court found there was a failure of consideration on the part of the Nursery for the following reasons: It did not furnish the number, size and variety of trees specified in the agreement; it did not furnish the replanting stock; it did not furnish any chemicals, fertilizers and other articles; it did not root prune the trees; and it did not provide technical training, supervision, and information. There is substantial evidence in the record to sustain the findings.

[Court here holds that the Uniform Negotiable Instruments Act, rather than the U.C.C., controls the facts of this case. The court further holds that the notes were not negotiable and if plaintiff is to prevail it cannot do so as a "holder in due course," but only as an assignee of the Nursery's contract right.] . . .

Significantly, the trial court found that the notes and franchise agreement constituted one integrated contract. This finding is substantiated by the recital concerning consideration in the note, and the absence of words of negotiability. Where there is a failure of consideration under a bilateral contract consisting of a breach by the assignor, such failure is a good defense to an action by the assignee whether it occurred before or after the assignment. Such a defense, although acquired after notice of the assignment, is based on a right of defendant inherent in the contract by its terms. Therefore, where payments under an executory contract are assigned, the debtor may set up failure of the assignor to fulfill his part of the contract though such failure occurs after the assignment, for the assignor cannot give another a larger right than he has himself. The trial court did not err in its ruling that failure of consideration constituted a valid defense to plaintiff's action. . . .

On appeal, plaintiff contends the defendants have derived a $20,000 benefit for which they have paid only $1,350.00, and defendants have been unjustly enriched. . . . Under any circumstances, a theory of unjust enrichment would be inappropriate in this case, for the matter of consideration was directly in issue. Since the notes were not negotiable instruments, there was no presumption that they were issued for a valuable consideration. Plaintiff, as assignee of the notes, had the burden to prove they were issued for a consideration from the Nursery. Plaintiff presented receipts acknowledging delivery of the trees, and then defendants sustained their burden, proving a failure of consideration, as found by the trial court. At this juncture, to recover any amount in excess of the payments received, plaintiff had the burden of proof as to the value of the consideration received by defendants from the Nursery. No evidence was adduced as to the value of the surviving trees at the time of delivery from the Nursery; and, therefore, plaintiff has failed to establish the value of the consideration received by defendants for their issuance of the notes.

Finally, plaintiff contends defendants should be estopped to assert the defense of failure of consideration by reason of their failure to advise plaintiff they were not going to pay. Plaintiff asserts that the Nursery filed a bankruptcy proceeding, and if plaintiff had been apprised of defendants' claim, it would have exerted greater pressure on the Nursery to collect the obligation. Plaintiff claims defendants' inaction and silence constitute a sufficient basis to invoke an estoppel.

". . . in order for silence to work an estoppel, there must be a legal duty to speak, or there must be something willful or culpable in the silence which allows another to place himself in an unfavorable position by reason thereof.

The facts revealed by the record do not support plaintiff's claim. The date the Nursery filed bankruptcy is not disclosed; however, defendants in their answer alleged it was in the spring of 1969. The claimed legal duty of the defendants to speak is not established. According to plaintiff's records, the last payment received from defendants was in January, 1967. Plaintiff sent defendants a series of letters, first demanding payment and later threatening legal action. . . . The evidence further indicated that the agreements between plaintiff and the Nursery provided that in the event any maker was forty-five or more days past due in payment, the note would be automatically repurchased by the Nursery. Plaintiff could have averted loss by enforcing its agreement with the Nursery requiring repurchase of the delinquent notes. Under the circumstances, the failure of defendants to respond to plaintiff's letters demanding payment did not establish a basis to invoke an estoppel.

[Judgment of Trial Court is affirmed.]

NOTES & QUESTIONS

1. In *Red Giant Oil Co. v. Lawlor*, 528 N.W.2d 524, 533 (Iowa 1995), the Supreme Court of Iowa summed it up nicely when it said:

> An assignment is a transfer to another of the whole of any property or right in the property. *Broyles v. Iowa Dep't of Social Servs.*, 305 N.W.2d 718, 721 (Iowa 1981). In such transfers, the assignee assumes the rights, remedies and benefits of the assignor. *Id.* at 723. On the other hand, the assignee also takes the property subject to all defenses to which the assignor is subject. *Van Maanen v. Van Maanen*, 360 N.W.2d 758, 762 (Iowa 1985); Iowa Code § 539.1. Choses in action whether for breach of contract or for tort are assignable in this state. *Fischer v. Klink*, 234 Iowa 884, 888, 14 N.W.2d 695, 698 (1944). In light of these rules and because insurers have available to them a variety of defenses — for example, coverage, fraud, and collusion — we fail to see why legally it should make any difference who sues the insurer — the insured or the insured's assignee.

2. Assume that there has been a valid assignment for value from R to E, and notice of this fact has been given to O. Now assume further that following this, R performs his duty, e.g., R delivers the goods that O had agreed to purchase from R; simultaneously, and with R's concurrence, O & R agree to revoke the assignment, and then O pays R for the goods. Does E have any right to payment from O? From R?

3. What kind of notice of the assignment should E give to O? Must it be in writing, or may it be oral? *See* 3 Williston, WILLISTON ON CONTRACTS § 437. The U.C.C. makes a radical departure from the common law as to the inability of O and R to modify their contract after notice of the assignment has been given. *See* U.C.C. § 9-318. Is this good or bad law in today's commercial setting?

4. The question has arisen whether O, by way of "counterclaim," may bring a cause of action against E. It should be noted that O may not obtain a judgment against E. The only way that O could obtain a judgment against E is if E had, expressly or impliedly, assumed R's duty to O, thus making O a third party beneficiary of E's promise to R.

O's "counterclaim" is really a claim for diminution of E's damages against O. The courts have distinguished "recoupment" (where O's claim against R arises out of the self-same contract, the right of which has been assigned to E) from "set off" (where O's claim against R arises not out of the assigned contract but out of an unrelated agreement or occurrence, e.g. an earlier contract between O & R that R allegedly breached).

In "recoupment," O may use R's breach to diminish his damages to E. This is true regardless of when the claim arose relative to the time that O receives notice of the assignment. In a "set off," O may use R's breach to diminish his liability to E if the claim for set-off accrues before O receives notice of the assignment. However, if the claim for set-off accrues after O receives notice of the assignment, it may not be so used.

> An assignee has traditionally been subject to defenses or set-offs existing before an account debtor is notified of the assignment. When the account debtor's defenses on an assigned claim arise from the contract between him and the assignor, it makes no difference whether the breach giving rise to the defense occurs before or after the account debtor is notified of the assignment. The account debtor may also have claims against the assignor which arise independently of that contract: an assignee is subject to all such claims which accrue before, and free of all those which accrue after, the account debtor is notified. . . . This is in accord with the general rule in sales transactions that the assignee takes his assignment subject to the purchaser's defenses, set-offs and counterclaims against the seller.

First New England Financial Corp. v. Woffard, 421 So. 2d 590, 595 (Fla. Dist. App. 1982).

> Conversely, an assignee's right against the obligor is subject to all of the limitations of the assignor's right, to all defenses thereto, and to all set-offs and counterclaims which would have been available against the assignor had there been no assignment, provided that these defenses and set-offs are based on facts existing at the time of the assignment.

Smith v. Cumberland Group, Limited, 687 A.2d 1167, 1172 (Pa. Super. 1997). *See also Maryland Cooperative Milk Producers v. Bell,* 206 Md. 168, 177-78, 110 A.2d 661, 665 (1955). *See* RESTATEMENT (SECOND) OF CONTRACTS § 336(2).

PROBLEM

If the assignment to E is one for value and O has a valid defense against the exercise of the right in E's hands, does E have any rights against R? For example, assume that O, for valuable consideration, was duty-bound to deliver goods worth $10,000 to R. R thereafter assigned his right to the goods to E in exchange for 100 shares of Acme corporation worth at the time $4,000. Thereafter O successfully resists E's claim because of a failure of consideration by R. Does E have a claim against R? If so, what is E's theory? If E is successful, what is his measure of damages — $10,000? $4,000?

F. DELEGATION OF DUTIES

We have already mentioned that technically "rights" are "assigned" and "duties" are "delegated." Admittedly, cases that reach appellate and supreme courts are there precisely because the parties used inexact language such as: "I hereby transfer the contract to X," or "I assign and set over my contract with Y to Z." If you, as a practicing attorney, are fortunate enough to be retained at the "planning" stage, such confusion should be able to be obviated.

The next question to be addressed is whether R may not only transfer his right to E, but also whether R may appoint E to perform his, i.e., R's, duty. Must O accept E's performance, or may O insist on receiving the return performance from R?

Our scenario can be graphically represented as follows:

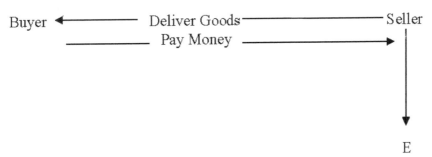

However, we are now concerned with whether Seller (the assignor) may appoint E to deliver the contracted-for goods. When analyzing whether duties may be effectively delegated, the names of the parties change. Buyer would be the "obligee" of seller's promise to deliver the goods. Seller becomes the "obligor" of that promise; seller is also the proposed "delegant" of that duty; and E is the proposed "delegate."

Therefore, directing our attention alone to seller's duty to deliver the goods and his proposal to appoint E to perform that duty, the parties could be denominated as follows:

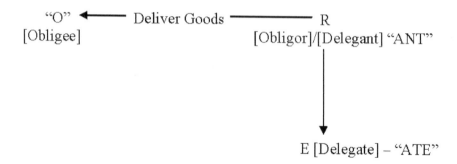

Henceforth in this chapter we will refer to the obligee of R's promise as "O"; the obligor of the duty to perform as "ANT"; and the proposed delegate, he/she who is being appointed to perform the duty for R, as "ATE."

So, once again, the essential question is: may ANT legally delegate, that is appoint, ATE to perform ANT's duty to O?

IMPERIAL REFINING CO. v. KANOTEX REFINING CO.
29 F.2d 193 (8th Cir. 1928)

BOOTH, Circuit Judge:

This is a writ of error to a judgment dismissing a cause, after an order had been entered sustaining a demurrer to the complaint, and after plaintiff had declined to plead further. The questions raised by the demurrer were: (1) whether the complaint stated facts sufficient to constitute a cause of action; and (2) [did the statute of limitations bar the action].

The complaint alleged in substance as follows: That the plaintiff, Imperial Refining Company, a corporation, had on May 28, 1919, made a written contract with Fern Oil Company, a joint-stock association, whereby plaintiff agreed to purchase from Fern Oil Company and that company agreed to sell to plaintiff for a period of one year commencing June 4, 1919, all of . . . the oil produced and saved from a certain oil and gas lease owned by the Fern Oil Company; that on the same day plaintiff assigned the contract and all its rights thereunder to the defendant herein, the Kanotex Refining Company, by written instrument duly signed by plaintiff, and duly accepted in writing by the Kanotex Company; that at the time when the contract and the assignment were made the Fern Oil Company was operating and developing the leased premises for oil and gas, and did thereafter obtain oil in paying quantities on the premises; that, after the assignment was made, defendant, acting under it and under the rights conferred by the contract, caused pipe line connections to be made to the leased premises, and made all necessary preparations to run and take the oil which was being produced at the time from the premises; that defendant, after making the pipe line connections, refused to run the oil then being produced; that as a result of the actions of defendant in making the pipe line connections, and then refusing to run the oil, the Fern Oil Company . . . sustained damages; that thereafter the Fern Oil Company . . . commenced suit in the state court of Oklahoma against plaintiff as the original promisor to recover damages for breach of the contract; that plaintiff herein immediately notified defendant herein of the suit brought by the Fern Oil

Company and requested defendant to defend the same; that, though defendant did not employ counsel to defend the suit, yet it did advise with plaintiff relative thereto, and furnished certain of its employees as witnesses at the trial, and its counsel was present at the trial; that plaintiff herein defended the suit with diligence, but nevertheless judgment was obtained against it in the amount of $18,000; . . . that plaintiff has paid and satisfied the judgment, and has paid the attorney's fees and costs incident to the suit; that by reason of the fact that defendant was the assignee of the contract with the Fern Oil Company, and succeeded to plaintiff's rights and obligations under the same, and by reason of the acts of defendant heretofore recited, plaintiff is entitled to recover from defendant the amount of the judgment, attorney's fees, and costs paid by plaintiff as before stated. Attached to the complaint as exhibits were copies of the contract with the Fern Oil Company, of the assignment to the defendant and of the journal entry of the judgment obtained against plaintiff in the state court.

[The Court then discusses the issue of whether the underlying contract between Fern Oil Company and Imperial Refining Co. was void for lack of mutuality of obligation, and therefore "no obligation in reference to it were (sic) assumed by the Kanotex Company." The court conceded that "unless the contract between the Imperial Company and the Fern Company was valid, no duty in reference thereto rested on the Kanotex Company under the assignment." The court concludes that Fern's promise to sell its entire supply was not an illusory promise, and that therefore both Fern and Imperial were mutually obligated.] . . .

The next question is: Was the defendant Kanotex Company under any obligation to the Imperial Company to carry out the provisions of the Fern Oil Company contract, by reason of the assignment of that contract to defendant by the Imperial Company? It is a general rule that the right of one party to a contract to its performance by the other may be assigned, absent any provision to the contrary in the contract or by statute, and excepting contracts involving relations of personal confidence or calling for personal services. 5 C.J. pp. 874–882, §§ 44-47. The contract in the case at bar did not forbid an assignment, and no statute is pointed out having such effect; nor did the contract fall within the excepted classes. That it was the intention of the parties to the assignment that the original contract should be carried out is apparent from the terms of the assignment. . . .

By this assignment from the Imperial Company to the Kanotex Company, the latter company acquired the right of the Imperial Company in the contract. This is conceded. But this was not the only effect of the assignment. The Imperial Company by the assignment not only transferred its rights in the contract, but it also delegated its duties, and the Kanotex Company by accepting the assignment accepted the delegation of the duties. It accepted the burdens with the benefits. As between the Imperial Company and the Kanotex Company, a primary duty rested upon the latter company to perform the contract, and the Imperial Company stood toward the Kanotex Company in the nature of a surety for the performance of the contract. We think the weight of authority sustains these views.

In 5 C.J. 976, it is said: "As between the assignee and the assignor, the assignee is bound to carry out the provisions of the assigned contract and in all respects to comply with the terms of the assignment, and the assignor may recover from him the damages he sustained by reason of the failure of the assignee to comply with the contract."

In *Cutting Packing Co. v. Packers' Exchange*, 86 Cal. 574, 25 P. 52, 21 Am. St. Rep. 63, 10 L.R.A. 369, the Cutting Company had contracted with one Blackwood to purchase from him certain apricots. The Cutting Company assigned its interest in the contract to Packers' Exchange. Blackwood refused to accept the Packers' Exchange in place of the Cutting Company, but delivered the apricots to the Cutting Company, according to the contract. The Cutting Company received the apricots and paid for them, and tendered them to the Packers' Exchange; but the latter refused to accept them. Thereupon the Cutting Company sold them to the best advantage, but sustained a loss, for which it sued Packers' Exchange. It was held that the original contract was assignable; that the assignment did not relieve the Cutting Company from its obligation to Blackwood; that the refusal of Blackwood did not relieve Packers' Exchange from its obligation to the Cutting Company under the assignment. The court in its opinion said:

> So far as the parties to this suit are concerned, the appellant [Packers' Exchange] contracted with the respondent [the Cutting Company] to accept and pay for the fruit Blackwood had contracted to deliver to the latter. It could make no difference, therefore, whether the fruit was delivered to the appellant by Blackwood directly or by the respondent. As between the parties to this suit, the appellant was bound to receive and accept the fruit, and it cannot relieve itself from this obligation by showing that Blackwood had refused to relieve the respondent from its obligation to him. . . . We therefore think it plain that as the plaintiff, as assignor, was still bound to Blackwood to pay the price stipulated in the contract, notwithstanding the assignment, and as the defendant, as assignee, assumed such obligation, the plaintiff, as between it and the defendant, stood in the nature of a surety for the latter for the performance of the obligation. If this be correct, it then follows that from the assignment an implied contract arose between the plaintiff and defendant, whereby the latter became bound to the former to receive and pay for the apricots, according to the terms of the original contract. . . .

From the foregoing discussion, we think it is plain that there was a duty under the Fern Oil Company contract on the part of the Imperial Company toward the Fern Company to carry out the terms of that contract, and that it is equally plain that there was also a duty, under the assignment of that contract, on the part of the Kanotex Company toward the Imperial Company to carry out the terms of the same contract. The allegations of the complaint are that the terms of the contract were not carried out. The Imperial Company thus became liable to the Fern Company, and in turn the Kanotex Company became liable to the Imperial Company. The Imperial Company was sued by the Fern Company. Its liability under the contract was established; judgment was obtained against it, and it paid the judgment. . . . Under these circumstances we think that the Kanotex Company is bound by the judgment obtained against the Imperial Company.

[The court concludes its opinion by holding that Imperial's cause of action against Kanotex was not barred by the statute of limitations.] . . .

Our conclusion is that the sustaining of the demurrer to the complaint and the entering of judgment dismissing the cause constituted error, and that the judgment should be reversed.

It is so ordered.

NOTES & QUESTIONS

1. When ANT properly delegates his delegable duty of performance to ATE, is ANT thereby relieved of his primary obligation to O? The *Imperial* opinion suggests yes. *Contra*, RESTATEMENT (SECOND) OF CONTRACTS § 318(3). What result if thereafter ANT informs O that ANT no longer considers himself obligated to O and that O should look only to ATE for the performance? *See* 4 CORBIN ON CONTRACTS § 870.

2. In *Epstein v. Gluckin*, 233 N.Y. 490, 135 N.E. 861, 862 (1922), Justice Cardozo held that an assignee of a vendee of land would not be denied the equitable relief of specific performance simply because of the supposed doctrine of "mutuality of remedy." The assignee had the assignor's right to that form of relief. In determining whether the assignee, by suing for specific performance, impliedly assumed any of the assignor's duties, the court stated:

> The assignee, by the very act of invoking the aid of equity, assumes the duty of performance, and subjects himself to any conditions of the judgment appropriate thereto. . . . At first the vendor had the obligation of the vendees, and of no one else. The obligation thus imposed has not been lost, but another has been added. Some one has at all times been charged with the duty of performance. The continuity of remedy is unbroken from contract to decree.

3. *Practice Points*: What if X, a party to a contract, simply assigns his "contract" or "all his rights under the contract" to Y, does Y thereby become duty-bound to perform X's duty to the other contracting party? In short, if Y becomes the recipient of a valuable contract right via assignment, does he thereby impliedly agree with X to also perform X's duties to the third party? Is it therefore possible that attractive "brown paper packages tied up with string" (with apologies to *The Sound of Music*) might not turn out to be one of the assignee's least "favorite things"? Referring again to *Imperial,* the opinion holds that the assignee has a duty to the assignor — Imperial — to fulfill Imperial's duty to Fern. Does it logically follow that Kanotex now has assumed a duty toward Fern to pay for the oil? If yes, on what theory? Do you see a third party beneficiary contract lurking in this fact pattern? *See* RESTATEMENT (SECOND) OF CONTRACTS § 328(2); U.C.C. § 2-210. But see *Langel v. Betz*, 250 N.Y. 159, 164 N.E. 890 (1928), where the court held that the mere assignment of a purchaser's right to buy real estate did not impose on the assignee any duty to pay for it. *See* Grismore, *Is the Assignee of a Contract Liable for the Non-Performance of Delegated Duties?*, 18 MICH. L. REV. 284 (1920); Calamari & Perillo, THE LAW OF CONTRACTS, § 18-27, at 759, n.60 (3d ed. 1987).

4. Would your answer to the previous question be any different if the assignment were gratuitous as opposed to being an assignment for value? In other words, is the obligee of the assignor's duty more likely to be found to be a third party beneficiary of the "assigned contract" when the assignment was one for value as opposed to having been merely gratuitous?

BRITISH WAGGON COMPANY v. LEA & CO.
Vol. V, Q.B.D. 149 (1880)

COCKBURN, C.J. This was an action brought by the plaintiffs to recover rent for the hire of certain railway waggons, alleged to be payable by the defendants to the plaintiffs, or one of them, under the following circumstances:

By an agreement in writing of the 10th of February, 1874, the Parkgate Waggon Company let to the defendants, who are coal merchants, fifty railway waggons for a term of seven years, at a yearly rent of 600£. a year, payable by equal quarterly payments. By a second agreement of the 13th of June, 1874, the company in like manner let to the defendants fifty other waggons, at a yearly rent of 625£., payable quarterly like the former.

Each of these agreements contained the following clause:

> The owners, their executors, or administrators, will at all times during the said term, except as herein provided, keep the said waggons in good and substantial repair and working order, and, on receiving notice from the tenant of any want of repairs, and the number or numbers of the waggons requiring to be repaired, and the place or places where it or they then is or are, will, with all reasonable despatch, cause the same to be repaired and put into good working order.

On the 24th of October, 1874, the Parkgate Company passed a resolution, under the 129th section of the Companies Act, 1862, for the voluntary winding up of the company. Liquidators were appointed, and by an order of the Chancery Division of the High Court of Justice, it was ordered that the winding-up of the company should be continued under the supervision of the Court.

By an indenture of the 1st of April, 1878, the Parkgate Company assigned and transferred, and the liquidators confirmed to the British Company and their assigns, among other things, all sums of money, whether payable by way of rent, hire, interest, penalty, or damage, then due, or thereafter to become due, to the Parkgate Company, by virtue of the two contracts with the defendants, together with the benefit of the two contracts, and all the interest of the Parkgate Company and the said liquidators therein; the British Company, on the other hand covenanting with the Parkgate Company "to observe and perform such of the stipulations, conditions, provisions, and agreements contained in the said contracts as, according to the terms thereof, were stipulated to be observed and performed by the Parkgate Company." On the execution of this assignment the British Company took over from the Parkgate Company the repairing stations, which had previously been used by the Parkgate Company for the repair of the waggons let to the defendants, and also the staff of workmen employed by the latter company in executing such repairs. It is expressly found that the British Company have ever since been ready and willing to execute, and have, with all due diligence, executed all necessary repairs to the said waggons. . . .

In this state of things the defendants asserted their right to treat the contract as at an end, on the ground that the Parkgate Company had incapacitated themselves [sic] from performing the contract, first, by going into voluntary liquidation, secondly, by assigning the contracts, and giving up the repairing stations to the British Company, between whom and the defendants there was no privity of contract, and whose services in substitution for those to be performed by the Parkgate Company under the contract, they the defendants were not bound to accept. The Parkgate Company not acquiescing in this view, it was agreed that the facts should be stated in a special case for the opinion of this Court, the use of the waggons by the defendants being in the meanwhile continued at a rate agreed on between the parties, without prejudice to either, with reference to their respective rights. . . .

The main contention on the part of the defendants, however, was that, as the Parkgate Company had, by assigning the contracts, and by making over their repairing stations to the British Company, incapacitated themselves to fulfill their obligation to keep the waggons in repair, that company had no right, as between themselves and the defendants, to substitute a third party to do the work they had engaged to perform, nor were the defendants bound to accept the party so substituted as the one to whom they were to look for performance of the contract; the contract was therefore at an end.

The authority principally relied on in support of this contention was the case of *Robson v. Drummond*, approved of by this court in *Humble v. Hunder*. In *Robson v. Drummond*, a carriage having been hired by the defendant of one Sharp, a coach-maker, for five years, at a yearly rent, payable in advance each year, the carriage to be kept in repair and painted once a year by the maker — Robson being then a partner in the business, but unknown to the defendant — on Sharp retiring from the business after three years had expired, and making over all interest in the business and property in the goods to Robson, it was held, that the defendant could not be sued on the contract — by Lord Tenterden on the ground that "the defendant might have been induced to enter into the contract by reason of the personal confidence which he reposed in Sharp, and therefore might have agreed to pay money in advance, for which reason the defendant had a right to object to its being performed by any other person;" and by Littledale and Parke, J.J., on the additional ground that the defendant had a right to the personal services of Sharp, and to the benefit of his judgment and taste, to the end of the contract.

In like manner, where goods are ordered of a particular manufacturer, another, who has succeeded to his business, cannot execute the order, so as to bind the customer, who has not been made aware of the transfer of the business, to accept the goods. The latter is entitled to refuse to deal with any other than the manufacturer whose goods he intended to buy. For this *Boulton v. Jones* is a sufficient authority. The case of *Robson v. Drummond* comes nearer to the present case, but is, we think, distinguishable from it. We entirely concur in the principle on which the decision in *Robson v. Drummond* rests, namely, that where a person contracts with another to do work or perform service, and it can be inferred that the person employed has been selected with reference to his individual skill, competency, or other personal qualification, the inability or unwillingness of the party so employed to execute the work or perform the service is a sufficient answer to any demand by a stranger to the original contract of the performance of it by the other party, and entitles the latter to treat the contract as at an end, notwithstanding that the person tendered to take the place of the contracting party may be equally well informed to do service. Personal performance is in such a case of the essence of the contract, which, consequently, cannot in its absence be enforced against an unwilling party.

But this principle appears to us inapplicable in the present instance, inasmuch as we cannot suppose that in stipulating for the repair of these waggons by the company — a rough description of work which ordinary workmen conversant with the business would be perfectly able to execute — the defendants attached any importance to whether the repairs were done by the company, or by any one with whom the company might enter into a subsidiary contract to do the work. All that the hirers, the defendants, cared for in this stipulation was that the waggons should be kept in repair; it was indifferent to them by whom the repairs should be done.

Thus if, without going into liquidation, or assigning these contracts, the company had entered into a contract with any competent party to do the repairs, and so had procured them to be done, we cannot think that this would have been a departure from the terms of the contract to keep the waggons in repair. While fully acquiescing in the general principle just referred to, we must take care not to push it beyond reasonable limits. And we cannot but think that, in applying the principle, the Court of Queen's Bench in *Robson v. Drummond* went to the utmost length to which it can be carried, as it is difficult to see how in repairing a carriage when necessary or painting it once a year, preference would be given to one coachmaker over another. Much work is contracted for, which it is known can only be executed by means of subcontracts; much is contracted for as to which it is indifferent to the party for whom it is to be done, whether it is done by the immediate party to the contract, or by someone on his behalf. In all these cases the maxim *Qui facit per alium facit per se* applies.

In the view we take of the case, therefore, the repair of the waggons, undertaken and done by the British Company under their contract with the Parkgate Company, is a sufficient performance by the latter of their engagement to repair under their contract with the defendants. Consequently, so long as the Parkgate Company continues to exist, and, through the British Company, continues to fulfill its obligation to keep the waggons in repair, the defendants cannot, in our opinion, be heard to say that the former company is not entitled to the performance of the contract by them, on the ground that the company have incapacitated themselves from performing their obligations under it, or that, by transferring the performance thereof to others, they have absolved the defendants from further performance on their part, . . .

We are therefore of opinion that our judgment must be for the plaintiffs for the amount claimed. . . .

NOTES & QUESTIONS

1. Is an obligation to give a patron dance lessons a delegable duty? Cf. *Seale v. Bates*, 145 Colo. 430, 359 P.2d 356 (1961).

2. Personal service contracts. In the classic case of *Taylor v. Palmer*, 31 Cal. 240 (1866), which involved a contract to grade a street in San Francisco and which raised the issues of whether the contract duties could be delegated, and whether the delegate, having done the work, might enforce the contract, the court said, pp. 247, 248:

> Aside from the discretion vested in the Board of Supervisors to reject all bids when they deem it for the public good, or the bid of any party who may have proved delinquent or unfaithful in any previous contract with the city, there is no restriction upon the capacity of the contractor. He is not expected nor required to perform the work in person. Were it so, street improvements in San Francisco would make slow progress. . . . All painters do not paint portraits like Sir Joshua Reynolds, nor landscapes like Claude Lorraine, nor do all writers write dramas like Shakespeare or fiction like Dickens. Rare genius and extraordinary skill are not transferable, and contracts for their employment are therefore personal, and cannot be assigned [really "delegated"]. But rare genius and extraordinary skills are not indispensable to the workman-like digging down of a sand hill

or the filling up of a depression to a given level, or the construction of brick sewers with manholes and covers, and contracts for such work are not personal, and may be assigned [really "delegated"]. *Cochran v. Collins*, 29 Cal. 129 (1865).

So, are "personal service contracts" "assignable"? It depends on what you mean.

Assume a contract where the owner of the Cleveland Cavaliers Professional Basketball Team has agreed to pay LeBron James $30,000,000 to play basketball for one season. Is this a "personal service contract"? It certainly appears so.

But breaking it down into duties and rights, is LeBron James's right to receive $30,000,000 assignable to a third party, T? Assuming no contractual provision between Owner and James, nor public policy prohibiting assignment, James may assign his right provided that the assignment:

(a) would not "materially change the duty of the owner" [the owner would simply have to make the checks payable to T instead of to LeBron James];

(b) would not "materially increase the burden or risk imposed on him," the owner, by the contract [the owner writes the same checks at the same times]; or

(c) would not "materially impair his [owner's] chance of obtaining" the valued return performance [LeBron James would continue to play as intensely as ever, so the argument goes, even though he will not be paid for the season.]

Hence, in this personal service contract LeBron James's right to payment might very well be assignable to T. RESTATEMENT (SECOND) OF CONTRACTS § 317(2).

As to LeBron James's duty to play for the Cleveland Cavaliers, this duty is not delegable to T. There is arguably only one LeBron James in the world, with his unparalleled talents. In short, he is unique. No one can take his place. He is the Luciano Pavarotti of the basketball court.

Similarly, may Owner assign his rights to LeBron James's unique services? Aside from a contractual prohibition, and more importantly aside from being banished forever, or worse, from Cleveland, Owner could assign his rights to James's services to another team, provided there would be no materially adverse effect on LeBron James. As to Owner's duty to pay $30,000,000, this duty is clearly delegable as the second person's checks, assuming they do not bounce, are as good as Owner's.

Therefore to say that a "personal service contract" is not "assignable" is to misspeak. It is more precise to say that personal, unique duties are not delegable. *See* 4 CORBIN ON CONTRACTS § 866.

3. Where the duties sought to be delegated are objectively measurable such as the duty to pay money, or the duty to perform work that can as well be performed by a delegate as by the delegant, the duties are delegable. If however, the contract calls for a specific person to do the work, no matter how pedestrian, that duty is not delegable. What about a substitute contracts professor for the semester? But what if he/she were better than the professor originally assigned to teach your class? Would the school's duty to teach contracts then be delegable?

4. Public policy on occasion mandates that a duty not be delegable. Similarly the parties, by an explicit contractual provision, may agree that their duties are not delegable, and courts should honor this. RESTATEMENT (SECOND) OF CONTRACTS § 318(1).

All other things being equal, would courts be more likely to find rights to be assignable rather than duties to be delegable? Why? What public policy or jurisprudential considerations militate toward a more restrictive view of one over the other? The RESTATEMENT (SECOND) OF CONTRACTS § 322(1) is instructive in this regard. It states:

> Unless the circumstances indicate the contrary, a contract term prohibiting assignment of "the contract" bars only the delegation to an assignee of the performance by the assignor of a duty or condition.

The U.C.C. is to the same effect. *See* U.C.C. § 2-210(3).

5. What if ANT, following the delegation of a delegable duty to ATE, informs O that he — ANT — is no longer liable, and then O begins accepting performance from ATE? Has ANT thereby become relieved of his primary duty to O? In other words, has ANT offered a novation to O and has O, by dealing with ATE, accepted the novation? Cf. *First Federal Savings & Loan Ass'n of Gary v. Arena*, 406 N.E.2d 1279 (Ind. App. 1980). RESTATEMENT (SECOND) OF CONTRACTS §329(2).

6. Would an otherwise delegable duty still be delegable from ANT to ATE if the facts were that the O had negotiated with both ANT and ATE before finally entering into a contract with ANT? In other words, although the contract between O and ANT does not expressly state, O preferred to contract with ANT. And now ANT wants ATE to perform his contractual obligation. If you were the judge, how would you rule? *See Macke Co. v. Pizza of Gaithersburg, Inc.*, 259 M.D. 479, 270 A.2d 645 (1970). If you, as the attorney drafting the contract, want to "wear both belt and suspenders," what language would you include in the contract on behalf of O, the obligee, to protect against the delegation of an otherwise delegable duty?

TABLE OF CASES

[References are to pages.]

[References are to pages.]

B

[References are to pages.]

[References are to pages.]

[References are to pages.]

[References are to pages.]

G

[References are to pages.]

[References are to pages.]

[References are to pages.]

N

O

[References are to pages.]

[References are to pages.]

[References are to pages.]

[References are to pages.]

[References are to pages.]

INDEX

[References are to pages.]

[References are to pages.]

[References are to pages.]

[References are to pages.]

[References are to pages.]